D0781622

Risk Management for Enterprises and Individuals Version 1.0

By

Etti Baranoff, Patrick L. Brockett and Yehuda Kahane

S-29698-CO-1

9 781936 126187

Risk Management for Enterprises and Individuals Version 1.0

Etti Baranoff, Patrick L. Brockett and Yehuda Kahane

Published by:

Flat World Knowledge, Inc.
1111 19th St NW, Suite 1180
Washington, DC 20036

© 2014 by Flat World Knowledge, Inc. All rights reserved. Your use of this work is subject to the License Agreement available here http://www.flatworldknowledge.com/legal.

No part of this work may be used, modified, or reproduced in any form or by any means except as expressly permitted under the License Agreement.

Brief Contents

Contents

About the Authors

ETTI BARANOFF

Dr. Etti Baranoff is an associate professor of risk management, insurance, and finance at the School of Business at Virginia Commonwealth University (VCU) in Richmond, Virginia, where she has taught since 1995. She has been in the insurance field for over thirty years. Prior to entering academia, she worked in the insurance industry and as a Texas insurance regulator. She began her insurance career as a pension administrator and market and product research analyst at American Founder's Life Insurance Company in Austin, Texas, in 1978. In 1982 she began a twelve-year career as a Texas insurance regulator, beginning with actuarial work for the rate promulgation of property/casualty lines of insurance, following with legislative research work on all topics.

Dr. Baranoff has spoken at many insurance and finance forums and won various awards for her research and teaching. She is a member of the prestigious Risk Theory Seminar and has published in prominent journals, including the *Journal of Risk and Insurance*, the *Journal of Banking and Finance*, the *Geneva Papers on Risk and Insurance*, the *Journal of Insurance Regulation*, *Best's Review*, and *Contingencies of the American Academy of Actuaries*, among others. She is also one of the authors of another textbook: *Risk Assessment* by the American Institute for CPCU.

Dr. Baranoff has authored or co-authored more than fifty papers relating to risk management and insurance. Her work, which considers issues such as capital structure, detection of potential insolvencies, asset allocation and performance, and market discipline, is all within the context of enterprise risk and enterprise risk management. She has received various honors and recognitions during her career, including five awards given by the International Insurance Society (2008, 2006, 2004, 1996, and 1995). She was recognized as the 2005 Distinguished Scholar by the VCU School of Business and was a seven-time winner of research awards given by the business school. She was also the recipient of the 1990 Spencer Scholarship Award (RIMS) and the 1989 Vestal Lemmon Presidential Scholarship at the University of Texas at Austin.

Along with her articles published in academic and nonacademic journals and periodicals, her textbooks, and countless presentations at various meetings and conferences, Dr. Baranoff is often quoted in major newspapers and has appeared on various TV stations on matters of insurance and risk management. Her presentations are available at the VCU School of Business Web site, which features a video, "On the Topic," about her expertise in risk management.

Dr. Baranoff has been a member of several professional societies, including the already noted Risk Theory Seminar (an invitation-only society), the Financial Management Association (FMA), the American Risk and Insurance Association (ARIA), the Western Risk and Insurance Association (WRIA), and the Southern Risk and Insurance Association (SRIA).

In addition to her PhD in finance with minors in insurance and statistics from the University of Texas at Austin in 1993 and her BA in economics and statistics from the University of Tel Aviv, Israel, in 1971, Dr. Baranoff also holds the fellow of Life Management Institute designation with distinction. She was a high school economics and social sciences teacher and earned a teaching certificate in social sciences from the University of Tel Aviv in 1974. She has served as an expert in a number of cases.

E-mail: ebaranoff@vcu.edu or ettib@earthlink.net.

Site: http://www.professorofinsurance.com.

PATRICK L. BROCKETT

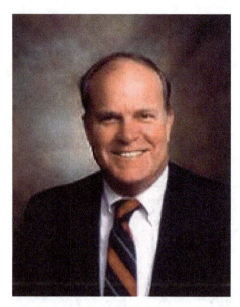

Dr. Patrick L. Brockett holds the Gus S. Wortham Memorial Chair in Risk Management and Insurance in the Department of Information, Risk, and Operations Management at the University of Texas at Austin. He is the director of the risk management program and the director of the Center for Risk Management and Insurance Research and holds a joint appointment as a full professor in the departments of Information, Risk, and Operations Management; Finance; and Mathematics. Prior to becoming the director of the risk management program, he served as the director of the actuarial science program at the University of Texas at Austin. He is the former director of the Center for Cybernetic Studies and is a fellow of the Institute of Risk Management, a fellow of the Institute of Mathematical Statistics, a fellow of the American Statistical Association, a fellow of the Royal Statistical Society, and a fellow of the American Association for the Advancement of Science.

Dr. Brockett has taught and done research in the fields of risk, insurance, and actuarial science for almost thirty years. His research articles have won awards from the American Risk and Insurance Association, the American Statistical Association, the Society of Actuaries, the International Insurance Society, and the Casualty Actuarial Society, as well as from the Faculty of Actuaries of Scotland and Institute of Actuaries in England. He is listed as one of the top ten most published researchers in the world in the seventy-five-year history of the *Journal of Risk and Insurance* (the premier academic journal in risk management and insurance in the world) in terms of the number of pages published. He was presented with the American Risk and Insurance Association Outstanding Achievement Award, won the Robert I. Mehr Award given by the American Risk and Insurance Association "for that journal article making a ten-year lasting contribution to risk management" and having "withstood the test of time," and won the Halmsted Prize for the Most Outstanding English Language Publication in Actuarial Science in the World, presented by the Society of Actuaries. He served as editor of the *Journal of Risk and Insurance* for nine years and in this capacity also became familiar with multiple aspects of insurance, including institutional details, market performance, agent behavior and responsibilities, and standard practice in the insurance industry.

Dr. Brockett worked with the Texas Department of Insurance on credit scoring and did a study for the Texas legislature on credit scoring as well. He currently serves as a member of the board of directors of the Texas Property and Casualty Guaranty Association. He is a past president of the American Risk and Insurance Association, the premier academic organization in risk management and insurance in the world. He has published four books or monographs and over 130 scientific research papers. He regularly teaches classes involving insurance and risk management. He received his PhD in mathematics in 1975 from the University of California at Irvine, California.

E-mail: utpatrickbrockett@gmail.com.

YEHUDA KAHANE

Dr. Yehuda Kahane is active in both the academic and business areas. He is a professor of insurance and finance, Faculty of Management, Tel Aviv University, and head of the Akirov Institute for Business and the Environment. He founded and served as the dean of the first academic school of insurance in Israel (now a part of Netanya Academic College). At Tel Aviv University he directed the Erhard Insurance Center and the actuarial studies program and coordinated the executive development program. He is a life and nonlife actuary.

Over more than forty years, Dr. Kahane has taught at universities around the globe, including the Wharton School at the University of Pennsylvania, the University of Texas at Austin, the Hebrew University of Jerusalem, the University of Florida, and the University of Toronto, among others. He founded and has directed the Israel CLU program. He has also organized and lectured in hundreds of seminars and conferences.

Dr. Kahane, the author of several books and numerous articles, was ranked among the most prolific researchers in insurance (*Journal of Risk and Insurance*, June 1990). In the late 1960s he was among the pioneers that applied multiple regressions for insurance rate making. In the early 1970s he developed the concept of balancing assets and liabilities of financial intermediaries, in works that are still quoted thirty years later. These studies laid the foundations for theories of insurance rate making, solvency, insurance regulation, and the vast area that is now known as ERM—enterprise risk management. He has major contributions to the theory and practice of loss reserving, agriculture and crop insurance, and the use of data mining in insurance.

Dr. Kahane also has a rich entrepreneurial experience. He is a co-founder, director, and major shareholder in Ituran Location and Control (ITRN). He was a co-initiator of the concept of "new" balanced pension funds in Israel and was the co-founder and co-owner of the managing firm of the first fund (Teshura) that became the fourth largest fund in Israel in 1995. He is highly involved in the formation and management of start-up companies in a variety of advanced and high-tech areas, specializing in seed money investments. He owns the Weizman Hi-Tech Incubator and is a co-owner of Capital Point Ltd. (traded on TASE), which owns Ofakim and Kazrin technological incubators. In addition, he is involved in many voluntary NGO activities, including the PIBF—Palestinian International Business Forum—and chairman of the Association of Visually Impaired People in Sharon District, Or Yarok—an association for prevention of traffic accident victims.

He started his business career in a large multinational corporation and in the management of various businesses. In addition, he served as a consultant on risk management, insurance, and actuarial and financial topics to the government, large organizations, and major companies both in Israel and internationally. Dr. Kahane has served on the Israeli Insurance Council and on several government committees on a variety of insurance-related topics.

Dr. Kahane earned a BA in economics and statistics in 1965, an MA in business administration, cum laude, in 1967, and a PhD in finance in 1973, all from the Hebrew University of Jerusalem. He has served as an associate editor of the leading journals on risk and insurance. He has taught courses in technological forecasting (the first teacher of this subject in Israel), finance, insurance, risk management, and actuarial topics. His research focus is on the portfolio implications for insurance, rate making, automobile insurance, natural hazards, pension and life insurance, reserving, and environmental risks.

E-mail: kahane@post.tau.ac.il.

Site: http://recanati.tau.ac.il/~kahane.

Acknowledgments

We would like to give special acknowledgment to Jeff Shelstad at Flat World Knowledge for his unequivocal support. This new publishing operation has proven outstanding.

We would also like to thank the following colleagues who have reviewed the text and provided comprehensive feedback and suggestions for improving the material:

- Saul Adelman, Miami University of Ohio
- Murat Binay, Drucker School of Management
- Yilin Chen, University of Georgia
- Cassadra Cole, Florida State University
- Juli-Ann Gasper, Creighton University
- Andre Liebenberg, University of Mississippi
- Robert Puelz, Southern Methodist University
- Peter Ritchken, Case Western University
- Stanley Ross, Bridgewater State College
- Jennifer Soost, Bethany Lutheran College
- Ajay Subramanian, Georgia State University
- Gil Taran, Carnegie Mellon University

Dedications

ETTI BARANOFF

To my family, to Steve, Dalit and Josh, Liat and Jeremy, Aviva, Sammy, Elie and Mia for making it all so wonderfully possible.

PAT BROCKETT

To Linda Golden, Angela Brockett, and Russell Brockett with all my love.

YEHUDA KAHANE

To my family, colleagues, and students all around the world. Let us create a safe, healthy, just, and sustainable world, with a healthy economy and ecology, while everybody is enjoying the process of change. The key to success is to have successors!

Preface

INTRODUCTION AND BACKGROUND

This textbook is designed to reflect the dynamic nature of the field of risk management as an introduction to intermediate-level students. With co-author experts Etti Baranoff, Patrick L. Brockett, and Yehuda Kahane, the timely issues of the field are kept alive. The catastrophes of the first decade of the new millennium, including the credit crisis of 2008–2009, are well depicted and used to illustrate the myriad of old and new risks of our times. With such major man-made and natural catastrophes, this field is of utmost importance for sustainability. The need to educate students to consider risks at every phase in a business undertaking is central, and this textbook provides such educational foundation.

This field requires timeliness as new risk management techniques and products are being developed in response to risks derived from innovations and sophistication. As such, this book allows the reader to be on the forefront of knowledge in the arena of risk management. Tomorrow's leaders in business and politics and tomorrow's citizens, consumers, and voters need to understand risks to make successful decisions. This book provides you with the background for doing so.

With the pedagogical enhancements of Flat World Knowledge and the ability to make changes dynamically, this textbook brings the best to educators. An important advantage of this book's publication format is that it can be updated in real time online as new risks appear (e.g., pandemic risk, financial crisis, terrorist attacks). Risk management consequences can be discussed immediately.

The management of risk is, essentially, the strategy for surviving and thriving in a volatile, uncertain, complex, and ambiguous world. Prior to the industrial revolution and the advanced communication age, decisions could be made easily using heuristics or "gut level feel" based on past experience. As long as the world faced by the decision maker was more or less the same as that faced yesterday, gut level decision making worked fairly well. The consequences of failure were concentrated in small locations. Entire villages were extinguished due to lack of crop risk planning or diseases. There were no systemic contagious interlocking risks, such as those that brought the financial markets to their knees worldwide in 2008–2009.

Today the stakes are higher; the decision making is more complex, and consequences more severe, global, and fundamental. Risk managers have become part of executive teams with titles, such as chief risk officer (CRO), and are empowered to bridge across all business activities with short-term, long-term, and far-reaching goals. The credit crisis revealed that lack of understanding of risks, and their combined and correlated ramifications has far-reaching consequences worldwide. The study of risk management is designed to give business stakeholders the weapons necessary to foresee and combat potential calamities both internal to the business and external to society overall. The "green movement" is an important risk management focus.

At the time of this writing (December 2009), more than 190 nations' leaders are gathered at the Copenhagen Climate Summit to come to some resolutions about saving Earth. The evolution into industrialized nations brought a sense of urgency to finding risk management solutions to risks posed by the supply chain of production with wastes flowing into the environment, polluting the air and waters. The rapid population growth in countries such as China and India that joined the industrialized nations accelerated the ecological destruction of the water and air and has impacted our food chain. The UN 2005 World Millennium Ecosystem Report—a document written by thousands of scientists—displays a gloomy picture of the current and expected future situation of our air, water, land, flora, and fauna. The environmental issue has become important on risk managers' agendas.

Other global worries that fall into the risk management arena are new diseases, such as the mutation in the H1N1 (swine) flu virus with the bird flu (50 percent mortality rate of infected). One of China's leading disease experts and the director of the Guangzhou Institute of Respiratory Diseases predicted that the combined effect of both H1N1 (swine) and the H5N1 (bird) flu viruses could become a disastrous deadly hybrid with high mortality due to its efficient transmission among people. With systemic and pervasive travel and communication, such diseases are no longer localized environmental risks and are at the forefront of both individuals' and firms' risks.

With these global risks in mind and other types of risks, as are featured throughout the textbook, this book enables students to work with risks effectively. In addition, you will be able to launch your professional career with a deep sense of understanding of the importance of the long-term handling of risks.

Critical to the modern management of risk is the realization that all risks should be treated in a holistic, global, and integrated manner, as opposed to having individual divisions within a firm treating the risk separately. Enterprise-wide risk management was named one of the top ten breakthrough ideas in business by the *Harvard Business Review* in 2004.[1] Throughout, this book also takes this enterprise risk management perspective as well.

FEATURES

- **An emphasis on the big picture—the Links section**. Every chapter begins with an introduction and a links section to highlight the relationships between various concepts and components of risk and risk management, so that students know how the pieces fit together. This feature is to ensure the holistic aspects of risk management are always upfront.

- **Every chapter is focused on the risk management aspects**. While many solutions are insurance solutions, the main objective of this textbook is to ensure the student realizes the fact that insurance is a risk management solution. As such there are details explaining insurance in many chapters—from the nature of insurance in Chapter 6, to insurance operations and markets in Chapter 7 and Chapter 8, to specifics of insurance contracts and insurance coverage throughout the whole text.

- **Chapter 1 and Chapter 2 are completely dedicated to explaining risks and risk measurement.**

- **Chapter 3 was created by Dr. Puneet Prakash to introduce the concepts of attitudes toward risk and the solutions.**

- **Chapter 4 and Chapter 5 provide risk management techniques along with financial risk management.**

- **Chapter 17–Chapter 22 focus on all aspects of risk management throughout the life cycle**. These can be used to study employee benefits as a special course.

- **Cases** are embedded within each chapter, and boxes feature issues that represent ethical dilemmas. Chapter 23 provides extra risk management and employee benefits cases.

- **Student-friendly**. A clear, readable writing style helps to keep a complicated subject from becoming overwhelming. Most important is the pedagogical structure of the Flat World Knowledge system.

CHAPTER 1
The Nature of Risk: Losses and Opportunities

In his novel *A Tale of Two Cities*, set during the French Revolution of the late eighteenth century, Charles Dickens wrote, "It was the best of times; it was the worst of times." Dickens may have been premature, since the same might well be said now, at the beginning of the twenty-first century.

When we think of large risks, we often think in terms of natural hazards such as hurricanes, earthquakes, or tornados. Perhaps man-made disasters come to mind—such as the terrorist attacks that occurred in the United States on September 11, 2001. We typically have overlooked financial crises, such as the credit crisis of 2008. However, these types of man-made disasters have the potential to devastate the global marketplace. Losses in multiple trillions of dollars and in much human suffering and insecurity are already being totaled as the U.S. Congress fights over a $700 billion bailout. The financial markets are collapsing as never before seen.

Many observers consider this credit crunch, brought on by subprime mortgage lending and deregulation of the credit industry, to be the worst global financial calamity ever. Its unprecedented worldwide consequences have hit country after country—in many cases even harder than they hit the United States.[1] The world is now a global village; we're so fundamentally connected that past regional disasters can no longer be contained locally.

We can attribute the 2008 collapse to financially risky behavior of a magnitude never before experienced. Its implications dwarf any other disastrous events. The 2008 U.S. credit markets were a financial house of cards with a faulty foundation built by unethical behavior in the financial markets:

1. Lenders gave home mortgages without prudent risk management to underqualified home buyers, starting the so-called subprime mortgage crisis.

2. Many mortgages, including subprime mortgages, were bundled into new instruments called mortgage-backed securities, which were guaranteed by U.S. government agencies such as Fannie Mae and Freddie Mac.

3. These new bundled instruments were sold to financial institutions around the world. Bundling the investments gave these institutions the impression that the diversification effect would in some way protect them from risk.

4. Guarantees that were supposed to safeguard these instruments, called credit default swaps, were designed to take care of an assumed few defaults on loans, but they needed to safeguard against a systemic failure of many loans.

5. Home prices started to decline simultaneously as many of the unqualified subprime mortgage holders had to begin paying larger monthly payments. They could not refinance at lower interest rates as rates rose after the 9/11 attacks.

FIGURE 1.1 Complete Picture of the Holistic Risk Puzzle

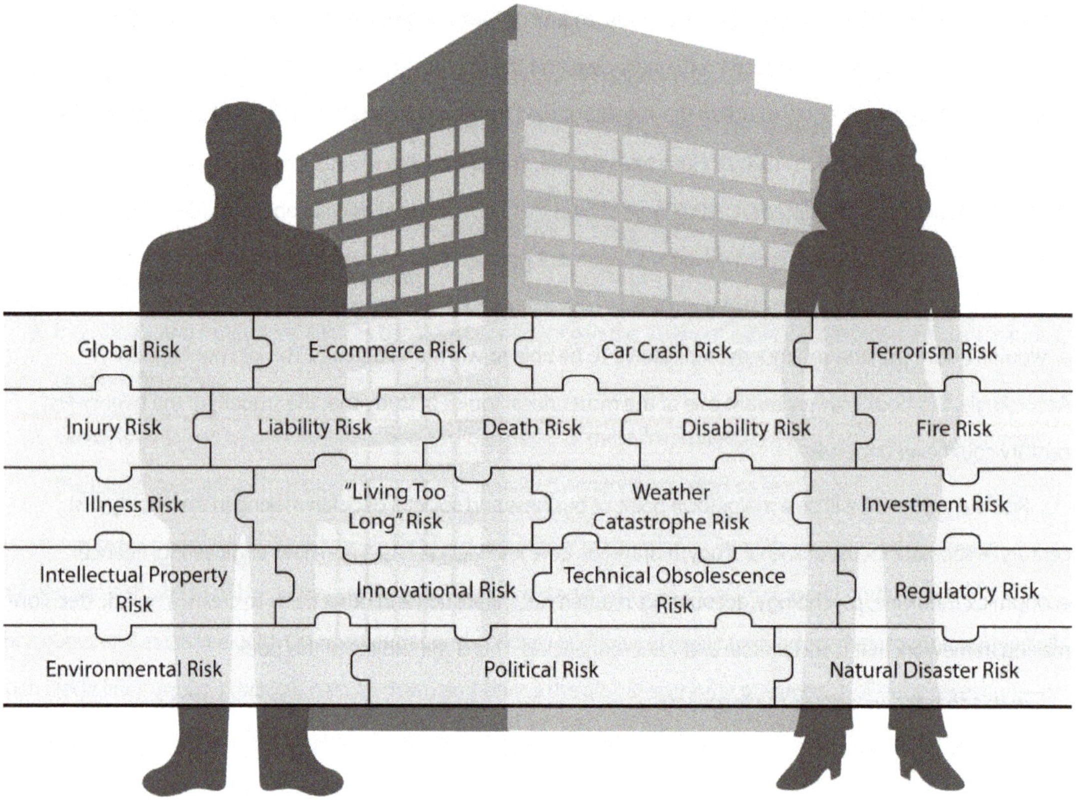

Global Risk	E-commerce Risk	Car Crash Risk	Terrorism Risk
Injury Risk	Liability Risk	Death Risk	Disability Risk	Fire Risk
Illness Risk	"Living Too Long" Risk	Weather Catastrophe Risk	Investment Risk
Intellectual Property Risk	Innovational Risk	Technical Obsolescence Risk	Regulatory Risk
Environmental Risk	Political Risk	Natural Disaster Risk

systemic financial risk

Risk that affects everything, as opposed to individuals being involved in risky enterprises.

Even in chapters that you may not think apply to the individual, such as commercial risk, the connection will highlight the underlying relationships among different risks. Today, management of personal and commercial risks requires coordination of all facets of the risk spectrum. On a national level, we experienced the move toward holistic risk management with the creation of the Department of Homeland Security after the terrorist attacks of September 11, 2001.[4] After Hurricane Katrina struck in 2005, the impasse among local, state, and federal officials elevated the need for coordination to achieve efficient holistic risk management in the event of a megacatastrophe.[5] The global financial crisis of 2008 created unprecedented coordination of regulatory actions across countries and, further, governmental involvement in managing risk at the enterprise level—essentially a global holistic approach to managing **systemic financial risk**. Systemic risk is a risk that affects everything, as opposed to individuals being involved in risky enterprises. In the next section, we define all types of risks more formally.

2. THE NOTION AND DEFINITION OF RISK

LEARNING OBJECTIVES

- In this section, you will learn the concept of risk and differentiate between risk and uncertainty.
- You will build the definition of risk as a consequence of uncertainty and within a continuum of decision-making roles.

The notion of "risk" and its ramifications permeate decision-making processes in each individual's life and business outcomes and of society itself. Indeed, risk, and how it is managed, are critical aspects of decision making at all levels. We must evaluate profit opportunities in business and in personal terms in terms of the countervailing risks they engender. We must evaluate solutions to problems (global, political, financial, and individual) on a risk-cost, cost-benefit basis rather than on an absolute basis. Because of risk's all-pervasive presence in our daily lives, you might be surprised that the word "risk" is hard to pin down. For example, what does a businessperson mean when he or she says, "This project should be rejected since it is too risky"? Does it mean that the amount of loss is too high or that the expected value of the loss is high? Is the expected profit on the project too small to justify the consequent risk exposure and the potential losses that might ensue? The reality is that the term "risk" (as used in the English language) is ambiguous in this regard. One might use any of the previous interpretations. Thus, professionals try to use different words to delineate each of these different interpretations. We will discuss possible interpretations in what follows.

2.1   Risk as a Consequence of Uncertainty

We all have a personal intuition about what we mean by the term "risk." We all use and interpret the word daily. We have all felt the excitement, anticipation, or anxiety of facing a new and uncertain event (the "tingling" aspect of risk taking). Thus, actually giving a single unambiguous definition of what we mean by the notion of "risk" proves to be somewhat difficult. The word "risk" is used in many different contexts. Further, the word takes many different interpretations in these varied contexts. In all cases, however, the notion of risk is inextricably linked to the notion of **uncertainty**. We provide here a simple definition of uncertainty: *Uncertainty is having two potential outcomes for an event or situation.*

Certainty refers to knowing something will happen or won't happen. We may experience no doubt in certain situations. Nonperfect predictability arises in uncertain situations. *Uncertainty* causes the emotional (or physical) anxiety or excitement felt in uncertain volatile situations. Gambling and participation in extreme sports provide examples. Uncertainty causes us to take precautions. We simply need to avoid certain business activities or involvements that we consider too risky. For example, uncertainty causes mortgage issuers to demand property purchase insurance. The person or corporation occupying the mortgage-funded property must purchase insurance on real estate if we intend to lend them money. If we knew, without a doubt, that something bad was about to occur, we would call it apprehension or dread. It wouldn't be risk because it would be predictable. Risk will be forever, inextricably linked to uncertainty.

As we all know, certainty is elusive. Uncertainty and risk are pervasive. While we typically associate "risk" with unpleasant or negative events, in reality some risky situations can result in positive outcomes. Take, for example, venture capital investing or entrepreneurial endeavors. *Uncertainty* about which of several possible outcomes will occur circumscribes the meaning of risk. Uncertainty lies behind the definition of risk.

While we link the concept of risk with the notion of uncertainty, risk isn't synonymous with uncertainty. A person experiencing the flu is not necessarily the same as the virus causing the flu. Risk isn't the same as the underlying prerequisite of uncertainty. **Risk** (intuitively and formally) has to do with consequences (both positive and negative); it involves having more than two possible outcomes (uncertainty).[6] The consequences can be behavioral, psychological, or financial, to name a few. Uncertainty also creates opportunities for gain and the potential for loss. Nevertheless, if no possibility of a negative outcome arises at all, even remotely, then we usually do not refer to the situation as having risk (only uncertainty) as shown in Figure 1.2.

uncertainty

Having two potential outcomes for an event or situation.

risk

Uncertainty about a future outcome, particularly the consequences of a negative outcome.

FIGURE 1.2 Uncertainty as a Precondition to Risk

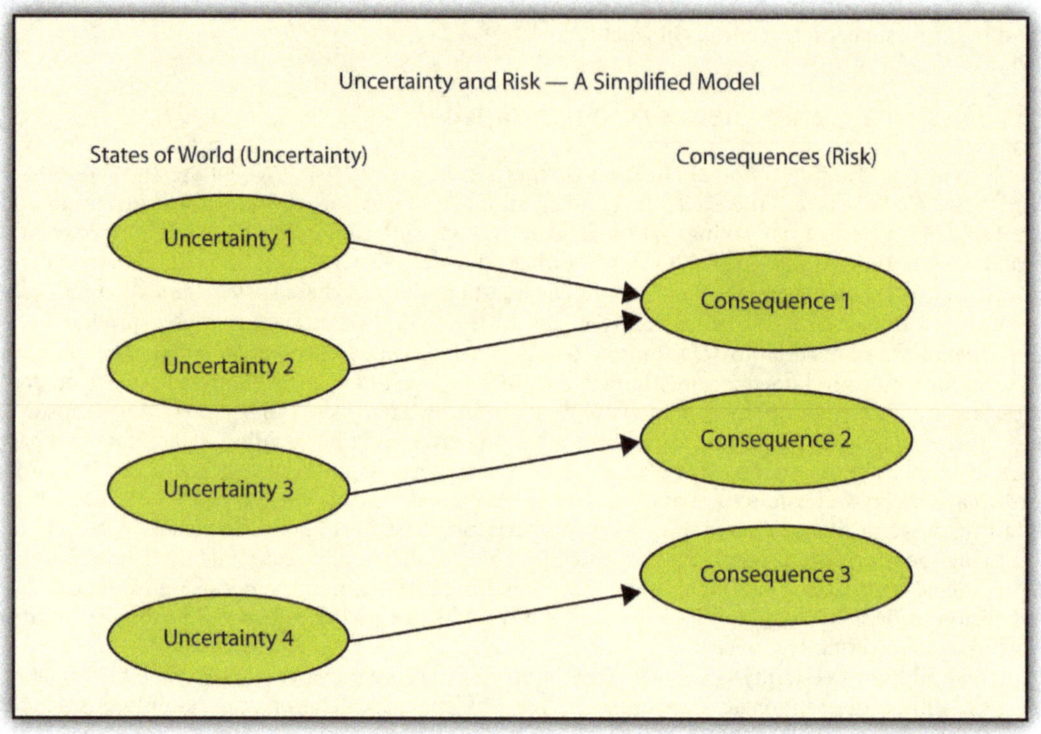

Uncertainty and Risk — A Simplified Model

States of World (Uncertainty)   Consequences (Risk)

TABLE 1.1 Examples of Consequences That Represent Risks

States of the World —Uncertainty	Consequences—Risk
Could or could not get caught driving under the influence of alcohol	Loss of respect by peers (non-numerical); higher car insurance rates or cancellation of auto insurance at the extreme.
Potential variety in interest rates over time	Numerical variation in money returned from investment.
Various levels of real estate foreclosures	Losses from financial instruments linked to mortgage defaults or some domino effect such as the one that starts this chapter.
Smoking cigarettes at various numbers per day	Bad health changes (such as cancer and heart disease) and problems shortening length and quality of life. Inability to contract with life insurance companies at favorable rates.
Power plant and automobile emission of greenhouse gasses (CO_2)	Global warming, melting of ice caps, rising of oceans, increase in intensity of weather events, displacement of populations; possible extinction or mutations in some populations.

In general, we widely believe in an a priori (previous to the event) relation between negative risk and profitability. Namely, we believe that in a competitive economic market, we must take on a larger possibility of negative risk if we are to achieve a higher return on an investment. Thus, we must take on a larger possibility of negative risk to receive a favorable rate of return. Every opportunity involves both risk and return.

2.2   The Role of Risk in Decision Making

In a world of uncertainty, we regard risk as encompassing the potential provision of both an opportunity for gains as well as the negative prospect for losses. See Figure 1.3—a Venn diagram to help you visualize risk-reward outcomes. For the enterprise and for individuals, risk is a component to be considered within a general objective of maximizing value associated with risk. Alternatively, we wish to minimize the dangers associated with financial collapse or other adverse consequences. The right circle of the figure represents mitigation of adverse consequences like failures. The left circle represents the opportunities of gains when risks are undertaken. As with most Venn diagrams, the two circles intersect to create the set of opportunities for which people take on risk (Circle 1) for reward (Circle 2).

FIGURE 1.3 Roles (Objectives) Underlying the Definition of Risk

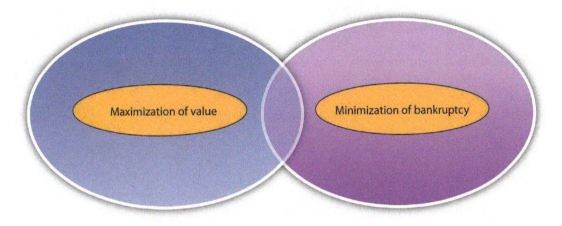

Identify the overlapping area as the set in which we both minimize risk and maximize value.

Figure 1.3 will help you conceptualize the impact of risk. Risk permeates the spectrum of decision making from goals of value maximization to goals of insolvency minimization (in game theory terms, maximin). Here we see that we seek to add value from the opportunities presented by uncertainty (and its consequences). The overlapping area shows a tight focus on minimizing the pure losses that might accompany insolvency or bankruptcy. The 2008 financial crisis illustrates the consequences of exploiting opportunities presented by risk; of course, we must also account for the risk and can't ignore the requisite adverse consequences associated with insolvency. Ignoring risk represents mismanagement of risk in the opportunity-seeking context. It can bring complete calamity and total loss in the pure loss-avoidance context.

We will discuss this trade-off more in depth later in the book. Managing risks associated with the context of minimization of losses has succeeded more than managing risks when we use an objective of value maximization. People model catastrophic consequences that involve risk of loss and insolvency in natural disaster contexts, using complex and innovative statistical techniques. On the other hand, risk management within the context of maximizing value hasn't yet adequately confronted the potential for catastrophic consequences. The potential for catastrophic human-made financial risk is most dramatically illustrated by the fall 2008 financial crisis. No catastrophic models were considered or developed to counter managers' value maximization objective, nor were regulators imposing risk constraints on the catastrophic potential of the various financial derivative instruments.

2.3   Definitions of Risk

We previously noted that risk is a *consequence* of uncertainty—it isn't uncertainty itself. To broadly cover all possible scenarios, we don't specify exactly what type of "consequence of uncertainty" we were considering as risk. In the popular lexicon of the English language, the "consequence of uncertainty" is that the observed outcome deviates from what we had expected. Consequences, you will recall, can be positive or negative. If the deviation from what was expected is negative, we have the popular notion of risk. "Risk" arises from a negative outcome, which may result from recognizing an uncertain situation.

If we try to get an *ex-post (i.e., after the fact) risk* measure, we can measure risk as the perceived variability of future outcomes. Actual outcomes may differ from expectations. Such variability of future outcomes corresponds to the economist's notion of risk. Risk is intimately related to the "surprise an outcome presents." Various actual quantitative risk measurements provide the topic of Chapter 2. Another simple example appears by virtue of our day-to-day expectations. For example, we expect to arrive on time to a particular destination. A variety of obstacles may stop us from actually arriving on time. The obstacles may be within our own behavior or stand externally. However, some uncertainty arises as to whether such an obstacle will happen, resulting in deviation from our previous expectation. As another example, when American Airlines had to ground all their MD-80 planes for government-required inspections, many of us had to cancel our travel plans and couldn't attend important planned meetings and celebrations. Air travel always carries with it the possibility that we will be grounded, which gives rise to uncertainty. In fact, we experienced this negative event because it was externally imposed upon us. We thus experienced a loss because we deviated from our plans. Other deviations from expectations could include being in an accident rather than a fun outing. The possibility of lower-than-expected (negative) outcomes becomes central to the definition of risk, because so-called losses produce the negative quality associated with not knowing the future. We must then manage the negative consequences of the uncertain future. This is the essence of risk management.

Our perception of risk arises from our perception of and quantification of uncertainty. In scientific settings and in actuarial and financial contexts, risk is usually expressed in terms of the probability of occurrence of adverse events. In other fields, such as political risk assessment, risk may be very qualitative or subjective. This is also the subject of Chapter 2.

KEY TAKEAWAYS

- Uncertainty is precursor to risk.
- Risk is a consequence of uncertainty; risk can be emotional, financial, or reputational.
- The roles of Maximization of Value and Minimization of Losses form a continuum on which risk is anchored.
- One consequence of uncertainty is that actual outcomes may vary from what is expected and as such represents risk.

DISCUSSION QUESTIONS

1. What is the relationship between uncertainty and risk?
2. What roles contribute to the definition of risk?
3. What examples fit under uncertainties and consequences? Which are the risks?
4. What is the formal definition of risk?
5. What examples can you cite of quantitative consequences of uncertainty and a qualitative or emotional consequence of uncertainty?

---

3. ATTITUDES TOWARD RISKS

LEARNING OBJECTIVES

- **In this section, you will learn that people's attitudes toward risk affect their decision making.**
- **You will learn about the three major types of "risk attitudes."**

risk averse

Refers to shying away from risks and preferring to have as much security and certainty as is reasonably affordable.

An in-depth exploration into individual and firms' attitudes toward risk appears in Chapter 3. Here we touch upon this important subject, since it is key to understanding behavior associated with risk management activities. The following box illustrates risk as a psychological process. Different people have different attitudes toward the risk-return tradeoff. People are **risk averse** when they shy away from risks and prefer to have as much security and certainty as is reasonably affordable in order to lower their discomfort level. They would be willing to pay extra to have the security of knowing that unpleasant risks would be removed from their lives. Economists and risk management professionals consider most people to be risk averse. So, why do people invest in the stock market where they confront the possibility of losing everything? Perhaps they are also seeking the highest value possible for their pensions and savings and believe that losses may not be pervasive—very much unlike the situation in the fall of 2008.

risk seeker

Someone who will enter into an endeavor as long as a positive long run return on the money is possible, however unlikely.

A **risk seeker**, on the other hand, is not simply the person who hopes to maximize the value of retirement investments by investing the stock market. Much like a gambler, a risk seeker is someone who will enter into an endeavor (such as blackjack card games or slot machine gambling) as long as a positive long run return on the money is possible, however unlikely.

Finally, an entity is said to be **risk neutral** when its risk preference lies in between these two extremes. Risk neutral individuals will not pay extra to have the risk transferred to someone else, nor will they pay to engage in a risky endeavor. To them, money is money. They don't pay for insurance, nor will they gamble. Economists consider most widely held or publicly traded corporations as making decisions in a risk-neutral manner since their shareholders have the ability to **diversify away risk**—to take actions that seemingly are not related or have opposite effects, or to invest in many possible unrelated products or entities such that the impact of any one event decreases the overall risk. Risks that the corporation might choose to transfer remain for diversification. In the fall of 2008, everyone *felt* like a gambler. This emphasizes just how fluidly risk lies on a continuum like that in Figure 1.3. Financial theories and research pay attention to the nature of the behavior of firms in their pursuit to maximize value. Most theories agree that firms work within risk limits to ensure they do not "go broke." In the following box we provide a brief discussion of people's attitudes toward risk. A more elaborate discussion can be found in Chapter 3.

Feelings Associated with Risk

Early in our lives, while protected by our parents, we enjoy security. But imagine yourself as your parents (if you can) during the first years of your life. A game called "Risk Balls" was created to illustrate tangibly how we handle and transfer risk.[7] See, for example, Figure 1.4 below. The balls represent risks, such as dying prematurely, losing a home to fire, or losing one's ability to earn an income because of illness or injury. Risk balls bring the abstract and **fortuitous** (accidental or governed by chance) nature of risk into a more tangible context. If you held these balls, you would want to dispose of them as soon as you possibly could. One way to dispose of risks (represented by these risk balls) is by transferring the risk to insurance companies or other firms that specialize in accepting risks. We will cover the benefits of transferring risk in many chapters of this text.

Right now, we focus on the risk itself. What do you actually *feel* when you hold the risk balls? Most likely, your answer would be, "insecurity and uneasiness." We associate risks with fears. A person who is risk averse—that is, a "normal person" who shies away from risk and prefers to have as much security and certainty as possible—would wish to lower the level of fear. Professionals consider most of us risk averse. We sleep better at night when we can transfer risk to the capital market. The capital market usually appears to us as an insurance company or the community at large.

As risk-averse individuals, we will often pay in excess of the expected cost just to achieve some certainty about the future. When we pay an insurance premium, for example, we forgo wealth in exchange for an insurer's promise to pay covered losses. Some risk transfer professionals refer to premiums as an exchange of a certain loss (the premium) for uncertain losses that may cause us to lose sleep. One important aspect of this kind of exchange: premiums are larger than are expected losses. Those who are willing to pay only the average loss as a premium would be considered risk neutral. Someone who accepts risk at less than the average loss, perhaps even paying to add risk—such as through gambling—is a risk seeker.

FIGURE 1.4   Risk Balls

risk neutral

When one's risk preference lies between the extremes of risk averse and risk seeking.

diversify away risk

To take actions that are seemingly not related or have opposite effects or to invest in many possible unrelated products or entities such that the impact of any one event decreases the overall risk.

fortuitous

A matter of chance.

KEY TAKEAWAY

- Differentiate among the three risk attitudes that prevail in our lives—risk averse, risk neutral, and risk seeker.

DISCUSSION QUESTIONS

1. Name three risk attitudes that people display.
2. How do those risk attitudes fits into roles that lie behind the definition of risks?

4.3 Property Loss Exposures—Property Pure Risk

consequential or indirect losses

A nonphysical loss such as loss of business.

property loss exposures

Losses associated with both real property such as buildings and personal property such as automobiles and the contents of a building.

Property owners face the possibility of both direct and indirect (consequential) losses. If a car is damaged in a collision, the direct loss is the cost of repairs. If a firm experiences a fire in the warehouse, the direct cost is the cost of rebuilding and replacing inventory. **Consequential or indirect losses** are nonphysical losses such as loss of business. For example, a firm losing its clients because of street closure would be a consequential loss. Such losses include the time and effort required to arrange for repairs, the loss of use of the car or warehouse while repairs are being made, and the additional cost of replacement facilities or lost productivity. **Property loss exposures** are associated with both real property such as buildings and personal property such as automobiles and the contents of a building. A property is exposed to losses because of accidents or catastrophes such as floods or hurricanes.

4.4 Liability Loss Exposures—Liability Pure Risk

liability loss

Loss caused by a third party who is considered at fault.

The legal system is designed to mitigate risks and is not intended to create new risks. However, it has the power of transferring the risk from your shoulders to mine. Under most legal systems, a party can be held responsible for the financial consequences of causing damage to others. One is exposed to the possibility of **liability loss** (loss caused by a third party who is considered at fault) by having to defend against a lawsuit when he or she has in some way hurt other people. The responsible party may become legally obligated to pay for injury to persons or damage to property. Liability risk may occur because of catastrophic loss exposure or because of accidental loss exposure. Product liability is an illustrative example: a firm is responsible for compensating persons injured by supplying a defective product, which causes damage to an individual or another firm.

4.5 Catastrophic Loss Exposure and Fundamental or Systemic Pure Risk

fundamental risk or systemic risk

Risks that are pervasive to and affect the whole economy, as opposed to accidental risk for an individual.

Catastrophic risk is a concentration of strong, positively correlated risk exposures, such as many homes in the same location. A loss that is catastrophic and includes a large number of exposures in a single location is considered a nonaccidental risk. All homes in the path will be damaged or destroyed when a flood occurs. As such the flood impacts a large number of exposures, and as such, all these exposures are subject to what is called a **fundamental risk**. Generally these types of risks are too pervasive to be undertaken by insurers and affect the whole economy as opposed to accidental risk for an individual. Too many people or properties may be hurt or damaged in one location at once (and the insurer needs to worry about its own solvency). Hurricanes in Florida and the southern and eastern shores of the United States, floods in the Midwestern states, earthquakes in the western states, and terrorism attacks are the types of loss exposures that are associated with fundamental risk. Fundamental risks are generally systemic and nondiversifiable.

FIGURE 1.5 A Photo of Galveston Island after Hurricane Ike

4.6 Accidental Loss Exposure and Particular Pure Risk

Many pure risks arise due to accidental causes of loss, not due to man-made or intentional ones (such as making a bad investment). As opposed to fundamental losses, noncatastrophic accidental losses, such as those caused by fires, are considered particular risks. Often, when the potential losses are reasonably bounded, a risk-transfer mechanism, such as insurance, can be used to handle the financial consequences.

In summary, exposures are units that are exposed to possible losses. They can be people, businesses, properties, and nations that are at risk of experiencing losses. The term "exposures" is used to include all units subject to some potential loss.

Another possible categorization of exposures is as follows:

- Risks of nature
  - Risks related to human nature (theft, burglary, embezzlement, fraud)
- Man-made risks
- Risks associated with data and knowledge
- Risks associated with the legal system (liability)—it does not create the risks but it may shift them to your arena
- Risks related to large systems: governments, armies, large business organizations, political groups
- Intellectual property

Pure and speculative risks are not the only way one might dichotomize risks. Another breakdown is between catastrophic risks, such as flood and hurricanes, as opposed to accidental losses such as those caused by accidents such as fires. Another differentiation is by systemic or nondiversifiable risks, as opposed to idiosyncratic or diversifiable risks; this is explained below.

4.7 Diversifiable and Nondiversifiable Risks

As noted above, another important dichotomy risk professionals use is between diversifiable and non-diversifiable risk. **Diversifiable risks** are those that can have their adverse consequences mitigated simply by having a well-diversified portfolio of risk exposures. For example, having some factories located in nonearthquake areas or hotels placed in numerous locations in the United States diversifies the risk. If one property is damaged, the others are not subject to the same geographical phenomenon causing the risks. A large number of relatively homogeneous independent exposure units pooled together in a portfolio can make the average, or per exposure, unit loss much more predictable, and since these exposure units are independent of each other, the per-unit consequences of the risk can then be significantly reduced, sometimes to the point of being ignorable. These will be further explored in a later chapter about the tools to mitigate risks. Diversification is the core of the modern portfolio theory in finance and in insurance. Risks, which are **idiosyncratic** (with particular characteristics that are not shared by all) in nature, are often viewed as being amenable to having their financial consequences reduced or eliminated by holding a well-diversified portfolio.

Systemic risks that are shared by all, on the other hand, such as global warming, or movements of the entire economy such as that precipitated by the credit crisis of fall 2008, are considered nondiversifiable. Every asset or exposure in the portfolio is affected. The negative effect does not go away by having more elements in the portfolio. This will be discussed in detail below and in later chapters. The field of risk management deals with both diversifiable and nondiversifiable risks. As the events of September 2008 have shown, contrary to some interpretations of financial theory, the idiosyncratic risks of some banks could not always be diversified away. These risks have shown they have the ability to come back to bite (and poison) the entire enterprise and others associated with them.

Table 1.3 provides examples of risk exposures by the categories of diversifiable and nondiversifiable risk exposures. Many of them are self explanatory, but the most important distinction is whether the risk is unique or idiosyncratic to a firm or not. For example, the reputation of a firm is unique to the firm. Destroying one's reputation is not a systemic risk in the economy or the market-place. On the other hand, market risk, such as devaluation of the dollar is systemic risk for all firms in the export or import businesses. In Table 1.3 we provide examples of risks by these categories. The examples are not complete and the student is invited to add as many examples as desired.

diversifiable risks

Risks whose adverse consequences can be mitigated simply by having a well-diversified portfolio of risk exposures.

idiosyncratic

Risks viewed as being amenable to having their financial consequences reduced or eliminated by holding a well-diversified portfolio.

TABLE 1.3 Examples of Risk Exposures by the Diversifiable and Nondiversifiable Categories

Diversifiable Risk—Idiosyncratic Risk	Nondiversifiable Risks—Systemic Risk
• Reputational risk	• Market risk
• Brand risk	• Regulatory risk
• Credit risk (at the individual enterprise level)	• Environmental risk
• Product risk	• Political risk
• Legal risk	• Inflation and recession risk
• Physical damage risk (at the enterprise level) such as fire, flood, weather damage	• Accounting risk
• Liability risk (products liability, premise liability, employment practice liability)	• Longevity risk at the societal level
• Innovational or technical obsolesce risk	• Mortality and morbidity risk at the societal and global level (pandemics, social security program exposure, nationalize health care systems, etc.)
• Operational risk	
• Strategic risk	
• Longevity risk at the individual level	
• Mortality and morbidity risk at the individual level	

4.8 Enterprise Risks

As discussed above, the opportunities in the risks and the fear of losses encompass the holistic risk or the enterprise risk of an entity. The following is an example of the enterprise risks of life insurers in a map in Figure 1.6.[9]

Since enterprise risk management is a key current concept today, the enterprise risk map of life insurers is offered here as an example. Operational risks include public relations risks, environmental risks, and several others not detailed in the map in Figure 1.4. Because operational risks are so important, they usually include a long list of risks from employment risks to the operations of hardware and software for information systems.

FIGURE 1.6 Life Insurers' Enterprise Risks

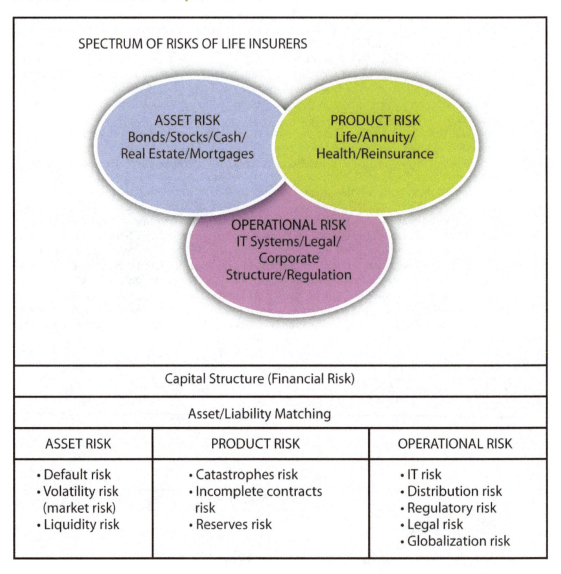

SPECTRUM OF RISKS OF LIFE INSURERS

ASSET RISK
Bonds/Stocks/Cash/
Real Estate/Mortgages

PRODUCT RISK
Life/Annuity/
Health/Reinsurance

OPERATIONAL RISK
IT Systems/Legal/
Corporate
Structure/Regulation

Capital Structure (Financial Risk)		
Asset/Liability Matching		
ASSET RISK	PRODUCT RISK	OPERATIONAL RISK
• Default risk • Volatility risk (market risk) • Liquidity risk	• Catastrophes risk • Incomplete contracts risk • Reserves risk	• IT risk • Distribution risk • Regulatory risk • Legal risk • Globalization risk

4.9 Risks in the Limelight

Our great successes in innovation are also at the heart of the greatest risks of our lives. An ongoing concern is the electronic risk (e-risk) generated by the extensive use of computers, e-commerce, and the Internet. These risks are extensive and the exposures are becoming more defined. The box "The Risks of E-exposures" below illustrates the newness and not-so-newness in our risks.

The Risks of E-exposures

Electronic risk, or e-risk, comes in many forms. Like any property, computers are vulnerable to theft and employee damage (accidental or malicious). Certain components are susceptible to harm from magnetic or electrical disturbance or extremes of temperature and humidity. More important than replaceable hardware or software is the data they store; theft of proprietary information costs companies billions of dollars. Most data theft is perpetrated by employees, but "netspionage"—electronic espionage by rival companies—is on the rise.

Companies that use the Internet commercially—who create and post content or sell services or merchandise—must follow the laws and regulations that traditional businesses do and are exposed to the same risks. An online newsletter or e-zine can be sued for libel, defamation, invasion of privacy, or misappropriation (e.g., reproducing a photograph without permission) under the same laws that apply to a print newspaper. Web site owners and companies conducting business over the Internet have three major exposures to protect: intellectual property (copyrights, patents, trade secrets); security (against viruses and hackers); and business continuity (in case of system crashes).

All of these losses are covered by insurance, right? Wrong. Some coverage is provided through commercial property and liability policies, but traditional insurance policies were not designed to include e-risks. In fact, standard policies specifically exclude digital risks (or provide minimal coverage). Commercial property policies cover physical damage to *tangible* assets—and computer data, software, programs, and networks are generally not counted as tangible property. (U.S. courts are still debating the issue.)

This coverage gap can be bridged either by buying a rider or supplemental coverage to the traditional policies or by purchasing special e-risk or e-commerce coverage. E-risk property policies cover damages to the insured's computer system or Web site, including lost income because of a computer crash. An increasing number of insurers are offering e-commerce liability policies that offer protection in case the insured is sued for spreading a computer virus, infringing on property or intellectual rights, invading privacy, and so forth.

Cybercrime is just one of the e-risk-related challenges facing today's risk managers. They are preparing for it as the world evolves faster around cyberspace, evidenced by record-breaking online sales during the 2005 Christmas season.

Sources: Harry Croydon, "Making Sense of Cyber-Exposures," National Underwriter, Property & Casualty/Risk & Benefits Management Edition, 17 June 2002; Joanne Wojcik, "Insurers Cut E-Risks from Policies," Business Insurance, 10 September 2001; Various media resources at the end of 2005 such as Wall Street Journal and local newspapers.

Today, there is no media that is not discussing the risks that brought us to the calamity we are enduring during our current financial crisis. Thus, as opposed to the megacatastrophes of 2001 and 2005, our concentration is on the failure of risk management in the area of speculative risks or the opportunity in risks and not as much on the pure risk. A case at point is the little media coverage of the devastation of Galveston Island from Hurricane Ike during the financial crisis of September 2008. The following box describes the risks of the first decade of the new millennium.

Risks in the New Millennium

While man-made and natural disasters are the stamps of this decade, another type of man-made disaster marks this period.[10] Innovative financial products without appropriate underwriting and risk management coupled with greed and lack of corporate controls brought us to the credit crisis of 2007 and 2008 and the deepest recession in a generation. The capital market has become an important player in the area of risk management with creative new financial instruments, such as Catastrophe Bonds and securitized instruments. However, the creativity and innovation also introduced new risky instruments, such as credit default swaps and mortgage-backed securities. Lack of careful underwriting of mortgages coupled with lack of understanding of the new creative "insurance" default swaps instruments and the resulting instability of the two largest remaining bond insurers are at the heart of the current credit crisis.

As such, within only one decade we see the escalation in new risk exposures at an accelerated rate. This decade can be named "*the decade of extreme risks with inadequate risk management.*" The late 1990s saw extreme risks with the stock market bubble without concrete financial theory. This was followed by the worst terrorist attack in a magnitude not experienced before on U.S. soil. The corporate corruption at extreme levels in corporations such as Enron just deepened the sense of extreme risks. The natural disasters of Katrina, Rita, and Wilma added to the extreme risks and were exacerbated by extraordinary mismanagement. Today, the extreme risks of mismanaged innovations in the financial markets combined with greed are stretching the field of risk management to new levels of governmental and private controls.

However, did the myopic concentration on terrorism risk derail the holistic view of risk management and preparedness? The aftermath of Katrina is a testimonial to the lack of risk management. The increase of awareness and usage of enterprise risk management (ERM) post–September 11 failed to encompass the already well-known risks of high-category hurricanes on the sustainability of New Orleans levies. The newly created holistic Homeland Security agency, which houses FEMA, not only did not initiate steps to avoid the disaster, it also did not take the appropriate steps to reduce the suffering of those afflicted once the risk materialized. This outcome also points to the importance of having a committed stakeholder who is vested in the outcome and cares to lower and mitigate the risk. Since the insurance industry did not own the risk of flood, there was a gap in the risk management. The focus on terrorism risk could be regarded as a contributing factor to the neglect of the natural disasters risk in New Orleans. The ground was fertile for mishandling the extreme hurricane catastrophes. Therefore, from such a viewpoint, it can be argued that September 11 derailed our comprehensive national risk management and contributed indirectly to the worsening of the effects of Hurricane Katrina.

Furthermore, in an era of financial technology and creation of innovative modeling for predicting the most infrequent catastrophes, the innovation and growth in human capacity is at the root of the current credit crisis. While the innovation allows firms such as Risk Management Solutions (RMS) and AIR Worldwide to provide models[11] that predict potential man-made and natural catastrophes, financial technology also advanced the creation of financial instruments, such as credit default derivatives and mortgage-backed securities. The creation of the products provided "black boxes" understood by few and without appropriate risk management. Engineers, mathematicians, and quantitatively talented people moved from the low-paying jobs in their respective fields into Wall Street. They used their skills to create models and new products but lacked the business acumen and the required safety net understanding to ensure product sustenance. Management of large financial institutions globally enjoyed the new creativity and endorsed the adoption of the new products without clear understanding of their potential impact or just because of greed. This lack of risk management is at the heart of the credit crisis of 2008. No wonder the credit rating organizations are now adding ERM scores to their ratings of companies.

The following quote is a key to today's risk management discipline: "Risk management has been a significant part of the insurance industry…, but in recent times it has developed a wider currency as an emerging management philosophy across the globe…. The challenge facing the risk management practitioner of the twenty-first century is not just breaking free of the mantra that risk management is all about insurance, and if we have insurance, then we have managed our risks, but rather being accepted as a provider of advice and service to the risk makers and the risk takers at all levels within the enterprise. It is the risk makers and the risk takers who must be the owners of risk and accountable for its effective management."[12]

KEY TAKEAWAYS

- You should be able to delineate the main categories of risks: pure versus speculative, diversifiable versus nondiversifiable, idiosyncratic versus systemic.
- You should also understand the general concept of enterprise-wide risk.
- Try to illustrate each cross classification of risk with examples.
- Can you discuss the risks of our decade?

DISCUSSION QUESTIONS

1. Name the main categories of risks.
2. Provide examples of risk categories.
3. How would you classify the risks embedded in the financial crisis of fall 2008 within each of cross-classification?
4. How does e-risk fit into the categories of risk?

5. PERILS AND HAZARDS

LEARNING OBJECTIVES

- In this section you will learn the terminology used by risk professionals to note different risk concepts.
- You will learn about causes of losses—perils and the hazards, which are the items increasing the chance of loss.

As we mentioned earlier, in English, people often use the word "risk" to describe a loss. Examples include hurricane risk or fraud risk. To differentiate between loss and risk, risk management professionals prefer to use the term **perils** to refer to "the causes of loss." If we wish to understand risk, we must first understand the terms "loss" and "perils." We will use both terms throughout this text. Both terms represent immediate causes of loss. The environment is filled with perils such as floods, theft, death, sickness, accidents, fires, tornadoes, and lightning—or even contaminated milk served to Chinese babies. We include a list of some perils below. Many important risk transfer contracts (such as insurance contracts) use the word "peril" quite extensively to define inclusions and exclusions within contracts. We will also explain these definitions in a legal sense later in the textbook to help us determine terms such as "residual risk retained."

perils
The causes of loss.

TABLE 1.4 Types of Perils by Ability to Insure

Natural Perils		Human Perils	
Generally Insurable	**Generally Difficult to Insure**	**Generally Insurable**	**Generally Difficult to Insure**
Windstorm	Flood	Theft	War
Lightning	Earthquake	Vandalism	Radioactive contamination
Natural combustion	Epidemic	Hunting accident	Civil unrest
Heart attacks	Volcanic eruption	Negligence	Terrorism
	Frost	Fire and smoke	
		Global	
		E-commerce	
		Mold	

Although professionals have attempted to categorize perils, doing so is difficult. We could talk about natural versus human perils. **Natural perils** are those over which people have little control, such as hurricanes, volcanoes, and lightning. **Human perils**, then, would include causes of loss that lie within individuals' control, including suicide, terrorism, war, theft, defective products, environmental contamination, terrorism, destruction of complex infrastructure, and electronic security breaches. Though some would include losses caused by the state of the economy as human perils, many professionals separate these into a third category labeled **economic perils**. Professionals also consider employee strikes, arson for profit, and similar situations to be economic perils.

We can also divide perils into insurable and noninsurable perils. Typically, noninsurable perils include those that may be considered catastrophic to an insurer. Such noninsurable perils may also encourage policyholders to cause loss. Insurers' problems rest with the security of its financial standing. For example, an insurer may decline to write a policy for perils that might threaten its own solvency (e.g., nuclear power plant liability) or those perils that might motivate insureds to cause a loss.

natural perils
Causes of losses over which people have little control.

human perils
Causes of losses that lie within individuals' control.

economic perils
Causes of losses resulting from the state of the economy.

5.1 Hazards

Risk professionals refer to **hazards** as conditions that increase the cause of losses. Hazards may increase the probability of losses, their frequency, their severity, or both. That is, **frequency** refers to the number of losses during a specified period. **Severity** refers to the average dollar value of a loss per occurrence, respectively. Professionals refer to certain conditions as being "hazardous." For example, when summer humidity declines and temperature and wind velocity rise in heavily forested areas, the likelihood of fire increases. Conditions are such that a forest fire could start very easily and be difficult to contain. In this example, low humidity increases both loss probability and loss severity. The more hazardous the conditions, the greater the probability and/or severity of loss. Two kinds of hazards—physical and intangible—affect the probability and severity of losses.

Physical Hazards

We refer to **physical hazards** as tangible environmental conditions that affect the frequency and/or severity of loss. Examples include slippery roads, which often increase the number of auto accidents; poorly lit stairwells, which add to the likelihood of slips and falls; and old wiring, which may increase the likelihood of a fire.

Physical hazards that affect property include location, construction, and use. Building locations affect their susceptibility to loss by fire, flood, earthquake, and other perils. A building located near a fire station and a good water supply has a lower chance that it will suffer a serious loss by fire than if it is in an isolated area with neither water nor firefighting service. Similarly, a company that has built a backup generator will have lower likelihood of a serious financial loss in the event of a power loss hazard.

Construction affects both the probability and severity of loss. While no building is fireproof, some construction types are less susceptible to loss from fire than others. But a building that is susceptible to one peril is not necessarily susceptible to all. For example, a frame building is more apt to burn than a brick building, but frame buildings may suffer less damage from an earthquake.

Use or occupancy may also create physical hazards. For example, buildings used to manufacture or store fireworks will have greater probability of loss by fire than do office buildings. Likewise, buildings used for dry cleaning (which uses volatile chemicals) will bear a greater physical hazard than do elementary schools. Cars used for business purposes may be exposed to greater chance of loss than a typical family car since businesses use vehicles more extensively and in more dangerous settings. Similarly, people have physical characteristics that affect loss. Some of us have brittle bones, weak immune systems, or vitamin deficiencies. Any of these characteristics could increase the probability or severity of health expenses.

Intangible Hazards

Here we distinguish between physical hazards and **intangible hazards**—attitudes and nonphysical cultural conditions can affect loss probabilities and severities of loss. Their existence may lead to physical hazards. Traditionally, authors of insurance texts categorize these conditions as moral and morale hazards, which are important concepts but do not cover the full range of nonphysical hazards. Even the distinction between moral and morale hazards is fuzzy.

Moral hazards are hazards that involve behavior that can be construed as negligence or that borders on criminality. They involve dishonesty on the part of people who take out insurance (called "insureds"). Risk transfer through insurance invites moral hazard by potentially encouraging those who transfer risks to cause losses intentionally for monetary gain. Generally, moral hazards exist when a person can gain from the occurrence of a loss. For example, an insured that will be reimbursed for the cost of a new stereo system following the loss of an old one has an incentive to cause loss. An insured business that is losing money may have arson as a moral hazard. Such incentives increase loss probabilities; as the name "moral" implies, moral hazard is a breach of morality (honesty).

Morale hazards, in contrast, do not involve dishonesty. Rather, morale hazards involve attitudes of carelessness and lack of concern. As such, morale hazards increase the chance a loss will occur or increase the size of losses that do occur. Poor housekeeping (e.g., allowing trash to accumulate in attics or basements) or careless cigarette smoking are examples of morale hazards that increase the probability fire losses. Often, such lack of concern occurs because a third party (such as an insurer) is available to pay for losses. A person or company that knows they are insured for a particular loss exposure may take less precaution to protect this exposure than otherwise. Nothing dishonest lurks in not locking your car or in not taking adequate care to reduce losses, so these don't represent morality breaches. Both practices, however, increase the probability of loss severity.

Many people unnecessarily and often unconsciously create morale hazards that can affect their health and life expectancy. Such hazards include excessive use of tobacco, drugs, and other harmful

---

hazards

Conditions that increase the cause of loss.

frequency

The number of losses during a specified period.

severity

The average dollar value of a loss per claim.

physical hazards

Tangible environmental conditions that affect the frequency and/or severity of loss.

intangible hazards

Attitudes and nonphysical cultural conditions can affect loss probabilities and severities of loss.

moral hazards

Hazards that involve behavior that can be construed as negligence bordering on criminality.

morale hazards

Hazards that involve attitudes of carelessness and lack of concern.

substances; poor eating, sleeping, and exercise habits; unnecessary exposure to falls, poisoning, electrocution, radiation, venomous stings and bites, and air pollution; and so forth.

Hazards are critical because our ability to reduce their effects will reduce both overall costs and variability. Hazard management, therefore, can be a highly effective risk management tool. At this point, many corporations around the world emphasize disaster control management to reduce the impact of biological or terrorist attacks. Safety inspections in airports are one example of disaster control management that intensified after September 11. See "Is Airport Security Worth It to You?" for a discussion of safety in airports.

Is Airport Security Worth It to You?

Following the September 11, 2001, terrorist attacks, the Federal Aviation Administration (now the Transportation Security Administration [TSA] under the U.S. Department of Homeland Security [DHS]) wrestled with a large question: how could a dozen or more hijackers armed with knives slip through security checkpoints at two major airports? Sadly, it wasn't hard. Lawmakers and security experts had long complained about lax safety measures at airports, citing several studies over the years that had documented serious security lapses. "I think a major terrorist incident was bound to happen," Paul Bracken, a Yale University professor who teaches national security issues and international business, told *Wired* magazine a day after the attacks. "I think this incident exposed airport security for what any frequent traveler knows it is—a complete joke. It's effective in stopping people who may have a cigarette lighter or a metal belt buckle, but against people who want to hijack four planes simultaneously, it is a failure."

Two days after the attacks, air space was reopened under extremely tight security measures, including placing armed security guards on flights; ending curbside check-in; banning sharp objects (at first, even tweezers, nail clippers, and eyelash curlers were confiscated); restricting boarding areas to ticket-holding passengers; and conducting extensive searches of carry-on bags.

In the years since the 2001 terrorist attacks, U.S. airport security procedures have undergone many changes, often in response to current events and national terrorism threat levels. Beginning in December 2005, the Transportation Security Administration (TSA) refocused its efforts to detect suspicious persons, items, and activities. The new measures called for increased random passenger screenings. They lifted restrictions on certain carry-on items. Overall, the changes were viewed as a relaxation of the extremely strict protocols that had been in place subsequent to the events of 9/11.

The TSA had to revise its airline security policy yet again shortly after the December 2005 adjustments. On August 10, 2006, British police apprehended over twenty suspects implicated in a plot to detonate liquid-based explosives on flights originating from the United Kingdom bound for several major U.S. cities. Following news of this aborted plot, the U.S. Terror Alert Level soared to red (denoting a severe threat level). As a result, the TSA quickly barred passengers from carrying on most liquids and other potentially explosives-concealing compounds to flights in U.S. airports. Beverages, gels, lotions, toothpastes, and semisolid cosmetics (such as lipstick) were thus expressly forbidden.

Less-burdensome modifications were made to the list of TSA-prohibited items not long after publication of the initial requirements. Nevertheless, compliance remains a controversial issue among elected officials and the public, who contend that the many changes are difficult to keep up with. Many contended that the changes represented too great a tradeoff of comfort or convenience for the illusion of safety. To many citizens, though, the 2001 terrorist plot served as a wake-up call, reminding a nation quietly settling into a state of complacency of the need for continued vigilance. Regardless of the merits of these viewpoints, air travel security will no doubt remain a hot topic in the years ahead as the economic, financial, regulatory, and sociological issues become increasingly complex.

Questions for Discussion

1. Discuss whether the government has the right to impose great cost to many in terms of lost time in using air travel, inconvenience, and affronts to some people's privacy to protect a few individuals.

2. Do you see any morale or moral hazards associated with the homeland security monitoring and actively searching people and doing preflight background checks on individuals prior to boarding?

3. Discuss the issue of personal freedom versus national security as it relates to this case.

Sources: Tsar's Press release at http://www.tsa.gov/public/display?theme=44&content=090005198018c27e. For more information regarding TSA, visit our Web site at http://www.TSA.gov; Dave Linkups, "Airports Vulnerable Despite Higher Level of Security," Business Insurance, 6 May 2002; "U.S. Flyers Still at Risk," National Underwriter Property & Casualty/Risk & Benefits Management Edition, 1 April 2002; Stephen Power, "Background Checks Await Fliers," The Wall Street Journal, 7 June 2002. For media sources related to 2006 terrorist plot, see http://en.wikipedia.org/wiki/2006_transatlantic_aircraft_plot#References.

KEY TAKEAWAYS

- You should be able to differentiate between different types of hazards.
- You should be able to differentiate between different types of perils.
- Can you differentiate between a hazard and a peril?

DISCUSSION QUESTIONS

1. What are perils?
2. What are hazards?
3. Why do we not just call perils and hazards by the name "risk," as is often done in common English conversations?
4. Discuss the perils and hazards in box "Is Airport Security Worth It to You?".

6. REVIEW AND PRACTICE

1. What are underlying objectives for the definition of risk?
2. How does risk fit on the spectrum of certainty and uncertainty?
3. Provide the formal definition of risk.
4. What are three major categories of risk attitudes?
5. Explain the categories and risk and provide examples for each category.
6. What are exposures? Give examples of exposures.
7. What are perils? Give examples of perils.
8. What are hazards? Give examples of hazards.
9. In a particular situation, it may be difficult to distinguish between moral hazard and morale hazard. Why? Define both terms.
10. Some people with complete health insurance coverage visit doctors more often than required. Is this tendency a moral hazard, a morale hazard, or simple common sense? Explain.
11. Give examples of perils, exposures, and hazards for a university or college. Define each term.
12. Give examples of exposure for speculative risks in a company such as Google.
13. Inflation causes both pure and speculative risks in our society. Can you give some examples of each?
14. Define holistic risk and enterprise risk and give examples of each.
15. Describe the new risks facing society today. Give examples of risks in electronic commerce.
16. Read the box "The Risks of E-exposures" in this chapter. Can you help the risk managers identify all the risk exposures associated with e-commerce and the Internet?
17. Read the box "Is Airport Security Worth It to You?" in this chapter and respond to the discussion questions at the end. What additional risk exposures do you see that the article did not cover?
18. One medical practice that has been widely discussed in recent years involves defensive medicine, in which a doctor orders more medical tests and X-rays than she or he might have in the past—not because of the complexity of the case, but because the doctor fears being sued by the patient for medical malpractice. The extra tests may establish that the doctor did everything reasonable and prudent to diagnose and treat the patient.

    a. What does this tell you about the burden of risk?
    b. What impact does this burden place on you and your family in your everyday life?
    c. Is the doctor wrong to do this, or is it a necessary precaution?
    d. Is there some way to change this situation?

19. Thompson's department store has a fleet of delivery trucks. The store also has a restaurant, a soda fountain, a babysitting service for parents shopping there, and an in-home appliance service program.

    a. Name three perils associated with each of these operations.

b. For the pure risk situations you noted in part 1 of this exercise, name three hazards that could be controlled by the employees of the department store.

c. If you were manager of the store, would you want all these operations? Which—if any—would you eliminate? Explain.

20. Omer Laskwood, the major income earner for a family of four, was overheard saying to his friend Vince, "I don't carry any life insurance because I'm young, and I know from statistics few people die at my age."

a. What are your feelings about this statement?

b. How does Omer perceive risk relative to his situation?

c. What characteristic in this situation is more important than the likelihood of Mr. Laskwood dying?

d. Are there other risks Omer should consider?

21. The council members of Flatburg are very proud of the proposed new airport they are discussing at a council meeting. When it is completed, Flatburg will finally have regular commercial air service. Some type of fire protection is needed at the new airport, but a group of citizens is protesting that Flatburg cannot afford to purchase another fire engine. The airport could share the downtown fire station, or the firehouse could be moved to the airport five miles away. Someone suggested a compromise—move the facilities halfway. As the council members left their meeting that evening, they had questions regarding this problem.

a. What questions would you raise?

b. How would you handle this problem using the information discussed in this chapter?

ENDNOTES

1. David J. Lynch, "Global Financial Crisis May Hit Hardest Outside U.S.," USA Today, October 30, 2008. The initial thought that the trouble was more a U.S. isolated trouble "laid low by a Wall Street culture of heedless risk-taking" and the thinking was that "the U.S. will lose its status as the superpower of the global financial system…. Now everyone realizes they are in this global mess together. Reflecting that shared fate, Asian and European leaders gathered Saturday in Beijing to brainstorm ahead of a Nov. 15 international financial summit in Washington, D.C."

2. In essence, a credit derivative is a financial instrument issued by one firm, which guarantees payment for contracts of another party. The guarantees are provided under a second contract. Should the issuer of the second contract not perform—for example, by defaulting or going bankrupt—the second contract goes into effect. When the mortgages defaulted, the supposed guarantor did not have enough money to pay their contract obligations. This caused others (who were counting on the payment) to default as well on other obligations. This snowball effect then caused others to default, and so forth. It became a chain reaction that generated a global financial market collapse.

3. This lack of risk management cannot be blamed on lack of warning of the risk alone. Regulators and firms were warned to adhere to risk management procedures. However, these warnings were ignored in pursuit of profit and "free markets." See "The Crash: Risk and Regulation, What Went Wrong" by Anthony Faiola, Ellen Nakashima, and Jill Drew, Washington Post, October 15, 2008, A01.

4. See http://www.dhs.gov/dhspublic/.

5. The student is invited to read archival articles from all media sources about the calamity of the poor response to the floods in New Orleans. The insurance studies of Virginia Commonwealth University held a town hall meeting the week after Katrina to discuss the natural and man-made disasters and their impact both financially and socially. The PowerPoint basis for the discussion is available to the readers.

6. See http://www.dhs.gov/dhspublic/.

7. Etti G. Baranoff, "The Risk Balls Game: Transforming Risk and Insurance Into Tangible Concept," Risk Management & Insurance Review 4, no. 2 (2001): 51–59.

8. L. Buchanan, "Breakthrough Ideas for 2004," Harvard Business Review 2 (2004): 13–16.

9. Etti G. Baranoff and Thomas W. Sager, "Integrated Risk Management in Life Insurance Companies," an award winning paper, International Insurance Society Seminar, Chicago, July 2006 and in Special Edition of the Geneva Papers on Risk and Insurance.

10. Reprinted with permission from the author; Etti G. Baranoff, "Risk Management and Insurance During the Decade of September 11," in The Day that Changed Everything? An Interdisciplinary Series of Edited Volumes on the Impact of 9/11, vol. 2.

11. http://www.rms.com, http://www.iso.com/index.php?option= com_content&task=view&id=932&Itemid=587, and http://www.iso.com/index.php?option= com_content&task=view&id=930&Itemid=585.

12. Laurent Condamin, Jean-Paul Louisot, and Patrick Maim, "Risk Quantification: Management, Diagnosis and Hedging" (Chichester, UK: John Wiley & Sons Ltd., 2006).

CHAPTER 2
Risk Measurement and Metrics

In Chapter 1, we discussed how risk arises as a consequence of uncertainty. Recall also that risk is not the state of uncertainty itself. Risk and uncertainty are connected and yet are distinct concepts.

In this chapter, we will discuss the ways in which we measure risk and uncertainty. If we wish to understand and use the concepts of risk and uncertainty, we need to be able to measure these concepts' outcomes. Psychological and economic research shows that emotions such as fear, dread, ambiguity avoidance, and feelings of emotional loss represent valid risks. Such feelings are thus relevant to decision making under uncertainty. Our focus here, however, will draw more on financial metrics rather than emotional or psychological measures of risk perception. In this chapter, we thus discuss measurable and quantifiable outcomes and how we can measure risk and uncertainty using numerical methods.

A "metric" in this context is a system of related measures that helps us quantify characteristics or qualities. Any individual or enterprise needs to be able to quantify risk before they can decide whether or not a particular risk is critical enough to commit resources to manage. If such resources have been committed, then we need measurements to see whether the risk management process or procedure has reduced risk. And all forms of enterprises, for financial profit or for social profit, must strive to reduce risk. Without risk metrics, enterprises cannot tell whether or not they have reached risk management objectives. Enterprises including businesses hold risk management to be as important as any other objective, including profitability. Without risk metrics to measure success, failure, or incremental improvement, we cannot judge progress in the control of risk.

Risk management provides a framework for assessing opportunities for profit, as well as for gauging threats of loss. Without measuring risk, we cannot ascertain what action of the available alternatives the enterprise should take to optimize the risk-reward tradeoff. The risk-reward tradeoff is essentially a cost-benefit analysis taking uncertainty into account. In (economic) marginal analysis terms, we want to know how many additional units of risk we need to take on in order to get an additional unit of reward or profit. A firm, for example, wants to know how much capital it needs to keep from going insolvent if a bad risk is realized.[1] Indeed, if they cannot measure risk, enterprises are stuck in the ancient world of being helpless to act in the face of uncertainty. Risk metrics allow us to measure risk, giving us an ability to control risk and simultaneously exploit opportunities as they arise. No one profits from establishing the existence of an uncertain state of nature. Instead, managers must measure and assess their enterprise's degree of vulnerability (risk) and sensitivity to the various potential states of nature. After reading this chapter, you should be able to define several different risk metrics and be able to discuss when each metric is appropriate for a given situation.

We will discuss several risk measures here, each of which comes about from the progression of mathematical approaches to describing and evaluating risk. We emphasize from the start, however, that measuring risk using these risk metrics is only one step as we assess any opportunity-risk issue. Risk metrics cannot stand alone. We must also evaluate how appropriate each underlying model might be for the occasion. Further, we need to evaluate each question in terms of the risk level that each entity is willing to assume for the gain each hopes to receive. Firms must understand the assumptions behind worst-case or ruin scenarios, since most firms do not want to take on risks that "bet the house." To this end, knowing the severity of losses that might be expected in the future (severity is the dollar value per claim) using forecasting models represents one aspect of quantifying risk. However, financial decision making requires that we evaluate severity levels based upon what an individual or a firm can comfortably endure (risk appetite). Further, we must evaluate the frequency with which a particular outcome will occur. As with the common English language usage of the term, frequency is the number of times the event is expected to occur in a specified period of time. The 2008 financial crisis provides an example: Poor risk management of the financial models used for creating mortgage-backed securities and credit default derivatives contributed to a worldwide crisis. The assessment of loss frequency, particularly managers' assessment of the *severity* of losses, was grossly underestimated. We discuss risk assessment using risk metrics in the pages that follow.

As we noted in Chapter 1, risk is a concept encompassing perils, hazards, exposures, and perception (with a strong emphasis on perception). It should come as no surprise that the metrics for measuring risk are also quite varied. The aspect of risk being considered in a particular situation dictates the risk measure used. If we are interested in default risk (the risk that a contracting party will be unable to live up to the terms of some financial contract, usually due to total ruin or bankruptcy), then one risk measure might be employed. If, on the other hand, we are interested in expected fluctuations of retained earnings for paying future losses, then we would likely use another risk measure. If we wish to know how much risk is generated by a risky undertaking that cannot be diversified away in the marketplace, then we would use yet another risk measure. Each risk measure has its place and appropriate application. One part of the art of risk management is to pick the appropriate risk measure for each situation.

In this chapter, we will cover the following:

1. Links

2. Quantification of uncertain outcomes via probability models

3. Measures of risk: putting it together

1.   LINKS

The first step in developing any framework for the measuring risk quantitatively involves creating a framework for addressing and studying uncertainty itself. Such a framework lies within the realm of probability. Since risk arises from uncertainty, measures of risk must also take uncertainty into account. The process of quantifying uncertainty, also known as probability theory, actually proved to be surprisingly difficult and took millennia to develop. Progress on this front required that we develop two fundamental ideas. The first is a way to quantify uncertainty (probability) of potential states of the world. Second, we had to develop the notion that the outcomes of interest to human events, the risks, were subject to some kind of regularity that we could predict and that would remain stable over time. Developing and accepting these two notions represented path-breaking, seminal changes from previous mindsets. Until research teams made and accepted these steps, any firm, scientific foundation for developing probability and risk was impossible.

Solving risk problems requires that we compile a puzzle of the many personal and business risks. First, we need to obtain quantitative measures of each risk. Again, as in Chapter 1, we repeat the Link puzzle in Figure 2.1. The point illustrated in Figure 2.1 is that we face many varied risk exposures, appropriate risk measures, and statistical techniques that we apply for different risks. However, most risks are interconnected. When taken together, they provide a holistic risk measure for the firm or a family. For some risks, measures are not sophisticated and easy to achieve, such as the risk of potential fires in a region. Sometimes trying to predict potential risks is much more complex, such as predicting one-hundred-year floods in various regions. For each type of peril and hazard, we may well have different techniques to measure the risks. Our need to realize that catastrophes can happen and our need to account for them are of paramount importance. The 2008–2009 financial crisis may well have occurred in part because the risk measures in use failed to account for the systemic collapses of the financial institutions. Mostly, institutions toppled because of a result of the mortgage-backed securities and the real estate markets. As we explore risk computations and measures throughout this chapter, you will learn terminology and understand how we use such measures. You will thus embark on a journey into the world of risk management. Some measures may seem simplistic. Other measures will show you how to use complex models that use the most sophisticated state-of-the-art mathematical and statistical technology. You'll notice also that many computations would be impossible without the advent of powerful computers and computation memory. Now, on to the journey.

FIGURE 2.1   Links between Each Holistic Risk Puzzle Piece and Its Computational Measures

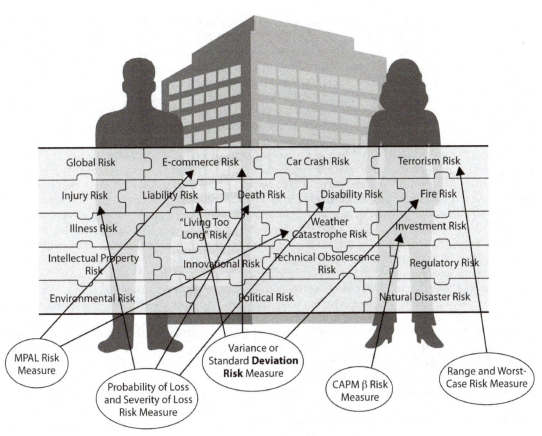

2. QUANTIFICATION OF UNCERTAINTY VIA PROBABILITY MODELS

LEARNING OBJECTIVES

- In this section, you will learn how to quantify the relative frequency of occurrences of uncertain events by using probability models.
- You will learn about the measures of frequency, severity, likelihood, statistical distributions, and expected values.
- You will use examples to compute these values.

As we consider uncertainty, we use rigorous quantitative studies of chance, the recognition of its empirical regularity in uncertain situations. Many of these methods are used to quantify the occurrence of uncertain events that represent intellectual milestones. As we create models based upon probability and statistics, you will likely recognize that probability and statistics touch nearly every field of study today. As we have internalized the predictive regularity of repeated chance events, our entire worldview has changed. For example, we have convinced ourselves of the odds of getting heads in a coin flip so much that it's hard to imagine otherwise. We're used to seeing statements such as "average life of 1,000 hours" on a package of light bulbs. We understand such a phrase because we can think of the length of life of a light bulb as being uncertain but statistically predictable. We routinely hear such statements as "The chance of rain tomorrow is 20 percent." It's hard for us to imagine that only a few centuries ago people did not believe even in the existence of chance occurrences or random events or in accidents, much less explore any method of quantifying seemingly chance events. Up until very recently, people have believed that God controlled every minute detail of the universe. This belief rules out any kind of conceptualization of chance as a regular or predictable phenomenon. For example, until recently the cost of buying a life annuity that paid buyers $100 per month for life was the same for a thirty-year-old as it was for a seventy-year-old. It didn't matter that empirically, the "life expectancy" of a thirty-year-old was four times longer than that of a seventy-year-old.[2] After all, people believed that a person's particular time of death was "God's will." No one believed that the length of someone's life could be judged or predicted statistically by any noticed or exhibited regularity across people. In spite of the advancements in mathematics and science since the beginning of civilization, remarkably, the development of measures of relative frequency of occurrence of uncertain events did not occur until the 1600s. This birth of the "modern" ideas of chance occurred when a problem was posed to mathematician Blaisé Pascal by a frequent gambler. As often occurs, the problem turned out to be less important in the long run than the solution developed to solve the problem.

The problem posed was: If two people are gambling and the game is interrupted and discontinued before either one of the two has won, what is a fair way to split the pot of money on the table? Clearly the person ahead at that time had a better chance of winning the game and should have gotten more. The player in the lead would receive the larger portion of the pot of money. However, the person losing could come from behind and win. It could happen and such a possibility should not be excluded. How should the pot be split fairly? Pascal formulated an approach to this problem and, in a series of letters with Pierre de Fermat, developed an approach to the problem that entailed writing down all possible outcomes that could possibly occur and then counting the number of times the first gambler won. The proportion of times that the first gambler won (calculated as the number of times the gambler won divided by the total number of possible outcomes) was taken to be the proportion of the pot that the first gambler could fairly claim. In the process of formulating this solution, Pascal and Fermat more generally developed a framework to quantify the relative frequency of uncertain outcomes, which is now known as probability. They created the mathematical notion of expected value of an uncertain event. They were the first to model the exhibited regularity of chance or uncertain events and apply it to solve a practical problem. In fact, their solution pointed to many other potential applications to problems in law, economics, and other fields.

From Pascal and Fermat's work, it became clear that to manage future risks under uncertainty, we need to have some idea about not only the possible outcomes or states of the world but also how likely each outcome is to occur. We need a **model**, or in other words, a symbolic representation of the possible outcomes and their likelihoods or relative frequencies.

model

A symbolic representation of the possible outcomes.

A Historical Prelude to the Quantification of Uncertainty Via Probabilities

Historically, the development of measures of chance (probability) only began in the mid-1600s. Why in the middle ages, and not with the Greeks? The answer, in part, is that the Greeks and their predecessors did not have the mathematical concepts. Nor, more importantly, did the Greeks have the psychological perspective to even contemplate these notions, much less develop them into a cogent theory capable of reproduction and expansion. First, the Greeks did not have the mathematical notational system necessary to contemplate a formal approach to risk. They lacked, for example, the simple and complete symbolic system including a zero and an equal sign useful for computation, a contribution that was subsequently developed by the Arabs and later adopted by the Western world. The use of Roman numerals might have been sufficient for counting, and perhaps sufficient for geometry, but certainly it was not conducive to complex calculations. The equal sign was not in common use until the late middle ages. Imagine doing calculations (even such simple computations as dividing fractions or solving an equation) in Roman numerals without an equal sign, a zero element, or a decimal point!

But mathematicians and scientists settled these impediments a thousand years before the advent of probability. Why did risk analysis not emerge with the advent of a more complete numbering system just as sophisticated calculations in astronomy, engineering, and physics did? The answer is more psychological than mathematical and goes to the heart of why we consider risk as both a psychological and a numerical concept in this book. To the Greeks (and to the millennia of others who followed them), the heavens, divinely created, were believed to be static and perfect and governed by regularity and rules of perfection—circles, spheres, the six perfect geometric solids, and so forth. The earthly sphere, on the other hand, was the source of imperfection and chaos. The Greeks accepted that they would find no sense in studying the chaotic events of Earth. The ancient Greeks found the path to truth in contemplating the perfection of the heavens and other perfect unspoiled or uncorrupted entities. Why would a god (or gods) powerful enough to know and create everything intentionally create a world using a less than perfect model? The Greeks, and others who followed, believed pure reasoning, not empirical, observation would lead to knowledge. Studying regularity in the chaotic earthly sphere was worst than a futile waste of time; it distracted attention from important contemplations actually likely to impart true knowledge.

It took a radical change in mindset to start to contemplate regularity in events in the earthly domain. We are all creatures of our age, and we could not pose the necessary questions to develop a theory of probability and risk until we shook off these shackles of the mind. Until the age of reason, when church reforms and a growing merchant class (who pragmatically examined and counted things empirically) created a tremendous growth in trade, we remained trapped in the old ways of thinking. As long as society was static and stationary, with villages this year being essentially the same as they were last year or a decade or century before, there was little need to pose or solve these problems. M. G. Kendall captures this succinctly when he noted that "mathematics never leads thought, but only expresses it."* The western world was simply not yet ready to try to quantify risk or event likelihood (probability) or to contemplate uncertainty. If all things are believed to be governed by an omnipotent god, then regularity is not to be trusted, perhaps it can even be considered deceptive, and variation is irrelevant and illusive, being merely reflective of God's will. Moreover, the fact that things like dice and drawing of lots were simultaneously used by magicians, by gamblers, and by religious figures for divination did not provide any impetus toward looking for regularity in earthly endeavors.

* M. G. Kendall, "The Beginnings of a Probability Calculus," in *Studies in the History of Statistics and Probability*, vol. 1, ed. E. S. Pearson and Sir Maurice Kendall (London: Charles Griffin & Co., 1970), 30.

2.1   Measurement Techniques for Frequency, Severity, and Probability Distribution Measures for Quantifying Uncertain Events

When we can see the pattern of the losses and/or gains experienced in the past, we hope that the same pattern will continue in the future. In some cases, we want to be able to modify the past results in a logical way like inflating them for the time value of money discussed in Chapter 4. If the patterns of gains and losses continue, our predictions of future losses or gains will be informative. Similarly, we may develop a pattern of losses based on theoretical or physical constructs (such as hurricane forecasting models based on physics or likelihood of obtaining a head in a flip of a coin based on theoretical models of equal **likelihood** of a head and a tail). Likelihood is the notion of how often a certain event will occur. Inaccuracies in our abilities to create a correct **distribution** arise from our inability to predict futures outcomes accurately. The distribution is the display of the events on a map that tells us the likelihood that the event or events will occur. In some ways, it resembles a picture of the likelihood and regularity of events that occur. Let's now turn to creating models and measures of the outcomes and their frequency.

likelihood

The probability that an event will occur in a specified amount of time.

distribution

The display of the events on a map that tells us the likelihood that the event or events will occur.

Measures of Frequency and Severity

Table 2.1 and Table 2.2 show the compilation of the number of claims and their dollar amounts for homes that were burnt during a five-year period in two different locations labeled Location A and Location B. We have information about the total number of claims per year and the amount of the fire losses in dollars for each year. Each location has the same number of homes (1,000 homes). Each location has a total of 51 claims for the five-year period, an average (or mean) of 10.2 claims per year, which is the frequency. The average dollar amount of losses per claim for the whole period is also the same for each location, $6,166.67, which is the definition of severity.

TABLE 2.1   Claims and Fire Losses for Group of Homes in Location A

Year	Number of Fire Claims	Number of Fire Losses ($)	Average Loss per Claim ($)
1	11	16,500.00	1,500.00
2	9	40,000.00	4,444.44
3	7	30,000.00	4,285.71
4	10	123,000.00	12,300.00
5	14	105,000.00	7,500.00
Total	51.00	314,500.00	6,166.67
Mean	10.20	62,900.00	6,166.67
	Average Frequency =	10.20	
	Average Severity =	6,166.67 for the 5-year period	

TABLE 2.2   Claims and Fire Losses ($) for Homes in Location B

Year	Number of Fire Claims	Fire Losses	Average Loss per Claim ($)
1	15	16,500.00	1,100.00
2	5	40,000.00	8,000.00
3	12	30,000.00	2,500.00
4	10	123,000.00	12,300.00
5	9	105,000.00	11,666.67
Total	51.00	314,500.00	6,166.67
Mean	10.20	62,900.00	6,166.67
	Average frequency =	10.20	
	Average severity =	6,166.67 for the 5-year period	

As shown in Table 2.1 and Table 2.2, the total number of fire claims for the two locations A and B is the same, as is the total dollar amount of losses shown. You might recall from earlier, the number of claims per year is called the frequency. The average frequency of claims for locations A and B is 10.2 per year. The size of the loss in terms of dollars lost per claim is called severity, as we noted previously. The average dollars lost per claim per year in each location is $6,166.67.

The most important measures for risk managers when they address potential losses that arise from uncertainty are usually those associated with frequency and severity of losses during a specified period of time. The use of frequency and severity data is very important to both insurers and firm managers concerned with judging the risk of various endeavors. Risk managers try to employ activities (physical construction, backup systems, financial hedging, insurance, etc.) to decrease the frequency or severity (or both) of potential losses. In Chapter 4, we will see frequency data and severity data represented. Typically, the risk manager will relate the number of incidents under investigation to a base, such as the number of employees if examining the frequency and severity of workplace injuries. In the examples in Table 2.1 and Table 2.2, the severity is related to the number of fire claims in the five-year period per 1,000 homes. It is important to note that in these tables the precise distribution (frequencies and dollar losses) over the years for the claims per year arising in Location A is different from distribution for Location B. This will be discussed later in this chapter. Next, we discuss the concept of frequency in terms of probability or likelihood.

Frequency and Probability

Returning back to the quantification of the notion of uncertainty, we first observe that our intuitive usage of the word probability can have two different meanings or forms as related to statements of uncertain outcomes. This is exemplified by two different statements:[3]

1. "If I sail west from Europe, I have a 50 percent chance that I will fall off the edge of the earth."
2. "If I flip a coin, I have a 50 percent chance that it will land on heads."

Conceptually, these represent two distinct types of probability statements. The first is a statement about probability as a degree of belief about whether an event will occur and how firmly this belief is held. The second is a statement about how often a head would be expected to show up in repeated flips of a coin. The important difference is that the first statement's validity or truth will be stated. We can clear up the statement's veracity for all by sailing across the globe.

The second statement, however, still remains unsettled. Even after the first coin flip, we still have a 50 percent chance that the next flip will result in a head. The second provides a different interpretation of "probability," namely, as a relative frequency of occurrence in repeated trials. This relative frequency conceptualization of probability is most relevant for risk management. One wants to learn from past events about the likelihood of future occurrences. The discoverers of probability theory adopted the relative frequency approach to formalizing the likelihood of chance events.

Pascal and Fermat ushered in a major conceptual breakthrough: the concept that, in repeated games of chance (or in many other situations encountered in nature) involving uncertainty, fixed relative frequencies of occurrence of the individual possible outcomes arose. These relative frequencies were both stable over time and individuals could calculate them by simply counting the number of ways that the outcome could occur divided by the total number of equally likely possible outcomes. In addition, empirically the relative frequency of occurrence of events in a long sequence of repeated trials (e.g., repeated gambling games) corresponded with the theoretical calculation of the number of ways an event could occur divided by the total number of possible outcomes. This is the model of equally likely outcomes or relative frequency definition of probability. It was a very distinct departure from the previous conceptualization of uncertainty that had all events controlled by God with no humanly discernable pattern. In the Pascal-Fermat framework, prediction became a matter of counting that could be done by anyone. Probability and prediction had become a tool of the people! Figure 2.2 provides an example representing all possible outcomes in the throw of two colored dice along with their associated probabilities.

FIGURE 2.2 Possible Outcomes for a Roll of Two Dice with the Probability of Having a Particular Number of Dots Facing Up

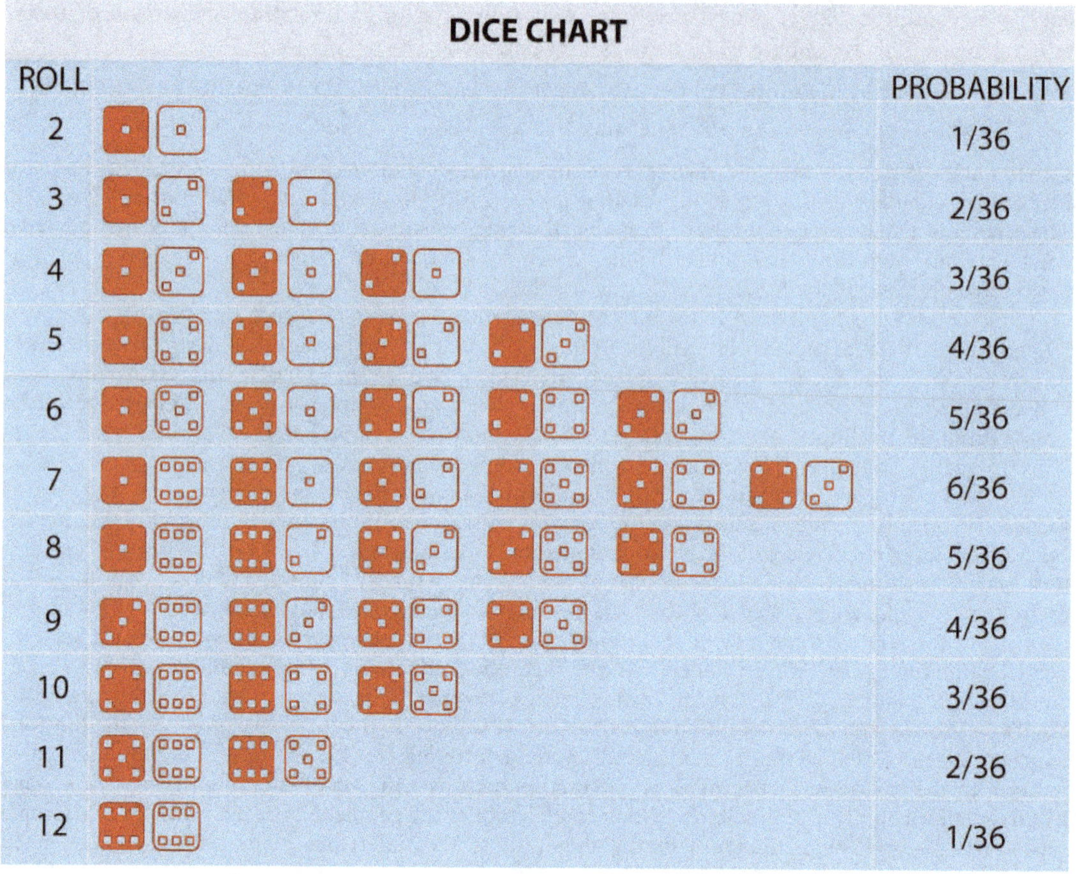

Figure 2.2 lists the probabilities for the number of dots facing upward (2, 3, 4, etc.) in a roll of two colored dice. We can calculate the probability for any one of these numbers (2, 3, 4, etc.) by adding up the number of outcomes (rolls of two dice) that result in this number of dots facing up divided by the total number of possibilities. For example, a roll of thirty-six possibilities total when we roll two dice (count them). The probability of rolling a 2 is 1/36 (we can only roll a 2 one way, namely, when both dice have a 1 facing up). The probability of rolling a 7 is 6/36 = 1/6 (since rolls can fall any of six ways to roll a 7—1 and 6 twice, 2 and 5 twice, 3 and 4 twice). For any other choice of number of dots facing upward, we can get the probability by just adding the number of ways the event can occur divided by thirty-six. The probability of rolling a 7 or an 11 (5 and 6 twice) on a throw of the dice, for instance, is (6 + 2)/36 = 2/9.

The notions of "equally likely outcomes" and the calculation of probabilities as the ratio of "the number of ways in which an event could occur, divided by the total number of equally likely outcomes" is seminal and instructive. But, it did not include situations in which the number of possible outcomes was (at least conceptually) unbounded or infinite or not equally likely.[4] We needed an extension. Noticing that the probability of an event, any event, provided that extension. Further, extending the theory to nonequally likely possible outcomes arose by noticing that the probability of an event—any event—occurring could be calculated as the relative frequency of an event occurring in a long run of trials in which the event may or may not occur. Thus, different events could have different, nonequal chances of occurring in a long repetition of scenarios involving the possible occurrences of the events. Table 2.3 provides an example of this. We can extend the theory yet further to a situation in which the number of possible outcomes is potentially infinite. But what about a situation in which no easily definable bound on the number of possible outcomes can be found? We can address this situation by again using the relative frequency interpretation of probability as well. When we have a continuum of possible outcomes (e.g., if an outcome is time, we can view it as a continuous variable outcome), then a curve of relative frequency is created. Thus, the probability of an outcome falling between two numbers x and y is the area under the frequency curve between x and y. The total area under the curve is one reflecting that it's 100 percent certain that some outcome will occur.

The so-called normal distribution or bell-shaped curve from statistics provides us with an example of such a continuous probability distribution curve. The bell-shaped curve represents a situation wherein a continuum of possible outcomes arises. Figure 2.3 provides such a bell-shaped curve for the profitability of implementing a new research and development project. It may have profit or loss.

FIGURE 2.3 Normal Distribution of Potential Profit from a Research and Development Project

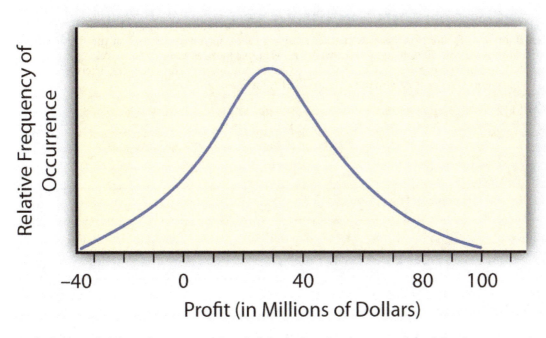

To find the probability of any range of profitability values for this research and development project, we find the area under the curve in Figure 2.3 between the desired range of profitability values. For example, the distribution in Figure 2.3 was constructed to have what is called a normal distribution with the hump over the point $30 million and a measure of spread of $23 million. This spread represents the standard deviation that we will discuss in the next section. We can calculate the area under the curve above $0, which will be the probability that we will make a profit by implementing the research and development project. We do this by reference to a normal distribution table of values available in any statistics book. The area under the curve is 0.904, meaning that we have approximately a 90 percent change (probability of 0.9) that the project will result in a profit.

In practice, we build probability distribution tables or probability curves such as those in Figure 2.2, Figure 2.3, and Table 2.3 using estimates of the likelihood (probability) of various different states of nature based on either historical relative frequency of occurrence or theoretical data. For example, empirical data may come from repeated observations in similar situations such as with historically constructed life or mortality tables. Theoretical data may come from a physics or engineering assessment of failure likelihood for a bridge or nuclear power plant containment vessel. In some situations, however, we can determine the likelihoods subjectively or by expert opinion. For example, assessments of political overthrows of governments are used for pricing political risk insurance needed by corporations doing business in emerging markets. Regardless of the source of the likelihoods, we can obtain an assessment of the probabilities or relative frequencies of the future occurrence of each conceivable event. The resulting collection of possible events together with their respective probabilities of occurrence is called a probability distribution, an example of which is shown in Table 2.3.

Measures of Outcome Value: Severity of Loss, Value of Gain

We have developed a quantified measure of the likelihood of the various uncertain outcomes that a firm or individual might face—these are also called probabilities. We can now turn to address the consequences of the uncertainty. The consequences of uncertainty are most often a vital issue financially. The reason that uncertainty is unsettling is not the uncertainty itself but rather the various different outcomes that can impact strategic plans, profitability, quality of life, and other important aspects of our life or the viability of a company. Therefore, we need to assess how we are impacted in each state of the world. For each outcome, we associate a value reflecting how we are affected by being in this state of the world.

As an example, consider a retail firm entering a new market with a newly created product. They may make a lot of money by taking advantage of "first-mover" status. They may lose money if the product is not accepted sufficiently by the marketplace. In addition, although they have tried to anticipate any problems, they may be faced with potential product liability. While they naturally try to make their products as safe as possible, they have to regard the potential liability because of the limited experience with the product. They may be able to assess the likelihood of a lawsuit as well as the consequences (losses) that might result from having to defend such lawsuits. The uncertainty of the consequences makes this endeavor risky and the potential for gain that motivates the company's entry into the new market. How does one calculate these gains and losses? We already demonstrated some calculations in the examples above in Table 2.1 and Table 2.2 for the claims and fire losses for homes in locations A and B. These examples concentrated on the consequences of the uncertainty about fires. Another way to compute the same type of consequences is provided in the example in Table 2.3 for the probability distribution for this new market entry. We look for an assessment of the financial consequences of the entry into the market as well. This example looks at a few possible outcomes, not only the fire losses outcome. These outcomes can have positive or negative consequences. Therefore, we use the opportunity terminology here rather than only the loss possibilities.

TABLE 2.3 Opportunity and Loss Assessment Consequences of New Product Market Entry

State of Nature	Probability Assessment of Likelihood of State	Financial Consequences of Being in This State (in Millions of Dollars)
Subject to a loss in a product liability lawsuit	.01	−10.2
Market acceptance is limited and temporary	.10	−.50
Some market acceptance but no great consumer demand	.40	.10
Good market acceptance and sales performance	.40	1
Great market demand and sales performance	.09	8

As you can see, it's not the uncertainty of the states themselves that causes decision makers to ponder the advisability of market entry of a new product. It's the consequences of the different outcomes that cause deliberation. The firm could lose $10.2 million or gain $8 million. If we knew which state would materialize, the decision would be simple. We address the issue of how we combine the probability assessment with the value of the gain or loss for the purpose of assessing the risk (consequences of uncertainty) in the next section.

Combining Probability and Outcome Value Together to Get an Overall Assessment of the Impact of an Uncertain Endeavor

fair value

The numerical average of the experience of all possible outcomes if you played a game over and over.

Early probability developers asked how we could combine the various probabilities and outcome values together to obtain a single number reflecting the "value" of the multitude of different outcomes and different consequences of these outcomes. They wanted a single number that summarized in some way the entire probability distribution. In the context of the gambling games of the time when the outcomes were the amount you won in each potential uncertain state of the world, they asserted that this value was the "**fair value**" of the gamble. We define fair value as the numerical average of the experience of all possible outcomes if you played the game over and over. This is also called the "expected value." Expected value is calculated by multiplying each probability (or relative frequency) by its respective gain or loss.[5] It is also referred to as the mean value, or the average value. If X denotes the value that results in an uncertain situation, then the expected value (or average value or mean value) is often denoted by $E(X)$, sometimes also referred to by economists as $E(U)$—expected utility—and $E(G)$—expected gain. In the long run, the total experienced loss or gain divided by the number of repeated trials would be the sum of the probabilities times the experience in each state. In Table 2.3 the expected value is $(.01) \times (-10.2) + (.1) \times (-.50) + (.4) \times (.1) + (.4) \times (1) + (.09) \times (8) = 1.008$. Thus, we would say the expected outcome of the uncertain situation described in Table 2.3 was $1.008 million, or $1,008,000.00. Similarly, the expected value of the number of points on the toss of a pair of dice calculated from example in Figure 2.2 is $2 \times (1/36) + 3 \times (2/36) + 4 \times (3/36) + 5 \times (4/36) + 6 \times (5/36) + 7 \times (6/36) + 8 \times (5/36) + 9 \times (4/36) + 10 \times (3/36) + 11 \times (2/36) + 12 \times (1/36) = 7$. In uncertain economic situations involving possible financial gains or losses, the mean value or average value or expected value is often used to express the expected returns.[6] It represents the expected return from an endeavor; however, it does not express the risk involved in the uncertain scenario. We turn to this now.

Relating back to Table 2.1 and Table 2.2, for locations A and B of fire claim losses, the expected value of losses is the severity of fire claims, $6,166.67, and the expected number of claims is the frequency of occurrence, 10.2 claims per year.

years are all treated equally so the average squared deviation from the mean is just the simple average of the five years squared deviations from the mean. We calculate the variance of the number of claims only.

TABLE 2.4 Variance and Standard Deviation of Fire Claims of Location A

Year	Number of Fire Claims	Difference between Observed Number of Claims and Mean Number of Claims	Difference Squared
1	11	0.8	0.64
2	9	−1.2	1.44
3	7	−3.2	10.24
4	10	−0.2	0.04
5	14	3.8	14.44
Total	51	0	26.8
Mean	10.2		= (26.8)/4 = 6.7
Variance 6.70			
Standard Deviation = Square Root (6.7) = 2.59			

TABLE 2.5 Variance and Standard Deviation of Fire Claims of Location B

Year	Number of Fire Claims	Difference between Observed Number of Claims and Mean Number of Claims	Difference Squared
1	15	4.8	23.04
2	5	−5.2	27.04
3	12	1.8	3.24
4	10	−0.2	0.04
5	9	−1.2	1.44
Total	51	0	54.8
Mean	10.2		=(54.8)/4 = 13.70
Variance 13.70			
Standard Deviation 3.70			

A problem with the variance as a measure of risk is that by squaring the individual deviations from the mean, you end up with a measure that is in squared units (e.g., if the original losses are measured in dollars, then the variance is measured in dollars-squared). To get back to the original units of measurement we commonly take the square root and obtain a risk measure known as the standard deviation, denoted by the Greek letter sigma (σ). To provide a more meaningful measure of risk denominated in the same units as the original data, economists and risk professionals often use this square root of the variance—the standard deviation—as a measure of risk. It provides a value comparable with the original expected outcomes. Remember that variance uses squared differences; therefore, taking the square root returns the measure to its initial unit of measurement.

Thus, the standard deviation is the square root of the variance. For the distribution in Table 2.3, we calculated the variance to be 7.445, so the standard deviation is the square root of 7.445 or $2.73 million. Similarly, the standard deviations of locations A and B of Table 2.1 and Table 2.2 appear in Tables 2.4 and 2.5. As you can see, the standard deviation of the sample for Location A is only 2.59, while the standard deviation of the sample of Location B is 2.70. The number of fire claims in Location B is more spread out from year to year than those in Location A. The standard deviation is the numeric representation of that spread.

If we compare one standard deviation with another distribution of equal mean but larger standard deviation—as when we compare the claims distribution from Location A with Location B—we could say that the second distribution with the larger standard deviation is riskier than the first. It is riskier because the observations are, on average, further away from the mean (more spread out and hence providing more "surprise" potential) than the observations in the first distribution. Larger standard deviations, therefore, represent greater risk, everything else being the same.

coefficient of variation

The standard deviation of a distribution divided by its mean.

Of course, distributions seldom have the same mean. What if we are comparing two distributions with different means? In this case, one approach would be to consider the **coefficient of variation**, which is the standard deviation of a distribution divided by its mean. It essentially trades off risk (as measured by the standard deviation) with the return (as measured by the mean or expected value). The coefficient of variation can be used to give us a relative value of risk when the means of the distributions are not equal.

The Semivariance

semivariance

The average square deviation of values in a distribution.

The above measures of risk gave the same attention or importance to both positive and negative deviations from the mean or expected value. Some people prefer to measure risk by the surprises in one direction only. Usually only negative deviations below the expected value are considered risky and in need of control or management. For example, a decision maker might be especially troubled by deviations below the expected level of profit and would welcome deviations above the expected value. For this purpose a "semivariance" could serve as a more appropriate measure of risk than the variance, which treats deviations in both directions the same. The **semivariance** is the average square deviation. Now you sum only the deviations below the expected value. If the profit-loss distribution is symmetric, the use of the semivariance turns out to result in the exact same ranking of uncertain outcomes with respect to risk as the use of the variance. If the distribution is not symmetric, however, then these measures may differ and the decisions made as to which distribution of uncertain outcomes is riskier will differ, and the decisions made as to how to manage risk as measured by these two measures may be different. As most financial and pure loss distributions are asymmetric, professionals often prefer the semi-variance in financial analysis as a measure of risk, even though the variance (and standard deviation) are also commonly used.

3.2   Value at Risk (VaR) and Maximum Probable Annual Loss (MPAL)

Value at Risk (VaR)

The worst-case scenario dollar value loss (up to a specified probability level) that could occur for a company exposed to a specific set of risks.

How do banks and other financial institutions manage the systemic or fundamental market risks they face? **VaR** modeling has become the standard risk measurement tool in the banking industry to assess market risk exposure. After the banking industry adopted VaR, many other financial firms adopted it as well. This is in part because of the acceptance of this technique by regulators, such as conditions written in the Basel II agreements on bank regulation.[8] Further, financial institutions need to know how much money they need to reserve to be able to withstand a shock or loss of capital and still remain solvent. To do so, they need a risk measure with a specified high probability. Intuitively, VaR is defined as the worst-case scenario dollar value loss (up to a specified probability level) that could occur for a company exposed to a specific set of risks (interest rates, equity prices, exchange rates, and commodity prices). This is the amount needed to have in reserve in order to stave off insolvency with the specified level of probability.

In reality, for many risk exposures the absolute "worst-case" loss that could be experienced is conceivably unbounded. It's conceivable that you could lose a very huge amount but it may be highly unlikely to lose this much. Thus, instead of picking the largest possible loss to prepare against, the firm selects a probability level they can live with (usually, they are interested in having their financial risk exposure covered something like 95 percent or 99 percent of the time), and they ask, "What is the worst case that can happen up to being covered 95 percent or 99 percent of the time?" For a given level of confidence (in this case 95 percent or 99 percent) and over a specified time horizon, VaR can measure risks in any single security (either a specific investment represented in their investment securities or loan from a specific customer) or an entire portfolio as long as we have sufficient historical data. VaR provides an answer to the question "What is the worst loss that could occur and that I should prepare for?"

In practice, professionals examine a historical record of returns for the asset or portfolio under consideration and construct a probability distribution of returns. If you select a 95 percent VaR, then you pick the lowest 5 percent of the distribution, and when multiplied by the asset or portfolio value, you obtain the 95 percent VaR. If a 99 percent VaR is desired, then the lowest 1 percent of the return distribution is determined and this is multiplied by the asset or portfolio value to obtain the 99 percent VaR.

FIGURE 2.6   The 95 percent VaR for the Profit and Loss Distribution of Figure 2.2

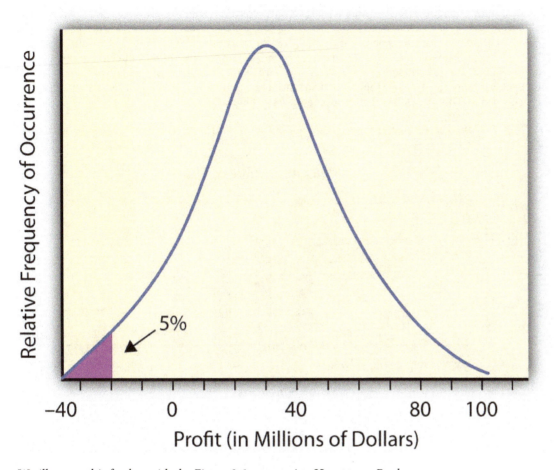

We illustrate this further with the Figure 2.6, concerning Hometown Bank.

3.3   Case: Hometown Bank Market Risk

Market risk is the change in market value of bank assets and liabilities resulting from changing market conditions. For example, as interest rates increase, the loans Hometown Bank made at low fixed rates become less valuable to the bank. The total market values of their assets decline as the market value of the loans lose value. If the loans are traded in the secondary market, Hometown would record an actual loss. Other bank assets and liabilities are at risk as well due to changing market prices. Hometown accepts equity positions as collateral (e.g., a mortgage on the house includes the house as collateral) against loans that are subject to changing equity prices. As equity prices fall, the collateral against the loan is less valuable. If the price decline is precipitous, the loan could become undercollateralized where the value of the equity, such as a home, is less than the amount of the loan taken and may not provide enough protection to Hometown Bank in case of customer default.

Another example of risk includes bank activities in foreign exchange services. This subjects them to currency exchange rate risk. Also included is commodity price risk associated with lending in the agricultural industry.

Hometown Bank has a total of $65.5 million in investment securities. Typically, banks hold these securities until the money is needed by bank customers as loans, but the Federal Reserve requires that some money be kept in reserve to pay depositors who request their money back. Hometown has an investment policy that lists its approved securities for investment. Because the portfolio consists of interest rate sensitive securities, as interest rates rise, the value of the securities declines.[9] Hometown Bank's CEO, Mr. Allen, is interested in estimating his risk over a five-day period as measured by the worst case he is likely to face in terms of losses in portfolio value. He can then hold that amount of money in reserve so that he can keep from facing liquidity problems. This problem plagued numerous banks during the financial crisis of late 2008. Allen could conceivably lose the entire $65.5 million, but this is incredibly unlikely. He chooses a level of risk coverage of 99 percent and chooses to measure this five-day potential risk of loss by using the 99 percent—the VaR or value at risk. That is, he wants to find the amount of money he needs to keep available so that he has a supply of money sufficient to meet demand with probability of at least 0.99. To illustrate the computation of VaR, we use a historical database to track the value of the different bonds held by Hometown Bank as investment securities. How many times over a given time period—one year, in our example—did Hometown experience negative price movement on their investments and by how much? To simplify the example, we will assume the entire portfolio is invested in two-year U.S. Treasury notes. A year of historical data would create approximately 250 price movement data points for the portfolio.[10] Of those 250 results, how frequently did the portfolio value decrease 5 percent or more from the beginning value? What was the frequency of times the portfolio of U.S. Treasury notes increased in value more than 5 percent? Hometown Bank can now construct a probability distribution of returns by recording observations of portfolio performance. This probability distribution appears in Figure 2.7.

FIGURE 2.7 Hometown Bank Frequency Distribution of Daily Price Movement of Investment Securities Portfolio

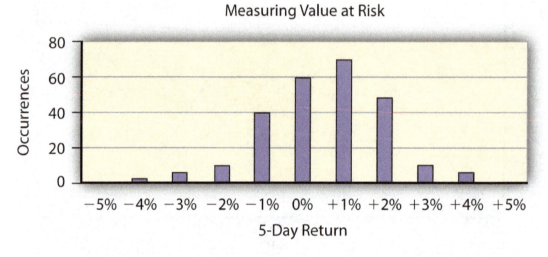

Sample Data

Date	Portfolio Value	Change from Beginning Value
12-31-06	$65,500,000	0
1-02-07	$64,300,000	−1.83%
1-03-07	$64,900,000	−0.16%
1-04-07	$64,100,200	−2.14%
1-07-07	$63,900,900	−2.44%
1-08-07	$64,500,000	−1.52%

The frequency distribution curve of price movement for the portfolio appears in Figure 2.4. From that data, Hometown can measure a portfolio's 99 percent VaR for a five-day period by finding the lower one percentile for the probability distribution. VaR describes the probability of potential loss in value of the U.S. Treasury notes that relates to market price risk. From the chart, we observe that the bottom 1 percent of the 250 observations is about a 5 percent loss, that is, 99 percent of the time the return is greater than −5 percent. Thus, the 99 percent VaR on the returns is −5 percent. The VaR for the portfolio is the VaR on the return times $65.5 million, or −.05 × ($65.5 million) = −$3,275,000. This answers the question of how much risk capital the bank needs to hold against contingencies that should only occur once in one hundred five-day periods, namely, they should hold $3,275,000 in reserve. With this amount of money, the likelihood that the movements in market values will cause a loss of more than $3,275,000 is 1 percent.

The risk can now be communicated with the statement: *Under normal market conditions, the most the investment security portfolio will lose in value over a five-day period is about $3,275,000 with a confidence level of 99 percent.*[11]

In the context of pure risk exposures, the equivalent notion to VaR is the Maximal Probable Annual Loss (MPAL). As with the VaR measure, it looks at a probability distribution, in this case of losses over a year period and then picks the selected lower percentile value as the MPAL. For example, if the loss distribution is given by Figure 2.3, and the 95 percent level of confidence is selected, then the MPAL is the same as the 95 percent VaR value. In insurance contexts one often encounters the term MPAL, whereas in finance one often encounters the term VaR. Their calculation is the same and their interpretation as a measure of risk is the same.

We also note that debate rages about perceived weaknesses in using VaR as a risk measure in finance. "In short, VaR models do not provide an accurate measure of the losses that occur in *extreme* events. You simply cannot depict the full texture and range of your market risks with VaR alone."[12] In addition, the VaR examines the size of loss that would occur only 1 percent of the time, but it does not specify the size of the shortfall that the company would be expected to have to make up by a distress liquidation of assets should such a large loss occur. Another measure called the expected shortfall is used for this. The interested reader is referred to Brockett and Ai[13] for this calculation.

3.4   CAPM's Beta Measure of Nondiversifiable Portfolio Risk

Some risk exposures affect many assets of a firm at the same time. In finance, for example, movements in the market as a whole or in the entire economy can affect the value of many individual stocks (and firms) simultaneously. We saw this very dramatically illustrated in the financial crisis in 2008–2009 where the entire stock market went down and dragged many stocks (and firms) down with it, some more than others. In Chapter 1 we referred to this type of risk as systematic, fundamental, or nondiversifiable risk. For a firm (or individual) having a large, well-diversified portfolio of assets, the total negative financial impact of any single idiosyncratic risk on the value of the portfolio is minimal since it constitutes only a small fraction of their wealth.

Therefore, the asset-specific idiosyncratic risk is generally ignored when making decisions concerning the additional amount of risk involved when acquiring an additional asset to be added to an already well-diversified portfolio of assets. The question is how to disentangle the systematic from the nonsystematic risk embedded in any asset. Finance professors Jack Treynor, William Sharpe, John Lintner, and Jan Mossin worked independently and developed a model called the Capital Asset Pricing Model (CAPM). From this model we can get a measure of how the return on an asset systematically varies with the variations in the market, and consequently we can get a measure of systematic risk. The idea is similar to the old adage that a rising tide lifts all ships. In this case a rising (or falling) market or economy rises (or lowers) all assets to a greater or lesser degree depending on their covariation with the market. This covariation with the market is fundamental to obtaining a measure of systematic risk. We develop it now.

Essentially, the CAPM model assumes that investors in assets expect to be compensated for both the time value of money and the systematic or nondiversifiable risk they bear. In this regard, the return on an asset A, R_A, is assumed to be equal to the return on an absolutely safe or risk-free investment, r_f (the time value of money part) and a **risk premium**, which measures the compensation for the systematic risk they are bearing. To measure the amount of this systematic risk, we first look at the correlation between the returns on the asset and the returns on a market portfolio of all assets. The assumption is that the market portfolio changes with changes in the economy as a whole, and so systematic changes in the economy are reflected by changes in the level of the market portfolio. The variation of the asset returns with respect to the market returns is assumed to be linear and so the general framework is expressed as

$$R_A = r_f + \beta A^*(R_m - r_f) + \varepsilon,$$

where ε denotes a random term that is unrelated to the market return. Thus the term $\beta_A \times (R_m - r_f)$ represents a systematic return and ε represents a firm-specific or idiosyncratic nonsystematic component of return.

Notice that upon taking variances, we have $\sigma^2_A = .\beta^2_A \times \beta^2_m, + \sigma^2_\varepsilon$, so the first term is called the systematic variance and the second term is the idiosyncratic or firm-specific variance.

The idea behind the CAPM is that investors would be compensated for the systematic risk and not the idiosyncratic risk, since the idiosyncratic risk should be diversifiable by the investors who hold a large diversified portfolio of assets, while the systematic or market risk affects them all. In terms of expected values, we often write the equation as

$$E[R_A] = r_f + \beta_A^*(E[R_m] - r_f),$$

risk premium

The premium over and above the actuarially fair premium that a risk-averse person is willing to pay to get rid of risk.

which is the so-called CAPM model. In this regard the expected rate of return on an asset $E[R_A]$, is the risk-free investment, r_f, plus a market risk premium equal to $\beta_A \times (E[R_m] - R_f)$. The coefficient β_A is called the market risk or systematic risk of asset A.

By running a linear regression of the returns experienced on asset A with those returns experienced on a market portfolio (such as the Dow Jones Industrial stock portfolio) and the risk-free asset return (such as the U.S. T-Bill rate of return), one can find the risk measure β_A. A regression is a statistical technique that creates a trend based on the data. An actual linear regression to compute future frequency and severity based on a trend is used in Chapter 4 for risk management analysis. Statistical books show[14] that $\beta_A = COV(R_A, R_m)/\beta^2_m$ where $COV(R_A, R_m)$ is the covariance of the return on the asset with the return on the market and is defined by

$$COV(R_A, R_m) = E[\{R_A, -E(R_A)\} \times \{ R_m, -E(R_m)\}],$$

that is, the average value of the product of the deviation of the asset return from its expected value and the market returns from its expected value. In terms of the correlation coefficient ρ_{Am} between the return on the asset and the market, we have $\beta_A = \rho_{Am} \times (\beta_A/\beta_m)$, so we can also think of beta as scaling the asset volatility by the market volatility and the correlation of the asset with the market.

The β (beta) term in the above equations attempts to quantify the risk associated with market fluctuations or swings in the market. A beta of 1 means that the asset return is expected to move in conjunction with the market, that is, a 5 percent move (measured in terms of standard deviation units of the market) in the market will result in a 5 percent move in the asset (measured in terms of standard deviation units of the asset). A beta less than one indicates that the asset is less volatile than the market in that when the market goes up (or down) by 5 percent the asset will go up (or down) by less than 5 percent. A beta greater than one means that the asset price is expected to move more rapidly than the market so if the market goes up (or down) by 5 percent then the asset will go up (or down) by more than 5 percent. A beta of zero indicates that the return on the asset does not correlate with the returns on the market.

KEY TAKEAWAYS

- Risk measures quantify the amount of surprise potential contained in a probability distribution.
- Measures such as the range and Value at Risk (VaR) and Maximal Probable Annual Loss (MPAL) focus on the extremes of the distributions and are appropriate measures of risk when interest is focused on solvency or making sure that enough capital is set aside to handle any realized extreme losses.
- Measures such as the variance, standard deviation, and semivariance are useful when looking at average deviations from what is expected for the purpose of planning for expected deviations from expected results.
- The market risk measure from the Capital Asset Pricing Model is useful when assessing systematic financial risk or the additional risk involved in adding an asset to an already existing diversified portfolio.

DISCUSSION QUESTIONS

1. Compare the relative risk of Insurer A to Insurer B in the following questions.
   a. Which insurer carries more risk in losses and which carries more claims risk? Explain.
   b. Compare the severity and frequency of the insurers as well.
2. The experience of Insurer A for the last three years as given in Problem 2 was the following::

Year	Number of Exposures	Number of Collision Claims	Collision Losses ($)
1	10,000	375	350,000
2	10,000	330	250,000
3	10,000	420	400,000

   a. What is the range of collision losses per year?
   b. What is the standard deviation of the losses per year?
   c. Calculate the coefficient of variation of the losses per year.
   d. Calculate the variance of the number of claims per year.
3. The experience of Insurer B for the last three years as given in Problem 3 was the following:

Year	Number of Exposures	Number of Collision Claims	Collision Losses
1	20,000	975	650,000
2	20,000	730	850,000
3	20,000	820	900,000

   a. What is the range of collision losses?
   b. Calculate the variance in the number of collision claims per year.
   c. What is the standard deviation of the collision losses?
   d. Calculate the coefficient of collision variation.
   e. Comparing the results of Insurer A and Insurer B, which insurer has a riskier book of business in terms of the range of possible losses they might experience?
   f. Comparing the results of Insurer A and Insurer B, which insurer has a riskier book of business in terms of the standard deviation in the collision losses they might experience?

4. REVIEW AND PRACTICE

1. The Texas Department of Insurance publishes data on all the insurance claims closed during a given year. For the thirteen years from 1990 to 2002 the following table lists the percentage of medical malpractice claims closed in each year for which the injury actually occurred in the same year.

Year	% of injuries in the year that are closed in that year
1990	0.32
1991	1.33
1992	0.86
1993	0.54
1994	0.69
1995	0.74
1996	0.76
1997	1.39
1998	1.43
1999	0.55
2000	0.66
2001	0.72
2002	1.06

Calculate the average percentage of claims that close in the same year as the injury occurs.

2. From the same Texas Department of Insurance data on closed claims for medical malpractice liability insurance referred to in Problem 1, we can estimate the number of claims in each year of injury that will be closed in the next 16 years. We obtain the following data. Here the estimated dollars per claim for each year have been adjusted to 2007 dollars to account for inflation, so the values are all compatible. Texas was said to have had a "medical malpractice liability crisis" starting in about 1998 and continuing until the legislature passed tort reforms effective in September 2003, which put caps on certain noneconomic damage awards. During this period premiums increased greatly and doctors left high-risk specialties such as emergency room service and delivering babies, and left high-risk geographical areas as well causing shortages in doctors in certain locations. The data from 1994 until 2001 is the following:

Injury year	Estimated # claims	Estimated $ per claim
1994	1021	$415,326.26
1995	1087	$448,871.57
1996	1184	$477,333.66
1997	1291	$490,215.19
1998	1191	$516,696.63
1999	1098	$587,233.93
2000	1055	$536,983.82
2001	1110	$403,504.39

a. Calculate the mean or average number of claims per year for medical malpractice insurance in Texas over the four-year period 1994–1997.

b. Calculate the mean or average number of claims per year for medical malpractice insurance in Texas over the four-year period 1998–2001.

c. Calculate the mean or average dollar value per claim per year for medical malpractice insurance in Texas over the four-year period 1994–1997 (in 2009 dollars).

d. Calculate the mean or average dollar value per claim per year for medical malpractice insurance in Texas over the four-year period 1998–2001 (in 2009 dollars).

e. Looking at your results from (a) to (e), do you think there is any evidence to support the conclusion that costs were rising for insurers, justifying the rise in premiums?

3. Referring back to the Texas Department of Insurance data on closed claims for medical malpractice liability insurance presented in Problem 5, we wish to see if medical malpractice was more risky to the insurer during the 1998–2001 period than it was in the 1994–1997 period. The data from 1994 until 2001 was:

Injury year	Estimated # claims	Estimated $ per claim
1994	1021	$415,326.26
1995	1087	$448,871.57
1996	1184	$477,333.66
1997	1291	$490,215.19
1998	1191	$516,696.63
1999	1098	$587,233.93
2000	1055	$536,983.82
2001	1110	$403,504.39

a. Calculate the standard deviation in the estimated payment per claim for medical malpractice insurance in Texas over the four-year period 1994–1997.

b. Calculate the standard deviation in the estimated payment per claim for medical malpractice insurance in Texas over the four-year period 1998–2001.

c. Which time period was more risky (in terms of the standard deviation in payments per claim)?

d. Using the results of (c) above, do you think the medical malpractice insurers raising rates during the period 1998–2001 was justified on the basis of assuming additional risk?

ENDNOTES

1. This is particularly true in firms like insurance companies and banks where the business opportunity they pursue is mainly based on taking calculated and judgment-based risks.

2. The government of William III of England, for example, offered annuities of 14 percent regardless of whether the annuitant was 30 or 70 percent; (Karl Pearson, *The History of Statistics In the 17th and 18th Centuries against the Changing Background of Intellectual, Scientific and Religious Thought* (London: Charles Griffin & Co., 1978), 134.

3. See Patrick Brockett and Arnold Levine Brockett, *Statistics, Probability and Their Applications* (W. B. Saunders Publishing Co., 1984), 62.

4. Nor was the logic of the notion of equally likely outcomes readily understood at the time. For example, the famous mathematician D'Alembert made the following mistake when calculating the probability of a head appearing in two flips of a coin (Karl Pearson, *The History of Statistics in the 17th and 18th Centuries against the Changing Background of Intellectual, Scientific and Religious Thought* [London: Charles Griffin & Co., 1978], 552). D'Alembert said the head could come up on the first flip, which would settle that matter, or a tail could come up on the first flip followed by either a head or a tail on the second flip. There are three outcomes, two of which have a head, and so he claimed the likelihood of getting a head in two flips is 2/3. Evidently, he did not take the time to actually flip coins to see that the probability was 3/4, since the possible equally likely outcomes are actually (H,T), (H,H), (T,H), (T,T) with three pairs of flips resulting in a head. The error is that the outcomes stated in D'Alembert's solution are not equally likely using his outcomes H, (T,H), (T,T), so his denominator is wrong. The moral of this story is that postulated theoretical models should always be tested against empirical data whenever possible to uncover any possible errors.

5. In some ways it is a shame that the term "expected value" has been used to describe this concept. A better term is "long run average value" or "mean value" since this particular value is really not to be expected in any real sense and may not even be a possibility to occur (e.g., the value calculated from Table 2.3 is 1.008, which is not even a possibility). Nevertheless, we are stuck with this terminology, and it does convey some conception of what we mean as long as we interpreted it as being the number expected as an average value in a long series of repetitions of the scenario being evaluated.

6. Other commonly used measures of profitability in an uncertain opportunity, other than the mean or expected value, are the mode (the most likely value) and the median (the number with half the numbers above it and half the numbers below it—the 50 percent mark).

7. Calculating the average signed deviation from the mean or expected value since is a useless exercise since the result will always be zero. Taking the square of each deviation for the mean or expected value gets rid of the algebraic sign and makes the sum positive and meaningful. One might alternatively take the absolute value of the deviations from the mean to obtain another measure called the absolute deviation, but this is usually not done because it results in a mathematically inconvenient formulation. We shall stick to the squared deviation and its variants here.

8. Basel Committee on Banking Supervision (BCBS), International Convergence of Capital Measurement and Capital Standards: A Revised Framework (Basel, Switzerland, 2004).

9. Valuation of bonds is covered in general finance text. Bond value = present value of coupons + present value of face value of bond.

10. The number 250 comes from a rough estimate of the number of days securities can be traded in the open market during any given year. Fifty-two weeks at five days per week yields 260 weekdays, and there are roughly ten holidays throughout the year for which the market is closed.

11. Philippe Jorion, *Value at Risk: The New Benchmark for Managing Financial Risk*, 2nd ed. (McGraw Hill, 2001), ch. 1. Chapter 1.

12. Gleason, chapter 12.

13. Patrick L. Brockett and Jing Ai, "Enterprise Risk Management (ERM)," in *Encyclopedia of Quantitative Risk Assessment and Analysis*, ed. E. Melnick and B. Everitt (Chichester, UK: John Wiley & Sons Ltd., 2008), 559–66.

14. See Patrick Brockett and Arnold Levine Brockett, *Statistics, Probability and Their Applications* (W. B. Saunders Publishing Co., 1984).

utility theory

A theory postulated in economics to explain behavior of individuals based on the premise people can consistently rank order their choices depending upon their preferences.

This notion that an individual derives satisfaction from wealth seems to work more often than not in economic situations. The economic theory that links the level of satisfaction to a person's wealth level, and thus to consumption levels, is called **utility theory**. Its basis revolves around individuals' preferences, but we must use caution as we apply utility theory.[3]

In this chapter, we will study the utility theory. If utility theory is designed to measure satisfaction, and since every individual always tries to maximize satisfaction, it's reasonable to expect (under utility theory) that each person tries to maximize his or her own utility.

Then we will extend utility to one of its logical extensions as applied to uncertain situations: expected utility (EU henceforth). So while utility theory deals with situations in which there is no uncertainty, the EU theory deals with choices individuals make when the outcomes they face are uncertain. As we shall see, if individuals maximize utility under certainty, they will also attempt to maximize EU under uncertainty.

However, individuals' unabashed EU maximization is not always the case. Other models of human behavior describe behavior in which the observed choices of an individual vary with the decision rule to maximize EU. So why would a mother jump into a river to save her child, even if she does not know how to swim? Economists still confront these and other such questions. They have provided only limited answers to such questions thus far.

Hence, we will touch upon some uncertainty-laden situations wherein individuals' observed behavior departs from the EU maximization principle. Systematic departures in behavior from the EU principle stem from "biases" that people exhibit, and we shall discuss some of these biases. Such rationales of observed behavior under uncertainty are termed "behavioral" explanations, rather than "rational" explanations—explanations that explore EU behavior of which economists are so fond.

In this chapter, we will apply the EU theory to individuals' hedging decisions/purchase of insurance. Let's start by asking, Why would anyone buy insurance? When most people face that question, they respond in one of three ways. One set says that insurance provides peace of mind (which we can equate to a level of satisfaction). Others respond more bluntly and argue that if it were not for regulation they'd never buy insurance. The second reply is one received mostly from younger adults. Still others posit that insurance is a "waste of money," since they pay premiums up front and insurance never pays up in the absence of losses. To all those who argue based upon the third response, one might say, would they rather have a loss for the sake of recovering their premiums? We look to EU theory for some answers, and we will find that even if governments did not make purchase of insurance mandatory, the product would still have existed. Risk-averse individuals would always demand insurance for the peace of mind it confers.

Thus we will briefly touch upon the ways that insurance is useful, followed by a discussion of how some information problems affect the insurance industry more than any other industry. "Information asymmetry" problems arise, wherein one economic agent in a contract is better informed than the other party to the same contract. The study of information asymmetries has become a full-time occupation for some economics researchers. Notably, professors George A. Akerlof, A. Michael Spence, and Joseph E. Stiglitz were awarded the Nobel Prize in Economics in 2001 for their analyses of information asymmetry problems.

1. LINKS

Preferences are not absolute but rather they depend upon market conditions, cultures, peer groups, and surrounding events. Individuals' preferences nestle within these parameters. Therefore, we can never talk in absolute terms when we talk about satisfaction and preferences. The 2008 crisis, which continued into 2009, provides a good example of how people's preferences can change very quickly. When people sat around in celebration of 2009 New Year's Eve, conversation centered on hopes for "making a living" and having some means for income. These same people talked about trips around the world at the end of 2007. Happiness and preferences are a dynamic topic depending upon individuals' stage of life and economic states of the world. Under each new condition, new preferences arise that fall under the static utility theory discussed below. Economists have researched "happiness," and continuing study is very important to economists.[4]

FIGURE 3.1   Links between the Holistic Risk Picture and Risk Attitudes

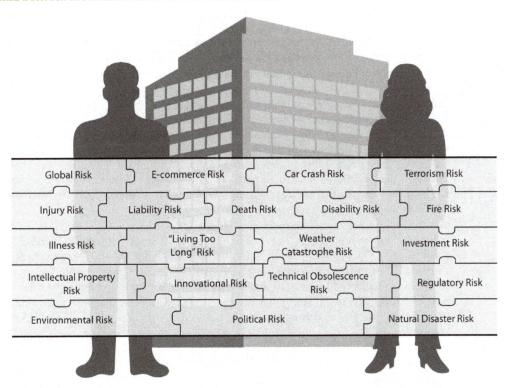

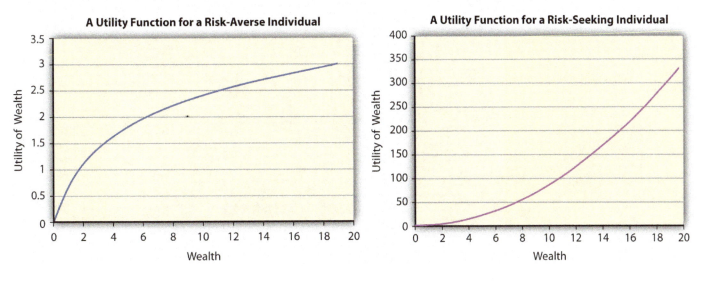

2. UTILITY THEORY

LEARNING OBJECTIVES

- In this section we discuss economists' utility theory.
- You will learn about assumptions that underlie individual preferences, which can then be mapped onto a utility "function," reflecting the satisfaction level associated with individuals' preferences.
- Further, we will explore how individuals maximize utility (or satisfaction).

utility theory

A theory postulated in economics to explain behavior of individuals based on the premise people can consistently order rank their choices depending upon their preferences.

positive theory

Theory that seeks to explain an individual's observed behavior and choices.

normative theory

Theory that dictates that people should behave in the manner prescribed by it.

utility function

A mathematical formulation that ranks the preferences of the individual in terms of satisfaction different consumption bundles provide.

ordinal utility

Utility that can only represent relative levels of satisfaction between two or more alternatives, that is, rank orders them.

cardinal utility

Utility that can represent the absolute level of satisfaction.

Utility theory bases its beliefs upon individuals' preferences. It is a theory postulated in economics to explain behavior of individuals based on the premise people can consistently rank order their choices depending upon their preferences. Each individual will show different preferences, which appear to be hard-wired within each individual. We can thus state that individuals' preferences are intrinsic. Any theory, which proposes to capture preferences, is, by necessity, abstraction based on certain assumptions. Utility theory is a **positive theory** that seeks to explain the individuals' observed behavior and choices.[5] This contrasts with a **normative theory**, one that dictates that people should behave in the manner prescribed by it. Instead, it is only since the theory itself is positive, after observing the choices that individuals make, we can draw inferences about their preferences. When we place certain restrictions on those preferences, we can represent them analytically using a **utility function**—a mathematical formulation that ranks the preferences of the individual in terms of satisfaction different consumption bundles provide. Thus, under the assumptions of utility theory, we can assume that people behaved as if they had a utility function and acted according to it. Therefore, the fact that a person does not know his/her utility function, or even denies its existence, does not contradict the theory. Economists have used experiments to decipher individuals' utility functions and the behavior that underlies individuals' utility.

To begin, assume that an individual faces a set of consumption "bundles." We assume that individuals have clear preferences that enable them to "rank order" all bundles based on desirability, that is, the level of satisfaction each bundle shall provide to each individual. This rank ordering based on preferences tells us the theory itself has **ordinal utility**—it is designed to study relative satisfaction levels. As we noted earlier, absolute satisfaction depends upon conditions; thus, the theory by default cannot have **cardinal utility**, or utility that can represent the absolute level of satisfaction. To make this theory concrete, imagine that consumption bundles comprise food and clothing for a week in all different combinations, that is, food for half a week, clothing for half a week, and all other possible combinations.

The utility theory then makes the following assumptions:

1. Completeness: Individuals can rank order all possible bundles. Rank ordering implies that the theory assumes that, no matter how many combinations of consumption bundles are placed in front of the individual, each individual can always rank them in some order based on preferences. This, in turn, means that individuals can somehow compare any bundle with any other bundle and rank them in order of the satisfaction each bundle provides. So in our example, half a week of food and clothing can be compared to one week of food alone, one week of clothing alone, or any such combination. Mathematically, this property wherein an individual's preferences enable him or her to compare any given bundle with any other bundle is called the **completeness** property of preferences.

2. More-is-better: Assume an individual prefers consumption of bundle A of goods to bundle B. Then he is offered another bundle, which contains more of everything in bundle A, that is, the new bundle is represented by αA where α = 1. The more-is-better assumption says that individuals prefer αA to A, which in turn is preferred to B, but also A itself. For our example, if one week of food is preferred to one week of clothing, then two weeks of food is a preferred package to one week of food. Mathematically, the more-is-better assumption is called the **monotonicity assumption** on preferences. One can always argue that this assumption breaks down frequently. It is not difficult to imagine that a person whose stomach is full would turn down additional food. However, this situation is easily resolved. Suppose the individual is given the option of disposing of the additional food to another person or charity of his or her choice. In this case, the person will still prefer more food even if he or she has eaten enough. Thus under the monotonicity assumption, a hidden property allows costless disposal of excess quantities of any bundle.

3. Mix-is-better: Suppose an individual is indifferent to the choice between one week of clothing alone and one week of food. Thus, either choice by itself is not preferred over the other. The **"mix-is-better" assumption** about preferences says that a mix of the two, say half-week of food mixed with half-week of clothing, will be preferred to both stand-alone choices. Thus, a glass of milk mixed with Milo (Nestlè's drink mix), will be preferred to milk or Milo alone. The mix-is-better assumption is called the "convexity" assumption on preferences, that is, preferences are convex.

4. Rationality: This is the most important and controversial assumption that underlies all of utility theory. Under the assumption of **rationality**, individuals' preferences avoid any kind of circularity; that is, if bundle A is preferred to B, and bundle B is preferred to C, then A is also preferred to C. Under no circumstances will the individual prefer C to A. You can likely see why this assumption is controversial. It assumes that the innate preferences (rank orderings of bundles of goods) are fixed, regardless of the context and time.

If one thinks of preference orderings as comparative relationships, then it becomes simpler to construct examples where this assumption is violated. So, in "beats"—as in A beat B in college football. These are relationships that are easy to see. For example, if University of Florida beats Ohio State, and Ohio State beats Georgia Tech, it does not mean that Florida beats Georgia Tech. Despite the restrictive nature of the assumption, it is a critical one. In mathematics, it is called the assumption of transitivity of preferences.

Whenever these four assumptions are satisfied, then the preferences of the individual can be represented by a **well-behaved utility function**.[6] Note that the assumptions lead to "a" function, not "the" function. Therefore, the way that individuals represent preferences under a particular utility function may not be unique. Well-behaved utility functions explain why any comparison of individual people's utility functions may be a futile exercise (and the notion of cardinal utility misleading). Nonetheless, utility functions are valuable tools for representing the preferences of an individual, provided the four assumptions stated above are satisfied. For the remainder of the chapter we will assume that preferences of any individual can always be represented by a well-behaved utility function. As we mentioned earlier, well-behaved utility depends upon the amount of wealth the person owns.

Utility theory rests upon the idea that people behave as if they make decisions by assigning imaginary utility values to the original monetary values. The decision maker sees different levels of monetary values, translates these values into different, hypothetical terms ("utils"), processes the decision in utility terms (not in wealth terms), and translates the result back to monetary terms. So while we observe inputs to and results of the decision in monetary terms, the decision itself is made in utility terms. And given that utility denotes levels of satisfaction, individuals behave as if they maximize the utility, not the level of observed dollar amounts.

While this may seem counterintuitive, let's look at an example that will enable us to appreciate this distinction better. More importantly, it demonstrates why utility maximization, rather than wealth maximization, is a viable objective. The example is called the "St. Petersburg paradox." But before we turn to that example, we need to review some preliminaries of uncertainty: probability and statistics.

completeness

Property in which an individual's preferences enable him/her to compare any given consumption bundle with any other bundle.

monotonicity assumption

The assumption that more consumption is always better.

mix-is-better assumption

The assumption that a mix of consumption bundles is always better than stand-alone choices.

rationality

The assumption that individuals' preferences avoid any kind of circularity.

well-behaved utility function

A representation of the preferences of the individual that satisfies the assumptions of completeness, monotonicity, mix-is-better, and rationality.

KEY TAKEAWAYS

- In economics, utility theory governs individual decision making. The student must understand an intuitive explanation for the assumptions: completeness, monotonicity, mix-is-better, and rationality (also called transitivity).
- Finally, students should be able to discuss and distinguish between the various assumptions underlying the utility function.

DISCUSSION QUESTIONS

1. Utility theory is a preference-based approach that provides a rank ordering of choices. Explain this statement.
2. List and describe in your own words the four axioms/assumptions that lead to the existence of a utility function.
3. What is a "util" and what does it measure?

3. UNCERTAINTY, EXPECTED VALUE, AND FAIR GAMES

LEARNING OBJECTIVES

- **In this section we discuss the notion of uncertainty. Mathematical preliminaries discussed in this section form the basis for analysis of individual decision making in uncertain situations.**
- **The student should pick up the tools of this section, as we will apply them later.**

As we learned in the chapters Chapter 1 and Chapter 2, risk and uncertainty depend upon one another. The origins of the distinction go back to the Mr. Knight,[7] who distinguished between risk and uncertainty, arguing that measurable uncertainty is risk. In this section, since we focus only on measurable uncertainty, we will not distinguish between risk and uncertainty and use the two terms interchangeably.

As we described in Chapter 2, the study of uncertainty originated in games of chance. So when we play games of dice, we are dealing with outcomes that are inherently uncertain. The branch of science of uncertain outcomes is probability and statistics. Notice that the analysis of probability and statistics applies only if outcomes are uncertain. When a student registers for a class but does not attend any lectures nor does any assigned work or test, only one outcome is possible: a failing grade. On the other hand, if the student attends all classes and scores 100 percent on all tests and assignments, then too only one outcome is possible, an "A" grade. In these extreme situations, no uncertainty arises with the outcomes. But between these two extremes lies the world of uncertainty. Students often do research on the instructor and try to get a "feel" for the chance that they will make a particular grade if they register for an instructor's course.

Even though we covered some of this discussion of probability and uncertainty in Chapter 2, we repeat it here for reinforcement. Figuring out the chance, in mathematical terms, is the same as calculating the probability of an event. To compute a probability empirically, we repeat an experiment with uncertain outcomes (called a random experiment) and count the number of times the event of interest happens, say n, in the N trials of the experiment. The empirical probability of the event then equals n/N. So, if one keeps a log of the number of times a computer crashes in a day and records it for 365 days, the probability of the computer crashing on a day will be the sum of all of computer crashes on a daily basis (including zeroes for days it does not crash at all) divided by 365.

For some problems, the probability can be calculated using mathematical deduction. In these cases, we can figure out the probability of getting a head on a coin toss, two aces when two cards are randomly chosen from a deck of 52 cards, and so on (see the example of the dice in Chapter 2). We don't have to conduct a random experiment to actually compute the mathematical probability, as is the case with empirical probability.

Finally, as strongly suggested before, subjective probability is based on a person's beliefs and experiences, as opposed to empirical or mathematical probability. It may also depend upon a person's state of mind. Since beliefs may not always be rational, studying behavior using subjective probabilities belongs to the realm of behavioral economics rather than traditional rationality-based economics.

So consider a lottery (a game of chance) wherein several outcomes are possible with defined probabilities. Typically, outcomes in a lottery consist of monetary prizes. Returning to our dice example of Chapter 2, let's say that when a six-faced die is rolled, the payoffs associated with the outcomes are $1 if a 1 turns up, $2 for a 2, ..., and $6 for a 6. Now if this game is played once, one and only one amount can be won—$1, $2, and so on. However, if the same game is played many times, what is the amount that one can *expect* to win?

Mathematically, the answer to any such question is very straightforward and is given by the expected value of the game.

In a game of chance, if $W_1, W_2, \ldots, W_N$ are the N outcomes possible with probabilities $\pi_1, \pi_2, \ldots, \pi_N$, then the expected value of the game (G) is

$$E(U) = \sum_{i=1}^{\infty} \pi_i U(W_i) = \frac{1}{2} \times \ln(2) + \frac{1}{4} \times \ln(4) + \ldots = \sum_{i=1}^{\infty} \frac{1}{2^i} \ln(2^i).$$

The computation can be extended to expected values of any uncertain situation, say losses, provided we know the outcome numbers and their associated probabilities. The probabilities sum to 1, that is,

$$\sum_{i=1}^{N} \pi_i = \pi_1 + \ldots + \pi_N = 1.$$

While the computation of expected value is important, equally important is notion behind expected values. Note that we said that when it comes to the outcome of a single game, only one amount can be won, either $1, $2, ..., $6. But if the game is played over and over again, then one can expect to win $E(G) = \frac{1}{6}1 + \frac{1}{6}2 \ldots + \frac{1}{6}6 = \$3.50$ per game. Often—like in this case—the expected value is not one of the possible outcomes of the distribution. In other words, the probability of getting $3.50 in the above lottery is zero. Therefore, the concept of expected value is a long-run concept, and the hidden assumption is that the lottery is played many times. Secondly, the **expected value** is a sum of the products of two numbers, the outcomes and their associated probabilities. If the probability of a large outcome is very high then the expected value will also be high, and vice versa.

Expected value of the game is employed when one designs a **fair game**. A fair game, actuarially speaking, is one in which the cost of playing the game equals the expected winnings of the game, so that net value of the game equals zero. We would expect that people are willing to play all fair value games. But in practice, this is not the case. I will not pay $500 for a lucky outcome based on a coin toss, even if the expected gains equal $500. No game illustrates this point better than the St. Petersburg paradox.

The paradox lies in a proposed game wherein a coin is tossed until "head" comes up. That is when the game ends. The payoff from the game is the following: if head appears on the first toss, then $2 is paid to the player, if it appears on the second toss then $4 is paid, if it appears on the third toss, then $8, and so on, so that if head appears on the nth toss then the payout is 2^n. The question is how much would an individual pay to play this game?

Let us try and apply the fair value principle to this game, so that the cost an individual is willing to bear should equal the fair value of the game. The expected value of the game *E(G)* is calculated below.

The game can go on indefinitely, since the head may never come up in the first million or billion trials. However, let us look at the expected payoff from the game. If head appears on the first try, the probability of that happening is $\frac{1}{2}$, and the payout is $2. If it happens on the second try, it means the first toss yielded a tail (T) and the second a head (H). The probability of TH combination $= \frac{1}{2} \times \frac{1}{2} = \frac{1}{4}$, and the payoff is $4. Then if H turns up on the third attempt, it implies the sequence of outcomes is TTH, and the probability of that occurring is $\frac{1}{2} \times \frac{1}{2} \times \frac{1}{2} = \frac{1}{8}$ with a payoff of $8. We can continue with this inductive analysis ad infinitum. Since expected is the sum of all products of outcomes and their corresponding probabilities, $E(G) = \frac{1}{2} \times 2 + \frac{1}{4} \times 4 + \frac{1}{8} \times 8 + \ldots = \infty$.

It is evident that while the expected value of the game is infinite, not even the Bill Gateses and Warren Buffets of the world will give even a thousand dollars to play this game, let alone billions.

Daniel Bernoulli was the first one to provide a solution to this paradox in the eighteenth century. His solution was that individuals do not look at the expected wealth when they bid a lottery price, but the expected utility of the lottery is the key. Thus, while the expected wealth from the lottery may be infinite, the expected utility it provides may be finite. Bernoulli termed this as the "moral value" of the

expected value

The sum of the products of two numbers, the outcomes and their associated probabilities.

fair game

Game in which the cost of playing equals the expected winnings of the game, so that net value of the game equals zero.

game. Mathematically, Bernoulli's idea can be expressed with a utility function, which provides a representation of the satisfaction level the lottery provides.

Bernoulli used $U(W) = \ln(W)$ to represent the utility that this lottery provides to an individual where W is the payoff associated with each event H, TH, TTH, and so on, then the expected utility from the game is given by

$$E(U) = \sum_{i=1}^{\infty} \pi_i U(W_i) = \frac{1}{2} \times \ln(2) + \frac{1}{4} \times \ln(4) + \ldots = \sum_{i=1}^{\infty} \frac{1}{2^i} \ln\left(2^i,\right)$$

which can be shown to equal 1.39 after some algebraic manipulation. Since the expected utility that this lottery provides is finite (even if the expected wealth is infinite), individuals will be willing to pay only a finite cost for playing this lottery.

The next logical question to ask is, What if the utility was not given as natural log of wealth by Bernoulli but something else? What is that about the natural log function that leads to a finite expected utility? This brings us to the issue of expected utility and its central place in decision making under uncertainty in economics.

KEY TAKEAWAYS

- Students should be able to explain probability as a measure of uncertainty in their own words.
- Moreover, the student should also be able to explain that any expected value is the sum of product of probabilities and outcomes and be able to compute expected values.

DISCUSSION QUESTIONS

1. Define probability. In how many ways can one come up with a probability estimate of an event? Describe.
2. Explain the need for utility functions using St. Petersburg paradox as an example.
3. Suppose a six-faced fair die with numbers 1–6 is rolled. What is the number you *expect* to obtain?
4. What is an actuarially fair game?

4. CHOICE UNDER UNCERTAINTY: EXPECTED UTILITY THEORY

LEARNING OBJECTIVES

- **In this section the student learns that an individual's objective is to maximize expected utility when making decisions under uncertainty.**
- **We also learn that people are risk averse, risk neutral, or risk seeking (loving).**

expected utility

A construct to explain the level of satisfaction a person gets when faced with uncertain choices.

We saw earlier that in a certain world, people like to maximize utility. In a world of uncertainty, it seems intuitive that individuals would maximize **expected utility**. This refers to a construct used to explain the level of satisfaction a person gets when faced with uncertain choices. The intuition is straightforward, proving it axiomatically was a very challenging task. John von Neumann and Oskar Morgenstern (1944) advocated an approach that leads us to a formal mathematical representation of maximization of expected utility.

We have also seen that a utility function representation exists if the four assumptions discussed above hold. Messrs. von Neumann and Morgenstern added two more assumptions and came up with an expected utility function that exists if these axioms hold. While the discussions about these assumptions[8] is beyond the scope of the text, it suffices to say that the expected utility function has the form

$$E(U) = \sum_{i=1}^{n} \pi_i u_i,$$

where u is a function that attaches numbers measuring the level of satisfaction u_i associated with each outcome i. u is called the Bernoulli function while E(U) is the von Neumann-Morgenstern expected utility function.

Again, note that expected utility function is not unique, but several functions can model the preferences of the same individual over a given set of uncertain choices or games. What matters is that such a function (which reflects an individual's preferences over uncertain games) exists. The expected utility theory then says if the axioms provided by von Neumann-Morgenstern are satisfied, then the individuals behave as if they were trying to maximize the expected utility.

The most important insight of the theory is that the expected value of the dollar outcomes may provide a ranking of choices different from those given by expected utility. The **expected utility theory** then says persons shall choose an option (a game of chance or lottery) that maximizes their expected utility rather than the expected wealth. That expected utility ranking differs from expected wealth ranking is best explained using the example below.

Let us think about an individual whose utility function is given by $u(W) = \sqrt{W}$ and has an initial endowment of $10. This person faces the following three lotteries, based on a coin toss:

expected utility theory

Theory that says persons will choose an option that maximizes their expected utility rather than their expected wealth.

TABLE 3.1 Utility Function with Initial Endowment of $10

Outcome (Probability)	Payoff Lottery 1	Payoff Lottery 2	Payoff Lottery 3
H (0.5)	10	20	30
T (0.5)	−2	−5	−10
E(G)	4	7.5	10

We can calculate the expected payoff of each lottery by taking the product of probability and the payoff associated with each outcome and summing this product over all outcomes. The ranking of the lotteries based on expected dollar winnings is lottery 3, 2, and 1—in that order. But let us consider the ranking of the same lotteries by this person who ranks them in order based on expected utility.

We compute expected utility by taking the product of probability and the associated utility corresponding to each outcome for all lotteries. When the payoff is $10, the final wealth equals initial endowment ($10) plus winnings = ($20). The utility of this final wealth is given by $\sqrt{20} = 4.472$. The completed utility table is shown below.

TABLE 3.2 Lottery Rankings by Expected Utility

Outcome (Probability)	Utility Lottery 1	Utility Lottery 2	Utility Lottery 3
H (0.5)	4.472	5.477	6.324
T (0.5)	2.828	2.236	0
E(U) =	3.650	3.856	3.162

The expected utility ranks the lotteries in the order 2–1–3. So the expected utility maximization principle leads to choices that differ from the expected wealth choices.

The example shows that the ranking of games of chance differs when one utilizes the expected utility (E[U]) theory than when the expected gain E(G) principle applies This leads us to the insight that if two lotteries provide the same E(G), the expected gain principle will rank both lotteries equally, while the E(U) theory may lead to unique rankings of the two lotteries. What happens when the E(U) theory leads to a same ranking? The theory says the person is indifferent between the two lotteries.

4.1 Risk Types and Their Utility Function Representations

What characteristic of the games of chance can lead to same E(G) but different E(U)? The characteristic is the "risk" associated with each game.[9] Then the E(U) theory predicts that the individuals' risk "attitude" for each lottery may lead to different rankings between lotteries. Moreover, the theory is "robust" in the sense that it also allows for attitudes toward risk to vary from one individual to the next. As we shall now see, the E(U) theory does enable us to capture different risk attitudes of individuals. Technically, the difference in risk attitudes across individuals is called "heterogeneity of risk preferences" among economic agents.

From the E(U) theory perspective, we can categorize all economic agents into one of the three categories as noted in Chapter 1:

- Risk averse
- Risk neutral
- Risk seeking (or loving)

We will explore how E(U) captures these attitudes and the meaning of each risk attitude next.

$$E(U) = \sum_{i=1}^{n} \pi_i u(W_i).$$

Consider the E(U) function given by $E(U) = \sum_{i=1}^{n} \pi_i u(W_i)$. Let the preferences be such that the addition to utility one gets out of an additional dollar at lower levels of wealth is always greater than the additional utility of an extra dollar at higher levels of wealth. So, let us say that when a person has zero wealth (no money), then the person has zero utility. Now if the person receives a dollar, his utility jumps to 1 util. If this person is now given an additional dollar, then as per the monotonicity (more-is-better) assumption, his utility will go up. Let us say that it goes up to 1.414 utils so that the increase in utility is only 0.414 utils, while earlier it was a whole unit (1 util). At 2 dollars of wealth, if the individual receives another dollar, then again his families' utility rises to a new level, but only to 1.732 utils, an increase of 0.318 units (1.732 − 1.414). This is increasing utility at a decreasing rate for each additional unit of wealth. Figure 3.2 shows a graph of the utility.

FIGURE 3.2 A Utility Function for a Risk-Averse Individual

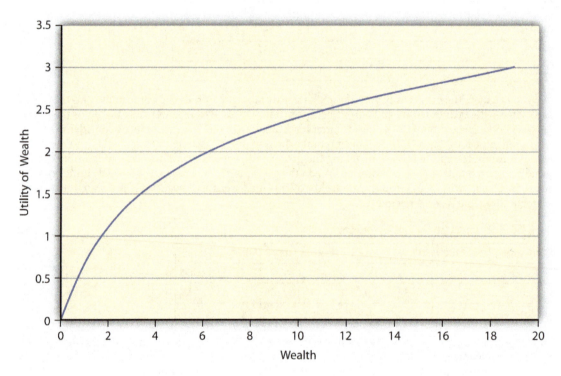

The first thing we notice from Figure 3.2 is its **concavity**, which means if one draws a chord connecting any two points on the curve, the chord will lie strictly below the curve. Moreover, the utility is always increasing although at a decreasing rate. This feature of this particular utility function is called **diminishing marginal utility**. Marginal utility at any given wealth level is nothing but the slope of the utility function at that wealth level.[10] $u'(W) > 0$, $u''(W) < 0$ $u(W) = \sqrt{W}, LN(W), -e^{-2W}$. The functional form depicted in Figure 3.2 is LN(W).

concavity

Property of a curve in which a chord connecting any two points on the curve will lie strictly below the curve.

diminishing marginal utility

Feature of a utility function in which utility is always increasing although at a decreasing rate.

The question we ask ourselves now is whether such an individual, whose utility function has the shape in Figure 3.2, will be willing to pay the **actuarially fair price (AFP)**, which equals expected winnings, to play a game of chance? Let the game that offers him payoffs be offered to him. In Game 1, tables have playoff games by Game 1 in Table 3.1 based on the toss of a coin. The AFP for the game is $4. Suppose that a person named Terry bears this cost upfront and wins; then his final wealth is $10 − $4 + $10 = $16 (original wealth minus the cost of the game, plus the winning of $10), or else it equals $10 − $4 − $2 = $4 (original wealth minus the cost of the game, minus the loss of $2) in case he loses. Let the utility function of this individual be given by $\sqrt{W}$. Then expected utility when the game costs AFP equals $0.5\sqrt{16} + 0.5\sqrt{4} = 3$ utils. On the other hand, suppose Terry doesn't play the game; his utility remains at $\sqrt{10} = 3.162$. Since the utility is higher when Terry doesn't play the game, we conclude that any individual whose preferences are depicted by Figure 3.2 will forgo a game of chance if its cost equals AFP. This is an important result for a concave utility function as shown in Figure 3.2.

Such a person will need incentives to be willing to play the game. It could come as a price reduction for playing the lottery, or as a premium that compensates the individual for risk. If Terry already faces a risk, he will pay an amount greater than the actuarially fair value to reduce or eliminate the risk. Thus, it works both ways—consumers demand a premium above AFP to take on risk. Just so, insurance companies charge individuals premiums for risk transfer via insurances.

An individual—let's name him Johann—has preferences that are characterized by those shown in Figure 3.2 (i.e., by a concave or diminishing marginal utility function). Johann is a risk-averse person. We have seen that a risk-averse person refuses to play an actuarially fair game. Such risk aversions also provide a natural incentive for Johann to demand (or, equivalently, pay) a risk premium above AFP to take on (or, equivalently, get rid of) risk. Perhaps you will recall from Chapter 1 that introduced a more mathematical measure to the description of risk aversion. In an experimental study, Holt and Laury (2002) find that a majority of their subjects under study made "safe choices," that is, displayed risk aversion. Since real-life situations can be riskier than laboratory settings, we can safely assume that a majority of people are risk averse most of the time. What about the remainder of the population?

We know that most of us do not behave as risk-averse people all the time. In the later 1990s, the stock market was considered to be a "bubble," and many people invested in the stock market despite the preferences they exhibited before this time. At the time, Federal Reserve Board Chairman Alan Greenspan introduced the term "irrational exuberance" in a speech given at the American Enterprise Institute. The phrase has become a regular way to describe people's deviations from normal preferences. Such behavior was also repeated in the early to mid-2000s with a real estate bubble. People without the rational means to buy homes bought them and took "nonconventional risks," which led to the 2008–2009 financial and credit crisis and major recessions (perhaps even depression) as President Obama took office in January 2009. We can regard external market conditions and the "herd mentality" to be significant contributors to changing rational risk aversion traits.

An individual may go skydiving, hang gliding, and participate in high-risk-taking behavior. Our question is, can the expected utility theory capture that behavior as well? Indeed it can, and that brings us to risk-seeking behavior and its characterization in E(U) theory. Since risk-seeking behavior exhibits preferences that seem to be the opposite of risk aversion, the mathematical functional representation may likewise show opposite behavior. For a risk-loving person, the utility function will show the shape given in Figure 3.3. It shows that the greater the level of wealth of the individual, the higher is the increase in utility when an additional dollar is given to the person. We call this feature of the function, in which utility is always increasing at an increasing rate, **increasing marginal utility**. It turns out that all **convex utility functions** look like Figure 3.3. The curve lies strictly below the chord joining any two points on the curve.[11] $u(W) = W^2, e^W$.

actuarially fair premium (AFP)

The expected loss in wealth to the individual.

increasing marginal utility

Feature of a utility function in which utility is always increasing at an increasing rate.

convex utility function

Utility function in which the curve lies strictly below the chord joining any two points on the curve.

FIGURE 3.3 A Utility Function for a Risk-Seeking Individual

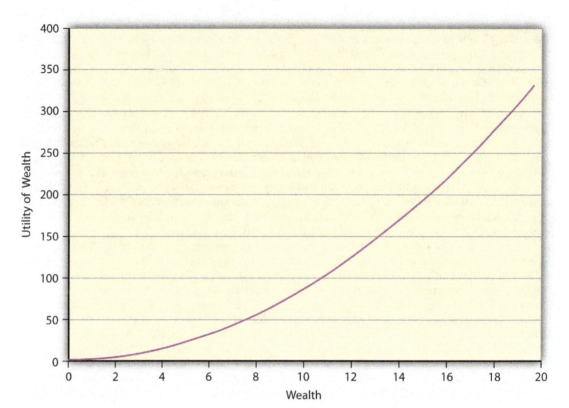

A risk-seeking individual will always choose to play a gamble at its AFP. For example, let us assume that the individual's preferences are given by $u(W) = W^2$. As before, the individual owns $10, and has to decide whether or not to play a lottery based on a coin toss. The payoff if a head turns up is $10 and −$2 if it's a tail. We have seen earlier (in Table 3.1) that the AFP for playing this lottery is $4.

The expected utility calculation is as follows. After bearing the cost of the lottery upfront, the wealth is $6. If heads turns up, the final wealth becomes $16 ($6 + $10). In case tails turns face-up, then the final wealth equals $4 ($6 − $2). People's expected utility if they play the lottery is $u(W) = 0.5 \times 16^2 + 0.5 \times 4^2 = 136$ utils.

On the other hand, if an individual named Ray decides not to play the lottery, then the $E(U) = 10^2 = 100$. Since the E(U) is higher if Ray plays the lottery at its AFP, he will play the lottery. As a matter of fact, this is the mind-set of gamblers. This is why we see so many people at the slot machines in gambling houses.

The contrast between the choices made by risk-averse individuals and risk-seeking individuals is starkly clear in the above example.[12] To summarize, a risk-seeking individual always plays the lottery at its AFP, while a risk-averse person always forgoes it. Their concave (Figure 3.1) versus convex (Figure 3.2) utility functions and their implications lie at the heart of their decision making.

Finally, we come to the third risk attitude type wherein an individual is indifferent between playing a lottery and not playing it. Such an individual is called risk neutral. The preferences of such an individual can be captured in E(U) theory by a linear utility function of the form $u(W) = aW$, where a is a real number > 0. Such an individual gains a constant marginal utility of wealth, that is, each additional dollar adds the same utility to the person regardless of whether the individual is endowed with $10 or $10,000. The utility function of such an individual is depicted in Figure 3.4.

FIGURE 3.4 **A Utility Function for a Risk-Neutral Individual**

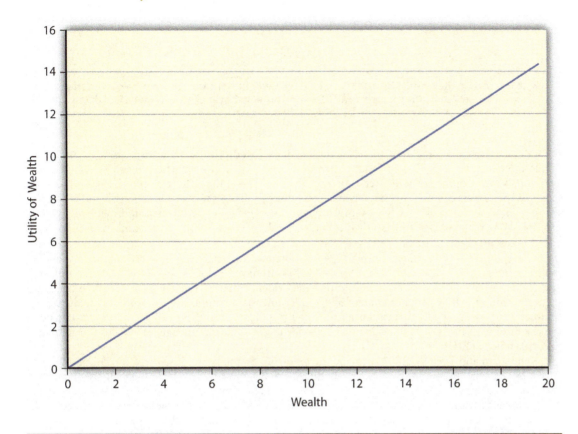

KEY TAKEAWAYS

- This section lays the foundation for analysis of individuals' behavior under uncertainty. Student should be able to describe it as such.
- The student should be able to compute expected gains and expected utilities.
- Finally, and most importantly, the concavity and convexity of the utility function is key to distinguishing between risk-averse and risk-seeking individuals.

DISCUSSION QUESTIONS

1. Discuss the von Neumann-Morgenstern expected utility function and discuss how it differs from expected gains.

2. You are told that $U(W) = W^2$ is a utility function with diminishing marginal utility. Is it correct? Discuss, using definition of diminishing marginal utility.

3. An individual has a utility function given by $(W) = \sqrt{W}$, and initial wealth of $100. If he plays a costless lottery in which he can win or lose $10 at the flip of a coin, compute his expected utility. What is the expected gain? Will such a person be categorized as risk neutral?

4. Discuss the three risk types with respect to their shapes, technical/mathematical formulation, and the economic interpretation.

5. BIASES AFFECTING CHOICE UNDER UNCERTAINTY

LEARNING OBJECTIVE

- In this section the student learns that an individual's behavior cannot always be characterized within an expected utility framework. Biases and other behavioral aspects make individuals deviate from the behavior predicted by the E(U) theory.

behavioral economics

Realm of academic study that deals with departures from E(U) maximization behavior.

Why do some people jump into the river to save their loved ones, even if they cannot swim? Why would mothers give away all their food to their children? Why do we have herd mentality where many individuals invest in the stock market at times of bubbles like at the latter part of the 1990s? These are examples of aspects of human behavior that E(U) theory fails to capture. Undoubtedly, an emotional component arises to explain the few examples given above. Of course, students can provide many more examples. The realm of academic study that deals with departures from E(U) maximization behavior is called **behavioral economics**.

While expected utility theory provides a valuable tool for analyzing how rational people should make decisions under uncertainty, the observed behavior may not always bear it out. Daniel Kahneman and Amos Tversky (1974) were the first to provide evidence that E(U) theory doesn't provide a complete description of how people actually decide under uncertain conditions. The authors conducted experiments that demonstrate this variance from the E(U) theory, and these experiments have withstood the test of time. It turns out that individual behavior under some circumstances violates the axioms of rational choice of E(U) theory.

Kahneman and Tversky (1981) provide the following example: Suppose the country is going to be struck by the avian influenza (bird flu) pandemic. Two programs are available to tackle the pandemic, A and B. Two sets of physicians, X and Y, are set with the task of containing the disease. Each group has the outcomes that the two programs will generate. However, the outcomes have different phrasing for each group. Group X is told about the efficacy of the programs in the following words:

- Program A: If adopted, it will save exactly 200 out of 600 patients.
- Program B: If adopted, the probability that 600 people will be saved is 1/3, while the probability that no one will be saved is 2/3.

Seventy-six percent of the doctors in group X chose to administer program A.

Group Y, on the other hand, is told about the efficacy of the programs in these words:

- Program A: If adopted, exactly 400 out of 600 patients will die.
- Program B: If adopted, the probability that nobody will die is 1/3, while the probability that all 600 will die is 2/3.

Only 13 percent of the doctors in this group chose to administer program A.

The only difference between the two sets presented to groups X and Y is the description of the outcomes. Every outcome to group X is defined in terms of "saving lives," while for group Y it is in terms of how many will "die." Doctors, being who they are, have a bias toward "saving" lives, naturally.

framing effect

The coding of alternatives, which makes individuals vary from E(U) maximizing behavior.

This experiment has been repeated several times with different subjects and the outcome has always been the same, even if the numbers differ. Other experiments with different groups of people also showed that the way alternatives are worded result in different choices among groups. The coding of alternatives that makes individuals vary from E(U) maximizing behavior is called the **framing effect**.

value function

A mathematical formulation that seeks to explain observed behavior without making any assumption about preferences.

In order to explain these deviations from E(U), Kahneman and Tversky suggest that individuals use a **value function** to assess alternatives. This is a mathematical formulation that seeks to explain observed behavior without making any assumption about preferences. The nature of the value function is such that it is much steeper in losses than in gains. The authors insist that it is a purely descriptive device and is not derived from axioms like the E(U) theory. In the language of mathematics we say the value function is convex in losses and concave in gains. For the same concept, economists will say that the function is risk seeking in losses and risk averse in gains. A Kahneman and Tversky value function is shown in Figure 3.5.

FIGURE 3.5 Value Function of Kahneman and Tversky

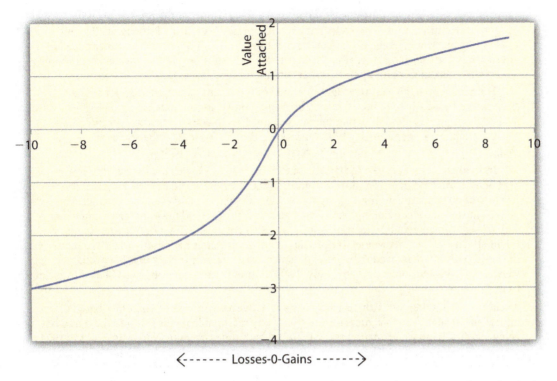

<------- Losses-0-Gains ------->

Figure 3.5 shows the asymmetric nature of the value function. A loss of $200 causes the individual to feel more value is lost compared to an equivalent gain of $200. To see this notice that on the losses side (the negative x-axis) the graph falls more steeply than the rise in the graph on the gains side (positive x-axis). And this is true regardless of the initial level of wealth the person has initially.

The implications of this type of value function for marketers and sellers are enormous. Note that the value functions are convex in losses. Thus, if $L is lost then say the value lost = $-\sqrt{L}$. Now if there are two consecutive losses of $2 and $3, then the total value lost feels like V (lost) = $-\sqrt{2} - \sqrt{3} = -1.414 - 1.732 = -3.142$. On the other hand if the losses are combined, then total loss = $5, and the value lost feels like $-\sqrt{5} = -2.236$. Thus, when losses are combined, the total value lost feels less painful than when the losses are segregated and reported separately.

We can carry out similar analysis on the Kahneman and Tversky function when there is a gain. Note the value function is concave in gains, say, $V(W) = \sqrt{W}$. Now if we have two consecutive gains of $2 and $3, then the total value gained feels like V (gain) = $\sqrt{2} + \sqrt{3} = 1.414 + 1.732 = 3.142$. On the other hand, if we combine the gains, then total gains = $5, and the value gained feels like $\sqrt{5} = 2.236$. Thus, when gains are segregated, the sum of the value of gains turns out to be higher than the value of the sum of gains. So the idea would be to report combined losses, while segregating gains.

Since the individual feels differently about losses and gains, the analysis of the value function tells us that to offset a small loss, we require a larger gain. So small losses can be combined with larger gains, and the individual still feels "happier" since the net effect will be that of a gain. However, if losses are too large, then combining them with small gains would result in a net loss, and the individual would feel that value has been lost. In this case, it's better to segregate the losses from the gains and report them separately. Such a course of action will provide a consolation to the individual of the type: "At least there are some gains, even if we suffer a big loss."

Framing effects are not the only reason why people deviate from the behavior predicted by E(U) theory. We discuss some other reasons next, though the list is not exhaustive; a complete study is outside the scope of the text.

availability bias

Tendency to work with whatever information is easily availability.

experience bias

Tendency to assign more weight to the state of the world that we have experienced and less to others.

anchoring bias

Tendency to base subjective assessments of outcomes on an initial estimate.

sunk cost

Money spent that cannot be recovered.

a. Overweighting and underweighting of probabilities. Recall that E(U) is the sum of products of two sets of numbers: first, the utility one receives in each state of the world and second, the probabilities with which each state could occur. However, most of the time probabilities are not assigned objectively, but subjectively. For example, before Hurricane Katrina in 2005, individuals in New Orleans would assign a very small probability to flooding of the type experienced in the aftermath of Katrina. However, after the event, the subjective probability estimates of flooding have risen considerably among the same set of individuals.

Humans tend to give more weight to events of the recent past than to look at the entire history. We could attribute such a bias to limited memory, individuals' myopic view, or just easy availability of more recent information. We call this bias to work with whatever information is easily availability an **availability bias**. But people deviate from E(U) theory for more reasons than simply weighting recent past more versus ignoring overall history.

Individuals also react to **experience bias**. Since all of us are shaped somewhat by our own experiences, we tend to assign more weight to the state of the world that we have experienced and less to others. Similarly, we might assign a very low weight to a bad event occurring in our lives, even to the extent of convincing ourselves that such a thing could never happen to us. That is why we see women avoiding mammograms and men colonoscopies. On the other hand, we might attach a higher-than-objective probability to good things happening to us. No matter what the underlying cause is, availability or experience, we know empirically that the probability weights are adjusted subjectively by individuals. Consequently, their observed behavior deviates from E(U) theory.

b. Anchoring bias. Often individuals base their subjective assessments of outcomes based on an initial "guesstimate." Such a guess may not have any reasonable relationship to the outcomes being studied. In an experimental study reported by Kahneman and Tversky in *Science* (1974), the authors point this out. The authors call this **anchoring bias**; it has the effect of biasing the probability estimates of individuals. The experiment they conducted ran as follows:

First, each individual under study had to spin a wheel of fortune with numbers ranging from zero to one hundred. Then, the authors asked the individual if the percent of African nations in the United Nations (UN) was lower or higher than the number on the wheel. Finally, the individuals had to provide an estimate of the percent of African nations in the UN. The authors observed that those who spun a 10 or lower had a median estimate of 25 percent, while those who spun 65 or higher provided a median estimate of 45 percent.

Notice that the number obtained on the wheel had no correlation with the question being asked. It was a randomly generated number. However, it had the effect of making people anchor their answers around the initial number that they had obtained. Kahneman and Tversky also found that even if the payoffs to the subjects were raised to encourage people to provide a correct estimate, the anchoring effect was still evident.

c. Failure to ignore sunk costs. This is the most common reason why we observe departures from E(U) theory. Suppose a person goes to the theater to watch a movie and discovers that he lost $10 on the way. Another person who had bought an online ticket for $10 finds he lost the ticket on the way. The decision problem is: "Should these people spend another $10 to watch the movie?" In experiments conducted suggesting exactly the same choices, respondents' results show that the second group is more likely to go home without watching the movie, while the first one will overwhelmingly (88 percent) go ahead and watch the movie.

Why do we observe this behavior? The two situations are exactly alike. Each group lost $10. But in a world of mental accounting, the second group has already spent the money on the movie. So this group mentally assumes a cost of $20 for the movie. However, the first group had lost $10 that was not marked toward a specific expense. The second group does not have the "feel" of a lost ticket worth $10 as a **sunk cost**, which refers to money spent that cannot be recovered. What should matter under E(U) theory is only the value of the movie, which is $10. Whether the ticket or cash was lost is immaterial. Systematic accounting for sunk costs (which economists tell us that we should ignore) causes departures from rational behavior under E(U) theory.

The failure to ignore sunk costs can cause individuals to continue to invest in ventures that are already losing money. Thus, somebody who bought shares at $1,000 that now trade at $500 will continue to hold on to them. They realized that the $1,000 is sunk and thus ignore it. Notice that under rational expectations, what matters is the value of the shares now. Mental accounting tells the shareholders that the value of the shares is still $1,000; the individual does not sell the shares at $500. Eventually, in the economists' long run, the shareholder may have to sell them for $200 and lose a lot more. People regard such a loss in value as a paper loss versus real loss, and individuals may regard real loss as a greater pain than a paper loss.

By no mean is the list above complete. Other kinds of cognitive biases intervene that can lead to deviating behavior from E(U) theory. But we must notice one thing about E(U) theory versus the value function approach. The E(U) theory is an axiomatic approach to the study of human behavior. If those axioms hold, it can actually predict behavior. On the other hand the value function approach is designed only to *describe* what actually happens, rather than what *should* happen.

KEY TAKEAWAYS

- Students should be able to describe the reasons why observed behavior is different from the predicted behavior under E(U) theory.
- They should also be able to discuss the nature of the value function and how it differs from the utility function.

DISCUSSION QUESTIONS

1. Describe the Kahneman and Tversky value function. What evidence do they offer to back it up?
2. Are shapes other than the ones given by utility functions and value function possible? Provide examples and discuss the implications of the shapes.
3. Discuss similarities and dissimilarities between availability bias, experience bias, and failure to ignore sunk costs.?

6.   RISK AVERSION AND PRICE OF HEDGING RISK

LEARNING OBJECTIVES

- **In this section we focus on risk aversion and the price of hedging risk. We discuss the actuarially fair premium (AFP) and the risk premium.**
- **Students will learn how these principles are applied to pricing of insurance (one mechanism to hedge individual risks) and the decision to purchase insurance.**

From now on, we will restrict ourselves to the E(U) theory since we can predict behavior with it. We are interested in the predictions about human behavior, rather than just a description of it.

The risk averter's utility function (as we had seen earlier in Figure 3.2) is concave to the origin. Such a person will never play a lottery at its actuarially fair premium, that is, the expected loss in wealth to the individual. Conversely, such a person will always pay at least an actuarially fair premium to get rid of the entire risk.

Suppose Ty is a student who gets a monthly allowance of $200 (initial wealth W_0) from his parents. He might lose $100 on any given day with a probability 0.5 or not lose any amount with 50 percent chance. Consequently, the expected loss (E[L]) to Ty equals 0.5($0) + 0.5($100) = $50. In other words, Ty's expected final wealth E (FW) = 0.5($200 − $0) + 0.5($200 − $100) = W_0 − E(L) = $150. The question is how much Ty would be willing to pay to hedge his expected loss of $50. We will assume that Ty's utility function is given by $U(W) = \sqrt{W}$ —a risk averter's utility function.

To apply the expected utility theory to answer the question above, we solve the problem in stages. In the first step, we find out Ty's expected utility when he does not purchase insurance and show it on Figure 3.6 (a). In the second step, we figure out if he will buy insurance at actuarially fair prices and use Figure 3.6 (b) to show it. Finally, we compute Ty's utility when he pays a premium P to get rid of the risk of a loss. P represents the maximum premium Ty is willing to pay. This is featured in Figure 3.6 (c). At this premium, Ty is exactly indifferent between buying insurance or remaining uninsured. What is P?

FIGURE 3.6 Risk Aversion

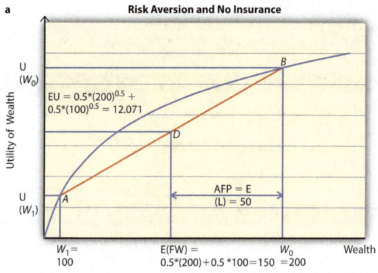

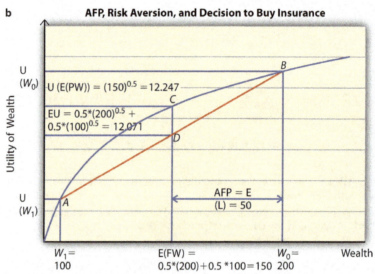

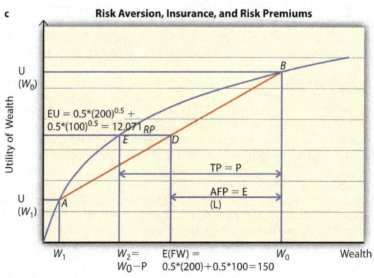

- Step 1: Expected utility, no insurance.

    In case Ty does not buy insurance, he retains all the uncertainty. Thus, he will have an expected final wealth of $150 as calculated above. What is his expected utility?

    The expected utility is calculated as a weighted sum of the utilities in the two states, loss and no loss. Therefore, $EU = 0.5\sqrt{(\$200 - \$0)} + 0.5\sqrt{(\$200 - \$100)} = 12.071$. Figure 3.6 (a) shows the point of E(U) for Ty when he does not buy insurance. His expected wealth is given by $150 on the x-axis and expected utility by 12.071 on the y-axis. When we plot this point on the chart, it lies at D, on the chord joining the two points A and B. A and B on the utility curve correspond to the utility levels when a loss is possible ($W_1 = 100$) and no loss ($W_0 = 200$), respectively. In case Ty does not hedge, then his expected utility equals 12.071.

    What is the actuarially fair premium for Ty? Note actuarially fair premium (AFP) equals the expected loss = $50. Thus the AFP is the distance between W_0 and the E (FW) in Figure 3.6 (a).

- Step 2: Utility with insurance at AFP.

    Now, suppose an insurance company offers insurance to Ty at a $50 premium (AFP). Will Ty buy it? Note that when Ty buys insurance at AFP, and he does not have a loss, his final wealth is $150 (Initial Wealth [$200] – AFP [$50]). In case he does suffer a loss, his final wealth = Initial Wealth ($200) – AFP ($50) – Loss ($100) + Indemnity ($100) = $150. Thus, after the purchase of insurance at AFP, Ty's final wealth stays at $150 regardless of a loss. That is why Ty has purchased a certain wealth of $150, by paying an AFP of $50. His utility is now given by $\sqrt{150} = 12.247$. This point is represented by C in Figure 3.6 (b). Since C lies strictly above D, Ty will always purchase full insurance at AFP. The noteworthy feature for risk-averse individuals can now be succinctly stated. A risk-averse person will always hedge the risk completely at a cost that equals the expected loss. This cost is the actuarially fair premium (AFP). Alternatively, we can say that a risk-averse person always prefers certainty to uncertainty if uncertainty can be hedged away at its actuarially fair price.

    However, the most interesting part is that a risk-averse individual like Ty will pay more than the AFP to get rid of the risk.

- Step 3: Utility with insurance at a price greater than AFP.

    In case the actual premium equals AFP (or expected loss for Ty), it implies the insurance company does not have its own costs/profits. This is an unrealistic scenario. In practice, the premiums must be higher than AFP. The question is how much higher can they be for Ty to still be interested?

    To answer this question, we need to answer the question, what is the maximum premium Ty would be willing to pay? The maximum premium P is determined by the point of indifference between no insurance and insurance at price P.

    If Ty bears a cost of P, his wealth stands at $200 – P. And this wealth is certain for the same reasons as in step 2. If Ty does not incur a loss, his wealth remains $200 – P. In case he does incur a loss then he gets indemnified by the insurance company. Thus, regardless of outcome his certain wealth is $200 – P.

    To compute the point of indifference, we should equate the utility when Ty purchases insurance at P to the expected utility in the no-insurance case. Note E(U) in the no-insurance case in step 1 equals 12.071. After buying insurance at P, Ty's certain utility is $\sqrt{200 - P}$. So we solve the equation $\sqrt{200 - P} = 12.071$ and get P = $54.29.

    Let us see the above calculation on a graph, Figure 3.6 (c). Ty tells himself, "As long as the premium P is such that I am above the E(U) line when I do not purchase insurance, I would be willing to pay it." So starting from the initial wealth W_0, we deduct P, up to the point that the utility of final wealth equals the expected utility given by the point E(U) on the y-axis. This point is given by $W_2 = W_0 - P$.

    The **Total Premium** (TP) = P comprises two parts. The AFP = the distance between initial wealth W_0 and E (FW) (= E [L]), and the distance between E (FW) and W_2. This distance is called the risk premium (RP, shown as the length ED in Figure 3.6 [c]) and in Ty's case above, it equals $54.29 – $50 = $4.29.

    The premium over and above the AFP that a risk-averse person is willing to pay to get rid of the risk is called the **risk premium**. Insurance companies are aware of this behavior of risk-averse individuals. However, in the example above, any insurance company that charges a premium greater than $54.29 will not be able to sell insurance to Ty.

    Thus, we see that individuals' risk aversion is a key component in insurance pricing. The greater the degree of risk aversion, the higher the risk premium an individual will be willing to pay. But the insurance price has to be such that the premium charged turns out to be less than or equal to the maximum premium the person is willing to pay. Otherwise, the individual will never buy full insurance.

total premium

The sum of the actuarially fair premium and the risk premium.

risk premium

The premium over and above the actuarially fair premium that a risk-averse person is willing to pay to get rid of risk.

Thus, risk aversion is a necessary condition for transfer of risks. Since insurance is one mechanism through which a risk-averse person transfers risk, risk aversion is of paramount importance to insurance demand.

The degree of risk aversion is only one aspect that affects insurance prices. Insurance prices also reflect other important components. To study them, we now turn to the role that information plays in the markets: in particular, how information and information asymmetries affect the insurance market.

KEY TAKEAWAYS

- In this section, students learned that risk aversion is the key to understanding why insurance and other risk hedges exist.
- The student should be able to express the demand for hedging and the conditions under which a risk-averse individual might refuse to transfer risk.

DISCUSSION QUESTIONS

1. What shape does a risk-averse person's utility curve take? What role does risk aversion play in market demand for insurance products?
2. Distinguish between risk premium and AFP. Show the two on a graph.
3. Under what conditions will a risk-averse person refuse an insurance offer?

7. INFORMATION ASYMMETRY PROBLEM IN ECONOMICS

LEARNING OBJECTIVE

- Students learn the critical role that information plays in markets. In particular, we discuss two major information economics problems: moral hazard and adverse selection. Students will understand how these two problems affect insurance availability and affordability (prices).

information asymmetry

A problem encountered when one party knows more than the other party in the contract.

adverse selection

Situation in which a person with higher risk chooses to hedge the risk, preferably without paying more for the greater risk.

We all know about the used-car market and the market for "lemons." Akerlof (1970) was the first to analyze how **information asymmetry** can cause problems in any market. This is a problem encountered when one party knows more than the other party in the contract. In particular, it addresses how information differences between buyers and the sellers (information asymmetry) can cause market failure. These differences are the underlying causes of **adverse selection**, a situation under which a person with higher risk chooses to hedge the risk, preferably without paying more for the greater risk. Adverse selection refers to a particular kind of information asymmetry problem, namely, hidden information.

A second kind of information asymmetry lies in the hidden action, wherein one party's actions are not observable by the counterparty to the contract. Economists study this issue as one of moral hazard.

7.1 Adverse Selection

Consider the used-car market. While the sellers of used cars know the quality of their cars, the buyers do not know the exact quality (imagine a world with no blue book information available). From the buyer's point of view, the car may be a lemon. Under such circumstances, the buyer's offer price reflects the *average* quality of the cars in the market.

When sellers approach a market in which average prices are offered, sellers who *know* that their cars are of better quality do not sell their cars. (This example can be applied to the mortgage and housing crisis in 2008. Sellers who knew that their houses are worth more prefer to hold on to them, instead of lowering the price in order to just make a sale). When they withdraw their cars from market, the average quality of the cars for sale goes down. Buyers' offer prices get revised downward in response. As a result, the new level of better-quality car sellers withdraws from the market. As this cycle continues, only lemons remain in the market, and the market for used cars fails. As a result of an information asymmetry, the bad-quality product drives away the good-quality ones from the market. This phenomenon is called adverse selection.

It's easy to demonstrate adverse selection in health insurance. Imagine two individuals, one who is healthy and the other who is not. Both approach an insurance company to buy health insurance policies. Assume for a moment that the two individuals are alike in all respects but their health condition. Insurers can't observe applicants' health status; this is private information. If insurers could find no way to figure out the health status, what would it do?

Suppose the insurer's price schedule reads, "Charge $10 monthly premium to the healthy one, and $25 to the unhealthy one." If the insurer is asymmetrically informed of the health status of each applicant, it would charge an average premium $\left(\frac{10+25}{2} = \$17.50\right)$ to each. If insurers charge an average premium, the healthy individual would decide to retain the health risk and remain uninsured. In such a case, the insurance company would be left with only unhealthy policyholders. Note that these less-healthy people would happily purchase insurance, since while their actual cost should be $25 they are getting it for $17.50. In the long run, however, what happens is that the claims from these individuals exceed the amount of premium collected from them. Eventually, the insurance company may become insolvent and go bankrupt. Adverse selection thus causes bankruptcy and market failure. What is the solution to this problem? The easiest is to charge $25 to all individuals regardless of their health status. In a **monopolistic market** of only one supplier without competition this might work but not in a competitive market. Even in a close-to-competitive market the effect of adverse selection is to increase prices.

How can one mitigate the extent of adverse selection and its effects? The solution lies in reducing the level of information asymmetry. Thus we find that insurers ask a lot of questions to determine the risk types of individuals. In the used-car market, the buyers do the same. Specialized agencies provide used-car information. Some auto companies certify their cars. And buyers receive warranty offers when they buy used cars.

Insurance agents ask questions and undertake individuals' risk classification according to risk types. In addition, leaders in the insurance market also developed solutions to adverse selection problems. This comes in the form of risk sharing, which also means partial insurance. Under partial insurance, companies offer products with **deductibles** (the initial part of the loss absorbed by the person who incurs the loss) and **coinsurance**, where individuals share in the losses with the insurance companies. It has been shown that high-risk individuals prefer full insurance, while low-risk individuals choose partial insurance (high deductibles and coinsurance levels). Insurance companies also offer policies where the premium is adjusted at a later date based on the claim experience of the policyholder during the period.

7.2 Moral Hazard

Adverse selection refers to a particular kind of information asymmetry problem, namely, hidden information. A second kind of information asymmetry lies in the hidden action, if actions of one party of the contract are not clear to the other. Economists study these problems under a category called the moral hazard problem.

The simplest way to understand the problem of "observability" (or clarity of action) is to imagine an owner of a store who hires a manager. The store owner may not be available to actually monitor the manager' actions continuously and at all times, for example, how they behave with customers. This inability to observe actions of the agent (manager) by the principal (owner) falls under the class of problems called the **principal-agent problem**.[13] Extension of this problem to the two parties of the insurance contract is straightforward.

Let us say that the insurance company has to decide whether to sell an auto insurance policy to Wonku, who is a risk-averse person with a utility function given by $U(W) = \sqrt{W}$. Wonku's driving record is excellent, so he can claim to be a good risk for the insurance company. However, Wonku can also choose to be either a careful driver or a not-so-careful driver. If he drives with care, he incurs a cost.

To exemplify, let us assume that Wonku drives a car carrying a market value of $10,000. The only other asset he owns is the $3,000 in his checking account. Thus, he has a total initial wealth of $13,000. If he drives carefully, he incurs a cost of $3,000. Assume he faces the following loss distributions when he drives with or without care.

monopolistic market

A market with only one supplier.

deductibles

Initial part of the loss absorbed by the person who incurs the loss.

coinsurance

Situation where individuals share in the losses with the insurance companies.

principal-agent problem

The inability of the principal (owner) to observe actions of the agent (manager).

TABLE 3.3 Loss Distribution

Drives with Care		Drives without Care	
Probability	**Loss**	**Probability**	**Loss**
0.25	10,000	0.75	10,000
0.75	0	0.25	0

Table 3.3 shows that when he has an accident, his car is a total loss. The probabilities of "loss" and "no loss" are reversed when he decides to drive without care. The E(L) equals $2,500 in case he drives with care and $7,500 in case he does not. Wonku's problem has four parts: whether to drive with or without care, (I) when he has no insurance and (II) when he has insurance.

We consider Case I when he carries no insurance. Table 3.4 shows the expected utility of driving with and without care. Since care costs $3,000, his initial wealth gets reduced to $10,000 when driving with care. Otherwise, it stays at $13,000. The utility distribution for Wonku is shown in Table 3.4.

TABLE 3.4 Utility Distribution without Insurance

Drives with Care		Drives without Care	
Probability	**U (Final Wealth)**	**Probability**	**U (Final Wealth)**
0.25	0	0.75	54.77
0.75	100	0.25	114.02

When he drives with care and has an accident, then his final wealth (FW) $(FW) = \$13,000 - \$3,000 - \$10,000 = \$0$, and the utility $= \sqrt{0} = 0$. In case he does not have an accident and drives with care then his final wealth $(FW) = (FW) = \$13,000 - \$3,000 - \$0 = \$10,000$ (note that the cost of care, $3,000, is still subtracted from the initial wealth) and the utility $= \sqrt{10,000} = 100$. Hence, E(U) of driving with care $= 0.25 \times 0 + 0.75 \times 100 = 75$. Let's go through it in bullets and make sure each case is clarified.

- When Wonku drives without care he does not incur cost of care, so his initial wealth = $13,000. If he is involved in an accident, his final wealth $(FW) = \$13,000 - \$10,000 = \$3,000$, and the utility $= \sqrt{3,000} = 54.77$. Otherwise, his final wealth $(FW) = \$13,000 - \$0 = \$13,000$ and the utility $= \sqrt{13,000} = 114.02$. Computing the expected utility the same way as in the paragraph above, we get $E(U) = 0.75 \times 54.77 + 0.25 \times 114.02 = 69.58$.

- In Case I, when Wonku does not carry insurance, he will drive carefully since his expected utility is higher when he exercises due care. His utility is 75 versus 69.58.

- In Case II we assume that Wonku decides to carry insurance, and claims to the insurance company. He is a careful driver. Let us assume that his insurance policy is priced based on this claim. Assuming the insurance company's profit and expense loading factor equals 10 percent of AFP (actuarially fair premium), the premium demanded is $2,750 = \$2,500(1 + 0.10)$. Wonku needs to decide whether or not to drive with care.

- We analyze the decision based on E(U) as in Case I. The wealth after purchase of insurance equals $10,250. The utility in cases of driving with care or without care is shown in Table 3.5 below.

TABLE 3.5 Utility Distribution with Insurance

Drives with Care		Drives without Care	
Probability	**U (FW)**	**Probability**	**U (FW)**
0.25	85.15	0.75	101.24
0.75	85.15	0.25	101.24

Notice that after purchase of insurance, Wonku has eliminated the uncertainty. So if he has an accident, the insurance company indemnifies him with $10,000. Thus, when Wonku has insurance, the following are the possibilities:

- He is driving with care

    - And his car gets totaled, his final wealth =
      $10,250 − $3,000 − $10,000 + $10,000 = $7,250$, and associated utility = $\sqrt{7250} = 85.15$.
    - And no loss occurs, his final wealth = $10,250 − $3,000 = $7,250$.

    So the expected utility for Wonku = 85.15 when he drives with care.

- He does not drive with care

    - And his car gets totaled, his final wealth = $10,250 − $10,000 + $10,000 = $10,250$, and associated utility = $\sqrt{10250} = 101.24$.
    - And no loss occurs, his final wealth = $10,250$ and utility = 101.24.

    So the expected utility for Wonku = 101.24 when he drives without care after purchasing insurance.

The net result is he switches to driving with no care.

Wonku's behavior thus changes from driving with care to driving without care after purchasing insurance. Why do we get this result? In this example, the cost of insurance is cheaper than the cost of care. Insurance companies can charge a price greater than the cost of care up to a maximum of what Wonku is willing to pay. However, in the event of asymmetric information, the insurance company will not know the cost of care. Thus, inexpensive insurance distorts the incentives and individuals switch to riskier behavior ex post.

In this moral hazard example, the probabilities of having a loss are affected, not the loss amounts. In practice, both will be affected. At its limit, when moral hazard reaches a point where the intention is to cheat the insurance company, it manifests itself in fraudulent behavior.

How can we solve this problem? An ideal solution would be continuous monitoring, which is prohibitively expensive and may not even be legal for privacy issues. Alternatively, insurance companies try and gather as much information as possible to arrive at an estimate of the cost of care or lack of it. Also, more information leads to an estimate of the likelihood that individuals will switch to riskier behavior afterwards. So questions like marital status/college degree and other personal information might be asked. Insurance companies will undertake a process called risk classification. We discuss this important process later in the text.

So far we have learned how individuals' risk aversion and information asymmetry explain behavior associated with hedging. But do these reasons also hold when we study why corporations hedge their risks? We provide the answer to this question next.

KEY TAKEAWAYS

- Students should be able to define information asymmetry problems, in particular moral hazard and adverse selection.
- They must also be able to discuss in detail the effects these phenomena have on insurance prices and risk transfer markets in general.
- Students should spend some effort to understand computations, which are so important if they wish to fully understand the effects that these computations have on actuarial science. Insurance companies make their decisions primarily on the basis of such calculations.

DISCUSSION QUESTIONS

1. What information asymmetry problems arise in economics? Distinguish between moral hazard and adverse selection. Give an original example of each.
2. What effects can information asymmetry have in markets?
3. Is risk aversion a necessary condition for moral hazard or adverse selection to exist? Provide reasons.
4. What can be done to mitigate the effect of moral hazard and adverse selection in markets/insurance markets?

8.   WHY CORPORATIONS HEDGE

LEARNING OBJECTIVE

- Why should corporations hedge? Financial theory tells us that in a perfect world, corporations are risk neutral. Students can learn in this section the reasons why large companies hedge risk, and, in particular, why they buy insurance.

Financial theory tells us that corporations are risk neutral. This is because only the systematic risk matters, while a particular company can diversify the idiosyncratic risk[14] away. If we think about a large company held by a large number of small shareholders like us, then we'd prefer that the company not hedge its risks. In fact, if we wanted to hedge those risks we can do it ourselves. We hold a particular company's shares because we are looking for those particular risks.

Look back at Figure 3.4. Since firms are risk neutral, their value function is the straight line that appears in the figure. Thus corporations will hedge risk only at their AFP, otherwise they will not. But we know that insurance companies cannot really sell policies at AFP, since they also have to cover their costs and profits. Yet we find that corporations still buy these hedging instruments at greater price than AFP. Therefore, to find a rationale for corporations hedging behavior, we have to move beyond the individual level utility functions of risk aversion.

The following are several reasons for companies hedging behavior:

optimal capital structure

A company's optimal mix of debt and equity financing.

1. Managers hedge because they are undiversified: Small shareholders like us can diversify our risks, but managers cannot. They invest their income from labor as well as their personal assets in the firm. Therefore, while owners (principals) are diversified, managers (agents) are not. Since managers are risk averse and they control the company directly, they hedge.

2. Managers want to lower expected bankruptcy costs: If a company goes bankrupt, then bankruptcy supervisors investigate and retain a part of the company's assets. The wealth gets transferred to third parties and constitutes a loss of assets to the rightful owners. Imagine a fire that destroys the plant. If the company wants to avoid bankruptcy, it might want to rebuild it. If rebuilding is financed through debt financing, the cost of debt is going to be very high because the company may not have any collateral to offer. In this case, having fire insurance can serve as collateral as well as compensate the firm when it suffers a loss due to fire.

3. Risk bearers may be in a better position to bear the risk: Companies may not be diversified, in terms of either product or geography. They may not have access to broader capital markets because of small size. Companies may transfer risk to better risk bearers that are diversified and have better and broader access to capital markets.

4. Hedging can increase debt capacity: Financial theory tells us about an **optimal capital structure** for every company. This means that each company has an optimal mix of debt and equity financing. The amount of debt determines the financial risk to a company. With hedging, the firm can transfer the risk outside the firm. With lower risk, the firm can undertake a greater amount of debt, thus changing the optimal capital structure.

5. Lowering of tax liability: Since insurance premiums are tax deductible for some corporate insurance policies, companies can lower the expected taxes by purchasing insurance.

6. Other reasons: We can cite some other reasons why corporations hedge. Regulated companies are found to hedge more than unregulated ones, probably because law limits the level of risk taking. Laws might require companies to purchase some insurance mandatorily. For example, firms might need aircraft liability insurance, third-party coverage for autos, and workers compensation. Firms may also purchase insurance to signal credit worthiness (e.g., construction coverage for commercial builders). Thus, the decision to hedge can reduce certain kinds of information asymmetry problems as well.

We know that corporations hedge their risks, either through insurance or through other financial contracts. Firms can use forwards and futures, other derivatives, and option contracts to hedge their risk. The latter are not pure hedges and firms can use them to take on more risks instead of transferring them outside the firm. Forwards and futures, derivatives, and option contracts present the firm with double-edged swords. Still, because of their complex nature, corporations are in a better position to use it than the individuals who mostly use insurance contracts to transfer their risk.

KEY TAKEAWAYS

- The student should be able to able to distinguish between individual demand and corporate demand for risk hedging.
- The student should be able to understand and express reasons for corporate hedging.

DISCUSSION QUESTIONS

1. Which risks matter for corporations: systematic or idiosyncratic? Why?
2. Why can't the rationale of hedging used to explain risk transfer at individual level be applied to companies?
3. Describe the reasons why companies hedge their risks. Provide examples.
4. What is an optimal capital structure?

9. REVIEW AND PRACTICE

1. What is risk? How is it philosophically different from uncertainty?
2. What is asymmetric information? Explain how it leads to market failures in an otherwise perfectly competitive market.
3. Explain the difference between moral hazard and adverse selection. Can one exist without the other?
4. What externalities are caused in the insurance market by moral hazard and adverse selection? How are they overcome in practice?
5. Do risk-averse individuals outnumber risk-seeking ones? Give an intuitive explanation.
6. Provide examples that appear to violate expected utility theory and risk aversion.
7. Give two examples that tell how the framing of alternatives affects peoples' choices under uncertainty.
8. Suppose you are a personal financial planner managing the portfolio of your mother. In a recession like the one in 2008, there are enormous losses and very few gains to the assets in the portfolio you suggested to your mother. Given the material covered in this chapter, suggest a few marketing strategies to minimize the pain of bad news to your mother.
9. Distinguish, through examples, between sunk cost, availability bias, and anchoring effect as reasons for departure from the expected utility paradigm.
10. Suppose Yuan Yuan wants to purchase a house for investment purposes. She will rent it out after buying it. She has two choices. Either buy it in an average location where the lifetime rent from the property will be $700,000 with certainty or buy it in an upscale location. However, in the upscale neighborhood there is a 60 percent chance that the lifetime income will equal $1 million and 40 percent chance it will equal only $250,000. If she has a utility function that equals $U(W) = \sqrt{W}$, Where would she prefer to buy the house?
11. What is the expected value when a six-sided fair die is tossed?
12. Suppose Yijia's utility function is given by LN(W) and her initial wealth is $500,000. If there is a 0.01 percent chance that a liability lawsuit will reduce her wealth to $50,000, how much premium will she be willing to pay to get rid of the risk?
13. Your professor of economics tells you, "The additional benefit that a person derives from a given increase of his stock of a thing decreases with every increase in the stock he already has." What type of risk attitude does such a person have?
14. Ms. Frangipani prefers Pepsi to Coke on a rainy day; Coke to Pepsi on a sunny one. On one sunny day at the CNN center in Atlanta, when faced with a choice between Pepsi, Coke, and Lipton iced tea, she decides to have a Pepsi. Should the presence of iced teas in the basket of choices affect her decision? Does she violate principles of utility maximization? If yes, which assumptions does she violate? If not, then argue how her choices are consistent with the utility theory.

15. Explain why a risk-averse person will purchase insurance for the following scenario: Lose $20,000 with 5 percent chance or lose $0 with 95 percent probability. The premium for the policy is $1,000.

16. Imagine that you face the following pair of concurrent decisions. First examine both decisions, then indicate the options you prefer:

Decision (i) Choose between

a. a sure gain of $240,

b. 25 percent chance to gain $1,000, and 75 percent chance to gain nothing.

Decision (ii) Choose between:

a. a sure loss of $750,

b. 75 percent chance to lose $1,000 and 25 percent chance to lose nothing.

Indicate which option you would choose in each of the decisions and why.[15]

17. Consider the following two lotteries:

a. Gain of $100 with probability 0.75; no gain ($0 gain) with probability 0.25

b. Gain of $1,000 with probability 0.05; no gain ($0 gain) with probability 0.95

Which of these lotteries will you prefer to play?

Now, assume somebody promises you sure sums of money so as to induce you to not play the lotteries. What is the sure sum of money you will be willing to accept in case of each lottery: a or b? Is your decision "rational"?

18. Partial insurance:[16] This problem is designed to illustrate why partial insurance (i.e., a policy that includes deductibles and coinsurance) may be optimal for a risk-averse individual.

Suppose Marco has an initial wealth of $1,000 and a utility function given by $U(W) = \sqrt{W}$. He faces the following loss distribution:

Prob	Loss
0.9	0
0.1	500

a. If the price per unit of insurance is $0.10 per dollar of loss, show that Marco will purchase full insurance (i.e., quantity for which insurance is purchased = $500).

b. If the price per unit of insurance is $0.11 per dollar of loss, show that Marco will purchase less than full insurance (i.e., quantity for which insurance is purchased is less than $500). Hint: Compute E(U) for full $500 loss and also for an amount less than $500. See that when he insures strictly less than $500, the EU is higher.

19. Otgo has a current wealth of $500 and a lottery ticket that pays $50 with probability 0.25; otherwise, it pays nothing. If her utility function is given by $U(W) = W^2$, what is the minimum amount she is willing to sell the ticket for?

20. Suppose a coin is tossed twice in a row. The payoffs associated with the outcomes are

Outcome	Win (+) or loss (−)
H-H	+15
H-T	+9
T-H	−6
T-T	−12

If the coin is unbiased, what is the fair value of the gamble?

21. If you apply the principle of framing to put a favorable spin to events in your life, how would you value the following gains or losses?

a. A win of $100 followed by a loss of $20

b. A win of $20 followed by a loss of $100

c. A win of $50 followed by a win of $60

d. A loss of $50 followed by a win of $60

22. Explain in detail what happens to an insurer that charges the same premium to teenage drivers as it does to the rest of its customers.

23. Corporations are risk neutral, yet they hedge. Why?

ENDNOTES

1. At one time, economists measured satisfaction in a unit called "utils" and discussed the highest number of utils as "bliss points"!

2. Economists are fond of the phrase *"ceteris paribus,"* which means all else the same. We can only vary one component of human behavior at a time.

3. The utility theory is utilized to *compare* two or more options. Thus, by its very nature, we refer to the utility theory as an "ordinal" theory, which rank orders choices, rather than "cardinal" utility, which has the ability to attach a number to even a single outcome where there are no choices involved.

4. An academic example is the following study: Yew-Kwang Ng, "A Case for Happiness, Cardinalism, and Interpersonal Comparability," *Economic Journal* 107 (1997): 1848–58. She contends that "modern economists are strongly biased in favour of preference (in contrast to happiness), ordinalism, and against interpersonal comparison. I wish to argue for the opposite." A more popular research is at *Forbes* on happiness research.

   Forbes magazine published several short pieces on happiness research. Nothing especially rigorous, but a pleasant enough read:

   - *"Money Doesn't Make People Happy,"* by Tim Harford.

     But marriage, sex, socializing and even middle age do.

     http://www.forbes.com/2006/02/11/ tim-harford-money_cz_th_money06_0214 harford.html

   - *"Shall I Compare Thee To A Summer's Sausage?"* by Daniel Gilbert.

     Money can't make you happy, but making the right comparisons can.

     http://www.forbes.com/2006/02/11/ daniel-gilbert-happiness_cx_dg_money06_0214 gilbert.html

   - *"Money, Happiness and the Pursuit of Both,"* by Elizabeth MacDonald.

     When it comes [to] money and happiness, economists and psychologists have got it all wrong.

     http://www.forbes.com/2006/02/11/ money-happiness-consumption_cz_em_money 06_0214pursuit.html

   - *"The Happiness Business,"* by Paul Maidment.

     There is more academic research than you can shake a Havana cigar at saying there is no correlation between wealth and happiness.

     http://www.forbes.com/2006/02/11/ happiness-economists-money_cx_pm_money 06_0214maidment.html

5. The distinction between normative and positive aspects of a theory is very important in the discipline of economics. Some people argue that economic theories should be normative, which means they should be prescriptive and tell people what to do. Others argue, often successfully, that economic theories are designed to be explanations of observed behavior of agents in the market, hence positive in that sense.

6. The assumption of convexity of preferences is not required for a utility function representation of an individual's preferences to exist. But it is necessary if we want that function to be well behaved.

7. See Jochen Runde, "Clarifying Frank Knight's Discussion of the Meaning of Risk and Uncertainty," *Cambridge Journal of Economics* 22, no. 5 (1998): 539–46.

8. These are called the *continuity* and *independence* assumptions.

9. At this juncture, we only care about that notion of risk, which captures the inherent variability in the outcomes (uncertainty) associated with each lottery.

10. Mathematically, the property that the utility is increasing at a decreasing rate can be written as a combination of restrictions on the first and second derivatives (rate of change of slope) of the utility function, $u'(W) > 0$, $u''(W) < 0$. Some functions that satisfy this property are $u(W) = \sqrt{W}$, $LN(W)$, $-e^{-aW}$.

11. The **convex curve** in Figure 3.2 has some examples that include the mathematical function $u(W) = W^2$, e^W.

12. Mathematically speaking, for a risk-averse person, we have $E(U[W]) \leq U[E(W)]$. Similarly, for a risk-seeking person we have $E(U[W]) \geq U[E(W)]$. This result is called Jensen's inequality.

13. The complete set of principal-agent problems comprises all situations in which the agent maximizes his own utility at the expense of the principal. Such behavior is contrary to the principal-agent relationship that assumes that the agent is acting on behalf of the principal (in principal's interest).

14. Systematic risk is the risk that everyone has to share, each according to his/her capacity. Idiosyncratic risk, on the other hand, falls only on a small section of the population. While systematic risk cannot be transferred to anyone outside since it encompasses all agents, idiosyncratic risk can be transferred for a price. That is why idiosyncratic risk is called diversifiable, and systematic is not. The economy-wide recession that unfolded in 2008 is a systematic risk in which everyone is affected.

15. This problem has been adopted from D. Kahneman and D. Lovallo, "Timid Choices and Bold Forecasts: A Cognitive Perspective on Risk Taking," *Management Science* 39, no. 1 (1993): 17–31.

16. Challenging problem.

CHAPTER 4

Evolving Risk Management: Fundamental Tools

In the prior chapters, we discussed risks from many aspects. With this chapter we begin the discussion of risk management and its methods that are so vital to businesses and to individuals. Today's unprecedented global financial crisis following the man-made and natural megacatastrophes underscore the urgency for studying risk management and its tools. Information technology, globalization, and innovation in financial technologies have all led to a term called "enterprise risk management" (ERM). As you learned from the definition of risk in Chapter 1 (see Figure 1.2), ERM includes managing pure opportunity and speculative risks. In this chapter, we discuss how firms use ERM to further their goals. This chapter and Chapter 5 that follows evolve into a more thorough discussion of ERM. While employing new innovations, we should emphasize that the first step to understanding risk management is to learn the basics of the fundamental risk management processes. In a broad sense, they include the processes of identifying, assessing, measuring, and evaluating alternative ways to mitigate risks.

The steps that we follow to identify all of the entity's risks involve measuring the frequency and severity of losses, as we discussed in Chapter 1 and computed in Chapter 2. The measurements are essential to create the risk map that profile all the risks identified as important to a business. The risk map is a visual tool used to consider alternatives of the risk management tool set. A risk map forms a grid of frequency and severity intersection points of each identified and measured risk. In this and the next chapter we undertake the task of finding risk management solutions to the risks identified in the risk map. Following is the anthrax story, which occurred right after September 11. It was an unusual risk of high severity and low frequency. The alternative tools for financial solutions to each particular risk are shown in the risk management matrix, which provides fundamental possible solutions to risks with high and low severity and frequency. These possible solutions relate to external and internal conditions and are not absolutes. In times of low insurance prices, the likelihood of using risk transfer is greater than in times of high rates. The risk management process also includes cost-benefit analysis.

The anthrax story was an unusual risk of high severity and low frequency. It illustrates a case of risk management of a scary risk and the dilemma of how best to counteract the risks.

How to Handle the Risk Management of a Low-Frequency but Scary Risk Exposure: The Anthrax Scare

The date staring up from the desk calendar reads June 1, 2002, so why is the Capitol Hill office executive assistant opening Christmas cards? The anthrax scare after September 11, 2001, required these late actions. For six weeks after an anthrax-contaminated letter was received in Senate Majority Leader Tom Daschle's office, all Capitol Hill mail delivery was stopped. As startling as that sounds, mail delivery is of small concern to the many public and private entities that suffered loss due to the terrorism-related issues of anthrax. The biological agent scare, both real and imagined, created unique issues for businesses and insurers alike since it is the type of poison that kills very easily.

Who is responsible for the clean-up costs related to bioterrorism? Who is liable for the exposure to humans within the contaminated facility? Who covers the cost of a shutdown of a business for decontamination? What is a risk manager to do?

Senator Charles Grassley (R-Iowa), member of the Senate Finance Committee at the time, estimated that the clean-up project cost for the Hart Senate Office Building would exceed $23 million. Manhattan Eye, Ear, and Throat Hospital closed its doors in late October 2001 after a supply-room worker contracted and later died from pulmonary anthrax. The hospital—a small, thirty-bed facility—reopened November 6, 2001, announcing that the anthrax scare closure had cost the facility an estimated $700,000 in revenue.

These examples illustrate the necessity of holistic risk management and the effective use of risk mapping to identify *any* possible risk, even those that may remotely affect the firm. Even if their companies aren't being directly targeted, risk managers must incorporate disaster management plans to deal with indirect atrocities that slow or abort the firms' operations. For example, an import/export business must protect against extended halts in overseas commercial air traffic. A mail-order-catalog retailer must protect against long-term mail delays. Evacuation of a workplace for employees due to mold infestation or biochemical exposure must now be added to disaster recovery plans that are part of loss-control programs. Risk managers take responsibility for such programs.

After a temporary closure, reopened facilities still give cause for concern. Staffers at the Hart Senate Office Building got the green light to return to work on January 22, 2002, after the anthrax remediation process was completed. Immediately, staffers began reporting illnesses. By March, 255 of the building's employees had complained of symptoms that included headaches, rashes, and eye or throat irritation, possibly from the chemicals used to kill the anthrax. Was the decision to reopen the facility too hasty?

Sources: "U.S. Lawmakers Complain About Old Mail After Anthrax Scare." Dow Jones Newswires, 8 May 2002; David Pilla, "Anthrax Scare Raises New Liability Issues for Insurers," A.M. Best Newswire, October 16, 2001; Sheila R. Cherry, "Health Questions Linger at Hart," Insight on the News, April 15, 2002, p.16; Cinda Becker, "N.Y. Hospital Reopens; Anthrax Scare Costs Facility $700,000," Modern Healthcare, 12 November 2001, p. 8; Sheila R. Cherry, "Health Questions Linger at Hart," Insight on the News, April 15, 2002, p. 16(2).

Today's risk managers explore all risks together and consider correlations between risks and their management. Some risks interact positively with other risks, and the occurrence of one can trigger the other—flood can cause fires or an earthquake that destroys a supplier can interrupt business in another side of the country. As we discussed in Chapter 1, economic systemic risks can impact many facets of the corporations, as is the current state of the world during the financial crisis of 2008.

In our technological and information age, every person involved in finding solutions to lower the adverse impact of risks uses risk management information systems (RMIS), which are data bases that provide information with which to compute the frequency and severity, explore difficult-to-identify risks, and provide forecasts and cost-benefits analyses.

This chapter therefore includes the following:

1. Links

2. The risk management function

3. Projected frequency and severity, cost-benefit analysis, and capital budgeting

4. Risk management alternatives: the risk management matrix

5. Comparing to current risk-handling methods

1. LINKS

Now that we understand the notion and measurement of risks from Chapter 1 and Chapter 2, and the attitudes toward risk in Chapter 3, we are ready to begin learning about the actual process of risk management. Within the goals of the firm discussed in Chapter 1, we now delve into how risk managers conduct their jobs and what they need to know about the marketplace to succeed in reducing and eliminating risks. Holistic risk management is connected to our complete package of risks shown in Figure 4.1. To complete the puzzle, we have to

1. identify all the risks,

2. assess the risks,

3. find risk management solutions to each risk, and

4. evaluate the results.

Risk management decisions depend on the nature of the identified risks, the forecasted frequency and severity of losses, cost-benefit analysis, and using the risk management matrix in context of external market conditions. As you will see later in this chapter, risk managers may decide to transfer the risk to insurance companies. In such cases, final decisions can't be separated from the market conditions at the time of purchase. Therefore, we must understand the nature of underwriting cycles, which are the business cycles of the insurance industry when insurance processes increase and fall (explained in Chapter 6). When insurance prices are high, risk management decisions differ from those made during times of low insurance prices. Since insurance prices are cyclical, different decisions are called for at different times for the same assessed risks.

Risk managers also need to understand the nature of insurance well enough to be aware of which risks are uninsurable. Overall, in this Links section, shown in Figure 4.1, we can complete our puzzle only when we have mitigated all risks in a smart risk management process.

FIGURE 4.1 Links between the Holistic Risk Picture and the Risk Management Alternative Solutions

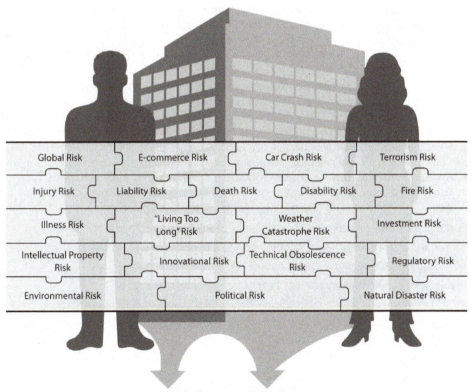

Risk Management Solutions

Pure Risk Solutions

	Low Frequency of Losses	High Frequency of Losses
Low Severity of Losses	Retention	Retention with Loss Control
High Severity of Losses	Transfer—Insurance/ Reinsurance (New: Cat bonds and securitization for catastrophe risk)	Avoidance

Activities

Other Influences

- Financial Condition
- Nature of Risk
- External Market Conditions
- Size of the Firm

Solutions for Other Risks

- Cash Flow Management using Value at Risk (VaR)
- Using derivative instruments such as futures, swaps, and options

2. THE RISK MANAGEMENT FUNCTION

LEARNING OBJECTIVE

■ **In this section you will learn about the big picture of all risk management steps.**

Traditionally, a firm's risk management function ensured that the pure risks of losses were managed appropriately. The risk manager was charged with the responsibility for specific risks only. Most activities involved providing adequate insurance and implementing loss-control techniques so that the firm's employees and property remained safe. Thus, risk managers sought to reduce the firm's costs of pure risks and to initiate safety and disaster management.

self-insuring

Retaining the risk within the firm.

Typically, the traditional risk management position has reported to the corporate treasurer. Handling risks by **self-insuring** (retaining risks within the firm) and paying claims in-house requires additional personnel within the risk management function. In a small company or sole proprietorship, the owner usually performs the risk management function, establishing policy and making decisions. In fact, each of us manage our own risks, whether we have studied risk management or not. Every time we lock our house or car, check the wiring system for problems, or pay an insurance premium, we are performing the same functions as a risk manager. Risk managers use agents or brokers to make smart insurance and risk management decisions (agents and brokers are discussed in Chapter 7).

The traditional risk manager's role has evolved, and corporations have begun to embrace enterprise risk management in which all risks are part of the process: pure, opportunity, and speculative risks. With this evolution, firms created the new post of chief risk officer (CRO). The role of CROs expanded the traditional role by integrating the firm's silos, or separate risks, into a holistic framework. Risks cannot be segregated—they interact and affect one another.

risk map

A visual tool used to consider alternatives of the risk management tool set.

In addition to insurance and loss control, risk managers or CROs use specialized tools to keep cash flow in-house, which we will discuss in Chapter 6 and Chapter 7. Captives are separate insurance entities under the corporate structure—mostly for the exclusive use of the firm itself. CROs oversee the increasing reliance on capital market instruments to hedge risk. They also address the entire **risk map**—a visual tool used to consider alternatives of the risk management tool set—in the realm of non-pure risks. For example, a cereal manufacturer, dependent upon a steady supply of grain used in production, may decide to enter into fixed-price long-term contractual arrangements with its suppliers to avoid the risk of price fluctuations. The CRO or the financial risk managers take responsibility for these trades. They also create the risk management guideline for the firm that usually includes the following:

- Writing a mission statement for risk management in the organization
- Communicating with every section of the business to promote safe behavior
- Identifying risk management policy and processes
- Pinpointing all risk exposures (what "keeps employees awake at night")
- Assessing risk management and financing alternatives as well as external conditions in the insurance markets
- Allocating costs
- Negotiating insurance terms
- Adjusting claims adjustment in self-insuring firms
- Keeping accurate records

Writing risk management manuals set up the process of identification, monitoring, assessment, evaluation, and adjustments.

In larger organizations, the risk manager or CRO has differing authority depending upon the policy that top management has adopted. Policy statements generally outline the dimensions of such authority. Risk managers may be authorized to make decisions in routine matters but restricted to making only recommendations in others. For example, the risk manager may recommend that the costs of employee injuries be retained rather than insured, but a final decision of such magnitude would be made by top management.

2.1 The Risk Management Process

A typical risk management function includes the steps listed above: identifying risks, assessing them, forecasting future frequency and severity of losses, mitigating risks, finding risk mitigation solutions, creating plans, conducting cost-benefits analyses, and implementing programs for loss control and insurance. For each property risk exposure, for example, the risk manager would adopt the following or similar processes:

- Finding all properties that are exposed to losses (such as real property like land, buildings, and other structures; tangible property like furniture and computers; and intangible personal property like trademarks)
- Evaluating the potential causes of loss that can affect the firms' property, including natural disasters (such as windstorms, floods, and earthquakes); accidental causes (such as fires, explosions, and the collapse of roofs under snow); and many other causes noted in Chapter 1;
- Evaluating property value by different methods, such as book value, market value, reproduction cost, and replacement cost
- Evaluating the firm's legal interest in each of the properties—whether each property is owned or leased
- Identifying the actual loss exposure in each property using loss histories (frequency and severity), accounting records, personal inspections, flow charts, and questionnaires
- Computing the frequency and severity of losses for each of the property risk exposures based on loss data
- Forecasting future losses for each property risk exposure
- Creating a specific risk map for all property risk exposures based on forecasted frequency and severity
- Developing risk management alternative tools (such as loss-control techniques) based upon cost-benefit analysis or insurance
- Comparing the existing solutions to potential solutions (traditional and nontraditional)—uses of risk maps
- Communicating the solutions with the whole organization by creating reporting techniques, feedback, and a path for ongoing execution of the whole process
- The process is very similar to any other business process.

KEY TAKEAWAYS

- The modern firm ensures that the risk management function is embedded throughout the whole organization.
- The risk management process follows logical sequence just as any business process will.
- The main steps in the risk management process are identifying risks, measuring risks, creating a map, finding alternative solutions to managing the risk, and evaluating programs once they are put into place.

DISCUSSION QUESTIONS

1. What are the steps in the pure risk management process?
2. Imagine that the step of evaluation of the risks did not account for related risks. What would be the result for the risk manager?
3. In the allocation of costs, does the CRO need to understand the holistic risk map of the whole company? Explain your answer with an example.

3. BEGINNING STEPS: COMMUNICATION AND IDENTIFICATION

LEARNING OBJECTIVE

- In this section you will learn how to identify risks and create a risk map to communicate the importance of each risk on a severity and frequency grid.

risk management policy statement

The primary tool to communicate risk management objectives.

Risk management policy statements are the primary tools to communicate risk management objectives. Forward-thinking firms have made a place for risk management policy statements for many years as leaders discuss the risk management process. Other tools used to relay objectives may include company mission statements, risk management manuals (which provide specific guidelines for detailed risk management problems, such as how to deal with the death or disability of a key executive), and even describe the risk manager's job description. Effective risk management objectives coincide with those of the organization generally, and both must be communicated consistently. Advertisements, employee training programs, and other public activities also can communicate an organization's philosophies and objectives.

3.1 Identifying Risks

The process of identifying all of a firm's risks and their values is a very detailed process. It is of extreme importance to ensure that the business is not ignoring anything that can destroy it. To illustrate how the process takes shape, imagine a business such as Thompson's department store that has a fleet of delivery trucks, a restaurant, a coffee shop, a restaurant, and a babysitting service for parents who are shopping. The risk manager who talks to each employee in the store usually would ask for a list of all the perils and hazards (discussed in Chapter 1) that can expose the operation to losses.

A simple analysis of this department store risk exposure nicely illustrates risk identification, which is a critical element of risk management. For the coffee shop and restaurant, the risks include food poisoning, kitchen fire, and injuries to customers who slip. Spilled coffee can damage store merchandise. For the babysitting service, the store may be liable for any injury to infants as they are fed or play or possibly suffer injuries from other kids. In addition to worry about employees' possible injuries while at work or damage to merchandise from mistreatment, the store risk manager would usually worry about the condition of the floors as a potential hazard, especially when wet. Most risk managers work with the architectural schematics of the building and learn about evacuation routes in case of fires. The location of the building is also critical to identification of risks. If the department store is in a flood-prone area, the risks are different than if the store were located in the mountains. The process involves every company stakeholder. Understanding the supply chain of movement of merchandise is part of the plan as well. If suppliers have losses, risk managers need to know about the risk associated with such delays. This example is a short illustration of the enormous task of risk identification.

Today's CRO also reviews the financial statement of the firm to ensure the financial viability within the financial risks, the asset risks and product risks the firm undertakes. We elaborate more on this aspect with examples in Chapter 5.

Risk Profiling

risk profiling

A process that evaluates all the risks of the organizations and measures the frequency and severity of each risk.

Discovering all risks, their assessments and their relationships to one another becomes critical to learning and understanding an organization's tolerance for risk. This step comes after a separate and thorough review of each risk. Holistic risk mapping is the outcome of **risk profiling**, a process that evaluates all the risks of the organizations and measures the frequency and severity of each risk. Different kinds of organizations pose very different types of risk exposures, and risk evaluations can differ vastly among industries. Boeing, for example, has a tremendous wrongful death exposure resulting from plane crashes. Intellectual property piracy and property rights issues could have a big impact upon the operations of an organization like Microsoft.

Risk Mapping: Creating the Model

The results of risk profiling can be graphically displayed and developed into a model. One such model is **risk mapping**.[1] Risk mapping involves charting entire spectrums of risk, not individual risk "silos" from each separate business unit. Risk mapping becomes useful both in identifying risks and in choosing approaches to mitigate them. Such a map presents a cumulative picture of all the risks in one risk management solution chart. Different facets of risk could include

- workers' compensation claims,
- earthquake or tornado exposure,
- credit risk,
- mold,
- terrorism,
- theft,
- environmental effects,
- intellectual property piracy, and
- a host of other concerns.

A risk map puts the risks a company faces into a visual medium to see how risks are clustered and to understand the relationships among risks. The risks are displayed on a severity and frequency grid after each risk is assessed. Risk maps can be useful tools for explaining and communicating various risks to management and employees. One map might be created to chart what risks are most significant to a particular company. This chart would be used to prioritize risk across the enterprise. Another map might show the risk reduction after risk management action is adopted, as we will show later in this chapter.[2]

Figure 4.2 presents an example of a holistic risk map for an organization examining the dynamics of frequency and severity as they relate to each risk. By assigning the probability of occurrence against the estimate of future magnitude of possible loss, risk managers can form foundations upon which a corporation can focus on risk areas in need of actions. The possible actions—including risk avoidance, loss control, and insurance (loss transfer)—provide alternative solutions during the discussion of the risk management matrix in this chapter.

Note that risk maps include plotting intersection points between measures of frequency (on an x-axis) and severity (on a y-axis) and visually plotting intersection points. Each point represents the relationship between the frequency of the exposure and the severity of the exposure for each risk measured.

Risk Identification and Estimates of Frequency and Severity

Strategies for risk mapping will vary from organization to organization. Company objectives arise out of the firm's risk appetite and culture. These objectives help determine the organization's risk tolerance level (see Chapter 3). As in the separate risk management process for each risk exposure, the first step in mapping risk is to identify the firm's loss exposures and estimate and forecast the frequency and severity of each potential risk. Figure 4.2 displays (for illustration purposes only) quantified trended estimates of loss frequency and severity that risk managers use as inputs into the risk map for a hypothetical small import/export business, Notable Notions. The risk map graph is divided into the four quadrants of the classical risk management matrix (which we discuss in detail later in this chapter). As we will see, such matrices provide a critical part of the way to provide risk management solutions to each risk.

risk mapping

Charting entire spectrums of risk, not individual risk "silos" from each separate business unit.

FIGURE 4.2 Notable Notions Risk Map

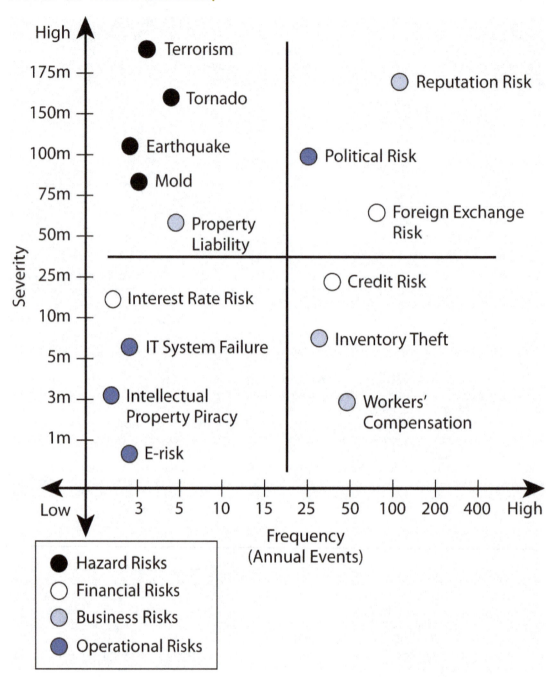

Plotting the Risk Map

Several sample risks are plotted in Notable Notions' holistic risk map.[3] This model can be used to help establish a risk-tolerance boundary and determine priority for risks facing the organization. Graphically, risk across the enterprise comes from four basic risk categories:

1. natural and man-made risks (grouped together under the hazard risks),
2. financial risks,
3. business risks, and
4. operational risks.

Natural and man-made risks include unforeseen events that arise outside of the normal operating environment. The risk map denotes that the probability of a natural and man-made frequency is very low, but the potential severity is very high—for example, a tornado, valued at approximately $160 million. This risk is similar to earthquake, mold exposure, and even terrorism, all of which also fall into the low-frequency/high-severity quadrant. For example, in the aftermath of Hurricane Katrina, the New Orleans floods, and September 11, 2001, most corporations have reprioritized possible losses related to huge man-made and natural catastrophes. For example, more than 1,200 World Bank employees were sent home and barred from corporate headquarters for several days following an anthrax scare in the mailroom.[4] This possibility exposes firms to large potential losses associated with an unexpected interruption to normal business operations. See the box in the introduction to this chapter "How to Handle the Risk Management of a Low-Frequency but Scary Risk Exposure: The Anthrax Scare".

Financial risks arise from changing market conditions involving

- prices,
- volatility,
- liquidity,
- credit risk,
- foreign exchange risk, and
- general market recession (as in the third and fourth quarter of 2008).

financial risks

Uncertainty regarding the outcome of financial decisions, as influenced by factors such as prices, volatility, liquidity, credit markets, currency exchange, and general market conditions.

The credit crisis that arose in the third and fourth quarters of 2008 affected most businesses as economies around the world slowed down and consumers retrench and lower their spending. Thus, risk factors that may provide opportunities as well as potential loss as interest rates, foreign exchange rates are embedded in the risk map. We can display the opportunities—along with possible losses (as we show in Chapter 5 in Figure 5.1).

In our example, we can say that because of its global customer base, Notable Notions has a tremendous amount of exposure to exchange rate risk, which may provide opportunities as well as risks. In such cases, there is no frequency of loss and the opportunity risk is not part of the risk map shown in Figure 4.2. If Notable Notions was a highly leveraged company (meaning that the firm has taken many loans to finance its operations), the company would be at risk of inability to operate and pay salaries if credit lines dried out. However, if it is a conservative company with cash reserves for its operations, Notable Notions' risk map denotes the high number (frequency) of transactions in addition to the high dollar exposure (severity) associated with adverse foreign exchange rate movement. The credit risk for loans did not even make the map, since there is no frequency of loss in the data base for the company. Methods used to control the risks and lower the frequency and severity of financial risks are discussed in Chapter 5.

One example of business risks is reputation risk, which is plotted in the high-frequency/high-severity quadrant. Only recently have we identified reputation risk in map models. Not only do manufacturers such as Coca-Cola rely on their high brand-name identification, so do smaller companies (like Notable Notions) whose customers rely on stellar business practices. One hiccup in the distribution chain causing nondelivery or inconsistent quality in an order can damage a company's reputation and lead to canceled contracts. The downside of reputation damage is potentially significant and has a long recovery period. Companies and their risk managers currently rate loss of good reputation as one of the greatest corporate threats to the success or failure of their organization.[5] A case in point is the impact on Martha Stewart's reputation after she was linked to an insider trading scandal involving the biotech firm ImClone.[6] The day after the story was reported in the *Wall Street Journal*, the stock price of Martha Stewart Living Omnimedia declined almost 20 percent, costing Stewart herself nearly $200 million.

Operational risks are those that relate to the ongoing day-to-day business activities of the organization. Here we reflect IT system failure exposure (which we will discuss in detail later in this chapter). On the figure above, this risk appears in the lower-left quadrant, low severity/low frequency. Hard data shows low down time related to IT system failure. (It is likely that this risk was originally more severe and has been reduced by backup systems and disaster recovery plans.) In the case of a nontechnology firm such as Notable Notions, electronic risk exposure and intellectual property risk are also plotted in the low-frequency/low-severity quadrant.

A pure risk (like workers' compensation) falls in the lower-right quadrant for Notable Notions. The organization experiences a high-frequency but low-severity outcome for workers' compensation claims. Good internal record-keeping helps to track the experience data for Notable Notions and allows for an appropriate mitigation strategy.

The location of each of the remaining data points on Figure 4.2 reflects an additional risk exposure for Notable Notions.

Once a company or CRO has reviewed all these risks together, Notable Notions can create a cohesive and consistent holistic risk management strategy. Risk managers can also review a variety of effects that may not be apparent when exposures are isolated. Small problems in one department may cause big ones in another, and small risks that have high frequency in each department can become exponentially more severe in the aggregate. We will explore property and liability risks more in Chapter 9 and Chapter 10.

KEY TAKEAWAYS

- Communication is key in the risk management processes and there are various mediums in use such as policy statement and manuals.
- The identification process includes profiling and risk mapping.

DISCUSSION QUESTIONS

1. Design a brief risk management policy statement for a small child-care company. Remember to include the most important objectives.
2. For the same child-care company, create a risk identification list and plot the risks on a risk map.
3. Identify the nature of each risk on the risk map in terms of hazard risk, financial risk, business risk, and operational risks.
4. For the child-care company, do you see any speculative or opportunity risks? Explain.

4. PROJECTED FREQUENCY AND SEVERITY AND COST-BENEFIT ANALYSIS—CAPITAL BUDGETING

LEARNING OBJECTIVES

- In this section we focus on an example of how to compute the frequency and severity of losses (learned in Chapter 2).
- We also forecast these measures and conduct a cost-benefit analysis for loss control.

risk management matrix

Matrix that provides alternative financial action to undertake for each frequency/severity combination on the risk map.

forecasting

Projecting the frequency and severity of losses into the future based on current data and statistical assumptions.

Dana, the risk manager at Energy Fitness Centers, identified the risks of workers' injury on the job and collected the statistics of claims and losses since 2003. Dana computed the frequency and severity using her own data in order to use the data in her risk map for one risk only. When we focus on one risk only, we work with the **risk management matrix**. This matrix provides alternative financial action to undertake for each frequency/severity combination (described later in this chapter). Dana's computations of the frequency and severity appear in Table 4.1. Forecasting, on the other hand, appears in Table 4.2 and Figure 4.3. **Forecasting** involves projecting the frequency and severity of losses into the future based on current data and statistical assumptions.

TABLE 4.1 Workers' Compensation Loss History of Energy Fitness Centers—Frequency and Severity

Year	Number of WC Claims	WC Losses	Average Loss per Claim
2003	2,300	$3,124,560	$1,359
2004	1,900	$1,950,000	$1,026
2005	2,100	$2,525,000	$1,202
2006	1,900	$2,345,623	$1,235
2007	2,200	$2,560,200	$1,164
2008	1,700	$1,907,604	$1,122
Total	12,100	$14,412,987	
	Frequency for the whole period		Severity for the whole period
Mean	2,017	$2,402,165	$1,191
(See Chapter 2 for the computation)			

TABLE 4.2 Workers' Compensation Frequency and Severity of Energy Fitness Centers—Actual and Trended

	WC Frequency	Linear Trend Frequency	WC Average Claim	Linear Trend Severity
2003	2,300	2,181	$1,359	$1,225
2004	1,900	2,115	$1,026	$1,226
2005	2,100	2,050	$1,202	$1,227
2006	1,900	1,984	$1,235	$1,228
2007	2,200	1,918	$1,422	$1,229
2008	1,700	1,852	$1,122	$1,230
2009	Estimated	1,786.67	Estimated	$1,231.53

FIGURE 4.3 Workers' Compensation Frequency and Severity of Energy Fitness Centers—Actual and Trended

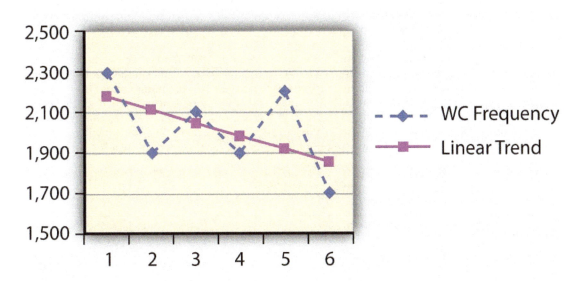

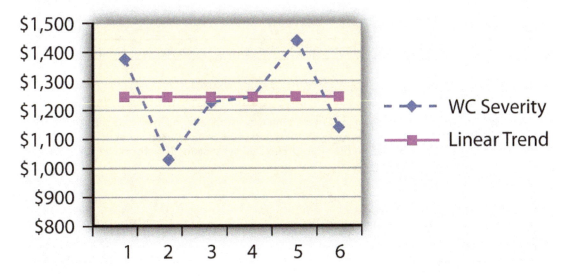

Dana installed various loss-control tools during the period under study. The result of the risk reduction investments appear to be paying off. Her analysis of the results indicated that the annual frequency trend has decreased (see the negative slope for the frequency in Figure 4.2). The company's success in decreasing loss severity doesn't appear in such dramatic terms. Nevertheless, Dana feels encouraged that her efforts helped level off the severity. The slope of the annual severity (losses per claim) trend line is 1.09 per year—and hence almost level as shown in the illustration in Figure 4.2. (See the Section 7 to this chapter for explanation of the computation of the forecasting analysis.)

4.1 Capital Budgeting: Cost-Benefit Analysis for Loss-Control Efforts

With the ammunition of reducing the frequency of losses, Dana is planning to continue her loss-control efforts. Her next step is to convince management to invest in a new innovation in security belts for the employees. These belts have proven records of reducing the severity of WC claim in other facilities. In this example, we show her cost-benefit analysis—analysis that examines the cost of the belts and compares the expense to the expected reduction in losses or savings in premiums for insurance. If the benefit of cost reduction exceeds the expense for the belt, Dana will be able to prove her point. In terms of the actual analysis, she has to bring the future reduction in losses to today's value of the dollar by looking at the present value of the reduction in premiums. If the present value of premium savings is greater than the cost of the belts, we will have a positive net present value (NPV) and management will have a clear incentive to approve this loss-control expense.

cash flow analysis

Analysis that looks at the amount of cash that will be saved and brings it into today's present value.

With the help of her broker, Dana plans to show her managers that, by lowering the frequency and severity of losses, the workers' compensation rates for insurance can be lowered by as much as 20–25 percent. This 20–25 percent is actually a true savings or benefit for the cost-benefit analysis. Dana undertook to conduct **cash flow analysis** for purchasing the new innovative safety belts project. A cash flow analysis looks at the amount of cash that will be saved and brings it into today's present value. Table 4.3 provides the decrease in premium anticipated when the belts are used as a loss-control technique.

The cash outlay required to purchase the innovative belts is $50,000 today. The savings in premiums for the next few years are expected to be $20,000 in the first year, $25,000 in the second year, and $30,000 in the third year. Dana would like to show her managers this premium savings over a three-year time horizon. Table 4.3 shows the cash flow analysis that Dana used, using a 6 percent rate of return. For 6 percent, the NPV would be ($66,310 – 50,000) = $16,310. You are invited to calculate the NPV at different interest rates. Would the NPV be greater for 10 percent? (The student will find that it is lower, since the future value of a lower amount today grows faster at 10 percent than at 6 percent.)

TABLE 4.3 **Net Present Value (NPV) of Workers' Compensation Premiums Savings for Energy Fitness Centers When Purchasing Innovative Safety Belts for $50,000**

Use a financial calculator

	Savings on Premiums	Present Value of $1 (at 6 percent)	Present Value of Premium savings
End of Year	End of Year		
1	$20,000	0.943	$18,860
2	$25,000	0.890	$22,250
3	$30,000	0.840	$25,200
Total present value of all premium savings			$66,310
Net present value = $66,310 − $50,000 = $16,310 > 0			

4.2 Risk Management Information System

Risk managers rely upon data and analysis techniques to assess and evaluate and thus to make informed decisions. One of the risk managers' primary tasks—as you see from the activities of Dana at Energy Fitness Centers—is to develop the appropriate data systems to allow them to quantify the organization's loss history, including

- types of losses,
- amounts,
- circumstances surrounding them,
- dates, and
- other relevant facts.

risk management information systems

Computerized data systems to allows a risk manager to quantify the organization's loss history.

We call such computerized quantifications a **risk management information system**, or RMIS. An RMIS provides risk managers with the ability to slice and dice the data in any way that may help risk managers assess and evaluate the risks their companies face. The history helps to establish probability distributions and trends analysis. When risk managers use good data and analysis to make risk reduction decisions, they must always include consideration of financial concepts (such as the time value of money) as shown above.

The key to good decision making lies in the risk managers' ability to analyze large amounts of data collected. A firm's **data warehousing** (a system of housing large sets of data for strategic analysis and operations) of risk data allows decision makers to evaluate multiple dimensions of risks as well as overall risk. Reporting techniques can be virtually unlimited in perspectives. For example, risk managers can sort data by location, by region, by division, and so forth. Because risk solutions are only as good as their underlying assumptions, RMIS allows for modeling data to assist in the risk exposure measurement process. Self-administered retained coverages have experienced explosive growth across all industries. The boom has meant that systems now include customized Web-based reporting capabilities. The technological advances that go along with RMIS allows all decision makers to maximize a firm's risk/reward tradeoff through data analysis.

data warehousing

A system of housing large sets of data for strategic analysis and operations.

KEY TAKEAWAY

- The student learned how to trend the frequency and severity measures for use in the risk map. When this data is available, the risk manager is able to conduct cost-benefit analysis comparing the benefit of adopting a loss-control measure.

DISCUSSION QUESTIONS

1. Following is the loss data for slip-and-fall shoppers' medical claims of the grocery store chain Derelex for the years 2004–2008.

    a. Calculate the severity and frequency of the losses.

    b. Forecast the severity and frequency for next year using the appendix to this chapter.

    c. If a new mat can help lower the severity of slips and falls by 50 percent in the third year from now, what will be the projected severity in 3 years if the mats are used?

    d. What should be the costs today for this mats to break even? Use cost-benefit analysis at 6 percent.

Year	Number of Slip and Fall Claims	Slip-and-Fall Losses
2004	1,100	$1,650,000
2005	900	$4,000,000
2006	700	$3,000,000
2007	1,000	$12,300,000
2008	1,400	$10,500,000

5. RISK MANAGEMENT ALTERNATIVES: THE RISK MANAGEMENT MATRIX

LEARNING OBJECTIVES

- **In this section you will learn about the alternatives available for managing risks based on the frequency and severity of the risks.**
- **We also address the risk manager's alternatives—transferring the risk, avoiding it, and managing it internally with loss controls.**

Once they are evaluated and forecasted, loss frequency and loss severity are used as the vertical and horizontal lines in the risk management matrix for one specific risk exposure. Note that such a matrix differs from the risk map described below (which includes all important risks a firm is exposed to). The risk management matrix includes on one axis, categories of relative frequency (high and low) and on the other, categories of relative severity (high and low). The simplest of these matrices is one with just four cells, as shown in the pure risk solutions in Table 4.4. While this matrix takes into account only two variables, in reality, other variables—the financial condition of the firm, the size of the firm, and external market conditions, to name a few—are very important in the decision.[7]

TABLE 4.4 The Traditional Risk Management Matrix (for One Risk)

Pure Risk Solutions		
	Low Frequency of Losses	High Frequency of Losses
Low Severity of Losses	Retention—self-insurance	Retention with loss control—risk reduction
High Severity of Losses	Transfer—insurance	Avoidance

5.1 The Risk Management Decision—Return to the Example

Dana, the risk manager of Energy Fitness Centers, also uses a risk management matrix to decide whether or not to recommend any additional loss-control devices. Using the data in Table 4.3 and Figure 4.3, Dana compared the forecasted frequency and severity of the worker's compensation results to the data of her peer group that she obtained from the Risk and Insurance Management Society (RIMS) and her broker. In comparison, her loss frequency is higher than the median for similarly sized fitness centers. Yet, to her surprise, EFC's risk severity is lower than the median. Based on the risk management matrix she should suggest to management that they retain some risks and use loss control as she already had been doing. Her cost-benefit analysis from above helps reinforce her decision. Therefore, with both cost-benefits analysis and the method of managing the risk suggested by the matrix, she has enough ammunition to convince management to agree to buy the additional belts as a method to reduce the losses.

To understand the risk management matrix alternatives, we now concentrate on each of the cells in the matrix.

5.2 Risk Transfer—Insurance

transfer of risk

Displacement of risk to a third, unrelated party.

The lower-left corner of the risk management matrix represents situations involving low frequency and high severity. Here we find **transfer of risk**—that is, displacement of risk to a third, unrelated party—to an insurance company. We discuss insurance—both its nature and its operations—at length in Chapter 6 and Chapter 7. In essence, risk transference involves paying someone else to bear some or all of the risk of certain financial losses that cannot be avoided, assumed, or reduced to acceptable levels. Some risks may be transferred through the formation of a corporation with limited liability for its stockholders. Others may be transferred by contractual arrangements, including insurance.

5.3 Corporations—A Firm

The owner or owners of a firm face serious potential losses. They are responsible to pay debts and other financial obligations when such liabilities exceed the firm's assets. If the firm is organized as a *sole proprietorship*, the proprietor faces this risk. His or her personal assets are not separable from those of the firm because the firm is not a separate legal entity. The proprietor has unlimited liability for the firm's obligations. General partners in a *partnership* occupy a similar situation, each partner being liable without limit for the debts of the firm.

Because a corporation is a separate legal entity, investors who wish to limit possible losses connected with a particular venture may create a corporation and transfer such risks to it. This does not prevent losses from occurring, but the burden is transferred to the corporation. The owners suffer indirectly, of course, but their loss is limited to their investment in the corporation. A huge liability claim for damages may take all the assets of the corporation, but the stockholders' personal assets beyond their stock in this particular corporation are not exposed to loss. Such a method of risk transfer sometimes is used to compartmentalize the risks of a large venture by incorporating separate firms to handle various segments of the total operation. In this way, a large firm may transfer parts of its risks to separate smaller subsidiaries, thus placing limits on possible losses to the parent company owners. Courts, however, may not approve of this method of transferring the liability associated with dangerous business activities. For example, a large firm may be held legally liable for damages caused by a small subsidiary formed to manufacture a substance that proves dangerous to employees and/or the environment.

5.4 Contractual Arrangements

Some risks are transferred by a guarantee included in the contract of sale. A noteworthy example is the warranty provided a car buyer. When automobiles were first manufactured, the purchaser bore the burden of all defects that developed during use. Somewhat later, automobile manufacturers agreed to replace defective parts at no cost, but the buyer was required to pay for any labor involved. Currently, manufacturers typically not only replace defective parts but also pay for labor, within certain constraints. The owner has, in effect, transferred a large part of the risk of purchasing a new automobile back to the manufacturer. The buyer, of course, is still subject to the inconvenience of having repairs made, but he or she does not have to pay for them.

Other types of contractual arrangements that transfer risk include leases and rental agreements, hold-harmless clauses[8] and surety bonds.[9] Perhaps the most important arrangement for the transfer of risk important to our study is insurance.

Insurance is a common form of planned risk transfer as a financing technique for individuals and most organizations. The insurance industry has grown tremendously in industrialized countries, developing sophisticated products, employing millions of people, and investing billions of dollars. Because of its core importance in risk management, insurance is the centerpiece in most risk management activities.

5.5   Risk Assumption

The upper-left corner of the matrix in Table 4.4, representing both low frequency and low severity, shows retention of risk. When an organization uses a highly formalized method of retention of a risk, it is said the organization has self-insured the risk. The company bears the risk and is willing to withstand the financial losses from claims, if any. It is important to note that the extent to which risk retention is feasible depends upon the accuracy of loss predictions and the arrangements made for loss payment. Retention is especially attractive to large organizations. Many large corporations use captives, which are a form of self-insurance. When a business creates a subsidiary to handle the risk exposures, the business creates a captive. As noted above, broadly defined, a captive insurance company is one that provides risk management protection to its parent company and other affiliated organizations. The captive is controlled by its parent company. We will provide a more detailed explanation of captives in Chapter 6. If the parent can use funds more productively (that is, can earn a higher after-tax return on investment), the formation of a captive may be wise. The risk manager must assess the importance of the insurer's claims adjusting and other services (including underwriting) when evaluating whether to create or rent a captive.

Risk managers of smaller businesses can become part of a **risk retention group**.[10] A risk retention group provides risk management and retention to a few players in the same industry who are too small to act on their own. In this way, risk retention groups are similar to group self-insurance. We discuss them further in Chapter 6.

risk retention group

A group that provides risk management and retention to a few players in the same industry who are too small to act on their own.

5.6   Risk Reduction

Moving over to the upper-right corner of the risk management matrix in Table 4.4, the quadrant characterized by high frequency and low severity, we find retention with loss control. If frequency is significant, risk managers may find efforts to prevent losses useful. If losses are of low value, they may be easily paid out of the organization's or individual's own funds. Risk retention usually finances highly frequent, predictable losses more cost effectively. An example might be losses due to wear and tear on equipment. Such losses are predictable and of a manageable, low-annual value. We described loss control in the case of the fitness center above.

Loss prevention efforts seek to reduce the probability of a loss occurring. Managers use **loss reduction** efforts to lessen loss severity. If you want to ski in spite of the hazards involved, you may take instruction to improve your skills and reduce the likelihood of you falling down a hill or crashing into a tree. At the same time, you may engage in a physical fitness program to toughen your body to withstand spills without serious injury. Using both loss prevention and reduction techniques, you attempt to lower both the probability and severity of loss.

Loss prevention's goal seeks to reduce losses to the minimum compatible with a reasonable level of human activity and expense. At any given time, economic constraints place limits on what may be done, although what is considered too costly at one time may be readily accepted at a later date. Thus, during one era, little effort may have been made to prevent injury to employees, because employees were regarded as expendable. The general notion today, however, is that such injuries are prevented because they have become too expensive. Change was made to adapt to the prevailing ideals concerning the value of human life and the social responsibility of business.

loss prevention

Efforts that seek to reduce the probability of a loss occurring.

loss reduction

Efforts to lessen loss severity.

5.7   Risk Avoidance

In the lower-right corner of the matrix in Table 4.4, at the intersection of high frequency and high severity, we find avoidance. Managers seek to avoid any situation falling in this category if possible. An example might be a firm that is considering construction of a building on the east coast of Florida in Key West. Flooding and hurricane risk would be high, with significant damage possibilities.

Of course, we cannot always avoid risks. When Texas school districts were faced with high severity and frequency of losses in workers' compensation, schools could not close their doors to avoid the problem. Instead, the school districts opted to self-insure, that is, retain the risk up to a certain loss limit.[11]

Not all avoidance necessarily results in "no loss." While seeking to avoid one loss potential, many efforts may create another. Some people choose to travel by car instead of plane because of their fear of flying. While they have successfully avoided the possibility of being a passenger in an airplane accident, they have increased their probability of being in an automobile accident. Per mile traveled, automobile deaths are far more frequent than aircraft fatalities. By choosing cars over planes, these people actually raise their probability of injury.

KEY TAKEAWAYS

- One of the most important tools in risk management is a road map using projected frequency and severity of losses of one risk only.
- Within a framework of similar companies, the risk manager can tell when it is most appropriate to use risk transfer, risk reduction, retain or transfer the risk.

DISCUSSION QUESTIONS

1. Using the basic risk management matrix, explain the following:
   a. When would you buy insurance?
   b. When would you avoid the risk?
   c. When would you retain the risk?
   d. When would you use loss control?
2. Give examples for the following risk exposures:
   a. High-frequency and high-severity loss exposures
   b. Low-frequency and high-severity loss exposures
   c. Low-frequency and low-severity loss exposures
   d. High-frequency and low-severity loss exposure

---

6. COMPARISONS TO CURRENT RISK-HANDLING METHODS

LEARNING OBJECTIVES

- **In this section we return to the risk map and compare the risk map created for the identification purpose to that created for the risk management tools already used by the business.**
- **If the solution the firm uses does not fit within the solutions suggested by the risk management matrix, the business has to reevaluate its methods of managing the risks.**

At this point, the risk manager of Notable Notions can see the potential impact of its risks and its best risk management strategies. The next step in the risk mapping technique is to create separate graphs that show how the firm is currently handling each risk. Each of the risks in Figure 4.4 is now graphed according to whether the risk is uninsured, retained, partially insured or hedged (a financial technique to lower the risk by using the financial instrument discussed in Chapter 6), or insured. Figure 4.4 is the new risk map reflecting the current risk management handling.

FIGURE 4.4 Notable Notions Current Risk Handling

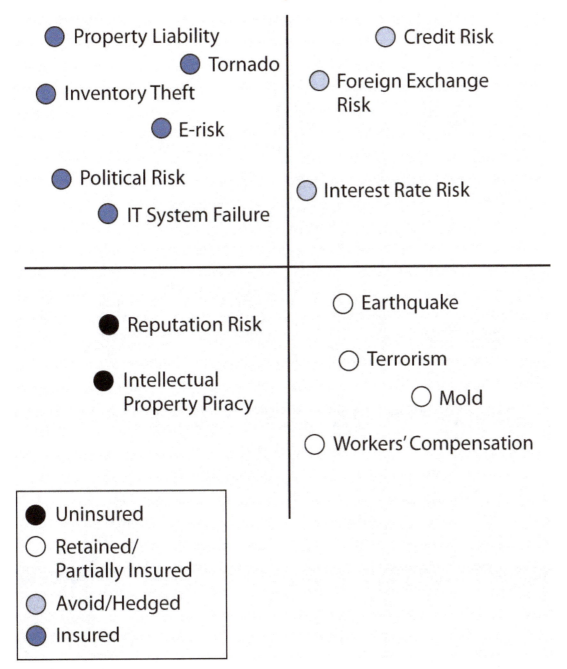

When the two maps, the one in Figure 4.2 and the one in Figure 4.4, are overlaid, it can be clearly seen that some of the risk strategies suggested in Table 4.4 differ from current risk handling as shown in Figure 4.4. For example, a broker convinced the risk manager to purchase an expensive policy for e-risk. The risk map shows that for Notable Notions, e-risk is low severity and low frequency and thus should remain uninsured. By overlaying the two risk maps, the risk manager can see where current risk handling may not be appropriate.

6.1   The Effect of Risk Handling Methods

We can create another map to show how a particular risk management strategy of the maximum severity that will remain after insurance. This occurs when insurance companies give only low limits of coverage. For example, if the potential severity of Notable Notions' earthquake risk is $140 million, but coverage is offered only up to $100 million, the risk falls to a level of $40 million.

Using holistic risk mapping methodology presents a clear, easy-to-read presentation of a firm's overall risk spectrum or the level of risks that are still left after all risk mitigation strategies were put in place. It allows a firm to discern between those exposures that after all mitigation efforts are still

1. unbearable,
2. difficult to bear, and
3. relatively unimportant.

In summary, risk mapping has five main objectives:

1. To aid in the identification of risks and their interrelations
2. To provide a mechanism to see clearly what risk management strategy would be the best to undertake
3. To compare and evaluate the firm's current risk handling and to aid in selecting appropriate strategies
4. To show the leftover risks after all risk mitigation strategies are put in place
5. To easily communicate risk management strategy to both management and employees

6.2 Ongoing Monitoring

The process of risk management is continuous, requiring constant monitoring of the program to be certain that (1) the decisions implemented were correct and have been implemented appropriately and that (2) the underlying problems have not changed so much as to require revised plans for managing them. When either of these conditions exists, the process returns to the step of identifying the risks and risk management tools and the cycle repeats. In this way, risk management can be considered a systems process, one in never-ending motion.

KEY TAKEAWAYS

- In this section we return to the risk map and compare the risk map created for the identification purpose to that created for the risk management tools already used by the business. This is part of the decision making using the highly regarded risk management matrix tool.
- If the projected frequency and severity indicate different risk management solutions, the overlay of the maps can immediately clarify any discrepancies. Corrective actions can be taken and the ongoing monitoring continues.

DISCUSSION QUESTIONS

1. Use the designed risk map for the small child-care company you created above. Create a risk management matrix for the same risks indentified in the risk map of question 1.
2. Overlay the two risk maps to see if the current risk management tools fit in with what is required under the risk management matrix.
3. Propose corrective measures, if any.
4. What would be the suggestions for ongoing risk management for the child-care company?

7. APPENDIX: FORECASTING

7.1 Forecasting of Frequency and Severity

When insurers or risk managers use frequency and severity to project the future, they use trending techniques that apply to the loss distributions known to them.[12] Regressions are the most commonly used tools to predict future losses and claims based on the past. In this textbook, we introduce linear regression using the data featured in Chapter 2. The scientific notations for the regressions are discussed later in this appendix.

TABLE 4.5 Linear Regression Trend of Claims and Losses of A

Year	Actual Fire Claims	Linear Trend For Claims	Actual Fire Losses	Linear Trend For Losses
1	11	8.80	$16,500	$10,900.00
2	9	9.50	$40,000	$36,900.00
3	7	10.20	$30,000	$62,900.00
4	10	10.90	$123,000	$88,900.00
5	14	11.60	$105,000	$114,900.00

FIGURE 4.5 Linear Regression Trend of Claims of A

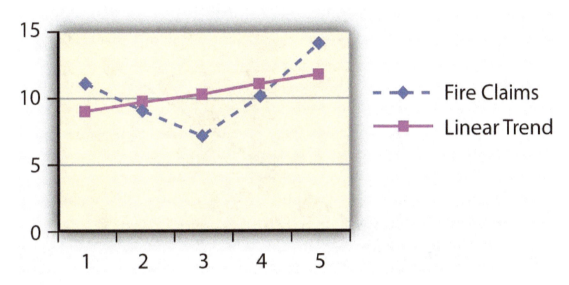

FIGURE 4.6 Linear Regression Trend of Losses of A

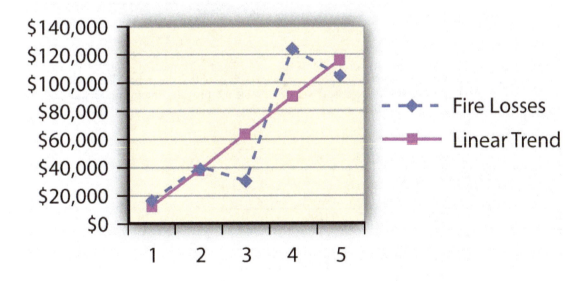

7.2 Using Linear Regression

Linear regression attempts to explain the relationship among observed values by applying a straight line fit to the data. The linear regression model postulates that

$$Y = b + mX + e$$

,where the "residual" e is a random variable with mean of zero. The coefficients a and b are determined by the condition that the sum of the square residuals is as small as possible. For our purposes, we do not discuss the error term. We use the frequency and severity data of A for 5 years. Here, we provide the scientific notation that is behind Figure 4.5 and Figure 4.6.

In order to determine the intercept of the line on the y-axis and the slope, we use m (slope) and b (y-intercept) in the equation.

Given a set of data with n data points, *the slope (m) and the y-intercept (b)* are determined using:

$$m = \frac{n\Sigma(xy) - \Sigma x \Sigma y}{n\Sigma(x^2) - (\Sigma x)^2}$$

$$b = \frac{\Sigma y - m\Sigma x}{n}$$

FIGURE 4.7 Showing the Slope and Intercept

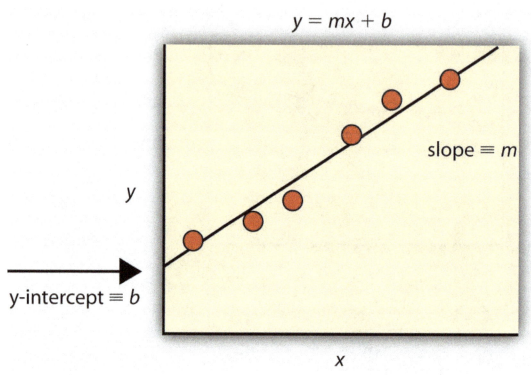

The graph is provided by Chris D. Odom, with permission.

Most commonly, practitioners use various software applications to obtain the trends. The student is invited to experiment with Microsoft Excel spreadsheets. Table 4.6 provides the formulas and calculations for the intercept and slope of the claims to construct the trend line.

TABLE 4.6 Method of Calculating the Trend Line for the Claims

	(1)	(2)	(3) = (1) × (2)	(4) = (1)2
	Year	Claims		
	X	Y	XY	X2
	1	11	11.00	1
	2	9	18.00	4
	3	7	21.00	9
	4	10	40.00	16
	n=5	14	70.00	25
Total	15	51	160	55
M = Slope = 0.7	$m = \dfrac{n\Sigma(xy) - \Sigma x \Sigma y}{n\Sigma(x^2) - (\Sigma x)^2}$			$= \dfrac{(5 \times 160) - (15 \times 51)}{(5 \times 55) - (15 \times 15)}$
b = Intercept = 8.1	$b = \dfrac{\Sigma y - m\Sigma x}{n}$			$= \dfrac{51 - (0.7 \times 15)}{5}$

Future Forecasts using the Slopes and Intercepts for A:

- Future claims = Intercept + Slope × (X)
- In year 6, the forecast of the number of claims is projected to be: {8.1 + (0.7 × 6)} = 12.3 claims
- Future losses = Intercept + Slope × (X)
- In year 6, the forecast of the losses in dollars is projected to be: {−15, 100 + (26,000 × 6)} = $140,900 in losses

The in-depth statistical explanation of the linear regression model is beyond the scope of this course. Interested students are invited to explore statistical models in elementary statistics textbooks. This first exposure to the world of forecasting, however, is critical to a student seeking further study in the fields of insurance and risk management.

8.   REVIEW AND PRACTICE

1. What are the adverse consequences of risk? Give examples of each.

2. What is a common process of risk management for property exposure of a firm?

3. How was the traditional process of risk management expanded?

4. The liability of those who own a corporation is limited to their investment, while proprietors and general partners have unlimited liability for the obligations of their business. Explain what relevance this has for risk management.

5. What are the three objectives of risk mapping? Explain one way a chief risk officer would use a risk map model.

6. Define the terms *loss prevention* and *loss reduction*. Provide examples of each.

7. What are the types of risks that are included in an enterprise risk analysis?

8. What has helped to expand risk management into enterprise risk management?

9. Following is the loss data for slip-and-fall shoppers' medical claims of the fashion designer LOLA for the years 2004–2008.

   a. Calculate the severity and frequency of the losses.

   b. Forecast the severity and frequency for next year using the appendix to this chapter.

   c. What would be the risk management solution if Lola's results are above the median of severity and frequency for the industry of the geographical location?

Year	Number of Slip-and-Fall Claims	Slip-and-Fall Losses
2004	700	$2,650,000
2005	1,000	$6,000,000
2006	700	$7,000,000
2007	900	$12,300,000
2008	1,400	$10,500,000

10. Brooks Trucking, which provides trucking services over a twelve-state area from its home base in Cincinnati, has never had a risk management program. Shawana Lee, Brooks Trucking's financial vice-president, has a philosophy that "lightning can't strike twice in the same place." Because of this, she does not believe in trying to practice loss prevention or loss reduction.

    a. If you were appointed its risk manager, how would you identify the pure-risk exposures facing Brooks?

    b. Do you agree or disagree with Shawana? Why?

11. Devin Davis is an independent oil driller in Oklahoma. He feels that the most important risk he has is small property damages to his drilling rig, because he constantly has small, minor damage to the rig while it is being operated or taken to new locations.

    a. Do you agree or disagree with Devin?

    b. Which is more important, frequency of loss or severity of loss? Explain.

12. Rinaldo's is a high-end jeweler with one retail location on Fifth Avenue in New York City. The majority of sales are sophisticated pieces that sell for $5,000 or more and are Rinaldo's own artistic creations using precious metals and stones. The raw materials are purchased primarily in Africa (gold, platinum, and diamonds) and South America (silver). Owing to a large amount of

international marketing efforts, Internet and catalog sales represent over 45 percent of the total $300 million in annual sales revenue. To accommodate his customers, Rinaldo will accept both the U.S. dollar and other foreign currencies as a form of payment. Acting as an enterprise risk manager consultant, create a risk map model to identify Rinaldo's risks across the four basic categories of business/strategic risk, operational risk, financial risk, and hazard risk.

ENDNOTES

1. Etti G. Baranoff, "Mapping the Evolution of Risk Management," *Contingencies* (July/August 2004): 22–27.

2. Lee Ann Gjertsen, "'Risk Mapping' Helps RM's Chart Solutions," *National Underwriter*, Property & Casualty/Risk & Benefits Management Edition, June 7, 1999.

3. The exercise is abridged for demonstrative purposes. An actual holistic risk mapping model would include many more risk intersection points plotted along the frequency/severity X and Y axes.

4. Associated Press Newswire, May 22, 2002.

5. "Risk Whistle: Reputation Risk," *Swiss Re* publication, http://www.swissre.com.

6. Geeta Anand, Jerry Arkon, and Chris Adams, "ImClone's Ex-CEO Arrested, Charged with Insider Trading," *Wall Street Journal*, June 13, 2002, 1.

7. Etti G. Baranoff, "Determinants in Risk-Financing Choices: The Case of Workers' Compensation for Public School Districts," *Journal of Risk and Insurance*, June 2000.

8. "A Hold Harmless Agreement is usually used where the Promisor's actions could lead to a claim or liability to the Promisee. For example, the buyer of land wants to inspect the property prior to close of escrow, and needs to conduct tests and studies on the property. In this case, the buyer would promise to indemnify the current property owner from any claims resulting from the buyer's inspection (i.e., injury to a third party because the buyer is drilling a hole; to pay for a mechanic's lien because the buyer hired a termite inspector, etc.). Another example is where a property owner allows a caterer to use its property to cater an event. In this example, the Catering Company (the "Promisor") agrees to indemnify the property owner for any claims arising from the Catering Company's use of the property." From Legaldocs, a division of U.S.A. Law Publications, Inc., http://www.legaldocs.com/docs/holdha_1.mv.

9. A surety bond is a three-party instrument between a surety, the contractor, and the project owner. The agreement binds the contractor to comply with the terms and conditions of a contract. If the contractor is unable to successfully perform the contract, the surety assumes the contractor's responsibilities and ensures that the project is completed.

10. President Reagan signed into law the Liability Risk Retention Act in October 1986 (an amendment to the Product Liability Risk Retention Act of 1981). The act permits formation of retention groups (a special form of captive) with fewer restrictions than existed before. The retention groups are similar to association captives. The act permits formation of such groups in the U.S. under more favorable conditions than have existed generally for association captives. The act may be particularly helpful to small businesses that could not feasibly self-insure on their own but can do so within a designated group. How extensive will be the use of risk retention groups is yet to be seen. As of the writing of this text there are efforts to amend the act.

11. Etti G. Baranoff, "Determinants in Risk-Financing Choices: The Case of Workers' Compensation for Public School Districts," *Journal of Risk and Insurance*, June 2000.

12. Forecasting is part of the Associate Risk Manager designation under the Risk Assessment course using the book: Baranoff Etti, Scott Harrington, and Greg Niehaus, *Risk Assessment* (Malvern, PA: American Institute for Chartered Property Casualty Underwriters/Insurance Institute of America, 2005).

CHAPTER 5
The Evolution of Risk Management: Enterprise Risk Management

In the first three chapters, we provided information to help you understand and measure risks, as well as to evaluate risk attitudes and risk behavior. Chapter 4 concentrated on risk management and methods for identifying, measuring, and managing risks. In this chapter we elaborate further on the management of risk, placing greater emphasis on the opportunities that risk represents. We emphasize *prudent* opportunities rather than actions motivated by greed. When trying to identify the main causes of the 2008–2009 credit crisis, the lack of risk management and prudent behavior emerge as key factors. However, even companies that were not part of the debacle are paying the price, as the whole economy suffers a lack of credit and consumers' entrenchment. Consumers are less inclined to buy something that they don't consider a necessity. As such, even firms with prudent and well-organized risk management are currently seeing huge devaluation of their stocks.[1]

In many corporations, the head of the ERM effort is the chief risk officer or CRO. In other cases, the whole executive team handles the risk management decision with specific coordinators. Many large corporations adopted a system called Six Sigma, which is a business strategy widely adopted by many corporations to improve processes and efficiency. Within this model of operation they embedded enterprise risk management. The ERM function at Textron follows the latter model. Textron's stock fell from $72 in January 2008 to $15 in December 2008. Let's recall that ERM includes every aspect of risks within the corporation, including labor negotiation risks, innovation risks, lack-of-foresight risks, ignoring market condition risks, managing self-interest and greed risks, and so forth. Take the case of the three U.S. auto manufacturers—GM, Chrysler, and Ford. Their holistic risks include not only insuring buildings and automobiles or worker's compensation. They must look at the complete picture of how to ensure survival in a competitive and technologically innovative world. The following is a brief examination of the risk factors that contributed to the near-bankrupt condition of the U.S. automakers: [2]

- Lack of foresight in innovation of fuel-efficient automobiles with endurance and sustainability of value.

- Too much emphasis on the demand for the moment rather than on smart projections of potential catastrophes impacting fuel prices, like hurricanes Katrina, Wilma, and Ike.

- They did not account for an increase in the worldwide demand for use of fuel.

- Inability to compete in terms of quality control and manufacturing costs because of the labor unions' high wage demands. Shutting down individual initiatives and smart thinking. Everything was negotiated rather than done via smart business decisions and processes.

- Allowing top management to stagnate into luxury and overspending, such as the personal planes in which they went to Washington to negotiate bailouts.

- The credit crisis of 2008 escalated the demise; it compounded the already mismanaged industry that didn't respond to consumers' needs.

Had risk management been a top priority for the automobile companies, perhaps they would face a different attitude as they approach U.S. taxpayers for their bailouts. ERM needs to be part of the mind-set of every company stakeholder. When one arm of the company is pulling for its own gains without consideration of the total value it delivers to stakeholders, the result, no doubt, will be disastrous. The players need to dance together under the paradigm that every action might have the potential to lead to catastrophic results. The risk of each action needs to be clear, and assuredness for risk mitigation is a must.

This chapter includes the following:

1. Links

2. Enterprise risk management within firm goals

3. Risk management and the firm's financial statement—opportunities within the ERM

4. Risk management using the capital markets

1. LINKS

While Chapter 4 enumerated all risks, we emphasized the loss part more acutely, since avoiding losses represents the essence of risk management. But, with the advent of ERM, the risks that represent opportunities for gain are clearly just as important. The question is always "How do we evaluate activities in terms of losses and gains within the firm's main goal of value maximization?" Therefore, we are going to look at maps that examine both sides—both gains and losses as they appear in Figure 5.1. We operate on the negative and positive sides of the ERM map and we look into opportunity risks. We expand our puzzle to incorporate the firm's goals. We introduce more sophisticated tools to ensure that you are equipped to work with all elements of risk management for firms to sustain themselves.

FIGURE 5.1 The Links to ERM with Opportunities and Risks

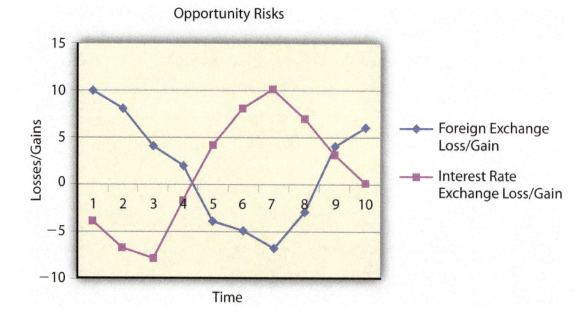

Let us emphasize that, in light of the financial crisis of 2008–2009, ERM is a needed mind-set for all disciplines. The tools are just what ERM-oriented managers can pull out of their tool kits. For example, we provide an example for the life insurance industry as a key to understanding the links. We provide a more complete picture of ERM in Figure 5.2.

FIGURE 5.2 **Links between the Holistic Risk Picture and Conventional Risk and ERM Tools**

Part C illustrates the interaction between parts A and B.

Part C Interaction between Risk and ERM Tools Spaces	RISKS		ERM TOOLS
	Capital structure risk	<====>	Capital structure risk management
	Asset/liability matching risk	<====>	Asset/liability matching risk management
	Asset risk	<====>	Asset risk management
	Product risk	<====>	Product risk management
	Operational risk	<====>	Operational risk management
	Capital Structure (Financial Risk) Management Tools		
	Asset/Liability Matching Management Tools		
Part B: Life Insurers' Enterprise Risk Management Tools	ASSET RISK Management Tools	PRODUCT RISK Management Tools	OPERATIONAL RISK Management Tools
	• Hedging/derivatives • Asset allocation management (active versus passive)	• Reinsurance • Reserving • Securitization • Diversification	• Control over agents and brokers • Organizational/corporate structure • Adherence to regulation • IT controls • Operational safety and loss controls

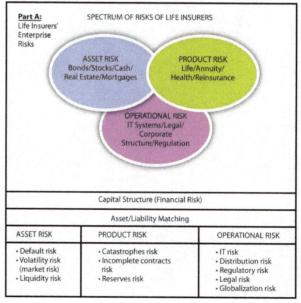

Part A: Life Insurers' Enterprise Risks	SPECTRUM OF RISKS OF LIFE INSURERS		
	Capital Structure (Financial Risk)		
	Asset/Liability Matching		
	ASSET RISK	PRODUCT RISK	OPERATIONAL RISK
	• Default risk • Volatility risk (market risk) • Liquidity risk	• Catastrophes risk • Incomplete contracts risk • Reserves risk	• IT risk • Distribution risk • Regulatory risk • Legal risk • Globalization risk

Source: Etti G. Baranoff and Thomas W. Sager, "Integrated Risk Management in Life Insurance Companies," a $10,000 award-winning paper, International Insurance Society Seminar, Chicago, July 2006 and in special edition of the Geneva Papers on Risk and Insurance Issues and Practice.

2. ENTERPRISE RISK MANAGEMENT WITHIN FIRM GOALS

LEARNING OBJECTIVES

- In this section you will learn how the ERM function integrates well into the firm's main theoretical and actual goal: to maximize value. We show a hypothetical example of ERM adding value to a firm.
- We also discuss the ambiguities regarding the firm goals.

As you saw in Chapter 4, risk management functions represent an integrated function within the organization. In Figure 4.2, we map every risk. While the enterprise risk management (ERM) function compiles the information, every function should identify risks and examine risk management tools. Finance departments may take the lead, but engineering, legal, product development, and asset management teams also have input. The individual concerned with the organization's ERM strategy is often given the position **chief risk officer (CRO)**. The CRO is usually part of the corporation's executive team and is responsible for all risk elements—pure and opportunity risks.

In this section, we illustrate in simple terms how the function integrates well into the firm's goal to maximize value. In terms of publicly traded corporations, maximizing value translates to maximizing the company's stock value. Even nonpublicly traded firms share the same goal. With nonpublicly traded firms, the market isn't available to explicitly recognize the company's true value. Therefore, people may interpret the term "firm's value" differently with public versus nonpublic companies. Instead of the simple stock value, nonpublic firms may well create value using inputs such as revenues, costs, or sources of financing (debt of equity). While "cash-rich" companies have greater value, they may not optimally use their money to invest in growth and future income. External variables, such as the 2008–2009 credit crisis, may well affect firm value, as can the weather, investors' attitudes, and the like. In 2008 and 2009, even strong companies felt the effects from the credit crisis. Textron and other well-run companies saw their values plummet.

The inputs for a model that determines value allow us to examine how each input functions in the context of all the other variables.[3] Once we get an appropriate model, we can determine firms' values and use these values to reach rational decisions. Traditionally, the drive for the firm to maximize value referred to the drive to maximize **stockholders' wealth**. In other words, the literature referred to the maximization of the value of the firm's shares (its **market value**, or the price of the stock times the number of shares traded, for a publicly traded firm). This approach replaces the traditional concept of profits maximization, or expected profit maximization, enabling us to introduce risky elements and statistical models into the decision-making process. We just have to decipher the particular model by which we wish to calculate the firm's value and to enumerate the many factors (including risk variables from the enterprise risk map) that may affect firm value. Actual market value should reflect all these elements and includes all the information available to the market. This is the efficient-markets hypothesis.

Recently, many developed countries have seen a tendency to change the rules of corporate governance. Traditionally, many people believed that a firm should serve only its shareholders. However, most people now believe that firms must satisfy the needs of all the stakeholders—including employees and their families, the public at large, customers, creditors, the government, and others. A company is a "good citizen" if it contributes to improving its communities and the environment. In some countries, corporate laws have changed to include these goals. This newer definition of corporate goals and values translates into a modified valuation formula/model that shows the firm responding to stakeholders' needs as well as shareholder profits. These newly considered values are the hidden "good will" values that are necessary in a company's risk management. We assume that a firm's market value reflects the combined impact of all parameters and the considerations of all other stakeholders (employees, customers, creditors, etc.) A firm's **brand equity** entails the value created by a company with a good reputation and good products. You may also hear the term a company's "franchise value," which is an alternative term for the same thing. It reflects positive corporate responsibility image.

2.1 Maximization of Firm's Value for Sustainability

Another significant change in a way that firms are valued is the special attention that many are giving to general environmental considerations. A case in point is the issue of fuel and energy. In the summer of 2008, the cost of gas rising to over $150 a barrel and consumers paying more than $4 at the pump for

chief risk officer (CRO)

Part of the executive team responsible for all risk elements in the organization.

stockholders' wealth

Value of equity held by the owners of a company plus income in the form of dividends.

market value

For a public firm, the price of the stock times the number of shares traded.

brand equity

The value created by a company with a good reputation and good products.

a gallon of gas, alternatives have emerged globally. At the time of writing this textbook, the cost of gas had dropped significantly to as low as $1.50 per gallon at the pump, but the memory of the high prices, along with the major financial crisis, is a major incentive to production of alternative energy sources such as wind and sun. Fuel cost contributed in large part to the trouble that the U.S. automakers faced in December because they had continued to produce large gas-guzzlers such as sport-utility vehicles (SUVs) with minimal production of alternative gas-efficient cars like the Toyota Prius and Yaris, the Ford Fusion hybrid, and the Chevrolet Avio. With the U.S. government bailout of the U.S. automobile industry in December 2008 came a string of demands to modernize and to innovate with electric cars. Further, the government made it clear that Detroit must produce competitive products already offered by the other large automakers such as Toyota and Honda (which offered both its Accord and its Civic in hybrid form).[4] Chevrolet will offer a plug-in car called the Volt in the spring of 2010 with a range of more than 80 mpg on a single charge. Chrysler and Ford plan to follow with their own hybrids by 2012.

sustainability

The capacity to maintain a certain process or state.

World population growth and fast growth among emerging economies have led us to believer that our environment has suffered immense and irrevocable damage.[5] Its resources have been depleted; its atmosphere, land, and water quickly polluted; and its water, forests, and energy sources destroyed. The 2005 United Nations Millennium Ecosystem report from 2005 provides a glimpse into our ecosystem's fast destruction. From a risk management point of view, these risks can destroy our universe, so their management is essential to **sustainability**. Sustainability, in a broad sense, is the capacity to maintain a certain process or state. It is now most frequently used in connection with biological and human systems. In an ecological context, sustainability can be defined as the ability of an ecosystem to maintain ecological processes and functions.[6] Some risk management textbooks regard the risk management for sustainability as the first priority, since doing business is irrelevant if we are destroying our planet and undoing all the man-made achievements.

To reflect these considerations in practical decision making, we have to further adjust the definition and measurement of business goals. To be sensible, the firm must add a long-term perspective to its goals to include sustainable value maximization.

2.2   How Risk Managers Can Maximize Values

In this section we demonstrate how the concept of a firm maximizing its value can guide risk managers' decisions. For simplicity's sake, we provide an example. Assume that we base firm valuation on its forecasted future annual cash flow. Assume further that the annual cash flow stays roughly at the same level over time. We know that the annual cash flows are subject to fluctuations due to uncertainties and technological innovations, changing demand, and so forth.[7] In order to explain the inclusion of risk management in the process, we use the following income statement example:[8]

TABLE 5.1   Example of an Income Statement Before Risk Management

Income	$1,000
Salaries	$800
Interest	$100
Total expenses	($900)
Profit	$100

We assume that the value of the firm is ten times the value of the profit,[9] or $1,000 in this very simple example (10 × $100).[10] Now, assume that the firm considers a new risk management policy in which $40 will be spent to improve safety (or insurance premiums). If all other factors are held constant, then the firm's profits will decrease, and the firm's value will also decrease. In other words, in the simplistic model of certainty, any additional expense would reduce the firm's value and managers would, therefore, regard the situation as undesirable. It seems that in general, almost all risk management activities would be undesirable, since they reduce the hypothetical firm's value. However, this analysis ignores some effects and, therefore, leads to incorrect conclusions. In reality, the risk manager takes an action that may improve the state of the firm in many directions. Recall our demonstration of the safety belts example that we introduced Chapter 4. Customers may increase their purchases from this firm, based on their desire to trade with a more secure company, as its chances of surviving sudden difficulties improve. Many also believe that, as the firm gains relief from its fears of risks, the company can improve long-term and continuous service. Employees would feel better working for a more secure company and could be willing to settle for lower salaries. In addition, bondholders (creditors) will profit from increased security measures and thus would demand lower interest rates on the loans they provide (this is the main effect of a high credit rating). Thus, risk management activity may affect a variety of parameters and change the expected profit (or cash flow) in a more complex way. We present the state of this hypothetical firm as follows:

TABLE 5.2 Example of an Income Statement after Risk Management

	Before Change	After Change	
Revenue	$1,000	1020	Customers satisfied with increased security increase purchases
Insurance expenses	0	40	
Salaries	800	760	Employees satisfied with less
Interest on bonds	100	95	Creditors appreciate the improved security
Expected reported profit	100	125	

The profit (or expected profit) of the company has risen. If the owners continue to demand a tenfold multiplication factor, then the firm's value increases from $1,000 to $1,250. The increase is a direct result of the new risk management policy, despite the introduction of the additional risk management or insurance costs. Note that the firm's value has increased because other stakeholders (besides the owners) have enjoyed a change of attitude toward the firm. The main stakeholders affected include the credit suppliers in the capital market, the labor market and the product customers' market. This did not happen as a result of improving the security of the stockholders but as a result of other parties benefiting from the firm's new policy.

In fact, the situation could be even more interesting, if, in addition, the owners would be interested in a more secure firm and would be willing to settle for a higher multiplier (which translates into lower rate of return to the owners).[11] For example, if the new multiplier is eleven, the value of the firm would go up to $1,375 (125 × 11), relative to the original value of $1,000, which was based on a multiplier of ten.

This oversimplified example sheds a light on the practical complexity of measuring the risk manager's performance, according to the modern approach. Top managers couldn't evaluate the risk manager's performance without taking into account all the interactions between all the parties involved. In reality, a precise analysis of this type is complicated, and risk managers would have a hard time estimating if their policies are the correct ones. Let us stress that this analysis is extremely difficult if we use only standard accounting tools, which are not sensitive enough to the possible interactions (e.g., standard accounting does not measure the fine changes that take place—such as the incremental effect of the new risk management policy on the sales, the salaries, or the creditors' satisfaction). We described this innovative approach in hope that the student will understand the nature of the problem and perhaps develop accounting tools that will present them with practical value.

Risk managers may not always clearly define their goals, because the firm's goals are not always clearly defined, especially for nonprofit organizations. Executives' complex personal considerations, management coalitions, company procedures, past decisions, hopes, and expectations enter into the mix of parameters defining the firm's goals. These types of considerations can encourage risk managers to take conservative action. For example, risk managers may buy too much insurance for risks that the firm could reasonably retain. This could result from holding the risk manager personally responsible for uninsured losses. Thus, it's very important not to create a conflict between the risk managers' interests and the firm's interests. For example, the very people charged with monitoring mortgage issuance risk, the mortgage underwriters and mortgage bankers, had a financial incentive (commissions) to issue the loans regardless of the intrinsic risks. The resulting subprime mortgage crisis ensued because of the conflict of interest between mortgage underwriters and mortgage bankers. This situation created the starting point for the 2008–2009 financial crisis.

Risk managers must ascertain—before the damage occurs—that an arrangement will provide equilibrium between resources needed and existing resources. The idea is to secure continuity despite losses. As such, the risk manager' job is to evaluate the firm's ability or capacity to sustain (absorb) damages. This job requires in-depth knowledge of the firm's financial resources, such as credit lines, assets, and insurance arrangements. With this information risk managers can compare alternative methods for handling the risks. We describe these alternative methods in the next section.

KEY TAKEAWAYS

- In this section you studied the interrelationship between firms' goals to maximize value and the contributions of the enterprise risk management function to such goals.
- We used a hypothetical income statement of a company.
- We also discussed the challenges in achieving firms' goals under stakeholders' many conflicting objectives.

DISCUSSION QUESTIONS

1. Discuss the different firm goals that companies seek to fulfill in the late 2000s.
2. How does the risk management function contribute to firm goals?
3. Find a company's income statement and show how the enterprise risk management functions contribute at least two actions to increase the firm's value.
4. How might firm stakeholders' goals conflict? How might such conflicting goals affect value maximization objectives?

3. RISK MANAGEMENT AND THE FIRM'S FINANCIAL STATEMENT—OPPORTUNITIES WITHIN THE ERM

LEARNING OBJECTIVES

- In this section you will learn the tasks of the enterprise risk managers (ERM) function as it relates to the balance sheet of the firm annual statement.
- The ERM function manages and ensures sustainability by preventing losses and providing opportunities within the risk matrix.
- Using hypothetical balance sheets, the student learns the actual ERM functions of both financial and nonfinancial firms.
- Our exploration of financial firms uncovers some of the causes of the 2008–2009 financial crisis.

balance sheet

Document that provides a snapshot of a firm's assets and liabilities.

financial statements

Income statements and balance sheets.

The enterprise risk manager or CRO must understand the risks inherent in both sides of the balance sheet of the firm's financial statements. A **balance sheet** provides a snapshot of a firm's assets and liabilities. We show a balance sheet for a nonfinancial firm in Table 5.3. Table 5.5 then shows a balance sheet for an insurance company. Firms must produce annual financial reports including their balance sheets and income statements. Together, we call income statements and balance sheets **financial statements**. While we focused in the section above on a simplified hypothetical income statement, now we focus on the assets and liabilities as they appear at a certain point. With this ammunition at hand, we will be able to explain why financial institutions created so many problems during the 2008–2009 credit crisis. You will be able to explain AIG's major problems and why the government ended up bailing it out, along with many other financial institutions. The question that you will be able to answer is, "What side of the balance sheet did AIG fail to manage appropriately?"

3.1 Nonfinancial Firm

First, we will work with a hypothetical, small, nonfinancial institution, such as a furniture manufacturer or high-tech hardware and software company. Table 5.3 shows the hypothetical assets, liabilities, and equity of this business.

TABLE 5.3 Hypothetical Retail and Wholesaler Fashion Apparel Balance Sheet—(Risks and ERM)

Assets		Liabilities and Owners' Equity		
Cash (loss of use risks)	$8,000	**Liabilities**		
Accounts Receivable (customers quality, foreign exchange and interest rate risks)	$28,000	Notes Payable (cash flow, foreign exchange and interest rate risks)		$50,000
		Accounts Payable and the mortgage on the building (real estate crisis, cash flow, and interest rate risks)		$90,000
Buildings (asset risk)	$100,000	*Total liabilities*		$140,000
Tools, furniture, inventory, and equipment (asset risk and opportunity asset risk in store design)	$27,000	**Owners' equity**		
		Capital Stock	$17,000	
		Retained Earnings	$6,000	
		Total owners' equity		$23,000
Total	$163,000	*Total*		$163,000

Based on Table 5.3, we can list some areas for which enterprise risk managers (ERMs) need to involve themselves for risk mitigation. Note, these loss risks do not. As part of the executive team, enterprise risk managers regard all activities, including any involvement in opportunity risks that carry the potential of gains as discussed in Chapter 1.

Examples of ERM activities generated from the assets and the liabilities on the balance sheet are as follows:

- *Building risk*: The ERM or CRO has to keep all company buildings safe and operational. Most, if not all, companies carry insurance on all real property. We will discuss the reasons later in the text. However, this represents only part of the CRO's activities. The risk management manual should give directions for how to take care of weather-related potential damages, or losses from fires or other perils. Furthermore, the risk manager should be involved in any discussions of how to convert some building parts into income–producing opportunities. This will entail carefully assessing potential cash flow streams from reliable and careful tenants, not only from their capacity to pay potential, but also from their capacity to keep losses at an absolute minimum. The CRO or ERM takes on the capital budgeting function and computes net present values with the appropriate risk factors, as shown in Chapter 4 with the example of the safety belts. They need to include some risk factors to measure tenant quality in terms of both paying the rent and maintaining the properties properly.

- *Accounts Receivables and Notes Due*: ERMs and CROs must create procedures to ensure that the accounts receivables can be collected and remain in good standing. This is key to sustainability—the ability to maintain expected cash flows. In addition, since the Fashion Apparel's customers are from other countries, the decision of what currency to use is very important. As far as currency risk is concerned, the risk officer must negotiate with the suppliers and designers to set a mutually beneficial currency. This mutually beneficial currency will provide a very important means to pay the firm's suppliers and global designers. The risk manager can use currency derivatives to hedge/mitigate the currency risk. Also, if the company uses credit to maintain inventory for the long term, the ERM procedures should include ways to handle interest rate risk on both sides. Such interest rate risk would affect both receivables and payments to vendors, designers, and suppliers. To ensure liquidity, many companies create interest-bearing credit lines from banks—as long as the interest rates are in line with what can be collected in the accounts receivable. The firm has to borrow money to create the cash flows to pay salaries and buy new inventory. At the same time, the firm receives interest from clients. These transactions create a need for interest-rate management while it is receiving interest from clients, there needs to be interest risk management, such as using swaps, which is explained in detail with an example in the next section of this chapter.

- If used correctly, the swap derivative can act as insurance to mitigate interest rate risk. The interest rate used for borrowing and lending must make sense in terms of the management of accounts receivable and notes due on the liabilities side of the balance sheet. See Figure 5.1 showing the gains and losses that can occur because of interest rate and currency risks. They can also provide opportunities if handled with appropriate risk management. Note that the ability to obtain lines of credit from banks and suppliers and extend credit to customers is an integral part of the working of the cash flow of the firm. Indeed the credit crisis of 2008–2009 occurred in part

capital structure

A firm's choice between debt and equity.

because banks and other creditors lost confidence in the counterparty's ability to pay, and the credit markets "froze." This led to insolvencies, declines in stock value, and a general recession.

- *Tools, furniture, and inventory.* ERMs must take account of the traffic flow in the show room because they will want to establish sustainability and opportunities to make money. They must ensure that halls provide safety designs as well as fashion statements and innovative and creative designs to enhance visibility of the merchandise. Thus, while the risk manager is involved in avoiding or reducing losses, he/she is also involved in the opportunities. For example, it may be risky to hang some of the merchandise from the ceilings with wind tunnels that accentuate the flow of the fabrics, but it may also increase sales dramatically if the right effects are achieved. CROs must manage the opportunity risk (the chance to make money) with the appropriate risk factors as they compute the capital budget.

- *Accounts Payable including the Mortgage on the Buildings → Capital Structure.* Until the real estate crisis of 2008, real estate investments were stable. However, the CRO, working with other managers, must decide whether to purchase large assets with debt or equity from investors. The financing method is very important and it is regarded as the **capital structure** of the firm—the choice between debt and equity. In this company, the Apparel Designer, the building was purchased with a large mortgage (debt). The mortgage amount due is not subject to reduction unless paid. But, the buildings can decline in value, and at the same time the company's net worth can be in jeopardy, with potentially catastrophic consequences. If our hypothetical example was a publicly traded company, it would have to show at the end of each year the true value of buildings—the market value. Under this scenario, with so much debt and so little owner's equity, the balance sheet can show the firm as insolvent. The CRO or risk manager must address the company's capital structure issue and point out the risks of taking large mortgages on buildings, since the properties may lose their value. The capital structure decision creates a need for managers to choose between financing property with debt versus equity. This tradeoff is a tricky one to negotiate. If the firm uses equity, it may be underinvested. If it uses debt, it runs the risk of insolvency. For example, we know that before the 2008 financial crisis, many firms used too much debt, leading to sustainability issues and liquidation, such as Circuit City.[12]

covenants

The details of the contracts and promises between the debt contract parties.

financial risk managers

Managers responsible for managing the risk of the investments and assets of a firm.

Capital structure decisions as well as the nature of debt and its **covenants** (the details of the contracts and promises between the debt contract parties), accounts receivables, and notes have been under the domain of the finance or treasury department of companies with a new breed of **financial risk managers**. These risk managers are responsible for managing the risk of the investments and assets of the firms using tools such as Value at Risk (VaR; discussed in Chapter 2) and capital markets instruments such as derivatives as explained in Chapter 2 and will be detailed in the next section of this chapter. Currently, the trend is to move financial risk management into the firm-wide enterprise risk management.

3.2 Financial Firm—An Insurer

Next, we move to the risk management function with regard to the balance sheet of financial institutions. We delve into an example of a hypothetical life insurance company. As you will see in the coming chapters, insurance companies are in two businesses: the insurance and investment businesses. The insurance side is the underwriting and reserving liabilities. **Underwriting** is the process of evaluating risks, selecting which risks to accept, and identifying potential adverse selection. **Reserving liabilities** involves the calculation of the amount that the insurer needs to set aside to pay future claims. It's equivalent to the debt of a nonfinancial firm. The investment side includes decisions about **asset allocation** to achieve the best rate of return on the assets entrusted to the insurer by the policyholders seeking the security. Asset allocation is the mix of assets held by an insurer; also, the allocation of assets is necessary to meet the timing of the claims obligations. This activity is called **asset-liabilities matching**. The matching is, in essence, to ensure **liquidity** so that when claims come due the firm has available cash to pay for losses.

When reviewing the **asset portfolio**, also referred to as the **investment portfolio** or **asset allocation** of an insurer, we see the characteristics of the assets needed to support the payment of claims of the specific insurer. Asset allocation is the mix of assets held by an insurer. A property or health insurer needs a quick movement of funds and cannot invest in many long-term investments. On the other hand, insurers that sell mostly life insurance or liability coverage know that the funds will remain for longer-term investment, as claims may not arrive until years into the future.

The firm maintains **liability accounts** in the form of reserves on balance sheets to cover future claims and other obligations such as taxes and premium reserves. The firm must maintain assets to cover the reserves and still leave the insurer with an adequate net worth in the form of **capital and surplus**. Capital and surplus represent equity on the balance sheet of a nonfinancial firm. We calculate the firm's net worth by taking the asset minus liabilities. For students who have taken a basic accounting course, the balance sheet of a firm will be very familiar. Table 5.4 provides the two sides of the balance sheet of an insurer in insurance terminology.

TABLE 5.4 Balance Sheet Structure of an Insurer

Assets	Liabilities
Portfolio of invested assets	Liabilities including reserves
Premiums, reinsurance, and other assets	Capital and surplus

The following is Table 5.5, which shows the investment portfolio or the asset allocation of a hypothetical life insurer within its balance sheet. The asset mix reflects the industry's asset distribution. Table 5.5 also shows the liabilities side of that insurer.

TABLE 5.5 A Hypothetical Balance Sheet of a Hypothetical Life Insurance Firm with Its Asset Allocation Mix (in Millions of Dollars)—Risks and ERM

Assets		Liabilities and Capital and Surplus	
Bonds: risks of junk bonds and nonperforming, mortgage-backed securities.	$1,800	Loans and advances	$10
Stocks: risks of the market fluctuations	990	Life insurance and annuities reserves [risk of catastrophes and miscalculations by actuaries (longevity risk) and lack of underwriting	950
Mortgages: risk of nonperforming mortgages, no liquidity	260	Pension fund reserves: risk of inability to keep the promises of the guarantees	1,200
Real Estate: risks of real estate collapse and lack of liquidity	50	Taxes payable	25
Policy Loans: risk of inability of policyholders to pay	110	Miscellaneous liabilities	650
Miscellaneous	120	Total Liabilities	2,835
		Capital and Surplus	$495
Total	3,330	Total	$3,330

The hypothetical life insurer in Table 5.5 represents a typical insurer in the United States with a larger percentage of investment in bonds and mortgages and less investment in stocks. The ERM joins the executive team and regards all activities, including firm undertakings in opportunity and financial risks.

underwriting

The process of evaluating risks, selecting which risks to accept, and identifying potential adverse selection.

reserving liabilities

Calculating the amount that the insurer needs to set aside to pay future claims.

asset allocation

The mix of assets held by an insurer.

asset-liabilities matching

Allocation of an insurer's assets to meet claims obligations as they become due.

liquidity

Degree to which assets can be used to meet a firm's obligations (the more liquid an asset, the easier it can be used to meet obligations).

asset portfolio

Details the assets that are to be matched to liabilities in the asset-liabilities matching process.

investment portfolio

Details the assets that are to be matched to liabilities in the asset-liabilities matching process..

asset allocation

The mix of assets held by an insurer.

liability accounts

Reserves held on balance sheets to cover future claims and other obligations, such as taxes and premium reserves.

capital and surplus

The equivalent of equity on the balance sheet of any firm—the net worth of the firm, or assets minus liabilities.

Therefore, the risk manager works also as a financial risk manager on the side of the insurer's asset allocation and capital structure questions. Examples of ERM activities generated from the assets and liabilities on the balance sheet are as follows:

■ *Risks from the liabilities*. The liabilities comprise mostly reserves for claims on the products sold by the life insurer. The products here are life and annuities (this insurance company does not sell health insurance). Most of the reserves are for these products. The reserves are computed by **actuaries**, who specialize in forecasting the losses and developing the losses' potential future impact on the insurers. Actuaries use mortality tables and life expectancy tables to estimate the future losses that the insurer must pay. **Mortality tables** indicate the percent of expected deaths for each age group. **Life expectancy** shows the length of life expected for people born in each year. Chapter 1 delves into this topic in detail. Usually, life insurance firms maintain a high level of expertise in selling products to people and categorizing them in similar risk levels. Insurance underwriters develop specialized expertise to ensure that the insurer does not sell the products too cheaply for the risks that the insurer accepts. As such, the enterprise risk manager depends on the actuarial and underwriting expertise to ensure the liabilities side of the business is well managed. If the reserve calculations miss the mark, the insurer can become insolvent very quickly and lose the capital and surplus, which is its net worth.[13]

■ *Risks from the asset mix*. The enterprise risk manager or CRO should ensure that the insurer's investment portfolio or asset mix can perform and sustain its value. Our hypothetical life insurer posted $1,800 million in bonds. The mix of these bonds is critical, especially during the recent 2008–2009 global crisis (described in Chapter 1). The amount of mortgage-backed securities (MBS) within the bonds is very critical, especially if these MBS are nonperforming and lose their value. As it turns out, the balance sheet we provided above represents a time before the credit crisis of 2008. This hypothetical insurer held 10 percent of its bonds in MBS and half of them turned into nonperforming assets by the end of 2008. This translates into $90 million of lost assets value in 2008. In addition, the stock market collapse took its toll and the 2008 market value of the stocks decreased by 30.33 percent. Investment professionals worked with a CRO to ensure a much lower decrease than the market indexes. They ensured that the stock portfolio was more conservative. If we assume that all other liabilities and assets did not suffer any additional loss, the capital and surplus of this hypothetical insurer will be almost wiped out at the end of 2008.[14]

$$\$495 - 90 - 330 = \$75 \text{ worth of capital and surplus}$$

As an insurer, the firm faces an outcome to the ERM function, since underwriting is a critical component for the insurer's sustainability. Here, the balance sheet would show that the insurer invested in mortgage-backed securities (MBS), not doing its underwriting work itself. The insurers allowed the investment professionals to invest in financial instruments that did not underwrite the mortgage holders prudently. If the CRO was in charge completely, he would have known how to apply the expertise of the liabilities side into the expertise of the assets side and would have demanded clear due diligence into the nature of MBS. Warren Buffet, the owner of insurance companies, said he did not trust MBS and did not invest in such instruments in his successful and thriving businesses. **Due diligence** examines every action and items in the financial statement of companies to ensure the data reflect true value.

actuaries

Individuals who specialize in forecasting the losses and developing the losses' potential future impact on the insurers.

mortality tables

Tables that indicate the percent of expected deaths for each age group.

life expectancy

Measure of the length of life expected for people born in each year.

due diligence

The process of examining every action and items in the financial statement of companies to ensure the data reflect true value.

KEY TAKEAWAYS

In this section you learned the following:

■ How the ERM function has to consider both sides of the balance sheet: assets and liabilities
■ How the ERM function ensures the survival of the firm and its net worth
■ How the ERM function can help in the due diligence for sustainability
■ The differences between the ERM function of a nonfinancial firm and a financial firm

---

DISCUSSION QUESTIONS

1. Find the balance sheet of a company such as Best Buy and analyze all the risk and ERM from the assets side and from the liabilities side. Create a list of actions for the ERM function.

2. Find the balance sheet of Bank of America from 2006 or 2007 and analyze all the risk and ERM from the assets side and from the liabilities side. Create a list of actions for the ERM function.

3. Introduce the 2008–2009 credit crisis to both companies in questions 1 and 2. Explain the impact on the net worth of these companies. What actions you would suggest to incorporate in the ERM function?

---

4. RISK MANAGEMENT USING THE CAPITAL MARKETS

LEARNING OBJECTIVES

- **In this section you will learn how the ERM function can incorporate the capital markets' instruments, such as derivatives.**
- **You also learn though a case how swaps can help mitigate the interest rate risk of a bank.**

Enterprise risk management has emerged from the following steps of maturation:

- Risk management using insurance as discussed briefly in Chapter 4 and will be the topic of the rest of the book
- Explosive growth in technology and communications
- Development of quantitative techniques and models to measure risk (shown in Chapter 2)
- Evolution of the financial markets and financial technology into hedging of risks

These mechanisms combine to create a direct connection between the firm's overall appetite for risk, as set in company objectives, and choosing appropriate corporate-level for solutions in mitigating risks.

4.1 Evolution of the Financial Markets

The last two or three decades have been a period of rapid financial innovation. Capital markets soared and with the growth came the development of derivatives. **Derivatives** can be defined as financial securities whose value is derived from another underlying asset. Our discussion will incorporate three basic tools used: forwards/futures, swaps, and options. Derivatives are noninsurance instruments used to hedge, or protect, against adverse movements in prices (in stocks or in commodities such as rice and wheat) or rates (such as interest rates or foreign exchange rates). For example, breakfast cereal manufacturer Frosty O's must have wheat to produce its finished goods. As such, the firm is continually vulnerable to sudden increases in wheat prices. The company's risk management objective would be to protect against wheat price fluctuations. Using derivatives, we will explore the different choices in how an enterprise risk manager might mitigate the unwanted price exposure.

derivatives

Financial securities whose value is derived from another underlying asset.

Forward/Future Purchase

Forwards and futures are similar in that they are agreements that obligate the owner of the instrument to buy or sell an asset for a specified price at a specified time in the future. **Forwards** are traded in the over-the-counter market, and contract characteristics can be tailored to meet specific customer needs. Farmers and grain elevator operators also use forwards to lock in a price for their corn or soybeans or wheat. They may choose to lock in the **basis**, which is the amount of money above and beyond the futures price. Alternatively, if they like (believe that the prices are at their highest likely levels) the futures' price levels, they can lock in the entire price. Food and beverage companies use forwards to lock in their costs for grains and fruits and vegetables. Quaker Oats, for example, locks in the prices on corn and oats using forward contracts with growers. Anheuser Busch depends upon forwards to lock in the price of hops, rice, and other grains used to make beer. Dole fruit companies use forwards to price out pineapples, raspberries, grapes, and other fruits.

forwards

Financial securities traded in the over-the-counter market whose characteristics can be tailored to meet specific customer needs.

basis

The amount of money above and beyond the futures price.

futures

Financial securities that trade on an exchange and that have standardized contract specifications.

Futures, on the other hand, trade on an exchange with standardized contract specifications. Forwards and futures prices derive from the spot, or cash market, which is "today's" price for a particular asset. An example of a spot contract would be your agreement to purchase a meal at a restaurant. The spot market is the quoted price on today's menu. A futures or forwards market would be the price you would have to pay if you wanted the same meal one year from today. Getting back to our cereal manufacturer, Frosty O's can either go to the spot market on an ongoing basis or use the forwards/futures market to contract to buy wheat in the future at an agreed-upon price. Buying in the spot market creates exposure to later price fluctuation. Buying in the forwards/futures market allows the manufacturer to guarantee future delivery of the wheat at a locked-in price. Hence, this strategy is known as a "lock it in" defense. Southwest Airlines' strategy to buy oil futures during the fuel crisis of 2007–2008 allowed them to be the only profitable airline. On the other side, Continental Airline is suffering from buying aviation fuel futures when the price of oil subsequently declined dramatically. Thus, the use of futures and forwards can create value or losses, depending upon the timing of its implementation.

Swaps

swaps

Agreements to exchange or transfer expected future variable-price purchases of a commodity or foreign exchange contract for a fixed contractual price today.

Swaps are agreements to exchange or transfer expected future variable-price purchases of a commodity or foreign exchange contract for a fixed contractual price today. In effect, Frosty O's buys wheat and swaps its expected "floating" price exposure for wheat at different times in the future for a fixed rate cost. For example, if Frosty O's normally buys wheat on the first of each month, the company will have to pay whatever the spot price of wheat is on that day. Frosty O's is exposed to market price fluctuations for each of the twelve months over a year's time period. It can enter into a transaction to pay a fixed monthly rate over a year's time period instead of whatever the floating spot rate may be each month. The net effect of the swap transaction is to receive the necessary wheat allotment each month while paying a fixed, predetermined rate. The swap rate quote would be fixed using the spot market and the one-year forward market for wheat. Thus Frosty O's eliminates any adverse price exposure by switching the "floating" price exposure for an agreed-upon fixed price. Swaps are used in the same manner to exchange floating interest rate liabilities for fixed-interest rate liabilities. Hence, this strategy is known as a "switch out of it" defense. We will show an elaborate swaps example at the end of this section.

Options

options

Agreements that give the right (but not the obligation) to buy or sell an underlying asset at a specified price at a specified time in the future.

Agreements that give the right (but not the obligation) to buy or sell an underlying asset at a specified price at a specified time in the future are known as **options**. Frosty O's can purchase an option to buy the wheat it needs for production at a given strike price. The strike price (also called exercise price) is the specified price set in the option contract. In this fashion, Frosty O's can place a ceiling on the price it will pay for the needed wheat for production in future time periods. Until the maturity date of the option passes, option holders can exercise their rights to buy wheat at the strike price. If the future spot price of wheat rises above the strike price, Frosty O's will execute its option to purchase the wheat at the lower strike price. If the future price of wheat falls below the strike price, the company will not exercise its option and will instead purchase wheat directly in the spot market. This differentiates the option contract from the futures contract. An option is the *right* to buy or sell, whereas a futures/forward contract is an *obligation* to buy of sell. The option buyer pays the cost of the option to buy wheat at the strike price—also known as the option premium. A call option grants the right to buy at the strike price. A put option grants the right to sell at the strike price. A call option acts like insurance to provide an upper limit on the cost of a commodity. A put option acts like insurance to protect a floor selling price for wheat. Hence, option strategies are known as "cap" and "floor" defenses.[15]

Individuals and companies alike use derivative instruments to hedge against their exposure to unpredictable loss due to price fluctuations. The increasing availability of different derivative products has armed enterprise risk managers (ERM) with new risk management tool solutions. An importer of raw materials can hedge against changes in the exchange rate of the U.S. dollar relative to foreign currencies. An energy company can hedge using weather derivatives to protect against adverse or extreme weather conditions. And a bank can hedge its portfolio against interest rate risk. All of these risk exposures interrupt corporate cash flow and affect earnings, capital, and the bottom line, which is the value of the firm. These solutions, however, create new risk exposures. Over-the-counter market-traded derivatives, which feature no exchange acting as counterparty to the trade, expose a company to credit risk in that the counter party to the contract may not live up to its side of the obligation.

4.2   Risk Management Using Capital Markets

Dramatic changes have taken place in the insurance industry in the past two to three decades. A succession of catastrophic losses has caused insurers and reinsurers to reevaluate their risk analyses. The reassessment effort was made in full realization that these disasters, as horrible as they were, may not be the last worst-case scenarios. Past fears of multiple *noncorrelated* catastrophic events occurring in a relatively short period of time are on the top of agendas of catastrophe risk modelers and all constituencies responsible for national disaster management. The affordability of coverage, along with reinsurers' credit quality concerns players who have lost large chunks of capital and surplus or equity to those disasters led to the first foray into using the capital markets as a reinsurance alternative.[16]

Securitization

Packaging and transferring the insurance risks to the capital markets through the issuance of a financial security is termed **securitization**.[17] The risks that have been underwritten are pooled together into a bundle, which is then considered an asset and the underwriter then sells its shares; hence, the risk is transferred from the insurers to the capital markets. Securitization made a significant difference in the way insurance risk is traded—by making it a commodity and taking it to the capital markets in addition to or instead of to the insurance/reinsurance market. Various insurance companies' risks for similar exposures in diversified locations are combined in one package that is sold to investors (who may also include insurers). Securitized catastrophe instruments can help a firm or an individual to diversify risk exposures when reinsurance is limited or not available. Because global capital markets are so vast, they offer a promising means of funding protection for even the largest potential catastrophes. Capital market solutions also allow the industry (insurers and reinsurers) to reduce credit risk exposure, also known as **counterparty risk**. This is the risk of loss from failure of a counterparty, or second party, in a derivatives contract to perform as agreed or contracted. Capital market solutions also diversify funding sources by spreading the risk across a broad spectrum of capital market investors. Securitization instruments are also called **insurance-linked securities (ISLs)**. They include catastrophe bonds, catastrophe risk exchange swaps, insurance-related derivatives/options, catastrophe equity puts (Cat-E-Puts), contingent surplus notes, collateralized debt obligations (CDOs),[18] and weather derivatives.

Catastrophe bonds, or CAT bonds, seek to protect the insurance industry from catastrophic events. The bonds pay interest and return principal to investors the way other debt securities do—as long as the issuer does not experience losses above an agreed-upon limit. Insurers can come to the capital market to issue bonds that are tied to a single peril, or even to a portfolio or basket of risks. Embedded in each issue is a risk trigger that, in the event of catastrophic loss, allows for forgiveness of interest and/or principal repayment.

securitization

Packaging and transferring the insurance risks to the capital markets through the issuance of a financial security.

counterparty risk

Risk of loss from failure of a counterparty, or second party, in a derivatives contract to perform as agreed or contracted.

insurance-linked securities

General term for securitization instruments.

catastrophe bonds

Bonds that seek to protect the insurance industry from catastrophic events.

The CAT Bond Story

Innovation is key to the success stories on Wall Street. In November 1996, Morgan Stanley & Co. was about to make history as the first to underwrite an insurance-related issue offered to the public: catastrophe bonds. California Earthquake Authority (CEA), a state agency providing homeowners insurance, needed capital and had sought Wall Street's assistance. Morgan Stanley proposed a simple structure: bonds paying a robust 10 percent interest but with a catastrophic loss trigger point of $7 billion. If CEA lost that much (or more) from any one earthquake, the investors would lose their principal.

The deal didn't happen because Berkshire Hathaway's insurance division, National Indemnity Co., offered to underwrite CEA's earthquake risk. Many speculate that Berkshire was intent on foiling investment banking firms' attempt to steal away traditional reinsurance business. The market didn't go away, however. By the time Katrina hit the Gulf Coast in 2005, the market had grown to an estimated $6 billion in value. The market kept growing since 1997 when $900 million worth of CAT bonds were sold. In June of that year, USAA, a San Antonio-based insurer, floated an issue of $477 million in the capital markets with a one-year maturity. The loss threshold was $1 billion. As long as a hurricane didn't hit USAA for more than the $1 billion over the one-year time period, investors would enjoy a hefty coupon of 11 percent and would get their principal back.

Reinsurer industry executives agreed upon only one thing: CAT bonds would radically change their business. With ongoing property development in catastrophe-prone areas, the insurance industry's exposure to huge losses is only increasing. S&P calculated that the probability of a $1 billion loss occurring in any given year is about 68 percent, while the probability of a $3 billion loss drops to about 31 percent. The chance of a $15 billion loss in a given year is about 4 percent. For example, Hurricane Ike produced losses of about $23 billion in 2008.

CAT bonds have been hailed for the following reasons: they add capacity to the market, fill in coverage gaps, and give risk managers leverage when negotiating with insurers by creating a competitive alternative. As the insurance industry cycles, and the next wave of disasters depletes reinsurance companies' capital and surplus, Wall Street will be poised to take advantage. During soft markets, CAT bonds are more expensive than traditional reinsurance. If reinsurance markets begin to harden, CAT bond issues are a practical alternative. However, some downside potential threaten. What happens when you have a loss, and the bonds are used to pay for the exposure? Andrew Beazley, active underwriter of Beazley Syndicate 623 in London, said, "Once you have a loss, the bonds will pay, but you still have the exposure. The question is whether you'll be able to float another bond issue to cover it the next time something happens. Reinsurers are expected to stick around and still write coverage after a loss, but can the same be said with CAT bond investors?" Apparently, the answer is "yes," as evidenced from the substantial growth of this risk capital from an estimated $4.04 billion in 2004 to approximately $6 billion in 2005. The biggest fear of the CAT bonds owners in the aftermath of Katrina did not materialize. The insured losses from Katrina did not exceed the agreed level.

Sources: Andrew Osterland, "The CATs Are out of the Bag," BusinessWeek, January 26, 1998; Douglas McLeod, "Cat Bonds to Grow: Increasing Frequency of Losses Will Contribute: S&P," Business Insurance, July 12 1999, 2; Mike Hanley, "Cat Bond Market Almost There," International Risk Management, 8, no. 1 (2001); Sam Friedman, "There's More than One Way to Skin a Cat," National Underwriter, Property & Casualty/Risk & Benefits Management Edition, May 8, 2000; Mark E. Ruquet "CAT Bonds Grew 17 Percent In '04" National Underwriter Online News Service, April 1, 2005; Richard Beales and Jennifer Hughes, "Katrina Misses Cat Bond Holders," Financial Times, August 31, 2005 at http://news.ft.com/cms/s/59e21066-1a66-11da-b7f5-00000e2511c8.html.

An example of a CAT bond is the issue by Oriental Land Company Ltd., owner and operator of Tokyo Disneyland. Oriental Land used CAT bonds to finance one facility providing earthquake coverage and the other to provide standby financing to continue a $4 billion expansion of the theme park. Each facility raised $100 million via the bond market to cover property risk exposure and subsequent indirect business interruption loss in case of catastrophic loss from an earthquake. The trigger event was for an earthquake, regardless of whether the event caused any direct physical damage to the park.[19] For more about how CAT bonds provide protection, see "The CAT Bond Story" in this chapter.

With **catastrophe equity puts (Cat-E-Puts)**, the insurer has the option to sell equity (e.g., preferred shares) at predetermined prices, contingent upon the catastrophic event. **Contingent surplus notes** are options to borrow money in case of a specific event. **Collateralized debt obligations (CDOs)** are securities backed by a pool of diversified assets; these are referred to as collateralized bond obligations (CBOs) when the underlying assets are bonds and as collateralized loan obligations (CLOs) when the underlying assets are bank loans.[20] **Weather derivatives** are derivative contracts that pay based on weather-related events. All are examples of financial market instruments that have been used to transfer risk and to provide risk-financing vehicles.[21]

Investors' advantages in insurance-linked securities are diversification, as these instruments allow noninsurance investors to participate in insurance-related transactions and above-average rates of return. Advantages to the issuers of such instruments include greater capacity and access to the capital markets. Insurance-linked securities provide issuers with more flexibility and less reliance on reinsurers. The presence of new instruments stabilizes reinsurance pricing and provides higher levels of risk transfer with cutting-edge understanding for both insurance and capital markets.

We have shown that enterprise risk management (ERM) for a corporation is indeed complex. Full enterprise-wide risk management entails folding financial risk management into the CRO's department responsibilities. A chief risk officer's role is multifaceted. Today, risk managers develop goals to widen the understanding of risk management so that employees take into account risk considerations in their day-to-day operations. Risk awareness has become imperative to the overall health of the organization. Sound practices must incorporate the advancements on the technology front so that companies can compete in the global environment. Viewing all integrated segments of risk from across the enterprise in a holistic manner facilitates a global competitive advantage.

4.3 Example: The Case of Financial Risk Management for the Hypothetical Hometown Bank

John Allen is the CEO of Hometown Bank.[22] Mr. Allen is addressing company-wide, long-range plans to incorporate risk management techniques to maximize his bank's financial performance and shareholder value.

Important note: This hypothetical case reflects a bank's activities in the early 2000s. It does not deal with the 2008–2009 credit crisis and it ramifications on many banks and the financial institutions globally.

History

In the early years of U.S. banking history, banks seemed to have the easiest job in the corporate world. All a bank manager had to do was receive deposits in the form of checking, savings, and deposit accounts (bank liabilities), and provide mortgage and other lending services (bank assets). Throughout the twentieth century, the banking industry prospered. For most of the post–World War II era the upward-sloping yield curve meant that interest rates on traditional thirty-year residential mortgage

---

catastrophe equity puts (Cat-E-Puts)

Financial instrument that gives an insurer the option to sell equity (e.g., preferred shares) at predetermined prices, contingent upon the catastrophic event.

contingent surplus notes

Options to borrow money in case of a specific event.

collateralized debt obligations (CDOs)

Securities backed by a pool of diversified assets.

weather derivatives

Derivative contracts that pay based on weather-related events.

loans exceeded rates on shorter-term savings and time deposits.[23] The positive net margin between the two rates accounted for banks' prosperity. All of this ended abruptly when the Federal Reserve changed its monetary policy in October 1979 to one of targeting bank reserves instead of interest rates. Figure 5.3 and Figure 5.4 provide a historical perspective of interest rates.

FIGURE 5.3   Thirty-Year Treasury Rates—Secondary Market

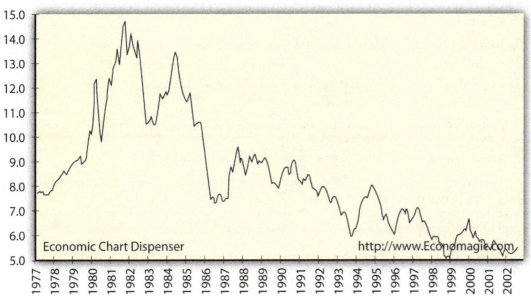

Source: http://www.Economagic.com. Economagic includes the original data source: U.S. Government, Federal Reserve Board of Governors historical monthly interest rate series.

FIGURE 5.4   Three-Month Treasury Bills Rates—Secondary Market

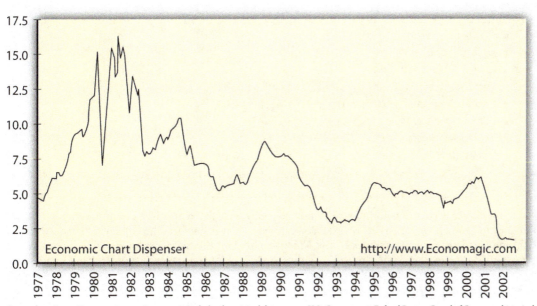

Source: http://www.Economagic.com. Economagic includes the original data source: U.S. Government, Federal Reserve Board of Governors historical monthly interest rate series.

Figure 5.3 and Figure 5.4 graphically present interest rate risk exposure that banks face. The noticeable change is the absolute pickup in interest rate volatility from 1979 forward. As Figure 5.4 shows, three-month T-bill interest rates reached above 16 percent in the early 1980s. Yet many banks' assets were locked into low-interest, long-term loans, mostly thirty-year mortgages. The financial crisis that followed the rapid rise in interest rates (on both short- and long-term liabilities) was catastrophic in proportion; many banks failed by positioning their loan portfolios incorrectly for the change in interest rates. Locked-in long-term mortgage loan rates provided insufficient cash inflows to meet the higher cash outflows required on deposits. Those that survived had to make major changes in their risk management style. Later we will introduce how a specific bank, Hometown Bank, manages its interest rate exposure using derivatives.

"Modern banks employ credit-scoring techniques to ensure that they are making good lending decisions, use analytical models to monitor the performance of their loan portfolios, and implement financial instruments to transfer out those credit risks with which they are not comfortable."[24] Bankers learned a costly lesson in the 1980s by not being adequately prepared for a changing interest rate environment. Risk management must be enterprise-wide and inclusive of all components of risk. Hometown Bank is a surviving bank, with lofty goals for the future. The current focus for CEO John Allen has three components:

1. Review the primary elements of Hometown's financial risks:
   - Interest rate risk—those risks associated with changes in interest rates
   - Market risk—risk of loss associated with changes in market price or value
   - Credit risk—risk of loss through customer default
2. Review Hometown's nonfinancial, or operational, risks: those risks associated with the operating processes or systems in running a bank
3. Monitor the success of risk mitigation techniques the bank employs

4.4 The Hypothetical Hometown Bank—Early 2000s

Hometown Bancorp was formed in 1985 as a financial holding company headquartered in Richmond, Virginia. Its only subsidiary is Hometown Bank, which was chartered in 1950 with the opening of its first branch in downtown Richmond. Hometown has experienced a steady growth of core assets: deposits, money market instruments, and marketable security investments. Table 5.6 shows Hometown's investment policy and lists allowable securities for their investment securities account.

TABLE 5.6 Hometown Bancorp Investment Policy, December 31, 2001

The securities portfolio is managed by the president and treasurer of the bank. Investment management is handled in accordance with the investment policy, which the board of directors approves annually. To assist in the management process, each investment security shall be classified as "held-for-maturity" or "available-for-sale." The investment policy covers investment strategies, approved securities dealers, and authorized investments. The following securities have been approved as investments:

- U.S. Treasury Securities
- Agency Securities
- Municipal Notes and Bonds
- Corporate Notes and Bonds
- GNMA, FNMA, and FHLMC mortgage-backed securities (MBS)
- Collateralized Mortgage Obligations (CMOs)
- Interest Rate Swaps
- Interest Rate Caps

All securities must be investment grade quality and carry a minimum rating of no less than single-A by Moody's or Standard & Poor's.

Asset growth has occurred both internally and externally with the acquisition of community banks and branches in Hometown's market. Market domain expanded to include the capital region (the city of Richmond and surrounding counties), the Tidewater region, the Shenandoah Valley region, and the northern Virginia markets. In March 2002, Hometown Bank opened its twenty-fifth branch, in Virginia Beach, Virginia. With total assets of approximately $785 million (as of December 2001), Hometown ranks as the eighth largest commercial bank in the state of Virginia. The network of branches offers a wide range of lending and deposit services to business, government, and consumer clients. The use of these deposits funds both the loan and investment portfolio of the bank. Principal sources of revenue are interest and fees on loans and investments and maintenance fees for servicing deposit accounts. Principal expenses include interest paid on deposits and other borrowings and operating expenses. Corporate goals include achieving superior performance and profitability, gaining strategic market share, and providing superior client service. Hometown has achieved its fifth consecutive year of record earnings. Table 5.7 shows Hometown's consolidated financial statements from 1999 to 2001.

TABLE 5.7 Hometown Bancorp and Subsidiaries Financial Statements (in Thousands)

	2001	2000	1999
Consolidated Balance Sheet			
Interest-earning assets			
Money market investments	$62,800	$49,600	$39,100
Investment securities	65,500	51,700	40,800
Loans	649,300	513,000	405,000
Allowance for loan losses	(11,300)	(7,600)	(6,000)
Premises, furniture, & equipment	14,900	11,700	10,000
Other real estate	3,800	3,000	2,500
Total assets	$785,000	$621,400	$491,400
Interest-bearing liabilities			
Deposits	$467,500	$369,300	$292,000
Other short-term borrowings	123,000	97,000	76,700
non-interest borrowings	117,000	92,400	73,000
Long-term debt	12,900	10,000	8,200
Total liabilities	$720,400	$568,700	$449,900
Shareholders' equity	64,600	$52,700	41,500
Total liabilities and shareholders equity	$785,000	$621,400	$491,400
Consolidated Income Statement			
Interest income	$55,000	$44,000	$34,700
Interest expense	(27,500)	(21,100)	(18,300)
Net interest income	$27,500	$22,900	$16,400
Provision for loan losses	(4,400)	(3,400)	(2,700)
Net interest income after provision	$23,100	$19,500	$13,700
noninterest income	4,400	2,800	1,900
Operating expenses	(16,900)	(14,300)	(10,100)
Income before taxes	$10,600	$8,000	$5,500
Taxes	(3,600)	(2,700)	(1,100)
Net Income	$7,000	$5,300	$4,400

4.5 The Challenges of Managing Financial Risk

Corporations all face the challenge of identifying their most important risks. Allen has identified the following broad risk categories that Hometown Bank faces:

- *Interest rate risk* associated with asset-liability management
- *Market risk* associated with trading activities and investment securities portfolio management; that is, the risk of loss/gain in the value of bank assets due to changes in market prices (VaR was computed for this Bank in Chapter 2).
- *Credit risk* associated with lending activities, including the risk of customer default on repayment (VaR was computed for this Bank in Chapter 2)
- *Operational risk* associated with running Hometown Bank and the operating processes and systems that support the bank's day-to-day activities

Here we only elaborate on the management of interest rate risk using swaps.

Interest Rate Risk

Hometown Bank's primary financial objective is to grow its assets. Net worth, also known as shareholder value, is defined as:

$$\text{Shareholders' Equity} \ = \ \text{Total Assets} \ - \ \text{Total Liabilities.}$$

Thus, when assets grow more than liabilities, shareholder value also increases. Hometown Bank's assets, as noted on its consolidated balance sheet in Table 5.7, primarily consist of loans; at year-end 2001, $649 million of Hometown's $785 million total assets were in the form of loans (see Table 5.8 for loan portfolio composition). Hometown obtains funding for these loans from its deposit base. Note that for Hometown Bank, as for all banks, deposit accounts are recorded as liabilities. Hometown Bank has an outstanding obligation to its deposit customers to give the money back. For Hometown, deposits make up $467.5 million, or 65 percent, of total outstanding liabilities. The mismatch between deposits and loans is each element's time frame. Hometown's main asset category, retail mortgage loans, has long-term maturities, while its main liabilities are demand deposits and short-term CDs, which have immediate or short-term maturities.

TABLE 5.8 Loan Portfolio Composition, Hometown Bancorp (in Thousands)

	2001 Amount ($)	%	2000 Amount ($)	%	1999 Amount ($)	%
Construction and land development						
Residential	32,465	5	30,780	6	28,350	7%
Commercial	32,465	5	25,650	5	20,250	5
Other	12,986	2	20,520	4	16,200	4
Mortgage						
Residential	331,143	51	241,110	47	182,250	45
Commercial	110,381	17	82,080	16	81,000	20
Commercial and industrial	32,465	5	41,040	8	24,300	6
Consumer	97,395	15	71,820	14	52,650	13
Total Loans Receivable	649,300	100	513,000	100	405,000	100

Hometown's net cash outflows represent payments of interest on deposits. Because of the deposits' short-term maturities, these interest payments are subject to frequent changes. Demand depositors' interest rates can change frequently, even daily, to reflect current interest rates. Short-term CDs are also subject to changes in current interest rates because the interest rate paid to customers changes at each maturity date to reflect the current market. If bank customers are not happy with the new rate offered by the bank, they may choose not to reinvest their CD. Interest rate risk for Hometown Bank arises from its business of lending long-term, with locked-in interest rates, while growing their loan portfolio with short-term borrowings like CDs, with fluctuating interest rates. This risk has increased dramatically because of the increase in interest rate volatility. During the period of January 2001 through October 2002, three-month treasury bills traded in a range from 6.5 percent to 1.54 percent. (Refer to Figure 5.3). During periods of inverted yield curves (where longer-term investments have lower interest rates than short-term investments), a bank's traditional strategy of providing long-term loans using deposits is a money-losing strategy. Note the normal yield curve and inverted yield curve inset below in Figure 5.5.

FIGURE 5.5 Yield Curves

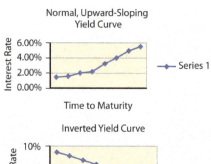

When interest rates are inverted, cash outflows associated with interest payments to depositors will exceed cash inflows from borrowers such as mortgage holders. For example, a home buyer with a thirty-year mortgage loan at 6 percent on $100,000 will continue to make principal and interest payments to Hometown at $597.65 per month. Interest cash flow received by Hometown is calculated at the 6 percent stated rate on the $100,000 loan. If short-term interest rates move higher, for example to 10 percent, Hometown will have interest cash outflows at 10 percent with interest cash inflows at only 6 percent. How will Hometown Bank deal with this type of interest rate risk?

Swaps as a Tool

An interest rate swap is an agreement between two parties to exchange cash flows at specified future times. Banks use interest rate swaps primarily to convert floating-rate liabilities (remember, customers will demand current market interest rates on their deposits—these are the floating rates) into fixed-rate liabilities. Exchanging variable cash flows for fixed cash flows is called a "plain vanilla" swap. Hometown can use a swap as a tool to reduce interest rate risk.

TABLE 5.9 Interest Rate Risks

U.S. Banks		European Banks	
Assets	Liabilities	Assets	Liabilities
Fixed rate loans	Floating rate deposits	Floating rate loans	Fixed rate deposits
Hometown Bank Average Rates			
7.25%	2.5%		
Risk: If interest rates go up, interest paid on deposits could exceed interest received on loans; a loss		**Risk**: If interest rates go down, interest received on loans could be less than interest paid on deposits; a loss	

European banks are the opposite of U.S. banks. European bank customers demand floating rate loans tied to LIBOR (London Interbank Offer Rate); their loans are primarily variable rate and their deposit base is fixed-rate time deposits. If two banks, one U.S. and one European, can agree to an exchange of their liabilities the result is the following:

TABLE 5.10 Objective of Mitigating Interest Rate Risks

U.S. Bank		European Bank	
Assets	Liabilities	Assets	Liabilities
Fixed	Fixed	Floating	Floating

The swap creates a match of interest-rate-sensitive cash inflows and outflows: fixed rate assets and liabilities for the U.S. bank and floating rate assets and liabilities for the European bank as shown in Table 5.10. The following steps show how Hometown Bank employs the financial instrument of a swap with SwissBank for $100 million of their mortgage loans as a risk management tool.

In our simplified example, Hometown agrees to swap with SwissBank cash flows equal to an agreed-upon fixed rate of 3 percent on $100 million, a portion of their total assets. The term is set for ten years. At the same time, SwissBank agrees to pay Hometown cash flows equal to LIBOR an indexed short-term floating rate of interest on the same $100 million. Remember, the contract is an agreement to exchange, or swap, interest payments only. The amount is determined by the desired amount of assets the two parties wish to hedge against interest rate risk. They agree to do this because, as explained above, it better aligns each bank's risk. They agree to swap to minimize interest-rate risk exposure. For Hometown Bank, when interest rates rise, the dollars they receive on the swap increase. This creates a gain on the swap that offsets the loss or supplements the smaller margins are available to the bank because of interest rate moves. Keep in mind that the interest margin may have been profitable at the time of the original transaction; however, higher interest rates have increased cash outflows of interest paid to depositors.

TABLE 5.11 Swap Cash Flow

Hometown Bank	Pays 5 percent fixed rate to	SwissBank
SwissBank	pays LIBOR to	Hometown Bank

Swap Example for Hometown Bank					
End of Year	LIBOR	Fixed-Rate	Interest Obligation of Hometown Bank	Interest Obligation of SwissBank	Net Cash Payment to Hometown
1	2.50%	3%	$100,000,000 × .03 = $3,000,000	$100,000,000 × .025 = $2,500,000	$(500,000)
2	3.00%	3%	$100,000,000 × .03 = $3,000,000	$100,000,000 × .03 = $3,00,000	$0
3	4.00%	3%	$100,000,000 × .03 = $3,000,000	$100,000,000 × .04 = $4,000,000	$1,000,000
4	4.50%	3%	$100,000,000 × .03 = $3,000,000	$100,000,000 × .045 = $4,500,000	$1,500,000
...					
10	5.50%	3%	$100,000 × .03 = $3,000,000	$100,000,000 × 0.55 = $5,500,000	$2,500,000

In our example in Table 5.11, we show what happens if interest rates increase. Over the sample four years shown, short-term interest rates move up from 2.50 percent to 4.50 percent. If Hometown Bank was not hedged with the interest rate swap, their interest expenses would increase as their deposit base would be requiring higher interest cash outflows. With the swap, Hometown Bank can offset the higher cash outflows on their liabilities (higher interest payments to depositors) with the excess cash payments received on the swap. The swap mitigates the risk of increasing interest rates.

Why, you might ask, would SwissBank agree to the swap? Remember, SwissBank has floating rate loans as the majority of their asset base. As interest rates rise, their cash inflows increase. This offsets their increasing cash flows promised to Hometown Bank. The risk of loss for SwissBank comes into play when interest rates decline. If interest rates were to decline below the fixed rate of 3 percent, SwissBank would benefit from the swap.

KEY TAKEAWAY

- In this section you learned about the use capital markets to mitigate risks and the many financial instruments that are used as derivatives to hedge against risks.

DISCUSSION QUESTIONS

1. What financial instrument might a jeweler use to cap his price for gold, the main raw material used in jewelry production?
2. If an insurance company invests in the stock market, what type of instrument would the insurer use to mitigate the risk of stock price fluctuations?
3. What are the benefits of securitization in the insurance/reinsurance industry?
4. It has been said that the most important thing in the world is to know what is most important now. What do you think is the most important risk for you now? What do you think will be the most important risk you will face twenty-five years from now?
5. Explain securitization and provide examples of insurance-linked securities.
6. Explain how swaps work to mitigate the interest rate risk. Give an example.

ENDNOTES

1. See explanation at http://www.Wikiperdia.org. see also "Executive Suite: Textron CEO Zeroes in on Six Sigma," USA Today, updated January 28, 2008.

2. Paul Ingrassia, "How Detroit Drove into a Ditch: The Financial Crisis Has Brought the U.S. Auto Industry to a Breaking Point, but the Trouble Began Long Ago," *Wall Street Journal*, October 25, 2008.

3. See references to Capital versus Risks studies such as Etti G. Baranoff and Thomas W. Sager, "The Impact of Mortgage-backed Securities on Capital Requirements of Life Insurers in the Financial Crisis of 2007–2008," *Geneva Papers on Risk and Insurance Issues and Practice*, The International Association for the Study of Insurance Economics 1018–5895/08, http://www.palgrave-journals.com/gpp; Etti G. Baranoff, Tom W. Sager, and Savas Papadopoulos, "Capital and Risk Revisited: A Structural Equation Model Approach for Life Insurers," *Journal of Risk and Insurance*, 74, no. 3 (2007): 653–81; Etti G. Baranoff and Thomas W. Sager, "The Interrelationship among Organizational and Distribution Forms and Capital and Asset Risk Structures in the Life Insurance Industry," *Journal of Risk and Insurance* 70, no. 3 (2003): 375; Etti G. Baranoff and Thomas W. Sager, "The Relationship between Asset Risk, Product Risk, and Capital in the Life Insurance Industry," *Journal of Banking and Finance* 26, no. 6 (2002): 1181–97.

4. See references to Capital versus Risks studies such as Etti G. Baranoff and Thomas W. Sager, "The Impact of Mortgage-backed Securities on Capital Requirements of Life Insurers in the Financial Crisis of 2007–2008," *Geneva Papers on Risk and Insurance Issues and Practice*, The International Association for the Study of Insurance Economics 1018–5895/08, http://www.palgrave-journals.com/gpp; Etti G. Baranoff, Tom W. Sager, and Savas Papadopoulos, "Capital and Risk Revisited: A Structural Equation Model Approach for Life Insurers," *Journal of Risk and Insurance*, 74, no. 3 (2007): 653–81; Etti G. Baranoff and Thomas W. Sager, "The Interrelationship among Organizational and Distribution Forms and Capital and Asset Risk Structures in the Life Insurance Industry," *Journal of Risk and Insurance* 70, no. 3 (2003): 375; Etti G. Baranoff and Thomas W. Sager, "The Relationship between Asset Risk, Product Risk, and Capital in the Life Insurance Industry," *Journal of Banking and Finance* 26, no. 6 (2002): 1181–97.

5. See environmental issues at http://environment.about.com/b/2009/01/20/obama-launches-new-white-house-web-site-environment-near-the-top-of-his-agenda.htm, http://environment.about.com/b/2009/01/12/billions-of-people-face-food-shortages-due-to-global-warming.htm, or http://environment.about.com/b/2009/01/20/obamas-first-100-days-an-environmental-agenda-for-obamas-first-100-days.htm.

6. http://en.wikipedia.org/wiki/Sustainability.

7. Capital budgeting is a major topic in financial management. The present value of a stream of projected income is compared to the initial outlay in order to make the decision whether to undertake the project. We discuss Net Present Value (NPV) in Chapter 4 for the decision to adopt safety belts. For more methods, the student is invited to examine financial management textbooks.

8. This example follows Doherty's 1985 *Corporate Risk Management*.

9. This assumes an interest rate for the cash flow of 10 percent. The value of the firm is the value of the perpetuity at 10 percent which yields a factor of ten.

10. This concept follows the net income (NI) approach, which was shown to have many drawbacks relative to the Net Operating Income (NOI) approach. See the famous Miller-Modigliani theorems in the financial literature of 1950 and 1960.

11. This happens if the corporate cost of capital decreases to about 9 percent from 10 percent.

12. Circuit City announced its liquidation in the middle of January 2009 after they could not find a buyer to salvage the company that specialized in electronics.

13. Insurers have a special accounting system called statutory accounting. Only insurers that are publicly traded are required to show the market value of their assets in a separate accounting system, called GAAP accounting (Generally Accepted Accounting Procedures). The assets and liabilities shown in Table 5.5 are based on the statutory accounting and the assets are booked at book value, rather than market value, except for the stocks. The differences between the two accounting systems are beyond the scope of this textbook. Nevertheless, the most important differences have to do with accrued liabilities and mark-to-market values of the assets. Statutory accounting does not require market values of bonds.

14. This was reflected in the stock market with insurers such as Hartford Life, Genworth Life, and AIG life insurance, for example. This decline, without a decline in the liabilities, lowered the capital amount of these insurers.

15. James T. Gleason, *The New Management Imperative in Finance Risk* (Princeton, NJ: Bloomberg Press, 2000), Chapter 4.

16. Michael Himick et al., *Securitized Insurance Risk: Strategic Opportunities for Insurers and Investors* (Chicago: Glenlake Publishing Co., Ltd., 1998), 49–59.

17. David Na, "Risk Securitization 101, 2000, CAS Special Interest Seminar" (Bermuda: Deloitte & Touche), http://www.casact.org/coneduc/specsem/catastrophe/2000/handouts/na.ppt.

18. A word of caution: AIG and its CDS without appropriate capitalization and reserves. The rating of credit rating agencies provided the security rather than true funds. Thus, when used inappropriately, the use of such instruments can take down giant corporations as is the case of AIG during the 2008 to 2009 crisis.

19. Sam Friedman, "There's More Than One Way to Skin a Cat," *National Underwriter*, Property & Casualty/Risk & Benefits, May 8, 2000.

20. Definition from Frank J. Fabozzi and Laurie S. Goodman, eds., *Investing in Collateralized Debt Obligations* (Wiley, 2001).

21. A comprehensive report by Guy Carpenter appears in "The Evolving Market for Catastrophic Event Risk," August 1998, http://www.guycarp.com/publications/white/evolving/evolv24.html.

22. Written by Denise Togger, printed with permission of the author. Denise Williams Togger earned her Bachelor of Science degree in economics in 1991 and her Master of Science in finance in 2002 from Virginia Commonwealth University. In fulfilling the MS degree requirements, she completed an independent study in finance focusing on enterprise risk management tools. Text and case material presented draws from curriculum, research, and her eighteen years experience in the investment securities industry. Most recently Denise served as a member of the risk management committee of BB&T Capital Markets as senior vice president and fixed-income preferred trader. BB&T Capital Markets is the capital markets division of BB&T Corporation, the nation's fourteenth largest financial holding company. It was featured as part of Case 4 in the original "Risk Management and Insurance" Textbook by Etti Baranoff, 2003, Wiley and Sons.

23. Anthony Saunders, Chapter 1 *Financial Institutions Management: A Modern Perspective*, 3rd ed. (New York: McGraw-Hill Higher Education, 2000), ch. 1.

24. Sumit Paul-Choudhury, "Real Options," *Risk Management Magazine*, September 2001, 38.

CHAPTER 6

The Insurance Solution and Institutions

In Part I of this book, we discussed the nature of risk and risk management. We defined risk, measured it, attempted to feel its impact, and learned about risk management tools. We statistically measured risk using the standard deviation and coefficient of variance, for example. We are going to emphasize the fact that risk decreases as the number of exposures increases as the most important foundation of insurance. This is called the law of large numbers. This law is critical to understanding the nature of risk and how it is managed. Once there are large numbers of accidental exposures, the next questions are (1) How does insurance work? and (2) What is insurable risk? This chapter responds to these questions and elaborates on insuring institutions.

The transfer of risk to insurers reduces the level of risk to society as a whole. In the transfer of risk to insurers, the risk of loss or no loss that we face changes. As we learned in Chapter 3, we pay premiums to get the security of no loss. When we transfer the risk, insurers take on some risk. To them, however, the risk is much lower; it is the risk of missing the loss prediction. The insurer's risk is the standard deviation we calculated in Chapter 2. The larger the number of exposures, the lower the risk of missing the prediction of future losses. Thus, the transfer of risk to insurers also lowers the risk to society as a whole through the law of large numbers. Even further, insurance is one of the tools that maintains our wealth and keeps the value of firms intact. As we elaborated in Chapter 5, people and firms work to maximize value. One essential element in maximizing the value of our assets is preservation and sustainability. If purchased from a credible and well-rated insurance company, insurance guarantees the preservation of assets and economic value. In this chapter, we will cover the following:

1. Links

2. Ideal requisites for insurability

3. Types of insurance and insurers

1. LINKS

The adverse, or negative, effects of most of the risks can be mitigated by transferring them to insurance companies. The new traveler through the journey of risk mitigation is challenged to ensure that the separate risks receive the appropriate treatment. In Figure 6.1, each puzzle piece represents a fragment of risk, each with its associated insurance solution or an indication of a noninsurance solution. Despite having all of the risks in one completed puzzle to emulate a notion of holistic risk, the insurance solutions are not holistic. Insurers sell separate policies that cover the separate risks. Each policy specifically excludes the coverage that another policy provides. For example, the auto policy excludes the coverage provided by the homeowners' policy. These exclusions are designed to prevent double dipping, or double coverage. Every risk has its unique policy or a few layers of coverages from various sources. For the risk of dying prematurely, we can purchase life insurance policies as well as receive coverage from Social Security. For the risk of becoming ill and not being able to pay for medical care, we have health insurance. For the risk of losing our income because of injury, we have disability insurance (or workers' compensation if the injury occurred on the job). Throughout this text, you will learn about all the policies and how to create an entire portfolio to complete the puzzle of the insurance solution within the risk management activities.

FIGURE 6.1 Links between the Holistic Risk Puzzle Pieces and Insurance Coverages

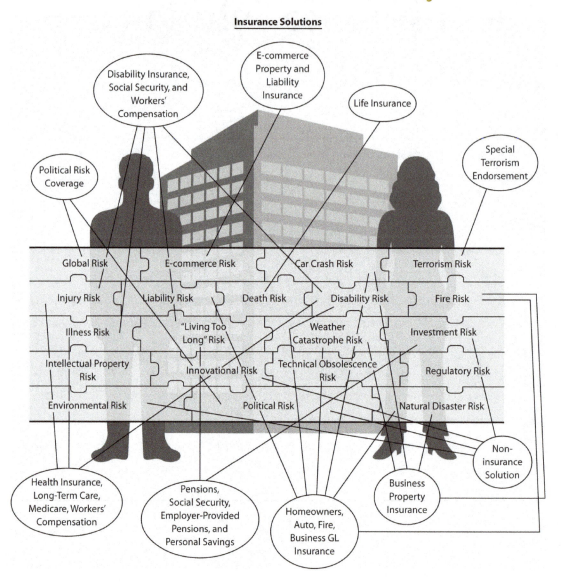

2. NATURE OF INSURANCE

LEARNING OBJECTIVES

In this section you will learn the following:

- **The law of large numbers as the essence of insurance**
- **How insurance is defined**

A brief survey of insurance literature reveals differences of opinion among authors concerning how the term *insurance* should be defined. Regardless, however, the literature agrees that insurance has to contain both of the following elements: (1) risk pooling and (2) risk transfer. The risk pooling creates a large sample of risk exposures and, as the sample gets larger, the possibility of missing future loss predictions gets lower. This is the law of large numbers, discussed further in the box below, "Law of Large Numbers." The combination of risk pooling and risk transfer (from the owner of the risk to a third, unrelated party) physically reduces the risk, both in number and in the anxiety it causes. As such, we regard **insurance** as a social device in which a group of individuals transfer risk to another party in such a way that the third party combines or pools all the risk exposures together. Pooling the exposures together permits more accurate statistical prediction of future losses. Individuals who transfer risk to a third-party are known as **insureds**. The third party that accepts the risks transferred by insureds is known as the **insurer**.

insurance

A social device in which a group of individuals transfer risk to another party in such a way that the third party combines or pools all the risk exposures together.

insureds

Individuals who transfer risk to a third-party.

insurer

The third party that accepts the risks transferred by insureds.

law of large numbers

As a sample of observations is increased in size, the relative variation about the mean declines.

The Law of Large Numbers

Availability of only small data sources (or sometimes none at all) is troublesome because most estimation techniques rely on numerous observations for accuracy. The benefit of many observations is well stated by the law of large numbers, an important statistical doctrine for the successful management of risk and the basic foundation for the existence of insurance in society.

The **law of large numbers** holds that, as a sample of observations increases in size, the relative variation about the mean declines. An example is given in Section 5. The important point is that, with larger samples, we feel more confident in our estimates.

If it were not for the law of large numbers, insurance would not exist. A risk manager (or insurance executive) uses the law of large numbers to estimate future outcomes for planning purposes. The larger the sample size, the lower the relative risk, everything else being equal. The pooling of many exposures gives the insurer a better prediction of future losses. The insurer still has some risk or variability around the average. Nevertheless, the risk of an insurer with more exposures is relatively lower than that of an insurer with fewer exposures under the same expected distribution of losses, as presented in Section 5.

The importance of the large number of exposures often prompts the question, What can smaller insurers do to reduce the uncertainty in predicting losses? Smaller insurers use the sharing of data that exists in the insurance industry. One such data collection and statistical analysis organization is the Insurance Services Office (ISO). In addition to being a statistical agent, this organization provides the uniform policy forms for the property/casualty industry (a small sample of these policies are in the appendixes at the end of the text). The ISO is both a data collection agent and an advisory organization to the industry on matters of rates and policy forms.

2.1 How Insurance Works

Insurance works through the following steps:

- Risk is transferred from an individual or entity (insured) to a third party (insurer).
- The third party (insurer) pools all the risk exposures together to compute potential future losses with some level of accuracy. The insurer uses various forecasting techniques, depending on the distribution of losses. One of the forecasting techniques was demonstrated in Chapter 4.
- The pooling of the risk leads to an overall reduction of risk in society because insurers' accuracy of prediction improves as the number of exposures increases.

- Insurers pool similar risk exposures together to compute their own risk of missing the prediction.
- Insurers discriminate via underwriting—the process of evaluating a risk and classifying it with similar risks (see the box below, "Fitting into a Lower Risk-Exposure Pooling Group"). Both the transfer of risk to a third party and the pooling lead to reduced risk in society as a whole and a sense of reduced anxiety.

Risk Transfer

insurer assumes risk

The insurer promises to pay whatever loss may occur as long as it fits the description given in the policy and is not larger than the amount of insurance sold.

Insurance is created by an insurer that, as a professional risk-bearer, assumes the financial aspect of risks transferred to it by insureds. The **insurer assumes risk** by promising to pay whatever loss may occur as long as it fits the description given in the policy and is not larger than the amount of insurance sold. The loss may be zero, or it may be many thousands of dollars. In return for accepting this variability in outcomes (our definition of risk), the insurer receives a premium. Through the premium, the policyholder has paid a certain expense in order to transfer the risk of a possible large loss. The insurance contract stipulates what types of losses will be paid by the insurer.

Most insurance contracts are expressed in terms of money, although some compensate insureds by providing a service. A life insurance contract obligates the insurer to pay a specified sum of money upon the death of the person whose life is insured. A liability insurance policy requires the insurer not only to pay money on behalf of the insured to a third party but also to provide legal and investigative services needed when the event insured against occurs. The terms of some health insurance policies are fulfilled by providing medical and hospital services (e.g., a semiprivate room and board, plus other hospital services) if the insured is ill or injured. Whether the insurer fulfills its obligations with money or with services, the burden it assumes is financial. The insurer does not guarantee that the event insured against will not happen. Moreover, it cannot replace sentimental value or bear the psychological cost of a loss. A home may be worth only $80,000 for insurance purposes, but it may have many times that value to the owner in terms of sentiment. The death of a loved one can cause almost unbearable mental suffering that is in no way relieved by receiving a sum of money from the insurer. Neither of these aspects of loss can be measured in terms of money; therefore, such risks cannot be transferred to an insurer. Because these noneconomic risks create uncertainty, it is apparent that insurance cannot completely eliminate uncertainty. Yet insurance performs a great service by reducing the financial uncertainty created by risk.

2.2   Insurance or Not?

finite risk programs

Financial methods that can be construed as financing risk assumptions.

In the real world, a clear definition of what is considered an insurance product does not always exist. The amount of risk that is transferred is usually the key to determining whether a certain accounting transaction is considered insurance or not. A case in point is the product called finite risk. It was used by insurers and reinsurers and became the center of a controversy that led to the resignation of Hank Greenberg, the former chairperson and chief executive officer (CEO) of American International Group (AIG) in 2006. **Finite risk programs** are financial methods that can be construed as financing risk assumptions. They began as arrangements between insurers and reinsurers, but they can also be arrangements between any business and an insurer. Premiums paid by the corporation to finance potential losses (losses as opposed to risks) are placed in an experience fund, which is held by the insurer. Over time, the insured pays for his or her own losses through a systematic payment plan, and the funds are invested for the client. This arrangement raises the question, Is risk transferred, or is it only an accounting transaction taking place? The issue is whether finite risk should be called insurance without the elements of insurance. The rule is that, if there is no transfer of at least 10 percent of the risk, regulators regard the transaction as a noninsurance transaction that has less favorable accounting treatment for losses and taxes.[1]

Risk Pooling (Loss Sharing)

In general, the bulk of the premium required by the insurer to assume risk is used to compensate those who incur covered losses. Loss sharing is accomplished through premiums collected by the insurer from all insureds—from those who may not suffer any loss to those who have large losses. In this regard, the losses are shared by all the risk exposures who are part of the pool. This is the essence of pooling.

Pooling can be done by any group who wishes to share in each other's losses. The pooling allows a more accurate prediction of future losses because there are more risk exposures. Being part of pooling is not necessarily an insurance arrangement by itself. As such, it is not part of the transfer of risk to a third party. In a pooling arrangement, members of the group pay each other a share of the loss. Even those with no losses at all pay premiums to be part of the pooling arrangement and enjoy the benefits of such an arrangement. For this purpose, actuaries, charged with determining appropriate rates (prices) for coverage, estimate the frequency and severity of losses and the loss distribution discussed in Chapter 2. These estimates are made for a series of categories of insureds, with each category intended to group insureds who are similar with regard to their likelihood. An underwriter then has the job of determining which category is appropriate for each insured (see the discussion in Chapter 7). Actuaries combine the information to derive expected losses. Estimates generally are based on empirical (in this case, observed) data or theoretical relationships, making them objective estimates. When the actuary must rely on judgment rather than facts, the estimates are termed *subjective*. In most cases, both objective and subjective estimates are used in setting rates. For example, the actuary may begin with industry—determined rates based on past experience and adjust them to reflect the actuary's instincts about the insurer's own expected experience. A life insurer may estimate that 250 of the 100,000 risk exposures of forty-year-old insureds it covers will die in the next year. If each insured carries a $1,000 policy, the insurer will pay out $250,000 in claims (250 × $1,000). To cover these claims, the insurer requires a premium of $2.50 from each insured ($250,000/100,000), which is the average or expected cost per policyholder. (An additional charge to cover expenses, profit, and the risk of actual losses exceeding expected losses would be included in the actual premium. A reduction of the premium would result from the insurer sharing its investment earnings with insureds.) In Chapter 7, we provide the loss development calculations that are performed by the actuary to determine the rates and calculate how much the insurer should keep on reserve to pay future expected claims. Chapter 7 also explains the relationship between rates and investment income of insurers.

2.3   Discrimination: The Essence of Pooling

In order for the law of large numbers to work, the pooled exposures must have approximately the same probability of loss (that is, it must follow the same probability distribution, as demonstrated in Chapter 2). In other words, the exposures need to be homogeneous (similar). Insurers, therefore, need to **discriminate**, or classify exposures according to expected loss. For this reason, twenty-year-old insureds with relatively low rates of mortality are charged lower rates for life insurance than are sixty-year-old insureds, holding factors other than age constant. The rates reflect each insured's expected loss, which is described in the box "Fitting into a Lower Risk-Exposure Pooling Group."

If the two groups of dissimilar risk exposures were charged the same rate, problems would arise. As previously stated, rates reflect average loss costs. Thus, a company charging the same rate to both twenty-year-old insureds and sixty-year-old insureds would charge the average of their expected losses. The pooling will be *across* ages, not *by* ages. Having a choice between a policy from this company and one from a company that charged different rates based on age, the sixty-year-old insureds would choose this lower-cost, single-rate company, while the young insureds would not. As a result, sixty-year-old policyholders would be overrepresented in the group of insureds, making the average rate insufficient. The sixty-year-old insureds know they represent higher risk, but they want to enjoy lower rates.

discriminate

Classify exposures according to expected loss.

Fitting into a Lower Risk-Exposure Pooling Group

Your insurance company relies on the information you provide. Your obligation to the insurance company is not only to provide correct information, but also to provide complete information in order to be placed with your appropriate risk pooling group. The similar exposure in the pooling group is essential for the risk to be insurable, as you saw in this chapter.

Because automobile insurance is an issue of great concern to most students, it is important to know how to handle the process of being placed in the appropriate risk pool group by an insurer. What do you need to tell the insurance agent when you purchase automobile insurance? The agent, usually the first person you talk to, will have routine questions: the make and model of the automobile, the year of manufacture, the location (where the car is parked overnight or garaged), and its usage (e.g., commuting to work). The agent will also ask if you have had any accidents or traffic violations in the past three to five years.

You might be tempted to tell the agent that you keep the automobile at your parents' home, if rates there are cheaper. You may also be tempted to tell the agent that you have not had any traffic violations, when actually you have had three in the past year. Certainly, your insurance premium will be lower if the agent thinks you have a clean record, but that premium savings will mean very little to you when the insurer notifies you of denial of coverage because of dishonesty. This occurs because you gave information that placed you in the wrong risk pool and you paid the wrong premiums for your characteristics.

Safe driving is the key to maintaining reasonable auto insurance premiums because you will be placed in the less risky pool of drivers. The possibility of being placed in a high-risk pool and paying more premiums can be reduced in other ways, too:

- Avoiding traffic violations and accidents helps reduce the probability of loss to a level that promotes the economic feasibility of premiums.
- Steering clear of sports cars and lavish cars, which place you in a group of similar (homogeneous) insureds. Furthermore, a car that is easily damaged or expensive to repair will increase your physical damage premiums.
- Costs can be reduced further if you use your car for pleasure only instead of driving to and from work. Riding the bus or in a friend's car will lower the probability of an accident, making you a more desirable policyholder. Living outside the city limits has a similar effect.
- Passing driving courses, maintaining a grade point average of at least B, and not drinking earn discounts on premiums.

This phenomenon of selecting an insurer that charges lower rates for a specific risk exposure is known as adverse selection because the insureds know they represent higher risk, but they want to enjoy lower rates. Adverse selection occurs when insurance is purchased more often by people and/or organizations with higher-than-average expected losses than by people and/or organizations with average or lower-than-average expected losses. That is, insurance is of greater use to insureds whose losses are expected to be high (insureds "select" in a way that is "adverse" to the insurer). On this basis alone, no problem exists because insurers could simply charge higher premiums to insureds with higher expected losses. Often, however, the insurer simply does not have enough information to be able to distinguish completely among insureds, except in cases of life insurance for younger versus older insureds. Furthermore, the insurer wants to aggregate in order to use the law of large numbers. Thus, some tension exists between limiting adverse selection and employing the law of large numbers.

Adverse selection, then, can result in greater losses than expected. Insurers try to prevent this problem by learning enough about applicants for insurance to identify such people so they can either be rejected or put in the appropriate rating class of similar insureds with similar loss probability. Many insurers, for example, require medical examinations for applicants for life insurance.

Some insurance policy provisions are designed to reduce adverse selection. The suicide clause in life insurance contracts, for example, excludes coverage if a policyholder takes his or her own life within a specified period, generally one or two years. The preexisting conditions provision in health insurance policies is designed to avoid paying benefits to people who buy insurance because they are aware, or should be aware, of an ailment that will require medical attention or that will disable them in the near future.[2]

KEY TAKEAWAYS

In this section you studied the following:

- The essence of insurance, which is risk transfer and risk pooling
- The necessity of discrimination in order to create pools of insureds
- The fact that insurance provides risk reduction

DISCUSSION QUESTIONS

1. What is the definition of insurance?
2. What is the law of large numbers? Why do insurers rely on the law of large numbers?
3. Why is it necessary to discriminate in order to pool?
4. Why are finite risk programs not considered insurance?

3. IDEAL REQUISITES FOR INSURABILITY

LEARNING OBJECTIVES

In this section you will learn the following:

- Why so many risks cannot be insured by private insurance companies
- The definition of insurable risks by private insurers
- Why catastrophes such as floods are not insurable risks by private insurers

Soon after the devastation of Hurricane Katrina became known, the Mississippi attorney general filed a lawsuit against insurers claiming that the flood should be covered by homeowner's insurance policies. The controversy over coverage was explored in the September 8, 2005, *New York Times* article, "Liability Issue: Wind or Water?" Is this question so open-ended?

Are all pure risks insurable by private (nongovernmental) insurers? No. The private insurance device is not suitable for all risks. Many risks are uninsurable. This section is devoted to a discussion of the requirements that must generally be met if a risk is to be insurable in the private market. As a practical matter, many risks that are insured privately meet these requirements only partially or, with reference to a particular requirement, not at all. Thus, in a sense, the requirements listed describe those that would be met by the ideal risk. Nevertheless, the bulk of the risks insured fulfill—at least approximately—most of the requirements. No private insurer can safely disregard them completely.[3] A risk that was perfectly suited for insurance would meet the following requirements:

1. The number of similar exposure units is large.
2. The losses that occur are accidental.
3. A catastrophe cannot occur.
4. Losses are definite.
5. The probability distribution of losses can be determined.
6. The cost of coverage is economically feasible.

The sixth requirement in the list above influences the consumer demand for insurance and looks at what is economically feasible from the perspective of potential insureds. The other requirements influence the willingness of insurers to supply insurance.

3.1 Many Similar Exposure Units

As noted, an insurance organization prefers to have a large number of similar units when insuring a possible loss exposure. The concepts of mass and similarity are thus considered before an insurer accepts a loss exposure. Some insurance is sold on exposures that do not possess the requirements of mass and similarity, but such coverage is the exception, not the rule. An example is insurance on the fingers of a concert pianist or on prize-winning racehorses. When there are no masses of exposures, the coverage is usually provided by specialty insurers. Lloyd's of London, for example, is known for insuring nonmass exposures such as Bruce Springsteen's voice. The types of insurers will be discussed in Chapter 7.

Mass

A major requirement for insurability is mass; that is, there must be large numbers of exposure units involved. For automobile insurance, there must be a large number of automobiles to insure. For life insurance, there must be a large number of persons. An automobile insurance company cannot insure a dozen automobiles, and a life insurance company cannot insure the lives of a dozen persons. How large is a "large group"? For insurance purposes, the number of exposure units needed in a group depends on the extent to which the insurer is willing to bear the risk of deviation from its expectations. Suppose the probability of damage to houses is 1/1,000. An insurer might assume this risk for 1,000 houses, with the expectation that one claim would be made during the year. If no houses were damaged, there would be a 100 percent deviation from expectations, but such a deviation would create no burden for the insurer. On the other hand, if two houses were damaged, the claims to be paid would be twice the expected number. This could be a severe burden for the insurer, assuming average or higher loss severities. By increasing the number of similar houses insured to 10,000, the expected number of losses increases to ten, but the stability of experience is increased. That is, there is a proportionately smaller deviation from expected losses than would exist with a group of 1,000 houses. Similarly, if the group is increased to 100,000 houses, the variation between actual and expected losses would be likely to increase in absolute terms, but it would decline proportionally. One additional loss from 100,000 houses is proportionally less than one additional loss from 10,000 houses and even less than one additional loss from 1,000 houses.

Similarity

The loss exposures to be insured and those observed for calculating the probability distributions must have similarities. The exposures assumed by insurers are not identical, no matter how carefully they may be selected. No two houses are identical, even though physically they may appear to be. They cannot have an identical location and, perhaps more important, they are occupied by different families. Nevertheless, the units in a group must be reasonably similar in characteristics if predictions concerning them are to be accurate. For example, homes with brick sidings are similar for insurance purposes.

Moreover, probability distributions calculated on the basis of observed experience must also involve units similar to one another. Observing the occupational injuries and illnesses of a group of people whose ages, health conditions, and occupations were all different would not provide a basis for calculating workers' compensation insurance rates. For example, clerical work typically involves much lower probabilities of work-related loss than do occupations such as logging timber or climbing utility poles. Estimates based on experience require that the exposure units observed be similar to one another. Moreover, such estimates are useful only in predicting losses for comparable exposures.

3.2 Accidental Losses

fortuitous

A matter of chance.

The risks assumed by an insurer must involve only the possibility, not the certainty, of loss to the insured. Insurable losses must be accidental or **fortuitous**; that is, they must be a matter of chance. Ideally, the insured should have no control or influence over the event to be insured. In fact, this situation prevails only with respect to limited situations. As mentioned in Chapter 1, intangible and physical hazards influence the probability of loss. Prediction of potential losses is based on a probability distribution that has been estimated by observing past experience. Presumably, the events observed were, for the most part, fortuitous occurrences. The use of such estimates for predicting future losses is based on the assumption that future losses will also be a matter of chance. If this is not the case, predictions cannot be accurate.

3.3 Small Possibility of Catastrophe

catastrophic loss

Loss that could imperil the insurer's solvency.

The possibility of catastrophic loss may make a loss exposure uninsurable. A **catastrophic loss** to an insurer is one that could imperil the insurer's solvency. When an insurer assumes a group of risks, it expects the group as a whole to experience some losses—but only a small percentage of the group members to suffer loss at any one time. Given this assumption, a relatively small contribution by each member of the group will be sufficient to pay for all losses. It is possible for a large percentage of all insureds to suffer a loss simultaneously; however, the relatively small contributions would not provide sufficient funds. Similarly, a single very large loss would also require large contributions. Thus, a requisite for insurability is that there must be no excessive possibility of catastrophe for the group as a whole. Insurers must be reasonably sure that their losses will not exceed certain limits. Insurers build up surpluses (net worth) and contingency reserves (funds for future claims) to take care of deviations of experience from the average, but such deviations must have practical limits. If losses cannot be predicted with reasonable accuracy and confidence, it is impossible to determine insurance premium rates, the size of surpluses, or the net worth required.

dependent loss

When loss to one exposure unit affects the probability of loss to another.

Catastrophic losses may occur in two circumstances. In the first, all or many units of the group are exposed to the same loss-causing event, such as war, flood, tornado, mudslide, forest fire, hurricane, earthquake, tsunami, terrorist attack, or unemployment. For example, if one insurer had assumed the risk of damage by wind (hurricane) for all houses in the Miami, Florida, area, it would have suffered a catastrophic loss in 1992 when many structures were damaged simultaneously by Hurricane Andrew (and in fact several insurers were unable to withstand the losses). The 2005 hurricanes, which caused the largest-ever insured losses, are an example of a megacatastrophe that affected many units. These are examples of exposure units that suffer from the same cause of loss because of geographic proximity. Exposure units are susceptible to **dependent loss** when loss to one exposure unit affects the probability of loss to another. Thus, fire at one location increases the probability of fire at other homes in the area: their experience is dependent. In the early days of insurance in the United States, many fire insurance companies concentrated their business in small areas near their headquarters. This worked in New York City, for example, until a major fire devastated large sections of the city in 1835. Because of their concentrated exposures, several insurers suffered losses to a large percentage of their business. The insurers were unable to pay all claims, and several went bankrupt.

A recent example of catastrophe exposure is the case of the risk of mold. Mold created a major availability and affordability issue in the homeowner's and commercial property insurance markets in the early 2000s. The *Wall Street Journal* article, "Hit With Big Losses, Insurers Put Squeeze on Homeowner Policies," reported massive exclusions of mold coverage because of the "avalanche of claims."[4]

A second type of catastrophe exposure arises when a single large value may be exposed to loss. September 11, 2001, represents such catastrophic loss. Tremendous value was concentrated in the towers of the World Trade Center. The possibility of a human-made catastrophe of such magnitude was not anticipated. Private insurers stopped short of calling the terrorist attacks "acts of war"—which would have been excluded from coverage—and honored the policies covering the World Trade Center and the lives of the victims. However, one consequence was the industry's action to immediately exclude terrorism coverage from new policies until the Terrorism Risk Insurance Act (TRIA) of 2002 provided stop-gap coverage from the federal government. When insurers and reinsurers (the insurers of the insurance companies) see the peril as having a far higher probability than previously perceived, they know that they can no longer accurately predict future losses, and their immediate reaction is to exclude the peril. Because of regulation and oversight (see Chapter 8), however, the industry cannot make policy changes instantaneously.[5] When private insurers can no longer provide coverage, a solution may be to create pools such as those described in the box below, "Who Should Insure Against Megacatastrophes?" More on this topic and on reinsurance will be explained in Chapter 7.

3.4 Definite Losses

Losses must be definite in time, place, and amount because, in many cases, insurers promise to pay in dollar amounts for losses if they occur during a particular time and in a particular geographical area. For example, the contract may cover loss by fire at a specified location. For this contract to be effective, it must be possible to determine when, where, and how much loss occurred. If this cannot be established, it is impossible to determine whether the loss is covered under the terms of the contract. The fact that pain and suffering is hard to measure in dollar terms increases the insurer's risk when calculating rates for liability insurance. One other reason the requirement of definiteness is essential is that it is necessary to accumulate data for future predictions. Unless such data can be accurate, they cannot provide the basis for useful predictions.

3.5 Determinable Probability Distribution

For an exposure to loss to be insurable, the expected loss must be calculable. Ideally, this means that there is a determinable probability distribution for losses within a reasonable degree of accuracy. Insurance premium rates are based on predictions of the future, which are expressed quantitatively as expected losses. Calculation of expected losses requires the use of estimated probability distributions (discussed in detail in Chapter 2).

Probability distributions based on experience are useful for prediction; however, only when it is safe to assume that factors shaping events in the future will be similar to those of the past. For this reason, mortality (death) rates during times of peace are inappropriate for estimating the number of insured deaths during times of war. Similarly, the introduction of new technologies such as foam blanketing makes past experience of fire damage a poor indicator of future experience. Yet, because the technology is new and no theory exists as to what the losses ought to be, actuaries have little information on which to base lower rates. The actuary must use subjective estimates as well as engineering information to develop proper rates.

When the probability distribution of losses for the exposure to be insured against cannot be calculated with reasonable accuracy, the risk is uninsurable. An example of purported uninsurability due to inability to predict losses is the nuclear power industry. Insurance experts convinced government officials in 1957 that the risk of loss caused by an incident at a nuclear power site was too uncertain (because of lack of experience and unknown maximum severity) for commercial insurers to accept without some government intervention. As a result, the government limited the liability of owners of nuclear power plants for losses that could arise from such incidents.

Who Should Insure against Megacatastrophes?

The incredible losses from hurricanes Wilma, Rita, and Katrina, including the breached levees in low-lying New Orleans and the subsequent bungled inaction by local, state, and federal authorities, opened a major public debate in the United States. On one level (which is not the focus of this text), the dialogue focused on who should have been first responder and what processes can be put in place to ensure that history does not repeat itself. The second topic of the debate (which we will focus on) was who should pay for such disasters in the future. The economic loss of Katrina and its aftermath was estimated to surpass $100 to $150 billion, large portions of which were not insured. As you will learn in Chapter 1, flood is insured only by the federal government through the National Federal Insurance Program, and the coverage limits are low, at $250,000. Many flooded homes and businesses in Louisiana and Mississippi did not carry this insurance. Even if they carried the coverage, the limits prevented recovery of their true property values. Residents had to resort to other assistance programs, some from the Federal Emergency Management Agency (FEMA).

The unprecedented economic loss is at the heart of the debate. Who should insure against such megacatastrophes in the future? The Insurance Information Institute (III) provided a summary of the proposals that were put forward during the public dialogue about how large-scale natural catastrophes should be managed in the post-9/11 era. The following are two main viewpoints:

1. Because the private industry cannot insure mega losses that are fundamentally uninsurable, the federal government should be the ultimate insurer. The federal government is already the national flood insurer and has been providing the terrorism stopgap coverage under the Terrorism Risk Insurance Act (TRIA). It makes sense that uninsurable risks be mitigated by the government. The insurance commissioners of Florida, California, and New York proposed a national catastrophe fund. Others suggested amendment to the federal tax code for insurers' reserves. The idea is that coverage would still be provided by insurers, but states would create pools, and above them, a third layer would be provided for national megacatastrophes by the federal government. Involvement by the federal government in case of large-scale losses has elements of the Terrorism Risk Insurance Act that was extended until the end of 2014.

2. Because we are living in a free market economy, the private sector is best suited to handle any disaster, large or small. The idea is to have less government, with relaxed regulation and taxation. The creativity of the private sector should prevail. The government should not compete with private insurance and reinsurance markets. In this scenario, insurers have more capacity and thus more actuarially sound predictions to set appropriate rates. To prove the point, the industry was able to sustain both 9/11 and Katrina (except that the industry has not been responsible for the flood damages). If the private industry takes over all potential mega losses, there does need to be great improvement, however, in catastrophe modeling. The industry will have to diversify and utilize the capital markets (see Chapter 3 about CAT bonds). It is predicted that the industry will ensure high-quality loss control in areas with potential disasters through building codes, strengthening of levees, and utilization of all possible disaster management techniques.

Questions for Discussion

1. Because large-scale human-made and natural disasters are not controllable by insurers, should the government pay for damages?

2. Because insurance is the business of insurers, should they handle their problems without being subsidized by taxpayers? What would be the outcome in terms of safety and loss controls?

Sources: This box relied on information from articles from the National Underwriter, Business Insurance, and the Insurance Information Institute (III) at http://www.iii.org.

3.6 Economic Feasibility

economically feasible

When the size of the possible loss must be significant to the insured and the cost of insurance must be small compared with the potential loss.

For insurance to be **economically feasible** for an insured, the size of the possible loss must be significant to the insured, and the cost of insurance must be small compared to the potential loss. Otherwise, the purchase of insurance is not practical. If the possible loss is not significant to those exposed, insurance is inappropriate. Cost-benefit analysis is needed for the insurers to determine if the rates can be feasible to insureds. Also, the analysis in Chapter 3 regarding the actuarially fair premiums a risk-averse individual would be willing to pay is important here. For catastrophic coverage, the insurer may determine through capital budgeting methods and cash flow analysis that it cannot provide low enough costs to make the coverage feasible for insureds.

Retention (bearing the financial loss by oneself) of many risks is almost automatic because the loss would not be a burden. If all the people who own automobiles were wealthy, it is doubtful that much automobile collision insurance would be written because such losses would not be significant to the wealthy owners. Insurance is feasible only when the possible loss is large enough to be of concern to the person who may bear the burden.

The possible loss must also be relatively large compared to the size of the premium. If the losses the insurer pays plus the cost of insurer operations are such that the premium must be very large in relation to the potential loss, insurance is not economically feasible. From the viewpoint of the insured, when the expected loss premium is high relative to the maximum possible loss, internal budgeting for the risk is preferable to insurance. The use of deductibles (a form of retention) to eliminate insurance reimbursement for frequent small losses helps make automobile collision premiums economically feasible. The deductible eliminates claims for small losses. Small automobile collision losses have such high probability and the cost of settling them is so great that the premium for covering them would be very large compared to the size of actual losses. For example, if a policy with a $200 deductible costs $85 more than one with a $500 deductible, you may consider $85 too large a premium for $300 of lower deductible. Insurance is best suited for risks involving large potential losses with low probabilities (described in Chapter 3). Large losses are key because insureds cannot pay them, and low probabilities for large losses make premiums relatively small compared with the possible losses. In other situations, insurance may not be economically feasible for the person or business facing risk.

3.7   Summary of Insurable Risks

Table 6.1 provides an analysis of the insurability characteristics of a few common perils and risks. The first column lists the requirements for insurability that we have just discussed. Note that the risk of flooding is not considered insurable because of its potential for catastrophe: many exposures can suffer losses in the same location. Thus, flooding is covered by the federal government, not by private insurers. Hurricanes, though similar to floods, are covered by private insurers, who obtain reinsurance to limit their exposure. After a catastrophe like Hurricane Andrew, however, many reinsurers became financially strapped or insolvent.

TABLE 6.1 Examples of Insurable and Uninsurable Risks

Flood	Fire	Disability	Terrorism	
Large number of similar exposure units	Yes	Yes	Yes	No
Accidental, uncontrollable	Yes	Yes	Yes	No (man-made, though not by the insured)
Potentially catastrophic	Yes	No	No	Yes
Definite losses	Yes	Yes	No	Yes
Determinable probability distribution of losses	Yes	Yes	Yes	No
Economically feasible	Depends	Depends	Depends	No
Insurable?	No	Yes	Yes	No

The second example in Table 6.1 is the peril/risk of fire. Fire is an insurable risk because it meets all the required elements. Even this peril can be catastrophic, however, if fires cannot be controlled and a large geographical area is damaged, such as the large fires in Colorado and Arizona in 2002. Disability is another type of peril that is considered insurable in most cases. The last example is the risk of terrorism. As noted above, it is no longer considered an insurable risk due to the catastrophic element associated with this peril since the September 11, 2001, attack.

Insurance companies use cost-benefit analysis to determine whether they should bring a new product to the market. In Chapter 4, you learned about the time value of money and computation for such decisions.

KEY TAKEAWAYS

In this section you studied that a risk perfectly suited for insurance meets the following requirements:

- The number of similar exposure units is large.
- The losses that occur are accidental.
- A catastrophe cannot occur.
- Losses are definite.
- The probability distribution of losses can be determined.
- The cost of coverage is economically feasible.

DISCUSSION QUESTION

Explain whether the following risks and perils are insurable by private insurers:

  a. A hailstorm that destroys your roof
  b. The life of an eighty-year-old man
  c. A flood
  d. Mold
  e. Biological warfare
  f. Dirty bombs

---

4. TYPES OF INSURANCE AND INSURERS

LEARNING OBJECTIVES

In this section you will learn the following:

- **The types of insurance**
- **The types of insurance company corporate structures**
- **Governmental insurance organizations**

Many types of insurance policies are available to families and organizations that do not wish to retain their own risks. The following questions may be raised about an insurance policy:

1. Is it personal, group, or commercial?
2. Is it life/health or property/casualty?
3. Is it issued by a private insurer or a government agency?
4. Is it purchased voluntarily or involuntarily?

4.1 Personal, Group, or Commercial Insurance

personal insurance

Insurance that is purchased by individuals and families for their risk needs. Such insurance includes life, health, disability, auto, homeowner, and long-term care.

group insurance

Insurance provided by the employer for the benefit of employees.

commercial insurance

Property/casualty insurance for businesses and other organizations.

life/health insurance

Insurance that covers exposures to the perils of death, medical expenses, disability, and old age.

Personal insurance is insurance that is purchased by individuals and families for their risk needs. Such insurance includes life, health, disability, auto, homeowner, and long-term care. **Group insurance** is insurance provided by the employer for the benefit of employees. Group insurance coverage includes life, disability, health, and pension plans. **Commercial insurance** is property/casualty insurance for businesses and other organizations.

An insurance company is likely to have separate divisions within its underwriting department for personal lines, group lines, and commercial business. The criterion to assign insureds into their appropriate risk pool for rating purposes is different for each type of insurance. Staff in the personal lines division are trained to look for risk factors (e.g., driving records and types of home construction) that influence the frequency and severity of claims among individuals and families. Group underwriting looks at the characteristics and demographics, including prior experience, of the employee group. The commercial division has underwriting experts on risks faced by organizations. Personnel in other functional areas such as claims adjustment may also specialize in personal, group, or commercial lines.

4.2 Life/Health or Property/Casualty Insurance

Life/health insurance covers exposures to the perils of death, medical expenses, disability, and old age. Private life insurance companies provide insurance for these perils, and individuals voluntarily decide whether or not to buy their products. Health insurance is provided primarily by life/health insurers but is also sold by some property/casualty insurers. All of these are available on an individual and a group basis. The Social Security program provides substantial amounts of life/health insurance on an involuntary basis.

Property/casualty insurance covers property exposures such as direct and indirect losses of property caused by perils like fire, windstorm, and theft. It also includes insurance to cover the possibility of being held legally liable to pay damages to another person. Before the passage of multiple-line underwriting laws in the late 1940s and early 1950s, property/casualty insurance had to be written by different insurers. Now they frequently are written in the same contract (e.g., homeowner's and commercial package policies, which will be discussed in later chapters).

A private insurer can be classified as either a life/health or a property/casualty insurer. Health insurance may be sold by either. Some insurers specialize in a particular type of insurance, such as property insurance. Others are affiliated insurers, in which several insurers (and sometimes noninsurance businesses) are controlled by a holding company; all or almost all types of insurance are offered by some company in the group.

4.3   Private or Government Insurance

Insurance is provided both by privately owned organizations and by state and federal agencies. Measured by premium income, the bulk of property/casualty insurance is provided by private insurers. Largely because of the magnitude of the Social Security program, however, government provides about one-third more personal insurance than the private sector. Our society has elected to provide certain levels of death, health, retirement, and unemployment insurance on an involuntary basis through governmental (federal and state) agencies. If we desire to supplement the benefit levels of social insurance or to buy property/casualty insurance, some of which is required, private insurers provide the protection.

4.4   Voluntary or Involuntary Insurance

Most private insurance is purchased voluntarily, although some types, such as automobile insurance or insurance on mortgages and car loans, are required by law or contracts. In many states, the purchase of automobile liability insurance is mandatory, and if the car is financed, the lender requires property damage coverage.

Government insurance is involuntary under certain conditions for certain people. Most people are required by law to participate in the Social Security program, which provides life, health, disability, and retirement coverage. Unemployment and workers' compensation insurance are also forms of involuntary social insurance provided by the government. Some government insurance, such as flood insurance, is available to those who want it, but no one is required to buy it.

4.5   Insurers' Corporate Structure

Stock Insurers

Stock insurers are organized in the same way as other privately owned corporations created for the purpose of making a profit and maximizing the value of the organization for the benefit of the owners. Individuals provide the operating capital for the company. Stock companies can be publicly traded in the stock markets or privately held. Stockholders receive dividends when the company is profitable.

Mutual Insurers

Mutual insurers are owned and controlled, in theory if not in practice, by their policyowners. They have no stockholders and issue no capital stock. People become owners by purchasing an insurance policy from the mutual insurer. Profits are shared with owners as **policyowners' dividends**. Company officers are appointed by a board of directors that is, at least theoretically, elected by policyowners. The stated purpose of the organization is to provide low-cost insurance rather than to make a profit for stockholders.

Research shows that mutual and stock insurers are highly competitive in the sense that neither seems to outperform the other. There are high-quality, low-cost insurers of both types. A wise consumer should analyze both before buying insurance.

Many mutual insurers in both the life/health and property/casualty fields are large and operate over large areas of the country. These large mutuals do a general business in the life/health and property/casualty insurance fields, rather than confining their efforts to a small geographic area or a particular type of insured. The largest property/casualty mutual insurer in the United States is State Farm, which was established in 1922 by George J. Mecherle, an Illinois farmer who turned to insurance sales. State Farm grew to be the leading auto and homeowner's insurer in the United States, with twenty-five regional offices, more than 79,000 employees, and nearly 70 million policies in force. Because of its

property/casualty insurance

Insurance that covers property exposures such as direct and indirect losses of property caused by perils such as fire, windstorm, and theft.

stock insurers

Insurers created for the purpose of making a profit and maximizing the value of the organization for the benefit of the owners.

mutual insurers

Insurers owned and controlled, in theory if not in practice, by their policyowners.

policyowners' dividends

Profits shared by insurance policyholders.

mutual status, State Farm is overcapitalized (holding relatively more surplus than its peer group or stock companies).

Demutualization

When top managers of a mutual company decide they need to raise capital, they may go through a process called demutualization. In the last decade, there was an increase in the number of companies that decided to demutualize and become stock companies. Policyholders, who were owners of the mutual company, received shares in the stock company. Part of the motive was to provide top management with an additional avenue of income in the form of stock options in the company. The demutualization wave in the life insurance industry reached its peak in December 2001, when the large mutual insurer, Prudential, converted to a stock company. The decade between the mid-1990s and mid-2000s saw the demutualization of twenty-two life insurance companies: Unum, Equitable Life, Guarantee Mutual, State Mutual (First American Financial Life), Farm Family, Mutual of New York, Standard Insurance, Manulife, Mutual Life of Canada (Clarica), Canada Life, Industrial Alliance, John Hancock, Metropolitan Life, Sun Life of Canada, Central Life Assurance (AmerUs), Indianapolis Life, Phoenix Home Life, Principal Mutual, Anthem Life, Provident Mutual, Prudential, and General American Mutual Holding Company (which was sold to MetLife through its liquidation by the Missouri Department of Insurance).[6]

4.6 Lloyd's of London: A Global Insurance Exchange

Lloyd's of London

The oldest insurance organization in existence.

Lloyd's of London is the oldest insurance organization in existence; it started in a coffeehouse in London in 1688. Lloyds conducts a worldwide business primarily from England, though it is also licensed in Illinois and Kentucky. It maintains a trust fund in the United States for the protection of insureds in this country. In states where Lloyd's is not licensed, it is considered a nonadmitted insurer. States primarily allow such nonadmitted insurers to sell only coverage that is unavailable from their licensed (admitted) insurers. This generally unavailable coverage is known as excess and surplus lines insurance, and it is Lloyd's primary U.S. business.

Lloyd's does not assume risks in the manner of other insurers. Instead, individual members of Lloyd's, called Names, accept insurance risks by providing capital to an underwriting syndicate. Each syndicate is made up of many Names and accepts risks through one or more brokers. Surplus lines agents—those who sell for excess and surplus lines insurers—direct business to brokers at one or more syndicates. Syndicates, rather than Names, make the underwriting decisions of which risks to accept. Various activities of Lloyd's are supervised by two governing committees—one for market management and another for regulation of financial matters. The syndicates are known to accept exotic risks and reinsure much of the asbestos and catastrophic risk in the United States. They also insure aviation.

The arrangement of Lloyd's of London is similar to that of an organized stock exchange in which physical facilities are owned by the exchange, but business is transacted by the members. The personal liability of individual Names has been unlimited; they have been legally liable for their underwriting losses under Lloyd's policies to the full extent of their personal and business assets. This point is sometimes emphasized by telling new male members that they are liable "down to their cufflinks" and for female members "down to their earrings." In addition to Names being required to make deposits of capital with the governing committee for financial matters, each Name is required to put premiums into a trust fund that makes them exclusively encumbered to the Name's underwriting liabilities until the obligations under the policies for which the premiums were paid have been fulfilled. Underwriting accounts are audited annually to ensure that assets and liabilities are correctly valued and that assets are sufficient to meet underwriting liabilities. Normally, profits are distributed annually. Following losses, Names may be asked to make additional contributions. A trust fund covers the losses of bankrupt Names. A supervisory committee has authority to suspend or expel members.

Seldom does one syndicate assume all of one large exposure; it assumes part. Thus, an individual Name typically becomes liable for a small fraction of 1 percent of the total liability assumed in one policy. Historically, syndicates also reinsured with each other to provide more risk sharing. The practice of sharing risk through reinsurance within the Lloyd's organization magnified the impact of heavy losses incurred by Lloyd's members for 1988 through 1992. Losses for these five years reached the unprecedented level of $14.2 billion. Reinsurance losses on U.S. business were a major contributor to losses due to asbestos and pollution, hurricanes Hugo and Andrew, the 1989 San Francisco earthquake, the Exxon *Valdez* oil spill, and other product liabilities.

The massive losses wiped out the fortunes of many Names. In 1953, Lloyd's consisted of 3,400 Names, most of whom were wealthy citizens of the British Commonwealth. By 1989, many less wealthy, upper-middle-class people had been enticed to become Names with unlimited liability, pushing the total number of Names to an all-time high of 34,000 in 400 syndicates. By mid-1994, only about 17,500 Names and 178 underwriting syndicates (with just ninety-six accepting new business) remained. As a result of the mammoth total losses (and bankruptcy or rehabilitation for many individual members), Lloyd's had reduced underwriting capacity and was experiencing difficulty in attracting new capital. What started in a coffeehouse was getting close to the inside of the percolator.

Among Lloyd's reforms was the acceptance of corporate capital. By mid-1994, 15 percent of its capital was from twenty-five corporations that, unlike individual Names, have their liability limited to the amount of invested capital. Another reform consisted of a new system of compulsory stop-loss insurance designed to help members reduce exposure to large losses. Reinsurance among syndicates has ceased.

Other forms of insurance entities that are used infrequently are not featured in this textbook.

4.7 Banks and Insurance

For decades, savings banks in Massachusetts, New York, and Connecticut have sold life insurance in one of two ways: by establishing life insurance departments or by acting as agents for other savings banks with insurance departments. Savings banks sell the usual types of individual life insurance policies and annuities, as well as group life insurance. Business is transacted on an over-the-counter basis or by mail. No agents are employed to sell the insurance; however, advertising is used extensively for marketing. Insurance is provided at a relatively low cost.

Many savings and loan associations have been selling personal property/casualty insurance (and some life insurance) through nonbanking subsidiaries. Commercial banks have lobbied hard for permission to both underwrite (issue contracts and accept risks as an insurer) and sell all types of insurance. Approximately two-thirds of the states have granted state-chartered banks this permission. At this time, national banks have not been granted such power.[7]

In November 1999, State Farm Mutual Automobile Insurance Company opened State Farm Bank. At the time of this writing, State Farm has banking services in eleven states—Alabama, Arizona, Colorado, Illinois, Indiana, Mississippi, Missouri, New Mexico, Nevada, Utah, and Wyoming—and plans to expand to all fifty states. The banking division benefits from State Farm's 16,000 agents, who can market a full range of banking products.[8]

The U.S. Supreme Court approved (with a 9–0 vote) the sale of fixed-dollar and variable annuities by national banks, reasoning that annuities are investments rather than insurance. Banks are strong in annuities sales.

4.8 Captives, Risk Retention Groups, and Alternative Markets

Risk retention groups and captives are forms of self-insurance. Broadly defined, a **captive insurance company** is a company that provides insurance coverage to its parent company and other affiliated organizations. The captive is controlled by its policyholder-parent. Some captives sell coverage to non-affiliated organizations. Others are comprised of members of industry associations, resulting in captives that closely resemble the early mutual insurers.

captive insurance company

A company that provides insurance coverage to its parent company and other affiliated organizations.

Forming a captive insurer is an expensive undertaking. Capital must be contributed in order to develop a net worth sufficient to meet regulatory (and financial stability) requirements. Start-up costs for licensing, chartering, and managing the captive are also incurred. And, of course, the captive needs constant managing, requiring that effort be expended by the firm's risk management department and/or that a management company be hired.

To justify these costs, the parent company considers various factors. One is the availability of insurance in the commercial insurance market. During the liability insurance crisis of the 1980s, for example, pollution liability coverage became almost nonexistent. Chemical and other firms formed captives to fill the void. Today, there is a big push for captives after the losses of September 11. Another factor considered in deciding on a captive is the opportunity cost of money. If the parent can use funds more productively (that is, can earn a higher after-tax return on investment) than the insurer can, the formation of a captive may be wise. The risk manager must assess the importance of the insurer's claims adjusting and other services (including underwriting) when evaluating whether to create a captive. Insurers' services are very important considerations. One reason to create a captive is to have access to the reinsurance market for stop-loss catastrophic coverage for the captive. One currently popular use of captives is to coordinate the insurance programs of a firm's foreign operations. An added advantage of captives in this setting is the ability to manage exchange rate risks as well as the pure risks more common to traditional risk managers. Perhaps of primary significance is that captives give their parents access to the reinsurance market.

Captive managers in Bermuda received many inquiries after September 11, 2001, as U.S. insurance buyers searched for lower rates. The level of reinsurance capacity is always a concern for captive owners because reinsurers provide the catastrophic layer of protection. In the past, reinsurance was rather inexpensive for captives.[9]

risk retention group

A group that provides risk management and retention to a few players in the same industry who are too small to act on their own.

A special form of self-insurance is known as a **risk retention group**.[10] An interesting example of the risk retention group in practice is the one formed recently by the airline industry, which suffered disproportional losses as a result of September 11, 2001. A risk retention group designed to cover passenger and third-party war risk liability for airlines gained regulatory approval in Vermont.[11] The risk retention group for airlines is named Equitime, and it was formed by the Air Transport Association (ATA), a Washington, D.C.-based trade group, and Marsh, Inc. (one of the largest brokerage firms worldwide). Equitime offers as much as $1.5 billion in combined limits for passenger and third-party war risk liability. Equitime's plan is to retain $300 million of the limit and reinsure the balance with the federal government. The capitalization of this risk retention group is through a private placement of stock from twenty-four airlines belonging to the ATA and about fifty members of the Regional Airline Association.[12]

governmental risk pools

Pools formed for governmental entities to provide group self-insurance coverage.

Alternative markets are the markets of all self-insurance programs. Captives and group captives will see steady growth in membership. In addition, **governmental risk pools** have been formed for governmental entities to provide group self-insurance coverage such as the Texas Association of School Boards (TASB), municipals risk pools, and other taxing-authorities pools. TASB, for example, offers to the Texas school districts a pooling arrangement for workers' compensation and property, liability, and health insurance. Public risk pools have a large association, the Public Risk Management Association (PRIMA), which provides support and education to public risk pools.[13]

4.9 Government Insuring Organizations

Federal and state government agencies account for nearly half of the insurance activity in the United States. Primarily, they fill a gap where private insurers have not provided coverage, in most cases, because the exposure does not adequately meet the ideal requisites for private insurance. However, some governmental programs (examples include the Maryland automobile fund, state workers' compensation, insurance plans, crop insurance, and a Wisconsin life plan) exist for political reasons. Government insurers created for political goals usually compete with private firms. This section briefly summarizes state and federal government insurance activities.

State Insuring Organizations

- All states administer unemployment compensation insurance programs. All states also have guaranty funds that provide partial or complete coverage in cases of insurance company failure from all insurers in the market. This ensures that the results of insolvencies are not borne solely by certain policyowners. Covered lines of insurance and maximum liability per policyowner vary by state. Financing is provided on a postloss assessment basis (except for preloss assessments in New York) by involuntary contributions from all insurance companies licensed in the state. An insurer's contributions to a particular state are proportionate to its volume of business in the state. No benefits are paid to stockholders of defunct insurers. The funds are responsible for the obligations of insolvent companies owed to their policyowners.

- Eighteen states have funds to insure worker's compensation benefits. Some funds are monopolistic, while others compete with private insurers.

- Several states provide temporary nonoccupational disability insurance, title insurance, or medical malpractice insurance. Many states provide medical malpractice insurance (discussed in upcoming chapters) through joint underwriting associations (JUAs), which provide coverage to those who cannot obtain insurance in the regular markets. The JUAs are created by state legislation. If a JUA experiences losses in excess of its expectations, it has the power to assess all insurers that write liability insurance in the state. However, rates are supposed to be set at a level adequate to avoid such assessments. Some states have also created JUAs for lawyers and other groups that have had difficulty finding insurance in the private market.

- Seven states along the Atlantic and Gulf coasts assure the availability of property insurance, and indirect loss insurance in some states, to property owners of coastal areas exposed to hurricanes and other windstorms. Insurance is written through beach and windstorm insurance plans that provide coverage to those who cannot obtain insurance in the regular markets, especially in areas prone to natural catastrophes and hurricanes. Compliance with building codes is encouraged for loss reduction.

- The state of Maryland operates a fund to provide automobile liability insurance to Maryland motorists unable to buy it in the private market. The Wisconsin State Life Fund sells life insurance to residents of Wisconsin on an individual basis similar to that of private life insurers. In recent years, several states have created health insurance pools to give uninsurable individuals access to health insurance. Coverage may be limited and expensive.

Federal Insuring Organizations

- The Social Security Administration, which operates the Social Security program, collects more premiums (in the form of payroll taxes) and pays more claims than any other insurance organization in the United States. The Federal Deposit Insurance Corporation insures depositors against loss caused by the failure of a bank. Credit union accounts are protected by the National Credit Union Administration. The Securities Investor Protection Corporation covers securities held by investment brokers and dealers.

- The Federal Crop Insurance Corporation provides open-perils insurance for farm crops. Policies are sold and serviced by the private market. The federal government provides subsidies and reinsurance.

- The Federal Crime Insurance Program covers losses due to burglary and robbery in both personal and commercial markets.

- Fair Access to Insurance Requirements (FAIR) plans have been established in a number of states under federal legislation. They are operated by private insurers as a pool to make property insurance available to applicants who cannot buy it in the regular market. Federal government reinsurance pays for excessive losses caused by riots and civil disorder.

- The National Flood Insurance Program provides flood insurance through private agents in communities that have met federal requirements designed to reduce flood losses. (See Chapter 1 for a description of the federal flood insurance.)

- The Veterans Administration provides several programs for veterans. Several federal agencies insure mortgage loans made by private lenders against losses due to borrowers failing to make payments. The Pension Benefit Guaranty Corporation protects certain retirement plan benefits in the event the plan sponsor fails to fulfill its promises to participants. The Overseas Private Investment Corporation (OPIC) protects against losses suffered by U.S. citizens through political risks in underdeveloped countries.

KEY TAKEAWAYS

In this section you studied the different types of insurance:

- Personal, group, or commercial
- Life/health or property/casualty
- Private insurer or a government agency?
- Purchased voluntarily or involuntarily?
- Insurers' Corporate structure: stock insurers; mutual insurers; Lloyd's of London; Banks and Insurance; Captives, Risk Retention Groups; Alternative Markets
- Government insuring organizations

DISCUSSION QUESTIONS

1. What types of insurance are available?
2. What are the main organizational structures adopted by insurance companies?
3. Why is the government involved in insurance, and what are the governmental insuring organizations listed in this section?
4. What is demutualization?

5.   APPENDIX: MORE EXPOSURES, LESS RISK

Assume that the riskiness of two groups is under consideration by an insurer. One group is comprised of 1,000 units and the other is comprised of 4,000 units. Each group anticipates incurring 10 percent losses within a specified period, such as a year. Therefore, the first group expects to have one hundred losses, and the second group expects 400 losses. This example demonstrates a binomial distribution, one where only two possible outcomes exist: loss or no loss. The average of a binomial equals the sample size times the probability of success. Here, we will define success as a loss claim and use the following symbols:

- n = sample size
- p = probability of "success"
- q = probability of "failure" = $1 - p$
- $n \times p$ = mean

For Group 1 in our sample, the mean is one hundred:

- $(1,000) \times (.10) = 100$

For Group 2, the mean is 400:

- $(4,000) \times (.10) = 400$

The standard deviation of a distribution is a measure of risk or dispersion. For a binomial distribution, the standard deviation is

$$\sqrt{n \times p \times q}.$$

In our example, the standard deviations of Group 1 and Group 2 are 9.5 and 19, respectively.

$$\sqrt{(1,000) \times (.1) \times (.9)} = 9.5$$

$$\sqrt{(4000) \times (.1) \times (.9)} = 19$$

Thus, while the mean, or expected number of losses, quadrupled with the quadrupling of the sample size, the standard deviation only doubled. Through this illustration, you can see that the proportional deviation of actual from expected outcomes decreases with increased sample size. The relative dispersion has been reduced. The coefficient of variation (the standard deviation divided by the mean) is often used as a relative measure of risk. In the example above, Group 1 has a coefficient of variation of 9.5/100, or 0.095. Group 2 has a coefficient of variation of 19/400 = 0.0475, indicating the reduced risk.

Taking the extreme, consider an individual ($n = 1$) who attempts to retain the risk of loss. The person either will or will not incur a loss, and even though the probability of loss is only 10 percent, how does that person know whether he or she will be the unlucky one out of ten? Using the binomial distribution, that individual's standard deviation (risk) is a much higher measure of risk than that of the insurer. The individual's coefficient of variation is .3/.1 = 3, demonstrating this higher risk. More specifically, the risk is 63 times (3/.0475) that of the insurer, with 4,000 units exposed to loss.

6.   REVIEW AND PRACTICE

1. How can small insurers survive without a large number of exposures?
2. Professor Kulp said, "Insurance works well for some exposures, to some extent for many, and not at all for others." Do you agree? Why or why not?
3. Insurance requires a transfer of risk. Risk is uncertain variability of future outcomes. Does life insurance meet the ideal requisites of insurance when the insurance company is aware that death is a certainty?
4. What are the benefits of insurance to individuals and to society?
5. What types of insurance exist? Describe the differences among them.
6. What are the various types of insurance companies?
7. What are the various types of insurance corporate structures?

8. Hatch's furniture store has many perils that threaten its operation each day. Explain why each of the following perils may or may not be insurable. In each case, discuss possible exceptions to the general answer you have given.

    a. The loss of merchandise because of theft when the thief is not caught and Hatch's cannot establish exactly when the loss occurred.

    b. Injury to a customer when the store's delivery person backs the delivery truck into that customer while delivering a chair.

    c. Injury to a customer when a sofa catches fire and burns the customer's living room. Discuss the fire damage to the customer's home as well as the customer's bodily injury.

    d. Injury to a customer's child who runs down an aisle in the store and falls.

    e. Mental suffering of a customer whose merchandise is not delivered on schedule.

9. Jack and Jill decide they cannot afford to buy auto insurance. They are in a class with 160 students, and they come up with the idea of sharing the automobile risk with the rest of the students. Their professor loves the idea and asks them to explain in detail how it will work. Pretend you are Jack and Jill. Explain to the class the following:

    a. If you expect to have only three losses per year on average (frequency) for a total of $10,000 each loss (severity), what will be the cost of sharing these losses per student in the class?

    b. Do you think you have enough exposures to predict only three losses a year? Explain.

ENDNOTES

1. The interested student should also explore it further. In the case of AIG, the finite risk arrangements were regarded as noninsurance transactions. In early 2006, AIG agreed to pay $1.64 billion to settle investigations by the Securities and Exchange Commission and New York State Attorney General Eliot Spitzer, who brought charges against AIG. This recent real-life example exemplifies how the careful treatment of the definition of insurance is so important to the business and its presentation of its financial condition. For more information on finite risk programs, see "Finite Risk Reinsurance," Insurance Information Institute (III), May 2005, at http://www.iii.org/media/hottopics/insurance/finite/; Ian McDonald, Theo Francis, and Deborah Solomon, "Rewriting the Books—AIG Admits 'Improper' Accounting Broad Range of Problems Could Cut $1.77 Billion Of Insurer's Net Worth A Widening Criminal Probe," *Wall Street Journal*, March 31, 2005, A1; Kara Scannell and Ian McDonald, "AIG Close to Deal to Settle Charges, Pay $1.5 Billion," *Wall Street Journal*, February 6, 2006, C1; Steve Tuckey, "AIG Settlement Leaves Out Life Issues," *National Underwriter Online News Service*, February 10, 2006. These articles are representative regarding these topics.

2. Recent health care reforms (HIPAA 1996) have limited the ability of insurers to reduce adverse selection through the use of preexisting-condition limitations.

3. Governmental insurance programs make greater deviations from the ideal requisites for insurability. They are able to accept greater risks because they often make their insurance compulsory and have it subsidized from tax revenues, while private insurers operate only when a profit potential exists. The nature of government insurance programs will be outlined later in this chapter.

4. Jeff D. Opdyke and Christopher Oster, "Hit With Big Losses, Insurers Put Squeeze on Homeowner Policies," *Wall Street Journal*, May 14, 2002.

5. Insurance is regulated by the states, a topic that will be covered in more detail in Chapter 7.

6. Arthur D. Postal, "Decision On Demutualization Cost Basis Sought," *National Underwriter*, Life and Health Edition, March 25, 2005. Accessed March 5, 2009. http://www.nationalunderwriter.com/lifeandhealth/nuonline/032805/L12decision.asp.

7. An exception: national commercial banks in communities of less than 5,000 have, for many years, had the right to sell insurance.

8. Mark E. Ruquet, "Insurer-Bank Integration Stampede Unlikely," *National Underwriter*, Property & Casualty/Risk & Benefits Management Edition, April 23, 2001.

9. Lisa S. Howard, "Tight Re Market Puts Heat On Fronts," *National Underwriter*, Property & Casualty/Risk & Benefits Management Edition, March 4, 2002.

10. President Reagan signed into law the Liability Risk Retention Act in October 1986 (an amendment to the Product Liability Risk Retention Act of 1981). The act permits formation of retention groups (a special form of captive) with fewer restrictions than existed before. The retention groups are similar to association captives. The act permits formation of such groups in the United States under more favorable conditions than have existed generally for association captives. The act may be particularly helpful to small businesses that could not feasibly self-insure but can do so within a designated group.

11. "Vermont Licenses Industry-Backed Airline Insurer," BestWire, June 11, 2002.

12. Sue Johnson, "Airline Captive May Be Formed in Second Quarter," *Best's Review*, March 2002. See also the document created by Marsh to explain the program along with other aviation protection programs (as of August 14, 2002) at http://www.marsh.se/files/Third%20Party%20War%20Liability%20Comparison.pdf.

13. For detailed information about PRIMA, search its Web site at http://www.primacentral.org/default.php.

CHAPTER 7
Insurance Operations

The decision to seek coverage is only the first of many important choices you will have to make about insurance. Whether you are acting as your own personal risk manager or on behalf of your business, it will help you to know how insurance companies work. This chapter will explain the internal operations of an insurance company and will dispel the notion that insurance jobs are all sales positions. The marketing aspect of insurance is important, as it is for any business, but it is not the only aspect. An interesting and distinctive characteristic of insurance is that it is really a business with two separate parts, each equally important to the success of the operation. One part is the insurance underwriting business; the other is the investment of the funds paid by insureds.

In this chapter we cover the following:

1. Links

2. Insurance operations: marketing, underwriting, and administration

3. Insurance operations: actuarial analysis and investments

4. Insurance operations: reinsurance, legal and regulatory issues, claims adjusting, and management

1. LINKS

As we have done in each chapter, we first link the chapter to the complete picture of our holistic risk management. As consumers, it is our responsibility to know where our premium money is going and how it is being used. When we transfer risk to the insurance company and pay the premium, we get an intangible product in return and a contract. However, this contract is for future payments in case of losses. Only when or if we have a loss will we actually see a return on our purchase of insurance. Therefore, it is imperative that the insurance company be there when we need it. To complete the puzzle of ensuring that our holistic risk management process is appropriate, we also need to understand how our insurance company operates. Because the risks are not transferred to just one insurer, we must learn about the operations of a series of insurers—the reinsurers that insure the primary insurers. The descriptions provided in this chapter are typical of most insurers. However, variations should be expected. To grasp how we relate to the operations of a typical insurer, look at Figure 7.1. The figure describes the fluid process of the operations within an insurer. Each function is closely linked to all the other functions, and none is performed in a vacuum. It is like a circular chain in which each link is as strong as the next one. Because insurers operate in markets with major influences, especially catastrophes (both natural and human-made), the external conditions affecting the insurers form an important part of this chapter. The regulatory structure of insurers is shown in the second part of the link in Figure 7.1, which separates the industry's institutions into those that are government-regulated and those that are non- or semiregulated. Regardless of regulation, however, insurers are subject to market conditions.

FIGURE 7.1 Links between the Holistic Risk Picture and Insurance Company Operations

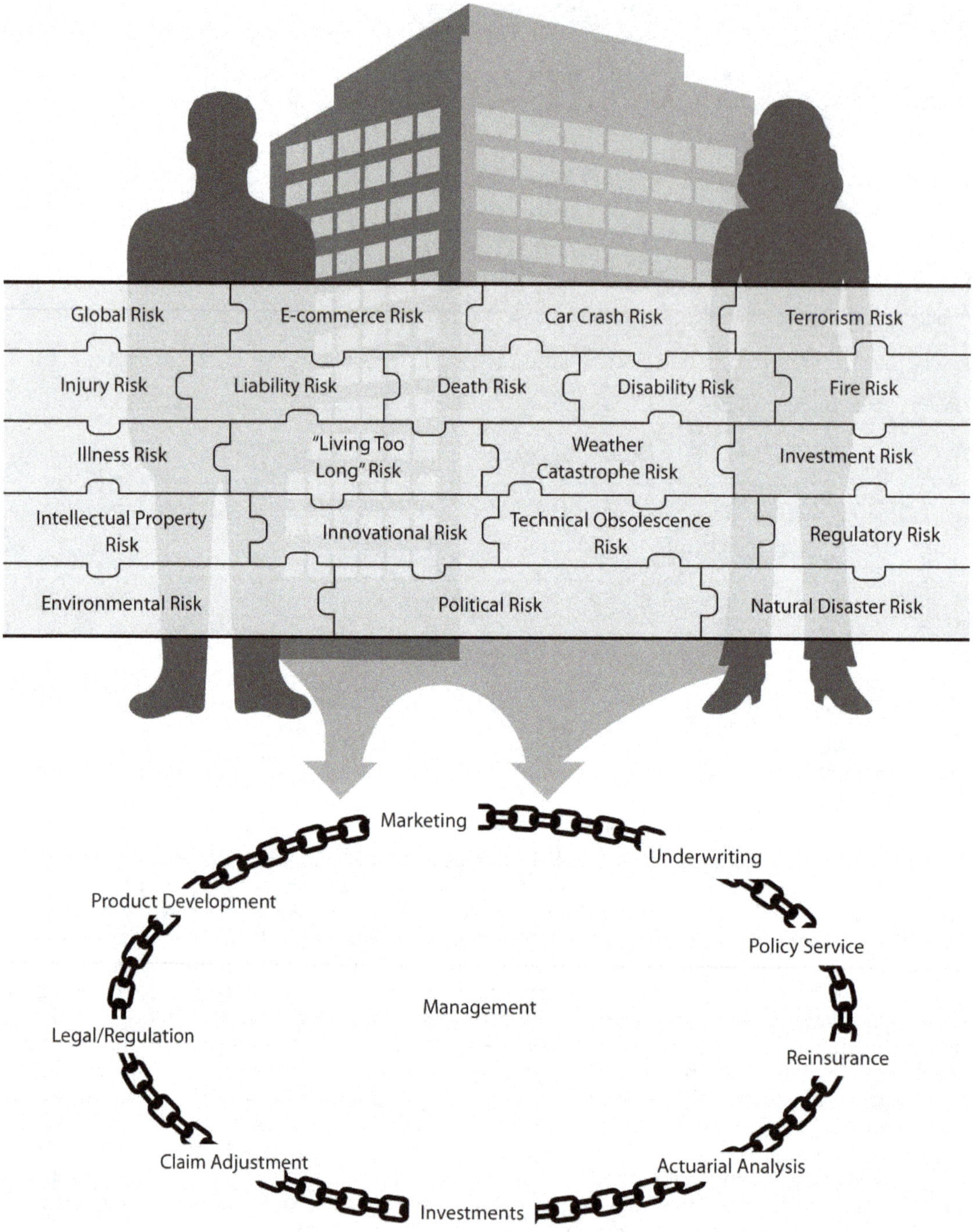

Thus, when we select an insurer, we need to understand not only the organizational structure of that insurance firm, we also need to be able to benefit from the regulatory safety net that it offers for our protection. Also important is our clear understanding of insurance market conditions affecting the products and their pricing. Major rate increases for coverage do not happen in a vacuum. While past losses are important factors in setting rates, outside market conditions, availability, and affordability of products are also very important factors in the risk management decision.

2.   INSURANCE OPERATIONS: MARKETING, UNDERWRITING, AND ADMINISTRATION

LEARNING OBJECTIVES

In this section we elaborate on the following:

- **Marketing activities within different segments of the insurance industry**
- **The various types of agency relationships**
- **How agents and brokers differ**
- **The major features of underwriting**

2.1   Marketing

We begin with marketing despite the fact that it is not the first step in starting a business. From a consumer's point of view, it is the first glimpse into the operations of an insurer. Insurance may be bought through agents, brokers, or (in some cases) directly from the insurer (via personal contact or on the Internet). An agent legally represents the company, whereas a broker represents the buyer and, in half of the states, also represents the insurer because of state regulations.[1] Both agents and brokers are compensated by the insurer. The compensation issue was brought to the limelight in 2004 when New York State Attorney General Eliot Spitzer opened an investigation of contingent commissions that brokers received from insurers; these contingent commissions were regarded as bid rigging. Contingent commissions are paid to brokers for bringing in better business and can be regarded as profit sharing. As a result of this investigation, regulators look for more transparency in the compensation disclosure of agents and brokers, and major brokerage houses stopped the practice of accepting contingency commission in the belief that clients view the practice negatively.[2]

In many states, **producer** is another name for both agents and brokers. This new name has been given to create some uniformity among the types of distribution systems. Because life/health insurance and property/casualty insurance developed separately in the United States, somewhat different marketing systems evolved. Therefore, we will discuss these systems separately.

producer

Another name for both agents and brokers.

Life/Health Insurance Marketing

Most life/health insurance is sold through agents, brokers, or (the newest term) producers, who are compensated by commissions. These commissions are added to the price of the policy. Some insurance is sold directly to the public without sales commissions. Fee-only financial planners often recommend such no-load insurance to their clients. Instead of paying an agent's commission, the client pays the planner a fee for advice and counseling and then buys directly from the no-load insurer. Unlike the agent, the planner has no incentive to recommend a high-commission product. Whether your total cost is lower depends on whether the savings on commissions offsets the planner's fee.

Some companies insist that their agents represent them exclusively, or at least that agents not submit applications to another insurer unless they themselves have refused to issue insurance at standard premium rates. Others permit their agents to sell for other companies, though these agents usually have a primary affiliation with one company and devote most of their efforts to selling its policies.

The two dominant types of life/health marketing systems are the general agency and the managerial (branch office) system.

General Agency System

A **general agent** is an independent businessperson rather than an employee of the insurance company and is authorized by contract with the insurer to sell insurance in a specified territory. Another major responsibility is the recruitment and training of subagents. Subagents usually are given the title of *agent* or *special agent*. Typically, subagents are agents of the insurer rather than of the general agent. The insurer pays commissions (a percentage of premiums) to the agents on both new and renewal business. The general agent receives an override commission (a percentage of agents' commissions) on all business generated or serviced by the agency, pays most of it to the subagents, and keeps the balance for expenses and profit. Agent compensation agreements are normally determined by the insurer.

In most cases, the general agent has an exclusive franchise for his or her territory. The primary responsibilities of the general agent are to select, train, and supervise subagents. In addition, general

general agent

An independent businessperson rather than an employee of the insurance company who is authorized by contract with the insurer to sell insurance in a specified territory.

agents provide office space and have administrative responsibilities for some customer service activities.

personal producing general agent

Agent who sells for one or more insurers, often with a higher-than-normal agent's commission and seldom hires other agents.

A large number of life/health insurers use personal producing general agents. A **personal producing general agent** sells for one or more insurers, often with a higher-than-normal agent's commission and seldom hires other agents. The extra commission helps cover office expenses. The trend is toward an agent representing several different insurers. This is desirable for consumers because a single insurer cannot have the best products for all needs. To meet a client's insurance needs more completely, the agent needs to have the flexibility to serve as a broker or a personal producing general agent for the insurer with the most desirable policy.

Managerial (Branch Office) System

branch manager

A company employee who is compensated by a combination of salary, bonus, and commissions related to the productivity of the office to which he or she is assigned.

A branch office is an extension of the home office headed by a branch manager. The **branch manager** is a company employee who is compensated by a combination of salary, bonus, and commissions related to the productivity of the office to which he or she is assigned. The manager also employs and trains agents for the company but cannot employ an agent without the consent of the company. Compensation plans for agents are determined by the company. All expenses of maintaining the office are paid by the company, which has complete control over the details of its operation.

Group and Supplemental Insurance Marketing

Group life, health, and retirement plans are sold to employers by agents in one of the systems described above or by brokers. An agent may be assisted in this specialized field by a group sales representative. Large volumes of group business are also placed through direct negotiations between employers and insurers. A brokerage firm or an employee benefits consulting firm may be hired on a fee-only basis by the employer who wishes to negotiate directly with insurers, thus avoiding commissions to the agent/broker. In these direct negotiations, the insurer typically is represented by a salaried group sales representative.

Supplemental insurance plans that provide life, health, and other benefits to employees through employer sponsorship and payroll deduction have become common. These plans are marketed by agents, brokers, and exclusive agents. The latter usually work on commissions; some receive salaries plus bonuses.

Property/Casualty Insurance Marketing

Like life/health insurance, most property/casualty insurance is sold through agents or brokers who are compensated on a commission basis, but some is sold by salaried representatives or by direct methods. The independent (American) agency system and the exclusive agency system account for the bulk of insurance sales.

Independent (American) Agency System

independent agent

Agent who usually represents several companies, pays all agency expenses, is compensated on a commission plus bonus basis, and makes all decisions concerning how the agency operates.

The distinguishing characteristics of the independent (American) agency system are the independence of the agent, the agent's bargaining position with the insurers he or she represents, and the fact that those who purchase insurance through the agent are considered by both insurers and agents to be the agent's customers rather than the insurer's. The **independent agent** usually represents several companies, pays all agency expenses, is compensated on a commission plus bonus basis, and makes all decisions concerning how the agency operates. Using insurer forms, the agent binds an insurer, sends underwriting information to the insurer, and later delivers a policy to the insured. The agent may or may not have the responsibility of collecting premiums. Legally, these agents represent the insurer, but as a practical matter they also represent the customer.

owns the x-date

Has the right to contact the customer when a policy is due for renewal.

An independent agent **owns the x-date**; that is, he or she has the right to contact the customer when a policy is due for renewal. This means that the insured goes with the agent if the agent no longer sells for the insurance company. This ownership right can be sold to another agent, and when the independent agent decides to retire or leave the agency, the right to contact large numbers of customers creates a substantial market value for the agency. This marketing system is also known as the American agency system. It is best recognized for the Big I advertisements sponsored by the Independent Insurance Agents & Brokers of America. These advertisements usually emphasize the independent agent's ability to choose the best policy and insurer for you. (Formerly known as the Independent Insurance Agents of America, the 106-year-old association recently added the "& Brokers" to more accurately describe its membership.[3])

Direct Writers and Exclusive Agents

Several companies, called **direct writers**,[4] market insurance through exclusive agents. **Exclusive agents** are permitted to represent only their company or a company in an affiliated group of insurance companies. A group is a number of separate companies operating under common ownership and management. This system is used by companies such as Allstate, Nationwide, and State Farm. These insurers compensate the agent through commissions that are lower than those paid to independent agents, partly because the insurer absorbs some expenses that are borne directly by independent agents. The insurer owns the x-date. The customer is considered to be the insurer's rather than the agent's, and the agent does not have as much independence as do those who operate under the independent agency system. Average operating expenses and premiums for personal lines of insurance tend to be lower than those in the independent agency system.

Some direct writers place business through **salaried representatives**, who are employees of the company. Compensation for such employees may be a salary and/or a commission plus bonus related to the amount and quality of business they secure. Regardless of the compensation arrangement, they are employees rather than agents.

Brokers

A considerable amount of insurance and reinsurance is placed through brokers. A **broker** solicits business from the insured, as does an agent, but the broker acts as the insured's legal agent when the business is placed with an insurer. In about half the states, brokers are required to be agents of the insurer. In the other states, brokers do not have ongoing contracts with insurers—their sole obligation is to the client. When it appears desirable, a broker may draft a specially worded policy for a client and then place the policy with an insurer. Some property/casualty brokers merely place insurance with an insurer and then rely on this company to provide whatever engineering and loss-prevention services are needed. Others have a staff of engineers to perform such services for clients. Modern brokerage firms provide a variety of related services, such as risk management surveys, information systems services related to risk management, complete administrative and claim services to self-insurers, and captive insurer management.

Brokers are a more significant part of the marketing mechanism in commercial property, liability, employee benefits, and marine insurance than in personal lines of insurance. Brokers are most active in metropolitan areas and among large insureds, where a broker's knowledge of specialized coverages and the market for them is important. Some brokerage firms operate on a local or regional basis, whereas others are national or international in their operations.

With today's proliferation of lines and services, it is extremely difficult for brokers to understand all the products completely. Brokers are always looking for unique product designs, but gaining access to innovative products and actually putting them into use are two different things. Generally, each broker selects about three favorite insurers. The broker's concern is the underwriting standards of their insurers. For example, a broker would like to be able to place a client who takes Prozac with an insurer that covers such clients.

Internet Marketing

With today's proliferation of **Internet marketing**, one can select an insurance product and compare price and coverage on the Internet. For example, someone interested in purchasing a life insurance policy can click on Insweb.com. If she or he is looking for health insurance, ehealthinsurance or other such Web sites present information and a questionnaire to fill out. The site will respond with quotes from insurers and details about the plans. The customer can then send contact information to selected insurers, who will begin the underwriting process to determine insurability and appropriate rates. The sale is not finalized through the Internet, but the connection with the agent and underwriters is made. Any Internet search engine will lead to many such Web sites.

Most insurance companies, like other businesses, set up their own Web sites to promote their products' features. They set up the sites to provide consumers with the tools to compare products and find the unique characteristics of the insurer. See the box, "Shopping for Insurance on the Internet" for a description of Internet sites.

Mass Merchandising

Mass merchandising is the selling of insurance by mail, telephone, television, or e-mail. Mass merchandising often involves a sponsoring organization such as an employer, trade association, university, or creditor; however, you are likely to be asked to respond directly to the insurer. Some mass merchandising mixes agents and direct response (mass mailing of information, for example, that includes a card the interested person can fill out and return); an agent handles the initial mailing and subsequently contacts the responding members of the sponsoring organization.

---

direct writers

Companies that market insurance through exclusive agents.

exclusive agents

Agents permitted to represent only their company or a company in an affiliated group of insurance companies.

salaried representatives

Employees of the company.

broker

Individual who solicits business from the insured and also acts as the insured's legal agent when the business is placed with an insurer.

Internet marketing

Selecting an insurance product and comparing price and coverage on the Internet.

mass merchandising

The selling of insurance by mail, telephone, television, or e-mail.

In some cases, you can save money buying insurance by mass merchandising methods. Direct response insurers, however, cannot provide the counseling you may receive from a good agent or financial planner.

Financial Planners

financial planner

Individual who facilitates some insurance sales by serving as a consultant on financial matters, primarily to high-income clients.

A **financial planner** facilitates some insurance sales by serving as a consultant on financial matters, primarily to high-income clients. An analysis of risk exposures and recommendations on appropriate risk management techniques, including insurance, are major parts of the financial planning process. A fee-only financial planner, knowledgeable in insurance, may direct you to good-quality, no-load insurance products when they are priced lower than comparable products sold through agents. You are already paying a fee for advice from the financial planner. Why also pay a commission to an insurance agent or broker?

In many instances, it is appropriate for the financial planner to send you to an insurance agent. Products available through agents may have a better value than the still limited supply of no-load products. Also, your financial planner is likely to be a generalist with respect to insurance, and you may need advice from a knowledgeable agent. In any event, financial planners are now part of the insurance distribution system.

Shopping for Insurance on the Internet

True to its name, Progressive was the first large insurer to begin selling insurance coverage via the Internet in the late 1990s. Other well-known names like Allstate and Hartford quickly followed suit. So-called aggregator sites like Insure.com, Quotesmith.com, Ehealthinsurance.com, and InsWeb.com joined in, offering one-stop shopping for a variety of products. To tap the potential of e-commerce, insurers have had to overcome one big challenge: how to sell complex products without confusing and driving away the customer. Therefore, the sale is not finalized on the Internet. The glimpse into the product is only the first step for comparative shopping.

An insurance application can be frustrating even when an agent is sitting across the desk explaining everything, but most people don't walk out in the middle of filling out a form. On the Internet, however, about half of those filling out a quote request quit because it is too complicated or time-consuming. Most of those who do finish are "just looking," comparing prices and services. Twenty-seven million shoppers priced insurance online in 2001, according to a recent study by the Independent Insurance Agents of America and twenty-six insurers, but less than 5 percent closed the deal electronically.

As shopping on the Internet becomes a boom business, each state department of insurance provides guidelines to consumers. For example, the Texas Department of Insurance issued tips for shopping smart on the Internet, as follows:

Insurance on the Internet—Shopping Tips and Dangers

- Be more cautious if the type of insurance you need recently became more expensive or harder to get and the policy costs far less than what other insurers charge.
- Don't succumb to high-pressure sales, last-chance deals of a lifetime, or suggestions that you drop one coverage for another without the chance to check it out thoroughly.
- Check with an accountant, attorney, financial adviser, a trusted friend, or relative before putting savings or large sums of money into any annuity, other investment, or trust.
- Get rate quotes and key information in writing and keep records.
- If you buy coverage, keep a file of all paperwork you completed online or received in the mail and signed, as well as any other documents related to your insurance, including the policy, correspondence, copies of advertisements, premium payment receipts, notes of conversations, and any claims submitted.
- Make sure you receive your policy—not a photocopy—within thirty days.

Sources: Lynna Goch, "What Works Online: Some Insurers Have Found the Key to Unlocking Online Sales," Best's Review, May 2002; Ron Panko, "IdentityWeb: Linking Agents and Customers," Best's Review, May 2002; Google search for "shopping for insurance on the Internet"; and http://www.tdi.state.tx.us/consumer/cpinsnet.html.

Professionalism in Marketing

Ideally, an agent has several years of experience before giving advice on complicated insurance matters. You will be interested in the agent's experience and educational qualifications, which should cover an extensive study of insurance, finance, and related subjects. A major route for life/health agents to gain this background is by meeting all requirements for the Chartered Life Underwriter (CLU) designation. The Chartered Financial Consultant (ChFC) designation from the American College (for information, see http://www.amercoll.edu/) is an alternative professional designation of interest to life/health agents. Property/casualty agents gain a good background by earning the Chartered Property and Casualty Underwriter (CPCU) designation granted by the American Institute for Property and Liability Underwriters (see http://www.aicpcu.org/). Another, broader designation with applications to insurance is Certified Financial Planner (CFP), awarded by the Certified Financial Planner Board of Standards (see http://www.cfp-board.org/).

2.2 Underwriting

Underwriting is the process of classifying the potential insureds into the appropriate risk classification in order to charge the appropriate rate. An **underwriter** decides whether or not to insure exposures on which applications for insurance are submitted. There are separate procedures for group underwriting and individual underwriting. For group underwriting, the group characteristics, demographics, and past losses are judged. Because individual insurability is not examined, even very sick people such as AIDS patients can obtain life insurance through a group policy. For individual underwriting, the insured has to provide evidence of insurability in areas of life and health insurance or specific details about the property and automobiles for property/casualty lines of business. An individual applicant for life insurance must be approved by the life insurance company underwriter, a process that is sometimes very lengthy. It is not uncommon for the application to include a questionnaire about lifestyle, smoking habits, medical status, and the medical status of close family members. For large amounts of life insurance, the applicant is usually required to undergo a medical examination.

Once the underwriter determines that insurance can be issued, the next decision is to apply the proper premium rate. Premium rates are determined for classes of insureds by the actuarial department. An underwriter's role is to decide which class is appropriate for each insured. The business of insurance inherently involves discrimination; otherwise, adverse selection would make insurance unavailable.

Some people believe that any characteristic over which we have no control, such as gender, race, and age, should be excluded from insurance underwriting and rating practices (although in life and annuity contracts, consideration of age seems to be acceptable). Their argument is that if insurance is intended in part to encourage safety, then its operation ought to be based on behavior, not on qualities with which we are born. Others argue that some of these factors are the best predictors of losses and expenses, and without them, insurance can function only extremely inefficiently. Additionally, some argument could be made that almost no factor is truly voluntary or controllable. Is a poor resident of Chicago, for instance, able to move out of the inner city? A *National Underwriter* article provided an interesting suggestion for mitigating negative characteristics: enclosing a personalized letter with an application to explain special circumstances.[5] For example, according to the article, "If your client is overweight, and his family is overweight, but living a long and healthy life, note both details on the record. This will give the underwriters more to go on." The article continues, "Sending letters with applications is long overdue. They will often shorten the underwriting cycle and get special risks—many of whom have been given a clean bill of health by their doctor or are well on their way to recovery—the coverage they need and deserve."

Over the years, insurers have used a variety of factors in their underwriting decisions. A number of these have become taboo from a public policy standpoint. Their use may be considered unfair discrimination. In automobile insurance, for instance, factors such as marital status and living arrangements have played a significant underwriting role, with divorced applicants considered less stable than never-married applicants. In property insurance, concern over redlining receives public attention periodically. **Redlining** occurs when an insurer designates a geographical area in which it chooses not to provide insurance, or to provide it only at substantially higher prices. These decisions are made without considering individual insurance applicants. Most often, the redlining is in poor urban areas, placing low-income inner-city dwellers at great disadvantage. A new controversy in the underwriting field is the use of genetic testing. In Great Britain, insurers use genetic testing to screen for Huntington's disease,[6] but U.S. companies are not yet using such tests. As genetic testing continues to improve, look for U.S. insurance companies to request access to that information as part of an applicant's medical history.

Two major areas of underwriting controversies are discussed in the box below, "Keeping Score—Is It Fair to Use Credit Rating in Underwriting?" and in "Insurance and Your Privacy—Who Knows?" in Chapter 8. The need for information is a balancing act between underwriting requirements and preserving the privacy of insureds. The tug-of-war between more and less information is a regulatory matter. The use of credit ratings in setting premiums illustrates a company's need to place insureds in the appropriate risk classification—a process that preserves the fundamental rules of insurance operations (discussed in Chapter 6). We will explore underwriting further in other chapters as we look at types of policies.

---

underwriting

The process of evaluating risks, selecting which risks to accept, and identifying potential adverse selection.

underwriter

Individual who decides whether or not to insure exposures on which applications for insurance are submitted.

redlining

When an insurer designates a geographical area in which it chooses not to provide insurance, or to provide it only at substantially higher prices.

Equal Credit Opportunity Act (ECOA)

Law requiring that the creditor give you a notice that tells you the specific reasons your application was rejected or the fact that you have the right to learn the reasons if you ask within sixty days.

Keeping Score—Is It Fair to Use Credit Rating in Underwriting?

Body-mass index, cholesterol level, SAT score, IQ: Americans are accustomed to being judged by the numbers. One important number that you may not be as familiar with is your credit score. Determined by the financial firm Fair, Isaac, and Co., a credit score (also known as a FICO score) is calculated from an individual's credit history, taking into account payment history, number of creditors, amounts currently owed, and similar factors.

Like your grade point average (GPA), your credit score is one simple number that sums up years of hard work (or years of goofing off). But while your GPA is unlikely to be important five years from now, your credit score will affect your major financial decisions for the rest of your life. This number determines whether you're eligible for incentive (low-rate) financing on new cars, how many credit card offers get stuffed in your mailbox each month, and what your mortgage rate will be. The U.S. Federal Trade Commission (FTC) issued a directive to consumers about the handling of credit scores. If you are denied credit, the FTC offers the following:

- If you are denied credit, the **Equal Credit Opportunity Act (ECOA)** requires that the creditor give you a notice that tells you the specific reasons your application was rejected or the fact that you have the right to learn the reasons if you ask within sixty days. If a creditor says that you were denied credit because you are too near your credit limits on your charge cards or you have too many credit card accounts, you may want to reapply after paying down your balances or closing some accounts. Credit scoring systems consider updated information and change over time.

- Sometimes, you can be denied credit because of information from a credit report. If so, the Fair Credit Reporting Act (FCRA) requires the creditor to give you the name, address, and phone number of the consumer reporting company that supplied the information. This information is free if you request it within sixty days of being turned down for credit. The consumer reporting company can tell you what's in your report, but only the creditor can tell you why your application was denied.

- If you've been denied credit, or didn't get the rate or credit terms you want, ask the creditor if a credit scoring system was used. If so, ask what characteristics or factors were used in that system, and the best ways to improve your application. If you get credit, ask the creditor whether you are getting the best rate and terms available and if you are not, ask why. If you are not offered the best rate available because of inaccuracies in your credit report, be sure to dispute the inaccurate information in your credit report.

Your credit score may also affect how much you'll pay for insurance. About half of the companies that write personal auto or homeowner's insurance now use credit data in underwriting or in setting premiums, and the bad credit penalty can be 20 percent or more. But it's not because they're worried that poor credit risks won't pay their insurance premiums. Rather, it's the strong relationship between credit scores and the likelihood of filing a claim, as study after study has borne out. Someone who spends money recklessly is also likely to drive recklessly, insurers point out; someone who is lazy about making credit card payments is apt to be lazy about trimming a tree before it causes roof damage. Often, a credit record is the best available predictor of future losses. Insurers vary on how much they rely on credit scoring—most consider it as one factor of many in setting premiums, while a few flat out refuse to insure anyone whose credit score is below a certain number—but almost all see it as a valuable underwriting tool. It's only fair, insurers say, for low-risk customers to pay lower premiums rather than subsidizing those more likely to file claims.

Consumer advocates disagree. Using credit scores in this manner is discriminatory and inflexible, they say, and some state insurance commissioners agree. Consumer advocate and former Texas insurance commissioner Robert Hunter finds credit scoring ludicrous. "If I have a poor credit score because I was laid off as a result of terrorism, what does that have to do with my ability to drive?" he asked at a meeting of the National Association of Insurance Commissioners in December 2001. Therefore, in 2004, twenty-four states have adopted credit scoring legislation and/or regulation that is based on a National Conference of Insurance Legislators (NCOIL) model law.

The debate over the use of credit scoring has spread across the country. More states are considering regulations or legislation to curb its use by insurers.

Questions for Discussion

1. Mr. Smith and Mr. Jones, both twenty-eight years old, have the same educational and income levels. Mr. Smith has one speeding ticket and a credit score of 600. Mr. Jones has a clean driving record and a credit score of 750. Who should pay more for automobile insurance?

2. After some investigation, you discover that Mr. Smith's credit score is low because his wife recently died after a long illness and he has fallen behind in paying her medical bills. Mr. Jones's driving record is clean because he hired a lawyer to have his many speeding tickets reduced to nonmoving violations. Who should pay more for auto insurance?

3. Considering the clear correlation between credit scores and losses, is credit scoring discriminatory?

4. Should credit scores count?

Sources: Barbara Bowers, "Giving Credit Its Due: Insurers, Agents, Legislators, Regulators and Consumers Battle to Define the Role of Insurance Scoring" and "Insurers Address Flurry of Insurance-Scoring Legislative Initiatives," Best's Review, May 2002; U.S. Federal Trade Commission at http://www.ftc.gov/ bcp/conline/pubs/credit/scoring.htm. See http://www.ncoil.org/ and all media outlets for coverage of this issue, which occurs very frequently.

2.3 Administration

After insurance is sold and approved by the underwriter, records must be established, premiums collected, customer inquiries answered, and many other administrative jobs performed. Administration is defined broadly here to include accounting, information systems, office administration, customer service, and personnel management.

Service

Service is the ultimate indicator on which the quality of the product provided by insurance depends. An agent's or broker's advice and an insurer's claim practices are the primary services that the typical individual or business needs. In addition, prompt, courteous responses to inquiries concerning changes in the policy, the availability of other types of insurance, changes of address, and other routine matters are necessary.

Another service of major significance that some insurers offer, primarily to commercial clients, is engineering and loss control. **Engineering and loss control** is concerned with methods of prevention and reduction of loss whenever the efforts required are economically feasible. Much of the engineering and loss-control activity may be carried on by the insurer or under its direction. The facilities the insurer has to devote to such efforts and the degree to which such efforts are successful is an important element to consider in selecting an insurer. Part of the risk manager's success depends on this element. Engineering and loss-control services are particularly applicable to workers' compensation and boiler and machinery exposures. With respect to the health insurance part of an employee benefits program, loss control is called cost containment and may be achieved primarily through managed care and wellness techniques.

service

The ultimate indicator upon which the quality of the product provided by insurance depends.

engineering and loss control

Methods of prevention and reduction of loss whenever the efforts required are economically feasible.

KEY TAKEAWAYS

In this section you studied the following:

- The marketing function of insurance companies differs for life/health and property/casualty segments.
- Agents represent insurers and may work under a general agency or managerial arrangement and as independent agents or direct writers.
- Brokers represent insureds and place policies with appropriate insurers.
- Internet marketing, mass merchandising campaigns, and financial planning are other methods of acquiring customers.
- Underwriting classifies insureds into risk categories to determine the appropriate rate.

DISCUSSION QUESTIONS

1. Would you rather shop for insurance on the Internet or call an agent?
2. Advertising by the Independent Insurance Agents & Brokers of America extols the unique features of the American agency system and the independent agent. Its logo is the Big I. Does this advertising influence your choice of an agent? Do you prefer one type of agent to others? If so, why?
3. What does an underwriter do? Why is the underwriting function in an insurance company so important?
4. Why are insurers using credit scoring in their underwriting? In what areas is it possible to misjudge a potential insured when using credit scoring? What other underwriting criteria would you suggest to replace the credit scoring criterion?

3. INSURANCE OPERATIONS: ACTUARIAL AND INVESTMENT

> ## LEARNING OBJECTIVES
>
> In this section we elaborate on the following:
>
> - **The role of actuarial analysis in insurance operations**
> - **The tools actuaries utilize to perform their work**
> - **The investments of insurers, or investment income—the other side of insurance operation**
> - **The fact that insurers are holders of large asset portfolios**

3.1 Actuarial Analysis

actuarial analysis

A highly specialized mathematic analysis that deals with the financial and risk aspects of insurance.

Actuarial analysis is a highly specialized mathematic analysis that deals with the financial and risk aspects of insurance. Actuarial analysis takes past losses and projects them into the future to determine the reserves an insurer needs to keep and the rates to charge. An **actuary** determines proper rates and reserves, certifies financial statements, participates in product development, and assists in overall management planning.

actuary

Individual who determines proper rates and reserves, certifies financial statements, participates in product development, and assists in overall management planning.

Actuaries are expected to demonstrate technical expertise by passing the examinations required for admission into either the Society of Actuaries (for life/health actuaries) or the Casualty Actuarial Society (for property/casualty actuaries). Passing the examinations requires a high level of mathematical knowledge and skill.

Prices and Reserves

Property/Casualty Lines—Loss Development

The rates or premiums for insurance are based first and foremost on the past experience of losses. Actuaries calculate the rates using various procedures and techniques. The most modern techniques include sophisticated regression analysis and data mining tools. In essence, the actuary first has to estimate the expected claim payments (equaling the net premium) then "loads" the figure by factors meant to accommodate the underwriting, management, and claims handling expenses. In addition, other elements may be considered, such as a loading to cover the uncertainty element.

In some insurance lines (called long tail lines), claims are settled over a long period; therefore, the company must estimate its future payments before it can determine losses. The payments still pending and will be paid in the future are held as a liability for the insurance company and are called loss reserves or pending (or outstanding) losses. Typically, the claims department personnel give their estimates of the amounts that are expected to be paid for each open claim file, and the sum of these case by case estimates makes up the case estimates reserve. The actuaries offer their estimates based on sophisticated statistical analysis of aggregated data. Actuaries sometimes have to estimate, as a part of the loss reserves, the payments for claims that have not yet been reported as well. These incurred but not yet reported claims are referred to by the initials IBNR in industry parlance.

The loss reserves estimation is based on data of past claim payments. Such data is typically presented in the form of a triangle. Actuaries use many techniques to turn the triangle into a forecast. Some of the traditional, but still popular, methods are quite intuitive. For pedagogical reasons, we shall demonstrate one of those methods below. A more sophisticated and modern concept is presented in the appendix to this chapter (Section 5) and reveals deficiencies of the traditional methods.

loss development

The calculation of how amounts paid for losses increase (mature) over time for the purpose of future projection.

A hypothetical example of one loss-reserving technique is featured here in Table 7.1 through Table 7.5. The technique used in these tables is known as a triangular method of loss development to the ultimate. The example is for illustration only. **Loss development** is the calculation of how amounts paid for losses increase (or mature) over time for the purpose of future projection. Because the claims are paid progressively over time, like medical bills for an injury, the actuarial analysis has to project how losses will be developed into the future based on their past development.

With property/casualty lines such as product liability, the insurer's losses can continue for many years after the initial occurrence of the accident. For example, someone who took certain weight-loss medications in 1994 (the "accident year") might develop heart trouble six years later. Health problems from asbestos contact or tobacco use can occur decades after the accident actually occurred.

Table 7.1 describes an insurance company's incurred losses for product liability from 1994 to 2000. **Incurred losses** are both paid losses plus known but not yet paid losses. Look at accident year 1996: over the first twelve months after those accidents, the company posted losses of $38.901 million related to those accidents. Over the next twelve months—as more injuries came to light or belated claims were filed or lawsuits were settled—the insurer incurred almost $15 million, so that the cumulative losses after twenty-four developed months comes to $53.679 million. Each year brought more losses relating to accidents in 1996, so that by the end of the sixty-month development period, the company had accumulated $70.934 million in incurred losses for incidents from accident year 1996. The table ends there, but the incurred losses continue; the ultimate total is not yet known.

To calculate how much money must be kept in reserve for losses, actuaries must estimate the ultimate incurred loss for each accident year. They can do so by calculating the rate of growth of the losses for each year and then extending that rate to predict future losses. First, we calculate the rate for each development period. In accident year 1996, the $38.901 million loss in the first development period increased to $53.679 million in the second development period. The loss development factor for the twelve- to twenty-four-month period is therefore 1.380 million (53.679/38.901), meaning that the loss increased, or developed, by a factor of 1.380 (or 38 percent). The factor for twenty-four- to thirty-six months is 1.172 (62.904/53.679). The method to calculate all the factors follows the same pattern: the second period divided by first period. Table 7.2 shows the factors for each development period from Table 7.1.

incurred losses

Paid losses plus known, but not yet paid losses.

TABLE 7.1 Incurred Losses for Accident Years by Development Periods (in Millions of Dollars)

Developed Months	Accident Year						
	1994	1995	1996	1997	1998	1999	2000
12	$37.654	$38.781	$38.901	$36.980	$37.684	$39.087	$37.680
24	53.901	53.789	53.679	47.854	47.091	47.890	
36	66.781	61.236	62.904	56.781	58.976		
48	75.901	69.021	67.832	60.907			
60	79.023	73.210	70.934				
72	81.905	79.087					
84	83.215						

TABLE 7.2 Loss Factors for Accident Years by Development Periods

Developed Months	Accident Year					
	1994	1995	1996	1997	1998	1999
12–24	1.431	1.387	1.380	1.294	1.250	1.225
24–36	1.239	1.138	1.172	1.187	1.252	
36–48	1.137	1.127	1.078	1.073		
48–60	1.041	1.061	1.046			
60–72	1.036	1.080				
72–84	1.016					
84–ultimate						

After we complete the computation of all the factors in Table 7.2, we transpose the table in order to compute the averages for each development period. The transposed Table 7.2 is in Table 7.3. The averages of the development factors are at the bottom of the table. You see, for example, that the average of factors for the thirty-six- to forty-eight-month development period of all accident years is 1.104. This means that, on average, losses increased by a factor of 1.104 (or 10.4 percent, if you prefer) in that period. That average is an ordinary mean. To exclude anomalies, however, actuaries often exclude the highest and lowest factors in each period, and average the remainders. The last line in Table 7.3 is the average, excluding the high and low, and this average is used in Table 7.4 to complete the triangle.

TABLE 7.3 Averages of the Incurred Loss Factors for Each Accident Year

Accident Year	Developed Months					
	12–24	24–36	36–48	48–60	60–72	72–84
1994	1.431	1.239	1.137	1.041	1.036	1.016
1995	1.387	1.138	1.127	1.061	1.080	
1996	1.380	1.172	1.078	1.046		
1997	1.294	1.187	1.073			
1998	1.250	1.252				
1999	1.225					
	12–24	24–36	36–48	48–60	60–72	72–84
Average	1.328	1.198	1.104	1.049	1.058	1.016
Average of last three years	1.256	1.204	1.093	1.049	1.058	1.016
Average of last four years	1.287	1.187	1.104	1.049	1.058	1.016
Average excluding high and low	1.328	1.199	1.103	1.046	1.058	1.016

In Table 7.4, we complete the incurred loss factors for the whole period of development. The information in bold is from Table 7.2. The information in italics is added for the later periods when incurred loss data are not yet available. These are the predictions of future losses. Thus, for accident year 1997, the bold part shows the factors from Table 7.2, which were derived from the actual incurred loss information in Table 7.1. We see from Table 7.4 that we can expect losses to increase in any forty-eight- to sixty-month period by a factor of 1.046, in a sixty- to seventy-two-month period by 1.058, and in a seventy-two- to eighty-four-month period by 1.016. The development to ultimate factor is the product of all estimated factors: for 1997, it is 1.046 × 1.058 × 1.016 × 1.02 = 1.147. Actuaries adjust the development-to-ultimate factor based on their experience and other information.[7]

To determine ultimate losses, these factors can be applied to the dollar amounts in Table 7.1. Table 7.5 provides the incurred loss estimates to ultimate payout for each accident year for this book of business. To illustrate how the computation is done, we estimate total incurred loss for accident year 1999. The most recent known incurred loss for accident year 1999 is as of 24 months: $47.890 million. To estimate the incurred losses at thirty-six months, we multiply by the development factor 1.199 and arrive at $57.426 million. That $57.426 million is multiplied by the applicable factors to produce a level of $63.326 million after forty-eight months, and $66.239 million after sixty months. Ultimately, the total payout for accident year 1999 is predicted to be $72.625 million. Because $47.890 million has already been paid out, the actuary will recommend keeping a reserve of $24.735 million to pay future claims. It is important to note that the ultimate level of incurred loss in this process includes incurred but not reported (IBNR) losses. **Incurred but not reported (IBNR)** losses are estimated losses that insureds did not claim yet, but they are expected to materialize in the future. This is usually an estimate that is hard to accurately project and is the reason the final projections of September 11, 2001, losses are still in question.

incurred but not reported (IBNR)

Estimated losses that insureds did not claim yet but are expected to materialize in the future.

TABLE 7.4 Development of the Triangles of Incurred Loss Factors to Ultimate for Each Accident Year

Developed Months	Accident Year						
	1994	1995	1996	1997	1998	1999	2000
12–24	**1.431**	**1.387**	**1.380**	**1.294**	**1.250**	**1.225**	1.328
24–36	**1.239**	**1.138**	**1.172**	**1.187**	**1.252**	1.199	1.199
36–48	**1.137**	**1.127**	**1.078**	**1.073**	1.103	1.103	1.103
48–60	**1.041**	**1.061**	**1.046**	1.046	1.046	1.046	1.046
60–72	**1.036**	**1.080**	1.058	1.058	1.058	1.058	1.058
72–84	**1.016**	1.016	1.016	1.016	1.016	1.016	1.016
84–ultimate*	1.020	1.020	1.020	1.020	1.020	1.020	1.020
Development to ultimate†	1.020	1.036	1.096	1.147	1.265	1.517	2.014

* Actuaries use their experience and other information to determine the factor that will be used from 84 months to ultimate. This factor is not available to them from the original triangle of losses.

† For example, the development to ultimate for 1997 is 1.046 × 1.058 × 1.016 × 1.02 = 1.147.

TABLE 7.5   Development of the Triangle of Incurred Losses to Ultimate (in Millions of Dollars)

Developed Months	Accident Year							Total
	1994	**1995**	**1996**	**1997**	**1998**	**1999**	**2000**	**Total**
12	$37.654	$38.781	$38.901	$36.980	$37.684	$39.087	$37.680	
24	53.901	53.789	53.679	47.854	47.091	47.890	**50.039**	
36	66.781	61.236	62.904	56.781	58.976	**57.426**	**60.003**	
48	75.901	69.021	67.832	60.907	**65.035**	63.326	66.167	
60	79.023	73.210	70.934	**63.709**	68.027	66.239	69.211	
72	81.905	79.087	**75.048**	67.404	71.972	70.080	73.225	
84	83.215	**80.352**	76.249	68.482	73.123	71.201	74.396	
Ultimate	**84.879**	**81.959**	77.773	69.852	74.586	72.625	**75.884**	537.559
Pd. to date	83.215	79.087	70.934	60.907	58.976	47.890	37.680	438.689
Reserve	1.664	2.872	6.839	8.945	15.610	24.735	38.204	98.870

The process of loss development shown in the example of Table 7.1 through Table 7.5 is used also for rate calculations because actuaries need to know the ultimate losses each book of business will incur. **Rate calculations** are the computations of how much to charge for insurance coverage once the ultimate level of loss is estimated, plus factors for taxes, expenses, and returns on investments.

Catastrophe (Cat) Modeling

Catastrophe (cat) modeling is composed of sophisticated statistical and technological mathematical equations and analysis that help predict future occurrences of natural and human-made disastrous events with large severity of losses. These models are relatively new and are made possible by the exponential improvements of information systems and statistical modeling over the years. Cat modeling relies on computer technology to synthesize loss data, assess historical disaster statistics, incorporate risk features, and run event simulations as an aid in predicting future losses. From this information, cat models project the impact of hypothetical catastrophes on residential and commercial properties.[8]

Cat modeling is concerned with predicting the future risk of catastrophes, primarily in the form of natural disasters. Cat modeling has its roots in the late 1980s and came to be utilized considerably following Hurricane Andrew in 1992 and the Northridge earthquake in 1994.[9] The parallel rapid sophistication of computer systems during this period was fortuitous and conducive to the growth of cat modeling. Today, every conceivable natural disaster is considered in cat models. Common hazard scenarios include hurricanes, earthquakes, tornados, and floods. One catastrophic event of increased concern in recent years is that of terrorism; some effort has been made to quantify the impact of this risk through cat models as well.[10]

Development of catastrophe models is complex, requiring the input of subject matter experts such as meteorologists, engineers, mathematicians, and actuaries. Due to the highly specialized nature and great demand for risk management tools, consulting firms have emerged to offer cat modeling solutions. The three biggest players in this arena are AIR Worldwide, Risk Management Solutions (RMS), and EQECAT.[11] The conclusions about exposures drawn from the models of different organizations are useful to insurers because they allow for better loss predictions of specific events.

Based on inputs regarding geographic locations, physical features of imperiled structures, and quantitative information about existing insurance coverage, catastrophe models render an output regarding the projected frequency, severity, and the overall dollar value of a catastrophic occurrence. From these results, it is possible to place property into appropriate risk categories. Thus, cat modeling can be extremely useful from an underwriting standpoint. Additionally, indications of high-dollar, high-severity risks in a particular region would certainly be influential to the development of premium rates and the insurer's decision to explore reinsurance options (discussed in the next section of this chapter). Cat models are capable of estimating losses for a portfolio of insured properties.[12] Clearly, the interest that property/casualty insurers have in loss projections from hurricane catastrophes in southern Florida would benefit from this type of modeling.

Reliance on cat models came under fire following the devastating back-to-back hurricane seasons of 2004 and 2005. Critics argued that the models that were utilized underestimated the losses. It is important to note that the insurance industry is not the only market for cat models; consequently, different methodologies are employed depending on the needs of the end-user. These methodologies might incorporate different assumptions, inputs, and algorithms in calculation.[13] The unusually active 2004 and 2005 hurricane seasons could similarly be considered outside a normal standard deviation and thus unaccounted for by the models. In response to criticisms, refinements by developers following

rate calculations

The computation of how much to charge for insurance coverage once the ultimate level of loss is estimated plus factors for taxes, expenses, and returns on investments.

catastrophe (cat) modeling

The use of computer technology to synthesize loss data, assess historical disaster statistics, incorporate risk features, and run event simulations as an aid in predicting future losses.

Hurricane Katrina included near-term projections providing probable maximum loss estimates using short-term expectations of hurricane activity.

Life and Annuity Lines

mortality tables

Tables that indicate the percent of expected deaths for each age group.

premium elements

The adjustments for various factors in life insurance premiums.

investment income

Returns from all the assets held by the insurers from both capital investment and from premiums.

For life insurance, actuaries use **mortality tables**, which predict the percentage of people in each age group who are expected to die each year. This percentage is used to estimate the required reserves and to compute life insurance rates. Life insurance, like other forms of insurance, is based on three concepts: pooling many exposures into a group, accumulating a fund paid for by contributions (premiums) from the members of the group, and paying from this fund for the losses of those who die each year. That is, life insurance involves the group sharing of individual losses. To set premium rates, the insurer must be able to calculate the probability of death at various ages among its insureds, based on pooling. Life insurers must collect enough premiums to cover mortality costs (the cost of claims). In addition to covering mortality costs, a life insurance premium, like a property/casualty premium, must reflect several adjustments, as noted in Table 7.6. The adjustments for various factors in life insurance premiums are known as **premium elements**. First, the premium is reduced because the insurer expects to earn **investment income**, or returns from all the assets held by the insurers from both capital investment and from premiums. Investment is a very important aspect of the other side of the insurance business, as discussed below. Insurers invest the premiums they receive from insureds until losses need to be paid. Income from the investments is an offset in the premium calculations. By reducing the rates, most of an insurer's investment income benefits consumers. Second, the premium is increased to cover the insurer's marketing and administrative expenses, as described above. Taxes are the third component; those that are levied on the insurer also must be recovered. Fourth, in calculating premiums, an actuary usually increases the premium to cover the insurer's risk of not predicting future losses accurately. The fifth element is the profits that the insurer should obtain because insurers are not "not for profit" organizations. All life insurance premium elements are depicted in Table 7.6 below. The actual prediction of deaths and the estimation of other premium elements are complicated actuarial processes.

TABLE 7.6 Term Premium Elements

Mortality Cost

− Investment income

+ Expense charge

+ Taxes

+ Risk change

+ Profit

= Gross premium charge

The mortality rate has two important characteristics that greatly influence insurer practices and the nature of life insurance contracts. First, yearly probabilities of death rise with age. Second, for practical reasons, actuaries set at 1.0 the probability of death at an advanced age, such as ninety-nine. That is, death during that year is considered a certainty, even though some people survive. The characteristics are illustrated with the mortality curve.

Mortality Curve

mortality curve

Curve that illustrates the relationship between age and the probability of death.

If we plot the probability of death for males by age, as in Figure 7.2, we have a mortality curve. The **mortality curve** illustrates the relationship between age and the probability of death. It shows that the mortality rate for males is relatively high at birth but declines until age ten. It then rises until age twenty-one and declines between ages twenty-two and twenty-nine. This decline apparently reflects many accidental deaths among males in their teens and early twenties, followed by a subsequent decrease. The rise is continuous for females older than age ten and for males after age twenty-nine. The rise is rather slow until middle age, at which point it begins to accelerate. At the more advanced ages, it rises very rapidly.

FIGURE 7.2 Male Mortality Curve

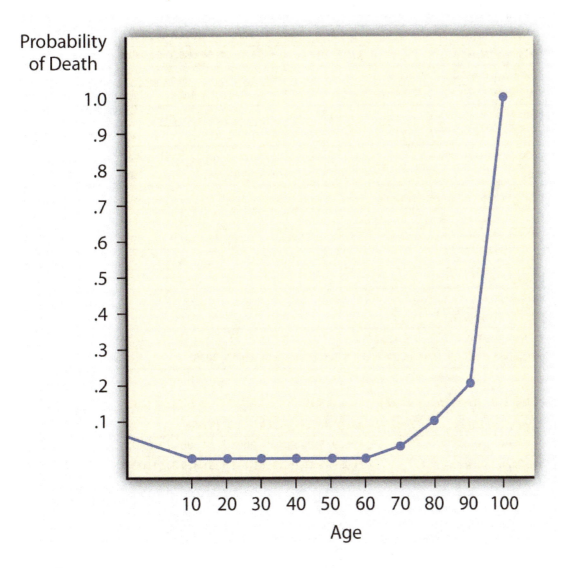

3.2   Investments

As noted above, insurance companies are in two businesses: the insurance business and the investment business. The insurance side is underwriting and reserving (liabilities), while the investment side is the area of securing the best rate of return on the assets entrusted to the insurer by the policyholders seeking the security. Investment income is a significant part of total income in most insurance companies. Liability accounts in the form of reserves are maintained on balance sheets to cover future claims and other obligations such as taxes and premium reserves. Assets must be maintained to cover the reserves and still leave the insurer with an adequate net worth in the form of capital and surplus. **Capital and surplus** are the equivalent of equity on the balance sheet of any firm—the net worth of the firm, or assets minus liabilities.

The investment mix of the life/health insurance industry is shown Table 7.7 and that of the property/casualty industry is shown in Table 7.8. As you can see, the assets of the life insurance industry in the United States were $4.95 trillion in 2007. This included majority investments in the credit markets, which includes bonds of all types and mortgage-backed securities of $387.5 billion. As discussed in Chapter 1 and the box below, "Problem Investments and the Credit Crisis," many of these securities were no longer performing during the credit crisis of 2008–2009. In comparison, the U.S. property casualty industry's asset holdings in 2007 were $1.37 trillion, with $125.8 billion in mortgage-backed securities. In Chapter 5, we included a discussion of risk management of the balance sheet to ensure that the net worth of the insurer is not lost when assets held are no longer performing. The capital and surplus of the U.S. property/casualty industry reached $531.3 billion at year-end 2007, up from $499.4 billion at year-end 2006. The capital and surplus of the U.S. life/health insurance industry was $252.8 billion in 2007, up from $244.4 billion in 2006.[14]

capital and surplus

The equivalent of equity on the balance sheet of any firm—the net worth of the firm, or assets minus liabilities.

TABLE 7.7 Life/Health Insurance Industry Asset Mix, 2003–2007 ($ Billions)

Life/Health Insurer Financial Asset Distribution, 2003–2007 ($ Billions)					
	2003	2004	2005	2006	2007
Total financial assets	**$3,772.8**	**$4,130.3**	**$4,350.7**	**$4,685.3**	**$4,950.3**
Checkable deposits and currency	47.3	53.3	47.7	56.1	58.3
Money market fund shares	151.4	120.7	113.6	162.3	226.6
Credit market instruments	2,488.3	2,661.4	2,765.4	2,806.1	2,890.8
Open market paper	55.9	48.2	40.2	53.1	57.9
U.S. government securities	420.7	435.6	459.7	460.6	467.7
Treasury	71.8	78.5	91.2	83.2	80.2
Agency and GSE[15] -backed securities	348.9	357.1	368.5	377.4	387.5
Municipal securities	26.1	30.1	32.5	36.6	35.3
Corporate and foreign bonds	1,620.2	1,768.0	1,840.7	1,841.9	1,889.7
Policy loans	104.5	106.1	106.9	110.2	113.9
Mortgages	260.9	273.3	285.5	303.8	326.2
Corporate equities	919.3	1,053.9	1,161.8	1,364.8	1,491.5
Mutual fund shares	91.7	114.4	109.0	148.8	161.4
Miscellaneous assets	74.7	126.6	153.1	147.1	121.6
Source: Board of Governors of the Federal Reserve System, June 5, 2008.					

Source: Insurance Information Institute, Accessed March 6, 2009, http://www.iii.org/media/facts/statsbyissue/life/.

TABLE 7.8 Property/Casualty Insurance Industry Asset Mix, 2003–2007 ($ Billions)

Property/Casualty Insurer Financial Asset Distribution, 2003–2007 ($ Billions)					
	2003	2004	2005	2006	2007
Total financial assets	**$1,059.7**	**$1,162.2**	**$1,243.8**	**$1,329.3**	**$1,373.6**
Checkable deposits and currency	34.6	25.9	21.0	29.9	42.7
Security repurchase agreements[16]	52.8	63.1	68.9	66.0	53.8
Credit market instruments	625.2	698.8	765.8	813.5	840.0
U.S. government securities	180.1	183.4	187.1	197.8	180.9
Treasury	64.7	71.3	69.2	75.8	55.1
Agency and GSE[17] -backed securities	115.4	112.1	117.9	122.0	125.8
Municipal securities	224.2	267.8	313.2	335.2	368.7
Corporate and foreign bonds	218.9	245.3	262.8	277.0	285.6
Commercial mortgages	2.1	2.4	2.7	3.5	4.8
Corporate equities	178.4	196.6	199.5	227.0	235.3
Trade receivables	79.3	79.6	82.1	87.0	85.4
Miscellaneous assets	85.0	93.0	100.7	99.0	108.7
Source: Board of Governors of the Federal Reserve System, June 5, 2008.					

Source: Insurance Information Institute, Accessed March 6, 2009, http://www.iii.org/media/facts/statsbyissue/life/.

The liabilities are composed mostly of reserves for loss payments. For the life insurance industry, the largest component of liabilities is reserves for pensions. Life reserves are the second-largest component. For property/casualty insurers, the reserves are for all lines of insurance, depending on the mix of products sold by each company.

Many conglomerate insurance corporations own their own investment firms and provide mutual funds. In this area, insurers, like other financial institutions, are subject to regulation by the states and by the Securities and Exchange Commission.

Problem Investments and the Credit Crisis

The greater risk faced by insurance companies is not the threat of going out of business due to insufficient sales volume, but the possibility that losses will be greater than anticipated and that they won't be covered through reserves and investment income. This further reinforces the importance of comprehending the nature of insureds' business and properly categorizing their risks on the underwriting side, while accurately capturing loss expectations on the actuarial side. Insuring common risks in high volume leads to more accuracy in predicting losses, but these risks do not vanish simply because they have been aggregated by the insurer. Unfortunately, this concept was not taken into consideration by several large investment banks and some insurance companies during the credit crisis beginning in 2007.

The credit crisis began when the U.S. housing bubble burst, setting off a protracted period characterized by increased valuation in real property, low interest rates, speculative investing, and massive demand for homes. During the housing bubble, low interest rates coupled with high liquidity were viewed as sufficiently favorable conditions to permit the extension of credit to high-risk (or subprime) borrowers. Many people who would otherwise not qualify for loans found themselves with mortgages and the homes of their dreams. Lenders protected themselves through the issuance of variable interest rate mortgages, whereby increased risk could be transferred to borrowers in the form of interest rate hikes. While this had the potential to put already high-risk (subprime) borrowers in an even worse position to meet their monthly obligations, borrowers counted on the very liquid nature of real estate during this period as a crutch to salvage their investments. Because home valuations and turnover were rising at such rapid rates, it was reasoned that financially strapped borrowers could simply sell and pay off their mortgages rather than face foreclosure.

The cycle of high turnover feeding into the housing bubble was halted when excess inventory of new homes and interest rate increases led to a downward correction of housing prices in 2005.[18] When lenders tried to pass these rate increases on to their buyers—many of whom had put little money down and had lived in their homes for less than a year—mortgage payments skyrocketed, even to the point of leaving buyers owing more than their homes were worth (negative equity). Home buying activity thus halted, leaving real estate a highly illiquid investment. The worst-case scenario was materializing, with foreclosures leaping to a staggering 79 percent in 2007, comprised of about 1.3 million homes.[19]

During the housing bubble, the concept of risk transfer was carried out to an egregious extent. Lenders recognized the inherent riskiness of their activities, but they compounded the problem by attempting to transfer this risk to the very source of it. In other cases, subprime loans were sold to investment banks, who bundled them into exotic investment vehicles known as mortgage-backed securities (MBSs). These securities, derived mainly from subprime mortgages, ordinarily would be comparable to junk bonds in their risk assessment. Nevertheless, by dividing them into different investment classifications and purchasing credit-default swap (CDS) insurance (discussed below), investment banks were able to acquire acceptable grades on MBSs from the major rating agencies.[20] Investment-grade MBSs were in turn marketed as collateralized debt obligations (CDOs) and other options and sold to institutional investors. Ultimately, this group was left holding the bag when foreclosures rippled through the system, rendering the derivative investments worthless. Thus, the lending pendulum swung in the opposite direction, making it difficult for normally creditworthy borrowers to secure even rudimentary business loans. The pass-the-buck mentality with respect to risk transfer precipitated this credit crunch, which came to be known as the credit crisis. Everyone wanted the risky mortgage-backed securities off their balance sheets without acknowledging the potential folly of investing in them in the first place.

As it relates to the insurance industry, recall that insurers must hold assets that are sufficient to cover their liabilities (as discussed in the previous section) at any given time. In much the same way that a mortgage holder is required to purchase mortgage insurance to protect the lender when equity accounts for less than 25 percent of the total value of his or her home, issuers of MBSs engage in what are called credit default swaps (CDSs) to reassure investors.[21] Insuring CDSs means that an insurer, rather than the MBS issuer, will deliver the promised payment to MBS investors in the event of default (in this case, foreclosure of the underlying mortgages).

AIG was one of the largest issuers of CDS insurance at the time of the credit crisis. The tightening of standards with respect to risk forced CDS insurers like AIG to hold liquid assets such that payouts could be made in the event that all of their CDS writings made claims. To illustrate, this burden would be the equivalent of all of a company's insured homeowners suffering total losses simultaneously. While this scenario was improbable, the capital had to be set aside as if it would occur. AIG found it impossible to shore up enough assets to match against its now enormous liabilities, plunging the company into dire financial straits. In September 2008, AIG was extended an $85 billion line of credit from the Federal Reserve,[22] adding to the list of companies bailed out by the U.S. government in the wake of the economic recession brought about by the credit crisis.

At the Senate Budget Committee hearing on March 2, 2009, Federal Reserve Board Chairman Ben Bernanke testified as to the role of failures in the regulatory environment that allowed AIG to accumulate so much bad debt on its books. Bernanke accused the company of exploiting the fact that there was no oversight of the financial products division and went on to say, "If there's a single episode in this entire 18 months that has made me more angry [than AIG], I can't think of one." He likened AIG to a "hedge fund … attached to a large and stable insurance company" that made "irresponsible bets" in explaining the firm's actions leading up to its financial meltdown. Bernanke called for the Obama administration to expand the powers of the Federal Deposit Insurance Corporation (FDIC) to address the problems of large financial institutions rather than focusing on banks alone.[23]

KEY TAKEAWAYS

In this section you studied the following:

- Actuarial analysis is used to project past losses into the future to predict reserve needs and appropriate rates to charge.
- Actuaries utilize loss development and mortality tables to aid in setting premium rates and establishing adequate reserves.
- Several adjustments are reflected in insurance premiums: anticipated investment earnings, marketing/administrative costs, taxes, risk premium, and profit.
- Insurers use catastrophe modeling to predict future losses.
- A major component of insurance industry profits is investment income from the payment of premiums.
- Investments are needed so that assets can cover insurers' significant liabilities (primarily loss reserves) while providing adequate capital and surplus.

DISCUSSION QUESTIONS

1. Why must insurance companies be concerned about the amount paid for a loss that occurred years ago?

2. Explain the process an actuary goes through to calculate reserves using the loss development triangle.

3. When does an actuary need to use his or her judgment in adjusting the loss development factors?

4. Compare the investment (asset) portfolio of the life/health insurance industry to that of the property/casualty insurance industry. Why do you think there are differences?

5. Use the assets and liabilities of property/casualty insurers in their balance sheets to explain why losses from an event like Hurricane Ike can hurt the net worth of insurers.

6. The following table shows the incurred losses of the Maruri Insurance Company for its liability line.

Development Months	Accident Year						
	1994	**1995**	**1996**	**1997**	**1998**	**1999**	**2000**
12	$27,634	$28,781	$28,901	$26,980	$27,684	$29,087	$27,680
24	$43,901	$43,777	$43,653	$37,854	$37,091	$37,890	
36	$56,799	$51,236	$52,904	$46,777	$48,923		
48	$65,901	$59,021	$57,832	$50,907			
60	$69,023	$63,210	$60,934				
72	$71,905	$69,087					
84	$73,215						

Using the example in this chapter as a guide, do the following:

    a. Create the loss development factors for this book of business.

    b. Calculate the ultimate reserves needed for this book of business. Make assumptions as needed.

    c. Read Section 5 and reevaluate your answer.

7. Read Section 5 and respond to the following:

    a. The table below shows the cumulative claim payments of the Enlightened Insurance Company for its liability line.

Accident Year	Development Year						
	0	**1**	**2**	**3**	**4**	**5**	**6**
2002	$27,634	$28,781	$28,901	$26,980	$27,684	$29,087	$27,680
2003	$43,901	$43,777	$43,653	$37,854	$37,091	$37,890	
2004	$56,799	$51,236	$52,904	$46,777	$48,923		
2005	$65,901	$59,021	$57,832	$50,907			
2006	$69,023	$63,210	$60,934				
2007	$71,905	$69,087					
2008	$73,215						

    b. Plot the numbers in the table on a graph where that horizontal axis represents the development period and the vertical axis represents the amounts. Can you describe the pattern in the form of a graph (a free-hand drawing)? If you know regression analysis, try to describe the graph by a nonlinear regression. Can you give your estimate for the ultimate payments (the total claims after many more years) for a typical accident year by just looking at the graph and without any mathematical calculations?

    c. Create the noncumulative (current) claim payments triangle (the difference between the years).

    d. Describe the differences you see between the cumulative plot and the noncumulative plot. Can you say something about the "regularity" of the pattern that you see in each plot? Do you get an "illusion" that the cumulative data are more predictable? When looking at the noncumulative curve, do you see any points that draw your attention actuarially?

    e. Can you say something about the possible trends of this portfolio?

    f. What are the disadvantages of using chain ladder approach, in comparison to the new actuarial approach?

    g. Compare your answer to discussion question 6 to the analysis of this question.

4. INSURANCE OPERATIONS: REINSURANCE, LEGAL AND REGULATORY ISSUES, CLAIMS, AND MANAGEMENT

LEARNING OBJECTIVES

In this section we elaborate on the following:

- **How reinsurance works and the protection it provides**
- **Contract arrangements in reinsurance transactions and methods of coverage**
- **The benefits of reinsurance**
- **The general legal aspects of insurance**
- **The claims adjustment process and the role of the claims adjuster**
- **The management function**

4.1 Reinsurance

reinsurance

An arrangement by which an insurance company transfers all or a portion of its risk under a contract (or contracts) of insurance to another company.

ceding insurer

The company transferring risk in a reinsurance arrangement.

assuming reinsurer

The company taking over the risk in a reinsurance arrangement.

treaty arrangement

Arrangement in which the original insurer is obligated to automatically reinsure any new underlying insurance contract that meets the terms of a prearranged treaty, and the reinsurer is obligated to accept certain responsibilities for the specified insurance.

facultative arrangement

Arrangement in which both the primary insurer and the reinsurer retain full decision-making powers with respect to each insurance contract.

Reinsurance is an arrangement by which an insurance company transfers all or a portion of its risk under a contract (or contracts) of insurance to another company. The company transferring risk in a reinsurance arrangement is called the **ceding insurer**. The company taking over the risk in a reinsurance arrangement is the **assuming reinsurer**. In effect, the insurance company that issued the policies is seeking protection from another insurer, the assuming reinsurer. Typically, the reinsurer assumes responsibility for part of the losses under an insurance contract; however, in some instances, the reinsurer assumes full responsibility for the original insurance contract. As with insurance, reinsurance involves risk transfer, risk distribution, risk diversification across more insurance companies, and coverage against insurance risk. Risk diversification is the spreading of the risk to other insurers to reduce the exposure of the primary insurer, the one that deals with the final consumer.

How Reinsurance Works

Reinsurance may be divided into three types: (1) treaty, (2) facultative, and (3) a combination of these two. Each of these types may be further classified as proportional or nonproportional. The original or primary insurer (the ceding company) may have a treaty with a reinsurer. Under a **treaty arrangement**, the original insurer is obligated to automatically reinsure any new underlying insurance contract that meets the terms of a prearranged treaty, and the reinsurer is obligated to accept certain responsibilities for the specified insurance. Thus, the reinsurance coverage is provided automatically for many policies. In a **facultative arrangement**, both the primary insurer and the reinsurer retain full decision-making powers with respect to each insurance contract. As each insurance contract is issued, the primary insurer decides whether or not to seek reinsurance, and the reinsurer retains the flexibility to accept or reject each application for reinsurance on a case-by-case basis. The combination approach may require the primary insurer to offer to reinsure specified contracts (like the treaty approach) while leaving the reinsurer free to decide whether to accept or reject reinsurance on each contract (like the facultative approach). Alternatively, the combination approach can give the option to the primary insurer and automatically require acceptance by the reinsurer on all contracts offered for reinsurance. In any event, a contract between the ceding company and the reinsurer spells out the agreement between the two parties.

When the reinsurance agreement calls for **proportional (pro rata) reinsurance**, the reinsurer assumes a prespecified percentage of both premiums and losses. Expenses are also shared in accord with this prespecified percentage. Because the ceding company has incurred operating expenses associated with the marketing, evaluation, and delivery of coverage, the reinsurer often pays a fee called a **ceding commission** to the original insurer. Such a commission may make reinsurance profitable to the ceding company, in addition to offering protection against catastrophe and improved predictability.

Nonproportional reinsurance obligates the reinsurer to pay losses when they exceed a designated threshold. **Excess-loss reinsurance**, for instance, requires the reinsurer to accept amounts of insurance that exceed the ceding insurer's retention limit. As an example, a small insurer might reinsure all property insurance above $25,000 per contract. The excess policy could be written per contract or per occurrence. Both proportional and nonproportional reinsurance may be either treaty or facultative. The excess-loss arrangement is depicted in Table 7.9. A proportional agreement is shown in Table 7.10.

In addition to specifying the situations under which a reinsurer has financial responsibility, the reinsurance agreement places a limit on the amount of reinsurance the reinsurer must accept. For example, the SSS Reinsurance Company may limit its liability per contract to four times the ceding insurer's retention limit, which in this case would yield total coverage of $125,000 ($25,000 retention plus $100,000 in reinsurance on any one property). When the ceding company issues a policy for an amount that exceeds the sum of its retention limit and SSS's reinsurance limit, it would still need another reinsurer, perhaps TTT Reinsurance Company, to accept a second layer of reinsurance.

TABLE 7.9   An Example of Excess-Loss Reinsurance

Original Policy Limit of $200,000 Layered as Multiples of Primary Retention	
$75,000	Second reinsurer's coverage (equal to the remainder of the $200,000 contract)
100,000	First reinsurer's limit (four times the retention)
25,000	Original insurer's retention

TABLE 7.10   An Example of Proportional Reinsurance

Assume 30–70 split, premiums of $10,000, expense of $2,000, and a loss of $150,000. Ignore any ceding commission.

	Total Exposure	Premium	Expenses	Net Premium*	Loss
Reinsurer	70%	7,000	1,400	5,600	105,000
Ceding Insurer	30%	3,000	600	2,400	45,000
Total	100	10,00	2,000	8,000	150,000
* Net premium = Premium–Expenses					

Benefits of Reinsurance

A ceding company (the primary insurer) uses reinsurance mainly to protect itself against losses in individual cases beyond a specified sum (i.e., its retention limit), but competition and the demands of its sales force may require issuance of policies of greater amounts. A company that issued policies no larger than its retention would severely limit its opportunities in the market. Many insureds do not want to place their insurance with several companies, preferring to have one policy with one company for each loss exposure. Furthermore, agents find it inconvenient to place multiple policies every time they insure a large risk.

In addition to its concern with individual cases, a primary insurer must protect itself from catastrophic losses of a particular type (such as a windstorm), in a particular area (such as a city or a block in a city), or during a specified period of operations (such as a calendar year). An **aggregate reinsurance** policy can be purchased for coverage against potentially catastrophic situations faced by the primary insurer. Sometimes they are considered excess policies, as described above, when the excess retention is per occurrence. An example of how an excess-per-occurrence policy works can be seen from the damage caused by Hurricane Andrew in 1992. Insurers who sell property insurance in hurricane-prone areas probably choose to reinsure their exposures not just on a property-by-property basis but also above some chosen level for any specific event. Andrew was considered one event and caused billions of dollars of damage in Florida alone. A Florida insurer may have set limits, perhaps $100 million, for its own exposure to a given hurricane. For its insurance in force above $100 million, the insurer can purchase excess or aggregate reinsurance.

Other benefits of reinsurance can be derived when a company offering a particular line of insurance for the first time wants to protect itself from excessive losses and also take advantage of the

proportional (pro rata) reinsurance

Situation in which the reinsurer assumes a prespecified percentage of both premiums and losses.

ceding commission

A fee paid by the reinsurer to the original insurer.

nonproportional reinsurance

Reinsurance that obligates the reinsurer to pay losses when they exceed a designated threshold.

excess-loss reinsurance

Reinsurance that requires the reinsurer to accept amounts of insurance that exceed the ceding insurer's retention limit.

aggregate reinsurance

Policy that can be purchased for coverage against potentially catastrophic situations faced by the primary insurer.

reinsurer's knowledge concerning the proper rates to be charged and underwriting practices to be followed. In other cases, a rapidly expanding company may have to shift some of its liabilities to a reinsurer to avoid impairing its capital. Reinsurance often also increases the amount of insurance the underlying insurer can sell. This is referred to as increasing capacity.

Reinsurance is significant to the buyer of insurance for a number of reasons. First, reinsurance increases the financial stability of insurers by spreading risk. This increases the likelihood that the original insurer will be able to pay its claims. Second, reinsurance facilitates placing large or unusual exposures with one company, thus reducing the time spent seeking insurance and eliminating the need for numerous policies to cover one exposure. This reduces transaction costs for both buyer and seller. Third, reinsurance helps small insurance companies stay in business, thus increasing competition in the industry. Without reinsurance, small companies would find it much more difficult to compete with larger ones.

Individual policyholders, however, rarely know about any reinsurance that may apply to their coverage. Even for those who are aware of the reinsurance, whether it is on a business or an individual contract, most insurance policies prohibit direct access from the original insured to the reinsurer. The prohibition exists because the reinsurance agreement is a separate contract from the primary (original) insurance contract, and thus the original insured is not a party to the reinsurance. Because reinsurance is part of the global insurance industry, globalization is also at center stage.

4.2 Legal and Regulatory Issues

In reality, the only tangible product we receive from the insurance company when we transfer the risk and pay the premium is a legal contract in the form of a policy. Thus, the nature of insurance is very legal. The wordings of the contracts are regularly challenged. Consequently, law pervades insurance industry operations. Lawyers help draft insurance contracts, interpret contract provisions when claims are presented, defend the insurer in lawsuits, communicate with legislators and regulators, and help with various other aspects of operating an insurance business.

4.3 Claims Adjusting

claims adjusting

The process of paying insureds after they sustain losses.

claims adjuster

The person who represents the insurer when the policyholder presents a claim for payment.

company adjuster

An employee of the insurer who handles claims.

independent adjuster

An employee of an adjusting firm that works for several different insurers and receives a fee for each claim handled.

Claims adjusting is the process of paying insureds after they sustain losses. The **claims adjuster** is the person who represents the insurer when the policyholder presents a claim for payment. Relatively small property losses, up to $500 or so, may be adjusted by the sales agent. Larger claims will be handled by either a **company adjuster**, an employee of the insurer who handles claims, or an independent adjuster. The **independent adjuster** is an employee of an adjusting firm that works for several different insurers and receives a fee for each claim handled.

A claims adjuster's job includes (1) investigating the circumstances surrounding a loss, (2) determining whether the loss is covered or excluded under the terms of the contract, (3) deciding how much should be paid if the loss is covered, (4) paying valid claims promptly, and (5) resisting invalid claims. The varying situations give the claims adjuster opportunities to use her or his knowledge of insurance contracts, investigative abilities, knowledge of the law, negotiation skills, and tactful communication. Most of the adjuster's work is done outside the office or at a drive-in automobile claims facility. Satisfactory settlement of claims is the ultimate test of an insurance company's value to its insureds and to society. Like underwriting, claims adjusting requires substantial knowledge of insurance.

Claim Practices

It is unreasonable to expect an insurer to be overly generous in paying claims or to honor claims that should not be paid at all, but it is advisable to avoid a company that makes a practice of resisting reasonable claims. This may signal financial trouble. Information is available about insurers' claims practices. Each state's insurance department compiles complaints data. An insurer that has more than an average level of complaints is best avoided.

4.4 Management

As in other organizations, an insurer needs competent managers to plan, organize, direct, control, and lead. The insurance management team functions best when it knows the nature of insurance and the environment in which insurers conduct business. Although some top management people are hired without backgrounds in the insurance business, the typical top management team for an insurer consists of people who learned about the business by working in one or more functional areas of insurance. If you choose an insurance career, you will probably begin in one of the functional areas discussed above.

KEY TAKEAWAYS

In this section you studied the following:

- Reinsurance acts as insurance for insurance companies, assuming responsibility for part of the losses of a ceding insurer by contract.
- Reinsurance may be treaty, facultative, or a combination arrangement.
- Treaty and facultative reinsurance arrangements may be proportional or nonproportional.
- Benefits of reinsurance include protection against excess losses and catastrophe for the ceding insurer, opening new business opportunities through increased capacity, financial stability from spreading risk, greater efficiencies for agents by allowing large risks to be placed with a single company, and increased competition by helping smaller companies remain in business.
- The nature of insurance is very legal, requiring lawyers to draft and interpret policies.
- Claims adjustment and management demand specialists with a great deal of knowledge about the insurance industry.

DISCUSSION QUESTIONS

1. Distinguish among the different types of reinsurance and give an example of each.
2. What are the advantages of reinsuring?
3. Explain the differences between company adjusters and independent adjusters. Given the choice, who would you prefer to deal with in managing your claim? Why?

5. APPENDIX: MODERN LOSS RESERVING METHODS IN LONG TAIL LINES

The actuarial estimation in loss reserving is based on data of past claim payments. This data is typically presented in the form of a triangle, where each row represents the accident (or underwriting) period and each column represents the development period. Table 7.11 represents a hypothetical claims triangle. For example, the payments for 2006 are presented as follows: $13 million paid in 2006 for development year 0, another $60 million paid in development year 1 (i.e., 2007 = [2006+1]), and another $64 million paid during 2008 for development year 2. Note, that each diagonal represents payments made during a particular calendar period. For example, the last diagonal represents payment made during 2008.

TABLE 7.11 A Hypothetical Loss Triangle: Claim Payments by Accident and Development Years ($ Thousand)

Accident Year	Development Year						
	0	1	2	3	4	5	6
2002	9,500	50,500	50,000	27,500	9,500	5,000	3,000
2003	13,000	44,000	53,000	33,500	11,500	5,000	
2004	14,000	47,000	56,000	29,500	15,000		
2005	15,000	52,000	48,000	35,500			
2006	13,000	60,000	64,000				
2007	16,000	47,000					
2008	17,000	?					

The actuarial analysis has to project how losses will be developed into the future based on their past development. The loss reserve is the estimate of all the payments that will be made in the future and is still unknown. In other words, the role of the actuary is to estimate all the figures that will fill the blank lower right part of the table. The actuary has to "square the triangle." The table ends at development year 6, but the payments may continue beyond that point. Therefore, the actuary should also forecast beyond the known horizon (beyond development year 6 in our table), so the role is to "rectanglize the triangle."

The actuary may use a great variety of triangles in preparing the forecast: the data could be arranged by months, quarters, or years. The data could be in current figure or in cumulative figures. The data could represent numbers: the number of reported claims, the number of settled claims, the number of still pending claims, the number of closed claims, and so forth The figures could represent claim payments such as current payments, payments for claims that were closed, incurred claim figures (i.e., the actual payments plus the case estimate), indexed figures, average claim figures, and so forth.

All actuarial techniques seek to identify a hidden pattern in the triangle, and to use it to perform the forecast. Some common techniques are quite intuitive and are concerned with identifying relationships between the payments made across consecutive developing years. Let us demonstrate it on Table 7.11 by trying to estimate the expected payments for accident year 2008 during 2009 (the cell with the question mark). We can try doing so by finding a ratio of the payments in development year 1 to the payments in development year 0. We have information for accident years 2002 through 2007. The sum of payments made for these years during development year 1 is $300,500 and the sum of payments made during development year 0 is $80,500. The ratio between these sums is 3.73. We multiply this ratio by the $17,000 figure for year 2008, which gives an estimate of $63,410 in payments that will be made for accident year 2008 during development year 1 (i.e., during 2009). Note that there are other ways to calculate the ratios: instead of using the ratio between sums, we could have calculated for each accident year the ratio between development year 1 and development year 0, then calculated the average ratio for all years. This would give a different multiplying factor, resulting in a different forecast.

In a similar way, we can calculate factors for moving from any other development period to the next one (a set of factors to be used for moving from each column to the following one). Using these factors, we can fill all other blank cells in Table 7.11. Note that the figure of $63,410 that we inserted as the estimate for accident year 2008 during development year 1 is included in estimating the next figure in the table. In other words, we created a recursive model, where the outcome of one step is used in estimating the outcome of the next step. We have created a sort of "chain ladder," as these forecasting methods are often referred to.

In the above example, we used ratios to move from one cell to the next one. But this forecasting method is only one of many we could have utilized. For example, we could easily create an additive model rather than a multiplicative model (based on ratios). We can calculate the average difference between columns and use it to climb from one cell to the missing cell on its right. For example, the average difference between the payments for development year 1 and development year 0 is $36,667 (calculated only for the figures for which we have data on both development years 0 and 1, or 2002 through 2007). Therefore, our alternative estimate for the missing figure in Table 7.11, the payments that are expected for accident year 2008 during 2009, is $53,667 ($17,000 plus $36,667). Quite a different estimate than the one we obtained earlier!

We can create more complicated models, and the traditional actuarial literature is full of them. The common feature of the above examples is that they are estimating the set of development period factors. However, there could also be a set of "accident period factors" to account for the possibility that the portfolio does not always stay constant between years. In one year, there could have been many policies or accidents, whereas in the other year, there could have been fewer. So, there could be another set of factors to be used when moving between rows (accident periods) in the triangle. Additionally, there could also be a set of calendar year factors to describe the changes made while moving from one diagonal to the other. Such effects may result from a multitude of reasons—for example, a legal judgment forcing a policy change or inflation that increases average payments. A forecasting model often incorporates a combination of such factors. In our simple example with a triangle having seven rows, we may calculate six factors in each direction: six for the development periods (column effects), six for the accident periods (row effects), and six for the diagonals (calendar or payment year effects). The analysis of such a simple triangle may include eighteen factors (or parameters). A larger triangle (which is the common case in practice) where many periods (months, quarters, and years) are used involves the estimation of too many parameters, but simpler models with a much smaller number of factors can be used (see below).

Although the above methods are very appealing intuitively and are still commonly used for loss reserving, they all suffer from major drawbacks and are not ideal for use. Let us summarize some of the major deficiencies:

- The use of factors in all three directions (accident year, development year, and payment year) may lead to contradictions. We have the freedom to determine any two directions, but the third is determined automatically by the first two.

- There is often a need to forecast "beyond the horizon"—that is, to estimate what will be paid in the development years beyond year six in our example. The various chain ladder models cannot do this.

- We can always find a mathematical formula that will describe all the data points, but it will lack good predictive power. At the next period, we get new data and a larger triangle. The additional new pieces of information will often cause us to use a completely different set of factors—including those relating to previous periods. The need to change all the factors is problematic, as it indicates instability of the model and lack of predictive power. This happens due to overparameterization (a very crucial point that deserves a more detailed explanation, as provided below).

- There are no statistical tests for the validity of the factors. Thus, it is impossible to understand which parameters (factors) are statistically significant. To illustrate, it is clear that a factor (parameter) based on a ratio between only two data points (e.g., a development factor for the sixth year, which will be based on the two figures in the extreme right corner of the Table 7.11 triangle) is naturally less reliable, although it may drastically affect the entire forecast.

- The use of simple ratios to create the factors may be unjustified because the relationships between two cells could be more complicated. For example, it could be that a neighboring cell is obtained by examining the first cell, adding a constant, and then multiplying by a ratio. Studies have shown that most loss reserves calculated with chain ladder models are suffering from this problem.

- Chain ladder methods create a deterministic figure for the loss reserves. We have no idea as to how reliable it is. It is clear that there is zero probability that the forecast will exactly foretell the exact future figure. But management would appreciate having an idea about the range of possible deviations between the actual figures and the forecast.

- The most common techniques are based on triangles with cumulative figures. The advantage of cumulative figures is that they suppress the variability of the claims pattern and create an illusion of stability. However, by taking cumulative rather than noncumulative figures, we often lose much information, and we may miss important turning points. It is similar to what a gold miner may do by throwing away, rather than keeping, the little gold nuggets that may be found in huge piles of worthless rocks.

- Many actuaries are still using triangles of incurred claim figures. The incurred figures are the sum of the actually paid numbers plus the estimates of future payments supplied by claims department personnel. The resulting actuarial factors from such triangles are strongly influenced by the changes made by the claims department from one period to the other. Such changes should not be included in forecasting future trends.

There are modern actuarial techniques based on sophisticated statistical tools that could be used for giving better forecasts while using the same loss triangles.[24] Let us see how this works without engaging in a complicated statistical discussion. The purpose of the discussion is to increase the understanding of the principles, but we do not expect the typical student to be able to immediately perform the analysis. We shall largely leave the analysis to actuaries that are better equipped with the needed mathematical and statistical tools.

A good model is evaluated by its simplicity and generality. Having a complex model with many parameters makes it complicated and less general. The chain ladder models that were discussed above suffer from this overparameterization problem, and the alternative models that are explained below overcome this difficulty.

Let us start by simply displaying the data of Table 7.11 in a graphical form in Figure 7.3. The green dots describe the original data points (the paid claims on the vertical axis and the development years on the horizontal axis). To show the general pattern, we added a line that represents the averages for each development year. We see that claim payments in this line of business tend to increase, reach a peak after a few years, then decline slowly over time and have a narrow "tail" (that is, small amounts are to be paid in the far future).

FIGURE 7.3 Paid Claims (in Thousands of Dollars) by Development Year

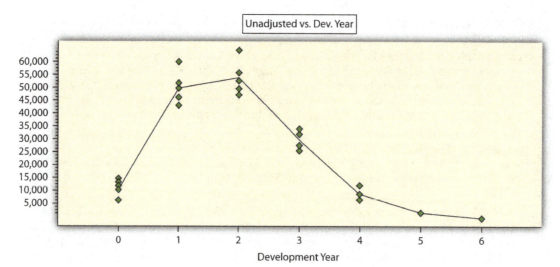

We can immediately see that the entire claims triangle can be analyzed in a completely different way: by fitting a curve through the points. One of these tools to enable this could be regression analysis. Such a tool can give us a better understanding of the hidden pattern than does the chain ladder method. We see that the particular curve in our case is nonlinear, meaning that we need more than two parameters to describe it mathematically. Four parameters will probably suffice to give a mathematical function that will describe the pattern of Figure 7.3. The use of such methods can reach a level of sophistication that goes beyond the scope of this book. It is sufficient to say that we can get an excellent mathematical description of the pattern with the use of only four to six parameters (factors). This can be measured by a variety of statistical indicators. The coefficient of correlation for such a mathematical formula is above 95 percent, and the parameters are statistically significant.

Such an approach is simpler and more general than any chain ladder model. It can be used to forecast beyond the horizon, it can be statistically tested and validated, and it can give a good idea about the level of error that may be expected. When a model is based on a few parameters only, it becomes more "tolerant" to deviations: it is clear that the next period payment will differ from the forecast, but it will not force us to change the model. From the actuary's point of view, claim payments are stochastic variables and should never be regarded as a deterministic process, so why use a deterministic chain ladder analysis?

It is highly recommended, and actually essential, to base the analysis on a noncumulative claims triangle. The statistical analysis does not offer good tools for cumulative figures; we do not know their underlying statistical processes, and therefore, we cannot offer good statistical significance tests. The statistical analysis that is based on the current, noncumulative claim figures is very sensitive and can easily detect turning points and changing patterns.

One last point should be mentioned. The key to regression analysis is the analysis of the residuals, that is, the differences between the observed claims and the figures that are estimated by the model. The residuals must be spread randomly around the forecasted, modeled, figures. If they are not randomly spread, the model can be improved. In other words, the residuals are the compass that guides the actuary in finding the best model. Traditional actuarial analyses based on chain ladder models regard variability as a corrupt element and strive to get rid of the deviations to arrive at a deterministic forecast. By doing so, actuaries throw away the only real information in the data and base the analysis on the noninformative part alone! Sometimes the fluctuations are very large, and the insurance company is working in a very uncertain, almost chaotic claims environment. If the actuary finds that this is the case, it will be important information for the managers and should not be hidden or replaced by a deterministic, but meaningless, forecast.

6.   REVIEW AND PRACTICE

1. How do agents and brokers differ?

2. After hearing the advice that it is usually best to buy life insurance from a person who has been in the business at least five years, a life insurance company general agent became upset and said rather vehemently, "How do you think we could recruit an agency force if everybody took your advice?" How would you answer that question?

3. Is the inherently discriminatory nature of underwriting acceptable from a public policy standpoint? Would shifting to a primarily behavior-based approach to risk assessment be feasible?

4. What actuarial adjustments are built into the pricing of life insurance premiums?

5. Occasionally, Insurer X will reinsure part of Insurer Y's risks, and Insurer Y will reinsure part of Insurer X's risks. Doesn't this seem like merely trading dollars? Explain.

6. What is the relationship between the following functions within an insurance company?

   a. Marketing and underwriting

   b. Underwriting and actuarial

   c. Actuarial and investment

   d. Legal and underwriting

   e. Claims and marketing

   f. Claims adjusting and actuarial

7. Your acquaintance, Nancy Barns, recently commented to you that she and her husband want to reevaluate their homeowner's insurance. Nancy said that it seemed the only time they ever had any contact with their present insurance agency was when a premium was due. Nancy asked if you knew of a good agency.

   a. Help Nancy set up standards to evaluate and choose a good agent.

   b. Review with her the standards of education and experience required of an agent, including the CPCU designation.

8. Read the box, "Problem Investments and the Credit Crisis", in this chapter and respond to the following questions:

   a. Use the asset and liabilities of life insurers in their balance sheets to explain why losses in mortgage-backed securities can hurt the net worth of insurers.

   b. Insurance brokers have been very busy since the troubles of AIG became public knowledge. Why are these brokers busier? What is the connection between AIG's troubles and the work of these brokers?

   c. What is the cause of AIG's problems? Explain in the context of assets and liabilities.

9. Respond to the following:

   a. If you have an auto policy with insurer XYZ that is deeply hurt by both mortgage-backed securities and Hurricane Ike, do you have any protection in case of losses to your own auto (not caused by another driver)? Explain in detail.

   b. If you have an auto policy with insurer XYZ that is deeply hurt by both mortgage-backed securities and Hurricane Ike, do you have any protection in case of losses to your own auto and to your body from an accident that was caused by another driver (you are not at fault)? Explain in detail.

10. You are reading the Sunday newspaper when you notice a health insurance advertisement that offers the purchase of insurance through the mail and the first month's coverage for one dollar. The insurance seems to be a real bargain.

    a. Are there any problems you should be aware of when buying insurance through the mail?

    b. Explain how you could cope with the problems you listed above if you did purchase coverage through the mail.

ENDNOTES

1. Etti G. Baranoff, Dalit Baranoff, and Tom Sager, "Nonuniform Regulatory Treatment of Broker Distribution Systems: An Impact Analysis for Life Insurers," *Journal of Insurance Regulations*, Regulations 19, no. 1 (Fall 2000): 94.

2. "2006: The Year When Changes Take Hold," *Insurance Journal*, January 2, 2006, accessed March 6, 2009, http://www.insurancejournal.com/magazines/west/2006/01/02/features/64730.htm; Steve Tuckey, "NAIC Broker Disclosure Amendment Changes Unlikely," *National Underwriter Online News Service*, April 15, 2005, accessed March 6, 2009, http://www.nationalunderwriter.com/pandc/hotnews/viewPC.asp?article=4_15_05_15_17035.xml; "NAIC Adopts Model Legislation Calling For Broker Disclosures Defers One Section for Further Consideration" at http://www.naic.org/spotlight.htm; Mark E. Ruquet, "MMC Says Contingent Fees No Longer A Plus" *National Underwriter Online News Service*, February 15, 2006.

3. Sally Roberts, "Big I Changes Name to Reflect Membership Changes," *Business Insurance*, May 6, 2002.

4. The term direct writer is frequently used to refer to all property insurers that do not use the Independent Agency System of distribution, but some observers think there are differences among such companies.

5. Paul P. Aniskovich, "Letters With Apps Can Make The Difference," *National Underwriter*, Life & Health/Financial Services Edition, November 12, 2001.

6. Catherine Arnold, "Britain Backs Insurers Use of Genetic Testing," *National Underwriter*, Life & Health/Financial Services Edition, November 27, 2000.

7. In this example, we do not introduce actuarial adjustments to the factors. Such adjustments are usually based on management, technology, marketing, and other known functional changes within the company. The book of business is assumed to be stable without any extreme changes that may require adjustments.

8. Claire Wilkinson, "Catastrophe Modeling: A Vital Tool in the Risk Management Box," Insurance Information Institute, February 2008, Accessed March 6, 2009, http://www.iii.org/media/research/catmodeling/.

9. Michael Lewis, "In Nature's Casino," *New York Times Magazine*, August 26, 2007, Accessed March 6, 2009; http://www.nytimes.com/2007/08/26/magazine/26neworleans-t.html.

10. AIR Worldwide, Accessed March 6, 2009, http://www.air-worldwide.com/ContentPage.aspx?id=16202.

11. Claire Wilkinson, "Catastrophe Modeling: A Vital Tool in the Risk Management Box," Insurance Information Institute, February 2008, Accessed March 6, 2009, http://www.iii.org/media/research/catmodeling/.

12. American Insurance Association, Testimony for the National Association of Insurance Commissioners (NAIC) 9/28/2007 Public Hearing on Catastrophe Modeling.

13. Claire Wilkinson, "Catastrophe Modeling: A Vital Tool in the Risk Management Box," Insurance Information Institute, February 2008, Accessed March 6, 2009, http://www.iii.org/media/research/catmodeling/.

14. Insurance Information Institute. *The Insurance Fact Book*, 2009, p 31, 36.

15. Government-sponsored enterprise.

16. Short-term agreements to sell and repurchase government securities by a specified date at a set price.

17. Government-sponsored enterprise.

18. "Getting worried downtown." *The Economist* November 15, 2007.

19. "U.S Foreclosure Activity Increases 75 Percent in 2007," RealtyTrac, January 29, 2008, Accessed March 6, 2009, http://www.realtytrac.com/ContentManagement/pressrelease.aspx?ChannelID=9&ItemID=3988&accnt=64847.

20. "Let the Blame Begin; Everyone Played Some Role—The Street, Lenders, Ratings Agencies, Hedge Funds, Even Homeowners. Where Does Responsibility Lie? (The Subprime Mess)," Business Week Online, July 30, 2007.

21. "The Financial Meltdown of AIG and Insurers Explained." Smallcap Network, October 27, 2008, http://www.smallcapnetwork.com/scb/the-financial-meltdown-of-aig-and-other-insurers-explained/2315/.

22. Edmund L. Andrews, Michael J. de la Merced, and Mary Williams Walsh, "Fed's $85 Billion Loan Rescues Insurer," *The New York Times*, September 17, 2008, Accessed March 6, 2009, http://www.nytimes.com/2008/09/17/business/17insure.html.

23. Arthur D. Postal, "Fed Chief Blasts AIG for Exploiting Reg System," *National Underwriter Online*, Property/Casualty Edition, March 3, 2009, Accessed March 6, 2009. http://www.propertyandcasualtyinsurancenews.com/cms/nupc/Breaking+News/2009/03/03-AIG-HEARING-dp.

24. The interested reader should seek out publications by Professor B. Zehnwirth, a pioneer of the approach described, in actuarial literature. One of the authors (Y. Kahane) has collaborated with him, and much actuarial work has been done with these tools. The approach is now well accepted around the world. The graph was derived using resources developed by Insureware Pty. (www.insureware.com).

CHAPTER 8
Insurance Markets and Regulation

The insurance industry, in fact, is one of the largest global financial industries, helping to propel the global economy. "In 2007, world insurance premium volume, for [property/casualty and life/health] combined, totaled $4.06 trillion, up 10.5 percent from $3.67 trillion in 2006," according to international reinsurer Swiss Re. The United States led the world in total insurance premiums, as shown in Table 8.1.

TABLE 8.1 Top Ten Countries by Life and Nonlife Direct Premiums Written, 2007 (Millions of U.S.$)*

Rank	Country	Nonlife Premiums[1]	Life Premiums	Total Premiums		
				Amount	Percentage Change from Prior Year	Percentage of Total World Premiums
1	United States[2]	$578,357	$651,311	$1,229,668	4.69%	30.28%
2	United Kingdom	349,740	113,946	463,686	28.16	11.42
3	Japan[3]	330,651	94,182	424,832	−3.31	10.46
4	France	186,993	81,907	268,900	7.47	6.62
5	Germany	102,419	120,407	222,825	10.09	5.49
6	Italy	88,215	54,112	142,328	1.27	3.50
7	South Korea[4]	81,298	35,692	116,990	16.28	2.88
8	The Netherlands	35,998	66,834	102,831	11.98	2.53
9	Canada[5]	45,593	54,805	100,398	14.74	2.47
10	PR China	58,677	33,810	92,487	30.75	2.28

* Before reinsurance transactions.

Source: Insurance Information Institute (III), accessed March 6, 2009, http://www.iii.org/media/facts/statsbyissue/international/.

The large size of the global insurance markets is demonstrated by the written premiums shown in Table 8.1. The institutions making the market were described in Chapter 6. In this chapter we cover the following:

1. Links

2. Markets conditions: underwriting cycles, availability and affordability, insurance and reinsurance markets

3. Regulation of insurance

1. LINKS

underwriting cycles

The movement of insurance prices through time.

insurance capacity

The quantity of coverage that is available in terms of limits of coverage.

As we have done in the prior chapters, we begin with connecting the importance of this chapter to the complete picture of holistic risk management. We will become savvy consumers only when we understand the insurance marketplace and the conditions under which insurance institutions operate. When we make the selection of an insurer, we need to understand not only the organizational structure of that insurance firm, but we also need to be able to benefit from the regulatory safety net available to protect us. Also important is our clear understanding of insurance market conditions affecting the products and their pricing. Major rate increases for coverage do not happen in a vacuum. As you saw in Chapter 4, past losses are the most important factor in setting rates. Market conditions, availability, and affordability of products are very important factors in the risk management decision, as you saw in Chapter 3. In Chapter 2, you learned that an insurable risk must have the characteristic of being affordable. Because of **underwriting cycles**—the movement of insurance prices through time (explained next in this chapter)—insurance rates are considered dynamic. In a hard market, when rates are high and **insurance capacity**, the quantity of coverage that is available in terms of limits of coverage, is low, we may choose to self-insure. Insurance capacity relates to the level of insurers' capital (net worth). If capital levels are low, insurers cannot provide a lot of coverage. In a soft market, when insurance capacity is high, we may select to insure for the same level of severity and frequency of losses. So our decisions are truly related to external market conditions, as indicated in Chapter 3.

The regulatory oversight of insurers is another important issue in our strategy. If we care to have a safety net of guarantee funds, which act as deposit insurance in case of insolvency of an insurer, we will work with a regulated insurer. In case of insolvency, a portion of the claims will be paid by the guarantee funds. We also need to understand the benefits of selecting a regulated entity as opposed to nonregulated one for other consumer protection actions such as the resolution of complaints. If we are unhappy with our insurer's claims settlement process and if the insurer is under the state's regulatory jurisdiction, the regulator in our state may help us resolve disputes.

FIGURE 8.1   Links between the Holistic Risk Picture and the Big Picture of the Insurance Industry Markets by Regulatory Status

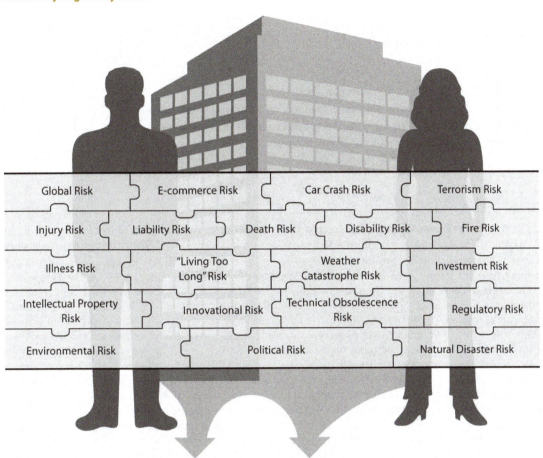

Global Risk	E-commerce Risk	Car Crash Risk	Terrorism Risk
Injury Risk	Liability Risk	Death Risk	Disability Risk	Fire Risk
Illness Risk	"Living Too Long" Risk	Weather Catastrophe Risk	Investment Risk
Intellectual Property Risk	Innovational Risk	Technical Obsolescence Risk	Regulatory Risk
Environmental Risk	Political Risk	Natural Disaster Risk

Regulated Insurance

- Private/Governmental
  - Private Insurers
    - Stock
    - Mutual
- U.S. Regulation
  - Solvency
  - Consumer protection
- Market Issues
  - Underwriting cycles—growth when prices are low

Nonregulated or Semiregulated Insurance

- Types of Insurers
  - Offshore reinsurers and Lloyd's of London
  - Self-insurance/captives
  - Excess and surplus lines
  - Public risk pools
- No U.S. Regulation
  - No solvency regulation
  - No consumer protection
- Market Issues
  - Underwriting cycles—growth when prices are high

As you can see, understanding insurance institutions, markets, and insurance regulation are critical to our ability to complete the picture of holistic risk management. Figure 8.1 provides the line of connection between our holistic risk picture (or a business holistic risk) and the big picture of the insurance industry and markets. Figure 8.1 separates the industry's institutions into those that are government-regulated and those that are non- or semiregulated. Regardless of regulation, insurers are subject to market conditions and are structured along the same lines as any corporation. However, some insurance structures, such as governmental risk pools or Lloyd's of London, do have a specialized organizational structure.

2. INSURANCE MARKET CONDITIONS

LEARNING OBJECTIVES

In this section we elaborate on the following:

- **Hard and soft insurance market conditions**
- **How underwriting standards are influenced by cyclical market conditions**
- **The significance of the combined ratio as an indicator of profitability**
- **Reinsurance organizations and the marketplace**

2.1 Property/Casualty Market Conditions

soft market

Condition that occurs when insurance losses are low and prices are very competitive.

hard market

Condition that occurs when insurance losses are above expectations and reserves no longer are able to cover all losses.

combined ratio

The loss ratio (losses divided by premiums) plus the expense ratio (expenses divided by premiums).

At any point in time, insurance markets (mostly in the property/casualty lines of insurance) may be in hard market or soft market conditions because of the underwriting cycle. **Soft market** conditions occur when insurance losses are low and prices are very competitive. **Hard market** conditions occur when insurance losses are above expectations (see loss development in Chapter 7) and reserves are no longer able to cover all losses. Consequently, insurers or reinsurers have to tap into their capital. Under these conditions, capacity (measured by capital level relative to premiums) is lowered and prices escalate. A presentation of the underwriting cycle of the property/casualty insurance industry from 1956 to 2008 is featured in Figure 8.2. The cycle is shown in terms of the industry's combined ratio, which is a measure of the relationship between premiums taken in and expenditures for claims and expenses. In other words, the **combined ratio** is the loss ratio (losses divided by premiums) plus the expense ratio (expenses divided by premiums). A combined ratio above one hundred means that, for every premium dollar taken in, more than a dollar was spent on losses and expenses. The ratio does not include income from investments, so a high number does not necessarily mean that a company is unprofitable. Because of investment income, an insurer may be profitable even if the combined ratio is over 100 percent. Each line of business has its own break-even point because each line has a different loss payment time horizon and length of time for the investment of the premiums. The break-even point is determined on the basis of how much investment income is available in each line of insurance. If a line has a longer tail of losses, there is a longer period of time for investment to accumulate.

FIGURE 8.2 Underwriting Cycles of the U.S. Property/Casualty Insurance Industry, 1970–2008*

* Peaks are hard markets; valleys are soft markets. † A.M. Best year-end estimate of 103.2; actual nine-month result was 105.6.

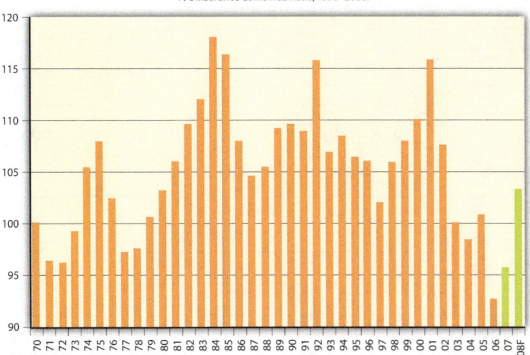

P/C Insurance Combined Ratio, 1970–2008F*

Source: Insurance Information Institute, 2009; A.M. Best; ISO, III

As you can see in Figure 8.2, the ups and downs are clearly visible across the whole industry for all lines of business. When the combined ratio is low, the industry lowers its underwriting standards in order to obtain more cash that can be invested—a strategy known as **cash flow underwriting**. The industry is regarded as competing itself to the ground, and underwriting standards are loose. The last soft market lasted about fifteen years, ending in the late 1990s. From 1986 to 1999, the combined ratio stayed in the range of 101.6 in 1997 to 109.6 in 1990, with only one jump in 1992 to a combined ratio of 115.7. Because the break-even point of the industry combined ratio is 107, the industry was doing rather well during that long period. It caused new decision makers (those without experience in underwriting cycles) to be less careful. In addition, computerized pricing models gave a false sense of security in making risk-selection and pricing decisions. Actual losses ended up causing rate increases, and the soft market changed into a true hard market.

During the 1990s, the soft market conditions lasted longer than usual because the industry had large capacity. There were speculations that the introduction of capital markets as an alternative to reinsurance (see Chapter 3) kept rates down. In April 2005, the Insurance Information Institute reported that the 2004 statutory rate of return on average surplus was 10.5 percent, up from 9.5 percent for calendar year 2003, 1.1 percent for 2002, and −2.3 percent for 2001 (one of the worst years ever). The 2004 recovery is the most remarkable underwriting recovery in modern history, with insurers slicing 17.6 points off the combined ratio in just three years. Additional improvement is shown in 2006, a year after Hurricane Katrina.

For each line of insurance, there is a level of combined ratio that determines whether the line is profitable or not. The level of combined ratio that is required for each line of business to avoid losing money is called the **break-even combined ratio level**. Depending on the investment income contribution of each line of insurance, the longer tail lines (such as general liability and medical malpractice) have a much larger break-even level. Fire and allied lines as well as homeowner's have the lowest break-even combined ratio levels because the level of investment income is expected to be lower. Thus, if the actual combined ratio for homeowner's is 106, the industry is experiencing negative results. The break-even for all lines of the industry is 107. If the industry's combined ratio is 103, the industry is reaping a profit. The largest break-even combined ratio is for the medical malpractice line, which is at 115; for general and product liability lines, it is 113; and for worker's compensation, it is 112. The lowest break-even combined ratio is 103 for homeowner's and 105 for personal auto.

The soft market climate of 2005 helped the industry recover from the devastation of hurricanes Katrina, Rita, and Wilma. Some even regard the impact of these major catastrophes as a small blip in

cash flow underwriting

Strategy pursued when the combined ratio is low, in which the industry lowers its underwriting standards in order to obtain more cash that can be invested.

break-even combined ratio level

The level of combined ratio that is required for each line of business to not lose money.

the underwriting results for the property/casualty industry, except for the reinsurers' combined ratio. Table 8.2 shows the adjusted amounts of loss for these catastrophes. Despite the high magnitude of these losses, market analysts projected a stable outlook for the property/casualty industry in 2006. In fact, the actual combined ratio for that year was the lowest observed in decades, at 92.6, as indicated in Figure 8.2.

TABLE 8.2 **The Ten Most Costly Catastrophes in the United States***

			Insured Loss (Millions of $)	
Rank	Date	Peril	Dollars when Occurred	In 2008 Dollars[6]
1	Aug. 2005	Hurricane Katrina	$41,100	$45,309
2	Aug. 1992	Hurricane Andrew	15,500	23,786
3	Sept. 2001	World Trade Center and Pentagon terrorist attacks	18,779	22,830
4	Jan. 1994	Northridge, CA, earthquake	12,500	18,160
5	Oct. 2005	Hurricane Wilma	10,300	11,355
6	Sept. 2008	Hurricane Ike	10,655[7]	10,655[8]
7	Aug. 2004	Hurricane Charley	7,475	8,520
8	Sept. 2004	Hurricane Ivan	7,110	8,104
9	Sept. 1989	Hurricane Hugo	4,195	7,284
10	Sept. 2005	Hurricane Rita	5,627	6,203

* Property coverage only. Does not include flood damage covered by the federally administered National Flood Insurance Program.

Source: Insurance Information Institute (III). Accessed March 6, 2009. http://www.iii.org/media/hottopics/insurance/catastrophes/.

In addition to the regular underwriting cycles, external market conditions affect the industry to a great extent. The 2008–2009 financial crisis impact on the property/casualty insurance industry is discussed in the box below.

The Property/Casualty Industry in the Economic Recession of 2008–2009

There's a fair chance that your bank has changed names—perhaps more than once—within the past twelve months. A year from now, it may do so again. While your liquid assets may be insured through the Federal Deposit Insurance Corporation (FDIC), it is understandable that such unpredictability makes you nervous. Quite possibly, you have suffered personally in the economic recession as well. You may have lost your job, watched investments erode, or even experienced home foreclosure. Investment banks, major retailers, manufacturers, and firms across many industries, large and small, have declared bankruptcy, turned to government subsidy, or collapsed altogether. In light of the bleak realities of the recession, you have no doubt reexamined the things in your life you have come to depend on for security. The question is raised, Should you also worry about the risks you are insured against? Should you worry about your insurance company? The outlook is more optimistic than you may think. Chances are, the home, auto, or commercial property insurer you are with today is the insure you will be with tomorrow (should you so desire).

It is now known that the 2008–2009 economic recession began in December of 2007. It is the longest recession the United States has experienced since 1981; should it extend beyond April 2009, it will be the longest recession in United States history since the Great Depression. At the time of writing, 3.6 million jobs have been lost during the course of the recession, leaving 12.5 million U.S. workers unemployed. The Bureau of Labor Statistics reported an unemployment rate of 8.1 percent in February of 2009, the highest since November of 1982. It is anticipated that unemployment will peak at 9 percent by the end of 2009. The Dow Jones industrial average lost 18 percent of its value and the S&P 500 declined by 20 percent as a result of the October 2008 market crash. In 2007, 1.3 million U.S. properties faced foreclosure, up a staggering 79 percent from 2006. This was just the tip of the iceberg, however, with foreclosures increasing by 81 percent in 2008, amounting to 2.3 million properties. Conditions like these have been damaging to homeowners and organizations alike. Firms that were weak going into the crisis have been decimated, while even resilient companies have seen profits and net worth shrink. With people out of jobs and homes, discretionary spending has contracted considerably. The effects on property and casualty insurers, though, have been less direct.

The property/casualty segment has been hurt by problems in the stock market, real estate, and auto industry primarily. Underwriting alone rarely produces an industry profit; investments account for most of the industry's positive returns. With stocks hit hard by the recession, even the conservative investments typically made by property/casualty insurers have posted poor returns. New home starts dropped 34 percent from 2005–2007, a net decline of 1.4 million units. To insurers, this represents revenues foregone in the form of premiums that could be collected on new business, potentially amounting to $1.2 billion. Auto and light trucks are projected to have the worst unit sales in 2009 since the late 1960s with a reduction of 6 million units. The effect of poor performance in underlying businesses is less pronounced on auto insurers than on home insurers but still substantial. Workers' compensation insurers (to be discussed in Chapter 16) have seen their exposure base reduced by the high unemployment rate.

Nonetheless, the industry attributes recent financial results more to basic market conditions than the economic recession. The combination of a soft market (recall the discussion in Chapter 8) and high catastrophe experience meant a reduction in profits and slow growth. Property/casualty industry profits were 5.4 billion in 2008, down considerably from 61.9 billion in 2007. The 2007 performance, however, was down slightly from an all-time record industry profit in 2006. The 2008 drop is less noteworthy in the wider context of historical annual profits, which are highly correlated with the fluctuating market cycles. Despite the dire economic condition, two important points are made clear: the insurance industry, on the whole, is operating normally and continues to perform the basic function of risk transfer. Insurers are able to pay claims, secure new and renewal business, and expand product offerings. The problems at American International Group (AIG) (discussed in Chapter 7) have been the exception to the rule. Low borrowing, conservative investments, and extensive regulatory oversight have also aided insurance companies in avoiding the large-scale problems of the crisis. All of these factors were inverted in the case of the imperiled banks and other financial institutions. Consider the following: between January 2008 and the time of this writing, forty-one bank failures were observed. This is in comparison to zero property/casualty insurer failures.

The $787 billion stimulus package authorized by the American Recovery and Reinvestment Act of 2009 is further expected to help matters. The program aims to save or create 3.5 million jobs. Of the stimulus, 24.1 percent of funding is intended for spending on infrastructure, 37.9 percent on direct aid, and 38 percent on tax cuts. Insurers will see no direct injection of capital and virtually no indirect benefits from the latter two components of the stimulus package. As it relates to infrastructure spending, however, workers' compensation insurers will be helped by the boost in employment. Considerable outlays on construction projects will also increase demand for commercial property insurance. Renewed investor confidence in the stock market would also enhance investment returns considerably. Just as insurers are indirectly harmed by the crisis, so too will they indirectly benefit from recovery efforts.

Of course, the success of the stimulus plan remains unproven, so the insurance industry must prepare for the uncertain future. In the current economic climate, investments cannot be relied upon as the major driver of industry profitability that they once were. This calls for even greater discipline in underwriting in order for companies to remain solvent. With the federal government taking an unusually active role in correcting deficiencies in the market, a new wave of regulation is inevitable. New compliance initiatives will be introduced, and existing protections may be stripped away. Still, the insurance industry may be uniquely equipped to cope with these challenges, as exemplified by the fundamental nature of their business: risk management. By practicing what they preach, insurers can be rewarded with insulation from the most detrimental effects of the recession and emerge as role models for their fellow financial institutions.

Sources: Dr. Robert P. Hartwig, "Financial Crisis, Economic Stimulus & the Future of the P/C Insurance Industry: Trends, Challenges & Opportunities," March 5, 2009, accessed March 9, 2009, http://www.iii.org/media/presentations/sanantonio/; United States Department of Labor, Bureau of Labor Statistics, "The Unemployment Situation: February 2009," USDL 09-0224, March 6, 2009, accessed March 9, 2009, http://www.bls.gov/news.release/archives/empsit_03062009.pdf; "U.S. FORECLOSURE ACTIVITY INCREASES 75 PERCENT IN 2007," RealtyTrac, January 9, 2008, accessed March 9, 2009, http://www.realtytrac.com/ContentManagement/pressrelease.aspx?ChannelID=9&ItemID= 3988&accnt=64847; Mark Huffman, "2008 Foreclosure Activity Jumps 81 Percent," ConsumerAffairs.com, January 15, 2009, accessed March 9, 2009, http://www.consumeraffairs.com/news04/2009/01/foreclosure_jumps.html.

2.2 Life/Health Market Conditions

The life and health insurance markets do not show similar underwriting cycles. As you saw in Chapter 7, the investment activity of the life/health industry is different from that of the property/casualty segment. In recent years, focus has shifted from traditional life insurance to underwriting of annuities (explained in Chapter 21). Net premiums for life/health insurers increased by 5.7 percent to $616.7 billion and investment income increased by 4.9 percent to $168.2 billion in 2007.[9] However, in recent years, many life insurance companies have invested in mortgage-backed securities with impact on their capital structure, as detailed in "Problem Investments and the Credit Crisis" of Chapter 7. These investments and the effects of the recession brought about a host of problems for the life/health industry in 2008 that have continued into 2009. You will read about such issues in "The Life/Health Industry in the

Economic Recession of 2008–2009" of Chapter 19. As of writing this chapter, the *Wall Street Journal* reported (on March 12, 2009) that life insurers "are being dragged down by tumbling markets and hope a government lifeline is imminent."[10]

Health insurance consists of coverage for medical expenses, disability, and long-term care (all covered in Chapter 22). Figure 8.3 shows how health insurance expenditures increased as a percentage of the gross domestic product in 2006 to 16 percent. Expenditures are projected to increase to 18.7 percent in 2014. In 2007, total health insurance premiums amounted to $493 billion.[11] As with life insurance, emphasis on product offerings in the health segment has seen a transition over time in response to the changing consumer attitudes and needs. The year 1993 marks the beginning of the shift into managed care plans, the features of which are again discussed in Chapter 22.

Despite the managed-care revolution of the 1990s, health care costs continued to increase with no relief in sight.[12] The role of health insurers in influencing insureds' decisions regarding medical treatment has been a topic of controversy for many years in the United States. Some Americans avoid seeking medical care due to the high health care costs and their inability to afford insurance. These and other issues have motivated health insurance reform efforts, the most recent of which have originated with new President Barack Obama. For an in-depth discussion, see "What is the Tradeoff between Health Care Costs and Benefits?" in Chapter 22.

FIGURE 8.3   National Health Expenditures Share of Gross Domestic Product, 1993–2014

(1) Marks the beginning of the shift to managed care. (2) Projected.

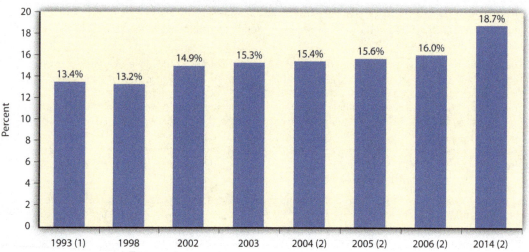

Source: Insurance Information Institute per the Centers for Medicare and Medicaid Services, Office of the Actuary; U.S. Department of Commerce, Bureau of Economic Analysis and Bureau of the Census.

2.3 Reinsurance Organizations and the Marketplace

Reinsurers, by the nature of their business, suffer to a greater extent when catastrophes hit. This fact requires better understanding of not only the reinsurance operations described in Chapter 7 but also the global reinsurance markets and their players.

The top ten reinsurance companies by gross premiums written for 2007 are provided in Table 8.3. Reinsurance is an international business out of necessity. The worldwide growth of jumbo exposures, such as fleets of wide-bodied jets, supertankers, and offshore drilling platforms, creates the potential for hundreds of millions of dollars in losses from one event. No single insurer wants this kind of loss to its income statement and balance sheet. One mechanism for spreading these mammoth risks among insurers is the international reinsurance market.

As you can see in Table 8.3, most of the largest reinsurers are based in Europe. The last two in the list are in Bermuda, an emerging growth market for reinsurance. The Bermuda insurance industry held $146 billion in total assets in 2000, according to the Bermuda Registrar of Companies. Insurers flock to Bermuda because it is a tax haven with no taxes on income, withholding, capital gains, premiums, or profits. It also has a friendly regulatory environment, industry talent, and many other reinsurers. After September 11, a new wave of reinsurers started in Bermuda as existing reinsurers lost their capacity. These reinsurers have since suffered substantial losses as a result of the catastrophic hurricanes of 2004 and 2005.[13]

TABLE 8.3 Top Ten Global Reinsurance Companies by Gross Premiums Written, 2007

Company	Country	Net Reinsurance Premiums Written (Millions of $)
Munich Re Co.	Germany	$30,292.9
Swiss Re Co.	Switzerland	27,706.6
Berkshire Hathaway Re	United States	17,398.0
Hannover Rueckversicherung AG	Germany	10,630.0
Lloyd's	United Kingdom	8,362.9
SCOR SE	France	7,871.7
Reinsurance Group of America, Inc.	United States	4,906.5
Transatlantic Holdings, Inc.	United States	3,952.9
Everest Reinsurance Co.	Bermuda	3,919.4
PartnerRe Ltd.	Bermuda	3,757.1

Source: Insurance Information Institute (III). The Insurance Fact Book 2009, p 42.

KEY TAKEAWAYS

In this section you studied the following:

- Insurance markets are described as either hard or soft depending on loss experience.
- Market cycles are cyclical and are indicated by the industry's combined ratio.
- Market cycles influence underwriting standards.
- Different lines of business have different break-even combined ratio levels to gauge their profitability.
- Reinsurers suffer exponentially greater losses in the event of a catastrophe, so they operate internationally to reduce tax burdens and regulatory obligations.

DISCUSSION QUESTIONS

1. Among the leading insurance markets in the world, which countries are the largest in life premiums and which are the largest in property/casualty premiums?
2. Explain the underwriting cycle. What causes it? When would there be a hard market? When would there be a soft market?
3. Insurance brokers were very busy in the fall of 2008, since the troubles of AIG became public knowledge. Also there were speculations that the property/casualty markets were becoming hard as a consequence of the credit crisis and the problems with mortgage-backed securities. What are hard markets? Why would there be such speculations? Explain in terms of the underwriting cycles and the breakeven combined ratio for each line of insurance.
4. Why did the world reinsurance market become hard in 2001?

3. INSURANCE REGULATION

LEARNING OBJECTIVES

In this section we elaborate on the following:

- **Why insurance is regulated and the objective of regulation**
- **How regulatory authority is structured**
- **The licensing requirements of insurers**
- **Specific solvency regulations**
- **The features of rate regulation, control of agents' activities, claims adjusting, and underwriting practices**
- **Arguments in the debate regarding state versus federal regulation**

Insurance delivers only future payment in case of a loss. Therefore, it has long been actively regulated. The nature of the product requires strong regulation to ensure the solvency of insurers when claims are filed. This is the big picture of the regulation of insurance in a nutshell. However, within this important overall objective are many areas and issues that are regulated as interim steps to achieve the main objective of the availability of funds to pay claims. Most of the regulation has been at the state level for many years. The possibility of federal involvement has also been raised, especially since the passage of the Gramm-Leach-Bliley Financial Services Modernization Act (GLBA) in 1999 and subsequent activities like the optional federal charter of insurers (discussed in the box "The State of State Insurance Regulation—A Continued Debate"). In August 2004, Representative Michael Oxley, chairperson of the House Financial Services Committee, and Representative Richard Baker, chairperson of the Subcommittee on Capital Markets, Insurance, and Government Sponsored Enterprises, released a draft of the State Modernization and Regulatory Transparency (SMART) Act. This proposal is also regarded as the insurance regulatory reform road map draft, and it has added fuel to the debate of state versus federal insurance regulation. The debate has taken many shapes, including a dual (federal/state) chartering system, similar to the banking industry's dual regulatory system that would allow companies to choose between the state system and a national regulatory structure.

Under the current state insurance regulation scheme, state legislatures pass insurance laws that form the basis for insurance regulation. Common forms of insurance regulatory laws are listed in Table 8.4. To ensure the smooth operation of insurance markets and the solvency of insurers, insurance laws are concerned not only with the operations and investments of insurers but also with licensing requirements for insurers, agents, brokers, and claims adjusters and with rates and policy forms and consumer protection. The laws provide standards of financial solvency, including methods of establishing reserves and the types of investments permitted. Provisions are made in the states' laws for the liquidation or rehabilitation of any insurance company in severe financial difficulty. Because solvency is considered to be affected by product pricing (setting rates), rate regulation is an important part of insurance regulation. Trade practices, including marketing and claims adjustment, are also part of the law. Legislation also creates methods to make certain types of insurance readily available at affordable (that is, subsidized) prices. In addition, the taxation of insurers at the state level is spelled out in the insurance code for each state.

TABLE 8.4 Common Types of Insurance Regulatory Laws

- Licensing requirements
- Solvency standards
- Liquidation/rehabilitiation provisions
- Rating (pricing) restrictions
- Trade practice requirements
- Subsidy programs
- Taxation

Every state has an insurance department to administer insurance laws; it is known as the **commissioner (or superintendent) of insurance**. In some states, the commissioner of insurance also acts as another official of the state government, such as state treasurer, state auditor, or director of banking. In most states, however, acting as commissioner of insurance is the person's sole responsibility. In some states, the commissioner is appointed; in others, he or she is elected. Most insurance departments have relatively few staff employees, but several are large, such as those in Texas, California, Illinois, Florida, and New York. The small departments are generally not equipped to provide effective regulation of such a powerful industry.

As indicated above, the most important part of regulation is to ensure solvency of insurers. Assisting in this objective are the regulatory efforts in the area of consumer protection in terms of rates and policy forms. Of course, regulators protect insureds from fraud, unscrupulous agents, and white-collar crime. Regulators also make efforts to make coverage available at affordable prices while safeguarding the solvency of insurers. Regulation is a balancing act and it is not an easy one. Because insurance is regulated by the states, lack of uniformity in the laws and regulation is of great concern. Therefore, the **National Association of Insurance Commissioners (NAIC)** deals with the creation of model laws for adoption by the states to encourage uniformity. Despite the major effort to create uniformity, interest groups in each state are able to modify the NAIC model laws, so those that are finally adopted may not be uniform across the states. The resulting maze of regulations is considered a barrier to the entry of new insurers. This is an introductory text, so insurance regulation will be discussed only briefly here. For the interested student, the NAIC Web site (http://www.naic.org) is a great place to explore the current status of insurance regulation. Each state's insurance department has its own Web site as well.

The state insurance commissioner is empowered to do the following:

- Grant, deny, or suspend licenses of both insurers and insurance agents
- Require an annual report from insurers (financial statements)
- Examine insurers' business operations
- Act as a liquidator or rehabilitator of insolvent insurers
- Investigate complaints
- Originate investigations
- Decide whether to grant all, part, or none of an insurer's request for higher rates
- Propose new legislation to the legislature
- Approve or reject an insurer's proposed new or amended insurance contract
- Promulgate regulations that interpret insurance laws

3.1 Licensing Requirements

An insurer must have a license from each state in which it conducts business. This requirement is for the purpose of exercising control. Companies chartered in a state are known as **domestic insurers**. Foreign insurers are those formed in another state; **alien insurers** are those organized in another country. The commissioner has more control over domestic companies than over foreign and alien ones (he or she has generally less control over insurers not licensed in the state).

An insurer obtains licenses in its state of domicile and each additional state where it plans to conduct insurance business. Holding a license implies that the insurer meets specified regulatory requirements designed to protect the consumer. It also implies that the insurer has greater business opportunities than nonlicensed insurers. A foreign insurer can conduct business by direct mail in a state without a license from that state. The insurer is considered nonadmitted and is not subject to regulation. Nonadmitted or nonlicensed insurers are also called **excess and surplus lines insurers**. They provide coverage that is not available from licensed insurers. That is, nonlicensed insurers are permitted to sell insurance only if no licensed company is willing to provide the coverage. Persons who hold special "licenses" as **surplus lines agents or brokers** provide access to nonadmitted insurers.

A license may be denied under certain circumstances. If the management is incompetent or unethical, or lacking in managerial skill, the insurance commissioner is prohibited from issuing a license. Because unscrupulous financiers have found insurers fruitful prospects for stock manipulation and the milking of assets, some state laws prohibit the licensing of any company that has been in any way associated with a person whose business activities the insurance commissioner believes are characterized by bad faith. For example, the *Equity Funding* case, in which millions of dollars in fictitious life insurance were created and sold to reinsurers, shows how an insurer can be a vehicle for fraud on a gigantic scale.[14] A more recent example is the story of Martin Frankel, who embezzled more than $200 million

commissioner (or superintendent) of insurance

State insurance department that administers insurance laws.

National Association of Insurance Commissioners (NAIC)

A group that deals with the creation of model laws for adoption by the states to encourage uniformity.

domestic insurers

A group that deals with the creation of model laws for adoption by the states to encourage uniformity.

alien insurers

Insurance companies organized in another country.

excess and surplus lines insurers

Companies that provide coverages that are not available from licensed insurers.

surplus lines agents or brokers

Persons who hold special licenses to provide access to nonadmitted insurers.

in the 1990s from small insurance companies in Arkansas, Mississippi, Missouri, Oklahoma, and Tennessee. Three insurance executives in Arkansas were charged in connection with the case.[15]

3.2 Financial Requirements

To qualify for a license, an insurer must fulfill certain financial requirements. Stock insurers must have a specified amount of capital and surplus (that is, net worth), and mutual insurers must have a minimum amount of surplus (mutual companies, in which the policyholders are the owners, have no stock and therefore do not show "capital" on their balance sheets). The amounts depend on the line of insurance and the state law. Typically, a multiple-line insurer must have more capital (and/or surplus) than a company offering only one line of insurance.[16] Insurers must also maintain certain levels of capital and surplus to hold their license. Historically, these requirements have been set in simple dollar values. During the 1990s, requirements for risk-based capital were implemented by the states.

3.3 Accounting Compliance

generally accepted accounting (GAP)

The acceptable system of accounting for publicly traded firms.

statutory accounting (SAP)

System of reporting of insurance that allows companies to account differently for accrued losses.

Insurance companies are required to submit uniform financial statements to the regulators. These statements are based on statutory accounting as opposed to the **generally accepted accounting (GAP)** system, which is the acceptable system of accounting for publicly traded firms. **Statutory accounting (SAP)** is the system of reporting of insurance that allows companies to account differently for accrued losses. The NAIC working groups modify the financial reporting requirements often. In 2002, in the wake of a series of corporate financial scandals, including those affecting Enron, Arthur Andersen, and WorldCom, the Sarbanes-Oxley (SOX) Act of 2002 was adopted. It is considered to be the most significant change to federal securities law in the United States in recent history. It mandates that companies implement improved internal controls and adds criminal and civil penalties for securities violations. SOX calls for auditor independence and increased disclosure regarding executive compensation, insider trading, and financial statements. This act has been successful at improving corporate governance.[17] Publicly traded stock insurance companies (as explained in Chapter 6) are required to comply with SOX. As a fallout of accounting problems at AIG in 2005, there have been proposals to amend the NAIC's model audit rule to require large mutual insurers and other insurers not currently under the act to comply as well. In addition, the issues uncovered in the investigation of AIG's finite reinsurance transactions led to consideration of new rules for such nontraditional insurance products.[18] The rules will require inclusion of some level of risk transfer in such transactions to counter accounting gimmicks that served only to improve the bottom line of a firm. As the student can see, new laws and regulations emerge in the wake of improper actions by businesses. Better transparency benefits all stakeholders in the market, including policyholders.

3.4 Solvency Regulations

unearned premiums

Premiums collected in advance of the policy period.

Regulating insurers is most important in the area of safeguarding future payment of losses. Solvency regulation may help but, in spite of the best efforts of insurance executives and regulators, some insurers fail. When an insurer becomes insolvent, it may be placed either in rehabilitation or liquidation. In either case, policyholders who have claims against the company for losses covered by their policies or for a refund of **unearned premiums**—premiums collected in advance of the policy period—may have to wait a long time while the wheels of legal processes turn. Even after a long wait, insurer assets may cover only a fraction of the amount owed to policyowners. In the aggregate, this problem is not large; only about 1 percent of insurers become insolvent each year.

Investment Requirements

The solvency of an insurer depends partly on the amount and quality of its assets, and how the assets' liquidity matches the needs of liquidity to pay losses. Because poor investment policy caused the failure of many companies in the past, investments are carefully regulated. The states' insurance codes spell out in considerable detail which investments are permitted and which are prohibited. Life insurers have more stringent investment regulations than property/casualty insurers because some of the contracts made by life insurers cover a longer period of time, even a lifetime or more.

Risk-Based Capital

For solvency regulation, the states' insurance departments and the NAIC are looking into the investment and reserving of insurers. During the 1990s, requirements for risk-based capital were implemented by the states. Remember that capital reflects the excess value a firm holds in assets over liabilities. It represents a financial cushion against hard times. **Risk-based capital** describes assets, such as equities held as investments, with values that may vary widely over time; that is, they involve more risk than do certain other assets. To account for variations in risks among different assets, commissioners of insurance, through their state legislators, have begun requiring firms to hold capital sufficient to produce a level that is acceptable relative to the risk profile of the asset mix of the insurer.[19] The requirements are a very important part of solvency regulation. The NAIC and many states also established an early warning system to detect potential insolvencies. Detection of potential insolvencies is a fruitful area of research. The interested student is invited to read the *Journal of Insurance Regulation* and *The Journal of Risk and Insurance* for articles in this area.[20]

risk-based capital

Assets, such as equities held as investments, with values that may vary widely over time.

Reserve Requirements

The investment requirements discussed above concern the nature and quality of insurer assets. The value of assets an insurer must hold is influenced by capital and surplus requirements and the regulation of reserves. Reserves are insurer liabilities that represent future financial obligations to policyholders. Reserves constitute the bulk of insurance company liabilities. See more about how to calculate reserves in Chapter 7.

Guaranty Funds Associations

All states have state guaranty fund associations for both property/casualty and life/health insurance. **State guaranty fund associations** are security deposit pools made up of involuntary contributions from solvent, state-regulated insurance companies doing business in their respective states to ensure that insureds do not bear the entire burden of losses when an insurer becomes insolvent. The guaranty association assesses each company on the basis of the percentage of its premium volume to cover the obligations to policyholders, as discussed later in this chapter.[21] Most guaranty associations limit the maximum they will reimburse any single insured, and most also provide coverage only to residents of the state.

state guaranty fund associations

Security deposit pools made up of involuntary contributions from state-regulated insurance companies to assure that insureds do not bear the entire burden of losses when an insurer becomes insolvent.

3.5 Policy and Rate Regulation

The state insurance commissioners have extensive power in approving policy forms and controlling the rates for insurance. Policy form and rate regulation is part of the regulatory activity, and it is a topic for open debate. Most states consider property/casualty rates not adequately regulated by market forces. Therefore, rates are regulated for auto, property, and liability coverages and workers' compensation. Minimum rates for individual life insurance and annuity contracts are regulated indirectly through limits imposed on assumptions used in establishing reserves. Competitive forces are the only determinants of maximum rates for individual life, individual annuity, and group life/health insurance. Rates for individual health insurance are regulated in some states. Individual disability and accident rates are controlled in some states by their refusal to approve policy forms in which at least a target level of premiums is not expected to be returned to the policyholder as benefits.

prior approval

Method of regulation in which an insurer or its rating bureau must file its new rates and have them approved by the commissioner before using them.

file-and-use

Method of regulation that allows an insurer to begin using a new rate as soon as it is filed with the commissioner.

open competition

Method of regulation that requires no rate filings by an insurer, as the underlying assumption is that market competition is a sufficient regulator of rates.

twisting

Inducing a policyholder to cancel one contract and buy another by misrepresenting the facts or providing incomplete policy comparisons.

rebating

Providing substantial value as an inducement to purchase insurance.

One type of property/casualty rate regulation is the prior approval approach. In states that use the **prior approval** method, an insurer or its rating bureau (such as the Insurance Services Office [ISO] discussed earlier) must file its new rates and have them approved by the commissioner before using them. Another approach called **file-and-use** allows an insurer to begin using a new rate as soon as it is filed with the commissioner. The commissioner can disapprove the new rate if it is determined to be undesirable within a specified period, generally thirty days. A few states have adopted open competition rating laws. **Open competition** requires no rate filings by an insurer because the underlying assumption is that market competition is a sufficient regulator of rates. Although results are mixed, studies of the effects of different types of rate regulation generally find no significant differences in the prices paid by consumers under different systems for the same service.

3.6 Control of Agent's Activities

Insurance laws also prohibit certain activities on the part of agents and brokers, such as twisting, rebating, unfair practices, and misappropriation of funds belonging to insurers or insureds. **Twisting** (also called *churning*) is inducing a policyholder to cancel one contract and buy another by misrepresenting the facts or providing incomplete policy comparisons. An unfair or misleading comparison of two contracts can be a disservice if it causes the insured to drop a policy he or she had for some time in order to buy another that is no better, or perhaps not as good. On the other hand, sometimes changing policies is in the best interest of the policyholder, and justified replacements are legal. Twisting regulations, therefore, may include the requirement that the resulting policy change be beneficial to the policyholder.

Rebating is providing (substantial) value as an inducement to purchase insurance; for example, the agent or broker shares his or her commission with the insured. Rebating is prohibited because:

- It is considered unfair competition among agents.
- Some knowledgeable consumers would buy a new policy each year when first-year commissions are larger than renewal commissions (higher lapse rates increase long-run cost).
- More sophisticated consumers could negotiate larger rebates than the less informed, and this would be unfair.[22]
- Agents may be encouraged to engage in unethical behavior by selling new policies over renewal policies because of the larger first-year commissions.

Some insurers adjust to rebating laws by offering their agents and brokers two or more series of contracts with the same provisions but with rates that reflect different levels of commissions. A particular insurer's "personal series," for example, may include a normal level of commissions. Its "executive series," however, may pay the agent or broker a lower commission and offer a lower rate to potential insureds. In competitive situations, the agent or broker is likely to propose the "executive series" in order to gain a price advantage. The Florida Supreme Court decided in 1986 that the antirebate law was unconstitutional. This decision had the potential to increase pressure on other states to reconsider the practice, but very little activity on the subject has occurred since then. California's Proposition 103 (passed in 1988), however, includes a provision to abandon the state's antirebate laws. In the settlement to resolve their Proposition 103 rollback obligations with the California state insurance department, insurers paid rebates to their 1989 customers.[23]

At the end of 2004, the NAIC adopted a fee disclosure amendment to the producer licensing model act in order to enhance the transparency of producer-fee arrangements. These changes were in response to the probe of broker activities by the New York State Attorney General's Office (mentioned in Chapter 7), which resulted in civil action against Marsh & McLennan. The firm was accused of rigging bids and taking incentive payments to steer business to insurers who were part of the conspiracy. Since the passage of the amendment, the top three insurance brokers have settled with their state regulators and agreed to stop the practice of collecting contingency fees. Most insurance and business newspapers reported extensively about the creation of an $850 million restitution fund for policyholders by Marsh & McLennan as part of the settlement. Many brokers changed their business models as well.[24] For example, Willis Group Holdings Ltd. abolished profit-based contingency fees and offered complete disclosure of all compensation earned from underwriters for all activities relating to placing the business. It also introduced a client bill of rights laying out its responsibilities as a client advocate and established internal controls.

Unfair Practices

Unfair practice is a catch-all term that can be applied to many undesirable activities of agents, claims adjusters, and insurers (including misleading advertisements). Unfair practices may lead to fines, removal of licenses, and—in extreme cases—to punitive damage awards by the courts. **Misappropriation of funds** refers to situations in which the agent keeps funds (primarily premiums) belonging to the company, the policyholder, or a beneficiary. For example, suppose an insured was killed by accident; his $1,000 life insurance policy had a double indemnity rider. In order to impress the beneficiary with the value of this rider, the insurer mailed two checks in the amount of $1,000 each to the agent for delivery. The agent gave one check to the beneficiary and then induced the beneficiary to endorse the second check to the agent, claiming that its issuance was in error, so it had to be cashed and the money returned to the insurer. The insurance department recovered the $1,000, paid it to the beneficiary, and revoked the agent's license.

unfair practice

A catch-all term that can be applied to many undesirable activities of agents, claim adjusters, and insurers.

misappropriation of funds

Situations in which the agent keeps funds belonging to the company, the policyholder, or a beneficiary.

3.7   Control of Claims Adjusting

Every insured has contact with an insurer's marketing system, most often through an agent. Regulation of agents, therefore, has a significant impact on most insureds. Only those who make claims on their policies, however, have contact with claims adjusters. This is the time when an insured may be vulnerable and in need of regulatory attention.

Insurance commissioners control claims adjusting practices primarily through policyholder complaints. Any insured who believes that the insurer improperly handled or denied a claim can contact the insurance commissioner's office with details of the transaction. The commissioner's office will investigate the complaint. Unfortunately for the insured, the commissioner's office cannot require an insurer to pay a claim, although a letter from the commissioner's office that the insured is "in the right" may be persuasive. The most common form of punishment for wrongdoing is either a reprimand or fine against the insurer. Some commissioners' offices keep track of the number of complaints lodged against insurers operating in the state and publish this information on a standardized basis (e.g., per $100,000 of premium volume).

3.8   Control of Underwriting Practices

We have discussed the ways in which insurer pricing practices are regulated. Closely tied to rate making is an insurer's underwriting function. Over the years, insurers have used a variety of factors in their underwriting decisions. A number of these have become taboo from a public policy standpoint. Their use may be considered unfair discrimination. The insurance commissioner's office has some authority to regulate against inappropriate underwriting practices. See the box "Insurance and Your Privacy—Who Knows?" for a discussion of the conflict between the underwriting needs and privacy. Also, the issue of the use of credit scoring in underwriting was discussed in the box "Keeping Score—Is It Fair to Use Credit Rating in Underwriting?" in Chapter 7. The discussions in the boxes are only examples of the vast array of underwriting issues under regulatory oversight. For more issues, visit the NAIC Web site at http://www.NAIC.org.

3.9   Impact of the Gramm-Leach-Bliley Act on Insurance Regulation

The **Gramm-Leach-Bliley Financial Services Modernization Act (GLBA)** of 1999 allowed financial institutions to consolidate their services, bringing sweeping changes for insurance as part of its provisions. Since the passage of the GLBA on November 12, 1999, insurance regulators have been working to maintain state regulation while complying with the new requirements under the act. One of the outcomes is the current debate regarding optional federal insurers' chartering debate (see the box "The State of State Insurance Regulation—A Continued Debate"). Insurers on both sides—the life and the property/casualty—have lobbied for different ways to create federally chartered insurance companies.[25] Many insurers today are global players. The regional mind-set of state regulation appears not to fit the needs of international players. Therefore, these insurers are pushing for federal charters.

Gramm-Leach-Bliley Financial Services Modernization Act (GLBA)

1999 law that allowed financial institutions to consolidate their services.

After the enactment of the GLBA, the NAIC issued a statement of intent to ensure the preservation of state regulation within the GLBA prerequisites. In this statement, the commissioners pointed out, "Fueled by enhanced technology and globalization, the world financial markets are undergoing rapid changes. In order to protect and serve more sophisticated but also more exposed insurance consumers of the future, insurance regulators are committed to modernize insurance regulation to meet the realities of an increasingly dynamic, and internationally competitive financial services marketplace" (see http://www.naic.org). Among the NAIC's commitments to change are the following:

- Amending state laws to include antiaffiliation statutes, licensure laws, demutualization statutes (discussed later in this chapter), and various essential consumer protections, including sales and privacy provisions.

- Streamlining and standardizing the licensing procedure for producers. One of the provisions of Gramm-Leach-Bliley requires U.S. jurisdictions to adopt uniform or reciprocal agent- and broker-licensing laws by November 2002 (three years after the enactment of the law). If this requirement is not met, a National Association of Registered Agents and Brokers will be created.[26] By leveraging work already done on the Producer Database and the Producer Information Network and by using the Insurance Regulatory Information Network (IRIN), the NAIC has already succeeded in meeting the requirements by having enough state legislatures pass bills permitting reciprocity among the states.

- Building on initiatives already underway concerning national companies, such as review of financial reporting, financial analysis and examination, and refining the risk-based approach to examining the insurance operations of financial holding companies.

- Implementing functional regulation and sharing regulatory information to encourage the execution of information-sharing agreements between the individual states and each of the key federal functional regulators.

speed-to-market

Expediting the introduction of new insurance products into the marketplace.

regulatory reengineering

A movement that promotes legislative uniformity.

market conduct reform

A movement that creates a process to respond to changing market conditions, especially relating to e-commerce.

As a result of GLBA, forty-one states enacted reciprocal producer licensing laws, eight states enacted uniform insurance product approval laws, and twenty-four states have enacted property casualty insurance rate deregulation as reported by the National Conference of Insurance Legislators (NCOIL).[27] In addition, the NAIC started to work on the **speed-to-market** concept of expediting the introduction of new insurance products into the marketplace (a process that had been too time-consuming). The idea is to develop state-based uniform standards for policy form and rate filings without loss of flexibility. Other areas of improvements are **regulatory reengineering**, a movement that promotes legislative uniformity, and **market conduct reform**, which creates a process to respond to changing market conditions, especially relating to e-commerce.

The debate regarding federal versus state insurance regulation has been heightened as a result of the 2008–2009 economic recession. As noted in the box "The State of Insurance Regulation—A Continued Debate," the National Insurance Consumer Protection and Regulatory Modernization Act is the most current proposal as of March 2009. It is anticipated that the work on regulatory changes will take years, but insurance companies are in national and global markets, and they are at a disadvantage compared with federally regulated industries such as banking and securities. The need to obtain approval for products from fifty states costs the insurance industry too much time. By contrast, securities firms bring new products to the market within ninety days, and banks do so almost immediately.

Insurance and Your Privacy—Who Knows?

Your insurer knows things about you that your best friend probably doesn't. If you have homeowner's, health, and auto coverage, your insurance provider knows how much money you make, whether you pay your bills on time, how much your assets are worth, what medications you're taking, and which embarrassing diseases you've contracted. Your personal identification numbers, such as your Social Security number and driver's license number, are in those files as well. If you pay your premiums online, your insurance company has a record of your bank account number, too.

Insurance companies can't function without this personal information. Underwriters must know your history to determine your level of coverage, risk pooling group, and rate classification. Adjusters, particularly in the workers' compensation and auto lines, need your identification numbers to gather information from outside providers so they can settle your claims promptly. And to stay competitive, insurers must be able to develop new products and market them to the people who might be interested—special "embarrassing diseases" coverage, perhaps?

But is this information safe? Many consumers who trust their insurance agents with personal information worry about it getting in the hands of the government, an identity thief, or—worst of all—a telemarketer. Insurance companies worry about how to balance protecting their customers' privacy with maintaining enough openness to perform their day-to-day business operations for those same customers.

Two pieces of federal legislation address the issue. The Health Insurance Portability and Accountability Act (HIPAA) of 1996 authorized the Department of Health and Human Services to set minimum standards for protection of health information and gave states the right to impose tougher standards. The Financial Services Modernization Act of 1999, better known as the Gramm-Leach-Bliley Act (GLBA), gave consumers more control over the distribution of their personal financial information.

Insurance is a state-regulated business, so insurance-specific regulations fall within the authority of state insurance commissioners. Thus far, thirty-six states plus the District of Columbia are following a model developed by the National Association of Insurance Commissioners (see the model law and updates on state activity at http://www.naic.org/1privacy). An important component of the NAIC's model is the opt-in provision for health information, which regulators consider to be more sensitive than financial information. As opposed to GLBA's opt-out provision, which gives insurers the right to share your financial information with outsiders unless you specifically tell them not to, NAIC's opt-in provision means insurers can't share your health history unless you specifically permit them to do so.

But the system is far from airtight. Under GLBA provisions, insurers do not need your permission to share your data with its affiliates—and in these days of mega conglomerations, an insurance company can have lots of affiliates. Insurers are even permitted to disclose, without your permission, protected (nonidentifying) financial information to third parties with whom they have a marketing agreement.

For their part, insurers fear that further restrictions on sharing information would affect their ability to provide timely quotes and claims settlements. Another major concern is a broker's ability to shop a policy around to find the best rate and coverage for his or her client. And while consumers might complain about the paperwork involved in opting-out, insurance companies have had to develop and implement privacy policies, train all staff who handle personal information, and set up new departments to handle the opt-out wishes of tens of millions of customers. It's estimated that GBLA compliance could cost the insurance industry as much as $2 billion.

Any federal or state privacy legislation must protect consumers' right to control what happens to their personal data, but it also must preserve insurers' ability to operate their businesses. Where should the line be drawn?

Questions for Discussion

1. How concerned are you about privacy? Are you more protective about your health or your financial information?

2. When companies have to spend money to comply with the law, it's generally the consumer who ends up paying. Would you accept slightly higher premiums to cover the costs of keeping your personal information private?

3. Why would increased privacy provisions make it difficult for brokers to give their customers the best service?

Sources: National Association of Insurance Commissioners, "NAIC Privacy of Consumer Financial and Health Information," http://www.naic.org/ 1privacy; American Civil Liberties Union, "Defending Financial Privacy," http://www.aclu.org /Privacy/PrivacyMain.cfm; American Insurance Association, "Industry Issues: Privacy," http://www.aiadc.org/IndustryIssues/Privacy.asp; Steven Brostoff, "Stakes Are High in Battle over Health Data Privacy," National Underwriter Property & Casualty/Risk & Benefits Management Edition, May 27, 2002; Mark E. Ruquet, "Privacy Is Still a Hot Topic for Agents," National Underwriter Property & Casualty/Risk & Benefits Management Edition, May 27, 2002; Lori Chordas, "Secret Identity," Best's Review, June 2002; Arthur D. Postal "Privacy Rules: A Success?" National Underwriter Property & Casualty/Risk & Benefits Management Edition, March 10, 2005, accessed March 6, 2009, http://www.propertyandcasualtyinsurancenews.com/cms/NUPC/Weekly%20Issues/Issues/2005/10/ p10bank_privacy?searchfor=Privacy%20Rules:%20A%20Success.

The State of State Insurance Regulation—A Continued Debate

Did it surprise you to learn that insurance companies—many of them billion-dollar firms that conduct business across the nation and even around the globe—are regulated by states rather than by the federal government? The state-based regulatory system was established by Congress more than fifty years ago, when most insurers were local or regional—your "good neighbors." Each state's regulations grew more or less independently, based on its own mix of population, weather conditions, and industry, until they were finally quite different from one another. For a long time, though, it didn't matter: Florida agents rarely sold hurricane insurance to Nebraska farmers, so what difference did it make if the rules were different?

These days, however, a Florida-based insurance company might sell insurance policies and annuities to Nebraska farmers, Louisiana shrimpers, and California surfers. But it would have to file the policies for approval from each state involved, a complicated course that can take more than a year. Meanwhile, Huge National Bank goes through a single federal-approval process to sell its investment products, and voilà: permission to market in all fifty states. The consumer, who doesn't have the opportunity to compare prices and benefits, is the ultimate loser.

For life insurers in particular, many of the products sold are investment vehicles. That puts life insurers in direct competition with banks and securities firms, which are federally chartered and can bring their products to market more quickly—and often at a competitive price, too, because they don't have to reformat to meet different requirements in different states.

Equitable market entry, faster review processes, and uniform rate regulation are the top goals for the many insurance groups who are calling for federal chartering as an option for insurance companies, as it has been for the banking industry for 140 years. In December 2001, Senator Charles E. Schumer introduced a bill, the National Insurance Chartering and Supervision Act, that uses the banking industry's dual state-federal regulatory system as a model. Under this bill, insurance companies could choose between state and federal regulation. The following February, Representative John J. LaFalce introduced the Insurance Industry Modernization and Consumer Protection Act, which also would create an optional federal charter for the companies but would keep the states in charge of overseeing insurance rates. (As of March 2009, neither bill had been scheduled for a vote.) In 2004, the State Modernization and Regulatory Transparency (SMART) Act was introduced as the national federal insurance standards conceptual framework (known also as the Oxley-Baker Roadmap) and also invoked major debate.

The 2008–2009 economic recession has renewed interest in optional federal chartering and federal involvement in insurance regulation among members of Congress. The National Insurance Consumer Protection and Regulatory Modernization Act, proposed by Representatives Mellisa Bean and Ed Royce, calls for a national regulatory system and supervision of nationally registered insurers, agencies, and producers; states would retain responsibility over state-licensed entities. The bill would also establish separate guaranty funds for the federally regulated insurers and create federal insurance offices in every state. A vocal critic of the proposal is the National Association of Professional Insurance Agents, who claims that the bill promotes deregulation similar in nature to the type of failed regulation of other financial institutions that brought about the economic recession. Agents for Change, a trade organization representing both life/health and property/casualty agents, applauds the bill as a progressive step that would help insurers to address the present-day needs of consumers.

The bailout of AIG by the federal government in the fall of 2008 escalated the talk about regulatory reform of the insurance industry. Further, there are talks about an active role nationally versus globally. Regardless of the form of the change, all observers talk about some reform with the new administration of President Obama and the makeup of Congress. There are serious talks about an office of insurance information within the Treasury and a greater federal role in insurance regulation and in solutions to systemic risk issues.

Some groups doubt the wisdom of federal involvement at all and urge a reform of the state system, arguing that state regulation is more attuned to the needs of the local consumer. Federal regulation, they contend, would merely add another layer of bureaucracy and cost that not only would hurt the consumer, but also might drive small, specialty insurers out of business while the larger global insurers opt for more uniformity afforded by federal regulation.

Members of Congress say that the issue will not be easily decided, and any reform will take years to accomplish. Nevertheless, all agree that some kind of change is needed. "No matter what side one takes in this long-standing debate, it has become clear to me that this is no longer a question of whether we should reform insurance regulation in the United States," said Representative Paul Kanjorski, a member of the House Committee on Financial Services. "Instead, it has become a question of how we should reform insurance regulation."

Sources: Steven Brostoff, "Optional Federal Chartering: Federal Chartering Hearings to Begin in June," National Underwriter Online News Service, May 16, 2002; Mark A. Hofmann, "Supporters of Federal Chartering Speak Out," Crain's, June 17, 2002; Steven Brostoff, "Battle Lines Being Drawn Over Federal Chartering Bill," National Underwriter Property & Casualty/Risk & Benefits Management Edition, February 25, 2002; Steven Brostoff, "Chartering Plans Have Much in Common," National Underwriter Property & Casualty/Risk & Benefits Management Edition, January 28, 2002; Lori Chordas, "State versus Federal: Insurers and Regulators Continue to Debate the Pros and Cons of Insurance Regulation," Best's Review, April 2002; Arthur D. Postal, "NAIC Calls SMART Act Totally Flawed," National Underwriter Online News Service, March 24, 2005, accessed March 6, 2009, http://www.propertyandcasualtyinsurancenews.com/cms/NUPC/Breaking%20News/2005/03/24-NAIC%20Calls %20SMART%20Act%20Totally%20Flawed?searchfor=totally%20flawed; Arthur D. Postal, "Agent Groups Split Over New OFC Bill," National Underwriter Online News Service, February 17, 2008, accessed March 6, 2009, http://www.propertyandcasualtyinsurancenews.com/cms/nupc/Breaking%20News/ 2009/02/17-AGENTS-dp; Business Insurance Insights, "Howard Mills Speaks about Federal Insurance Regulation," published February 2009, accessed March 6, 2009, http://www.businessinsurance.com/cgi-bin/page.pl?pageId=987; and many more articles in the insurance media from the period between 2004 and 2005 regarding reaction to the proposed SMART Act.

KEY TAKEAWAYS

In this section you studied the following:

- Insurance is actively regulated to ensure solvency.
- Insurance is regulated at the state level by insurance commissioners; the National Association of Insurance Commissioners (NAIC) encourages uniformity of legislation across different states.
- An insurer must have a license from each state in which it conducts business, or conduct business through direct mail as a nonadmitted insurer.
- Features of solvency regulations include investment rules, risk-based minimum capital, reserve requirements, and guaranty fund association contributions.
- Rates are controlled for auto, property, liability, and workers' compensation insurance.
- Regulation of agents' activities is enforced to protect the consumer.
- Claims adjusting practices are influenced through policyholder complaints to the state insurance commission.
- Underwriting practices are scrutinized because they are inherently discriminatory.
- There is much debate over the merits of the existing state regulatory system versus that of federal regulation.

DISCUSSION QUESTIONS

1. Describe the main activities of insurance regulators.
2. What methods are used to create uniformity in insurance regulation across the states?
3. What is the function of the states' guarantee funds?
4. Describe the efforts put forth by the National Association of Insurance Commissioners to preserve state insurance regulation after the passage of the Gramm-Leach-Bliley Financial Services Modernization Act (GLBA).

---

4.   REVIEW AND PRACTICE

1. What are the reasons for the high combined ratios of the commercial lines of property/casualty business in 2001?

2. Describe the emerging reinsurance markets. Why are they developing in Bermuda?

3. What is the difference between each of the following?

   a. Admitted and nonadmitted insurers

   b. Regulated and nonregulated insurers

   c. Surplus lines writers and regulated insurers

   d. "File and use" and "prior approval" rate regulation

   e. "Twisting" and "rebating"

4. The Happy Life Insurance Company is a stock insurer licensed in a large western state. Its loss reserves are estimated at $9.5 million and its unearned premium reserves at $1.7 million. Other liabilities are valued at $1.3 million. It is a mono-line insurer that has been operating in the state for over twenty years.

   a. What concern might the commissioner have if most of Happy Life Insurance Company's assets are stocks? How might regulation address this concern?

   b. If Happy Life Insurance Company fails to meet minimum capital and surplus requirements, what options are available to the commissioner of insurance? How would Happy Life Insurance Company's policyholders be affected? How would the policyholders of other life insurers in the state be affected?

5. Harry is a risk manager of a global chain of clothing stores. The chain is very successful, with annual revenue of $1 billion in 2001. After the record hurricane seasons of 2004 and 2005, his renewal of insurance coverages became a nightmare. Why was renewal so difficult for him?

6. Read the box "Insurance and Your Privacy—Who Knows?" in this chapter and respond to the following questions in addition to the questions that are in the box.

    a. What are privacy regulations?

    b. Why do you think state regulators have been working on adopting such regulation?

    c. What is your opinion about privacy regulation? What are the pros and cons of such regulation?

7. What are risk-based capital requirements, and what is their purpose?

8. How do stock insurers differ from mutuals with respect to their financial requirements?

ENDNOTES

1. Includes accident and health insurance.

2. Nonlife premiums include state funds; life premiums include an estimate of group pension business.

3. April 1, 2007–March 31, 2008.

4. April 1, 2007–March 31, 2008.

5. Life business expressed in net premiums.

6. Adjusted to 2008 dollars by the Insurance Information Institute.

7. Estimated.

8. "Weiss: Life Profits Jump 42 Percent," *National Underwriter*, Life & Health/Financial Services Edition, March 15, 2005.

9. Insurance Information Institute (III), *Insurance Fact Book 2009*, 19.

10. Scott Patterson and Leslie Scism, "The Next Big Bailout Decision: Insurers," *Wall Street Journal*, March 12, 2009, A1.

11. Insurance Information Institute (III), *Insurance Fact Book 2009*, 23.

12. Ron Panko, "Healthy Selection: Less Than a Decade After the Managed-Care Revolution Began in Earnest, New Styles of Health Plans Are on the Market. Proponents See Them As the Next Major Trend in Health Insurance," *Best's Review*, June 2002.

13. David Hilgen, "Bermuda Bound—Bermuda: Insurance Oasis in the Atlantic," and "Bermuda Bound—The New Bermudians," *Best's Review*, March 2002.

14. Raymond Dirks and Leonard Gross, *The Great Wall Street Scandal* (New York: McGraw-Hill Book Company, 1974).

15. "Three Executives Charged in Frankel Case," *Best's Review*, February 2002.

16. The theory behind this requirement is that a company offering all lines of insurance may have greater variations of experience than a company engaged in only one or a few lines and therefore should have a greater cushion of protection for policyholders. It seems reasonable to believe, however, that the opposite may be the case; bad experience in one line may be offset by good experience in another line.

17. Andrew Balls, "Greenspan Praises Corporate Governance Law," *Financial Times*, May 16, 2005, http://www.ft.com/cms/s/0/e7dc1c70-c568-11d9-87fd-00000e2511c8.html?nclick_check=1 (accessed March 6, 2009).

18. Jim Connolly, "AIG Mess Spurring Move to Tighten Insurer Rules," *National Underwriter Online News Service*, May 17, 2005, http://www.propertyandcasualtyinsurancenews.com/cms/NUPC/Breaking%20News/2005/05/16-CONNOLLY-jc?searchfor=AIG%20Mess%20Spurring%20Move%20to%20Tighten%20Insurer%20Rules (accessed March 6, 2009).

19. See the discussion of risk-based capital laws at http://www.naic.org. The requirement and formulas are continuously changing as the NAIC continues to study the changing environment. The basic formula prior to 1996, the Life RBC formula, comprised four components related to different categories of risk: asset risk (C-1), insurance risk (C-2), interest rate risk (C-3), and business risk (C-4). Each of the four categories of risk is a dollar figure representing a minimum amount of capital required to cover the corresponding risk. The final formula is the following:

$$\text{RBC Authorized Capital} = (C-4) + \text{Square Root of } [(C-1+C-3)^2 + (C-2)^2].$$

20. For some examples, see Etti G. Baranoff, Tom Sager, and Tom Shively, "Semiparametric Modeling as a Managerial Tool for Solvency," *Journal of Risk and Insurance*, September 2000; and Etti G. Baranoff, Tom Sager, and Bob Witt, "Industry Segmentation and Predictor Motifs for Solvency Analysis of the Life/Health Insurance Industry," *Journal of Risk and Insurance*, March 1999.

21. New York is the only state that funds the guaranty fund prior to losses from insolvent insurers.

22. John S. Moyse, "Legalized Rebating—A Marketing View," *Journal of the American Society of CLU* 40, no. 5 (1986): 57.

23. "Four More California Insurers Settle on Prop. 103 Rebates," *National Underwriter*, Property & Casualty/Risk & Benefits Management Edition, March 18, 1996. The article explains, "Prop. 103 rebates are determined by applying a formula contained in administrative regulation RH-291 into which a company's verifiable financial data is inserted. The purpose of the regulations is to determine rebate amounts so as not to conflict with the California Supreme Court's ruling in Calfarm v. Deukmejian that rebates may not deprive an insurer of a fair rate of return. After the California Supreme Court upheld the regulations in 1994, insurance companies appealed to the U.S. Supreme Court, which in February 1995 refused to review the case. Commissioner Quackenbush re-adopted the regulations in March, 1995."

24. Steven Brostoff, "Hearing Bares Insurers' Charter Split," *National Underwriter Online News Service*, June 12, 2002.

25. Irene Weber, "No Sale Despite Gramm-Leach-Bliley," *Best's Review*, May 2002.

26. "NCOIL to Congress: Smart Act Unwarranted," Albany, New York, September 11, 2004.

27. E. E. Mazier, "Chartering Plans: They all Have Much in Common," *National Underwriter*, Property & Casualty/Risk & Benefits Management Edition, January 28, 2002.

CHAPTER 9
Fundamental Doctrines Affecting Insurance Contracts

The insurance **contract (or policy)** we receive when we transfer risk to the insurance company is the only physical product we receive at the time of the transaction. As described in the Risk Ball Game in Chapter 1, the contract makes the exchange tangible. Now that we have some understanding of the nature of risk and insurance, insurance company operations, markets, and regulation, it is time to move into understanding the contracts and the legal doctrines that influence insurance policies. Because contracts are subject to disputes, understanding their nature and complexities will make our risk management activities more efficient. Some contracts explicitly spell out every detail, while other contracts are considered incomplete and their interpretations are subject to arguments.[1] For example, in a health contract, the insurer promises to pay for medicines. However, as new drugs come to market every day, insurers can refuse to pay for an expensive new medication that was not on the market when the contract was signed. An example is Celebrex, exalted for being easier on the stomach than other anti-inflammatory drugs and a major favorite of the "young at heart" fifty-plus generation. Many insurers require preauthorization to verify that the patient has no other choices of other, less expensive drugs.[2] The evolution of medical technology and court decisions makes the health policy highly relational to the changes and dynamics in the marketplace.

Relational contracts, we can say, are contracts whose provisions are dynamic with respect to the environment in which they are executed. Some contracts are known as **incomplete contracts** because they contain terms that are implicit, rather than explicit. In the previous example, the dynamic nature of the product that is covered by the health insurance policy makes the policy "incomplete" and open to disputes. Fallen Celebrex rival, Vioxx, is a noted example. New Jersey–based Merck & Co., Inc., faces more than 7,000 lawsuits claiming that its blockbuster drug knowingly increased risk of heart attack and stroke. This chapter also delves into the structure of insurance contracts in general and insurance regulations as they all tie together. We will explore the following:

1. Links

2. Agency law, especially as applied to insurance

3. Basic contractual requirements

4. Important distinguishing characteristics of insurance contracts

1. LINKS

At this point in the text, we are still focused on broad subject matters that connect us to our holistic risk and risk management puzzle. We are not yet drilling down into specific topics such as homeowner's insurance or automobile insurance. We are still in the big picture of understanding the importance

contract (or policy)

Document received when one transfer risks to the insurance company; is the only physical product received at the time of the transaction.

relational contracts

Contracts whose provisions are dynamic with respect to the environment in which they are executed.

incomplete contracts

Contracts that contain terms that are implicit rather than explicit.

of clarity in insurance contracts and the legal doctrines that influence those contracts, and the agents or brokers who deliver the contracts to us. If you think about the contracts like the layers of an onion that cover the core of the risk, you can apply your imagination to Figure 9.1.[3] We know now that each risk can be mitigated by various methods, as discussed in prior chapters. The important point here is that each activity is associated with legal doctrines culminating in the contracts themselves. The field of risk and insurance is intertwined with law and legal implications and regulation. No wonder the legal field is so connected to the insurance field as well as many pieces of legislation.

FIGURE 9.1   Links between the Holistic Risk Picture, the Insurance Contract, and Regulation

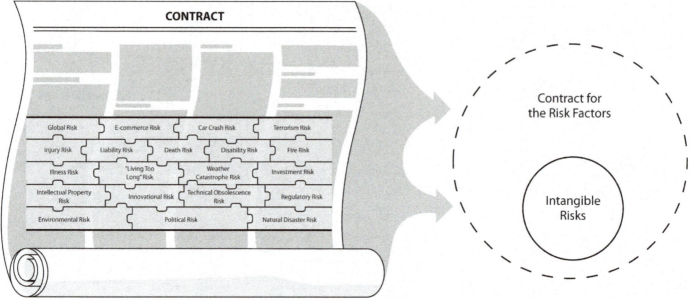

Source: Etti G. Baranoff, "The Risk Balls Game: Transforming Risk and Insurance Into Tangible Concepts," Risk Management & Insurance Review 4, no. 2 (2001): 51–59.

You, the student, will learn in this text that the field of insurance encompasses many roles and careers, including legal ones. As the nature of the contract, described above, becomes more incomplete (less clear or explicit), more legal battles are fought. These legal battles are not limited to disputes between insurers and insureds. In many cases, the agents or brokers are also involved. This point is emphasized in relation to the dispute over the final settlement regarding the World Trade Center (WTC) catastrophe of September 11, 2001.[4] The case at hand was whether the collapse of the two towers should be counted as one insured event (because the damage was caused by a united group of terrorists) or two insured events (because the damage was caused by two separate planes some fifteen minutes apart). Why is this distinction important? Because Swiss Re, one of the principal reinsurers of the World Trade Center, is obligated to pay damages up to $3.5 billion per insured event. The root of the dispute involves explicit versus incomplete contracts, as described above. The leaseholder, Silverstein Properties, claimed that the broker, Willis Group Holdings, Ltd., promised a final contract that would interpret the attack as two events. The insurer, Swiss Re, maintained that it and Willis had agreed to a type of policy that would explicitly define the attack as one event. Willis was caught in the middle and, as you remember, brokers represent the insured. Therefore, a federal judge had to choose an appropriate way to handle the case. The final outcome was that for some insurers, the event was to be counted as two events.[5] This story is only one of many illustrations of the complexities of relationships and the legal doctrines that are so important in insurance transactions.

2. AGENCY LAW: APPLICATION TO INSURANCE

LEARNING OBJECTIVES

In this section we elaborate on the following:

- **The law of agency relative to principals and agents and its role in insurance**
- **The implications of binding authority for agents, their principals, and the insured**
- **How the agency relationship is influenced by the concepts of waiver and estoppel**

2.1 Agents

Insurance is sold primarily by agents. The underlying contract, therefore, is affected significantly by the legal authority of the agent, which in turn is determined by well-established general legal rules regarding agency.

The **law of agency**, as stated in the standard work on the subject, "deals basically with the legal consequences of people acting on behalf of other people or organizations."[6] Agency involves three parties: the principal, the agent, and a third party. The **principal** (insurer) creates an agency relationship with a second party by authorizing him or her to make contracts with third parties (policyholders) on the principal's behalf. The second party to this relationship is known as the **agent**, who is authorized to make contracts with a third party.[7] The source of the agent's authority is the principal. Such authority may be either expressed or implied. When an agent is appointed, the principal expressly indicates the extent of the agent's authority. The agent also has, by implication, whatever authority is needed to fulfill the purposes of the agency. By entering into the relationship, the principal implies that the agent has the authority to fulfill the principal's responsibilities, implying **apparent authority**. From the public's point of view, the agent's authority is whatever it appears to be. If the principal treats a second party as if the person were an agent, then an agency is created. Agency law and the doctrines of waiver and estoppel have serious implications in the insurance business.

Binding Authority

The law of agency is significant to insurance in large part because the only direct interaction most buyers of insurance have with the insurance company is through an agent or a broker, also called a **producer** (see the National Association of Insurance Commissioners' Web site at http://www.naic.org and licensing reforms as part of the Gramm-Leach-Bliley Act prerequisites discussed in Chapter 8).[8] Laws regarding the authority and responsibility of an agent, therefore, affect the contractual relationship.

One of the most important agency characteristics is binding authority. In many situations, an agent is able to exercise **binding authority**, which secures (binds) coverage for an insured without any additional input from the insurer. The agreement that exists before a contract is issued is called a **binder**. This arrangement, described in the offer and acceptance section presented later, is common in the property/casualty insurance areas. If you call a GEICO agent in the middle of the night to obtain insurance for your new automobile, you are covered as of the time of your conversation with the agent. In life and health insurance, an agent's ability to secure coverage is generally more limited. Rather than issuing a general binder of coverage, some life insurance agents may be permitted to issue only a conditional binder. A **conditional binder** implies that coverage exists only if the underwriter ultimately accepts (or would have accepted) the application for insurance. Thus, if the applicant dies prior to the final policy issuance, payment is made if the applicant would have been acceptable to the insurer as an insured. The general binder, in contrast, provides coverage immediately, even if the applicant is later found to be an unacceptable policyholder and coverage is canceled at that point.

Waiver and Estoppel

The agent's relationship between the insured and the insurer is greatly affected by doctrines of waiver and estoppel.

law of agency

Law that deals basically with the legal consequences of people acting on behalf of other people or organizations.

principal

Individual who creates an agency relationship with a second party by authorizing him or her to make contracts with third parties (policyholders) on the principal's behalf.

agent

Individual who is authorized to make contracts with a third party.

apparent authority

The implied authority of the agent to fulfill the principal's responsibilities.

producer

Another name for both agents and brokers.

binding authority

Authority that secures (binds) coverage for an insured without any additional input from the insurer.

binder

The agreement that exists before a contract is issued.

conditional binder

Agreement that implies that coverage exists only if the underwriter ultimately accepts (or would have accepted) the application for insurance.

waiver

The intentional relinquishment of a known right.

Waiver is the intentional relinquishment of a known right. To waive a right, a person must know he or she has the right and must give it up intentionally. If an insurer considers a risk to be undesirable at the time the agent assumes it on behalf of the company, and the agent knows it, the principal (the insurer) will have waived the right to refuse coverage at a later date. This situation arises when an agent insures a risk that the company has specifically prohibited.

Suppose, for example, that the agent knew an applicant's seventeen-year-old son was allowed to drive the covered automobile and also knew the company did not accept such risks. If the agent issues the policy, the company's right to refuse coverage on this basis later in the policy period has been waived.

In some policies, the insurer attempts to limit an agent's power to waive its provisions. A business property policy, for example, may provide that the terms of the policy shall not be waived, changed, or modified except by endorsement issued as part of the policy.

Unfortunately for the insurer, however, such stipulations may not prevent a waiver by its agent. For example, the business property policy provides that coverage on a building ceases after it has been vacant for over sixty days. Let's suppose that the insured mentions to the agent that one of the buildings covered by the policy has been vacant sixty days, but also adds that the situation is only temporary. If the agent says, "Don't worry, you're covered," the right of the insurer to deny coverage in the event of a loss while the building is vacant is waived. The policy may provide that it cannot be orally waived, but that generally will not affect the validity of the agent's waiver. From the insured's point of view, the agent is the company and the insurer is responsible for the agent's actions.

private pension

When the investment portion or cash accumulation of a permanent life insurance policy is elevated to a position of a retirement account.

This point came to a head in the mid-1990s when many life insurance companies were confronted by class-action lawsuits that accused their agents of selling life insurance as a **private pension**[9] —that is, when the investment portion or cash accumulation of a permanent life insurance policy is elevated to a position of a retirement account. There were also large numbers of complaints about misrepresentation of the interest rate accumulation in certain life insurance policies called universal life, which was discussed at length in Chapter 1.[10] The allegations were that insurers and their agents "furnished false and misleading illustrations to whole life insurance policyholders, failing to show that policies would need to be active over twenty years to achieve a 'comparable interest rate' on their premium dollars and used a 'software on-line computer program' and other misleading sales materials to do so."[11] These were dubbed **vanishing premiums policies** because the policyholders were led to believe that after a certain period of time, the policy would be paid in full, and they would no longer have to make premium payments.[12] Though no vanishing-premium case has been tried on the merits, litigation costs and settlement proceedings have cost companies hundreds of millions of dollars. Many large insurers such as Prudential, Met Life,[13] Money, Northwestern Life, Life of Virginia, and more were subject to large fines by many states' insurance regulators and settled with their policyholders. Prudential's settlement with 8 million policyholders will cost the company more than $3.5 billion.[14]

vanishing premiums policies

Policies that policyholders were led to believe would be paid in full after a certain period of time, and they would no longer have to make premium payments.

compliance officer

Individual charged with overseeing all sales materials and ensuring compliance with regulations and ethics.

Many of these companies created the new position of **compliance officer**, who is charged with overseeing all sales materials and ensuring compliance with regulations and ethics.[15] Meanwhile, states focused on modifying and strengthening market conduct regulations. See the box "Enforcing the Code—Ethics Officers" for a review of insurers' efforts regarding ethics and for ethical discussion questions. Ultimately, the insurer may hold the agent liable for such actions, but with respect to the insured, the insurer cannot deny its responsibilities. "The vexing problem of vanishing premiums has proven to be an expensive lesson for insurance companies on the doctrine of **respondeat superior**—a Latin phrase referring to the doctrine that the master is responsible for the actions taken by his or her servant during the course of duty."[16] Neither insurers nor regulators consider an agency relationship as an independent contractor relationship.

respondeat superior

A Latin phrase referring to the doctrine that the master is responsible for the actions taken by his or her servant during the course of duty.

estoppel

Situation that occurs when the insurer or its agent has led the insured into believing that coverage exists, and as a consequence, it means that the insurer cannot later claim that no coverage existed.

Estoppel occurs when the insurer or its agent has led the insured into believing that coverage exists and, as a consequence, the insurer cannot later claim that no coverage existed. For example, when an insured specifically requests a certain kind of coverage when applying for insurance and is *not* told it is not available, that coverage likely exists, even if the policy wording states otherwise, because the agent implied such coverage at the time of sale, and the insurer is estopped from denying it.

Agency by Estoppel

An agency relationship may be created by estoppel when the conduct of the principal implies that an agency exists. In such a case, the principal will be estopped from denying the existence of the agency (recall the binding authority of some agents). This situation may arise when the company suspends an agent, but the agent retains possession of blank policies. People who are not agents of a company do not have blank policies in their possession. By leaving them with the former agent, the company is acting as if he or she is a current agent. If the former agent issues those policies, the company is estopped from denying the existence of an agency relationship and will be bound by the policy.

If an agent who has been suspended sends business to the company that is accepted, the agency relationship will be ratified by such action and the company will be estopped from denying the contract's existence. The company has the right to refuse such business when it is presented, but once the business is accepted, the company waives the right to deny coverage on the basis of denial of acceptance.

Enforcing the Code—Ethics Officers

In the minds of much of the public, insurance agents are up there with used-car dealers and politicians when it comes to ethical conduct. A May 2002 survey by Golin/Harris International, a public relations firm based in Chicago, ranked insurance second only to oil and gas companies as the least trustworthy industry in America. The factors that make an industry untrustworthy, Golin/Harris Marketing Director Ellen Ryan Mardiks told Insure.com, include perceptions that "these industries are distant or detached from their customers, are plagued by questionable ethics in their business practices, are difficult or confusing to deal with, or act primarily in self-interest." Rob Anderson, Director for Change at Golin/Harris, provided the following list of corporate citizenship drivers:

1. Ethical, honest, responsible, and accountable business practices/executives
2. Company treats employees well and fairly
3. Company's products/services positively enhance people's lives
4. Company's values/business practices are consistent with an individual's own beliefs
5. Company listens to and acts on customer and community input before making business decisions
6. Company gets involved with and invests in the community other than in a crisis
7. Company demonstrates a long-term commitment to a cause or issue
8. Company's support for a cause or issue has led to positive improvement and change
9. Company donates a fair share of its profits, goods, or services to benefit others
10. Company's employees are active in the community

He notes that the two most critical things a company must do are to be seen as an "ethical and honest" company and as "treating employees well and fairly."

How people might describe insurance companies is evidenced by the horror stories told on Web sites like screwedbyinsurance.com and badfaithinsurance.com. Of course, every industry has its detractors (and its detractors have Web sites), but insurance can be a particularly difficult sell. Think about it: in life, homeowner's, property/casualty, and auto, the best-case scenario is the one in which you pay premiums for years and never get anything back.

Trust is important in a business of intangibles. The insurance industry's image of trustworthiness took a big hit in the mid-1990s, when some of the biggest companies in the industry, including Prudential, Met Life, and New York Life, were charged with unethical sales practices. The class-action lawsuits were highly publicized, and consumer mistrust soared. The American Council of Life Insurers responded by creating the Insurance Marketplace Standards Association (IMSA)—not to placate the public, which remains mostly unaware of the program—but to set and enforce ethical standards and procedures for its members. IMSA's ethics are based on six principles:

- To conduct business according to high standards of honesty and fairness and to render that service to its customers that, in the same circumstances, it would apply to or demand for itself
- To provide competent and customer-focused sales and service
- To engage in active and fair competition
- To provide advertising and sales materials that are clear as to purpose and honest and fair as to content
- To provide for fair and expeditious handling of customer complaints and disputes
- To maintain a system of supervision and review that is reasonably designed to achieve compliance with these principles of ethical market conduct

IMSA members don't simply pledge allegiance to these words; they are audited by an independent assessor to make sure they are adhering to IMSA's principles and code. The members, who also must monitor themselves continually, found it more efficient to have one person or one division of the company in charge of overseeing these standards. Thus was born the ethics officer, sometimes called the compliance officer.

Actually, ethics officers have been around for some time, but their visibility, as well as the scope of their duties, has expanded greatly in recent years. Today, insurance companies have an ethics officer on staff. In large companies, this person might hold the title of vice president and oversee a staff that formulates policy for ethics and codes of conduct and is charged with educating employees. The ethics officer may also be responsible for creating and implementing privacy policies in accordance with the Gramm-Leach-Bliley Act. Ethics officers' mandate is to make sure that each employee in the company knows and follows the company's ethical guidelines.

Sources: Vicki Lankarge, "Insurance Companies Are Not to Be Trusted, Say Consumers," Insure.com, May 30, 2002; http://www.insure.com/gen/ trust502.html; Insurance Marketplace Standards Association, http://www.imsaethics.org; Barbara Bowers, "Higher Profile: Compliance Officers Have Experienced Elevated Status within Their Companies Since the Emergence of the Insurance Marketplace Standards Association," Best's Review, October 2001; Lori Chordas, "Code of Ethics: More Insurers Are Hiring Ethics Officers to Set and Implement Corporate Mores," Best's Review, March 2001.

KEY TAKEAWAYS

In this section you studied the following:

- Agents work on behalf of a principal (insurer) in establishing a contract with a third party (the insured)
- Principals fulfill their responsibilities by imparting binding authority to their agents to secure coverage with insureds
- Agents may provide coverage for risks that the insurer prohibits, waiving the principal's right of refusal later

DISCUSSION QUESTIONS

1. Describe how agents can bring major liability suits from consumers against their insurers. Do you think insurers should really be liable for the actions of their agents?
2. Explain the concepts of waiver and estoppel, and provide an example of each.
3. Henrietta Hefner lives in northern Minnesota. She uses a wood-burning stove to heat her home. Although Ms. Hefner has taken several steps to ensure the safety of her stove, she does not tell her insurance agent about it because she knows that most wood-burning stoves represent uninsurable hazards. Explain to Ms. Hefner why she should tell her insurance agent about the stove.

3. REQUIREMENTS OF A CONTRACT

LEARNING OBJECTIVES

In this section we elaborate on general requirements of contracts:

- **Offer, acceptance, and consideration**
- **Competent parties**
- **Legal purpose**
- **Legal form**

When an agent sells an insurance policy, he or she is selling a contract. A contract is an agreement enforceable by law. For any such agreement to be legally enforceable, it must meet the following minimum requirements:

- There must be an offer and an acceptance
- There must be consideration
- The parties to the contract must be competent
- Its purpose must be legal
- The contract must be in legal form

3.1 Offer and Acceptance

offer and acceptance

The process of two parties entering into a contract.

Offer and acceptance is the process of two parties entering into a contract; an agreement is reached only after offer and acceptance between the contracting parties. If the party to whom the offer was made requests a change in terms, a counteroffer is made, which releases the first offerer from the terms of the original offer. In the making of insurance contracts, the buyer usually offers to buy and the insurer accepts or rejects the offer. When you call an insurance agent for insurance on your new automobile and the agent provides coverage, there is an offer to buy and the agent has accepted the offer on behalf of his or her company. As stated previously, this acceptance is called a binder. The offer may be verbal, as in this case, or it may be in the form of a written application. This process differs for life and health insurance.

3.2 Consideration

A contract also requires the exchange of consideration. **Consideration** is the price each party demands for agreeing to carry out his or her part of the contract. The value of the consideration is usually unimportant, but lack of consideration will cause the contract to be regarded as a gift and therefore unenforceable. In many cases, insurance contracts stipulate that the consideration is both in the form of premium and certain conditions specified in the policy. Such conditions may include maintenance of a certain level of risk, timely notice of loss, and periodic reports to insurers of exposure values. Conditions will be explained in detail in parts III and IV of the text in the descriptions of insurance contracts. Consideration, therefore, does not necessarily imply dollars.

consideration
The price each party demands for agreeing to carry out his or her part of the contract.

3.3 Competent Parties

Another essential element for a contract is that the parties to the contract must be **competent parties**, or of undiminished mental capacity. Most people are competent to contract, but there are exceptions. Mentally ill or intoxicated persons are not recognized as competent. Minors may enter into contracts, but such contracts may be voided (or terminated). Upon reaching majority (age eighteen in some states, age twenty-one in others), the young person may ratify or reject the contract. If ratified, the contract would then have the same status as one originally entered into by competent parties.

A minor who enters into an insurance contract, therefore, may void it during infancy or when he or she reaches majority. Ratification of a policy at the age of majority can be accomplished (by oral or written communication) either explicitly or implicitly (by continuing the policy). Some states have laws giving minors the power to enter into binding life insurance contracts on their own lives as young as age fourteen.

competent parties
Individuals of undiminished mental capacity.

3.4 Legal Purpose

A contract must have a **legal purpose**—that is, it must not be for the performance of an activity prohibited by law. If it does not, enforcing the contract would be contrary to public policy. A contract by a government employee to sell secret information to an agent of an enemy country, for example, would not have a legal purpose and would be unenforceable. For the same reason, a contract of insurance to cover losses caused by the insured's own arson would be illegal and contrary to public policy, and thus unenforceable.

legal purpose
Not be for the performance of an activity prohibited by law.

3.5 Legal Form

Contracts may be either oral or written; they must, however, follow a specific **legal form**, or appropriate language. Legal form may vary from state to state. As noted, some insurance contracts are—at least initially—oral. Most states do not have laws directly prohibiting oral contracts of insurance. They do, however, require that some contract forms (the written version of standardized insurance policy provisions and attachments) be approved by the state before being offered for sale.

Moreover, the nature and general content of some policies are specified by law. Most states require that certain provisions be included in life and health insurance contracts. Thus, although some contracts may be oral, insurance contracts must—for the most part—be in writing, and they must conform to the requirements of the states in which they are sold.

legal form
Appropriate language.

KEY TAKEAWAYS

In this section, you studied the following:

- Contracts feature an offer, acceptance, and consideration; an insured must offer to buy and consider the premiums/policy conditions, and the agent must accept the offer (provide coverage) in order for an insurance contract to be enacted
- Parties to a contract must be competent; mentally ill and intoxicated persons are not competent to contract
- A contract must be for a legal purpose only
- Contracts may be oral or written, but they must follow legal form

DISCUSSION QUESTIONS

1. What are the requirements of a contract? Provide an example.
2. A talented high school senior is entered into the National Basketball Association Draft, selected by a team, and ultimately signs a play contract. Why might this contract be disputed as unenforceable?
3. Following construction of a storage shed on his property, a homeowner refuses to pay the builder the full amount agreed upon orally for performance of this service. Can the builder sue the homeowner and collect damages for breach of contract? Why or why not?

4. DISTINGUISHING CHARACTERISTICS OF INSURANCE CONTRACTS

LEARNING OBJECTIVES

In this section we elaborate on the following:

- **The concept and importance of utmost good faith in insurance contracts**
- **The feature of adhesion and why it plays a significant role in the event of contract disputes**
- **The importance of indemnity and how it is enforced**
- **The personal nature of insurance contracts**

In addition to the elements just discussed, insurance contracts have several characteristics that differentiate them from most other contracts. Risk managers must be familiar with these characteristics in order to understand the creation, execution, and interpretation of insurance policies. Insurance contracts are the following:

- Based on utmost good faith
- Contracts of adhesion
- Contracts of indemnity
- Personal

4.1 Based on Utmost Good Faith

uberrimae fidei

Utmost good faith.

When an insurer considers accepting a risk, it must have accurate and complete information to make a reasonable decision. Should the insurer assume the risk and, if so, under what terms and conditions? Because insurance involves a contract of **uberrimae fidei**, or utmost good faith, potential insureds are held to the highest standards of truthfulness and honesty in providing information for the underwriter. In the case of contracts other than for insurance, it is generally assumed that each party has equal knowledge and access to the facts, and thus each is subject to requirements of "good faith," not "utmost good faith." In contrast, eighteenth-century ocean marine insurance contracts were negotiated under circumstances that forced underwriters to rely on information provided by the insured because they could not get it firsthand. For example, a ship being insured might be unavailable for inspection because it was on the other side of the world. Was the ship seaworthy? The underwriter could not inspect it, so he (they were all men in those days) required the insured to warrant that it was. If the warranty was not strictly true, the contract was voidable. The penalty for departing from utmost good faith was having no coverage when a loss occurred. Today, the concept of utmost good faith is implemented by the doctrines of (1) representations and (2) concealment.[17]

Representations

When people are negotiating with insurers for coverage, they make statements concerning their exposures, and these statements are called **representations**. They are made for the purpose of inducing insurers to enter into contracts; that is, provide insurance. If people misrepresent **material facts**—information that influences a party's decision to accept the contract—insurers can void their contracts and they will have no coverage, even though they do have insurance policies. In essence, the contracts never existed.

Note that "material" has been specified. If an insurer wants to void a contract it has issued to a person in reliance upon the information she provided, it must prove that what she misrepresented was material. That is, the insurer must prove that the information was so important that if the truth had been known, the underwriter would not have made the contract or would have done so only on different terms.

If, for example, you stated in an application for life insurance that you were born on March 2 when in fact you were born on March 12, such a misrepresentation would not be material. A correct statement would not alter the underwriter's decision made on the incorrect information. The policy is not voidable under these circumstances. On the other hand, suppose you apply for life insurance and state that you are in good health, even though you've just been diagnosed with a severe heart ailment. This fact likely would cause the insurer to charge a higher premium or not to sell the coverage at all. The significance of this fact is that the insurer may contend that the policy never existed (it was void), so loss by any cause (whether related to the misrepresentation or not) is not covered. Several exceptions to this rule apply, as presented in chapters discussing specific policies. In the case of life insurance, the insurer can void the policy on grounds of material misrepresentation only for two years, as was discussed in Chapter 1.

It is not uncommon for students to misrepresent to their auto insurers where their cars are garaged, particularly if premium rates at home are lower than they are where students attend college. Because location is a factor in determining premium rates, where a car is garaged is a material fact. Students who misrepresent this or other material facts take the chance of having no coverage at the time of a loss. The insurer may elect to void the contract.

Concealment

Telling the truth in response to explicit application questions may seem to be enough, but it is not. One must also reveal those material facts about the exposure that only he or she knows and that he or she should realize are relevant. Suppose, for example, that you have no insurance on your home because you "don't believe in insurance." Upon your arrival home one afternoon, you discover that the neighbor's house—only thirty feet from yours—is on fire. You promptly telephone the agency where you buy your auto insurance and apply for a homeowner's policy, asking that it be put into effect immediately. You answer all the questions the agent asks but fail to mention the fire next door. You have intentionally concealed a material fact you obviously realize is relevant. You are guilty of **concealment** (intentionally withholding a material fact), and the insurer has the right to void the contract.

If the insurance company requires the completion of a long, detailed application, an insured who fails to provide information the insurer neglected to ask about cannot be proven guilty of concealment unless it is obvious that certain information should have been volunteered. Clearly, no insurance agent is going to ask you when you apply for insurance if the neighbor's house is on fire. The fact that the agent does not ask does not relieve you of the responsibility.

In both life and health insurance, most state insurance laws limit the period (usually one or two years) during which the insurer may void coverage for a concealment or misrepresentation. Other types of insurance contracts do not involve such time limits.

4.2   Contracts of Adhesion

Insurance policies are contracts of **adhesion**, meaning insureds have no input in the design of a policy's terms. Unlike contracts formulated by a process of bargaining, most insurance contracts are prepared by the insurer and then accepted or rejected by the buyer. The insured does not specify the terms of coverage but rather accepts the terms as stipulated. Thus, he or she adheres to the insurer's contract. That is the case for personal lines. In most business lines, insurers use policies prepared by the Insurance Services Office (ISO), but in some cases contracts are negotiated. These contracts are written

representations

Statements concerning an insured's exposures.

material facts

Information that influences a party's decision to accept a contract.

concealment

Intentionally withholding a material fact.

adhesion

Situation in which insureds have no input in the design of a policy's terms.

by risk managers or brokers who then seek underwriters to accept them, whereas most individuals go to an agent to request coverage as is.

The fact that buyers usually have no influence over the content or form of insurance policies has had a significant impact on the way courts interpret policies when there is a dispute.[18] When the terms of a policy are ambiguous, the courts favor the insured because it is assumed that the insurer that writes the contract should know what it wants to say and how to state it clearly. Further, the policy language generally is interpreted according to the insured's own level of expertise and situation, not that of an underwriter who is knowledgeable about insurance. When the terms are not ambiguous, however, the courts have been reluctant to change the contract in favor of the insured.

A violation of this general rule occurs, however, when the courts believe that reasonable insureds would expect coverage of a certain type. Under these conditions, regardless of the ambiguity of policy language (or lack thereof), the court may rule in favor of the insured. Courts are guided by the expectations principle (or reasonable expectations principle), which may be stated as follows:

> *The objectively reasonable expectations of applicants and intended beneficiaries regarding the terms of insurance contracts will be honored even though painstaking study of the policy provisions would have negated those expectations.*[19]

expectations principle

The event of a dispute, courts will read insurance policies as they would expect the insured to do.

In other words, the **expectations principle** holds that, in the event of a dispute, courts will read insurance policies as they would expect the insured to do. Thus, the current approach to the interpretation of contracts of adhesion is threefold: first, to favor the insured when terms of the contract drafted by the insurer are ambiguous; second, to read the contract as an insured would; third, to determine the coverage on the basis of the reasonable expectations of the insured.

4.3 Indemnity Concept

indemnity

The insurer agrees to pay no more (and no less) than the actual loss suffered by the insured.

Many insurance contracts are contracts of indemnity. **Indemnity** means the insurer agrees to pay no more (and no less) than the actual loss suffered by the insured. For example, suppose your house is insured for $200,000 at the time it is totally destroyed by fire. If its value at that time is only $180,000, that is the amount the insurance company will pay.[20] You cannot collect $200,000 because to do so would exceed the actual loss suffered. You would be better off after the loss than you were before. The purpose of the insurance contract is—or should be—to restore the insured to the same economic position as before the loss.

The indemnity principle has practical significance both for the insurer and for society. If insureds could gain by having an insured loss, some would deliberately cause losses. This would result in a decrease of resources for society, an economic burden for the insurance industry, and (ultimately) higher insurance premiums for all insureds. Moreover, if losses were caused intentionally rather than as a result of chance occurrence, the insurer likely would be unable to predict costs satisfactorily. An insurance contract that makes it possible for the insured to profit by an event insured against violates the principle of indemnity and may prove poor business to the insurer.

The doctrine of indemnity is implemented and supported by several legal principles and policy provisions, including the following:

- Insurable interest
- Subrogation
- Actual cash value provision
- Other insurance provisions

Insurable Interest

insurable interest

Financial interest in life or property that is subject to loss.

If a fire or auto collision causes loss to a person or firm, that person or firm has an insurable interest. A person not subject to loss does not have an insurable interest. Stated another way, **insurable interest** is financial interest in life or property that is subject to loss. The law concerning insurable interest is important to the buyer of insurance because it determines whether the benefits from an insurance policy will be collectible. Thus, all insureds should be familiar with what constitutes an insurable interest, when it must exist, and the extent to which it may limit payment under an insurance policy.

Basis for Insurable Interest

Many situations constitute an insurable interest. The most common is ownership of property. An owner of a building will suffer financial loss if it is damaged or destroyed by fire or other peril. Thus, the owner has an insurable interest in the building.

A mortgage lender on a building has an insurable interest in the building. For the lender, loss to the security, such as the building being damaged or destroyed by fire, may reduce the value of the loan. On the other hand, an unsecured creditor generally does not have an insurable interest in the general assets of the debtor because loss to such assets does not directly affect the value of the creditor's claim against the debtor.

If part or all of a building is leased to a tenant who makes improvements in the leased space, such improvements become the property of the building owner on termination of the lease. Nevertheless, the tenant has an insurable interest in the improvements because he or she will suffer a loss if they are damaged or destroyed during the term of the lease. This commonly occurs when building space is rented on a "bare walls" basis. To make such space usable, the tenant must make improvements.

If a tenant has a long-term lease with terms more favorable than would be available in the current market but that may be canceled in the event that the building is damaged, the tenant has an insurable interest in the lease. A bailee—someone who is responsible for the safekeeping of property belonging to others and who must return it in good condition or pay for it—has an insurable interest. When you take your clothes to the local dry-cleaning establishment, for example, it acts as a bailee, responsible for returning your clothes in good condition.

A person has an insurable interest in his or her own life and may have such an interest in the life of another.[21] An insurable interest in the life of another person may be based on a close relationship by blood or marriage, such as a wife's insurable interest in her husband. It may also be based on love and affection, such as that of a parent for a child, or on financial considerations. A creditor, for example, may have an insurable interest in the life of a debtor, and an employer may have an insurable interest in the life of a key employee.

When Insurable Interest Must Exist

The time at which insurable interest must exist depends on the type of insurance. In property insurance, the interest must exist at the time of the loss. As the owner of a house, one has an insurable interest in it. If the owner insures himself against loss to the house caused by fire or other peril, that person can collect on such insurance only if he still has an insurable interest in the house at the time the damage occurs. Thus, if one transfers unencumbered title to the house to another person before the house is damaged, he cannot collect from the insurer, even though the policy may still be in force. He no longer has an insurable interest. On the other hand, if the owner has a mortgage on the house that was sold, he will continue to have an insurable interest in the amount of the outstanding mortgage until the loan is paid.

As a result of the historical development of insurance practices, life insurance requires an insurable interest only at the inception of the contract. When the question of insurable interest in life insurance was being adjudicated in England, such policies provided no cash surrender values; the insurer made payment only if the person who was the subject[22] of insurance died while the policy was in force. An insured who was also the policyowner and unable to continue making premium payments simply sacrificed all interest in the policy.

This led to the practice of some policyowners/insureds selling their policies to speculators who, as the new owners, named themselves the beneficiaries and continued premium payments until the death of the insured. This practice is not new but appears to have grown, as reported in the *Wall Street Journal*.[23] Life-settlement companies emerged recently for seniors. **Life-settlement companies** buy life insurance policies from senior citizens for a percentage of the value of the death benefits. These companies pay the premiums and become the beneficiary when the insured passes away. This is similar to **viatical-settlement companies**, which buy life insurance policies from persons with short life expectancies, such as AIDS patients in the 1990s. An example of a life-settlement company is Stone Street Financial, Inc., in Bethesda, Maryland, which bought the value of $500,000 of life insurance for $75,775 from an older person. The person felt he was making money on the deal because the policy surrender value was only $5,000. Viatical settlement companies ran into trouble after new drug regimens extended the lives of AIDS patients, and investors found themselves waiting years or decades, instead of weeks or months, for a return on their investments. In contrast, life-settlement companies contend that, because there is no cure for old age, investors cannot lose in buying the policies from people over sixty-five years old with terminal illnesses such as cancer, amyotrophic lateral sclerosis (Lou Gehrig's disease), and liver disease.[24] These companies don't sell to individual investors, but rather package the policies they buy into portfolios for institutional investors. According to Scope Advisory GmbH (Berlin), which rates life-settlement companies, "Institutional investments helped increase the face

life-settlement companies

Firms that buy life insurance policies from senior citizens for a percent of the value of the death benefits.

viatical-settlement companies

Firms that buy life insurance policies from persons with short life expectancies.

value of life insurance policies traded through the life settlement market to about $10 billion in 2004, from $3 billion in 2003."[25] There is a regulatory maze regarding these arrangements.[26]

Because the legal concept of requiring an insurable interest only at the inception of the life insurance contract has continued, it is possible to collect on a policy in which such interest has ceased. For example, if the life of a key person in a firm is insured, and the firm has an insurable interest in that key person's life because his or her death would cause a loss to the firm, the policy may be continued in force by the firm even after the person leaves the firm. The proceeds may be collected when he or she dies. This point was brought to light with the publication of the *Wall Street Journal* story "Big Banks Quietly Pile Up 'Janitors' Insurance."[27] The article reports that banks and other large employers bought inexpensive life coverage—or **janitor's insurance**—on the lives of their employees. This practice did not require informing the employees or their families. Coverage was continued even after the employees left the company. Upon the death of the employees, the employer collected the proceeds and padded their bottom-line profits with tax-free death benefits. Many newspapers reported the story as a breach of ethical behavior. *The Charlotte Observer* (North Carolina) reported that employers were not required to notify workers of **corporate-owned life insurance (COLI)** policies in which employers own life insurance policies on employees. However, the newspaper continued, "some of the Charlotte area's biggest companies said they have notified all employees covered by the policies, but declined to say how they informed the workers. Use of COLI policies has raised outcries from human rights activists and prompted federal legislation calling for disclosure."[28] The National Association of Insurance Commissioners (NAIC) formed a special working group to study these issues. Dissatisfaction with the janitor insurance scandal led the state of Washington to instate a law requiring employers to obtain written permission from an employee before buying life insurance on the employee's life. Key employees can still be exempt from the law. In 2005, members of the U.S. House of Representative also proposed legislation to limit such practices.[29]

Extent to which Insurable Interest Limits Payment

In the case of property insurance, not only must an insurable interest exist at the time of the loss, but the amount the insured is able to collect is limited by the extent of such interest. For example, if you have a one-half interest in a building that is worth $1,000,000 at the time it is destroyed by fire, you cannot collect more than $500,000 from the insurance company, no matter how much insurance you purchased. If you could collect more than the amount of your insurable interest, you would make a profit on the fire. This would violate the principle of indemnity. An exception exists in some states where valued policy laws are in effect. These laws require insurers to pay the full amount of insurance sold if property is totally destroyed. The intent of the law is to discourage insurers from selling too much coverage.

In contrast to property insurance, life insurance payments are usually not limited by insurable interest. Most life insurance contracts are considered to be **valued policies**,[30] or contracts that agree to pay a stated sum upon the occurrence of the event insured against, rather than to indemnify for loss sustained. For example, a life insurance contract provides that the insurer will pay a specified sum to the beneficiary upon receipt of proof of death of the person whose life is the subject of the insurance. The beneficiary does not have to prove that any loss has been suffered because he or she is not required to have an insurable interest.

Some health insurance policies provide that the insurance company will pay a specified number of dollars per day while the insured is hospitalized. Such policies are not contracts of indemnity; they simply promise to make cash payments under specified circumstances. This makes such a contract "incomplete," as discussed in the introduction to this chapter. This also leads to more litigation because there are no explicit payout amounts written into the contract while improvements in medical technology change the possible treatments daily.

Although an insurable interest must exist at the inception of a life insurance contract to make it enforceable, the amount of payment is usually not limited by the extent of such insurable interest. The amount of life insurance collectible at the death of an insured is limited only by the amount insurers are willing to issue and by the insured's premium-paying ability.[31] The life insurance payout amount is expressed explicitly in the contract. Thus, in most cases, it is not subject to litigation and arguments over the coverage. The amount of the proceeds of a life insurance policy that may be collected by a creditor-beneficiary, however, is generally limited to the amount of the debt and the premiums paid by the creditor, plus interest.[32]

janitor's insurance

Inexpensive life insurance coverage.

corporate-owned life insurance (COLI)

Policies in which employers own life insurance policies on employees.

valued policies

Contracts to pay a stated sum upon the occurrence of the event insured against, rather than to indemnify for loss sustained.

Subrogation

The principle of indemnity is also supported by the right of subrogation. **Subrogation** gives the insurer whatever claim against third parties the insured may have as a result of the loss for which the insurer paid. For example, if your house is damaged because a neighbor burned leaves and negligently permitted the fire to get out of control, you have a right to collect damages from the neighbor because a negligent wrongdoer is responsible to others for the damage or injury he or she causes. (Negligence liability will be discussed in later chapters.) If your house is insured against loss by fire, however, you cannot collect from both the insurance company and the negligent party who caused the damage. Your insurance company will pay for the damage and is then subrogated (that is, given) your right to collect damages. The insurer may then sue the negligent party and collect from him or her. This prevents you from making a profit by collecting twice for the same loss.

The right of subrogation is a common law right the insurer has without a contractual agreement. It is specifically stated in the policy, however, so that the insured will be aware of it and refrain from releasing the party responsible for the loss. The standard personal auto policy, for example, provides that

> *if we make a payment under this policy and the person to or for whom payment was made has a right to recover damages from another, that person shall subrogate that right to us. That person shall do whatever is necessary to enable us to exercise our rights and shall do nothing after loss to prejudice them.*
>
> *If we make a payment under this policy and the person to or for whom payment is made recovers damages from another, that person shall hold in trust for us the proceeds of the recovery and shall reimburse us to the extent of our payment.*

Actual Cash Value

This clause is included in many property insurance policies. An insured generally does not receive an amount greater than the actual loss suffered because the policy limits payment to actual cash value. A typical property insurance policy says, for example, that the company insures "to the extent of actual cash value…but not exceeding the amount which it would cost to repair or replace…and not in any event for more than the interest of the insured."

Actual cash value is not defined in the policy, but a generally accepted notion of it is the replacement cost at the time of the loss, less physical depreciation, including obsolescence. For example, if the roof on your house has an expected life of twenty years, roughly half its value is gone at the end of ten years. If it is damaged by an insured peril at that time, the insurer will pay the cost of replacing the damaged portion, less depreciation. You must bear the burden of the balance. If the replacement cost of the damaged portion is $2,000 at the time of a loss, but the depreciation is $800, the insurer will pay $1,200 and you will bear an $800 expense.

Another definition of actual cash value is **fair market value**, which is the amount a willing buyer would pay a willing seller. For auto insurance, where thousands of units of nearly identical property exist, fair market value may be readily available. Retail value, as listed in the National Automobile Dealers Association (NADA) guide or the Kelley Blue Book, may be used. For other types of property, however, the definition may be deceptively simple. How do you determine what a willing buyer would be willing to pay a willing seller? The usual approach is to compare sales prices of similar property and adjust for differences. For example, if three houses similar to yours in your neighborhood have recently sold for $190,000, then that is probably the fair market value of your home. You may, of course, believe your house is worth far more because you think it has been better maintained than the other houses. Such a process for determining fair market value may be time-consuming and unsatisfactory, so it is seldom used for determining actual cash value. However, it may be used when obsolescence or neighborhood deterioration causes fair market value to be much less than replacement cost minus depreciation.

Property insurance is often written on a **replacement cost** basis, which means that there is no deduction for depreciation of the property. With such coverage, the insurer would pay $2,000 for the roof loss mentioned above and you would not pay anything. This coverage may or may not conflict with the principle of indemnity, depending on whether you are better off after payment than you were before the loss. If $2,000 provided your house with an entirely new roof, you have gained. You now have a roof that will last twenty years, rather than ten years. On the other hand, if the damaged portion that was repaired accounted for only 10 percent of the roof area, having it repaired would not increase the expected life of the entire roof. You are not really any better off after the loss and its repair than you were before the loss.

When an insured may gain, as in the case of having a loss paid for on a replacement cost basis, there is a potential moral hazard. The insured may be motivated to be either dishonest or careless. For

subrogation

Situation that gives the insurer whatever claim against third parties the insured may have as a result of the loss for which the insurer paid.

actual cash value

The replacement cost at the time of the loss, less physical depreciation including obsolescence.

fair market value

The amount a willing buyer would pay a willing seller.

replacement cost

Indemnification for a property loss with no deduction for depreciation.

example, if your kitchen has not been redecorated for a very long time and looks shabby, you may not worry about leaving a kettle of grease unattended on the stove. The resulting grease fire will require extensive redecoration as well as cleaning of furniture and, perhaps, replacement of some clothing (assuming that the fire is extinguished before it gets entirely out of control). Or you may simply let your old house burn down. Insurers try to cope with these problems by providing in the policy that, when the cost to repair or replace damage to a building is more than some specified amount, the insurer will pay not more than the actual cash value of the damage until actual repair or replacement is completed. In this way, the insurer discourages you from destroying the house in order to receive a monetary reward. Arson generally occurs with the intent of financial gain. Some insurers will insure personal property only on an actual cash value basis because the opportunity to replace old with new may be too tempting to some insureds. Fraudulent claims on loss to personal property are easier to make than are fraudulent claims on loss to buildings. Even so, insurers find most insureds to be honest, thus permitting the availability of replacement cost coverage on most forms of property.

Other Insurance Provisions

other insurance provisions

Clauses in in insurance contracts is to prevent insureds from making a profit by collecting from more than one insurance policy for the same loss.

The purpose of **other insurance provisions** in insurance contracts is to prevent insureds from making a profit by collecting from more than one insurance policy for the same loss. For example, if you have more than one policy protecting you against a particular loss, there is a possibility that by collecting on all policies, you may profit from the loss. This would, of course, violate the principle of indemnity.

Most policies (other than life insurance) have some provision to prevent insureds from making a profit from a loss through ownership of more than one policy. The homeowner's policy, for example, provides a clause about other insurance, or pro rata liability, that reads as follows:

> *If a loss covered by this policy is also covered by other insurance, we will pay only the proportion of the loss that the limit of liability that applies under this policy bears to the total amount of insurance covering the loss.*

Suppose you have a $150,000 homeowners policy with Company A, with $75,000 personal property coverage on your home in Montana, and a $100,000 homeowners policy with Company B, with $50,000 personal property coverage on your home in Arizona. Both policies provide coverage of personal property anywhere in the world. If $5,000 worth of your personal property is stolen while you are traveling in Europe, because of the "other insurance" clause, you cannot collect $5,000 from each insurer. Instead, each company will pay its pro rata share of the loss. Company A will pay its portion of the obligation ($75,000/$125,000 = 3/5) and Company B will pay its portion ($50,000/$125,000 = 2/5). Company A will pay $3,000 and Company B will pay $2,000. You will not make a profit on this deal, but you will be indemnified for the loss you suffered. The proportions are determined as follows:

Amount of insurance, Company A	$75,000
Amount of insurance, Company B	$50,000
Total amount of insurance	$125,000
Company A pays $\frac{75,000}{125,000} \times 5,000 =$	$3,000
Company B pays $\frac{50,000}{125,000} \times 5,000 =$	$2,000
Total paid	$5,000

4.4 Personal

personal

Insuring against loss to a person, not to the person's property.

Insurance contracts are **personal**, meaning they insure against loss to a person, not to the person's property. For example, you may say, "My car is insured." Actually, you are insured against financial loss caused by something happening to your car. If you sell the car, insurance does not automatically pass to the new owner. It may be assigned,[33] but only with the consent of the insurer. The personal auto policy, for example, provides that your rights and duties under this policy may not be assigned without our written consent.

As you saw in Chapter 7, underwriters are as concerned about who it is they are insuring as they are about the nature of the property involved, if not more so. For example, if you have an excellent driving record and are a desirable insured, the underwriter is willing to accept your application for insurance. If you sell your car to an eighteen-year-old male who has already wrecked two cars this year, however, the probability of loss increases markedly. Clearly, the insurer does not want to assume that kind of risk without proper compensation, so it protects itself by requiring written consent for assignment.

Unlike property insurance, life insurance policies are freely assignable. This is a result of the way life insurance practice developed before policies accumulated cash values. Whether or not change of ownership affects the probability of the insured's death is a matter for conjecture. In life insurance, the policyowner is not necessarily the recipient of the policy proceeds. As with an auto policy, the subject of the insurance (the life insured) is the same regardless of who owns the policy. Suppose you assign your life insurance policy (including the right to name a beneficiary) to your spouse while you are on good terms. Such an assignment may not affect the probability of your death. On the other hand, two years and two spouses later, the one to whom you assigned the policy may become impatient about the long prospective wait for death benefits. Changing life insurance policyowners may not change the risk as much as, say, changing auto owners, but it could (murder is quite different from stealing). Nevertheless, life insurance policies can be assigned without the insurer's consent.

Suppose you assign the rights to your life insurance policy to another person and then surrender it for the cash value before the insurance company knows of the assignment. Will the person to whom you assigned the policy rights also be able to collect the cash value? To avoid litigation and to eliminate the possibility of having to make double payment, life insurance policies provide that the company is not bound by an assignment until it has received written notice. The answer to this question, therefore, generally is no. The notice requirements, however, may be rather low. A prudent insurer may hesitate to pay off life insurance proceeds when even a slight indication of an assignment (or change in beneficiary) exists.

KEY TAKEAWAYS

In this section you studied the following:

- Insurance contracts are contracts of utmost good faith, so potential insureds are held to the highest standards of truthfulness and honesty in providing information (making representations) to the underwriter
- Insurance contracts are contracts of adhesion because the insured must accept the terms as stipulated; in disputes between insureds and insurers, this feature has led courts generally to side with insureds where policy ambiguity is concerned
- Insurance contracts are contracts of indemnity (the insurer will pay no more or no less than the actual loss incurred); indemnity is supported by the concepts of the following:

  - Insurable interest
  - Subrogation
  - Actual cash value provisions
  - Other insurance provisions

- Insurance contracts are personal, meaning that people are insured against losses rather than property; insurers often require written consent of assignment when insureds wish to assign coverage with the transfer of property

DISCUSSION QUESTIONS

1. Assume that you are a key employee and that your employer can buy an insurance policy on your life and collect the proceeds, even if you are no longer with the firm at the time of your death. Clearly, if you leave the firm, your employer no longer has an insurable interest in your life and would gain by your death. Would this situation make you uncomfortable? What if you learned that your former employer was in financial difficulty? Do you think the law should permit a situation of this kind? How is this potential problem typically solved? Relate your situation to the janitor's insurance stories described in this chapter.

2. Does the fact that an insurance policy is a contract of adhesion make it difficult for insurers to write it in simple, easy-to-understand terms? Explain.

3. If your house is destroyed by fire because of your neighbor's negligence, your insurer may recover from your neighbor what it previously paid you under its right of subrogation. This prevents you from collecting twice for the same loss. But the insurer collects premiums to pay losses and then recovers from negligent persons who cause them. Isn't that double recovery? Explain.

4. If you have a $100,000 insurance policy on your house but it is worth only $80,000 at the time it is destroyed by fire, your insurer will pay you only $80,000. You paid for $100,000 of insurance but you get only $80,000. Are you being cheated? Explain.

5. Who makes the offer in insurance transactions? Why is the answer to this question important?

5. REVIEW AND PRACTICE

1. Walter Brown owns a warehouse in Chicago. The building would cost $400,000 to replace at today's prices, and Walter wants to be sure he's properly insured. He feels that he would be better off if he had two $250,000 replacement cost property insurance policies on the warehouse because "then I'll know if one of the insurers is giving me the runaround. Anyhow, you have to get a few extra dollars to cover expenses if there's a fire—and I can't get that from one company."

    a. If the building is totally destroyed by fire, how much may Walter collect without violating the concept of indemnity?

    b. What is Walter's insurable interest? Does it exceed the value of the building?

2. During the application process for life insurance, Bill Boggs indicated that he had never had pneumonia, when the truth is that he did have the disease as a baby. He fully recovered, however, with no permanent ill effects. Bill was unaware of having had pneumonia as a baby until, a few weeks after he completed the application, his mother told him about it. Bill was aware, however, that he regularly smoked three or four cigarettes a day when he answered a question on the application about smoking. He checked a block indicating that he was not a smoker, realizing that nonsmokers qualified for lower rates per $1,000 of life insurance. The insurer could have detected his smoking habit through blood and urine tests. Such tests were not conducted because Bill's application was for a relatively small amount of insurance compared to the insurer's average size policy. Instead, the insurer relied on Bill's answers being truthful.

    Twenty months after the issuance of the policy on Bill Bogg's life, he died in an automobile accident. The applicable state insurance law makes life insurance policies contestable for two years. The insurer has a practice of investigating all claims that occur during the contestable period. In the investigation of the death claim on Bill Boggs, the facts about Bill's case of pneumonia and his smoking are uncovered.

    a. Will Bill's statements on the application be considered misrepresentations? Discuss what you know about misrepresentations as they could apply in this case.

    b. Because the cause of Bill's death was unrelated to his smoking habit, his beneficiary will not accept the insurer's offer to return Bill's premiums plus interest. The beneficiary is insisting on pursuing this matter in court. What advice do you have for the beneficiary?

3. A smart college senior accepted a job. After the celebration in a bar, he caused an accident. The employer wanted to change the contract and not hire him. Do you think the senior has grounds to dispute the decision?

4. An insurance company denied a claim. Three years earlier, the insurer paid for a similar claim. What concept of the law can help the insured? Explain.

5. Michelle Rawson recently moved to Chicago from a rural town. She does not tell her new auto insurance agent about the two speeding tickets she got in the past year. What problem might Michelle encounter? Explain.

6. You cannot assign your auto policy to a purchaser without the insurer's consent, but you can assign your life insurance policy without the insurer's approval. Is this difference really necessary? Why or why not?

ENDNOTES

1. The origin of the analysis of the type of contracts is founded in transaction cost economics (TCE) theory. TCE was first introduced by R. H. Coase in "The Nature of the Firm," *Economica*, November 1937, 386–405, reprinted in Oliver E. Williamson, ed., *Industrial Organization* (Northampton, MA: Edward Elgar Publishing, 1996); Oliver E. Williamson, *The Economic Institution of Capitalism* (New York: Free Press, 1985); application to insurance contracts developed by Etti G. Baranoff and Thomas W. Sager, "The Relationship Among Asset Risk, Product Risk, and Capital in the Life Insurance Industry," *Journal of Banking and Finance* 26, no. 6 (2002): 1181–97.

2. Testimonials and author's personal experience.

3. The idea of using Risk Balls occurred to me while searching for ways to apply transaction costs economic theory to insurance products. I began thinking about the risk embedded in insurance products as an intangible item separate from the contract that completes the exchange of that risk. The abstract notion of risk became the intangible core and the contract became the tangible part that wraps itself around the core or risk.

4. This issue was discussed at length in all financial magazines and newspapers since September 11, 2001.

5. The December 9, 2004, *BestWire* article, "Tale of Two Trials: Contract Language Underlies Contradictory World Trade Center Verdicts," explains that "the seemingly contradictory jury verdicts from two trials as to whether the Sept. 11, 2001, destruction of the World Trade Center was one event or two for insurance purposes is not so surprising when the central question in both trials is considered: Did the language in the insurance agreements adequately define what an occurrence is?" http://www3.ambest.com/Frames/FrameServer.asp?AltSrc =23&Tab=1&Site=news&refnum=70605 (accessed March 7, 2009).

6. J. Dennis Hynes, *Agency and Partnership: Cases, Materials and Problems*, 2nd ed. (Charlottesville, VA: The Michie Company, 1983), 4.

7. It is important to note the difference between an agent who represents the insurer and a broker who represents the insured. However, because of state insurance laws, in many states brokers are not allowed to operate unless they also obtain an agency appointment with an insurer. For details, see Etti G. Baranoff, Dalit Baranoff, and Tom Sager, "Nonuniform Regulatory Treatment of Broker Distribution Systems: An Impact Analysis for Life Insurers," *Journal of Insurance Regulations* 19, no. 1 (2000): 94.

8. Steven Brostoff, "Agent Groups Clash On License Reform," *National Underwriter Online News Service*, June 20, 2002.

9. Donald F. Cady, "'Private Pension' Term Should Be Retired," *National Underwriter*, Life & Health/Financial Services Edition, March 1, 1999.

10. Allison Bell, "Met Settles Sales Practices Class Lawsuits," *National Underwriter*, Life & Health/Financial Services Edition, August 23, 1999.

11. Diane West, "Churning Suit Filed Against NW Mutual," *National Underwriter*, Life & Health/Financial Services Edition, October 14, 1996.

12. James Carroll, "Holding Down the Fort: Recent Court Rulings Have Shown Life Insurers That They Can Win So-called 'Vanishing-Premium' Cases," *Best's Review*, September 2001.

13. Amy S. Friedman, "Met Life Under Investigation in Connecticut," *National Underwriter*, Life & Health/Financial Services Edition, January 26, 1998.

14. Lance A. Harke and Jeffrey A. Sudduth, "Declaration of Independents: Proper Structuring of Contracts with Independent Agents Can Reduce Insurers' Potential Liability," *Best's Review*, February 2001.

15. Barbara Bowers, "Higher Profile: Compliance Officers Have Experienced Elevated Status Within Their Companies Since the Emergence of the Insurance Marketplace Standards Association," *Best's Review*, October 2001, http://www3.ambest.com/ Frames/FrameServer.asp?AltSrc=23&Tab=1&Site=bestreview&refnum=13888 (accessed March 7, 2009); and "Insurance Exec Points to Need For Strong Ethical Standards," *National Underwriter Online News Service*, May 19, 2005.

16. Lance A. Harke and Jeffrey A. Sudduth, "Declaration of Independents: Proper Structuring of Contracts with Independent Agents Can Reduce Insurers' Potential Liability," *Best's Review*, February 2001.

17. Warranties are no longer as prevalent. However, they are stringent requirements that insureds must follow for coverage to exist. They were considered necessary in the early days of marine insurance because insurers were forced to rely on the truthfulness of policyholders in assessing risk (often, the vessel was already at sea when coverage was procured, and thus inspection was not possible). Under modern conditions, however, insurers generally do not find themselves at such a disadvantage. As a result, courts rarely enforce insurance warranties, treating them instead as representations. Our discussion here, therefore, will omit presentation of warranties. See Kenneth S. Abraham, *Insurance Law and Regulation: Cases and Materials* (Westbury, NY: Foundation Press, 1990) for a discussion.

18. Some policies are designed through the mutual effort of insurer and insured. These "manuscript policies" might not place the same burden on the insurer regarding ambiguities.

19. See Robert E. Keeton, *Basic Text on Insurance Law* (St. Paul, MI: West Publishing Company, 1971), 351. While this reference is now almost forty years old, it remains perhaps the most popular insurance text available.

20. In some states, a valued policy law requires payment of the face amount of property insurance in the event of total loss, regardless of the value of the dwelling. Other policy provisions, such as deductibles and coinsurance, may also affect the insurer's effort to indemnify you.

21. Although a person who dies suffers a loss, he or she cannot be indemnified. Because the purpose of the principle of insurable interest is to implement the doctrine of indemnity, it has no application in the case of a person insuring his or her own life. Such a contract cannot be one of indemnity.

22. The person whose death requires the insurer to pay the proceeds of a life insurance policy is usually listed in the policy as the insured. He or she is also known as the cestuique vie or the subject. The beneficiary is the person (or other entity) entitled to the proceeds of the policy upon the death of the subject. The owner of the policy is the person (or other entity) who has the authority to exercise all the prematurity rights of the policy, such as designating the beneficiary, taking a policy loan, and so on. Often, the insured is also the owner.

23. Lynn Asinof, "Is Selling Your Life Insurance Good Policy in the Long-Term?" *Wall Street Journal*, May 15, 2002.

24. Ron Panko, "Is There Still Room for Viaticals?" *Best's Review*, April 2002.

25. "Life Settlement Group Sets Premium Finance Guidelines," *National Underwriter Online News Service*, April 5, 2005; "Firm to Offer Regular Life Settlement Rating Reports," *National Underwriter Online News Service*, April 21, 2005; and Jim Connolly, "Institutions Reshape Life Settlement Market," *National Underwriter*, Life/Health Edition, September 16, 2004.

26. Allison Bell, "Life Settlement Firms Face Jumbled Regulatory Picture," *National Underwriter*, Life/Health Edition, September 16, 2004.

27. Theo Francis and Ellen E. Schultz, "Big Banks Quietly Pile Up 'Janitors' Insurance,'" *Wall Street Journal*, May 2, 2002.

28. Sarah Lunday, "Business Giants Could Profit from Life Insurance on Workers," *The Charlotte* (North Carolina) *Observer*, May 12, 2002: "Some of Charlotte's biggest companies—Bank of America Corp., Wachovia Corp. and Duke Energy Corp. included—stand to reap profits from life insurance policies purchased on current and former workers. In some cases, the policies may have been purchased without the workers or their families ever knowing."

29. Arthur D. Postal, "House Revives COLI Bill," *National Underwriter Online News Service*, May 12, 2005.

30. Some property insurance policies are written on a valued basis, but precautions are taken to ensure that values agreed upon are realistic, thus adhering to the principle of indemnity.

31. Life and health insurance companies have learned, however, that overinsurance may lead to poor underwriting experience. Because the loss caused by death or illness cannot be measured precisely, defining overinsurance is difficult. It may be said to exist when the amount of insurance is clearly in excess of the economic loss that may be suffered. Extreme cases, such as the individual whose earned income is $300 per week but who may receive $500 per week in disability insurance benefits from an insurance company while he or she is ill, are easy to identify. Life and health insurers engage in financial underwriting to detect overinsurance. The requested amount of insurance is related to the proposed insured's (beneficiary's) financial need for insurance and premium-paying ability.

32. This is an area in which it is difficult to generalize; the statement made in the text is approximately correct. The point is that the creditor-debtor relationship is an exception to the statement that an insurable interest need not exist at the time of the death of the insured and that the amount of payment is not limited to the insurable interest that existed at the inception of the contract. For further discussion, see Kenneth Black, Jr., and Harold Skipper, Jr., *Life Insurance*, 12th ed. (Englewood Cliffs, NJ: Prentice-Hall, 1994), 187–88.

33. A complete assignment is the transfer of ownership or benefits of a policy.

CHAPTER 10
Structure and Analysis of Insurance Contracts

As discussed in Chapter 9, an insurance policy is a contractual agreement subject to rules governing contracts. Understanding those rules is necessary for comprehending an insurance policy. It is not enough, however. We will be spending quite a bit of time in the following chapters discussing the specific provisions of various insurance contracts. These provisions add substance to the general rules of contracts already presented and should give you the skills needed to comprehend any policy.

In Chapter 10, we offer a general framework of insurance contracts, called policies. Because most policies are somewhat standardized, it is possible to present a framework applicable to almost all insurance contracts. As an analogy, think about grammar. In most cases, you can follow the rules almost implicitly, except when you have exceptions to the rules. Similarly, insurance policies follow comparable rules in most cases. Knowing the format and general content of insurance policies will help later in understanding the specific details of each type of coverage for each distinct risk. This chapter covers the following:

1. Links

2. Entering into the contract: applications, binders, and conditional and binding receipts

3. The contract: declarations, insuring clauses, exclusions and exceptions, conditions, and endorsements and riders

1. LINKS

By now, we assume you are accustomed to connecting the specific topics of each chapter to the big picture of your holistic risk. This chapter is wider in scope. We are not yet delving into the specifics of each risk and its insurance programs. However, compared with Chapter 9, we are drilling down a step further into the world of insurance legal documents. We focus on the open-peril type of policy, which covers all risks. This means that everything is covered unless specifically excluded, as shown in Figure 10.1. Nevertheless, the open-peril policy has many exclusions and more are added as new risks appear on the horizon. For the student who is first introduced to this field, this unique element is an important one to understand. Most insurance contracts in use today do not list the risks that are covered; rather, the policy lets you know that everything is covered, even new, unanticipated risks such as anthrax (described in the box "How to Handle the Risk Management of a Low-Frequency but Scary Risk Exposure: The Anthrax Scare?" in Chapter 4). When the industry realizes that a new peril is too catastrophic, it then exerts efforts to exclude such risks from the standardized, regulated policies. Such efforts are not easy and are met with resistance in many cases. As you learned in Chapter 6, catastrophic risks are not insurable by private insurers; therefore, they are excluded from the policies. In 2005, the topic of wind versus water was of concern as a result of hurricanes Katrina and Rita. Despite the devastation, all damages caused by flood water were excluded from the policies because floods are considered catastrophic. Another case in point is the terrorism exclusion that became moot after President Bush signed the Terrorism Risk Insurance Act (TRIA) in 2002.

FIGURE 10.1   Links between the Holistic Risk Puzzle and the Insurance Contract

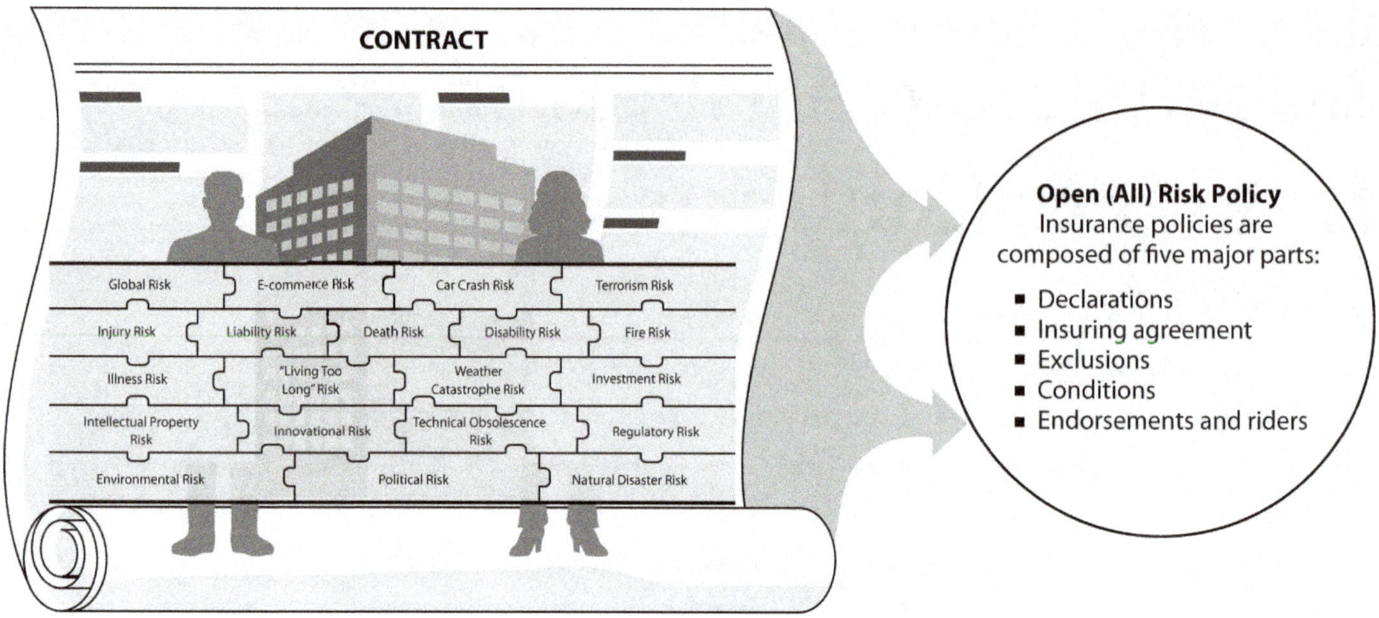

Another important element achieved by exclusions, in addition to excluding the uninsurable risk of catastrophes, is duplication of coverage. Each policy is designed not to overlap with another policy. Such duplication would violate the contract of indemnity principal of insurance contracts. The homeowner's liability coverage excludes automobile liability, workers' compensation liability, and other such exposures that are nonstandard to home and personal activities. These specifics will be discussed in later chapters, but for now, it is important to emphasize that exclusions are used to reduce the moral hazard of allowing insureds to be paid twice for the same loss.

Thus, while each insurance policy has the components outlined in Figure 10.1, the exclusions are the part that requires in-depth study. Exclusions within exclusions in some policies are like a maze. We not only must ensure that we are covered for each risk in our holistic risk picture, we must also make sure no areas are left uncovered by exclusions. At this point, you should begin to appreciate the complexity of putting the risk management puzzle together to ensure completeness.

2.   ENTERING INTO THE CONTRACT

LEARNING OBJECTIVES

In this section we elaborate on the following:

- **The preliminary steps of entering into an insurance contract**
- **The roles assumed by applications and binders in the offer and acceptance process**

You may recall from Chapter 9 that every contract requires an offer and an acceptance. This is also true for insurance. The offer and acceptance occur through the application process.

2.1   Applications

application

An offer to buy insurance

Although more insurance is sold rather than bought, the insured is still required to make an **application**, which is an offer to buy insurance. The function of the agent is to induce a potential insured to make an offer. As a practical matter, the agent also fills out the application and then asks for a signature after careful study of the application. The application identifies the insured in more or less detail, depending on the type of insurance. It also provides information about the exposure involved.

For example, in an application for an automobile policy, you would identify yourself; describe the automobile to be insured; and indicate the use of the automobile, where it will be garaged, who will drive it, and other facts that help the insurer assess the degree of risk you represent as a policyholder. Some applications for automobile insurance also require considerable information about your driving and claim experience, as well as information about others who may use the car. In many cases, such as life insurance, the written application becomes part of the policy. Occasionally, before an oral or written property/casualty application is processed into a policy, a temporary contract, or binder, may be issued.

2.2 Binders

As discussed in Chapter 9, property/casualty insurance coverage may be provided while the application is being processed. This is done through the use of a binder, which is a temporary contract to provide coverage until the policy is issued by the agent or the company.

In property/casualty insurance, an agent who has binding authority can create a contract between the insurance company and the insured. Two factors influence the granting of such authority. First, some companies prefer to have underwriting decisions made by specialists in the underwriting department, so they do not grant binding authority to the agent. Second, some policies are cancelable; others are not. The underwriting errors of an agent with binding authority may be corrected by cancellation if the policy is cancelable. Even with cancelable policies, the insurer is responsible under a binder for losses that occur prior to cancellation. If it is not cancelable, the insurer is obligated for the term of the contract.

The binder may be written or oral. For example, if you telephone an agent and ask to have your house insured, the agent will ask for the necessary information, give a brief statement about the contract—the coverage and the premium cost—and then probably say, "You are covered." At this point, you have made an oral application and the agent has accepted your offer by creating an oral binder. The agent may mail or e-mail a written binder to you to serve as evidence of the contract until the policy is received. The written binder shows who is insured, for what perils, the amount of the insurance, and the company with which coverage is placed.

In most states, an oral binder is as legal as a written one, but in case of a dispute it may be difficult to prove its terms. Suppose your house burns after the oral binder has been made but before the policy has been issued, and the agent denies the existence of the contract. How can you prove there was a contract? Or suppose the agent orally binds the coverage, a fire occurs, and the agent dies before the policy is issued. Unless there is evidence in writing, how can you prove the existence of a contract? Suppose the agent does not die and does not deny the existence of the contract, but has no evidence in writing. If the agent represents only one company, he or she may assert that the company was bound and the insured can collect for the loss. But what if the agent represents more than one company? Which one is bound? Typically, the courts will seek a method to allocate liability according to the agent's common method of distributing business. Or if that is not determinable, relevant losses might be apportioned among the companies equally. Most agents, however, keep records of their communication with insureds, including who is to provide coverage.

2.3 Conditional and Binding Receipts

Conditional and binding receipts in life insurance are somewhat similar to the binders in property/casualty insurance but contain important differences. If you pay the first premium for a life insurance policy at the time you sign the application, the agent typically will give you either a conditional receipt or a binding receipt. The **conditional receipt** does not bind the coverage of life insurance at the time it is issued, but it does put the coverage into effect retroactive to the time of application if one meets all the requirements for insurability as of the date of the application. A claim for benefits because of death prior to issuance of the policy generally will be honored, but only if you were insurable when you applied. Some conditional receipts, however, require the insured to be in good health when the policy is delivered.

In contrast, a claim for the death benefit under a **binding receipt** will be paid if death occurs while one's application for life insurance is being processed even if the deceased is found not to be insurable. Thus, the binding receipt provides interim coverage while your application is being processed, whether or not you are insurable. This circumstance parallels the protection provided by a binder in property/casualty insurance.[1]

conditional receipt

Policy that does not bind the coverage of life insurance at the time it is issued, but it does put the coverage into effect retroactive to the time of application if one meets all the requirements for insurability as of the date of the application.

binding receipt

Policy that will be paid if death occurs while one's application for life insurance is being processed, even if the deceased is found not to be insurable.

KEY TAKEAWAYS

In this section you studied that the act of entering into an insurance contract, like all contracts, requires offer and acceptance between two parties:

- The insurance application serves as the insured's offer to buy insurance.
- An agent may accept an application through oral or written binder in property/casualty insurance and through conditional receipt or a binding receipt in life/health insurance

DISCUSSION QUESTIONS

1. What is the difference between a conditional receipt and a binding receipt?
2. You apply for homeowners insurance and are issued a written binder. Before your application has been finalized, your house burns down in an accidental fire. Are you covered for this loss? What about in the case of an oral binder?
3. Dave was just at his insurance agent's office applying for health insurance. On his way home from the agent's office, Dave had a serious accident that kept him hospitalized for two weeks. Would the health insurance policy Dave just applied for provide coverage for this hospital expense?

3. THE CONTRACT

LEARNING OBJECTIVES

In this section we elaborate on the following major elements of insurance contracts:

- **Declarations**
- **Insuring agreement**
- **Exclusions**
- **Conditions**
- **Endorsements and riders**

Having completed the offer and the acceptance and met the other requirements for a contract, a contract now exists. What does it look like? Insurance policies are composed of five major parts:

- Declarations
- Insuring agreement
- Exclusions
- Conditions
- Endorsements and riders

These parts typically are identified in the policy by headings. (A section titled "definition" is also becoming common.) Sometimes, however, they are not so prominently displayed, and it is much more common to have explicit section designations in property/casualty contracts than it is in life/health contracts. Their general intent and nature, however, has the same effect.

3.1 Declarations

Generally, the declarations section is the first part of the insurance policy. Some policies, however, have a cover (or jacket) ahead of the declarations. The cover identifies the insurer and the type of policy.

Declarations are statements that identify the person(s) or organization(s) covered by the contract, give information about the loss exposure, and provide the basis upon which the contract is issued and the premium determined. This information may be obtained orally or in a written application. The declarations section may also include the period of coverage and limitations of liability. (The latter may also appear in other parts of the contract.)

Period of Coverage

All insurance policies specify the **period of coverage**, or the time duration for which coverage applies. Life and health policies may provide coverage for the entire life of the insured, a specified period of years, or up until a specified age. Health policies and term life policies often cover a year at a time. Most property insurance policies are for one year or less (although longer policies are available). Perpetual policies remain in force until canceled by you or the insurer. Liability policies may be for a three-month or six-month period, but most are for a year. Some forms of automobile insurance may be written on a continuous basis, with premiums payable at specified intervals, such as every six months. Such policies remain in force as long as premiums are paid or until they are canceled. Whatever the term during which any policy is to be in force, it will be carefully spelled out in the contract. During periods when insureds may expect a turn to hard markets in the underwriting cycles, they may want to fix the level of premiums for a longer period and will sign contracts for longer than one year, such as three years.

Limitations of Liability

All insurance policies have clauses that place **limitations of liability** (maximum amount payable by the insurance policy) on the insurer. Life policies promise to pay the face amount of the policy. Health policies typically limit payment to a specified amount for total medical expenses during one's lifetime and have internal limits on the payment of specific services, such as a surgical procedure. Property insurance policies specify as limits actual cash value or replacement value, insurable interest, cost to repair or replace, and the face amount of insurance. Limits exist in liability policies for the amount payable per claim, sometimes per injured claimant, sometimes per year, and sometimes per event. Remember the example in Chapter 9 of the dispute between the leaseholder and the insurer over the number of events in the collapse of the World Trade Center (WTC) on September 11, 2001. The dispute was whether the attack on the WTC constituted two events or one. Defense services, provided in most liability policies, are limited only to the extent that litigation falls within coverage terms and the policy proceeds have not been exhausted in paying judgments or settlements. Because of the high cost of providing legal defense in recent years, however, attempts to limit insurer responsibility to some dollar amount have been made.

Retained Losses

In many situations, it is appropriate not to transfer all of an insured's financial interest in a potential loss. Loss retention benefits the insured when losses are predictable and manageable. For the insurer, some losses are better left with the insured because of moral hazard concerns. Thus, an insured might retain a portion of covered losses through a variety of policy provisions. Some such provisions are deductibles, coinsurance in property insurance, copayments in health insurance, and waiting periods in disability insurance. Each is discussed at some length in later chapters. For now, realize that the existence of such provisions typically is noted in the declarations section of the policy.

3.2 Insuring Clauses

The second major element of an insurance contract, the **insuring clause** or agreement, is a general statement of the promises the insurer makes to the insured. Insuring clauses may vary greatly from policy to policy. Most, however, specify the perils and exposures covered, or at least some indication of what they might be.

Variation in Insuring Clauses

Some policies have relatively simple insuring clauses, such as a life insurance policy, which could simply say, "The company agrees, subject to the terms and conditions of this policy, to pay the amount shown on page 2 to the beneficiary upon receipt at its Home Office of proof of the death of the insured." Package policies are likely to have several insuring clauses, one for each major type of coverage and each accompanied by definitions, exclusions, and conditions. An example of this type is the personal automobile policy, described in Chapter 1.

---

declarations

Statements that identify the person(s) or organization(s) covered by a contract, give information about the loss exposure, and provide the basis upon which the contract is issued and the premium determined.

period of coverage

The time duration for which coverage applies.

limitations of liability

The maximum amount payable by an insurance policy.

insuring clause

A general statement of the promises the insurer makes to the insured.

Some insuring clauses are designated as the "insuring agreement," while others are hidden among policy provisions. Somewhere in the policy, however, it states that the "insurer promises to pay…." This general description of the insurer's promises is the essence of an insuring clause.

Open-Perils versus Named-Perils

The insuring agreement provides a general description of the circumstances under which the policy becomes applicable. The circumstances include the covered loss-causing events, called **perils**. They may be specified in one of two ways.

perils

The causes of loss.

A **named-perils policy** covers only losses caused by the perils listed in the policy. If a peril is not listed, loss resulting from it is not covered. For example, one form of the homeowner's policy, HO-2, insures for direct loss to the dwelling, other structures, and personal property caused by eighteen different perils. Only losses caused by these perils are covered. Riot or civil commotion is listed, so a loss caused by either is covered. On the other hand, earthquake is not listed, so a loss caused by earthquake is not covered.

named-perils policy

Policy that covers only losses caused by the perils listed in the policy.

An **open-perils policy** (formerly called "all risk") covers losses caused by all perils except those excluded. This type of policy is most popular in property policies. It is important to understand the nature of such a policy because the insured has to look for what is not covered rather than what is covered. The exclusions in an open-perils policy are more definitive of coverage than in a named-perils policy. Generally, an open-perils policy provides broader coverage than a named-perils policy, although it is conceivable, if unlikely, that an open-perils policy would have such a long list of exclusions that the coverage would be narrower.

open-perils policy

Policy that covers losses caused by all perils except those excluded.

As noted in the Links section, many exclusions in property policies have been in the limelight. After September 11, 2001, the terrorism exclusion was the first added exclusion to all commercial policies but was rescinded after the enactment of TRIA in 2002 and its extensions. The mold exclusion was another new exclusion of our age. The one old exclusion that received major attention in 2005 in the wake of hurricanes Katrina and Rita is the flood exclusion in property policies. Flood coverage is provided by the federal government and is limited in its scope (see Chapter 1). Additional exclusions will be discussed further in Chapter 11 and Chapter 12. In the 1980s, pollution liability was excluded after major losses. As noted in Chapter 6, most catastrophes would be excluded because they are not considered insurable by private insurers. A most common exclusion, as noted above, is the war exclusion. The insurance industry decided not to trigger this exclusion in the aftermath of September 11. For a closer look, see the box below, "The Risk of War".

Policies written on a named-perils basis cannot cover all possible causes of loss because of "unknown peril." There is always the possibility of loss caused by a peril that was not known to exist and so was not listed in the policy. For this reason, open-perils policies cover many perils not covered by named-perils policies. This broader coverage usually requires a higher premium than a named-perils policy, but it is often preferable because it is less likely to leave gaps in coverage. The anthrax scare described in Chapter 4 is an example of an unknown peril that was covered by the insurance industry's policies.

Very few, if any, policies are "all risk" in the sense of covering every conceivable peril. Probably the closest approach to such a policy in the property insurance field is the comprehensive glass policy, which insures against all glass breakage except those caused by fire, war, or nuclear peril. Most life insurance policies cover all perils except for suicide during the first year or the first two years. Health insurance policies often are written on an open-perils basis, covering medical expenses from any cause not intentional. Some policies, however, are designed to cover specific perils such as cancer (discussed in Chapter 2). Limited-perils policies are popular because many people fear the consequences of certain illnesses. Of course, the insured is well-advised to be concerned with (protect against) the loss, regardless of the cause.

The Risk of War

"This means war!" was a frequent refrain among angry Americans in the days after September 11, 2001. Even President George W. Bush repeatedly referred to the terrorist attacks on the World Trade Center and the Pentagon as an "act of war." One politician who disagreed with that choice of words was Representative Michael Oxley.

By definition and by U.S. law, war is an act of violent conflict between two nations. The hijackers, it was soon determined, were working not on behalf of any government but for the al Qaeda network of terrorists. Thus, a week after the attacks, Oxley, chairperson of the Financial Services Committee of the U.S. House of Representatives, sent a letter to the National Association of Insurance Commissioners urging the insurance industry not to invoke war risk exclusions to deny September 11 claims.

Most insurers had already come to the same conclusion. Generally, auto, homeowner's, commercial property, business interruption, and (in some states) worker's compensation policies contain act-of-war exclusions, meaning that insurance companies can refuse to pay claims arising from a war or a warlike act. To illustrate, the standard commercial property policy form provided by the Insurance Services Office contains the following exclusions:

1. War, including undeclared or civil war
2. Warlike action by a military force, including action in hindering or defending against an actual or expected attack, by any government, sovereign or other authority using military personnel or other agents
3. Insurrection, rebellion, revolution, usurped power, or action taken by governmental authority in hindering or defending against any of these

Wars are not considered insurable events: they are unpredictable, intentional, and potentially catastrophic. (Recall the discussion in Chapter 6 on insurable and uninsurable risks.) The risks of war are simply too great for an insurance company to accept.

The war exclusion clause has given rise to few lawsuits, but in each case the courts have supported its application "only in situations involving damage arising from a genuine warlike act between sovereign entities." *Pan American World Airways v. Aetna Casualty and Surety Co.*, 505 F2d 989 (1974), involved coverage for the hijacking and destruction of a commercial aircraft. The Second Circuit Court of Appeals held that the hijackers, members of the Popular Front for the Liberation of Palestine, were not "representatives of a government," and thus the war exclusion did not apply. The insurers were liable for the loss. A war exclusion claim denial was upheld in *TRT/FTC Communications, Inc. v. Insurance Company of the State of Pennsylvania*, 847 F. Supp. 28 (Del. Dist. 1993), because the loss occurred in the context of a declared war between the United States and Panama—two sovereign nations.

With some $50 billion at stake from the September 11 attacks, it wouldn't have been surprising if some insurers considered taking a chance at invoking the war exclusion clause. Instead, companies large and small were quick to announce that they planned to pay claims fairly and promptly. "We have decided that we will consider the events of September 11 to be 'acts of terrorism,' not 'acts of war,'" said Peter Bruce, Senior Executive Vice President of Northwestern Mutual Life Insurance. The industry agreed.

Sources: "Insurers: WTC Attack Not Act of War," Insurance-Letter, September 17, 2001, http://www.cybersure.com/godoc/1872.htm; Jack P. Gibson et al., "Attack on America: The Insurance Coverage Issues," International Risk Management Institute, Inc., September 2001, http://www.imri.com; Tim Reason, "Acts of God and Monsters No Longer Covered: Insurers Say Future Policies Will Definitely Exclude Terrorist Attacks," CFO.com, November 19, 2001, http://www.cfo.com/article/1,5309,5802%7C%7CA%7C736%7C8,00.html; Susan Massmann, "Legal Background Outlined for War Risk Exclusion," National Underwriter Online News Service, September 18, 2001; "Northwestern Mutual Won't Invoke War Exclusion on Claims," The (Milwaukee) Business Journal, September 14, 2001.

Exposures to Loss

Generally, the exposures to be covered are also defined (broadly speaking) in the insuring agreement. For example, the liability policy states that the insurer will pay "those sums the insured is legally obligated to pay for damages…." In addition, "the Company shall have the right and duty to defend…." The exposures in this situation are legal defense costs and liability judgments or settlements against the insured.

In defining the exposures, important information, such as the basis of valuation and types of losses covered, is needed. Various valuation methods have already been discussed. Actual cash value and replacement cost are the most common means of valuing property loss. Payments required of defendants, either through mutually acceptable settlements or court judgments, define the value of liability losses. The face value (amount of coverage) of a life insurance policy represents the value paid upon the insured's death. Health insurance policies employ a number of valuation methods, including an amount per day in the hospital or per service provided, or—more likely—the lesser of the actual cost of the service or the customary and prevailing fee for this service. Health maintenance organizations promise the provision of services, as such, rather than a reimbursement of their cost.

direct loss

The value of property that is physically destroyed or damaged, not including the loss caused by inability to use the property.

consequential or indirect losses

A nonphysical loss such as loss of business.

business interruption

Losses that occur when an organization is unable to sell its goods or services and/or unable to produce goods for sale because of direct or indirect loss.

contingent business interruption

Loss caused by property damage not owned by the business.

extra expense losses

Additional costs incurred by organizations that choose to continue operating following property damage.

property damage

Liability that includes responsibility both for the physical damage to property and the loss of use of property.

bodily injury

Physical injury to a person, including the pain and suffering that may result.

personal injury

Nonphysical injury to a person, including damage caused by libel, slander, false imprisonment, and the like.

punitive damages

Awards intended to punish an offender for exceptionally undesirable behavior.

The types of covered losses are also generally stated in the insuring agreement. Many property insurance policies, for example, cover only direct loss. **Direct loss** to property is the value that is physically destroyed or damaged, not the loss caused by inability to use the property. Other policies that cover loss of use of property without physical damage to the property are called **consequential or indirect loss**. In the aftermath of Hurricane Rita, many Texas coastal residents who evacuated encountered indirect loss without damage to their homes. This included the evacuation of Galveston and Houston. Coverage for these losses was disputed by insurers, such as Allstate, that tried to exclude these indirect losses. In addition, in the introduction to this chapter, it was explained how important the consequential loss coverage was to the businesses that suffered indirectly from the September 11 attacks. A report released by PricewaterhouseCoopers in New York City noted that business interruption claims came from a wide scope of industries, including financial services, communications, media, and travel industries, that were not in the attack zone.[2] Many remote businesses were disrupted when the world transportation networks were paralyzed. It was estimated that losses up to $10 billion were caused by these indirect effects.[3]

Business interruption losses occur when an organization is unable to sell its goods or services, and/or unable to produce goods for sale because of direct or indirect loss. Generally, these losses are due to some property damage considered direct loss. Such lost revenues typically translate into lost profits. The 1992 Chicago flood, for example, required that Marshall Fields downtown store close its doors for several days while crews worked to clean up damage caused by the flood waters.[4] When loss is caused by property damage not owned by the business, it is considered a **contingent business interruption**. If Marshall Fields reduced its orders to suppliers of its goods, for instance, those suppliers may experience contingent business interruption loss caused by the water damage, even though their own property was not damaged.

Alternatively, some organizations choose to continue operating following property damage, but they are able to do so only by incurring additional costs known as **extra expense losses**. These costs also reduce profits. Continuing with the 1992 Chicago flood example, consider the various accounting firms who could not use their offices the second week in April. With the upcoming tax filing deadline, these firms chose to rent additional space in other locations so they could meet their clients' needs. The additional rental expense (and other costs) resulted in reduced profits to the accounting firms. Yet a variety of service organizations, including accountants, insurance agents, and bankers, prefer to incur such expenses in order to maintain their reputation of reliability, upon which their long-term success and profits depend. Closing down, even temporarily, could badly hurt the organization.

Individuals and families too may experience costs associated with loss of use. For example, if your home is damaged, you may need to locate (and pay for) temporary housing. You may also incur abnormal expenses associated with the general privileges of home use, such as meals, entertainment, telephones, and similar conveniences. Likewise, if your car is unavailable following an accident, you must rent a car or spend time and money using other forms of transportation. Thus, while a family's loss of use tends to focus on extra expense, its effect may be as severe as that of an organization.

Liability policies, on the other hand, may cover liability for property damage, bodily injury, personal injury, and/or punitive damages. **Property damage** liability includes responsibility both for the physical damage to property and the loss of use of property. **Bodily injury** is the physical injury to a person, including the pain and suffering that may result. **Personal injury** is the nonphysical injury to a person, including damage caused by libel, slander, false imprisonment, and the like. **Punitive damages** are damages assessed against defendants for gross negligence, supposedly for the purpose of punishment and to deter others from acting in a similar fashion. Examples of punitive damages in recent cases and their ethical implications are featured in the box "Are Punitive Damages out of Control?"

Are Punitive Damages out of Control?

In December 2005, a California jury delivered a guilty verdict and awarded $172 million in damages against Wal-Mart Stores, Inc., for not giving the appropriate lunch breaks to its thousands of employees. The verdict included $57.3 million in general damages and $115 million in punitive damages. Wal-Mart planned to appeal. In 2002, a California state court judge awarded $30 million against grocery chain Kroger, where six employees had been verbally harassed by a store manager. The verdict was reduced to a mere $8.25 million when the upper court decided it was "grossly excessive." A jury in Laredo, Texas, awarded $108 million to Mexican heiress Cristina Brittingham Sada de Ayala in a lawsuit against her stepmother for failing to repay a $34 million loan. A Utah jury ordered State Farm to pay a policyholder $145 million in punitive damages for handling a claim in bad faith and inflicting emotional distress. A Los Angeles jury ordered tobacco giant Philip Morris to pay Betty Bullock $28 billion in punitive damages.

The Bullock award of $28 billion (which was lowered to $28 million and is still being appealed by Philip Morris) is by itself almost five times the combined amount of the top ten largest jury awards to individuals and families in 2001. Though a Department of Justice study showed that only a small percentage of cases are awarded punitive damages, and that the majority of awards are under $40,000, the number and amounts of punitive awards have been geometrically increasing since the high of $10,000 in 1959.

Some people argue that a fine is the best way to punish a corporation for acting wrongly. For example, the 1994 case against McDonald's that won an elderly woman $2.7 million for spilling hot coffee in her lap is commonly seen as the beginning of our frivolous lawsuit period. What the jury heard, but most people did not, was that McDonald's purposely kept its coffee at least forty degrees hotter than most restaurants did, as a cost-saving measure to extract more coffee from the beans; that more than 700 people had filed complaints of scalding coffee burns over the previous decade; and that McDonald's knew their coffee was dangerously hot, yet had no plans to turn the heat down or postwarning signs. The woman in the case suffered third-degree burns to her groin, thighs, and buttocks that required skin grafts and a lengthy hospital stay. She filed suit against McDonald's only after the company refused to pay her medical bills. Even the famous multimillion-dollar award was reduced on appeal to $480,000.

The true problem, many say, is not the size of such awards but the method by which we determine them. Punitive damages are not truly "damages" in the sense of compensation for a loss or injury but rather a fine, levied as punishment. In determining the amount of a punitive award, a jury is instructed to consider whether the defendant displayed reckless conduct, gross negligence, malice, or fraud—but in practice, a jury award often depends on how heart-tugging the plaintiff seems to be versus how heartless the big bad corporation appears.

Questions for Discussion

1. Were the facts behind the McDonald's lawsuit news to you? Do they change your opinion about this landmark case? What would you have done if you had been on the jury?

2. Betty Bullock, who has lung cancer, had been a regular smoker for forty years and blamed Philip Morris for failing to warn her about smoking risks. Do you think Philip Morris is responsible? Do you think learning more about the case might change your opinion?

3. Exxon was ordered to pay $125 million in criminal fines for the *Exxon Valdez* oil spill. In a separate trial, a civil jury hit Exxon with a $5 billion punitive award. Is it fair for a company to pay twice for the same crime?

4. Are juries—composed of people who have no legal training, who know only about the case they are sitting on, who may be easily swayed by theatrical attorneys, and who are given only vague instructions—equipped to set punitive damage awards? Should punitive awards be regulated?

Sources: Kris Hudson, "Wal-Mart Workers Awarded $172 Million," Wall Street Journal, December 23, 2005, B3; Olson, speech at the Manhattan Institute conference, "Crime and Punishment in Business Law," May 8, 2002, reprinted at http://www.manhattan-institute.org/html/cjm_15.htm; "Surprise: Judges Hand Out Most Punitive Awards," Wall Street Journal, June 12, 2000, 2b; Steven Brostoff, "Top Court to Review Punitive Damages," National Underwriter Online News Service, June 27, 2002; "McFacts about the McDonalds Coffee Lawsuit," Legal News and Views, Ohio Academy of Trial Lawyers, http://lawandhelp.com/q298-2.htm, Michael Bradford, "Phillip Morris to Continue Appeal of Punitives Award," Business Insurance, December 19, 2002; http://www.altria.com/media/03_06_04_03_00_Bullock.asp for update on the Bullock case.

3.3   Exclusions and Exceptions

Whether the policy is open-perils or named-perils, the coverage it provides cannot be ascertained without considering the **exclusions**, which are those perils, risks, losses, and properties that are not covered in an all-risk policy. Exclusions represent the third major part of an insurance policy and explicitly identify losses not covered by the policy. Usually, an insured may not know what the policy covers until he or she finds out what it does not cover. Unfortunately, this is not always an easy task. In many policies, exclusions appear not only under the heading "Exclusions" in one or more places but also throughout the policy and in various forms. When we delve into homeowners policies in Chapter 1, you will be amazed at the many exclusions, and exclusions to exclusions, that you will encounter. The homeowners policy section I (which provides property coverage) has two lists of exclusions identified as such, plus others scattered throughout the policy. The last sentence in the description of loss of use coverage, for example, says, "We do not cover loss or expense due to cancellation of a lease or agreement." In other words, such loss is excluded. In "Perils Insured Against," the policy at one point says, "We insure for risks of physical loss to the property.... Except," followed by a list of losses or loss causes. Under the heading "Additional Coverages," several types of coverage are listed and then the following sentence appears: "We do not cover loss arising out of business pursuits...." Thus, such loss is excluded.

A policy may exclude specified locations, perils, property, or losses. Perhaps a discussion of the exclusions in some policies and the reasons for them will be helpful.

exclusions

Perils, risks, losses, and properties that are not covered in an all-risk policy.

Reasons for Exclusions

Let us review the reasons for the existence of exclusions. As noted in Chapter 6, one reason exclusions exist is to avoid financial catastrophe for the insurer, which may result if many dependent exposures are insured or if a single, large-value exposure is insured. Because war would affect many exposures simultaneously, losses caused by war are excluded in most policies in order to avoid insuring catastrophic events. Exclusions also exist to limit coverage of nonfortuitous (that is, not accidental) events. Losses that are not accidental make prediction difficult, cause coverage to be expensive, and represent circumstances in which coverage would be contrary to public policy. As a result, losses caused intentionally (by the insured) are excluded. So, too, are naturally occurring losses that are expected. Wear and tear, for instance, is excluded from coverage. Adverse selection and moral hazard are limited by these exclusions.

Adverse selection is limited further by use of specialized policies and endorsements that standardize the risk. That is, limitations (exclusions) are placed in standard policies for exposures that are nonstandard. Those insureds who need coverage for such nonstandard exposures purchase it specifically. For example, homeowner's policies limit theft coverage on jewelry and furs to a maximum amount ($2,500). Exposures in excess of the maximum are atypical, representing a higher probability (and severity) of loss than exists for the average homeowner. Insureds who own jewelry and furs with values in excess of the maximum must buy special coverage (if desired).

An important element is the point emphasized in the Links section at the beginning of the chapter. Some exclusions exist to avoid duplication of coverage by policies specifically intended to insure the exposure. As noted above, homeowners liability coverage excludes automobile liability, workers' compensation liability, and other such exposures that are nonstandard to home and personal activities. Other policies specifically designed to cover such exposures are available and commonly used. To duplicate coverage would diminish insurers' ability to discriminate among insureds and could result in moral hazard if insureds were paid twice for the same loss. A policy clause, termed **other insurance clause** (discussed in Chapter 9), addresses the potential problem of duplicating coverage when two or more similar policies cover the same exposure. Through this type of provision, the insurer's financial responsibility is apportioned so that payment in excess of the insured's loss is avoided.

These reasons for exclusions are manifested in limitations on the following:

- Locations
- Perils
- Property
- Losses

The following is a discussion of the purposes of limiting locations, perils, property, and losses.

Excluded Locations

Some types of coverage are location-specific, such as to buildings. Other policies define the location of coverage. Automobile policies, for example, cover the United States and Canada. Mexico is not covered because of the very high auto risk there. In addition, some governmental entities in Mexico will not accept foreign insurance. Some property policies were written to cover movable property anywhere in the world except the Eastern bloc countries, likely because of difficulty in adjusting claims. With the breakup of the Communist bloc, these limitations are also being abandoned. Yet coverage may still be excluded where adjusting is difficult and/or the government of the location has rules against such foreign insurance. For a discussion of political risk—unanticipated political events that disrupt the earning or profit-making ability of an enterprise—see Chapter 11.

Excluded Perils

Some perils are excluded because they can be covered by other policies or because they are unusual or catastrophic. The earthquake peril, for example, requires separate rating and is excluded from homeowners policies. This peril can be insured under a separate policy or added by endorsement for an extra premium. Many insureds do not want to pay the premium required, either because they think their property is not exposed to the risk of loss caused by an earthquake or because they expect that federal disaster relief would cover losses. Given the choice of a homeowners policy that excluded the earthquake peril and one that included earthquake coverage but cost $50 more per year, they would choose the former. Thus, to keep the price of their homeowners policies competitive, insurers exclude the earthquake peril. It is excluded also because it is an extraordinary peril that cannot easily be included with the other perils covered by the policy. It must be rated separately.

As noted above, perils, such as those associated with war, are excluded because commercial insurers consider them uninsurable. Nuclear energy perils, such as radiation, are excluded from most policies because of the catastrophic exposure. Losses to homeowners caused by the nuclear meltdown

---

other insurance clause

Provision in a policy that apportions the insurer's financial responsibility so that payment in excess of the insured's loss is avoided.

at Three Mile Island in 1979, which forced homeowners to evacuate the damaged property in the area, were not covered by their homeowners insurance. Losses due to floods are excluded and were a topic of much discussion after hurricanes Katrina and Rita. Losses due to wear and tear are excluded because they are inevitable rather than accidental and thus not insurable. Similarly, inherent vice, which refers to losses caused by characteristics of the insured property, is excluded. For example, certain products, such as tires and various kinds of raw materials, deteriorate with time. Such losses are not accidental and are, therefore, uninsurable.

Excluded Property

Some property is excluded because it is insurable under other policies. Homeowners policies, as previously stated, exclude automobiles because they are better insured under automobile policies. Other property is excluded because the coverage is not needed by the average insured, who would, therefore, not want to pay for it.

Liability policies usually exclude damage to or loss of others' property in the care, custody, or control of the insured because property insurance can provide protection for the owner against losses caused by fire or other perils. Other possible losses, such as damage to clothing being dry cleaned, are viewed as a business risk involving the skill of the dry cleaner. Insurers do not want to assume the risk of losses caused by poor workmanship or poor management.

Excluded Losses

Losses resulting from ordinance or law—such as those regulating construction or repair—are excluded from most property insurance contracts. Policies that cover only direct physical damage exclude loss of use or income resulting from such damage. Likewise, policies covering only loss of use exclude direct losses. Health insurance policies often exclude losses (expenses) considered by the insurer to be unnecessary, such as the added cost of a private room or the cost of elective surgery.

3.4   Conditions

The fourth major part of an insurance contract is the conditions section. **Conditions** enumerate the duties of the parties to the contract and, in some cases, define the terms used. Some policies list them under the heading "Conditions," while others do not identify them as such. Wherever the conditions are stated, you must be aware of them. You cannot expect the insurer to fulfill its part of the contract unless you fulfill the conditions. Remember that acceptance of these conditions is part of the consideration given by the insured at the inception of an insurance contract. Failure to accept conditions may release the insurer from its obligations. Many conditions found in insurance contracts are common to all. Others are characteristic of only certain types of contracts. Some examples follow.

conditions

Clauses in a policy that enumerate the duties of the parties to the contract and, in some cases, define the terms used.

Notice and Proof of Loss

All policies require that the insurer be notified when the event, accident, or loss insured against occurs. The time within which notice must be filed and the manner of making it vary. The homeowners policy, for example, lists as one of the insured's duties after loss to "give immediate notice to us or our agent" and to file proof of loss within sixty days. A typical life insurance policy says that payment will be made "upon receipt…of proof of death of the insured." A health policy requires that "written proof of loss must be furnished to the Company within twelve months of the date the expense was incurred." The personal auto policy says, "We must be notified promptly of how, when, and where the accident or loss happened."

In some cases, if notice is not made within a reasonable time after the loss or accident, the insurer is relieved of all liability under the contract. A beneficiary who filed for benefits under an accidental death policy more than two years after the insured's death was held in one case to have violated the notice requirement of the policy.[5] The insurer is entitled to such timely notice so it can investigate the facts of the case. Insureds who fail to fulfill this condition may find themselves without protection when they need it most—after a loss.

Suspension of Coverage

suspension of coverage

Release of the insurer from liability.

voidance of coverage

Termination of coverage under an insurance policy.

Because there are some risks or hazardous situations insurers want to avoid, many policies specify acts, conditions, or circumstances that will cause the **suspension of coverage** or, in other words, that will release the insurer from liability. The effect is the same as if the policy were canceled or voided, but when a policy is suspended, the effect is only temporary. When a **voidance of coverage** is incurred in an insurance contract, coverage is terminated. Protection resumes only by agreement of the insured and insurer. Suspension, in contrast, negates coverage as long as some condition exists. Once the condition is eliminated, protection immediately reverts without the need for a new agreement between the parties.

Some life and health policies have special clauses that suspend coverage for those in military service during wartime. When the war is over or the insured is no longer in military service, the suspension is terminated and coverage is restored. The personal auto policy has an exclusion that is essentially a suspension of coverage for damage to your auto. It provides that the insurer will not pay for loss to your covered auto "while it is used to carry persons or property for a fee," except for use in a share-the-expense car pool. The homeowners policy (form 3) suspends coverage for vandalism and malicious mischief losses if the house has been vacant for more than thirty consecutive days. A property insurance policy may suspend coverage while there is "a substantial increase in hazard."

You can easily overlook or misunderstand suspensions of coverage or releases from liability when you try to determine coverage provided by a policy. They may appear as either conditions or exclusions. Because their effect is much broader and less apparent than the exclusion of specified locations, perils, property, or losses, it is easy to underestimate their significance.

Cooperation of the Insured

All policies require your cooperation, in the sense that you must fulfill certain conditions before the insurer will pay for losses. Because the investigation of an accident and defense of a suit against the insured are very difficult unless he or she will cooperate, liability policies have a specific provision requiring cooperation after a loss. The businessowners policy, for example, says, "The insured shall cooperate with the Company, and upon the Company's request, assist in…making of settlements; conducting of suits…."

It is not unusual for the insured to be somewhat sympathetic toward the claimant in a liability case, especially if the claimant is a friend. There have been situations in which the insured was so anxious for the claimant to get a large settlement from the insurer that the duty to cooperate was forgotten. If you do not meet this condition and the insurer can prove it, you may end up paying for the loss yourself. This is illustrated by the case of a mother who was a passenger in her son's automobile when it was involved in an accident in which she was injured. He encouraged and aided her in bringing suit against him. The insurer was released from its obligations under the liability policy, on the grounds that the cooperation clause was breached.[6] The purpose of the cooperation clause is to force insureds to perform the way they would if they did not have insurance.

Protection of Property after Loss

Most property insurance policies contain provisions requiring the insured to protect the property after a loss in order to reduce the loss as much as possible. An insured who wrecks his or her automobile, for example, has the responsibility for having it towed to a garage for safekeeping. In the case of a fire loss, the insured is expected to protect undamaged property from the weather and other perils in order to reduce the loss. You cannot be careless and irresponsible just because you have insurance. Yet the requirement is only that the insured be reasonable. You are not required to put yourself in danger or to take extraordinary steps. Of course, views of what is extraordinary may differ.

Examination

A provision peculiar to some disability income policies gives the insurer the right to have its physician examine the insured periodically during the time he or she receives benefits under the policy. This right cannot be used to harass the claimant, but the insurer is entitled to check occasionally to see if he or she should continue to receive benefits. Property insurance policies have a provision that requires the claimant to submit to examination under oath, as well as make records and property available for examination by representatives of the insurance company.

3.5   Endorsements and Riders

Sometimes (maybe often), but not always, an insurance policy will include a fifth major part: the attachment of endorsements or riders. *Riders* and *endorsements* are two terms with the same meaning. Riders are used with life/health policies, whereas endorsements are used with property/casualty policies. A **rider** makes a change in the life/health insurance policy to which it is attached; an **endorsement** makes a change in the property/casualty insurance policy to which it is attached. It may increase or decrease the coverage, change the premium, correct a statement, or make any number of other changes.

The endorsement guaranteeing home replacement cost, for example, provides replacement cost coverage for a dwelling insured by a homeowners policy, regardless of the limit of liability shown in the declarations. This keeps the amount of insurance on the dwelling up-to-date during the term of the policy. A waiver of premium rider increases the benefits of a life insurance policy by providing for continued coverage without continued payment of premiums if the insured becomes totally disabled. Endorsements and riders are not easier to read than the policies to which they are attached. Actually, the way some of them are glued or stapled to the policy may discourage you from looking at them. Nevertheless, they are an integral part of the contract you have with the insurer and cannot be ignored. When their wording conflicts with that in exclusions or other parts of the contract, the rider or endorsement takes precedence, negating the conflict.

Insurers continually add and change endorsements and riders to the policies as market conditions change and the needs are altered. For example, the commercial insurance units of Travelers Indemnity and Aetna Casualty and Surety provided an endorsement to protect contractors against third-party bodily injury and property damage claims arising out of accidental releases of pollutants they bring to job sites.[7] Some features included were no time limits, full policy limits, and defense cost in addition to the basic full limits.

An example of a rider to life insurance policies is the estate tax repeal rider. This rider, which exemplifies the need to modify policies as tax laws change, was created in response to the Economic Growth and Tax Relief Reconciliation Act of 2001 (EGTRRA 2001). Under this act, the federal estate tax will be phased out completely by 2010 but would return in 2011 unless Congress votes to eliminate it. If Congress eliminates the tax, the rider would let holders of the affected policies surrender the policies without paying surrender charges.[8]

Another example of a rider relates to long-term care (LTC) insurance (discussed in Chapter 2). Most long-term care policies include a rider offering some sort of inflation protection, generally 5 percent annually.[9]

rider

Attachment to a life/health insurance policy that changes the terms of the policy.

endorsement

Attachment to a the property/casualty insurance policy that changes the terms of the policy.

KEY TAKEAWAYS

In this section you studied the five basic parts of insurance contracts:

- Declarations—specify periods of coverage, place limitations on liability, and stipulate the insured's loss retention provisions
- Insuring agreement—statement of general promise made to the insured; determines whether policy covers named-perils or open-perils; provides exposures to be covered and types of losses
- Exclusions—state what losses/causes of loss the policy does not cover because of limitations on locations, perils, property, and losses
- Conditions—define the duties of the parties to the contract; notice and proof of loss mandates, suspension of coverage triggers, cooperation of the insured requirement, protection of property after loss measures, and physical examination right
- Endorsements and riders—optional elements that change the terms of property/casualty and life/health policies; take precedence when they conflict with other parts of the contract

DISCUSSION QUESTIONS

1. What are the main reasons for exclusions and for endorsements and riders in insurance policies?
2. What is the significance of an open-perils policy? In deciding between a named-perils policy and an open-perils policy, what factors would you consider? Define both terms and explain your answer.
3. In Chapter 1 on automobile insurance, you will find that portable stereos and tape decks are excluded from coverage. What do you think the insurance company's rationale is for such an exclusion? What are other reasons for insurance policy exclusions? Give examples of each.
4. Lightning struck a tree in the Gibsons' yard, causing it to fall over and smash the bay window in their living room. The Gibsons were so distraught by the damage that they decided to go out for dinner to calm themselves. After dinner, the Gibsons decided to take in a movie. When they returned home, they discovered that someone had walked through their broken bay window and stolen many of their valuable possessions. The Gibsons have a homeowners policy that covers both physical damage and theft. As the Gibsons' insurer, do you cover all their incurred losses? Why or why not?
5. Your careless driving results in serious injury to Linda Helsing, a close personal friend. Because she knows you have liability insurance and the insurer will pay for damages on your behalf, she files suit against you. Would it be unreasonable for your insurer to expect you not to help Linda pursue maximum recovery in every conceivable way? Explain.

4. REVIEW AND PRACTICE

1. Describe a few exclusions and a few endorsements and riders.
2. Joe Phelps is a chemistry aficionado. For his twenty-ninth birthday last month, Joe's wife bought him an elaborate chemistry set to use in their attached garage. The set includes dangerous (flammable) substances, yet Joe does not notify his homeowner's insurer. What problem might Joe encounter?
3. Joe has another insurance problem. He had an automobile accident last month in which he negligently hit another motorist while turning right on red. The damage was minor, so Joe just paid the other motorist for the repairs. Fearing the increase in his auto insurance premiums, Joe did not notify his insurer of the accident. Now the other motorist is suing for whiplash. What is Joe's problem, and why?
4. "A Federal Reserve Board survey showing that banks are still making commercial real estate loans for 'high profile' properties does not tell the whole story of the impact of problems in the terrorism insurance market, insurance industry officials contend" (Steven Brostoff, "Loans Still Coming Despite Terror Risks," *National Underwriter*, Property & Casualty/Risk & Benefits Management Edition, June 3, 2002).
    a. Relate this story to the terrorism exclusion information you found in this chapter.
    b. What is the actual problem?
5. "States approving terrorism exclusions for commercial property insurance are a help to the insurance industry, but two critical exposures aren't excluded from terrorism—workers' compensation and fire following a terrorist event" ("Even with Exclusions, Insurers Still Exposed to Workers' Comp, Fire Losses," *Best's Insurance News*, January 10, 2002.) What can be the impact on insurers' bottom line when such exclusions are not adopted?
6. Kevin Kaiser just replaced his old car with a new one and is ready to drive the new car off the lot. He did not have collision insurance on the old car, but he wants some on the new one. He calls his friend Dana Goldman, who is an insurance agent. "Give me the works, Dana. I want the best collision coverage you have." Soon after he drives the car away from the lot, he is struck by an eighteen-wheeler and the new car is totaled.

    Kevin then discovers that he has collision insurance with a $500 deductible, which he must pay. He is upset because to him "the works" meant full insurance for all losses he might have due to collision. Dana had thought that he wanted more cost-efficient coverage and had used the deductible to lower the premium. The applicable state law and insurer underwriting practices allow deductibles as low as $250, although they can be much higher.

    a. Kevin wants to take Dana to court to collect the full value of the auto. What would you advise him?
    b. What does this tell you about oral contracts?
7. What are the shortcomings of limited-peril health insurance policies, such as coverage for loss caused solely by cancer, from a personal risk management point of view?

8. A. J. Jackson was very pleased to hear the agent say that she was covered the moment she finished completing the application and paid the agent the first month's premium for health insurance. A. J. had had some health problems previously and really didn't expect to be covered until after she had taken her physical and received notice from the company. The agent said that the conditional binder was critical for immediate coverage. "Of course," said the agent, "this coverage may be limited until the company either accepts or rejects your application." The agent congratulated A. J. again for her decision. A. J. began to wonder the next morning exactly what kind of coverage, if any, she had.

   a. What kind of coverage did A. J. have?

   b. Did her submission to the agent of the first month's premium have any impact on her coverage? Why?

   c. If you were the agent, how would you have explained this coverage to A. J.?

9. LeRoy Leetch had a heck of a year. He suffered all the following losses. Based on what you know about insurance, which would you expect to be insurable and why?

   a. LeRoy's beloved puppy, Winchester, was killed when struck by a school bus. He has losses of burial expenses, the price of another puppy, and his grief due to Winchester's death.

   b. LeRoy has an expensive collection of rare clocks. Most are kept in his spare bedroom and were damaged when a fire ignited due to faulty wiring. The loss is valued at $15,000.

   c. Heavy snowfall and a rapid thaw caused flooding in LeRoy's town. Damage to his basement was valued at $2,200.

   d. Weather was hard on the exterior of LeRoy's house as well. Dry rot led to major damage to the first-story hardwood floors. Replacement will cost $6,500.

10. When you apply for a life insurance policy, agent Dawn Gale says, "If you will give me your check for the first month's premium now, the policy will cover you now if you are insurable." Is this a correct statement, or is Dawn just in a hurry to get her commission for selling you the policy? Explain.

ENDNOTES

1. In a few states, the conditional receipt is construed to be the same as the binding receipt. See William F. Meyer, *Life and Health Insurance Law: A Summary*, 2nd ed. (Cincinnati: International Claim Association, 1990), 196–217.

2. "9/11 Business Interruption Claims Analysis," *National Underwriter Online News Service*, February 20, 2002.

3. Diana Reitz, "9/11 Spotlights Business Interruption Threat—What Is the Art and Science of Establishing the Accurate Limit of Coverage?" *National Underwriter*, Property/Casualty Edition, April 16, 2004, http://www.propertyandcasualtyinsurancenews.com/cms/NUPC/Weekly%20Issues/Issues/2004/15/p15911spotlights?searchfor= (accessed March 8, 2009).

4. In April 1992, part of Chicago's underground tunnel system was flooded when the river pushed back a wall far enough to cause a rapid flow of water into the tunnels. Water levels rose high enough to damage stored property, force electrical supplies to be shut off, and cause concern about the stability of structures built above the tunnels.

5. *Thomas v. Transamerica Occidental Life Ins. Co.*, 761 F. Supp. 709 (1991).

6. *Beauregard v. Beauregard, 56* Ohio App. 158, 10 N.E.2d 227 (1937).

7. "Travelers Construction Offers New Pollution Endorsements," *National Underwriter*, Property & Casualty/Risk & Benefits Management Edition, March 10, 1997.

8. "Hartford Introduces Estate-Tax Repeal Rider," *National Underwriter Online News Service*, April 1, 2002; "Lincoln Life Expands Estate Tax Safety Net on Life Insurance" *National Underwriter Online News Service*, Oct. 12, 2001.

9. Jack Crawford, "Inflation Protection: Is the LTC Industry on the Right Path?" *National Underwriter*, Life & Health/Financial Services Edition, January 21, 2002.

CHAPTER 11
Property Risk Management

At this point you should feel somewhat comfortable with most of the overall picture of risk, but despite the many examples of risk management and types of coverage you have seen, the details of each coverage are not explicit yet. In this chapter, we will elaborate on property risks, including electronic commerce, or e-commerce, risk and global risk exposures. In Chapter 12, we will elaborate on liability risks overall and the particulars of e-commerce liability. Home coverage that includes both property and liability coverage will be discussed in detail in Chapter 1. Auto coverage will be discussed in Chapter 1. Chapter 13 and Chapter 14 focus on personal lines coverage. Chapter 15 and Chapter 16 take us into the world of commercial lines coverage and workers' compensation. In this part of the text, you will be asked to relate sections of the actual policies provided in the appendixes at the end of the textbook to loss events. Our work will clarify many areas of property and liability of various risks, including the most recent e-commerce risk exposures and the fundamental global risk exposure. In this chapter, we cover the following:

1. Links

2. Property risks

3. E-commerce property risks

4. Global risks

1. LINKS

The most important part of property coverage is that you, as the first party, are eligible to receive benefits in the event you or your business suffers a loss. In contrast, liability coverage, discussed in Chapter 12, pays benefits to a third party if you cause a loss (or if someone causes you to have a loss, his or her liability insurance would pay benefits to you). In this chapter we focus on the first type: coverage for you when your property is damaged or lost.

In personal lines coverage such as homeowners and auto policies, the property coverage for losses you sustain, as the owner of the property, is only part of the policies. In commercial lines, you may use a packaged multilines policy that includes both commercial property and commercial general liability policies. In this chapter we focus only on the part of the policies relating to the property coverage for first-party damages to you. As part of your holistic risk and risk management, it is important to have an appreciation of this part of the coverage.

As we develop the holistic risk management program, you now realize that you need a myriad of policies to cover all your property exposures, including that of e-commerce, and another myriad of policies to protect your liability exposures. In some cases, property and liability coverages are packaged together, such as in homeowners and auto policies, but what is actually covered under each? Our objective is to untangle it all and show how to achieve a complete risk management picture. To achieve complete holistic risk management, we have to put together a hierarchy of coverages for various exposures, perils, and hazards—each may appear in one or another policy—as shown in Figure 11.1 (see the shaded risk pieces of the puzzle that indicate property or first-party-type risks applicable to this chapter). In addition to understanding this hierarchy, we need to have a vision of the future. E-commerce risk, considered one of the emerging risks, is explored in this chapter. Hazards derived from global exposure are other important risks that receive special attention in this chapter.

FIGURE 11.1 Links between Property Risks and Insurance Contracts

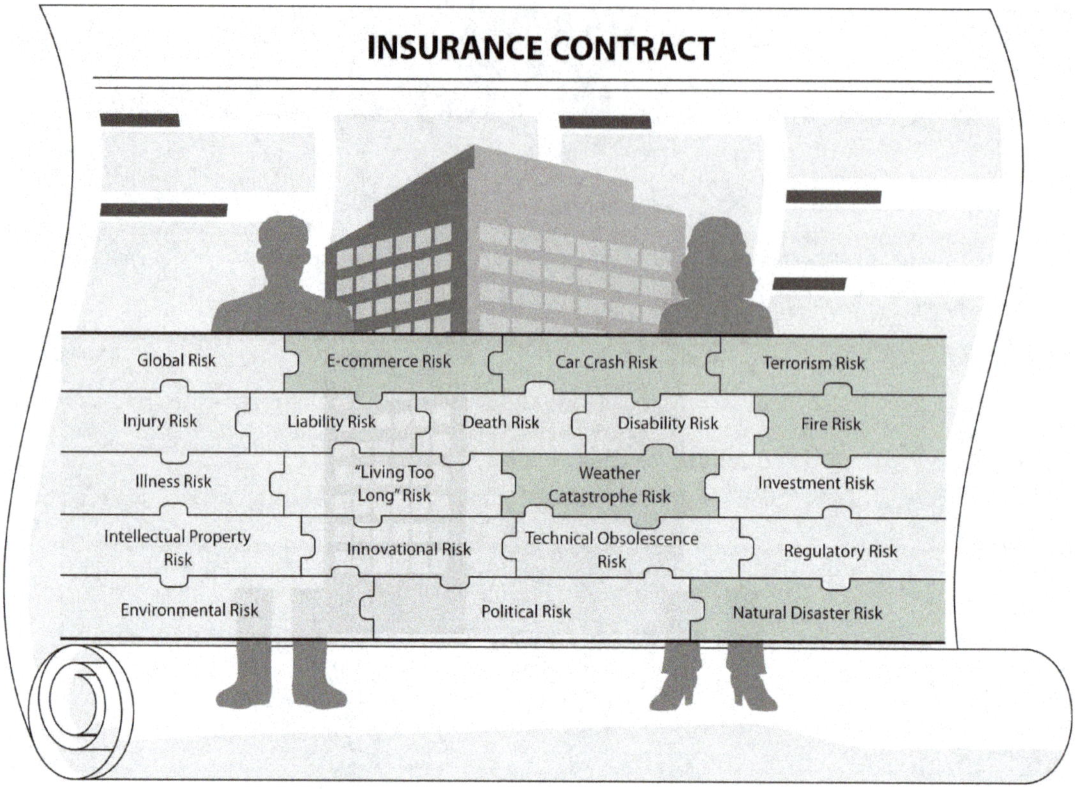

2. PROPERTY RISKS

LEARNING OBJECTIVES

In this section we elaborate on the following:

- **How insurable property is classified**
- **The ways in which valuation, deductibles, and coinsurance clauses influence property coverage and premiums**

Property can be classified in a number of ways, including its mobility, use value, and ownership. Sometimes these varying characteristics affect potential losses, which in turn affect decisions about which risk management options work best. A discussion of these classifying characteristics, including consideration of the hot topic of electronic commerce (e-risk) exposures and global property exposures, follows.

Physical property generally is categorized as either real or personal. **Real property** represents permanent structures (realty) that if removed would alter the functioning of the property. Any building, therefore, is real property. In addition, built-in appliances, fences, and other such items typically are considered real property.

Physical property that is mobile (not permanently attached to something else) is considered **personal property**. Included in this category are motorized vehicles, furniture, business inventory, clothing, and similar items. Thus, a house is real property, while a stereo and a car are personal property. Some property, such as carpeting, is not easily categorized. The risk manager needs to consider the various factors discussed below in determining how best to manage such property.

Why is this distinction between real and personal property relevant? One reason is that dissimilar properties are exposed to perils with dissimilar likelihoods. When flood threatens a house, the opportunities to protect it are limited. Yet the threat of flood damage to something mobile may be thwarted by movement of the item away from flood waters. For example, you may be able to drive your car out of the exposed area and to move your clothes to higher ground.

A second reason to distinguish between real and personal property is that appropriate valuation mechanisms may differ between the two. We will discuss later in this chapter the concepts of actual

---

physical property

Consists of real or personal property.

real property

Permanent structures (realty) that if removed would alter the functioning of the property.

personal property

Physical property that is mobile (not permanently attached to something else).

cash value and replacement cost new. Because of moral hazard issues, an insurer may prefer to value personal property at actual cash value (a depreciated amount). The amount of depreciation on real property, however, may outweigh concerns about moral hazard. Because of the distinction, valuation often varies between personal and real property.

When property is physically damaged or lost, the cost associated with being unable to use that property may go beyond the physical loss. Indirect loss and business interruption losses discussed in the box "Business Interruption with and without Direct Physical Loss" provides a glimpse into the impact of this coverage on businesses and the importance of the appropriate wording in the policies. In many cases, only loss of use of property that is directly damaged leads to coverage; in other cases, the loss of property itself is not a prerequisite to trigger loss of use coverage. As a student in this field, you will become aware of the importance of the exact meaning of the words in the insurance policy.

2.1   General Property Coverage

The first **standard fire policy (SFP)** came into effect during the late 1800s and came to be described as the generally accepted manner of underwriting for property loss due to fire. Two revisions of the SFP were made in 1918 and 1943. Most recently, the SFP has largely been removed from circulation, replaced by homeowners policies for residential property owners, discussed in Chapter 1, and the commercial package policy (CPP), featured in Chapter 1. The SFP was simple and relatively clear. Most of its original provisions are still found in current policies, updated for the needs of today's insured. In light of the changes regarding terrorism exclusion that occurred after September 11, 2001 (discussed in Chapter 1), the topic of standard fire policies came under review. The issue at hand is that, under current laws, standard fire policies cannot exclude fires resulting from terrorism or nuclear attacks without legislative intervention.[1]

standard fire policy (SFP)

The generally accepted method of insuring against property loss due to fire until being replaced by homeowners policies and commercial insurance options.

Business Interruption with and without Direct Physical Loss

When there is a direct physical loss, insurance coverage for business interruption is more likely to exist than when the interruption is not from direct physical loss. The New Orleans hotels that suffered damage due to flooding and wind caused by Hurricane Katrina on August 30, 2005, are more likely to have had business interruption coverage. The oil industry, including its refineries and rigs that were shut down as both hurricanes Katrina and Rita ripped through the Gulf Coast, also had insurance coverage for business interruption. The stop in oil production was associated with a physical loss. Not all business interruptions are covered by insurance. The economic losses suffered by many New York businesses during the New York City transportation strike of December 2005 were not a direct loss from physical damage. As such, these businesses did not have insurance to cover the losses. Nonrelated causes of loss that affect the continued viability of businesses usually do not have insurance remedies. The avian flu pandemic is expected to disrupt many businesses' activities indirectly. Employees are expected to be afraid to show up for work, and some industries—such as shipping—will be vulnerable. A key problem in these cases would be lack of insurance coverage.

In the past, some policyholders submitted business-interruption claims for nondirect economic loss. They were not successful in court. A case in point is the lawsuit filed in August 2002 by the luxury hotel chain Wyndham International against half a dozen of its insurers and the brokerage firm Marsh & McLennan. Wyndham claimed that it had suffered $44 million in lost revenue following the terrorist acts of September 11, 2001, and that the insurers had acted in bad faith in failing to pay the corporation's business-interruption claims. The Wyndham properties that reported September 11-related losses included hotels in Chicago and Philadelphia and three Puerto Rico beach resorts. Wyndham owns no properties in downtown New York City.

September 11 was the wake-up call. It's estimated that some $10 billion in claims have been filed for business-interruption losses, much of them far away from Ground Zero. With the Federal Aviation Administration—ordered closing of airports nationwide, the travel industry bore major losses. Resort hotels like Wyndham's saw business fall dramatically.

Are losses recoverable if the business sustained no physical damage? It depends, of course, on the policy. Most small and midsize businesses have commercial policies based on standard forms developed by the Insurance Services Office (ISO). The ISO's customary phrase is that the suspension of business to which the income loss relates must be caused by "direct physical loss of or damage to property at the premises described in the Declarations." Larger companies often have custom-written manuscript policies that may not be so restrictive. Whatever the wording is, it is likely to be debated in court.

Sources: Michael Bradford, "Hotels Start Recovery Efforts in Wake of Katrina Losses," Business Insurance, October 10, 2005, accessed March 15, 2009, http://www.businessinsurance.com/cgi-bin/article.pl?articleId=17714&a=a&bt=Hotels+Start+Recovery+Efforts; Michael Bradford, "Storms Slap Energy Sector with Losses as High as $8 Billion," Business Insurance, October 3, 2005, accessed March 15, 2009, http://www.businessinsurance.com/cgi-bin/article.pl?articleId=17640&a=a&bt=storms+slap+energy; Daniel Hays, "No Coverage Likely for N.Y. Transit Strike," National Underwriter Online News Service, December 20, 2005, accessed March 15, 2009, http://www.propertyandcasualtyinsurancenews.com/cms/NUPC/Breaking%20News/

2005/12/20-STRIKE-dh?searchfor=transit%20strike; Mark E. Ruquet, "Business Policies May Not Cover Pandemics," National Underwriter Online News Service, December 7, 2005, accessed March 15, 2009, http://www.propertyandcasualtyinsurancenews.com/cms/NUPC/Breaking%20News/2005/12/ 07-PANDEMIC-mr?searchfor= policies%20may%20not%20cover%20pandemics; Mark Ruquet, "Avian Flu Could Send Shipping Off Course," National Underwriter Online News Service, December 12,2005, accessed March 15, 2009, http://www.propertyandcasualtyinsurancenews.com/cms/NUPC/ Breaking%20News/2005/12/12-AVIAN-AON-mr?searchfor=avian%20flu; Sam Friedman, "9/11 Boosts Focus on Interruption Risks," National Underwriter, Property & Casualty/Risk & Benefits Management Edition, April 29, 2002; Joseph B. Treaster, "Insurers Reluctant to Pay Claims Far Afield from Ground Zero," New York Times, September 12, 2002; John Foster, "The Legal Aftermath of September 11: Handling Attrition and Cancellation in Uncertain Times," Convene, the Journal of the Professional Convention Management Association, December 2001; Daniel Hays, "Zurich Loses Ruling in a 9/11 Case," National Underwriter Online News Service, February 11, 2005, accessed March 15, 2009, http://www.propertyandcasualtyinsurancenews.com/cms/NUPC/Breaking%20News/2005/02/ 11-Zurich%20Loses%20Ruling%20In%20A%209-11%20Case?searchfor=.

From Coast to Coast: Who Is Responsible for Earthquake and Flood Losses?

No region of the United States is safe from environmental catastrophes. Floods and flash floods, the most common of all natural disasters, occur in every state. The Midwest's designated Tornado Alley ranges from Texas to the Dakotas, though twisters feel free to land just about anywhere. The Pacific Rim states of Hawaii, Alaska, Washington, Oregon, and California are hosts to volcanic activity, most famously the May 1980 eruption of Mount St. Helens in southwestern Washington, which took the lives of more than fifty-eight people. California is also home to the San Andreas Fault, whose seismic movements have caused nine major earthquakes in the past one hundred years; the January 1994 Northridge quake was the most costly in U.S. history, causing an estimated $20 billion in total property damage. (By comparison, the famous San Francisco earthquake of 1906 caused direct losses of $24 million, which would be about $10 billion in today's dollars.) Along the Gulf and Atlantic coasts, *natural disaster* means hurricanes. Insurers paid out more money for Hurricane Katrina in 2005 than they collected in premiums in twenty-five years from Louisiana insureds. California insurers paid out more in Northridge claims than they had collected in earthquake premiums over the previous thirty years. The year 2005 saw an unprecedented number of losses because of hurricanes Katrina, Rita, and Wilma. The record number of hurricanes included twenty-seven named storms. The insured losses from Hurricane Katrina alone were estimated between $40 and $60 billion, while the economic losses were estimated to be more than $100 billion. Theses losses are the largest catastrophic losses in U.S. history, surpassing Hurricane Andrew's record cost to the industry of $20.9 billion in 2004 dollars. This record also surpasses the worst human-made catastrophe of September 11, 2001, which stands at $34.7 billion in losses in 2004 dollars.

Fearing that the suffering housing, construction, and related industries would impair economic growth, state government stepped in. The state-run California Earthquake Authority was established in 1996 to provide coverage to residential property owners in high-risk areas. Disaster insurance then went to the federal level. In the aftermath of Katrina, in December 2005, a proposal for a national catastrophe insurance program was pushed by four big state regulators during the National Insurance Commissioners meeting in Chicago. The idea was to change the exclusion in the policies and allow for flood coverage, while calling for a private-state-federal partnership to fund megacatastrophe losses and the creation of a new all-perils homeowners policy that would cover the cost of flood losses.

Questions for Discussion

1. Lee is in favor of government-supported disaster reinsurance because it encourages economic growth and development. Chris believes that it encourages overgrowth and overdevelopment in environmentally fragile areas. Whose argument do you support?

2. The Gulf Coast town you live in has passed a building code requiring that new beachfront property be built on stilts. If your house is destroyed by a hurricane, rebuilding it on stilts will cost an extra $25,000. The standard homeowners policy excludes costs caused by ordinance or laws regulating the construction of buildings. Is this fair? Who should pay the extra expense?

3. Jupiter Island, located off the coast of south Florida, is the wealthiest town in the country. Its 620 year-round residents earn an average of just over $200,000 per year, per person. Thus, a typical household of two adults, two children, a housekeeper, a gardener/chauffeur, and a cook boasts an annual income of some $1.4 million. What is the reasoning for subsidizing hurricane insurance for residents of Jupiter Island?

4. In light of your understanding of the uninsurable nature of catastrophes, who should bear the financial burden of natural disasters?

Sources: Insurance Information Institute at http://www.iii.org; Steve Tuckey, "A National Cat Program? Insurers Have Doubts," National Underwriter Online News Service, December 5, 2005, accessed March 15, 2009, http://www.propertyandcasualtyinsurancenews.com/cms/NUPC/ Breaking%20News/2005/12/05-CAT-st?searchfor=national%20cat%20program; Mark E. Ruquet, "Towers Perrin: Katrina Loss $55 Billion," National Underwriter Online News Service, October 6, 2005, accessed March 15, 2009, http://www.propertyandcasualtyinsurancenews.com/cms/NUPC/ Breaking%20News/2005/10/06-TOWERSP-mr?searchfor =towers%20perrin%20katrina; "Louisiana Hurricane Loss Cancels 25 Years of Premiums,"

National Underwriter, January 6, 2006, accessed March 15, 2009, http://www.propertyandcasualtyinsurancenews.com/cms/NUPC/ Breaking%20News/2006/01/06-LAIII-ss?searchfor=louisiana%20hurricane; Insurance Information Institute, "Earthquakes: Risk and Insurance Issues," May 2002, http://www.iii.org/media/hottopics/insurance/earthquake/; Jim Freer, "State to Help Those Seeking Property, Casualty Insurance," The South Florida Business Journal, March 15, 2002.

2.2   Types of Property Coverage and Determination of Payments

Once it is determined that a covered peril has caused a covered loss to covered property, several other policy provisions are invoked to calculate the covered amount of compensation. As noted earlier, the topic of covered perils is very important. Catastrophes such as earthquakes are not considered covered perils for private insurance, but in many cases catastrophes such as hurricanes and other weather-related catastrophes are covered. The box "From Coast to Coast: Who Is Responsible for Earthquake and Flood Losses?" is designed to stimulate discussions about the payment of losses caused by catastrophes. Important provisions in this calculation are the valuation clause, deductibles, and coinsurance.

Valuation Clause

The intent of insurance is to indemnify an insured. Payment on an actual cash value basis is most consistent with the indemnity principle, as discussed in Chapter 9. Yet the deduction of depreciation can be both severe and misunderstood. In response, property insurers often offer coverage on a replacement cost new (RCN) basis, which does not deduct depreciation in valuing the loss. Rather, **replacement cost new** is the value of the lost or destroyed property if it were bought new or rebuilt on the day of the loss.

replacement cost

Indemnification for a property loss with no deduction for depreciation.

Deductibles

The cost of insurance to cover frequent losses (as experienced by many property exposures) is high. To alleviate the financial strain of frequent small losses, many insurance policies include a deductible. A deductible requires the insured to bear some portion of a loss before the insurer is obligated to make any payment. The purpose of deductibles is to reduce costs for the insurer, thus making lower premiums possible. The insurer saves in three ways. First, the insurer is not responsible for the entire loss. Second, because most losses are small, the number of claims for loss payment is reduced, thereby reducing the claims processing costs. Third, the moral and morale hazards are lessened because there is greater incentive to prevent loss when the insured bears part of the burden.[2]

The small, frequent losses associated with property exposures are good candidates for deductibles because their frequency minimizes risk (the occurrence of a small loss is nearly certain) and their small magnitude makes retention affordable. The most common forms of deductibles in property insurance are the following:

1. Straight deductible
2. Franchise deductible
3. Disappearing deductible

A **straight deductible** requires payment for all losses less than a specified dollar amount. For example, if you have a $200 deductible on the collision coverage part of your auto policy, you pay the total amount of any loss that does not exceed $200. In addition, you pay $200 of every loss in excess of that amount. If you have a loss of $800, therefore, you pay $200 and the insurer pays $600.

straight deductible

One that requires payment for all losses less than a specified dollar amount.

A **franchise deductible** is similar to a straight deductible, except that once the amount of loss equals the deductible, the entire loss is paid in full. This type of deductible is common in ocean marine cargo insurance, although it is stated as a percentage of the value insured rather than a dollar amount. The franchise deductible is also used in crop hail insurance, which provides that losses less than, for example, 5 percent of the crop are not paid, but when a loss exceeds that percentage, the entire loss is paid.

franchise deductible

One that pays the entire amount in full once the amount of loss equals the deductible.

The major disadvantage with the franchise deductible from the insurer's point of view is that the insured is encouraged to inflate a claim that falls just short of the amount of the deductible. If the claims adjuster says that your crop loss is 4 percent, you may argue long and hard to get the estimate up to 5 percent. Because it invites moral hazard, a franchise deductible is appropriate only when the insured is unable to influence or control the amount of loss, such as in ocean marine cargo insurance.

disappearing deductible

One whose amount decreases as the amount of the loss increases.

The disappearing deductible is a modification of the franchise deductible. Instead of having one cut-off point beyond which losses are paid in full, a **disappearing deductible** is a deductible whose amount decreases as the amount of the loss increases. For example, let's say that the deductible is $500 to begin with; as the loss increases, the deductible amount decreases. This is illustrated in Table 11.1.

TABLE 11.1 How the Disappearing Deductible Disappears

Amount of Loss ($)	Loss Payment ($)	Deductible ($)
500.00	0.00	500.00
1,000.00	555.00	445.00
2,000.00	1,665.00	335.00
4,000.00	3,885.00	115.00
5,000.00	4,955.00	5.00
5,045.00	5,045.00	0.00
6,000.00	6,000.00	0.00

At one time, homeowners policies had a disappearing deductible. Unfortunately, it took only a few years for insureds to learn enough about its operation to recognize the benefit of inflating claims. As a result, it was replaced by the straight deductible.

The small, frequent nature of most direct property losses makes deductibles particularly important. Deductibles help maintain reasonable premiums because they eliminate administrative expenses of the low-value, common losses. In addition, the nature of property losses causes the cost of property insurance per dollar of coverage to decline with the increasing percentage of coverage on the property. That is, the first 10 percent value of the property insurance is more expensive than the second (and so on) percent value. The cost of property insurance follows this pattern because most property losses are small, and so the expected loss does not increase in the same proportion as the increased percentage of the property value insured.

Coinsurance

coinsurance clause

Clause that requires one to carry an amount of insurance equal to a specified percentage of the value of property in order to be paid the full amount of loss incurred and that stipulates a proportional payment of loss for failure to carry sufficient insurance.

A **coinsurance clause** has two main provisions: first, it requires you to carry an amount of insurance equal to a specified percentage of the value of the property if you wish to be paid the amount of loss you incur in full, and second, it stipulates a proportional payment of loss for failure to carry sufficient insurance. It makes sense that if insurance coverage is less than the value of the property, losses will not be paid in full because the premiums charged are for lower values. For property insurance, as long as coverage is at least 80 percent of the value of the property, the property is considered fully covered under the coinsurance provision.

What happens when you fail to have the amount of insurance of at least 80 percent of the value of your building? Nothing happens until you have a partial loss. At that time, you are subject to a penalty. Suppose in January you bought an $80,000 policy for a building with an actual cash value of $100,000, and the policy has an 80 percent coinsurance clause, which requires at least 80 percent of the value to be covered in order to receive the actual loss. By the time the building suffers a $10,000 loss in November, its actual cash value has increased to $120,000. The coinsurance limit is calculated as follows:

$$\frac{\text{Amount of insurance carried}}{\text{Amount you agreed to carry}} \times \text{Loss}$$

$$= \frac{\$80,000}{\$96,000 \, (80\% \, of \, \$120,000)} \times \$10,000 = \$8,333.33$$

The amount the insurer pays is $8,333.33. Who pays the other $1,666.67? You do. Your penalty for failing to carry at least 80 percent of the actual value is to bear part of the loss. You will see in Chapter 1 that you should buy coverage for the value of the home and also include an inflation guard endorsement so that the value of coverage will keep up with inflation.

What if you have a total loss at the time the building is worth $120,000, and you have only $80,000 worth of coverage? Applying the coinsurance formula yields the following:

$$\frac{\$80,000}{\$96,000} \times \$120,000 = \$99,999.99$$

You would not receive $99,999.99, however, because the total amount of insurance is $80,000, which is the maximum amount the insurer is obligated to pay. When a loss equals or exceeds the amount of insurance required by the applicable percentage of coinsurance, the coinsurance penalty is not part of the calculation because the limit is the amount of coverage. The insurer is not obligated to pay more than the face amount of insurance in any event because a typical policy specifies this amount as its maximum coverage responsibility.

You save money buying a policy with a coinsurance clause because the insurer charges a reduced premium rate, but you assume a significant obligation. The requirement is applicable to values only at the time of loss, and the insurer is not responsible for keeping you informed of value changes. That is your responsibility.

KEY TAKEAWAYS

In this section you studied the general features of property coverage:

- Insurable property is classified as either real or personal property, and this classification affects the property's exposure to risks and basis for valuation
- Coverage amounts depend on valuation as either actual cash value or replacement cost new
- The use of deductibles reduces the cost of claims, the frequency of claims, and moral hazard; common forms of deductibles are straight, franchise, and disappearing
- A coinsurance clause requires insureds to carry an amount of insurance equal to a specified percentage of the value of the property in order to be paid the full amount of an incurred loss; otherwise insureds will be subject to penalty in the form of bearing a proportional amount of the loss

DISCUSSION QUESTIONS

1. What is the difference between real and personal property? Why do insurers make a distinction between them?
2. What is a deductible? Provide illustrative examples of straight, franchise, and disappearing deductibles.
3. What is the purpose of coinsurance? How does the policyholder become a coinsurer? Under what circumstances does this occur?

3. E-COMMERCE PROPERTY RISKS

LEARNING OBJECTIVES

In this section we elaborate on the following:

- **The increased frequency and severity of e-commerce property risks**
- **Five major categories of e-commerce property risks**
- **Loss-control steps that can reduce e-commerce property risks**
- **Availability of insurance as a means of transferring e-commerce property risks**

This chapter, as noted above, introduces areas that are growing in importance in the world of insurance. Almost every home, family, and business has risk exposures because of the use of computers, the Internet, and the Web; we refer to this as **e-commerce property risk**. Think about your own courses at the university. Each professor emphasizes his or her communication with you on the Web site for the course. You use the Internet as a research tool. Every time you log on, you are exposed to risks from cyberspace. Most familiar to you is the risk of viruses. But there are many additional risk exposures from electronic business, both to you as an individual and to businesses. Businesses with a Web presence are those that offer professional services online and/or online purchasing. Some businesses are business to consumer (BTC); others are business to business (BTB).

Regardless of the nature of the use of the Internet, cyber attacks have become more frequent and have resulted in large financial losses. According to the 2002 Computer Security Institute/Federal Bureau of Investigation (CSI/FBI) Computer Crime and Security Survey, Internet-related losses increased from $100 million in 1997 to $456 million in 2002.[3] The 6th Annual CyberSource fraud survey indicated a $700 million increase (37 percent) in lost revenue in 2004, from an estimated $2.6 billion in 2003. Small and medium businesses were hit the hardest. These losses are in line with fast revenue growth from e-commerce.[4]

Businesses today are becoming aware of their e-commerce risk exposures. In every forum of insurers' meetings and in every insurance media, e-risk exposure is discussed as one of the major "less

e-commerce property risk

Business risk exposures due to of the use of computers, the Internet, and the Web.

understood" risk exposures.[5] In this chapter, we discuss the hazards and perils of e-commerce risk exposure to the business itself as the first party. In Chapter 12, we will discuss the liability side of the risk exposure of businesses due to the Internet and online connections. Next, we discuss the hazards and perils of electronic business in general.

3.1 Causes of Loss in E-Commerce

The 2004 CSI/FBI survey provided many categories of the causes of losses in the computer/electronic systems area. By frequency, the 2004 order of causes of losses were: virus (78 percent); insider abuse of net access (59 percent); laptop/mobile thefts (49 percent); unauthorized access to information (39 percent); system penetration (37 percent); denial of service (17 percent); theft of proprietary information (10 percent); and sabotage, financial fraud, and telecom fraud (less than 10 percent). This list does not account for the severity of losses in 2004; however, the 269 respondents to this section of the survey reported losses reaching $141.5 million.

The 2004 CSI/FBI survey covered a wide spectrum of risk exposure in e-commerce, for both first-party (property and business interruption) and third-party (liability losses, covered in Chapter 12) losses. As you can see from this summary of the survey and other sources, the causes of **e-commerce property risks** are numerous. We can group these risks into five broad categories:

- Hardware and software thefts (information asset losses and corruption due to hackers, vandalism, and viruses)
- Technological changes
- Regulatory and legal changes
- Trademark infringements
- Internet-based telephony crimes

Hardware and Software Thefts

Companies have rapidly become dependent on computers. When a company's computer system is down, regardless of the cause, the company risks losing weeks, months, or possibly years of data. Businesses store the majority of their information on computers. Customer databases, contact information, supplier information, order forms, and almost all documents a company uses to conduct business are stored on the computer system. Losses from theft of proprietary information, sabotage of data networks, or telecom eavesdropping can cause major losses to the infrastructure base of a business, whether it is done by outside hackers or by insider disgruntled employees.

Hackers and crackers can cause expensive, if not fatal, damage to a company's computer systems. **Hackers** are virtual vandals who try to poke holes in a company's security network.[6] Hackers may be satisfied with defacing Web sites, while **crackers** are vandals who want to break in to a company's security network and steal proprietary information for personal gain. Potential terrorists are usually classified as crackers. Their objective is to hit specific companies in order to bring systems down, steal data, or modify data to destroy its integrity. **Insiders** are internal employees upset with the company for some reason, perhaps because of a layoff or a failure to get an expected promotion. Inside access to the company computer network, and the knowledge of how to use it, gives this group the potential to cause the most damage to a business.

A **virus** is a program or code that replicates itself inside a personal computer or a workstation with the intent to destroy an operating system or control program. When it replicates, it infects another program or document.[7]

Technological Changes

Another risk companies face in the cyber world is the rapid advancement of technology. When a company updates its computer system, its software package, or the process for conducting business using the computer system, business is interrupted while employees learn how to conduct business using the new system. The result of this downtime is lost revenue.

Regulatory and Legal Changes

Almost as quickly as the Internet is growing, the government is adding and changing applicable e-commerce laws. In the past, there were few laws because the Internet was not fully explored nor fully understood, but now, laws and regulations are mounting. Thus, companies engaged in e-commerce face legal risks arising from governmental involvement. An example of a law that is likely to change is the tax-free Internet sale. There is no sales tax imposed on merchants (and hence the consumer) on

e-commerce property risk

Business risk exposures due to of the use of computers, the Internet, and the Web.

hackers

Virtual vandals who try to poke holes in a company's security network.

crackers

Vandals who want to break in to a company's security network and steal proprietary information for personal gain.

insiders

Internal employees who vandalize a company because they are upset with it for some reason.

virus

Program or code that replicates itself inside a personal computer or a workstation with the intent to destroy an operating system or control program.

Internet sales between states partly because the government has not yet determined how states should apportion the tax revenue. As the volume of online purchases increases, so do the consequences of lost sales tax revenue from e-commerce.

Lack of qualified lawyers to handle cases that arise out of e-commerce disputes is another new risk. There are many areas of e-law that lawyers are not yet specialized in. Not only are laws complex and tedious, they are also changing rapidly. As a result, it is difficult for lawyers to stay abreast of each law that governs and regulates cyberspace.

Trademarks Infringements

Domain name disputes are a serious concern for many businesses. In most cases, disputes over the rights to a domain name result from two specific events. **Domain name hijacking** occurs when an individual or a business reserves a domain name that uses the trademark of a competitor. The other event arises when a business or an individual reserves the well-recognized name or trademark of an unrelated company as a domain name with the intent of selling the domain name to the trademark holder. Seeking compensation for the use of a registered domain name from the rightful trademark holder is known as **cybersquatting**.[8]

A recent case involving cybersquatting is *People for the Ethical Treatment of Animals v. Doughney*. In August 2001, the Fourth Circuit Court of Appeals held that the defendant, Michael Doughney, was guilty of service mark infringement and unfair competition, and had violated the Anti-Cybersquatting Consumer Protection Act (ACPA). Doughney had created a Web site at http://www.peta.org, which contained the registered service mark PETA. People for the Ethical Treatment of Animals (PETA) is an animal rights organization that opposes the exploitation of animals for food, clothing, entertainment, and vivisection. When users typed in http://www.peta.org, they expected to arrive at the site for People for the Ethical Treatment of Animals. Instead, they surprisingly arrived at People Eating Tasty Animals, a "resource for those who enjoy eating meat, wearing fur and leather, hunting, and the fruits of scientific research." The site contained links to a number of organizations that held views generally opposing those of PETA.[9] On two occasions, Doughney suggested that if PETA wanted one of his domains, or objected to his registration, it could "make me an offer" or "negotiate a settlement."

Web site hijacking occurs when a Web site operator knowingly deceives the user by redirecting the user to a site the user did not intend to view. A recent case, *Ford Motor Company v. 2600 Enterprises et al.*, caught attention in December 2001 when 2600 Enterprises automatically redirected users from a Web site they operate at a domain name directing profanity at General Motors to the Web site operated by Ford at http://www.ford.com. The defendants redirected users by programming an embedded link, which utilized Ford's mark, into the code of the defendants' Web site.[10] Domain-name hijacking, cybersquatting, and Web site hijacking for the sake of parody or satire is protected by the First Amendment, but sometimes the pranksters' only purpose is to harass or extract profit from the trademark owner.[11]

Internet-Based Telephony Crimes

One of the fastest-growing communication technologies is Internet-based telephony—known as voice-over-Internet protocol (VoIP). The National Institute of Standards and Technology warned that this technology has "inherent vulnerabilities"[12] because firewalls are not designed to help in securing this industry, which is grew by $903 million in 2005, up from $686 million in 2004.

3.2 Risk Management of E-Commerce Exposures

Businesses can take loss-control steps to reduce the e-commerce property and business interruption risks by using the following:

- Security products and processes
- System audits
- Antivirus protection
- Backup systems and redundancies
- Data protection and security
- Passwords
- Digital signatures
- Encryption
- Firewalls
- Virtual private network (VPN)

domain name hijacking

When an individual or a business reserves a domain name that uses the trademark of a competitor.

cybersquatting

Seeking compensation for the use of a registered domain name from the rightful trademark holder.

Web site hijacking

When a Web site operator knowingly deceives the user by redirecting the user to a site the user did not intend to view.

Businesses today buy electronic security systems and develop many steps to reduce the risk of data and hardware losses. Firms conduct regular system audits to test for breaches in network security. Auditors attempt to break into various components of the company computer system, including the operating systems, networks, databases, servers, Web servers, and business processes in general, to simulate attacks and discover weaknesses.[13] Managed security services provide an option for virus protection. They include both antivirus protection and firewall installation.

Regular system backup processes and off-site systems saved many businesses hurt by the September 11 attacks. One advantage of keeping backup data files off-site is having clean data in case of damage in the original files from viruses, hackers, and crackers. Because security may be breached from people within the company, Internet access is generally available only to authorized internal and external users via the use of passwords. E-mails are easy to intercept and read as they travel across the Internet. Attaching a digital signature allows the recipient to discern whether the document has been altered.[14] Another method to protect e-mails is encryption. **Encryption** allows the sender of an e-mail to scramble the contents of the document. Before the recipient can read the message, he or she needs to use a password for a private key. Encryption is used for confidential communications.

A firewall is another loss-control solution that protects the local area network (LAN) or corporate network from unauthorized access. A **firewall** protects a network from intrusion by preventing access unless certain criteria are met. Another loss-control technique is the virtual private network, which connects satellite offices with a central location. A **virtual private network (VPN)** allows remote users to gain secure access to a corporate network. VPNs provide endless opportunities for telecommuters, business travelers, and multiple independent offices of a bigger company.

E-Commerce Property Insurance

According to the 2004 CSI/FBI Computer Crime and Security Survey described above, only 28 percent of 320 respondents had any external insurance policies to help manage cyber security risks. Traditional property insurance covers physical damage to tangible property due to an insured peril. Electronic data can be considered property in most instances, but standard commercial insurance policies, discussed in Chapter 1, contain exclusions that "explicitly invalidate coverage for exposures in relation to the use of technology."[15] Some insurers now offer customized e-commerce insurance policies that expand the areas of coverage available for e-commerce property risk. ISO has an e-commerce endorsement that modifies insurance provided under commercial property coverage. Under this endorsement,

> *insurers will pay for the cost to replace or restore electronic data which has suffered loss or damage by a Covered Cause of Loss…including the cost of data entry, re-programming and computer consultation services.*

The endorsement has four sections. Section I describes the electronic data coverage. Section II defines the period of coverage as well as the coverage of business income, extra expenses, and resumption of e-commerce activity. Section III classifies covered and excluded perils; exclusions include mechanical breakdown; downtime due to viruses, unless the computer is equipped with antivirus software; errors or omissions in programming or data processing; errors in design, maintenance, or repair; damage to one computer on the network caused by repair or modification of any other computer on the network; interruption as a result of insufficient capacity; and unexplained failure. Section IV of the endorsement is for other provisions, explained in Chapter 10.

In addition to this endorsement, a few insurers have created a variety of e-commerce policies. Some of the companies include ACE USA, Chubb, AIG, the Fidelity and Deposit Companies (members of Zurich Financial Services Group), Gulf Insurance Group, Legion Indemnity Company, and Lloyd's of London. This list is by no means inclusive.[16] These companies provide not only first-party e-commerce property and business interruption coverage, but also liability coverage for third-party liability risks. The liability coverage will be discussed in Chapter 12. Because e-commerce does not see geographical boundaries, many policies provide worldwide e-commerce coverage.

---

encryption

Allows the sender of an e-mail to scramble the contents of the document.

firewall

Device that protects a network from intrusion by preventing access unless certain criteria are met.

virtual private network (VPN)

Network that connects satellite offices with a central location and allows remote users to gain secure access to a corporate network.

KEY TAKEAWAYS

In this section you studied the emerging exposure of e-commerce property risk:

- E-commerce property risks fall under five categories: hardware and software thefts, technological changes, regulatory and legal changes, trademark infringements, and Internet-based telephony crimes
- Cyber attacks have become more frequent and more costly in the financial losses they cause
- Hackers, crackers, insiders, and viruses are major causes of hardware and software theft and data losses
- Technological advancements cause downtime while employees learn how to use new systems and components
- Frequent additions to and changes in existing e-commerce laws creates compliance risks and lack of qualified lawyers to handle disputes.
- Domain name hijacking, cybersquatting, and Web site hijacking are all ways of infringing legitimate companies' trademarks
- Voice-over-Internet protocol (VoIP) has inherent vulnerabilities due to the absence of effective security measures
- Loss-control steps that can reduce e-commerce property risks include security products, system audits, backup systems, and data protection
- While electronic data is considered property, it is typically excluded from standard commercial insurance policies, thus leading to the rise of customized e-commerce policies and endorsements

DISCUSSION QUESTIONS

1. What are the risk exposures of e-commerce?
2. How should the property risk of e-commerce be managed?
3. Describe the parts of an e-commerce endorsement.
4. What are some of the potential e-commerce property losses that businesses face?

4. GLOBAL PROPERTY EXPOSURES

LEARNING OBJECTIVES

In this section we elaborate on the following:

- **Global risk exposures in the international competitive landscape**
- **Risk control measures for reducing common global risks**
- **Insurance options for global risk exposures**

As with the Internet, global exposure is rapidly growing for many companies. This forces management to think about the unique problems that arise when companies cross national borders, also known as **global risk**. Political Risk Services (http://www.prsonline.com/), an organization that ranks countries for their instability, attaches a major cost to each country. This highlights the importance of understanding the countries that businesses decide to enter. In a survey conducted by the insurance broker Aon[17] of Fortune 1,000 companies in the United States, 26 percent of the respondents felt comfortable with their political risk exposure and 29 percent felt comfortable with their global financial or economic risk exposure. While most respondents felt comfortable with their property/casualty coverages, only a small percentage felt comfortable with their political risk protection. The survey was conducted during May 2001, before the September 11 attack. In 2005, Aon provided a map of the political and economic risk around the world. The climate around the world has changed with the war in Iraq, a part of the world surrounded by major economic and political hot spots.

Political risk can be defined as unanticipated political events that disrupt the earning or profit-making ability of an enterprise. In "The Risk Report: Managing Political Risks," insurance expert Kevin M. Quinley describes some of the perils that can affect a global organization: nationalization, privatization, expropriation (property taken away by the host nation according to its laws), civil unrest, revolution, foreign exchange restrictions, labor regulations, kidnapping, terrorism, seizure, and forfeiture.

global risk

The unique problems that arise when companies cross national borders.

political risk

Unanticipated political events that disrupt the earning or profit-making ability of an enterprise.

Some of the risks are considered political risks, others are economic risks. Table 11.2 explains some of these risks. In summary, the main categories of global risk exposure are as follows:

- Destabilized international political environment
- Heightened terrorism risk
- Legal risk due to changes in local laws
- Lack-of-data risk
- Currency inconvertibility risk
- Cultural barriers risks

According to the Risk Report, the nature of the risks has changed. Twenty years ago, the major risk was in the area of nationalization of capital assets, while the perils of today are more related to economic integration and the power of international financial markets. Experts agree that political risk looms larger after September 11, the war in Iraq, and the instability in the Middle East. Following the September 11 attack, Marsh and all large brokerage firms began providing political risk assessment services to clients worldwide.[18] The consulting includes formulating and reviewing crisis management plans for events such as natural disasters, product recalls, and terrorism. The plans are comprehensive, and they are integrated throughout the enterprise.

TABLE 11.2 Ten Ways to Tune Up Management of Political Risks

1. Look closely at foreign operations—current or planned—and identify all possible political risks.
2. Examine the locale of each foreign operation and stratify them along a risk continuum, according to susceptibility of political risks.
3. Explore "public" political risk insurance coverage through facilities such as MIGA and OPIC.
4. Allow plenty of lead time for procuring insurance for political risk coverage.
5. Seek multiyear policies or coverage for as long a time frame as possible. Keep tightlipped about the existence of any political risk coverage you obtain.
6. Engage an insurance broker who is specialized in procuring political risk coverage.
7. Invest in infrastructure in host countries and cultivate a strong track record of being a good corporate citizen.
8. Fine-tune security and anti-hijacking procedures to address the potential loss from kidnapping, ransom, extortion, or terrorism.
9. Make sure that retention of any political risks is accompanied by realistic funding mechanisms.
10. Strive to bring the same thoroughness to political risk management as the organization brings to more mainstream risks such as fire, flood, earthquake, and workers' compensation.

Reproduced with permission of the publisher, International Risk Management Institute, Inc., Dallas, Texas, from the Risk Report, copyright International Risk Management Institute, Inc., author Kevin Quinley CPCU, ARM. Further reproduction prohibited. For subscription information, phone 800-827-4242. Visit http://www.IRMI.com for practical and reliable risk and insurance information.

4.1 Legal Risk

Often, the decision to undertake operations in a particular country is made apart from any risk management considerations. Although the legal environment may have been carefully reviewed from the standpoint of firm operations, little information may have been obtained about insurance requirements and regulations. For example, in many countries, social insurance is much broader than in the United States and there are few, if any, alternatives available to the risk manager. The risk manager may be forced by regulations to purchase local coverage that is inadequate in covered perils or limits of liability. Particularly in less-developed countries, there simply may not be adequate insurance capacity to provide desirable amounts and types of coverage. The risk manager then must decide whether or not to ignore the regulations and use nonadmitted coverage.

Nonadmitted coverage involves contracts issued by a company not authorized to write insurance in the country where a risk exposure is located. **Admitted insurance** is written by companies authorized to write insurance in the country where a risk exposure is located. Nonadmitted contracts have advantages to some U.S. policyholders: they are written in English; use U.S. dollars for premiums and claims, thus avoiding exchange rate risk; utilize terms and conditions familiar to U.S. risk managers; and provide flexibility in underwriting. However, such contracts may be illegal in some countries, and the local subsidiary may be subject to penalties if the contracts' existence becomes known. Further, premium payment may not be tax deductible, even in countries where nonadmitted coverage is permitted. If nonadmitted insurance is purchased where it is prohibited, claim payments must be made to the parent corporation, which then has to find a way to transfer the funds to the local subsidiary.

Coverage is also affected by the codification of the legal system in the other countries. The Napoleonic code, for example, is used in France, Belgium, Egypt, Greece, Italy, Spain, and several other countries. Under this legal system, liability for negligence is not treated in the same way as liability is treated under the United States system of common law; any negligence not specifically mentioned in the code is dismissed. The common law system is based on legal precedent, and the judges play a much more significant role.

4.2   Data Risk

Another problem facing the international risk manager is the collection of adequate statistical information. Economic and statistical data commonly available in the United States may simply be nonexistent in other parts of the world. For example, census data providing an accurate reflection of mortality rates may not be available. Even in industrialized countries, statistics may need careful scrutiny because the method used to produce them may be vastly different from that typical to the risk manager's experience. This is particularly true of rate-making data. Data may also be grossly distorted for political reasons. Officially stated inflation rates, for instance, are notoriously suspect in many countries.

Faced with this lack of reliable information, the risk manager has little choice but to proceed with caution until experience and internal data collection can supplement or confirm other data sources. Contacts with other firms in the same industry and with other foreign subsidiaries can provide invaluable sources of information.

Data collection and analysis are a problem not only in this broad sense. Communication between the corporate headquarters and foreign operations becomes difficult due to language barriers, cultural differences, and often a sense of antagonism about a noncitizen's authority to make decisions. Particularly difficult under these circumstances are the identification and evaluation of exposures and the implementation of risk management tools. Loss control, for instance, is much more advanced and accepted in the United States than in most other countries. Encouraging foreign operations to install sprinklers, implement safety programs, and undertake other loss-control steps is generally quite difficult. Further, risk managers of U.S.-based multinational firms may have difficulty persuading foreign operations to accept retention levels as high as those used in the United States. Retention simply is not well accepted elsewhere.

4.3   Currency Risk

Any multinational transaction, where payments are transferred from one currency to another, is subject to exchange rate risk. Under the current system of floating exchange rates, the rate of currency exchange between any two countries is not fixed and may vary substantially over time. Currency exchange risk is in the area of liquidity and convertibility between currencies. The risk exposure is the inability of the global firm to exchange the currency and transfer out of hostile countries. How this kind of risk can be mitigated is explained in Chapter 5.

4.4   Cultural Differences Risk

As we are very acutely aware after the September 11, 2001, attacks, cultural differences are at the root of much of the trouble around the world. But this is not only in hostile events. When a business expands abroad, one of the first actions is the study of the local culture of doing business. If you ever were in the market in old Jerusalem, you may have experienced the differences in shopping. You learn very quickly that a merchant never expects you to buy the item for the quoted price. The haggling may take a long time. You may leave and come back before you buy the item you liked for less than half the originally quoted price. This is the culture. You are expected to bargain and negotiate. Another cultural difference is the "connection" or "protection." Many business moves will never happen without the right connection with the right people in power.

nonadmitted coverage

Contracts issued by a company not authorized to write insurance in the country where a risk exposure is located.

admitted insurance

Contracts written by companies authorized to write insurance in the country where a risk exposure is located.

Labor laws reflect another interesting cultural difference. In some countries, it is common to employ very young children—an act that is against the law in the United States. The families in these countries depend heavily on the income of their children. But an American business in such a country may be faced with an ethical dilemma: should it employ children or adhere to U.S. practices and labor laws?[19] Islamic finance is very different from finance in the Western world; for example, in Islam, interest payments are not permitted. With the expanded involvement of many businesses in the Middle East and Islamic countries, many academics, as well as businesspeople, are learning about the special ways to conduct business there.

4.5 Global Risk Management

The steps in global risk management include processes to reduce risk and develop loss-control policies, along with obtaining the appropriate insurance. Table 11.2 lists ways to manage political risks. The steps include learning the culture of the country and becoming a good corporate citizen, learning about the reality of the country, and finding ways to avoid political and legal traps. In the area of insurance, the global firm first looks for public insurance policies. The U.S. government established an insurance program administered through the Overseas Private Investment Corporation (OPIC) in 1948. The types of coverage available include expropriation, confiscation, war risks, civil strife, unfair calling of guarantees, contract repudiation, and currency inconvertibility. These are shown in Table 11.2. OPIC insurance is available only in limited amounts and only in certain developing countries that have signed bilateral trade agreements with the United States for projects intended to aid development. Some private insurers, however, also provide political risk insurance. Private insurers do not have the same restrictions as OPIC, but country limits do exist to avoid catastrophe (dependent exposure units). Additional types of coverage, such as kidnap, ransom, and export license cancellation, are also provided by private insurers. Poor experience in this line of insurance has made coverage more difficult and costly to obtain.

After September 11, some insurers pulled out of the political risk market, while others took the opportunity to expand their global coverage offerings. A Canadian insurer reported that the demand for insurance for employee political risk and kidnap and ransom for a dozen global companies increased by 100 percent.[20] Zurich North America and Chubb expanded their political risk insurance offerings to the Asian market.[21] The private insurance market's ability to meet the demand has been strengthening each year because customers require broader coverage with longer terms, up to ten years. Other companies expanding into the market are Bermuda's Sovereign Risk, AIG, and Reliance, among others.

Until recently, long-term political risk insurance was available mostly from international government agencies such as the Washington-based Multilateral Investment Guarantee Corporation (MIGA), a member of the World Bank Group; OPIC; the United Kingdom's Export Credit Guarantee Department; and the French government's export credit agency, Coface. But now the private market has been competing in the longer-term coverages and has opened coverage to losses caused by war and currency inconvertibility. Capacity and limits increased as reinsurance became more readily available in this area of global risks. Lloyd's of London, for example, offered about $100 million in limits in 2002, a huge increase from the $10 million it could provide in 1992, according to Investment Insurance International, the specialist political risk division of Aon Group. AIG has increased its limits to $30 million per risk, while the rest of the private market had about $55 million to work with.

Coverage is even available in Israel, where major concerns about security made investors and businesspeople nervous. A political risk team at Lloyd's (MAP Underwriting) developed a policy to address those concerns.[22] The policy gives peace of mind to businesses that believe in the economic future of Israel by protecting the effects of "war and other political violence on their investments, property and personnel." This specific coverage includes acts of war.

As noted in Table 11.2, some global firms use captives for this exposure. Captives were discussed in Chapter 6.

KEY TAKEAWAYS

In this section you studied global risk exposures that arise from the increasingly international nature of business operations:

- Political risk results from unanticipated governmental destabilization that disrupts an enterprise's profit-making ability
- Legal attitudes with respect to insurance can be very different in other parts of the world, leading many international companies to turn to nonadmitted coverage
- International data-gathering may be limited, suspect, or inconsistent with domestic techniques, so internal collection efforts and collaboration among businesses is often required
- Volatile currencies can create unfavorable exchange rates
- Cultural differences, especially as reflected in labor laws, pose ethical dilemmas for companies with opposing views in conducting business
- Public insurance policies available through groups like the Overseas Private Investment Corporation (OPIC) and the Multilateral Investment Guarantee Corporation (MIGA) provide options for mitigating global risks such as expropriation, confiscation, war risks, civil strife, and currency inconvertibility
- Private insurers have increased political risk insurance offerings such as coverage for kidnap, ransom, and export license cancellation in response to greater demand

DISCUSSION QUESTIONS

1. What is different about international property exposures compared with U.S. property exposures?
2. Why might an American company operating in a foreign country choose to purchase nonadmitted coverage?
3. Describe the steps of political risk management.

5. REVIEW AND PRACTICE

1. Assume you live on the Texas Gulf Coast, where hurricane damage can be extensive. Also assume that you own a two-story frame home valued at $120,000. You insured the house for $80,000, which was your purchase price four years ago. If you had a total loss, what reimbursement would you receive from your insurer? What if you had a loss of $10,000? (Assume an 80 percent coinsurance provision.)

2. Erin Lavinsky works for the Pharmacy On-Line company in Austin, Texas. She uses her business computer for personal matters and has received a few infected documents. She was too lazy to update her Norton Utilities and did not realize that she was sending her infected material to her coworkers. Before long, the whole system collapsed and business was interrupted for a day until the backup system was brought up. Respond to the following questions:

    a. Describe the types of risk exposures that Pharmacy On-Line is facing as a result of e-commerce.

    b. If Pharmacy On-Line purchased the ISO endorsement in Chapter 26, would it be covered for the lost day?

    c. Describe what other risk exposures could interrupt the business of Pharmacy On-Line.

3. What is a standard policy? Why is a standard policy desirable (or undesirable)?

4. Marina Del Ro Shipping Company expanded its operations to the Middle East just before September 11, 2001. Respond to the following questions:

    a. What are the global risk exposures of Marina Del Ro?

    b. What should Marina Del Ro do to mitigate these risks in terms of noninsurance and insurance solutions?

5. Provide an example of a business interruption loss and of an extra expense loss in the e-commerce endorsement.

ENDNOTES

1. For more information, read the article "Standard Fire Policy Dates Back to 19th Century," featured in *Best's Review*, April 2002.

2. For example, residents of a housing development had full coverage for windstorm losses (that is, no deductible). Their storm doors did not latch properly, so wind damage to such doors was common. The insurer paid an average of $100 for each loss. After doing so for about six months, it added a $50 deductible to the policies as they were renewed. Storm door losses declined markedly when insureds were required to pay for the first $50 of each loss.

3. Richard Power, "Computer Security Issues & Trends," Vol. VIII, Mo I. The survey was conducted by the Computer Security Institute (CSI) with the participation of the San Francisco Federal Bureau of Investigation's Computer Intrusion Squad. Established in 1974, CSI has thousands of members worldwide and provides a wide variety of information and education programs to assist in protecting the information assets of corporations and governmental organizations. For more information, go to http://online.sju.edu/resource/justice-studies/top-criminal-justice-misconceptions-television, http://justicenews.hubpages.com/hub/Common-Misconceptions-About-Criminal-Justice, and http://www.mccarthymartin.com/blog/2013/09/misconceptions-about-immigrants-and-the-criminal-justice-system.shtml.

4. The 6th Annual CyberSource Fraud Survey was sponsored by CyberSource Corporation and undertaken by Mindwave Research. The survey was fielded September 17 through October 1, 2004, and yielded 348 qualified and complete responses (versus 333 the year before). The sample was drawn from a database of companies involved in electronic commerce activities. Copies of the survey are available by visiting http://www.cybersource.com/fraudreport/.

5. For example, see Lee McDonald," Insurer Points out Risks of E-Commerce," *Best's Review*, February 2000; Ron Lent, "Electronic Risk Gives Insurers Pause," *National Underwriter*, Property & Casualty/Risk & Benefits Management Edition, May 7, 2001; Caroline Saucer, "Technological Advances: Web Site Design Provides Clues to Underwriting Online Risks," *Best's Review*, December 2000.

6. George S. Sutcliffe, Esq., *E-Commerce and Insurance Risk Management* (Boston: Standard Publishing Corp., 2001), 13.

7. Adapted from the online glossary of Symantec, a worldwide provider of Internet security solutions, at http://www.symantec.com/avcenter/refa.html.

8. George S. Sutcliffe, Esq., *E-Commerce and Insurance Risk Management* (Boston: Standard Publishing Corp., 2001), 13.

9. *People for the Ethical Treatment of Animals* v. Doughney, No. 00-1918 (4th Cir2001); http://www.phillipsnizer.com/internetlib.htm.

10. *Ford Motor Company v. 2600 Enterprises et al.*, 177 F. Supp. 2d 661, 2001, U.S. District Court Lexis 21302 (E.D. Michigan2001); http://www.phillipsnizer.com/int-trademark.htm.

11. Monte Enbysk, "Hackers and Vandals and Worms, Oh My!" Microsoft bCentral newsletter, http://www.bcentral.com.

12. Simon London, "Government Warns Users on Risks of Internet-Based Telephony: Voip Is Growing in Popularity as the Technology Proliferates, but Inherent in the Service, Warns the Government, Is Increased Security and Privacy Flaws," *Financial Times*, February 6, 2005, http://www.ft.com/cms/s/0/5fca499c-7554-11d9-9608-00000e2511c8.html (accessed March 15, 2009).

13. Kevin Coleman, "How E-Tailers and Online Shoppers Can Protect Themselves," KPMG.

14. George S. Sutcliffe, Esq., *E-Commerce and Insurance Risk Management* (Boston: Standard Publishing Corp., 2001), 13.

15. "New Policy Offered to Cover Tech Risks," *National Underwriter Online News Service*, July 2, 2002; Stand Alone E-Commerce Market Survey, by IRMI at http://www.irmi.com/Expert/Articles/2001/Popups/Rossi02-1.aspx.

16. George S. Sutcliffe, Esq., *E-Commerce and Insurance Risk Management* (Boston: Standard Publishing Corp., 2001), 13.

17. Mark E. Ruquet, "Big Firms Worry About Coverage for Political Risks Abroad," *National Underwriter Online News Service*, August 9, 2001. The Aon survey asked 122 risk managers, chief financial officers, and others in similar positions of responsibility to assess various aspects of their overseas risks. The surveys were done by telephone and in some cases over the Internet.

18. "Marsh to Begin Crisis Consulting Led by Anti-Terror Expert," *National Underwriter Online News Service*, October 12, 2001; see Aon services at http://www.aon.com/risk_management/political_risk.jsp; see Willis services at http://www.willis.com/Services/Political%20Risk.aspx.

19. Etti G. Baranoff and Phyllis S. Myers, "Ethics in Insurance," Academy of Insurance Education, Washington, D.C., instructional video with supplemental study guide (video produced by the Center for Video Education, 1997.)

20. Daniel Hays, "Insurer Finds Good Market in Political Risk," *National Underwriter Online News Service*, November 28, 2001.

21. "Zurich North America Expands Political Risk Insurance to Asian Market," *National Underwriter Online News Service*, April 6, 2002; John Jennings, "Political Risk Cover Demand Surges: Insurers," *National Underwriter*, Property & Casualty/Risk & Benefits Management Edition, April 27, 1998.

22. "Armed-Conflict Risks Covered," *National Underwriter, Property & Casualty/Risk & Benefits Management Edition*, June 11, 2001. Many Internet sites deal with global risk. For example, Global Risk International at http://www.globalrisk.uk.com/ offers counterterrorist training, kidnap and ransom management, close protection, and surveillance.

CHAPTER 1 2

The Liability Risk Management

As noted in Chapter 11, liability risk is the risk that we may hurt a third party and will be sued for bodily injury or other damages. Most of us have heard about auto liability; pollution liability; product liability; medical malpractice; and the professional liability of lawyers, accountants, company directors and officers, and more. In the early 2000s, the United States was mired in the accounting scandals of Enron and WorldCom. In the mid-2000s, AIG added its name to the list of lawsuits and criminal allegations with accounting improprieties that padded company results. Shareholders and participants in the 401(k) plans of these companies filed lawsuits, some of which were class-action suits. In February 2005, President Bush signed a bill to redirect class-action lawsuits in excess of $5 million and with geographically dispersed plaintiffs from state courts to federal courts.[1] Cases of this type are expected to continue to emerge. In 2008, the credit crisis began and the allegations of misconduct and negligence by directors and officers are expected to bring about a large numbers of lawsuits.

While liability insurance is for unintentional actions, the fear of having to pay liability claims because of the errors and omissions of accountants and the directors and officers of companies have caused insurance rates in these types of coverage to jump dramatically. The relationships between behavior and coverage will be strongly demonstrated in this chapter, which will cover the following:

1. Links

2. Nature of the liability exposure

3. Major sources of liability

4. Liability issues and possible solutions

1.   LINKS

As discussed in the Links section in Chapter 11, liability coverage is coverage for a third party that may suffer a loss because of your actions. It also covers you in case you are hurt or your property is damaged because of someone else's actions, such as the actions of the accountants and executives of Enron, WorldCom, and AIG. The harmed parties are investors and the employees of these companies who lost all or part of their investments or pensions. In personal lines coverage, such as homeowners and auto policies, the liability of property damage or bodily injury you may inflict on others is covered up to a limit. In commercial lines, you may use a packaged multilines policy that also includes liability coverage. In this chapter, we focus only on the liability sections of these policies.

As part of your holistic risk management program, you now realize that you need a myriad of policies to cover all your liability exposures. In many cases, both the property and liability are in the same policies, but what liability coverage is actually included in each policy? As we delve further into insurance policies, we find many types of liability coverage. As you will see in this chapter, businesses have a vast number of liabilities: product, errors and omissions, professional, directors and officers, e-commerce, medical, employment, employee benefits, and more. The aftermath of September 11, 2001, revealed additional liabilities from terrorism. Liability risk exposure is scary for any individual or business, especially in such a litigious society as the United States. Nonetheless, it is important to have the recourse when someone has been wronged, for example, during the scandals of accounting irregularities and management fraud.

To better understand the complete holistic risk management process, it is imperative for us to understand all sections of the liability coverages in all the policies we hold. Figure 12.1 shows the connection among the types of coverage and the complete puzzle of risk. At this point we are drilling down into a massive type of risk exposure, which is covered by a myriad of policies. Our ability to connect them all allows us to complete the picture of our holistic risk.

FIGURE 12.1 Links between Liability Risks and Insurance Contracts

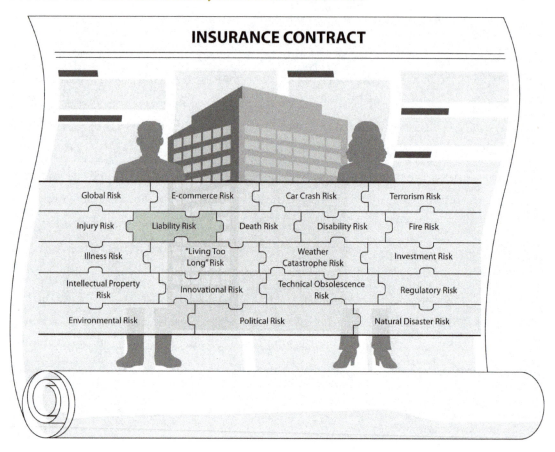

2. NATURE OF THE LIABILITY EXPOSURE

LEARNING OBJECTIVES

In this section we elaborate on the following:

- **How legal liability is defined and determined**
- **Types of monetary compensation for liability damages**
- **The role of negligence in liability**
- **Defenses against liability**
- **Modifications to liability, as they are generally determined**

Legal liability is the responsibility, based in law, to right some wrong done to another person or organization. Several aspects of this definition deserve further discussion. One involves the remedy of liability. A **remedy** is compensation for a person who has been harmed in some way. A person who has been wronged or harmed may ask the court to remedy or compensate him or her for the harm. Usually, this will involve monetary compensation, but it could also involve some behavior on the part of the person who committed the wrong, or the **tortfeasor**. For example, someone whose water supply has been contaminated by a polluting business may request an injunction against the business to force the cessation of pollution. A developer who is constructing a building in violation of code may be required to halt construction based on a liability lawsuit.

When monetary compensation is sought, it can take one of several forms. **Special damages** (or economic damages) compensate for those harms that generally are easily quantifiable into dollar measures. These include medical expenses, lost income, and repair costs of damaged property. Those harms that are not specifically quantifiable but that require compensation all the same are called **general damages** (or **noneconomic damages**). Examples of noneconomic or general damages include pain and suffering, mental anguish, and loss of consortium (companionship). The third type of monetary liability award is punitive damages, which was discussed in "Are Punitive Damages out of Control?" in Chapter 10. In this chapter, we will continue to discuss the controversy surrounding the use of punitive damages. **Punitive damages** are considered awards intended to punish an offender for exceptionally undesirable behavior. Punitive damages are intended not to compensate for actual harm incurred but rather to punish.

A second important aspect of the definition of liability is that it is based in law. In this way, liability differs from other exposures because it is purely a creation of societal rules (laws), which reflect social norms. As a result, liability exposures differ across societies (nations) over time. In the United States, liability is determined by the courts and by laws enacted by legislatures.

The risk of liability is twofold. Not only may you become liable to someone else and suffer loss, but someone else may become liable to you and have to pay you. You need to know about both sides of the coin, so to speak. Your financial well-being or that of your organization can be adversely affected by your responsibility to others or by your failure to understand their responsibility to you. If you are the party harmed, you would be the **plaintiff** in litigation. The party being sued in litigation is the **defendant**. In some circumstances the parties will be both plaintiffs and defendants.

---

legal liability

The responsibility, based in law, to right some wrong done to another person or organization.

remedy

Compensation for a person who has been harmed in some way.

tortfeasor

A person who commits a wrong.

special damages (economic damages)

Compensation for harms that generally are easily quantifiable into dollar measures.

general damages

Compensation for harms that are not specifically quantifiable but that require compensation all the same.

noneconomic damages

Compensation for harms that are not specifically quantifiable but that require compensation all the same.

punitive damages

Awards intended to punish an offender for exceptionally undesirable behavior.

plaintiff

The party harmed in litigation.

defendant

The party being sued in litigation.

2.1 Basis of Liability

The liability exposure may arise out of either statutory or common law, as shown in Figure 12.2. **Statutory law** is the body of written law created by legislatures. **Common law**, on the other hand, is based on custom and court decisions. In evolving common law, the courts are guided by the doctrine of *stare decisis* (Latin for "to stand by the decisions"). Under the doctrine of **stare decisis**, once a court decision is made in a case with a given set of facts, the courts tend to adhere to the principle thus established and apply it to future cases involving similar facts. This practice provides enough continuity of decision making that many disputes can be settled out of court by referring to previous decisions. Some people believe that in recent years, as new forms of liability have emerged, continuity has not been as prevalent as in the past.

FIGURE 12.2 **Basis of Liability Risk**

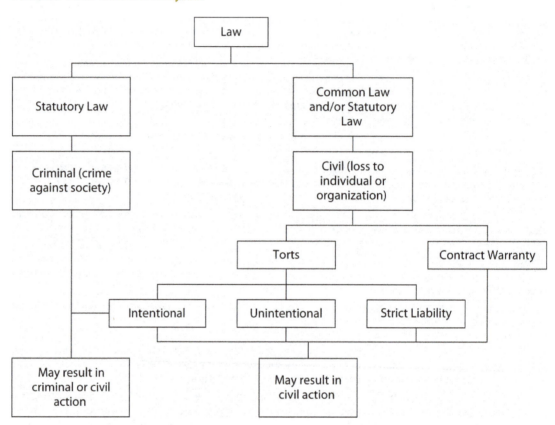

As illustrated in Figure 12.2, the field of law includes criminal law and civil law. **Criminal law** is concerned with acts that are contrary to public policy (crimes), such as murder or burglary. **Civil law**, in contrast, deals with acts that are not against society as a whole, but rather cause injury or loss to an individual or organization, such as carelessly running a car into the side of a building. A civil wrong may also be a crime. Murder, for instance, attacks both society and individuals. Civil law has two branches: one concerned with the law of contracts and the other with the law of torts (explained in the next paragraph). Civil liability may stem from either contracts or torts.

---

statutory law

The body of written law created by legislatures.

common law

Body of law based on custom and court decisions.

stare decisis

Principle that once a court decision is made in a case with a given set of facts, the courts tend to adhere to the principle thus established and apply it to future cases involving similar facts.

---

criminal law

Law concerned with acts that are contrary to public policy (crimes), such as murder or burglary.

civil law

Law that deals with acts that are not against society as a whole but rather cause injury or loss to an individual or organization.

Contractual liability occurs when the terms of a contract are not carried out as promised by either party to the contract. When you sign a rental agreement for tools, for example, the agreement may provide that the tools will be returned to the owner in good condition, ordinary wear and tear excepted. If they are stolen or damaged, you are liable for the loss. As another example, if you offer your car for sale and assure the buyer that it is in perfect condition, you have made a warranty. A **warranty** is a guarantee that property or service sold is of the condition represented by the seller. If the car is not in perfect condition, you may be liable for damages because of a breach of warranty. This is why some sellers offer goods for sale on an "as is" basis; they want to be sure there is no warranty.

A **tort** is "a private or civil wrong or injury, other than breach of contract, for which the court will provide a remedy in the form of an action for damages."[2] That is, all civil wrongs, except breach of contract, are torts. A tort may be intentional if it is committed for the purpose of injuring another person or the person's property, or it may be unintentional. Examples of intentional torts include libel, slander, assault, and battery, as you will see in the contracts provided as appendixes at the end of this book. While a risk manager may have occasion to be concerned about liability arising from intentional torts, the more frequent source of liability is the unintentional tort. By definition, unintentional torts involve negligence.

If someone suffers bodily injury or property damage as a result of your negligence, you may be liable for damages. Negligence refers to conduct or behavior. It may be a matter of doing something you should not do, or failing to do something you should do. **Negligence** can be defined as a failure to act reasonably, and that failure to act causes harm to others. It is determined by proving the existence of four elements (sometimes people use three, combining the last two into one). These four elements are the following:

- A duty to act (or not to act) in some way
- Breach of that duty
- Damage or injury to the one owed the duty
- A causal connection, called a **proximate cause**, between the breach of a duty and the injury

An example may be helpful. When a person operates an automobile, that person has a duty to obey traffic rules and to drive appropriately for the given conditions. A person who drives while drunk, passes in a no passing zone, or drives too fast on an icy road (even if within set speed limits) has breached the duty to drive safely. If that person completes the journey without an incident, no negligence exists because no harm occurred. If, however, the driver causes an accident in which property damage or bodily injury results, all elements of negligence exist, and legal liability for the resulting harm likely will be placed on the driver.

A difficult aspect of proving negligence is showing that a breach of duty has occurred. Proof requires showing that a reasonable and prudent person would have acted otherwise. Courts use a variety of methods to assess reasonableness. One is a cost-benefit approach, which holds behavior to be unreasonable if the discounted value of the harm is more than the cost to avoid the harm[3] —that is, if the present value of the possible loss is greater than the expense required to avoid the loss. In this way, courts use an efficiency argument to determine the appropriateness of behavior.

A second difficult aspect of proving negligence is to show a proximate cause between the breach of duty and resulting harm. Proximate cause has been referred to as an unbroken chain of events between the behavior and harm. The intent is to find the relevant cause through assessing liability. The law is written to encourage behavior with consideration of its consequences.

Liability will not be found in all the circumstances just described. The defendant has available a number of defenses, and the burden of proof may be modified under certain situations.

Defenses

A number of defenses against negligence exist, with varying degrees of acceptance. A list of defenses is shown in Table 12.1. One is assumption of risk. The doctrine of **assumption of risk** holds that if the plaintiff knew of the dangers involved in the act that resulted in harm but chose to act in that fashion nonetheless, the defendant will not be held liable. An example would be a bungee cord jumper who is injured from the jump. One could argue that a reasonable person would know that such a jump is very dangerous. If applicable, the assumption of risk defense bars the plaintiff from a successful negligence suit. The doctrine was particularly important in the nineteenth century for lawsuits involving workplace injuries, where employers would defend against liability by claiming that workers knew of job dangers. With workers' compensation statutes in place today, the use of assumption of risk in this way is of little importance, as you will see in Chapter 1. Many states have also abolished the assumption of risk doctrine in automobile liability cases, disallowing the defense that a passenger assumed the risk of loss if the driver was known to be dangerous or the car unsafe.

---

contractual liability

When the terms of a contract are not carried out as promised by either party to the contract.

warranty

A guarantee that property or service sold is of the condition represented by the seller.

tort

A private or civil wrong or injury, other than breach of contract, for which the court will provide a remedy in the form of an action for damages.

negligence

Failure to act reasonably, where such failure to act causes harm to others.

proximate cause

A causal connection.

assumption of risk

Doctrine that holds that if the plaintiff knew of the dangers involved in the act that resulted in harm, but chose to act in that fashion nonetheless, the defendant will not be held liable.

TABLE 12.1   Defenses against Liability

- Assumption of risk
- Contributory negligence
- Comparative negligence
- Last clear chance
- Sovereign, familial and charitable immunity

contributory negligence

Situation that disallows any recovery by the plaintiff if the plaintiff is shown to be negligent to any degree in not avoiding the relevant harm.

A second defense found in just a few states is the doctrine of **contributory negligence**, which disallows any recovery by the plaintiff if the plaintiff is shown to be negligent to any degree in not avoiding the relevant harm. Thus, the motorist who was only slightly at fault in causing an accident may recover nothing from the motorist who was primarily at fault. In practice, a judge or jury is unlikely to find a plaintiff slightly at fault where contributory negligence applies. Theoretically, however, the outcome is possible.

comparative negligence

Situation in which the court compares the relative negligence of the parties and apportions recovery on that basis.

The trend today is a shift away from the use of contributory negligence. Instead, most states follow the doctrine of comparative negligence. In **comparative negligence**, the court compares the relative negligence of the parties and apportions recovery on that basis. At least two applications of the comparative negligence rule may be administered by the courts. Assume that, in the automobile example, both motorists experienced damages of $100,000, and that one motorist was 1 percent at fault, the other 99 percent at fault. Under the **partial comparative negligence** rule, only the individual less than 50 percent at fault in causing harm receives compensation. The compensation equals the damages multiplied by the percentage not at fault, or $99,000 ($100,000 × .99) in our example. Under the **complete comparative negligence** rule, damages are shared by both parties in relation to their levels of responsibility for fault. The motorist who was 1 percent at fault still receives $99,000, but must pay the other motorist $1,000 ($100,000 × .01), resulting in a net compensation of $98,000. Because few instances exist when a party is completely free of negligence, and because society appears to prefer that injured parties be compensated, comparative negligence has won favor over contributory negligence. An important question, though, is how the relative degrees of fault are determined. Generally, a jury is asked to make such an estimate based on the testimony of various experts. Examples of the application of contributory and comparative negligence are shown in Table 12.2.

partial comparative negligence

Rule under which only the individual less than 50 percent at fault in causing harm receives compensation.

complete comparative negligence

Rule under which both parties share damage in relation to their levels of responsibility for fault.

TABLE 12.2   Contributory and Comparative Negligence

Assume that two drivers are involved in an automobile accident. Their respective losses and degrees of fault are as follows:		
	Losses ($)	Degree of Fault
Dan	16,000	.60
Kim	22,000	.40

Their compensation would be determined as follows:			
	Contributory	Partial Comparative*	Complete Comparative**
Dan	0	0	7,200
Kim	0	13,200	13,200
* Only when party is less at fault than the other is compensation available. Here Dan's fault exceeds Kim's.			
** Complete comparative negligence forces an offset of payment. Kim would receive $6,000 from Dan ($13,200 ± 7,200).			

last clear chance

Doctrine under which a plaintiff who assumed the risk or contributed to an accident through negligence is not barred from recovery if the defendant had the opportunity to avoid the accident but failed to do so.

Last clear chance is a further defense to liability. Under the **last clear chance** doctrine, a plaintiff who assumed the risk or contributed to an accident through negligence is not barred from recovery if the defendant had the opportunity to avoid the accident but failed to do so. For instance, the motorist who could have avoided hitting a jaywalker but did not had the last clear chance to prevent the accident. The driver in this circumstance could not limit liability by claiming negligence on the part of the plaintiff. Today, the doctrine has only minor application. It may be used, however, when the defendant employs the defense of contributory negligence against the plaintiff.

Last in this list of defenses is immunity. Where **immunity** applies, the defendant has a complete defense against liability merely because of status as a protected entity, professional, or other party. For example, governmental entities in the United States were long protected under the doctrine of sovereign immunity. Sovereign immunity held that governments could do no wrong and therefore could not be held liable. That doctrine has lost strength in most states, but it still exists to some degree in certain circumstances. Other immunities extend to charitable organizations and family members. Like sovereign immunity, these too have lost most of their shield against liability.

Modifications

Doctrines of defense are used to prevent a successful negligence (and sometimes strict liability) lawsuit. Other legal doctrines modify the law to assist the plaintiff in a lawsuit. Some of these are discussed here and are listed in Table 12.3.

TABLE 12.3   Modifications of Negligence

- Res Ipsa Loquitur
- Strict liability
- Vicarious liability
- Joint and several liability

Rules of negligence hold that an injured person has the burden of proof; that is, he or she must prove the defendant's negligence in order to receive compensation. Courts adhere to these rules unless reasons exist to modify them. In some situations, for example, the plaintiff cannot possibly prove negligence. The court may then apply the doctrine of **res ipsa loquitur** ("the thing speaks for itself"), which shifts the burden of proof to the defendant. The defendant must prove innocence. The doctrine may be used upon proof that the situation causing injury was in the defendant's exclusive control, and that the accident was one that ordinarily would not happen in the absence of negligence. Thus, the event "speaks for itself."

Illustrations of appropriate uses of res ipsa loquitur may be taken from medical or dental treatment. Consider the plaintiff who visited a dentist for the extraction of wisdom teeth and was given a general anesthetic for the operation. Any negligence that may have occurred during the extraction could not be proved by the plaintiff, who could not possibly have observed the negligent act. If, upon waking, the plaintiff has a broken jaw, res ipsa loquitur might be employed.

Doctrines with similar purposes to res ipsa loquitur may be available when a particular defendant cannot be identified. Someone may be able to prove by a preponderance of evidence, for example, that a certain drug caused an adverse reaction, but that person may be unable to prove which company manufactured the particular bottle consumed. Courts may shift the burden of proof to the defendants in such a circumstance.[4]

Liability may also be strict (or, less often, absolute) rather than based on negligence. That is, if you have property or engage in an activity that is considered ultra-dangerous to others, you may become liable on the basis of **strict liability** without regard to fault. In some states, for example, the law holds owners or operators of aircraft liable with respect to damage caused to persons or property on the ground, regardless of the reasonableness of the owner's or operator's actions. Similarly, if you dam a creek on your property to build a lake, you will be liable in most situations for injury or damage caused if the dam collapses and floods the area below. In product liability, discussed later in this chapter, a manufacturer may be liable for harm caused by use of its product, even if the manufacturer was reasonable in producing it. Thus, the manufacturer is strictly liable.

In some jurisdictions, the owner of a dangerous animal is liable by statute for any harm or damage caused by the animal. Such liability is a matter of law. If you own a pet lion, you may become liable for damages regardless of how careful you are. Similarly, the responsibility your employer has in the event you are injured or contract an occupational disease is based on the principle of liability without fault.[5] Both situations involve strict liability.

In addition, liability may be vicarious. That is, the **vicarious liability** of one person may be based on the tort of another, particularly in an agency relationship. An employer, for example, may be liable for damages caused by the negligence of an employee who is on duty. Such an agency relationship may result in vicarious liability for the principal (employer) if the agent (employee) commits a tort while acting as an agent. The principal need not be negligent to be liable under vicarious liability. The employee who negligently fails to warn the public of slippery floors while waxing them, for instance, may cause his or her employer to be liable to anyone injured by falling. Vicarious liability will not, however, shield the wrongdoer from liability. It merely adds a second potentially liable party. The employer and employee in this case may both be liable. Recall the case of vanishing premiums described in Chapter 9. Insurers were found to have liability because of the actions of their agents.

immunity
A complete defense against liability because of status as a protected entity, professional, or other party.

res ipsa loquitur ("The thing speaks for itself")
Doctrine that shifts the burden of proof to the defendant.

strict liability
Liability without regard to fault.

vicarious liability
Situation in which the liability of one person may be based on the tort of another.

joint and several liability

Situation that exists when a plaintiff is permitted to sue any of several defendants individually for the full harm incurred.

A controversial modification to negligence is the use of the joint and several liability doctrine. **Joint and several liability** exists when the plaintiff is permitted to sue any of several defendants individually for the full harm incurred. Alternatively, the plaintiff may sue all or a portion of the group together. Under this application, a defendant may be only slightly at fault for the occurrence of the harm, but totally responsible for paying for it. The classic example comes from a case in which a Disney World patron was injured on a bumper car ride.[6] The plaintiff was found 14 percent contributory at fault; another park patron was found 85 percent at fault; Disney was found 1 percent at fault. Because of the use of the joint and several liability doctrine, Disney was required to pay 86 percent of the damages (the percentage that the plaintiff was not at fault). Note that this case is an exceptional use of joint and several liability, not the common use of the doctrine.

KEY TAKEAWAYS

In this section you studied the general notion of liability and the related legal aspects thereof:

- Legal liability is the responsibility to remedy a wrong done to another
- Special damages, general damages, and punitive damages are the types of monetary remedies applied to liability
- Liability exposure arises out of statutory law or common law and cases are heard in criminal or civil court
- Negligent actions may result in liability for losses suffered as a result
- Liability through negligence is proven through existence of a duty to act (or not act) in some way, breach of the duty, injury to one owed the duty, and causal connection between breach of duty and injury
- Defenses against liability include assumption of risk, contributory negligence, comparative negligence, last clear chance, and immunity
- Modifications to help the plaintiff in a liability case include res ipsa loquitur, strict liability, vicarious liability, and joint and several liability

DISCUSSION QUESTIONS

1. Distinguish between criminal law and civil law.
2. Distinguish between strict liability and negligence-based liability.
3. What is the impact of res ipsa loquitur on general doctrines of liability? What seems to be the rationale for permitting use of this modification?
4. Considering the factors involved in establishing responsibility for damages based on negligence, what do you think is your best defense against such a suit?

3. MAJOR SOURCES OF LIABILITY

LEARNING OBJECTIVES

In this section we elaborate on the following:

- **The liabilities of property owners and property owners' duties to others**
- **Sources of liability for tenants**
- **Liability in activities and conduct, such as automobile liability, professional liability, product liability, and more**

Individuals, families, firms, and other organizations are exposed to countless sources of liability. These may be related to the property they own or control, or to their activities (including using an automobile, providing professional services, manufacturing products, or being involved in e-commerce).

3.1 Property

You have a duty to the public not only with regard to your activities but also in connection with real and personal property you own or for which you are responsible. The duty—the degree of care—varies with the circumstances. The owner or tenant of premises, for example, does not owe the same duty to each person who enters the property. The highest degree of care is owed to invitees, whereas the standard of care is less for licensees and lowest for trespassers.

A **trespasser** is a person who enters the premises of another without either express or implied permission from a person with the right to give such permission. Generally, the only duty owed to a trespasser is to refrain from taking steps to harm him or her. There are several exceptions to this, the most important concerning trespassing children. This exception is discussed in connection with the doctrine of attractive nuisance.

A **licensee** is a person who enters premises with permission but (1) not for the benefit of the person in possession, or (2) without a reasonable expectation that the premises have been made safe. If your automobile breaks down and you ask the owners of the nearest house to use their telephone, the permission you receive to enter the house makes you a licensee. Because a licensee is the party who receives the benefit of entering the property, he or she is entitled to a minimum degree of care by the owner or tenant. An owner or tenant must avoid harm to licensees and must warn licensees of any dangerous activity or condition of the property. They need not make the place safer, however, than it is normally.

An **invitee** is a person who enters the premises with permission and for the benefit of the person in possession. The invitee is entitled to a higher degree of care than a licensee. Thus, a customer in a store is an invitee, whether or not he or she makes a purchase. The property owner is expected to maintain safe premises for invitees and to warn of dangers that cannot be corrected.

For the most part, it is a person's reasonable expectation that determines his or her status. If you reasonably expect that the premises have been made safe for you, you are an invitee. For example, if I invite you to a party at my home, you are an invitee. If you should reasonably expect to accept the premises as is without special effort on the part of the possessor, then you are a licensee. The distinction between a licensee and an invitee is not always clear because it depends on reasonable expectations. Further, the courts have tended in recent years to place little weight on these distinctions. The question becomes, What is reasonable of the property owner? Generally, the owner has the responsibility to provide a reasonably safe environment.

In one case, a guest who fell on a slippery floor was awarded damages against the homeowner. In another case, a visitor fell down steps that were not properly lighted because a worker had failed to turn on a light. Although it was the worker who was negligent, the homeowner had to pay because the worker was his representative. Thus, the property owner's liability was vicarious; he was not negligent, but his employee was. In another case, a homeowner repaired a canopy and then hired a painter. When the painter crawled onto the canopy, the canopy collapsed. The homeowner was held liable for the injuries sustained.

Tenant's Liability to the Public

If you are a tenant, you cannot assume that the owner alone will be liable for defects in the premises. In many cases, the injured party will sue both the owner and the tenant. Furthermore, the owner may shift responsibility to the tenant by means of a hold-harmless clause in the lease. A **hold-harmless agreement** is a contractual provision that transfers financial responsibility for liability from one party to another. This is particularly important to understand because many tenants who sign a lease do not realize they are assuming such liability by contract. A typical clause is as follows:

> ... That the lessor shall not be liable for any damage, either to person or property, sustained by the lessee or by any other person, due to the building or any part thereof, or any appurtenances thereof, becoming out of repair, or due to the happening of any accident in or about said building, or due to any act or neglect of any tenant or occupant of said building, or of any other person.

The gist of this clause is to transfer the financial aspects of the landlord's potential liability to the tenant.

Tenant's Liability to Owner

If your negligence results in damage to premises you lease, you may be liable to the owner. The fact that the owner has insurance to cover the damage does not mean you will not be required to pay for the loss. After the insurer pays the owner, the insurer receives subrogation of the owner's right to recover damages, meaning that the insurer is given legal recourse against you for any liability you may have to the owner.

trespasser
A person who enters the premises of another without either express or implied permission from a person with the right to give such permission.

licensee
A person who enters premises with permission but (1) not for the benefit of the person in possession, or (2) without a reasonable expectation that the premises have been made safe.

invitee
A person who enters the premises with permission and for the benefit of the person in possession.

hold-harmless agreement
A contractual provision that transfers financial responsibility for liability from one party to another.

Animals

Ownership of pets and other animals may also result in liability. Anyone owning an animal generally is responsible for damage or injury that the animal may cause. In many jurisdictions, if the owner acted reasonably in controlling the animal, no liability will result. For example, in many places, a pet dog that has been friendly and tame need not be leashed. Once that dog has bitten someone, however, more control is required. If the dog bites a second person, the owner is likely to be held liable for the harm. In this case, the owner had forewarning.

Likewise, anyone owning dangerous animals such as lions or poisonous snakes is held to a higher standard of care. In this case, strict liability may be applied. Knowledge of the potential danger already exists; thus, the owner must be given strong incentives to prevent harm.

In a recent, highly visible California case, a thirty-three-year-old woman was mauled to death by a 123-pound English mastiff/Presa Canary Island crossbreed. The owners were found guilty of second degree murder by the jury, but the judge, in a surprise move, changed the ruling.[7] This case illuminates statistics from the Center for Disease Control and Prevention in Atlanta, which reports ten to twenty deaths annually from dog bites. Lawmakers in various states enacted laws concerning dogs. The insurance industry also reacted to curtail the losses caused by dogs. In the Insurance Services Office (ISO) homeowners policy (see Chapter 24 in this textbook) there are "special provisions that excludes liability coverage for any insured for bodily injury arising out of the actions of a dangerous or vicious, and out of the insureds failure to keep the dangerous dog leashed or tethered or confined in a locked pen with a top or locked fenced yard. The owners are required to control the dogs and assure the safety of passersby."[8]

Attractive Nuisance

attractive nuisance

Anything that is (1) artificial, (2) attractive to small children, and (3) potentially harmful.

In some cases, small children are attracted by dangerous objects or property. In such circumstances, the owner has a special duty toward the children, especially if they are too young to be responsible for their own safety. This is called the doctrine of attractive nuisance. An **attractive nuisance** is anything that is (1) artificial, (2) attractive to small children, and (3) potentially harmful. People who own power lawn mowers, for example, must be especially watchful for small children who may be injured through their own curiosity. If you leave your mower running while you go in the house to answer the telephone and there are small children in the neighborhood who may be attracted to the mower, you may be held financially responsible for any harm they experience. The most common attractive nuisance is the swimming pool. Although some courts have held that those who own swimming pools are not necessarily babysitters for the community, it appears that pool owners do have the duty of keeping children out. There have been many cases in which children entered a neighbor's pool without permission and drowned. The result is a suit for damages and in many cases a verdict in favor of the plaintiff.

Hazardous Waste

An increasingly important area of potential liability involving property derives from the possibility that land may be polluted, requiring cleanup and/or compensation to parties injured by the pollution. Because of significant legislation passed in the 1970s and 1980s, the cleanup issue may be of greater concern today than previously.

In 1980, the U.S. Congress passed the Comprehensive Environmental Response, Compensation, and Liability Act (known as either CERCLA or Superfund). This act places extensive responsibilities on organizations involved in the generation, transportation, storage, and disposal of hazardous waste. Responsibility generally involves cleaning or paying to clean polluted sites that are dangerous to the public. Estimates of total program costs run from $100 billion to $1 trillion, giving an indication of the potential severity of liability judgments. Any purchaser of realty (or creditor for that purchase) must be aware of these laws and take steps to minimize involvement in Superfund actions. A small amendment to the law was signed by President George W. Bush on January 11, 2002. Under the Small Business Liability Relief and Brownfields Revitalization Act, certain small contributors to Superfund sites were taken out of the liability system. The new law creates incentives for developers to purchase and restore abandoned urban sites known as brownfields.[9]

The area of pollution liability is very complex. Decisions have been made regularly in pollution cases. In a pollution case that went to the Ohio Supreme Court, Goodyear Tire & Rubber Co. sought to recover the cost of environmental cleanups at some of its sites from its insurers.[10] The insurers claimed that the coverage was excluded under the pollution exclusions provisions. The court sided with Goodyear, however, ordering that Goodyear be allowed to choose—from the pool of triggered policies—a single primary policy against which to make a claim.

3.2 Activities and Conduct

People also may be liable for damages caused by their own actions or those of someone else. In negligence suits, you will be judged on how a "reasonable" person in the same or similar circumstances with your training and ability would have acted. You will be judged according to different criteria for non-negligence suits.

Automobile Liability

Ownership and operation of an automobile is probably the most common source of liability any individual will encounter. Details about this liability will be given in Chapter 1.

As the driver of an automobile, you are responsible for its careful and safe operation. If you do not operate it in a reasonable and prudent fashion and someone is injured as a result of such lack of care, you may be held liable for damages. If, for example, you carelessly drive through a stop sign and run into another car, you may be liable for the damage done.

Through either direct or vicarious liability, the owner of an automobile may be responsible for the damage it causes when driven by another person. In some states, the **family purpose doctrine** makes the owner of the family car responsible for whatever damage it does, regardless of which member of the family may be operating the car at the time of the accident. The theory is that the vehicle is being used for a family purpose, and the owner, as head of the family, is therefore responsible.

Many parents assume responsibility for their children's automobile accidents without realizing they are doing so. In some states, minors between the ages of sixteen and eighteen are issued driver's licenses only if their applications are signed by a parent or guardian. What many parents do not realize is that by signing the application, they may assume responsibility for damage arising from the child's driving any automobile. Ordinarily, a child is responsible for his or her own torts, but the parent may become liable by contract.

Vicarious liability is possible in other settings as well. If you lend your car to a friend, Sid Smith, so he can go buy a case of liquor for a party you are having, he will be your agent during the trip and you may be held responsible if he is involved in an accident. Your liability in this case is vicarious; you are responsible for Smith's negligence. On the other hand, if Smith is not a competent driver, you may be held directly liable for putting a dangerous instrument in his hands. In such a case, it is your own negligence for which you are responsible.

A special problem for employers is the risk known as **nonownership liability**, in which an employer is held liable for an injury caused by an employee using his or her own property when acting on the employer's behalf. If an employee offers to drop the mail at the post office as he or she drives home from work, the firm may be held liable if the employee is involved in an accident in the process. This possibility is easily overlooked because the employer may not be aware that employees are using their cars for company business.

Professional Liability

Members of a profession claim to have met high standards of education and training, as well as of character and ethical conduct. They are expected to keep up with developments in their field and maintain the standards established for the profession. As a result, the duty a professional owes to the public is considerably greater than that owed by others. Along with this duty, of course, comes liability for damage caused by failure to fulfill it. People expect more from a professional, and when they do not get it, some sue for damages.

As noted above, improper accounting activities to fatten the bottom line by publicly traded firms is becoming an all-too-prevalent headline in the news. With fraud rampant, it appears that this chapter will not be closed for a long time. The lack of trust of investors, small or large, in the accounting profession and corporate leadership in the United States led to the creation of the Sarbanes-Oxley Act of 2002, as discussed in Chapter 8. The failures of the dot.com companies brought about an "onslaught of securities litigation, increasing claims for directors, officers and accountants' professional liability insurers."[11]

Errors and Omissions

Professionals' mistakes can result in professional liability claims. The insurance protection for this risk is **errors and omissions (E&O) liability coverage**. In light of the Enron/Arthur Anderson debacle and the WorldCom fraud, it is no wonder that the price for E&O has skyrocketed.[12]

family purpose doctrine

Doctrine that makes the owner of a family car responsible for whatever damage it does, regardless of which member of the family may be operating the car at the time of the accident.

nonownership liability

Situation in which an employer is held liable for an injury caused by an employee using his or her own property when acting on the employer's behalf.

errors and omissions (E&O) liability coverage

Insurance protection for mistakes made by professionals that result in professional liability claims.

Directors and Officers

The outcome of all these accounting irregularities and the pure fraud that was alleged also has caused the rates of directors and officers (D&O) liability coverage to soar.[13] Headlines such as "Insurers Likely to Balk at WorldCom D&O Coverage,"[14] "Lawsuits Send D&O Premiums Soaring,"[15] and "D&O Mkt. Could Face Catastrophic Year"[16] were just some examples of the reflection of the accounting, telecom, and Enron scandals.

class-action lawsuits

Lawsuits filed on behalf of many plaintiffs.

In 2005, with added allegations against AIG, there was increased regulatory scrutiny of corporate activities, and insurers became more selective in their underwriting. *BestWire* reported in 2005 that "typically, D&O insurers offer three types of coverage: The first is coverage provided directly to directors and officers who aren't indemnified by their companies; the second is coverage to companies for settlements, judgments and defense costs; and the third is coverage for securities-related claims made directly against companies."[17] AIG has been one of the largest providers of D&O coverage. In 2005, it tested its coverage on its own directors and officers.[18] As described in earlier chapters, AIG's stock price was hurt because of irregularities in the way the insurer accounted for the sale of finite risk and other loss mitigation products. These actions also led to **class-action lawsuits** (lawsuits filed on behalf of many plaintiffs) from the employees who invested in their company through their 401(k) accounts (discussed in Chapter 2).[19]

Medical Malpractice

The risks to which physicians and surgeons are exposed illustrate the position of a professional. In taking cases, doctors represent that they possess—and the law imposes upon them the duty of possessing—the degree of learning and skill ordinarily possessed by others in their profession. If medical doctors fail to use reasonable care and diligence, and they fail to use their best judgment in exercising their skill and applying their knowledge, they are guilty of **malpractice**.

malpractice

Failure by a professional to use reasonable care and diligence, and/or failure to use one's best judgment in exercising skill and applying knowledge.

Two cases demonstrate the risk to which medical doctors are exposed. A plastic surgeon who made his patient look worse instead of better had to pay $115,000 for the damage. A court awarded $4.5 million to a girl suffering acute kidney failure as a result of malpractice.

Unlike the days when a family had one doctor who took care of almost all health problems, the modern health care system is specialized; many patients are dealing primarily with doctors they do not know. Faith in, and friendship with, the family doctor has been displaced by impersonal, brief contact with a specialist who may be more efficient than friendly. Furthermore, publicity about fraud by some doctors under the Medicare and Medicaid programs and about the amount of unneeded medical procedures (often performed as a defense against lawsuits) has reduced the prestige of the medical profession. As a result, there has been a decrease in confidence and an increase in willingness to sue.

Some of the increase in lawsuits, however, has been caused by a combination of unrealistic expectations based on news about modern medical miracles and the belief by some that people are entitled to perfect care. When they do not get it, they feel entitled to compensation.

One result of the surge in medical malpractice suits has been a scarcity of professional liability insurance in the private market and a dramatic increase in the cost of protection for both doctors and hospitals. These costs, of course, are passed along by most doctors to the consumer. They represent one factor contributing to rising health care costs.

Another result is the rise of defensive medicine. Doctors and hospitals are guided not only by what is good for the patient but also by their own interests in preventing liability losses. The latter, of course, leads to practices that may not be medically necessary and that increase the size of the patient's bill. The total effect of defensive medicine on the cost of health care is difficult to determine, but it is likely significant.

Medical malpractice lawsuits continued to soar into the new millennium and the availability of coverage became scarce in many states. Unable to find liability coverage, many doctors in risky specialties such as obstetrics and neurosurgery simply left the business. Medical liability rates nearly doubled in some areas, and insurers left many states. In 2005, rates continued to climb but at a slower rate.[20] Some published studies in 2004 and 2005 concluded that lawsuits against doctors were not necessarily the cause of med-mal rate increases.[21] For more details, see the box, "The Medical Malpractice Crisis" later in this chapter.

Operations

operations liability

Liability arising from the ownership, maintenance, and use of premises and conduct of activity.

Many firms are exposed to liability from their operations. Contractors are particularly susceptible to **operations liability**, or liability arising from the ownership, maintenance, and use of premises and conduct of activity. Because they perform most of their work away from their premises, contractors' greatest liability exposure is on the job rather than arising from their own premises. Bystanders may be injured by equipment, excavations may damage the foundation of adjacent buildings, blasting operations may damage nearby property or injure someone. If harm is caused while performing the job, as opposed to a negligently completed job, the liability may be an operations one.

E-Commerce Liability

As was discussed in detail in Chapter 11, e-commerce poses not only property and interruption of business risks but also third-party liability arising from the following:[22]

- Invasion of privacy and identity theft
- Employee-related risks and harassment
- Intellectual property risks such as copyright, trademark infringement, defamation, encryption, and discovery
- Publishing and advertising risks
- Service denial risks (contractual risks)
- Professional risks (errors and omissions risks)

Online privacy issues continue to top headlines. According to the respondents of a survey conducted by the Yankee Group, a consulting firm focusing on global e-commerce and wireless markets, 83 percent of online consumers are somewhat or very concerned about their privacy on the Internet.[23] According to a Fox News/Opinion Dynamics Poll, 69 percent of those polled said they're "very concerned" about their ability to keep personal information, such as medical and financial records, confidential. While nearly two-thirds of Americans said they have access to the Internet at work, home, or school, only 7 percent believed their most personal information is secure from the prying eyes of hackers or bosses.[24] The reputation of the business is at stake if customers' information does not remain private and protected. Invasion of privacy is an issue of major public concern, as noted in the box "Insurance and Your Privacy—Who Knows?" in Chapter 8. Businesses often collect data about their customers or Web site visitors by having them fill out an online form or by making the user register for permission to use the site. This information, if not protected, can create liability when the privacy of the customer is breached. When so much information is released on the Internet, there are many opportunities for committing public defamation and opening the door to lawsuits.

Another e-commerce liability risk is raised with encryption, that is, the coding of Internet messages so information cannot be read by an interceptor. Because the terrorists responsible for the September 11 attacks in New York City and Washington, D.C., presumably communicated via encrypted Internet messages, some lawmakers renewed calls for restricting the use of encryption and for giving law enforcement unrestricted access to codes, or keys, for unlocking the encrypted text.

Employee privacy and the monitoring of employees' e-mail by employers are also key privacy issues. The courts appear to be on the employer's side by agreeing that employers have the right to monitor employee e-mails. In the case of *United States of America v. Eric Neil Angevine*, the Tenth Circuit Court of Appeals held that, when the computer is provided to an employee (in this case, a university professor) by the employer, the employee should not have privacy expectations.[25] Liability falls on the employer if an employee uses e-mail while at work to commit a federal crime or send a threat. The entire computer system can be subject to seizure (Federal Computer Seizure guidelines). A firm is liable for any e-mails sent by employees; the e-mails are written proof of what the employee promised. The company can also be held liable for any sexually harassing e-mails sent by employees.

Because a business derives much of its value from the uniqueness of its intellectual property, including trade secrets, copyrights, and trademarks, infringement of these properties opens the firm to liability lawsuits. There is increasing liability risk associated with statements posted on the Internet. Traditional publishing methods require many different people to proofread the document, checking for potentially harmful statements. None of this is required to place information online. This point is stressed by many professors when students are asked to write reports or do research. The validity of the material on the Internet is as good as the trust you have in the reputation of the source of the material. In the commercial world, advertising on the Internet brought both state and federal agencies into the act of protecting consumers from false Web-based advertisements. In the early 2000s, the Securities and Exchange Commission (SEC) sued to enjoin an illegal offer and sale of securities over America Online and the Internet without a prospectus, and the Department of Transportation fined Virgin Atlantic Airways for failing to disclose the full price of flights on its home page. The Food and Drug Administration (FDA) is also looking into online advertisements for pharmaceuticals. The National Association of Attorneys General (NAAG) has formed a thirty-eight-state task force to develop enforcement guidelines for combating illegal activity online. The Federal Trade Commission (FTC) has been involved in cleaning the Internet of false advertising by finding the perpetrators and fining them with large penalties. An example is the advertisers of Super Nutrient Program and Fat Burner Pills, who had to pay $195,000 in penalties.[26]

Denial of service liability is caused when a third party cannot access a promised Web site. This may be a major contractual liability.[27] For example, if a hacker penetrated a company's Web site and caused a shutdown, customers and other businesses may file lawsuits contending that their inability to access the site caused them to suffer losses. These losses are different from the first-party losses of the attacked company discussed in Chapter 11. The attacked company is covered under first-party insurance of property and business interruption income or special e-commerce endorsement. Finally, the professional liability of errors and omissions may cause a third party to have a loss of income. This may occur when an Internet provider fails or security software fails to perform.

The possible liabilities outlined above are not a complete list. Many of the causes of losses described in Chapter 11 may be causes for liabilities as well. The important point is that e-commerce exposes businesses to liabilities not anticipated prior to the electronic age. These liabilities may not be covered in the traditional commercial liability policy.

Product Manufacture

Product liability is one of the most widely debated sources of risk for a firm. The basis for **product liability** may be negligence, warranty, or strict liability in tort relating to defects causing injury in products sold to the public.

Product liability is a somewhat unusual aspect of common law because its development has occurred primarily within the twentieth century. One explanation for this late development is the doctrine of privity. The privity doctrine required a direct contractual relationship between a plaintiff and a defendant in a products suit. Thus, a consumer injured by a product had a cause of action only against the party from whom the product was purchased. The seller, however, likely had no control over the manufacture and design of the product, thus limiting potential liability. Consumers' only recourse was to claim a breach of warranty by the seller; this cause of action is still available.[28]

Once the privity doctrine was removed, negligence actions against manufacturers surfaced. Demonstrating a manufacturer's negligence is difficult, however, because the manufacturer controls the production process. You may recall that the doctrine of res ipsa loquitur becomes relevant in such a circumstance, placing the burden of proof on the manufacturer.

By 1963, members of the judiciary for the United States seemed to have concluded that consumers deserved protection beyond res ipsa loquitur. Thus developed strict liability in products, as stated by Justice Traynor:

> *A manufacturer is strictly liable in tort when an article he places on the market, knowing that it is to be used without inspection for defects, proves to have a defect that causes injury to a human being.[29]*

These three doctrines of breach of warranty, negligence, and strict liability are available today as causes of action by a consumer in a product liability cases. Each is briefly described below.

Breach of Warranty

Many products are warranted suitable for a particular use, either expressly or by implication. The statement on a container of first-aid spray, "This product is safe when used as directed…," is an express warranty. If you use a product as directed and suffer injury as a result, **breach of warranty** has occurred and the manufacturer may be held liable for damages. On the other hand, if you use the product other than as directed and injury results, the warranty has not been breached. Directions on a container may create an implied warranty. A statement such as "Apply sparingly to entire facial surface" implies that the product is not harmful for such use, thus creating an implied warranty. If the product is harmful even when the directions are followed, the warranty has been breached.

Negligence

When a firm manufactures a product, sells a commodity, or acts in one of the other points in the marketing chain, it has a duty to act reasonably in protecting users of the commodity from harm. Failure to fulfill this duty constitutes negligence and may provide the basis for liability if harm results. According to Noel and Phillips, "Negligence in products cases is most likely to involve a failure to warn or to warn adequately of foreseeable dangers, a failure to inspect fully or test, a failure in either design or production to comply with standards imposed by law or to live up to the customary standards of the industry." For example, failure to warn that the paint you sell may burn the skin unless removed immediately may result in injury to the buyer and a liability for the seller. The product liability exposure can extend over the life of a product, which may be a very long time in the case of durable goods. A number of proposals have been made both nationally and at the state level to limit the time period during which such responsibility exists.

product liability

Situation in which a manufacturer may be liable for harm caused by use of its product, even if the manufacturer was reasonable in producing it.

breach of warranty

Situation arising when an individual uses a product as directed and suffers injury as a result.

Strict Liability

A firm may be held liable for damage caused by a product even though neither negligence nor breach of warranty is established. This is called strict liability.

The doctrine of strict liability has been applied primarily based on the description provided in 1965 by the American Law Institute in section 402 of the Second Restatement of Torts. It reads as follows:

1. One who sells any product in a defective condition unreasonably dangerous to the user or consumer or to his property is subject to liability for physical harm thereby caused to the ultimate user or consumer, or to his property, if

    a. the seller is engaged in the business of selling such a product, and

    b. it is expected to and does reach the user or consumer without substantial change in the condition in which it is sold.

2. The rule stated in Subsection (1) applies although

    a. the seller has exercised all possible care in the preparation and sale of his product, and

    b. the user or consumer has not bought the product from or entered into any contractual relation with the seller.

The important aspects of this description are that the product was sold in a defective condition, which makes it unreasonably dangerous, thereby causing physical harm to the ultimate user. Thus, the manufacturer and/or seller of the product may be held liable even if "all possible care in the preparation and sale" of the product was undertaken, and even if the injured party was not the buyer. Because of the extent of this liability, it is not surprising that manufacturers hope to eliminate or at least limit the use of strict liability.

As already discussed, product liability suits were rare prior to the 1960s, and awards were small by today's standards. Two legal changes altered the scope of the product liability system. First came the abolition of the privity rule. With the expansion of trade to include wholesalers and retailers, especially with respect to automobiles, the concept of privity seemed inappropriate. Then, in 1963, strict liability was brought to the arena of products cases. With strict liability, an injured party could receive damages by showing that the product was inherently dangerous and also defective. The result was a subtle shift from focus on the manufacturer's behavior to the product's characteristics.[30]

Since 1963, the United States has seen a rapid increase in product liability litigation. One of the most difficult and common forms of litigation today involves strict liability due to defective warnings. Another source of consternation is the mass tort area (also referred to as class-action lawsuits), in which thousands of people are injured by the same product or set of circumstances, such as the Dalkon Shield and asbestos products. Some users of the Dalkon Shield, an intrauterine contraceptive device (IUD), experienced severe medical problems allegedly due to the defective nature of the product. Another cause for mass tort is asbestos. Asbestos is an insulation material made of tiny fibers that, when inhaled, may cause respiratory ailments. Thousands of workers using asbestos in the 1930s and 1940s have been diagnosed with various forms of cancer. Their injuries led to class-action lawsuits. In 2005, Congress was in the process of passing legislation to create a special fund for the victims of asbestos exposure. The proposal was highly debated and the constitutionality of the potential new law questioned. The proposed bill was to provide a no fault $140 billion asbestos compensation trust fund in place of the existing litigation-based system of compensating victims of asbestos-related diseases.[31]

The increase in product liability litigation and awards is believed to have been a major cause of the liability insurance crisis of the mid-1980s. The cost of insurance increased so much that some firms have gone out of business, while others have discontinued production of the items that seem to be causing the trouble. In some circumstances, the discontinuance of a product line may not be very newsworthy. In others, however, the results could be quite detrimental. The threat of lawsuits, for instance, appears to have been the impetus for several vaccine manufacturers to leave the business. Merck & Co. is now the sole U.S. producer of the combined measles, mumps, and rubella (MMR) vaccine. In other circumstances, companies have not only terminated the manufacture of products but have filed for bankruptcy. Johns Manville Corporation, an asbestos manufacturer, and A. H. Robbins, a producer of the Dalkon Shield IUD, are two examples of companies who filed for Chapter 11 bankruptcy to get out from under liability suits.

The largest liability cases are the tobacco liability cases that started in the 1990s and are continuing with large awards given to the plaintiffs, who are victims of cancer and other illnesses caused by smoking cigarettes. A case that stands out is the one against R. J. Reynolds Tobacco Holdings, Inc., where the Kansas judge, not the jury, levied a $15 million punitive damages awards to the amputee David Burton. The punitive damage awards were fifteen times larger than the $196,416 compensatory award.[32] Note also the major case against Philip Morris discussed in the box "Are Punitive Damages out of Control?" in Chapter 10.

The tobacco cases did not end in courts. The states brought lawsuits themselves. The states forced the industry to the negotiating table, and the tobacco industry settled for $368 billion in 1997, four years after the battle began. Some of the stories of the hurt, loss, and misery caused by cigarette smoking and the lawsuits are described in *The People vs. Big Tobacco* by the Bloomberg News team of Carrick Mollenkamp, Adam Levy, Joseph Menn, and Jeffrey Rothfeder (Princeton, NJ: Bloomberg Press, 1998) and *Cornered: Big Tobacco at the Bar of Justice*, by Peter Pringle (New York: Henry Holt Co., 1998).

As the courts provide large awards to plaintiffs and the tobacco companies find ways to curtail the damage,[33] the next wave of lawsuits may be expected to target the food industry because of obesity. This topic is discussed in the box "Obesity and Insurance—Litigation or Self-Discipline?" in this chapter.

Completed Operations

Closely related to product liability is liability stemming from activities of the firm in installing equipment or doing other jobs for hire off its own premises, called **completed operations liability**. Defective workmanship may cause serious injury or property damage, for which the firm may be held liable.

Contingent Liability

Generally, a firm that hires an independent contractor is not liable for damage or injury caused by the contractor. There are a number of exceptions to this general rule, however, resulting in contingent liability. **Contingent liability** occurs in situations where the firm is liable for an independent contractor's negligence because the firm did not use reasonable care in selecting someone competent. If the activity to be performed by an independent contractor is inherently dangerous, the firm is strictly liable for damages and cannot shift its liability to the contractor. The fact that the contractor agrees to hold the firm harmless will not relieve it from liability. A firm that hires an independent contractor to do a job and then interferes in details of the work may also find itself liable for the contractor's negligence.

Liquor Liability

Many states have liquor laws—or **dramshop laws**—which impose special liability on anyone engaged in any way in the liquor business. Some apply not only to those who sell liquor but also to the owner of the premises on which it is sold. The laws are concerned with injury, loss of support, and damage to property suffered by third parties who have no direct connection with the store or tavern. For example, if liquor is served to an intoxicated person or a minor and the person served causes injury or damage to a third party, the person or firm serving the liquor may be held liable. In some cases, liability has been extended to employers providing alcohol at employee parties.

completed operations liability

Liability stemming from activities of the firm in installing equipment or doing other jobs for hire off its own premises.

contingent liability

Situation in which a firm is liable for an independent contractor's negligence because the firm did not use reasonable care in selecting someone competent.

dramshop laws

Laws that impose special liability on anyone engaged in any way in the liquor business.

Obesity and Insurance—Litigation or Self-Discipline?

Business Insurance reported in January 2005 that obesity claims against fast-food giant McDonald's were revived. The McDonald's case was the most celebrated 2002 class-action lawsuit. The plaintiffs were a group of teenagers who sued the chain for causing their obesity. Following a dismissal, a federal appeals court reinstated the claims that McDonald's used deceptive advertising to mask the health risks associated with its foods. While a U.S. district court judge threw out the complaint in 2003, parts of the dismissed suits were upheld. The obesity cases have not stopped with this fast-food restaurant. In a 2003 California lawsuit against Kraft Foods, the manufacturer of Oreo cookies was asked by the plaintiff to cease its target marketing until the cookies no longer contained trans fat. This lawsuit was later withdrawn, but it did affect the actions of Kraft. In another high-profile lawsuit, McDonald's french fries were the focus of the suit. The plaintiffs accused the fast-food chain of misleading the public by using beef fat while promoting them as vegetarian fries. The case was eventually settled in 2002 for $12.5 million and McDonald's posted an apology.

These are examples of the problems with the food-obesity-liability triangle. The Centers for Disease Control (CDC) estimates that 60 percent of Americans are overweight, defined as a body mass index score (a ratio of weight to height) of 25 or above. Forty million people are considered obese, with a BMI of 30 or more.*

Flab has become a national crisis. In December 2001, then-surgeon general David Satcher predicted that obesity would soon surpass smoking as the leading cause of preventable deaths in the United States. Overweight people are ten times more likely to develop diabetes and six times more likely to have heart disease. Excess weight is linked to gallbladder disease, gout, respiratory problems, and certain types of cancer. Estimates of the annual health care costs of obesity run as high as $100 billion. With major pressure on health care systems and a growing number of our citizens' quality of life deteriorating, is obesity the next crisis, destined to eclipse tobacco in magnitude for liability?

Question for Discussion

Is obesity a disease that needs medical intervention, in your opinion, or a lifestyle issue that calls for self-discipline? Is it a case of self-discipline or a topic for litigation?

* Check your BMI with the CDC's Web calculator: http://www.cdc.gov/nccdphp/dnpa/bmi/calc-bmi.htm.

Sources: Karen Shideler, "Rising Cost of Obesity in America Hurts Us All," The Wichita Eagle, October 27, 2002; "Weight Management and Health Insurance," American Obesity Association, http://www.obesity.org; "Overweight and Obesity," Centers for Disease Control, http://www.cdc.gov/ nccdphp/dnpa/obesity/index.htm; Libby Copeland, "Snack Attack: after Taking On Big Tobacco, Social Reformer Jabs at a New Target—Big Fat," Washington Post, November 3, 2002, F01; Nanci Hellmich, "Weighing the Cost of Obesity," USA Today, January 20, 2002; reports by the Insurance Information Institute in 2005 such as "Obesity, Liability & Insurance" and various articles from the media in 2005.

KEY TAKEAWAYS

In this section you studied the various ways that individuals, families, firms, and other entities are exposed to liability in property and in activities and conduct:

- Property owners' duties vary with respect to invitees, licensees, and trespassers; children must be specially considered when property is an attractive nuisance.
- Tenants face liability to the public and to property owners.
- Property considered hazardous waste has the potential to be an environmental liability.
- The most common source of liability in activities/conduct is the activity of operating an automobile, which also invites vicarious and nonownership liabilities.
- Doctors, lawyers, accountants, and other professionals are exposed to professional liability in errors in omissions, activities of directors and officers, and medical malpractice.
- Contractors are susceptible to operations liability.
- E-commerce entails liability risks such as invasion of privacy, intellectual property risks, and contractual service denials.
- The basis for product liability may be negligence, warranty, or strict liability.
- Completed operations, contingent liability, and liquor liability are other sources of liability in activities and conduct.

DISCUSSION QUESTIONS

1. Explain why a trampoline in a backyard is considered an attractive nuisance.
2. Ceci Willis sells books door to door. What responsibilities do you owe her when she visits your home? How would the circumstances change if you were the book seller and Ceci came to your home as a potential buyer? What if you owned several pet panthers?
3. Describe when strict liability applies in products. What is the practical effect of this doctrine?
4. Monique rents a one-bedroom apartment. Because she does not own the property, does this mean she is not liable for any injuries that might occur in her home? Give an example of a situation where she would be responsible.
5. When Vivienne and Paul Jensen's daughter Heather turned sixteen, they signed a form allowing her to get a driver's license. Two weeks after she received her license, Heather crashed the family car into a tree. He friend Rebecca, who was in the passenger seat, was severely injured. Explain why Heather's parents are responsible in this case. What are the consequences to them of this liability?

4. POSSIBLE SOLUTIONS

LEARNING OBJECTIVES

In this section we elaborate on the following:

- **Methods within the legal system of alleviating liability by limiting use and improvements of defenses or reducing incentives to sue**
- **Risk management for e-commerce liabilities**

A number of suggestions have been made to alleviate the problems of product liability and malpractice (professional) liability. Some would limit the right to use or improve the defendant's defenses; others would reduce the incentive to sue or provide an alternative to legal action.

In both areas, proposals would limit the compensation available to plaintiffs' attorneys. Most plaintiffs compensate their attorneys with a percentage (typically one third) of their award, called a **contingency fee**. The advantage of a contingency fee system is that low-income plaintiffs are not barred from litigation because of inability to pay legal fees. A disadvantage is that lawyers have incentives to seek very large awards, even in situations that may appear only marginally appropriate for litigation. Reduced contingency fee percentages and/or caps on lawyer compensation have been recommended as partial solutions to increases in the size of liability awards and the frequency of litigation itself. Similarly, shorter **statutes of limitation**, which determine the time frame within which a claim must be filed, have also been proposed as a means to reduce the number of liability suits.

Placing caps on the amount of damages available and eliminating the collateral source rule are recommendations that focus on the size of liability payments. Caps on damages typically limit recovery either for general damages or for punitive damages. Often, when actually awarded, general and punitive damages far exceed the special damages; thus, they dramatically increase the size of the award and can add significant uncertainty to the system.

The **collateral source rule** is a legal doctrine that prevents including information about a plaintiff's financial status and/or compensation of losses from other sources in the litigation. In a setting in which a plaintiff has available payments from workers' compensation or health insurance, for example, the jury is not made aware of these other payments when determining an appropriate liability award. Thus, the plaintiff may receive double recovery.

Another prominent recommendation is to abolish or limit the use of joint and several liability. As previously described, joint and several liability has the potential to hold a slightly-at-fault party primarily responsible for a given loss. The extent of the use of the doctrine, however, is disputed.

contingency fee

A percentage (typically one third) of the award to a plaintiff, collected by the attorney only if the plaintiff prevails.

statutes of limitation

Laws that determine the time frame within which a claim must be filed.

collateral source rule

A legal doctrine that prevents including information about a plaintiff's financial status and/or compensation of losses from other sources in the litigation.

4.1 Risk Management of E-Commerce Liabilities

The first step in the risk management process of e-commerce liability in particular is the development of privacy procedures. This is done to protect consumers and avoid personal injury of defamation of another person or entity.

The transfer of e-commerce liability risk is not commonly covered under the usual general liability policy, which is discussed in Chapter 1. The commercial general liability policy does not cover all of the liabilities that result from loss of electronic information. Therefore, in the risk management process, the risk manager should look into separate e-commerce policies. An e-commerce liability policy generally will include, in Section I, the definitions of claims, defense costs, the named insured, an Internet site that is noted on the declaration page, policy period, and so forth. Section II usually includes the exclusions. As would be expected, bodily injury and property damage are excluded because they are usually covered under the general liability policy. Additional exclusions are fraud, antitrust activities, breach of contract, employment practices, product liability, patent infringement, lotteries, loyalties, securities, governmental actions, prior claims, and prior pending litigation. Section III emphasizes that the coverage is the liability of only Internet-related activities. The limit of liability is set in the declaration page. The last sections of the policy include additional details relating to reporting of notice, defense and settlement, other insurance, and more.[34]

E-commerce liability policies are not standardized. Some provide more coverage while others are more limited. The interested student can find many examples on the Internet and in *E-Commerce Insurance and Risk Management* by George Sutcliffe (Boston: Standard Publishing Corp., 2001).

The Medical Malpractice Crisis

The Insurance Information Institute stated in its May 2005 "Medical Malpractice" report the following:

- The cost of medical malpractice insurance is rising. This hard market began in 2000 following a long period of flat prices. Fewer insurers in the field is one of the causes of rate increases.
- Rate increases led the medical community to lobby for limits on noneconomic damages and other reforms.

How did the situation get so bad? Doctors blame insurance companies for skyrocketing premiums. Insurers blame personal-injury attorneys who work on contingency. The American Medical Association blames jurors who award exorbitant punitive damages. In fact, much of the problem can be traced to ordinary business cycles and a bit of coincidence. Some studies in no way attribute lawsuits to the premium increases. The 1970s saw sweeping changes in both medicine and jurisprudence; broader liability rulings and rapid advances in medical technologies coparented a rash of record-breaking lawsuits. Insurers raised premiums, and when lawsuits declined in the 1980s, malpractice insurance again became a profit center for insurers—so much so that by the mid-1990s, the field became very competitive. The competition among insurers led to price wars, but lowering premiums depleted the insurers' reserves just as malpractice lawsuits began escalating again.

Horror stories abound of frivolous lawsuits on the plaintiff's side, appalling negligence on the defendant's, and exorbitant jury awards in the middle. As in the 1970s, many think the answer lies in legislative reform. Twenty states now have medical malpractice caps on jury awards. West Virginia is proposing a state-managed liability plan. Pennsylvania has banned "forum shopping," in which lawyers file their suits in jurisdictions where juries tend to award huge damages; lawsuits now must be tried in the county where the malpractice took place. Mississippi, too, has recently instituted sweeping medical malpractice reform law, including a provision against forum shopping. The Bush administration urged Congress to pass a bill that would limit noneconomic damage awards to $250,000, limit punitive damage awards, place limits on the time allowed for injured patients to file a lawsuit, and establish a fee schedule for lawyers' contingency fees. A provision would also provide liability protection for pharmaceutical firms. In May 2005, the American Medical Association (AMA) reported a decline in medical malpractice claims and improved physician recruitment and retention resulting from some states' tort reforms.

Sources: The Insurance Information Institute is a good source for special timely reports. In addition, see Joseph B. Treaster, "Rise in Insurance Forces Hospitals to Shutter Wards," New York Times, August 25, 2002; Steven Brostoff, "Medical Malpractice Reform Bill Draws Praise From Insurers," National Underwriter, Property & Casualty/Risk & Benefits Management Edition, October 7, 2002; Rachel Zimmerman and Christopher Oster, "Insurers' Price Wars Contributed to Doctors Facing Soaring Costs," Wall Street Journal, June 24, 2002; Lori Chordas, "A Downward Spiral: Medical Malpractice Insurance Is Losing Its Place as a Top Performing Line of Business in the Property/Casualty Industry," Best's Review, August 2001; "Report: Suits Don't Cause Higher Med Mal Premiums" National Underwriter Online News Service, March 11, 2005, accessed March 16, 2009, http://www.propertyandcasualtyinsurancenews.com/cms/NUPC/Breaking%20News/2005/03/11-Report%20Suits%20 Dont%20Cause%20Higher%20Med%20Mal%20Premiums? searchfor=suits%20cause%20higher%20premiums; Arthur D. Postal and Matt Brady, "President To Unveil Tort Reform Proposals," National Underwriter Online News Service, January 4, 2005, accessed March 16, 2009, http://www.propertyandcasualtyinsurancenews.com/cms/NUPC/Breaking%20News/2005/01/05-President%20To%20 Unveil%20Tort%20Reform%20Proposals?searchfor=tort%20reform%20proposals.

KEY TAKEAWAYS

In this section you studied suggestions for reducing liability losses from legal and risk management perspectives:

- Reduction in attorneys' contingency fees would reduce the financial incentive of trying liability suits
- Shorter statutes of limitation on claims would reduce the overall number of liability cases
- Placing caps on the amount of damages and eliminating the collateral source rule are efforts designed to limit award amounts
- In e-commerce liability, privacy procedures should first be developed
- Risk can be transferred through special e-commerce liability policies

DISCUSSION QUESTIONS

1. How might elimination of the collateral source rule and a shortened statute of limitations affect the availability and affordability of liability insurance?
2. How does the contingency fee system work?
3. How might the contingency fee system affect the frequency and severity of liability exposures?

5. REVIEW AND PRACTICE

1. Betsy Boomer does not own a car and she must rely on friends for transportation. Last month, Betsy asked Freda Farnsworth to drive her to the store. Freda is known to be a reckless driver, but Betsy is not in a position to be choosy. On the way to the store, Freda is distracted by Betsy and hits a telephone pole. The car, of course, is damaged, and Betsy is injured. Describe Freda's possible liability and the various defenses to or modifications of liability that her lawyer may try to employ in her defense.

2. Your neighbor's English bulldog, Cedric, is very friendly, but you wouldn't know it by looking at him. Last Monday, the substitute mail carrier met Cedric as he was approaching the mailbox. Because the mail carrier is afraid of even small dogs, he collapsed from fright at the sight of Cedric approaching, fell to the ground, and broke his left arm. A motorist, who observed this situation while driving by, rammed the neighbor's parked car. The parked car then proceeded down the street through two fences, finally stopping in Mrs. Smith's living room.

    a. Is there a case for litigation involving your neighbor?

    b. Where does the motorist's liability fit into this picture?

3. Your neighbor's small children run wild all day, every day, totally ignored by their parents. You have forcibly ejected them from your swimming pool several times but they return the next day. Your complaints to their parents have had no effect. Do you think it is fair to hold you responsible for the safety of these children simply because your swimming pool is an attractive nuisance? Are their parents being negligent? Can you use their possible negligence in your defense in the event one of the children drowns in your pool and they sue you for damages?

4. In an interesting case in Arizona, *Vanguard Insurance Company v. Cantrell v. Allstate Insurance Company*, 1973 C.C.H. (automobile) 7684, an insurer was held liable for personal injuries inflicted on a storeowner when its insured robbed the store and fired a warning shot to scare the owner. The robber's aim was bad, and he hit the owner. Because he had not intended to harm the owner, the insured convinced the court that the exclusion under a homeowners policy of intentional injury should not apply.

    a. What reasoning might the court have applied to reach this decision?

    b. Do you agree with this decision? Why or why not?

5. A physician or surgeon may become liable for damages on the basis of contract or negligence. Why is the latter more common than the former? What does your answer to this question tell you about managing your liability risks?

6. Most states have a vicarious liability law regarding the use of an automobile. For instance, California and New York hold the owner liable for injuries caused by the driver's negligence, whereas Pennsylvania and Utah make the person furnishing an automobile to a minor liable for that minor's negligence. Ohio, Indiana, Texas, Hawaii, and Rhode Island make the parent, guardian, or signer of the minor's application for a license liable for the minor's negligence.

    a. Why do states differ in their approach to this situation?

    b. Do you agree with one of these approaches? Explain.

    c. If you are a resident of a state that has no such vicarious liability statute, does this mean you are unaffected by these laws? Why or why not?

7. Bigz Communications Corp, a small telecommunication company, provides long-distance phone service and Internet dial-up connections. What types of e-commerce liability does such a firm face?

8. In *Steyer v. Westvaco Corporation*, 1979 C.C.H. (fire & casualty) 1229, and in *Grand River Lime Company v. Ohio Casualty Insurance Company* 1973 C.C.H. (fire and casualty) 383, industrial operators were held liable for damages caused by their discharge of pollutants over a period of years, even though they were not aware of the damage they were causing when discharging the pollutants.

    a. How might this decision affect the public at large?

    b. What impact will it have on liability insurance?

    c. Because the discharge of pollutants was intentional, should it be insurable at all?

9. Erin Lavinsky works for the Pharmacy On-Line company in Austin, Texas. She likes to work on private matters on her business computer and has received a few infected documents. She was too lazy to update her Norton Utilities and did not realize that she was sending her infected material

to her coworkers. Before long, the whole system collapsed and business was interrupted for a day until the backup system was brought up.

a. Describe the types of liability risk exposures Pharmacy On-Line is facing as a result of Erin's action.

b. If Pharmacy On-Line purchased the ISO e-commerce liability endorsement, would it be covered for the liability?

c. If Erin penetrated into the system and obtained information about the customers, and if she later sold that information to a competitor, what would be the liability ramifications? Is there insurance coverage for this breach of privacy issue?

ENDNOTES

1. For class-action lawsuits, see major business and insurance journals during February 2005. Examples include Allison Bell, "Industry Welcomes Class-Action Victory," *National Underwriter Online News Service*, February 10, 2005; Jim Drinkard, "Bush to Sign Bill on Class-Action Suits," *USA Today*, February 18, 2005, http://www.usatoday.com/money/2005-02-17-lawsuits-usat_x.htm (accessed March 16, 2009). For AIG stories, see all media outlets in 2005, for example, "401(k) Participants File Class-Action Suit Against AIG," *BestWire*, May 13, 2005. Also, review many articles in the media during the fall of 2008 and the winter of 2009.

2. H. J. Black, *Black's Law Dictionary*, 5th ed. (St. Paul, MI: West Publishing Company, 1983), 774.

3. This was first stated explicitly by Judge Learned Hand in *U.S. v. Carroll Towing Co.*, 159 F. 2d 169 (1947).

4. Two such theories are called enterprise liability and market share liability. Both rely on the plaintiff's inability to prove which of several possible companies manufactured the particular product causing injury when each company makes the same type of product. Under either theory, the plaintiff may successfully sue a "substantial" share of the market without proving that any one of the defendants manufactured the actual product that caused the harm for which compensation is sought.

5. Workers' compensation is discussed in Chapter 1.

6. *Walt Disney World Co. v. Wood*, 489 So. 2d 61 (Fla. 4th Dist. Ct. Appl. 1986), upheld by the Florida Supreme Court (515 So. 2d 198, 1987).

7. Coverage of the story is available in all media stories in the beginning of June 2002.

8. Diane Richardson, "Bite Claims Can Dog Insurance Companies," *National Underwriter*, Property & Casualty/Risk & Benefits Management Edition, May 14, 2001; Daniel Hays, "Insurers Feel the Bite of Policyholders' Big Bad Dogs," *National Underwriter Online News Service*, January 31, 2001.

9. Steven Brostoff, "New Brownfields Law Falls Short of Sought-After Superfund Reforms," *National Underwriter* Property & Casualty/Risk & Benefits Management Edition, March 25, 2002.

10. Rodd Zolkos, "Ohio High Court Favors Policyholder in Pollution Case," *Business Insurance*, June 27, 2002.

11. Mark E. Ruquet, "Accountants Under Scrutiny Even Before Enron Failure," *National Underwriter*, Property & Casualty/Risk & Benefits Management Edition, February 25, 2002.

12. Mark E. Ruquet, "Accountants Paying More for E&O Coverage," *National Underwriter*, Property & Casualty/Risk & Benefits Management Edition, February 25, 2002.

13. The citations are too many to list because the issues develop daily. Review information in *National Underwriter*, *Best's Review*, and *Business Insurance* to learn more. Some parts of these Web sites are open only to subscribers, so students are encouraged to use their library's subscriptions to search these publications.

14. *Best Wire*, July 1, 2002.

15. *National Underwriter Online News Service*, June 17, 2002.

16. Lisa S. Howard, *National Underwriter*, Property & Casualty/Risk & Benefits Management Edition, February 25, 2002.

17. "D&O Coverage Evolve in Unstable Regulatory Climate," *BestWire*, May 23, 2005, http://www3.ambest.com/Frames/FrameServer.asp?AltSrc=23&Tab=1&Site=news&refnum=74599 (accessed March 16, 2009). This article and those in footnotes 14 to 16 are a few examples. During the early to mid-2000s, the student can find related stories in every media outlet.

18. Dave Lenckus, "AIG Set to Test Its Own Cover," *Business Insurance*, May 16, 2005, http://www.businessinsurance.com/cgi-bin/article.pl?articleId=16843&a=a&bt=AIG+Set+to+Test+Its+Own+Cover (accessed March 16, 2009).

19. Michael Ha, "AIG Center of Class-Action Lawsuit," *National Underwriter Online News Service*, May 13, 2005, http://www.propertyandcasualtyinsurancenews.com/cms/NUPC/Weekly   %20Issues/Issues/2005/20/News/P20AIGUPDATE?searchfor= (accessed March 16, 2009).

20. Steven Brostoff, "Malpractice Cover Worries Docs: AHA," *National Underwriter Online News Service*, June 26, 2002; Daniel Hays, "Another Malpractice Insurer Leaving Florida," *National Underwriter Online News Service*, June 24, 2002; "Study: Tort Costs Still Edging Up, Albeit More Slowly," *National Underwriter Online News Service*, January 17, 2005,   http://www.propertyandcasualtyinsurancenews.com/cms/NUPC/Breaking%20News/2005/01/17-Study%20Tort%20Costs%20Still%20Edging%20Up%20Albeit%20More%20Slowly?searchfor=tort%20costs%20edging%20up (accessed March 16, 2009).

21. Rachel Zimmerman and Christopher Oster, "Insurers' Price Wars Contributed to Doctors Facing Soaring Costs; Lawsuits Alone Didn't Inflate Malpractice Premiums," *Wall Street Journal*, June 24, 2002; "Report: Suits Don't Cause Higher Med Mal Premiums," *National Underwriter Online News Service*, March 11, 2004, http://www.propertyandcasualtyinsurancenews.com/cms/NUPC/Breaking%20News/2005/03/11-Report%20Suits%20Dont%20Cause%20Higher%20Med%20Mal%20Premiums?searchfor=suits%20cause%20higher%20premiums (accessed March 16, 2009).; Arthur D. Postal, "More Conflict over What Raises Med-Mal Rates," *National Underwriter Online News Service*, May 23, 2005, http://www.propertyandcasualtyinsurancenews.com/cms/NUPC/Breaking%20News/2005/05/23-TORT-dp?searchfor=conflict%20raises%20rates (accessed March 16, 2009).

22. George Sutcliffe, *E-Commerce and Insurance Risk Management* (Boston: Standard Publishing Corp., 2001); 2004 CSI/FBI Computer Crime and Security Survey at GoCSI.com.

23. "Online Privacy Continues to Be a Major Concern for Consumers," research report, the Yankee Group, July 27, 2001. For its 2001 Interactive Consumer (IAC) report, the Yankee Group surveyed approximately 3,000 online consumers.

24. Richard S. Dunham "Who's Worried About Online Privacy? Who Isn't?" *Business Week Online*, June 28, 2000, in http://www.businessweek.com/bwdaily/dnflash/june2000/nf00628c.htm?scriptFramed.

25. Thomas Jackson, "Protecting Your Company Assets and Avoiding Risk in Cyberspace," online newsletter of legal firm Phillips Nizer Benjamin Krim & Ballon LLP, July 16, 1996.

26. Thomas Jackson, "Protecting Your Company Assets and Avoiding Risk in Cyberspace," online newsletter of legal firm Phillips Nizer Benjamin Krim & Ballon LLP, July 16, 1996.

27. George Sutcliffe, *E-Commerce and Insurance Risk Management* (Boston: Standard Publishing Corp., 2001); 2004 CSI/FBI Computer Crime and Security Survey at GoCSI.com.

28. Dix W. Noel and Jerry J. Phillips, *Products Liability in a Nutshell* (St. Paul, MI: West Publishing Co., 1981).

29. *Greeman v. Yuba Power Products*, inc., 377 P.2d 897 (Cal 1963).

30. Many people consider strict product liability to be anything but a subtle shift from negligence. For a discussion of the difference, however, see *Barrett v. Superior Court (Paul Hubbs)*, 272 Cal. Rptr. 304 (1990).

31. "Asbestos Trust Could Face Constitutional Challenges," *BestWire*, May 23, 2005; Mark A. Hofmann, "Amendments Delay Vote on Asbestos Trust Fund Bill," *Business Insurance*, May 16, 2005; Matt Brady, "House Dems Ask Study Of Asbestos Fund Concept," *National Underwriter Online News Service*, May 13, 2005; Jerry Geisel, "Insurer Groups Oppose Asbestos Legislation," *Business Insurance*, April 19, 2005.

32. Michael Bradford, "Tobacco Firms Facing String of Legal Defeats," *Business Insurance*, July 1, 2002.

33. Vanessa O'Connell, "*Lifting Clouds*: New Tactics at Philip Morris Help Stem Tide of Lawsuits: As It Revamps Legal Team, Cigarette Giant Also Gains in Appeals-Court Rulings, Some Big Battles Still Loom," *Wall Street Journal*, May 11, 2005, A1.

34. This discussion is based on Safety 'Net Internet Liability Policy by Chubb Group of Insurance Companies and Executive Risk Indemnity, Inc.

CHAPTER 13

Multirisk Management Contracts: Homeowners

Historically, fires were the most damaging cause of loss. In "Shaped by Risk: The Fire Insurance Industry in America 1790–1920" by Dalit Baranoff, the author describes the major conflagrations in the United States that engulfed parts of cities such as Chicago in 1871.[1] Losses from fire cost society dearly. The cost for firefighting in the 2003 southern California fires alone was estimated to be $2 billion in insured losses.[2] The Rhode Island Station Club fire that took so many lives and the Chicago E2 Club panic led to improved fire codes. It has always been the case that major fire catastrophes prompted improved fire codes. Even though, statistically, nightclub fires account for only 0.3 percent of all fires, their fatality rate is disproportionately high.[3] In February 2009, Australia experienced the country's highest ever loss of life from bushfires when over 1.1 million acres across eastern Victoria burned for days. At least 210 people were reported killed and over 500 more were treated for injuries. An estimated 7,500 residents were rendered homeless, with over 2,000 homes burned in the bushfires. A combination of intense, dry heat, lighting, and arson has been posited as the catalyst for this national disaster. While the complete toll of the tragedy cannot be quantified, insurers anticipate $2 billion in losses, and the Australian government has pledged aid to the victims.[4]

As you saw in previous chapters, fires are not the only cause of catastrophes. Catastrophes are caused by weather, geology, and humans. The last quarter of 2005 broke all records in weather-related catastrophes in the United States, with hurricanes Katrina, Rita, and Wilma responsible for combined insured losses in excess of $42 billion by some estimates. The economic losses are estimated to exceed $150 billion. Much of the uninsured losses were driven by floods from water surges in the Gulf Coast and the subsequent breaches of New Orleans levees. Katrina has been described as "by far the most devastating catastrophe ever to hit the insurance industry, with insured losses at $34.4 billion and counting—surpassing 1992's Hurricane Andrew."[5] As noted in Chapter 11, because of Katrina and Rita, Louisiana homeowners 2005 insurance claim payments are estimated to be as high as all homeowners premiums paid in the previous twenty-five years. In Mississippi, the claims are estimated to be as high as the sum of all premiums for the preceding seventeen years.[6]

The Insurance Services Office (ISO) defines *catastrophe* as an event in which losses total at least $25 million. As you have learned, large losses lead to availability and affordability problems. The industry may even decide to pull out of a specific market and not renew policies; the state governments, however, may prevent this action. In the case of the Colorado fires, the state senate passed a bill prohibiting insurers from refusing to issue fire insurance policies within a wildfire disaster area.[7] Regulatory protection appeared to be necessary.

If disaster struck your home, no doubt you would be devastated. Lesser risks, too, can be distressing. For example, if a friend is hurt while visiting your home, who will pay her medical bills? As your invitee, she might be forced, through her health insurer, to sue you. These and many other pure risks associated with your home are very real. A partial listing of home risks is shown in Table 13.1. They need to be managed carefully. One of the most important risk management tools to finance such losses is the homeowners policy. We will discuss this coverage in detail. The policy includes both property and liability coverages.

TABLE 13.1   **Risks of Your Home**

1. Liability
2. Damage to, or destruction of, the home
3. Loss of use of the home
4. Loss of, or damage to, personal property
5. Defective title

The chapter includes discussion of the following:

1. Links

2. Packaging coverages, homeowners policy forms, the Special Form (HO-3)

3. Endorsements

4. Other risks: flood and title risks

5. Personal liability umbrella policies

6. Shopping for homeowners insurance

1. LINKS

At this point in our study, we are drilling down into specific coverages. We first stay within the personal property/casualty line of the home coverage. The current policies combine both property and liability coverage in one package. In the next chapter, we will drill down into the automobile policy, which also combines liability and property coverage in a single packaged policy.

As part of our holistic risk management, we need to be assured that the place we call home is secure. Whether we buy our home or rent it, we care about its security and the safety of our possessions. We also want to safeguard our possessions from lawsuits by having some liability coverage within these policies. If we feel that the limits are not high enough, we can always obtain an umbrella policy—liability coverage for higher limits than is available in specific lines of insurance—which is discussed later in this chapter. How the risk management of our home fits into the big picture of a family holistic risk management portfolio is featured in Case 1 at the back of this textbook.

Your risk management decision will take specific factors regarding your home and external conditions into account, as you saw in Chapter 4. Your specific homeowner pricing factors such as the type of material used for the siding of the house, distance from a fire station, age of the house, and location of the house are very critical. You may decide to use higher deductibles, lower limits, and fewer riders. How rating factors are used and the issue of redlining—the alleged practice of insurers charging higher premiums and providing less coverage for homeowners insurance in inner cities—is discussed in the box "Redlining: Urban Discrimination Myth or Reality?" The risks within your holistic risk management puzzle that homeowners insurance protects against are highlighted in Figure 13.1 below.

FIGURE 13.1   Links between Holistic Risk Pieces and Homeowners Insurance Policies

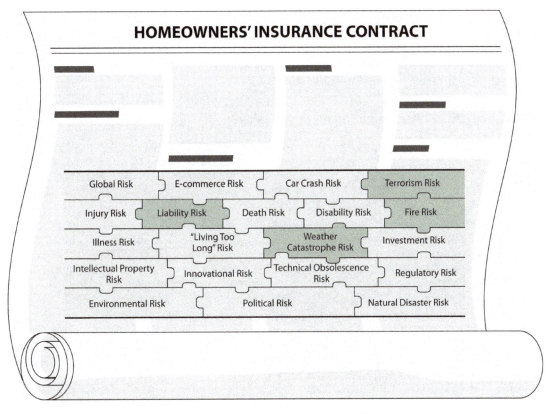

As you learned in Chapter 10 and Chapter 11, most of the homeowners policies are open peril: everything that is not specifically excluded is covered. Thus, the concepts you have learned until now are coming together in one specific type of coverage. To better complete our holistic risk management puzzle, we need to understand how to read and interpret an open peril policy such as the Homeowners Special Form (HO-3) discussed in this chapter.

2.   PACKAGING COVERAGE, HOMEOWNERS POLICY FORMS, AND THE SPECIAL FORM (HO-3)

LEARNING OBJECTIVES

In this section we elaborate on the following:

- **Types of homeowners policies**
- **The Homeowners Special Form (HO-3)**
- **Structure of the HO-3 and explanation of policy language**
- **How to determine loss levels**

Homeowners policies are similar to automobile policies in that they combine several types of coverage into one policy. They are a combination of property and liability insurance, along with a little health insurance for guests and residence employees. The persons insured vary from coverage to coverage and place to place.

package policies

Another name for homeowners policies, so called because they combine different types of coverage that were previously provided by several policies and a number of endorsements.

Homeowners policies are sometimes referred to as **package policies** because they combine different types of coverage that were previously provided by several policies and a number of endorsements. Before the availability of homeowners policies, someone trying to replicate coverage would have needed to buy a standard fire policy with a dwelling, building, and contents broad form; a personal property floater; and a comprehensive personal liability policy. In today's homeowners policies, packaging reduces cost and premiums by reducing administrative and marketing costs. It also provides broader protection and eliminates many gaps in coverage.

Redlining: Urban Discrimination Myth or Reality?

The alleged practice of discrimination against inner-city residents by insurers, dubbed redlining, has been a hot topic for two decades. During the 1990s, class-action lawsuits and allegations by consumer advocacy organizations plagued the insurance industry. Because redlining is a form of racial discrimination, these allegations have the potential to tarnish an insurer's reputation. As a result, most insurers have preferred to settle such cases out of court and thus avoid admitting any wrongdoing.

The SMART proposal discussed in Chapter 8 reintroduced the redlining debate in 2005, with most consumer organizations calling it an "act against the consumer protection strides achieved so far in many states." Consumers saw fault in the proposed act because it did not contain elements for creating a federal office for consumer protection to sustain the achievements reached by consumers in various states. Some states passed important consumer protection acts, activities that were accelerated by New York Attorney General Eliot Spitzer's investigations of the insurance industry.

The redlining debate is also a topic featured in local newspapers. The March 2006 edition of *Palo Alto Online* included a report that focused on the problem of insurers singling out specific zip codes for higher rates or denial of coverage. Residents in zip code 94303 are those who feel they should not be singled out. They are angry at being confused with people living in a poorer neighborhood. Nationwide Mutual Insurance Company of Columbus, Ohio, has settled several such lawsuits in recent years. In 2000, Nationwide reached an agreement with Housing Opportunities Made Equal (HOME), a fair housing advocacy organization that had brought a lawsuit accusing the company of discriminating against black homeowners in urban neighborhoods of Richmond, Virginia. The insurer paid HOME $17.5 million to drop the suit and agreed to provide more services in underserved urban areas. Two years earlier, Nationwide paid $3.5 million to settle a class-action lawsuit alleging redlining in Toledo, Ohio. In a similar case, the same company paid almost $500,000 to homeowners in Lexington, Kentucky. Nationwide admitted no wrongdoing in either case.

Do these settlements mean that redlining really occurs? The evidence is inconclusive. Studies conducted by the Ohio Insurance Department and the National Association of Insurance Commissioners (NAIC), which looked at Ohio and Missouri homeowners, found little evidence that redlining existed. While the NAIC study found that average premiums were usually higher in high-minority urban neighborhoods in Missouri, it pointed out that "loss costs also appear to be higher in urban and minority areas and there is no indication that urban and minority homeowners pay higher premiums relative to the claim payments they receive." The Ohio Insurance Department also concluded that "it appears that companies in Ohio use the same underwriting standards throughout the state and do not unfairly discriminate."

A report by the Massachusetts Affordable Housing Alliance paints a less rosy picture. In 1996, Massachusetts passed an antiredlining law, but in the four years after its passage, the state saw only modest improvement in availability of insurance in the state's most underserved zip codes, where 62 percent of homes were covered by the state-run insurer of last resort in 2000. Part of the problem, according to the report, was the predominance of flat-roofed triple-decker houses in these neighborhoods, which insurers said were more likely to suffer expensive water damage than pitched-roof houses.

Real or not, the redlining issue is not going away any time soon. Recently, it has become the focus of debate over federal chartering of insurance companies (see Chapter 8). Current proposed legislation would require national insurers to file annual reports identifying the communities in which they sell insurance policies and the types of policies sold in these communities. The law would bar them from refusing to insure a property because of its location.

Questions for Discussion

1. Do insurers have an ethical responsibility to minimize race, gender, age, and other discrimination in underwriting, even if actuarially appropriate?

2. Does society benefit by limitation on insurer practices? Or is society negatively affected by higher insurance costs overall?

3. Could and should insurers be forced to find less socially significant factors for pricing and underwriting?

Sources: Various articles in National Underwriter and Business Insurance in 2005 with a summary in "Top Ten 2005 Stories #8—SMART Sparks Tough Talk, Not Action," National Underwriter, January 6, 2006, http://www.propertyandcasualtyinsurancenews.com/cms/NUPC/Weekly%20Issues/Issues/2005/48/2005%20Top%2010%20Stories/P48-2005-TOP10-SMART?searchfor=SMART%20sparks%20tough%20talk%20not%20action (accessed March 20, 2009); Jocelyn Dong, "Palo Alto 94303: In Unusual Zip-Code Area, a No Man's Land of Mistaken Identity," Palo Alto Weekly Online Edtion, March 23, 2005, http://www.paloaltoonline.com/weekly/morgue/2005/2005_03_23.zipcode23.shtml (accessed March 20, 2009); Amanda Levin, "Nationwide Settles Virginia Redlining Suit," National Underwriter, Property & Casualty/Risk & Benefits Management Edition, May 1, 2000; Tony Attrino, "Nationwide Settles Redlining Suit In Ohio," National Underwriter, Property & Casualty/Risk & Benefits Management Edition, April 27, 1998; L. H. Otis, "Ohio, Missouri Studies Fail to Confirm Redlining Fears," National Underwriter, Property & Casualty/Risk & Benefits Management Edition, August 19, 1996; John Hillman, "Study Says Mass. Homeowners Insurers Underserve Some Neighborhoods," Best's Insurance News, November 8, 2002; Steven Brostoff, "(A) Key Dem. Readies Federal Charter Bill," National Underwriter Online News Service, February 6, 2002.

2.1 Homeowners Policy Forms

First we will look at the different kinds of homeowners policies shown in Table 13.2. Then we will examine the homeowners special form in some detail.

TABLE 13.2 Homeowners Policy Forms*

HO-1.	Basic form	HO-4.	Contents broad form
HO-2.	Broad form	HO-6.	Condominium unit owners form
HO-3.	Special form	HO-8.	Modified coverage

* The numbering and content vary in some states.

FIGURE 13.2 Homeowners Policy Structure

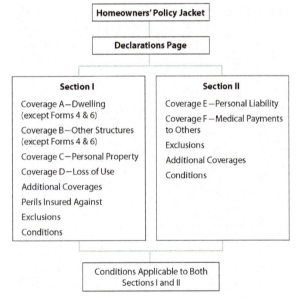

As shown in Figure 13.2, each policy consists of three parts: a declarations page, a homeowners policy jacket, and a policy form attached to the jacket. The **declarations page** identifies the specifics that are unique to the insured, such as the covered location, and also lists policy limits, period of coverage, the name of the insurer, and similar information. The policy jacket includes general, universal provisions, such as the title of the coverage, and acts to bind together the remaining policy parts. The policy form is the substance of the contract, spelling out the specific coverage provisions. The insured can choose from the several types of forms that are available.

Following the declarations page, the balance of each form is divided into two sections. Section I pertains to direct and indirect property losses related to the dwelling, other structures, personal property, and loss of use. A stated deductible ($250 in most states), which can be increased, applies to Section I coverages. Section II includes personal liability coverage for you and medical payments to others. Each section lists the coverages provided, the perils insured against, and the exclusions and conditions applicable to that section. Finally, conditions applicable to both sections are listed. Table 13.3 outlines the coverages in Section I, the amounts of insurance for each type of coverage, and the perils included for the various forms (ISO forms are discussed here). Note that the limit for coverages B, C, and D is a specified percentage of the amount of insurance on the dwelling (coverage A) in forms 1, 2, and 3.

declarations page

Part of a policy that identifies the specifics that are unique to the insured, such as the covered location, and also lists policy limits, period of coverage, the name of the insurer, and similar information.

Thus, when you decide on the amount of insurance to have on your house, you have automatically selected the amount for other coverages. If additional amounts of coverage are needed, they are available with payment of additional premium. Forms 4 (for tenants) and 6 (for condominium unit owners) do not cover a dwelling or other structures; the amount for coverage D is based on that selected for coverage C (personal property).

The basic amount for Section II (coverages E and F) is the same for all forms but can be increased with the payment of additional premium. The insuring agreements, exclusions, and conditions for Section II are the same for all forms. The basic differences among the forms are in the property coverages provided in Section I. Forms 4 and 6 do not include insurance on the dwelling and other structures because form 4 is for tenants and form 6 is for condominium owners. The latter have an interest in the building in which they live as well as related structures, but such property is insured on behalf of the owner and all occupants in a common separate policy. Limited coverage for permanent appliances is provided in Part A. Form 8 is for older homes that may involve special hazards. The valuation provision used in form 8 on the building is actual cash value, not replacement cost new. The perils covered represent another basic difference among the forms. Some are named perils while others are open perils. Note that form 8 has a much shorter list of covered perils than the others do.

TABLE 13.3 Section 1: Homeowners Coverage

Coverage	Form HO-2	Form HO-3	Form HO-4	Form HO-6	Form HO-8
A	15,000 minimum	15,000 minimum	Not included	$1,000 minimum	Varies by company
B	10% of A	10% of A	Not included	Not included	10% of A
C	50% of A	50% of A	$6,000 minimum	$6,000 minimum	50% of A
D	20% of A	20% of A	20% of C	40% of C	10% of A
Perils Covered under Section 1					
	Fire or lightning windstorm or hail	Open perils A, B, & D	Contents same as HO-2 (except glass breakage)	Contents same as HO-2.	Fire or lightning
	Explosion	Contents same as HO-2		Also covers improvements (e.g., carpet, wallpaper) up to $1,000	Windstorm or hail
	Riot or civil commotion				Explosion
	Aircraft				Riot or civil commotion
	Vehicles				Aircraft
	Smoke				Vehicles
	Vandalism or malicious mischief				Smoke
	Theft				Vandalism or malicious mischief
	Glass breakage				Theft (limited)
	Falling objects				Volcanic eruption
	Weight of ice, snow, or sleet				
	Collapse				
	Accidental discharge of overflow of water or steam				
	Rupture of heating or A-C system				
	Freezing pluming and heating or A-C				
	Artificially generated electricity				
	Volcanic eruption				
Note: Form HO-5 provided contents and real property coverage on an open perils basis. that coverage is now available through endorsement HO-15 to the HO-3 form, eliminating the need for HO-5. HO-1 provided a list of perils similar to that of HO-8 (i.e., shorter than the others), and is no longer in use in most states."					

2.2   The Special Form (HO-3)

We will examine form HO-3 in some detail because it is representative of the various forms and is the most popular homeowners policy. We will, in effect, take a guided tour through the policy using the most recent ISO HO-3 policy form in Chapter 24 (the form is HO 00 03 10 0005 01). Our purpose is to familiarize you with its structure and content so you will know what to look for and how to find the coverages and exclusions in any homeowners policy. Your own policy may differ slightly from the one provided in the appendix due to state and company variations. The basic coverage, however, is the same.

Insuring Agreement and Definitions

The insuring agreement and definitions parts of the policy follow the declarations page. They are the same in all homeowners forms. The insuring agreement says,

> *We will provide the insurance described in this policy in return for the premium and compliance with all applicable provisions of this policy.*

Two aspects of this agreement should be noted. First, the portion following the words "in return for" is the consideration that is vital to the contract. Unless you comply with the provisions of the policy, the consideration is incomplete. The insurer is saying, "If you comply with the provisions, we will provide the insurance described in the policy." Second, you must look further in the policy to find out what insurance is described. Before you can determine this, you must know the meaning of the terms used in the policy. Words or phrases printed in bold letters are defined in detail under the heading "definitions." Because definitions are crucial to an understanding of the scope of coverage, these terms are listed separately in Table 13.4. Several other terms are defined in the body of the policy. Armed with this terminology, you are prepared to examine the following parts of Section I:

1. Coverages
2. Perils insured against
3. Exclusions
4. Conditions

Section I—Coverages

Coverage A—Dwelling

residence premises

The home being insured.

The dwelling on the **residence premises** (i.e., the home being insured) plus structures attached to the dwelling, such as an attached garage, are insured in coverage A. Also covered are materials and supplies on or adjacent to the residence premises for use in the construction, alteration, or repair of the dwelling or other structures. Land is not included.

TABLE 13.4 Essential Policy Terms

1. Bodily injury
2. Business
3. Insured
4. Insured location
5. Occurrence
6. Property damage
7. Residence employee
8. Residence premises

Coverage B—Other Structures

The exposures insured in coverage B are structures on the residence premises that are separated from the dwelling, such as a detached garage. Coverage B does not apply to any structure used for business purposes or rented to any person not a tenant of the dwelling, unless used solely as a private garage. The location of this exclusion and the way it is stated illustrate two important points made in Chapter 6. First, exclusions are not always called exclusions. They may appear following "we do not cover," or "except." Second, they may appear anywhere in the policy, not just under the heading "Exclusions."

Coverage C—Personal Property

This part of the policy says,

> *We cover personal property owned or used by any insured while it is anywhere in the world.*

Note that this definition includes property you own as well as that belonging to others while you are using it. If you borrow your neighbor's lawnmower, it is protected by your insurance as if it were yours.

If the insured requests, coverage C applies to personal property owned by others while it is "on the part of the residence premises occupied by an insured" and to property of guests and residence employees while at any residence occupied by an insured. For example, if you store the property of a friend at your residence premises, you can cover the property under your policy, even if you are not using the friend's property. Or if a guest at your vacation house (not the residence premises) has property damaged while visiting you there, that property too can be covered.

Property usually situated at an insured's residence other than the residence premises (such as the vacation house described above) is subject to a limit of 10 percent of coverage C or $1,000, whichever is greater. Coverage C, remember, is 50 percent of coverage A unless specifically amended to provide some other amount. Protection of $100,000 for coverage A thus results in a $50,000 limit for coverage C. Ten percent of coverage C in this case is $5,000, which is greater than $1,000, and therefore is the limit on personal property usually kept at a residence other than the residence premises. If you, as a member of your parents' household, rent a room at school, the personal property normally kept in your school room is subject to this limit. Property brought there for a special occasion, perhaps when your sister drives up for a visit, is not subject to this limit.

Two provisions in coverage C merit careful attention. One is a special limit of liability and the other is property not covered. Under the **special limit of liability**, dollar limits are placed on some property for loss caused by any peril, and on other property for loss caused by theft. These special limits should call your attention to any gaps in coverage if you have the kind of property listed. Note that, for some items, you can be reimbursed up to $2,500, while for others, such as money in any form (bank notes, coins, even value cards and smart cards), the limit is $200. You may want to cover the gaps with a scheduled personal property endorsement added to your policy. This endorsement is explained later in the chapter.

Most of the exclusions and limitations have the purpose of standardizing the risk, with coverage available by endorsement or in other policies. For example, much of the property not covered is related to conduct of a business and therefore is not suited for homeowners coverage. A business-related policy or endorsement should be used to cover those items.

Some exclusions are of greater interest to a typical full-time college student than others. An example is the exclusion from coverage of compact discs and players when used in a motor vehicle. These items would be included in the automobile policy, sometimes under a special endorsement. As you know by now, if a certain item is covered by another policy, such as the automobile policy discussed in Chapter 14, it would be excluded from the homeowners policy to avoid duplication. Note also that if you rent your room in a private home, the landlord's homeowners policy does not cover your belongings. Your parents' homeowners policy may.

Coverage D—Loss of Use

Loss of use coverage protects you from losses sustained if the premises cannot be lived in as a result of a direct loss to either the premises or neighboring premises. **Additional living expense** is coverage provided if a loss covered under Section I of the homeowners policy renders the residence uninhabitable. An example is the large additional living expenses paid to homeowners whose homes where plagued with toxic mold and needed lengthy remediation. If a similar loss makes the part of the residence rented to others uninhabitable, the policy pays for its fair rental value. If a civil authority prohibits you from using the premises as a result of direct damage to neighboring premises by a peril insured against in this policy, both additional living expense and fair rental value loss will be paid for a period not exceeding two weeks. The two-week limit does not apply except for loss of use due to actions by a civil authority.

An important characteristic of coverage D is that it covers only additional expenses. A family forced out of its home for a week due to fire damage will not receive payment for all expenses incurred during that week. Suppose that the family normally spends $250 a week on groceries, but had to pay $400 while away from the damaged premises. Only the difference, $150, plus other added expenses would be compensable.

Additional Coverages

You might think that every conceivable source of loss in connection with your home and personal property has been covered, modified, or excluded. Such is not the case.

Twelve additional items of coverage are provided under the additional coverages section of the policy. First is debris removal, which provides payment for the cost of removing (under Part A) debris of covered property damaged by a covered peril and the cost of removing ash, dust, or particles from a volcanic eruption that has caused direct property loss. Part B under (1) is for fallen trees, which will pay up to $1,000 for the removal from residence premises of trees that fall due to the weight of ice, snow, and sleet. This additional protection is needed because other coverages provide only for the cost of repair or replacement of damaged property, not for the cost of hauling away the debris that blocks a driveway in the residence premises or a ramp for a handicapped person.

special limit of liability

Situation in which dollar limits are placed on some property for loss caused by any peril and on other property for loss caused by theft.

loss of use

Coverage that protects a policyholder from losses sustained if the premises cannot be lived in as a result of a direct loss to either the premises or neighboring premises.

additional living expense

Coverage provided if a loss covered under Section I of the homeowners policy renders the residence uninhabitable.

Several provisions in the additional coverages section of the policy are intended to encourage the insured to take steps that reduce the size of a loss after it has occurred. One is a reasonable repair, which provides payment for repairs made solely to protect property from further damage. For example, a temporary patch in the roof, following a covered loss, would be paid to prevent more extensive damages inside while awaiting permanent repairs. The conditions section (later in the policy) further stipulates that if the insured fails to protect property in this way, some further damage might not be covered.

Similarly, property removed from premises endangered by a covered peril is covered while removed "against loss from any cause" for no more than thirty days. If this provision were not included, you might be better off to leave personal property in your house while it burned to the ground rather than remove it and risk having it damaged or destroyed by a peril other than those included in the policy.

The insurer also promises to pay fire department service charges incurred to save or protect covered property from a covered peril. Up to $500 per loss, without application of a deductible, is available.

Trees, shrubs, and other plants are also addressed in additional coverages. Loss to these items on the residence premises is covered if caused by one of several named perils. You should note that windstorm, ice, insects, and disease are not among the covered perils. No more than $500 per tree, shrub, or plant is available, with a total limit of 5 percent of coverage A.

Many of us have as many credit cards as we have books and DVDs. The homeowners policy will pay up to $500 for such loss under the credit card, fund transfer card, forgery, and counterfeit money coverage. The $500 limit is for loss caused by any single person, regardless of the number of cards or other instruments involved. No deductible applies to this coverage.

Many of us may also belong to an association of property owners (e.g., condominium projects). As members, we may be assessed charges for damage to association property. The loss assessment provision in the additional coverages section of the homeowners policy provides up to $1,000 to cover such charges. This provision has its greatest applicability in the condominium unit owners form (HO-6), but it is included in all of the homeowners forms.

The additional coverages section also provides for direct physical loss to covered property due to two situations previously considered as perils: collapse of a building and loss caused to or by glass or safety glazing material. The definition and covered causes of collapse are outlined in this provision. Coverage is more narrowly defined for loss caused by collapse than had been the case when it was included under the open perils protection to real property. The glass coverage actually is slightly broader than that found in previous versions of the policy.

The tenth additional coverage found in the HO-3 is for landlord's furnishings. Up to $2,500 coverage is available to cover a landlord's appliances and other property located in an apartment on the residence premises that is usually available for rental. The same perils that are available for coverage C apply to this protection, except that theft is excluded.

Section I—Perils Insured Against

Coverages A and B—Dwelling and Other Structures

Under this heading, the policy says,

> *We insure against risk of direct loss to property described in Coverages A and B.*

The most important aspect of the agreement is that coverage is for open perils (sometimes also referred to as "for all risk"), but a close second is the limiting phrase "we do not insure, however, for loss…." Three exceptions to coverage follow this phrase. Through these exceptions, the coverage, while it is for open perils, does not protect for all losses under all circumstances. The first exception is for collapse other than as provided in additional coverages noted above. The second exception lists six circumstances in which protection is not afforded under the policy. In general, these circumstances relate to especially hazardous situations or nonfortuitous events, such as theft in a dwelling under construction or loss due to wear and tear. One of these circumstances deals with losses arising from mold, fungus, and wet rot, which are covered only if hidden within walls or ceilings and caused from accidental discharge of water or steam. This coverage is available only for those states that did not adopt the ISO endorsement adding mold as a new exclusion.[8]

Coverage C—Personal Property

Unlike the open perils protection for the dwelling and other structures, personal property is covered against direct loss on a named perils basis, including the following:

- Fire or lightning

- Windstorm or hail
- Explosion
- Riot or civil commotion
- Aircraft
- Vehicles
- Smoke
- Vandalism or malicious mischief
- Theft
- Falling objects
- Weight of ice, snow, or sleet
- Accidental discharge or overflow of water or steam
- Sudden and accidental tearing apart, cracking, burning, or bulging of a water heating or transporting appliance
- Freezing
- Sudden and accidental damage from artificially generated electrical current
- Volcanic eruption

Most of these perils are listed along with some explanation of what they involve, as well as specific exclusions. For example, damage by windstorm or hail to personal property in a building is not covered unless the opening is caused by wind or hail. Therefore, if hail broke a window and damaged property inside, the loss would be covered. If the window was left open, however, damage to property would not be covered. Similarly, furnishings, equipment, and other personal property are covered only if such property is inside a fully enclosed building. So, if your curtains are damaged by a windstorm while the window is left open, coverage C of HO-3 will not pay for the loss.

Smoke damage is covered if it is sudden and accidental, but not if it is caused by smoke from agricultural smudging or industrial operations. If, for example, your oil furnace malfunctions and spreads smoke throughout the house, the insurer will pay for redecorating and having smoky furniture and clothing cleaned. On the other hand, if you hang your clothing outside on the clothesline and it needs cleaning because of exposure to emissions from a coal-burning power plant, you will have to pay for any resulting loss.

Theft includes damages caused by attempted theft as well as loss of property from a known location when it is likely that the property has been stolen. If someone damages your bicycle in an attempt to steal it, such damage is covered. The second part of the theft definition is sometimes referred to as mysterious disappearance. Suppose, for example, you leave your camera at your table in McDonald's, go to the counter for another cup of coffee, return to your table, and find the camera gone. Was it stolen, or did it leave under its own power? It was probably stolen, so the loss is covered. **Mysterious disappearance** coverage requires that there be loss of property from a known place in such a fashion that theft is the likely cause.

Several exceptions to the theft coverage are enumerated in the policy. First, the HO-3 does not include loss caused by theft committed by any insured. This appears strange until you consider how many people are included in the definition of insured, which includes any resident relative and anyone under age twenty-one in the care of one of these resident relations.

Second, theft in or from a dwelling under construction or of materials and supplies for use in the construction is excluded because the risk is too great. Theft from any part of a residence rented by an insured to someone other than an insured is also excluded. If you rent a room to an outsider, for example, and he or she steals something from that room, the loss is not covered.

The third exception is one particularly important to typical college-age students. Unless an insured is residing there, theft from a residence owned by, rented by, rented to, or occupied by an insured, other than the residence premises, is excepted. Property of students kept at school, however, is covered as long as the student has been there within forty-five days. If you go home for winter break and your dorm room (or apartment) is broken into, your property is covered if you were not gone more than forty-five days at the time of the theft, subject of course to other policy exclusions and limitations.

Falling objects is the next listed peril. If a tree falls on your canoe, the damage is covered because the tree is a falling object. This peril does not include loss to property contained in a building, however, unless the roof or an exterior wall of the building is first damaged by a falling object. If you drop a hammer on a piece of china, the loss is not covered. If the roof is damaged by a falling tree that, in turn, damages the china, the loss is covered. Similarly, damage to personal property caused by the weight of ice, snow, or sleet or the collapse of part or all of a building is covered.

Loss caused by accidental discharge or overflow of water or steam from a plumbing, heating, air conditioning, or automatic fire protective sprinkler system, or from a household appliance, is covered.

mysterious disappearance

Coverage that requires that there be loss of property from a known place in such a fashion that theft is the likely cause.

Water could leak from a washing machine, for example, and cause damage to a painting hung on the wall of a room below. Sudden and accidental tearing, cracking, burning, or bulging of a steam or hot water heating system, an air conditioning or automatic fire protective sprinkler system, or a hot water heater could damage not only the premises but personal property. Such loss is covered.

Loss caused by freezing of a plumbing, heating, air conditioning, or automatic fire protective sprinkler system, or of a household appliance, is covered. This does not include loss on the residence premises while the dwelling is unoccupied, unless you arrange to maintain heat in the building or shut off the water supply and drain the system. If you leave your home during the winter for several weeks or months, losses caused by cold weather will not be covered unless you take the same precautions as would a prudent person who did not have insurance.

Damage to some property caused by a short circuit in your electrical system is covered. Excluded is loss to a tube, transistor, or similar electronic component. Thus, damage to your television or personal computer is not covered.

Section I—Exclusions

Because we have already noted so many exceptions and limitations, you would think that an exclusion section is hardly worthwhile. Nevertheless, additional items are listed as general exclusions from Section I coverages, nine exclusions under Part A, and three under Part B. These are listed in Table 13.5.

TABLE 13.5 Listed Exclusions

A	B
1. Ordinance or law	1. Weather
2. Earth movement	2. Acts or decisions including groups, organizations, or governmental body
3. Water damage	3. Faulty, inadequate, or defective plans, design, material, or maintenance
4. Power failure	
5. Neglect	
6. War	
7. Nuclear hazard	
8. Intentional loss	
9. Governmental action	

Some of these exclusions deserve comment. The law in your city, for example, may provide that a building that does not comply with the building code is permitted to stand, but if it is damaged by fire or other peril to the extent of 50 percent of its value, it must be demolished. The first exclusion listed under Part A of Table 13.5 says, in effect, "We will pay for the loss caused directly by an insured peril, but not one caused by an ordinance." If your garage does not meet building code requirements and is damaged by fire to such an extent that it must be razed, the insurer will pay only for the first damage (the fire). You will bear the rest of the loss (the demolition).

If earth movement damages your house, the loss will not be paid. If, however, the damage is not total, and fire, explosion, or breakage of glass follows the earth movement, the additional loss caused by those perils is covered. Of course, determining the property value following earth movement is not an easy task. Homeowners who want earthquake protection can purchase an endorsement for an additional premium. This endorsement is discussed later in the chapter.

The water damage exclusion is not identical to the earth movement exclusion, but it works in the same way. That is, it excludes loss caused by specified water damage and then says, "direct loss by fire, explosion, or theft resulting from water damage is covered." Specified exclusions are for flood, backup of sewers or drains, water seepage below the ground, and overflow of a sump.

Under the fourth exclusion listed under Part A in Table 13.5, loss caused by power failure off the residence premises is not covered. If the power failure results in the occurrence of a covered peril, however, loss caused by the covered peril is covered. Thus, if lightning strikes a power station, cutting off electricity that heats your greenhouse, loss caused by frost to your plants is not covered. On the other hand, the freezing and bursting of your pipes, as a covered peril, is covered.

The neglect exclusion can be confusing, especially because neglect is not defined in the policy. People often negligently cause damage to their homes, such as smokers who fall asleep with lit cigarettes in their hands. However, negligence is not neglect, and these incidents are not excluded. Rather, the exclusion has the purpose of encouraging insureds to act at the time of loss to minimize severity. You are not expected to run into a burning building to recover property. However, you are expected to make temporary repairs to holes in the roof caused by wind damage in order to prevent further damage by rain before permanent repairs can be made.

The war and nuclear hazard exclusions require little explanation. Their purpose in the homeowners policy, of course, is to avoid the catastrophe potential.

Insurers have added the last exclusions under Part A and those in Part B in recent years because of several court decisions providing broader coverage than insurers intend. The intentional loss exclusion is directed toward court decisions that permitted insureds not guilty of any misrepresentation or concealment to collect for arson damage caused by another insured. The purpose is to discourage arson, or at least to avoid paying for it.

The remaining exclusions in the list in Table 13.5 are motivated by the doctrine of concurrent causation. According to the **concurrent causation** doctrine, when a loss is caused simultaneously (concurrently) by two or more perils, and at least one is not excluded, the loss is covered. The doctrine has been used most frequently in cases where earth movement, aggravated by negligent construction, engineering, or architecture of the building or weather conditions, was the cause of loss. Courts considered the negligence of third parties a concurrent peril, not excluded, resulting in coverage.[9] Insurers are responding to the concurrent causation doctrine by excluding weather conditions; acts or decisions of governmental bodies; and faulty, inadequate, or defective planning, zoning, development, surveying, design, specifications, workmanship, repair, construction, renovation, remodeling, grading, compaction, and the like.

concurrent causation

Doctrine that states when a loss is caused simultaneously (concurrently) by two or more perils, and at least one is not excluded, the loss is covered.

Section I—Conditions

As you have seen, there are several ways to place bounds around coverages provided by the policy:

- Special limits of liability, as in coverage C
- Listing property not covered, as in coverage C
- Listing losses not covered, as in additional coverages and perils insured against

Another place where coverages may be limited is the conditions section. Conditions outline your duties, the company's duties and options, what happens in the event of a dispute between you and the company about the amount of a loss and the position of mortgagees and bailees.[10] Table 13.6 lists the conditions in Section I of the policy.

TABLE 13.6 Section I—Conditions

A. Insurable interest and limit of liability
B. Duties after loss
C. Loss settlement
D. Loss to a pair or set
E. Appraisal
F. Other insurance or service agreement
G. Suit against us
H. Our option
I. Loss payment
J. Abandonment of property
K. Mortgage clause
L. No benefit to bailee
M. Nuclear hazard clause
N. Recovered property
O. Volcanic eruption period
P. Policy period
Q. Concealment or fraud
R. Loss payable clause

Because the contract is conditional (meaning that your rights depend on fulfillment of certain duties), you must be familiar with the conditions. Your failure to fulfill a duty may result in a loss not being paid. This point is emphasized by condition G, which provides that you cannot bring legal action against the insurer unless you have complied with the policy provisions and the action is started within one year after the occurrence causing loss or damage.[11] Two other duties warrant further discussion: duties after loss and loss settlement.

Duties after Loss

When a loss occurs, you must do the following:

1. Give immediate notice to the company or its agent.
2. Notify the police in case of theft.
3. Notify credit card companies, if applicable.
4. Protect the property from further damage, make reasonable and necessary repairs to protect it, and keep an accurate record of repair expenditures. If, for example, a falling tree makes a hole in the roof of your house, you should have temporary repairs made immediately to prevent water damage to the house and its contents in case of rain. The insurer will pay for such repairs, as noted in the additional coverages.
5. Cooperate with the insurer's investigations of the claim.
6. Prepare an inventory of damaged personal property showing the quantity, description, actual cash value, and amount of loss.
7. Exhibit the damaged property as often as required and submit to examination under oath.
8. Submit to the company, within sixty days of its request, a signed, sworn statement of loss that shows the time and cause of loss, your interest and that of all others in the property, all encumbrances on the property, other insurance that may cover the loss, and various other information spelled out in the policy.

Preparing an inventory (duty 6) after a loss is, for most people, a very difficult task. Generally, the loss adjuster for the insurance company will help you, but that does not ensure a complete inventory. The only way to deal with this problem is before a loss. You should have an inventory not only before a loss but at the time you buy insurance so that you will know how much insurance you need. Often insureds will use photographs or videotapes of their homes and belongings to supplement an inventory. An up-to-date inventory of your household furnishings and personal belongings can help you do the following:

- Determine the value of your belongings and your personal insurance needs
- Establish the purchase dates and cost of major items in case of loss
- Identify exactly what was lost (most people cannot recall items accumulated gradually)
- Settle your insurance claim quickly and efficiently
- Verify uninsured losses for income tax deductions

Loss Settlement

Personal property losses are paid on the basis of actual cash value at the time of loss, not exceeding the cost to repair or replace the property. Carpeting, domestic appliances, awnings, outdoor antennas, and outdoor equipment, whether or not attached to buildings, are paid on the same basis. Typically, anything permanently attached to a building is considered to be part of the building. You would expect such losses to be settled in the same way as buildings. But the phrase "whether or not attached to buildings" makes them coverage C (personal property) losses rather than coverage A or B (real property).

The provision for settling losses to buildings may be confusing, but it is similar to the coinsurance calculations shown in Chapter 11. Here is how it works: if the total amount of coverage equals at least 80 percent of the current replacement cost of your home (e.g., at least $80,000 on a $100,000 structure), you are paid the full cost of replacing or repairing the damage up to the policy limits. There is no deduction for depreciation.

On the other hand, if the amount of coverage is less than 80 percent of the replacement cost, the insurer will pay the larger of (1) the actual cash value, which is replacement cost minus depreciation, or (2) that proportion of the cost to repair or replace, without deduction for depreciation, which the total amount of insurance on the building bears to 80 percent of its replacement cost. An example, similar to that provided in Chapter 11, may help clarify what the policy says. Suppose that at the time of a $20,000 loss, your home has a replacement value of $100,000. And suppose you have $70,000 worth of insurance on it. The loss could be settled as follows:

$$\frac{\text{Amount of Insurance carried}}{80\% \text{ of replacement cost}} \times \text{loss} = \text{payment}$$

$$\frac{\$70,000}{\$80,000} \times \$20,000 = \$17,500$$

If, however, the actual cash value of the loss—replacement cost minus depreciation—was greater than $17,500, you would be paid the larger amount. This example demonstrates that, unless there is no depreciation, you would usually have to bear part of the loss if the coverage is less than 80 percent of the value of the building. On the other hand, if construction of the house was completed the day before the loss occurred, depreciation would be zero, actual cash value would equal replacement cost, and the loss would be paid in full. In most cases, of course, depreciation is greater than zero, so actual cash value is less than replacement cost.

Clearly, you are well advised to carry an amount of insurance equal to at least 80 percent of the replacement value of your house. But even if you do, what happens in the event of a total loss? If you have $80,000 insurance on your $100,000 house and it burns to the ground, you will lose $20,000. Remember that insurance works best against high-value, low-probability losses. It may be valuable to know also that replacement cost estimates do not include the value of foundations or land, both of which are not insured.

Furthermore, if you have $80,000 insurance at the beginning of this year, will that be 80 percent of the value of your house later in the year? If housing values in your area are increasing, you should (1) consider adding an **inflation guard endorsement** to your policy, which increases the amount of insurance automatically every year, or (2) increase the amount of insurance to between 90 and 100 percent of replacement value and keep the amount up to date every time you pay the premium. That will ensure being paid in full for partial losses and provide more complete protection against a total loss. Some insurers also offer a replacement cost guarantee endorsement whereby replacement cost is covered, even if it exceeds the limit of liability.

Determining Coverages

If you are like most people, the previous discussion has provided you with some new information. Even so, the homeowners policy still remains a puzzle, with pieces that do not seem to fit. How do you determine what coverage you have? Different people will find alternative methods of breaking a puzzle's code. We offer one method here that may help get you started. Figure 13.3 is a visual representation of the verbal path that follows.

FIGURE 13.3 Determining Coverages

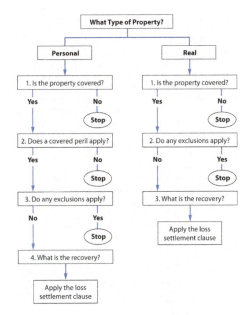

To determine coverage once loss has occurred, ask yourself which type of property (real or personal) is involved in the loss. If both, consider each type separately.

If real property is involved, be certain it is covered by the policy by consulting the declarations page to see if a premium was paid for coverage A. Next, check the exclusions listed under Section I—Perils Insured Against for coverages A and B, as well as those listed under Section I—Exclusions. If no exclusion applies, refer to the provisions of the loss settlement clause to determine how much of the loss will be compensated.

When the loss involves personal property, the process is slightly more complicated. First, make certain that the property is covered by referring to the special limits of liability and property not covered provisions of coverage C under Section I—Property Coverages. You hope the property is not listed here. Next, look at Section I—Perils Insured Against for coverage C for a listing of covered loss-causing events. If the loss was caused by a peril that is not listed, no coverage exists. If loss was caused by a covered peril, refer to Section I—Exclusions for limitations on protection. Last, apply the provisions of the loss settlement clause to determine how much you will be paid for the loss. An illustration

inflation guard endorsement

Endorsement that increases the amount of insurance automatically every year, or increases the amount of insurance to between 90 and 100 percent of replacement value and keeps the amount up to date every time the policyholder pays the premium.

of how a hypothetical family, the Smith family, determines the homeowners coverage needed and the rate comparison is provided in Case 1 of Chapter 23.

Section II—Liability Coverages

As discussed in Chapter 12, many of our daily activities may result in our involvement in litigation. The liability exposures that are standard to homeowners are covered in the homeowners policy. The coverage includes defense costs. This liability protection is found in coverage E. Medical expenses incurred by others in circumstances that might result in litigation may—or may not—be provided in coverage F.

Coverage E—Personal Liability

The insuring agreement for coverage E includes two promises by the insurer: to pay damages for which the insured is legally liable and to "provide a defense at our expense by counsel of our choice, even if the suit is groundless, false, or fraudulent." Both promises are of significant value, given the frequency of lawsuits, the size of awards, and the cost of defense. Note that the coverage is on an open perils basis; therefore, all events not excluded from coverage are included. One limitation is that damages must be either bodily injury or property damage, not a nonphysical personal injury such as libel. (Coverage for nonphysical personal injuries is discussed later in the chapter.) Note the exact wording of the policy:

> *A. Coverage E—Personal Liability*
>
> *If a claim is made or a suit is brought against an "insured" for damages because of "bodily injury" or "property damage" caused by an "occurrence" to which this coverage applies….*

In addition, defense is provided only until the amount paid by the insurer for damages (court judgments or negotiated settlements) equals the limit of liability. Thereafter, the insured is responsible for defense. Therefore, deciding on a sufficient amount for coverage E is best done by considering both the exposure to liability and to extended litigation.

Coverage F—Medical Payments

You may at times be wise to pay for medical expenses of other people without requiring that they prove you're at fault. You may, for instance, feel morally obligated, or you may merely hope to avoid litigation by remaining on friendly terms with the injured person.

Coverage F of the homeowners policy provides funds for such events. Specifically, medical expenses will be paid if incurred within three years of an accident and arising out of one of five possible situations. This coverage differs from that found in your auto policy. In the auto policy, medical expense coverage is for you and your passengers. Here (in a homeowners policy), the coverage is for losses incurred by others. The covered situations are as follows:

a. That of a person on the insured location with the permission of an insured

b. That of a person off the insured location if the bodily injury arises out of a condition on the insured location

c. One caused by the activities of an insured

d. One caused by a residence employee in the course of employment by the insured

e. One caused by an animal owned by or in the care of an insured

Expenses incurred by regular residents of the residence premises, except for residence employees, are not covered. The insured, spouse, and children living at the residence, and others living there, are excluded so that this policy does not become a first-party health insurance policy for them.

Section II—Exclusions

The exclusions to Section II coverage in the homeowners policy are found in the following separate subsections:

a. Motor vehicle liability

b. Watercraft liability

c. Aircraft liability

d. Hovercraft liability

e. Further exclusions to both coverage E and coverage F

f. Exclusions to coverage E only

g. Exclusions to coverage F only

Section II exclusions E, F, and G are listed in Table 13.7. All the exclusions fit the general purposes of exclusions discussed in Chapter 10. Among the group of exclusions shared by coverages E and F, for instance, is the exclusion for acts that were not accidental. Also, war, as a catastrophic exposure, is excluded, as are communicable disease, sexual molestation, corporal punishment, and mental abuse. Substance abuse is also excluded. Premises that are owned by, rented to, or rented by an insured, but are not insured locations, are also excluded.

As you can see in Table 13.7, there are six more exclusions to coverage E. The first is exclusion of liability of losses charged against the insured as a member of an association or corporation. This is to omit coverage of most contractually assumed liabilities, which are nonfortuitous risks. Duplicate coverage is avoided in the fourth exclusion, where payments for bodily injury are available from various work-related laws. The last two exclude coverage for catastrophic nuclear exposure and coverage for bodily injury to the named insured.

Four exclusions apply to coverage F. The first is for medical payments to resident employees while away from the residence premises and arising out of events not related to employment duties. The second is where other available compensation exists. Third is the nuclear exclusion. The fourth exclusion clarifies the intention of omitting protection for the named insured and resident relatives, all of whom are assumed to be covered by health insurance.

TABLE 13.7   Liability Exclusions for ISO HO-3 Policy (2003)—Appendix A

E. **Coverage E—Personal Liability and Coverage F—Medical Payments to Others**

Coverages **E** and **F** do not apply to the following:

1. Expected or intended injury
2. "Business"
3. Professional services
4. "Insured's" premises not an "insured location"
5. War
6. Communicable disease
7. Sexual molestation, corporal punishment, or physical or mental abuse
8. Controlled substance

F. **Coverage E—Personal Liability**

Coverage **E** does not apply to the following:

1. Liability:

   a. For any loss assessment charged against you as a member of an association, corporation, or community of property owners, except as provided in **D** (see Chapter 24). Loss Assessment under Section **II**—Additional Coverages.

   b. Under any contract or agreement entered into by an "insured." However, this exclusion does not apply to written contracts

      1. that directly relate to the ownership, maintenance, or use of an "insured location"; or

      2. where the liability of others is assumed by you prior to an "occurrence," unless excluded in a. above or elsewhere in this policy.

2. "Property damage" to property owned by an "insured." This includes costs or expenses incurred by an "insured" or others to repair, replace, enhance, restore, or maintain such property to prevent injury to a person or damage to property of others, whether on or away from an "insured location,"

3. "Property damage" to property rented to, occupied or used by, or in the care of an "insured." This exclusion does not apply to "property damage" caused by fire, smoke, or explosion.

4. "Bodily injury" to any person eligible to receive any benefits voluntarily provided or required to be provided by an "insured" under any

   a. worker's compensation law,

   b. nonoccupational disability law, or

   c. occupational disease law.

5. "Bodily injury" or "property damage" for which an "insured" under this policy

   a. is also an insured under a nuclear energy liability policy issued by the

      1. Nuclear Energy Liability Insurance Association,

      2. Mutual Atomic Energy Liability Underwriters,

      3. Nuclear Insurance Association of Canada,

      or any of their successors, or

   b. would be an insured under such a policy but for the exhaustion of its limit of liability

6. "Bodily injury" to you or an "insured" as defined under Definitions **5.a**. or **b**.

   This exclusion also applies to any claim made or suit brought against you or an "insured":

   a. to repay or

   b. Share damages with

   another person who may be obligated to pay damages because of "bodily injury" to an "insured."

G. **Coverage F—Medical Payments to Others**

Coverage **F** does not apply to "bodily injury":

1. To a "residence employee" if the "bodily injury":

    a. Occurs off the "insured location"; and

    b. Does not arise out of or in the course of the "residence employee's" employment by an "insured";

2. To any person eligible to receive benefits voluntarily provided or required to be provided under any:

    a. Workers' compensation law;

    b. Nonoccupational disability law; or

    c. Occupational disease law;

3. From any:

    a. Nuclear reaction;

    b. Nuclear radiation; or

    c. Radioactive contamination;

    all whether controlled or uncontrolled or however caused; or

    d. Any consequence of any of these; or

4. To any person, other than a "residence employee" of an "insured," regularly residing on any part of the "insured location."

Section II—Additional Coverages

Section II of the homeowners policy provides four additional coverage:

a. Claim expenses

b. First-aid expenses

c. Damage to property of others

d. Loss assessment

The claim expenses and first-aid expenses coverages stipulate what the insurer will pay. Claim expenses refer generally to costs associated with litigation, such as premiums on bonds and prejudgment interest assessed against the insured, other than the actual cost of defense. First-aid expenses are those associated with bodily injury liability as covered under the policy and therefore are not limited to the conditions required for medical payments to apply, but they do require the possibility of an insured's liability. The coverage for damage to the property of others is an added (small) benefit to cover others' property losses when you are not liable. You may, at times, feel a moral obligation to pay for someone's property damage, even though you are not legally liable for such damage. This is similar to times when you feel a moral obligation to pay for someone's medical expenses (coverage F). When you are using someone else's property, coverage may exist in Section I, but what about the friend's coat that is damaged by your dog? You are not using the coat, and you'd rather not be sued for it. **Damage to property of others** in form HO-3 provides up to $500 for losses to property belonging to someone other than the insured on the insured's premises, but for which the insured is not liable. Coverage applies even when loss is caused intentionally by an insured who is under thirteen years old, such as when a child throws a rock through a window. These types of intentional activities might be excluded under the liability coverage if the courts consider the child able to "intend" harm. The loss assessment provision is the same as that found in Section I, except that it covers liability assessments instead of property assessments.

damage to property of others

Coverage that provides up to $500 for losses to property belonging to someone other than the insured on the insured's premises, but for which the insured is not liable.

Section II—Conditions

Just as Section I contains a set of limiting conditions, Section II contains a set of conditions that limit and clarify coverage. Section II conditions are listed in Table 13.8.

TABLE 13.8 Homeowners Section II Conditions

> A. Limit of liability
> B. Severability of insurance
> C. Duties after "occurrence"
> D. Duties of an injured person—coverage F—medical payments to others
> E. Payment of claim—coverage F—medical payments to others
> F. Suit against us
> G. Bankruptcy of an "insured"
> H. Other insurance
> I. Policy period
> J. Concealment or fraud

"Limit of liability" clarifies that the maximum coverage available is the amount shown in the declarations. "Severability of insurance" provides coverage separately to each insured, although the total available for any one occurrence is the limit shown in the declarations. "Duties after loss" and "duties of an injured person" are similar to the duties stipulated in the Section I conditions, as is the "suit against us" condition. "Payment of claim, in regard to coverage F," merely emphasizes that payment is made without regard to fault. The "bankruptcy of an insured" condition requires that the insurer be responsible for payment even if the insured has been relieved of his or her obligation due to bankruptcy. Finally, the "other insurance clause" makes coverage E "excess," meaning the policy pays only after another coverage is exhausted. However, if the other coverage has a similar provision, then the allocation is determined as discussed in Chapter 10. For example, if both policies provide the same level of coverage, each carrier will pay half of the loss.

Sections I and II—Conditions

Seven conditions apply to the entire contract. Four are discussed below. Refer to the ISO sample HO-3 policy in Chapter 24 for the conditions not discussed here.

Cancellation

For various reasons, either the insured or the insurer may want to terminate the policy prior to the end of the policy period. You may cancel the policy at any time by giving the insurer written notice. State insurance regulations, however, have increasingly limited the cancellation privileges of insurers. Four situations exist under which the insurer may cancel the policy.

First, nonpayment of premium is a justified reason for cancellation. Second, a new policy in effect less than sixty days may be canceled for any reason with thirty days written notice. Third, in Section C, a material misrepresentation or substantial change (increase) in risk will permit cancellation with a thirty-day written notice. For example, an insured who began to store large amounts of flammables on the premises after purchasing the policy may cause the insurer to cancel the coverage when such use becomes known to the insurer.

Nonrenewal

In Section D, Nonrenewal, the insurer (under the most recent ISO HO-3 in Chapter 24) promises the following: "We will not fail to renew this policy except for one of the reasons referred to in C. Cancellation above. We may refuse to renew for one of the listed reasons by mailing the 'insured' named in the Declarations at the mailing address shown in the policy or at a forwarding address, written notice at least 30 days prior to the expiration date of this policy."

Assignment

Because of the personal nature of insurance, policy rights of ownership are not transferable (assignable) without the written permission of the insurer. As a result, when you sell your house, you cannot automatically transfer the insurance on it to the new owner.

Subrogation

Various provisions that limit overindemnification were discussed in Chapter 9. One of these was subrogation, whereby the insured is required to transfer to the insurer any rights to recovery available from a third party. The transfer is made only to the extent of payment made by the insurer. For example, if part of an airplane detaches and falls on your house, the resulting damage is covered within the limits of your policy because it is a "falling object." Payment is limited by the loss settlement clause and deductible. If you did not have insurance, you likely would attempt to collect from the airline. The insurer, upon payment of your loss, has your right to sue the airline. Generally, the insured will be reimbursed for any out-of-pocket expenses not covered by insurance (such as deductibles and coinsurance) from any amount the insurer collects from the third party. If such collection exceeds the amount paid by the insurer to the insured, then that, too, is the property of the insured. An additional point worth emphasizing is that the insured is precluded from interfering with the insurer's subrogation rights by, for example, settling with a negligent party without the insurer's consent.

KEY TAKEAWAYS

In this section you studied the features of homeowners policies, with particular focus on the Special Form (HO-3):

- Homeowners policies package broad coverages into a single contract
- There are six homeowners policy forms. The focus here is on HO-3 only.
- Homeowners policies are structured as follows: declarations page, section I, section II, and conditions applicable to both sections I and II.
    - Declarations page—specifics that are unique to insured (covered location, policy limits, period of coverage, etc.)
    - Section I coverages—direct and indirect property losses related to the dwelling, other structures, personal property, and loss of use:
        - Coverage A—dwelling
        - Coverage B—other structures
        - Coverage C—personal property
        - Coverage D—loss of use
        - Additional coverages—debris removal, reasonable repair, collapse, and the like
        - Perils insured against—open perils (coverages A–C)
        - Exclusions—nine under A, three under B, concurrent causation, catastrophic exposures
        - Conditions—several items clarifying and limiting coverage if not satisfied
    - Section II coverages—liability
        - Coverage E—personal liability
        - Coverage F—medical payments to others
        - Exclusions—six under E, four under F, losses nonaccidental, catastrophic exposures, liabilities that would be covered by other forms of insurance
        - Additional coverages—claim expenses, first-aid expenses, damage to property of others, loss assessment
        - Conditions—several items clarifying and limiting coverage if not satisfied
    - Conditions applicable to sections I and II—cancellation, nonrenewal, assignment, subrogation
- Provisions of loss settlement clause (under conditions) are used to determine how much of a loss will be compensated.

DISCUSSION QUESTIONS

1. Name three exclusions in Section I of the homeowners policy, and describe why each exclusion is appropriate.

2. Provide an example of a loss covered under Section II of the homeowners policy.

3. Will the inflation guard endorsement alone ensure that you have enough insurance on your home? Why or why not? Discuss the application of the endorsement.

4. What part of the homeowners policy provides coverage when damage to your home makes it unlivable? Explain how this coverage works.

5. The Rupnicks' home was damaged in a fire, forcing them to stay at a nearby hotel for two weeks while repairs were being done. Due to the circumstances, the Rupnicks ate out every day, doubling the amount they would normally spend on food at home during a two-week period to $400. When the Rupnicks filed a claim for damages under their HO-3, they included the $400 cost of eating out as an expense resulting from the fire. How will the insurer respond to this claim for food? Explain.

6. What is the justification for the provision that damage to your home (coverages A and B) will be paid on a replacement basis up to the limits of your coverage if you have coverage equal to 80 percent of replacement cost, but on a less favorable basis if you have a smaller amount of insurance? Do you think this provision is reasonable?

7. What are a policyholder's duties after a loss?

8. Diane has her home and personal property insured under an HO-3 policy and is covering the actual value of the home. She has no endorsements. Indicate whether each of the following losses is covered and indicate what section of the HO-3 policy supports your answer.

    a. A fire damaged the home, destroying two of the end tables in the living room.

    b. The fire also destroyed Diane's fur coat, which was valued at $100,000, and her three computers, valued at $1,500 each.

    c. The house sustained smoke damage from a nearby industrial plant.

    d. A windstorm destroyed five trees in the large yard.

    e. A windstorm caused a tree to fall on the roof. The roof is a total loss.

    f. Diane's dog bit a neighbor's daughter.

    g. Diane hurt her teammate while playing soccer. The teammate was in the hospital for three days.

    h. During a skiing trip, Diane left the fireplace burning in her cabin when she went out. The cabin was destroyed in the fire.

    i. Diane rented a snowmobile on the same trip and collided with a skier. He sued her for $50,000.

    j. Diane is a self-employed dietician who works at home. A client sued her for $30,000.

    k. Diane entertained members of her bridge club and served a wonderful buffet lunch. Three guests became ill and sued Diane for damages. The court awarded each $15,000.

    l. In light of all the losses sustained by Diane, she asked you about improving her coverage. What would you suggest that she do? Think about everything that would improve her coverage using your newly acquired knowledge. Pretend she did not cover the actual value of her home. What would you suggest she do?

3. ENDORSEMENTS

LEARNING OBJECTIVES

In this section we elaborate on endorsements that supplement coverage in the HO-3:

- **Earthquake**
- **Personal property replacement cost**
- **Scheduled personal property**
- **Business pursuits**
- **Personal injury**
- **Mold**

3.1 Earthquake Endorsement

This endorsement can be added to your policy to cover losses such as those suffered by residents of the San Francisco Bay area when a 1989 earthquake caused damage of $20.3 billion. Unfortunately, only approximately 10 percent of the damage was covered by insurance, despite the frequency of earthquakes in California. The low reimbursement rate is due to several factors, including the failure of the majority of homeowners to purchase the endorsement and the effect of a deductible of 2 percent (in some states, 10 percent) of the insurance applicable separately to dwellings and other structures. A minimum deductible of $250 applies to any one loss. The endorsement covers damage caused by earth movement, including earthquakes, landslides, and volcanic eruptions.

3.2 Personal Property Replacement Cost Endorsement

Coverage C of HO-3 pays for loss on an actual cash-value basis, which means replacement cost minus depreciation. Except for something you bought very recently, you are underinsured from the replacement cost point of view. For example, your four-year-old large-screen television might cost $700 to replace today. If it has depreciated 10 percent per year, the insurer will pay you $420 in the event it is stolen or destroyed this year. You will have to find another $280 if you want to replace it. You can protect yourself from this unfavorable development by adding a personal property replacement cost endorsement to your homeowners policy. In the event of a loss, it will pay you the lowest of the following:

- The full cost of replacement (if replacement cost exceeds $500, actual replacement must occur)
- The cost incurred to repair or restore the item
- The limit of coverage C
- Any special limit stipulated in the policy
- Any limit separately added by endorsement

3.3 Scheduled Personal Property Endorsement

Some of the special limits that apply to personal property may be too low for you. Your jewelry or furs, for example, may be worth far more than the $1,000 limit. Such property can be listed and specifically insured to provide adequate coverage against all risks by adding the scheduled personal property endorsement. Another alternative is to pay an extra premium amount to have the main policy's limit for a particular category of personal property, such as jewelry, watches, and furs, increased. (Note, however, that this leaves your coverage on a named-perils basis rather than changing it to open perils.) The insurer may require an appraisal at your expense before agreeing to a specified value.

3.4 Business Pursuits Endorsement

Personal liability coverage and medical payments to others coverage does not apply to bodily injury or property damage arising out of business pursuits of any insured or out of rendering or failing to render professional services. The business pursuits exclusion does not apply, however, to activities that are ordinarily incident to nonbusiness pursuits. For example, your liability exposure in connection with an occasional garage sale would be covered. If you conduct garage sales regularly, however, such activity is a business pursuit and liability coverage does not apply. Liability stemming from rental operations, except for the occasional rental of your residence or rental to no more than two people, is also excluded. Normal part-time employment, such as an after-school job, is not considered a business pursuit. But what about regular, full-time summer employment as a lifeguard? Such employment could be considered a business pursuit. The business pursuits endorsement eliminates these exclusions.

3.5 Personal Injury Endorsement

The liability coverage of your homeowners policy provides protection against losses caused by bodily injury or property damage for which you may be responsible. Bodily injury is defined as bodily harm, sickness, or disease. It does not include the following, which are considered to be personal injury and are added by the personal injury endorsement:

- False arrest, detention, or imprisonment, or malicious prosecution
- Libel, slander, defamation of character, or violation of the right of privacy
- Invasion of the right of private occupation, wrongful eviction, or wrongful entry

Could you become liable for personal injury? Suppose you write a letter to the editor of the local paper in which you make a defamatory statement about a person. You could be sued for libel. Or suppose you make an oral defamatory statement about someone. You could be sued for slander.

3.6 Mold Endorsement

mold exclusions

Endorsement adopted by many states to lower the cost of homeowners insurance, particularly mold claims.

The endorsements of 2002 relate to the **mold exclusions** adopted by many states to lower the cost of homeowners insurance, and particularly mold claims. The ISO "Limited Fungi, Wet or Dry Rot, or Bacteria Coverage" endorsement adds an exclusion to the HO-3 policy (see Chapter 24). This endorsement specifies coverage limits per incidence of mold that are lower than the limits available under the HO-3. The endorsement specifies the following definitions:

SECTION I—PERILS INSURED AGAINST *in form* **HO 00 03**:

A. Coverage A—Dwelling and Coverage B—Other Structures

Paragraph **2.c.(5)** *is deleted and replaced by the following:*

(5) *Caused by constant or repeated seepage or leakage of water or the presence or condensation of humidity, moisture or vapor, over a period of weeks, months or years unless such seepage or leakage of water or the presence or condensation of humidity, moisture or vapor and the resulting damage is unknown to all insureds and is hidden within the walls or ceilings or beneath the floors or above the ceilings of a structure.*

Paragraph **2.c.(6)(c)** *is deleted and replaced by the following:*

(c) *Smog, rust or other corrosion;*

B. Coverage C—Personal Property

12. Accidental Discharge or Overflow of Water or Steam

Paragraph **b.(4)** *is deleted and replaced by the following:*

(4) *Caused by constant or repeated seepage or leakage of water or the presence or condensation of humidity, moisture or vapor, over a period of weeks, months or years unless such seepage or leakage of water or the presence or condensation of humidity, moisture or vapor and the resulting damage is unknown to all insureds and is hidden within the walls or ceilings or beneath the floors or above the ceilings of a structure.*

The following exclusion is added:

SECTION I—EXCLUSIONS

*Exclusion **A.10**. is added.*

10. Fungi, Wet or Dry Rot, or Bacteria

Fungi, Wet or Dry Rot, or Bacteria meaning the presence, growth, proliferation, spread or any activity of fungi, wet or dry rot, or bacteria.

This exclusion does not apply:

A. *When fungi, wet or dry rot, or bacteria results from fire or lightning; or*

B. *To the extent coverage is provided for in the Fungi, Wet or Dry Rot, or Bacteria Additional Coverage under Section **I**—Property Coverages with respect to loss caused by a Peril Insured Against other than fire or lightning.*

Direct loss by a Peril Insured Against resulting from fungi, wet or dry rot, or bacteria is covered.

The only other coverage is what is provided under Additional Coverage as bought by the insured and specified in the following table:

These limits of liability apply to the total of all loss or costs payable under this endorsement, regardless of the number of "occurrences," the number of claims made, or the number of locations insured under this endorsement and listed in this schedule.

1.	Section I—Property Coverage Limit of Liability for the Additional Coverage "Fungi," Wet or Dry Rot, or Bacteria	$
2.	Section **II**—Coverage **E** Aggregate Sublimit of Liability for "Fungi." Wet or Dry Rot, or Bacteria	$
* Entries may be left blank if shown elsewhere in this policy for this coverage.		

Including sections of the endorsement here is a way to provide the student with some explanation of how to read the endorsement in Chapter 24.

KEY TAKEAWAYS

In this section you studied common endorsements that may be added to the HO-3 for additional coverages and coverage of perils that would otherwise be excluded:

- Earthquake endorsement—covers damage caused by earth movement such as landslides, earthquakes, and volcanic eruptions
- Personal property replacement cost—pays the lowest of full cost of replacement, cost incurred to repair/restore item, limit of coverage C, any special limit stipulated in policy, and any limit separately endorsed to policy
- Scheduled personal property—specifies greater limits on particularly valuable personal property
- Business pursuits—applies personal liability and medical payments to others coverage to insureds' business pursuits and professional services
- Personal injury—liability coverage for false arrest, false detention, false imprisonment, malicious prosecution, libel, slander, defamation of character, and the like
- Mold—coverage for fungi, wet or dry rot, or bacteria

DISCUSSION QUESTIONS

1. Why might a homeowners policy provide coverage for losses arising out of business pursuits, even by endorsement?
2. Other than the added cost, what is a drawback to paying extra premium to have the main policy's limit for a particular category of personal property increased?
3. Would you be willing to pay a higher premium for mold coverage as a standard peril in the HO-3 rather than obtain this coverage by endorsement only? In other words, are insurers doing policyholders a favor in excluding mold and offering coverage only by endorsement? Why or why not?

4.   OTHER RISKS

LEARNING OBJECTIVES

In this section we elaborate on the following:
- **Flood exposure and options for flood insurance**
- **Title risk as mitigated through title insurance policies**

Two major risks that are too significant to be retained and cannot be avoided are the possibility of losses by flood or title defect.

4.1   Flood Risk

Homeowners policies exclude loss caused by flood for two reasons: it is considered catastrophic, and it is due to the problem of adverse selection because only those living in flood-prone areas would buy the coverage. This major gap in coverage can be filled by purchasing a flood insurance policy available through the National Flood Insurance Program (NFIP), a federal program that provides flood insurance to flood-prone communities. Communities must apply to the program so that citizens can become eligible to buy flood insurance policies. In addition, the communities must undertake certain required loss-control activities under a program administered by the Federal Insurance Administration. Flood insurance is required by law in order to get secured financing to buy, build, or improve structures in areas that are designated Special Flood Hazard Areas (SFHAs).[12]

The policy covers losses that result directly from river and stream and coastal and lakeshore flooding. Structures that are covered by flood insurance include most types of walled and roofed buildings that are principally above ground and affixed to a permanent site. The contents of a fully enclosed building are also eligible for coverage; however, flood insurance policies do not automatically provide this coverage. It must be specifically requested. Commercial structures, multiple-family dwellings, and single-family residences are also eligible for coverage.

Flood insurance provides coverage for structures and (if covered) personal property or contents on an actual cash value basis. Flood policies do not offer replacement coverage for contents. If a single-family residence is insured for 80 percent of its replacement cost, damage to the structure will be reimbursed on a replacement cost basis.

Two layers of coverage are available. The first is emergency coverage, available to residents of flood-prone communities as soon as the community enters the program. The rates are partially subsidized by the federal government.

Once a flood rate map is completed, a second, or regular, layer of coverage is available at actual rather than subsidized rates. Insurance under the regular program is available only to communities that have passed required ordinances and have undergone studies by the Army Corps of Engineers.

In September 1994, Congress enacted the National Flood Insurance Reform Act.[13] One of the major provisions of the act was to provide for a substantial increase in the amount of flood insurance coverage available. However, after Hurricane Katrina and the floods in New Orleans, these limits appeared too low for the total devastating losses. The rates of flood insurance cost and coverage are shown in Table 13.9.

The Act also increased the waiting period from five to thirty days before a flood insurance policy is effective. This thirty-day waiting period begins the day after the application for flood insurance is made. This is a measure to reduce potential adverse selection from individuals who may be downriver from rising flood waters. The waiting period does not apply to the initial purchase of flood insurance coverage when the purchase is in connection with the making, increasing, extension, or renewal of a loan.

TABLE 13.9 National Flood Insurance Cost and Coverage as of May 2008

For nonresidential, see: http://www.floodsmart.gov/floodsmart/pages/choose_your_policy/policy_rates.jsp Flood Quick-Quote: **Residential** Rates Effective May 1, 2008

Moderate-to-Low Risk Areas

RESIDENTIAL: Preferred Risk Policy (ZONES B, C, X)

(PRE-/POST-FIRM)

A residential policy, based on preferred rates for qualified structures in moderate-to-low risk areas. A Preferred Risk Policy offers two types of coverage: Building & Contents and Contents Only.

Building & Contents			Contents Only [14] , [15]		
Coverage	Annual Premium [16] , [17]		Coverage	Annual Premium [18]	
	Without Basement or Enclosure	With Basement or Enclosure		Contents above Ground (More Than One Floor)	All Other Locations (Basement Only Not Eligible)
$20,000/ $8,000	$119	$144	$8,000	$39	$58
$30,000/ $12,000	$148	$173	$12,000	$53	$80
$50,000/ $20,000	$196	$221	$20,000	$81	$113
$75,000/ $30,000	$230	$260	$30,000	$93	$130
$100,000/ $40,000	$257	$287	$40,000	$105	$147
$125,000/ $50,000	$277	$307	$50,000	$117	$164
$150,000/ $60,000	$296	$326	$60,000	$129	$181
$200,000/ $80,000	$326	$361	$80,000	$153	$201
$250,000/ $100,000	$348	$388	$100,000	$177	$221

Note: Residential condominium associations are not eligible for the Preferred Risk Policy. Individual residential condominium units in residential condominium buildings are eligible for the Preferred Risk Policy. In addition, individual residential condominium unit owners in nonresidential condominium buildings are only eligible for contents coverage. The deductibles apply separately to building and contents. Building deductible, $500. Contents deductible, $500.

To qualify for replacement cost claim settlement, a single-family dwelling must be the insured's primary residence and be insured to the maximum amount of insurance available under the program or no less than 80 percent of the replacement cost at the time of loss. Please refer to the policy or manual for further explanation and requirements.

RESIDENTIAL: Standard Rated Policy (ZONES B, C, X)
(PRE-/POST-FIRM)

A residential policy, based on standard rates, for moderate-to-low risk areas offers three types of coverage: Building and Contents, Building Only, and Contents Only.

Building and Contents		Building Only		Contents Only	
Coverage	Annual Premium[19]	Coverage	Annual Premium[20]	Coverage	Annual Premium[21]
$35,000/$10,000	$434	$35,000	$314	$10,000	$155
$50,000/$15,000	$611	$50,000	$431	$15,000	$215
$75,000/$20,000	$724	$75,000	$484	$20,000	$275
$100,000/$30,000	$813	$100,000	$536	$30,000	$312
$125,000/$40,000	$903	$125,000	$589	$40,000	$349
$150,000/$50,000	$992	$150,000	$641	$50,000	$386
$250,000/$100,000	$1,385	$250,000	$849	$100,000	$571

Higher deductible limits are available, up to $5,000 for single-family properties.

The community rating system (CRS) is a voluntary incentive program that recognizes and encourages community floodplain management activities that exceed the minimum NFIP requirements. As a result, flood insurance premium rates are discounted to reflect the reduced flood risk resulting from the community actions. To learn more about CRS and to see if your community participates, go to FEMA's CRS Web page, at http://www.fema.gov/business/nfip/crs.shtm.

Note: Single-family dwellings that are primary residences and insured to the maximum amount of insurance available under the program or no less than 80 percent of the replacement cost at the time of loss may qualify for replacement cost claim settlement. All other buildings and contents will be adjusted based on their actual cash value (depreciated cost). Please refer to the policy for further explanation and requirements.

High-Risk Areas
RESIDENTIAL: Standard Rated Policy (A ZONES)

A residential policy, based on standard rates, for high-risk areas offers three types of coverage: Building and Contents, Building Only, and Contents Only.

Building and Contents		Building Only		Contents Only	
Coverage	Annual Premium[22]	Coverage	Annual Premium[23]	Coverage	Annual Premium[24]
$35,000/$10,000	$509	$35,000	$403	$10,000	$145
$50,000/$15,000	$686	$50,000	$528	$15,000	$201
$75,000/$20,000	$887	$75,000	$676	$20,000	$256
$100,000/$30,000	$1,143	$100,000	$825	$30,000	$367
$125,000/$40,000	$1,399	$125,000	$974	$40,000	$479
$150,000/$50,000	$1,653	$150,000	$1,122	$50,000	$590
$250,000/$100,000	$2,766	$250,000	$1,701	$100,000	$1,148

These example premiums were calculated for a post-FIRM home, built at base flood elevation in a zone AE. Your building may be different; check with your insurance agent for a rate specific to your building's risk.

The community rating system (CRS) is a voluntary incentive program that recognizes and encourages community floodplain management activities that exceed the minimum NFIP requirements. As a result, flood insurance premium rates are discounted to reflect the reduced flood risk resulting from the community actions. To learn more about CRS and to see if your community participates, go to FEMA's CRS Web page, at http://www.fema.gov/business/nfip/crs.shtm.

Note: Single-family dwellings that are primary residences and insured to the maximum amount of insurance available under the program or no less than 80 percent of the replacement cost at the time of loss may qualify for replacement cost claim settlement. All other buildings and contents will be adjusted based on their actual cash value (depreciated cost) Please refer to the policy for further explanation and requirements.

The National Flood Insurance Reform Act added an optional extension for mitigation insurance to help policyholders rebuild their substantially, repetitively damaged homes and businesses according to the floodplain management code, including their community's flood proofing and mitigation regulations. This was previously unavailable under the flood insurance policy; however, substantially damaged structures were still required to be rebuilt according to the floodplain management code.

Flood insurance may be required by law, such as under the Federal Housing Authority (FHA), Veterans Affairs (VA), and federally insured bank or savings and loan association mortgage agreements. Under a provision in the National Flood Insurance Reform Act of 1994, if a lender discovers at any time during the term of a loan that a building is located in a special flood hazard area, the lender must notify the borrower that flood insurance is required. If the borrower fails to respond, the lender must purchase coverage on behalf of the borrower.

Flood insurance can be purchased through any licensed property or casualty insurance agent or from some direct writing insurers. Some insurers actually issue the flood insurance policies, in partnership with the federal government, as a service and convenience for their policyholders. In those instances, the insurer handles the premium billing and collection, policy issuance, and loss adjustment on behalf of the federal government. These insurers are called Write Your Own (WYO) insurers. Another important result of the National Flood Insurance Reform Act of 1994 involves the availability of Federal Disaster Relief funds following a flood disaster. Individuals who live in communities located in special flood hazard areas that participate in the National Flood Insurance Program and who do not buy flood insurance no longer are eligible for automatic federal disaster aid for property losses suffered as a result of a flood.

Federal Disaster Assistance

Federal disaster funds are given to victims of floods for assistance in rebuilding their lives. The Federal Disaster Fund is usually activated when an area is declared a disaster by the president. The funds are provided to the victims at a low interest rate. The example in Figure 13.4 was designed by the Federal Emergency Management Agency to educate residents of flood-prone areas about the value of obtaining flood insurance. Questions regarding flood coverage in the aftermath of hurricanes Katrina and Rita prompted FEMA's press release shown in the box "Insurance Coverage for Flood and Wind-Driven Rain."

FIGURE 13.4   A $50,000 Flood Damage Repair Cost Comparison

Insurance Coverage for Flood and Wind-Driven Rain

Press Release, October 22, 2005.

BATON ROUGE, La.—To receive appropriate financial coverage for water damage sustained from hurricanes Katrina and/or Rita, the definition of the type of damage is necessary. The U.S. Department of Homeland Security's Federal Emergency Management Agency (FEMA) and the State of Louisiana are offering the following guidelines to better understand flood and wind-driven rain damage.

The simple definition of a flood is an excess of water on land that is normally dry. The National Flood Insurance Program includes in their definition inland tidal waters; unusual and rapid accumulation or runoff of surface waters **from any source**; collapse or subsidence of land along the shore of a lake or similar body of water as a result of erosion or undermining caused by waves or currents of water exceeding anticipated cyclical levels that result in a flood.

Homeowner, renter and business owner insurance policies **DO NOT** cover flooding. Generally, policies will cover wind, rain, hail, *wind-driven rain*, and lightning damage. A separate flood insurance policy is needed to protect homes, businesses and personal property against flood damage. If a home, business or other residence is in a FEMA-identified high risk flood zone, a separate flood insurance policy should have been required on a mortgage transaction.

Rain, wind-driven rain, and hail damage are not in the same damage category as floods. Wind-driven rain damage, regardless of the cause, is a covered peril like wind or lightning, which may have caused an opening in which rain has entered and caused water damage to the home or personal property.

If people affected by hurricanes Katrina and/or Rita have suffered both flood and wind-driven rain damage, it should be reported to the flood insurance carrier as well as to the homeowner, tenant, or business owner insurance carrier. It is likely that a separate adjuster will be assigned for each claim. Adjusters should communicate with each other to coordinate information prior to final settlement.

To get more information about the insurance coverage, visit the Louisiana Department of Insurance online at http://www.ldi.state.la.us or call toll-free at 1-800-259-5300. For questions about the National Flood Insurance Program, call your insurance agent or 1-800-427-4661 or log onto http://www.floodsmart.gov to learn more.

Source: FEMA Web site at http://www.fema.gov/news/newsrelease.fema?id=19938, accessed March 20, 2009.

4.2 Title Risk

title defect

A claim against property that has not been satisfied.

A **title defect** is a claim against property that has not been satisfied. One example of such a claim is a lien filed by an unpaid worker or materials supplier. Another example is a spouse whose signature does not appear on the deed signed by the other spouse when the property was sold. The claim is based on the spouse's community property interest in the couple's real property, regardless of who originally paid for it.

If there is a defect in the title to your property, an informed buyer will insist that it be removed (cleared) before the title is acceptable, even though it may have originated many years ago. The clearing process can be time-consuming and expensive. A title insurance policy protects the home buyer against loss caused by a defect in the title that existed at the time the policy was issued. It does not cover defects that come into existence after the policy is issued. The insurer says,

> *If anything was wrong with the title to this property at the time this policy was issued, we will defend you and pay for the loss caused when it is discovered, within policy limits.*

Before making this promise, the insurer attempts to determine if defects exist. If any are found, they are described in the policy and excluded from coverage, or a policy is not issued until they have been removed. A single premium is paid for the policy, and it remains in force indefinitely. As a general rule, it cannot be assigned. When title to the property is transferred, the purchaser must buy his or her own title insurance policy if protection is desired.

KEY TAKEAWAYS

In this section you studied losses by flood or title defect and their insurance solutions:

- Flood is excluded from homeowners policies because it is considered catastrophic and due to the problem of adverse selection.
- The federal government offers flood insurance, through the National Flood Insurance Program (NFIP), to flood-prone communities.
- Flood insurance is required by law to secure financing to buy, build, or improve structures in special flood hazard areas (SFHAs) and under federally insured bank or savings and loan association mortgage agreements.
- Flood insurance offers replacement cost coverage for a residence and actual cash value only for personal property.
- Emergency coverage is available at partially subsidized rates as soon as a community enters the National Flood Insurance Program; regular coverage at actual rates is available to communities that have passed required ordinances.
- Federal disaster funds are distributed to victims of floods when an area is declared a disaster.
- Clearing title defects can be costly and time-consuming.
- Title insurance protects a home buyer against loss caused by a title defect that existed at the time the policy was issued.

DISCUSSION QUESTIONS

1. Is advertising flood insurance through the National Flood Insurance Program encouraging adverse selection? Why or why not?
2. What is the significance of WYO insurers with respect to flood insurance?
3. Should there be limits on the number of insurable losses or the amount of compensation to which a single insured is eligible to claim under a flood policy?
4. What might cause a title defect?
5. What protection is provided by title insurance, and who receives that protection?

5. PERSONAL UMBRELLA LIABILITY POLICIES

LEARNING OBJECTIVES

In this section we elaborate on the use of umbrella liability policies as an extra layer of liability protection. Umbrella liability policies protect against catastrophic losses by providing high limits over underlying coverage. There are no standard umbrella policies as there are in auto and home insurance. All, however, have the following characteristics in common:

- **They are excess over a basic coverage**
- **They are broader than most liability policies**
- **They require specified amounts and kinds of underlying coverage**
- **They have exclusions**

5.1 Excess and Broad

Unlike other liability policies, umbrella policies do not provide first-dollar coverage. They pay only after the limits of underlying coverage, such as your auto or homeowners policy, have been exhausted. Furthermore, they cover some exposures not covered by underlying coverage. A typical umbrella policy covers personal injury liability, for example, whereas auto and homeowners policies do not. When there is no underlying coverage for a covered exposure, however, a deductible is applied. Some personal umbrella liability policies have deductibles (also called the retained limit) as small as $250, but deductibles of $5,000 or $10,000 are not uncommon.

5.2 Minimum Underlying Coverage

Buyers of umbrella coverage are required to have specified minimum amounts of underlying coverage. If you buy a personal umbrella policy, for example, you may be required to have at least $100,000/$300,000/$50,000[25] (or a single limit of $300,000) auto liability coverage and $300,000 personal liability coverage (Section II in your homeowners policy). If you have other specified exposures, such as aircraft or boats excluded by your homeowners policy, the insurer will require underlying coverage of specified minimum limits. Clearly, an umbrella liability policy is not a substitute for adequate basic coverage with reasonable limits.

5.3 Exclusions

Umbrella policies are broad, but they are not without limitations. Typically, they exclude the following:

- Obligations under workers' compensation, unemployment compensation, disability benefits, or similar laws
- Owned or rented aircraft, watercraft excluded by the homeowners policy, business pursuits, and professional services, unless there is underlying coverage
- Property damage to any property in the care, custody, or control of the insured, or owned by the insured
- Any act committed by or at the direction of the insured with intent to cause personal injury or property damage
- Personal injury or property damage for which the insured is covered under a nuclear energy liability policy

KEY TAKEAWAYS

In this section you studied the following features of personal umbrella liability policies:

- Umbrella liability policies protect against catastrophic losses by providing high limits over underlying coverage.
- Umbrella policies are excess and broad in coverage provided.
- Buyers must have specified minimum amounts of underlying coverage to be eligible.
- Several exclusions exist in umbrella policies.

DISCUSSION QUESTIONS

1. Under what conditions should a homeowner consider the purchase of a personal umbrella policy?
2. Are there any common features among the exclusions in umbrella liability policies?
3. Why might the deductibles for umbrella policies be so high?

6. SHOPPING FOR HOMEOWNERS INSURANCE

LEARNING OBJECTIVE

- **In this section we elaborate on strategies for acquiring the most suitable insurance at the lowest relative cost**

You can buy insurance for your home from many different sources, and premiums can vary greatly. As with any kind of purchase, price is not the sole consideration, but the possibility of saving 40 or 50 percent a year on your home insurance is worth some effort. The range of prices may not be as great where you live, but there is likely enough variation to justify shopping around. The startling difference between high and low prices clearly demonstrates that it pays to shop for home insurance.

There are three steps to shopping for homeowners coverage:

- Figure out what you have
- Figure out what you want
- Collect your quotes and information about insurers before making your final decision

These steps are illustrated in the case of the Smith family mentioned earlier in the chapter. You will need to inventory your possessions and organize all the information the insurer will need. Taking photos of your property and keeping the photos in a safe place away from your home is a good method of maintaining an inventory list. Figure 13.5 shows the information about your property that you will need to provide to your insurer, including details such as construction (brick, frame), access to fire hydrants, location, age, and security. The location of the property is important and may cause you to have to pay higher premiums. The issue of redlining—higher premiums for homes in inner cities—is discussed in the box "Redlining: Urban Discrimination Myth or Reality?"

FIGURE 13.5 Homeowners Insurance Quotation Worksheet

Applicant: _____

Address of property to be insured: _____

Number of losses in last 3 years if covered by insurance: _____

Dwelling:

Number of apartments or households in building: _____

Construction:				Major Options	
(frame, brick, etc.)	_____	Age of dwelling	_____	Central air	_____
Number of stories	_____	Age of roof	_____	Cen. vacuum	_____
Number of rooms	_____	Age/type of furnace	_____	Cen. bur. al.	_____
Total square feet	_____			Smoke dec.	_____
				Other	_____

Owner occupant   ☐ Yes   ☐ No

Inside city limits   ☐ Yes   ☐ No

Outside city limits   ☐ Yes   ☐ No

Current Dwelling Replacement Cost	Current Market Value of Dwelling & Land	Purchase Price of Dwelling
Name of Fire Department	Distance from Hydrant/Station	

Cost of Your Insurance _____

Annual Premium _____

Property Coverage & Amount (% of replacement cost)

			Company Name _____	Company Name _____
A.	Dwelling	_____	$	$
B.	Appurtenant structures	_____	$	$
C.	Unscheduled personal property	_____	$	$
D.	Additional living expense	_____	$	$

Liability Coverage & Amount

E.	Personal liability (bodily injury and property damage)	_____	$	$
F.	Medical payments	_____	$	$
	Deductible amount		$	$
	Scheduled personal property		$	$
	Other coverage(s)		$	$
Total Annual Premium			$	$
	Installment charges		$	$
Total Annual Cost of Homeowners' Insurance			$	$

Next, you need to decide what insurance you want and the amounts of coverage, for example:

- Coverage A (dwelling) $100,000
- Coverage E (liability) $25,000
- Coverage F (medical payments) $500 per person

You will also need to choose your deductibles, such as $100, $250, and $500, and limits on coverages E and F, such as $100,000 or $300,000 on coverage E.

Finally, collect quotes from potential insurers. You might choose a couple of online or direct-mail insurers, some independent agents, and some exclusive-agency companies. Taking into account any differences in coverage, compare annual premiums and decide which company will provide what you want at the best price, as is demonstrated in Case 1 of Chapter 23.

KEY TAKEAWAYS

In this section you studied the general notion of liability and the related legal aspects thereof:

- It is worth shopping around for home insurance because savings can amount to 40 to 50 percent per year.
- The first step in seeking coverage is to perform a thorough inventory of possessions and gather information pertinent to an insurer.
- The second step is deciding on the insurance, the amounts of coverage desired, and the deductibles.
- The final step is to collect quotes from potential insurers.

DISCUSSION QUESTIONS

1. What might account for cost differentials between policies that offer the same limits of coverage?
2. In your experience, is cost the bottom line when it comes to the purchase of insurance? Does service factor into the decision?

7.   REVIEW AND PRACTICE

1. Why might auto policies exclude compact disks and players?
2. Identify the major factors that determine the cost of a homeowners policy.
3. Bill has a homeowners policy with form HO-3. His home has a replacement value of $80,000, and the contents are worth $45,000 at replacement cost or $35,000 at actual cash value. He has a detached greenhouse with heat and humidity control that houses his prized collection of exotic flowers. The flowers are valued at $11,000, and the greenhouse would cost $7,500 to replace at today's prices. His policy has the following coverages:

Dwellings	$60,000
Unscheduled personal property	$30,000
Personal liability, per occurrence	$25,000

A property coverage deductible of $250 per occurrence applies. Analyze each of the following situations in light of the above information. Determine all applicable coverage(s) and limit(s), and explain all factors that might affect the coverage provided by the policy.

   a. A windstorm causes $20,000 in repair cost damages to the house, and subsequent wind-blown rain causes damage to the contents of the house—$18,000 in replacement cost or $11,000 at actual cash value. The greenhouse is a total loss, as are the exotic plants. Debris removal of the greenhouse to satisfy the city's health laws costs $350, and further debris removal to clear the way for repairs costs another $280. Two maple trees valued at $600 each are blown down, and their removal costs another $400. Bill must move his family to a nearby rental home for two months while repairs are made to the house. Rental costs are $600 per month, utilities at the rental house are $150 more per month, and the mortgage payments of $550 per month continue to be payable. It costs Bill another $80 per month to commute to work and to drive his children to school. The telephone company charges him $50 to change his telephone to the rental unit and back to his home again.

   b. After Bill and his family return to their home, faulty wiring installed during repair causes a short and a small fire. All the family clothing has to be washed because of smoke damage, at a cost of $1,200. Repair to the walls requires an additional $4,700. What might be the effect of subrogation in this case?

4. What is the mortgage clause in the HO-3 policy?

5. Ms. Gotcheaux's home in San Francisco was damaged by an earthquake. The earthquake caused a gas line to explode and a fire broke out, completely destroying the house. Ms. Gotcheaux's homeowners policy explicitly excludes coverage for any damage caused by earth movement. Nevertheless, she files a claim with her insurer under her HO-3 policy. As Ms. Gotcheaux's insurer, how would you handle her claim?

6. Brenda Joy is an accountant in a small Kansas town. She works out of her home, which has a replacement value of $125,000 and an actual cash value of $105,000. Brenda purchased an HO-3 with the following limits:

Coverage A:	$110,000, $250 deductible
Coverage E:	$300,000
Coverage F:	$5,000

Discuss the application of Brenda's HO-3 to the following losses.

   a. One of Brenda's clients sues her for negligent accounting advice. The lawsuit alleges damages of $75,000.

   b. A friend of Brenda's visits at Brenda's home and trips over a stack of books Brenda laid on the floor temporarily. Brenda takes the friend to the hospital, where treatment costs $645.

   c. Brenda is the star pitcher for the local softball team. Unfortunately, Brenda's game was off last month and she beaned an opponent. The opponent's attorney filed a notice of claim against Brenda, asserting damages of $500,000.

   d. Neighborhood children often run through Brenda's yard. Recently, a group did just that, with one child falling over a rock hidden in the grass. The child needed stitches and an overnight stay in the hospital. It is not clear if the child's parents will sue.

7. Where are exclusions found in the homeowners insurance policy? List some standard exclusions.

8. Lisbeth is a college student living in a dorm. She has a television, DVD player, stereo, and a number of CDs and DVDs. She also has a lot of expensive clothing. Her parents' homeowners policy provides $120,000 of protection for coverage A. Do you think Lisbeth should get her own policy to cover her personal property?

9. As a newly graduated lawyer, Quinn Krueger was able to find a well-paying job and, as a result, could afford a large enough mortgage to buy a nice house. The mortgage company required that Quinn also purchase a homeowners policy, and so Quinn obtained an HO-3 with $95,000 on coverage A (the replacement cost value), $60,000 for coverage C, $100,000 on coverage E, and $2,000 on coverage F. How would Quinn's insurer react to the following losses? Explain.

   a. Coming home late one night, Quinn accidentally drives her car into the corner of her attached garage. Damage to the garage involves repairs of $2,300. The car needs repairs costing $3,200.

   b. Quinn owns an electric guitar and likes to play it loudly. Neighbors sue Quinn for nuisance, claiming damages of $25,000 (the reduction in the value of their house).

   c. Heavy snowfall, followed by rapid melting, results in high water levels. Quinn finds herself dealing with an overflow in her basement. It causes $2,700 in damage to personal property and requires repairs of $1,700 to the basement.

   d. Thieves are not common in Quinn's neighborhood, but police believe that a group of crafty criminals broke into her house. The break-in damages the doorway, requiring $685 in repairs. The thieves take a Persian rug valued at $8,300, a television worth $500, jewelry assessed at $3,000, a CD player costing $450, and silverware worth $1,200.

10. Homeowners insurance pays medical expenses under what circumstances?

ENDNOTES

1. Dalit Baranoff, "Shaped by Risk: Fire Insurance in America 1790–1920," Ph.D. dissertation, Johns Hopkins University, 2003.

2. Mark E. Ruguet, "Fire Fight Est. $67 M, Total $2 B," *National Underwriter Online News Service*, November 3, 2003.

3. David R. Blossom, "Club Fires Spur Major Changes In Fire Codes," *National Underwriter*, January 20, 2005, http://www.propertyandcasualtyinsurancenews.com/cms/NUPC/Weekly%20Issues/Issues/2005/03/p03club_fires?searchfor=club%20fires (accessed March 20, 2009).

4. See Victoria Police, "Bushfires Death Toll," February 24, 2009, http://www.police.vic.gov.au/content.asp?Document_ID=19190 (accessed February 26, 2009); Cheryl Critchley, "Hospitals Stretched as 500 Treated for Burns," *Daily Telegraph*, February 10, 2009, http://www.news.com.au/dailytelegraph/story/0,22049,25031406-5001021,00.html (accessed February 26, 2009); John Huxley, "Horrific, but Not the Worst We've Suffered," *Sydney Morning Herald*, February 11, 2009, http://www.smh.com.au/national/horrific-but-not-the-worst-weve-suffered-20090210-83ib.html (accessed February 26, 2009); Erin Cassar, "Doctors Treating Bushfire Burns Victims Around the Clock," ABC News, February 9, 2009, http://www.abc.net.au/news/stories/2009/02/09/2486698.htm (accessed February 26, 2009).

5. Sam Friedman, "Katrina Leads Pack of Record Hurricanes Worst Disaster Ever Combines with Rita, Wilma to Cause $45.2 Billion in Losses," *National Underwriter*, January 10, 2006, accessed March 20, 2009, http://www.propertyandcasualtyinsurancenews.com/cms/NUPC/Weekly%20Issues/Issues/2005/48/2005%20Top%2010%20Stories/P48-2005-TOP10-Hurricanes?searchfor=worst%20disaster%20ever;.

6. "Record Homeowners Insurance Claim Payments from 2005 Hurricanes Equal to 25 Years of Louisiana Homeowners Premiums, Says I.I.I. $12.4 Billion in Homeowners Insurance Claims to Be Paid in Louisiana Alone; Homeowners Insurers Will Begin Reassessment of Risk in State," Insurance Information Institute (III). January 5, 2006, accessed March 20, 2009, http://www.iii.org/media/updates/press.748181/.

7. Joanne Wojcik, "Colorado Bill Would Bar Nonrenewals in Wildfire Areas," *Business Insurance*, July 11, 2002.

8. E. E. Mazier, "Alabama OKs ISO Mold Endorsement," *National Underwriter Online News Service*, February 26, 2002: "In terms of property coverage, Alabama homeowners will have a choice of three limits—$10,000, $25,000 or $50,000—on claims payouts within a policy year…. The limits for liability are $50,000 and $100,000…. Liability coverage would apply if, for example, a guest developed an illness due to exposure to mold in the host's home." See also Michael Ha, "Maryland Regulator OKs Mold Exclusion," *National Underwriter Online News Service*, July 8, 2003.

9. *Safeco Insurance Co. of America v. Guyton*, 692 F.2d 551 (1982), and *Premier Insurance Co. v. Welch*, 140 Cal.App.3d 420 (1983).

10. A mortgagee is the lending agency; when you borrow money to buy a home, you sign a note and a mortgage. You are the mortgagor who executes a mortgage in favor of the mortgagee. A bailee is a person who holds another person's property; the bailor is the person who leaves his or her property with the bailee.

11. If the one-year time limit conflicts with state law, the law prevails. In South Carolina, for example, it is six years.

12. Federal Emergency Management Agency, Accessed March 20, 2009, http://www.fema.gov/nfip/nfip.htm.

13. Federal Insurance and Mitigation Administration (FIMA) is part of the Federal Emergency Management Agency (FEMA). The National Flood Insurance Program (NFIP) is under FEMA: http://www.fema.gov/nfip/laws.htm (accessed March 20, 2009).

14. Add the $50.00 Probation Surcharge, if applicable.

15. Contents-only policies are not available for contents located in basement only.

16. Premium includes Federal Policy Fee of $13.00.

17. Premium includes ICC premium fee of $6.00. Deduct this amount if the risk is a condominium unit.

18. Premium includes Federal Policy Fee of $13.00.

19. Includes a federal policy fee of $35 and ICC premium.

20. Includes a federal policy fee of $35 and ICC premium.

21. Includes a federal policy fee of $35 only.

22. Includes a federal policy fee of $35 and ICC premium.

23. Includes a federal policy fee of $35 and ICC premium.

24. Higher deductible limits are available, up to $5,000 for single-family properties.

25. Automobile limits are explained in Chapter 14. These values represent $100,000 coverage per person for bodily injury liability and $300,000 total for all bodily injury liability per accident. Property damage liability coverage is $50,000 per accident.

Multirisk Management Contracts: Auto

Automobiles are an essential part of American society. In the beginning of the new millennium, there were approximately 156 million cars, vans, trucks, and sport-utility vehicles insured in the United States. The expenditures for auto insurance have declined in recent years, as shown in Table 14.1. Factors contributing to the decrease are safer cars, better safety devices, and less fraud and theft. These factors are somewhat diminished by overall increases in litigation and medical costs, as indicated in the private passenger auto insurance losses of Table 14.2[1]

TABLE 14.1 Average Expenditures on Auto Insurance, United States, 1997–2006

Year	Average Expenditure	Percentage Change	Year	Average Expenditure	Percentage Change
1997	$705	2.0%	2002	$786	8.3%
1998	$703	−0.3	2003	$830	5.6
1999	$685	−2.6	2004	$842	1.4
2000	$690	0.7	2005	$831	−1.3
2001	$726	5.2	2006	$817	−1.7

Source: © 2007 National Association of Insurance Commissioners. Source: Insurance Information Institute (III), accessed March 21, 2009, http://www.iii.org.

According to the U.S. Department of Transportation's National Highway Traffic Safety Administration, an auto accident death occurs, on average, every twelve minutes, and an injury occurs every eleven seconds. Vehicle occupants accounted for 74 percent of traffic deaths in 2007.[2]

Drunk driving (driving while intoxicated [DWI] or driving under the influence [DUI]) contributes dramatically to fatalities on the road. In 2007, 12,998 traffic deaths were related to drunk driving. Most states have DWI or DUI laws that include lower blood-alcohol level tolerances for drivers under the age of twenty-one.[3]

TABLE 14.2 Auto Insurance Claims Frequency and Severity for Bodily Injury, Property Damage, Collision, and Comprehensive, 1998–2007

Liability				
	Bodily Injury[4]		Property Damage[5]	
Year	Claim Frequency[6]	Claim Severity[7]	Claim Frequency[8]	Claim Severity[9]
1998	1.26	$9,437	3.97	$2,240
1999	1.23	9,646	4.00	2,294
2000	1.20	9,807	3.98	2,393
2001	1.16	10,149	3.97	2,471
2002	1.15	10,400	3.92	2,552
2003	1.16	10,662	3.87	2,606
2004	1.14	11,079	3.78	2,624
2005	1.10	11,423	3.67	2,693
2006	1.03	12,020	3.49	2,811
2007	1.00	12,296	3.54	2,869

Physical Damage[10]				
	Collision		Comprehensive[11]	
Year	Claim Frequency[12]	Claim Severity[13]	Claim Frequency[14]	Claim Severity[15]
1998	5.39	$2,273	2.93	$1,078
1999	5.73	2,352	2.80	1,116
2000	5.61	2,480	2.89	1,125
2001	5.53	2,525	3.11	1,152
2002	5.48	2,728	2.91	1,250
2003	5.17	2,919	2.75	1,331
2004	4.88	3,073	2.45	1,420
2005	5.05	3,062	2.37	1,456
2006	4.88	3,189	2.39	1,529
2007	5.14	3,131	2.46	1,519
Source: ISO.				
* For all limits combined. Data are for paid claims.				

Source: "Automobile Insurance Overview," Insurance Information Institute, accessed March 21, 2009, http://www.iii.org/media/facts/statsbyissue/auto/.

To alleviate the economic risk of getting hurt or hurting someone else in an automobile accident, the law in most states requires automobile owners to buy automobile insurance. In this chapter we will learn about the following:

1. Links

2. The fault system and financial responsibility laws

3. Ensuring auto insurance availability

4. Types of automobile policies and the personal automobile policy (PAP)

5. Auto insurance premium rates

1. LINKS

At this point in our study, we are still in the realm of different types of personal lines coverages. As with the homeowners policy, the automobile policy combines both property and liability coverage in one package. The liability part is now at the front of the policy rather than the property part, as is the case in the homeowners policy.

As part of our holistic risk management, we need to be sure that when we are on the road we are covered. If we hurt anyone, we may be sued for every penny we and our parents ever earned. If we get hurt or damage our own cars, we may not be able to get to work, or we may be out of work for a long time. As you saw in the statistics above, car accidents do occur and no one is immune to them.

FIGURE 14.1 Links between Holistic Risk Pieces and Auto Policies

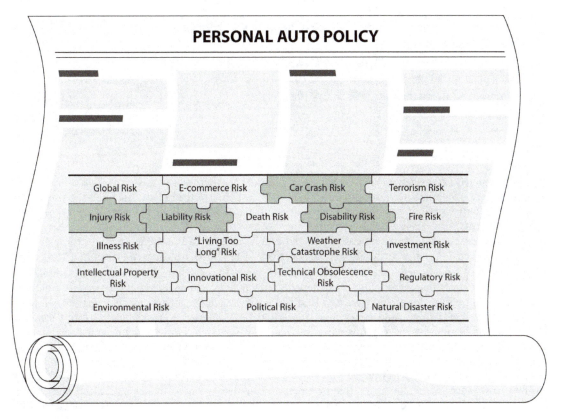

The personal auto line prices are not increasing as quickly as in the beginning of the new millennium. Of course, the premium level for each driver depends on the specific pricing factors for private passenger automobiles such as location, classification, car make, and so forth. Regardless of your individual rating factors, you know by now that external market conditions affect your risk management decision (as you saw in Chapter 8). When rates are high, for example, you may decide to use higher deductibles for your automobile coverage.

In addition to understanding how the market conditions affect our risk management decision in the area of automobile insurance, the concepts we studied thus far will be helpful in quickly capturing the essence of auto coverage and the particulars of the wording in the policy. Here, we need to know not only what coverage we have but also what is required by the various state laws. You will have the opportunity to delve into an actual policy (Chapter 25) and complete your understanding of this important and costly risk. Figure 14.1 connects this topic to our holistic risk puzzle. An example of the automobile coverage of the Smith family mentioned in Chapter 13 is provided in Case 1 of Chapter 23. The case shows how a family creates a complete risk management portfolio.

2. THE FAULT SYSTEM AND FINANCIAL RESPONSIBILITY LAWS

LEARNING OBJECTIVES

In this section we elaborate on the following:

- **The functioning of no-fault compensation systems for automobile accidents**
- **Forms of no-fault systems**
- **Arguments in favor of and against no-fault laws**
- **The purpose of financial responsibility laws**
- **How financial responsibility laws are satisfied**

2.1 The Fault System

personal injury protection (PIP) and medical payments (Med Pay)

Compensation paid to insureds for medical expenses, lost wages, replacement service costs, and funeral expenses incurred as a result of an automobile accident.

no-fault

Insurance laws under which benefits are provided by insurers without regard to who caused the accident.

pure no-fault

Theoretical insurance laws that would pay only specific damages (economic losses, such as medical expenses and lost wages), but these would be unlimited.

An issue debated extensively over the past several decades is whether or not to maintain a fault-based compensation mechanism for automobile accidents. In response to the debate, over half the states have passed mandatory first-party benefits (also known as no-fault) laws. Subject to various limitations, such laws require that insurers compensate insureds for the insureds' medical expenses, lost wages, replacement service costs, and funeral expenses incurred as a result of an automobile accident; these are collectively referred to as **personal injury protection (PIP) and medical payments (Med Pay)** Under **no-fault** laws, benefits are provided by insurers without regard to who caused the accident.

Under the no-fault concept, first-party benefits such as PIP are provided without regard to fault as a way to avoid legal battles. If you were involved in a multicar accident where tort law applied, a lawsuit between the parties likely would result. The suit would be an attempt to place blame for the accident, thereby also placing financial responsibility for the losses incurred. Under the no-fault concept, each injured party would receive compensation from his or her own insurance company. There would be no need to expend resources in determining fault. Furthermore, the worry of being hit by someone who does not have automobile liability insurance would be eliminated. You already have a form of limited no-fault insurance in the coverages that compensate for damage to your car (discussed later in the chapter). The no-fault PIP or Med Pay benefits extend first-party coverage to expenses associated with bodily injury.

No-fault automobile laws are not uniform, yet they typically fall into three categories. Table 14.3 lists the laws in each state. **Pure no-fault** exists only theoretically and would abolish completely the opportunity to litigate over automobile accidents. Only specific damages (economic losses, such as medical expenses and lost wages) would be available under pure no-fault, but these would be unlimited. Michigan's no-fault law is closer to pure no-fault than are the laws of other no-fault states.

TABLE 14.3 State Auto Insurance Laws Governing Liability Coverage (Financial Responsibility Laws), 2009

"True" No-Fault	First-party Benefits		Restrictions on Lawsuits		Thresholds for Lawsuits	
	Compulsory	Optional	Yes	No	Monetary	Verbal
Colorado	X		X		X	
Florida	X		X			X
Hawaii	X		X		X	
Kansas	X		X		X	
Kentucky	X		X	X	X	
Massachusetts	X		X		X	
Michigan	X		X			X
Minnesota	X		X		X	
New Jersey	X		X	X		X
New York	X		X			X
North Dakota	X		X		X	
Pennsylvania	X		X	X		X
Utah	X		X		X	
Puerto Rico	X		X		X	
Add-on						
Arkansas		X		X		
Delaware	X			X		
D.C.		X	X	X		
Maryland	X			X		
New Hampshire		X		X		
Oregon	X			X		
South Dakota		X		X		
Texas		X		X		
Virginia		X		X		
Washington		X		X		
Wisconsin		X		X		
"Choice" no-fault state. Policyholder can choose a policy on the no-fault system or traditional tort liability. Verbal threshold for the Basic Policy contains lower amounts of coverage. The District of Columbia is neither a true no-fault or add-on state. Drivers are offered the option of no-fault or fault-based coverage, but in the event of an accident, a driver who originally chose no-fault benefits has sixty days to decide whether to receive those benefits or file a claim against the other party.						

Source: American Insurance Association as appeared in the I.I.I. Insurance Fact Book, 2002, p. 49.

Michigan's plan, however, is an example of a modified no-fault law. Under a **modified no-fault** plan, rights to litigate are limited but not eliminated; generally, suit can be brought against an automobile driver only when serious injury has resulted from the accident or special damages exceed a given dollar amount, called a threshold. For nonserious injuries and those resulting in losses below the threshold, only no-fault benefits are available. Serious injuries, or those resulting in losses in excess of the dollar-value threshold, permit the injured party to take legal action, including claims for general damages (such as pain and suffering).

In states that adopted modified no-fault laws, as shown in Table 14.3, there are two types of modification: (1) the verbal threshold, which describes the types of injuries for which the party at fault is considered liable, as in Florida, Michigan, New Jersey, New York, and Pennsylvania, and (2) the monetary threshold, which has a monetary limit under which no fault is assigned. When the claim is over this amount (the threshold in Massachusetts, for example, is $2,000), the at-fault system kicks in.

modified no-fault

Insurance plan, in which rights to litigate are limited but not eliminated; generally, suit can be brought against an automobile driver only when serious injury has resulted from the accident or special damages exceed a given dollar amount.

add-on plans

Auto insurance plans that offer compensation to an injured motorist through the individual's own insurer.

Some states do not limit rights to litigate but do require that insurers offer first-party coverage similar to what is available in no-fault states. An injured party can be compensated from his or her own insurer. The insurer in turn can sue the negligent driver. Rights to litigate are not affected. Auto plans that offer compensation to an injured motorist through the individual's own insurer are called **add-on plans** or expanded first-party coverage.

No-Fault Appraised

Interest in no-fault grew from the belief that the tort system is slow, erratic in its results, and expensive considering the portion of the premium dollar used to compensate persons injured in automobile crashes.[16] If the tort system could be bypassed, all the expenses of the process—including costs of defense and plaintiff's counsel—could be eliminated. This would make more dollars available for compensation at no additional cost to insureds and perhaps even reduce the cost of insurance. Proponents of no-fault assert that enough money is spent on automobile insurance to compensate all crash victims, but that the tort system wastes funds on the question of fault. Therefore, the concept of fault should be abandoned and the funds should be used more effectively. Furthermore, proponents argue that evidence is weak (if it exists at all) that insurance premiums actually reflect loss potentials and therefore work to deter unsafe driving.

Opponents of no-fault argue that it is simply compulsory health insurance with restrictions on tort action. They observe that workers' compensation was designed to reduce litigation by abandoning employers' liability but that, in recent times, litigation in that field has been increasing. Opponents of no-fault assert that many people who favor no-fault do so primarily because they expect it will be cheaper than the present system when, in fact, it may cost more. A study by the Rand Corporation explains that opponents to the no-fault system argue that the system will reduce drivers' incentives to drive carefully, and, in so doing, accident rates will increase.[17]

2.2 Financial Responsibility Laws

financial responsibility law

Law that acts to induce motorists to buy auto liability insurance so victims of their negligence will receive compensation.

Every state has some kind of **financial responsibility law** that acts to induce motorists to buy auto liability insurance so victims of their negligence will receive compensation. A typical law requires evidence of financial responsibility when a driver is involved in an accident or is convicted of a specified offense, such as driving while intoxicated. The simplest way to prove such responsibility is to have an auto liability insurance policy with specified limits that meet or exceed the minimum limits set by various state legislatures. The financial responsibility laws in the various states are shown in Table 14.4. Insurers and consumer advocacy groups recommend a minimum of $100,000 of bodily injury protection per person and $300,000 per accident to avoid paying from your pocket in case of liability.[18]

TABLE 14.4 **Automobile Financial Responsibility/Compulsory Limits by State, 2009**

State	Insurance Required	Minimum Liability Limits[19]
Alabama	BI & PD Liab	25/50/25
Alaska	BI & PD Liab	50/100/25
Arizona	BI & PD Liab	15/30/10
Arkansas	BI & PD Liab, PIP	25/50/25
California	BI & PD Liab	15/30/5[20]
Colorado	BI & PD Liab	25/50/15
Connecticut	BI & PD Liab, UM, UIM	20/40/10
Delaware	BI & PD Liab, PIP	15/30/10
D.C.	BI & PD Liab, UM	25/50/10
Florida	PD Liab, PIP	10/20/10[21]
Georgia	BI & PD Liab	25/50/25
Hawaii	BI & PD Liab, PIP	20/40/10
Idaho	BI & PD Liab	25/50/15
Illinois	BI & PD Liab, UM	20/40/15
Indiana	BI & PD Liab	25/50/10
Iowa	BI & PD Liab	20/40/15
Kansas	BI & PD Liab, PIP, UM	25/50/10
Kentucky	BI & PD Liab, PIP	25/50/10
Louisiana	BI & PD Liab	10/20/10[22]
Maine	BI & PD Liab, UM, UIM	50/100/25[23]
Maryland	BI & PD Liab, PIP,[24] UM	20/40/15
Massachusetts	BI & PD Liab, PIP, UM	20/40/5
Michigan	BI & PD Liab, PIP	20/40/10
Minnesota	BI & PD Liab, PIP, UM, UIM	30/60/10
Mississippi	BI & PD Liab	25/50/25
Missouri	BI & PD Liab, UM	25/50/10
Montana	BI & PD Liab	25/50/10
Nebraska	BI & PD Liab	25/50/25
Nevada	BI & PD Liab	15/30/10
New Hampshire	FR only, UM	25/50/25
New Jersey	BI & PD Liab, PIP, UM	15/30/5[25]
New Mexico	BI & PD Liab	25/50/10
New York	BI & PD Liab, PIP, UM	25/50/10[26]
North Carolina	BI & PD Liab, UM, UIM	30/60/25
North Dakota	BI & PD Liab, PIP, UM	25/50/25
Ohio	BI & PD Liab	12.5/25/7.5
Oklahoma	BI & PD Liab	25/50/25
Oregon	BI & PD Liab, PIP, UM	25/50/10
Pennsylvania	BI & PD Liab, PIP	15/30/5
Rhode Island	BI & PD Liab, UM	25/50/25[27]
South Carolina	BI & PD Liab, UM	25/50/25
South Dakota	BI & PD Liab, UM	25/50/25
Tennessee	BI & PD Liab	25/50/10[28]

State	Insurance Required	Minimum Liability Limits[19]
Texas	BI & PD Liab	25/50/25[29]
Utah	BI & PD Liab, PIP	25/65/15[30]
Vermont	BI & PD Liab, UM, UIM	25/50/10
Virginia	BI & PD Liab, UM	25/50/20
Washington	BI & PD Liab	25/50/10
West Virginia	BI & PD Liab, UM	20/40/10
Wisconsin	FR only, UM	25/50/10
Wyoming	BI & PD Liab	25/50/20

Source: Property Casualty Insurers Association of America; state departments of insurance.

unsatisfied judgment funds

State organizations that provide compensation in situations when an injured motorist obtains a judgment against the party at fault but cannot collect because the party has neither insurance nor resources.

compulsory auto liability insurance law

Law that requires automobile registrants to have specified liability insurance in effect at all times.

Several states also have **unsatisfied judgment funds** to provide compensation in situations when an injured motorist obtains a judgment against the party at fault but cannot collect because the party has neither insurance nor resources. The maximum amount the injured party may claim from the fund is usually the same as that established by the state's financial responsibility law. When the fund pays the judgment, the party at fault becomes indebted to the fund and his or her driving privilege is suspended until the fund is reimbursed.

Financial responsibility laws increased the percentage of drivers with auto liability insurance, but many drivers remained uninsured. Therefore, about half the states require evidence of insurance prior to licensing the driver or the vehicle. Unfortunately, in many such states, only about 80 or 90 percent of the drivers maintain their insurance after licensing. Even a compulsory auto liability insurance law does not guarantee that you will not be injured by a financially irresponsible driver. A **compulsory auto liability insurance law** requires automobile registrants to have specified liability insurance in effect at all times; however, numerous drivers find ways to operate motor vehicles without insurance.

KEY TAKEAWAYS

In this section you studied the major features of no-fault compensation systems and financial responsibility laws for automobile accidents:

- In the traditional at-fault system, an injured party is compensated by the liability coverage of the at-fault driver.
- Under no-fault laws, benefits are provided by insurers without regard to who caused the accident.
- No-fault takes three forms: pure no-fault, modified no-fault, and add-on plans.
- No-fault is backed by the belief that the tort system is slow and erratic and adds unnecessary expense in determining fault.
- Critics say that no-fault is a form of compulsory health insurance and reduces drivers' incentives to drive carefully (thereby increasing accidents and premium costs).
- Financial responsibility laws induce motorists to buy auto liability insurance so that victims of their negligence will be compensated.
- State legislatures set minimum limits that must be carried in auto liability insurance.
- Unsatisfied judgment funds assist injured motorists who cannot collect from financially irresponsible liable parties.

DISCUSSION QUESTIONS

1. Discuss the forms of automobile no-fault laws presented in this chapter.
2. What are the advantages and disadvantages of no-fault laws presented in this chapter?
3. Explain the difference between a monetary threshold and a verbal threshold for no-fault laws.
4. What is the purpose of financial responsibility laws?
5. Automobile financial responsibility laws require you to have some minimum amount of auto liability insurance. If the purpose of liability insurance is to protect you from loss caused by your negligence, why should the law force you to buy it? Do you think this is a decision for you to make? Explain.

3. ENSURING AUTO INSURANCE AVAILABILITY

LEARNING OBJECTIVES

In this section we elaborate on the residual or shared market for auto liability insurance, including the following:

- **Auto insurance plans**
- **Reinsurance facilities**
- **Joint underwriting associations (JUAs)**
- **The Maryland State Fund**

The assumption underlying laws requiring motorists to buy automobile liability insurance is that it is available. Unfortunately, some drivers cannot buy insurance through the usual channels because, as a group, their losses are excessive. As a result, people injured by such drivers might not be able to collect anything for their losses. Presumably, this problem can be solved by charging higher premium rates for such drivers, as is the case of insurers providing coverage to the so-called **substandard market**, in which some companies offer limited auto coverage to high-risk drivers at high premium rates. These insurers can do so because of the availability of computerized systems permitting them to calculate the rates for smaller groups of insureds.

The **residual market (shared market)** exists to provide insurance to people who cannot buy it through the usual channels; it is created by state law. Methods of creating this market are listed in Table 14.5. The private passenger percentage of cars that are insured by the shared market was largest in North Carolina in 2006 with 23.2 percent market share. This was followed by Massachusetts with 4.8 percent. In New York, the share of the residual market fell by 28 percent in 2006 to 1.7 percent, mostly as a result of legal changes.[31]

TABLE 14.5 **Auto Insurance Residual Market**

Auto Insurance Plans	Joint Underwriting Associations
Reinsurance Facilities	Maryland State Fund

3.1 Auto Insurance Plans

Auto insurance plans were formerly called assigned risk plans because they operate on an assignment basis. In **auto insurance plans**, drivers who cannot buy auto liability insurance through the usual channels can apply to be assigned to an insurer who must sell them coverage that meets the requirements of the financial responsibility law. Every company writing auto insurance in the state is a member of the plan and each must take its share of such business. If a company writes 10 percent of the auto insurance business in the state, it has to accept 10 percent of the qualified applicants. In spite of generally higher rates than those found in the voluntary market, auto insurance plans have caused significant losses to the auto insurance industry.

3.2 Reinsurance Facilities

Where there is a **reinsurance facility**—as in Massachusetts, North Carolina, New Hampshire, and South Carolina—every auto insurer is required to issue auto insurance to any licensed driver who applies and can pay the premium; in return, insurers can transfer the burden of bad risks to a pool to which all auto insurers belong. As members of the pool, insurers share in both premiums and losses. The insured generally knows nothing about this arrangement; like all other insureds, he or she receives a policy issued by the company to which he or she applied. In some states, however, a specific insurer is designated to service the policy or pay for losses of a given insured; then the insured likely knows his or her status in the facility.

substandard market

Insurance market in which some companies offer limited auto coverage to high-risk drivers at high premium rates.

residual market (shared market)

Insurance market created by state law that exists to provide insurance to people who cannot buy it through the usual channels.

auto insurance plans

Arrangement in which drivers who cannot buy auto liability insurance through the usual channels can apply to be assigned to an insurer who must sell them coverage that meets the requirements of the financial responsibility law.

reinsurance facility

State plan in which every auto insurer is required to issue auto insurance to any licensed driver who applies and can pay the premium; in return, insurers can transfer the burden of bad risks to a pool to which all auto insurers belong.

3.3 Joint Underwriting Associations

joint underwriting association (JUA)

State plan in which all automobile insurers are members and the association is, in effect, an insurance industry company.

Where there is a **joint underwriting association (JUA)**—as in Florida, Hawaii, and Missouri—all automobile insurers in the state are members and the association is, in effect, an insurance industry company. Several insurers are appointed as servicing carriers to act as agents for the association. An applicant for insurance who cannot meet underwriting requirements in the regular market is issued a policy by the servicing carrier on behalf of the association; as far as the policyholder is concerned, the association is his or her insurer. Premiums and losses are shared by all the auto insurers in the state, similar to the auto insurance plan. The JUA differs from an auto insurance plan in that only designated servicing carriers can issue coverage to participants.

3.4 Maryland State Fund

This government-operated residual market company provides coverage to drivers who cannot obtain insurance through the regular market. In spite of high premiums, however, it has suffered heavy losses. Originally, it was to bear such losses itself (through taxation), but the law now requires that the private insurance industry subsidize the fund.

KEY TAKEAWAYS

In this section you studied the issue of affordability in auto insurance and options in the residual market for individuals unable to obtain insurance through the usual channels:

- In auto insurance plans, drivers can apply to be assigned to an insurer who must sell them coverage that meets the requirements of the financial responsibility laws of that state.
- Reinsurance facilities are designed to accept risk pools from insurers issuing policies to very high-risk drivers.
- Where there is a joint underwriting association (JUA), all automobile insurers in the state are members and the association is like an insurance industry company.
- The Maryland State Fund is subsidized by the private insurance industry.

DISCUSSION QUESTIONS

1. Larry, a twenty-four-year-old graduate student with three speeding tickets on his record, is considered high-risk and cannot get normal automobile insurance coverage. The state where he lives requires automobile insurance before he can register his car. Explain his options for purchasing insurance coverage.
2. Do you think high-risk drivers should be able to obtain auto insurance at all?
3. Explain the various structures of the residual markets.
4. How are the residual markets funded?

4. TYPES OF AUTOMOBILE POLICIES AND THE PERSONAL AUTOMOBILE POLICY

LEARNING OBJECTIVES

In this section we elaborate on the following:

- **The basic types of automobile policies**
- **The structure of the personal automobile policy (PAP) in detail**
- **The types of coverage provided through the PAP**

4.1 Types of Automobile Policies

There are two general types of auto insurance policies: commercial use (discussed in Chapter 15) and personal use, which is discussed in this chapter. The Insurance Services Office (ISO) has developed standard forms for each category.

Some insurers issue the standard policies; others issue policies that are similar but not identical. Variations result from competition that motivates insurers to try to differentiate their products. The personal automobile policy (PAP, discussed below) is the newest of the policies for personal use automobiles and has nearly displaced other personal use forms. You will probably buy a PAP or a policy similar to it, so we will discuss it in detail.

Bear in mind, however, that your policy may differ in some significant ways from the PAP. The major differences are in the perils covered, persons insured, exclusions and definitions, and the presence of personal injury protection (PIP) coverage or no-fault provisions that are required in some states. To understand your own coverage, therefore, be sure to read the specifics of your policy.

The Personal Automobile Policy (PAP)

The **personal automobile policy (PAP)** is the automobile insurance contract purchased by most individuals, whether to meet financial responsibility laws or just to protect against the costs associated with auto accidents. A copy of the Insurance Services Office's sample PAP is provided in Chapter 25 at the end of the text. It begins with a declarations page, general insuring agreement, and list of important definitions. These are followed by the policy's six major parts:

personal automobile policy (PAP)

The automobile insurance contract purchased by most individuals.

- Part A—Liability coverage
- Part B—Medical payments coverage
- Part C—Uninsured motorists coverage
- Part D—Coverage for damage to your auto
- Part E—Duties after an accident or loss
- Part F—General provisions

Each of the first four parts has its own insuring agreement, exclusions, and other insurance provisions, but most conditions are in parts E and F. In a sense, each of the first four parts is (almost) a separate policy, and the PAP is a package that brings them all together. Each part is made effective by indicating in the declarations that the premium has been paid for that specific part and the coverage applies. When you receive your policy, check the declarations to be sure they show a premium for all the coverages you requested, and see that the information relating to your policy is correct.

Parts E and F apply to the entire policy. As we discuss each part, you will find reference to the specimen policy in Chapter 25 helpful.

Declarations

The declarations identify you by name and address and show the term of the policy, the premiums charged, the coverages provided, and the limits of liability of the coverages. You—and your spouse, if you are married—are the named insured(s). A description of the automobile(s) covered—by year, name, model, identification or serial number, and date of purchase—is included. The loss payee for physical damage to the automobile is listed to protect the lender who has financed the automobile's purchase, and the garaging address is shown. The latter is an important underwriting factor. Loss frequency and severity vary from one area (called territory by rate makers) to another. For example, losses are generally greater in urban than in rural areas. Although many people drive all over the country, most driving is done within a rather short distance of the place the car is typically garaged. Thus, the place where it is garaged affects the premium.

Where is your car garaged if your home is in a rural area but you are attending a university in a large city or different state? It would be wise to talk to your agent about this question. He or she will—or should—know what the insurer's interpretation is about identifying the proper garaging location. You, of course, want to avoid misrepresenting a material fact, an action that could void the policy.

Definitions

Definitions are crucial elements of insurance policies because the meaning of a term may determine in a particular instance whether or not you have coverage. Any term found in quotations in the policy is defined. Some are defined in the definitions section, others within the separate coverage sections.

Those found in the definitions section include the following. "You" and "your" refer to the "named insured" shown in the declarations, and the spouse if a resident of the same household. "We," "us," and "our" refer to the insurance company. A private passenger auto is deemed to be owned by a person if it is leased under a written agreement to that person for a continuous period of at least six months. If you refer to the PAP in Chapter 25, you will see that the most recent ISO PAP is as of 2003. This PAP defines "you" and "your" with a limitation on spouses that leave the residence; these spouses are not covered.

> *"If the spouse ceased to be resident of the same household during the policy period or prior to the inception of this policy, the spouse will be considered 'you' and 'your' under this policy but only until the earlier of: (1) the end of 90 days following the spouse's change of residency, (2) the effective date of another policy listing the spouse as a named insured, or (3) the end of the policy period."*

"Bodily injury" (page 1, section D) occurs when there is bodily harm, sickness, or disease, including a resulting death. "Property damage" (in section H) involves physical damage to, destruction of, or loss of use of tangible property. A "business" includes trade, profession, or occupation. "Family member" (in section F) means a resident of your household related to you by blood, marriage, or adoption. This includes a ward or foster child. "Occupying" (in section G) means in; upon; and getting in, on, out, or off. It may seem ridiculous to define a common word such as "occupying," but a reading of the exclusions for medical payments coverage shows how crucial the definition may be. A recent example provides a helpful illustration. A woman walked to her car, and, while unlocking the door, was struck by another vehicle. The insurer included this scenario under the category of "occupying."

"Trailer" means a vehicle designed to be pulled by a private passenger auto or pickup, panel truck, or van. It also means a farm wagon or farm implement being towed by one of the vehicles listed.

"Your covered auto" (in section J) includes the following:

- Any vehicle shown in the declarations
- A "newly acquired auto."
- Any "trailer" you own
- Any auto or trailer you do not own while used as a temporary substitute for any other vehicle described in this definition that is out of normal use because of its breakdown, repair, servicing, loss, or destruction

Section K defines "newly acquired auto" and the various provisions regarding such an auto.

Liability Coverage—Part A

In the PAP, the liability insuring agreement can be paraphrased as follows:

> *We will pay damages for "bodily injury" or "property damage" for which any "insured" becomes legally responsible because of an auto accident. Damages include prejudgment interest awarded against the "insured." We will settle or defend, as we consider appropriate, any claim or suit asking for these damages. In addition to our limit of liability, we will pay all defense costs we incur...*

In the liability part of the PAP, the policy defines "insured" as the following:

1. You or any family member, for the ownership, maintenance, or use of any auto or trailer.

2. Any person using your covered auto.

3. For your covered auto, any person or organization, but only with respect to legal responsibility for acts or omissions of a person for whom coverage is afforded under this part.

4. For any auto or trailer other than your covered auto, any person or organization, but only with respect to legal responsibility for acts or omissions of you or any family member for whom coverage is afforded under this part. This provision applies only if the person or organization does not own or hire the auto or trailer.

In a situation where the owner of the car lends you the covered auto to take children to the church picnic, you become a covered person, according to definition 2. The policy will cover your liability in connection with an accident on the way to the picnic. It will also, according to definition 3, cover any liability the church may have in connection with the accident if the kids get hurt. If, on the other hand, I borrow the other person's car to take the children to the church picnic, I am a covered person according to definition 1, and the church's liability for any accident I might have is covered by definition 4. In both situations, coverage for the organization stems from the fact that the driver is a covered person. It is important to understand that it does not matter who is driving the covered car; as long as the driver has permission to drive the car, he or she is covered under the policy. The coverage for the car is the first insurance company that pays for the accident. If the liability is larger, the other driver's policy picks up the rest of the liability.

Defense

Section A of Part A of the liability coverage quoted above indicates that legal defense is not part of the limits of liability. Defense costs often run into the thousands of dollars, making this a significant benefit of liability insurance. If you are found liable, the insurer pays on your behalf to the plaintiff(s), up to the limit(s) of liability under the policy. The insurer's responsibility to defend ends when that limit is reached (is paid in award or settlement to third-party claimants).

The insurer retains the right to settle claims without the insured's approval if it finds this expedient. Such action keeps many cases out of court and reduces insurance claims expenses. It can cause dissatisfaction, however, if the insured did not expect to have to settle.

Exclusions

The wording of the insuring agreement of Part A provides for open perils liability coverage. All events resulting in automobile liability, therefore, are covered unless specifically excluded. Some exclusions apply to unprotected persons and others apply to noncovered vehicles. The exclusions, listed in Table 14.6, can be discussed in terms of the purposes of exclusions presented in Chapter 9.

As in the homeowner's policy, intentionally caused (nonfortuitous) harm is always excluded. As before, several exclusions exist to prevent duplicate coverage, which would result in overindemnification. Property damage to owned or used property, for instance, ought to be covered under other property insurance contracts, such as a homeowner's policy, and is therefore excluded in the PAP. As noted in the homeowners coverage, bodily injury to an employee of the covered person who is eligible for workers' compensation benefits is excluded. Anyone using a motor vehicle as a taxi, for example, represents greater risk than one who does not. Thus, persons using a vehicle as a public livery or conveyance are excluded from coverage. Because persons employed in the automobile business represent a significant risk while in their employment status, they too are excluded. You can understand that the insurer prefers not to provide coverage to the mechanic while he or she is test-driving your car. The automobile business is expected to have its own automobile policy, with rates that reflect its unique hazards.

Certain other occupations require the use of vehicles that are hazardous regardless of who operates them. Large garbage trucks, for example, are difficult to control. Insurers do not provide liability protection while you operate such a vehicle. Insurers, however, do not exclude all business uses of motor vehicles. Specifically excepted from the exclusion are private passenger autos (e.g., those of traveling salespeople), owned pickups or vans, trailers used with any of these vehicles, and any vehicle used in a farming or ranching business.

TABLE 14.6 Personal Auto Policy, Part A Exclusions (PAP 2003)*

Exclusions
A. We do not provide Liability Coverage for any "insured":

    1. Who intentionally causes "bodily injury" or "property damage."

    2. For "property damage" to property owned or being transported by that "insured."

    3. For "property damage" to property:

        a. Rented to;

        b. Used by; or

        c. In the care of;

   that "insured."

      This Exclusion (A.3.) does not apply to "property damage" to a residence or private garage.

    4. For "bodily injury" to an employee of that "insured" during the course of employment. This Exclusion (A.4.) does not apply to "bodily injury" to a domestic employee unless worker's compensation benefits are required or available for that domestic employee.

    5. For that "insured's" liability arising out of the ownership or operation of a vehicle while it is being used as a public or livery conveyance. This Exclusion (A.5.) does not apply to a share-the-expense car pool.

    6. While employed or otherwise engaged in the "business" of:

        a. Selling;

        b. Repairing;

        c. Servicing;

        d. Storing; or

        e. Parking;

   vehicles designed for use mainly on public highways. This includes road testing and delivery. This Exclusion (A.6.) does not apply to the ownership, maintenance, or use of "your covered auto" by:

        a. You;

        b. Any "family member"; or

        c. Any partner, agent, or employee of you or any "family member."

* See Chapter 25.

Insurers also standardize the risk through exclusion of coverage while "using a vehicle without a reasonable belief that that person is entitled to do so." The insurance company rates the policy according to the insured's characteristics, which include who the insured allows to use the covered auto. A thief, or someone without permission to use the covered auto, does not reflect these characteristics. Questions sometimes arise when an insured's child allows a friend to use the covered car, despite parents' admonitions to the contrary. Court rulings are mixed on the application of the exclusion in such a situation. Generally, such persons represent greater risks. The use of a motor vehicle with less than four wheels also represents a greater risk than one with at least four wheels. It too is excluded.

To prevent catastrophic exposure, the PAP excludes persons covered under nuclear energy liability policies. This exclusion is a standard provision in all liability policies.

The final two exclusions are confusing. Their purpose is to prevent insureds from obtaining more coverage than was purchased. Thus, no coverage applies for accidents arising out of ownership, maintenance, or use of a motor vehicle you own or have available for regular use if it is not a declared auto in the declarations section of the policy. If such protection were available, you would need to purchase coverage on only one vehicle instead of on all your owned vehicles. The second exclusion is the same, except that it applies to motor vehicles owned by or available for the regular use of family members. This last exclusion does not apply to you. Remember that "you" is the named insured and the named insured's spouse. Thus, if the named insured uses a noncovered vehicle owned by a family member (perhaps a son or daughter living at home), liability coverage exists. On the other hand, the family member who owns the noncovered vehicle is not protected while driving the undeclared auto.

Supplementary Payments

In addition to the limit for liability, the insurer will pay up to $250 for the cost of bail bonds required because of an accident if the accident results in bodily injury or property damage covered by the policy. Note that this would not cover the cost of a bond for a traffic ticket you receive when there is no accident. Premiums on appeal bonds and bonds to release attachments are paid in any suit the insurer defends. Interest accruing after a judgment is entered, and reasonable expenses incurred at the insurer's request are paid. Up to $200 a day for loss of earnings because of attendance at hearings or trials is also available.

Single or Split Limits

Although liability coverage under the PAP usually is subject to a single, aggregate limit (called a combined single limit [CSL]), it can be divided by use of an endorsement into two major subparts: bodily injury liability and property damage liability. Bodily injury liability applies when the use of your car results in the injury or death of pedestrians, passengers of other vehicles, or passengers of your automobile. Property damage liability coverage applies when your car damages property belonging to others. Although the first thing you probably think about under this coverage is the other person's car (and you are right), this coverage could also cover street signs, fences, bicycles, telephone poles, houses, and other types of property. Remember, however, that it does not apply to your house or to other property you own because you cannot be legally liable to yourself.

If you choose a **single limit** of liability to cover all liability, including both property damage and bodily injury, then the insurer will pay on your behalf for all losses up to this limit for any single accident, whether they are property-related or bodily injury-related. The only limit you are concerned with in this case is the single, or aggregate, limit. Once all losses equal this limit, you will have to bear the burden of any further liability.

If you choose a **split limit** of liability, a set of two limits will be specifically applied to bodily injury, and a single, aggregate limit will be applied to property damage. For the bodily injury limits, one limit applies per person, per accident, and a second limit is the total the insurer will pay for your liability to all persons injured in an accident. The limit for property damage is shown separately. For example, your limits are shown as follows:

| Bodily injury | $150,000 each person, $300,000 each accident |
| Property damage | $50,000 each accident |

In insurance jargon, these limits would be described as 150/300/50. An example will help illustrate how the split limits work. If you caused an accident in which only one person was injured, the coverage is limited to $150,000 for that person. If the accident involved six people, each person is covered up to $150,000, but the total for all six injured people combined cannot exceed $300,000. So if all are badly injured, the limit for the accident may not be sufficient. In this case (and as discussed in Chapter 13), an umbrella policy with high limits—such as $1 million—may be very valuable.

Alternatively, a single limit, say, $300,000, can be purchased to cover all liabilities from any one accident. Whether you have single or split limits, the need for adequate limits is imperative, as noted above. Also note the clarifying language in "limit of liability," which states that the amount shown is the maximum payable, regardless of the number of covered persons, claims made, vehicles or premiums shown in the declarations, or vehicles involved in the auto accident. If two vehicles shown in the declarations are involved in the same accident, twice the limit of liability will not be available. At least, this is the intent of the insurer. Various state courts have interpreted the policy differently, permitting what is called stacking. **Stacking** may occur when a single auto policy covers two vehicles, and the court interprets this situation to yield a limit of liability equal to double the amount shown in the policy declarations.

Out-of-State Coverage

Part A also has provisions for out-of-state coverage and other insurance. The out-of-state provision takes care of a situation in which your liability limits comply with the financial responsibility or compulsory insurance law in your state but are inadequate in another state. It provides that, under such circumstances, your policy will provide at least the minimum amounts and types of coverage required by the state in which you are driving. Suppose you have limits of 15/25/15 ($15,000/$25,000/$15,000), the minimum required in the state where your car is garaged. If you are driving in a state that requires 25/50/20 ($25,000/$50,000/$20,000) and are involved in an accident, your insurer will interpret your policy as if it had the higher limits. Thus, even though you have to meet only the requirements where you live, your policy will provide the limits you need in any state or province in which you may be driving.

Financial Responsibility

This one sentence states, "When this policy is certified as future proof of financial responsibility, this policy shall comply with the law to the extent required." The requirements in each state are shown in Table 14.4.

single limit

Coverage under which the insurer will pay on your behalf for all losses up to a specified limit for any single accident, whether the losses are property-related or bodily injury-related.

split limit

Coverage under which the insurer applies a set of two limits to bodily injury, and an single, aggregate to property damage.

stacking

Situation that arises when a single auto policy covers two vehicles, and the court interprets this situation to yield a limit of liability equal to double the amount shown in the policy declarations.

Other Insurance

The liability coverage of the PAP is excess with regard to a nonowned vehicle. In the event of a loss while you are driving a friend's car, your insurer will pay only the amount by which a claim (or judgment) exceeds the limits of your friend's auto insurance. In such a situation, your friend's insurance is **primary coverage**, or the first payee in a situation where two or more coverages apply, and your insurance is excess coverage. This means that coverage on the vehicle is always primary. If two excess policies apply, then the "other insurance" provision calls for a pro rata distribution of liability. For example, if you were driving a friend's car whose insurance had expired and you were an insured under two policies (as, perhaps, a resident relative of two insureds who bought separate policies on their vehicles), these two policies would share in any liability attributable to you on a pro rata basis. This example, however, is quite unusual.

primary coverage

Coverage for the first payee in a situation where two or more coverages apply.

Medical Payments Coverage—Part B

Medical payments coverage, which is optional in some states and from some insurers, overlaps family health insurance coverage. You may consider it unnecessary if you have excellent health insurance. Your own family health insurance does not cover nonfamily members riding in your vehicle, so it is narrower than is medical payments coverage. If you are liable, however, Part A will provide coverage. If not, your passengers may have their own health insurance.

Insuring Agreement

Under Part B, the insurer agrees to pay reasonable expenses incurred within three years from the date of an accident for necessary medical and funeral services because of bodily injury caused by an accident and sustained by a covered person. A covered person means you or any family member, while occupying, or as a pedestrian when struck by, a motor vehicle designed for use mainly on public roads or a trailer of any type. It also includes any other person occupying your covered auto.

Note that you or a family member would be covered by your PAP medical payments protection while occupying a nonowned car, but other passengers in the vehicle are not. No benefits are paid if you are struck by a machine not designed for use on the highway, such as a farm tractor.

Exclusions

Medical payments coverage is similar to liability coverage because it is provided on an open perils basis within the category of automobile use. Seven of the exclusions to Part A (liability) are nearly identical to exclusions found in Part B (medical payments). These exclusions are as follows:

- While occupying a motor vehicle with less than four wheels
- While occupying your covered auto when it is being used as a public livery or conveyance
- While occupying any vehicle located for use as a residence or premises
- During the course of employment if workers' compensation is available
- While occupying or when struck by any vehicle (other than your covered auto) that is (a) owned by you or (b) furnished or available for your regular use
- While occupying or when struck by any vehicle (other than your covered auto) that is (a) owned by any family member or (b) furnished or available for the regular use of any family member
- While occupying a vehicle without a reasonable belief that the insured is entitled to do so
- While occupying a vehicle when it is being used in the business or occupation of a covered person, unless the vehicle is a private passenger auto, pickup, or van owned by the insured or trailer used with one of these means of transportation
- Caused by the consequence of nuclear weapons, war, civil war, insurrection, or rebellion or revolution
- Consequence of nuclear reaction to radiation or radioactive contamination
- While occupying any vehicle located inside a facility designed for racing, for the purpose of (a) competing in or (b) practicing or preparing for any prearranged or organized racing or speed contest

Limit of Liability

The limit of liability for medical payments is on a per person basis, such as $5,000 per person. This is the maximum limit of liability for each person injured in any one accident. If you have two autos insured, with a medical payments limit for each shown on the declarations page, you cannot add all (stack) the limits together. It may appear that you have $10,000 in medical payments coverage because you have $5,000 on each vehicle, but such is not intended by the insurer.

When there is other applicable auto medical payments insurance, your policy will pay on a pro rata basis. With respect to nonowned automobiles, however, the PAP is excess; that is, it pays only after the limits of all other applicable insurance have been exhausted.

Other Insurance

Any amounts payable by this coverage are reduced by any amounts payable for the same expenses under Part A (liability) or Part C (uninsured motorists). Thus, a passenger in your car who is injured cannot recover under both liability and medical payments coverages for the same losses. Nor can you recover expenses under both medical payments and the uninsured motorists coverages. Injured parties are entitled to indemnity but not double payment.

Uninsured Motorists Coverage—Part C

Uninsured motorists coverage pays for bodily injuries (and property damage in some states) caused by an accident with another vehicle whose driver is negligent and (1) has no liability insurance or less than that required by law, (2) was a hit-and-run driver, or (3) is a driver whose insurance company is insolvent. Covered persons include you or any family member, any other person occupying your covered auto, and any other person entitled to recovery because of bodily injury to a person in the first two categories. An example of "any other person entitled to recovery" is one who has suffered loss of companionship as a result of a spouse (who was in one of the first two categories) being injured in an accident.

Minimum coverage is the amount required to comply with your state's financial responsibility or compulsory insurance law. You can, however, purchase additional coverage up to the limit you purchased under Part A. In addition, if you purchase increased amounts of uninsured motorists coverage, you are eligible to buy underinsured motorists coverage, which is discussed later in this chapter.

uninsured motorists coverage

Insurance that pays for bodily injuries (and property damage in some states) caused by an accident with another vehicle whose driver is negligent and (1) has no liability insurance or less than that required by law, (2) was a hit-and-run driver, or (3) is a driver whose insurance company is insolvent.

Uninsured Motor Vehicle

Because you can recover expenses under Part C of the PAP only if you are involved in an accident with a negligent driver of an uninsured motor vehicle, the definition of such a vehicle is crucial. The policy defines it as a land motor vehicle or trailer of any type, with the following specifications:

- One to which no bodily injury liability bond or policy applies at the time of the accident
- One to which there is a bodily injury liability bond or policy in force, but the limit of liability is less than that specified by the financial responsibility law in the state where your covered auto is garaged
- A hit-and-run vehicle whose operator/owner cannot be identified and that hits you or any family member, a vehicle you or any family member are occupying, or your covered auto
- One to which a bodily injury liability bond or policy applies at the time of the accident, but the company denies coverage or is insolvent

However, an uninsured motor vehicle does not include any of the following vehicles or types of equipment:

- Owned by, furnished, or available for the regular use of you or any family member
- Owned or operated by a self-insurer under any applicable motor vehicle law, except a self-insurer who is or becomes insolvent
- Owned by any governmental unit or agency
- Operated on rails or crawler treads
- Designed mainly for use off public roads and used while not on public roads
- While located for use as a residence or premises

Exclusions

Perhaps because the definition of an uninsured motor vehicle is so limited, only four exclusions apply to Part C. Like the prior two parts, uninsured motorists coverage excludes losses:

a. Involving an undeclared motor vehicle owned by you or any family member
b. While using a vehicle without reasonable belief of permission
c. When there is other coverage, such as workers' compensation or disability benefits
d. Not applicable to punitive damages

In addition, exclusion B1 denies payment to a covered person "if that person or the legal representative settles the bodily injury claim without our consent." Just because a negligent driver is an uninsured motorist, he or she is not free from liability. The insurer, therefore, does not want its subrogation rights to be adversely affected by agreements between the insured and negligent driver, which could include collusive and fraudulent situations.

On the other hand, the auto insurer does not want to make uninsured motorists payments available through subrogation to a workers' compensation or disability benefits insurer. If the accident occurred during the course of employment and resulted in workers' compensation benefits, the compensation insurer might seek such subrogation. Exclusion C prevents this type of activity.

Last, the coverage is not intended to pay for punitive damages, which are excluded. Additionally, the insuring agreement is specific in promising to pay compensatory damages only. Punitive damages are not compensatory.

Other Provisions

The limit of liability provision for uninsured motorists coverage is nearly the same as for medical payments (although the actual limit is usually quite different). The other insurance provision is the same as that for parts A and B, namely, pro rata for your covered auto and excess for a nonowned auto. In the event of a dispute concerning the right to recover damages or their amount, either party—you or the insurer—can demand binding arbitration. Local rules about procedure and evidence apply.

There are provisions for other insurance and for arbitration. The arbitration section specifies that if the insured and the insurer do not agree about the amounts of entitled recovery of damages, both parties can arbitrate. But both must agree to arbitration and may not be forced to arbitrate.

underinsured motorists coverage

Insurance that fills in the coverage gap that arises when the negligent party meets the financial responsibility law of the state, but the auto accident victim has losses in excess of the negligent driver's liability limit.

Underinsured motorists coverage fills in the coverage gap that arises when the negligent party meets the financial responsibility law of the state, but the auto accident victim has losses in excess of the negligent driver's liability limit. In such circumstances, when the negligent driver meets the legal insurance requirements but is legally responsible for additional amounts, the driver is not an uninsured motorist. The negligent driver may not have available other noninsurance resources to pay for the loss, leaving the injured party to bear the financial strain. Underinsured motorists coverage permits the insured to purchase coverage for this situation.

You may purchase underinsured motorists coverage in amounts up to the amount of liability (Part A) protection you purchased. The same amount of uninsured motorists coverage must also be purchased. The underinsured motorists coverage will pay the difference between the at-fault driver's liability and the at-fault driver's limit of liability insurance, up to the amount of underinsured motorists coverage purchased. For example, assume that you were hit by another motorist and that you incurred damages of $60,000. Further assume that the other driver is found liable for the full amount of your loss, but that driver carries insurance of only $30,000, which meets the financial responsibility law requirement. An underinsured motorists coverage equal to your limit of liability coverage, say, $100,000, would cover the remaining $30,000 of loss above the at-fault driver's insurance. Your total payment, however, could not exceed the underinsured motorists coverage limit of liability. If your loss were $115,000; therefore, you would receive $30,000 from the at-fault driver's insurer and $70,000 from your own insurer. The remaining $15,000 loss is still the responsibility of the at-fault driver, but you may have difficulty collecting it.

Coverage for Damage to Your Auto—Part D

Part D of the PAP is first-party property insurance. The insurer agrees to pay for direct and accidental loss to your covered auto and to any other nonowned auto used by you or a family member, subject to policy limitations and exclusions. Automobile equipment, generally meaning those items normally used in the auto and attached to or contained in it, is also covered. All of this is subject to a deductible.

You have the option of buying coverage for your automobile on an open perils basis by purchasing both collision and comprehensive (also called other-than-collision) coverage. You may instead opt to buy just collision (although it may be difficult to find a company to provide just collision coverage) or just other-than-collision, or neither. A premium for the coverage must be stated in the declarations for coverage to apply. The distinction between the two coverages may be important because collision protection generally carries a higher deductible than other-than-collision coverage.

collision

The upset (turning over) of a covered auto or nonowned auto, or striking another object.

comprehensive (or other-than-collision)

Any type of nonexcluded loss-causing event other than collision.

Collision means the upset (turning over) of the covered auto or nonowned auto, or striking another object. Every type of nonexcluded loss-causing event other than collision is considered **comprehensive (other-than-collision)**. To help you identify certain ambiguous perils as either collision or other-than-collision, a list is provided in the policy. You might mistakenly take this list as one of exclusions. Rather, the perils shown in Table 14.7 are other-than-collision perils and are therefore covered along with other nonexcluded perils if other-than-collision coverage applies. For example, loss caused by an exploded bomb is neither collision nor among the events listed as examples of other-than-collision. Because breakage of glass may occur in a collision or by other means, the insurer will allow you to consider the glass breakage as part of the collision loss, negating dual deductibles.

TABLE 14.7   Other-Than-Collision Losses

1. Missiles and falling objects
2. Fire
3. Theft or larceny
4. Explosion
5. Windstorm
6. Hail, water, or flood
7. Malicious mischief, or vandalism
8. Riot or civil commotion
9. Contact with bird or animal
10. Breakage of glass

In addition to the items listed in Table 14.7, the insurer will pay up to $20 per day (to a maximum of $600) for transportation expenses in the event your covered auto is stolen. Transportation expenses would include car rental or the added cost of public transportation, taxis, and the like. You are entitled to expenses beginning forty-eight hours after the theft and ending when your covered auto is returned to you or its loss is paid. You must notify the police promptly if your covered auto is stolen.

Some insurers offer towing and labor coverage for an additional premium. If your car breaks down, this coverage pays the cost of repairing it at the place where it became disabled or towing it to a garage. The limit of liability is $25 and a typical premium is $4 or $5. Considering the fact that you may be able to get towing service and many other services for about the same cost from automobile associations, adding towing and labor to your policy may not be a bargain. Furthermore, if your car is disabled by collision or other-than-collision loss, the cost of towing it to the garage will be paid under those coverages.

Exclusions

Two of the exclusions found in Part D (the first and third) have already been discussed. The remaining exclusions are dominated by limitations on the coverage for automobile equipment. Part D exclusions are listed in Table 14.8. One important exclusion reflects the high frequency of theft losses to certain equipment. Exclusion 4 omits coverage for electronic equipment, including radios and stereos, tape decks, compact disk systems, navigation systems, Internet access systems, personal computers, video entertainment systems, telephones, televisions, and more. These exclusions do not apply to electronic equipment that is permanently installed in the car.

Overall, custom furnishings in pickups and vans and loss to awnings or cabanas and equipment designed to create additional living facilities are excluded. Such equipment represents nonstandard exposures for which insurance can be bought through endorsement.

TABLE 14.8   Personal Auto Policy, Part D Exclusions—ISO PAP 2003

Exclusions
We will not pay for:
1. Loss to "your covered auto" or any "nonowned auto," which occurs while it is being used as a public or livery conveyance. This Exclusion (1.) does not apply to a share-the-expense car pool.
2. Damage due and confined to:
a. Wear and tear;
b. Freezing;
c. Mechanical or electrical breakdown or failure; or
d. Road damage to tires.
This Exclusion (2.) does not apply if the damage results from the total theft of "your covered auto" or any "nonowned auto."

EXCLUSIONS

3. Loss due to or as a consequence of:

     a. Radioactive contamination;

     b. Discharge of any nuclear weapon (even if accidental);

     c. War (declared or undeclared);

     d. Civil war;

     e. Insurrection; or

     f. Rebellion or revolution.

4. Loss to any electronic equipment that reproduces, receives, or transmits audio, visual, or data signals. This includes but is not limited to:

     a. Radios and stereos;

     b. Tape decks;

     c. Compact disk systems;

     d. Navigation systems;

     e. Internet access systems;

     f. Personal computers;

     g. Video entertainment systems;

     h. Telephones;

     i. Televisions;

     j. Two-way mobile radios;

     k. Scanners; or

     l. Citizens band radios.

This Exclusion (4.) does not apply to electronic equipment that is permanently installed in "your covered auto" or any "nonowned auto."

5. Loss to tapes, records, disks or other media used with equipment described in Exclusion 4.

6. A total loss to "your covered auto" or any "nonowned auto" due to destruction or confiscation by governmental or civil authorities.

This Exclusion (6.) does not apply to the interests of Loss Payees in "your covered auto."

7. Loss to:

     a. A "trailer," camper body, or motor home, which is not shown in the Declarations; or

     b. Facilities or equipment used with such "trailer," camper body or motor home. Facilities or equipment include but are not limited to:

         1. Cooking, dining, plumbing or refrigeration facilities;

         2. Awnings or cabanas; or

         3. Any other facilities or equipment used with a "trailer," camper body, or motor home.

This Exclusion (7.) does not apply to a:

     a. "Trailer," and its facilities or equipment, which you do not own; or

     b. "Trailer," camper body, or the facilities or equipment in or attached to the "trailer" or camper body, which you:

         1. Acquire during the policy period; and

         2. Ask us to insure within 14 days after you become the owner.

8. Loss to any "nonowned auto" when used by you or any "family member" without a reasonable belief that you or that "family member" are entitled to do so.

9. Loss to equipment designed or used for the detection or location of radar or laser.

10. Loss to any custom furnishings or equipment in or upon any pickup or van. Custom furnishings or equipment include but are not limited to:

     a. Special carpeting or insulation;

     b. Furniture or bars;

     c. Height-extending roofs; or

     d. Custom murals, paintings or other decals or graphics.

This Exclusion (10.) does not apply to a cap, cover, or bedliner in or upon any of "your covered auto" which is a pickup.

EXCLUSIONS

11. Loss to any "nonowned auto" being maintained or used by any person while employed or otherwise engaged in the "business" of:

    a. Selling;

    b. Repairing;

    c. Servicing;

    d. Storing; or

    e. Parking;

    vehicles designed for use on public highways. This includes road testing and delivery.

12. Loss to "your covered auto" or any "nonowned auto" located inside a facility designed for racing, for the purpose of:

    a. Competing in; or

    b. Practicing or preparing for;

    any prearranged or organized racing or speed contest.

13. Loss to, or loss of use of, a "nonowned auto" rented by:

    a. You; or

    b. Any "family member";

    if a rental vehicle company is precluded from recovering such loss or loss of use, from you or that "family member," pursuant to the provisions of any applicable rental agreement or state law.

Recall that trailers you own, whether declared or not, are defined as covered autos. To obtain property insurance on those trailers, they must be declared (permitting the insurer to charge a premium). Nonfortuitous losses are also excluded. Certain losses are expected or preventable, such as damage due to wear and tear, freezing, mechanical or electrical breakdown, and road damage to tires. Exclusion 7 denies coverage for loss or destruction because the government seized the vehicle. This exclusion follows the development of new laws associated with illegal drug trafficking and the handling of hazardous waste.

Prior to revisions in 1986, the PAP covered damage to nonowned autos (including temporary substitutes) for liability only. If you were driving a friend's car or a rental vehicle, the old policy would cover damage to that vehicle only if you were legally liable. The 1986 form provided property damage coverage for nonowned autos in Part D, negating the requirement that you be liable. The 1989 form went one step further by including temporary substitutes (cars used because the declared vehicle is out of commission) in Part D rather than Part A.

The amount of coverage available for nonowned autos, however, is limited to the maximum available (actual cash value) on any declared auto. In addition, a deductible likely applies, and three exclusions relevant to nonowned autos have been added. First, a nonowned auto used without reasonable belief or permission to do so is not covered. Second, a nonowned vehicle damaged while being driven by someone performing operations associated with the automobile business (servicing, repairing, etc.) is not covered. Last, if the nonowned auto is driven by anyone in any business operation (other than a private passenger auto or trailer driven by you or any family member), the auto is not covered.

Other Provisions

The limit of liability is the lesser of the actual cash value of the stolen or damaged property or the amount necessary to repair or replace it. The insurer reserves the right to pay for the loss in money or repair or replace the damaged property. There are limits, however, as described in the policy: $500 for a nonowned auto and $1,000 for equipment designed solely for the reproduction of sounds. For payment of loss, the insurer will repair or replace the damaged property. If the stolen property is returned damaged, the insurer will repair it.

The no benefit to bailee provision says, "This insurance shall not directly or indirectly benefit any carrier or other bailee for hire." If your car is damaged or stolen while in the custody of a parking lot or transportation company, your insurer will pay you and then have the right of subrogation against a negligent bailee. If other insurance covers a loss, your insurer will pay its share on a pro rata basis. If there is a dispute concerning the amount of loss, either you or the insurer may demand an appraisal, which is binding on both parties. As a practical matter, appraisal is seldom used by an insured because the cost is shared with the insurer.

The other insurance provision is pro rata except for nonowned autos, which is excess. In prior coverages, nonowned autos were included in the liability part, not Part D. As in other parts of the policy, there is an appraisal section for evaluating the value of the loss.

Duties After an Accident or Loss—Part E

When an accident or loss occurs, you must notify the company promptly, indicating how, when, and where it happened. Notice should include the names and addresses of any injured persons and any witnesses. You can notify your agent or call the company. You must also comply with the following conditions:

- Cooperate with the insurer in the investigation, settlement, or defense of any claim or suit
- Promptly send the company copies of any notices or legal papers received in connection with the accident or loss
- Submit, as often as reasonably required and at the insurer's expense, to physical exams by physicians it selects, as well as examinations under oath
- Authorize the company to obtain medical reports and other pertinent records
- Submit a proof of loss when required by the insurer

A person seeking uninsured motorists coverage must also notify the police promptly if a hit-and-run driver is involved and send copies of the legal papers if a suit is brought. The requirement that you notify the police concerning a hit-and-run driver is to discourage you from making such an allegation when, in fact, something else caused your accident. If, for example, you do not have coverage for damage to your auto but you do have uninsured motorists coverage, you may be tempted to use the latter after you fail to negotiate a sharp curve in the road. Having to report a hit-and-run driver to the police may deter you from making such an assertion.

If an accident causes damage to your car, or if it is stolen, you must also fulfill the following duties:

- Take reasonable steps after loss to protect the auto and its equipment from further loss (the company will pay for reasonable cost involved in complying with this requirement)
- Notify the police promptly if your car is stolen
- Permit the company to inspect and appraise the damaged property before its repair or disposal

The first duty listed means that you cannot just walk off and abandon your automobile after an accident. If you do, it may very well be stripped as an abandoned car. The second duty, prompt notification of the police in the event of theft, increases the probability that stolen property will be recovered. This requirement also reduces the moral hazard involved; people have been known to sell a car and then report it stolen. The third duty, permitting company appraisal, allows the insurer to inspect and appraise the loss before repairs are made in order to keep costs down. If you could simply take your damaged car to a repair shop, have the work done, and then send the bill to the insurance company, costs would increase immensely. The most common question you hear upon entering many (if not most) repair shops is, "Do you have insurance?"

General Provisions—Part F

Several general provisions apply to the whole contract. Following is a brief summary of each.

- Bankruptcy or insolvency of a covered person shall not relieve the insurer of any obligations under the policy. The fact that you are bankrupt does not relieve the insurance company of its obligation to pay a third-party claimant or you.
- Changes in the policy can be made only in writing and may affect the premium charged. If the form is revised to provide more coverage without a premium increase, the policy you have will automatically provide it.
- The insurer does not provide any coverage for any insured who made fraudulent statements or engaged in fraudulent conduct in connection with any accident or loss for which coverage is sought under the policy.
- An insured cannot start legal proceedings against the insurer until there has been full compliance with all the terms of the policy.
- If a person who receives payment from the insurer has the right to recover damages from another, the insurer has the right to subrogation. Such a person must help the insurer to exercise its rights and do nothing after a loss to prejudice them. This would apply, for example, to a passenger in your car who is injured, receives payment under the medical payments coverage, and has the right to recover damages from a liable third party or a first-party health insurer. The company's subrogation right, however, does not apply under the damage to your auto coverage against any person using your covered auto with a reasonable belief that he or she has the right to do so. If it were not for this provision, a person who borrowed your car with your permission and had a wreck would wind up paying for the damage if he or she was at fault.

- The policy's territorial limits are the United States, its territories and possessions, Puerto Rico, and Canada. Note that this does not include Mexico. If you are going to drive your car in Mexico, it is imperative that you buy Mexican insurance. You will have ample opportunity to do so almost anywhere once you cross the border. Also, the coverage is limited to the policy period only.

- You can cancel the policy by returning it to the insurer or providing advance written notice of the date that cancellation is to take effect.

- The insurer can cancel the policy at any time for nonpayment of premium. During the first sixty days the policy is in effect, the insurer can cancel upon ten days' notice for any reason, unless the policy is a renewal or continuation policy. After the first sixty days or if the policy is a renewal or continuation policy, the insurer can cancel only for nonpayment of premium or if your driver's license, or the license of any driver who lives with you or customarily uses your covered auto, is suspended or revoked. In such instances, twenty days' notice must be given. If your state requires a longer notice period or special requirements concerning notice, or modifies any of the stated reasons for termination, the insurer will comply.

- Transfer of the interest in the policy may not be assigned without the insurer's written consent, except when the insured dies. The surviving spouse or the legal representative of the insured will have coverage until the end of the policy period.

- If you have another policy issued by the company and both apply to the same accident, the maximum limit under all the policies will not exceed the highest applicable limit of liability under any one policy. In other words, you cannot stack them. If a policy has a single limit for liability of $300,000 and another policy you have with the same company has a single limit of $200,000, your total coverage—if both apply to the same accident—is $300,000.

Insuring Other Vehicles

A miscellaneous type vehicle endorsement can be added to the PAP to insure motorcycles, mopeds, motor scooters, golf carts, motor homes, and other vehicles. The endorsement does not cover snowmobiles; they require a separate endorsement. The miscellaneous type vehicle endorsement can be used to provide all the coverages of the PAP, including liability, medical payments, uninsured motorists, and physical damage coverage. With a few exceptions, the PAP provisions and conditions applicable to these coverages are the same for the endorsement.

No-Fault Coverages

The liability coverage in the PAP protects you against loss if you are responsible to someone else for bodily injury or property damage because of an accident that was your fault. All the other coverages pay benefits without regard to fault. Thus, they could be referred to as no-fault coverages. This term, however, generally refers to legally required coverage added to the auto policy to compensate you and members of your family who are injured in an auto accident. This coverage, as discussed earlier, is called personal injury protection (PIP).

In some states, the PIP provides only medical payments, whereas in other states it will also replace part of your income if you are disabled in an auto accident. It may also include payments to replace uncompensated personal services, such as those of the parent who maintains the home. If you operate your vehicle in a no-fault state, your coverage will conform to the state law. Usually, there is an aggregate limit per person per accident for all benefits provided by the PIP.

KEY TAKEAWAYS

In this section you studied the components of the personal automobile policy (PAP), the auto insurance contract purchased by most people:

- The PAP is structured as follows: declarations page, general insuring agreement, definitions, and parts A–F.
  - Declarations—identify the insured by name and address; specify term of policy, premiums charged, coverages provided, and limits of liability
  - Definitions—describe any term of policy in quotations
  - Part A—liability coverage: pays for bodily injury and property damage for which insured is responsible at single or split limits (subject to exclusions), provides legal defense, and makes supplementary payments
  - Part B—medical payments coverage: pays for necessary medical or funeral expenses because of bodily injury to a covered person, subject to exclusions, limits of liability, and other insurance
  - Part C—uninsured motorists coverage: pays for bodily injury caused by another vehicle whose driver has no or inadequate insurance or was a hit-and-run, subject to exclusions and other provisions
  - Part D—coverage for damage to your auto: pays for direct and accidental loss to the covered auto(s) on open perils basis through collision and comprehensive options, subject to exclusions and other provisions
  - Part E—duties after an accident or loss: must notify insurer immediately and meet other conditions
  - Part F—general provisions: general conditions applying to entire contract
- Insurance on miscellaneous vehicles available by endorsement.
- All coverages other than liability pay benefits without regard to fault.

DISCUSSION QUESTIONS

1. Who is insured under the liability coverage of the PAP? Who gets paid in case of a loss?
2. Explain the difference between a single limit for liability and split limits.
3. Morton Jones currently has a PAP with only bodily injury and property damage liability coverages. While hurrying home one evening, Mr. Jones smashed through his garage door. There was damage to his car and extensive damage to the garage and its contents. Will Mr. Jones be able to collect for these damages under his PAP? Explain.
4. The deductible for other-than-collision is usually smaller than for collision coverage. Does this make sense to you? How do you account for it?
5. The insuring agreement for Part D of the PAP shown in Chapter 25 lists perils that are covered under other-than-collision coverage. Explain the meaning of this list and what protection is afforded under the policy for loss caused by one of the perils. Explain further the coverage for loss caused by a peril neither listed in the insuring agreement nor considered collision (such as lightning damage).
6. Evelyn's car skidded on a wet road and hit another car. She was able to get out of her car and assist the passenger in the other car until an ambulance and the police arrived. She felt okay, so she signed a form refusing medical treatment. Then she called a tow truck to take her car to a repair shop and took a taxi home. Now that the accident is over, what does Evelyn need to do to meet the conditions of her PAP?
7. Joyce owns a Ford Explorer; her friend Sharon owns a Jeep. Joyce has coverage from State Farm and Sharon from ERIE. Both of them have exactly the same coverages and use the PAP. They have a single liability limit of $250,000 and the same limit for uninsured motorists. They have a $250 deductible for collision and a $100 deductible for other-than-collision. They have towing and labor and car rental reimbursement.

   Please respond to the following questions:

   a. Joyce borrowed Sharon's Jeep when her Explorer was in the shop to replace recalled tires. While driving the Jeep, she was seriously injured by an uninsured drunk driver. The Jeep is a total loss. How much will be paid by each policy if it is determined that Joyce has $370,000 of bodily injury loss? Explain the process of the payment. Whose insurance company pays first and whose insurance company pays second? What amount is covered by each insurer for all the damage in this case? Find the justification for the coverages (if possible) in the PAP.

   b. In this case, the drunk driver destroyed his car. Would he get any reimbursement? Explain.

   c. Now that Sharon has no car and Joyce is in the hospital, Sharon is driving the Explorer. With her three children in the car, Sharon slid off an icy road and hit a tree. She was not injured, but the kids were taken to the emergency room for a few hours. The Explorer was damaged. What coverages will take care of these losses? Explain and find the justification in the PAP.

5. AUTO INSURANCE PREMIUM RATES

LEARNING OBJECTIVE

- In this section we elaborate on how auto insurance premiums are influenced and perceptions thereof.

Pricing factors of auto insurance include the make of the car, age of the car, whether the car is driven to and from work, age and gender of the driver, marital status, and location of the car. The location is critical because in some markets, insurers are pulling out due to large losses. These factors are underwriting factors. Additionally, the driving record is an important factor in classifying a driver as a preferred driver or substandard risk. The industry uses the data presented in Table 14.1 and Table 14.2[32] in the introduction to this chapter. Fraudulent claims also affect rates; see the box "How to Combat Insurance Fraud?" for a discussion.

How to Combat Insurance Fraud?

Does your car have any dings or scratches on its exterior? Any car older than a few months probably has a few. Small scratches usually aren't worth getting fixed on their own, but what if you had a minor accident? Couldn't you just ask the body shop to include the cost of repairing the scratches in its repair estimates? The insurer is a big company; it won't even feel the effects of another couple of hundred dollars on your claim. Or will it?

Fraud is very costly to society as a whole. The Insurance Information Institute estimates that fraud accounts for 10 percent of the property/casualty insurance industry's losses with loss adjustment costs of about $30 per year. The states are making efforts to combat insurance fraud. The key state laws against insurance fraud and the number of states that adopted each law are listed below.

- Insurance fraud classified as crime—"A fraudulent act is committed if information in insurance applications is falsified in an attempt to obtain lower premium rates, or to inflate the amount of loss in a claim." This law was adopted by all the states. Alabama, Hawaii, and Oregon adopted this law for workers' compensation, healthcare insurance, or auto insurance only.

- Immunity statutes—"Individuals or organizations are exempt from libel or unfair trade practices lawsuits which could be brought against them for releasing information on prior claims." All states adopted this law. In Alabama, Hawaii, Mississippi, Rhode Island, and Wyoming, it applies to workers' compensation, arson, or auto insurance only.

- Fraud bureaus—"The main purpose of the bureau is to set up documented criminal cases that can be readily prosecuted. Some bureaus have law enforcement powers." All states have instituted fraud bureaus for all lines or limited lines of insurance, with the exception of Alabama, Illinois, Indiana, Michigan, Oregon, Tennessee, Vermont, and Wyoming.

- Mandatory insurer fraud plan—The plan has to include remedial actions. Only twenty states adopted this plan.

- Mandatory auto photo inspection—This is designed to eliminate claims for damage sustained prior to the issuance of a policy and the purchase of insurance for nonexistent vehicles. This law was adopted by five states.

Occupying an entire floor of a New Jersey skyscraper, ISO ClaimSearch, a sophisticated computer system, cross-references millions of claims every second. When a claim is entered, ClaimSearch automatically finds relevant public and insurance-related information about the claimant. In addition to flagging multiple claims, the system allows in-depth searches that help find links among claimants, doctors, and lawyers. When ClaimSearch investigators believe they have found a fraud case, they turn their information over to law enforcement. In 2001, for example, the Hudson County, New Jersey, prosecutor indicted 172 people for allegedly staging automobile accidents and filing false medical claims for more than $5 million. Nationwide, insurance fraud prosecutions and convictions are on the increase. According to the Washington, D.C.-based Coalition Against Insurance Fraud, state insurance fraud bureaus have doubled their criminal convictions of insurance scams since 1995.

The Insurance Research Council reported that fraud and inflated descriptions of injuries added between $4.8 to $6.8 billion to the cost of auto insurance in 2007. However, the laws described above act to lower the cost of fraud. For example, the overall loss ratio for private passenger auto insurance in New York fell from 0.86 in 2002 to 0.61 in 2003. This reduction points to the success of new laws that fight the padding of claims.

Questions for Discussion

1. How far should the insurer go in its investigations of claims?

2. What should be the insurer's response when it finds out about overcharging for a claim?

3. What is the relationship between some of the forms of no-fault laws and fraud in auto insurance? Do you think reform would combat fraud?

Sources: Insurance Information Institute, The Insurance Fact Book, 2009, 160–162; Insurance Information Institute, "Insurance Fraud," February 2009, accessed March 21, 2009, http://www.iii.org/media/hottopics/insurance/fraud/; "IRC Study: Details Billions in Injury Fraud," National Underwriter Online News Service, January 13, 2005; Ron Panko, "Making a Dent in Auto Insurance Fraud: Computer Technology Drives Auto Insurers' Efforts to Stall Fraud Rings," Best's Review, October 2001.

Data show that younger drivers and male drivers cause more accidents. In 2006, drivers age twenty-one to twenty-four were responsible for 11.2 percent of accidents with fatalities and for 10.7 percent of all reported accidents. For drivers age twenty and younger, the ratios were alarming, with 6.4 percent of the driving population responsible for 13 percent of the fatal accidents and 16.6 percent of all reported accidents. The data are from the National Safety Council, as cited by the Insurance Information Institute. The national safety data estimated that there were 202.8 million licensed drivers in 2006; 50.1 percent of them were male who accounted for about 74 percent of all accidents with fatalities and 58 percent of total reported accidents.[33]

The general public's perception is that auto insurance rating is unfair. California drivers decided to take matters into their own hands and in 1988 passed Proposition 103, legislation that set strict guidelines for insurance pricing activities. Proposition 103 also called for an elected insurance commissioner and provided that commissioner with expanded powers. A major selling point of this legislation to voters was the imposition of limitations on insurer use of geography as a rating factor. Specifically, Proposition 103 requires insurers to set prices primarily based on driving record, years of driving experience, and annual miles driven. Insurers are further restricted in their ability to incorporate age, gender, and zip code in their rating process.

It is important to note that there are also discounts for drivers, including ones for good students, nondrinkers, second car, driver training, and safety devices. Furthermore, having more than one car and not using it to drive to work but for pleasure use only is cheaper than driving the car to and from work.

As noted in Chapter 13, which discussed the homeowners policy, regulators in each state created well-designed booklets that inform consumers of the specific requirements in their states and the different rates for a typical automobile in many major locations. When purchasing auto insurance, it is advisable to read the booklet or explore the Internet for the best rates and the rating of insurers.

KEY TAKEAWAYS

In this section you studied pricing factors affecting auto insurance premiums and problems with some of those factors:

- Typical pricing factors include make, age, and use of the car; age, gender, location, driving record, and marital status of the driver.
- Young male drivers account for a disproportionately large percentage of accidents.
- California Proposition 103 in 1988 limited the use of geography, age, and gender as rating factors in that state.
- Discounts are available for good students, nondrinkers, those who have taken driver training, and others.

DISCUSSION QUESTIONS

1. Do you think it is socially desirable to do away with age, gender, and marital status as classification factors for auto insurance premium rates? Why or why not? What would be the implication if everyone paid the same rate?

2. Why might insurers allow for a good student discount? Is this factor any more legitimate to use in rating than marital status, for example? Explain.

6. REVIEW AND PRACTICE

1. What is considered a loss under the liability in the PAP?

2. What arguments are used in favor of and in opposition to the no-fault system?

3. What persons are insured for medical payment under the PAP? Who gets paid in case of a loss?

4. The Helsings (who have a PAP) are involved in an automobile accident that was not their fault on their way home from a dinner party. Although they are unharmed, their car is disabled. The police recommend that they leave the car by the side of the road and take a taxi home. When the Helsings return to the scene of the accident, they find that their car has been stripped down to the chassis. The Helsings submit a claim to their insurance agent for the entire loss. Are the Helsings covered under the PAP? Explain. What if the Helsings had not contacted the police and leaving the car was their own idea?

5. Chris Malmud says, "Buying uninsured motorists coverage is an awkward substitute for life and health insurance. Besides that, it protects you only in certain situations. I'd rather spend my money on more and better life and health insurance." Do you agree? Why or why not?

6. Barney has a PAP with liability limits of 25/50/15 and collision coverage with a $200 deductible. While pulling his boat and trailer—which are not listed in the policy's declarations—to the lake, he loses control, sideswipes the car he is passing with his trailer, and then rams a farmer's tree with his car. The losses are as follows:

Barney (medical expenses)	$1,300
Barney's girlfriend (medical expenses)	$2,450
Driver of other car	
Lost income	$10,000
Medical expenses	$13,500
Mental anguish	$20,000
	$43,500
Passenger of other car	
Lost income	$5,500
Medical expenses	$3,400
	$8,900
Barney's car	$4,000
Barney's boat	$800
Barney's trailer	$500
Farmer's tree	$300
Other driver's Mercedes	$29,800

Using the PAP in Chapter 25, explain what will and will not be paid by Barney's insurance contract, and why.

7. If you permit a friend to drive your car, does he or she have protection under your policy? How will losses be shared if your friend has a PAP on his or her own auto and negligently causes an accident while driving your car?

8. While attending classes at her college, Lisa parks her Corvette on the street and locks it. When she returns, it is gone. She reports its loss to her insurer and notifies the police immediately. Because she must commute to school and to work, she rents a car for $180 per week, or $28 per day for any part of a week. Twenty-three days after her car disappeared, it is recovered. It has been driven over 12,000 miles, its right rear fender has been destroyed in an accident, and the interior has been vandalized. The low estimate for repair of the exterior and interior damage is $23,000. The actual cash value of her car is $16,000. Lisa has a PAP with other-than-collision coverage and a $200 deductible. Explain her coverage to her, noting what she can expect to recover from her insurer, and why.

9. Assume your car was rear-ended by another motorist, incurring property damages of $10,000 and bodily injury of $50,000. Further assume that the other driver is found liable for the full amount of your loss, but he carries liability insurance of 10/20/10, which meets the financial responsibility law requirement. Unfortunately, he has no assets or ability to pay. How much can

you get from his insurance? What can you do to collect the full amount? Is there coverage you could have bought?

10. Allissa owns a home worth $500,000 and a car worth $35,000. Currently, the liability limits of her personal auto policy are 200/400/100. Does she have enough automobile liability insurance? Explain what her coverage levels mean and what could happen if she was responsible for a car accident that exceeded these limits.

ENDNOTES

1. Insurance Information Institute (III), *The Insurance Fact Book, 2009*, 57, 62; http://www.iii.org/media/facts/statsbyissue/auto/ (accessed March 21, 2009).

2. Insurance Information Institute (III), *The Insurance Fact Book, 2009*, 136–137.

3. Insurance Information Institute (III), *The Insurance Fact Book, 2009*, 72–74.

4. Excludes Massachusetts and most states with no-fault automobile insurance laws.

5. Excludes Massachusetts, Michigan, and New Jersey.

6. Claim Frequency is claims per one hundred earned car years. A car year is equal to 365 days of insured coverage for a single vehicle.

7. Includes loss adjustment expenses.

8. Claim frequency is claims per one hundred earned car years. A car year is equal to 365 days of insured coverage for a single vehicle.

9. Claim severity is the size of the loss measured by the average amount paid for each claim.

10. Excludes Massachusetts, Michigan, and Puerto Rico. Based on coverage with a $500 deductible.

11. Excludes wind and water losses.

12. Claim frequency is claims per one hundred earned car years. A car year is equal to 365 days of insured coverage for a single vehicle.

13. Claim severity is the size of the loss measured by the average amount paid for each claim.

14. Claim frequency is claims per one hundred earned car years. A car year is equal to 365 days of insured coverage for a single vehicle.

15. Claim severity is the size of the loss measured by the average amount paid for each claim.

16. See Jeffrey O'Connell, "No-Fault Auto Insurance: Back by Popular (Market) Demand," *San Diego Law Review* 26 (1989). Most studies regarding these aspects of fault-based laws are now old. Emphasis has turned recently to premium levels, as discussed.

17. David S. Loughran, "The Effect of No-Fault Automobile Insurance on Driver Behavior and Automobile Accidents in the United States," http://www.rand.org/cgi-bin/Abstracts/e-getabbydoc.pl?MR-1384-ICJISBN: 0-8330-3021-3, MR-1384-ICJ. Copyright © 2001 RAND. This research was conducted within the RAND Institute for Civil Justice.

18. Insurance Information Institute (III), *The Insurance Fact Book, 2009*, 66–67.

19. The first two numbers refer to bodily injury liability limits and the third number to property liability. For example, 20/40/10 means coverage up to $40,000 for all persons injured in an accident, subject to a limit of $20,000 for one individual and $10,000 coverage for property damage.

20. Low-cost policy limits for low-income drivers in the California Automobile Assigned Risk Plan are 10/20/3.

21. Instead of policy limits, policyholders can satisfy the requirement with a combined single limit policy. Amounts vary by state.

22. Minimum coverage requirements will increase to 15/30/25 on January 1, 2010.

23. In addition, policyholders must also carry at least $1,000 for medical payments.

24. May be waived for the policyholder but is compulsory for passengers.

25. Basic policy (optional) limits are 10/10/5. Uninsured and underinsured motorist coverage not available under the basic policy but uninsured motorist coverage is required under the standard policy.

26. In addition, policyholders must have 50/100 for wrongful death coverage.

27. Instead of policy limits, policyholders can satisfy the requirement with a combined single limit policy. Amounts vary by state.

28. Instead of policy limits, policyholders can satisfy the requirement with a combined single limit policy. Amounts vary by state.

29. Minimum coverage requirements will increase to 30/60/30 on January 1, 2011.

30. Instead of policy limits, policyholders can satisfy the requirement with a combined single limit policy. Amounts vary by state.

31. Insurance Information Institute (III), *The Insurance Fact Book, 2009*, 57, 62; http://www.iii.org/media/facts/statsbyissue/auto/ (accessed March 21, 2009).

32. For all limits combined. Data are for paid claims.

33. Insurance Information Institute, *The Insurance Fact Book, 2009*, 138–139.

CHAPTER 15

Multirisk Management Contracts: Business

In the preceding four chapters, you read about property and liability exposures generally and how families insure home and auto exposures specifically. Now, we will delve briefly into business, or commercial, insurance. Commercial insurance is a topic for an extensive separate course, but its importance has been reflected to a great extent throughout the previous chapters. Employers who take unnecessary risks or who do not practice prudent risk management may not only cause job losses, they may also cause the loss of pensions and important benefits such as health insurance (discussed in later chapters).

As members of the work force, we drive our employers' cars and spend many of our waking hours operating machines and computers on business premises. Risks are involved in these activities that require insurance coverage. A case in point is the damage caused by mold in many commercial buildings and schools as well as in homes. Mold can cause headaches, discomfort, and more serious problems. Employers' property coverage was of great help in remedying the problem. However, as a result of the many claims, insurers have excluded mold coverage or provided very low limits. This and more pertinent issues in different types of commercial coverage will be discussed in this chapter. Issues such as the complexities of directors and officers coverage due to the improper behavior of executives in many large corporations, like AIG, Enron, and WorldCom, are discussed in this chapter, as are the dispute over the limits of coverage of the World Trade Center. The interested student is invited to study in depth and explore the risk and insurance news media for current commercial coverage issues. Also, Case 3 in Chapter 23 relates to the types of commercial coverage embedded in integrated risk programs. The programs described in the case use similar commercial packaged policies that are described in this chapter, which covers the following:

1. Links

2. Commercial package policy and commercial property coverages

3. Other property coverages

4. Commercial general liability policy and commercial umbrella liability policy

5. Other liability risks

FIGURE 15.1 Links between the Holistic Risk Puzzle and Commercial Insurance

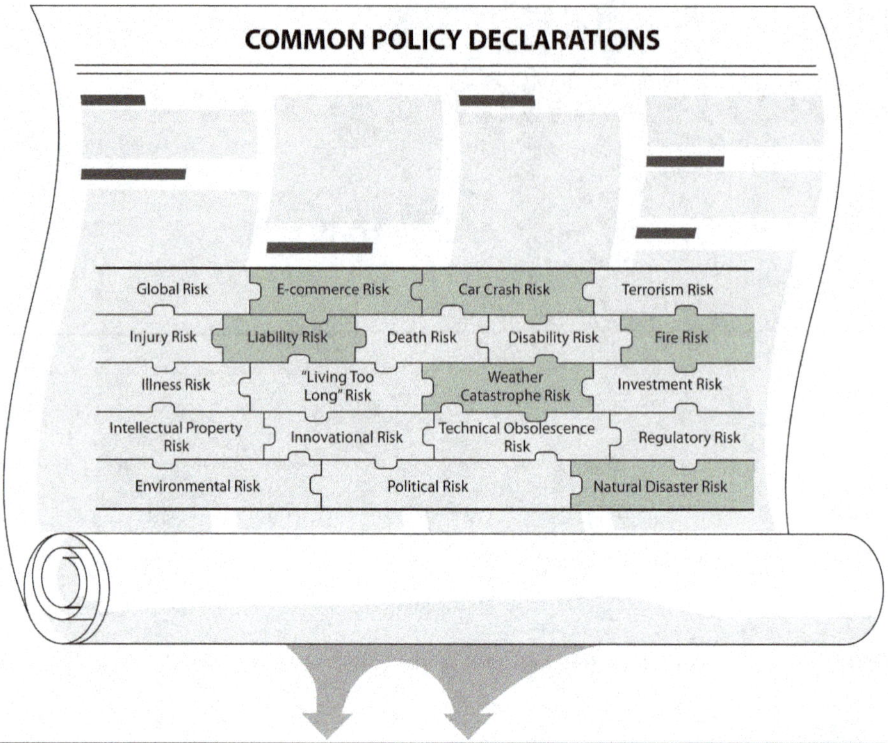

COMMON POLICY DECLARATIONS

Global Risk	E-commerce Risk	Car Crash Risk	Terrorism Risk
Injury Risk	Liability Risk	Death Risk	Disability Risk	Fire Risk
Illness Risk	"Living Too Long" Risk	Weather Catastrophe Risk	Investment Risk
Intellectual Property Risk	Innovational Risk	Technical Obsolescence Risk	Regulatory Risk
Environmental Risk	Political Risk	Natural Disaster Risk

COMPANY NAME AREA	PRODUCER NAME AREA

NAMED INSURED: _____

MAILING ADDRESS: _____

POLICY PERIOD: FROM _____ TO _____ AT 12:01 A.M. STANDARD
TIME AT YOUR MAILING ADDRESS SHOWN ABOVE: _____

| BUSINESS DESCRIPTION | |

IN RETURN FOR THE PAYMENT OF THE PREMIUM, AND SUBJECT TO ALL THE TERMS OF
THIS POLICY, WE AGREE WITH YOU TO PROVIDE THE INSURANCE AS STATED IN THIS

THIS POLICY CONSISTS OF THE FOLLOWING COVERAGE PARTS FOR WHICH A PREMIUM IS INDICATED. THIS PREMIUM MAY BE SUBJECT TO ADJUSTMENT.

	PREMIUM
BOILER AND MACHINERY COVERAGE PART	$
CAPITAL ASSETS PROGRAM (OUTPUT POLICY) COVERAGE PART	$
COMMERCIAL AUTOMOBILE COVERAGE PART	$
COMMERCIAL GENERAL LIABILITY COVERAGE PART	$
COMMERCIAL INLAND MARINE COVERAGE PART	$
COMMERCIAL PROPERTY COVERAGE PART	$
CRIME AND FIDELITY COVERAGE PART	$
EMPLOYMENT-RELATED PRACTICES LIABILITY COVERAGE PART	$
FARM COVERAGE PART	$
LIQUOR LIABILITY COVERAGE PART	$
POLLUTION LIABILITY COVERAGE PART	$
PROFESSIONAL LIABILITY COVERAGE PART	TOTAL: $

Premium shown is payable: $ at inception. $

FORMS APPLICABLE TO ALL COVERAGE PARTS (SHOW NUMBERS):
_____
_____
_____
_____
_____

Countersigned: _____   By: _____
                        (Date)   (Authorized Representative)

NOTE OFFICERS' FACSIMILE SIGNATURES MAY BE INSERTED HERE, ON THE POLICY COVER OR ELSEWHERE AT THE COMPANY'S OPTION.

Source: ISO Common Policy Declarations Form IL DS 00 09 08. Includes copyrighted material of Insurance Services Office, Inc., with its permission.

1. LINKS

At this point in our study, we are drilling further down into specific, more complex coverages of the commercial world. Many types of coverage are customized to the needs of the business, but many more use the policies designed by the Insurance Services Office (ISO), which have been approved in most states. We have moved from the narrow realm of personal line coverages, but the basic premises are still the same. The business risks shown in Figure 15.1 do not clearly differentiate between commercial risk and personal hazards. The perils of fire and windstorm do not separate personal homes from commercial buildings, as we saw from the devastation of hurricanes Katrina, Rita, and Wilma in 2005. Our business may be sued for mistakes we make as employees because the business is a separate legal entity. We cannot separate between the commercial world and our personal world when it comes to completing our risk management puzzle to ensure holistic coverage.

Figure 15.1 shows how the picture of our risk puzzles connects to the types of commercial coverage available as a package from the ISO. We use the common policy declarations page, which illustrates the mechanism of this packaged policy. This program permits businesses to select among a variety of insurance options, like a cafeteria where we can choose the items we want to eat and reject those we do not. The program is considered a package because it combines both property and liability options in the same policy, as well as additional coverages as listed in the common policy declarations page in Figure 15.1. Within each of the property and liability coverages are various options available to tailor protection to the particular needs of the insured, as you will see in this chapter.

2. COMMERCIAL PACKAGE POLICY AND COMMERCIAL PROPERTY COVERAGES

LEARNING OBJECTIVES

In this section we elaborate on the following commercial property insurance solutions:

- **Introduction and overview of the commercial package policy (CPP)**
- **The commercial property policy of the CPP**
- **The building and personal property (BPP) form of the commercial property policy and business interruption coverage (BIC)**
- **Causes of loss options in the BPP and BIC**
- **Major features of BPP and BIC**

The commercial package policy (CPP) program was started by the Insurance Services Office (ISO) in 1986. Every policy includes three standard elements: the cover page, common policy conditions, and common declarations (shown in Figure 15.1). It is important to elaborate on the declaration page because it provides a visual aid of the various coverages that can be selected by a business, depending on needs. Some businesses may not need specific parts of the package, but all the elements are listed for the choice of the potential insured. More specifically, the package may include the following commercial coverage elements: boiler and machinery, capital assets program, commercial automobile, commercial general liability, commercial inland marine, commercial property, crime and fidelity, employment-related practices liability, farm liability, liquor liability, pollution liability, and professional liability. Some of these coverages were discussed in prior chapters. The rest of the coverages will be described here.

Most commercial organizations have similar property exposures. Common business property exposures, along with business income exposures, can be insured through the **commercial property policy** form of the commercial package policy. The liability module of the commercial package policy is the **commercial general liability (CGL) policy**. It replaced the liability coverage previously available through the comprehensive general liability policy. In 1986, the CGL was made part of the new modular approach introduced by the ISO in the form of the CPP.

2.1 Commercial Property Coverages

The commercial property policy form of the CPP begins with property declarations and conditions. These provisions identify the covered location, property values (and limits), premiums, deductibles, and other specific aspects of the coverage. These pages make the insurance unique for a given

commercial property policy

Policy that provides insurance for direct physical loss to business property and income.

commercial general liability (CGL) policy

The liability module of the commercial package policy.

policyholder by identifying that policyholder's specific exposures. The information in the declarations must be accurate for the desired protection to exist. The remainder of the commercial property coverage consists of the following:

- The building and personal property (BPP) coverage form
- One of three causes of loss forms for the BPP
- Business income coverage (BIC) form
- Endorsements

Direct Property Coverage: The Building and Personal Property (BPP) Form

The BPP provides coverage for direct physical loss to buildings and/or contents as described in the policy. Separate sections with distinct limits of insurance are available for both buildings and contents to account for differing needs of insureds. Some insureds will be tenants who do not need building coverage. Others will be landlords who have limited or no need for contents coverage. Many insureds, of course, will need both in varying degrees.

Covered Property

What constitutes a building and business personal property may appear obvious. The insurer, however, must be very precise in defining its intent because, as you know, insurance is a contract of adhesion. Ambiguities, therefore, are generally construed in favor of the insured. Figure 15.2 lists the items defined as buildings. Figure 15.3 lists those items defined as business personal property.

FIGURE 15.2 Building as Defined in ISO Building and Personal Property Coverage Form (Sample)

> a. **Building,** meaning the building or structure described in the Declarations, including:
> (1) Completed additions;
> (2) Fixtures, including outdoor fixtures;
> (3) Permanently installed:
>   (a) Machinery and
>   (b) Equipment;
> (4) Personal property owned by you that is used to maintain or service the building or structure or its premises, including:
>   (a) Fire-extinguishing equipment;
>   (b) Outdoor furniture;
>   (c) Floor coverings; and
>   (d) Appliances used for refrigerating, ventilating, cooking, dishwashing or laundering;
> (5) If not covered by other insurance:
>   (a) Additions under construction, alterations and repairs to the building or structure;
>   (b) Materials, equipment, supplies and temporary structures, on or within 100 feet of the described premises, used for making additions, alterations or repairs to the building or structure.

Source: ISO Commercial Property Building and Personal Property Coverage Form CP 00 10 06 07. Includes copyrighted material of Insurance Services Office, Inc., with its permission.

FIGURE 15.3 Business Personal Property as Defined in ISO Building and Personal Property Coverage Form (Sample)

> **b. Your Business Personal Property** located in or on the building described in the Declarations or in the open (or in a vehicle) within 100 feet of the described premises, consisting of the following unless otherwise specified in the Declarations or on the Your Business Personal Property – Separation Of Coverage form:
> (1) Furniture and fixtures;
> (2) Machinery and equipment;
> (3) "Stock";
> (4) All other personal property owned by you and used in your business;
> (5) Labor, materials or services furnished or arranged by you on personal property of others;
> (6) Your use interest as tenant in improvements and betterments. Improvements and betterments are fixtures, alterations, installations or additions:
>   (a) Made a part of the building or structure you occupy but do not own; and
>   (b) You acquired or made at your expense but cannot legally remove;
> (7) Leased personal property for which you have a contractual responsibility to insure, unless otherwise provided for under Personal Property Of Others.

Source: ISO Commercial Property Building and Personal Property Coverage Form CP 00 10 06 07. Includes copyrighted material of Insurance Services Office, Inc., with its permission.

In addition to limiting coverage by defining building and business personal property, the BPP lists specific property that is excluded from protection. These items are listed in Figure 15.4. Reasons for exclusions in insurance were discussed earlier. Note in Figure 15.4 and in the corresponding section in the policy the exclusion of "electronic data, except as provided under additional coverages." In part f (4) of Additional Coverages, discussed below and in Figure 15.5, the electronic data that is covered is limited to a loss of up to $2,500 sustained in one year. The low limit on electronic equipment and data losses have propelled many businesses to buy the e-commerce endorsement discussed in Chapter 11. This exclusion is not always noticed by businesses. To ensure adequate coverage, insurers began to offer education programs to risk managers about their cyber-risk exposures.

FIGURE 15.4 Listed Property Not Covered as Defined in ISO Building and Personal Property Coverage Form (Sample)

2. **Property Not Covered**

Covered Property does not include:

a. Accounts, bills, currency, food stamps or other evidences of debt, money, notes or securities. Lottery tickets held for sale are not securities;

b. Animals, unless owned by others and boarded by you, or if owned by you, only as "stock" while inside of buildings;

c. Automobiles held for sale;

d. Bridges, roadways, walks, patios or other paved surfaces;

e. Contraband, or property in the course of illegal transportation or trade;

f. The cost of excavations, grading, backfilling or filling;

g. Foundations of buildings, structures, machinery or boilers if their foundations are below:

(1) The lowest basement floor; or

(2) The surface of the ground, if there is no basement;

h. Land (including land on which the property is located), water, growing crops or lawns;

i. Personal property while airborne or waterborne;

j. Bulkheads, pilings, piers, wharves or docks;

k. Property that is covered under another coverage form of this or any other policy in which it is more specifically described, except for the excess of the amount due (whether you can collect on it or not) from that other insurance;

l. Retaining walls that are not part of a building;

m. Underground pipes, flues or drains;

n. Electronic data, except as provided under the Additional Coverage, Electronic Data. Electronic data means information, facts or computer programs stored as or on, created or used on, or transmitted to or from computer software (including systems and applications software), on hard or floppy disks, CD-ROMs, tapes, drives, cells, data processing devices or any other repositories of computer software which are used with electronically controlled equipment. The term computer programs, referred to in the foregoing description of electronic data, means a set of related electronic instructions which direct the operations and functions of a computer or device connected to it, which enable the computer or device to receive, process, store, retrieve or send data. This paragraph, **n.**, does not apply to your "stock" of prepackaged software;

o. The cost to replace or restore the information on valuable papers and records, including those which exist as electronic data. Valuable papers and records include but are not limited to proprietary information, books of account, deeds, manuscripts, abstracts, drawings and card index systems. Refer to the Coverage Extension for Valuable Papers And Records (Other Than Electronic Data) for limited coverage for valuable papers and records other than those which exist as electronic data;

p. Vehicles or self-propelled machines (including aircraft or watercraft) that:

(1) Are licensed for use on public roads; or

(2) Are operated principally away from the described premises.

This paragraph does not apply to:

(a) Vehicles or self-propelled machines or autos you manufacture, process or warehouse;

(b) Vehicles or self-propelled machines, other than autos, you hold for sale;

(c) Rowboats or canoes out of water at the described premises; or

(d) Trailers, but only to the extent provided for in the Coverage Extension for Non-owned Detached Trailers;

Source: ISO Commercial Property Building and Personal Property Coverage Form CP 00 10 06 07. Includes copyrighted material of Insurance Services Office, Inc., with its permission.

Additional Coverages and Coverage Extensions

In addition to paying for repair or replacement of the listed property when caused by a covered peril, the BPP pays for other related costs. The BPP also extends coverage under specified conditions. These coverage additions and extensions are listed in Figure 15.5.

The value of these additional and extended coverages can be significant. Debris removal, for example, is a cost that is often overlooked by insureds, but can involve thousands of dollars. Recent tornadoes in the midwestern United States caused heavy property damage, and for many insureds, the most significant costs involved removal of tree limbs and other debris.

An interesting additional coverage is **pollutant cleanup and removal**, a provision that specifies the conditions under which, and the extent to which, protection for cleanup costs are paid by the insurer. Because of large potential liabilities, coverage is narrowly defined as those situations caused by a covered loss, and only for losses at the described premises. The amount of available protection is also limited.

The extended coverages primarily offer protection for properties not included in the definition of covered buildings and personal property. The intent is to provide specific and limited insurance for these properties, which is why they are separated from the general provision. Newly acquired property and property of others, for instance, involve exposures distinct from the general exposures, and they require special attention in the coverage extensions. Some of the coverage extensions offer protection against loss from a short list of causes to property otherwise excluded. Outdoor equipment is an example of property otherwise excluded.

FIGURE 15.5 Additional Coverage and Coverage Extension as Listed in ISO Building and Personal Property Coverage Form

Additional Coverages
a. Debris Removal
b. Preservation of Property
c. Fire Department Service Charge
d. Pollutant Clean Up and Removal
e. Increased Cost of Construction
f. Electronic Data—up to $2,500

Coverage Extensions
a. Newly Acquired or Constructed Property
b. Personal Effects and Property of Others
c. Valuable Papers and Records (Other than Electronic Data)
d. Property Off-Premises
e. Outdoor Property
f. Non-owned Detached Trailers

pollutant cleanup and removal

A provision that specifies the conditions under which, and the extent to which, protection for cleanup costs are paid by the insurer.

Valuation

As has been discussed in prior chapters, property insurance payments may be made on either a replacement cost new (RCN) basis or an actual cash value (ACV) basis. If the insured chooses actual cash value, then the provision 7 valuation of section E, loss conditions, applies. The valuation provision involves a number of parts.[1] Parts (b) through (e) explain the insurer's intent for valuation in situations involving RCN when ACV may be difficult to measure or inappropriate. Part (b), for instance, permits payment at RCN for relatively small losses: those valued at $2,500 or less.

If the insured chooses replacement cost new, this optional coverage must be designated in the declarations. Further, the insured ought to recognize the need for higher limits than if ACV is used. Typically, the insurer does not charge a higher rate for RCN coverage; however, more coverage is needed, which translates into a higher premium. For RCN to be paid, the insured must actually repair or replace the covered property. Otherwise, the insurer will pay on an ACV basis.

Limits of Insurance

As just discussed, you need to be cautious when selecting an amount of insurance that will cover your potential losses. The insurer will not pay more than the limit of insurance, except for the coverage extensions and coverage additions (fire department charges, pollution cleanup, and electronic data). In addition to concern over having a sufficient amount of insurance to cover the value of any loss, some insureds need to worry about violation of the coinsurance provision, which is found under section F, additional conditions of the BPP. The policy provides examples of coinsurance. An example of underinsurance in the policy is provided in Table 15.1 below.

TABLE 15.1 Example of Underinsurance in ISO Building and Personal Property Coverage Form (Sample)

Example #1 (Underinsurance)		
When:	The value of the property is:	$250,000
	The Coinsurance percentage for it is:	80%
	The Limit of Insurance for it is:	$100,000
	The Deductible is:	$250
	The amount of loss is:	$40,000
Step **(1)**:	$250,000 × 80% = $200,000	
	(the minimum amount of insurance to meet your Coinsurance requirements)	
Step **(2)**:	$100,000 ÷ $200,000 = .50	
Step **(3)**:	$40,000 × .50 = $20,000	
Step **(4)**:	$20,000 − $250 = $19,750	
We will pay no more than $19,750. The remaining $20,250 is not covered.		

Source: ISO Commercial Property Building and Personal Property Coverage Form CP 00 10 06 07. Includes copyrighted material of Insurance Services Office, Inc., with its permission.

agreed value option

Requires the policyholder to buy insurance equal to 100 percent of the value of the property, as determined at the start of the policy.

The BPP policy continues to include a coinsurance provision as a major condition of coverage. For most insureds, however, there is a choice to override the coinsurance clause with an agreed value option, found in section G of optional coverages. The **agreed value option** requires the policyholder to buy insurance equal to 100 percent of the value of the property, as determined at the start of the policy. If the insured does so, then the coinsurance provision does not apply and all losses are paid in full, up to the limit of insurance. The wording in the policy is shown in Figure 15.6.

FIGURE 15.6 Agreed Value Option in ISO Building and Personal Property Coverage Form (Sample)

1. Agreed Value
   a. The Addition Condition, Coinsurance, does not apply to Covered Property to which this Optional Coverage applies. We will pay no more for loss of or damage to that property than the proportion that the Limit of Insurance under this Coverage Part for the property bears to the Agreed Value shown for it in the Declarations.
   b. If the expiration date for this Optional Coverage shown in the Declarations is not extended, the Additional Condition, Coinsurance, is reinstated and this Optional Coverage expires.
   c. The terms of this Optional Coverage apply only to loss or damage that occurs:
      (1) On or after the effective date of this Optional Coverage; and
      (2) Before the Agreed Value expiration date shown in the Declarations or the policy expiration date, whichever occurs first.

Source: ISO Commercial Property Building and Personal Property Coverage Form CP 00 10 06 07. Includes copyrighted material of Insurance Services Office, Inc., with its permission.

inflation guard option

Provides for automatic periodic increases in insurance limits; the intent is to keep pace with inflation.

The agreed value option, however, does not ensure that the policyholder will have sufficient limits of insurance to cover a total loss, especially in times of high inflation. To ward off unwanted retention of loss values above the limit of insurance, the insured can purchase the inflation guard option found in section G, optional coverages (which is discussed in Chapter 13). The **inflation guard option** provides for automatic periodic increases in insurance limits; the intent is to keep pace with inflation. The amount of the annual increase is shown as a percentage in the declarations.

Causes of Loss

We have just described some major elements of the BPP form. A full understanding of the coverage requires a thorough reading and consideration of the impact of each provision. As for which perils are covered, the property section of the CPP offers three options: the basic causes of loss form, the broad causes of loss form, and the special causes of loss form.

Causes of Loss—Basic Form

The **basic causes of loss form** is a named-perils option of the commercial property policy that covers eleven named perils (see Figure 15.7). Some perils are defined and others are not. When exists, the common use of the term, supplemented by court opinions, will provide its meaning.

Fire, for example, is not defined because it has a generally accepted legal meaning. Insurance policies cover only certain fires. While excessive heat may be sufficient for the fire protection to apply, oxidation that results in a flame or glow is typically required. Further, the flame must be hostile, not within some intended container. For instance, if you throw something into a fireplace, intentionally or not, that fire is not hostile and the loss likely is not covered.

A review of the policy and Chapter 13, where many of these same perils were discussed as they apply to homeowners coverage, may clarify which loss situations are payable on the basic causes of loss form. Review of the exclusions is just as important.

FIGURE 15.7   Causes of Loss Forms, ISO Commercial Property Policy

Basic Form	Broad Form
• fire	Basic form perils, plus:
• lightning	• weight of snow, ice, or sleet
• explosion	• water damage
• windstorm or hail	• falling objects
• smoke	• breakage of glass
• aircraft or vehicles	
• riot or civil commotion	
• vandalism	
• sinkhole collapse	
• volcanic action	

Exclusions found in the basic causes of loss form can be categorized as follows:

- Ordinance of law
- Earth movement
- Governmental action
- Nuclear hazards
- Power failure
- War and military action
- Water damage
- Fungus, wet rot, dry rot, and bacteria
- Other, involving primarily steam, electrical, and mechanical breakdown

Most of these exclusions involve events with catastrophic potential, such as floods (the water exclusion).

Causes of Loss—Broad Form

The **broad causes of loss form** is a named-perils option of the commercial property policy that covers fifteen named perils. It differs from the basic form in adding some perils, as listed in Figure 15.7. Geography may dictate, to some extent, preference for the broad form because of its ice and snow coverage. Also note that the water damage peril is for the "sudden and accidental leakage of water or steam that results from the breaking or cracking of part of an appliance or system containing water or steam (not a sprinkler system)." It does not cover floods or other similar types of catastrophic water damage.

In addition to adding these perils, the broad form includes a provision to cover collapse caused by the named perils or by hidden decay; hidden insect or vermin damage; weight of people or personal

basic causes of loss form
A named-perils option of the commercial property policy that covers eleven named perils.

broad causes of loss form
A named-perils option of the commercial property policy that covers fifteen named perils.

property; weight of rain that collects on a roof; or use of defective materials in construction, remodeling, or renovation. While this "collapse" additional coverage does not increase the amount of coverage available (as the other additional coverages do), it does expand the list of covered-loss situations.

The mold exclusion was discussed in prior chapters. The exact wording of the exclusion is excerpted from the ISO Causes of Loss—Broad Form in Figure 15.8.

FIGURE 15.8 Mold Exclusion as Listed in the ISO Causes of Loss—Broad Form (Sample)

> **h. "Fungus," Wet Rot, Dry Rot And Bacteria**
>
> Presence, growth, proliferation, spread or any activity of "fungus," wet or dry rot or bacteria.
>
> But if "fungus," wet or dry rot or bacteria results in a "specified cause of loss," we will pay for the loss or damage caused by that "specified cause of loss."
>
> This exclusion does not apply:
>
> 1. When "fungus," wet or dry rot or bacteria results from fire or lightning; or
>
> 2. To the extent that coverage is provided in the Additional Coverage – Limited Coverage For "Fungus," Wet, Rot, Dry Rot And Bacteria with respect to loss or damage by a cause of loss other than fire or lightning.

Source: ISO Commercial Property Causes of Loss—Broad Form CP 10 20 06 07. Includes copyrighted material of Insurance Services Office, Inc., with its permission.

The additional coverage in the policy permits a coverage limit for mold for up to only $15,000, as noted in Additional Coverage—Limited Coverage For "Fungus," Wet, Rot, Dry Rot And Bacteria.

> *The coverage described under D.2. of this Limited Coverage is limited to $15,000. Regardless of the number of claims, this limit is the most we will pay for the total of all loss or damage arising out of all occurrences of Covered Causes of Loss (other than fire or lightning) and Flood which take place in a 12-month period (starting with the beginning of the present annual policy period). With respect to a particular occurrence of loss which results in 'fungus,' wet or dry rot or bacteria, we will not pay more than a total of $15,000 even if the 'fungus,' wet or dry rot or bacteria continues to be present or active, or recurs, in a later policy period.[2]*

Business income coverage will be discussed in the next section. For now, it is important to note that, under the mold exclusion and extension of coverage, business interruption income is provided for only thirty days. The days do not need to be consecutive.

Returning to the topic of cause of loss, it is very important to have a clear definition of what is considered a cause of loss for the limits of coverage. Whether or not the peril caused one loss or two separate losses is imperative in understanding the policy. A case in point is that of the complex decisions regarding whether the loss of the two World Trade Center buildings was one loss or two separate losses from two separate causes of loss. The stakes were very high, at $3.5 billion of limit. To understand the issue more clearly, see the box "Liability Limits: One Event or Two?"

Liability Limits: One Event or Two?

Did the September 11 terrorist attacks on the World Trade Center constitute one loss or two? The resolution to this question is far from simple. Controversy surrounding this issue illustrates the ambiguities inherent in some business insurance contracts.

When the two hijacked airplanes struck the World Trade Center towers on the morning of September 11, 2001, the insurance and reinsurance contracts for the property were still under binder agreements. Thus, the wording of the binder agreements became the central issue of this case. At the time of the attacks, real estate executive Larry A. Silverstein's company had only recently acquired a ninety-nine-year lease on the World Trade Center and had not yet finalized insurance coverage, which provided up to $3.5 billion in property and liability damage per occurrence. With policies of such size, which have large reinsurance requirements, it is not uncommon for the final policies not to be in place when the insured begins operations.

The United Kingdom-based reinsurer Swiss Re had agreed to underwrite 22 percent of coverage on the property once the loss exceeded $10 million, translating into $3.5 billion per occurrence in this case. After the attacks, Swiss Re argued that its preliminary agreement with the lessee defined occurrence as "all losses or damages that are attributable directly or indirectly to one cause or one series of similar causes" and that "all such losses will be added together and the total amount of such losses will be treated as one occurrence irrespective of the period of time or area over which such losses occur." Silverstein, however, argued that each of the airplane crashes was a separate occurrence and his company was due more than $7 billion for the two attacks.

The fuzziness of the language has been very problematic. This led to two opposing verdicts in separate court cases. In Phase I, the insurers prevailed. In Phase II, Silverstein did. The first jury found that "the form used by broker Willis Group Holdings Ltd., rather than a rival form used by Travelers or other forms, and that the Willis form, known as WilProp 2000, had specific language that defined what happened to the World Trade Center as a single occurrence." Under this WilProp form, occurrence means "all losses or damages that are attributable directly or indirectly to one cause or to one series of similar causes. All such losses are added together and the total amount of such losses is treated as one occurrence irrespective of the period of time or area over which such losses occur."

In the second case, the jury agreed with Silverstein that there were two occurrences, at least as defined by the temporary insurance agreements that bound the group of insurers that were involved in the second case. As a result of the second ruling, Silverstein had an open door to collect "as much as twice the $1.1 billion aggregate insured amount per occurrence for which the nine insurers were liable."

These two contradictory rulings stem from three tests:

1. The cause test—The question is, Was there more than one cause underlying the loss? As such, it can be determined that the fall of the twin towers resulted from one conspiracy by Osama bin Laden.

2. The effect test (less prevalent)—The question is, Was there more than one distinct loss? As such, the test looks at each injury or damage to determine the number of losses.

3. Unfortunate events test—This test combines the cause test with elements of the effect test; here, proximity of the cause of loss is important. Because there were two planes causing the loss, the loss is regarded as two separate losses.

The World Trade Center cases were heard in a federal court—the U.S. District Court for the Southern District of New York in Manhattan. Ultimately, however, the matter was settled out of court. In March of 2007, New York Insurance Superintendent Eric Dinallo requested that two representatives from Silverstein Properties and each of the seven insurers involved in the WTC settlement dispute attend a meeting with the state insurance department to bring closure to the ongoing litigation. After weeks of tense negotiations, then-New York Governor Eliot Spitzer and Superintendent Dinallo announced on May 23, 2007, that an agreement between the parties had been successfully brokered. Travelers, Zurich, Swiss RE, Employers Insurance of Wausau, Allianz Global, Industrial Risk Insurers, and Royal Indemnity Company agreed to settle all outstanding court cases and related proceedings for a total of $2 billion. Spitzer and Dinallo described this as the largest settlement in regulatory history. Specific amounts paid each company were not disclosed due to confidentiality agreements. The resolution to this dispute removes the last major obstacle to World Trade Center redevelopment as planned by Silverstein Properties and the New York and New Jersey Port Authority.

To address the underlying problem in the long-delayed loss settlement, Superintendent Dinallo issued a bulletin on October 16, 2008, requiring insurers to provide contract certainty for coverage agreements. This contract certainty called for contract language in insurance policies to be firmed up within thirty days of issuance and the delivery of the policy before, on, or promptly after the policy's inception date. This would ensure that policy provisions, like the question as to whether the destruction of the twin towers was one insured event or two, are definitively established before a loss. Insurance carriers were given twelve months from the date of Dinallo's bulletin to bring policies and procedures into compliance with the rule. When asked by the Risk and Insurance Management Society (RIMS) what would happen if carriers failed to meet the compliance deadline, the New York Insurance Department responded that it would "consider regulations spelling out more detailed rules. Regulations have the force of law and penalties can be assessed on licensees." Willis Group Holdings Chairman and CEO Joe Plumeri praised the contract certainty rule, saying, "There is absolutely no excuse for policies to be delivered months after their inception, an all too commonplace practice in this business.... We're in the business of keeping promises, and the insurance industry as a whole can do no less. We believe that the industry should police itself, take a principled approach to doing business, and adopt these measures as soon as possible."

The protracted settlement of the World Trade Center destruction provides a high-profile example of the problems that can arise due to uncertain policy terms. This is not typically an issue with most insurance policies written on standardized forms approved by the state insurance department. In the case of large commercial clients, excess and surplus lines, and reinsurance markets, however, it is likely to come up due to complexity of business scope, degree of risk, and lack of regulatory authority. Should the contract certainty rule in New York prove successful in curtailing disputes, RIMS anticipates that additional states will follow suit in passing similar requirements.

Questions for Discussion

1. Which ruling do you agree with in this complex case? What is the justification for the ruling against the leaseholder in this case, and the one in favor of the leaseholder? Do you think this ruling is ethical in light of the massive loss?

2. In ethical terms, who should really suffer the burden of the attack on America on September 11? Should it be any private citizen or the private insurance industry?

Sources: E. E. Mazier, "Swiss Re Presses 'One Attack' Theory," National Underwriter, Property & Casualty/Risk & Benefits Management Edition, October 29, 2001; E. E. Mazier, "Experts View Swiss Re WTC Lawsuit as Unprecedented Legal Quagmire," National Underwriter Online News Service, October 31, 2001; Mark E. Ruquet, "Insurers to Lose WTC Case: Agent Univ.," National Underwriter Online News Service, July 22, 2002; E. E. Mazier, "Judges Sends WTC Claim to Jury Trial," National Underwriter, Property & Casualty/Risk & Benefits Management Edition, June 10, 2002; E. E. Mazier, "Judge Rules WTC Terror Is One Event," National Underwriter Online News Service, September 25, 2002; E. E. Mazier, "Swiss Re Silverstein WTC Case in Shambles," National Underwriter Online News Service, September 27, 2002; "Tale of Two Trials: Contract Language Underlies Contradictory World Trade Center Verdicts," BestWire, December 9, 2004, accessed March 27, 2009, http://www3.ambest.com/Frames/FrameServer.asp?AltSrc=23&Tab=1&Site=news&refnum=70605; Mark E. Ruquet, "Spitzer Spearheads $2 Billion WTC Insurance Settlement," National Underwriter, Property & Casualty/Risk & Benefits Management Edition, May 23, 2007, accessed March 29, 2009, www.property-casualty.com/News/2007/5/Pages/Spitzer-Spearheads--2-Billion-WTC-Insurance-Settlement.aspx; Mark E. Ruquet, "WTC Deal Gets Dinallow Off on Right Foot," National Underwriter, Property & Casualty/Risk & Benefits Management Edition, June 18, 2007, accessed March 29, 2009, www.property-casualty.com/Issues/2007/24/Pages/WTC-Deal-Gets-Dinallo-Off-On-Right-Foot.aspx; Daniel Hays, "New N.Y. Regulation Calls For Policy Contract Certainty," National Underwriter, Property & Casualty/Risk & Benefits Management Edition, October 16, 2008, accessed March 29, 2009, www.property-casualty.com/News/2008/10/Pages/New-N-Y--Regulation-Calls-For-Policy-Contract-Certainty.aspx; Daniel Hays, "RIMS Reacts to N.Y. Contract Certainty Regulation," National Underwriter, Property & Casualty/Risk & Benefits Management Edition, October 22, 2008, accessed March 29, 2009, www.property-casualty.com/News/2008/10/Pages/RIMS-Reacts-To-N-Y--Contract-Certainty-Regulation.aspx; Mark E. Ruquet, "Willis CEO Applauds N.Y. Move On Contract Certainty," National Underwriter, Property & Casualty/Risk & Benefits Management Edition, October 17, 2008, accessed March 29, 2009, http://www.property-casualty.com/News/2008/10/Pages/Willis-CEO-Applauds-N-Y--Move-On-Contract-Certainty.aspx; See all media coverage at the end of 2004 and afterward.

Causes of Loss—Special Form

special causes of loss form

An open perils or all risk coverage option for the commercial property policy.

The **special causes of loss form** is an open perils or all risk coverage option for the commercial property policy. That is, instead of listing those perils that are covered, the special form provides protection for all causes of loss not specifically excluded. In this form, then, the exclusions define the coverage. Remember that all those exclusions listed in the basic form, except for the "other" category and some aspects of the water damage exclusion, apply to the special form.

Most of the additional exclusions found in the special form relate either to catastrophic potentials or to nonfortuitous events. Among the catastrophe exclusions are boiler or machinery explosions. Nonfortuitous exclusions relate to items such as wear and tear, smoke from agricultural smudging, and damage to a building interior caused by weather conditions, unless the building exterior is damaged first.

Some experts believe that the greatest benefit of the special form over the broad form is coverage against theft. You may recall that theft is not a listed peril in the broad or the basic form. Coverage of theft from any cause, however, is too costly for most policyholders. The special form, therefore, includes some limitations on this protection. For instance, employee dishonesty and loss of property that appears to have been stolen but for which there is no physical evidence of theft ("mysterious disappearance") are not covered. In addition, certain types of property such as patterns, dyes, furs, jewelry, and tickets are covered against theft only up to specified amounts. The special form also provides coverage for property in transit.

Consequential Property Coverage: Business Income Coverage (BIC)

In addition to the cost of repairing and/or replacing damaged or lost property, a business is likely to experience some negative consequences of being unable to use the damaged or lost property, which was noted in previous chapters. Those negative consequences typically involve reduced revenues (sales) or increased expenses, both of which reduce net income (profit). The commercial property policy provides coverage for net income losses through the **business income coverage (BIC)** form. The BIC protects against both business interruption and extra expense losses.

business income coverage (BIC)

Protects against both business interruption and extra expense losses.

Business Interruption

When operations shut down (are interrupted) because of loss to physical property, a business likely loses income. The definition of business income in the BIC is provided in Figure 15.9.

Normal operating expenses are those costs associated with the activity of the business, not the materials that may be consumed by the business. Included among operating expenses are payroll, heat and lighting, advertising, and interest expenses.

The intent of the BIC is to maintain the insured's same financial position with or without a loss. Payment, therefore, does not cover all lost revenues because those revenues generally cover expenses, some of which will not continue. Yet because some expenses continue, coverage of net income alone is insufficient. An example of a BIC loss is given in "Business Income Coverage (BIC) Hypothetical Loss."

It is important to note the wording in the policy. The coverage applies only to business interruption for damages to the property in the declaration. More specifically, the policy states,

FIGURE 15.9   Business Income as Defined in the ISO Business Income (and Extra Expense) Coverage Form (Sample)

> **A. Coverage**
>   **1. Business Income**
>   Business Income means the:
>   **a.** Net Income (Net Profit or Loss before income taxes) that would have been earned or incurred; and
>   **b.** Continuing normal operating expenses incurred, including payroll.

Source: ISO Commercial Property Business Income (and Extra Expense) Coverage Form CP 00 30 06 07. Includes copyrighted material of Insurance Services Office, Inc., with its permission.

We will pay for the actual loss of Business Income you sustain due to the necessary 'suspension' of your 'operations' during the 'period of restoration.' The 'suspension' must be caused by direct physical loss of or damage to property at premises which are described in the Declarations and for which a Business Income Limit of Insurance is shown in the Declarations. The loss or damage must be caused by or result from a Covered Cause of Loss. With respect to loss of or damage to personal property in the open or personal property in a vehicle, the described premises include the area within 100 feet of the site at which the described premises are located.[3]

Under this policy, businesses that sustained losses because of the economic backlash and fear after September 11, 2001, would not be covered for their loss of income. For discussion of this issue, read the box "Business Interruption with and without Direct Physical Loss" in Chapter 11.

As noted above in the discussion of the BPP policy, this part of the commercial package also limits coverage for interruption to computer operations under Section 4, as presented in Figure 15.10.

FIGURE 15.10 Interruption of Computer Operations Coverage Limitation in the ISO Business Income (and Extra Expense) Coverage Form (Sample)

4. Additional Limitation – Interruption Of Computer Operations

a. Coverage for Business Income does not apply when a "suspension" of "operations" is caused by destruction or corruption of electronic data, or any loss or damage to electronic data, except as provided under the Additional Coverage – Interruption Of Computer Operations.

b. Coverage for Extra Expense does not apply when action is taken to avoid or minimize a "suspension" of "operations" caused by destruction or corruption of electronic data, or any loss or damage to electronic data, except as provided under the Additional Coverage – Interruption Of Computer Operations.

c. Electronic data means information, facts or computer programs stored as or on, created or used on, or transmitted to or from computer software (including systems and applications software), on hard or floppy disks, CD-ROMs, tapes, drives, cells, data processing devices or any other repositories of computer software which are used with electronically controlled equipment. The term computer programs, referred to in the foregoing description of electronic data, means a set of related electronic instructions which direct the operations and functions of a computer or device connected to it, which enable the computer or device to receive, process, store, retrieve or send data.

Source: ISO Commercial Property Business Income (and Extra Expense) Coverage Form CP 00 30 06 07. Includes copyrighted material of Insurance Services Office, Inc., with its permission.

In Additional Coverage, the amount available for interruption of computer operation is $2,500. No wonder many businesses today purchase the e-commerce endorsement or buy the new policies from the companies described in Chapter 11 and Chapter 12.

Extra Expense

In addition to losing sales, a business may need to incur various expenses following property damage in order to minimize further loss of sales. These extra expenses are also covered by the BIC. A bank, for example, could not simply shut down operations if a fire destroyed its building because the bank's customers rely on having ready access to financial services. As a result, the bank is likely to set up operations at a temporary location (thus reducing the extent of lost revenues) while the damaged property is being repaired. The rent at the temporary location plus any increase in other expenses would be considered covered extra expenses.

Causes of Loss

The same three perils options available for the BPP are also available for the BIC. Because the BIC requires that the covered income loss results from direct physical loss or damage to property described in the declarations, most insureds choose the same causes of loss form for both the BPP and the BIC. Now, we show a more detailed example of a hypothetical loss that occurred during the Chicago flood in 1992.

Business Income Coverage (BIC) Hypothetical Loss

In the spring of 1992, Chicago experienced an unusual flood apparently caused by damage to an underground tunnel system. Many firms were required to shut down offices in the damaged area. Among them were large accounting organizations, just two weeks before the tax deadline of April 15. Thus, the losses were magnified by the fact that the flood occurred during the tax season. Assume the following hypothetical conditions for one of those firms.

Preloss Financial Information	
Average monthly revenues	$500,000
Average April revenues (stated in 1992 dollars)	$700,000
Average monthly payroll	$300,000
Average April payroll	$550,000
Monthly heat, electricity, water	$25,000
Monthly rent for leased office	$45,000
Monthly interest expense	$10,000
Monthly marketing expense	$15,000
Monthly other expenses	$10,000
Net income in April	$45,000

Postloss Financial Information for April 1992	
Revenues	$600,000
Payroll	$540,000
Utilities	$30,000
Rent on downtown space	$0
Rent for temporary space	$50,000
Interest expense	$10,000
Marketing expense	$22,000
Other expenses	$20,000
Net loss	($72,000)

This firm experienced both a reduction in revenue and an increase in expenses. The resulting profit (net income) loss is the covered loss in the BIC. For this example, the loss equals $117,000, the sum of the income not received ($45,000) that would have been expected without a loss, plus the actual lost income ($72,000) incurred. Such a substantial loss for a two-week period is not unusual.

Coinsurance

The coinsurance provision of the BIC is one of the more confusing parts of any insurance policy. Its purpose is the same as that discussed earlier, which is to maintain equity in pricing. Its application is also similar. The difficulty comes in defining the underlying value of the full exposure, which is needed to apply any coinsurance provision. Following in Table 15.2 is an underinsurance example from a BIC policy. More examples are provided in the policy sample.

TABLE 15.2 Example of Underinsurance in ISO Business Income (and Extra Expense) Coverage Form (Sample)

Example #1 (Underinsurance)		
When:	The Net Income and operating expenses for the 12 months following the inception, or last previous anniversary date, of this policy at the described premises would have been:	$400,000
	The Coinsurance percentage is:	50%
	The Limit of Insurance is:	$150,000
	The amount of loss is:	$80,000
Step (1):	$400,000 × 50% = $200,000	
	(the minimum amount of insurance to meet your Coinsurance requirements)	
Step (2):	$150,000 ÷ $200,000 = .75	
Step (3):	$80,000 × .75 = $60,000	
We will pay no more than $60,000. The remaining $20,000 is not covered.		

Source: ISO Commercial Property Business Income (and Extra Expense) Coverage Form CP 00 30 06 07. Includes copyrighted material of Insurance Services Office, Inc., with its permission.

Remember that a BIC loss equals net income plus continuing operating expenses. Coinsurance, however, applies to net income plus all operating expenses, a larger value. The amount of insurance required to meet the coinsurance provision is some percentage of this value, with the percentage determined by what the insured expects to be the maximum period of interruption. If a maximum interruption of six months is expected, for example, the proper coinsurance percentage is 50 percent (6/12). If it is nine months, a coinsurance percentage of 75 percent (9/12) is appropriate.

Because of the complexity of the coinsurance provision, however, many insureds choose an agreed value option. This option works under the same principles as those discussed with regard to the BPP. Using the example illustrated in "Business Income Coverage (BIC) Hypothetical Loss," we can demonstrate the application of the coinsurance provision. Coinsurance requirements apply to net income plus operating expenses ($95,000 plus $405,000 per month on average, or $6,000,000 for the year). If a 50 percent coinsurance provision is used because the expected maximum period of interruption is six months, then the amount of insurance required is $3,000,000 (0.50 × $6,000,000). If the April figures are representative (which is really not the case with a tax accounting office), then a six-month interruption would result in a much lower loss.

Other Options

The BIC includes a number of options designed to modify coverage for the insured's specific needs. Three options that affect the coinsurance provision are the monthly limit of indemnity, maximum period of indemnity, and payroll endorsements. For better understanding, the student is invited to read the policy in addition to reading the following explanations.

The **monthly limit of indemnity** negates the coinsurance provision of business income coverage; instead, a total limit is listed, as is the percentage of that limit available each month. The policy uses the example of a $120,000 limit and ¼ monthly amount. For this example, only $30,000 (¼ × $120,000) is available each month. An organization with stable earnings and expectations of a short period of restoration would likely find this option worthwhile.

The **maximum period of indemnity** option also negates the coinsurance provision of the BIC; instead, this option limits the duration of coverage to 120 days (or until the limit is reached, whichever comes first). Both the maximum period of indemnity and the monthly limit of indemnity address the fact that the standard policy cannot be used with a coinsurance provision of less than 50 percent (six months).

monthly limit of indemnity

Negates the coinsurance provision of business income coverage; instead, a total limit is listed, as is the percentage of that limit available each month.

maximum period of indemnity

Option also negates the coinsurance provision of the BIC; instead, this option limits the duration of coverage to 120 days (or until the limit is reached, whichever comes first).

Instead of negating the coinsurance provision, as do the two options just discussed, the **payroll endorsement** allows the insured to deduct some or all payroll expenses from the value of operating expenses before calculating the coinsurance requirement. Doing so allows the insured to purchase less insurance (and usually pay lower premiums) and still meet the coinsurance provision. It also excludes payroll from covered expenses, however, so the insured must feel confident that payroll would not be maintained during a shutdown. A common payroll endorsement includes ninety days of payroll expense in the coinsurance calculation (and BIC coverage), assuming that a short shutdown might allow the insured to continue to pay employees. For a longer shutdown, termination of employment might be more cost effective.

payroll endorsement

Allows the insured to deduct some or all payroll expenses from the value of operating expenses before calculating the coinsurance requirement.

KEY TAKEAWAYS

In this section you studied the commercial package policy (CPP) and the commercial property component of the CPP:

- The commercial package policy (CPP) is a modular business insurance option that bundles coverages such as commercial property, commercial general liability, commercial inland marine, professional liability, and more, into a single policy.
- The CPP contains the standard elements: cover page, common policy conditions, and common declarations.
- Common business property exposures are insured through the commercial property policy of the CPP.
- Property declarations and conditions of the commercial property policy form identify the covered location, property values and limits, premiums, deductibles, and other items.
- The commercial property policy's building and personal property (BPP) form provides coverage for direct physical loss to buildings and contents and additional or extended coverages, per the insured's valuation provision up to the limits of insurance and subject to listed exclusions.
- Three causes of loss options are available in the BPP: basic (eleven named perils), broad (fifteen named perils), and special (open perils), all subject to exclusions.
- The commercial property policy provides coverage of net income losses as a result of being unable to use damaged or lost property through the business income coverage (BIC) form.
- BIC protects against business interruption and extra expense losses.
- The BIC offers the same three cause of loss options as the BPP.
- Both the BPP and the BIC are subject to coinsurance provisions; this can be modified in the BIC through use of the monthly limit of indemnity, maximum period of indemnity, and payroll endorsements.

DISCUSSION QUESTIONS

1. What types of property are covered in the BPP? What are some examples of excluded property, and why are they excluded?

2. How can an insured get around the coinsurance provision in the BPP? Why might an insured prefer to do this?

3. What kinds of losses are covered in the BIC? Provide examples.

4. The building where Alpha Mortgage Company's office was located received minor smoke damage, forcing the company to relocate its operations for one month. Assuming standard BIC coverage and the following hypothetical conditions, what amount of benefits could the company expect to receive?

Preloss Financial Information	
Average monthly revenues	$220,000
Average monthly payroll	$100,000
Monthly heat, electricity, water	$25,000
Monthly rent for leased office	$25,000
Monthly interest expense	$10,000
Monthly marketing expense	$5,000
Monthly other expenses	$5,000

Postloss Financial Information for One Month	
Revenues	$170,000
Payroll	$100,000
Utilities	$30,000
Rent on leased office	$0
Rent for temporary space	$50,000
Interest expense	$0
Marketing expense	$6,000
Other expenses	$12,000

5. The Bravo Multiplex Movie Theater has a BIC coverage limit of $200,000 with a coinsurance percentage of 50 percent. Over the previous one-year period, the theater's net income and operating expenses totaled $400,000. If Bravo is forced to shut down one of its eight theaters for six months (incurring a total loss of $60,000), how much will BIC cover? Does the company have enough insurance? Do they have other options?

6. Assume that the Steinman Shoe Station owns the $1 million building in which it operates, maintains inventory and other business properties in the building worth $700,000, and often has possession of people's property up to a value of $50,000 while they are being repaired. For each of the following losses, what, if anything, will Steinman's BPP insurer pay? Limits are $1 million on coverage A and $800,000 on coverage B. The broad causes-of-loss form is used and there was no e-commerce endorsement. Explain your answers.

    a. Wind damage rips off tiles from the roof, costing $20,000 to replace. The actual cash value is $17,000.

    b. An angry arsonist starts a fire. The building requires repairs of $15,000, $17,000 of inventory is destroyed, and $2,000 of other people's property is burned.

    c. A water pipe bursts, destroying $22,000 of inventory and requiring $10,000 to repair the pipe.

    d. The computer system crashes for three days.

7. Steinman also bought a BIC with a limit of $250,000 and a 50 percent coinsurance clause. No other endorsements are used. A limited income statement for last year is shown below.

Revenues	$2,000,000
Less:	
Cost of goods sold	$800,000
Utilities	$200,000
Payroll	$400,000
Other expenses	$300,000
	$1,700,000
Profit	**$300,000**

  a. How much in expenses does Steinman expect to be noncontinuing in the event of a shutdown? Explain.
  b. What is the longest shutdown period Steinman would expect following a loss?
  c. If a three-month closing occurred following the roof collapsing due to the weight of snow, what do you think would be the loss? Explain.

3. OTHER PROPERTY COVERAGES

LEARNING OBJECTIVES

In this section we elaborate on the different types of optional property coverage available in the CPP offering insurance on property otherwise excluded or to meet the special needs of businesses:

- **The Crime and Fidelity insurance program**
- **Inland marine (IM) insurance**
- **Boiler and machinery (B&M) insurance**
- **The Capital Assets Program**
- **The business owners policy (BOP)**

The commercial package policy is designed to accommodate separate and sometimes special property needs of insureds. Refer again to Figure 15.1.

3.1 Commercial Crime and Fidelity Coverage

The program includes enhancements that protect businesses and government entities against the following:

- Employee theft
- Burglary
- Other workplace crimes

Historically, crime losses have been insured separately from other property losses. Perhaps the separation was intended to standardize the risk; exposure to crime loss may involve quite different loss-control needs and frequency and severity estimates from those associated with exposure to fire, weather damage, or other BPP type losses. Furthermore, within the crime coverage, employee dishonesty has typically been insured separately from other property crimes, likely also in an effort to recognize variations in risk and loss-control needs between the two. Employee dishonesty protection began as a bond (called a **fidelity bond**), which was a guarantee provided to employers by each employee promising loyalty and faithfulness and stipulating a mechanism for financial recovery should the promise be broken. As a result, bonding companies developed to protect against employee crimes, while insurers expanded their coverage separately to protect against other property-related crimes.

Today, ISO has a Crime and Fidelity insurance program.[4] The ISO enhancements include coverage for losses caused by employee theft of the following:

- Money
- Securities

fidelity bond

A guarantee provided to employers by each employee promising loyalty and faithfulness and stipulating a mechanism for financial recovery should the promise be broken.

- Other property of the insured
- Clients' property on the clients' premises

Also available is coverage for additional perils, including the following:

- Forgery or alteration of negotiable instruments
- Loss through transferring money and securities by fraudulent telephone or fax instructions
- Extortion threats targeting the insured's property

3.2 Inland Marine

inland marine (IM) insurance

Covers nonwater forms of transportation such as rails and trucking.

ocean marine insurance

Coverage for property while being transported by water (including coverage for the vessels doing the transporting).

You may recall that the BPP covers personal property while it is located at the described premises. Many businesses, however, move property from one location to another or have specialized personal property that requires insurance coverage not intended by the BPP. These needs are often met by inland marine (IM) insurance. Despite its name, **inland marine (IM) insurance** covers nonwater forms of transportation such as rails and trucking.

Inland marine insurance is an outgrowth of **ocean marine insurance**, which is coverage for property while being transported by water (including coverage for the vessels doing the transporting). IM tends to be broad coverage, often on an open-perils basis and generally for replacement cost. Exclusions tend to involve nonfortuitous events, such as wear and tear and intentionally caused loss. The protection IM provides is for inland transportation and specialized equipment.

3.3 Boiler and Machinery Coverage

When a boiler or similar piece of machinery explodes, the cost tends to be enormous. Typically, the entire building is destroyed, as are surrounding properties. Anyone in or near the building may be killed or badly injured. Furthermore, the overwhelming majority of such explosions can be prevented through periodic inspection and excellent maintenance. As a result, a boiler inspection industry developed, which ultimately became an inspection and insurance industry.

boiler and machinery (B&M) insurance

Protects against loss that results from property damage to the insured's own property and to nonowned property caused by explosions or other sudden breakdowns of boilers and machinery.

Boiler and machinery (B&M) insurance protects against loss that results from property damage to the insured's own property and to nonowned property caused by explosions or other sudden breakdowns of boilers and machinery. (Bodily injury liability coverage can be added by endorsement.) The bulk of the premium, however, goes toward costs of inspection and loss control. Any business that uses a boiler or similar type of machinery needs to consider purchase of this coverage because the potential loss is large while the probability of loss is low if proper care is maintained.

3.4 Capital Assets Program

The Insurance Services Office introduced "the ISO Capital Assets Program—a manufacturer's output type policy—that enables insurers to provide large and medium commercial accounts superior coverage and pricing flexibility for buildings and business personal property."[5]

Capital Assets Program

Provides businesses coverage on a blanket, replacement-cost basis without a coinsurance provision to sufficiently large accounts.

The **Capital Assets Program** provides businesses coverage on a blanket, replacement-cost basis without a coinsurance provision to sufficiently large accounts. The program also provides options to value property at actual cash value, agreed value, or (for buildings) functional replacement cost. Under the program, "Business income and extra expense coverages are written into the form and can be activated by entries on the policy declaration page."

3.5 Business Owners Policy

business owners policy (BOP)

Provides a comprehensive policy that would omit the need for small businesses to make numerous decisions while also incorporating coverage on exposures often overlooked.

In 1976, the ISO developed its first business owners policy, which was designed for small businesses in the office, mercantile, and processing categories and for apartment houses and condominium associations. The intent of the **business owners policy (BOP)** was to provide a comprehensive policy that would omit the need for small businesses to make numerous decisions, while also incorporating coverage on exposures often overlooked. The original BOP was one policy covering both property and liability exposures. The current program incorporates the BOP into the commercial package policy through separate property and liability policies designed for small businesses. When these coverages are combined, they provide protection nearly identical to the old BOP policy.

The property portion of the business owners program covers both direct and consequential losses, combining the types of coverage found in the BPP and BIC. An inflation guard is standard, as is a seasonal fluctuation for personal property. The inflation guard increases the building's coverage limit by some stated percentage automatically each year. The **seasonal fluctuation** permits recovery of lost personal property up to 125 percent of the declared limit, as long as the average value of the personal property over the prior twelve months is not greater than the limit. For organizations with fluctuating stock values, this provision is helpful. Coverage is on a replacement cost new basis without a coinsurance provision.

The policy also provides business income loss for one year of interruption without a stated dollar limit or coinsurance requirement. Many small businesses are prone to ignore this exposure, which is why the coverage is included automatically.

Coverage can be purchased either on a named-perils or an open-risk basis. The named-perils form covers the causes of loss listed in Figure 15.7, which are the same perils available in other coverage forms. One additional peril, transportation, is also covered in the BOP. The transportation peril affords some inland marine protection.

The business owners program was released by the ISO in June 2002.[6] It expanded some risk categories eligible for coverage with a new section, "Commercial Lines Manual." The BOP includes "computer coverage, business income from dependent properties coverage, and fire extinguisher system recharge expense." There are some new optional endorsements, such as "coverage for food contamination, water backup and sump overflow, functional building and personal property valuation, liquor liability, employee benefits liability, and several coverage and exclusion options for pollution liability."[7]

seasonal fluctuation

Permits recovery of lost personal property up to 125 percent of the declared limit, as long as the average value of the personal property over the prior twelve months is not greater than the limit.

KEY TAKEAWAYS

In this section you studied the separate, special property needs of insureds that can be resolved through the CPP:

- The Crime and Fidelity insurance program provides employers with coverage for a variety of forms of employee theft.
- Inland marine insurance covers nonwater forms of commercial transportation.
- Boiler and machinery (B&M) insurance protects against loss from property damage to the insured's own property and to nonowned property caused by explosions or other breakdowns of boilers and machinery.
- The Capital Assets Program provides large and medium commercial accounts businesses coverage on a blanket, replacement-cost basis without a coinsurance provision and options to value property at actual cash value, agreed value, or, functional replacement cost.
- The business owners policy (BOP) provides comprehensive coverage for small businesses through separate property and liability policies incorporating both the BPP and BIC.

DISCUSSION QUESTIONS

1. What is a fidelity bond?
2. What is inland marine insurance?
3. What are the advantages of using a business owners policy?
4. What protection is provided by boiler and machinery (B&M) insurance?
5. What does the Capital Assets Program provide?

4. COMMERCIAL GENERAL LIABILITY POLICY AND COMMERCIAL UMBRELLA LIABILITY POLICY

> ### LEARNING OBJECTIVES
>
> In this section we elaborate on commercial liability insurance solutions:
> - **The five sections of the commercial general liability (CGL) policy**
> - **Features of the commercial umbrella liability policy**

4.1 Commercial General Liability Policy

As discussed in Chapter 12, businesses have a wide variety of liability exposures. Many of these are insurable through the CGL.

CGL Policy Format

The format of the CGL is very similar to that of the BPP and BIC. The CGL contract includes the following:

- CGL declaration form
- CGL coverage form
- Any appropriate endorsements, such as the mold exclusion

The CGL itself is comprised of the following five sections:

1. Coverages
2. Who is an insured
3. Limits of insurance
4. CGL conditions
5. Definitions

claims-made basis

A policy that limits the period in which the claims for injuries need to be made.

Coverage is available either on an occurrence or on a claims-made basis. **Claims-made basis** is a policy that limits the period in which the claims for injuries need to be made. Under such a program, claims for injuries that occurred thirty years ago cannot be covered. The claim needs to be filed (made) during the coverage period for injuries that occur during the same period or the designated retroactive time. This limitation is the result of insurers having to pay for asbestos injuries that occurred years before knowledge of the exposure outcome was discovered. Insurers that provided coverage for those injuries thirty years ago were required to pay regardless of when the claims were made. Claims for past unforeseen injuries were not included in the loss development (discussed in Chapter 7) and caused major unexpected losses to the insurance industry. If the claims-made option is chosen, a sixth section is incorporated into the policy, the extended reporting periods provision.

Coverages

The CGL provides three types of coverage:

1. Bodily injury and property damage liability
2. Personal and advertising injury liability
3. Medical payments

Each coverage involves its own insuring agreement and set of exclusions. Each also provides a distinct limit of insurance, although an aggregate limit may apply to the sum of all costs under each coverage for the policy period. Other aggregates also apply, as discussed in the policy limits section below.

Coverage A—Bodily Injury and Property Damage Liability

The CGL provides open-perils coverage for the insured's liabilities due to bodily injury or property damage experienced by others. The bodily injury or property damage must arise out of an occurrence, which is "an accident, including continuous or repeated exposure to substantially the same general harmful conditions." If the commercial general liability policy is a claims-made **policy**, the event causing liability must take place after a designated **retroactive date**, and a claim for damages must be made during the policy period. Under the claims-made policy, an insured's liability is covered (assuming no other applicable exclusions) if the event causing liability occurs after some specified retroactive date and the claim for payment by the plaintiff is made within the policy period. This differs from an **occurrence policy**, which covers liability for events that take place within the policy period, regardless of when the plaintiff makes a claim. The claims-made policy may lessen the insurer's uncertainty about likely future payments because the time lag between premium payments and loss payments generally is smaller with claims-made than with occurrence.

If the claims-made policy is purchased, a retroactive date must be defined. In addition, an extended reporting period must be included for the policy to be legal. The **extended reporting period** applies if a claims-made policy is canceled and provides coverage for claims brought after the policy period has expired for events that occurred between the retroactive date and the end of the policy period. An example is shown in Table 15.3. The standard extended reporting form is very limited, so insureds may purchase additional extensions.

claims-made basis

A policy that limits the period in which the claims for injuries need to be made.

retroactive date

Date after which an event causing liability must take place in order to be covered.

occurrence policy

Covers liability for events that take place within the policy period, regardless of when the plaintiff makes a claim.

extended reporting period

Provides coverage for claims brought after the policy period has expired for events that occurred between the retroactive date and the end of the policy period.

TABLE 15.3   Claims-Made Coverage Example

Assume a policy purchased on January 1, 1990, that provides $1,000,000 per occurrence of claims-made coverage with a retroactive date of January 1, 1988, and a one-year policy period. Further assume that the policy was canceled on December 31, 1990, and that the insured purchased a one-year extended reporting period.

The following losses occur:

Amount	Date of Injury	Date of Claim	Insurer Responsibility
$100,000	3/15/88	3/15/89	–0[8]
$100,000	3/15/88	3/15/90	100,000[9]
$100,000	3/15/90	3/15/91	100,000[10]
$100,000	3/15/90	3/15/92	–0[11]
$100,000	3/15/91	3/15/91	–0[12]

The claims-made policy was introduced (first in medical malpractice insurance, later in other policies) in response to increased uncertainty about future liabilities. As explained above, an occurrence policy could be sold today, and liability associated with it could be determined thirty years later or more. With changing legal and social norms, the inability of insurers to feel confident with their estimates of ultimate liabilities (for pricing purposes) led them to develop the claims-made coverage.

Bodily injury (BI) is defined as bodily injury, sickness, or disease sustained by a person, including death resulting from any of these at any time. **Property damage (PD)** is defined as (a) physical injury to tangible property, including all resulting loss of use of that property, or (b) loss of use of tangible property that is not physically injured.

In addition to covering an insured's liability due to bodily injury or property damage, the insurer promises to defend against suits claiming such injuries. The cost of defense is provided in addition to the limits of insurance available for payment of settlements or judgments, as is payment of interest that accrues after entry of the judgment against the insured. The insurer, however, has the general right to settle any suit as it deems appropriate. Furthermore, the insurer's obligation to defend against liability ends when it has paid out its limits for any of the coverages in settlements or judgments.

So far, this coverage sounds extremely broad, and it is. A long list of exclusions, however, defines the coverage more specifically. Figure 15.11 provides the list of exclusions.

bodily injury (BI)

Bodily injury, sickness, or disease sustained by a person, including death resulting from any of these at any time.

property damage (PD)

Physical injury to tangible property, including all resulting loss of use of that property, or loss of use of tangible property that is not physically injured.

FIGURE 15.11 Exclusions to Coverage A—Bodily Injury and Property Damage Liability in the ISO Commercial General Liability Policy

a. Expected or Intended Injury—"bodily injury" or "property damage" expected or intended from the standpoint of the insured.

b. Contractual Liability

c. Liquor Liability

d. Workers' Compensation and Similar Laws

e. Employer's Liability

f. Pollution

g. Aircraft, Auto or Watercraft

h. Mobile Equipment

i. War

j. Damage to Property you own, rent, or occupy, including any costs or expenses incurred by you, Premises you sell, give away or abandon, Property loaned to you; Personal property in the care, custody or control of the insured;

k. Damage to Your Product

l. Damage to Your Work

m. Damage to Impaired Property or Property Not Physically Injured

n. Recall of Products, Work or Impaired Property

o. Personal and Advertising Injury

We can discuss the exclusions as they relate to the four general reasons for exclusions, as presented earlier. Several relate to situations that may be nonfortuitous. Exclusion (a), which denies coverage for intentionally caused harm, clearly limits nonfortuitous events. Exclusion (b), an exclusion of contractually assumed liability, also could be considered a nonfortuitous event because the insured chose to enter into the relevant contract. Pollution liability (exclusion f), likewise, may arise from activities that were known to be dangerous. Damage to the insured's own products or work (exclusions k and l) indicates that the insurer is not willing to provide a product warranty to cover the insured's poor workmanship, a controllable situation.

A number of exclusions are intended to standardize the risk and/or to limit duplicate coverage when other coverage does or should exist. Liquor liability (exclusion c), for instance, is not standard across insureds. Entities with a liquor exposure must purchase separate coverage to protect against it. Likewise, we know that workers' compensation and employers' liability (exclusions d and e) all are covered by specialized contracts. Separate policies also exist for autos, aircraft, watercraft, and mobile equipment (exclusions g and h) because these risks will not be standard for organizations with similar general liability exposures.

The category of property owned by or in the care, custody, and control of the insured is also excluded (exclusion m). These exposures are best handled in a property insurance policy, in part because the insured cannot be liable to itself for damage, and in part because the damage should be covered whether or not it is caused by the insured's carelessness.

Some exclusions apply because of the catastrophic potential of certain situations. In addition to the possible nonfortuitous occurrence of pollution losses, the potential damages are catastrophic. Cost estimates to clean hazardous waste sites in the United States run into the hundreds of billions of dollars, as discussed in Chapter 12. Similarly, war-related injuries (exclusion i) are likely to affect thousands, possibly hundreds of thousands of people simultaneously.

The war risk practically defines catastrophe because it affects so many people from a single situation, not too unlike a product recall (exclusion n). Most manufacturers produce tens of thousands of products in each batch. If a recall is necessary, the whole batch generally is affected. This situation also has some element of nonfortuity, in that the insured has some control over deciding upon a recall, although limited separate coverage is available for this exposure. A memorable example occurred when Johnson & Johnson recalled all of its Tylenol products following the lethal tampering of several boxes.

Even though Johnson & Johnson undertook the recall to prevent future injury (and possible liability), its insurer denied coverage for the recall costs. Insureds can buy an endorsement for product recall.

Another exclusion is the fungi and bacteria exclusion. CGL has a mold exclusion that applies to bodily injury and property damage only. The endorsement states that payment for liability is excluded for the following:

d. "Bodily injury" or "property damage," which would not have occurred, in whole or in part, but for the actual, alleged or threatened inhalation of, ingestion of, contact with, exposure to, existence of, or presence of, any "fungi" or bacteria on or within a building or structure, including its contents, regardless of whether any other cause, event, material or product contributed concurrently or in any sequence to such injury or damage

e. Any loss, cost or expenses arising out of the abating, testing for, monitoring, cleaning up, removing, containing, treating, detoxifying, neutralizing, remediating or disposing of, or in any way responding to, or assessing the effects of, "fungi" or bacteria, by any insured or by any other person or entity[13]

Coverage B—Personal and Advertising Injury Liability

Coverage A provides protection against physical injury or damage due to the insured's activities. Despite the many exclusions, it provides broad coverage for premises, products, completed work, and other liabilities. It does not provide protection, however, against the liabilities arising out of nonphysical injuries. Coverage B does provide that protection. The policy states,

> "We will pay those sums that the insured becomes legally obligated to pay as damages because of 'personal and advertising injury' to which this insurance applies. We will have the right and duty to defend the insured against any 'suit' seeking those damages. However, we will have no duty to defend the insured against any 'suit' seeking damages for 'personal and advertising injury' to which this insurance does not apply. We may, at our discretion, investigate any offense and settle any claim or 'suit' that may result.[14] "

The exclusions for Coverage B, Personal and Advertising Injury Liability, are listed in Figure 15.12.

The exclusions eliminate intentional acts (nonaccidental acts), acts that occurred before the coverage began, criminal acts, and contractual liability. False statements and failure to conform to statements and infringements of copyrights and trademarks are also excluded. As in other coverages, electronic chat rooms and Internet businesses are excluded (see Chapter 12). In this context, insureds in the Internet and media businesses are completely excluded from coverage B under the 2001 CGL policy. The particular exclusion of unauthorized use of another's name and product was also noted in Chapter 12. Because pollution and pollution related-risks are considered catastrophic, they are excluded as well.

FIGURE 15.12 Exclusions to Coverage B—Personal and Advertising Injury Liability in the ISO Commercial General Liability Policy

a. Knowing Violation of Rights of Another

b. Material Published with Knowledge of Falsity

c. Material Published Prior to Policy Period

d. Criminal Acts

e. Contractual Liability

f. Breach of Contract

g. Quality or Performance of Goods — Failure to Conform to Statements

h. Wrong Description of Prices

i. Infringement of Copyright, Patent, Trademark, or Trade Secret

j. Insureds in Media and Internet-Type Businesses

k. Electronic Chatrooms or Bulletin Boards

l. Unauthorized Use of Another's Name or Product

m. Pollution

n. Pollution-Related

Coverage C—Medical Payments

We have discussed medical payments coverage in both the homeowners and auto policies. The CGL medical payments coverage is similar to what is found in the homeowners policy. It provides payment for first aid; necessary medical and dental treatment; and ambulance, hospital, professional nursing, and funeral services to persons other than the insured. The intent is to pay these amounts to people injured on the insured's premises or due to the insured's operations, regardless of fault. That is, medical payments coverage is not a liability protection.

The medical payments coverage is not intended to provide health insurance to the insured nor to any employees of the insured (or anyone eligible for workers' compensation). Nor will it duplicate coverage provided in other sections of the CGL or fill in where Coverage A excludes protection. War is also excluded. A list of exclusions to Coverage C is provided in Figure 15.13.

FIGURE 15.13 Exclusions to Coverage C—Medical Payment in the ISO Commercial General Liability Policy

a. Any Insured

b. Hired Person

c. Injury on Normally Occupied Premises

d. Workers Compensation and Similar Laws

e. Athletics Activities

f. Products-Completed Operations Hazard

g. Coverage A Exclusions

h. War

Supplementary Payments

Supplementary payments are for bodily injury, property damage, and personal injury coverage. The insurer pays for the claim or suit, the cost for bonds up to $250, all expenses for investigations it conducts, and "all reasonable expenses incurred by the insured." As long as the list of conditions detailed in the policy is met, the insurer pays all attorneys' fees that it incurs in the defense of the insured. The obligation to defend and to pay for attorneys' fees and necessary litigation expenses as supplementary payments ends when the insurer has reached the applicable limit of insurance in the payment of judgments or settlements.

Who Is an Insured?

Section II of the CGL is very specific and detailed in defining whose liability is covered. The following are insureds:

- An individual
- A partnership or joint venture
- A limited liability company
- An organization other than a partnership, joint venture, or limited liability company
- A trust

The volunteer workers of the business are also insured. However, none of the employees or volunteer workers are insureds for bodily injury or personal and advertising injury to the insured or damage to property that is owned or occupied by the insured.

Limits of Insurance

The limits of insurance, as you know by now, define the maximum responsibility of the insurer under specified situations. A portion of the declaration for CGL is shown in Figure 15.14.

FIGURE 15.14 Section of the ISO Commercial General Liability Declaration Page ((Sample))

LIMITS OF INSURANCE		
EACH OCCURRENCE LIMIT	$ _____	
DAMAGE TO PREMISES		
RENTED TO YOU LIMIT	$ _____	Any one premises
MEDICAL EXPENSE LIMIT	$ _____	Any one person
PERSONAL ADVERTISING INJURY LIMIT	$ _____	Any one person or organization
GENERAL AGGREGATE LIMIT	$ _____	
PRODUCTS/COMPLETED OPERATIONS AGGREGATE LIMIT	$ _____	

Source: ISO Commercial General Liability Coverage Form CG 00 0110 01. Includes copyrighted material of Insurance Services Office, Inc., with its permission.

The policy clarifies the limits of insurance shown in the declarations and the applicable rules. The general aggregate limit is the most that the insurer pays for the sum of

- medical expenses under Coverage C, plus
- damages under Coverage A, except damages because of "bodily injury" or "property damage" included in the "products-completed operations hazard," plus
- damages under Coverage B

The limits are paid regardless of the number of insureds, claims made, or suits brought, or persons or organizations making claims or bringing suits. The limits apply separately to each consecutive annual period.

CGL Conditions

Like all other policies, the CGL includes an extensive conditions section, primarily outlining the duties of the insured and insurer. Subrogation, other insurance, proper action in the event of loss, and similar provisions are spelled out in the conditions section.

Definitions

Words used in insurance policies might not have the same interpretation as when they are used in other documents or conversations. To specify its intent, insurers define significant terms (remember that insurance is a contract of adhesion, so ambiguities are read in the manner most favorable to the insured). Some defined terms in the CGL have already been discussed, including "bodily injury," "property damage," "personal injury," "advertising injury," and "occurrence." In total, twenty-two terms are defined in the CGL. Like the rest of the policy, a full interpretation of coverage requires reading and analyzing these definitions. The problems that arise out of interpretation of the CGL policy wording is discussed in the box "Liability Limits: One Event or Two?"

4.2 Commercial Umbrella Liability Policy

Today, $1,000,000 of liability coverage, the standard limit for a CGL, is insufficient for many businesses. Furthermore, liabilities other than those covered by the CGL may be of significant importance to a business. To obtain additional amounts and a broader scope of coverage, a business can purchase a commercial umbrella liability policy.

The **umbrella liability policy** provides excess coverage over underlying insurance. Except for excluded risks, it also provides excess over a specified amount, such as $25,000, for which there is no underlying coverage. Typically, you are required to have specified amounts of underlying coverage, such as the CGL with a $1,000,000 limit and automobile insurance with the same limit. When a loss occurs, the basic contracts pay within their limits and then the umbrella policy pays until its limits are exhausted. If there is no underlying coverage for a loss covered by the umbrella, you pay the first $25,000 (or whatever is the specified retention), and the umbrella insurer pays the excess.

The umbrella policy covers bodily injury, property damage, personal injury, and advertising injury liability, similar to what is provided in the CGL. Medical expense coverage is not included. The limits of coverage, however, are intended to be quite high, and the exclusions are not as extensive as those found in the CGL. Most businesses find umbrella liability coverage an essential part of their risk management operations.

> **umbrella liability policy**
>
> Provides excess coverage over underlying insurance. Except for excluded risks, it also provides excess over a specified amount, for which there is no underlying coverage.

KEY TAKEAWAYS

In this section you studied the commercial general liability component of the CPP and the umbrella liability option:

- The CGL format is similar to the BPP and BIC; it consists of the declaration form, coverage form, and any endorsements.
- Five sections make up the CGL: coverages, who is an insured, limits of insurance, conditions, and definitions.
  - Coverages are available on either an occurrence or a claims-made basis for bodily injury and property damage, personal and advertising injury, and medical payments, each subject to many exclusions.
  - The insureds can be an individual, a partnership/joint venture, limited liability company, an other organization, or a trust.
  - The limits of insurance provide clarification for limits shown in declarations and applicable rules as follows: paid regardless of number of insureds, claims made, suits brought, or persons/organizations making claims or bringing suits.
  - Conditions outlines the duties of the insured and insurer.
  - Definitions describes any term of policy in quotation marks.
- The standard limits for CGL may be inadequate for many businesses.
- The umbrella liability policy provides excess coverage above and beyond underlying insurance.
- The umbrella policy has the same coverages as the CGL except medical expense.

DISCUSSION QUESTIONS

1. Provide an example of expenses that would be covered under each of the three CGL coverages.
2. What responsibility does a CGL insurer have with regard to litigation expenses for a lawsuit that, if successfully pursued by the plaintiff, would result in payment of damages under the terms of the policy?
3. How does personal injury differ from bodily injury?
4. Who needs an umbrella liability policy? Why?
5. Assume that the Baker-Leetch Pet Store has a CGL with a $1,000,000 aggregate limit. The policy commences July 1, 2008, and ends June 30, 2009.

   a. If claims-made, the retroactive date is July 1, 2007, and a one-year extended reporting period applies. Under both occurrence and claims-made scenarios, would the following losses be covered? The pet shop sold a diseased gerbil in August 2007. The gerbil ultimately infected the owner's twenty cats and dogs (kept for breeding purposes), who all died. The owner filed a lawsuit against Baker-Leetch in September 2008. What if the lawsuit were filed in September 2009? September 2010?

   b. The pet shop provided dog training in July 2008 and guaranteed the results of the training. In December 2008, one of the trained dogs attacked a mail carrier, causing severe injuries. The mail carrier immediately sued Baker-Leetch.

   c. The pet store sold an inoculated rare and expensive cat in October 2008. The cat contracted a disease in October 2009 that would not have occurred if the animal truly had been properly inoculated. The owners sued in December 2009.

---

5.   OTHER LIABILITY RISKS

LEARNING OBJECTIVES

In this section we elaborate on additional liability risks and insurance solutions:

- **Auto liability**
- **Professional liability**
- **Employment practices liability**

What about the business liability exposures not covered by the CGL? Space limitations prohibit discussing all of them, but several merit some attention: automobile, professional liability, and workers' compensation. Workers' compensation is discussed in more detail in Chapter 16.

5.1   Automobile Liability

If the business is a proprietorship and the only vehicles used are private passenger automobiles, the personal auto policy or a similar policy is available to cover the automobile exposure. If the business is a partnership or corporation or uses other types of vehicles, other forms of automobile insurance must be purchased if the exposure is to be insured. The coverages are similar to the automobile insurance discussed in Chapter 14.

5.2   Professional Liability

The nature and significance of the professional liability risk were discussed in Chapter 12. Most professionals insure this exposure separately with malpractice insurance, errors and omissions insurance, or directors and officers (D&O) insurance. These liability coverages were discussed in Chapter 12. You are urged to review the current conditions of the D&O coverage featured in the box "Directors and Officers Coverage in the Limelight."

Directors and Officers Coverage in the Limelight

William Webster had enjoyed a long and distinguished career in public service, most notably as the only person ever to head both the FBI (under President Carter) and the CIA (under President Reagan). The onetime U.S. District Court judge retired from public office in 1991, at age sixty-seven, and devoted his time to practicing law in Washington, D.C., and sitting on the boards of several large corporations. One of them was U.S. Technologies, which develops and supports emerging Internet companies. But in July 2002, Webster was told the company could no longer provide adequate liability insurance to its directors and officers. He resigned.

All publicly traded companies must have a board of directors, a group of people elected by the stockholders to govern the company. Generally, the board is charged with selecting and supervising the executive officers, setting overall corporate policy, and overseeing the preparation of financial statements. This role leaves directors vulnerable to lawsuits from shareholders, creditors, customers, or employees on charges such as abuse of authority, libel or slander, and—the biggest concern these days—financial mismanagement. Board members at many corporations became concerned about their personal liability and started taking a closer look at the insurance known as directors and officers (D&O) coverage that is supposed to protect them.

Not surprisingly, the corporate scandals of 2001 and 2002–2004 had driven up the cost of D&O insurance. Following WorldCom's June 2002 announcement that it had "inappropriately classified" nearly $4 billion in expenses, D&O insurers pulled back from covering not just WorldCom but also its banks, its suppliers, and its business customers. Another reason for the shrinking D&O insurance pool was the late 1990s trend toward astronomical settlements in class-action securities lawsuits. By 2002, high-risk companies—in the aircraft, financial, health care, technology, and telecommunications industries—were paying triple what they used to for D&O, if they could find coverage at all.

Directors and officers were made even more vulnerable with the passage of the Sarbanes-Oxley Act in July 2002. With this key piece of legislation, Congress hoped to restore the public's confidence in U.S. financial markets by holding chief executives, directors, and outside auditors more responsible—even criminally liable—for the accuracy of financial reports. Sarbanes-Oxley was passed just one month after Enron's outside auditor, the accounting firm Arthur Andersen, was convicted on obstruction of justice charges for its role in the financial fraud.

The days of shortage in D&O availability and affordability ended as the market softened. According to the 2005 Directors and Officers Liability Survey conducted by the Tillinghast business of Towers Perrin, the 2005 standardized premium index (that was created in 1974) decreased about 8 percent in the D&O coverage cost. The average index decreased from its highest level of 1,237 in 2003 to 1,010 in 2005. The only business classes that reported an increase from 2004 were durable goods, education, health services, and nonbanking financial services. The report also indicated that coverage limits and deductibles remained level.

The leading insurers for the line are: Chubb (21 percent) and AIG (35 percent). Interestingly, AIG, one of the major players in this line of insurance, saw its own 2005 D&O rates increasing in the midst of allegations of its improper accounting.

Sources: Roberto Ceniceros, "WorldCom Adds to D&O Ills," Business Insurance, July 8, 2002; Rodd Zolkos and Mark A. Hofmann, "Crises Spur Push for Reform," Business Insurance, July 15, 2002; Richard B. Schmitt, Michael Schroeder, and Shailagh Murray, "Corporate-Oversight Bill Passes, Smoothing Way for New Lawsuits," Wall Street Journal, July 26, 2002; Carrie Coolidge, "D&O Insurance Gets Closer Scrutiny," Forbes, November 22, 2002; 2005 Survey of Directors and Officers Liability by the Tillinghast business of Towers Perrin is available at http://www.iii.org and http://www.Towersperrin.Com/Tillinghast/Publications/Reports/2005_DO/DO_2005_Exec_Sum.pdf, accessed March 27, 2009; Matt Scroggins, "AIG Board Panel to Oversee Director Indemnification," Business Insurance, May 25, 2005; Regis Coccia, "AIG to Pay Directors' Expenses Amid Suits and Probes," Business Insurance, May 16, 2005.

5.3 Employment Practices Liability

Employment-Related Practices Liability Program

Covers insureds' liability for claims arising out of an injury to an employee because of an employment-related offense, as well as providing legal defense for the insured.

The ISO's Employment-Related Practices Liability Program, which is available to all ISO-participating insurance companies, was filed with state insurance regulators for approval effective April 1, 1998.[15] It was the newest line introduced in more than twenty years. Because of an increase in the number of lawsuits filed for sexual harassment and many more employment-related liability suits, the coverage became imperative to most businesses. The ISO is considered a baseline program. "The [**Employment-Related Practices Liability Program**] covers insureds' liability for claims arising out of an injury to an employee because of an employment-related offense, as well as providing legal defense for the insured. Injury may result from discrimination that results in refusal to hire; failure to promote; termination; demotion; discipline or defamation. Injury also can include coercion of an employee to perform an unlawful act; work-related sexual harassment; or verbal, physical, mental or emotional abuse."

The ISO program excludes the following:

1. Criminal, fraudulent, or malicious acts

2. Violations of the accommodations requirement of the Americans with Disabilities Act

3. Liability of the perpetrator of sexual harassment

4. Injury arising out of strikes and lockouts, employment termination from specified business decisions, and retaliatory actions taken against whistleblowers

The program makes available a number of optional coverages:

1. Extending the claims-reporting period to three years

2. Extending coverage beyond managers and supervisors to all of a firm's employees

3. Insuring organizations that are newly formed or acquired by the insured during the policy period for ninety days

4. Insuring persons or organizations with financial control over the insured or the insured's employment-related practices

---

KEY TAKEAWAYS

In this section you studied business liability exposures not covered by the CGL:

- In a proprietorship, if the only vehicles used are private passenger automobiles, the personal auto policy is available; if the business uses other types of vehicles, other forms of automobile insurance must be purchased.

- Most professionals insure professional liability exposure with malpractice insurance, errors and omissions insurance, or directors and officers insurance (D&O).

- The Employment-Related Practices Liability Program covers liability for injury to employees because of employment-related offenses and provides legal defense for the insured; injury may result from discrimination that results in refusal to hire, failure to promote, termination, demotion, discipline, or defamation.

DISCUSSION QUESTIONS

1. How does malpractice differ from errors and omissions?

2. The Employment-Related Practices Liability Program is concerned with what kind of injury to employees?

---

6. REVIEW AND PRACTICE

1. How does the insured choose a limit of insurance for the BIC?

2. What are the primary differences among the three causes of loss forms available in the commercial property policy? Why not always choose the special form?

3. When would the monthly limit of indemnity, maximum period of indemnity, or payroll endorsement be appropriate?

4. Hurricane Iniki in 1992 caused extensive damage to one of the Hawaiian Islands. A significant loss in tourist activity resulted. Assume the Kooey Hotel experienced $500,000 in damage to its property. Furthermore, assume Kooey typically brought in $100,000 of revenue per month, on which it incurred $80,000 of fixed and variable expenses. For two months following Iniki, the Kooey Hotel was shut down, but still incurred expenses of $50,000. The hotel spent $15,000 more than usual on advertising before reopening. Based on this information, what would be the insurable consequential losses of the Kooey Hotel from Hurricane Iniki? What can be done to reduce those losses?

5. Compare occurrence and claims-made policies.

6. Assume the Koehn Kitchen Corporation, a manufacturer of kitchen gadgets, experiences the following losses:

   a. A consumer chops off his finger while using Koehn's Cutlery Gizmo. The consumer sues Koehn for medical expenses, lost income, pain and suffering, and punitive damages.

   b. An employee of Koehn is injured while delivering goods to a wholesaler. The employee sues for medical expenses and punitive damages.

   c. Koehn uses toxic substances in its manufacturing process. Neighbors of its plant bring suit against Koehn, claiming that a higher rate of stillbirths is occurring in the area because of Koehn's use of toxins. (Consider the variation that an explosion emitted the toxins rather than normal business operations.)

d. Koehn's Mighty Mate Slicing Machine must be recalled because of a product defect. The recall causes massive losses.

e. Based on information in this chapter, which parts of any of these losses are covered by Koehn's CGL? Explain your answer.

7. Provide a detailed rationale for excluding pollution, auto accidents, and liquor liability in the CGL.

8. What is a BOP? What does it cover?

9. The Goldman Cat House is a pet store catering to the needs of felines. The store is a sole proprietorship, taking in revenues of approximately $1,700,000 annually. Products available include kittens, cat food, cat toys, cages, collars, cat litter and litter boxes, and manuals on cat care. One manual was written by the store owner, who also makes up his own concoction for cat litter. All other goods are purchased from national wholesalers. Two part-time and two full-time employees work for Goldman. Sometimes the employees deliver goods to Goldman customers.

a. Identify some of Goldman Cat House's liability exposures.

b. Would Goldman be best advised to purchase an occurrence-based or claims-made liability policy?

c. What liability loss-control techniques would you recommend for Goldman?

ENDNOTES

1. A detailed description of this part of the policy is beyond the scope of this text.

2. ISO Commercial Property Causes of Loss—Broad Form CP 10 20 06 07. Includes copyrighted material of Insurance Services Office, Inc., with its permission.

3. ISO Commercial Property Business Income (and Extra Expense) Coverage Form CP 00 30 06 07. Includes copyrighted material of Insurance Services Office, Inc., with its permission.

4. ISO press release at http://www.iso.com/products/2200/prod2241.html (accessed March 27, 2009).

5. ISO press release at http://www.iso.com/press_releases/2002/01_22_02.html, January 22, 2002 (accessed March 27, 2009).

6. "New ISO Offering for Smaller Businesses," *National Underwriter Online News Service*, June 3, 2002. The press release by ISO "ISO's NEW BUSINESSOWNERS PROGRAM SIMPLIFIES RATING AND EXPANDS COVERAGE ELIGIBILITY—ISO IntegRater™ and AscendantOne™ Updated for the New BOP" is available at http://www.iso.com/press_releases/2002/06_03_02.html.

7. Businessowners Endorsement: BP 05 11 01 02 (N/A To Standard Fire Policy States); Businessowners Endorsement: BP 05 12 02 (Applies In Standard Fire Policy States); Businessowners Endorsement: BP 05 13 01 02.

8. The claim precedes the coverage period. No coverage exists under this policy.

9. The event follows the retroactive date and the claim is brought during the policy period.

10. The event follows the retroactive date and the claim is brought in the extended reporting period.

11. The claim follows the end of the reporting period.

12. Even though the claim is brought within the extended reporting period, the event occurs.

13. ISO Commercial General Liability Coverage Form CG 00 0110 01. Includes copyrighted material of Insurance Services Office, Inc., with its permission.

14. ISO Commercial General Liability Coverage Form CG 00 0110 01. Includes copyrighted material of Insurance Services Office, Inc., with its permission.

15. ISO press release as of August 19, 1997, at http://www.iso.com/press_releases/1997/08_19_97.html, (accessed March 31, 2009), http://www.iso.com/Press-Releases/1997/ISO-INTRODUCES-FIRST-STANDARDIZED-INSURANCE-PROGRAM-FOR-EMPLOYMENT-PRACTICES-LIABILITY.html.

CHAPTER 16

Risks Related to the Job: Workers' Compensation and Unemployment Compensation

Workers' compensation is a state-mandated coverage that is exclusively related to the workplace. Unemployment compensation is also a mandated program required of employers. Both are considered social insurance programs, as is Social Security. Social Security is featured in Chapter 18 as a foundation program for employee benefits (covered in Chapter 19 through Chapter 22). Social insurance programs are required coverages as a matter of law. The programs are based only on the connection to the labor force, not on need. Both workers' compensation and unemployment compensation are part of the risk management of businesses in the United States. The use of workers' compensation as part of an integrated risk program is featured in Case 3 of Chapter 23.

Workers' compensation was one of the coverages that helped the families who lost their breadwinners in the attacks of September 11, 2001. New York City and the state of New York suffered their largest-ever loss of human lives. Because most of the loss of life occurred while the employees were at work, those injured received medical care, rehabilitation, and disability income under the New York workers' compensation system, and families of the deceased received survivors' benefits. The huge payouts raised the question of what would happen to workers' compensation rates. The National Council on Compensation Insurance (NCCI) predicted a grim outlook then, but by 2005, conditions improved as frequency of losses declined and the industry's reserves increased.[1] The workers' compensation line has maintained this strong reserve position and has been helped by a continual downward trend in loss frequency. Consequently, the industry reported a combined ratio of 93 percent in 2006 and projects a 99 percent combined ratio for 2007. This indicates positive underwriting results. However, medical claims severity (in contrast to frequency) has continued to grow, as shown in Figure 16.1.

Workers' compensation is considered a social insurance program. Another social insurance program is the unemployment compensation offered in all the states. This chapter includes a brief explanation of this program as well. To better understand how workers' compensation and unemployment compensation work, this chapter includes the following:

1. Links

2. Workers' compensation laws and benefits

3. How benefits are provided

4. Workers' compensation issues

5. Unemployment compensation

FIGURE 16.1 **Changes in the Distribution of Medical versus Indemnity Claims in Workers' Compensation***

* 2007p: Preliminary based on data valued as of December 31, 2007; 1987, 1997: Based on data through December 31, 2006, developed to ultimate; based on the states where NCCI provides rate-making services, excludes the effects of deductible policies

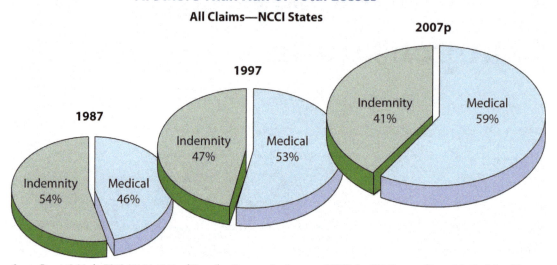

Source: Dennis C. Mealy, FCAS, MAAA, National Council on Compensation Insurance (NCCI), Inc. Chief Actuary, "State of the Line" Annul Issues Symposium (AIS), May 8, 2008, Accessed March 28, 2009, https://www.ncci.com/documents/AIS-2008-SOL-Complete.pdf. © 2008 NCCI Holdings, Inc. Reproduced with permission.

1. LINKS

At this point in our study, we look at the coverage employers provide for you and your family in case you are hurt on the job (workers' compensation) or lose your job involuntarily (unemployment compensation). As noted above, these coverages are mandatory in most states. Workers' compensation is not mandatory in New Jersey and Texas (although most employers in these states provide it anyway). In later chapters, you will see the employer-provided group life, health, disability, and pensions as part of noncash compensation programs. These coverages complete important parts of your holistic risk management. You know that, at least for work-related injury, you have protection, and that if you are laid off, limited unemployment compensation is available to you for six months. These coverages are paid completely by the employer; the rates for workers' compensation are based on your occupational classification.

In some cases, the employer does not purchase workers' compensation coverage from a private insurer but buys it from a state's monopolistic fund or self-insures the coverage. For unemployment compensation, the coverage, in most cases, is provided by the states.[2] Regardless of the method of obtaining the coverage, you are assured by statutes to receive the benefits.

As with the coverages discussed in Chapter 13 to Chapter 15, external market conditions are a very important indication of the cost of coverage to your employer. When rates increase dramatically, many employers will opt to self-insure and use a third-party administrator (TPA) to manage the claims. In workers' compensation, loss control and safety engineering are important parts of the risk management process. One of the causes of loss is ergonomics, particularly as related to computers. See the box "Should Ergonomic Standards Be Mandatory?" for a discussion. You would like to minimize your injury at work, and your employer is obligated under federal and state laws to secure a safe workplace for you.

Thus, in your pursuit of a holistic risk management program, workers' compensation coverage is an important piece of the puzzle that completes your risk mitigation. The coverages you receive are only for work-related injuries. What happens if you are injured away from work? This will be discussed in later chapters. One trend is integrated benefits, in which the employer integrates the disability and medical coverages of workers' compensation with voluntary health and disability insurance. Integrated benefits are part of the effort to provide twenty-four-hour coverage regardless of whether an injury occurred at work or away from work. Currently, nonwork-related injuries are covered for medical procedures by the employer-provided health insurance and for loss of income by group disability insurance. Integrating the benefits is assumed to prevent double dipping (receiving benefits under workers' compensation and also under health insurance or disability insurance) and to ensure security of coverage regardless of being at work or not. (See the box "Integrated Benefits: The Twenty-Four-Hour Coverage Concept.") Health and disability coverages are provided voluntarily by your employer, and it is your responsibility to seek individual coverages when the pieces that are offered are insufficient to complete your holistic risk management. Figure 16.2 shows how your holistic risk pieces relate to the risk management parts available under workers' compensation and unemployment compensation.

FIGURE 16.2   Links between Holistic Risk Pieces and Workers' Compensation and Unemployment Compensation

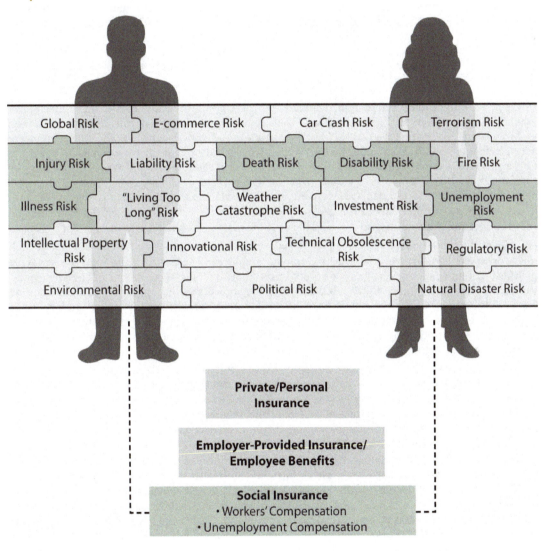

2. WORKERS' COMPENSATION LAWS AND BENEFITS

LEARNING OBJECTIVES

In this section we elaborate on the following:

- **History of workers' compensation**
- **Legal enactment of workers' compensation**
- **Benefits provided under workers' compensation**

workers' compensation

A system to enforce a series of state laws that requires employers to pay workers for their work-related injuries and illnesses with no relationship to who caused the injury or illness.

common law defenses

The three arguments that employers utilized to avoid assuming responsibility for employees' work-related injuries prior to the establishment of of workers' compensation laws: the fellow-servant rule, the assumption of risk doctrine, and the contributory negligence doctrine.

fellow-servant rule

Defense under which an employee injured as a result of the conduct of a fellow worker cannot recover damages from the employer.

assumption of risk doctrine

Defense providing that an employee who knew, or should have known, of unsafe conditions of employment assumed the risk by remaining on the job.

contributory negligence

Defense arguing that an employee was injured through negligence of the employer but was also partly at fault.

employers' liability

Portion of a worker's compensation policy that protects against potential liabilities not within the scope of the workers' compensation law, yet arising out of employee injuries.

Each state and certain other jurisdictions, such as the District of Columbia and other U.S. territories, has a **workers' compensation** system to enforce a series of state laws that requires employers to pay workers for their work-related injuries and illnesses with no relationship to who caused the injury or illness.

2.1 History and Purpose

In the nineteenth century, before implementation of workers' compensation laws in the United States, employees were seldom paid for work-related injuries. A major barrier to payment was that a worker had to prove an injury was the fault of his or her employer to recover damages. The typical employee was reluctant to sue his or her employer out of fear of losing the job. For the same reason, fellow workers typically refused to testify on behalf of an injured colleague about the circumstances surrounding an accident. If the injured employee could not prove fault, the employer had no responsibility. The injured employee's ability to recover damages was hindered further by the fact that even a negligent employer could use three **common law defenses** to disavow liability for workers' injuries: the fellow-servant rule, the doctrine of assumption of risk, and the doctrine of contributory negligence.

Under the **fellow-servant rule**, an employee who was injured as a result of the conduct of a fellow worker could not recover damages from the employer. The **assumption of risk doctrine** provided that an employee who knew, or should have known, of unsafe conditions of employment assumed the risk by remaining on the job. Further, it was argued that the employee's compensation recognized the risk of the job. Therefore, he or she could not recover damages from the employer when injured because of such conditions. If an employee was injured through negligence of the employer but was partly at fault, the employee was guilty of **contributory negligence**. Any contributory negligence, regardless of how slight, relieved the employer of responsibility for the injury.

These defenses made recovery of damages by injured employees nearly impossible and placed the cost of work-related injuries on the employee. As a result, during the latter part of the nineteenth century, various **employer liability laws** were adopted to modify existing laws and improve the legal position of injured workers. The system of negligence liability was retained, however, and injured employees still had to prove that their employer was at fault to recover damages.

Even with modifications, the negligence system proved costly to administer and inefficient in protecting employees from the financial burdens of workplace injuries.[3] The need for more extensive reform was recognized, with many European countries instituting social insurance programs during the latter half of the 1800s. Beginning with Wisconsin in 1911,[4] U.S. jurisdictions developed the concept of workers' compensation that compensated workers without the requirement that employers' negligence must be proved (that is, with strict employer liability). Costs were borne directly by employers (generally in the form of workers' compensation insurance premiums) and indirectly by employees who accepted lower wages in exchange for benefits. To the extent, if any, that total labor costs were increased, consumers (who benefit from industrialization) shared in the burden of industrial accidents through higher prices for goods and services. Employees demanded higher total compensation (wages plus benefits) to engage in high-risk occupations, resulting in incentives for employers to adopt safety programs. By 1948, each jurisdiction had similar laws.

In compromising between the interests of employees and those of employers, the originators of workers' compensation systems limited the benefits available to employees to some amount less than the full loss. They also made those benefits the sole recourse of the employee against the employer for work-related injuries. This give-and-take of rights and duties between employers and employees is termed **quid pro quo** (Latin for "this for that"). The intent was for the give and take to have an equal value, on average. You will see in our discussion of current workers' compensation issues that some doubt exists as to whether equity has been maintained. An exception to the sole recourse concept exists in some states for the few employees who elect, prior to injury, not to be covered by workers' compensation. Such employees, upon injury, can sue their employer; however, the employer in these instances retains the three defenses described earlier.

In addition to every state and territory having a workers' compensation law, there are federal laws applicable to longshore workers and harbor workers, to nongovernment workers in the District of Columbia, and to civilian employees of the federal government. Workers' compensation laws differ from jurisdiction to jurisdiction, but they all have the purpose of ensuring that injured workers and their dependents will receive benefits without question of fault.

quid pro quo

(Latin phrase meaning "this for that")—give-and-take of rights and duties between employers and employees.

Integrated Benefits: The Twenty-Four-Hour Coverage Concept

Are your wrists painful? Or numb? (If you think about it long enough, you'll convince yourself they're one or the other.) Perhaps you have a repetitive stress injury or carpal tunnel syndrome. Maybe it's now painful enough that you need to take a few days off. But wait—you use a computer at work, so this could be a work-related injury. Better go talk to the risk manager about filing a workers' compensation claim. But wait—you spend hours at home every night playing computer games. If this is an off-hours injury, you should call your health maintenance organization (HMO) for an appointment with your primary care physician so you can arrange for short-term disability. But wait—when your boss is not looking, you surf the Internet at work. What do you do?

If you worked for Steelcase, Inc., an office-furniture manufacturer based in Grand Rapids, Michigan, your wrists might still hurt, but you would not have to worry about who to call. Steelcase used to handle its medical benefits like most companies do: the risk management department handled workers' compensation; the human resources department handled health insurance, short-term disability, and long-term disability; and four separate insurers provided the separate coverages. Several events caused top management to rethink this disintegrated strategy: rising medical costs, a slowdown in the economy that forced a look at cost-saving measures, and the results of a survey showing that employees simply did not understand their benefits. "The employees hammered us in terms of not understanding who to call or what they get," Steelcase manager Libby Child told Employee Benefit News in June 2001.

In 1997, Steelcase became one of the first U.S. companies to implement an integrated benefits program. It combined long- and short-term disability, workers' compensation, medical case management, and Family and Medical Leave Act administration, and outsourced the record-keeping duties. Now a disabled employee—whether the injury is work-related or not—can make one phone call and talk to a representative who collects information, files any necessary claims, and assigns the worker to a medical case manager. The case manager ensures that the employee is receiving proper medical treatment and appropriate benefits and helps him or her return to work as soon as possible.

The integrated plan has been a hit with employees, who like the one-call system, and with managers because lost-time days decreased by one-third after the program was implemented. Steelcase's financial executives are happy, too: the combined cost of short-term disability, long-term disability, and workers' compensation dropped 13 percent in the program's first three years.

In California, however, results with integrated benefits have been mixed. The California state legislature authorized three-year pilot programs in four counties to study the effectiveness of twenty-four-hour health care in the early 1990s, a time when workers' compensation premiums were inordinately expensive for employers. By the time the programs were under way, these costs had become more competitive. Thus, most employers viewed a change to integrated benefits as simply too risky in relation to the traditional workers' compensation system. Nonetheless, then California Insurance Commissioner (and current California Lieutenant Governor) John Garamendi championed the concept of integrated benefits. Garamendi maintains that placing workers' compensation and health coverage under managed care has the potential to save California $1 billion through reductions in administrative and legal expenses, fraud, and medical costs.

With Steelcase and other pioneers proving the success of integrated benefits, it is a wonder that all companies have not jumped on the bandwagon. Many are, but there are still some obstacles to overcome:

- The shift from paper record keeping to computer databases raises concerns over privacy.
- Risk managers and human resources personnel may have turf wars over the combination of their duties.

- To fully integrate and to be able to generate, meaningful data, all computer systems must be compatible and their operators trained; however, human resource departments and the treasurer (where risk management resides) may not have the same systems.
- Workers' compensation is provided by property/casualty insurers, while health and disability are provided by life/health insurers, so integration may be complicated.
- Regulations vary widely for workers' compensation and employee benefits.

In the past few years, many companies, large and small, have taken the leap toward integrating benefits. Recent converts include Pacific Bell; San Bernardino County in California; Pitney Bowes; and even an insurance company, Nationwide. Several organizations specializing in the twenty-four-hour coverage concept have also emerged. Notably, the Integrated Benefits Institute (IBI) merges health, absenteeism, and disability management under one banner and provides consulting services. Integrated Benefits LLC is another brokerage firm in this area operating in the Carolinas, and United 24 has produced success bringing together managed care, workers' compensation, and disability insurance for Wisconsin employers. For any business that wants to reduce sick time off and disability benefits—which cost the average company 14.3 percent of payroll—the issue of integrating benefits is not "whether" but "when."

Sources: Diana Reitz, "It's Time to Resume the 24-Hour Coverage Debate," National Underwriter Property & Casualty/Risk & Benefits Management Edition, February 8, 1999; Annmarie Geddes Lipold, "Benefit Integration Boosts Productivity and Profits," Workforce.com, accessed March 31, 2009, http://www.workforce.com/section/02/feature/23/36/89/; Karen Lee, "Pioneers Return Data on Integrated Benefits," Employee Benefit News, June 2001; Lee Ann Gjertsen, "Brokers Positive on Integrated Benefits," National Underwriter, Property & Casualty/Risk & Benefits Management Edition, July 7, 1997; Leo D. Tinkham, Jr., "Making the Case for Integrated Disability Management," National Underwriter, Life & Health/Financial Services Edition, May 13, 2002; Phyllis S. Myers and Etti G. Baranoff, "Workers' Compensation: On the Cutting Edge," Academy of Insurance Education, Washington, D.C., instructional video with supplemental study guide, video produced by the Center for Video Education, 1997.

2.2 Coverage

Coverage under workers' compensation is either inclusive or exclusive. Further, it is compulsory or elective, depending on state law. A major feature is that only injuries and illnesses that "arise out of and in the course of employment" are covered.

Inclusive or Exclusive

Inclusive laws list all the types of employment that are covered under workers' compensation; **exclusive laws** cover all the types of employment under workers' compensation except those that are excluded. Typically, domestic service and casual labor (for some small jobs) are excluded. Agricultural workers are excluded in nineteen jurisdictions, whereas their coverage is compulsory in twenty-seven jurisdictions and entirely voluntary in four jurisdictions. Some states limit coverage to occupations classified as hazardous. The laws of thirty-nine states apply to all employers in the types of employment covered; others apply only to employers with more than a specified number of employees. Any employer can comply voluntarily.

Compulsory or Elective

In all but two states, the laws regarding workers' compensation are compulsory. In these two states (New Jersey and Texas) with **elective laws**, either the employer or the employee can elect not to be covered under workers' compensation law. An employer who opts out loses the common law defenses discussed earlier. If the employer does not opt out but an employee does, the employer retains those defenses as far as that employee is concerned. If both opt out, the employer loses the defenses. It is unusual for employees to opt out because those who do must prove negligence in order to collect and must overcome the employer's defenses.

An employer who does not opt out must pay benefits to injured employees in accordance with the requirements of the law, but that is the employer's sole responsibility. Thus, an employee who is covered by workers' compensation cannot sue his or her employer for damages because workers' compensation is the employee's **sole remedy** (also called exclusive remedy). (In fact, workers' compensation is losing its status as the employee's sole remedy against the employer. Later in this chapter, we will discuss some of the current methods used by employees to negate the exclusive remedy rule.) By coming under the law, the employer avoids the cost of litigation and the risk of having to pay a large judgment in the event an injured employee's suit for damages is successful.

In Texas, 65 percent of employers opted to stay in the system despite the fact that workers' compensation is not mandatory.[5] It is likely that as insurance rates rise, more companies will opt to stay out of the system. Nearly all employers that opt out reduce their likelihood of being sued by providing an alternative employee benefit plan that includes medical and disability income benefits as well as

---

inclusive laws

Laws that list all the types of employment covered under workers' compensation.

exclusive laws

Laws that cover all the types of employment under workers' compensation except those that are excluded.

elective laws

State laws providing that either the employer or the employee may elect not to be covered under workers' compensation law.

sole remedy

Provides that employees cannot (in most circumstances) sue their employers for work-related injuries, regardless of fault, when covered by workers' compensation.

accidental death and dismemberment benefits for work-related injuries and illnesses.[6] In addition, the employer purchases employer's liability insurance to cover the possibility of being sued by injured employees who are not satisfied with the alternative benefits.

Proponents of an opt-out provision argue that competition from alternative coverage provides market discipline to lower workers' compensation insurance prices. Furthermore, greater exposure to common law liability suits may encourage workplace safety. Opponents see several drawbacks of opt-out provisions:

- Some employers may fail to provide medical benefits or may provide only modest benefits, resulting in cost shifting to other segments of society.
- The right of the employee to sue may be illusory because some employers may have few assets and no liability insurance.
- Employees may be reluctant to sue the employer, especially when the opportunity to return to work exists or if family members may be affected.
- Safety incentives may not be enhanced for employers with few assets at risk.

Covered Injuries

To limit benefits to situations in which a definite relationship exists between an employee's work and the injury, most laws provide coverage only for injuries "arising out of and in the course of employment." This phrase describes two limitations. First, the injury **must arise out of employment**, meaning that the job environment was the cause. For example, the family of someone who has a relatively stress-free job but dies of cardiac arrest at work would have trouble proving the work connection and therefore would not be eligible for workers' compensation benefits. On the other hand, a police officer or firefighter who suffers a heart attack (even while not on duty) is presumed in many states to have suffered from work-related stress.

The second limitation on coverage is that the injury must occur **while in the course of employment**. That is, the loss-causing event must take place while the employee is on the job in order to be covered by workers' compensation. An employee injured while engaged in horseplay, therefore, might not be eligible for workers' compensation because the injury did not occur while the employee was "in the course of employment." Likewise, coverage does not apply while traveling the normal commute between home and work. Along these same lines of reasoning, certain injuries generally are explicitly excluded, such as those caused by willful misconduct or deliberate failure to follow safety rules, those resulting from intoxication, and those that are self-inflicted.

Subject to these limitations, all work-related injuries are covered, even if they are due to employee negligence. In addition, every state provides benefits for **occupational disease**, which is defined in terms such as "an injury arising out of employment and due to causes and conditions characteristic of, and peculiar to, the particular trade, occupation, process or employment, and excluding all ordinary diseases to which the general public is exposed."[7] Some states list particular diseases covered, whereas others simply follow general guidelines.

2.3   Benefits

Workers' compensation laws provide for four types of benefits: medical, income replacement, survivors' benefits, and rehabilitation.

Medical

All laws provide unlimited medical care benefits for accidental injuries. Many cases do not involve large expenses, but it is not unusual for medical bills to run into many thousands of dollars. Medical expenses resulting from occupational illnesses may be covered in full for a specified period of time and then terminated. Unlike nonoccupational health insurance, workers' compensation does not impose deductibles and coinsurance to create incentives for individuals to control their demand for medical services.

When you study health care in Chapter 21 and Chapter 22, you will become very familiar with managed care. To save on the escalating costs of medical care in workers' compensation, the medical coverage also uses managed care. Briefly, managed care limits the choice of doctors. The doctors' decisions are reviewed by the insurer, and many procedures require preapproval. Along with many other states, Texas passed legislation in 2005 that incorporates managed care in the workers' compensation system.[8] Under these systems, doctors who take care of injured employees under workers' compensation coverage are asked to try to get the employees back to work as soon as possible. The return-to-work objective is to ensure employees' presence at work under any capacity, thus incurring less workers' compensation losses. The industry is attempting to monitor itself for managing the care in a more

occupational disease

An injury arising out of employment and due to causes and conditions characteristic of, and peculiar to, the particular trade, occupation, process, or employment, and excluding all ordinary diseases to which the general public is exposed.

cost-saving manner.[9] One area that causes major increases in the workers' compensation rate is the cost of drugs. In 2006, medical costs per lost time claim increased 8.6 percent over the prior year, compared to a 4 percent increase in the medical consumer price index (CPI).[10] Figure 16.3 shows the costs of medical claims under workers' compensation from 1995 to 2007. As you can see, the severity of medical claims (losses per claim) has outpaced the medical CPI every year since.

FIGURE 16.3 Workers' Compensation Medical Severity*

* 2007p: Preliminary based on data valued as of December 31, 2007; Medical severity 1995–2006: Based on data through December 31, 2006, developed to ultimate; based on the states where NCCI provides ratemaking services, excludes the effects of deductible policies

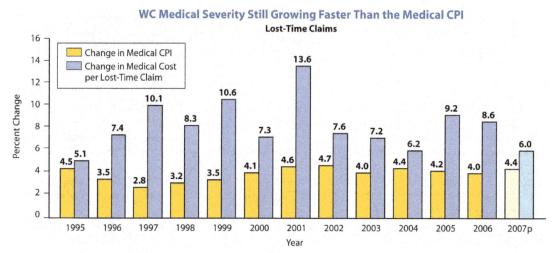

Source: Dennis C. Mealy, FCAS, MAAA, National Council on Compensation Insurance (NCCI), Inc. Chief Actuary, "State of the Line" Annul Issues Symposium (AIS), May 8, 2008, Accessed March 28, 2009, https://www.ncci.com/documents/AIS-2008-SOL-Complete.pdf. © 2008 NCCI Holdings, Inc. Reproduced with permission.

Income Replacement

indemnity benefits Reimburse insureds for actual costs incurred for health care up to covered limits in traditional fee-for-service plans.	All workers' compensation laws provide an injured employee with a weekly income while disabled as the result of a covered injury or disease. Income replacement benefits under workers' compensation are commonly referred to by industry personnel as **indemnity benefits**. The amount and duration of indemnity payments depend on the following factors: - Whether the disability is total or partial, and temporary or permanent - The employee's compensation - Each state's maximum duration of benefits - The waiting period - Cost-of-living adjustments

Degree and Length of Disability

Total disability refers to the condition of an employee who misses work because he or she is unable to perform any of the important duties of the occupation. Partial disability, on the other hand, means the injured employee can perform some but not all, of the duties of his or her occupation. In either case, disability may be permanent or temporary. Permanent total disability means the injured person is not expected to be able to work again. Temporary total disability means the injured employee is expected to be able to return to work at some future time.[11]

temporary partial benefits

Payments made to an injured employee can perform some, but not all, work duties.

Partial disability may be either temporary or permanent. Temporary partial payments are most likely to be made following a period of temporary total disability. A person who can perform some but not all work duties qualifies for **temporary partial benefits**. Such benefits are based on the difference between wages earned before and after an injury. They account for a minor portion of total claim payments.

Most laws specify that the loss of certain body parts constitutes **permanent partial disability**. Benefits expressed in terms of the number of weeks of total disability payments are usually provided in such cases and are known as **scheduled injuries**. For example, the loss of an arm might entitle the injured worker to two hundred weeks of total disability benefits; the loss of a finger might entitle him or her to thirty-five weeks of benefits. No actual loss of time from work or income is required because the assumption is that loss of a body part causes a loss of future income.

Of the fifteen largest classes of occupation, clerical jobs see the highest number of lost time claims. However, this by far the largest occupational class by payroll. The actual frequency of claims as a percentage of payroll dollars is among the lowest for clerical workers. Historically, trucking has seen the highest frequency of claims by payroll. Overall, the frequency of lost-time-only claims has declined, which is the good news in the workers' compensation field. The largest drop is in the convalescent/nursing home claims. The least decline is in the drivers/chauffeurs and college professional classifications.

Amount of Benefits

Weekly benefits for death, disability, and (often) disfigurement are primarily based on the employee's average weekly wage (average earned income per week during some specified period prior to disability) multiplied by a replacement ratio, expressed as a percentage of the average weekly wage. Jurisdictions also set minimum and maximum weekly benefits.

The replacement percentage for disability benefits ranges from sixty in one jurisdiction to seventy in two others, but in most jurisdictions it is 66⅔. The percentage reflects the intent to replace income after taxes and other work-related expenses because workers' compensation benefits are not subject to income taxation. In Virginia, for example, the compensation rate is adjusted each year on July 1. Effective July 1, 2008, the maximum rate was $841, and the minimum rate was $210.25. The cost of living increase will be 4.2 percent, effective October 1, 2008.[12] In Texas, the maximum temporary income benefit for 2009 is $750 and the minimum is $112.[13] Twenty jurisdictions lower their permanent partial maximum payment per week below their maximum for total disability. For these jurisdictions, the average permanent partial maximum is 66⅔ percent of their total disability maximum. With respect to death benefits, thirty-one jurisdictions use 66⅔ percent in determining survivors' benefits for a spouse only; five of these use a higher percentage for a spouse plus children. The range of survivors' benefits for a spouse plus children ranges from 60 percent in Idaho to 75 percent in Texas. Examples of Texas benefits calculations are demonstrated in hypothetical incomes in Table 16.1 A to D. In Texas, temporary income benefits equal 70 percent of the difference between a worker's average weekly wage and the weekly wage after the injury. If a worker's average weekly wage was $500, and an injury caused the worker to lose all of his or her income, temporary income benefits would be $350 a week.

TABLE 16.1 Hypothetical Examples of Texas Workers' Compensation Income Calculations

A. Calculation of Temporary Income Benefits	
Average weekly wage (hypothetical)	$400
Less: wage after injury	0
Equals	$400
Temporary income benefit (70 percent the "equals" amount)	$280
B. Calculation of Supplemental Income Benefits	
Average weekly wage	$400
80 percent of weekly wage	$320
Less: the current wage	0
Equals	$320
Supplemental benefit (80 percent of the "equals" amount)	$256
C. Calculation of Lifetime Income Benefits for Disability with a Loss of Limb	
Average weekly wage	$400
Lifetime income benefit (75 percent of weekly wage)	$300
D. Calculation of Death Benefits	
Average weekly wage	$400
Death benefit (75 percent of weekly wage)	$300

The next example is demonstrated in Table 16.1 B for temporary income after returning to work part-time. In Texas, an injured worker may get lifetime income benefits if the worker has an injury or illness

permanent partial disability

The loss of certain body parts.

scheduled injuries

Injuries covered under permanent partial disability.

that results in the loss of the hands, feet, or eyesight, or if the worker meets the conditions of the Texas Workers' Compensation Act. Table 16.1 C provides an example of benefits for lifetime in such a case.

Duration of Benefits

In thirty-nine jurisdictions, no limit is put on the duration of temporary total disability. Nine jurisdictions, however, allow benefits for less than 500 weeks; two specify a 500-week maximum. The limits are seldom reached in practice because the typical injured worker's condition reaches "maximum medical improvement," which terminates temporary total benefits earlier. Maximum medical improvement is reached when additional medical treatment is not expected to result in improvement of the person's condition.

In forty-three jurisdictions, permanent total benefits are paid for the duration of the disability and/ or lifetime. These jurisdictions generally do not impose a maximum dollar limit on the aggregate amount that can be paid.

Waiting Periods

Every jurisdiction has a waiting period before indemnity payments (but not medical benefits) for temporary disability can begin; the range is from three to seven days. The waiting period has the advantages of giving a financial incentive to work, reducing administrative costs, and reducing the cost of benefits. If disability continues for a specified period (typically, two to four weeks), benefits are retroactive to the date disability began. Moral hazard is created among employees who reach maximum medical improvement just before the time of the retroactive trigger. Some employees will malinger long enough to waive the waiting period. Hawaii does not allow retroactive benefits.

Cost-of-Living Adjustment

Fifteen jurisdictions have an automatic cost-of-living adjustment (COLA) for weekly benefits. In some cases, the COLA takes effect only after disability has continued for one or two years. Because benefit rates are usually set by law, those rates in jurisdictions that lack automatic increases for permanent benefits become out of date rapidly during periods of inflation.

Survivors' Benefits

In the event of a work-related death, all jurisdictions provide survivor income benefits for the surviving spouse and dependent children, as well as a burial allowance. The survivor income benefit for a spouse plus children is typically (in thirty jurisdictions) 66⅔ percent of the worker's average weekly wage. Several jurisdictions provide additional income for one child only. Table 16.1 D provides an example of the death benefits in Texas. Burial benefits pay up to $2,500 of the worker's funeral expenses. Burial benefits are paid to the person who paid the worker's funeral expenses. The death benefits in New York were discussed earlier in this chapter. In the example case for Texas, the replacement of lost income is 75 percent, as shown in Table 16.1 D.

Rehabilitation

Most people who are disabled by injury or disease make a complete recovery with ordinary medical care and return to work able to resume their former duties. Many workers, however, suffer disability of such a nature that something more than income payments and ordinary medical services is required to restore them, to the greatest extent possible, to their former economic and social situation. Rehabilitation is the process of accomplishing this objective and involves the following:

- Physical-medical attention in an effort to restore workers as nearly as possible to their state of health prior to the injury
- Vocational training to enable them to perform a new occupational function
- Psychological aid to help them adjust to their new situation and be able to perform a useful function for society

About one-fourth of the workers' compensation laws place this responsibility on the employer (or the insurer, if applicable). Most of the laws require special maintenance benefits to encourage disabled workers to cooperate in a rehabilitation program. Nearly all states reduce or stop income payments entirely to workers who refuse to participate.

KEY TAKEAWAYS

In this section you studied the history of workers' compensation, related laws, and benefits provided:

- Traditionally, employers used three common law defenses against liability for injury to workers: the fellow-servant rule, assumption of risk doctrine, and contributory negligence doctrine.
- Workers' compensation was developed as a compromise that would force employers to cover employees' injuries regardless of cause, in exchange for this being the employees' sole remedy.
- Workers' compensation laws are inclusive or exclusive, compulsory or elective.
- Covered injuries must arise out of and in the course of employment or be occupational diseases.
- Benefits provided under workers' compensation are medical, income replacement, survivors' benefits, and rehabilitation.
  - Medical—unlimited as of the date of occurrence
  - Income replacement—usually at 66⅔ percent of the average weekly wage, subject to state maximum, lifetime maximum, and degree and length of disability
  - Survivor's benefits—income benefits and burial allowances
  - Rehabilitation—physical, vocational, and psychological care necessary to restore (to the greatest extent possible) injured workers to their former economic and social situation

DISCUSSION QUESTIONS

1. Explain the former common law defenses employers utilized to avoid liability for employees' on-the-job injuries.
2. What are the arguments for and against allowing employers to opt out of the workers' compensation systems in Texas and New Jersey?
3. Given the rapid increases in workers' compensation costs, would you argue that other states should return to offering an opt-out provision? (*Note*: In the early days of workers' compensation laws in the United States, opt-out provisions were common because of concern about whether making workers' compensation mandatory was constitutional—now, not an issue.)
4. A worker is entitled to workers' compensation benefits when disability "arises out of and in the course of employment." A pregnant employee applies for medical and income benefits, alleging that her condition arose out of and in the course of the company's annual Christmas party. Is she entitled to benefits? Why or why not?

3.   HOW BENEFITS ARE PROVIDED

LEARNING OBJECTIVES

In this section we elaborate on the following ways that workers' compensation benefits are distributed:

- **Private insurance**
- **Residual markets**
- **State funds**
- **Self-insurance**
- **Second-injury funds**

Workers' compensation laws hold the employer responsible for providing benefits to injured employees. Employees do not contribute directly to this cost. In most states, employers may insure with a private insurance company or qualify as self-insurers. In some states, state funds act as insurers. Following is a discussion of coverage through insurance programs and through the residual markets (part of insurance programs for difficult-to-insure employers), self-insurance, and state funds.

3.1 Workers' Compensation Insurance

Employers' risks can be transferred to an insurer by purchasing a workers' compensation and employers' liability policy.

Coverage

The workers' compensation and employers' liability policy has three parts. Under part I, Workers' Compensation, the insurer agrees

> *to pay promptly when due all compensation and other benefits required of the insured by the workers' compensation law.*

The policy defines "workers' compensation law" as the law of any state designated in the declarations and specifically includes any occupational disease law of that state. The workers' compensation portion of the policy is directly for the benefit of employees covered by the law. The insurer assumes the obligations of the insured (that is, the employer) under the law and is bound by the terms of the law as well as the actions of the workers' compensation commission or other governmental body having jurisdiction. Any changes in the workers' compensation law are automatically covered by the policy.

Four limitations, or "exclusions," apply to part 1. These limitations include any payments in excess of the benefits regularly required by workers' compensation statutes due to (1) serious and willful misconduct by the insured; (2) the knowing employment of a person in violation of the law; (3) failure to comply with health or safety laws or regulations; or (4) the discharge, coercion, or other discrimination against employees in violation of the workers' compensation law. In addition, the policy refers only to state laws and that of the District of Columbia; thus, coverage under any of the federal programs requires special provisions.

Part 2 of the workers' compensation policy, **Employers' Liability**, protects against potential liabilities not within the scope of the workers' compensation law, yet arising out of employee injuries. The insurer agrees to pay damages for which the employer becomes legally obligated because of

employers' liability

Portion of a worker's compensation policy that protects against potential liabilities not within the scope of the workers' compensation law, yet arising out of employee injuries.

> *bodily injury by accident or disease, including death at any time resulting there from … by any employee of the insured arising out of and in the course of his employment by the insured either in operations in a state designated in … the declarations or in operations necessary or incidental thereto.*

Examples of liabilities covered under part 2 are those to employees excluded from the law, such as domestic and farm laborers. Part 2 might also be applicable if the injury is not considered work-related, even if it occurs on the job.

Part 3 of the workers' compensation policy provides Other States Insurance. Previously, this protection was available by endorsement. Part 1 applies only if the state imposing responsibility is listed in the declarations. To account for the case of an employee injured while working out of state who may be covered by that state's compensation law, the **Other States Insurance** part of the workers' compensation policy allows the insured to list states (perhaps all) where the employees may have potential exposure. Coverage is extended to these named locales.

Other States Insurance

Portion of a worker's compensation policy that allows the insured to list states (perhaps all) where the employees may have potential exposure.

Cost

Based on Payroll

The premium for workers' compensation insurance typically is based on the payroll paid by the employer. A charge is made for each $100 of payroll for each classification of employee. This rate varies with the degree of hazard of the occupation.[14] Large employers can elect to have experience rating, which takes a company's prior losses into account in determining its current rates.

Factors Affecting Rate

The rate for workers' compensation insurance is influenced not only by the degree of hazard of the occupational classification but also by the nature of the law and its administration and, of course, by prior losses. If the benefits of the law are high, rates will tend to be high. If they are low, rates will tend to be low. Moreover, given any law, no matter its benefits level, its administration will affect premium rates. If those who administer the law are conservative in their evaluation of borderline cases, premium rates will be lower than in instances where administrators are less circumspect in parceling out employers' and insurers' money. Most laws provide that either the claimant or the insurer may appeal a decision of the administrative board in court on questions of law, but if both the board and the courts are inclined toward generosity, the effect is to increase workers' compensation costs.

Workers' compensation may be a significant expense for the employer. Given any particular law and its administration, costs for the firm are influenced by the frequency and severity of injuries suffered by workers covered. The more injuries, the more workers will be receiving benefits. The more severe such injuries are, the longer such benefits must be paid. It is not unusual to find firms in hazardous industries having workers' compensation costs running from 10 to 30 percent of payroll. This can be a significant component of labor costs. Whatever their size, however, these costs are only part of the total cost of occupational injury and disease. The premium paid is the firm's direct cost, but indirect costs of industrial accidents, such as lost time, spoiled materials, and impairment of worker morale, can be just as significant. These costs can be reduced by loss prevention and reduction, and by self-insuring the risk.

Loss Prevention and Reduction

Most industrial accidents are caused by a combination of physical hazard and faulty behavior. Once an accident begins to occur, the ultimate severity is largely a matter of chance. Total loss costs are a function of accident frequency and severity as explained in prior chapters. Frequency is a better indicator of safety performance than severity because chance plays a greater part in determining the seriousness of an injury than it does in determining frequency.

Accident Prevention

The first consideration is to reduce frequency by preventing accidents. Safety must be part of your thinking, along with planning and supervising. Any safety program should be designed to accomplish two goals: (1) reduce hazards to a minimum, and (2) develop safe behavior in every employee. A safety engineer from the workers' compensation insurer (or a consultant for the self-insured employer) can give expert advice and help the program. He or she can identify hazards so they can be corrected. This involves plant inspection, job safety analysis, and accident investigation.

The safety engineer can inspect the plant to observe housekeeping, machinery guarding, maintenance, and safety equipment. He or she can help the employer organize and implement a safety training program to develop employee awareness and safe practices. He or she can analyze job safety to determine safe work methods and can set job standards that promote safety. The insurer usually provides employers with accident report forms and instructions on accident investigation. This is essential because every accident demonstrates a hazardous condition or an unsafe practice, or both. The causes of accidents must be discovered so that the information can assist in future prevention efforts. Inspections, job safety analysis, and accident investigations that lead consistently to corrective action are the foundations of accident prevention. The box "Should Ergonomic Standards Be Mandatory?" discusses the issues of job safety in the area of posture and position in the workplace.

Loss Reduction

Accident frequency cannot be reduced to zero because not all losses can be prevented. After an employee has suffered an injury, however, action may reduce the loss. First, immediate medical attention may save a life. Moreover, recovery will be expedited. This is why many large plants have their own medical staff. It is also why an employer should provide first-aid instruction for its employees. Second, the insurer along with the employer should manage the care of the injured worker, including referrals to low-cost, high-quality medical providers. Third, injured workers should take advantage of rehabilitation. Rehabilitation is not always successful, but experience has shown that remarkable progress is possible, especially if it is started soon enough after an injury. The effort is worthwhile from both the economic and humanitarian points of view. All of society benefits from such effort.

Residual Market

Various residual market mechanisms, such as assigned risk pools and reinsurance facilities, allow employers that are considered uninsurable access to workers' compensation insurance. This is similar to the structure discussed earlier for automobile insurance. Usually employers with large losses, as depicted by high experience ratings, are considered high risk. These employers encounter difficulty in finding workers' compensation coverage. The way to obtain coverage is through the residual or involuntary market (a market where insurers are required to provide coverage on an involuntary basis). Insurers are required to participate, and insureds are assigned to an insurer in various ways.

As reported in the NCCI "State of the Line" report, Figure 16.4 provides the workers' compensation residual market premiums from 1985 to 2006; Figure 16.5 provides the residual market combined ratio for the same period.

**state-operated workers'
compensation funds**

State government agencies
responsible for collecting
workers' compensation
founds and distributing
benefits.

Eighteen jurisdictions have **state-operated workers' compensation funds** in which the state government is responsible for collecting workers' compensation founds and distributing benefits. In six of these, the state fund is exclusive; that is, employers are not permitted to buy compensation insurance from a private insurance company but must insure with the state fund or self-insure.[15] Where the state fund is competitive (that is, optional), employers may choose to self-insure or to insure through either the state fund or a private insurer.

3.2 Employer's Risk

Industrial accidents create two possible losses for employers. First, employers are responsible to employees covered by the workers' compensation law for the benefits required by law. Second, they may become liable for injuries to employees not covered by the law.[16] The risks associated with these exposures cannot be avoided without suspending operations—hardly a practical alternative.

Where permitted, self-insurance of this exposure is common. Self-insurance is desirable, in part because of the predictability afforded by legislated benefits. In addition, employers can buy coverage (called excess loss insurance) for very large losses similar to the commercial umbrella liability policy discussed in Chapter 15 .

FIGURE 16.4 Residual Market Premiums as of December 31, 2007

* NCCI Plan states plus DE, IN, MA, MI, NJ, NC

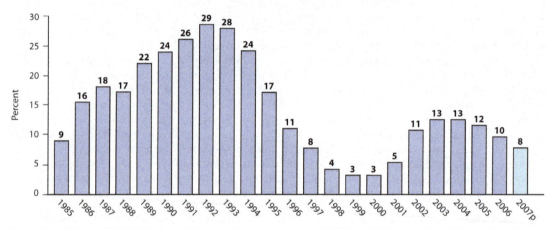

Source: Dennis C. Mealy, FCAS, MAAA, National Council on Compensation Insurance (NCCI), Inc. Chief Actuary, "State of the Line" Annul Issues Symposium (AIS), May 8, 2008, Accessed March 28, 2009, https://www.ncci.com/documents/AIS-2008-SOL-Complete.pdf. © 2008 NCCI Holdings, Inc. Reproduced with permission.

FIGURE 16.5 Residual Market Combined Ratio as of December 31, 2007

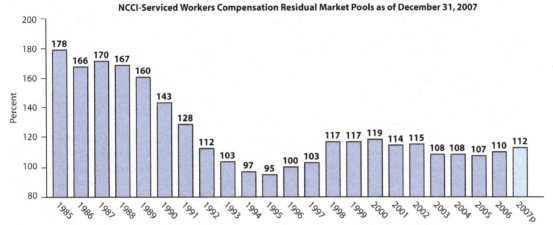

Source: Dennis C. Mealy, FCAS, MAAA, National Council on Compensation Insurance (NCCI), Inc. Chief Actuary, "State of the Line" Annul Issues Symposium (AIS), May 8, 2008, Accessed March 28, 2009, https://www.ncci.com/documents/AIS-2008-SOL-Complete.pdf. © 2008 NCCI Holdings, Inc. Reproduced with permission.

3.3 Self-Insurance

Most state workers' compensation laws permit an employer to retain the workers' compensation risk if it can be proven that the employer is financially able to pay claims. Some states permit the risk to be retained only by employers who furnish a bond guaranteeing payment of benefits.

The major question for the self-insurance of the workers' compensation risk is whether the firm has a large enough number of exposure units (employees) that its losses are reasonably stable and can be predicted with some accuracy. Clearly, an employer with ten employees cannot make an accurate prediction of workers' compensation benefit costs for next year. Such costs may be zero one year and several thousand dollars another year. On the other hand, as the number of employees of the firm increases, workers' compensation losses become more stable and predictable. Just how stable losses must be in order for self-insurance to be feasible depends on the employer's ability and willingness to pay for losses that exceed expectations. The employer's ability to pay for loss is a second important factor considered by regulators in determining whether or not to permit self-insurance. Captives are also used by many employers for this coverage. Of course, all types of self-insurance require the use of stop-loss coverage through reinsurance. The reinsurance is best for use with captives, as explained in Chapter 6. Smaller employers can join together with others, usually from the same industry, and create a group self-insurance program. Under these programs, each employer is responsible for paying the losses of the group when necessary—such as in the case of a member's insolvency. The employer's risk is not transferred; only the payment of losses is shared through the pooling mechanism discussed in Chapter 6. Group self-insurance members buy stop-loss coverage and are required to obtain regulatory approval for their existence.

Insurance or Self-Insurance?

Is your firm large enough to self-insure, and if it is, can you save money by doing so? Unless you have at least several hundred employees and your workers' compensation losses have a low correlation with other types of retained exposures, self-insurance is not feasible. The low correlation implies diversification of the retained risk exposures. Unless self-insurance will save money, it is not worthwhile. Most employers who decide to self-insure use third-party administrators to administer the claims or contract with an insurer to provide administrative services only.

What are the possible sources for saving money? Ask yourself the following questions about your present arrangement:

- Does your insurer pay benefits too liberally?
- Does it bear the risk of excessive losses?
- Does it bear the risk of employers' liability?
- Does it administer the program?
- How large is the premium tax paid by the insurer?
- How large is the insurer's profit on your business?

- What is your share of losses in the assigned risk plan that the insurer pays into?
- Can the third-party administrator be a good buffer in disputes with angry employees?

As a self-insured firm, you will still provide the benefits specified by the workers' compensation law(s) in the state(s) where you operate. Therefore, self-insuring reduces benefits only if you or your outside self-insurance administrator will settle claims more efficiently than your insurer.

Unless your firm is very large, you probably would decide to buy stop-loss insurance for excessive losses, and you would buy insurance for your employer's liability (part B of a workers' compensation insurance policy). Would you administer the self-insured program? Most likely, you would hire an outside administrator. In either case, the administrative expenses might be similar to those of your insurer. As a self-insurer, you would save the typical premium tax of between 2 and 3 percent that your insurer is required to pay to the state(s) where you do business. Profits are difficult to calculate because the insurer's investment income must be factored in along with premiums, benefit payments, expenses, and your own opportunity cost of funds. If you do not pay premiums ahead, you can use the cash flow for other activities until they are used to pay for losses. While the workers' compensation line of business produces losses in some years and profits in others, over a period of several years, you would expect the insurer to make a profit on your business. You could retain this profit by self-insuring.

Firms that do not qualify for insurance based on normal underwriting guidelines and premiums can buy insurance through an assigned risk plan, that is, the residual market. Because of inadequate rates and other problems, large operating losses are often realized in the residual market. These losses become an additional cost to be borne by insurers and passed on to insureds in the form of higher premiums. Assigned risk pool losses are allocated to insurers on the basis of their share of the voluntary (nonassigned risk) market by state and year. These losses can be 15 to 30 percent or more of premiums for employers insured in the voluntary market. This burden can be avoided by self-insuring. Many firms have self-insured for this reason, resulting in a smaller base over which to spread the residual market burden.

experience-rated premiums

When a group's own claims experience affects the cost of coverage for group insurance.

retrospective plan

Worker's compensation policy that involves payment of a premium between a minimum and a maximum, depending on the insured's loss experience.

If your firm is large enough to self-insure, your workers' compensation premium is **experience rated**. What you pay this year is influenced by your loss experience during the past three years. The extent to which your rate goes up or down to reflect bad or good experience depends on the credibility assigned by the insurer. This statistical credibility is primarily determined by the size of your firm. The larger your firm, the more your experience influences the rate you pay during succeeding years.

If an employer wants the current year's experience rating to influence what it pays for workers' compensation coverage this year, you can insure on a **retrospective plan**. It involves payment of a premium between a minimum and a maximum, depending on your loss experience. Regardless of how favorable your experience is, you must pay at least the minimum premium. On the other hand, regardless of how bad your experience is, you pay no more than the maximum. Between the minimum and the maximum, your actual cost for the year depends on your experience that year.

Several plans with various minimum and maximum premium stipulations are available. If you are conservative with respect to risk, you will prefer a low minimum and a low maximum, but that is the most expensive. Low minimum and high maximum is cheaper, but this puts most of the burden of your experience on you. If you have an effective loss prevention and reduction program, you may choose the high maximum and save money on your workers' compensation insurance.

In choosing between insurance and self-insurance, you should consider the experience rating plans provided by insurers, as well as the advantages and disadvantages of self-insurance. The process of making this comparison will undoubtedly be worthwhile.

3.4 State Funds

A third method of ensuring benefit payments to injured workers is the state fund. State funds are similar to private insurers except that they are operated by an agency of the state government, and most are concerned only with benefit payments under the workers' compensation law and do not assume the employers' liability risk. This usually must be insured privately. The employer pays a premium (or tax) to the state fund and the fund, in turn, provides the benefits to which injured employees are entitled. Some state funds decrease rates for certain employers or classes of employers if their experience warrants it.

Cost comparisons between commercial insurers and state funds are difficult because the state fund may be subsidized. In some states, the fund may exist primarily to provide insurance to employers in high-risk industries—for example, coal mining—that are not acceptable to commercial insurers. In any case, employers who have access to a state fund should consider it part of the market and compare its rates with those of private insurers.

3.5 Second-Injury Funds

Nature and Purpose

If two employees with the same income each lost one eye in an industrial accident, the cost in workers' compensation benefits for each would be equal. If one of these employees had previously lost an eye, however, the cost of benefits for him or her would be much greater than for the other worker (probably more than double the cost). Obviously, the loss of both eyes is a much greater handicap than the loss of one. To encourage employment in these situations, second-injury funds are part of most workers' compensation laws. When an employee suffers a second injury, the employee is compensated for the disability resulting from the combined injuries; the insurer (or employer) who pays the benefit is then reimbursed by a **second-injury fund** for the amount by which the combined disability benefits exceed the benefit that would have been paid only for the last injury.

Financing

Second-injury funds are financed in a variety of ways. Some receive appropriations from the state. Others receive money from a charge made against an employer or an insurer when a worker who has been killed on the job does not leave any dependents. Some states finance the fund by annual assessments on insurers and self-insurers. These assessments can be burdensome.

> **second-injury fund**
>
> Fund that reimburses an insurer (or employer) that pays a workman's compensation benefit to an employee who suffers more than one job-related injury.

KEY TAKEAWAYS

In this section you studied the ways workers' compensation benefits are provided through insurance programs, residual markets, self-insurance, and state funds:

- Employers' risks can be transferred to a workers' compensation and employers' liability policy, which pays for the benefits injured workers are entitled to under workers' compensation law and for expenses incurred as a result of liability on the part of the employer.
- Workers' compensation insurance premiums are based on payroll and experience (which is in turn influenced by loss prevention and reduction efforts).
- Employers considered uninsurable can obtain workers' compensation insurance through the residual market, made of assigned risk pools and reinsurance facilities.
- Some jurisdictions have state-operated workers' compensation funds as either the only source of workers' compensation coverage or as an alternative to the private market.
- Large employers with sufficient financial resources may be able to self-insure and thus pay for workers' compensation.
- Second-injury funds are set up to reimburse employers for payment to injured workers who suffer subsequent injuries that more than double the cost of providing them with compensation.

DISCUSSION QUESTIONS

1. How are workers' compensation rates influenced?
2. Under what circumstances should an employer retain workers' compensation risk?
3. How does a retrospective premium plan work?
4. What is the purpose of second-injury funds?

4. WORKERS' COMPENSATION ISSUES

LEARNING OBJECTIVES

In this section we elaborate on several issues that workers' compensation insurers must contend with, including the following:

- **Cost drivers and reform**
- **Erosion of exclusive remedy**
- **Scope of coverage**

As noted by the National Council of Compensation Insurance (NCCI), despite the improved results of the workers' compensation line, the following are challenging issues faced by the industry:

- Catastrophes such as terrorism
- Cost drivers and reform
- Capacity
- Adequate reserves
- Privacy
- Erosion of exclusive remedy and scope of coverage
- Mental health claims
- Black lung
- The Americans with Disabilities Act (ADA)
- Ergonomics

Coverage for terrorism is a major issue for workers' compensation. The problem has been somewhat alleviated by the relaunch of the Terrorism Risk Insurance Act (TRIA) of 2002 as the Terrorism Risk Insurance Program Reauthorization Act (TRIPRA), which provides protection until December 31, 2014. It is not a permanent solution, so the stakeholders are working on permanent solutions, including overall catastrophe pools.

As noted earlier, medical inflation, in addition to increased benefits through reforms in the states and attorney fees, have cost the system a substantial amount of extra expenses and caused escalation in the combined ratio for the workers' compensation line. All medical care costs have, for decades, grown much faster than the overall consumer price index (CPI). Workers' compensation medical care costs are of special concern. The high reimbursement rate (100 percent of allowable charges) by workers' compensation relative to lower rates (generally 80 to 90 percent) in nonoccupational medical plans creates a preference for workers' compensation among employees and medical care providers who influence some decisions about whether or not a claim is deemed work-related. The managed care option mentioned above is used, but because medical inflation is so high, the system cannot resolve the issue on its own.

Attorney involvement varies substantially among the states. It is encouraged by factors such as the following:

- The complexity of the law
- Weak early communication to injured workers
- Advertisements by attorneys
- Failure to begin claim payments soon after the start of disability
- Employee distrust of some employers and insurers
- Employee concern that some employers will not rehire injured workers
- The subjective nature of benefit determination (e.g., encouraging both parties to produce conflicting medical evidence concerning the degree of impairment)

The solution may be a system that settles claims equitably and efficiently through promoting agreement and the employee's timely return to work. Reforms in states such as California, Florida, Tennessee, and Wisconsin are examples of positive effects and cost controls. Wisconsin's system is an example characterized by prompt delivery of benefits, low transaction costs, and clear communication between employers and employees.

The workers' compensation combined ratio per calendar year since 1990 is shown in Figure 16.6. The combined ratio has declined since its peak of 122 in 2001.

FIGURE 16.6 Workers' Compensation Combined Ratios

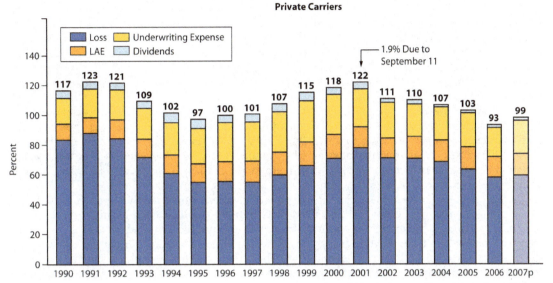

Source: Dennis C. Mealy, FCAS, MAAA, National Council on Compensation Insurance (NCCI), Inc. Chief Actuary, "State of the Line" Annul Issues Symposium (AIS), May 8, 2008, accessed March 28, 2009, https://www.ncci.com/documents/AIS-2008-SOL-Complete.pdf. © 2008 NCCI Holdings, Inc. Reproduced with permission.

As for the whole property/casualty industry, investment income results kept declining. The low interest rates took a toll on this long-tail line, requiring underwriting profits in order to provide returns to investors. The poor investment results are shown in Figure 16.7.

FIGURE 16.7 Workers' Compensation Ratios of Investment Gain and Other Income to Premium

* Adjusted to include realized capital gains to be consistent with 1992 and after. Investment gain on insurance transactions includes other income.

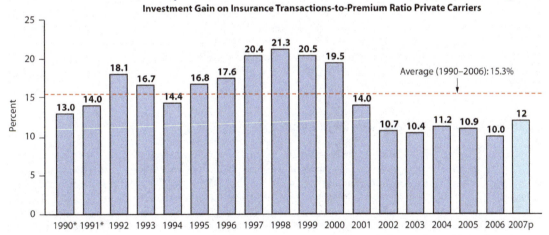

Source: Dennis C. Mealy, FCAS, MAAA, National Council on Compensation Insurance (NCCI), Inc. Chief Actuary, "State of the Line" Annul Issues Symposium (AIS), May 8, 2008, accessed March 28, 2009, https://www.ncci.com/documents/AIS-2008-SOL-Complete.pdf. © 2008 NCCI Holdings, Inc. Reproduced with permission.

The next issue, privacy, has been discussed in prior chapters. This is an issue engulfing the whole industry and is relevant to the workers' compensation line because of the medical and health components of this coverage. How to protect individuals' health information from being identified and transmitted is the industry's concern.

Employers, of course, benefit from having their liabilities limited to what is stipulated in workers' compensation laws. When the benefits received by workers are a close approximation of what would be received under common law, employees receive a clear advantage as well from the law. Today, however, there is a perception that workers' compensation provides inadequate compensation for many injuries. With high awards for punitive and general damages (neither available in workers' compensation) in tort claims, workers often perceive the exclusivity of compensation laws as inequitable.

As a result, workers attempt to circumvent the exclusivity rule. One method is to claim that the employer acts in a dual capacity, permitting the employee an action against the employer in the second relationship as well as a workers' compensation claim. For example, an employee injured while using a product manufactured by another division of the company might seek a products liability claim against the employer. Dual capacity has received limited acceptance. Consider the case of an employee of Firestone tires who uses the employer's commercial auto with Firestone tires to make deliveries. If a tire exploded, the employee has a workers' compensation claim as well as a case against the manufacturer of the tire—his own employer.

A second means of circumventing the exclusivity of workers' compensation is to claim that the employer intentionally caused the injury. Frequently, this claim is made with respect to exposure to toxic substances. Employees claim that employers knew of the danger but encouraged employees to work in the hazardous environment anyway. This argument, too, has received limited acceptance, and litigation of these cases is costly. Further, their mere existence likely indicates at least a perception of faults in the workers' compensation system.

A third circumvention of the exclusivity of workers' compensation is the third-party over action. It begins with an employee's claim against a third party (not the employer). For example, the employee may sue a machine manufacturer for products liability if the employee is injured while using the manufacturer's machine. In turn, the third party (the manufacturer in our example) brings an action against the employer for contribution or indemnification. The action against the employer might be based on the theory that the employer contributed to the loss by failing to supervise its employees properly. The end result is an erosion of the exclusive remedy rule—as if the employee had sued the employer directly.

Another current issue in workers' compensation is the broadening of the scope of covered claims. The original intent of workers' compensation laws was to cover only work-related physical injuries. Later, coverage was extended to occupational illnesses that often are not clearly work-related. Claims for stress and cases involving mental health claims, especially after September 11, are on the increase.

The Supreme Court in 2002 clarified that only the inability to perform daily living activities is a disability under the Americans with Disabilities Act (ADA) and not the inability to perform a job. The ADA forbids employers with more than fifteen employees from discriminating against disabled persons in employment. Disabled persons are those with physical or mental impairments limiting major life activities such as walking, seeing, or hearing. The ADA requires that employee benefits, as a privilege of employment, be provided in a nondiscriminatory manner as well. Employees with disabilities must be given equal access to medical expense insurance coverage and disability coverage. If the medical plan does not cover certain treatment needed by persons with disabilities, such as vision care, the employer does not have to add vision care treatment. However, if vision care is provided by the plan, then vision care must also be offered to employees with disabilities. In addition, specific disabilities, such as vision impairment, or disability in general, cannot be excluded from coverage.

The other issue regarding repetitive activities that cause stress and carpal tunnel syndrome is still under consideration at the time of writing this text, as noted in "Should Ergonomic Standards be Mandatory?

Should Ergonomic Standards Be Mandatory?

In the waning days of the Clinton administration, the Occupational Safety and Health Administration (OSHA) issued sweeping new guidelines for ergonomics in the workplace. Ergonomics refers to the design and arrangement of workplace equipment in order to maximize worker safety, health, comfort, and efficiency. The new standards, which applied to all industries and nearly all types of businesses, both large and small, placed the ergonomic burden on employers (and, through them, on the states' workers' compensation insurance industry, which would be responsible for implementing the new rules). Every company was required to set up a program to manage ergonomics, including worker training, analysis and elimination of risk factors, and identification of musculoskeletal disorder (MSD) injuries. Of most concern to the insurance industry was a provision that mandated a set level of compensation for MSD injuries. By requiring compensation for ergonomic injuries to be between 90 and 100 percent of a worker's salary, OSHA was infringing on state workers' compensation systems, which awarded injured workers only 67 percent, on average, of their salaries up to a certain maximum.

Controversial from the start, the ergonomic standards were overturned by Congress in April 2001 just after George W. Bush took office. Working with the insurance industry, OSHA has since launched a voluntary program to reduce ergonomic injuries.

A review of OSHA activities (available at its Web site, http://www.osha.gov/SLTC/ergonomics/index.html) reveals that OSHA developed a "four-pronged comprehensive approach to ergonomics designed to quickly and effectively address musculoskeletal disorders (MSDs) in the workplace." The following are four segments of OSHA's strategy for reducing injuries and illnesses from MSDs in the workplace:

- Guidelines
- Outreach and assistance
- Enforcement
- National advisory committee

The new guidelines include more cooperation with business, including technical support and an education campaign. However, not everyone is pleased with the new voluntary standards; labor advocates reject them as not providing enough protection for workers. OSHA has issued updates to its guidelines tailored to different industries in response to these criticisms. If you visit OSHA's Web site, you can view the educational component of the voluntary program for yourself. Along with a description of potential hazards and solutions, the site contains pictures (some animated) of both the correct and incorrect ways to undertake various work activities. Figure 16.8, taken from OSHA's Web site, is designed to illustrate the correct posture of a baker in a grocery store.

FIGURE 16.8   FIGURE 16.8 OSHA's Basics of Neutral Working Postures

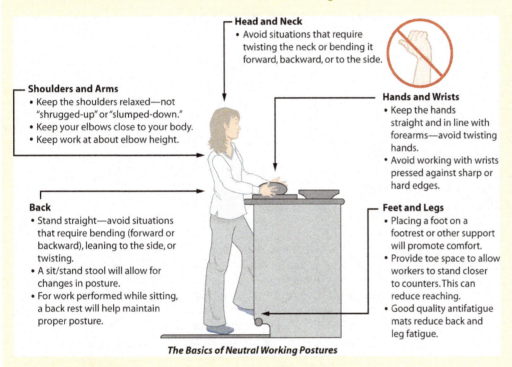

Head and Neck
- Avoid situations that require twisting the neck or bending it forward, backward, or to the side.

Shoulders and Arms
- Keep the shoulders relaxed—not "shrugged-up" or "slumped-down."
- Keep your elbows close to your body.
- Keep work at about elbow height.

Hands and Wrists
- Keep the hands straight and in line with forearms—avoid twisting hands.
- Avoid working with wrists pressed against sharp or hard edges.

Back
- Stand straight—avoid situations that require bending (forward or backward), leaning to the side, or twisting.
- A sit/stand stool will allow for changes in posture.
- For work performed while sitting, a back rest will help maintain proper posture.

Feet and Legs
- Placing a foot on a footrest or other support will promote comfort.
- Provide toe space to allow workers to stand closer to counters. This can reduce reaching.
- Good quality antifatigue mats reduce back and leg fatigue.

The Basics of Neutral Working Postures

Questions for Discussion

1. Can too much workplace regulation put employees out of work? In the face of hard-to-meet standards, might some employers decide not to stay in business or to move their businesses to a country without such strict rules?

2. Is it ethically correct to require the same workplace standards from small start-up companies and large, well-established ones?

3. Should the states be the only entities allowed to set workers' compensation rules? Why not the federal government?

4. Do voluntary programs work, or do they allow businesses to get away with ignoring workers' injuries?

Sources: Steven Brostoff, "Senate Sidesteps Ergonomics Mandate," National Underwriter, Property & Casualty/Risk & Benefits Management Edition, July 29, 2002; Bruce C. Wood, "Federal Regs Threaten State WC System," National Underwriter, Property & Casualty/Risk & Benefits Management Edition, August 19, 2002; Mark A. Hofmann, "Senate Committee Approves Ergo Rule Bill," Business Insurance, June 19, 2002, accessed March 31, 2009, http://dev.businessinsurance.com/cgi-bin/news.pl?id=999; Steven Brostoff, "Ergonomic Rule Bill Moves," National Underwriter Online News Service, June 19, 2002; Steven Brostoff, "Insurance Groups Support Ergo Plan," National Underwriter, Online News Service, August 27, 2002; Arlene Ryndak and Julie L. Gackenbach, "Congress Should Not Tie OSHA's Hands on Ergonomic Regulations," National Underwriter, Property & Casualty/Risk & Benefits Management Edition, May 20, 2002; "Risk Managers, Insurers Get a Break on Ergonomics," National Underwriter, Property & Casualty/Risk & Benefits Management Edition, April 22, 2002; Steven Brostoff, "New Ergonomics Bill Draws Insurer Ire," National Underwriter, Property & Casualty/Risk & Benefits Management Edition, April 29, 2002; Caroline McDonald, "Insurers: New OSHA Ergo Plan Okay," National Underwriter Online News Service, April 5, 2002; OSHA's Web site at http://www.osha.gov/SLTC/ergonomics/index.html (accessed March 28, 2009).

KEY TAKEAWAYS

In this section you studied the major issues faced by workers' compensation insurers:

- High reimbursement rates of medical costs contribute to the poor combined ratio of workers' compensation.
- Attorney involvement in the cases of injured workers inflates costs.
- Perceptions of workers' compensation as inadequate in indemnifying injured employees encourages workers to circumvent the exclusivity rule.
- Broadening the scope of workers' compensation coverage increases the number of claims.

DISCUSSION QUESTIONS

1. Why might workers' compensation be viewed as preferential to nonoccupational health coverage? Does this create any incentives for anyone within the system?
2. In what ways can the exclusivity rule be circumvented by employees?
3. Do you disagree with any of the ways that the scope of workers' compensation coverage has been broadened over the years? Explain.

5. UNEMPLOYMENT COMPENSATION

LEARNING OBJECTIVES

In this section we elaborate on the following features of unemployment compensation:

- **State unemployment laws**
- **Coverage provided**
- **Financing of unemployment compensation**
- **Administration of unemployment compensation**

unemployment compensation

Government programs that pay weekly cash benefits to workers who are involuntarily unemployed.

While workers' compensation is quasi-social private insurance of significant concern to its many stakeholders, unemployment compensation is a purely social insurance program. Because of the high risk associated with projecting future rates of unemployment and associated claims, private insurers are not willing to provide this type of insurance. **Unemployment compensation** programs pay weekly cash benefits to workers who are involuntarily unemployed. The following sections cover state laws, coverage, how benefits are financed, and administration of unemployment compensation.

5.1 State Laws

State unemployment compensation programs were established as a result of federal legislation. However, each state creates, finances, and administers its own law. Like workers' compensation, the law transfers to the employer at least part of the financial element of a risk faced by the employee. Unlike most workers' compensation programs, however, the firm's risk manager has no choice with regard to how the risk is handled. Neither private insurance nor self-insurance is permitted. Management can reduce the cost, however, by stabilizing the firm's employment and preventing payment of unjustified benefits.

Employers Subject to Tax

The federal tax applies to firms that have one or more employees in each of twenty weeks during a calendar year, or firms that pay $1,500 or more in wages during any calendar quarter. As of January 1987, coverage was extended to agricultural employers that have ten or more employees in each of twenty weeks during the year or that pay $20,000 or more in wages during any calendar quarter. New provisions to include domestic and municipal employees, as well as employees of nonprofit organizations, have also been added.

5.2   Coverage

The federal law established minimum standards for coverage and benefits. Unless a state law meets the standards, no tax offset is permitted. Every state meets the standards, and in many cases they are exceeded. Today, all states cover state and local government employees, several cover farm workers, and a few cover domestic workers. About 97 percent of the civilian labor force is covered. In some cases, unemployment compensation is self-insured in a pool, as is the case with the unemployment compensation of employees of many Texas school districts that opted to use the pool administered by the Texas Association of School Boards.[17]

Unemployment compensation is designed to relieve workers in certain industries and occupations of part of the economic burden of temporary unemployment. Three aspects of benefit payments are important: (1) amount and duration, (2) qualifications for benefits, and (3) disqualifications.

Amount and Duration

The amount of the weekly benefit payment a worker may receive through unemployment compensation varies according to the **benefit formula** in the law of each state. Usually, the amount is about one-half of the worker's full-time weekly pay within specified limits. The maximum is low and is easily accessible on the Web site of your state unemployment compensation agency (usually a division of the employment commission). Some states provide an additional allowance for certain dependents of the unemployed worker. With the passage of the 1986 Tax Reform Act, all unemployment benefits became fully taxable to the recipient for federal income tax purposes.

Most state laws have a waiting period—typically one week—between the time an unemployed worker files a claim for benefits and the time benefit payments begin. This is designed to place the burden of short-term temporary unemployment on the worker as well as to decrease the cost of the plan, thereby making possible greater coverage of more significant unemployment losses.

In most states, the maximum number of weeks that benefits can be paid is twenty-six. A federal-state program of extended benefits may continue payments for another thirteen weeks during periods of high unemployment, such as occurred in the early 1990s. In an economic emergency, federal funding may continue payments for another twenty-six weeks.

Qualifications for Benefits

To qualify for benefits, unemployed workers must fulfill certain conditions. They must first be involuntarily unemployed. Once they are involuntarily unemployed, they are required to register for work at a public employment office and file a claim for benefits. They must have been employed in a job covered by the state unemployment compensation law.[18] They must have earned a specified amount of pay or worked for a specified length of time, or both. They must be able to work (this is important in order to differentiate unemployment benefits from disability benefits), available for work, and willing to take a suitable job if it is offered to them. In most states, an unemployed worker who is sick and therefore unable to work is not entitled to unemployment compensation benefits. Some states permit payments to disabled workers under a separate disability program.[19]

Disqualifications

Unemployed workers may be disqualified from benefits even if they meet the qualifications described above. As noted above, most state laws disqualify those who quit voluntarily without good cause or who were discharged for just cause. Those who refuse to apply for or accept suitable work, or are unemployed because of a work stoppage caused by a labor dispute, may be disqualified. Other causes for disqualification are receiving pay from a former employer, receiving workers' compensation benefits, receiving Social Security benefits, or being deemed an independent contractor and therefore not an employee.

The effect of disqualification varies from state to state. In some cases, it means that the unemployed worker receives no benefits until he or she has again qualified by being employed for a specified length of time in covered work. In other cases, disqualification results in an increase in the waiting period. Some state laws not only increase the waiting period but also decrease the benefits.

benefit formula

Calculation used to determine the amount of the weekly benefit payment a worker may receive through unemployment compensation.

5.3 How Benefits Are Financed

Noncontributory

Federal Unemployment Tax Act (FUTA)

Law that places a tax on employers at the rate of 6.2 percent of workers' pay in covered jobs, excluding anything over $7,000 paid to a worker in a year for the purpose of financing unemployment compensation.

Most unemployment compensation insurance is *noncontributory*: employers pay all the cost in most states.[20] The **Federal Unemployment Tax Act (FUTA)** places a tax on employers at the rate of 6.2 percent of workers' pay in covered jobs, excluding anything over $7,000 paid to a worker in a year for the purpose of financing unemployment compensation. Up to 5.4 percent can be offset by employers who pay a state tax or have been excused through experience rating. So, in effect, the federal tax may be only (6.2 − 5.4 =) 0.8 percent. Revenue from this tax is deposited in the Federal Unemployment Trust Fund and credited to the state for the payment of benefits under its plan. Each state has its own trust fund. The remaining part of the federal tax goes into general federal revenues. Congress appropriates money for grants to the states for their administration of the program. If appropriations for this purpose are less than the federal share of the payroll tax, then the remainder of such revenue is put into a reserve fund for aid to the states in payment of benefits when state reserves are low.

Experience Rating

All states have experience rating; that is, they reduce the contribution of employers whose workers have little unemployment. The theory of this rating system is that it encourages employers to reduce unemployment and stabilize employment to the extent that they can. One other effect, however, is to make employers interested in disqualifying workers who apply for benefits because the benefits paid out of their account reflect their experience under the plan.[21] This has led to considerable discussion of disqualification standards and administration and to many hearings and disputes.

5.4 Administration

The federal portion of the unemployment compensation insurance program is administered by the Employment and Training Administration in the Department of Labor. Every state has its own employment security agency. Some are independent; others are in the State Department of Labor or some other state agency. Typically, the agency is also responsible for the administration of state employment search offices. There are more than 2,500 such offices in the United States where claims for benefits may be filed. Claimants apply for benefits and register for employment at the same time. The function of the office is to find employment for claimants or provide benefits.

KEY TAKEAWAYS

In this section you studied the following features of unemployment compensation, a pure social insurance program:

- State unemployment programs pay weekly cash benefits to workers who are involuntarily unemployed.
- Unemployment compensation is established by federal legislation, but it is administered by each state.
- Applies to employers with one or more employees in each of twenty weeks of a year or paying at least $1,500 in wages per year.
- Usually pays qualified, involuntarily unemployed workers half their weekly pay, subject to a waiting period and a maximum duration.
- Financed through taxes on employers between 0.8 to 6.2 percent and subject to experience rating.
- The federal portion of the program is administered by the Employment and Training Administration of the Department of Labor.

DISCUSSION QUESTIONS

1. Who is qualified to receive unemployment compensation? Who is not qualified?
2. Ann and Dick both have excellent jobs in Boston. She is transferred to Los Angeles. Dick quits his job so he can go with her. Should he receive unemployment compensation benefits? Why or why not?
3. Do unemployment compensation benefits help stabilize our economy? Explain your answer.

6. REVIEW AND PRACTICE

1. The Baylor Crane Construction Company is a Virginia-based builder with 1,750 full-time and 300 part-time employees. The company provides all the social insurance benefits required by law and most other employee benefits plans. Last year, Baylor suffered high severity of losses when the top five floors of a high rise collapsed in Virginia Beach during strong winds. Three workers sustained severe injuries and Johnny Kendel, the 64-year-old supervisor, was killed. All of the injured workers are back at work except for Tom Leroy, who is still on disability; his prognosis is not good.

   a. Compare the benefits provided by workers' compensation and unemployment compensation.

   b. Compare the method of financing of workers' compensation and unemployment compensation.

   c. Describe the benefits of each of the injured and killed employees.

2. Is the rationale for workers' compensation laws the same as that for no-fault auto insurance plans?

3. Loretta works at the ticket counter of a major airline. While lifting an oversized piece of luggage onto the scale, she strained her back. Assuming Loretta's injury was severe enough to temporarily disable her, what kind of benefits can she expect to receive through workers' compensation?

4. What are the advantages and disadvantages of mandatory participation by employers in the workers' compensation system? Explain your answer as it affects both employers and employees.

5. Lorenzo, a construction worker, was hit by a car while working alongside a busy highway. His average weekly wage before the accident was $500. The state he lives in provides workers' compensation benefits at a replacement ratio of 66.7 percent, with a maximum benefit of $400 a week.

   a. If Lorenzo is temporarily and totally disabled for twelve weeks, how much compensation can he expect to receive?

   b. What if he is permanently and partially disabled (with a maximum of 66.7 percent of the total allowed by his state in such situations)?

6. As risk manager for Titanic Corporation, you want to embark on a stringent work safety program that would cost the business at least $500,000 per year for the next three years and $300,000 per year thereafter. Workers' compensation losses average about $600,000 per year, and you estimate that you can reduce them by one-third. Your plan is opposed by the financial vice president as a "bleeding heart" program that is not even close to being cost efficient.

   a. In light of your knowledge of workers' compensation costs, employers' liability exposures, and trends in court decisions, what arguments can you make in favor of the safety program?

   b. Give some examples of activities you might include in this safety program.

7. The frequency of workers' compensation claims due to stress has increased. How can the law provide for legitimate stress claims while reducing illegitimate ones?

8. Jeanne quits her job because her boss continually makes advances directed toward her. She applies for unemployment compensation benefits while she looks for another job, but her former employer challenges her benefits on the grounds that her unemployment was voluntary because she quit her job with his firm.

   a. What do you think her chances of collecting benefits are?

   b. Do you think she should be able to collect?

   c. Could an employer make a workplace so hostile as to force resignations in order to escape unemployment compensation costs?

9. Do you think the experience rating of unemployment compensation contributions helps stabilize employment? Why or why not?

10. Franco Chen, a production foreman for Acme Machine Company, was discussing an unusual situation with Bill Johnson, a line supervisor. "Bill, I've got a bit of a problem. That new applicant for the number 7 drill press job seems to be just the person we need. He has the skill and experience to handle the job. The fact that he has sight in only one eye doesn't affect his ability to perform adequately. Yet I am worried about two things. First, he said he lost his sight in the bad eye because of a steel shaving from a drill press ten years ago. That bothers me about this job,

with a possibility of a reoccurrence. Second, I know that management would be upset if he lost his only good eye because he would be totally blind and the workers' compensation settlement would be much higher for him than for a less experienced worker with two good eyes. It's a hard decision for me to make." Bill replied, "I don't know much about the technical aspects of that problem, but I think I would hire the experienced fellow. In fact, the Americans with Disabilities Act requires that we not discriminate against him."

a. What obligation (if any) does the company have toward the new worker, if he is hired, to make his workplace extra safe?

b. How much added workers' compensation risk will the company be assuming by hiring the worker with one good eye rather than a worker with normal vision?

ENDNOTES

1. Dennis C. Mealy, FCAS, MAAA, Chief Actuary, NCCI, Inc., "State of the Line," May 8, 2008; Orlando, Florida, 2008; NCCI Holdings, Inc.

2. Exceptions are taxing governmental entities, such as the school districts in Texas, that may be allowed to self-insure unemployment compensation. They have a pool administered by the Texas Association of School Boards.

3. A counterargument is postulated in D. Edward and Monroe Berkowitz, "Challenges to Workers' Compensation: A Historical Analysis," in *Workers' Compensation Adequacy, Equity & Efficiency*, ed. John D. Worral and David Appel (Ithaca, NY: ILR Press, 1985). The authors contend that workers were becoming successful in suing employers. Thus, workers' compensation developed as an aid to employers in limiting their responsibilities to employees.

4. For a detailed history of workers' compensation laws, see the *Encyclopedia of Economic and Business History*, http://eh.net/encyclopedia/fishback.workers.compensation.php//eh.net/encyclopedia/.

5. Daniel Hays, "Despite Option, More Texas Firms Offer Comp," *National Underwriter Online News Service*, February 1, 2002. The results were obtained through a survey of 2,808 employers between August and October 2001 following the passage of a measure that outlawed the use of preinjury liability waivers by employees.

6. Employee benefits are discussed in Chapter 19 to Chapter 20. Alternative coverage never exactly duplicates a state's workers' compensation benefits.

7. Various concepts and statistics in this chapter are based on research described in S. Travis Pritchett, Scott E. Harrington, Helen I. Doerpinghaus, and Greg Niehaus, *An Economic Analysis of Workers' Compensation in South Carolina* (Columbia, SC: Division of Research, College of Business Administration, University of South Carolina, 1994).

8. Steve Tuckey, "Texas Legislature OKs Comp Reform," *National Underwriter Online News Service*, May 31, 2005.

9. Dale Chadwick and Peter Rousmaniere, "Managing Workers' Comp: The Workers' Compensation Managed-Care Industry Is Doing a Better Job of Monitoring Itself, but It Needs to Figure out What to Do with the Information," *Best's Review*, November 2001, http://www3.ambest.com/Frames/FrameServer.asp?AltSrc=23&Tab=1&Site=bestreview&refnum=13969 (accessed March 31, 2009).

10. Dennis C. Mealy, FCAS, MAAA, National Council on Compensation Insurance, Inc. (NCCI) Chief Actuary, "State of the Line" Annul Issues Symposium (AIS), May 8, 2008, https://www.ncci.com/documents/AIS-2008-SOL-Complete.pdf (accessed March 28, 2009).

11. The amount of weekly income benefits is the same for both permanent and temporary total disability.

12. See Virginia Workers' Compensation Commission Web site at http://www.vwc.state.va.us/ (accessed March 28, 2009).

13. See Texas Workers' Compensation Commission Web site at http://www.twcc.state.tx.us (accessed March 28, 2009) for the details regarding the Texas benefits. Each state workers' compensation commission has a Web site that shows its benefit amounts.

14. Rates are made for each state and depend on the experience under the law in that state. Thus, the rate for the same occupational classification may differ from state to state.

15. Three of the six permit self-insurance exclusive funds are called monopolistic state funds.

16. For example, many workers' compensation laws exclude workers hired for temporary jobs, known as casual workers. Injured employees who are classified as casual workers are not entitled to benefits under the law but may recover damages from the employer if they can prove that their injuries were caused by the employer's negligence. The employer's liability risk with regard to excluded employees is the same as it would be if there was no workers' compensation law.

17. This is firsthand information by the author, who was employed by the Texas Association of School Boards in 1994–1995.

18. An unemployed federal civilian or ex-serviceperson may be entitled to benefits under the conditions of a state law for determining benefit eligibility. The amount he or she may receive will be the same as if federal pay had been covered under the state law. Costs of the benefits are paid by the federal government.

19. Several states have compulsory temporary disability insurance laws to provide income benefits for disabled workers who are not receiving unemployment benefits. Some of these plans pay partial benefits to workers receiving workers' compensation benefits. Others exclude these workers.

20. Employees contribute in Alabama, Alaska, and New Jersey.

21. This does not necessarily mean that employers try to cheat employees out of benefits. There are many borderline cases in which there is room for argument about whether or not the unemployed worker is really *involuntarily* unemployed. Experience rating emphasizes the fact that employers pay the cost of benefits and motivates them to be interested in disqualifications. As in other human relations situations, one can find examples of bad behavior by both employers and employees.

CHAPTER 17
Life Cycle Financial Risks

In Part III, we concentrated on the risks to properties and liabilities, and we concluded with Chapter 16 about the risks in employment. We now begin a discussion of the life cycle and the quality of life risks. This chapter is a general overview of the life cycle risks that will be dealt with in greater detail in the following chapters. Dealing with life risks involves enormous sums of money (roughly speaking, about 40 percent of personal income). The handling of these risks is done by large organizations: the government, pension funds, saving plans, financial institutions, and insurance companies. These institutions directly employ a very large number of people, and they are connected to a large number of other employees (agents, adjusters, doctors, lawyers, suppliers). We will show that the handling of these risks is strongly correlated with some of the key macroeconomic parameters such as national savings, interest rates, the growth of the economy, and demographic developments. This will be done largely from a global perspective.

In this chapter, we shall give a general survey of the risks that are associated with our lives. We will characterize them, offer estimates as to their probabilities, and assess their impact. There are three major classes of risks associated with the life cycle: the risks associated with a premature death; the risks associated with long life (old age, longevity); and the risks associated with our well-being (health risks, disabilities, loss of earning capacity, and unemployment). Most of these risks are related to our physical well-being. However, the last one may be related to external economic parameters, like unemployment. Due to increases in life expectancy, old-age risks are becoming the dominant focus. We will discuss the major changes taking place in areas such as employment patterns, financial instruments, saving patterns, life expectancy, demography, societal forms, dependency ratios, family structure, and the like. To complete the picture and to broaden our horizons, we shall conclude the chapter by discussing important demographic trends that follow technological waves and affect the life cycle risks.

This chapter includes the following topics:

1. Links

2. Risks related to mortality

3. Risks related to longevity

4. Risks related to health and disability

5. Global trends and their impact on demography and the life cycle risks

1. LINKS

We are in the midst of immense technological developments that are drastically transforming the world we live in every ten to fifteen years. Technological waves are affecting every aspect of our lives: family structure; the social and political structure; the economy; and the way we live, work, eat, spend time, consume, learn, travel, and communicate. Shocks resonate throughout the system as a consequence of accelerated changes. The old tools are quickly becoming outdated. As a result, we need new instruments to deal with the new environment. During the search for new instruments, we also produce very risky behaviors that bring about financial crises, as is the case of the credit crisis and subsequent economic recession beginning in 2008. Thus, innovation and creativity sometimes involve greater levels of risk taking and the potential of systemic breakdowns of the economic systems (see Chapter 1).

Technological waves do not spread evenly over the world. They are typically delayed at certain invisible border lines. These border lines can be depicted by the geographical distribution of countries by their developmental stage (see Figure 17.1). The border lines typically coincide with the border lines of civilizations (the cultural and religious features that tie a certain region together). Many indicators show the level of development that a country has reached: mortality, GDP per capita, and health indicators, for example. On the world map, they all follow quite similar patterns, as we can see in Figure 17.1, which depicts the distribution of phones (number of lines per 1,000 people) and life expectancy at birth. These rankings generally agree with the ranking by many other indicators.

FIGURE 17.1   Links between the Holistic Risk Picture and Global Technological Development

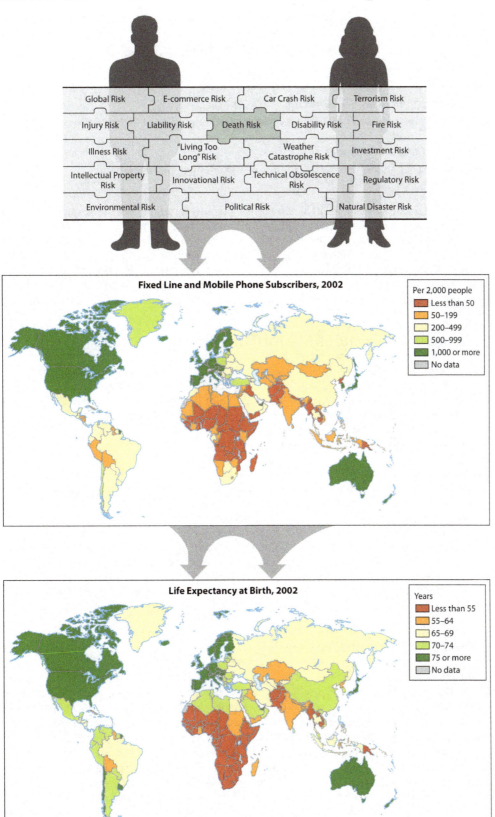

2.   THE RISKS RELATED TO MORTALITY

LEARNING OBJECTIVES

In this section we elaborate on the risk of a premature death:

- **The ways that mortality risk causes loss**
- **The use of mortality tables and life expectancy tables in assessing the probabilities of premature death**
- **Mortality changes over time**
- **Quantifying the intensity of the risk through the economic value of a person**

mortality risk

Life cycle risk of premature death.

Our lives involve uncertainties and risks. Sometimes, the uncertainty relates to the question of whether an event will occur (What if I become disabled? Will I reach retirement age?). In other cases, an event, such as death, will definitely occur; therefore, the risk relates to the *timing* of the event (all people will die, but we don't know when). The risk management of individuals is strongly related to mortality because it determines the probabilities of dying and surviving. It is also related to words and concepts like *life expectancy* and to the measurement of the financial threats created by the life cycle risks. In the following section, we shall further explore the topic of **mortality risk**: the risk of premature death.

2.1   Financial Implications of Mortality Risk

Speaking in terms of the financial threats and ignoring the very real psychological and emotional elements, we can say that the financial risk of a premature death is mainly borne by the dependents of the deceased person because they relied on the income stream generated by the deceased. The risk of old age is mainly borne by the person whose life is being assessed—that is, the need to guarantee the livelihood of that person. The cut-off point to distinguish between a premature death and old age depends on the particular person and family. We shall arbitrarily take a common retirement age, say, sixty-five, as the borderline.

The distinction between different effects of mortality risk was made at the beginning of the twentieth century. Human beings, like machines, were assessed according to their ability to contribute to the economy. A machine is expected to operate during its economic lifetime; it may, however, break down before it reaches its life expectancy, causing its owner to suffer a loss of future income streams. A machine may exceed its economic life, and this situation brings about increased maintenance costs. It may have a deficient production capacity due to some malfunctioning, and this situation involves increased costs and a lower level of production. The analogy between human beings and machines certainly raises ethical questions, and it may be disliked by most readers, but it is a practical approach that may help us characterize the risks and quantify them *purely from a financial perspective*. Like any other risk, we shall try to assess the probabilities and the intensity of occurrences.

2.2   The Risk of Premature Death

premature death

Dying prior to certain age (commonly, the expected retirement age).

economic loss

In mortality risk, the financial loss experienced by those that depended on a deceased person and the lost future income that would have been earned if the person had not died.

A **premature death** will be defined as dying prior to a certain age (commonly, the expected retirement age). The death of a person typically results in a variety of losses: the direct loss is to the dying person because the person is unable to continue enjoying what he or she was doing and still wished to do. Family members and friends suffer a psychological and emotional loss from the disappearance of their loved one. However, the **economic loss** is mainly felt by people who depended financially on the deceased person (e.g., spouse, children, parents) and who lost the future income that would have been earned if the person had not died. Of course, there are also business interests that could be damaged; for example, the employing firm that lost a key person who held particularly important know-how or who had exceptionally important and strong ties with suppliers, customers, or regulators. Another common type of loss is that of a partnership that lost a key partner, a situation that may endanger the continuation of the business.

2.3 Calculating the Probability of Death: Mortality Tables and Life Tables

The probability of dying within a defined period is obtained using a mortality table or a life table. In the following section, we shall extend what was said in Chapter 7 concerning mortality. The risk depends, of course, on the individual features of the particular person: genetics, age, health condition, profession, ethnic origin, lifestyle, hobbies, and so forth. We are typically unable to tell in advance who will die, when, and how. Nonetheless, we can use population statistics to get estimates of these probabilities. You will recall the law of large numbers from Chapter 6, which provided predictions of future losses with greater accuracy as the sample of people become larger. So when actuaries look at large populations, they are able to provide scientific estimates of the probabilities of dying in each age cohort. They can tell us the probability that a person celebrating the x birthday will die before reaching the next birthday (at age $x + 1$). By common actuarial notation, this probability is denoted by q_x. The mortality table, which we discussed in Chapter 7, expresses these probabilities for all age groups.

To recap the discussion on the mortality table and mortality curve in Chapter 7, the mortality rate for males is relatively high at birth, but it declines until age ten. It then rises to a peak between the ages of eighteen to twenty-two (often attributed to risk-taking behavioral patterns) and declines between the ages of twenty-three and twenty-nine. The rise is continuous for females above age ten and for males after age twenty-nine. The rise is rather slow until middle age, at which point it begins to accelerate. At the more advanced ages, it rises very rapidly.

A **life table (or survival table)** reflects either the probability of survival (one minus the probability of dying), or the number of people surviving at each age. Mortality tables and life tables are essential tools in the hands of actuaries. The actuary needs only one of the tables for making all the required calculations since one table can be derived from the other. A life table can be constructed by following a cohort of people that were born during a particular year over a long period of time and recording all deaths until the last one dies (generation life table). Such an approach is naturally not practical because the follow-up has to continue over a century and creates enormous technical problems: replacing researchers, following people wandering all over the globe, and so forth. Moreover, the results could be of some historical interest but of little practical value because they are influenced by the extreme technological changes (including nutrition, health standards, employment, etc.) that have taken place over time.

The most common way to generate a life table is to use the current mortality rates q_x (as reflected in a mortality table). A life table shows how many people, l_x, are expected to survive at each age x, out of the initial population. The life table typically starts with a round figure, like an initial population of 1,000,000 people at a particular age. Relying on the law of large numbers and statistical data, the computations (which are beyond the scope of this text) are made to determine the number of people still living at each age out of the entire population.

Life tables (and mortality tables) are constructed for particular purposes; therefore, they are based on specifically chosen populations: people from a particular geographical region, people with special occupations, males and females, retired or preretired populations, widows and widowers, people with or without certain diseases or disabilities, and more. Of special interest are tables for an insured population versus an uninsured population. Many types of mortality tables and life tables exist because they are calculated from different populations according to the particular needs of the actuaries. There are tables for urban or rural populations, tables for people in certain professions, tables for smokers versus nonsmokers, and the like. Notably, tables exist for the entire population or for only an insured population. Insured populations tend to be healthier because they are typically employed and pass medical screenings as a condition of insurability. Therefore, their mortality rates tend to be significantly lower than those of uninsured populations. Such tables are called **select tables**. In contrast, **ultimate tables** are used to make mortality calculations without the selection effects of medical examination. It is noteworthy that the selection of the period for which a life table is calculated is important because we do not like to have a table that is based on the mortality pattern during a year of plague. To obtain reliable figures, we need fairly large populations and databases, and we have to take great care in data processing.

The typical table used for many actuarial calculations in the United States is known as the Ultimate 2001 Commissioners Standard Ordinary (CSO) Mortality Table. The 2001 mortality table was revised in 2006, as discussed in the "New Mortality Tables" box later. Table 17.1 presents the life table that is derived from the Ultimate 2001 CSO Table. Recall from Chapter 7 that the mortality rates for males and females are different. This fact has implications for the pricing of products used to mitigate mortality risk, as discussed in "Should Life Insurance Rates Be Based on Gender?" also in this chapter.

life table

Shows how many people are expected to survive at each age out of an initial population.

select tables

The figures of a mortality table that relate to an insured population where the possible effects of medical examinations used for selecting the terms of insurance may influence the findings.

ultimate

The figures of a mortality table that relate to an insured population where the possible effects of medical examinations used for selecting the terms of insurance do not influence the findings.

TABLE 17.1 Life Table Depicting the Number of Survivors at Age x out of an Initial Population of 1,000,000 People

Age	Males	Females	Age	Males	Females	Age	Males	Females
0	1,000,000	1,000,000	39	969,354	980,702	78	556,428	663,795
1	999,030	999,520	40	967,861	979,496	79	524,957	639,513
2	998,471	999,170	41	966,264	978,223	80	491,853	613,900
3	998,081	998,910	42	964,534	976,873	81	457,355	586,975
4	997,812	998,711	43	962,644	975,427	82	421,594	558,148
5	997,602	998,521	44	960,574	973,876	83	385,109	527,478
6	997,393	998,341	45	958,279	972,201	84	348,327	495,402
7	997,173	998,161	46	955,739	970,383	85	311,603	462,077
8	996,954	997,952	47	952,967	968,394	86	275,280	427,675
9	996,734	997,742	48	949,947	966,195	87	239,793	393,038
10	996,505	997,533	49	946,783	963,780	88	205,659	357,354
11	996,276	997,313	50	943,451	961,101	89	173,426	321,236
12	996,007	997,084	51	939,903	958,140	90	143,617	285,251
13	995,678	996,815	52	936,087	954,873	91	116,666	250,473
14	995,290	996,516	53	931,903	951,254	92	93,048	218,701
15	994,822	996,187	54	927,309	947,259	93	72,780	188,765
16	994,215	995,838	55	922,208	942,873	94	55,746	160,141
17	993,480	995,450	56	916,518	938,065	95	41,746	132,867
18	992,615	995,042	57	910,213	932,783	96	30,509	107,136
19	991,682	994,614	58	903,259	927,009	97	21,795	84,031
20	990,710	994,156	59	895,789	920,706	98	15,187	63,991
21	989,720	993,689	60	887,736	913,902	99	10,299	48,495
22	988,730	993,212	61	878,983	906,581	100	6,778	36,118
23	987,722	992,715	62	869,366	898,712	101	4,316	26,159
24	986,704	992,219	63	858,717	890,273	102	2,676	18,368
25	985,668	991,703	64	846,944	881,246	103	1,611	12,450
26	984,613	991,168	65	834,036	871,587	104	939	8,104
27	983,511	990,612	66	819,983	861,259	105	528	5,036
28	982,360	990,018	67	804,838	850,218	106	286	2,968
29	981,211	989,394	68	788,668	838,408	107	148	1,652
30	980,082	988,741	69	771,436	825,773	108	73	864
31	978,965	988,069	70	753,199	812,264	109	34	423
32	977,859	987,348	71	733,789	797,797	110	15	192
33	976,754	986,588	72	713,133	782,264	111	6	80
34	975,630	985,779	73	690,798	765,602	112	2	31
35	974,479	984,911	74	666,882	747,763	113	1	11
36	973,300	983,956	75	641,488	728,696	114	0	3
37	972,054	982,942	76	614,603	708,365	115	0	1
38	970,752	981,851	77	586,282	686,739	Total	71,119,302	81,344,455

Sources: Processed by the authors from the American Academy of Actuaries CSO Task Force Report, June 2002, http://www.actuary.org/life/ CSO_0702.asp (accessed April 4, 2009); 2001 CSO Ultimate Table. Used with permission.

In Table 17.1, we see that the number of male survivors at age twenty-five is 985,668. This means that about 98.57 percent of the newborn males survived until the age of 25, and that about 1.43 percent (the difference) of the males are expected to die prior to reaching this age. The number of survivors at age sixty-five is 834,036. We can say that the probability of a twenty-five-year-old male surviving until age sixty-five is 84.6 percent (834,036/985,668). In other words, 14.5 percent of the twenty-five-year-old males will not reach age sixty-five. We can do similar calculations for people in other age groups. Comparable figures taken from a life table that was relevant a few decades ago show much higher probabilities of dying.

Using a modern life table leads to a very important conclusion: about 10 to 15 percent of males in the working ages of 20 to forty-five years will die before reaching retirement. If we would have made a similar calculation with a typical life table from the 1960s, we would have reached a figure around 20 to 25 percent! In other words, the probability of dying prior to retirement age declined by approximately half during the last fifty years in most developed countries.

In the United States, only 0.8 percent of females die before they reach age twenty-five (from the life table, 1 − [991,703/1,000,000]). About 88 percent of females at the age of twenty-five will reach age sixty-five (871,587/991,703). This means that about 12 percent of the females will die before retirement. Some other western countries have even higher survival probabilities: often 92 to 94 percent of young females in a developed country are expected to attain age sixty-five. In the 1960s and 1970s, the parallel probability would have been only around 82 to 85 percent.

Mortality Changes over Time

The twentieth century has been a period of unprecedented changes in mortality patterns. Most countries experienced enormous improvements (a drastic decline) in mortality rates. The chart in Figure 17.2 compares the q_x values in the mortality tables over two decades (2001 versus 1980). We see that the q_x values declined dramatically. The rate of change is not uniform, however, among various age groups and by gender. What seems to be a very drastic decline of the death probabilities at age ninety-five and above is just a technical result of extending the end of the mortality table from age ninety-nine in 1980 to 120 in 2001. The revisions to the CSO mortality table reflecting historical improvements in the mortality rate is discussed in the box "New Mortality Tables."

FIGURE 17.2 **Mortality Changes as Reflected by Comparisons of the 1980 and 2001 CSO Tables**

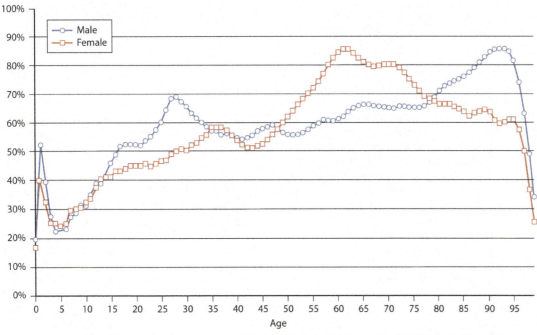

Source: American Academy of Actuaries; http://www.actuary.org/life/cso/appendix_b_jun02.xls (accessed April 4, 2009). Used with permission.

New Mortality Tables

Mortality improvements are critical to setting life insurance premiums and reserves (life insurance is a risk management solution for the financial component of life cycle risks and is the subject of Chapter 19). As mortality rates improve, you may be able to think of yourself as relatively younger as you age. According to the most up-to-date mortality tables, American adults can expect to live, on average, two to four years longer than their parents. The 2001 CSO Preferred Class Structure Mortality Table was adopted by the National Association of Insurance Commissioners in September 2006, a modification of the mortality table issued in 2001.

Age is a very important factor when life insurers assess the classification of an insurance applicant. Others include gender, tobacco use, and health. Like the 1980 tables, the 2001 tables are categorized by gender and show that women as a group live several years longer than men do. (See "Should Life Rates Be Based on Gender?" later in this chapter). Subtables separate tobacco users from nonusers and reflect the decrease in male smokers since 1980 but a slight increase in female smokers. Mortality rates for female smokers in their fifties and sixties are now higher than they were in 1980. Women in that group can expect to pay higher life insurance premiums when the new tables are adopted. Note that race is not a category in the mortality tables. Race-based discrimination is not permitted.

Changes in aggregate health status are difficult to determine (and the tables do not even try), but it is generally accepted that any improvements are offset by more and better medical testing. That is, if more seventy-year-olds are diagnosed with prostate cancer in 2002 than there were in 1982, it is possible the cancer rate has increased—but also true that the detection test is more widely given these days, and that men in 1982 were more likely to die of other causes before even reaching that age. One factor that has clearly worsened since 1980—in fact, it has more than doubled—is the nation's rate of obesity. Since overweight people are very likely to develop health problems as they grow older, most life insurers will charge higher premiums or even decline to cover people who weigh 30 percent or more above their ideal weight (see "Obesity and Insurance—Litigation or Self-Discipline?" in Chapter 12).

Other factors contributing to America's overall life expectancy have clearly progressed in the last twenty years: medical breakthroughs, including antibiotics and vaccines; public health and environmental efforts; and increased standards of living such as better housing and safer foods. Thanks to developments like these and more, the general mortality rate in the United States has improved about 1 percent per year since early last century. If this trend holds, in 2020 you can take another three years off your age.

Sources: Dr. Rick Rogers, "Will Mortality Improvements Continue?" National Underwriter, Life & Health/Financial Services Edition, August 26, 2002; American Academy of Actuaries, "June 2002 CSO Task Force Report," June 2002, accessed April 4, 2009, http://www.actuary.org/life/cso_0702.htm; National Association of Insurance Commissioners, "Recognition of the 2001 CSO Mortality Table for Use in Determining Minimum Reserve Liabilities and Nonforfeiture Benefits Model Regulation," http://www.naic.org/1papers/models/htms/cso-summary.htm; Insurance Information Institute, "Life Insurance Premium Rates to Continue Downward Trend," October 5, 2005, accessed April 4, 2009, http://www.iii.org/media/updates/archive/press.744841/; Donna L. Hoyert, Ph.D., Hsiang-Ching Kung, Ph.D., and Betty L. Smith, B.S. Ed., "Deaths: Preliminary data for 2003," Division of Vital Statistics, National Data Statistics Report 53, no. 15 (2005).

2.4   Estimating the Economic Value of Life

What is the economic loss value associated with the case of death? It is hard to answer the question without touching on deep ethical questions.[1] There are no objective market values that can be referred to, and there are no mechanisms in which one could purchase a substitute at a given price. Therefore, we have to find indirect ways to estimate the hard-to-measure economic value of a human life, while ignoring psychological or emotional elements that are typically attached to death.

The estimation of the value of human life is needed for private and business purposes. From the private point of view, there is often the need to assess how much financial protection a family needs in case of a breadwinner's death. From a practical business point of view, there are a variety of needs. For example, there is often a need to assess the loss that an organization will suffer when a key employee dies or to estimate the cash needed to buy out the share of a partner in the case of a partner's death. We shall focus on the estimation of the economic value of a person from the family's point of view.

A theoretical correct measurement method may be related to sophisticated theories about personal consumption and savings; however, we do not delve into these theories here. Instead, we focus on the estimated value of human life from the dependents' point of view. In principle, there are two alternative ways to estimate the value: one is to estimate the value of the income stream that the deceased person would have had if she or he had survived. The alternative way is to estimate the financial needs of the surviving heirs.

Assessing Economic Value by Lost Future Income Streams

Here, we try to estimate the economic value of a human life by calculating the value of the future income stream that will be lost in case of the person's death. For that purpose, there is a need to estimate the future income stream. The forecast should be limited to a certain period (say, an expected retirement age) when these income streams are expected to discontinue anyhow, even if the person survived beyond that period.

The risk manager must find a way to create a similar cash flow to replace the lost income once the person dies. Because the timing of the death cannot be predicted, it is common to calculate the present value of the income stream to derive a single number (present value was explained in Chapter 4). If we hold this amount and invest it at the same interest rate that is used for the computation of the present value, we can generate the same cash flow whenever it is needed. The use of the present value concept is practical because it can also give us one figure for the estimated economic value of the person.

The purpose of the discussion is to get an idea of the order of magnitude of the value of the lost income stream and to gain certain insights concerning the needs of a typical person. Therefore, we are making some simplifying assumptions: we shall assume a person is expected to retire at age sixty-five and has an expected constant annual income level of $1 (or a constant annual income) to work and earn money beyond retirement age. This approach replaces a more specific calculation for a particular person. Such a calculation would have to forecast the future development of the personal income stream and would involve a prediction of career patterns, promotions, future tax rates, price levels, and so forth.

The importance of the present value technique lies in its use as a tool for planning the needed financial protection against the case of a premature death. The present value of a future stream of earnings is affected by interest rates and by time. The values in Table 17.2 can be used to get a rough estimate for the economic value of our lives, and thus to set the financial protection plan for a family. At 3 percent interest, the economic value of a person in the twenty- to forty-year-old range (or forty-five to twenty-five years to retirement) is about 17.9 to 25.1 times the annual income, or roughly twenty times the assumed fixed annual income. At higher interest rates, say, 6 percent, the present value figure is lower. The present value at 6 percent for the same person would be 13.5 to 16.3 times the annual income, or we could say roughly fifteen times the annual income.

TABLE 17.2 Present Value of a Future Earnings Stream at 0, 3, and 6 Percent Interest for Period to Retirement

Duration or Time to Retirement	Age	Discount Rate		
(Years)	(Years)	0%	3%	6%
5	60	5	4.7	4.5
15	50	15	12.3	10.3
25	40	25	17.9	13.5
35	30	35	21.4	14.5
45	20	45	25.1	16.3

In other words, the economic value of a person with $100,000 annual income is about $2 million (twenty times the income) when the calculation is made under the assumption that we can invest the money at 3 percent, or it is only $1.5 million (fifteen times the annual income) at 6 percent interest. These figures remain steady for almost any age within the range of twenty to forty years. The amount of needed protection declines only at older ages. This present value technique serves as the basis for certain rules of thumb that are often used in the insurance industry and state that the economic value of a person is a certain multiplier of the annual income.[2]

Nevertheless, common life insurance literature talks about death benefits that are only five to seven times one's income. A possible explanation to this alarming discrepancy between the needed amount of protection and the actual one may be related to other forms of protection held by U.S. families. One should not deduce that there is a need to run and buy insurance covering fifteen or twenty times the annual income in case of a premature death. One should consider existing properties and other sources of protection (Social Security, pension plans, savings—all discussed in later chapters) that may be included in the portfolio. A person needs to buy protection only for the uncovered balance. Other explanations may be related to the subjective preferences of families: the desire or need to prefer current consumption over future savings, natural optimism, and so forth. These topics are related to complex economic theories that are not handled in this book.

In real life, an income level does not remain constant over long periods. However, the above instrument can also be used for the case that the income stream *grows* at a constant rate. Income growth (and inflation) has the opposite effect compared to discounting. If we assume, for example, that the cash flow grows at an annual rate of 3 percent, and the relevant interest rate is 6 percent, we can assume instead a constant income stream and discount it at a net interest rate of approximately 3 percent (i.e., 6 percent minus the 3 percent growth rate). This is a good approximation. Note that using this method with fast-growing income streams results in a low net interest rate, which in turn increases sharply the present value of the stream. To handle streams that are not constant and do not grow at a constant rate, one must perform a detailed present value calculation, a technique beyond the scope of this text.

Discounting in the present value method makes the distant future cash flows less significant. The present value of $1 received forty-five years from now is only $0.26 at an interest rate of 3 percent, and it is only $0.07 with a discount factor of 6 percent (refer to the appendixes at the back of the text for computation tables to aid in such analyses). Because of that, our unrealistic assumption that the annual income is constant over time is not that important because the future income streams have a smaller effect on the total present value of the lifetime income stream.

Another implication of this effect is that the economic value of our life is roughly similar for a wide range of ages. For example, at 6 percent interest, the present value of the stream for twenty-five years is only somewhat lower than the value of a stream for forty-five years (13.5 versus 16.3). If we assume that people plan to retire at age sixty-five, this means that the lost value for a person who dies at age twenty (loss of forty-five years) is not much higher than that of a person who dies at the age of forty (loss of twenty-five years).

Assessing Economic Value by Needs Analysis

An alternative way to estimate the financial loss in case of a premature death is to estimate the needs of the surviving members of the family who depended on the deceased person. The particular needs differ from one family to another; however, certain needs are quite common when the person is a breadwinner for the family. A detailed example of a hypothetical needs analysis with respect to the risk of premature death is presented in the appendix to this chapter.

Most insurance companies and insurance agents are equipped with software to prepare a family needs analysis like that described in the appendix. These programs are useful as a marketing tool by the agents, but they could be used by families in designing their plans. Many students are unmarried and therefore do not acknowledge the importance of family needs planning. Moreover, people tend to avoid thinking about what could happen in case of their death or their spouse's death. However, it is of utmost importance to do so once in a while (at least every ten years) and to keep updating it in accordance with changing personal status and needs (children, marriage, divorce, etc.). It will save many worries for you and your family in case something does go wrong in your life.

The financial planning process means creating a cash flow plan that could easily be translated to present values. It is expected that this method gives a more accurate estimate of financial needs and results in somewhat lower values than the ones obtained by the first approach (the present value of the lost income stream). This expectation is based on the assumption that the lost income approach overestimates the needs (mainly due to the fact that the dead person stops consuming). It is noteworthy that this hypothesis is not supported by practical experience, and we often find that the two methods result in very similar figures. The reason for this could be found in the empirical evidence that there is a very strong correlation between the family income and consumption. People get used to a standard of living that is strongly connected to the family's disposable income, and therefore the financial needs tend to reflect the current consumption pattern of the family while the breadwinner is still alive.

The above discussion has shown that the risk of death prior to retirement age is substantial. The probability of occurrence in developed countries could be around 10 to 12 percent for males and around 8 percent for females. As the present value estimation reveals, the amount of loss is typically around fifteen to twenty times annual income. Therefore, it is not surprising that many institutions are dealing with these risks and offer some sources of financial protection. Such arrangements will be the topic of Chapter 19.

KEY TAKEAWAYS

In this section you studied mortality, the risk of premature death:

- Mortality risk is borne mainly by the dependents of the deceased.
- Mortality tables and life tables can be used to determine the probability of a person dying before a certain age or surviving to a certain age.
- Mortality rates of the insured populations tend to be better than those of the uninsured populations.
- Actuarially, 8 to 15 percent of the population will die prior to retirement age.
- Mortality risk can be quantified by determining the economic value of a person through either the present value of the stream of lost income method or a family needs analysis.
- The economic value of life is said to be fifteen to twenty times one's permanent annual income (or higher when interest rates approach zero).
- The economic value of life is inversely related to interest rates.

DISCUSSION QUESTIONS

1. What are life tables used for? How are life tables distinguished from mortality tables?
2. Who primarily bears the risk associated with premature death?
3. Describe briefly some of the changes in mortality patterns that have been observed over the years.
4. Explain how present value can be utilized to estimate the economic value of life.
5. What does it mean to you that your mortality risk may be between 8 and 12 percent? Is this a risk whose probability is so low that you don't worry about it? Or are the consequences of its occurrence such that it must be dealt with regardless of its likelihood?

3. THE RISKS RELATED TO LONGEVITY

LEARNING OBJECTIVES

In this section we elaborate on the following:

- **Risks associated with living past the retirement age**
- **Measurement of life expectancy**
- **Why life expectancies are changing**
- **The significance of conditional life expectancies**
- **The role of interest rates in retirement planning**
- **The roles of individuals and governments in retirement planning**

Old-age issues have many aspects: social, psychological, economic, and political. In this text, we focus mainly on the risk management and financial aspect of old age. In the previous discussion, we showed the probability of reaching the old-age group. If we define the group of aged people as those that exceed a common retirement age (like sixty-five), we can easily find the probability of reaching this age by using a life table. We concluded that the probability of a young person reaching retirement age is about 88 percent for males and about 92 percent for females. In the following section, we shall first analyze the probabilities and then discuss the measurement of the financial burden associated with longevity risk. The financial burden is the amount of money that is needed to finance the retirement period. Therefore, we need an estimate for the expected length of this period. Such a measurement can be derived from the life table, and it is related to the concept of life expectancy. Hence, in the following sections we shall discuss survival probabilities and life expectancy figures.

3.1 Survival Probabilities

Survival probabilities can be derived from Table 17.1 of the previous section. We can see that out of the initial population of 1,000,000 people at age zero, about 985,668 people will be living at age twenty-five. At age sixty-five, the expected number of survivors is 834,036. We can say that the probability of a twenty-five-year-old male surviving to age sixty-five is 84.6 percent (834,036/985,668). About 59 percent of all the people that have reached age sixty-five are expected to survive beyond eighty years old (491,853 out of 834,036). In the 1950s, this figure was substantially lower, typically below 40 percent. The survival rates in less-developed countries are by far smaller, and in many cases are very close to zero.

Longevity risk can be defined simply as the risk of living too long such that one's advanced age hinders one's ability to continue adequately providing for oneself. To characterize the risk, we have to show also the costs involved in aging. Old age may bring about severe financial implications for the individual. Surviving for many years after retirement involves high costs of current maintenance (housing, clothing, food, entertainment, and the like) and frequently involves increased medical expenses (hospitalization, senior citizen housing, special care, and the like). Retired people often do not have the resources needed to finance these costs. They often lack current income sources and do not have sufficient properties. Moreover, they often face difficulties in generating adequate income from the properties they do hold. The risk of extended life without sufficient financial resources could be severe and more frequent than people think. Surveys often show that aged people have far lower income than they used to have during their employment period, and many report financial stresses.

longevity risk

Life cycle risk of living too long, such that one's advanced age hinders one's ability to continue adequately providing for oneself.

In the following section, we shall give a general review of the cost of aging, from the individual's point of view. Like the cost of premature death, we have to talk in general terms about populations and averages rather than relate to particular individuals. The first term to be discussed is life expectancy (at birth). We shall then discuss the average number of postretirement years.

3.2 Life Expectancy

life expectancy

Measures the average length of life in a population; in a stable population, it would be an approximation of the average age of deceased people.

The financial burden of aging is a direct function of the number of years that the individual will live beyond retirement. A common term that is related to the issue is **life expectancy**. Although this term is commonly used in the literature, there are misunderstandings concerning its meaning. Thus, we start by explaining this measure. Life expectancy measures the average length of life in a population. In a stable population, it would be an approximation of the average age of deceased people.

Life expectancy figures are calculated from the life table. Assume for a moment that mortality has a strange pattern: all people are expected to die during the year and to die immediately before they touch the birthday cake just prior to the next birthday. From the life table, actuaries can determine the total number of years that the cohort of people presented has lived (which is simply the sum of all l_x values from age zero to the end of the life table). If this figure is divided by the number of people that were assumed to be alive at age zero, the average age of death, or life expectancy, is the result. Actuaries do make a small correction to this figure: we have assumed that all people die at the end of the year, whereas people normally die throughout the year, so we have to deduct 0.5 from the average figure we got. We can deduce from the life table in Table 17.1 that all 1,000,000 males of the cohort are expected to live a total of 77,119,302 years, or 77.119 years per person on the average. Deducting 0.5, we see that life expectancy at birth as determined from the life table is 76.6 years. Similarly, life expectancy for females is 80.8 years. These values are based on the CSO table and are higher than the life expectancy of the general population.

Life expectancy depends, of course, on the nutrition, sanitation, life style, genetics, and general well-being of the population. Therefore, it is no wonder that it is chosen as one of the leading indicators for the developmental stage of a country. Because of that, we have this measure for most countries in the world, including the least-developed countries.

In a cross-section analysis, World Health Organization (WHO) statistics show that life expectancy for the entire population (males and females) is below sixty for less developed countries (in some countries it could even be as low as forty). On the other hand, developed and advanced countries experience life expectancy figures around seventy-seven to eighty-two (for the entire population). Will life expectancy continue to increase at the same rate in the future? Is there a limit to the human life span? These are critical questions for retirement planning. Scientists cannot give us a definite answer yet. Some claim that the body cells are designed to last only for a certain period; for example, heart cells are assumed to have a limited number of beats, perhaps 2 billion. Others believe that we are on the verge of deciphering the mechanism that determines the aging of cells, and we will learn the way to control it. Meanwhile, we experience a continuous increase in life expectancy due to the cumulative effect of gradual improvements in a wide variety of medical technologies. Modern medicine can replace failing organs through transplants, open clogged arteries, and administer drugs that immunize against and cure many diseases.

Human society is the only one among all animals that values longevity as a goal. It is not improbable that this value will be challenged in the future, and that societies finding it difficult to cope with the soaring costs of retirement and of health-related expenses will put constraints on medical treatment to aged people. This involves ethical problems that go far beyond the scope of this discussion.

During the last century, the developed countries have experienced an unprecedented increase in longevity. This increasing life expectancy is in direct correlation to the sharp reduction in mortality rates. At the beginning of the twentieth century, life expectancy at birth (corrected for mortality in the first few months after birth) was around forty-five to fifty years in most currently developed countries. A century later, at the beginning of the twenty-first century, life expectancy is around seventy-six years for males and approximately eighty years for females. In other words, life expectancy at birth has increased on the average by one year for every three to four calendar years! In 1900, the life expectancy of white males and females in the United States was 48.2 and 51.1, respectively. The parallel figures in 2002 are 75.1 and 80.3, respectively. The figures for the entire population differ, of course, from the figures of the CSO tables, which are based on the insured population, which in turn is typically healthier than the general population. Therefore, the life expectancy found in the CSO tables tends to be higher than that of the general population. The latest findings from the U.S. Census Bureau provide an excellent illustration of the life expectancy improvements in the United States over time, as seen in Table 17.3.[3]

TABLE 17.3   **Expectation of Life at Birth for the U.S. Population as Measured in Various Points in Time (1970–2005)**

Year	Total Population	Male	Female
1970	70.8	67.1	74.7
1975	72.6	68.8	76.6
1980	73.7	70.0	77.4
1985	74.7	71.1	78.2
1990	75.4	71.8	78.8
1995	75.8	72.5	78.9
2000	77.0	74.3	79.7
2005	77.8	75.2	80.4

Source: U.S. National Center for Health Statistics, National Vital Statistics Reports (NVSR), Deaths: Final Data for 2005, Vol. 56, No. 10, April 24, 2008, Accessed April 5, 2009, http://www.census.gov/compendia/statab/tables/09s0100.xls.

Conditional Life Expectancy

Longevity risk relates to the duration of the postretirement period, and for that purpose we need to consider **conditional life expectancy**—that is, the life expectancy after retirement (or some other relevant age). These figures are calculated from the life table in a similar way to life expectancy at birth. For example, to calculate the conditional life expectancy at age fifty-five, we have to sum all l_x values in the life table (Table 17.1 in the previous section) from age fifty-five to the end of the table to get the number of years lived by the cohort of the people aged fifty-five. This sum must then be divided by l_{55}, the initial number of people in that age. Again, since we used the rough assumption that all people die exactly at their birthdays, even though they die randomly throughout the year, we have to make a correction. Simply deducting half a year (0.5) from the average, we get the life expectancy.

Table 17.4 presents the average number of remaining years of life for the U.S. population. These figures are calculated in the same way as explained above, but they are calculated for the entire U.S. population and not from the 2001 CSO mortality table (Table 17.1 in the previous section) and would therefore be different.

conditional life expectancy
Life expectancy after retirement.

TABLE 17.4 Average Number of Remaining Years of Life by Sex and Age (2005)

Age (Years)	Entire Population	Male	Female
0	77.8	75.2	80.4
1	77.4	74.7	79.9
5	73.5	70.8	76.0
10	68.5	65.9	71.0
15	63.6	61.0	66.1
20	58.8	56.2	61.2
25	54.1	51.6	56.3
30	49.3	47.0	51.5
35	44.6	42.3	46.6
40	39.9	37.7	41.9
45	35.3	33.2	37.2
50	30.9	28.9	32.7
55	26.7	24.8	28.3
60	22.6	20.8	24.0
65	18.7	17.2	20.0
70	15.2	13.8	16.2
75	12.0	10.8	12.8
80	9.2	8.2	9.8
85	6.8	6.1	7.2
90	5.0	4.4	5.2
95	3.6	3.2	3.7
100	2.6	2.3	2.6

Source: processed by the authors from U.S. National Center for Health Statistics, National Vital Statistics Reports (NVSR), U.S. Decennial Life Tables for 1999–2001, United States Life Tables, vol. 57, no. 1, August 5, 2008, Accessed April 5, 2009, http://www.census.gov/compendia/statab/tables/09s0101.xls.

3.3 Financial Implications of Longevity Risk

To estimate the financial needs to confront the risk of longevity, we must look more carefully at the meaning of life expectancy. We will assume a very basic model, where people join the labor force at the age of twenty and retire at the age of sixty-five. In addition, assume that life expectancy is seventy-five and is not expected to change, and that interest rates can be ignored. Assume also that the annual consumption of a retired person is similar to that of a working person (a realistic assumption in view of studies showing that the total consumption is quite stable, although its composition changes significantly with age). These basic parameters seem to generate a simple retirement model: during forty-five years of work, people are supposed to accumulate sufficient funds to cover an additional ten years, that is, put aside about 10/45, or 22 percent, of their annual income.

There are two major flaws in this basic model, and both of them stem from a misinterpretation of the concept of life expectancy. First, relying on an average number (life expectancy) may be fine for a financial institution that holds a large portfolio of many insured people. An individual, however, is not supposed to plan her insurance needs according to average figures and must instead prepare for the extreme cases. Life expectancy is an average figure. A high proportion of retired people will live far longer than the assumed life expectancy (age seventy-five). What will all these people do when the funds are depleted at the end of the assumed ten-year postretirement period?

Second, when people refer to life expectancy, they commonly refer to the published figure, which is life expectancy at birth (the average age of death). The remaining life expectancy is a complicated function of age. If life expectancy at birth is seventy-five years, the remaining life expectancy at the age of sixty-five may be substantially higher than ten years insofar as those who reach age sixty-five have survived the childhood diseases, the motorcycle accidents, the risks of military service, and so forth. The U.S. Vital Statistics, for example, show that the life expectancy at birth of white males in 2005 was 75.2 (see Table 17.3). However, the remaining (conditional) life expectancy at age sixty-five is not just ten years, but rather 17.2 years, as shown in Table 17.4 above.

The above figures mean that when the U.S. white male in our model reaches retirement, he had better have sufficient funds for 17.2 years, on the average, rather than just ten years, as the model has assumed (and this figure is subject to the first comment about the use of averages in personal planning). Putting aside savings for 17.2 years over forty-five years of assumed employment is almost double the calculation that assumed a 10/45 ratio.

The problem of females is even more pressing in practice. Females are the biologically more resilient gender, and their life expectancy at birth is typically greater than that of males. In 2005, for example, life expectancy at birth for white U.S. females was 80.4 (compared to only 75.2 for males). However, females tend to retire earlier than men, say, at the age of sixty, and the remaining life expectancy at that age is twenty-four years. Earlier retirement, however, also means a shorter working period, perhaps only forty years. Traditionally, many women also spend a few years out of the wage-earning labor force to raise the family. The average working period for women can actually be reduced to thirty years or less. One needs to be a financial magician to be able to accumulate enough savings to finance a postretirement period of twenty-four years over approximately thirty years of work. The longevity differences between men and women are reflected in prices for life insurance, as discussed in "Should Life Insurance Rates Be Based on Gender" below.

Should Life Insurance Rates Be Based on Gender?

As a group, young male drivers cause more automobile insurance losses than do young female drivers. A few states, however, no longer allow automobile insurers to charge different rates for males and females. Similarly, over a decade ago, the Supreme Court ruled that employers using annuities to fund retirement benefits could no longer collect higher contributions from women, who were expected to live longer than men, in order to make equal annuity payments during retirement. Employers continuing to pay retirement benefits through annuities were forced by the Supreme Court to use unisex tables. That is, the mortality rates of men and women were pooled to produce an average life expectancy greater than that for men alone and less than that for women alone. Retirement benefits went up for the women and down for the men involved.

Should life insurance rates be made gender neutral as well? The quotes displayed here were requested from Insweb (http://www.insweb.com), an online insurance quotes and distribution company, in August 2005. They show that the premiums for a ten-year term life insurance policy (described in Chapter 19) of $250,000 for a twenty-five-year-old male of perfect health and family history, weight appropriate to height, and no tobacco use, are higher than those for a female with the same attributes. For example, the rate is $13.18 per month for a male as opposed to $11.90 for a female, as shown in the table of quotes below. For newer quotes for your specific age and needs, you can check on line.

When we compare a particular man to a particular woman of the same age and seemingly the same state of insurability (health, lifestyle, occupation, financial condition, and so forth), the man may outlive the woman, but, as you know, insurers pool cohorts of insureds rather than the individual. Insurers observe difference in average experience for large groups of males and females to justify different life rates based on gender, arguing that doing so creates actuarial equity. That is, premiums should differ because expected outcomes (death benefits multiplied by probabilities) are different for groups of males and females. In the past two decades, the gender mortality gap has begun to close. While female longevity has risen, male life spans have increased at a faster rate, due in part to medical advances in treating conditions like heart disease, which traditionally kills more men than women. Recently, companies have begun to incorporate data from the early 1990s. Yet even with a smaller gap between men's and women's longevity, insurance rates for women are still lower than for equally aged and healthy men.

Questions for Discussion

1. Is it ethical for life insurers to charge different rates for men and women? If it is not legal to charge different rates based on race, why should gender be different?

2. Does this practice represent unreasonable discrimination (sometimes called "social inequity") against males based on a factor over which they have no control?

3. Given the possibility that the gap between male and female mortality may close during the next few decades, is it really fair to charge different rates to men and women for a policy that runs twenty, thirty, or more years?

Monthly Premium for a 10-year Level Term Life Policy*								
Male	**25**	**30**	**35**	**40**	**45**	**50**	**55**	**60**
100,000	$8.76	8.76	9.01	10.88	13.01	17.94	24.57	33.25
250,000	13.18	13.18	13.39	15.73	22.10	28.00	41.65	62.48
500,000	20.83	20.83	21.25	25.08	32.63	46.55	73.10	112.63
1,000,000	27.13	27.13	26.97	33.93	55.68	87.87	141.95	221.00
Female	**25**	**30**	**35**	**40**	**45**	**50**	**55**	**60**
100,000	$8.33	8.33	8.50	10.03	11.48	14.71	18.45	26.35
250,000	11.90	11.90	12.11	14.45	19.55	25.71	30.23	43.50
500,000	17.85	17.85	18.28	22.53	26.54	37.85	53.13	78.20
1,000,000	32.04	31.45	32.30	29.58	46.11	67.86	102.00	152.15

* Quotes based on a composite of participating carriers, which have at least an A rating by S&P. Your rate may differ due to your health, smoking, or other activities. Rates subject to underwriting and state availability. InsWeb is a service offered by InsWeb Insurance Services, Inc., a licensed agency in most states (CA #0C24350).

Source: InsWeb, rates effective as of August, 2005, used with permission Sources: Ron Panko, "Closing the Gender Gap," Best's Review, August 2000, accessed April 4, 2009, http://www3.ambest.com/Frames/FrameServer.asp?AltSrc=23&Tab=1&Site=bestreview&refnum=10974; Insweb, http://www.insweb.com, accessed August 2005.

3.4   Interest Rate Considerations in Retirement Planning

The rough retirement model that has been discussed so far ignores the interest rate, changes in the purchasing power of money, and changes in the general standard of living. It must be corrected to deal with these factors, which can be done in an accurate actuarial manner, but the following less accurate way gives a better general picture.

A retirement plan has the advantage that its financing can be spread over a relatively long period: the employment period and the retirement period. Over such a long period, interest rates cannot be ignored. Thus, we shall examine some simple interest rate calculations. Imagine a person saves $1 per year over forty-five years. The amount saved by the end of the period (the future value of the stream of savings—as discussed in Chapter 4) depends on the interest rate. If the money is saved at 0 percent interest, the person will accumulate $45. At 2 percent interest, the amount saved by the end of the period will be $72. (The first dollar gained interest for forty-five years, the second for forty-four years, and so forth.) In other words, interest added approximately 60 percent to the $45 principal. At 4 percent, the amount jumps to $121, meaning that for each dollar saved, the (compounded) interest contributes approximately another $2. At 6 percent, the interest effect is even more impressive: each dollar saved brings in close to $4 in interest. With such a high interest rate, the total amount of the savings at the end of the period is about $212, approximately five times larger than the amount saved. These computations are summarized in Table 17.5 below.

TABLE 17.5   The Effect of Interest Rates on the Accumulation of Retirement Savings

(Future Value of an Annuity)	Interest Rate			
Saving Period (Years to Retirement)	**0%**	**2%**	**4%**	**6%**
1	1.0	1.0	1.0	1.0
15	15.0	17.3	20.0	23.3
25	25.0	32.0	41.6	54.9
35	35.0	50.0	73.7	111.4
45	45.0	71.9	121.0	212.7

This simple illustration demonstrates that the interest rate cannot be ignored in long-range planning. One must make a decision: Who should work for retirement—oneself or the interest rate? And the answer is obvious. Being able to finance retirement throughout forty-five years, at an interest rate of 6 percent, means that the financial burden that we discussed earlier could be about five times smaller than with zero percent interest.

There are a couple of caveats to the above discussion:

1. Compounding has a strong effect when the savings period is long. One must start the retirement planning at a young age in order to leave enough time for compounding to have a significant effect. A shorter savings period drastically cuts the contribution of the interest in the saved fund. Unfortunately, most young people joining the labor force do not think about their retirement and by the time they start thinking about it, they have to do most of the saving by themselves without much support from the interest rate.

2. Significant effects are reached only with high interest rates. Factors like inflation or a continuous increase in the standard of living operate in the opposite direction to the incoming interest rate. Deducting such factors from the interest rate and accumulating the savings at the lower real (net) effective interest rate results in lower real savings at the end of the period.

From the individual's point of view, the interest rate is an exogenous parameter. However, there is a very strong connection between retirement savings and market interest rates. The above discussion demonstrates that people are expected to save a substantial part of their income just to finance their retirement. These savings are a major component of the aggregated national savings, which in turn affect economic growth and the market interest rate.[4]

The Financial Risk Issue

The interest rate is a major economic parameter that affects and is affected by a variety of complicated political and economic processes. These processes are becoming very complex in the current "flat world" global economy, and they create frequent changes and fluctuations in the interest rates. This introduces a substantial financial risk factor into financial and retirement planning. It is hard to predict future interest rates in the world markets without a reliable, complex econometric model. One feature, though, seems to be quite certain: most developed countries are going to suffer a reduction in the numbers of the working-age population, and they will therefore experience a concomitant decline in the growth potential. The developing countries, on the other hand, will have substantial population and industrial growth, but they will probably soon be facing constraints on their growth due to market limitations. This may indicate that the real interest rates will not exceed, for example, 3 percent in the long run and that the risk factor resulting from interest rate uncertainties is significant.

Some countries have successfully stabilized their social insurance systems (as will be discussed at length in Chapter 18) by directly and indirectly guaranteeing interest rates. The current trend, however, puts the entire burden of interest risks on individuals. This element requires special treatment in the risk management of our personal risks. Low interest rates means that, on the average, the retirement of most people will be financed mainly by the direct contribution (by employers, employees, and the government), and only a relatively small part will be financed by interest accumulation. And the result will be that the burden of financing the retirement system will remain quite heavy.

In the United States, the government does not guarantee market interest rates, but it does influence them through monetary policy. The Federal Reserve (the Fed), for example, directly controls the federal funds rate. This is the rate that private banks charge each other for loans, and it is manipulated to alter the supply of money. The federal funds rate is a determinant of the prime rate, or the interest rate that banks charge their most credit-worthy customers. On the other hand, the rate that banks pay customers on their savings investments will generally be something below the prime rate (so that positive returns on lending activities are not canceled out). In light of the 2008–2009 economic recession, the Fed adjusted the federal funds rate to a target between 0 and 0.25 percent on December 16, 2008, in a radical move designed to increase lending.[5] In response, prime was lowered to 3.25 percent.[6] While this was good news for people holding outstanding bank notes, mortgages, or credit card debt, it was bad news for those counting on interest rates to help fund their retirements. Of course, banks are hardly the only source of interest rate returns for individuals saving for retirement.

Interest rates higher than those offered through private banks are available to individuals investing in mutual funds, money market accounts, corporate debt, and other long- and short-term investment vehicles. The interest rate will vary considerably depending on the source, but there is a national indicator often used as a benchmark in rate making: the U.S. Treasury bill (T-bill). T-bills are government bonds paying guaranteed, fixed interest rates. Because the government cannot default on its loan obligations, the yield on a T-bill can be said to be a risk-free rate of return. Thus, investments in the private sector must offer a risk premium to entice investors into taking on greater risk. No one would invest in risky private securities if the same return was available from risk-free government bonds. The ten-year annual T-bill rate for 2008 was 3.66 percent. In comparison, the rate on AAA-rated corporate bonds was 5.63 percent. The average ten-year annual T-bill rate since 2000 has been 4.6 percent. However, this compares with a 6.7 percent average for the decade of the 1990s.[7]

The crux of this discussion is that investing for retirement entails its own longevity risk due to interest rates. Consider, for example, an individual who retired in 1999 at the age of sixty-five. What if he were born ten years later and retired in 2009 at the age of sixty-five? Examining interest rates alone, it is hard to imagine this retiree being better off today than if he retired ten years ago. The boom period of the 1990s produced much higher returns, on balance, than are available today. Certainly, one's personal investment savvy is an important factor in the performance of his portfolio. However, when even the risk-free rate of return yielded 2 percent more during the 1990s, it is easy to see how a conservative, unsophisticated investor would be in a better position if he had to rely on his retirement savings in that decade. Equity investments, too, performed better in the 1990s than in the 2000s. The Dow Jones Industrial Average trended upward for the entire 1990s, peaking on the last day of the decade. The 2000s has seen more volatility in the Dow and a sharp dropoff in 2007.[8] Diversification can improve one's portfolio, but in a time when both the equity and bond markets are not what they once were, it may be impossible to restore what was lost. Indeed, many individuals who felt secure in building their nest eggs for retirement in the 1990s and again in the mid 2000s have seen those gains erased by the 2008–2009 recession when the Dow lost 50 percent of its value by March 2009. Some of the specific effects will be discussed in Chapter 21. In short, just as longevity risk can be equated as the risk of living too long, so too can it be examined from the standpoint of investing for too long in volatile markets. We cannot control when we are born, nor can we predict the future, so saving for retirement is a delicate balance involving short- and long-term investment mixes and asset diversification.

The Retirement Age

Most countries do not have a mandatory retirement age but some do. Given the great importance of the retirement age in determining Social Security and other pension arrangements (see Chapter 18 and Chapter 21), and due to the significant implications for socioeconomic issues, it is time to reexamine this parameter. We do not intend to go into the complex issue of the optimal retirement age, but it is clear that this topic justifies a deep and thorough study from a balanced social, political, and economic point of view.

Deferment of Retirement

One possible way to mitigate the increased longevity problem is by deferring the retirement age.[9] When retirement ages were first determined by the government of Germany in 1873, less than 40 percent of the people survived to the age of sixty-five. Today, 80 to 85 percent of males and more than 90 percent of females in developed countries live to that age and beyond. People reaching the age of sixty-five today are often in good physical and mental shape and are often willing to continue working. Some countries are actively moving toward the deferment of the retirement age, and some are already accepting a retirement age of sixty-seven. However, this trend conflicts with another major force of the declining demand for labor.[10] The present production capacity of developed countries is large, and it can be achieved with only part of the potential labor force. To mitigate the effects of the resulting growth of unemployment, some European countries are reducing the monthly working hours of employees. There is an inevitable clash between the forces driving toward a higher retirement age and the pressures on young populations that have to join the labor force.

Longevity is one of the most important risks that affect our economies. Planners of retirement systems typically focus on the economic and financial aspects and often ignore the basic demographic considerations. Nonetheless, the drastic changes in longevity and life expectancies should not be ignored.

KEY TAKEAWAYS

In this section you studied the following about longevity, the risk of living too long:

- Old age may invite increased hardships through higher costs, reduced income, and health problems.
- Modern medicine, better living conditions, and genetics are all contributing to greater life expectancies.
- Actuarially, 85 to 92 percent of the population will reach retirement age.
- Historically, life expectancy at birth has increased on the average by one year for every three to four calendar years.
- Conditional life expectancies must be considered in retirement planning—not just one's life expectancy at birth but one's probability of surviving to each incremental age.
- Males should be prepared to fund and additional fifteen to twenty of living expenses after retirement.
- Females can expect a longer postretirement period than males.
- Compounding interest rates have the power to reduce the financial burden of retirement planning.
- The earlier one begins saving for retirement, the longer interest rates can be taken advantage of to help finance future living expenses.
- The reality of low real interest rates (adjusted for cost-of-living increases and inflation) is that most people must finance their retirements through active, direct contributions (rather than relying on interest and time).

DISCUSSION QUESTIONS

1. Who bears the risks associated with living too long?
2. Why is living too long considered a risk? Assuming that one's health is not failing, isn't longevity a good thing?
3. Why can't people simply plan in their working years to put aside enough money to cover an additional ten or fifteen years of retirement?
4. What is unreliable about the life expectancy figure for one's year of birth as a predictive tool?
5. What is the relationship between aggregated retirement savings and interest rates? What problems might this relationship create?

4. THE RISKS RELATED TO HEALTH AND DISABILITY

LEARNING OBJECTIVES

In this section we elaborate on the following:

- **Why health risks are the most difficult of the life cycle risks to manage**
- **Global health statistics regarding medicine**
- **Cost as a function of medical care**
- **Where health costs are focused throughout one's lifetime**

4.1 Health and Age-Related Processes

Health and disability risk is the third category of life cycle risks. They can be defined as the risks that our physical and mental well-being will be diminished throughout our lifetime. In the case of disease or disability, one will have to pay for increased costs (hospitalization, surgery, doctors, medicines, and prolonged courses of treatment), while still having to finance the regular living expenses, like food, housing, and debt payments for oneself and for the other members of the household.

With costs escalating, health care is becoming the number one retirement-related problem in the developed economies. As with all other risks, the most effective treatment seems to be prevention, which can be accomplished through dieting, exercising, preemptive medicine, and a variety of other ways. Indeed, some of the sicknesses of old age stem from behavior during our youth and could probably be treated at that time.

health and disability risk

Life cycle risk that physical and mental well-being will be diminished throughout one's lifetime.

On average, some of the lifetime health-related costs are concentrated around the very young ages, but most are concentrated around the final years. Thus, due to the increased life expectancy and the fact that older people often suffer from all manner of medical problems, health costs are becoming associated more and more with retirement problems.

Global Health Statistics

World Health Organization (WHO) statistics show a positive correlation between the development level of the economy and the percentage of gross domestic product (GDP) spent on health-related costs. Typically, health-related expenditures reach 6 to 13 percent of GDP in developed nations such as United States, compared to 2 to 9 percent in the less-developed countries. In terms of per capita figures, the gap is very noticeable: an average annual per capita expenditure of $20 to $200 in the less-developed countries, compared to $1,800 to $4,000 in developed economies (the dollar values used conversions of the local currencies at international dollar rates).

The World Bank and the Global Health Organization suggested a new index to measure the global burden of disease: disability adjusted life years (DALY). It combines weighted information about morbidity and mortality, and it is expressed in terms of the numbers of healthy years lost. Each state of health is assigned a disability weighting on a scale from zero (perfect health) to one (death). To calculate the burden of a certain disease, the disability weighting is multiplied by the number of years lived in that health state and is added to the number of years lost due to that disease. Years of life in childhood and old age are assigned lower values in the weighting process. DALY is discounted to better reflect future burdens (an annual interest rate of 3 percent interest is assumed). It is not a perfect indicator and has a substantial degree of subjective judgment and uncertainty,[11] but it is a fairly useful instrument for describing a complex problem by a single measure. A complementary measure is the quality adjusted life years (QALY), which measures the years lived in good health and is used to calculate healthy adjusted life expectancy (HALE). Published by the WHO for the entire population at birth, the HALE figures run in the range of thirty-five to forty-five years for the least-developed countries, around fifty to sixty years for more developed countries, and around sixty-five to seventy-five years for most progressive nations. The difference between the life expectancy and HALE is a measure of the average equivalent number of years lost due to bad health and disability.

The expectation of lost healthy years at birth does not show a clear-cut distinction between the least-developed and most-developed countries. In some of the least-developed countries with the poorest health conditions, the number of years lost due to poor health can be fairly low—even three to four years—simply because life expectancy itself is very low (thirty-five to forty years). In others, it can be as high as eight to eleven years, compared to a life expectancy of around sixty to sixty-five years. In the developed countries, the variation of this figure is somewhat lower, and the expectation of lost healthy years at birth runs around six to nine years. A better measure might be the ratio between the expected lost years and the life expectancy at birth. For the developed countries, this figure typically runs around 10 percent, compared to 15 to 18 percent for the least-developed countries.

The main problem is that a substantial part of the years lost due to poor health occurs during the retirement period. A better analysis would be found in the ratio of lost years to life expectancy at retirement (although some lost years relate to the preretirement period). Calculating these ratios with WHO data for the life expectancy of sixty-year-old males shows that these ratios are very high (67 to 100 percent) in the least-developed countries and in the 35 to 45 percent range for developed economies. These ratios show that health concerns are becoming a major part of the retirement issue.

4.2 The Future of Medicine and Costs

About half of all deaths of adult males and about a quarter of all deaths of adult females are due to cardiovascular diseases, hypertension, and renal diseases. Another quarter of all deaths of adult males and about half of all deaths of adult females are related to cancer. In other words, about three-quarters of the deaths of the adult population are related to these two major groups of sickness. Major breakthroughs in these areas may lead to a remarkable decline of death rates, and this may lead to a further substantial increase in life expectancy (a reduction of mortality probabilities in all age groups by half can increase life expectancy at birth by about five years).

Important advances in medicine are expected in the future due to the improved knowledge and understanding of genetics and complex biochemical processes, better screening devices, smarter surgical technologies, and improved care (and maybe even due to improved understanding of the balance between body and spirit). All these will affect a variety of medical problems such as cancer, heart diseases, diabetes, strokes, neurology and gerontology, metabolic diseases, and more. Certain factors may interfere, delay, and even stop the development of such conditions. Among these factors could be economic and financial forces, global epidemics of new diseases, contamination and pollution, and political factors.

The sophistication of medical procedures cannot arrive without increased costs. Part of these increases is concentrated at the young ages. There are many conflicting factors; some tend to increase health costs for the young population, while others decrease them. For example, in developed countries, highly paid women may prefer not to have repeated pregnancies, and the use of surrogates for having children may increase. Technological developments may even enable families to conceive and nurture a fetus outside the human womb. On the other hand, genetic testing is becoming much more precise, so fewer families will have children suffering from physical and mental disabilities. (On the other hand, the ability to save the very young fetus may increase the prevalence of other birth defects.)

For the older part of the population, most factors operate in one direction: toward a continuous increase in medical and health costs. Among these are a variety of surgical procedures meant to replace or fix problems of aging or failing organs (transplants, angioplasty), special aids (hearing aids, dentures, vision support, mobility instruments), and new expensive drugs. In developed countries, conditions such as diabetes, obesity, and depression are becoming more prevalent as contributing factors in the causes of death for older age groups. Diseases that once killed people (like Tuberculosis and Polio) long before the above conditions could have a significant health impact have all but been eradicated.

4.3   The Probability of Health Risks

Particular health-related risk management solutions will be handled in greater detail in Chapter 22, but at this point we would like to say a few words about the probabilities. Unlike the mortality and longevity cases, we have no health and disability tables from which the relevant probabilities could be derived. There is an objective difficulty in getting the detailed data needed for the analysis of such a complex issue. Unlike death, disability is often a reversible event; it could be partial or full, and it could be temporary or permanent. Moreover, the event may be defined in a variety of ways: medical (e.g., the loss of a particular limb), psychological, or functional (there are people with severe disabilities—such as blindness—who can function better than many other healthy people). We can only hope that technological developments will enable us in the near future to use better databases and resolve these issues. Due to these reasons it is difficult to create the equivalent of mortality tables or life tables for the health area and, thus, estimates of the probabilities. However, the first steps have already been made in that direction with the WHO resources described previously.

The Effects of Smoking

The probabilities of dying and surviving depend greatly on the particular population studied in a given mortality table. Recall that the 2001 CSO mortality table is based on the insured population in the United States. However, the study was divided also into two subpopulations: smokers and nonsmokers. Some selected figures were taken from the statistics to demonstrate the potential wide differences between the mortality and survival rates of two distinct populations. Simultaneously, we can get some important and useful information about the potential impact of smoking.

TABLE 17.6 **The Number of Survivors at Age x out of an Initial Population of 1,000,000 (Ultimate Figures) as Derived from the USA 2001 CSO Table**

Age	Male		Female	
	Nonsmoker	Smoker	Nonsmoker	Smoker
0	1,000,000	1,000,000	1,000,000	1,000,000
15	994,822	994,822	996,187	996,187
20	990,790	990,165	994,176	993,937
30	980,995	974,651	989,048	986,419
40	970,024	954,815	980,487	971,858
50	948,455	913,895	963,645	941,426
60	898,373	824,017	920,087	861,264
65	848,793	744,298	880,502	793,026
70	772,499	636,113	824,182	703,167
80	514,495	353,797	630,748	446,153
90	154,508	79,032	298,023	150,271
99	11,361	4,302	51,122	19,743

Sources: Processed by the authors from the American Academy of Actuaries CSO Task Force Report, June 2002, http://www.actuary.org/life/

CSO_0702.asp (accessed April 4, 2009); 2001 CSO Ultimate Table.

As derived from Table 17.6, the probability of a nonsmoking male surviving to age sixty-five is 84.8 percent, whereas that of a smoker is only 74.4 percent. In other words, the probability of dying before the age of sixty-five is 15.2 percent for nonsmokers and 25.6 percent for smokers. Smoking takes an even greater toll at higher ages. The probability of survival to age eighty is 51.4 percent for a nonsmoking man, while that of a smoker is only 35.4 percent. The probabilities for females can easily be derived from the above table. The differences between smoking and nonsmoking females are also high, although slightly lower than those for males.

KEY TAKEAWAYS

In this section you studied the following risks to health throughout one's lifetime:

- Because the health and disability life cycle risk is ever-present, it occurs often and with some severity.
- Global health statistics reveal a positive correlation between the development level of the economy and the percentage of GDP spent on health-related costs.
- The World Health Organization's disability adjusted life years (DALY) combines weighted information about morbidity and mortality to express the numbers of healthy years lost for a given population.
- Cost rises with the sophistication of medicine.
- Health costs are concentrated at different points in a lifespan (most notably the extremes).

DISCUSSION QUESTIONS

1. When are the majority of health-related risks borne in a lifetime?
2. What relationship would you expect to see between the figures produced at the same time by DALY and HALE on a given population?
3. Do you think smoking is the sole reason why life expectancies of smokers are lower than those of nonsmokers? Why might smokers have reduced life expectancies that are not reflected by the mortality table?

---

5. GLOBAL TRENDS AND THEIR IMPACT ON DEMOGRAPHY AND THE LIFE CYCLE RISKS

LEARNING OBJECTIVES

In this section we elaborate on the following:

- **International demographic features as presented by population pyramids**
- **The effects of technology on populations and what this means for life cycle risks**
- **The implications of the ranking of countries by size and analysis of demographic growth for the future of retirement systems and the management of life cycle risks**
- **The implications of dependency ratios**

5.1 Demographic Changes Affecting Life Cycle Risks

In this section we focus on the impact of the technological waves described in the Links on demography, the social structure, and our health.[12] These waves are responsible for the growing cost of the age-related processes that mainly affect well-being during the retirement period and the need to countermeasure them by early preventive treatment. They will also affect the future retirement systems. The current retirement systems (in the form of nationalized social insurance programs and union pension funds, discussed in Chapter 18 and Chapter 19) are becoming products of the past in urgent need of major revisions. Popular solutions to the retirement problems are expected to become unsuitable to the populations they serve (as expressed by the rapid erosion of the value of saving plans around the globe at the end of 2008).

Although retirement may not seem to be the most pressing of issues in developing economies, it needs to be addressed without delay. Retirement systems are key to financing the other, more immediately imminent problems of these economies. The future retirement system will likely take the form of mandatory privatized plans, to be supported by some form of governmental social security system that will take care of special cases that cannot be handled by the private sector. This approach has already been successfully adopted by some nations (see "Does Privatization Provide a More Equitable Solution" and "The Future of Social Security" in Chapter 18).

5.2   Changing Mortality and Birth Patterns

The development of a country triggers major changes in birth and mortality patterns, which, in turn, results in dramatic changes in life expectancy, the age structure of the population, and dependency ratios. Developed countries enjoy declines in both mortality and birth rates, better sanitation and health, improved nutrition, increased use of hospitals, greater accessibility to doctors, and more. During the development phase of a country, birth rates and fertility rates decline as well, but at a much slower pace than mortality. It often takes a few decades for the number of births per mother to reach a significantly lower level. This outcome is not just a technical matter of faster spread and wider use of contraceptives, but a deeper cultural (and religious) issue. The World Health Organization (WHO) statistics show that in many less-developed countries, the use of contraceptives is limited to just 5 to 15 percent of the population, compared to about three-quarters of the population in the developed countries. The interaction with declining mortality means that the number of births declines slowly, but the number of surviving children per mother grows rapidly. The average number of births per woman can be around five to six in the least-developed countries, and this fertility rate slowly declines to around two births per woman. At fertility rates around two per mother, the natural growth of a population stops (or even turns into a slow decline). The fertility ratio continues to drop to around 1.5 and lower—meaning that these populations are shrinking, unless there is a significant inflow of immigrants in a country.

The immediate result of these trends of mortality and birth patterns is the experiences of "baby booms." This is expressed by growth in the number of surviving children. In the absence of major migration, the population structure is quite predictable for several decades (almost a century, in fact). During the first few years, there is remarkable growth in the number of school-aged children, and two decades later, a substantial increase in the figures for university students, then another four decades of a large work force, followed by a few decades with a large population of retired people. The baby boom turns into a geriatric boom! Together with the decreasing mortality of adults, there is drastic growth in the number of people needing some old age services. Concurrently, by the time the baby boomers get old, the gradually declining birth rates would reach the point of lowest proportion (and often also the absolute number) of young children. Figure 17.3 offers a schematic explanation for the baby boom phenomenon.

Population Pyramids

The mortality and birth patterns described above affect the age structure of the population. This is best perceived through a population pyramid, a graphical presentation of the age structure (distributions) of the population (in percentages or in absolute numbers). Because the age structure of a population is typically quite similar for males and females, the graph is almost symmetrical and looks like a pyramid. The population pyramid is essential for the understanding of dependency ratios and retirement policy problems. We will discuss these issues after describing at some length the changing patterns of population pyramids in countries that are experiencing rapid technological changes.

An examination of almost any agrarian economy typically shows a pyramid with a very large base (many young children) and a very pointed top (a very small number of old people). In such populations, the older people (over age sixty) are typically less than 5 percent of the population, whereas children below the age of fifteen can constitute around 40 percent. High mortality rates are also the main reason for the fast shortening of the bars at the higher age groups. These patterns characterize the pyramids of some of the countries that are expected to be among the top twenty largest countries by population within the first half of the twenty-first century. The pyramid for Ethiopia, with its very wide base, in Figure 17.4 serves as example of this general pattern. Those for Congo (Kinshasa), Nigeria, Pakistan, and the Philippines are quite similar.

FIGURE 17.3 **Changing Birth and Mortality Patterns in Developed Economies**

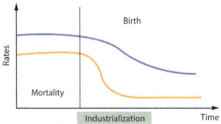

FIGURE 17.4 Age Pyramid for Ethiopia, 2000

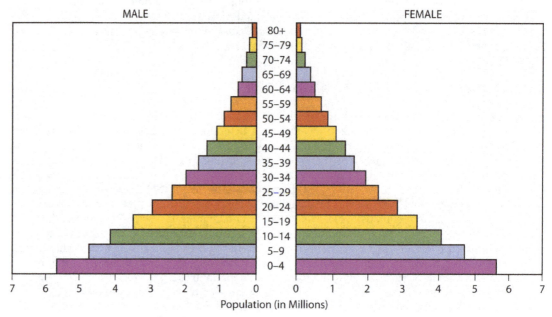

Source: U.S. Census Bureau, International Data Base.

Observing the development of the population pyramid of a country undergoing an industrial revolution immediately reveals the changing pattern. During the first years, the youngest age group (the base of the pyramid) gets wider due to the sudden reduction in mortality rates, which is not accompanied by an immediate decline in birth rates. The U.S. Bureau of the Census forecasts for Ethiopia in 2025 are presented in Figure 17.5. A comparison to the diagram in Figure 17.4 demonstrates the differences. Note the widening of the base of the pyramid due to the increased number of surviving children. The next age groups do not decline as fast as before due to the drastic reduction in infant mortality. Thus, the length of the bars does not decline as time passes. Note also the widening of the bars at the older ages at the top of the pyramid due to the generally declining mortality.

FIGURE 17.5 Age Pyramid for Ethiopia, 2025

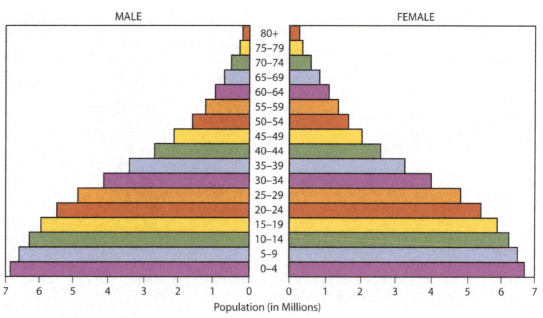

Source: U.S. Census Bureau, International Data Base.

FIGURE 17.6 Population Pyramid Summary for India, 2000–2050

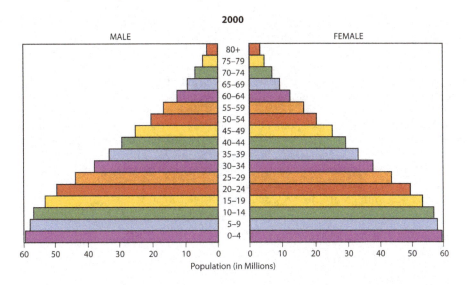

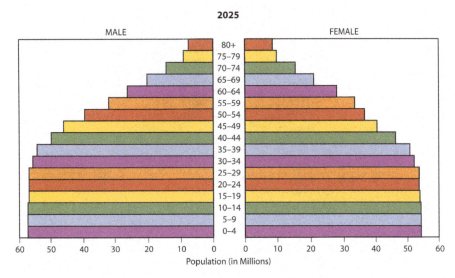

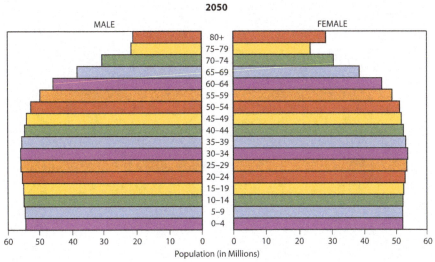

Source: U.S. Census Bureau, International Data Base.

A few decades later, as birth rates start to decline, the baby boom comes to an end, and the base of the pyramid gets narrower. Some of the developing countries are already showing this pattern, as demonstrated by India in Figure 17.6, from 2000 to 2025, and to 2050. Figure 17.6 shows how declining mortality rates quickly lead to a situation where most people who survived the early years continue to live for many years thereafter. Therefore, at any future point in time, the bars describing young age groups move upward (as the group gets older), but the length of the bar remains fairly constant. This makes the pyramid less and less pointed in appearance. After a few decades, when birth rates are significantly lower, the lower part of the pyramid becomes rectangular, or pillar-shaped.

The drastic decrease of births creates a situation in which we see a fully reversed age pyramid. Japan serves as an excellent example of this point. Similar patterns can be seen in western European countries. The pyramid of Germany serves as a good example of a country in which older people (above age sixty) are typically more than one-fifth, and sometimes even one-quarter of the entire population. The populations in France, Italy, and the United Kingdom follow similar patterns.

Two large countries deserve special mention. China has an age structure similar to that of a matured, developed country, but it has not experienced the natural evolutionary baby boom (see Figure 17.7). This is the result of the very strictly enforced birth control introduced by the Chinese government in recent decades. On the other hand, the United States, still has a rectangular-shaped population pyramid rather than an inverted pyramid (see Figure 17.8). The main reason for this anomaly is the absorption of many new immigrants into the population of the United States.

FIGURE 17.7 Population Pyramid Summary for China, 2000–2050

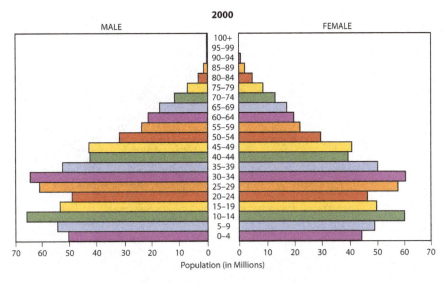

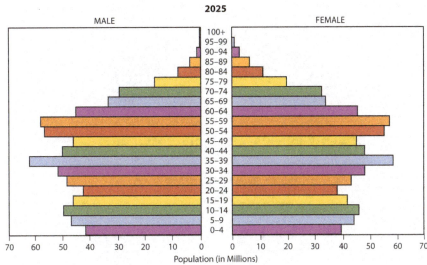

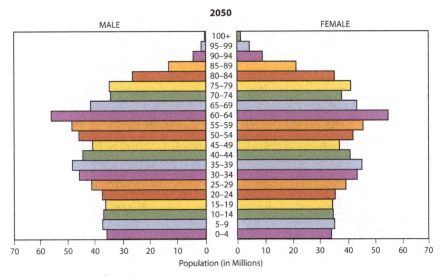

Source: U.S. Census Bureau, International Data Base.

FIGURE 17.8 Population Pyramid Summary for the United States, 2000–2050

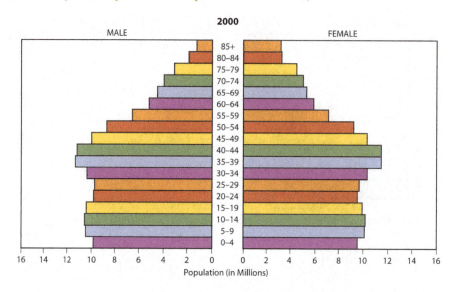

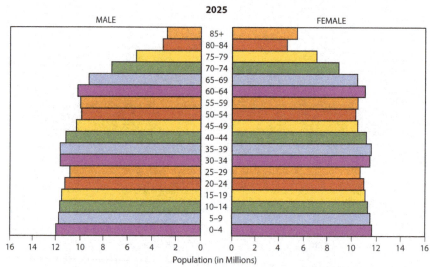

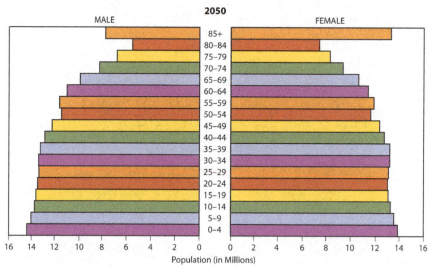

Source: U.S. Census Bureau, International Data Base.

Population and Dependency Ratios

The population structure is often translated into dependency ratios; that is, the ratios of dependents (children and people beyond working age) to the number of people in the working-age group. These ratios are quite stable over time, despite the drastically changing population structure. People in the working-age groups are typically one-half to two-thirds of the population, as you can see in the U.S. population pyramid of Figure 17.8. In agricultural countries, the number of children is large, but the number of elderly people is small. Dependency ratios tend to be around 75 to 100 percent. Countries in the middle have even lower dependency ratios (around 50 percent and sometimes even less). This is the result of complex trends: the birth rate and number of children has already declined, the number of elderly people has not yet increased substantially, and the baby boomers are already working adults.

The ratio between the older people and the younger ones is a more sensitive measure of the developmental stage. It changes dramatically: the ratio of people aged sixty-five or over to children below age five, for example, can be 3.5 to 4.0 in developed countries, compared to only 0.3 to 0.5 in the least-developed countries. This ratio gives a better idea of the future retirement problems: because most children are expected to survive until retirement, it shows how many retired people will have to be supported by one person in the working-age groups. It has been suggested that, in China, one child will eventually have to take care of two parents, four grandparents, and eight great-grandparents!

5.3   Effects on Employment Patterns

The 2007–2008 global economic recession and increased unemployment rates may be symptomatic to the changes driven by the technological changes of our time. One can no longer expect to be engaged in the same occupation throughout one's lifetime. Most people will have to change their occupations and professions several times during their careers and will change workplaces quite frequently throughout their lives. In such an environment, a traditional retirement arrangement based on a particular work place, with limited mobility, becomes inappropriate. Firms will be created, experience mergers and acquisitions, go through major reorganization, and sometimes collapse within fairly short periods if they are not capable of continuously adapting to the new markets, new competitors, new products, and new methods. The dramatic changes throughout the world's financial markets are the signs of a transition that will completely reshape the retirement systems of the world and handling of life cycle risks.

In this mobile and volatile work world, we will probably have to get used to continuously high unemployment rates, and may therefore need to structure a new system that enables unemployed people to survive during periods of joblessness at working age. Furthermore, the design of optimal retirement systems that will meet our needs in later years requires a good understanding of social, economic, and demographic trends that are by-products of profound technological changes with the power to completely reshape our environment, our needs, and our way of thinking.

Today, we recognize single-parent families, zero-parent families, same-sex families, blended families, virtual families, families of convenience, and more. A large proportion of women are being attracted to employment outside of their homes. The old concept that a man must be the primary bread-winner of the family, while the spouse is supposed to take care of the home, is dying. Both men and women work and take turns taking care of the home and family. A traditional retirement system, based mainly on the husband financing his wife's old age, is no longer relevant or valid.

In the heated public debates of recent years on the problems of Social Security (the topic of our next chapter), pension plans (the topic of Chapter 21), retirement systems, and the aging population, the financial viability of social insurance programs in modern economies (and especially in the United States) has been the focus of particular attention. Whatever the arguments in the debate, our environment is clearly changing rapidly and dramatically, and current popular solutions to retirement problems are expected to become obsolete very soon. If we are to prepare for completely new challenges, we have to ensure that the solutions are feasible for people over a relatively long period. This requires a good understanding of future economic and social trends.

KEY TAKEAWAYS

In this section you studied the following global demographic trends in relation to life cycle risks:

- Population distributions across different age ranges are changing in relation to technological changes in a country.
- Population pyramids can be used to represent the age structure of a population in any country.
- Older age groups increase in number and the youngest age groups decrease in number with the maturation of countries, when mortality rates improve and the adoption of technology becomes more widespread.
- The ranking of countries by size and the analysis of demographic growth has implications for the future of retirement systems and the management of life cycle risks.
- Dependency ratios express the ratio of dependents (children and people beyond working age) to the number of people in the working-age group.

DISCUSSION QUESTIONS

1. What effects are contributing to the inversion of population pyramids?
2. What are dependency ratios? What is their significance with respect to life cycle risks?
3. Describe briefly some of the population figures. What implication does this hold for future income needs?
4. Do you agree that the demographic changes across different countries are a response to predictable trends? Why or why not?

6. APPENDIX: HOW MUCH LIFE INSURANCE TO BUY?

In this section, the income continuation needs for a single-parent family, the Dowds, will be evaluated to see how much life insurance is necessary. Although the various types of life insurance products will be discussed at length in Chapter 19, this exercise is intended to satisfy the needs analysis approach to dealing with mortality risk. The risk management component of the financial planning process will be used to look at the family's present resources, income needs, and insurance needs in the event of the wage earner's death. Coverages for property and casualty, health, disability, and retirement are covered in Case 1 of Chapter 23.

6.1 Data Collection

The Dowd family has three members:

- Sharon, age thirty-five
- Liz, age six
- Bob, age four

Liz and Bob see a pediatrician at least once a year. Sharon had a routine checkup about six months ago. All three are apparently healthy.

Financial Situation

Sharon is a branch bank manager whose gross yearly income is $50,000. Her former husband lives in another state and does not pay alimony or contribute to child support.

A balance sheet and cash flow statement are important in evaluating Sharon's current ability to meet her needs and in establishing postloss objectives. Sharon has constructed Table 17.7 and Table 17.8. On the balance sheet, you may wonder why the value of furniture and other personal property is only $10,000. The sums listed are liquidation values; these items probably have a replacement value between $30,000 and $40,000. But our concern, in the event of Sharon's death, is how much the items would sell for if they had to be liquidated to meet family income needs. Unlike houses and automobiles, limited demand exists for used furniture and clothing.

TABLE 17.7 **Sharon Dowd's Balance Sheet (End of Year Market Value)**

Assets	
Checking account	$ 500
Certificates of deposit	3,000
Life insurance cash values	4,500
401(k) retirement plan (vested value)	15,000
Automobile	10,000
House	85,000
Furniture and other personal property	10,000
Total	$ 128,000
Liabilities	
Credit card balances	$ 1,000
Other household account balances	500
Automobile loan balance	8,000
Life insurance loan against cash values	4,000
Home mortgage balance	75,000
Total	$ 88,500
Net Worth	$ 39,500

TABLE 17.8 **Sharon Dowd's Annual Cash Flow Statement**

Income	
Sharon's salary	$50,000
Investment income	*
Total cash flow	$ 50,000
Taxes	
Social Security	$ 3,825
Federal income	$4,300
State income	$1,700
Total SS and income taxes	$9,825
Disposable personal income	$40,175
Expenses	
State sales taxes	$1,300
Personal property taxes (home and auto)	$1,175
$401(k) retirement savings contribution	$2,000
Dependent medical & dental insurance	$1,500
House payments, including homeowner's insurance	$8,900
Utilities	$2,700
Food	$3,200
Automobile payments and expenses	$3,600
Child care	$4,500
Clothes	$1,800
Miscellaneous expenses	$9,000
Total	$39,675
Savings	$500
* Investment earnings of approximately $1,500 are being reinvested in the certificates of deposit and 401(k) plan.	

The family has four types of basic resources in addition to the assets shown in Table 17.7. These resources are provided by the following:

- Social Security (discussed in Chapter 18; for now, simply consider it a source of income)
- Sharon's employer
- Individual insurance
- Personal savings and investments

Based on Sharon's earnings history, we estimate that the following Social Security
benefits would be available to her and/or the children in the event of her death. Survivor benefits are expected (based on the current Social Security law) to keep pace with inflation.

Sharon's death: $255 burial allowance plus $600 per month survivor benefits to each child until each is age 18 (or age 19 if still a full-time high school student)

Sharon's employee benefit plan at the bank where she works provides her and the children with the benefits outlined in Table 17.9 (such benefits will be described in Chapter 19 to Chapter 22).

TABLE 17.9 Sharon Dowd's Employee Benefits

Group Life Insurance

- Term insurance equal to two times annual salary for active employees
- $5,000 term insurance for retirees

Short-Term Disability

Paid sick leave equal to income for 90 days

Long-Term Disability

Long-term disability (LTD) income to age 70 equal to two-thirds of annual salary in last year of employment, minus total Social Security and employer-provided pension benefits; 90-day waiting period; no adjustment for inflation.

Group Comprehensive Preferred Provider Medical Care

- $200 annual deductible per family member
- 90 percent coinsurance for preferred providers; 75 percent coinsurance for nonnetwork providers
- $1 million aggregate lifetime limit
- Stop-loss provision after $1,000 out-of-pocket coinsurance expenses per person per year
- Benefits terminate upon job termination or retirement

Dental Coverage

- $50 per person annual deductible; no deductible on preventive care
- 80 percent coinsurance
- $1,000 per person per year limit
- $1,000 per person lifetime limit on orthodontic work
- $50,000 aggregate family lifetime limit on other care
- Benefits terminate upon job termination or retirement

401(k) Plan

Employer matches 50 percent of employee contributions up to a maximum employee contribution of 6 percent of basic pay, subject to the annual maximum limit on 401(k) contributions.

Defined-Benefit Pension Plan

Pension at age sixty-five equal to 40 percent of average final three years salary, minus half of primary Social Security retirement benefit, with no provision for benefits to increase after retirement. Early retirement is allowed between ages 60 and 65, subject to a reduction in benefits. Reductions equal 4 percent for each year the retiree is below age sixty-five.

Individual Coverage

Sharon has a $15,000 whole life insurance policy that her parents purchased when she was young and turned over to Sharon when she finished college. Sharon recently borrowed most of the policy's $4,500 cash value to help make the down payment on the family home. She purchased credit life insurance to cover the balance of her automobile loan. She has not purchased life or disability insurance associated with her home mortgage.

Personal Savings and Investments

At the present time, Sharon's personal savings and investments are small, consisting of $3,000 in certificates of deposit at her bank and a $15,000 vested value in her 401(k) plan. Her yearly savings of $500 are 1 percent of her gross income. In addition, she is contributing 4 percent of gross income to her 401(k) plan, and her employer matches 50 percent of this amount. If these saving rates can be continued over time and earn reasonable returns, her total savings and investments will grow quickly.

6.2 Objectives

In Case of Death

In the event of her premature death, Sharon would like her children to live with her sister, Kay, and Kay's husband, Robert, who have expressed a willingness to assume these responsibilities. However, Sharon has not formally created a legal document expressing this wish. Kay and Robert have three small children of their own, and Sharon would not want her children to be a financial burden to them. Taking care of her children's nonfinancial needs is all that Sharon expects from Kay and Robert.

Sharon's values influence her objectives. Her parents paid almost all her expenses, including the upkeep of a car while she earned a bachelor's degree. Sharon recognizes that her children are currently benefiting from her above-average income. When they reach college, she wants them to concentrate on their studies and enjoy extracurricular activities without having to work during the academic year. They would be expected to work during the summers to earn part of their spending money for school. Sharon decides that, if she dies prematurely, she wants to provide $12,000 per year before taxes for each child through age seventeen, when they will graduate from high school, both having been born in August. During their four years of college, Sharon wants $18,000 per year available for each child. She realizes that inflation can devastate a given level of income in only a few years. Thus, she wants her expressed objectives to be fulfilled in real (uninflated) dollars. We will present a simple planning solution to this problem.

6.3 Alternative Solutions/Exposure Evaluation

The next step in the financial planning process requires determining the following:

- The amount of money required to meet Sharon's objectives
- Any gaps that exist between what is desired and Sharon's current financial resources
- Alternatives available to fill the gaps

Money Required for Death

Determination of the amount of money required to meet Sharon's objectives for her children in the event of her premature death is complicated by the following:

- We do not know when Sharon will die.
- The family's income needs extend into the future possibly eighteen years (assuming Sharon dies now and income is provided until her younger child is age twenty-two).
- Social Security will make its payments monthly over fourteen of the eighteen years.
- Sharon's two life insurance policies (and any new policies) would most likely make lump-sum payments at the time of her death, although her objective calls for the provision of support over many years.
- Lump sums may be liquidated over the period of income need, but we need to be sure the money does not run out before the period ends.
- The effects of inflation must be recognized.

Life Insurance Planning and Need Analysis

With some simplifying assumptions, these problems can be solved by a technique that we will call **life insurance planning**. The technique is static in the sense that it considers only the worst possible scenario: Sharon dies this year. Also, the technique does not recognize various changes (e.g., remarriage and a third child) that could occur at some point during the planning period.

Figure 17.9 reflects the assumption that Sharon dies today by showing Liz's and Bob's current ages on the left, on the horizontal axis. The figure continues until Sharon's objectives are met when Bob is assumed to complete college at age twenty-two.

life insurance planning

A technique that considers only the worst possible scenario.

below as a life insurance resource. Sharon's net needs after recognizing existing resources are as follows:

Total needs		$277,800
Resources (minus):		
Net worth	$ 39,500	
Group life insurance	$100,000	
Individual life insurance	$11,000	
Credit life insurance	$8,000	$158,500
Net needs		$119,300

Solutions

Sharon could resolve this $119,300 shortage in one of three ways. First, she could reevaluate her objectives, decide to lower the amount of financial support for Liz and Bob, and calculate a lower total. Second, she could decide to tighten her budget and increase her savings/investment program. Third, she could buy an additional life insurance policy in the amount of, let's say, $125,000. Life insurance premiums would vary upward from approximately $175 for next year for an annual renewable term policy to higher amounts for other types of insurance. Buying additional life insurance is probably Sharon's best option. Savings as an alternative to life insurance is not a good solution because she could die before contributing much to her savings program. Nevertheless, she should continue to save.

Other Life Insurance Planning Issues

Sharon's situation certainly does not cover all planning possibilities. For example, a person with a disabled child might want to extend the family dependency period far beyond age twenty-two. Another person might want to contribute to a spouse's support for the remainder of his or her life. In this case, a good option is using the life insurance planning technique to quantify the need up to an advanced age, such as sixty-five, and getting price quotations on a life annuity for the remainder of the person's lifetime.

7. REVIEW AND PRACTICE

1. Why is the time period observed in life table calculation important?

2. How can the economic value of life be calculated? What does the result mean?

3. What income streams should be taken into consideration when assessing economic value by the PV method?

4. Using the PV method, what is the economic value of a forty-year-old man who earns an average annual income of $130,000 for his lifetime at an interest rate of 3 percent?

5. Why might the results of the family needs analysis and the PV method of determining economic value be so similar?

6. If both the PV value and needs analysis methods produce similar results with respect to a person's economic value, why aren't life insurance products typically made available at these amounts?

7. Do you see any fundamental problems with the methods of estimating economic value, other than ethical considerations?

8. Distinguish between select and ultimate tables.

9. Mary Koonce describes herself as an optimist who does not wish to dwell on the unpleasant what-ifs in life. She is urged by her financial planner to perform a family needs analysis to insure against the risk of premature death. Mary insists this is unnecessary because she already made such an assessment ten years ago and has a life insurance policy guaranteeing a $250,000 death benefit. Mary is divorced, has two teenage sons and a seven-year-old daughter, and purchased her first home a year ago. Do you agree with Mary's judgment regarding her needs analysis? If you were her financial advisor, what would you tell her?

10. In light of the significant demographic changes taking place in global populations, do world governments have a greater responsibility to provide for the retirement of their aged citizens, directly or indirectly? Why or why not?

11. Can you conclude from the World Health Organization statistics on medical costs that greater spending on health and wellness has a positive impact on longevity and/or mortality? Why or why not?

ENDNOTES

1. There could be substantial gaps between objective and subjective values, there could be differences between the point of view of the individual versus that of a government, and so forth.

2. See Y. Kahane, *Life Insurance, Pension Funds, and Retirement Saving Programs: A Handbook for Business and Personal Financial Planning* (Isreal: Ateret Publishing House, 1983). Published in Hebrew.

3. U.S. Census Bureau, "The 2009 Statistical Abstract," The National Data Book, http://www.census.gov/compendia/statab/cats/births_deaths_marriages_divorces/life_expectancy.html (accessed April 4, 2009).

4. Martin Feldstein, "Social Security, Induced Retirement, and Aggregate Capital Accumulation," *Journal of Political Economy* 82, no. 5 (September/October 1974): 905–26.

5. Board of Governors of the Federal Reserve System, "Press Release," December 16, 2008, http://www.federalreserve.gov/newsevents/press/monetary/20081216b.htm (accessed March 10, 2009).

6. *Wall Street Journal*, Market Data Center: Money Rates, March 9, 2009. http://online.wsj.com/mdc/public/page/2_3020-moneyrate.html. Accessed March 10. 2009.

7. Board of Governors of the Federal Reserve System, "Federal Reserve Statistical Release: Selected Interest Rates," http://www.federalreserve.gov/releases/h15/data.htm (accessed March 10, 2009).

8. Dow Jones Indexes, "The Dow Through History and Interactive Timeline," http://www.djaverages.com/ (accessed March 10, 2009).

9. Orio Giarini, *Dialogue on Wealth and Welfare, Report to the Club of Rome* (Oxford, England: Pergamon Press, 1980).

10. Orio Giarini and Patrick M. Liedtke, *The Employment Dilemma: The Future of Employment* (Geneva, Switzerland: Dossiers of the Geneva Association, 1997).

11. Trude Arnesen and Erik Nord, "The Value of DALY Life: Problems with Ethics and Validity of Disability Adjusted Life Years," *British Medical Journal* 319 (1999): 1423–25.

12. This section is based on Yehuda Kahane, "Technological Changes, the Reversal of Age Pyramids and the Future of Retirement Systems," European Papers on the New Welfare, February 2006, no. 4, pp. 17–47.

13. It is feasible that all furniture, jewelry, and so on would be liquidated. In a two-parent family, the surviving spouse might want to retain the house and all furnishings.

CHAPTER 18
Social Security

The mandatory coverage for life cycle events risk is Social Security. As noted in Chapter 16, Social Security is a major social insurance program that was created in 1935 as an outcome of the Great Depression. Originally, this program was a compulsory pension plan known as Old Age Insurance (OAI). Later, survivors' benefits were added and the program became known as Old Age and Survivors' Insurance (OASI). When disability benefits were added, it became Old Age, Survivors', and Disability Insurance (OASDI), and, with the addition of hospital and medical benefits, it became the Old Age, Survivors', Disability, and Hospital Insurance (OASDHI) program. Social Security is not need-based and depends on a person's employment history. Its objective is to provide a "floor of protection" or a "reasonable level of living." Figure 18.1 illustrates the idea of a "floor of protection." Social Security is the foundation on which retirement, survivors', and disability benefits should be designed. In addition, the program is the foundation for health benefits for the retired population under Medicare Part A (hospitals), Part B (doctors), Part C (managed care medicine), and Part D (the new drug program). The discussion of Social Security is positioned here, in this chapter of the text, to emphasize the importance of Social Security as the foundation for employer-provided benefits, such as group life, disability, and health insurance and retirement programs.

Most U.S. workers—full-time, part-time, self-employed, and temporary employees—are part of the Social Security program. Every employer and employee is required to contribute in the form of payroll taxes. Social Security provides income in the event of retirement, disability, or death. It also provides medical expense benefits for disabled or retired persons and their specified dependents.[1] The 2008 Social Security Trustees reported that income to the combined OASDI Trust Funds amounted to $785 billion in 2007. During that year, an estimated 163 million people had earnings covered by Social Security and paid payroll taxes, and the trust funds paid benefits of more than $585 billion to almost 50 million beneficiaries.[2]

The Medicare program is the second largest social insurance program in the United States, with 44.1 million beneficiaries and total expenditures of $432 billion in 2007.[3]

This chapter includes the following discussion points:

1. Links

2. Definition of social insurance, eligibility, benefits, financing, and program administration

3. Medicare

4. Social Security issues and global trends in social security

FIGURE 18.1 The Links between Life Cycle Risks and Social Security Benefits

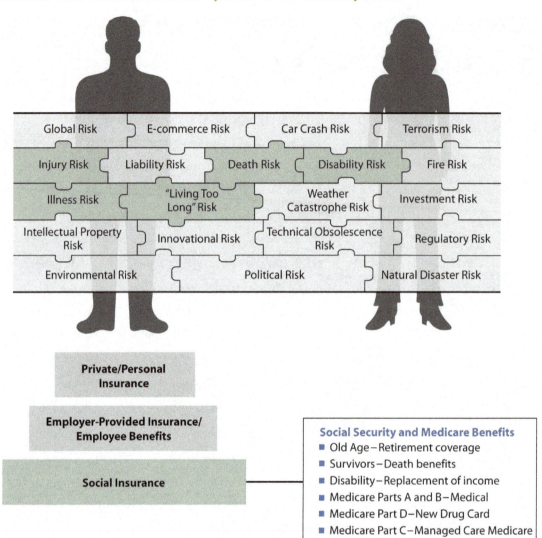

1. LINKS

At this point in our study, we get into the foundation of different types of coverage for many of the life cycle, injury, and illness risks. In Chapter 19 to Chapter 20 we will talk about the risk management of all life cycle risks, but in this chapter, we will discuss a basic mandatory package of coverages that is tied to belonging to the work force in the United States. Social Security's mandatory coverages comprise the first step in building the pyramid of coverages to ensure our complete holistic risk management process. Figure 18.1 depicts Social Security as the basic foundation of coverages for life cycle risks, which are part of our holistic risk picture.

As before, for our holistic risk management we need to look at all sources of coverage available. Understanding each component of the coverages from the various sources is critical to completing the picture and ensuring that we have adequately managed all our risks. Social insurance programs (including workers' compensation and unemployment compensation discussed in Chapter 16) play an important role in financial planning and should be considered when assessing the risk of economic loss due to premature death, disability, or retirement. The amount each individual must save for such situations is effectively reduced by the expected benefits from social insurance programs. The Social Security Administration (SSA) sends an annual statement to all workers that includes earnings history and projected future benefits. Table 18.1 provides the estimated average income by beneficiary category as of December 2008.

TABLE 18.1 Estimated Average Monthly Benefits Payable as of December 2008

Estimated Effect of a 5.8% COLA on Average Benefits				
Type of Benefit or Family		Before 5.8% COLA	After 5.8% COLA	Increase
Benefit type	All retired workers	$1,090	$1,153	$63
	All disabled workers	1,006	1,064	58
Family type	Aged couple	1,773	1,876	103
	Surviving child(ren) only[4]	936	991	55
	Widowed mother and 2 children	2,268	2,399	131
	Aged widow(er) alone	1,051	1,112	61
	Disabled worker, spouse, and one or more children	1,695	1,793	98
Note: The above estimates are based on actual benefit data through September 2008.				

Source: Social Security Administration, October 16, 2008, Accessed April 5, 2009, http://www.ssa.gov/OACT/COLA/colaeffect.html.

2. DEFINITION, ELIGIBILITY, BENEFITS, AND FINANCING OF SOCIAL SECURITY

LEARNING OBJECTIVES

In this section we elaborate on Social Security, one of the three social insurance programs in the United States:

- **Who is eligible to receive benefits under Social Security**
- **The old age, survivors', and disability benefits provided by Social Security**
- **How benefit amounts are computed**
- **How the Social Security system is funded**
- **Administration of the program**

2.1 Definition of Social Insurance

Many governmental programs are designed to provide economic security for individuals and families. Both public assistance (also referred to as welfare programs) and social insurance programs are organized and undertaken by the government and have the broad social purpose of reducing want and destitution. However, social insurance is different from public assistance: **social insurance** is an insurance program that is compulsory for nearly all Americans, eligibility criteria and benefits are specified by law, and financing is wholly or partially covered by the employer. Unlike public assistance, employers and employees pay into the social insurance system to earn their rights to benefits. Some examples of social insurance programs include workers' compensation and unemployment compensation, which were covered in Chapter 16, as well as Social Security.

Welfare benefits are financed through general revenues that come from both federal and state funds. Benefits received from welfare are not based on contributions made by or on behalf of the recipients. Medicaid is an example of a welfare benefit based solely on need. While public assistance programs have a role in providing economic security, they are not insurance programs. The insurance principles of assessing and pooling risk do not apply to welfare programs.

social insurance

An insurance program that is compulsory for nearly all Americans with eligibility criteria and benefits specified by law and financed wholly or partially through employment taxes.

OASDHI

Old age (or retirement), survivors, disability, and health insurance (or Medicare) benefits, which include hospital insurance and supplemental medical insurance.

Social Security

Social insurance program in the United States guaranteeing old age, survivors, disability (OASD) and health insurance (HI) benefits to eligible citizens who have contributed to the program.

The types of benefits available from Social Security are apparent from the acronym **OASDHI**: old age (or retirement), survivors', disability, and health (or Medicare) benefits, which include hospital insurance and supplemental medical insurance. The program can be separated into two broad parts. The first part of OASDHI is the old-age, survivors', and disability (OASD) insurance program known as **Social Security**. The second part of the OASDHI program is Medicare (HI).

We will begin the discussion about Social Security and Medicare with a description of each social program, its benefits, and its eligibility requirements. Following the general discussion is an explanation of how the programs are financed. We will introduce the two programs separately because there are many differences between Social Security and Medicare. We begin with the eligibility requirements and then discuss the benefits available to eligible employees.

2.2 Coverage and Eligibility Requirements

Today, nearly all employees in private industry, most self-employed persons, and members of the armed forces are covered by Social Security. Coverage is compulsory for more than 90 percent of all workers in the United States, meaning that Social Security taxes must be paid on their wages. The major exceptions are railroad workers, who are covered by the Railroad Retirement Act, and federal government employees, who were covered by other programs before 1984. Prior to 1984, state and local government bodies could elect not to cover certain employees under Social Security. With few exceptions, this option is no longer allowed. Municipal governments that elected out prior to 1984 do have the option to join the Social Security program voluntarily. Ministers are covered automatically unless they request a waiver on religious grounds. Members of religious sects whose beliefs prohibit acceptance of benefits are exempt.

Eligibility

To be eligible to receive benefits, a worker must achieve insured status. There are three levels of insured status: fully insured, currently insured, or disability insured. If the worker's status is fully insured, most types of Social Security benefits are payable. If the worker does not have enough work tenure to be fully insured, he or she may be currently insured or disability insured, which still allows eligibility for some survivor benefits or disability benefits.

fully insured

Status achieved by a Social Security beneficiary once forty credits of coverage are earned, or when the beneficiary has a minimum of six credits of coverage and, if greater, at least as many quarters of coverage as there are years elapsing after 1950 (or after age twenty-one, if later)

currently insured

Status achieved by a Social Security beneficiary having at least six credits in the thirteen-quarter period ending with the quarter of death.

disability insured

Status achieved by a Social Security beneficiary having twenty credits in the ten years before disability begins; less rigorous disability requirements apply to a beneficiary who is under age thirty-one or blind.

A person must be in the work force for a minimum number of quarters during which his or her earnings meet minimum criteria. The required earnings per quarter in 2008 was a minimum of $1,050, and in 2009 that amount increased to $1,090. The amount is adjusted every year. An employee can earn a maximum of four credits per year, even if he or she did not work the full four quarters, as long as he or she made enough even in one month (4 × $1,050). A Social Security beneficiary is **fully insured** once forty credits of coverage are earned, or when the beneficiary has a minimum of six credits of coverage and, if greater, at least as many quarters of coverage as there are years elapsing after 1950 (or after age twenty-one, if later). For example, a person age twenty-five who has six credits of coverage is fully insured, whereas a person age forty needs nineteen credits to be fully insured. **Currently insured** status is achieved if the Social Security beneficiary has at least six credits in the thirteen-quarter period ending with the quarter of death. **Disability insured** status is gained by the Social Security beneficiary having twenty credits in the ten years before disability begins. Less rigorous disability requirements apply to a beneficiary who is under age thirty-one or blind.

Types of Benefits

As noted, Social Security pays four types of benefits: old-age (or retirement), survivors', disability, and Medicare. Following is a more detailed description of each of these benefits.

Retirement (Old-Age) Benefits

A fully insured worker is eligible to receive benefits, including retirement income benefits. A spouse or divorced spouse of a retired worker is entitled to a monthly benefit if he or she is (1) at least age sixty-two, or (2) caring for at least one child of the retired worker (under age sixteen, or disabled if disability began before age twenty-two). A dependent child, grandchild, or great-grandchild of a retired worker who is (1) under age eighteen; (2) a full-time student between the ages of eighteen and nineteen; or (3) disabled, if disability began before age twenty-two, is also entitled to a benefit. Table 18.2 summarizes these benefits.

TABLE 18.2 **Who Gets Monthly Benefits If a Fully Insured Worker Retires?**

- Retired worker who is at least sixty-two years old
- Spouse of retired worker who either (1) has a child under age sixteen or a disabled child in his or her care or (2) is at least sixty-two years old; applies also to divorced spouse if the marriage lasted at least ten years
- Dependent child of retired worker, either under age eighteen, under nineteen if a full-time student, or disabled before age twenty-two

Normal retirement age for the purposes of Social Security ranges from sixty-five (for people born before 1938) to sixty-seven (for those born in or after 1960). A fully insured worker is entitled to receive **full retirement benefits** at the normal retirement age for Social Security, or reduced benefits as early as age sixty-two. A schedule of the new retirement ages is shown in Table 18.3.

TABLE 18.3 **Schedule of Normal Social Security Retirement Ages**

Year of Birth	Age
1937 and prior	65
1938	65 and 2 months
1939	65 and 4 months
1940	65 and 6 months
1941	65 and 8 months
1942	65 and 10 months
1943–1954	66
1955	66 and 2 months
1956	66 and 4 months
1957	66 and 6 months
1958	66 and 8 months
1959	66 and 10 months
1960 and later	67
Notes:	
1. Persons born on January 1 of any year should refer to the normal retirement age for the previous year.	
2. For the purpose of determining benefit reductions for early retirement, widows and widowers whose entitlement is based on having attained age sixty should add two years to the year of birth shown in the table.	

Sources: Processed by the authors from the American Academy of Actuaries CSO Task Force Report, June 2002, http://www.actuary.org/life/ CSO_0702.asp (accessed April 4, 2009); 2001 CSO Ultimate Table.

Early Retirement

Early retirement benefits are permanently reduced in amount because the expected benefit payout period is longer than it would have been starting from normal retirement age. In the case of **early retirement**, a benefit is reduced 5/9 of 1 percent for each month before the normal retirement age for Social Security benefits. The earliest a person can retire, with benefits, is age sixty-two. Beyond thirty-six months, the benefit is reduced 5/12 of 1 percent per month.

For example, assume that the normal retirement age is exactly age sixty-seven and that a person decides to retire at exactly age sixty-two. There are a total of sixty months of reduction to the worker's expected benefit. The reduction for the first thirty-six months is 5/9 of 1 percent times 36, or 20 percent. The reduction for the remaining twenty-four months is 5/12 of 1 percent times 24, or 10 percent. Thus, in this example, the total benefit reduction is 30 percent.

normal retirement age

The age at which full retirement benefits become available to retirees; age sixty-five in most private retirement plans.

full retirement benefits

What fully insured beneficiaries of Social Security are entitled to receive at the normal retirement age (or reduced benefits as early as age sixty-two)

early retirement

In the case of Social Security, can be taken as early as age sixty-two; results in reduction of benefit benefit by 5/9 of one percent for each month before the normal retirement age and a reduction of 5/12 percent beyond 36 months.

Late Retirement

Likewise, postponing retirement past Social Security's normal retirement age—**late retire-ment**—results in a permanently increased benefit amount to compensate for the shortened length of the payout period and to encourage older workers to continue working full-time. No delayed retirement credit is granted for retiring past age sixty-nine.

Survivors' Benefits

Social Security **survivors' benefits** protect the surviving dependents of a fully or currently insured deceased worker. The surviving spouse is entitled to monthly income payments if caring for a child who is under age sixteen or a child who is disabled by a disability that began before age twenty-two. A child of a fully or currently insured deceased worker is entitled to benefits if he or she (1) is under age eighteen, is disabled by a disability that began before age twenty-two, or is age eighteen or nineteen and a full-time student attending an elementary or secondary school; (2) was dependent on the deceased worker; and (3) is not married. Table 18.4 summarizes who gets monthly benefits if a fully insured or currently insured worker dies.

TABLE 18.4 Who Gets Monthly Benefits If a Fully Insured Worker Dies?

- Dependent child of deceased worker
- Aged widow(er) who is at least sixty years old
- Young widow(er) caring for a dependent child under age sixteen or a disabled child
- Disabled widow(er) who is disabled and fifty years or older (converted to aged widow[er] on attainment of age sixty-five)
- Parent who was a dependent of the deceased worker and is at least sixty-two years old

A widow or widower of a fully insured deceased worker is qualified for benefits at age fifty if disabled, and otherwise at age sixty. A divorced spouse also qualifies if he or she was married to the worker for at least ten years and has not remarried. A parent of a fully insured deceased worker is entitled to benefits if he or she (1) is at least age sixty-two, (2) was receiving at least half of his or her support from the child, (3) has not remarried since the child's death, and (4) is not entitled to a retirement or disability benefit equal to or larger than this survivors' benefit.

In addition to these monthly benefits, a small lump-sum death benefit of $255 is paid upon the death of a worker who is fully or currently insured. It is paid to the spouse living with the worker at the time of death, or a spouse otherwise entitled, or children entitled as described above. In the absence of a spouse or children, the death benefit is not paid. It is the only benefit that has not increased since the Social Security legislation was passed in 1935.

Disability Benefits

A fully insured worker who has a medically determinable physical or mental condition that prevents any substantial gainful work is entitled to monthly **disability benefits** after a waiting period of five full months if he or she is under age sixty-five and has been disabled for twelve months, is expected to be disabled for at least twelve months, or has a disability that is expected to result in death. A spouse or child of a disabled worker is entitled to a monthly benefit upon meeting the same qualifications as those previously listed in connection with retirement benefits. Table 18.5 shows who gets monthly benefits if a fully insured worker is disabled. Note that, to receive benefits, the worker must be eligible by being fully insured or meeting the disability insured status. A nonblind person earning more than $980 in 2009 is considered to be engaging in substantial gainful activities and is not eligible for Social Security benefits. The amount of earnings allowable if the person is blind is $1,640 in 2009. These amounts are indexed annually to increases in the national wage index.[5] It is extremely difficult to qualify to receive Social Security disability benefits.

Disability benefits may be stopped if the disabled worker refuses to participate in rehabilitation. They may be reduced if disability benefits are received from workers' compensation or under a federal, state, or local law. As reported in the 2008 Trustees Report, "On December 31, 2007, about 850,000 persons were receiving monthly benefits from the OASI Trust Fund because of their disabilities or the disabilities of children. This total includes 25,000 mothers and fathers (wives or husbands under age sixty-five of retired-worker beneficiaries and widows or widowers of deceased insured workers) who met all other qualifying requirements and were receiving unreduced benefits solely because they had disabled-child beneficiaries (or disabled children aged sixteen or seventeen) in their care. Benefits paid from this trust fund to the persons described above totaled $7,293 million in calendar year 2007."[6]

late retirement

In the case of Social Security, results in a permanently increased benefit amount to compensate for the shortened length of the pay-out period and to encourage older workers to continue working full-time; has no effect for retirement beyond age sixty-nine

survivors' benefits

Feature of Social Security that protects the surviving dependents of a fully or currently insured deceased worker; eligible recipients include dependent children, widows at least sixty years old, widows caring for dependent children under age sixteen or disabled children, disabled widows 50 years old and younger, and parents at least sixty-two years old considered dependents.

disability benefits

Available to a fully insured worker (and eligible dependents) in Social Security who has a medically determinable physical or mental condition preventing any gainful work after a waiting period of five full months if he or she is under age sixty-five and has been disabled for twelve months, is expected to be disabled for at least twelve months, or has a disability that is expected to result in death.

TABLE 18.5 Who Gets Monthly Benefits If a Fully Insured Worker Is Disabled?

- Disabled worker who had been working recently in covered employment prior to disability
- Spouse of disabled worker who either (1) has a child under age sixteen or a disabled child in his or her care or (2) is at least sixty-two years old; applies also to divorced spouse if the marriage lasted at least ten years
- Dependent child of disabled worker

Primary Insurance Amount

The **primary insurance amount (PIA)** is the basic unit used to determine the amount of monthly Social Security benefits. PIA is computed from a person's average indexed monthly earnings. In the calculation of **average indexed monthly earnings (AIME)**, workers' earnings for prior years, up to the maximum Social Security wage base (see Table 18.12 for the OASDI annual wage base), are adjusted to what they would have been if wage levels in earlier years had been the same as they are now. This is the indexed amount.

The Social Security Administration provides an illustration of retirement benefits using examples. Table 18.6 shows the examples of two workers retiring in 2009—one at age sixty-two, the earliest age possible, and the other at age sixty-five, the normal retirement age. It is important to note the differences in the application of the PIA formula to the worker retiring at age sixty-two. If a worker retires at normal retirement age, the PIA benefits are calculated as if the person retired at age sixty-two and are modified with cost of living adjustments.

primary insurance amount (PIA)

The basic unit used to determine the amount of monthly Social Security benefits.

average indexed monthly earnings (AIME)

Adjusts workers' earnings from prior years (up to the maximum wage base) to what they would have been if wage levels in earlier years had been the same as they are now in computing a beneficiary's primary insurance amount from Social Security.

TABLE 18.6 Benefit Calculation Examples for Workers Retiring in 2009

	Earnings before and after indexing					
	Case A, Born in 1947			Case B, Born in 1943		
Year	Nominal Earnings	Indexing Factor	Indexed Earnings	Nominal Earnings	Indexing Factor	Indexed Earnings
1969	$5,511	6.8556	$37,781	$4,803	5.7798	$27,761
1970	5,802	6.5315	37,896	5,434	5.5066	29,923
1971	6,113	6.2190	38,017	6,023	5.2431	31,579
1972	6,733	5.6639	38,135	6,906	4.7751	32,977
1973	7,177	5.3304	38,256	7,612	4.4940	34,208
1974	7,627	5.0313	38,374	8,327	4.2418	35,322
1975	8,223	4.6815	38,496	9,208	3.9469	36,343
1976	8,817	4.3793	38,612	10,102	3.6921	37,297
1977	9,374	4.1317	38,730	10,964	3.4833	38,191
1978	10,150	3.8277	38,851	12,097	3.2271	39,038
1979	11,072	3.5198	38,971	13,426	2.9675	39,841
1980	12,106	3.2290	39,090	14,918	2.7223	40,611
1981	13,365	2.9337	39,208	16,718	2.4733	41,349
1982	14,144	2.7806	39,328	17,941	2.3442	42,058
1983	14,878	2.6514	39,448	19,121	2.2353	42,742
1984	15,800	2.5042	39,566	20,559	2.1112	43,405
1985	16,523	2.4019	39,686	21,752	2.0250	44,047
1986	17,064	2.3326	39,804	22,715	1.9666	44,671
1987	18,207	2.1928	39,924	24,491	1.8487	45,276
1988	19,161	2.0899	40,044	26,033	1.7619	45,868
1989	19,978	2.0103	40,161	27,403	1.6948	46,443
1990	20,963	1.9215	40,281	29,016	1.6200	47,005
1991	21,809	1.8525	40,401	30,449	1.5618	47,555
1992	23,000	1.7617	40,519	32,380	1.4853	48,093
1993	23,266	1.7467	40,638	33,016	1.4726	48,619
1994	23,961	1.7010	40,758	34,262	1.4341	49,135
1995	24,994	1.6355	40,877	36,003	1.3788	49,642
1996	26,293	1.5592	40,997	38,142	1.3145	50,139
1997	27,908	1.4733	41,116	40,761	1.2421	50,628
1998	29,453	1.4000	41,234	43,301	1.1803	51,108
1999	31,185	1.3261	41,354	46,136	1.1180	51,580
2000	33,004	1.2566	41,473	49,126	1.0594	52,044
2001	33,888	1.2273	41,591	50,740	1.0347	52,502
2002	34,326	1.2151	41,710	51,689	1.0244	52,953
2003	35,266	1.1861	41,830	53,396	1.0000	53,396
2004	37,011	1.1334	41,950	56,336	1.0000	56,336
2005	38,474	1.0934	42,069	58,866	1.0000	58,866
2006	40,356	1.0454	42,187	62,054	1.0000	62,054
2007	42,307	1.0000	42,307	65,369	1.0000	65,369
2008	44,051	1.0000	44,051	68,383	1.0000	68,383
		Highest—35 total	1,415,637		Highest—35 total	1,677,907
		AIME	3,370		AIME	3,995

Source: Social Security Administration, October 16, 2008, Accessed April 4, 2009, http://www.ssa.gov/OACT/ProgData/retirebenefit1.html.

We will use the examples provided by the Social Security Administration as a learning tool here. First, we focus on the calculation of the AIME. For each case, we see the columns labeled "nominal earnings." Indexing brings nominal earnings up to near-current wage levels. For each case, the table shows columns of earnings before and after Indexing. The highest thirty-five years of indexed earnings and the corresponding average monthly amounts of such earnings are used for the benefit computation. The result is the AIME. The indexing requires some special computation. Consequently, there is no easy way to make an estimate of one's PIA. It is not as simple as finding average wages and consulting a table. The Social Security Administration has computerized wage histories for all workers, and the PIA calculation is made when an application for benefits is processed. The Social Security Administration furnishes annually the calculation of each insured's PIA. If a person has not received the statement, the Social Security Administration will furnish a record of the historical Social Security earnings and PIA upon request. The Social Security Administration Web site also has an online calculator.

After the AIME is determined, an individual's PIA in 2009 would be determined by the formula in Table 18.7. The formula shows that Social Security benefit levels, expressed as **replacement ratios**, are weighted in favor of lower-income workers. Here, a replacement ratio is defined as the Social Security benefit divided by the AIME.

replacement ratios

Expression of Social Security benefit levels weighted in favor of lower-income workers; calculated as the benefit divided by the AIME.

TABLE 18.7   PIA Formula for an Individual in 2009

For an individual who first becomes eligible for old-age insurance benefits or disability insurance benefits in 2009, or who dies in 2009 before becoming eligible for benefits, his or her PIA is the sum of
▪ (a) 90 percent of the first $744 of his or her average indexed monthly earnings, plus
▪ (b) 32 percent of his or her average indexed monthly earnings over $744 and through $4,483, plus
▪ (c) 15 percent of his or her average indexed monthly earnings over $4,483.
Round this amount to the next lower multiple of $0.10 if it is not already a multiple of $0.10.

Source: Social Security Administration, October 16, 2008, Accessed April 4, 2009, http://www.ssa.gov/OACT/COLA/piaformula.html for 2009.

The three AIME ranges represented in the formula are known as bend points. The **bend points** represent the dollar amounts at which the primary insurance amount formula for Social Security benefits changes. The bend points increase as average wages in the economy increase. This is shown in Table 18.8. The bend points in 2009 are $744 and $4,483, as you can see in Table 18.7. These bend points apply to workers who become eligible for benefits (at age sixty-two) in 2009. A table of bend points for past years is available at http://www.ssa.gov.

bend points

The AIME ranges in the Social Security benefit formula representing the dollar amounts at which the primary insurance amount calculation changes.

TABLE 18.8   Examples of PIA Calculations for the 2009 Retirement Cases Illustrated in [Unsupported Reference Type:] Case A—Retirement at Age Sixty-Two and Case B—Retirement at Age 65

| Case | AIME | Formula Bend Points | | Formula Applied to AIME |
		First	Second	
A	$3,370	$744	$4,483	.9(744) + .32(3370 − 744) = **$1,509.92**
B	3,995	627	3,779	.9(627) + .32(3779 − 627) + .15(3995 − 3779) = **$1,605.34**

Source: Social Security Administration, October 16, 2008, Accessed April 5, 2009, http://www.ssa.gov/OACT/ProgData/retirebenefit2.html.

Table 18.8 illustrates the straightforward calculation for the worker in Case A who retires at age sixty-two. For the worker who retires in 2009 at age sixty-five, the bend points are the same as those in 2006 (as if he or she retired at age sixty-two). Thereafter, the benefits are adjusted to reflect the COLA of 3.3 percent, 2.3 percent, and 5.8 percent, respectively. The resulting PIA is $1,605.34.

Other Factors Affecting Benefit Amounts

As described above, the AIME determines the PIA of a retired or disabled worker; the benefit levels for other beneficiaries are a percentage of the PIA. If an individual qualifies as both a worker and as the spouse of a worker, the beneficiary will receive whichever PIA is greater, but not both. Other factors may also affect the benefit amount.

The maximum family benefit is the maximum monthly amount that can be paid on a worker's earnings record. The formula for the maximum family benefit, shown in Table 18.9, is based on the worker's primary insurance amount (PIA). The maximum PIA for the family is computed based on the bend points shown in Table 18.9. When the family reaches its maximum family benefit, the worker's benefit is not reduced but the benefits of the survivors or dependents are reduced proportionately. There is also a minimum PIA for very-low-wage workers who have been covered by Social Security for at least ten years. This attempts to address the broad social purpose of Social Security: reducing want and destitution by providing an adequate income to insured workers.[7]

TABLE 18.9 The PIA Formula for Maximum Family Benefit, 2009

For the family of a worker who becomes age sixty-two or dies in 2009 before attaining age sixty-two, the total amount of benefits payable is computed so that it does not exceed

- (a) 150 percent of the first $950 of the worker's PIA, plus
- (b) 272 percent of the worker's PIA over $950 through $1,372, plus
- (c) 134 percent of the worker's PIA over $1,372 through $1,789, plus
- (d) 175 percent of the worker's PIA over $1,789.

This total amount is then rounded to the next lower multiple of $0.10 if it is not already a multiple of $0.10.

Source: Social Security Administration, October 16, 2008, Accessed April 5, 2009, http://www.ssa.gov/OACT/COLA/familymax.html.

Cost of Living Adjustment (COLA)

automatic cost-of-living adjustments (COLAs)

Increases Social Security benefit amounts annually in relation to increases in the consumer price index.

Social Security benefit amounts are increased annually by **automatic cost-of-living adjustments (COLAs)** linked to increases in the consumer price index (CPI). In addition, workers receiving Social Security disability income may have Social Security benefits reduced to offset other disability benefits received from governmental programs, such as workers' compensation, to reduce the moral hazard of malingering. Legislation enacted in 1973 provides for automatic cost-of-living adjustments (COLAs). The theory is to prevent inflation from eroding the value of Social Security and Supplemental Security Income (SSI) benefits. The COLA for 2008 is 5.8 percent for both Social Security benefits and SSI payments, as you can see in Table 18.10.

TABLE 18.10 Automatic Social Security Cost of Living Adjustments (COLAs)

Social Security Cost-of-Living Adjustments					
Year	COLA	Year	COLA	Year	COLA
1975	8.0%	1990	5.4%	2005	4.1%
1976	6.4%	1991	3.7%	2006	3.3%
1977	5.9%	1992	3.0%	2007	2.3%
1978	6.5%	1993	2.6%	2008	5.8%
1979	9.9%	1994	2.8%		
1980	14.3%	1995	2.6%		
1981	11.2%	1996	2.9%		
1982	7.4%	1997	2.1%		
1983	3.5%	1998	1.3%		
1984	3.5%	1999	2.5%[8]		
1985	3.1%	2000	3.5%		
1986	1.3%	2001	2.6%		
1987	4.2%	2002	1.4%		
1988	4.0%	2003	2.1%		
1989	4.7%	2004	2.7%		

Source: Social Security Administration, October 16, 2008, Accessed April 5, 2009, http://www.ssa.gov/OACT/COLA/colaseries.html.

Many people retire before or after the normal retirement age, which affects the PIA for those individuals. For an individual retiring past the normal retirement age, the final benefit amount is higher than the PIA formula reveals, as illustrated in the example of Case B in Table 18.8.

The Earnings Test

earnings test

Reduces the Social Security benefit for a retiree who is younger than normal retirement age and whose annual earned income exceeds the retirement earnings exempt amount.

The Social Security retirement benefit may be reduced for a retiree who is younger than normal retirement age and whose annual earned income exceeds the retirement earnings exempt amount; this provision is called the **earnings test**. Its purpose is to limit monthly cash benefits for retirees who have earned income and to reduce the cost of the Social Security program. As Table 18.11 shows, a beneficiary attaining the normal retirement age after 2002 is exempt from reduction of Social Security benefits regardless of the amount of earned income. The earning test applies only to early retirement.

TABLE 18.11 Annual Retirement Earnings Test Exempt Amounts for Persons Under the Normal Retirement Age

Annual Retirement Earnings Test Exempt Amounts		
Year	Lower Amount [9]	Higher Amount [10]
2000	$10,080	$17,000
2001	10,680	25,000
2002	11,280	30,000
2003	11,520	30,720
2004	11,640	31,080
2005	12,000	31,800
2006	12,480	33,240
2007	12,960	34,440
2008	13,560	36,120
2009	14,160	37,680

Source: Social Security Administration, October 16, 2008, Accessed April 5, 2009, http://www.ssa.gov/OACT/COLA/rtea.html

In 2008, a beneficiary under the normal retirement age would lose $1 of benefits for every $2 earned above $13,560. The beneficiary would also lose $1 for every $3 above the higher exempt amount, $36,120.

2.3 Financing of Benefits

Taxation

Social Security benefits are financed through payroll taxes paid by employers and employees and by a special tax on earnings paid by the self-employed. The tax rate for employers and employees is 6.2 percent for OASDI, up to a maximum amount of earnings called the **wage base level**, as shown in Table 18.12, and 1.45 percent for HI (Medicare Part A) on all earnings. The tax rates scheduled under current law are shown in Table 18.13. Those who elect Medicare Part B coverage pay monthly premiums via deductions from their Social Security benefits checks.

Social Security taxes, sometimes called FICA taxes (after the Federal Insurance Contributions Act of 1939), are automatically withheld on wages up to a set amount and are adjusted annually for inflation. Any wages earned over this wage base are not taxed for Social Security, although Medicare Part A taxes are still deducted.

The tax rates are intended to remain constant (the last hike was in 1990), but the taxable wage base is adjusted annually to reflect increases in average wages. As you can see in Table 18.12, the 2008 annual wage base was $102,000, and it is $106,800 in 2009, meaning employers, employees, and the self-employed paid OASDI taxes on individual wages up to the wage base. If wages increase 5 percent the following year, the tax rates would remain the same but the taxable wage base would increase by 5 percent, thus increasing total Social Security tax revenue (all else being equal). Wages beyond the threshold are not subject to the OASDI tax, but they are subject to the Medicare Part A tax.

Social Security benefits are subject to income taxes. More specifically, taxes are payable on 50 percent of the Social Security benefit by single persons whose taxable incomes (including 50 percent of Social Security benefits and any interest on tax-exempt bonds) are between $25,000 and $34,000 (between $32,000 and $44,000 for married couples filing joint returns). If income exceeds $34,000 for single persons (or $44,000 for married couples filing jointly), up to 85 percent of the Social Security benefit received at retirement as income is taxable.

wage base level

Specifies the maximum amount of earnings on which Social Security taxation applies.

TABLE 18.12 OASDI Annual Wage Base for Tax Purposes

Contribution and Benefit Bases, 1937–2009					
Year(s)	**Amount**	**Year(s)**	**Amount**	**Year(s)**	**Amount**
1937–1950	$3,000	1981	$29,700	1996	$62,700
1951–1954	3,600	1982	32,400	1997	65,400
1955–1958	4,200	1983	35,700	1998	68,400
1959–1965	4,800	1984	37,800	1999	72,600
1966–1967	6,600	1985	39,600	2000	76,200
1968–1971	7,800	1986	42,000	2001	80,400
1972	9,000	1987	43,800	2002	84,900
1973	10,800	1988	45,000	2003	87,000
1974	13,200	1989	48,000	2004	87,900
1975	14,100	1990	51,300	2005	90,000
1976	15,300	1991	53,400	2006	94,200
1977	16,500	1992	55,500	2007	97,500
1978	17,700	1993	57,600	2008	102,000
1979	22,900	1994	60,600	2009	106,800
1980	25,900	1995	61,200		

Note: **Amounts for 1937–1974 and for 1979–1981 were set by statute; all other amounts were determined under automatic adjustment provisions of the Social Security Act.**

Source: Social Security Administration, January 15, 2009, Accessed April 5, 2009, http://www.ssa.gov/OACT/COLA/cbb.html.

TABLE 18.13 Tax Rates Paid on Wages and Earnings

Calendar Years	Tax Rates as a Percentage of Taxable Earnings						
	Tax Rate for Employees and Employers, Each			Tax Rate for Self-Employed Persons			
	OASI	DI	Total	OASI	DI	Total	
2000 and later	5.300	0.900	6.200	10.6000	1.8000	12.400	

Calendar Years	Tax Rates as a Percentage of Taxable Earnings					
	Rate for Employees and Employers, Each			Rate for Self-Employed Persons		
	OASDI	Medicare A	Total	OASDI	Medicare A	Total
1990 and later	6.200	1.450	7.650	12.400	2.900	15.300

Trust Funds

The funds collected from payroll taxes are allocated among three trust funds. One trust fund is for retirement and survivors' benefits; the second is for disability insurance; and the third is for hospital insurance, or Medicare Part A. Medicare Parts B and D, supplementary medical benefits, are financed by monthly premiums from persons enrolled in the program, along with amounts appropriated from the general revenue of the federal government. These funds are deposited in a fourth trust fund, the supplementary medical insurance trust fund.

The Social Security system is primarily a **pay-as-you-go system**, meaning that current tax revenues are used to pay the current benefits of Social Security recipients. This is quite different from financing with traditional, private insurance, where funds are set aside in advance to accumulate over time and benefits are paid to those who contributed to the fund.

Income to the trust funds consists of the following:

- Employment taxes paid by employees, their employers, and self-employed persons
- Income from the taxation of benefits
- Interest on investments made by the program
- Other income such as donations and Treasury reimbursements

pay-as-you-go system

The nature of Social Security, in which current tax revenues are used to pay the current benefits of recipients.

2.4 Administration

The Social Security program is administered by the Social Security Administration, an agency of the United States Department of Health and Human Services. Local service is provided by offices located in the principal cities and towns of the fifty states and Puerto Rico. Applications for Social Security numbers and the various benefits as well as enrollment for the medical insurance plan (discussed next) are processed by the district office. The administration is set up to help beneficiaries in catastrophic times, as was evident following Hurricane Katrina. Because so many people were displaced, the Social Security Administration created emergency offices and stations to continue immediate payments to the evacuees.[11]

Disability determination—the decision whether or not an applicant for disability benefits is disabled as defined in the law—is made by a state agency (usually the vocational rehabilitation agency) under agreements between the state and the secretary of the Department of Health and Human Services. Qualification for hospital and medical benefits is determined by the district office, but claims for such benefits are processed through private insurer intermediaries under contract with the Social Security Administration.

The first decision concerning a person's qualification for benefits under the various parts of the program is made at the local level. Simple, effective procedures exist for appeal by any applicant for whom the decision is unsatisfactory. There is no charge for such appeals, and the agency strives to provide courteous assistance to the claimant.

KEY TAKEAWAYS

In this section you studied the features of Social Security, a compulsory social insurance program paying old age, survivors', and disability (OASD) benefits:

- A person must be in the work force a minimum number of quarters, during which earnings must meet minimum amounts to be eligible for Social Security benefits.
- The level of benefit depends on a worker's status as fully insured, currently insured, or disability insured.
- Fully insured workers, their aged spouses, and dependent children are eligible to receive retirement (old-age) benefits beginning at the worker's retirement age (which depends on birth year) and disability benefits.
- Benefits are reduced in the case of early retirement and increased in the case of late retirement.
- A fully insured worker under age sixty-five with a medical condition that prevents substantial gainful work can receive **disability benefits** after a waiting period if he or she has been disabled for twelve months, is expected to be disabled at least twelve months, or has a disability expected to result in death.
- Survivors (aged spouses, disabled spouses, and dependents) of deceased fully, currently, or disability insured workers are also eligible to receive old-age survivors' or disability benefits.
- The primary insurance amount (PIA), computed from average indexed monthly earnings (AIME) up to the Social Security wage base, is used to determine the amount of monthly benefits.
- The PIA formula is weighted to help lower-income workers at three different bend points—the sum of these amounts equals the monthly benefit, with COLAs made annually.
- Benefits are subject to (1) a monthly maximum that can be paid on a worker's earnings record, at which survivors' benefits are reduced proportionately, and (2) an earnings test, whereby benefits are reduced for retirees whose earned income exceeds the retirement earnings exempt amount.
- Social Security benefits are financed through payroll taxes on employers and employees at 6.2 percent (OASDI) and 1.45 percent (HI) up to the wage base level (adjusted annually).
- Benefits are paid through the Social Security trust fund, which is made up of employment tax revenues, benefit income tax revenues, interest on investments, and other income.
- The Social Security program is a pay-as-you-go system administered by the Social Security Administration (part of the Department of Health and Human Services), with offices to handle applications in each state.

disability benefits

Available to a fully insured worker (and eligible dependents) in Social Security who has a medically determinable physical or mental condition preventing any gainful work after a waiting period of five full months if he or she is under age sixty-five and has been disabled for twelve months, is expected to be disabled for at least twelve months, or has a disability that is expected to result in death.

DISCUSSION QUESTIONS

1. How does a worker become fully insured under Social Security? What benefits are fully insured workers entitled to?

2. Explain the concept of arriving at AIME. How do you compute the PIA?

3. How does the earnings test affect Social Security benefits?

4. Social Security benefits are financed largely through payroll taxes. The more you earn (up to the maximum earnings base), the more tax you pay. Income benefits, however, favor lower-income workers. Explain why lower-income people are favored.

5. The Baylor Crane Construction Company is a Virginia-based builder with 1,750 full-time and 300 part-time employees. The company provides all the social insurance programs required by law and most standard employee benefits plans. Last year, Baylor Crane suffered a high severity of losses when the top five floors of a high rise collapsed in Virginia Beach during strong winds. Luckily, most workers escaped injuries, except six workers who stayed to secure the building. Three of them sustained severe injuries and Johnny Kendle, the sixty-four-year-old supervisor, was killed. The injured workers are back at work except for Tom Leroy, who is still on disability. His prognosis is not good.

    a. What social insurance programs are provided by the company?

    b. Compare the benefits provided by each of the social programs.

6. Dan Wolf, Duncan Smith, and Jim Lavell are employees of the Happy Wood Company. Fifteen months ago, Dan Wolf was injured when a log fell on him and hurt his back. He has not been able to work since. Duncan Smith, who had fifteen years of service with the company, was killed in that accident. He left a wife and five children. About a month later, Jim Lavell injured his back at home and he, too, has been unable to work since the accident.

    a. Based on the benefits of the social insurance programs you described above, compare the type of benefits Dan, Duncan, and Jim (or their families) are receiving.

    b. What are the eligibility conditions that must be met to receive these benefits?

---

3. MEDICARE

LEARNING OBJECTIVES

In this section we elaborate on the portion of the Social Security program known as Medicare:

- **Medicare Part A—hospital insurance**
- **Medicare Part B—supplementary medical insurance**
- **Medicare Part C—managed care medical insurance**
- **Medicare Part D—prescription medication insurance**
- **Beneficiary costs under all Medicare parts**

3.1 Medicare Part A: Hospital Insurance Program

Medicare Part A

Benefit of Social Security that provides hospital-related benefits of: inpatient hospital services, posthospital home health services, and hospice care.

Anyone who is eligible for Social Security or railroad retirement benefits at age sixty-five is also eligible for Medicare Part A—hospital insurance benefits. No premium is required because workers have already paid Medicare A taxes. A worker does not have to retire to be covered for hospital benefits; however, Medicare is the secondary payer for persons who continue to work between ages sixty-five and sixty-nine and have medical coverage through their employers. Individuals age sixty-five and over who are not eligible for Social Security or railroad retirement benefits may enroll in Medicare Part A by paying premiums. The **Medicare Part A** plan provides the following hospital-related benefits:

- In-patient hospital services
- Posthospital home health services
- Hospice care

For Medicare Part A, the deductible paid by the beneficiary was $1,068 in 2009, up $44 from the deductible of $1,024 in 2008.

3.2 Medicare Parts B, C, and D: Supplementary Medical Insurance Program

Anyone eligible for Part A, the basic hospital benefits plan, and anyone age sixty-five or over is eligible for Medicare Part B—medical benefits, Medicare Part C—managed care benefits, and Medicare Part D—drug benefits. Those receiving Social Security or railroad retirement benefits are enrolled automatically unless they elect not to be covered. The monthly premium paid by beneficiaries enrolled in **Medicare Part B**, which covers physician services, out-patient hospital services, certain home health services, durable medical equipment, and other items, is $96.40 in 2009, the same as in 2008.

Charges that are not covered through Medicare parts A and B include routine physical examinations; routine care of the eyes, ears, and feet; prescription drugs; most immunizations; and cosmetic surgery. Coverage for such options may be available through Medicare Part C, discussed below. Doctors must bill Medicare directly, rather than having patients file Medicare claims. Some physicians and surgeons accept as full payment the amount that Medicare considers reasonable, but others charge patients an additional fee. However, doctors are limited in the additional amount they may charge patients.

Medicare Part C, also known as Medicare+Choice, was authorized by the Balanced Budget Act of 1997. Through Medicare Part C, eligible participants can elect to receive the benefits of Medicare Parts A and B through private health plans, in addition to certain items not covered by Medicare Parts A and B. These supplemental benefits might include dental care, vision care, and health club memberships. Medicare Part C may also cover routine physical examinations, unlike Parts A and B, thereby encouraging preventive care. Medicare+Choice became known as Medicare Advantage plans with the addition of prescription drug coverage through the Medicare Prescription Drug, Improvement, and Modernization Act of 2003. Medicare Part C enrollees are limited to a network of benefit providers, a feature similar to managed care health plans (discussed in Chapter 22). Going outside the network causes some expenses to be passed on to participants.

Medicare Advantage plans are offered to eligible persons through managed care, preferred provider organization (PPO), private fee-for-service, and specialty arrangements. You will learn about all of these concepts in Chapter 22. Membership cards are issued to Medicare Part C participants by plan providers. Because the range of covered services varies among Medicare Advantage providers, premiums for Medicare Part C benefits are not fixed by the Social Security Administration. Participants typically pay an amount equal to Medicare Part B premiums plus an additional charge for the added benefits of Medicare Part C. Medicare Advantage providers who choose to cover less for certain benefits than would be paid by Medicare Parts A and B typically lower out-of-pocket costs for plan participants so that they do not pay more for proportionately less coverage. Providers are compensated by the government. Additionally, benefit formulas that overpay providers of Medicare Advantage plans relative to traditional Medicare benefits result in a net extra benefit value for participants.

Medicare Part D is the Medicare Prescription Drug, Improvement, and Modernization Act of 2003 (P.L. 108–173), enacted December 8, 2003. It requires the Social Security Administration to undertake a number of additional Medicare-related responsibilities. Under Medicare Part D, the Social Security Administration and the Centers for Medicare & Medicaid Services (CMS) work together to provide persons with limited income and resources with extra help paying for their prescription drugs. The start date of this program was January 1, 2006. Insurance companies and other private companies work with Medicare to provide a choice of plans that cover both brand-name and generic drugs. To enroll, a beneficiary must have Medicare Part A and/or Medicare Part B. The combination of Part C Medicare Advantage plans with Part D prescription drug benefits are known as Medicare Advantage Prescription Drug (MAPD) plans.

Medicare D premiums are not set in stone. For example, the Center for Medicare and Medicaid Services released the following in September 2005: "The average Part D monthly premium will be $32, about 14 percent lower than had been projected, with plans in virtually all areas of the country available for a premium of under $20 or even less. The drug benefit will provide help with prescription drug costs that for many beneficiaries will exceed the premium cost."[12]

Table 18.14 details how the drug card works. For those with limited income and resources, there is a way to qualify for extra help that will cover between 85 and almost 100 percent of drug costs. Most people who are eligible for this extra help pay no premiums, no deductibles, and no more than $5 for each prescription. The amount of extra help depends on income and resources. In the beginning of 2006, the help promised was not in place, so the states helped those in need.

Medicare Part B

Benefit of Social Security that provides physician services, outpatient services, certain home health services, durable medical equipment, and other items.

Medicare Part C

Allows eligible participants to receive the benefits of Medicare Parts A and B through private health plans, in addition to certain items not covered by Medicare Parts A and B.

Medicare Part D

Benefit of Social Security created through the Medicare Prescription Drug, Improvement and Modernization Act of 2003 that provides assistance for costs relating to prescription medications.

TABLE 18.14 How Does Medicare Part D—the "Drug Card"—Work?

Steps:

1. You pay the first $250 per year for your prescriptions—the "deductible." (It is paid on an annual basis.)
2. After you pay the $250 yearly deductible, you pay 25 percent of your yearly drug costs, from $250 to $2,250, and the plan pays the other 75 percent of these costs, then
3. You pay 100 percent of your drug costs from $2,251 until your out-of-pocket costs reach $3,600, then
4. You pay 5 percent of your drug costs (or a small copayment) for the rest of the calendar year after you have spent $3,600 out-of-pocket and your plan pays the rest.

Here is an example:

	$250 Deductible	$250–$2,250	$2,251 Until You Reach $3,600 in Out-of-Pocket Cost	After $3,600 in Out-of-Pocket Costs
What you pay	$250	25% up to $500	$2,850*	5%
What your plan pays	$0	75% up to $1,500	$0	95%
Total drug spending	$250	$2,250	$5,100	

***$250 deductible + $500 (25% of $250 to $2,250) + $2,850 = $3,600 out of pocket cost.**

Source: http://www.medicare.gov/MPCO/Static/Resources.asp#HowPlansWork

The benefits provided under all Medicare parts are listed in Table 18.15.

TABLE 18.15 All Medicare Parts (A to D)

Medicare has four parts:

1. Hospital insurance (Part A) helps pay for in-patient hospital care and certain follow-up services.
2. Medical insurance (Part B) helps pay for doctors' services, out-patient hospital care, and other medical services.
3. Medicare Advantage plans (Part C) are available in many areas. People with Medicare Parts A and B can choose to receive all of their health care services through a provider organization under Part C.
4. Prescription drug coverage (Part D) helps pay for medications doctors prescribe for medical treatment.

Source: Social Security Administration, SSA Publication No. 05-10024, January 2009, ICN 454930, Accessed April 5, 2009, http://www.ssa.gov/pubs/10024.html#aboutbenefits.

KEY TAKEAWAYS

In this section you studied the features of Medicare, a compulsory social insurance program paying hospital insurance (HI) benefits:

- Anyone eligible for Social Security benefits at age sixty-five is also eligible for Medicare Part A, which provides hospital-related benefits: in-patient hospital service, posthospital home health service, and hospice care.
- Anyone age sixty-five and older who is eligible for Medicare Part A is also eligible for Medicare Part B, which provides physician, out-patient hospital, some home health services, and more. Medicare B requires premiums and is voluntary.
- Medicare Part C (Medicare Advantage) offers coverage of Medicare Parts A and B plus supplemental services through private health plans. Medicare Part C requires premiums and is voluntary.
- Medicare Part D, effective in 2006, was an enhancement to the Medicare program and provides assistance in paying prescription drug costs and discounts. Medicare D requires premiums and is voluntary.
- No premium is required for Medicare Part A because workers pay for it through employment taxes, but premiums are required for Parts B and D
- Annual deductibles apply to all parts of Medicare

DISCUSSION QUESTIONS

1. What is the difference between Medicare Part A and Medicare Part B?
2. Explain the concept of Medicare Part D.
3. Medicare costs have turned out to be much greater than expected when the program was first enacted. The number of people eligible for Medicare and the benefit amounts have increased through the years. For example, Medicare covers not only medical expenses for eligible retirees but also kidney dialysis and kidney transplants for persons of all ages.

   a. Why does Medicare have deductibles, coinsurance, and limitations on benefits that create gaps in coverage for insureds?

   b. Considering the fact that many older people worry about what is not covered by Medicare, do you think the gaps should be eliminated?

4. ISSUES AND GLOBAL TRENDS IN SOCIAL SECURITY

LEARNING OBJECTIVES

In this section we elaborate on the following:

- **Reasons for funding gaps in Social Security and Medicare**
- **Current actuarial projections**
- **International views on social insurance**
- **The trend toward privatization**

4.1 Issues in Social Security

During the 2000 presidential election campaign, Social Security financing was the most heated issue, with the debate focusing on privatization and moving away from the pay-as-you-go system. When the stock market was booming and everyone believed they could do better by investing their own funds, the idea of moving away from the current system became very appealing; however, their tune changed after the large decline in the stock market. The immediate big issue in early 2006 was how to help those who could not pay the deductibles and coinsurance for the new drug program. The major funding problems are still at issue.

Social Security and Medicare were originally designed to operate with advance funding, but for many years they have operated on an unfunded, pay-as-you-go basis. As a result, this generation of workers is paying for the benefits of current beneficiaries. Social Security taxes have increased much faster than the general level of prices and even faster than the cost of health care during the past two decades.

As described in the box "Does Privatization Provide a More Equitable Solution?" and depicted in Figure 18.2, the number of retired workers has increased faster than the number of those working. In 1945, there were forty-two workers per retiree. Currently, this has decreased to approximately three workers per retiree and is expected to decline to two by 2020. The Social Security funding burden is being borne by a shrinking sector of society because birth rates have declined and longevity has increased. This trend will continue as the baby boomers move out of the work force and into retirement. Retired workers are concerned about the certainty of their benefits and future required tax rates. The current generation of taxpayers has serious doubts about the ability of the Social Security system to deliver benefits at current inflation-adjusted levels.

Such doubts are understandable, considering recent problems of the OASI program, which is by far the largest part of the system. Each year, the trustees of the Social Security and Medicare trust funds report on the funds' status and their projected condition over the next seventy-five years. The 2008 Annual Reports continue to show that both Social Security and Medicare need serious reform.[13] Both programs face a long-term financing gap. Closing the gap between monies going into the Social Security and Medicare funds and monies coming out of the funds will be a challenge. It will force the government to come up with innovative solutions to fixing the long-term deficits.

As Figure 18.3 shows, the OASDI and HI trust funds are expected to be adequately financed for only the next ten years (depending on the actuarial assumptions).[14] Figure 18.4 shows the deficits of the Medicare Parts B and D trust funds. The deficits are expected to grow rapidly.

FIGURE 18.2 Number of Workers per OASDI Beneficiary

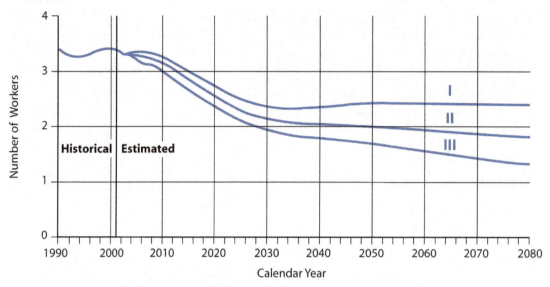

Source: OASDI Trustees Report, http://www.ssa.gov/OACT/COLA/CBB.html.

FIGURE 18.3 Long-Range OASI and DI Annual Income Rates and Cost Rates (as a Percentage of Taxable Payroll), Trustees Report 2008

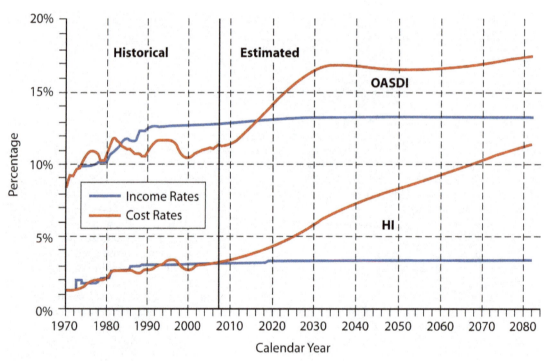

Source: Social Security and Medicare Board of Trustees, "A Summary of the 2008 Annual Reports," April 22, 2008, http://www.ssa.gov/OACT/TRSUM/trsummary.html (accessed April 5, 2009).

FIGURE 18.4   OASDI and HI Income Shortfall to Pay Scheduled Benefits, and the 75 Percent General Fund Revenue Contribution to SMI (Percentage of GDP), Trustees Report 2008

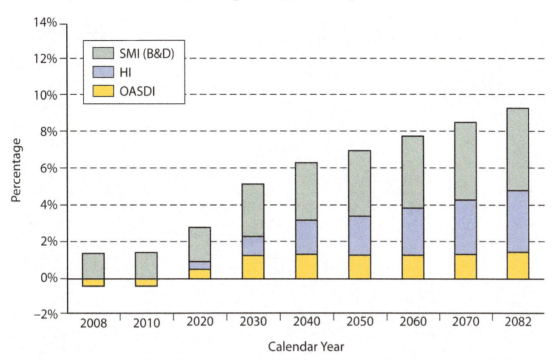

Source: Social Security and Medicare Board of Trustees, "A Summary of the 2008 Annual Reports," April 22, 2008, http://www.ssa.gov/OACT/ TRSUM/trsummary.html (accessed April 5, 2009).

Whether the objective of the Social Security program should be to provide a "floor of protection" or a "reasonable level of living" remains debatable. Reform will require agreement, however, by politicians and the public on not only what benefits citizens are entitled to, but what benefits taxpayers are willing to fund. See the box "The Future of Social Security," for a discussion of this topic.

4.2   Global Trends in Social Security Systems

In many countries, financing the government social security system has become increasingly difficult for several reasons. Benefit levels have increased in many nations, to the point where the tax rates necessary to support benefits are at an all-time high. For example, free or very-low-cost medical care may be available to everyone, disability benefits may require little proof of inability to work, and generous disability payments may result in the moral hazard of malingering. Demographic trends in other industrialized nations mirror those in the United States: the population is aging, so fewer workers finance the pay-as-you-go system for retirees. The declining birth rate suggests that this trend is unlikely to be reversed. In addition, other governments also face the problem of growing budget deficits. Governments in some developing countries may be perceived as unable to administer the social security system fairly and efficiently.

Experts anticipate a shift from public sector social insurance plans to private sector plans, especially for retirement benefits. Private sector organizations, particularly insurance companies, have successfully managed retirement savings and income for decades and are in a position to improve management and funding practices. Several countries have already begun to privatize the social security system, namely, Chile, Peru, Mexico, Italy, and Japan. In Chile (beginning in 1981) and Peru (in 1993), for example, workers are required to contribute to their own retirement fund, and contributions are invested by a private pension fund manager selected by the worker. In both these countries, the prefunded privatized system appears to be working well. Some countries also are moving toward privatized medical care systems.

The trend toward privatization is worldwide, including both industrialized and developing countries. The potential for market expansion for insurers and other financial institutions is tremendous.

Does Privatization Provide a More Equitable Solution?

> *The threat to the stability of Social Security has been apparent for decades. For years, political leaders have agreed that something must be done.... We can postpone action no longer. Social Security is a challenge now; if we fail to act, it will become a crisis. We must save Social Security and we now have the opportunity to do so.*

With these words, on May 2, 2001, President George W. Bush established the Presidential Commission to Strengthen Social Security.

The crisis President Bush was referring to is the declining numbers of new workers paying into the Social Security system. Fewer births and longer life expectancies are causes. In 1940, when the first benefits were paid, there were more than forty workers paying for each retiree receiving benefits. In 1960, there were five workers for each retiree. Today, there are 3.4 workers paying for each beneficiary. With the baby boom generation set to retire over the next few decades, that number is expected to fall even further. The Presidential Commission's report estimates that the ratio will be 2.2:1 in 2025 and just 2:1 by 2050.

These demographic changes mean that the burden of paying for Social Security will fall ever more heavily on the younger generation of workers. When polled, 41 percent of young people (ages eighteen to thirty-four) said that they do not expect to receive Social Security benefits at today's level when they retire, while 31 percent expected to receive no benefits at all.

Certainly, current benefit levels cannot be maintained without raising Social Security withholding taxes or extending the normal retirement age. But is it fair to tax younger workers more heavily to pay for their parents' retirement? Will there even be any money left for their own retirement? One solution that has been proposed is individual investment accounts that would allow individuals to invest a percentage of their Social Security savings themselves. Proponents of privatization argue that it would allow greater returns than the traditional Social Security system.

In the heady days of soaring stock prices and budget surpluses, just before President Bush created the commission, privatization was a popular solution. Workers, it was argued, could invest their Social Security funds in the stock market and see great returns. Low-wage workers would become shareholders in the U.S. economy and be able to accumulate wealth. Money would flow into the economy.

With the economic recession that began in 2008, privatization has lost momentum. But even when the plan was first proposed, it faced opposition on a number of grounds. The pay-as-you-go system is a guaranteed benefit. With many retirees depending on Social Security as their main source of income, this guarantee is crucial. But what happens if an individual invested unwisely? Proponents of a private system argue that an education campaign, along with requirements for diversification and safeguards against high-risk investments, should prevent such losses.

Another argument against privatization is the distortion it could cause in the stock market. With a large number of funds flowing into mutual funds from Social Security investors, prices might be driven up artificially. Government-approved mutual funds would receive a huge windfall in fees.

Most young people, who politicians have argued would benefit the most from privatization, do not support changing the Social Security system but would rather see the existing system strengthened. A majority polled say that "making sure that people receive a decent, guaranteed monthly retirement benefit" is a higher priority than "making sure that people receive a better rate of return."

Questions for Discussion

1. Who should be responsible for the welfare of the retired population? The current workers or the retirees (who should save for it)?

2. Is it appropriate for the government to mandate forced savings in private accounts in lieu of the pay-as-you-go Social Security system? Would this action change the nature of the requirements from taxes to private saving?

3. If part of the individual accounts would be administered by the government, is it ethical for the government to essentially become a major shareholder in private companies?

Sources: Key findings from Hart Research Poll, July 24, 1998; "Young Americans and Social Security: A Public Opinion Study Conducted for the 2030 Center by Peter D. Hart, Research Associates," July 1999, accessed April 5, 2009, http://www.commondreams.org/pressreleases/july99/072299a.htm; President's Commission to Strengthen Social Security, "Final Report: Strengthening Social Security and Creating Personal Wealth for All Americans," December 21, 2001 (this document includes all appendixes and Estimates of Financial Effects for Three Models Developed by the President's Commission to Strengthen Social Security, prepared by the Office of the Chief Actuary, Social Security Administration, May 2, 2001); Gary Burtless, "Social Security Privatization and Financial Market Risk," Center on Social and Economic Dynamics, Working Paper No. 10, February 2000; Social Security Administration, "Little Change in Social Security Solvency (Trustees Recommend Timely Action)," March 23, 2005, accessed April 5, 2009, http://www.ssa.gov/pressoffice/pr/trustee05-pr.htm.

The Future of Social Security

A quick glance at Figure 18.3 shows that the costs of Social Security are rising faster than the payments into the system. In the 2008 Annual Report to Congress, the Trustees announced the following:

- The projected point at which tax revenues will fall below program costs comes in 2011
- The projected point at which the trust funds will be exhausted comes in 2041
- The projected actuarial deficit over the seventy-five-year, long-range period is 3.54 percent of taxable payroll
- Over the seventy-five-year period, the trust funds require additional revenue, equivalent to $4.3 trillion in today's dollars to pay all scheduled benefits.

Figure 18.3 and Figure 18.4 are from the 2008 OASDI Trustees Report on the current and projected financial condition of all the Social Security programs. (The six trustees of the board are the Secretary of the Treasury, the Secretary of Labor, the Secretary of Health and Human Services, the Commissioner of Social Security, and two members appointed by the president.) The programs are financed through four separate trust funds: the Old-Age and Survivors Insurance (OASI) Trust Fund, Disability Insurance (DI), and two for Medicare.

To project future effects on the bottom line, the trustees review available evidence and gather expert opinion about all the factors that affect income and expenditures: demographic (birth rate, mortality, immigration); economic (unemployment rates, inflation); and program-specific (retirement patterns, disability incidence). The trustees make both short-range (ten-year) and long-range (seventy-five-year) predictions.

Traditional solutions to the looming Social Security and Medicare budget crisis have focused on increasing these taxes and cutting benefits. President G. W. Bush, in his State of the Union address on January 31, 2006, called for a bipartisan committee to find a solution to the impending major shortfall as the baby boom generation begins retirement. President Bush and many members of Congress believed the answer was privatization—allowing workers to invest some or all of their own (private) Social Security funds in the stock market, which historically yields greater returns over long investment periods than Treasury securities do. Beliefs in an ownership society and personal responsibility lie behind this objective. After Chile's successful move to privatization in 1981, almost every South American country has followed suit, with positive results. Countries from Singapore to Hungary have also converted successfully. With the economic recession of 2008 and the arrival of a new administration, focus has shifted from Social Security as a major political issue. But there are many arguments on both sides, and it remains to be seen how the Social Security system will be preserved.

Sources: Merrill Matthews, Jr., "A 12-Step Plan for Social Security Reform," National Center for Policy Analysis, June 4, 1998, http://www.ncpa.org/ba/ ba267.html (accessed April 4, 2009); Social Security Administration, the 2008 OASDI Trustees Report, June 11, 2008, http://ssa.gov/OACT/TR/TR08/ trTOC.html (accessed April 4, 2009).

KEY TAKEAWAYS

In this section you studied problems with the Social Security program in the United States and examples of global trends in administering social insurance:

- During the past two decades, Social Security taxes have increased faster than the general level of prices and the cost of health care.
- Extended life expectancies and lower birth rates have resulted in the funding burden being borne by a shrinking sector of society (three workers per retiree).
- Seventy-five-year actuarial projections issued annually by the Social Security and Medicare trustees show long-term funding deficits, with the program running out of money in the next thirty-two years.
- Global problems with social insurance institutions mirror those of the United States.
- Privatization of social security has worked well in Chile and Peru.
- The trend toward at least partial privatization and prefunding is worldwide.

DISCUSSION QUESTIONS

1. Do you think Social Security coverage should be voluntary? Explain.
2. Would you favor privatization of the Social Security retirement program, as other countries have done? Explain.
3. What solutions, other than privatization, would alleviate some of the funding problems of Social Security in the United States?
4. Should Medicare be expanded to cover everyone for a broad array of medical services, without regard to age or work history? Do you favor expanding Medicare into a national health insurance plan?

5. REVIEW AND PRACTICE

1. How is Social Security financed?

2. From time to time, you may hear that Social Security is in financial trouble and that you may not receive the benefits you expect. Do you think this is true? If it is true, what should be done about it?

3. C. J. Abbott worked hard all his life and built up a successful business. His daily routine involves helping with management decisions in the business, even though the majority of it is now owned and managed by his sons. He continues to draw a salary from the company sufficient to cover his expenses each month. C. J. is fully insured under Social Security and applied for benefits at age sixty-two. However, he does not presently receive, nor has he ever received, Social Security benefits. He celebrated his sixty-fourth birthday last May.

    a. Why hasn't C. J. received any Social Security benefits? Does this tell you anything about how much he is earning at the business?

    b. Why do you think C. J. continues to work?

    c. Will C. J.'s benefits be increased for his work beyond age sixty-five? (Assume that he starts drawing benefits at age seventy.)

    d. What is the logic behind the provision in the Social Security law that leads to a fully insured individual like C. J. not receiving Social Security retirement benefits after age sixty-five?

4. Your father-in-law was employed by a state agency for forty years before his retirement last year. He was not covered by Social Security on his state job. During the last five years of his career with the state government, however, you employed him on a part-time basis to do some surveying work on a housing development for which you had an engineering contract. You withheld Social Security tax from his wages and turned his share, plus yours as his employer, over to the government.

5. When your father-in-law retired, he applied for Social Security retirement benefits. Several months later, he was notified that he was not entitled to benefits because the work he did for you was in the family and not bona fide employment. The implication in the notice he received was that the job you gave him was designed to qualify him for Social Security benefits rather than to provide him with real employment.

    a. What should your father-in-law do?

    b. How can you help him?

6. Does the economic recession beginning in 2007 tell you anything about the merits, or the risks, of shifting Social Security funding to individual private accounts?

ENDNOTES

1. All statistics in this chapter are from the Social Security Administration (http://www.ssa.gov) and the Department of Health and Human Service's Medicare site (http://www.medicare.gov).

2. OASDI Board of Trustees, "Status of the Social Security Program: A Summary of the 2008 Annual Social Security," http://ssa.gov/OACT/TR/TR08/II_highlights.html#76455 (accessed April 4, 2009).

3. Boards of Trustees, Federal Hospital Insurance and Federal Supplementary Medical Insurance Trust Funds, 2008, Annual Report, http://www.cms.hhs.gov/ReportsTrustFunds/ (accessed April 4, 2009).

4. Family with one or more children excludes surviving parent or guardian who is ineligible to receive benefits.

5. Social Security Administration, "If You Are Blind or Have Low Vision—How We Can Help," SSA Publication No. 05-10052, January 2009, ICN 462554, http://www.ssa.gov/pubs/10052.html (accessed April 4, 2009).

6. Social Security Administration, The 2008 OASDI Trustees Report, Section VI(G): Analysis of Benefit Disbursements from the OASI Trust Fund with Respect to Disabled Beneficiaries, June 11, 2008, Accessed April 4, 2009, http://ssa.gov/OACT/TR/TR08/VI_OASIforDI.html#97986.

7. To be eligible for "special minimum" benefits, a worker must earn at least a certain portion (25 percent in years 1990 and before, and 15 percent in years following 1990) of the "old law" contribution and benefit base.

8. The COLA for December 1999 was originally determined as 2.4 percent based on CPIs published by the Bureau of Labor Statistics. Pursuant to Public Law 106-554; however, this COLA is effectively now 2.5 percent.

9. Applies in years before the year of attaining NRA.

10. Applies in the year of attaining NRA for months prior to such attainment.

11. Social Security Administration, "Social Security Responds to Hurricane Katrina, Agency Issues More Than 30,000 Emergency Checks to Date," Social Security Press Release, September 9, 2005, Accessed April 5, 2009, http://www.ssa.gov/pressoffice/pr/katrina-pr.html.

12. "Medicare Premiums and Deductibles for 2006," CMS Office of Public Affairs, September 16, 2005, http://www.cms.hhs.gov/apps/media/press/release.asp?Counter=1557, Accessed April 5, 2009.

13. Social Security and Medicare Board of Trustees' Summary of the 2008 Annual Reports on the status of the Social Security and Medicare Programs. The goal of the public trustees is to approach the current state of Social Security and Medicare in a nonpartisan way. They aim to ensure the integrity of the reports, both in methods of preparation and in the credibility of the information they contain. Realizing that numerous assumptions must be made to predict the future condition of the funds, the trustees prepare these reports because they believe the reports paint the most reliable picture available today. This summary is available online at http://www.ssa.gov/OACT/TRSUM/trsummary.html.

14. 2005 OASDI Trustees Report, Section II: Overview, http://www.ssa.gov/OACT/TR/TR02/II_highlights.html#76460.

CHAPTER 19

Mortality Risk Management: Individual Life Insurance and Group Life Insurance

Following Social Security as a foundation to managing the life cycle risks of old age, sickness, accidents, and death, we begin our expedition into the products that help in solving these risks. In this chapter we delve into the life insurance products and the life insurance industry as one separate from the property/casualty insurance industry. As you saw in Chapter 7, the accumulation of a reserve and the pricing of life insurance and annuities are based on mortality tables and life expectancy tables. The health insurance products use morbidity tables and loss data for calculating health and disability rates. In this chapter we will learn about the different life insurance products available—term life, whole life, universal life, variable life, and universal variable life products. The way these products fit into the risk management portfolio of the Smith family is featured in Case 1 of Chapter 23. This chapter concentrates on the life products themselves.

While mortality rates keep improving (as we discussed in Chapter 17), extreme health catastrophes can reverse the trend for brief periods. At various points in human history, mortality rates worsened as extreme health catastrophes occurred. For example, the mortality rate changed dramatically in 1918 when millions of people died from the flu pandemic. The potential for an avian flu pandemic in 2006 led to estimated life insurance claims of up to $133 billion under the most extreme scenario. The young and the elderly are those affected most by the flu. Because these age cohorts usually have less life insurance coverage, the general mortality impact may be even greater than the life claims estimates.[1]

Life insurance can be thought of as a contract providing a hedge against an untimely death. When purchasing life insurance, the policyowner buys a contract for the future delivery of dollars. This also provides liquidity. The death, whenever it occurs, will create , such as funeral costs and debt payment, and estate taxes if the estate is large enough, that must be paid immediately. Most people, no matter how wealthy, will not have this much cash on hand. Life insurance provides the necessary liquidity because its payment is triggered by death. Smart decisions about life insurance require understanding both the nature of life insurance and the different types of products available. In this chapter we cover the most widely used products.

The topics covered in this chapter include the following:

1. Links

2. How life insurance works

3. Life insurance products: term insurance, universal life, variable life, variable universal life, and current assumption whole life

4. Taxation, major policy provisions, riders, and adjusting life insurance for inflation

5. Group life insurance

1. LINKS

For our holistic risk management, we need to look at all sources of coverages available. Understanding each type of coverage will complete our ability to manage our risk. In this chapter we delve into the various types of life insurance coverage that are available in the market. Some focus on covering the risk of mortality alone, while others also offer a savings element along with covering the risk of dying. This means that at any point in time, there is a cash value to the policy. This savings element is critical to the choices we make among policies such as whole life, universal life, or universal variable life policies. Our savings with insurance companies, via life products or annuities, makes this industry one of the largest financial intermediaries globally. As explained in Chapter 7, the investment part of the operation of an insurer is as important as the underwriting part. Investments allow insurance companies to postprofits even when underwriting at a loss. In the life/health industry, investments are crucial to both financial performance and solvency. (Read how the industry is affected by poor investment returns in the box "The Life/Health Industry in the Economic Recession of 2008–2009" which appears later in this chapter.)

FIGURE 19.1 **The Links between Holistic Risk Puzzle Pieces and Life Insurance Policies**

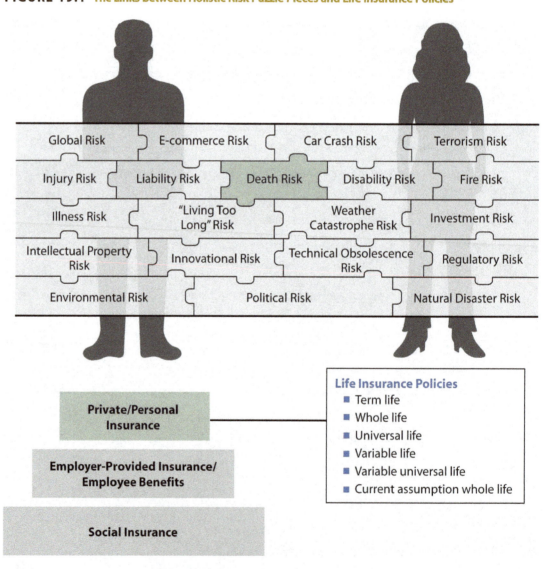

In this chapter, we drill down into the life insurance policies, but this is just a piece of the products puzzle that helps us complete the bigger picture of our risks. All of the steps of the three-step structure in Figure 19.1 include some elements of death benefits coverage. In this chapter we delve into the top step for the different types of individual life coverage. Figure 19.1 provides us with the connection between the life policies of this chapter and the holistic risk picture.

2.   HOW LIFE INSURANCE WORKS

LEARNING OBJECTIVES

In this section we elaborate on the manner in which life insurance products are able to pay the promised benefit:

- **The concept of pooling in life insurance**
- **Adjustments reflected in life insurance premiums**
- **The cost-prohibitive nature of renewable term life insurance over time**
- **Level premiums in whole life policies**
- **How level premiums create reserve and protection**

Life insurance, like other forms of insurance, is based on three concepts: pooling many exposures into a group, accumulating a fund through contributions (premiums) from the members of the group, and paying from this fund for the losses of those who die each year. That is, life insurance involves the group sharing of individual losses. The individual transfers the risk of dying to the pool by paying the premiums. To set premium rates, the insurer must be able to calculate the probability of death at various ages among its insureds, based on pooling. The simplest illustration of pooling is one-year term life insurance. If an insurer promises to pay $100,000 at the death of each insured who dies during the year, it must collect enough money to pay the claims. If past experience indicates that 0.1 percent of a group of young people will die during the year, one death may be expected for every 1,000 persons in the group. If a group of 300,000 is insured, 300 claims (300,000 × .001) are expected. Because each contract is for $100,000, the total expected amount of death claims is $30 million (300 claims × $100,000). To collect enough premiums to cover mortality costs (the cost of claims), the insurer must collect $100 per policyowner ($30 million in claims / 300,000 policyowners).

2.1   Other Premium Elements

In addition to covering mortality costs, a life insurance premium must reflect several adjustments. First, the premium is reduced to recognize that the insurer expects to earn investment income on premiums paid in advance. In this manner, most of an insurer's investment income benefits consumers. Second, the premium is increased to cover the insurer's marketing and administrative expenses. Taxes levied on the insurer must also be recovered. In calculating premiums, an actuary usually increases the premium to cover the insurer's risk and expected profits. Risk charges cover any deviations above the predicted level of losses and expenses. The major **premium elements** for term life insurance and the actual prediction of deaths and the estimation of other premium elements are complicated actuarial processes (see Chapter 7).

The mortality curve discussed in Chapter 7 and Chapter 17 also shows why life insurance for a term of one year costs relatively little for young people. The probability that a death benefit payment will be made during that year is very low. The mortality curve also indicates why the cost of **yearly renewable term life insurance**, purchased on a year-by-year basis, becomes prohibitive for most people's budgets beyond the middle years. The theory of insurance is that the losses of the few can be paid for by relatively small contributions from the many. If, however, a large percentage of those in the group suffer losses (say, because all members of the group are old), the burden on one's budget becomes too great, substantial adverse selection is experienced, and the insurance mechanism fails.

2.2   Level-Premium Plan

The mortality curve shows that yearly renewable term life insurance, where premiums increase each year as mortality increases, becomes prohibitively expensive at advanced ages. For example, the mortality table shows a mortality rate of 0.06419 for a male age seventy-five. Thus, just the mortality element of the annual premium for a $100,000 yearly renewable term life insurance policy would be $6,419 (0.06419 × $100,000). At age ninety, ignoring other premium elements and adverse selection, the mortality cost would be $22,177 (0.22177 × −$100,000). From a budget perspective, this high cost, coupled

premium elements

Adjustments made in life insurance rates for items such as investment income, marketing/administrative costs, taxes, and actuarial risks.

yearly renewable term life insurance

Term life insurance purchased on a year-by-year basis.

with adverse selection, can leave the insurer with a group of insureds whose mortality is even higher than would be anticipated in the absence of adverse selection. Healthy people tend to drop the insurance, while unhealthy people try to pay premiums because they think their beneficiaries may soon have a claim. This behavior is built into renewal rates on term insurance, resulting in renewal rates that rise substantially above rates for new term insurance for healthy people of the same age. A system of spreading the cost for life insurance protection, over a long period or for the entire life span, without a rise in premiums, is essential for most individuals. This is the function of level-premium life insurance.

level premium

In life insurance, a premium that remains constant throughout the premium-paying period instead of rising from year to year.

A **level premium** remains constant throughout the premium-paying period, instead of rising from year to year. Mathematically, the level premium is the amount of the constant *periodic payment* over a specified period (ending before the specified date in the event of death); it is equivalent to a hypothetical *single premium* that could be paid at the beginning of the contract, discounting for interest and mortality. The hypothetical single premium at the beginning can be thought of as similar to a mortgage that is paid for by periodic level premiums.

As Figure 19.2 shows, the level premium for an ordinary (whole) life policy (which provides lifetime protection) is issued at age twenty-five in the illustration and is greater during the early years than are the premiums for a yearly renewable term policy for the same period. The excess (see the shaded area between age twenty-five and a little before age fifty in Figure 19.2) and its investment earnings are available to help pay claims as they occur. This accumulation of funds, combined with a decreasing amount of true insurance protection (which is the net amount at risk to the insurance mechanism), makes possible a premium that remains level even though the probability of death rises as the insured grows older. In later years, the true cost of insurance protection (the probability of death at a particular age times the decreased amount of protection) is paid for by the level premium plus a portion of the investment earnings produced by the policy's cash value. In summary, the level premium is higher than necessary to pay claims and other expenses during the early years of the contract, but less than the cost of protection equal to the total death benefit during the later years. The concept of a level premium is basic to an understanding of financing death benefits at advanced ages.

cash value

Accumulated funds of level premium life insurance policies as that can be utilized to meet various savings needs.

The accumulation of funds is a mathematical side effect of leveling the premium to accommodate consumers' budgets. Beginning in the 1950s, however, insurers began to refer to the accumulated funds of level premium life insurance policies as **cash value** that could meet various savings needs. Today, the payment of premiums greater than the amount required to pay for a yearly renewable term policy often is motivated, at least in the minds of consumers, by the objective of creating savings or investment funds.

FIGURE 19.2 **Yearly Renewable Term Premium and Level Premium for Ordinary Life (Issued at Age Twenty-Five)**

Based on nonsmoker rates for a $50,000 policy with a selected company.

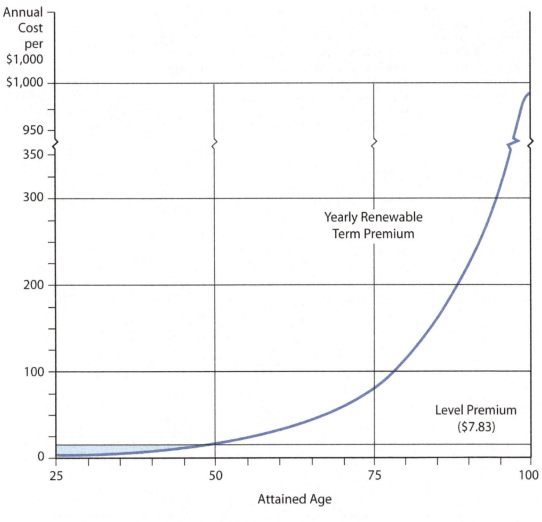

Premiums that exceed the cost of yearly renewable term life insurance.

Effects of the Level Premium Plan

From an economic standpoint, the level premium plan does two things. First, the insurer offers an installment payment plan with equal payments over time. Second, the level premium policies are made up of two elements: protection and investment.

As discussed, although the periodic premium payments exceed death benefits and other expenses for an insured group during the early years of the policy, they fall short during later years (see Figure 19.2); consequently, the insurer accumulates a **reserve** to offset this deficiency. The insurer's reserve is similar in amount, but not identical, to the sum of cash values for the insured group. The reserve is a liability on the insurer's balance sheet, representing the insurer's obligation and reflecting the extent to which future premiums and the insurer's assumed investment income will not be sufficient to cover the present value of future claims on a policy. At any point, the present value of the reserve fund, future investment earnings, and future premiums are sufficient to pay the present value of all future death claims for a group of insureds. When an insured dies, the insurer is obligated to pay the beneficiary the face amount (death benefit) of the policy. Part of this payment is an amount equal to the reserve.

reserve

In life insurance, funds accumulated to offset the deficiency of periodic premium payments falling short of providing promised death benefits in later years of a policy.

net amount at risk

For the insurer, the difference between the funding reserve at any point in time and the face amount of the policy.

protection element

For the insured, the difference between the funding reserve at any point in time and the face amount of the policy.

The difference between the reserve at any point in time and the face amount of the policy is known as the **net amount at risk** for the insurer and as the **protection element** for the insured. As Figure 19.2 illustrates, this element declines each year because the reserve (investment or cash value) increases. The protection/net-amount-at-risk element is analogous to decreasing term insurance. All level premium life policies have a combination of cash value and protection.

The amount at risk for the insurer (that is, the protection element) decreases as the cash value element increases with age; thus, less true insurance (protection) is purchased each year. This decreasing amount of insurance is one of the reasons why the annual cost of pure insurance (that is, the protection element) to the insurer is less than the sum of the level premium plus investment earnings, even at advanced ages when mortality rates significantly exceed the premium per $1,000 of death benefit. Over time, the growing amount of investment earnings (due to increasing cash value) more than offsets the inadequacy of the level premium. The periodic addition of part of these investment earnings to cash value explains why the cash value in the policy continues to grow throughout the life of the contract (see Figure 19.3).

FIGURE 19.3 **Proportion of Protection and Cash Value in Ordinary Life Contract (Issued to a Male Age Twenty-Five)**

This graph shows the cash value (investment) figures for a selected ordinary life policy. The insurer's reserve would be slightly higher than the cash value in the early contract years.

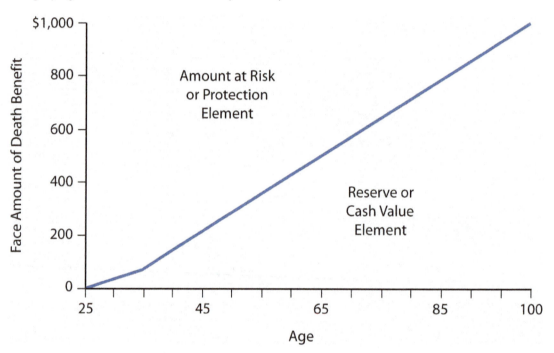

From an insurer's perspective, the reserve is a liability that will have to be paid when the insured either dies or surrenders the policy. The separation of a whole life policy into protection and investment elements is an economic or personal finance concept rather than an actuarial one. Actuaries deal with large groups of insureds rather than individual policies; they look at an individual policy as an indivisible contract.

The cash value is classified as an asset on the policyholder's personal balance sheet because it is the policy owner's money. There are three ways to realize the cash value:

1. Surrender (discontinue) the policy and receive the cash value as a refund

2. Take a loan for an amount not to exceed the cash value

3. Leave the cash value in the contract and eventually let it mature as part of the death claim

KEY TAKEAWAYS

In this section you studied mechanisms that allow for the provision of life insurance:

- The concept of pooling is critical to life insurance because the losses of the few can be paid for by relatively small contributions from the many.
- Life insurance premiums are adjusted for investment income, marketing/administrative costs, taxes, and actuarial risks.
- Yearly renewable term life insurance is cost-prohibitive in later years due to adverse selection and the increased probability of death.
- In whole life policies, the level premium is higher than necessary to pay claims and other expenses during the early years of the contract, but less than the cost of protection equal to the total death benefit during the later years.
- Level premium policies allow for cash value accumulation.
- The difference between the reserve and the face amount of the life insurance policy is the net amount at risk for the insurer and the protection element for the insured.
- Insureds may realize their cash value by surrendering the policy, taking out a loan, or letting the policy mature as part of the policy's death benefit.

DISCUSSION QUESTIONS

1. Why does yearly renewable term life become cost prohibitive over time?
2. Explain why an investment (cash value) segment becomes part of a level premium life insurance contract.
3. Explain the nature of the reserve an insurer accumulates in connection with its level premium life insurance policies.
4. What are the options with cash surrender value?

3.   LIFE INSURANCE MARKET CONDITIONS AND LIFE INSURANCE PRODUCTS

LEARNING OBJECTIVES

In this section we elaborate on the following:

- **Market condition in 2008–2009**
- **Term life insurance**
- **Whole life insurance**
- **Universal life insurance**
- **Variable life insurance**
- **Variable universal life insurance**
- **Current assumption whole life insurance**

3.1 Market Conditions

The life insurance industry is one of the largest industries in the world. Premiums for life, health, and annuity grew by 5.7 percent from $583.6 billion in 2006 to $616.7 billion in 2007 in the United States.[2] This section concentrates on the life products sold to individuals. A comprehensive summary of these products is available in Table 19.1. The trend is toward lower life insurance rates for all types of life insurance products. Improvements in mortality rates have accounted for lower expected rates. This improvement was also highlighted in Chapter 17. The life/health industry's condition deteriorated during the economic recession beginning in December 2007. These problems are detailed in the box "The Life/Health Industry in the Economic Recession of 2008–2009."

The Life/Health Industry in the Economic Recession of 2008–2009

Unlike property/casualty carriers, the prosperity of life insurance companies is closely linked to the health of the broader financial network. Investments make up a significant portion of industry profits, and they are the driving component behind product delivery. Because of the economic recession, life annuities promising minimum payments (discussed extensively in Chapter 21) are particularly strained; in many cases, their guarantees are no longer supported by underlying investments. Those underlying investments consist of stocks, commercial mortgages, mortgage-backed securities (or MBSs, which were covered in the box "Problem Investments and the Credit Crisis" in Chapter 7), and corporate bonds. Market devaluation, default, or interest rate reductions have harmed all of these funding sources. Consider that the asset mix of life insurers in 2007 included $387.5 billion worth of MBSs; by way of comparison, the property and casualty insurance industry held $125.8 billion.

Recall from Chapter 5 and Chapter 7 that insurers' net worth is expressed in the form of capital and surplus (assets minus liabilities). Insurers must have capital that is sufficient to satisfy their liabilities (mainly in the form of loss reserves). In 2008, surplus declined by 4.7 percent for the top one hundred life insurers. This drop was mitigated somewhat, however, by successfully raising new capital in 2008. Nonetheless, investors will be none too pleased with the return on equity ratio of −0.3 percent, down from 12.8 percent in 2007. With little bargaining power, the industry may be able to raise new capital in the future only at less-than-favorable terms. Conning Research and Consulting estimates that surplus for the entire industry could be off by as much as 24 percent in 2008. Low interest rates and investments that are not simply depressed, but highly volatile, are cited as the reasons for the industry's shrinking assets and surplus.

Twelve life insurers, including MetLife, Hartford Financial Group, and Prudential, have applied for aid through the government's Troubled Asset Relief Program (TARP). TARP, signed into law October 2, 2008, pledges $700 billion worth of federal spending toward the purchase of assets and equities of imperiled financial institutions. As of this writing, the U.S. Treasury has decided to include insurers in the TARP program. (AIG is a special case, in a class all its own.) At the end of 2008, unrealized losses amounted to $30 billion for MetLife, $15 billion for Hartford, and $11 billion for Prudential. Nonetheless, company officials insist that their firms are adequately capitalized to meet current liabilities.

On February 27, 2009, in line with previous moves by fellow rating agencies Fitch and Moody's, Standard & Poor's (S&P) lowered its financial strength and credit ratings on ten groups of U.S. life insurers and seven life insurance holding companies, respectively. Organizations implicated include Metlife, Hartford, Genworth Financial, Prudential, and Pacific LifeCorp. S&P's analysis focused on poor investment performance, equity declines, and company earnings volatility. On the bright side, Massachusetts Mutual Life, New York Life Insurance, and Northwestern Mutual in particular have retained triple-A financial strength ratings as of this writing. After these downgrades, the American Council of Life Insurers (ACLI) lobbied the National Association of Insurance Commissioners (NAIC) for lower capital and reserve requirements. The ACLI, a trade organization of 340 member companies accounting for 93 percent of the life insurance industry's U.S. assets, said that their proposal would give a financial cushion and restore some operating flexibility. The NAIC denied the request on January 29, 2009, with president and New Hampshire insurance commissioner Roger Sevigny stating, "So far the insurance industry is in much better condition than most of the rest of the financial services sector because of strong state solvency regulations."

With respect to the health segment, there has been a longstanding assumption that health care was a recession-proof industry due to the fact that people become ill and need medical services regardless of economic circumstances. The current recession is casting doubt on this notion. As of this writing, 60 percent of Americans have health insurance through employer-sponsored plans. The recent advent of high-deductible health plans and their adoption by employers has increased personal responsibility for covering health care expenses traditionally paid by insurers. (Both employer-sponsored health options and high-deductible health plans are covered in Chapter 22.) Financially strapped employees are thus forced to choose between paying for medical services or paying their mortgages. On the one hand, the delaying and avoidance of medical services by insureds could bode well for health insurers' loss experience. At the same time, however, with unemployment rates at their highest since 1982, the overall insured population has decreased over the course of the recession. To quantify, the Center for American Progress estimates that 4 million Americans have lost their health insurance since the recession began; up to 14,000 people could be losing coverage every day. The Center correlates each 1 percentage point rise in the unemployment rate with 2.4 million Americans losing employer-sponsored health insurance. Individual health insurance plans are an option, but they are frequently cost-prohibitive to the unemployed unless they are young and in the healthy pool. Those who do remain insured but reduce their consumption of medical services have less demand for health insurance. Consequently, they could drop all but the most basic and necessary health coverage options. Therefore, it is difficult to imagine potential improvements in loss experience offsetting the effects of a shrinking population of insureds.

As further evidence, consider that the top eight health insurance plans in the United States cover 58 percent of the insured population. These insurers have faced challenges over the course of the recession. For example, UnitedHealth Group saw the profit margins on its Health Care Services unit fall from 9.3 percent to 6.6 percent between September 30, 2007, and June 30, 2008. This may not seem significant, but stable profit margins help to contain premium costs in health insurance. The top eight plans have also experienced slowdowns in enrollment growth, a trend that could see enrollment contract as the recession persists.

In response to recessionary pressures, the life/health industry has scaled back on aggressive product development efforts to save costs and meet changing consumer demands. Life insurers are reporting an increasing preference among clients for term rather than permanent insurance. Insureds are also cutting the face value of their policies to reduce premiums. President of Genworth Retirement Services Chris Grady stressed, "The industry has to develop simple retirement income solutions, simple processes and simple marketing" to cope with current market conditions. To their advantage, life insurers' needs for new capital are partially subsidized by highly liquid premium revenues. Fortunately, the fundamental drive for the security provided by life insurance is strong, and especially so during uncertain times. As for health insurance, the Deloitte Center for Health Solutions expects that individuals will delay primary and preventive care, people with high-deductible health plans will put off making payments, and medical debt bankruptcies will rise. Insurers will adjust by shifting more costs to insureds in the form of higher premiums, deductibles, and copayments and by enacting stricter policy provisions.

On March 12, 2009, the *Wall Street Journal* reported that the Dow Jones Wilshire U.S. Life Insurance Index had fallen 59 percent for the year to date. For the life/health segment, the recession did not hit full-force until the fourth quarter of 2008 due to high losses from investments. Because of accounting rules, the impact of these losses may not be realized on insurers' books until late 2009 into 2010. FBR Capital Markets estimated that realized credit losses over the preceding two years could top $19.2 billion, exceeding the industry's projected excess capital of $17.5 billion through 2010. If such a shortfall materializes, it will entail raising new capital, government intervention, or dissolution of distressed companies. Going forward, Conning Research and Consulting predicts significant consolidation within the industry. With life insurers holding a reported 18 percent of all outstanding corporate bonds, the health of capital markets is highly dependent on the activities of life insurers. The 63 percent decline in private bond and equity purchases by life companies in the fourth quarter of 2008 certainly contributed to the depression of capital markets, which is projected to persist until investment activity improves. Similarly, with health care expenditures accounting for 17 percent of gross domestic product (GDP), recovery of the overall U.S. economy is projected to be influenced by the performance of the health industry. The Obama administration has targeted health care as a major area of reform, and the American Recovery and Reinvestment Act of 2009 contains some provisions for health care. These and other efforts will be discussed in Chapter 22.

Sources: "Analysis Shows Industry Income Down Sharply," National Underwriter Life/Health Edition, March 5, 2009, http://www.lifeandhealthinsurancenews.com/News/2009/3/Pages/Analysis-Shows-Industry- Income-Down-Sharply.aspx, accessed March 12, 2009; "Recession's Impact to Stay with Life Insurance Industry for Some Time, Study Says," Insurance & Financial Advisor (IFA), January 15, 2009, http://www.ifawebnews.com/articles/2009/01/15/news/life/doc496b5d961a699473705621.txt, accessed March 12, 2009; "Conning Research: Life Insurance Industry Forecast—Financial Crisis Will Impact Industry Results Through 2010," Reuters, January 7, 2009, http://www.reuters.com/article/ pressRelease/idUS141575+07-Jan-2009+PRN20090107, accessed March 12, 2009; Scott Patterson and Leslie Scism, "The Next Big Bailout Decision: Insurers," Wall Street Journal, March 12, 2009, A1; Stephen Taub, "S&P Less Sure of Life Insurance Industry," CFO, February 27, 2009, http://www.cfo.com/article.cfm/13209064/?f=rsspage, accessed March 12, 2009; Keith L. Martin, "State Regulators Deny Life Insurance Industry Request to Lower Capital and Surplus Standards," Insurance & Financial Advisor (IFA), February 2, 2009, http://www.ifawebnews.com/articles/2009/ 02/02/news/life/doc49836329444a1723733499.txt, accessed March 12, 2009; Catherine Arnst, "Health Care: Not So Recession-Proof," BusinessWeek, March 25, 2008, http://www.businessweek.com/technology/content/mar2008/ tc20080324_828167.htm?chan=top+news_top+news+index_top+story, accessed March 12, 20009; Meha Ahmad, "Job Losses Leave More Americans Without Health Insurance," Life and Health Insurance Foundation for Education, January 13, 2009, http://www.lifehappens.org/blog/p,154/ #more-154, accessed March 12, 2009; Mary Beth Lehman, "Report: 4 Million Americans Lost Health Insurance Since Recession Began," Business Review, February 22, 2009; http://www.bizjournals.com/albany/stories/2009/02/16/daily58.html, accessed March 12, 2009; "Top Health Plans Feel Recession According to Mark Farrah Associates," Reuters, February 19, 2009, http://74.125.47.132/search?q=cache:CK-PYvd3vZUJ:http://www.reuters.com/ article/pressRelease/idUS225967%2B19- Feb-2009%2BBW20090219+health+insurance+industry+recession&cd= 21&hl=en&ct=clnk&gl=us, accessed March 12, 2009; Linda Koco, "All Product Eyes Will Fix on the Economy in 2009," National Underwriter Life/Health Edition, January 5, 2009, http://www.lifeandhealthinsurancenews.com/Issues/2009/January%205%202009/Pages/All-Product-Eyes-Will-Fix-On-The-Economy-In-2009.aspx, accessed March 12, 2009; Scott Patterson, "Insurers Face More Losses," Wall Street Journal, March 12, 2009, http://blogs.wsj.com/marketbeat/2009/03/ 12/insurers-face-more-losses/, accessed March 12, 2009.

3.2   Term Insurance

Term life insurance provides protection for a specified period, called the policy's term (or duration). When a company issues a one-year term life policy, it promises to pay the face amount of the policy in the event of death during that year.

term life insurance

Provides coverage for a specified period, called the policy's term (or duration).

Duration

lapse rates

In term life insurance, failure to renew policies.

The length of term policies varies; common terms are one, five, ten, fifteen, and twenty years. Term policies are often not renewable beyond age sixty-five or seventy because of adverse selection that increases with age. Increasingly, however, yearly renewable term policies are renewable to age ninety-five or one hundred, although it would be unusual for a policy to stay in effect at advanced ages because of the amount of the premium. Yearly renewable term policies are subject to high **lapse rates** (that is, failure to be renewed) and low profitability for the insurer.

Short-term life insurance policies involve no investment element. Long-term contracts (e.g., term to age sixty-five), when accompanied by a level premium, can accumulate a small cash value element in the early years, but this is depleted during the latter part of the term because then the cost of mortality exceeds the sum of the level premium and the investment earnings. Two options are typically available with term insurance sold directly to individuals: renewability and convertibility.

TABLE 19.1 Characteristics of Major Types of Life Insurance Policies

	Distinguishing Feature	Premiums	Cash Value	Death Benefit
Term life	Provides protection for a specific period (term)	Fixed, but increase at each renewal	None, thus no provision for loans or withdrawals	Pays face amount of policy if death occurs within term
Whole life	Lifetime protection: as long as premiums are paid, policy stays in force	Fixed	Guaranteed	Pays face amount if policy is in force when death occurs
Universal life	Guaranteed minimum interest rate on the investments accumulated in the accounts. Interest rates are based on bonds only (not stocks) and can be higher than the minimum guaranteed	Flexible, set by policyholder; used to pay mortality rates and expenses, then remainder is invested	Depends on the account value minus surrender charges	Option A: maintains level death benefit Option B: face amount increases as accumulated cash value grows
Variable life	The "mutual fund" policy, intended to keep death benefits apace with inflation; technically, a security as well as insurance	Fixed	Not guaranteed; depends on investment performance of stocks	Minimum face amount that can be greater as cash value changes
Variable universal life	Combines the premium and death benefit flexibility of a universal life policy with the investment choices in stocks of variable life	Flexible, as in universal life	Not guaranteed; depends on investment performance of stocks	Same options are universal life

Renewability

renewability option

In term life insurance, gives the right to renew the policy for a specified number of additional periods of protection at a predetermined schedule of premium rates without new evidence of insurability.

If the policyholder wishes to continue the protection for more than one term, the insurer will require a new application and new evidence of insurability. The risk of being turned down may be handled by purchasing renewable term insurance. The **renewability option** gives the policyholder the right to renew the life insurance policy for a specified number of additional periods of protection, at a predetermined schedule of premium rates, without new evidence of insurability. Renewability protects insurability for the period specified. After that period has elapsed, the insured must again submit a new application and prove insurability.

Each time the policy is renewed, the premium increases because of the insured's increasing age. Because the least healthy tend to renew and the most healthy tend to discontinue, the renewable feature increases the cost of protection. The renewable feature, however, is valuable in term life insurance.

Convertibility

A term life policy with a **convertibility option** provides the right to convert the term policy to a whole life or another type of insurance, before a specified time, without proving insurability. If, for example, at age twenty-eight you buy a term policy renewable to age sixty-five and convertible for twenty years, you may renew each year for several years and then, perhaps at age thirty-six, decide you prefer cash value life insurance. Your motivation may be that the premium, though higher than that of the term policy at the age of conversion, will remain the same year after year; the policy can be kept in force indefinitely; or you may want to include cash values among your investments. If you become uninsurable or insurable only at higher-than-standard (called substandard) rates, you will find the convertibility feature very valuable.

Most life insurance conversions are made at **attained age premium rates**, meaning that the premium for the new policy is based on the age at the time of the conversion. The insured or policyowner pays the same rate as anyone else who can qualify for standard rates based on good health and other insurability factors. The option results in no questions about your insurability.

Death Benefit Pattern

The death benefit in a term policy remains level, decreases, or increases over time. Each pattern of protection fits specific needs. For example, a decreasing term policy may be used as collateral for a loan on which the principal is being reduced by periodic payments. An increasing amount of protection helps maintain purchasing power during inflation. The increasing benefit is likely to be sold as a rider to a level benefit policy.

Mortgage protection insurance is decreasing term insurance; with each mortgage payment, the face value of the insurance decreases to correspond to the amount of the loan that is outstanding. Otherwise, mortgage protection is like other decreasing term policies.[3] Credit life insurance is similar to mortgage protection. In **credit life insurance**, the death benefit changes, up or down, as the balance changes on an installment loan or other type of consumer loan.

Premium Patterns

An insurer's rates for nonsmokers may be 40 percent or so lower than those for smokers. Rates for women are less than for men (see the box "Should Life Insurance Rates Be Based on Gender?" in Chapter 17). The yearly renewable term contract usually has a table of premiums that increase each year as the insured ages and as time elapses since insurability was established.

Reentry term allows the insured to demonstrate insurability periodically, perhaps every five years, and qualify for a new (lower) select category of rates that are not initially loaded for adverse selection. If the insured cannot qualify for the new rates, usually because of worsening health, he or she can either pay the higher rates of the initial premium table (ultimate rates) or drop the policy and try to find better rates with another insurer.

Summary: Features of Term Life

In summary, in term life we see the following features (see also Table 19.1):

- Death benefits: level or decreasing
- Cash value: none
- Premiums: increase at each renewal
- Policy loans: not allowed
- Partial withdrawals: not allowed
- Surrender charges: none

3.3 Whole Life Insurance

Whole life insurance, as its name suggests, provides for payment of the face value upon death regardless of when the death may occur. As long as the premiums are paid, the policy stays in force. Thus, whole life insurance is also referred to as permanent insurance. This ability to maintain the policy throughout one's life, instead of a specific term, is the key characteristic of whole life insurance.

There are three traditional types of whole life insurance: (1) ordinary or straight life, (2) limited-payment life, and (3) single-premium life. The differences among them is in the arrangements for premium payment. (See Chapter 26 for a sample straight whole life policy.)

---

convertability option

In term life insurance, provides the right to convert the policy to a whole life or another type of insurance before a specified time without proving insurability.

attained age premium rates

In life insurance conversion, when the premium for the new policy is based on the age at the time of the conversion.

mortgage protection insurance

Decreasing term insurance; with each mortgage payment, the face value of the insurance decreases to correspond to the amount of the loan that is outstanding.

credit life insurance

Provides that the death benefit changes, up or down, as the balance changes on an installment loan or other type of consumer loan.

reentry term

In life insurance, allows the insured to re-demonstrate insurability periodically, perhaps every five years, and qualify for a new (lower) select category of rates that are not initially loaded for adverse selection.

whole life insurance

Provides for payment of the face value upon death regardless of when the death may occur; "permanent insurance"

Straight Life

straight life

Form of whole life insurance where premiums are paid in equal periodic amounts over the life of the insured.

The premiums for a **straight life** policy are paid in equal periodic amounts over the life of the insured. The rate is based on the assumption that the insured will live to an advanced age (such as age ninety or 100). In effect, the insured is buying the policy on an installment basis and the installments are spread over the balance of the lifetime, as explained earlier in our discussion of the level premium concept. This provides the lowest possible level outlay for permanent protection.

As shown in Figure 19.3, the level premium policy consists of a protection element and a cash value element. The cash value builds over time, and eventually, when the insured is ninety or one hundred, the cash value will equal the face value of the policy. If the insured is still alive at this advanced age, the insurer will pay the death benefit as if death occurred. By this time, no real insurance element exists. The options available with regard to this value are discussed later in this chapter. A basic straight life policy typically has a face amount (death benefit) that remains level over the lifetime. The pattern can change, however, by using dividends to buy additional amounts of insurance or by purchasing a cost-of-living adjustment rider.

Limited-Payment Life

limited-payment life

Form of whole life insurance that offers lifetime protection but limits premium payments to a specified period of years or to a specified age; after premiums have been paid during the specified period, the policy remains in force for the balance of life without further premium payment.

Like straight life, **limited-payment life** offers lifetime protection but limits premium payments to a specified period of years or to a specified age. After premiums have been paid during the specified period, the policy remains in force for the balance of the insured's life without further premium payment. The policy is "paid up." A twenty-pay life insurance policy becomes paid up after premiums have been paid for twenty years, a life-paid-up-at-sixty-five becomes paid up at age sixty-five, and so on (see Figure 19.4). The shorter premium payment period appeals to some buyers. For example, a life-paid-up-at-sixty-five policy ends premiums around the time many people expect to begin living on retirement pay. If the insured dies before the end of the premium-paying period, premium payments stop and the face amount is paid. These policies are mainly sold as business insurance where there is a need to pay fully for a policy by a certain date, such as the time an employee will retire.

Single-Premium Life

single premium life

Form of life insurance where the only premium paid is an amount equal to the present value of future benefits, with discounts both for investment earnings and mortality.

Whole life insurance may be bought for a single premium—the ultimate in limited payment. Mathematically, the **single premium** is the present value of future benefits, with discounts both for investment earnings and mortality. Cash and loan values are high compared with policies bought on the installment plan (see Figure 19.4). Single-premium life insurance is bought almost exclusively for its investment features; protection is viewed as a secondary benefit of the transaction.

FIGURE 19.4 **Protection and Cash Value Elements for Single-Premium and Installment Forms of Cash Value Life Insurance**

Note: Hypothetical values not drawn to scale.

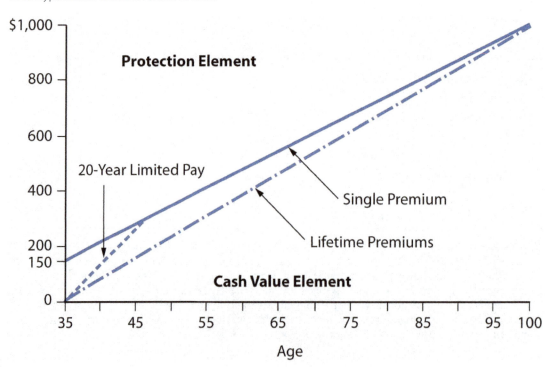

Investment Aspects

The typical buyer of life insurance, however, does not expect to pay income taxes on proceeds from his or her policy. Instead, the expectation is for the policy to mature eventually as a death claim. At that point, all proceeds (protection plus cash value) of life insurance death claims are exempt from income taxes under Section 101(a)(1). In practice, most policies terminate by being lapsed or surrendered prior to death as needs for life insurance change.

Life insurers offer participation in portfolios of moderate-yield investments, such as high-grade industrial bonds, mortgages, real estate, and common stock, in which cash values are invested with potentially no income tax on the realized investment returns. Part of each premium, for all types of cash value life insurance, is used to make payments on the protection element of the contract, but the protection element also has an expected return. This return is equal to the probability of death multiplied by the amount of protection. Thus, the need to pay for protection in order to gain access to the cash value element of a single-premium or other investment-oriented plan should not be viewed as a consumer disadvantage if there is a need for additional life insurance protection. The participation (dividend) feature of a policy has a major effect on its cost and worth.

Participation Feature

Mutual life insurers have always sold their term and cash value life products on a participation basis. Stock life companies have also made limited use of participating policies. Participating whole life contracts pay **dividends** for the purpose of refunding higher-than-necessary premiums and sharing company profits with policyowners. Thus, as investment returns escalate above previous expectations, or as mortality rates decline, the policyowners share in the success of the insurer.

Dividends allow the sharing of current profits from investments, mortality assumptions, expense estimates, and lapse experience with the policyholder. Investment returns usually have more influence on the size of dividends than do the other factors. The fact that insurer investment portfolios tend to have many medium- and long-term bonds and mortgages that do not turn over quickly creates a substantial lag, however, between the insurer's realization of higher yields on new investments and the effect of those higher yields on average portfolio returns that affect dividends.

Participating whole life insurance continues to be a major product line for mutual insurers. Sales illustrations are used by agents in presenting the product to the consumer. For products with the participation feature, dividends projected for long periods into the future are a significant part of the sales illustration. Generally, the illustrations are based on the current experience of the insurer with respect to its investment returns, mortality experience, expenses, and lapse rates.

Summary: Features of Whole Life

In summary, in whole life we see the following features (see also Table 19.1):

- Death benefits: fixed level
- Cash value: guaranteed amounts
- Premiums: fixed level
- Policy loans: allowed
- Partial withdrawals: not allowed
- Surrender charges: none

3.4 Universal Life Insurance

Universal life insurance contracts were introduced to the market in 1979 to bolster the profits of stock insurance companies. **Universal life insurance** policies offer competitive investment features and the flexibility to meet changing consumer needs. When expense charges (such as mortality rates) are set at reasonable levels, the investment part of the universal life contract can be competitive on an after-tax basis with money market mutual funds, certificates of deposit, and other short-term instruments offered by investment companies, banks, and other financial institutions. Most insurers invest funds from their universal life contracts primarily in short-term investments so they can have the liquidity to meet policyholder demands for cash values. Some other insurers use investment portfolios that are competitive with medium- and long-term investment returns. A key feature of the product is its flexibility. The policyowner can do the following:

- Change the amount of premium periodically
- Discontinue premiums and resume them at a later date without lapsing the policy
- Change the amount of death protection (subject to restrictions)

dividends

Paid by participating whole life contracts to insureds for the purpose of refunding higher-than-necessary premiums and sharing company profits with policyowners.

dividends

Paid by participating whole life contracts to insureds for the purpose of refunding higher-than-necessary premiums and sharing company profits with policyowners.

universal life insurance

Offer competitive investment features and the flexibility to meet changing consumer needs by allowing policyholder to change the amount of premium periodically, discontinue premiums and resume them at later date without lapsing the policy, and change the amount of death protection.

Universal life was introduced during a period of historically high, double-digit interest rates. Sales illustrations often projected high investment returns for many years into the future, resulting in illustrated cash values that surpassed those of traditional cash value policies. Traditional policy illustrations projected dividends and cash values using average investment returns for a portfolio of securities and mortgages purchased during periods of low, medium, and high interest rates. Consumers were attracted to the high new money rates of the early 1980s, which resulted in universal life growing to a sizable market, with $146.3 billion of face amount in 2000. The share of the market declined when interest rates declined and it increased as the stock market became bearish.

Separation of Elements

Traditional cash value life insurance products do not clearly show the separate effect of their mortality, investment, and expense components. The distinguishing characteristic of universal life contracts is a clear separation of these three elements. This is called **unbundling**. The separation is reported at least annually, by a disclosure statement. The **disclosure statement** shows the following:

- The gross rate of investment return credited to the account[4]
- The charge for death protection
- Expense charges
- The resulting changes in accumulation value and in cash value

This transparency permits seeing how the policy operates internally, after the fact.

The insurer maintains separate accounting for each policyowner. The account has three income items:

- New premiums paid
- Guaranteed interest credited
- Excess interest credited

The cash outflow items, from a consumer perspective, consist of the following:

- A mortality charge for death protection
- Administrative and marketing expenses
- Withdrawals or loans

The difference between cash income and outflow in universal life becomes a new contribution to (or deduction from) the **accumulation value** account. Visualize this as the level of liquid in an open container where the three income items flow in at the top and the outflow items are extracted through a spigot at the bottom. Accounting usually occurs on a monthly basis, followed by annual disclosure of the monthly cash flows. The steps in the periodic flow of funds for a universal life policy are shown in Figure 19.5. The first premium is at least a minimum amount specified by the insurer; subsequent premiums are flexible in amount, even zero if the cash value is large enough to cover the current cost of death protection and any applicable expense charges.

Administrative and marketing expense charges are subtracted each period. Some policies do not make explicit deductions. Instead, they recover their expenses by lowering investment credits or increasing mortality charges (limited by guaranteed maximums). Another periodic deduction is for mortality. The policyowner decides whether withdrawals (that is, partial surrenders of cash values) or policy loans are made. They cannot exceed the current cash value. If the entire cash value is withdrawn, the contract terminates. Withdrawals and loans reduce the death benefit as well as the cash value.

After deductions at the beginning of each accounting period for expenses, mortality, and withdrawals, the accumulation value is increased periodically by the percentage that reflects the insurer's current investment experience (subject to a guaranteed minimum rate) for the portfolio underlying universal life policies.

The difference between the accumulation value and what can be withdrawn in cash (the cash value) at any point in time is determined by surrender expenses. *Surrender expenses* and other terms will become clearer as aspects of universal life are discussed in more detail in the next chapter sections.

unbundling

Feature of universal life that clearly shows the separate effect of mortality, investment, and expense components.

disclosure statement

In universal life, annually reporting of the gross rate of investment return credited to the account, the charge for death protection, expense charges, and the resulting changes in accumulation value and in cash value.

accumulation value

The value of the annuity contract during the accumulation period; consists of premiums plus investment earnings minus expenses.

Death Benefit Options

Figure 19.6 shows two death benefit options that are typically available. Type A keeps a level death benefit by making dollar-for-dollar changes in the amount of protection as the investment (cash value account) increases or decreases. This option is expected to produce a pattern of cash values and protection like that of a traditional, ordinary life contract. When a traditional, straight life contract is issued, the policy stipulates exactly what the pattern of cash values will be and guarantees them. In universal life contracts, there are illustrations of cash values for thirty years or so, assuming the following:

- A specified level of premium payments
- A guaranteed minimum investment return
- Guaranteed maximum mortality rates

Another column of this type of illustration shows values based on current investment and mortality experience. Company illustration practices also usually provide a column of accumulation and cash values based on an intermediate investment return (that is, a return between the guaranteed and current rates).

FIGURE 19.5 **Flow of Funds for Universal Life Insurance**

* This accumulation value is zero for a new policy.

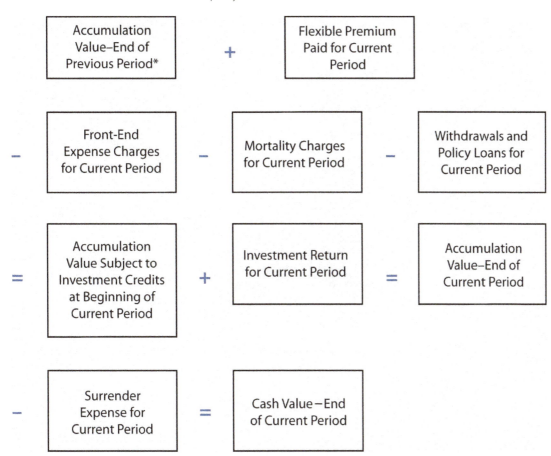

The type B option is intended to produce an increasing death benefit. The exact amount of increase depends on future nonguaranteed changes in cash value, as described in the discussion of type A policies. The type B alternative is analogous to buying a yearly, renewable level term insurance contract and creating a separate investment account.

With either type, the policyowner may use the contract's flexibility to change the amount of protection as the needs for insurance change. Like traditional life insurance contracts, additional amounts of protection require evidence of insurability, including good health, to protect the insurer against adverse selection. Decreases in protection are made without evidence of insurability. The insurer simply acknowledges the request for a different death benefit by sending notification of the change. The contract will specify a minimum amount of protection to comply with federal tax guidelines. These guidelines must be met to shelter the contract's investment earnings (commonly called inside interest buildup) from income taxes.

FIGURE 19.6 Two Universal Death Benefit Options

* Cash values may decrease and even go to zero, for example, due to low investment returns or inadequate premium payments.

Type A – Level Death Benefit

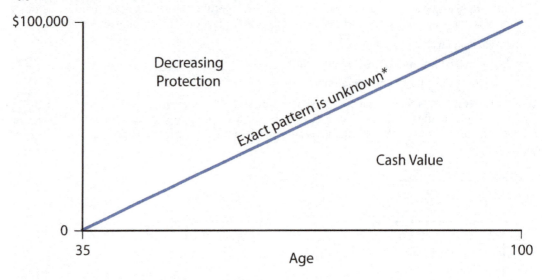

Type B – Increasing Death Benefit

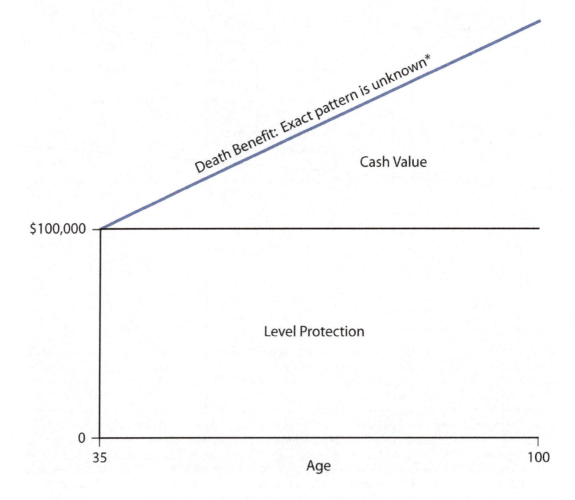

Cost-of-living adjustment (COLA) riders and options to purchase additional insurance are available from most insurers, as you will see at end of this chapter. **COLA riders** increase the death benefit annually, consistent with the previous year's increase in the consumer price index (CPI). Thus, if inflation is 3 percent, a $100,000 type A policy reflects a $103,000 death benefit in the second year. Of course, future mortality charges will reflect the higher amount at risk to the insurer, resulting in higher costs of death protection and lower cash values, unless premiums or investment returns increase concomitantly. Options to purchase additional insurance give the contractual right to purchase stipulated amounts of insurance at specified future ages (generally limited to age forty) and events (e.g., the birth of a child) without evidence of insurability.

Premium Payments

Most universal policies require a minimum premium in the first policy year. In subsequent years, the amount paid is the policyowner's decision, subject to minimums and maximums set by insurers and influenced by Internal Revenue Service (IRS) rules.

Mortality Charges

Almost all universal life insurance policies specify that mortality charges be levied monthly. The charge for a particular month is determined by multiplying the current mortality rate by the current amount of protection (net amount at risk to the insurer). The **current mortality rate** can be any amount determined periodically by the insurer as long as the charge does not exceed the guaranteed maximum mortality rate specified in the contract. Maximum mortality rates typically are those in the conservative 1980 CSO Mortality Table. Updated mortality tables were adopted in 2006 based on the 2001 CSO Mortality Table, as discussed in "New Mortality Tables" of Chapter 17.

The current practice among most insurers is to set current mortality rates below the specified maximums. Mortality charges vary widely among insurers and may change after a policy is issued. Consumers should not, however, choose an insurer solely based on a low mortality charge. Expense charges and investment returns also factor into any determination of a policy's price. It is also unwise to choose a policy solely on the basis of low expenses or high advertised gross investment returns.

Expense Charges

Insurers levy expense charges to help cover their costs of marketing and administering the policies. The charges can be grouped into **front-end expenses** and **surrender expenses** (back-end expenses). Front-end expenses are applied at the beginning of each month or year. They consist of some combination of: (1) a percentage of new premiums paid (e.g., 5 percent, with 2 percent covering premium taxes paid by the insurer to the state); (2) a small flat dollar amount per month or year (e.g., $1.50 per month), and (3) a larger flat dollar amount in the first policy year (e.g., $50). Universal life policies began with high front-end expenses, but the trend has been toward much lower or no front-end expenses due to competition among companies. Those that levy front-end expenses tend to use only a percentage of premium load in both first and renewal policy years. Policies with large front-end loads seldom levy surrender expenses.

As most early issuers of universal policies lowered their front-end charges, they added surrender charges. Whereas front-end expenses reduce values for all insureds, surrender expenses transfer their negative impact to policyowners who terminate their policies. Surrender charges help the insurer recover its heavy front-end underwriting expenses and sales commissions. Questions exist about whether or not they create equity between short-term and persisting policyholders. A few insurers issue universal policies with neither front-end nor surrender charges. These insurers, of course, still incur operating expenses. Some lower operating expenses by distributing their products directly to consumers or through financial planners who charge separate fees to clients. These no-load products still incur marketing expenses for the insurers that must promote (advertise) their products through direct mail, television, and other channels. They plan to recover expenses and make a profit by margins on actual mortality charges (current charges greater than company death claim experience) and margins on investment returns (crediting current interest rates below what the company is earning on its investment portfolio). Thus, even no-load contracts have hidden expense loads. Expense charges of all types, like current mortality rates, vary widely among insurers. Advertised investment returns are likely to vary in a narrower range.

Investment Returns

Insurers reserve the right to change the current rate of return periodically. Some guarantee a new rate for a year; others commit to the new rate only for a month or a quarter.

COLA riders

Increase the death benefit of universal life annually, consistent with the previous year's increase in the consumer price index.

current mortality rate

In universal life, can be any amount determined periodically by the insurer as long as the charge does not exceed the guaranteed maximum mortality rate specified in the contract.

front-end expenses

In universal life, expenses applied at the beginning of each month or year consisting of some combination of (1) a percentage of new premiums paid, (2) a small flat dollar amount per month or year, and (3) a larger flat dollar amount in the first policy year.

surrender expenses

In universal life, marketing and administrative expenses applied when policies are terminated.

indexed investment strategy

Ties the rate of return on cash values in life insurance to a published index, such as rates on ninety-day U.S. Treasury bills or Moody's Bond Index.

new money rate

In life insurance, credits the cash value account with the return an insurer earns on its latest new investments.

The **indexed investment strategy** used by some insurers ties the rate of return on cash values to a published index, such as rates on 90-day U.S. Treasury bills or Moody's Bond Index, rather than leaving it to the insurer's discretion and its actual investment portfolio returns. This approach also provides a guarantee between 4 and 5 percent.

Some insurers use a new money rate for universal contracts. As explained earlier, the **new money rate** approach credits the account with the return an insurer earns on its latest new investments. The practice dictates investment of universal life funds in assets with relatively short maturities in order to match assets with liabilities. When short-term rates are relatively high, such as in the early 1980s, the new money approach produces attractive returns. When short-term returns drop, as they did after the mid-1980s, the approach is not attractive, as noted earlier.

Summary: Features of Universal Life

- In summary, in universal life, we see the following features (see also Table 19.1):
- Death benefits: level or increasing
- Cash value: guaranteed minimum cash value plus additional interest when rates are higher than guaranteed
- Premiums: flexible
- Policy loans: yes, but the interest credited to the account is reduced
- Partial withdrawals: allowed
- Surrender charges: yes

3.5 Variable Life Insurance

variable life insurance

Provides the opportunity to invest funds in the stock market; created to overcome policyholder fears that inflation will erode life insurance values.

To overcome policyholder fears that inflation will erode life insurance values, **variable life insurance** provides the opportunity to invest funds in the stock market.

The theory of variable life insurance (and variable annuities) is that the prices of the stock and other equities purchased by the insurer for this product will provide insureds with access to any investment vehicle available in the marketplace and will not be limited to fixed-income products. Investments supporting variable life insurance are held in one or more account(s) separate from the general accounts of the insurer. This distinguishes them from investments underlying other life and health insurance contracts.

Each variable life consumer has a choice of investing in a combination of between five and twenty different separate accounts with varying investment objectives and strategies. For example, you might add more short-term stability by placing part of your money in a short-term bond fund while maintaining a significant equity element in one or more common stock funds. Each separate account makes investments in publicly traded securities that have readily determined market values. Market values are needed to determine the current values of cash/accumulation values and death benefits. Cash values vary daily, and death benefits vary daily, monthly, or annually.

Variable life transfers all investment risks to the policyowner. Unlike universal life, for example, which guarantees the fixed-dollar value of your accumulation fund and a minimum return, variable insurance products make no guarantee of either principal or returns. All the investment risk (upside or downside) is yours. Cash values (but not death benefits) can go to zero as a result of adverse investment experience.

How It Works

The *Model Variable Life Insurance Regulation*, produced by the National Association of Insurance Commissioners, sets guidelines that help establish the form of the product. Certain basic characteristics can be identified.

Variable life is, in essence, a whole life product that provides variable amounts of benefit for the entire life. It requires a level premium; therefore, the out-of-pocket contributions do not change with changes in the cost of living. This limits the extent to which death benefits can increase over time because no new amounts of insurance can be financed by defining the premium in constant dollars. All increases in death benefits must come from favorable investment performance.

Contracts specify a minimum death benefit, called the face amount. In one design, this minimum stays level during the life of the contract. Another design uses increasing term insurance to provide automatic increases of 3 percent per year for fourteen years, at which point the minimum face amount becomes level at 150 percent of its original face value. Assuming continuation of premium payments, the face amount can never go below the guaranteed minimum.

Each separate account is, in essence, a different mutual fund. For example, one contract offers five investment accounts: (1) guaranteed interest, (2) money market, (3) a balance of bonds and stocks, (4) conservative common stock, and (5) aggressive common stock. The policyowner could allocate all net premiums (new premiums minus expense and mortality charges) to one account or divide them among any two or more accounts. Currently, approximately 75 percent of separate account assets are in common stocks. Some policies limit the number of changes among the available accounts. For example, some contracts set a limit of four changes per year. Administrative charges may accompany switches among accounts, especially when one exceeds the limit. Because the changes are made inside a life insurance product where investment gains are not subject to income taxes (unless the contract is surrendered), gains at the time of transfer among accounts are not taxable.

It is assumed that investments in the underlying separate accounts will earn a modest compound return, such as 4 percent. This **assumed rate of return** is generally a rate necessary to maintain the level of cash values found in a traditional fixed-dollar straight life contract. Then, if actual investment returns exceed the assumed rate, (1) cash values increase more than assumed, and (2) these increases are used partly to purchase additional death benefits.

The additional death benefits are usually in the form of term insurance. The amount of term insurance can change (upward or downward) daily, monthly, or yearly, depending on the provisions of the contract. The total death benefit, at a point in time, becomes the amount of traditional straight life insurance that would be supported by a reserve equal to the policy's current cash value.

If separate account values fall below the assumed rate, (1) the cash value falls, and (2) one-year term elements of death protection are automatically surrendered. The net result is a new death benefit that corresponds to the amount of straight life that could be supported by the new cash value, subject to the minimum death benefit. These variable aspects are what give the contract its name. The nature of variable life insurance, with one-year term additions, is depicted in Figure 19.7.

Policy loans and contract surrenders can be handled by transferring funds out of the separate account. Loans are typically limited to 90 percent of the cash value at the time of the latest loan. Surrenders are equal to the entire cash value minus any applicable surrender charge.

Some variable contracts are issued on a participating basis. Because investment experience is reflected directly in cash values, dividends reflect only unanticipated experience with respect to mortality and operating expenses.

assumed rate of return

In variable life insurance, generally is a rate necessary to maintain the level of cash values found in a traditional fixed-dollar straight life contract.

FIGURE 19.7   Hypothetical Values for a Variable Life Insurance Contract

Note: The relationship depicted between the actual cash value and the total death benefit is approximate. It has not been drawn precisely to scale.

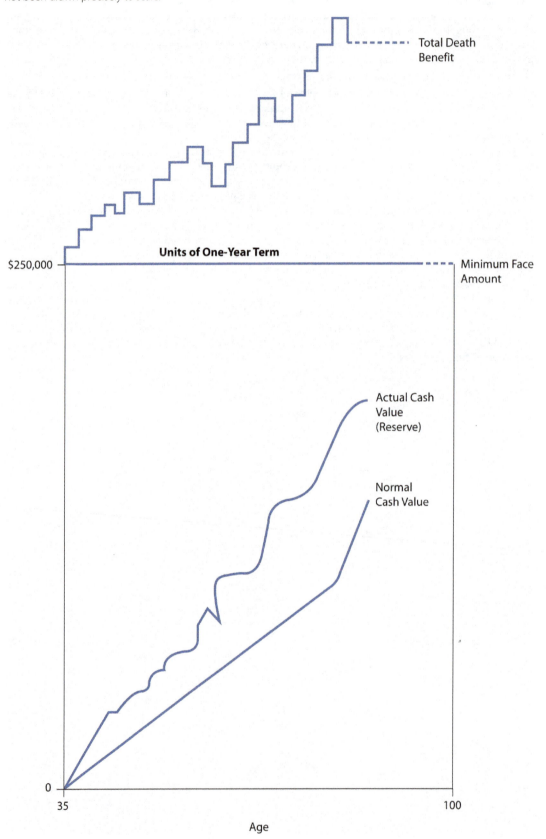

Variable life insurance is technically a security as well as insurance. Therefore, it is regulated by the Securities and Exchange Commission (SEC)—which enforces the Investment Company Act of 1940, the Securities Act of 1933, and the Securities Exchange Act of 1934—as well as by state insurance departments. The SEC requires that an applicant be given a **prospectus** before being asked to sign an application for variable life. The prospectus explains the risks and usually illustrates how the death benefit and cash values would perform if future investment experience results in returns of 0, 4, 6, 8, 10, and 12 percent. Returns also can be illustrated based on historical experience of the Standard and Poor's 500 Stock Price Index. Because the product is a security, it can be sold only by agents who register with and pass an investments examination given by the National Association of Security Dealers.

A midrange assumption (e.g., 4 percent) produces a contract that performs exactly like traditional straight life insurance. The 0 percent return would produce the minimum face amount; the cash value would be below normal for a period and go to zero at an advanced age. Because cash values cannot be negative, the policy would continue from the time the cash values reach zero until the death without cash values. At death, the minimum face amount would be paid. The 8 and 12 percent returns would produce cash values that grow much faster than those normal for an ordinary life policy; the total death benefit would continue to grow above the minimum face amount. These examples all assume continuous payment of the fixed annual premium.

Summary: Features of Variable Life

The cash value in a variable life policy fluctuates with the market value of one or more separate accounts. Death benefits, subject to a minimum face amount, vary up or down as the cash value changes. Success in achieving the objective of maintaining a death benefit that keeps pace with inflation depends on the validity of the theory that certain investments are good inflation hedges. All investment risks are borne by the policyowner rather than by the insurer. The issuer of a variable life policy assumes only mortality and expense risks.

In summary, in variable life we see the following features (see also Table 19.1):

- Death benefits: guaranteed minimum plus increases from investments
- Cash value: minimum not guaranteed; depends on investment performance
- Premiums: fixed level
- Policy loans: yes
- Partial withdrawals: not allowed
- Surrender charges: yes

3.6 Variable Universal Life Insurance

In 1985, variable universal life was marketed for the first time. **Variable universal life insurance** combines the premium and death benefit flexibility of a universal policy design with the investment choices of variable life. This policy is also called flexible premium variable life insurance. Some insurers allow all premiums to vary after the first year of the contract. Others specify minimum premiums that would, if paid, continue death protection at least through age sixty-five. Premiums can exceed these minimums. Single-premium policies are also available.

Like the universal life policyowner, the variable universal life policyowner decides periodically whether to decrease death protection (subject to the contract's minimum face amount) or increase death benefits (subject to evidence of insurability). One design specifies a fixed face amount, like the type A design of universal life (see Figure 19.6), and allows investment experience to affect only cash values. Another design, like variable life, allows the total amount of protection to increase when cash values exceed their normal level for a straight life contract.

As with variable life, the assets backing variable universal policies are invested in separate accounts. The choices are like those for variable life policies, and the policyowner continues to assume all investment risks. The flow of funds due to expenses, mortality charges, and policy loans for both variable and variable universal work like those in universal policies. The outlook for the sale of variable universal policies is bright because the contract combines the following:

- The premium flexibility of universal life
- The death benefit flexibility of universal life
- Greater investment flexibility than universal life
- The disclosure of universal and variable life
- The ability to withdraw cash values as policy loans without any tax penalties (this is an advantage in comparison to annuities rather than to other types of life insurance)

prospectus

Statement issued by insurers as required by the SEC explaining the risks of variable life and illustrates how the death benefit and cash values would perform if future investment experience results in returns of 0, 4, 6, 8, 10, and 12 percent.

variable universal life insurance

Combines the premium and death benefit flexibility of a universal policy design with the investment choices of variable life.

Separate accounts are not general assets of an insurer. Therefore, they are protected in the event of the insurer's insolvency. The major drawback of variable universal life, as with variable life, is the transfer of all investment risk to the policyowner.

Summary: Features of Variable Universal Life

In summary, in variable universal life, we see the following features:

- Death benefits: guaranteed minimum plus increases from investments
- Cash value: minimum not guaranteed; depends on investment performance
- Premiums: flexible
- Policy loans: allowed
- Partial withdrawals: allowed
- Surrender charges: yes

3.7   Current Assumption Whole Life Insurance

current assumption whole life insurance

Works like universal life, except, similar to traditional whole life contracts, the premiums are fixed.

In most respects, **current assumption whole life insurance** policies work like universal life. The major difference is that, similar to traditional whole life contracts, the premiums are fixed. These policies do not have the flexible premium arrangements characteristic of universal life. Some current assumption designs emphasize low premiums (e.g., $6 per year per $1,000 at age twenty-five) and expect the premiums, with periodic adjustments, to be paid over the entire lifetime. Low-premium policies emphasize protection and appeal primarily to families or businesses with modest incomes. Medium- and high-premium alternatives for the same initial face amount might have premiums of $10 and $15, respectively. They emphasize cash values in the protection/investment mix and reduce the chances of the insurer having to request higher premiums to avoid the contract lapsing in later years.

After a current assumption contract is issued, the outlook for prospective (future) mortality and expenses can result in periodic increases or decreases in premiums. Some insurers adjust premiums annually; others make changes at three- or five-year intervals.

vanishing premiums provision

In higher premium versions of current assumption life insurance, allow the policyowner to stop premium payments and essentially have a nonguaranteed, paid-up contract for the initial face amount.

The higher-premium versions of current assumption policies usually include a contract provision allowing the policyowner to stop premium payments and essentially have a nonguaranteed, paid-up contract for the initial face amount. This **vanishing premiums provision** is triggered when the cash-value account has a balance equal to a net single premium for this amount of death benefit at the attained age. The net single premium is determined with current (at the time of vanish) investment and mortality assumptions. If future experience with the insurer's investments and mortality turns out to be less favorable, the single premium may prove to be insufficient. The policyowner could either resume premium payments or let the policy lapse. Thus, the policyowner retains some financial risk even for higher-premium current assumption policies where premiums have vanished. See the discussion of vanishing premiums in Chapter 7.

interest-sensitive whole life

Another name for current assumption life insurance, emphasizing the product's participatory investment feature.

As is characteristic of universal life policies, minimum guaranteed interest rates are typically 4.0, 4.5, or 5.0 percent. Current assumption whole life is technically a nonparticipating policy, as is most universal life. Like universal life, however, it shares the insurer's investment and mortality expectations with the insured (through excess interest credits). It is sometimes referred to as **interest-sensitive whole life** because of its participatory investment feature. The accumulation value and cash value are determined in the same manner as was described earlier for universal life policies.

The death benefit is usually a fixed, level amount, analogous to a type A universal life contract. Some insurers, however, offer an alternative death benefit equal to the original stated face amount plus the accumulation fund balance, analogous to a type B universal life design.

An annual disclosure statement shows the current investment credit, mortality charge, any applicable expenses, and surrender charges. Although the premium is not flexible, the current assumption product provides far more flexibility and transparency for consumers than is available in traditional whole life policies.

Summary: Features of Current Assumption Life

In summary, in current assumption life, we see the following features:

- Death benefits: fixed
- Cash value: guaranteed minimum plus excess interest (like universal life)
- Premiums: vary according to experience, but no higher than a set maximum
- Policy loans: yes

- Partial withdrawals: allowed
- Surrender charges: yes

KEY TAKEAWAYS

In this section you studied about the life insurance industry's market condition in 2008–2009 and the following life insurance products:

- Term life insurance—provides protection for a specified period; is renewable (at increased premiums) and convertible and has a death benefit that is level, increasing, or decreasing depending on need
- Whole life insurance—provides for payment of the face value upon death regardless of when the death may occur (permanent)
  - Straight life—premiums paid in equal periodic amounts over the life of the insured
  - Limited-payment life—offers lifetime protection but limits premium payments to a specified period of years or to a specified age (policy becomes paid up)
  - Single premium life—pay the present value of future benefits, with discounts both for investment earnings and mortality (mainly investment vehicle); investment returns on cash value provide tax-free earnings; dividends that refund higher-than-necessary premiums are issued to policyholders
- Universal life insurance—allows the policyholder the flexibility to change the amount of the premium periodically, discontinue premiums and resume them at a later date without lapsing the policy, and change the amount of death protection
  - Allows loans and policy withdrawals
  - Death benefit can be level or increasing
  - Guaranteed minimum cash value, plus additional interest possible
  - Flexible premiums
  - Levies mortality and expense charges
- Variable life insurance—provides the opportunity to invest funds in the stock market
  - Choice of investing in combination of between five to twenty separate accounts with different objectives and strategies
  - No guarantee in cash values
  - Guaranteed minimum death benefit, increase comes from investment performance
  - Requires fixed level premiums
  - Allows policy loans, limited to 90 percent of cash value; does not permit withdrawals
- Variable universal life insurance—combines the premium and death benefit flexibility of a universal policy design with the investment choices of variable life
  - Premiums can vary after first year of contract, be single premium, or extend death protection
  - Policyholder can decrease or increase death benefits
  - Investment choices and risk are the same as variable life
  - Expenses and mortality changes are handled like universal life
  - Policy loans are allowed and are handled like universal life
- Current assumption whole life insurance—features are similar to universal life, except premiums are fixed like traditional whole life
  - Emphasize low-level premium paid over the life of the contract
  - Higher premium versions include a provision allowing the policyholder to stop paying premiums to have a nonguaranteed paid-up contract for face value

DISCUSSION QUESTIONS

1. What are the causes of the deteriorating market condition of the life insurance industry during the 2008–2009 recession?

2. Would you expect one-year term insurance that is renewable and convertible to require a higher premium than one-year term insurance without these features? Explain.

3. In what way is the reentry feature of term insurance desirable to policyholders? Is it a valuable policy feature after you become unhealthy?

4. How may the participating whole life policy share higher-than-expected investment earnings?

5. Explain how universal life policies transfer mortality risk (subject to a limit) to you. Does the provision that creates this risk have an advantage that may allow you to participate in your insurer's good fortunes?

6. Compare term life to universal life and to variable life insurance in terms of (a) death benefits, (b) cash value, (c) premium, and (d) policy loans.

7. What elements of a universal life contract are separated or unbundled relative to their treatment in a traditional life insurance policy? How does a disclosure statement help implement the separation and create transparency?

8. Explain the two death benefit options that are available to you when you purchase a universal life or current assumption policy.

9. What is the major difference between a current assumption life policy and a universal life policy? Why might a life insurer prefer issuing current assumption policies?

10. What is the objective of variable life insurance? Can this objective be achieved through a variable universal life policy with a level face amount (i.e., one like a type A universal life contract)?

11. Who bears the investment risk in variable life and universal variable life policies? How does this differ from investment risks borne by the buyer of a universal life policy?

4. TAXATION, MAJOR POLICY PROVISIONS, RIDERS, AND ADJUSTING LIFE INSURANCE FOR INFLATION

LEARNING OBJECTIVES

In this section we elaborate on the following:

- **Tax treatment of life insurance benefits**
- **Provisions from two sample life insurance policies: whole life and universal life**
- **Descriptions of different life insurance policy riders**
- **How life insurance needs can be adjusted for inflation**

4.1 Taxation

In the United States, we typically pay individual life insurance premiums out of funds on which we previously had paid income taxes. That is, premiums are paid from after-tax income. Therefore, there are no income taxes on the death benefit proceeds.

In general, when premiums are paid from after-tax income, death benefits are not part of the beneficiary's or anyone else's gross income.[5] Therefore, whether the death is soon or long after purchasing a $100,000 life insurance policy, the named beneficiary, regardless of relationship, would not incur any federal income taxes on the proceeds, including gains within the cash value portion of the policy. Nontaxable proceeds also include nonbasic benefits such as term riders, accidental death benefits, and paid-up additions. There are some exclusions, but a discussion of the exclusions is beyond the scope of this text. Some life insurance policies include dividends, and these policyholder dividends are excluded from federal income taxation. The federal government reasons that dividends constitute the return of an original overcharge of premiums. The premiums were paid with after-tax dollars, so any portion of those premiums, returned as a dividend, must have already been taxed as well. More will be said about dividends later in this chapter.

Except for single-premium life insurance, the purchase of most life insurance is motivated primarily by a need for death protection. The availability of private life insurance reduces pressures on government to provide welfare to families that experience premature deaths of wage earners. Furthermore, life insurance is owned by a broad cross section of U.S. society. This, along with effective lobbying by life insurers, may help explain the tax treatment of life insurance.

4.2   Major Policy Provisions

The major policy provisions are listed in Table 19.2 for the sample whole life policy in Chapter 26 and in Table 19.3 for the sample universal life policy in Chapter 27. Most of the explanations of the provisions relate to these sample policies, but they also apply to other whole life and universal life policies of other insurers. For more comprehensive comparisons of each of the provisions, you are invited to study the policies themselves.

TABLE 19.2   **Main Policy Provisions in the Whole Life Policy in [Unsupported Reference Type:]**

These provisions apply to most types of life insurance policies. The bolded provision is the only one unique to whole life.	
Policy identification	Payment of benefits provisions
Schedule of benefits	Premium provisions
Schedule of premiums	Dividend provisions
Schedule of insurance and values	Guaranteed value provisions
Definitions	Policy loan provisions
Ownership provisions	General provisions

TABLE 19.3   **Main Policy Provisions of the Universal Life Policy in [Unsupported Reference Type:]**

These provisions apply to most types of life insurance policies. Those unique to universal life are bolded.	
Policy identification	Ownership provisions
Schedule of benefits	**Death benefit and death benefit options provisions**
Schedule of premiums	Payment of benefits provisions
Monthly deductions	Premium provisions
Schedule of surrender charges	Guaranteed value provisions
Cost of insurance rates and monthly charges	General provisions
Definitions	Policy loan provisions
	General provisions

Both sample policies begin with a cover page (similar to any policy's declarations page) indicating the amounts of coverage and premiums. Because universal life has flexible premiums, the page also includes the monthly deduction statement. The second page in both policies relates to guarantees. In the whole life policy, the guaranteed cash value is shown along with other options (discussed later); in the universal life policy, a schedule of surrender charges and the maximum monthly cost of insurance rates, as explained in the universal life section above, is provided.

The next section defines the terms in both of the sample policies. The definitions are preceded by an explanation of ownership.

Policy Ownership

The whole and universal life policies have similar ownership sections. **Ownership** refers to rights. The owner of a life insurance policy has rights, such as the right to assign the policy to someone else, to designate the beneficiary, to make a policy loan, or to surrender the policy for its cash value. When filling out the initial policy application, the policyowner designates whether the rights should stay with the insured or be assigned to another person, such as a spouse or perhaps to a trust. The **ownership provision**, sometimes simply labeled rights, shows this designation.

Death Benefits and Death Benefits Options Provisions

This section is unique to universal life policy, as would be expected from the lengthy explanation above regarding the two options of death benefits. In Chapter 27, you can see the wording of these options, the amounts of coverage, and changes to the amounts.

The **changes in basic amount provision** specifies the conditions under which a policyowner can change the total face amount of the policy. Any requested decreases take place on a monthly anniversary date and reduce the most recent additions to coverage (if any) before affecting the initial face amount. Requests for increases in coverage must be made on a supplemental application and are subject to evidence of insurability.

Payment of Benefits Provisions

This section applies to both the sample whole life and the sample universal life policies and to other policies in general. The purpose of the **payment of benefits provision** is to enable the owner of the policy to designate to whom the proceeds shall be paid when the insured dies. If no beneficiary is named, the proceeds will go to the owner's estate. A **revocable beneficiary** can be changed at will by the policyowner. Most people prefer the revocable provision. **Irrevocable beneficiary** designations, on the other hand, can be changed only with the consent of the beneficiary. For example, a divorced spouse, as part of a property settlement, may be given an irrevocable interest in life insurance on his or her former spouse. The former spouse, as the insured and policyowner, would be required to continue premium payments but could not make a policy loan or other changes that would diminish the rights of the irrevocable beneficiary.

A beneficiary must survive the insured in order to be entitled to the proceeds of the policy. It is customary, therefore, to name one or more beneficiaries who are entitled to the proceeds in the event that the primary (first-named) beneficiary does not survive the insured. These are known as secondary or tertiary **contingent beneficiaries**. Such beneficiaries are named and listed in the order of their priority.

If the insured and the primary beneficiary die in the same accident and none of the evidence shows who died first, there is a question as to whether the proceeds shall be paid to the estate of the primary beneficiary or to a contingent beneficiary. In states where the Uniform Simultaneous Death Act has been enacted, the proceeds are distributed as if the insured had survived the beneficiary. Where this act is not in effect, the courts have usually reached the same conclusion. If no contingent beneficiary has been named, the proceeds go to the estate of the policyowner, thus subjecting the proceeds to estate taxes, probate costs, and the claims of creditors. Probate costs are levied by the court that certifies that an estate has been settled properly. Probate costs (but not estate taxes) are avoided when benefits go to a named beneficiary.

A similar problem arises when the primary beneficiary survives the insured by only a short period. In such a case, the proceeds may be depleted by taxes and costs associated with the beneficiary's estate settlement or because an annuity-type settlement option had been selected. This problem can be solved by adding a **common disaster provision (or survivorship clause)**, which provides that the beneficiary must survive the insured by a specified period of time (e.g., seven to thirty days) or must be alive at the time of payment to be entitled to the proceeds. If neither of these conditions is fulfilled, the proceeds go to a contingent beneficiary or to the estate of the policyowner if a contingent beneficiary has not been named.

Policyowners should designate the beneficiary clearly. No questions should exist about the identity of the beneficiary at the time of the insured's death. In designating children as beneficiaries, one must keep in mind that a minor is not competent to receive payment. In the event of the death of the insured prior to the maturity of a beneficiary child, a guardian may have to be appointed to receive the proceeds on behalf of the child. As a general rule, policyowners should avoid naming minors as beneficiaries. Where the objective is a substantial estate to benefit a child or children, the preferable approach would be to name a trust as beneficiary. The child or children (the ones already born and those to be born or join the family unit after a divorce and remarriage) could be the beneficiary(ies) of the trust.

---

ownership

In life insurance, refers to rights policyholders have over their policies such as the right to assign the policy to someone else, to designate the beneficiary, to make a policy loan, or to surrender the policy for its cash value.

ownership provision (labeled rights)

A provision filled out by the policyowner stating where the rights of the policy should be assigned (e.g., insured, spouse, or a trust).

changes in basic amount provision

In life insurance, specifies the conditions under which a policyowner can change the total face amount of the policy.

payment of benefits provision

In life insurance, enables the owner of the policy to designate to whom the proceeds shall be paid when the insured dies.

revocable beneficiary

Life insurance beneficiary that can be changed at will by the policyowner.

irrevocable beneficiary

Life insurance beneficiary that cannot be changed only with the consent of the beneficiary.

contingent beneficiaries

In life insurance, beneficiaries who are entitled to the proceeds in the event that the primary (first-named) beneficiary does not survive the insured.

common disaster provision (or survivorship clause)

Provides that the beneficiary of a life insurance policy must survive the insured by a specified period of time or must be alive at the time of payment to be entitled to the proceeds.

Payment Methods

Life insurance is designed to create a sum of money that can be used when the insured dies or the owner surrenders a cash value policy. In the early days of life insurance, the only form in which the death proceeds or cash value of a policy were paid was in a lump sum. Because a lump-sum payment is not desirable in all circumstances, several additional **settlement options (or settlement plans**; also called payment plans) have been developed and are now included in most policies. The owner may select an option in advance or leave the choice to the beneficiary. The owner may also change the option from time to time if the beneficiary designation is revocable. The payment plans have the following methods for death proceeds:

- Interest method—the beneficiary leaves the proceeds with the insurer and collects only the interest
- Fixed years method—even distribution of the proceeds over a certain number of years
- Life income method—even distribution of the proceeds over the life of the beneficiary
- Fixed amount method—even distribution of the proceeds until depleted
- Joint life income method—even distribution of the proceeds over the life of the beneficiary, with continued distribution to his or her beneficiary at the same or reduced level
- One-sum method—a lump-sum distribution
- Other method, as agreed upon

settlement options (or settlement plans)

Allows the policyholder or beneficiary of a life insurance contract to stipulate, from a variety of options, how the death benefit will be provided.

Premium Provisions

This section also applies to both the whole and the universal life policies. Premiums are payable on the due date on a monthly, quarterly, semiannual, or annual basis. The first premium must be paid in advance, while the insured is in good health and otherwise insurable. Subsequent premiums are due in advance of the period to which they apply. Insurance companies send a notice to the policyowner indicating when the premium is due. The time horizon over which premiums are payable depends on the type of policy (e.g., through age ninety-nine for a straight life policy), and it is stated on the cover page. Note in the sample universal life policy of Chapter 27 that the premium limitations section allows the insurer to refund any overpayment of premiums. As you know, such possibility may occur because of the flexible premium allowed for universal life policies.

Grace Period

The law requires that the contract contain a provision entitling the policyowner to a **grace period** within which payment of a past-due premium (excluding the first premium) must be accepted by the insurer. The grace period is thirty-one days in the whole life sample in Chapter 26. Although the premium is past due during this period, the policy remains in force. If the insured dies during the grace period, the face amount of the policy minus the amount of the premium past due will be paid to the beneficiary. If the premium is not paid during the grace period of a traditional policy, a nonforfeiture option (to be discussed later) becomes effective. The purpose of the grace period is to prevent unintentional lapses. If it were not for this provision, an insured whose premium was paid one day late would have to prove his or her insurability in order to have the policy reinstated.

In variable, universal, and other flexible-premium policies, the grace period is usually sixty days, as seen in the universal life policy in Chapter 27. This has meaning only when the cash value is not large enough to cover expense and mortality deductions for the next period. Most insurers notify the policyowner of such a situation. The cash surrender value in the first few policy years may be zero due to surrender charges. In that event, most universal and variable policies also contain a grace period exception clause. This clause states that during a specified period of time (generally the first few policy years, even if the policy has a negative surrender value), as long as at least the stated minimum premium has been paid during the grace period, the policy will continue in force.

grace period

Period of time within which payment of a past-due insurance premium (excluding the first premium) must be accepted by the insurer.

Nonpayment of Premium, Accumulation to Avoid Lapse, and Automatic Premium Loans

The nonpayment of premium, accumulation to avoid lapse, and automatic premium loans sections apply only to whole life policies, as should be clear from the nature of inflexible premiums. Regarding **automatic premium loans**, if the owner selects this option, at the end of the grace period, loans are taken automatically from the cash value to pay the premiums. The owner is charged interest and can cancel this provision at any time.

automatic premium loans

If selected by a life insurance policyholder, provides that loans are taken automatically from the policy's cash value to pay premiums at the end of a policy grace period.

Reinstatement

reinstatement provision

Provides that unless a life insurance policy has been surrendered for cash, it may be reinstated at any time within five (in some cases, three, ten, or more) years after premium payments were stopped.

This section applies to both sample policies. If the grace period has expired with a premium still due, the policy is considered to have lapsed. A policyowner who wants to reinstate the policy rather than apply for new insurance must follow certain requirements. The **reinstatement provision** provides that, unless the policy has been surrendered for cash, it may be reinstated at any time within five (in some cases, three, ten, or more) years after premium payments were stopped. Payment of all overdue premiums on the policy and other indebtedness to the insurer, plus interest on these items, is required along with payment of the current premium. Usually, the insured must provide satisfactory evidence of current insurability. This provision is shown in the sample whole life policy in Chapter 26, and in the universal life sample in Chapter 27.

Evidence of insurability may be as strict in the case of reinstatement as it is for obtaining new life insurance. The insurer may be interested in health, occupation, hobbies, and any other factors that may affect the probability of early death. For recently lapsed policies, most insurers require only a personal health statement from the insured. Universal and variable policies typically provide reinstatement without requiring payment of back premiums, as noted in Chapter 27. In this event, the cash value of the reinstated policy equals the amount provided by the premium paid, after deductions for the cost of insurance protection and expenses.

Premium Adjustment When the Insured Dies

premium refund provision

In whole life policies only, after the death of the insured, the insurers refund any premium paid but unearned for the term.

In whole life policies only, after the death of the insured, the insurers refund any premium paid but unearned. For example, if an annual premium was paid on January 1 and the insured died on September 30, 25 percent (reflecting the remaining three months of the year) of the premium would be refunded. Most insurers explain their practice in a contract **premium refund provision**.

Dividend Options

Participating policies of mutual insurers, such as State Farm, share in the profits the insurer earns because of lower-than-anticipated expenses, lower-than-expected mortality, and greater-than-expected investment earnings. The amounts returned to policyowners are called dividends. Dividends also involve the return of any premium overpayment. Dividends are payable annually on the policy anniversary. They are not guaranteed, but they are a highly significant element in many policies.

dividend options

When purchasing a participating life insurance policy, the policyowner can choose how the dividend money will be distributed from among several choices.

When purchasing a participating life insurance policy, the policyowner can choose how the dividend money should be spent from one or more of the following **dividend options** (see Chapter 26):

- Applied toward the next premium
- Used to buy paid-up additional insurance
- Left with the insurer to accumulate interest
- Paid to the policyholder

The majority of companies offer these four options. The selection of the appropriate dividend option is an important decision.

Guaranteed Values Provisions

nonforfeiture options

In whole life insurance, guarantees that a policyholder who decides to cancel the policy can either take cash for the surrender (cash) value or continue the policy in force as extended term insurance and paid-up insurance.

This section illustrates the major differences between the whole life and universal life policies. A whole life policy guarantees that a policyholder who decides to cancel the policy can either take cash for the surrender (cash) value or continue the policy in force as extended term insurance and paid-up insurance. These provisions are also called **nonforfeiture options** in other policies. The sample whole life policy lists these amounts in the Schedule of Insurance and Values in Chapter 26.

As pointed out earlier, the cash value life plan results in the accumulation of a savings (or cash value element, from the insured's perspective) that usually increases as each year passes. If the contract is terminated, the policyholder can receive the cash value, or the policy can be converted to **extended term insurance** or **paid-up insurance**. Under the extended term insurance option, the death benefit continues at its previous level for as long as the cash value supports this amount of term insurance (like a single premium life). Under the paid-up insurance option, it is as if there is a new policy providing a lower lifetime death benefit than the old one did. The death benefits are paid up completely without an expiration date. Both extended term and paid-up options are nonforfeiture options.

With universal, current assumption, and variable universal life policies, the policyowner may discontinue premium payments at any time without lapsing the policy, as long as the surrender value is sufficient to cover the next deduction for the cost of insurance and expenses. In the universal life policy, there is a description of the account value at the end of the first month. It is 95 percent of the initial premium less the monthly deduction. Thereafter, adjustments take the interest rate into account. The following sections are covered in the sample universal life in Chapter 27:

- Account value
- Monthly deduction
- Cost of insurance
- Monthly cost of insurance rates
- Interest (guaranteed at 4 percent in the sample policy)
- Cash surrender value
- Withdrawals
- Surrender charges
- Basis of computation, which includes the table of surrender charges

Policy Loan Provisions

Policy loan provisions apply to both the whole life and the universal life policies. The owner can borrow an amount up to the cash value from the insurer at a rate of interest specified in the policy, and up to the account value in universal life. In the sample universal life policy in Chapter 27, the interest rate is set at 8 percent. In the whole life policy, the majority of insurers use a fixed rate of interest or a variable rate, as indicated in the sample whole life policy in Chapter 26.

General Provisions

Both the whole life and the universal life sample policies conclude with general-provision sections that include the following:

- The contract
- Annual report (universal life only)
- Projection of benefits and values (universal life only)
- Annual dividend (universal life only)
- Dividend options (universal life only as part of this section; see dividends for whole life above as a separate section)
- Assignment
- Error in age or sex
- Incontestability
- Limited death benefits (suicide clause)

The Contract

The written policy and the attached application constitute the entire agreement between the insurer and the policyowner. Because of this contract provision, agents cannot, orally or in writing, change or waive any terms of the contract. Statements in the application are considered representations, rather than warranties. This means that only those material statements that would have caused the insurer to make a different decision about the issuance of the policy, its terms, or premiums will be considered valid grounds to void the contract.

Annual Report and Projection of Benefits and Values

As would be expected from the discussion above, the changes in the universal life values require reporting to the policyowner on a regular basis. The annual report and projection of benefits and values state the obligation of the insurer to provide such annual reports. The projection of death benefits is not

extended term insurance

Nonforfeiture option where the death benefit of a whole life policy continues at its previous level for as long as the cash value supports this amount of term insurance.

paid-up insurance

Nonforfeiture option where death benefits are paid up completely without expiration date, as if a new policy providing a lower death benefit was in place.

policy loan provisions

Apply to whole life and the universal life policies and allow the owner to borrow an amount up to the cash value from the insurer at a rate of interest specified in the policy and up to the account value in universal life.

automatic. The policyowner can request it and may be charged $25, as shown in the sample policy in Chapter 27.

Assignment

assignment provision

Provides that the insurer will not be bound by any policy assignment until it has received notice, that any indebtedness to the company shall have priority over any assignment, and that the company is not responsible for the validity of any assignment.

As mentioned, the owner of a life insurance policy can transfer part or all of the rights to someone else. The **assignment provision** provides, however, that the company will not be bound by any assignment until it has received notice, that any indebtedness to the company shall have priority over any assignment, and that the company is not responsible for the validity of any assignment. This provision helps the company avoid litigation about who is entitled to policy benefits, and it protects the insurer from paying twice. As you can see in the sample policies in chapters 26 and 27, the "assignment may limit the interest of the beneficiary."

Errors in Age and Sex

misstatement of age or sex

Provision in life insurance policies that if age or sex has been misstated in a life insurance policy, the amount of the insurance will be adjusted to that which the premium paid would have covered correctly.

Age and sex have a direct bearing on the cost of life insurance. Therefore, they are material facts. Thus, the **misstatement of age or sex** would ordinarily provide grounds, within the contestable period, for rescinding the contract. Most state laws, however, require that all policies include a provision that if age or sex has been misstated, the amount of the insurance will be adjusted to that which the premium paid would have covered correctly.

Incontestability

incontestable provision

Makes a life insurance contract incontestable after it has been in force for two years during the lifetime of the insured.

A typical **incontestable provision** makes a contract incontestable after it has been in force for two years during the lifetime of the insured. If the insured dies before the end of the two years, the policy is contestable on the basis of material misrepresentations, concealment, and fraud in the application. If the insured survives beyond the contestable period, the policy cannot be contested even for fraud. An exception is fraud of a gross nature, such as letting someone else take the medical exam. While the incontestable clause may force the insurer to do considerably more investigating (part of the underwriting process) before contracts are issued than would otherwise be the case, and perhaps does result in some claims being paid that should not be, it is important to the honest policyowner who wants to be confident that his or her insurance proceeds will be paid upon death.

Limited Death Benefits (Suicide Clause)

suicide clause

In life insurance, states that the insured is not to be paid death benefits in case of death by suicide within two years of the policy being in place.

In both sample policies, the insured is not to be paid death benefits in case of suicide within two years. (In some policies, the duration is only one year.) This is sometimes called the **suicide clause**. As you can see in the sample universal life policy in Chapter 27, when coverage is increased, the additional insurance is subject to a new suicide exclusion period. If the company wishes to deny a claim on the grounds that death was caused by suicide during the period of exclusion, it must prove conclusively that the death was suicide.

4.3 Life Insurance Riders

Attachmenst to a life/health insurance policy that change the terms of the policy.

Through the use of **riders**, life insurance policies may be modified to provide special benefits. Under specified circumstances, these riders may waive premiums if the policyholder becomes disabled, provide disability income, provide accidental death benefits, guarantee issuance of additional life insurance, and pay accelerated death benefits (before death).

Waiver of Premium

waiver of premium rider

In life insurance, provides that premiums due after commencement of an insured's total disability shall be waived for a period of time.

The **waiver of premium rider** is offered by all life insurance companies and is included in about half of the policies sold. Some companies automatically provide it without charging an explicit amount of additional premium. The rider provides that premiums due after commencement of the insured's total disability shall be waived for a period of time. A waiting period of six months must be satisfied first. In flexible premium contracts such as universal and variable universal life, the waiver of premium provision specifies that the target premium to keep the policy in force will be credited to the insured's account during disability.[6] If a premium was paid after disability began and before the expiration of a waiting period, the premium is refunded. When disability begins before a certain age, usually age sixty, premiums are waived as long as the insured remains totally disabled.

Definition of Disability

To qualify for disability benefits, the disability must be total and permanent and must occur prior to a specified age. Disability may be caused by either accidental injury or sickness; no distinction is made. Typically, for the first two years of benefit payments, the insured is considered totally disabled whenever he or she, because of injury or disease, is unable to perform the duties of the regular occupation.

Beyond two years, benefits usually continue only if the insured is unable to perform the duties of any occupation for which he or she qualified by reason of education, training, and experience. A minority of insurers uses this more restrictive definition from the beginning of the waiver period. Most insurers and courts interpret the definition liberally. Most riders define blindness or loss of both hands, both feet, or one hand and one foot as presumptive total disability. Typically, disability longer than six months is considered to be permanent. Circumstances may later contradict this assumption because proof (generally in the form of a physician's statement) of continued disability is usually required once a year up to age sixty-five.

Disability Income

The **disability income rider** provides a typical income benefit of $10 per month per $1,000 of initial face amount of life insurance for as long as total disability continues and after the first six months of such disability, provided it commences before age fifty-five or 60. Disability payments are usually made for the balance of the insured's life as long as total disability continues. Under some contracts, payments stop at age sixty-five and the policy matures as an endowment, but this is less favorable than continuation of income benefits.

The definitions of disability for these riders are like those for waiver of premium provisions. Most disability income insurance is now sold either through a group plan (e.g., see Chapter 22 and Case 2 of Chapter 23) or as separate individual policies. Most life insurers do not offer this rider.

Accidental Death Benefit

The **accidental death benefit (or double indemnity) rider** is sometimes called double indemnity. It usually provides that double the face amount of the policy will be paid if the insured's death is caused by accident, and sometimes triple the face amount if death occurs while the insured is riding as a paying passenger in a public conveyance.[7] Figure 19.8 illustrates the accidental death benefit rider.

A typical definition of accidental death is, "Death resulting from bodily injury independently and exclusively of all other causes and within ninety days after such injury." Certain causes of death are typically excluded: suicide, violations of the law, gas or poison, war, and certain aviation activities other than as a passenger on a scheduled airline. This rider is usually in effect until the insured is age seventy.

Guaranteed Insurability Option

Many insurers will add a **guaranteed insurability option (GIO)** to policies for an additional premium. This gives the policyowner the right to buy additional amounts of insurance, usually at three-year intervals up to a specified age, without new proof of insurability. The usual age of the last option is forty; a small number of insurers allow it up to age sixty-five. The amount of each additional purchase is usually equal to or less than the face amount of the original policy. If a $50,000 straight or interest-sensitive life policy with the GIO rider is purchased at age twenty-one, the policyowner can buy an additional $50,000 every three years thereafter to age forty, whether or not the insured is still insurable. By age forty, the total death benefit would equal $350,000. The new insurance is issued at standard rates on the basis of the insured's attained age when the option is exercised. The GIO rider ensures one's insurability. It becomes valuable if the insured becomes uninsurable or develops a condition that would prevent the purchase of new life insurance at standard rates.

disability income rider

In life insurance, provides a typical income benefit of $10 per month per $1,000 of initial face amount of life insurance for as long as an insured's total disability continues and after the first six months of such disability, provided it commences before age fifty-five or sixty.

accidental death benefit (or double indemnity) rider

In life insurance, usually provides that double the face amount of the policy will be paid if the insured's death is caused by accident, and, sometimes, triple the face amount if death occurs while the insured is riding as a paying passenger in a public conveyance.

FIGURE 19.8 Accidental Death Benefits Rider

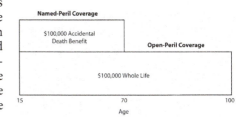

guaranteed insurability (GIO) option

In life insurance, gives the policyowner the right to buy additional amounts of insurance, usually at three-year intervals up to a specified age, without new proof of insurability.

Accelerated Death Benefits

accelerated death benefits

Triggered by either the occurrence of a catastrophic (dread) illness or the diagnosis of a terminal illness, resulting in payment of a portion of a life insurance policy's face amount prior to death.

Some medical conditions regularly result in high medical expenses for the insured and his or her family or other caregivers. The need for funds may significantly exceed benefits provided by medical and disability insurance because of deductibles, coinsurance, caps on benefits, and exclusions, and (perhaps primarily) because of having purchased inadequate coverage. **Accelerated death benefits** are triggered by either the occurrence of a catastrophic (dread) illness or the diagnosis of a terminal illness, resulting in payment of a portion of a life insurance policy's face amount prior to death.

The accelerated benefits are also called living benefits, or terminal illness rider. Usually, the terminally ill insured can receive up to 50 percent of the death benefits to improve quality of life before death. Often, the coverage is provided without an additional premium. The benefit can usually be claimed when two doctors agree that the insured has six months or less to live. When the insured desires greater amounts, he or she may use a viatical settlement company to transfer the ownership of the policy to a third party in return for a higher percentage of the death benefits, perhaps 80 percent. A more detailed discussion of viaticals is provided in the box "Do Viatical and Life Settlements Have a Place in Today's Market?"

Catastrophic Illness Coverage

catastrophic illness rider

In life insurance, provides that a portion (usually 25 to 50 percent) of the face amount of the policy is payable upon diagnosis of specified illnesses.

When a **catastrophic illness rider** is added to a life insurance policy (usually requiring an additional premium), a portion (usually 25 to 50 percent) of the face amount is payable upon diagnosis of specified illnesses. The named illnesses differ among insurers but typically include organ transplantation.

As benefits are paid under either a catastrophic or terminal illness rider, the face amount of the basic policy is reduced an equal amount, and an interest charge applies in some policies. Cash values are reduced either in proportion to the death benefit reduction or on a dollar-for-dollar basis.

4.4 Adjusting Life Insurance for Inflation

Participating policies, current assumption whole life policies, and universal life policies recognize inflation in a limited manner. Participating contracts can respond to inflation through dividends. Dividends can be used each year to purchase additional amounts of paid-up life insurance, but these small amounts of additional protection seldom keep pace with inflation.

Interest-sensitive contracts partly recognize inflation by crediting investment earnings directly to cash values. We say "partly recognize" because cash values in these policies are primarily invested in short-term debt instruments like government securities and in short-term corporate bonds, and the interest rates for these have an expected inflation component at the time they are issued. The expected inflation component is there because, in addition to a basic return on the money being loaned and an increase to reflect financial risks of failure, investors in debt instruments require an incremental return to cover their projections of future inflation rates. Thus, contracts with direct crediting of insurer investment returns to cash values give some recognition to inflation. The recognition is weak, however, for two reasons. First, the protection element of these contracts does not respond quickly, or at all for type A contracts, to inflation.[8] The protection element is expressed in fixed dollars and, as a storehouse of value and purchasing power, the dollar certainly is not ideal. Second, in a portfolio of primarily debt instruments, all except newly purchased parts reflect inflation expectations formed in the past. These expectations can grossly underestimate current and future rates of inflation.

Buy More Life Insurance

As long as you are insurable, you can buy more life insurance as your needs increase. What if you become uninsurable? You can protect yourself against that possibility by buying a policy with a guaranteed insurability option; however, this has drawbacks. First, the option is limited to a specified age, such as forty, and you may need more insurance after that age. Second, you must buy the same kind of insurance as the policy you have. Third, the premium will be higher due to your age.

Buy a Cost-of-Living Rider or Policy

inflation rider (or cost-of-living)

Automatically increases the amount of life insurance as the consumer price index rises.

Another alternative is the **inflation rider (or cost-of-living)**, which automatically increases the amount of insurance as the consumer price index (CPI) rises. It provides term insurance in addition to the face amount of your permanent or term policy up to a point, such as age fifty-five for the insured. If, for example, you have a $100,000 whole life policy and the CPI goes up 5 percent this year, $5,000 of one-year term insurance is automatically written for next year at the premium rate for your age. You are billed for it along with the premium notice for your basic policy. Because your premium increases with each increase in coverage, you may conclude that you bear the risk of keeping your coverage up with inflation. Keep in mind that no evidence of insurability is required. You do not have to accept (and pay for) the additional insurance if you don't want it. If you refuse to exercise the option, however, it is no longer available. In other words, you can't say, "I'm short of funds this year, but I will exercise the option next year." Table 19.4 illustrates how the inflation rider option would affect your total amount of insurance if you had bought a $100,000 whole life policy in 1995 and the inflation rate was 5 percent every year.

TABLE 19.4 Inflation Rider Option (at 5 Percent Annual Inflation)

Year	Consumer Price Index	Basic Insurance Amount	Option Amount	Total Death Benefit
1995	1.00000	$100,000		$100,000
1996	1.05000	100,000	$5,000	105,000
1997	1.10250	100,000	10,250	110,250
1998	1.15763	100,000	15,763	115,763
1995	1.21551	100,000	21,551	121,551
1996	1.27628	100,000	27,628	127,628
1997	1.34010	100,000	34,010	134,010
1998	1.40710	100,000	40,710	140,710
1999	1.47746	100,000	47,746	147,746
2000	1.55133	100,000	55,133	155,133
2001	1.62889	100,000	62,889	162,889
2002	1.71034	100,000	71,034	171,034
2003	1.79586	100,000	79,586	179,586
2004	1.88565	100,000	88,565	188,565
2005	1.97993	100,000	97,993	197,993
2006	2.07893	100,000	107,893	207,893
2007	2.18287	100,000	118,287	218,287
2008	2.29202	100,000	129,202	229,202
2009	2.40662	100,000	140,662	240,662
2010	2.52659	100,000	152,659	252,659
2011	2.65330	100,000	165,330	265,330

Buy a Variable or Variable Universal Life Policy

The face amount of variable life and variable universal life (except for the level face amount type) policies fluctuates with the performance of one or more separate accounts. You have the option of directing most of your premiums into common stock accounts where long-run returns are expected to offset CPI increases.

If you buy a variable life policy, you assume the risk that the equity markets may be going down at the same time that the CPI is going up. Should you buy a variable life policy? The answer depends on you. How much investment risk are you willing to take in coping with inflation?

KEY TAKEAWAYS

In this section you studied taxation of life insurance, major policy provisions, common life insurance riders, and accommodations to life insurance for inflation:

- There is no taxation on death benefits in life insurance (nor on dividends in participating policies).
- Life insurance provisions comparing the whole life to universal life policies in chapters 26 and 27.

    1. Ownership provision—(whole and universal life) spells out policyholder's rights
    2. Changes in basic amount provision (universal life) specifies conditions under which policyowner can change total face amount of the policy
    3. Payment of benefits provision—lets policyholder state the names and types of beneficiaries (and contingent beneficiaries)
    4. Settlement options—let owner state how death benefit will be provided
    5. Premium provisions—describe grace period through which policy will be enforced when a payment is missed, terms of reinstatement of a lapsed policy, premium refund when insured dies, and so forth
    6. Dividend provisions—in participating policies, dividends can be applied toward next premium, used to buy paid-up additions, left to accumulate interest, or paid to policyholder
    7. Guaranteed values provision—in whole life, guarantees cash surrender or continuance of policy as extended term, paid-up insurance if policyholder cancels
    8. Policy loan provisions—allow owner to borrow up to cash/account value in whole life and universal life
    9. General provisions—concern the contract, assignment, error in age or sex, incontestability, limited death benefits, and so forth

- Life insurance riders:

    1. Waiver of premium—allows premiums to be discontinued for a period of time in the event of insured's total disability
    2. Disability income—pays a benefit in the event of insured's total disability
    3. Accidental death benefit—double indemnity for death caused by accident
    4. Guaranteed insurability—allows insured to purchase additional insurance at intervals without new evidence of insurability
    5. Accelerated death benefits—allows insured to receive up to 50 percent of death benefit to improve quality of life before death
    6. Catastrophic illness—pays portion of face amount upon insured's diagnosis of specified illness

- Effects of inflation can be managed by using dividends to purchase additional amounts of paid-up insurance, buying a cost-of-living rider, or buying variable insurance or variable universal life insurance.

DISCUSSION QUESTIONS

1. The premium on Bill Brown's traditional whole life policy was due September 1. On September 15, he mailed a check to the insurance company. On September 26, he died. When the insurance company presented the check to the bank for collection, it was returned because there were insufficient funds in Bill's account. Does the company have to pay the claim presented by Bill's beneficiary? Why or why not? What provisions might result in payment?

2. If you don't need life insurance now but realize you may need it sometime in the future, would you be interested in buying a guaranteed insurability option, if it were available, without buying a policy now? Why or why not?

3. Describe the nature of what is purchased by the dividend on a life insurance policy when it is used to buy paid-up additions.

4. What desirable features characterize the policy loan provision of a cash value life insurance policy relative, for example, to borrowing money from a bank? How do policy loans affect death benefits?

5. Can you think of any ways that the terms of an accidental death benefit rider might encourage moral hazard?

6. When the dollar value of your home increases because of inflation, the insurer normally automatically increases the amount of insurance on your dwelling and its contents. Why does your life insurer require evidence of insurability before allowing you to increase the face value of your universal life insurance policy? (Assume no cost-of-living rider or guaranteed insurability rider.) How do you explain this difference between insuring homes and human lives?

5.   GROUP LIFE INSURANCE

LEARNING OBJECTIVES

In this section we elaborate on life insurance offered as group coverage by employers:

- **Life insurance plans typically offered by employers**
- **Benefit determination in group life**
- **Supplementary types of group life insurance coverage**
- **When employer obligations are terminated**
- **Tax implications of group life insurance**

Group life insurance is the oldest of the employer-sponsored group insurance benefits, dating from 1912. The most common type of group life insurance offered by employers is yearly renewable term coverage. It is the least expensive form of protection the employer can provide for employees during their working years. Due to a shorter average life expectancy, older employees and males have relatively higher premium rates. The premium for the entire group is the sum of the appropriate age- or sex-based premium for each member of the group. Obviously, a particular employee's premium will increase yearly with age. However, if younger employees continue to be hired, the lower premium for new hires can offset increases due to aging employees hired some years earlier. Also, if young employees replace older ones, premiums will tend to stabilize or decrease. This flow of covered lives helps maintain a fairly stable average total premium for the employer group.

5.1   Benefits

Most group term life insurance provides death benefit amounts equal to the employee's annual salary, one and one-half times the salary, or twice the salary. Some provide three or four times the salary, but some states and many insurers set limits on maximum benefits. Some provide a flat amount, such as $10,000 or $50,000. Other employers base the amount on the position of the employee, but they have to be careful to adhere to nondiscrimination laws. An amount equal to some multiplier of the salary is most common and reduces the possibilities of discrimination. Insurers' underwriting limitations are usually related to the total volume of insurance on the group.

Additional amounts of term life insurance may be available on a supplemental basis. Employers sponsor the supplemental plan, and employees usually pay the entire premium through payroll deductions. This allows employees to increase life insurance based on their individual needs. Supplemental coverages are usually subject to insurability evidence to avoid adverse selection. Accidental death and dismemberment insurance is also part of added benefits. This coverage provides an additional principal sum paid for accidental death. The death must occur within ninety days of the accident. The coverage also comes in multipliers of salary. The dismemberment part of the coverage is for loss of limb or eyesight. Dependent life insurance is available for low amounts for burial and funeral expenses. Benefits are minimal for children and spouses. Most employers also add waiver of premiums so that, in the event the employee becomes disabled, premiums are waived. Added benefits are also called voluntary coverage because the employee always pays for the coverage.

Beneficiary designation is determined by the insured persons; in some states, the employer may not be the beneficiary. The beneficiary can choose from the settlement options detailed previously. Any mistake in age made by the employer is corrected by a premium adjustment; this is different for individual coverage, which adjusts the death benefit. There is a grace period of thirty days for the premiums.

Life insurance policies have changed to meet the changing needs of policyholders. Many life insurance policies today allow benefits to be paid early in the event that the insured has a terminal illness or must pay catastrophic medical expenses, as noted previously. The insured must provide evidence that life expectancy is less than six months or one year or provide proof of catastrophic illness such as cancer or liver failure. The insured can then receive living benefits or accelerated death benefits rather than the traditional death benefit. Living benefits are limited in amount, typically from 25 to 50 percent of the face amount of the life insurance policy. The balance of the benefit (minus insurer expenses) is paid to beneficiaries after the death of the insured. Generally, adding the living benefits rider does not increase total group costs, and employers and employees do not pay more for the option.

Because living benefits may not provide enough funds to the terminally ill person, some may prefer to sell their policy to a viatical settlement company or to a life settlement program, which gives more funds up front, up to 80 percent of the face amount. Viatical settlements used to be very controversial; see the box "Do Viatical and Life Settlements Have a Place in Today's Market?"

Many group plans terminate an employee's group life insurance benefit when he or she retires. Those that allow employees to maintain coverage after retirement usually reduce substantially the amount of insurance available. If an employee is insurable at retirement, additional life insurance may be purchased on an individual basis. Alternatively, the employee can use the convertibility option in most group plans (regardless of the reason that employment terminates) to buy an equal or lower amount of permanent life insurance with level premiums based on the employee's attained age. Conversion takes place without having to demonstrate evidence of insurability. Because of potential adverse selection and the rapid increase in mortality rates after middle age, the costs of conversion are high as well.

Taxation of the group life is subject to IRS section 79, which states that the employer's premium contribution of up to $50,000 of death coverage is not considered income to the employee for income tax purposes. For any premiums for an amount of death benefits greater than $50,000, the employee has to pay taxes on the premiums as an income for income tax purposes. The premiums for the income calculations are based on the Uniform Premium Table I (revised in 1999 for lower rates), which is shown in Table 19.5.

TABLE 19.5 Uniform Premium Table I

Age	Cost per Month per $1,000 of Coverage
24 and under	$.05
25–29	$.06
30–34	$.08
35–39	$.09
40–44	$.10
45–49	$.15
50–54	$.23
55–59	$.43
60–64	$.66
65–69	$1.27
70 and over	$2.06

group universal life insurance

Usually offered as a supplement to a separate program of group term benefits.

Group universal life insurance is available from many employers. This insurance is usually offered as a supplement to a separate program of group term benefits. Universal life premiums are paid by employees and are administered through payroll deduction. A substantial amount of coverage (e.g., twice the annual salary, up to a maximum of $100,000 in face amount) is available without evidence of insurability. Low administrative expenses and low agents' commissions usually result in reasonably priced insurance. Group universal life insurance plans have become increasingly popular with both employers and employees. Employers are able to sponsor a life insurance plan that covers workers during their active years and into retirement at little or no cost to the employer. For example, the employer's expense may be limited to the costs of providing explanatory material to new employees, making payroll deductions of premiums, and sending a monthly check for total premiums to the insurer. Group universal life insurance is also popular with employees, largely because of the flexibility of the product.

Do Viatical and Life Settlements Have a Place in Today's Market?

Viatical settlements involve the sale of an existing life insurance policy by a terminally ill person to a third party. Viaticals saw their heyday during the late 1980s as AIDS patients with little time left sought funds to live out their final days or months with dignity. Numerous companies were formed in which individuals invested in the life insurance policies of AIDS patients, essentially betting on the short life expectancy of the policyholder. The investor would give the insured about 80 percent of the death benefits expecting to generate a large return in less than a year when the insured passed away and the proceeds would be collected by the investor/beneficiary.

With the advent of protease inhibitors in the mid-1990s, the life expectancy of people with AIDS increased dramatically. AIDS viaticals no longer looked like such a good investment. But the industry has not disappeared. Today, companies selling viaticals seek out individuals with other terminal illnesses, such as cancer or Amyotrophic Lateral Sclerosis (ALS, otherwise known as Lou Gehrig's disease).

Viatical settlements are possible because ownership of life insurance may be transferred at its owner's discretion. Viatical settlement firms typically buy insurance policies worth $10,000 and more from individuals with one to four years left to live. Both individual and employer-provided life insurance (group life) policies can be sold. Once sold, the new owner pays the premiums. The former owner uses the settlement money for anything from health expenses to taking that last dream vacation.

The option to receive a portion of the life proceeds before death is not new. The accelerated benefit option in life policies allows terminally ill policyholders access to the death benefits of their policies before they die. In such a case, a percentage of the face value (usually 50 percent or less) is paid in a lump sum to the policyholder. The rest of the insurance is paid to the beneficiary at the time of death. The low amount available under the accelerated benefit option is the impetus to the development of the viatical settlement companies. With transfer of ownership, the insured can get much more than 50 percent of the policy amount. According to Conning estimates, for a policy with a death benefit of $1.5 million, the typical payment would be $450,000 with a commission to the producer of close to $75,000.

While viatical settlements can provide greatly needed funds to terminally ill individuals, they are not without pitfalls. They pay less than the face value of the policy, but they usually provide higher amounts than the cash value of a policy. Settlement money may be subject to taxation, while life insurance benefits are not. Because beneficiaries may contest the sale of life insurance, which will reduce their inheritance, their advance approval is required. Senior citizens whose beneficiaries have died, however, often have no reason to continue paying premiums and may let their policies lapse anyway. In this case, selling their policy may provide them with funds they would otherwise never see.

Today, life settlements have supplanted viatical settlements in industry headlines. Life settlements are similar to viaticals, with the distinguishing feature that the insureds relinquishing their policies need not have a catastrophic illness (although in some jurisdictions, viaticals are defined broadly enough that there is no practical distinction between viatical and life settlements). Nonetheless, life settlements are marketed toward insureds with actuarially short conditional life expectancies, such as individuals over the age of sixty-five. This feature makes life settlements controversial, like their viatical cousins.

The regulatory climate of life and viatical settlements is tumultuous. Each state has a different view toward buyer practices, and regulatory standards range from nonexistent to draconian. Because sales are secondary-market transactions, some states impose no regulation over settlements. Agents and brokers may also be unlicensed. On the other hand, some states enforce onerous requirements on life settlement dealings. For example, the Ohio Department of Insurance (DoI) nearly drove life settlement dealings out of the state by calling for detailed information about brokers' transactions. The "self-audit data call" asked for over ninety data elements about life settlement contracts, including sensitive health and personal information about insureds. Brokers doing business in the state claimed the scope of the data call was highly burdensome and that compliance meant a potential violation of Health Insurance Portability and Accountability Act (HIPAA) privacy laws (discussed in Chapter 20). Nevertheless, noncompliant brokers were faced with the threat of losing their licenses to conduct business in Ohio. The DoI also wanted life settlement brokers to attest to the accuracy of their data call responses, a caveat that could expose them to litigation by insureds for misrepresentation. Ultimately, the Ohio DoI rescinded its data call request in March 2009 in light of significant criticism by the industry.

In the defense of states with strict regulatory protocols, the life settlement market is far from infallible. A variation known as stranger-originated life insurance (STOLI) has emerged as a new form of life settlement where senior citizens of high net worth become insureds for large death benefits. Premiums are paid by investors who become the owners and beneficiaries of these policies. The seniors usually receive a certain percentage of the death benefits. Because death benefits are not taxable, the life insurance industry is worried that the tax exemption may be lost if investors are the beneficiaries rather than family members. STOLI is a source of controversy because insureds may encounter tax liabilities, have their privacy compromised, and diminish their ability to buy more life insurance coverage in the future. The main problem is the insurable interest issue in some States.

The inconsistent regulatory environment is such that some life settlement transactions are completely illegitimate, as in the case of National Life Settlements (NLS), L.L.C. The company is alleged to have collected over $20 million from life settlement investors without purchasing any actual policies, according to bank records. NLS had compensated unlicensed brokers and agents in $3 million worth of commissions but returned only a fraction of the amount collected from investors over three years. The Texas State Securities Board seized the assets of NLS pending outcome of the legal investigation.

In an effort to improve industry transparency and ethical conduct, the National Association of Insurance Commissioners (NAIC) and National Conference of Insurance Legislators (NCOIL) proposed separate life settlements model acts in December 2007. The model acts put forth marketing standards, uniform purchase agreements, bans on STOLI, insureds' limited rights of termination, and sanctions for offenders. As of this writing, twenty-eight states have enacted legislation based on the model acts or their own standards governing life settlements and licensing requirements.

The life settlement business is growing and offering increasingly sophisticated financing arrangements. About $15 billion in life insurance policies were sold via life settlements in 2006, per the Life Insurance Settlement Association. An Internet search for "life settlement" will turn up countless organizations specializing in the service. Maturation of the industry and more standardized regulatory oversight are likely to improve the public's perception of life settlement and its reputation. Consumers are cautioned to be leery of STOLI dealings; conduct life settlements only through institutionally owned and funded entities; clarify all tax implications; and scrutinize contracts for features such as rescission periods, HIPAA compliance provisions, and next-of-kin notifications to protect their interests in life settlement transactions.

Questions for Discussion

1. Is it ethical to profit from someone else's misfortune by buying his or her life insurance at a discount?
2. Are life settlements a good idea for the policyholder? What are their advantages and disadvantages?
3. Do you think there is a need for viatical or life settlements when accelerated benefits are available?

Sources: Ron Panko, "Is There Still Room for Viaticals?" Best's Review, April 2002, http://www3.ambest.com/Frames/FrameServer.asp?AltSrc=23&Tab=1&Site=bestreview&refnum=16722, accessed April 11, 2009; Lynn Asinof, "Is Selling Your Life Insurance Good Policy in the Long Term?" Wall Street Journal, May 15, 2002; Karen Stevenson Brown, "Life Insurance Accelerated Benefits," http://www.elderweb.com/, accessed April 11, 2009; National Association of Insurance Commissioners, http://www.naic.org, accessed April 11, 2009; Life Partners, Inc., http://www.lifepartnersinc.com, accessed April 11, 2009; "Life Settlements—Top Ten Questions," New York State Insurance Department, http://www.ins.state.ny.us/que_top10/que_life_set.htm, accessed March 15, 2009; Trevor Thomas, "Feature: Ohio Department Shelves Demand for Detailed Data on Settlements," National Underwriter Life/Health Edition, March 9, 2009, http://www.lifeandhealthinsurancenews.com/Exclusives/2009/03/Pages/Feature-Ohio-shelves-demand-for-detailed-data-on-settlements.aspx, accessed March 15, 2009; Kevin M. McCarty, Commissioner, Florida Office of Insurance Regulation, "Stranger-Originated Life Insurance (STOLI) and the Use of Fraudulent Activity to Circumvent the Intent of Florida's Insurable Interest Law," January 2009, http://www.floir.com/pdf/stolirpt012009.pdf, accessed March 15, 2009; Trevor Thomas, "Life Settlement Firm Bought No Policies," National Underwriter Life/Health Edition, February 19, 2009, http://www.lifeandhealthinsurancenews.com/News/2009/2/Pages/Texas-Life-Settlement-Firm-Bought-No-Policies.aspx, accessed March 15, 2009; "Regulatory and Compliance Update," Life Settlement Solutions, Inc., February 2009, http://www.lifesettlementsmarketwatch.com/regulatory_compliance.html, accessed March 15, 2009; Alan Breus, "Virtues and Evils of Life Settlement," Planned Giving Design Center, http://www.pgdc.com/pgdc/virtues-and-evils-life-settlement, accessed March 15, 2009; Rachel Emma Silverman, "Letting an Investor, Bet on When You'll Die, New Insurance Deals Aimed at Wealthy Raise Concerns; Surviving a Two-Year Window," Wall Street Journal, May 26, 2005, D1.

KEY TAKEAWAYS

In this section you studied important aspects of group life insurance offered through employers:

- Yearly renewable term coverage is offered most often by employers to employees; group premium rates are based on the sum of the age- and sex-based premium for each member.
- Benefits are based on employee's salary or position, up to state and insurer maximums allowed.
- Supplemental coverage, subject to individual evidence of insurability, may be offered; accidental death/dismemberment, waiver of premium in event of disability, and dependent life insurance are typical forms.
- Employees select beneficiaries; beneficiaries choose settlement options.
- Living benefits riders are allowed and do not generally increase group costs.
- Group life typically ends when the employee retires, but the policy is convertible.
- Group premiums are tax-free for up to $50,000 of the benefit.
- Group universal life insurance may be offered as a supplemental program and is popular because of its affordability and flexibility.

DISCUSSION QUESTIONS

1. How is yearly renewable term life insurance made more affordable under a group arrangement?
2. Build a group life insurance program for Spookies Grocery Store using what you learned in this section, the section immediately preceding it, and Case 2 of Chapter 23. You can also ask a family member to give you their employer's employee benefits handbook if you are not currently employed.
3. On which factors is the underwriting and pricing of group life based?
4. How are age mistakes made by employers in group life coverage corrected? How does this differ from policies offered on an individual basis?
5. What options for continuing coverage does a retiree covered under a group life policy have?

---

6. REVIEW AND PRACTICE

1. George and Mary Keys are very excited over the news that they are to be parents. Since their graduation from college three years ago, they have purchased a new house and a new car. They owe $130,000 on the house and $8,000 on the car. Their only life insurance consists of $75,000 of term coverage on George and $50,000 on Mary. This coverage is provided by their employers as an employee benefit. Their personal balance sheet shows a net worth (assets minus liabilities) of $80,000. George is rapidly moving up within his company as special projects engineer. His current annual salary is $60,000. In anticipation of the new arrival, George is considering the purchase of additional life insurance. He feels that he needs at least $500,000 in coverage, but his budget for life insurance is somewhat limited. The couple has decided that Mary will stay at home with the new baby and put her career on hold for ten years or so while this baby and perhaps a later sibling or two are young.

    a. As George's agent, advise him as to the type(s) of life insurance that seem(s) most appropriate for his situation.

    b. George indicates to you that his financial situation will change in five years when he receives a one-time payment of approximately $100,000 from his uncle's estate. In what way would this information affect the type of life insurance you recommend to George?

2. Your wealthy Aunt Mabel, age sixty-four, recently talked to you, her life insurance agent, regarding her desire to see that her great-niece has the funds to attend college. Aunt Mabel is in very good health and expects to live for many years to come. She does not know if she should put aside money in certificates of deposit at the bank, buy more insurance on herself, or choose some other plan of action. She simply knows that her great-niece will need at least $80,000 to pay for her college education in ten years. What type of investment and/or insurance program would you recommend for her? Why?

3. Clancy knew he could not meet the physical requirements for insurability, so he had his twin brother, Clarence, take the physical examination in his place. A policy was issued, and three years later, Clancy died. The insurance company claims manager learned that Clancy's twin took the examination in his place and refused to pay the claim. Clancy's beneficiary sued the company for the proceeds, claiming that the two-year contestable period had expired. Did the company have to pay? Why or why not?

4. Phil Pratt has decided that the lowest-premium form of life insurance is definitely the best buy. Consequently, he has purchased a $250,000 yearly renewable term life insurance policy as his only life insurance. Explain why you agree or disagree with Phil's philosophy.

    a. Will his decision have any possible adverse effects in later years?

    b. Are there any realistic alternatives available to him without making premiums too high at a young age?

5. Betty Bick, age forty, is considering the purchase of a limited-payment participating life insurance policy that would be paid up when she turns sixty. She plans to work until then and does not wish to pay any premiums after she retires, but she definitely wants whole life insurance protection. Betty earns $45,000 per year as a branch manager for a commercial bank. As a single mother she has been unable to accumulate much wealth. At this time, Betty has two dependent children ages ten and fourteen.

    a. Explain to her any alternatives that would meet the criteria she has established.

    b. Why do you think her choice is a good (or bad) one? What additional information would you like to have before feeling confident about your answer?

6. Lane Golden has just purchased a universal life insurance policy from Midwest Great Life. Initially, Lane pays a first-month premium of $100. Her policy has (1) a front-end load of $2.00 per month; (2) a surrender charge equal to 100 percent of the minimum first-year premiums of $1,200 ($100 per month), decreasing 20 percent of the original surrender charge per year until it disappears after five years; (3) a current monthly mortality rate of $0.15 per $1,000 of protection (amount at risk); and (4) a current monthly investment return of 0.667 percent. Her policy is a type B, with a level $100,000 protection element.

   a. Construct a flow of funds statement, like the one in Figure 19.6, for the first month of Lane's policy.

   b. Explain why her accumulation value and cash value will be equal if she continues her policy for more than five years.

7. Mary and Henry both have universal life insurance policies with the same company. Mary wants to keep her death benefits level, while Henry wants to increase his death benefits over time. How will their insurer meet their different death benefit needs?

8. The following insureds have accidental death benefit riders on their life insurance policies. Discuss why you think this rider will or will not pay the beneficiary in each of the following situations.

   a. The insured dies from a fall through a dormitory window on the tenth floor. The door to his room is locked from the inside, and the window has no ledge. There is no suicide note. He had not appeared despondent before his death.

   b. The insured dies in a high-speed single-car automobile accident on a clear day and with no apparent mechanical malfunction in the vehicle. He had been very depressed about his job and had undergone therapy with a counselor, during which he had discussed suicide; however, there is no note.

   c. The insured contracts pneumonia after she is hospitalized due to injuries received from a fall from a ladder while rescuing a cat from a tree. She has a history of pneumonia and other serious respiratory problems. She dies of pneumonia thirty days after the fall.

ENDNOTES

1. Insurance Information Institute (III), "Moderate Avian Flu Pandemic Similar to 1957 and 1968 Outbreaks Could Cost U.S. Life Insurers $31 Billion in Additional Claims," Press Release, January 17, 2006, http://www.iii.org/media/updates/press.748721/ (accessed April 10, 2009).

2. Insurance Information Institute (III), *The Insurance Fact Book*, 2009, 19.

3. Before buying a mortgage protection policy, consider the pros and cons of paying off your mortgage at the time of death. Will your spouse's income be sufficient to meet the mortgage payments? Is the interest rate likely to be attractive in the future? Will the after-tax interest rate be less than the rate of growth in the value of the house, resulting in favorable leverage?

4. The advertised rate of return credited to the account is likely to be higher than the true rate of return being earned on the cash value element of the contract. This issue was discussed at length in Chapter 9 regarding vanishing premiums and market conduct.

5. Tax law changes in 1988 made single-premium surrenders and policy loans undesirable because any gain over net premiums becomes taxable immediately. Furthermore, gains are subject to an additional 10 percent tax penalty if the policyowner is less than age fifty-nine and a half. Thus, the tendency of single-premium buyers is to let the policy mature as a death claim. At that time there are no adverse income tax effects.

6. An alternative to the waiver of premium rider for flexible premium contracts waives only the amount required to cover mortality cost and expense deductions.

7. Policies with flexible face amounts usually issue the accidental death rider for a fixed amount equal to the basic policy's initial face amount.

8. Small recognition in total death benefits exists in type B universal policies because any increases in cash value as a result of higher interest rates are added to a level amount of protection. Dividends may be used to buy additional amounts of insurance, but the relationship to inflation is weak.

CHAPTER 20
Employment-Based Risk Management (General)

The mandatory benefits that employees obtain through the workplace—worker's compensation, unemployment compensation, and Social Security—were discussed in earlier chapters. In this chapter we move into the voluntary benefits area of group insurance coverages offered by employers. We begin with an overall explanation of the employee benefits field and group insurance in this chapter. Our first step is to delve into the specific group benefits provided by employers through insurance or self-insurance. In addition to being regulated by the states as insurance products, employee benefits are also regulated by the federal government (under the Employee Retirement Income Security Act of 1974), especially when the employer self-insures and is not subject to state insurance regulation. Because many tax incentives are available to employers that provide employee benefits, there are many nondiscrimination laws and specific limitations on the tax advantages. Employee benefits are regulated by the Department of Labor and the Internal Revenue Service (IRS).

To ensure your clear understanding of the main features of employee benefits, this chapter includes a general discussion of group insurance. The second part of the chapter includes a discussion of group life, group disability, and cafeteria plans. Some federal laws affecting employee benefits, such as the Americans with Disabilities Act, the Age Discrimination in Employment Act, and the Pregnancy Discrimination Act, are also covered. Chapter 22 delves into the most expensive noncash benefit, health care coverage. All types of managed care plans will be discussed along with the newest program of defined contribution health care plans, the health savings accounts. Relating to health insurance are long-term care and dental care, also discussed in Chapter 22. Two important federal laws, the Health Insurance Portability and Accountability Act (HIPAA) of 1996 and the Consolidated Omnibus Budget Reconciliation Act (COBRA) of 1986, will also be explained in Chapter 22. Chapter 21 is devoted to employer-provided qualified pension plans under the Employee Retirement Income Security Act (ERISA) of 1974 and subsequent reforms such as the Tax Reform Act of 1986 and the most recent Economic Growth Tax Reform and Reconciliation Act (EGTRRA) of 2001 (EGTRRA). Chapter 21 also describes deferred compensation plans such as 403(b), 457, the individual retirement account (IRA), and the Roth IRA. We will focus on qualified retirement plans, in which the employer contributes on the employee's behalf and receives tax benefits, while the employee is not taxed until retirement.

The field of employee benefits is a topic of more than one full course. Therefore, your study in this and the following two chapters, along with the employee benefits Case 2 of Chapter 23, is just a short introduction to the field. This chapter covers the following:

1. Links

2. Overview of employee benefits and employer objectives

3. Nature of group insurance

4. The flexibility issue, cafeteria plans, and flexible spending accounts

5. Federal regulation compliance, benefits continuity and portability, and multinational employee benefit plans

1. LINKS

At this point in our study, we are ready to discuss what the employer is doing for us in the overall process of our holistic risk management. Employers became involved in securing benefits for their employees during the industrial era, when employees left the security of their homes and families and moved to the cities. The employer became the caretaker for health needs, burial, disability, and retirement. As the years passed, the government began giving employers tax incentives to continue to provide these so-called fringe benefits. Today, these benefits are called noncash compensation and are very significant in the completeness of our risk management puzzle.

As noted in our complete risk management puzzle of Figure 20.1, we need to have coverage for the risks of health, premature death, disability, and living too long. These benefits and more are provided by most employers to their full-time employees. These types of coverage are the second step in the pyramid structure in the figure. Benefits offered by employers are critical in the buildup of our insurance coverages. As you will see in the next section of this chapter, there is no individual underwriting when we are covered in the group contract of our employer. As such, for some employees with health issues, the group life, disability, and health coverages are irreplaceable.

Two important federal laws will be discussed later in this chapter. COBRA provides for continuing health care coverage when an employee leaves a job or a breadwinner dies, and HIPAA enforces coverage for preexisting conditions when a person changes jobs. The reader can realize the enormous importance of this coverage in the holistic picture of risk management.

In our drill down into the specific pieces of the puzzle, we will again learn in this chapter that each risk is covered separately and that coverages from many sources protect each risk. It is up to us to pull together these separate pieces to provide a complete risk management portfolio. Whether the employer pays all or requires us to participate in the cost of the different types of coverage, the different coverages are important to consider and do not allow us a complete understanding of the holistic risk management process if they are not. Better yet, some of the benefits provide wonderful tax breaks that should be clearly recognized.

FIGURE 20.1   Links between Holistic Risk Pieces and Employee Benefits

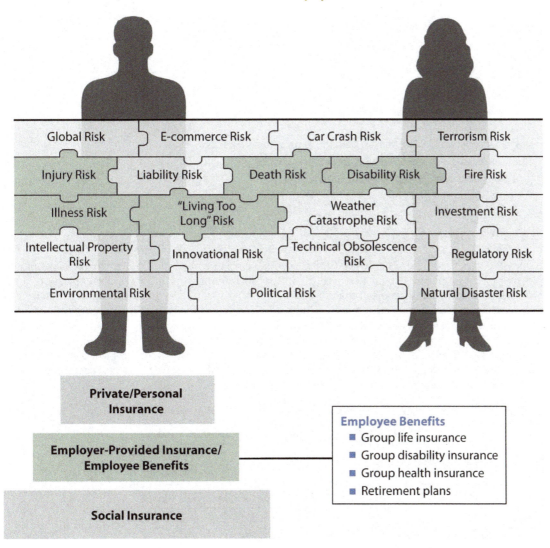

2. OVERVIEW OF EMPLOYEE BENEFITS AND EMPLOYER OBJECTIVES

LEARNING OBJECTIVES

In this section we elaborate on the general subject of noncash compensation to employees known as employee benefits:

- **The significance of employee benefits to total compensation**
- **Tax incentives associated with employee benefits**
- **Considerations in employee benefit plan design**

2.1 Overview of Employee Benefits

employee benefits

All noncash compensation items sponsored by employers for their employees; includes group insurance, educational assistance, legal assistance, childcare, discounts, and so forth.

Noncash compensation, or **employee benefits**, today is a large portion of the employer's cost of employment. The Employee Benefit Research Institute (EBRI), an important research organization in the area of employee benefits, reported that, in 2007, employers spent $1.5 trillion on major voluntary and mandatory employee benefit programs, including $693.9 billion for retirement programs, $623.1 billion for health benefit programs, and $138 billion for other benefit programs.[1] The complete picture of employee benefits costs over the years is provided in Table 20.1 As you can see in this table, benefits make up a significant amount of the pay from employers, equating to 18.6 percent of total compensation in 2007. The largest shares of the benefits go toward legally required benefits (social insurance), paid leave, and health insurance.

TABLE 20.1 **Employer Spending on Noncash Compensation, 1960–2007**

	1960	1970	1980	1990	2000	2007
	($ billions)					
Total compensation	$296.5	$617.1	$1,651.1	$3,337.5	$5,781.8	$7,810.7
Wages and salaries[2]	$272.8	$551.5	$1,377.4	$2,754.0	$4,829.8	$6,355.7
Total benefits	$23.6	$65.5	$273.7	$583.5	$952.6	$1,454.9
Retirement income benefits	$14.1	$40.1	$160.1	$292.9	$458.8	$693.9
Social Security (OASDI)	$5.6	$16.2	$55.6	$137.3	$233.3	$307.5
Private employers	$4.9	$13.1	$55.3	$63.8	$113.5	$199.9
Public employers	$3.7	$10.8	$49.2	$91.8	$112.0	$186.4
State and local governments	$1.8	$5.1	$19.1	$33.0	$39.6	$69.2
Federal governments	$1.9	$5.7	$30.1	$58.8	$72.4	$117.2
Civilian retirement	$0.8	$2.0	$15.9	$28.7	$41.3	$54.3
Military retirement	$0.8	$3.2	$12.5	$27.5	$28.2	$60.2
Railroad retirement	$0.3	$0.5	$1.7	$2.6	$2.9	$2.7
Health benefits	$3.4	$14.6	$73.0	$211.9	$399.6	$623.1
Medicare hospital insurance	$0.0	$2.3	$11.6	$33.5	$67.0	$88.5
Group health insurance	$3.4	$12.1	$61.0	$176.9	$331.4	$532.1
Military medical insurance[3]	$0.0	$0.2	$0.4	$1.5	$1.2	$2.5
Other benefits	$6.1	$10.8	$40.6	$78.6	$94.2	$138.0
Unemployment insurance	$3.0	$3.8	$17.2	$24.5	$29.8	$42.5
Workers' compensation	$2.0	$4.6	$19.3	$46.9	$52.0	$78.2
Group life insurance	$1.1	$2.4	$4.1	$7.2	$12.4	$17.3

© 2009, Employee Benefit Research Institute, reprinted with permission Source: Employee Benefit Research Institute tabulations of data from the U.S. Department of Commerce, Bureau of Economic Analysis, National Income and Product Accounts of the United States. http://www.bea.doc.gov/bea/ dn/nipaweb/index.asp. For additional years of data, see EBRI's Databook on Employee Benefits, chapter 2, which contains data in current dollars and inflation-adjusted dollars: http://www.ebri.org/pdf/publications/books/databook/DB.chapter%2002.pdf.

As noted above, employee benefits have tax incentives. Some benefits such as health care, educational assistance, legal assistance, child care, discounts, parking, cafeteria facility, and meals are deductible to the employer and completely tax exempt to the employees. Retirement benefits, both the contributions and earnings on the contributions, are tax deductible to the employer and tax deferred to the employees until their retirement. Some of the benefits paid by employees themselves are tax deferred, such as investment in 401(k) plans (discussed in Chapter 21). Other benefits are partially tax exempt, such as group life. The employee is not required to pay taxes on the cost of life insurance up to coverage in the amount of $50,000 in death benefits. For greater amounts of death benefits, the employer's contributed premiums are counted as taxable income to the employee. The largest expense comes in the form of health benefits, with $532.1 billion out of $1,454.9 billion of the total benefits spent by employers in 2007 (see Table 20.1). Health benefits receive the most favorable tax exemption of all employee benefit programs.

When we do not pay taxes, the government is forgoing income. Each year, the White House Office of Management and Budget calculates the amounts forgone by the tax benefits. EBRI reports that the foregone taxes from employer-provided benefits are projected to amount to $1.05 trillion for 2009 through 2013.[4]

With the tax incentives comes a very stringent set of rules for nondiscrimination to ensure that employers provide the benefits to all employees, not only to executives and top management. The most stringent rules appear in the Employee Retirement Income Security Act, which will be explored in Chapter 21 in the discussion of pensions. Keep in mind that employee benefits are a balance of tax incentives as long as employers do not violate **nondiscrimination rules** and act in good faith for the protection of the employees in their fiduciary capacity. The efforts to protect employees in cases of bankruptcies are featured in the box "Your Employer's Bankruptcy: How Will It Affect Your Employee Benefits?" Ways to detect mismanagement of certain benefit plan funding are described in the box "Ten Warning Signs That Pension Contributions Are Being Misused."

nondiscrimination rules

Rules set forth by the IRS stipulating that employee benefit plans must be for the benefit of all employees, not just executives and top management in order to qualify for tax incentives.

2.2   Employer Objectives

The first step in managing an effective employee benefits program, as with the other aspects of risk management discussed in Part I of the text, is setting objectives. Objectives take into account both (1) the economic security needs of employees and (2) the financial constraints of the employer. Without objectives, a plan is likely to develop incrementally into a haphazard program. An employer who does not have an on-staff specialist in this field would be wise to engage an employee benefits consulting firm.

Employers can use several methods to set objectives for benefit plans. They may investigate what other organizations in the region or within the industry are doing and then design a competitive package of their own to recruit and retain qualified employees. Benefits may be designed to compete with plans offered for unionized workers. Employers may survey employees to find out what benefits are most desired and then design the benefits package with employees' responses in mind.

Employer objectives are developed by answering questions such as the following:

- Who is eligible for each type of benefit?
- Should seniority, position, salary, and other characteristics influence the amount of each employee's benefit? (Care in observing nondiscrimination rules is very important in this area.)
- How might a specific benefit affect employee turnover, absenteeism, and morale?
- How should benefits be funded? (Should the employer buy insurance or self-insure?)
- Should the benefits program be designed to adjust to the differing needs of employees?
- How do laws and regulations influence benefit plan design?
- To what extent should tax preferences affect plan design?

In answering questions like these, management must keep in mind the effect of its benefits decisions on the organization's prime need to operate at an efficient level of total expenditures with a competitive product price. Efficiency requires management of total labor costs, wages plus benefits. Thus, if benefits are made more generous, this change can have a dampening effect on wages, all else being equal. Financial constraints are a major factor in benefit plan design. It is critical to note that health insurance is a key benefit employees expect and need. As shown in Table 20.1, group health insurance is a major part of the average compensation in the United States. Most people regard the employer as responsible to provide this very expensive benefit, which is discussed in detail in Chapter 22 (unless and until proposed changes are enacted by the Obama administration, that is).

KEY TAKEAWAYS

In this section you studied the following general features of employee benefits and important considerations for employers:

- Employee benefits make up a significant portion of total compensation to employees.
- Employers and employees enjoy tax deferrals, exemptions, and deductions on benefit expenditures.
- The economic needs of employees and the financial constraints of employers must be balanced in designing benefit programs.

DISCUSSION QUESTIONS

1. What is the significance of adherence to nondiscrimination rules in employee benefit plan design?
2. What are some of the tax incentives available to employers who provide employee benefits?
3. Which benefit is the most costly to the employer?
4. Which benefit receives the most favored tax exemption?
5. What methods do employers use to set objectives for a benefits plan?

3. NATURE OF GROUP INSURANCE

LEARNING OBJECTIVES

In this section we elaborate on the following insurance aspects of employee benefits:

- **Administration of group insurance**
- **Ways of providing group insurance**
- **How premiums are paid**
- **Key underwriting determinants for placing a group insurance program and for pricing a group insurance program**
- **Cost advantages of group coverage**
- **Cost features of group coverage**
- **Tax treatment of payments and benefits**

Individuals receive economic security from individually purchased insurance and from group insurance. Both types of coverage may provide protection against economic loss caused by death, disability, or sickness. To the covered person, the differences between the two types of coverage (shown in Table 20.2) may not be noticeable.

TABLE 20.2 Comparison of Group Insurance and Individual Insurance

	Individual Insurance Contract	Group Insurance Contract
Administration/ contract	Issued to the person insured	Master contract issued to employer or a trust; each employee is issued a certificate of insurance (not a contract)
Underwriting	Evidence of insurability	Characteristic of the group to minimize adverse selection and administrative costs
Eligibility	At inception of contract	Related to employment periods
Experience rating/pricing	Experience of the insurance company	Experience of the large group

3.1   Administration

The administration of group insurance differs from individual insurance because the contract is made with the employer rather than with each individual. The employer receives a **master contract** that describes all the terms and conditions of the group policy. The employer, in turn, provides each insured employee with a **certificate of insurance** as evidence of participation. **Participants** in the benefit plan may include employees, their dependents (including a spouse and children under a specified age, such as twenty-one, when enrolled in school), retirees, and their dependents. Participants receive a booklet describing the plan, distributed by the employer at the time the plan goes into effect or when eligibility begins, whichever is later.

Administration of group insurance also differs from individual insurance because the employer may be responsible for the record keeping ordinarily done by the insurer, especially if the group is large. Administration is simplified by the employer paying periodic premiums directly to the insurer. If employees are required to contribute toward the premium, the employer is responsible for collection or payroll deduction of employee contributions, as well as for payment to the insurer of the total group premium amount.

Many large employer plans are **self-insured**, and employers, rather than insurers, pay claims and bear the risk that actual claims will exceed expected claims. Some employers with self-insured plans also administer the benefits themselves. However, insurers and **third-party administrators (TPAs)** administer many (even large) self-funded plans under an **administrative services only (ASO)** contract. The employer transfers record keeping and claim payment functions to the insurer or TPA, paying about 5 to 10 percent of the normal premium for administrative services.

master contract

In group insurance, document issued to employer describing all the terms and conditions of the group policy.

certificate of insurance

Provided by employers to insured employees as evidence of participation in a group insurance plan.

participants

In a group benefit plan may include employees; their dependents (including a spouse and children under a specified age, such as twenty-one, when enrolled in school); retirees; and their dependents.

self-insured

When large employers with sufficient means pay claims in a group insurance arrangement and bear the risk that actual claims will exceed expected claims.

third-party administrators (TPAs)

Unaffiliated party contracted to administer self-funded group insurance plans.

administrative services only (ASO)

Arrangement under which an insurer or third-party administrator (TPA) handles record keeping and claim payment functions for employers sponsoring self-insured group insurance plans, who pay 5 to 10 percent of the normal premium for these services.

stop-loss insurance

A form of reinsurance or
excess insurance for
self-insured group insurance
plans whereby an insurer or
third-party administrator
(TPA) provides protection
against unexpectedly high
claims.

specific stop loss

Stop-loss insurance for
self-insured group insurance
plans that provides a limit per
claim above which the
employer is not responsible.

aggregate stop loss

Stop-loss insurance for
self-insured group insurance
plans that provides a limit on
the total claims in a year for
which the employer is
responsible.

group underwriting

Does not involve an
application to the insurer by
each participant or a medical
examination (except in some
very small employer groups);
the employer makes one
application for the entire
group, and, instead of
selecting individual insureds,
the insurer makes an
underwriting decision based
on group characteristics.

In addition, the employer may purchase **stop-loss insurance** from the same or another insurer through the TPA for protection against unexpectedly high claims. Stop-loss coverage is a form of reinsurance or excess insurance for self-insured plans. The two basic forms of coverage are **specific stop loss**, in which a limit is set per claim, and **aggregate stop loss**, in which a limit is set for the total claims in a year. The insurer reimburses the employer for claim amounts above the limit, also called the attachment point. Purchase of an ASO contract and stop-loss insurance gives the employer the potential cash flow and expense advantage of self-funding, while reducing the employer's administrative burden and potential for catastrophic risk.

3.2 Underwriting

Individually purchased life and health insurance contracts involve individual underwriting. The purchaser files an application and, in some cases, takes a medical examination. On the basis of this and other information, the underwriter decides whether or not to issue insurance, and on what terms. The merits of each application are decided individually. **Group underwriting** does not involve an application to the insurer by each participant, or a medical examination (except in some very small employer groups). The group as a whole is being underwritten. The employer makes one application for the entire group and, instead of selecting individual insureds, the insurer makes an underwriting decision based on group characteristics.

Characteristics of the Group as Key Underwriting Determinants

Reason for the Group's Existence

It is imperative that the group was not created for insurance purposes. Insurance should be incidental to the group's formation. Under state laws, the following are eligible groups for group insurance:

- Individual employer groups
- Negotiated trusteeships
- Trade associations
- Labor union groups
- Multiple-employer trusts (METs) or multiple-employer welfare arrangements

Some, mostly smaller, employers may have trouble finding an insurance carrier willing to service their group if one or more individuals are in ill health. Many of these firms, however, have access to group insurance by participating in a multiple-employer trust (MET). The MET makes available to small employers, often in the same industry group and with as few as one or two employees each, benefits similar to those available to large groups. METs are often organized for a trade association, union, or other sponsoring organization by an insurer or third-party administrator. When small employers come together through a MET to purchase insurance, they have access to group underwriting treatment, products, and services similar to those available to large employers.

Financial Stability of the Employer

Insurers prefer to work with firms that will exist from year to year and be able to pay the premium. Because the cash flow is very fast in group insurance such as health insurance, financial stability is critical to underwriters accepting the business. This requirement is really fundamental to all types of underwriting, not only group underwriting.

Your Employer's Bankruptcy: How Will It Affect Your Employee Benefits?

The Department of Labor's Employee Benefits Security Administration (EBSA) administers the Employee Retirement Income Security Act (ERISA) of 1974, which governs retirement plans (including profit sharing and 401(k) plans) and welfare plans (including health, disability, and life insurance plans). ERISA also includes the health coverage continuation and accessibility provisions of the Consolidated Omnibus Budget Reconciliation Act (COBRA) and the Health Insurance Portability and Accountability Act (HIPAA).

EBSA educates and assists the nation's 200 million participants and beneficiaries in pension, health, and other employee benefit plans and the more than 3 million sponsors of those plans. In carrying out its responsibility to protect participants' and beneficiaries' benefits, EBSA has targeted populations of plan participants who are potentially exposed to the greatest risk of loss. One such group of individuals is the group of participants and beneficiaries of plans whose sponsor has filed for bankruptcy. In such cases, EBSA provides the following.

If an employer declares bankruptcy, it will generally take one of two forms: reorganization under Chapter 11 of the Bankruptcy Code or liquidation under Chapter 7. A Chapter 11 (reorganization) usually means that the company continues in business under the court's protection while attempting to reorganize its financial affairs. A Chapter 11 bankruptcy may or may not affect your pension or health plan. In some cases, plans continue to exist throughout the reorganization process. In a Chapter 7 bankruptcy, the company liquidates its assets to pay its creditors and ceases to exist. Therefore, it is likely your pension and health plans will be terminated. When your employer files for bankruptcy, you should contact the administrator of each plan or your union representative (if you are represented by a union) to request an explanation of the status of your plan or benefits. The summary plan description will tell how to get in touch with the plan administrator. Questions that you may want to ask include the following:

- Will the plan continue or will it be terminated?
- Who will act as plan administrator of the health and pension plans during and after the bankruptcy, and who will be the trustee in charge of the pension plan?
- If the pension plan is to be terminated, how will accrued benefits be paid?
- Will COBRA continuation coverage be offered to terminated employees?
- If the health plan is to be terminated, how will outstanding health claims be paid, and when will certificates of creditable coverage (showing, among other things, the dates of enrollment in your employer's health plan) be issued?

Prior Experience of the Plan

This factor is important not only in accepting a group for coverage but also in pricing the group plan. Insurers look at past losses—the frequency, severity, and length of illnesses or disabilities—when deciding whether to accept a business and then how to price it. Pricing factors will be discussed later in this section.

Size of the Group

As you recall from the first two chapters of this text, the law of large numbers is very important to the functioning of insurance. Therefore, large groups can be rated on their own experience, while small groups have to be rated based on the insurer's experience with groups of similar type and size.

Source and Method of Premium Payment

Insurance laws may require that a minimum percentage of the group be enrolled in the benefit plan to ensure that there are enough healthy employees and dependents to help offset the high claims that can be expected from unhealthy employees or dependents. Every group, insured or self-insured, can anticipate enrollment by the unhealthy. The likelihood of achieving minimum participation (meaning at least 75 percent) is increased by **employer sharing of costs**. Most states and insurers require that noncontributory plans, in which employees do not pay for the cost of their coverage, enroll 100 percent of employees. In contributory plans, where employees pay all or part of the premium amount, 75 percent of employees must participate. This helps protect the plan from adverse selection.

employer sharing of costs

When an employer pays some portion of group insurance premiums; in group benefit plans where employees pay all or part of the premium amount, 75 percent of employees must participate to protect the plan from adverse selection.

Stability of the Group

To avoid the problems associated with high employee turnover, employers use waiting periods or probationary periods before insurance coverage begins. There are some advantages to turnover, however; for one, the age composition does not get older when more new employees join the plan.

Persistency of the Group

Group business is costly for the insurer in the first year. An employer that changes carriers every year is an undesirable client. Insurers look for a more permanent relationship with employers.

Method of Determining Benefits

To avoid adverse selection, employers are required under nondiscrimination laws to offer the same benefits package to all employees. In reality, many groups provide flexible benefit programs, which allow employee input into the amount of each benefit, and **supplemental plans**, which allow employees to purchase additional amounts of a specific benefit on a fully contributory basis. These options undoubtedly invite adverse selection, which is reflected in higher rates for flexible and supplemental benefits. However, given the diversity in needs among single, married, divorced, younger, older, male, and female employees in the typical group, the advantages of giving employees a voice in benefit decisions may well outweigh the cost of some adverse selection. Flexible benefit programs, also known as cafeteria plans, are discussed later in this chapter.

supplemental plans

Specific, additional group insurance coverages and amount that employees can purchase on a fully contributory basis.

Supplemental plans allow employees to choose additional group insurance coverage paid for entirely by the employees themselves. For example, supplemental life coverage can allow an employee to increase the face amount of group life insurance coverage, and supplemental group disability coverage can allow for a cost-of-living benefit increase for periods of long-term disability. In recent years, the use of supplemental plans has grown, largely due to the flexibility they provide to employees at little or no cost to employers, other than facilitating the payroll deductions.

The potential for adverse selection may be greater with supplemental benefits than with nonsupplemental benefits. Because employees pay the premium for supplemental coverage, it is likely that those who anticipate that they need the benefit are more willing to participate. Despite this, supplemental plans are popular because they allow employees to tailor benefits to meet their individual needs through a convenient payroll deduction plan.

Provisions for Determining Eligibility

Generally, employees are first eligible for benefits either immediately upon hiring or following a three- to six-month **probationary period**. Following hiring or the probationary period (whichever the employer requires), the employee's **eligibility period** usually extends for thirty-one days, during which employees may sign up for group insurance coverage. This period is called **open enrollment**. In order for coverage to become effective, most group plans require that the employee be actively at work on the day that coverage would normally become effective. Being at work provides some evidence of good health and helps reduce adverse selection.

Enrollment after the eligibility period usually means that the employee will have to provide evidence of insurability. The employee may have to complete a questionnaire or have a medical examination to show that he or she is in good health. This provision helps reduce adverse selection. Most employers allow only full-time employees to participate in the benefit plan. (The definition of *full-time* differs from employer to employer; the minimum may be as low as twenty hours per week, but it is more often thirty-two to thirty-five hours). To lower adverse selection, part-time employees are not included (some part-time employees join the work force only for the benefits). Some employers provide minimal benefits for part-time employees, such as burial cost only instead of full death benefits.

Administrative Aspects

The most important part of this requirement is to what extent the employer plans to help in the enrollment and claims process.

3.3 Pricing

Some employers pay the entire cost of the group insurance premium. These are **noncontributory plans**. In **contributory plans**, employees pay part of the cost. Frequently, group life and disability insurance plans are noncontributory, but they require the employees to contribute if other family members are covered. Health insurance is more likely to be contributory because of rising premiums, a situation described in the box "What Is the Tradeoff between Health Care Cost and Benefits?" in Chapter 22. The employer makes the premium payment to the insurer; contributory amounts, if any, are deducted from the employee's paycheck.

Important factors in underwriting for pricing are (1) the age and gender composition of the group, (2) the industry represented by the group, and (3) the geographical location of the group.

Group insurance is usually less expensive than individual insurance for several reasons: (1) with group coverage, the insurer deals with one insured instead of many, streamlining marketing costs; (2) the employer takes care of much of the administrative detail; (3) commission scales on group business are lower than they are on individual policies; (4) medical examinations are not needed because the employees are at least healthy enough to work; (5) the employer collects the premiums and pays the insurer in one lump sum, which is more efficient for the insurer; and (6) the employer often does some monitoring to eliminate false or unnecessary claims for health care benefits. In addition, group insurance theory maintains that the replacement by younger employees of employees who retire or quit keeps average mortality and morbidity rates from rising to prohibitive levels. That is, a flow of persons through the group tends to keep average costs down. This is often true when the number of employees in a group is growing, but it is less true for an organization that is downsizing.

Group life and health insurance rates are usually quoted by insurers as one monthly rate (e.g., $0.15 per $1,000 of coverage in the case of life insurance) for all employees. This rate is based on a weighted average, taking into account the age, sex, and accompanying mortality and morbidity rates for each employee in the group. Because mortality and morbidity rates increase with age, life insurance rates are quoted in age brackets. Someone in the thirty-one to thirty-five age bracket will pay slightly more than someone in the the twenty-six to thirty bracket. Thus, groups with a higher proportion of older people will have relatively higher premiums.

---

probationary period

Three- to six-month period through which a newly hired worker must be employed before becoming eligible for group benefits.

eligibility period

Timeframe (usually thirty-one days) during which employees may sign up for group insurance coverage.

open enrollment

The process of employees selecting group insurance coverage during the eligibility period.

noncontributory plan

Pension plan funded only by employer contributions.

contributory plan

Pension plan that requires the employee to pay all or part of pension fund contributions.

Most small organizations (e.g., those with fewer than fifty employees) have their entire premium based on pooled claims experience for similar-size firms. However, larger employers are likely to have **experience-rated premiums** in which the group's own claims experience affects the cost of coverage, as described in Chapter 16 for worker's compensation. Experience rating allows employer groups to benefit directly from their own good claims experience, and it provides a direct economic incentive for risk managers to control claims.

With experience rating, the weight or credibility given to a group's own experience increases with the number of participants. The experience of smaller groups (e.g., those with fewer than 500 or 1,000 employees) is not considered sufficiently statistically credible or reliable to determine premiums completely. Therefore, insurers use a weighted average of the group's loss experience and the pooled experience for groups of similar size and characteristics in developing the claims charge. For example, the group's actual loss experience may be weighted at 70 percent of the claims charge, and the pooled experience for groups of similar attributes may carry a weight of 30 percent. If the group had a loss experience of $80,000 and the pool experience was $100,000, then the claims charge for the experience-rated premium would be $86,000 per year. A larger group would have more statistically reliable experience and might receive an 80 percent weighting for its own experience and a 20 percent weighting for the pooled experience, resulting in a claims charge of $84,000. Thus, the larger the group, the more credit the group receives for its own claims experience. The experience-rated claims charge makes up the bulk of the total premium due, but the final experience-rated premium also includes administrative charges and fees.

Premiums for larger organizations, however, may reflect only the group's own loss experience. With prospective experience rating, the group's claims experience for the previous few years, plus an inflation factor, partly or completely determines the premium for the current year. A retrospective experience rating plan uses loss experience to determine whether premium refunds (or dividends) should be paid at the end of each policy year.

Group insurance premiums paid by the employer are a deductible business expense and are not taxable income to employees except for amounts of term life insurance in excess of $50,000 per person and all group property-liability insurance. Employee premium contributions are not tax deductible, except if they are allowed to be used in a cafeteria program under a premium conversion plan or flexible spending account (FSA), discussed later in this chapter. The other tax-sheltered accounts available under health savings account (HSA) plans are discussed in Chapter 22. Proceeds paid from group life insurance at death are not taxable income to the beneficiary, as noted in Chapter 19, but are included in the estate of the insured, if he or she is the owner, for federal estate tax purposes.

Group disability insurance (discussed in Chapter 22) premiums paid by the employer are also a deductible business expense for the employer, and they do not result in an immediate tax liability for the employee. If an employee receives disability benefits, the portion paid for by the employer is taxable to the employee. For example, if the employer pays one-third of the premium amount for disability coverage, and if the employee becomes disabled and receives benefits, one-third of the benefits are taxable income to the employee. Benefits attributable to coverage paid for by the employee with after-tax dollars are not taxable. Thus, in this example, two-thirds of the disability benefit amount would not be taxable income. Explaining taxation of disability income to employees can be a challenge for the benefits manager. However, many employers are successful in conveying the importance of after-tax premium payment to the level of benefits if disability occurs. The tax savings on the premiums are very small relative to the tax savings on the disability benefits.

Ten Warning Signs That Pension Contributions Are Being Misused

Increasingly, employees are asked to make voluntary or mandatory contributions to retirement and other benefit plans. This is particularly true for 401(k) savings plans (as will be discussed in Chapter 21). These plans allow you to deduct from your paycheck a portion of pretax income every year, invest it, and pay no taxes on those contributions until the money is withdrawn at retirement.

An antifraud campaign by the Department of Labor uncovered a small fraction of employers who abused employee contributions by either using the money for corporate purposes or holding on to the money too long. Here are ten warning signs that your pension contributions are being misused.

1. Your 401(k) or individual account statement is consistently late or comes at irregular intervals.
2. Your account balance does not appear to be accurate.
3. Your employer failed to transmit your contribution to the plan on a timely basis.
4. You notice a significant drop in account balance that cannot be explained by normal market ups and downs.
5. Your 401(k) or individual account statement does not reflect a contribution from your paycheck.
6. Investments listed on your statement are not what you authorized.

experience-rated premiums

When a group's own claims experience experience affects the cost of coverage for group insurance.

7. Former employees are having trouble getting their benefits paid on time or in the correct amounts.

8. You notice unusual transactions, such as a loan to the employer, a corporate officer, or one of the plan trustees.

9. Investment managers or consultants change frequently and without explanation.

10. Your employer has recently experienced severe financial difficulty.

If you think the plan trustees or others responsible for investing your pension money have been violating the rules, you should call or write the nearest field office of the U.S. Department of Labor's Employee Benefits Security Administration (EBSA). The Labor Department has authority to investigate complaints of fund mismanagement. If an investigation reveals wrongdoing, the department can take action to correct the violation, including asking a court to compel plan trustees and others to put money back in the plan. Courts can also impose penalties of up to 20 percent of the recovered amount and bar individuals from serving as trustees and plan money managers.

If you suspect that individuals providing services to the plans have gotten loans or otherwise taken advantage of their relationship to the plan, the Employee Plans Division of the Internal Revenue Service may want to take a closer look. The Internal Revenue Service is authorized to impose tax penalties on people involved in unlawful party-in-interest transactions.

Cases of embezzlement or stealing of pension money, kickbacks, or extortion should be referred to the Federal Bureau of Investigation or the Labor Department field office in your area. If illegal activities are discovered, the case can be referred to the U.S. Department of Justice for prosecution. Criminal penalties can include fines or prison sentences, or both.

Federal pension law makes it unlawful for employers to fire or otherwise retaliate against employees who provide the government with information about their pension funds' investment practices.

Sources: Portions reprinted from "10 Warning Signs," U.S. Department of Labor, Employee Benefits Security Administration, http://www.dol.gov/ebsa/ publications/10warningsigns.html, accessed April 12, 2009; "What You Should Know About Your Retirement Plan," a handbook from the U.S. Department of Labor, at http://www.dol.gov/ebsa/publications/wyskapr.html, accessed April 12, 2009. This booklet is available online. You can find explanation of all qualified retirement plans discussed in this chapter.

KEY TAKEAWAYS

In this section you studied the following:

- Employers handle many administrative aspects of group insurance that are normally dealt with by insurers.
- Employers may purchase group insurance from a private insurer or they may self-insure programs.
- Employers and employees may share in the cost of insurance premiums, and it is an important underwriting issue.
- Key underwriting determinants of accepting a group for insurance and pricing the group insurance include the reason for the group's existence, the employer's financial stability and persistency, prior experience of the plan, the size of the group, the source and/or method of premium payment, stability of the group, eligibility provisions, geographical location, industry, and employees mix.
- Group insurance is less expensive than individual insurance due to streamlined marketing costs, employer responsibilities, and lack of medical examinations.
- Monthly life and health insurance rates in group plans are weighted to account for age, sex, mortality, and morbidity features of employees in the group.
- Large employers can pay experience-rated premiums based on employer's own experience.
- Group health insurance premiums paid by the employer are tax deductible and not taxable income to employees; benefits are not taxable to the employees as well.
- Employee premium contributions are not tax deductible unless they are used in cafeteria plans under premium conversion arrangements or flexible spending accounts.
- Benefits attributable to coverage paid for by employees with after-tax dollars are not taxable.

DISCUSSION QUESTIONS

1. What is the difference between the probationary period and the eligibility period in group insurance?
2. What factors do underwriters consider when accepting an employer group plan?
3. Describe several group insurance underwriting requirements that reduce the potential for adverse selection.
4. What are the factors for pricing a group plan?
5. Why might a large employer self-insure?
6. How do employers protect themselves from the risk of catastrophic financial loss when they self-insure a benefits program?
7. Under what circumstances are benefits that are received by employees under a group arrangement considered taxable income?

---

4. THE FLEXIBILITY ISSUE, CAFETERIA PLANS, AND FLEXIBLE SPENDING ACCOUNTS

LEARNING OBJECTIVES

In this section we elaborate on the flexible features of employee benefits, including the following:

- **How flexible benefits allow employees to have choices**
- **The major components of cafeteria plans**
- **The tax incentives of premium conversion plans**
- **Savings made possible by flexible spending accounts (FSAs)**

4.1 The Flexibility Issue

Employers have been interested in **flexible benefit plans** since the early 1970s. These plans give the employee the ability to choose from among an array of benefits or cash and benefits. Few flexible plans were adopted until tax issues were clarified in 1984. At that time, it became clear that employees could choose between taxable cash income and nontaxable benefits without adversely affecting the favorable tax status of a benefit plan. These are the cafeteria plans and flexible spending account (FSA) rules. Rules regarding these plans have continued to change, resulting in some employer hesitancy to adopt them. Despite the uncertain legislative environment, flexible plans became very popular in the mid-1980s, particularly among large employers. Employers are attracted to flexible benefit plans because, relative to traditional designs, they do the following:

- Increase employee awareness of the cost and value of benefit plans
- Meet diverse employee economic security needs
- Help control total employer costs for the benefit plan
- Improve employee morale and job satisfaction

How flexible benefit plans accomplish these goals will become clear through discussion of cafeteria plans and flexible spending accounts.

flexible benefit plans

Give the employee choices among an array of benefits or cash to choose from.

4.2 Cafeteria Plans

cafeteria plan

Allow employees to select the types and amounts of desired benefits using flex credits and usually involves five elements: flexible benefit credits, minimum levels of certain benefits, optional benefits, cash credits, and tax deferral.

core plus cafeteria plan

Requires selection of basic employee benefits such as group life insurance and long-term disability, while giving the employee a choice among some health plans, additional disability coverage, dental coverage, and so forth.

premium conversion plan

Allows employees to purchase additional coverage in a cafeteria plan with pretax dollars through a payroll deduction.

modular cafeteria plan

A less-flexible cafeteria plan that includes a few packages available for employees to choose from.

Flexible benefit plans are frequently called **cafeteria plans** because they allow selection of the types and amounts of desired benefits. A cafeteria plan usually involves five elements: flexible benefit credits, minimum levels of certain benefits, optional benefits, cash credits, and tax deferral.

In a cafeteria plan, the employer generally allows each employee to spend a specified number of flexible credits, usually expressed in dollar amounts. The options in a cafeteria plan have to include a choice whether or not to take cash in lieu of benefits. The cash element is necessary in order for the plan to be considered a cafeteria plan for tax purposes. There may be a **core plus cafeteria plan** where basic benefits are required, such as $50,000 death benefits in a group life insurance and basic group long-term disability. The employee then has a choice among a few health plans, more disability coverage, dental coverage, and more. The additions are paid with the flexible credits. If there are not enough credits, the employee can pay the additional cost through payroll deduction on a pretax basis using a **premium conversion plan**. Usually, employees pay for dependents' health care on a pretax basis using the premium conversion plan.

Another cafeteria plan may be the **modular cafeteria plan**. This type of cafeteria plan includes a few packages available to the employees to choose from. It is less flexible than the core plus plan and requires less administrative cost. The number of credits assigned each year may vary with employee salary, length of service, and age. Cafeteria plans are included under Section 125 of the Internal Revenue Code. Qualified benefits in a cafeteria plan are any welfare benefits excluded from taxation under the Internal Revenue Code. The flexible spending account (explained later) is also part of a cafeteria plan. Long-term care is not included, while a 401(k) plan is included.

Benefit election must be made prior to the beginning of the plan year and cannot be changed during the plan year unless allowed by the plan; they can be changed because of changes in the following:

1. Legal marital status
2. Number of dependents
3. Employment status
4. Work schedule
5. Dependent status under a health plan for unmarried dependents
6. Residence or worksite of the employee, spouse, or dependent

The employer may restrict employee benefit choice to some degree because the employer has a vested interest in making sure that some minimal level of economic security is provided to employees. For example, the organization might be embarrassed if the employee did not elect health coverage and was subsequently unable to pay a large hospital bill. Most flexible benefit plans specify a minimum level of certain benefits judged to be essential, such as those in a core plus plan. For example, a core of medical, death, and disability benefits may be specified for all employees. The employee can elect to opt out of a core benefit by supplying written evidence that similar benefits are available from another source, such as the spouse's employer or the military retirement system.

Cafeteria plans also help control employer benefit costs. Employers set a dollar amount on benefit expenditures per employee, and employees choose within that framework. This maximizes employee appreciation because employees choose what they want, and it minimizes employer cost because employers do not have to increase coverage for all employees in order to satisfy the needs of certain workers.

Cafeteria plans have been especially effective in controlling group medical expense insurance costs. Employees often are offered several alternative medical plans, including health maintenance organizations (HMOs) and preferred provider organizations (PPOs), plans designed to control costs (discussed in Chapter 22). In addition, employees may be charged lower prices for traditional plans with more cost containment features. For example, a comprehensive medical insurance plan may have an option with a $100 deductible, 90 percent coinsurance, a $1,000 out-of-pocket or stop-loss provision, and a $1 million maximum benefit. A lower-priced comprehensive plan may offer the same maximum benefit with a $2,000 deductible, 80 percent coinsurance, and a $4,000 stop-loss provision. The employee uses fewer benefit credits to get the lower option plan, and the cost-sharing requirements likely reduce claim costs, too. Likewise, long-term disability insurance choices attach lower prices per $100 of monthly benefit with an option that insures 50 percent of income rather than 60 or 70 percent. Here again, lower prices attract employees to options with more cost sharing, and the cost sharing helps contain claims.

Cafeteria plans are well suited to meet the needs of a demographically diverse work force. The number of women, single heads of households, and dual-career couples in the work force (as discussed in Chapter 17) has given rise to the need for different benefit options. A single employee with no dependents may prefer fewer benefits and more cash income. Someone covered by medical benefits through a spouse's employer may prefer to use benefit dollars on more generous disability coverage.

An older worker with grown children may prefer more generous medical benefits and fewer life insurance benefits. Clearly, economic security needs vary, and job satisfaction and morale may improve by giving employees some voice in how benefits, a significant percentage of total compensation, are spent.

However, both higher administrative costs and adverse selection discourage employers from implementing cafeteria plans. Record keeping increases significantly when benefit packages vary for each employee. Computers help, but they do not eliminate the administrative cost factor. Communication with employees is both more important and more complicated because employees are selecting their own benefits and all choices must be thoroughly explained. Employers are careful to explain but not to advise about benefit choices because then the employer would be liable for any adverse effect of benefit selection on the employee.

Cafeteria plans may have some adverse selection effects because an employee selects benefits that he or she is more likely to need. Those with eye problems, for example, are more likely to choose vision care benefits, while other employees may skip vision care and select dental care to cover orthodontia. The result is higher claims per employee selecting each benefit. Adverse selection can be reduced by plan design and pricing. The employer may require, for example, that employees who select vision care must also choose dental care, thus bringing more healthy people into both plans. Pricing helps by setting each benefit's unit price high enough to cover the true average claim cost per employee or dependent, while trying to avoid excessive pricing that would discourage the enrollment of healthy employees.

4.3   Flexible Spending Accounts

Flexible spending accounts (FSAs) allow employees to pay for specified benefits (which are defined by law) with before-tax dollars. In the absence of a flexible spending account, the employee would have purchased the same services with after-tax dollars. An FSA can either add flexibility to a cafeteria plan or can accompany traditional benefit plans with little other employee choice. The employer may fund the FSA exclusively, the employee may fund the account through a salary reduction agreement, or both may contribute to the FSA.

The employee decides at the beginning of each year how much money to personally contribute to the FSA, and then he or she signs a salary reduction agreement for this amount. The legal document establishing the employer's program of flexible spending accounts specifies how funds can be spent, subject to the constraints of Section 125 in the Internal Revenue Code. For example, the simplest kind of FSA is funded solely by an employee salary reduction agreement and covers only employee contributions to a group medical insurance plan. The salary reduction agreement transforms the employee contribution from after-tax dollars to before-tax dollars, often a significant savings. A more comprehensive FSA, for example, may allow the employee to cover medical premium contributions, uninsured medical expenses, child care, and legal expenses. Dependent care is a nice addition in the FSA. The catch with an FSA plan is that the employee forfeits to the employer any balance in the account at year-end. This results in flexible spending accounts primarily being used to prefund highly predictable expenses on a before-tax basis.

Employees also pay their portion of the health premium in a premium conversion plan, which allows the funds to be collected on a pretax basis. These are usually the premiums for dependents.

flexible spending account (FSAs)

Allow employees to pay for specified benefits (defined by law) and out-of-pocket medical expenses using before-tax dollars contributed to the account at the beginning of the year; any funds not used by year-end are forfeited.

KEY TAKEAWAYS

In this section you studied the following ways that employee benefit plans can give flexibility to diverse employee groups at low cost to employers:

- Flexible benefit programs like cafeteria plans and flexible spending accounts allow the employee to choose from among an array of benefits or cash and benefits.
- Flexible benefit plans allow employers to retain the tax advantages of group coverage, give employees more choice, increase employee awareness and morale, and control costs.
- Cafeteria plans allow employees to spend flex credits on a selection of types of benefits at desired amounts.
- Cafeteria plans must have an option for cash in lieu of benefits.
- Some basic types of coverage (such as choice of death benefits, health plans, disability, dental, etc.) may be required in cafeteria plans.
- Employees can purchase additional coverage on a pretax basis under a premium conversion plan after exhausting flexible credits.
- Flexible spending accounts (FSAs) allow employees to pay for eligible out-of-pocket health care costs with before-tax dollars.
- FSAs may be part of a cafeteria plan selection or they can accompany traditional nonflexible benefit plans.
- Funds (from the employer or employee) must be contributed to an FSA at the beginning of the year and exhausted by year-end (use it or lose it).

DISCUSSION QUESTIONS

1. Cafeteria plans have become increasingly popular. What factors contributed to the increased use of these plans?
2. How might a flexible benefit plan achieve desirable goals for your employer as well as for you?
3. Create examples of core plus and modular cafeteria plans that include many benefits and cash.
4. Under what circumstances can employees change flexible benefit elections during the year?
5. In what ways are costs controlled by allowing employees more choice among benefits?
6. How can adverse selection be combated in benefit selection?
7. How are FSAs funded? What are the limitations of FSAs?

5. FEDERAL REGULATION COMPLIANCE, BENEFITS CONTINUITY AND PORTABILITY, AND MULTINATIONAL EMPLOYEE BENEFIT PLANS

LEARNING OBJECTIVES

In this section we elaborate on regulatory and multinational issues in employee benefits, including the requirements of the following pieces of legislation:

- **The Age Discrimination in Employment Act (ADEA)**
- **The Civil Rights Act**
- **The Americans with Disabilities Act (ADA)**
- **The Family Medical Leave Act (FMLA)**
- **The Consolidated Omnibus Budget Reconciliation Act (COBRA)**
- **The Health Insurance Portability and Accountability Act (HIPAA)**

5.1 Federal Regulation: Compliance with Nondiscrimination Laws

As noted above, the administration and design of group employee benefit plans have been affected by federal regulation through ERISA, EGTRRA 2001 (discussed in Chapter 21), the Age Discrimination in

Employment Act, the Civil Rights Act (which includes pregnancy nondiscrimination), and the Americans with Disabilities Act. The Social Security Act was discussed in Chapter 18; the Health Maintenance Organization Act will be discussed in Chapter 22, along with medical care delivery systems. Federal legislation is concerned with nondiscrimination in coverage and benefit amounts for plan participants. Some legislation relating to health care in general that also affects group underwriting practices is described in the box "Laws Affecting Health Care." Individuals called to military duty and the families they leave behind have certain rights regarding group health and pension coverages. These rights are discussed in the box "Individual Coverage Rights When Called to Military Duty."

Age Discrimination in Employment Act

The **Age Discrimination in Employment Act (ADEA)** was first passed in 1967 and is known primarily for eliminating mandatory retirement on the basis of age. That is, employees cannot be forced to retire at any age, with the exception of some executives who may be subject to compulsory retirement. Employee benefits are also affected by the ADEA because the law was amended to require that benefits must be continued for older workers. Most benefits can be reduced to the point where the cost of providing benefits for older workers is no greater than for younger workers except health care benefits. The act makes this an option; employers are not required to reduce benefits for older workers. Employers choosing to reduce some benefits for older workers generally do not reduce benefits except for workers over age sixty-five, even though reductions prior to age sixty-five may be legally allowed based on cost.

> **Age Discrimination in Employment Act (ADEA)**
>
> Eliminated mandatory retirement on the basis of age by employers.

The employer may reduce benefits on a benefit-by-benefit basis based on the cost of coverage, or may reduce them across the board based on the overall cost of the package. For example, with the benefit-by-benefit approach, the amount of life insurance in force might be reduced at older ages to compensate for the extra cost of term coverage at advanced ages. Alternatively, several different benefits for an older worker might be reduced to make the total cost of the older worker's package commensurate with the cost of younger workers' packages.

Life and disability insurance may be reduced for older workers. Acceptable amounts of life insurance reductions are specified by law. For example, employees age sixty-five to sixty-nine may be eligible for life insurance benefit amounts equal to 65 percent of the amounts available to eligible employees under age sixty-five; employees age seventy to seventy-four may receive only 45 percent. Disability benefits provided through sick leave plans may not be reduced on the basis of age. Reductions in benefit amounts for short-term disability insured plans are allowed, but they are relatively uncommon in actual practice. Long-term disability benefits may be reduced for older workers through two methods. Benefit amounts may be reduced and the duration may remain the same, or benefit duration may be curtailed and amounts remain the same. This is justified on the basis of cost because the probability of disability and the average length of disability increase at older ages.

Medical benefits may not be reduced for older employees. Employers must offer older workers private group medical benefits that are equal to those offered to younger participants, even if active workers over age sixty-five are eligible for Medicare. Medicare is the secondary payer for active employees over age sixty-five, covering only those expenses not covered by the primary payer, the employee's group medical insurance.

The Civil Rights Act

Traditionally, employee benefit plans have not been required to provide benefits for pregnancy and other related conditions. Including disability and medical benefits for pregnancy can significantly increase costs. However, in 1978 the **Civil Rights Act** was amended to require employers to provide the same benefits for pregnancy and related medical conditions as are provided for other medical conditions. If an employer provides sick leave, disability, or medical insurance, then the employer must provide these benefits in the event of employee pregnancy. Spouses of employees must also be treated equally with respect to pregnancy-related conditions. This federal regulation applies only to plans with more than fifteen employees, but some states impose similar requirements on employers with fewer employees.

> **Civil Rights Act**
>
> Requires employers to provide the same benefits for pregnancy and related medical conditions as are provided for other medical conditions.

Americans with Disabilities Act

As described in Chapter 13, the 1990 **Americans with Disabilities Act (ADA)** forbids employers with more than fifteen employees from discriminating against disabled persons in employment. Disabled persons are those with physical or mental impairments limiting major life activities such as walking, seeing, or hearing. The ADA has important implications for employee benefits. The ADA is not supposed to disturb the current regulatory system or alter industry practices such as underwriting. Under ADA, therefore, disabled employees must have equal access to the same health benefits as other employees with the same allowances for coverage limitations. The guidelines allow blanket preexisting conditions, but they do not include disability-based provisions. For example, if the medical plan does

> **Americans with Disabilities Act (ADA)**
>
> Forbids employers with more than fifteen employees from discriminating against disabled persons in employment.

not cover vision care, the employer does not have to offer vision care treatment to disabled employees. However, if vision care is provided by the plan, then vision care must also be offered to employees with disabilities. Recent Supreme Court cases clarified the intent of the ADA. Most important is the clarification that the ADA is concerned with a person's ability to perform regular daily living activities and not his or her ability to perform a specific job.

Family Medical Leave Act

Family Medical Leave Act (FMLA)

Requires an employer with fifty or more employees to grant an eligible employee (one who has been employed by the employer for at least twelve months) up to a total of twelve weeks of unpaid leave during any twelve-month period for one or more of the following reasons: the birth and care of the employee's newborn child, for placement with the employee of a child for adoption or foster care, to care for an immediate family member (spouse, child, or parent) with a serious health condition, to take medical leave when the employee is unable to work because of a serious health condition.

Under the **Family Medical Leave Act (FMLA)** of 1993, an employer with fifty or more employees must grant an eligible employee (one who has been employed by the employer for at least twelve months) up to a total of twelve work weeks of unpaid leave during any twelve-month period for one or more of the following reasons:

- For the birth and care of the employee's newborn child
- For placement with the employee of a child for adoption or foster care
- To care for an immediate family member (spouse, child, or parent) with a serious health condition
- To take medical leave when the employee is unable to work because of a serious health condition

This law may sometimes create conflicting interpretations, especially in relationship to workers' compensation and disability leaves. Employee benefits administrators are advised to track the leave taken by employees under different programs and ensure compliance with the law.[5] Compliance issues require clarifications; a recent Supreme Court decision clarified that only material denial of the FMLA statute should trigger penalties.[6]

5.2 Benefits Continuity and Portability

Continuity: COBRA

Consolidated Omnibus Budget Reconciliation Act (COBRA)

Directs that employers of more than twenty employees who maintain a group medical plan must allow certain minimum provisions for continuation of benefit coverage.

The Consolidated Omnibus Budget Reconciliation Act (**COBRA**) of 1986 directs that employers of more than twenty employees who maintain a group medical plan must allow certain minimum provisions for continuation of benefit coverage. COBRA's continuation provisions require that former employees, their spouses, divorced spouses, and dependent children be allowed to continue coverage at the individual's own expense upon the occurrence of a qualifying event (one that otherwise would have resulted in the loss of medical insurance). The qualifying events are listed in Table 20.3. Most terminations of employment, except for gross misconduct, activate a thirty-one-day right to convert the health insurance that the employee or dependent had before the qualifying event (vision and dental benefits need not be offered). The employer can charge for the cost of conversion coverage, but the charge cannot exceed 102 percent of the cost of coverage for employees, generally (including the portion the employer paid). Some events require coverage continuation for eighteen months, and others require thirty-six months of coverage.

TABLE 20.3 COBRA Qualifying Events for Continuation of Health Insurance

1. Voluntary (and in some cases, involuntary) termination of employment
2. Employee's death
3. Reduction of hours worked resulting in coverage termination
4. Divorce or legal separation from an employee
5. Entitlement by an employee for Medicare
6. Dependent child ceases to meet dependent child definition
7. Employer filing for Chapter 11 bankruptcy

Note: **For each event, it is assumed that the person was covered for group medical benefits immediately prior to the qualifying event.**

The employee has a valuable right with COBRA because continuation of insurance is provided without evidence of insurability. In addition, the group rate may be lower than individual rates in the marketplace. However, COBRA subjects employers to adverse selection costs and administrative costs beyond the additional 2 percent of premium collected. Many terminated healthy employees and dependents will immediately have access to satisfactory insurance with another employer, but many unhealthy employees may not. This is because of the preexisting condition clauses that many group insurance plans have (though this is less of a concern since the passage of HIPAA, as you will see below). After September 11, Congress worked on creating subsidies for the payment of COBRA premiums to laid-off employees. This law was part of the 2002 trade legislation. As of 2003, the law provides subsidies of 65 percent of the premiums to people who lose their jobs because of foreign competition.[7] The American Recovery and Reinvestment Act (ARRA) of 2009—intended as a stimulus against the economic recession—contains significant provisions regarding COBRA benefits (similar to the 2002 trade legislation) for involuntarily terminated workers. This and other features of ARRA are discussed in the box "Laws Affecting Health Care." The application of COBRA for military reservists called to active duty is explained in the box "Individual Coverage Rights When Called to Military Duty."

Retiree Eligibility for Group Medical Benefits

Most active, permanent, full-time employees are eligible for group coverage. Employers that offer group medical insurance are required to offer it to active workers over age sixty-five, under the Age Discrimination in Employment Act (ADEA) discussed above. For these employees, Medicare becomes a secondary payer. Some employers choose to offer continuation of group medical benefits to employees who have retired. This coverage is like Medigap insurance (discussed in Chapter 22), where Medicare is the primary payer and the group plan is secondary. Typically, the retiree plan is less generous than the plan for active workers because it is designed simply to fill in the gaps left by Medicare.

Historically, employers have paid medical premiums or benefits for retirees out of current revenues, recognizing the expense in the period that it was paid out. However, in 1993 the Financial Accounting Standards Board (FASB 106) began phasing in a requirement that employers recognize the present value of future retiree medical expense benefits on the balance sheet during the employees' active working years rather than the old pay-as-you-go system. The negative effect of these new rules on corporate earnings has been significant. Consequently, most employers have been cutting back on health benefits promised to retirees, and only about a third of the companies that had retiree health care in 1990 still had them a decade later.

Portability: HIPAA

Title I of the Health Insurance Portability and Accountability Act (**HIPPA**) of 1996 protects employees who change jobs from having to start a new waiting period before a preexisting condition is covered. For example, before HIPAA, a person with diabetes might not want to change jobs, even for a much better position, because it would mean going for a time without coverage for daily insulin shots and possible complications of the illness. Many employees were trapped in such situations before HIPAA. After the enactment of HIPAA, a person with diabetes could change jobs, and health insurance providers, without fear of losing coverage on that specific condition.

HIPAA provides protection for both group and individual health insurance. In essence, it provides **portability** of coverage: when an employee leaves one job and starts a new job, the coverage of health insurance under the new employer's program cannot exclude benefits for preexisting condition, as long as the break in health coverage is no longer than sixty-three days. Portability does not mean carrying the actual coverage of the old employer to the new one, but rather carrying forward the qualification for preexisting conditions. For example, Joe was employed by Company A for ten years and had health coverage under that employer. He accepted a job offer from Company B. One month before changing his job, he broke his leg in a skiing accident. Under HIPAA, the new company cannot limit coverage for the injured leg. If Joe needs surgery on this leg in three months, the health coverage under Company B will pay for the surgery. Before HIPAA, Joe would have had to stay covered under his old employer, paying the full amount himself through COBRA, until the preexisting condition period of the new employer was met. That could have been six months, a year, or even longer.

Under HIPAA, an employer can impose only up to twelve months preexisting conditions exclusions for regular enrollment and up to eighteen months for late enrollment. During an exclusion period, the health plan has to pay for all other conditions except the preexisting condition. Prior group health coverage applies to these limits. Thus, if an employee's only previous group health coverage was for six months with Company A, the preexisting conditions exclusion from new Company B would last for just six additional months rather than the full twelve. Under HIPAA, a preexisting condition is defined as a condition for which the employee received any treatment within the six-month period before enrolling with the new employer.

The details of HIPAA are complex, but the gist is that an employee without a break in health coverage will never have to meet a preexisting condition period more than once in a lifetime, if at all. When an employee leaves a job, the employer is required to provide a certificate of health coverage. This certificate is then taken to the next employer to ensure that no preexisting conditions are imposed on the employee. Employers who neglect to give the certificate are subject to penalties of $100 per day. More on HIPAA and other recent health care-related laws is featured in the box "Laws Affecting Health Care." Further, the application of HIPAA for military reservists called to active duty is detailed in the box "Individual Coverage Rights When Called to Military Duty."

Health Insurance Portability and Accountability Act (HIPPA)

Protects employees who change jobs from having to start a new waiting period before a preexisting condition is covered.

portability

Carrying forward the qualification for preexisting conditions.

Laws Affecting Health Care

The Health Insurance Portability and Accountability Act (HIPAA)

The Health Insurance Portability and Accountability Act (HIPAA) provides rights and protections for participants and beneficiaries in group health plans. HIPAA was signed into law on August 21, 1996, and became effective for all plans and issuers beginning June 1, 1997. The act protects workers and their families by doing the following:

- Limiting exclusions for preexisting medical conditions
- Providing credit against exclusion periods for prior health coverage and a process for showing periods of prior coverage to a new group health plan or health insurance issuer
- Providing new rights that allow individuals to enroll for health coverage when they lose other health coverage, get married, or add a new dependent
- Prohibiting discrimination in enrollment and in premiums charged to employees and their dependents based on health status-related factors
- Guaranteeing availability of health insurance coverage for small employers and renewability of health insurance coverage for both small and large employers

Newborns' and Mothers' Health Protection Act

The Newborns' and Mothers' Health Protection Act of 1996 requires plans that offer maternity coverage to pay for at least a forty-eight-hour hospital stay following childbirth (a ninety-six-hour stay in the case of a cesarean section). It was signed into law on September 26, 1996, and became effective for group health plans for plan years beginning on or after January 1, 1998.

All group health plans that provide maternity or newborn infant coverage must include a statement in their summary plan description advising individuals of the Newborns' Act requirements: a mother may not be encouraged to accept less than the minimum protections available to her under the Newborns' Act, and an attending provider may not be induced to discharge a mother or newborn earlier than forty-eight or ninety-six hours after delivery.

Women's Health and Cancer Rights Act

The Women's Health and Cancer Rights Act (WHCRA) contains protections for patients who elect breast reconstruction in connection with a mastectomy. It was signed into law on October 21, 1998, and became effective immediately. WHCRA requires that any plan offering mastectomy coverage must also include coverage for the following:

- Reconstruction of the breast on which the mastectomy was performed
- Surgery and reconstruction of the other breast to produce a symmetrical appearance
- Prostheses and physical complications at all stages of mastectomy, including lymphedemas

Under WHCRA, mastectomy benefits may be subject to annual deductibles and coinsurance consistent with those established for other benefits under the plan or coverage. Group health plans covered by the law must notify individuals of the coverage required by WHCRA upon enrollment, and annually thereafter.

Mental Health Parity Act

The Mental Health Parity Act (MHPA), signed into law on September 26, 1996, requires that annual or lifetime dollar limits on mental health benefits be no lower than any such dollar limits for medical and surgical benefits offered by a group health plan or health insurance issuer offering coverage in connection with a group health plan. The law does not apply to benefits for substance abuse or chemical dependency.

American Recovery and Reinvestment Act

Signed by President Barack Obama on February 17, 2009, the American Recovery and Reinvestment Act (ARRA, or H.R. 1) authorizes $787 billion in federal spending toward infrastructure, direct aid, and tax cuts as a stimulus for the U.S. economy in recession. Within the framework of that objective, it includes provisions affecting health care. H.R. 1 allows up to nine months of COBRA premiums to be subsidized at 65 percent for workers involuntarily terminated between September 1, 2008, and December 31, 2009, whose income is under $125,000 for individuals or $250,000 for families (to receive full benefits). Workers involuntarily terminated during this period who could not initially afford COBRA continuation are given an additional sixty days to elect COBRA coverage through the subsidy. This provision is designed to help an estimated 7 million people maintain health insurance and is expected to account for $24.7 billion of the ARRA funds. H.R. 1 also directs about $338 million in Medicare payment reductions for teaching hospitals, hospice care, and long-term-care hospitals. In another provision, the act aims to invest $19 billion in health information technology, thus encouraging the use of electronic health records for the exchange of patient health information. Ideally, this would see 90 percent of doctors and 70 percent of hospitals convert to electronic health records over the next decade, saving taxpayers $12 billion in the long run. Finally, ARRA sets aside $1.1 billion for federal agencies to draw upon for conducting studies on cost-benefit comparisons of various health care treatments.

Sources: Publications of the U.S. Department of Labor, Employee Benefits Security Administration at http://www.dol.gov/ebsa/faqs/faq_consumer_hipaa.html; "Link to H.R. 1 Conference Report Summary," National Underwriter Online News Service, February 13, 2009, http://www.lifeandhealthinsurancenews.com/News/2009/2/Pages/Link-To-HR-1-Conference-Report-Summary.aspx, accessed March 13, 2009; Allison Bell, "Obama Signs H.R. 1," National Underwriter, Life/Health Edition, February 19, 2009, http://www.lifeandhealthinsurancenews.com/News/2009/2/Pages/House-Passes-HR-1-Ball-On-To-Senate.aspx, accessed March 13, 2009.

Individual Coverage Rights When Called to Military Duty

With so many U.S. armed forces in Iraq and Afghanistan, the Department of Labor answers the following questions about the benefits-related rights and responsibilities of those called to active duty and their civilian employers.

My family had health coverage through my employer when I was called for active duty in the military. What are my rights concerning health coverage now?

If you are on active duty for more than thirty days, you and your dependents should be covered by military health care. For more information on these programs, contact your military unit.

In addition, two laws protect your right to continue health coverage under an employment-based group health plan. The Consolidated Omnibus Budget Reconciliation Act (COBRA) provides health coverage continuation rights to employees and their families after an event such as a reduction in employment hours. Also, the Uniformed Services Employment and Reemployment Rights Act (USERRA) of 1994 is intended to minimize the disadvantages that occur when a person needs to be absent from civilian employment to serve in the uniformed services.

Both COBRA and USERRA generally allow individuals called for active duty to continue coverage for themselves and their dependents under an employment-based group health plan for up to eighteen months. If military service is for thirty or fewer days, you and your family can continue coverage at the same cost as before your short service. If military service is longer, you and your family may be required to pay as much as 102 percent of the full premium for coverage. You should receive a notice from your plan explaining your rights.

The Health Insurance Portability and Accountability Act (HIPAA) may give you and your family rights to enroll in other group health plan coverage if it is available to you (e.g., if your spouse's employer sponsors a group health plan). You and your family have this opportunity to enroll regardless of the plan's otherwise applicable enrollment periods. However, to qualify, you must request enrollment in the other plan (e.g., your spouse's plan) within thirty days of losing eligibility for coverage under your employer's plan. After special enrollment is requested, coverage is required to be made effective no later than the first day of the first month following your request for enrollment. If you are on active duty more than thirty days, coverage in another plan through special enrollment is often cheaper than continuation coverage because the employer often pays part of the premium. For more information on the interaction of COBRA and HIPAA, see IRS Notice 98-12: "Deciding Whether to Elect COBRA Health Care Continuation Coverage After the Enactment of HIPAA," on the Employee Benefits Security Administration (EBSA) Web site at http://www.dol.gov/ebsa, which can be found at the link Publications. You can also call toll-free (1.866.444.EBSA[3272]) for a free copy.

Note. When considering your health coverage options, you should examine the scope of the coverage (including benefit coverage and limitations, visit limits, and dollar limits); premiums; cost-sharing (including co-payments and deductibles); and waiting periods for coverage.

My family and I had health coverage under my employer's group health plan before I was called on active duty. We let this coverage lapse while I was away and took military health coverage. When I return to my employer from active duty, what are our rights to health coverage under my old plan?

Under USERRA, you and your family should be able to reenter your employer's health plan. In addition, your plan generally cannot impose a waiting period or other exclusion period if health coverage would have been provided were it not for military service. The only exception to USERRA's prohibition of exclusions is for an illness or injury determined by the Secretary of Veterans Affairs to have been incurred in, or aggravated during, performance of service in the uniformed services, which is covered by the military health plan.

While I am on active duty, is my employer required to continue to make employer contributions to my 401(k) plan?

There is no requirement for your employer to make contributions to your 401(k) plan while you are on active duty. However, once you return from military duty and are reemployed, your employer must make the employer contributions that would have been made if you had been employed during the period of military duty. If employee contributions are required or permitted under the plan, the employee has a period equal to three times the period of military duty or five years, whichever ends first, to make up the contributions. If the employee makes up the contributions, the employer must make up any matching contributions. There is no requirement that the employer contributions include earnings or forfeitures that would have been allocated to the employee had the contributions been made during his or her military service.

Sources: Adapted from "Reservists Being Called to Active Duty," U.S. Department of Labor, Employee Benefits Security Administration, December 2007, http://www.dol.gov/ebsa/newsroom/fsreservists.html, accessed April 13, 2009.

5.3 Multinational Employee Benefit Plans

expatriates

U.S. citizens working outside the United States.

Multinational corporations manage the human resource risk across national boundaries. The most common concern of multinational employers is the benefit needs of **expatriates**, U.S. citizens working outside the United States. However, the employer is also concerned with managing benefits for employees who are not U.S. citizens but who are working in the United States. In addition, benefits must be considered for employees who are not U.S. citizens and who work outside the United States.

The corporation designs multinational benefit policy to achieve several objectives. First, the plans need to be sufficient to attract, retain, and reward workers in locations around the world where a corporate presence is required. The plan needs to be fair for all employees within the corporation itself, within the industry, and within the country where employees are located. In addition, the multinational benefit policy needs to facilitate the transfer of workers across national boundaries whenever necessary with a minimum of overall transaction costs.

international benefit network

Can be used to cover employees across countries under one master insurance contract when employers provide benefits in several international locations.

Typically, the multinational employer tries to protect the expatriate from losing benefits when the employee transfers outside the United States. A premium may be paid at the time of the move to compensate the employee for international relocation. The corporation often provides the expatriate with the same life, long-term disability, medical, and pension benefits as those provided to their U.S. employees. However, in some cases the employee may receive medical care or short-term disability benefits like those of the host country. When employers provide benefits in several international locations, they may use an **international benefit network** to cover employees across countries under one master insurance contract. This can simplify international benefit administration. The employer must also consider the social insurance systems of the host country and coordinate coverage as necessary with the employee's home country's system.

Cultural and regulatory factors differ among countries and affect benefit design, financing, and communication. This makes international employee benefits management a dynamic and challenging field. With the continued globalization of business in the new millennium, career opportunities in international benefits management are likely to grow.

KEY TAKEAWAYS

In this section you studied federal legislation affecting employee benefit plans and employment changes as well as international employee benefits coverage and concerns:

- The Age Discrimination in Employment Act (ADEA) stipulates that benefits must be continued for older workers, but it allows proportional reduction of some benefits.
- The Civil Rights Act requires employers to provide the same benefits for pregnancy and related medical conditions as are provided for other medical conditions.
- The Americans with Disabilities Act (ADA) states that disabled employees must have equal access to the same health benefits as other employees, with the same allowances for coverage limitations.
- The Family Medical Leave Act (FMLA) states that employers must give eligible employees up to twelve weeks of unpaid leave during any twelve-month period for qualifying reasons.
- COBRA requires employers to allow employees, their spouses, and their dependents to continue health coverage at the individual's expense (up to 102 percent of group coverage and in the event that medical coverage would otherwise end) for eighteen to thirty-six months without new evidence of insurability.
- HIPAA protects employees who change jobs from having to start a new waiting period before a preexisting condition is covered.
- Multinational employee benefit plans covering noncitizen employees and expatriates must be sufficient to attract, retain, and reward workers; must be fair for all parties affected; and must facilitate transfer of workers internationally when necessary and at minimum cost.

DISCUSSION QUESTIONS

1. Recall the discussion of integrated benefits in Chapter 16. How do you think a good integrated benefits program would be coordinated with workers' compensation, FMLA, and ADA? See the box, "Integrated Benefits: The Twenty-Four-Hour Coverage Concept" in Chapter 16.
2. In what ways can the FMLA create conflicting interpretations?
3. The intent behind the passage of COBRA was to reduce the number of uninsured persons. How does COBRA work to achieve this objective?
4. Now that we have HIPAA, do we need COBRA? Give an example.
5. The Meridian Advertising Agency has 1,340 employees in six states. The main office is in Richmond, Virginia. Meridian has employed Dan Smith for the last ten years. Three months ago, Dan had a foot injury for which he is still being treated. He recently accepted a job offer from a Washington, D.C., advertising agency. Before Dan leaves, Meridian's human resources department invites him for an exit interview. If you were Meridian's employee benefits specialist, what would you tell Dan about his rights? Explain to Dan about COBRA and HIPAA.
6. If Phoebe, who has a heart condition, leaves her current job (which provides group health benefits) for another one with similar benefits, will she immediately be covered for her heart condition? What if she is laid off from her job and does not find another job for eight months?
7. Mandy's employer will not provide coverage for claims relating to her chronic asthma until she satisfies the group health plan's twelve month preexisting condition exclusion period. Nine months into the job, Mandy obtains employment elsewhere. The new employer also imposes a twelve-month exclusion period for preexisting conditions. When will Mandy's condition be covered by her new employer?
8. Why might the benefits manager of a multinational corporation use an international benefits network?

6. REVIEW AND PRACTICE

1. What are the main ways in which group insurance differs from individual insurance?
2. Why is group insurance proportionately less expense than individual insurance?

3. Rosa Sanchez, single, age twenty-five, received two job offers after college graduation. Both were with organizations that she respected, and the nature of the work at each place sounded very interesting to her. One job was with a larger, well-established firm and offered $22,000 per year in salary plus noncontributory benefits worth $7,000 per year. The other job was with a small business and offered a salary of $30,000 per year without employer voluntary benefits (the employer is required to pay for social insurance programs). Rosa's mother suggested that she make the choice between the two jobs based on which offered better total compensation.

   a. What factors should Rosa consider in determining the better package? Which package do you think maximizes her total compensation?

   b. Which employer is economically better off (all else being equal), the one offering salary plus benefits or the one offering salary only? Explain your answer.

4. Henry Zantow, the comptroller for Kado Industries, was discussing the supposed advantages of a true cafeteria plan versus a traditional plan with Lloyd Olsen. Lloyd agreed with Henry that a cafeteria plan certainly seemed the better of the two plans. Both Henry and Lloyd looked at each other and in the same breath said, "I wonder why anyone would choose a traditional plan?"

   a. What is your answer to this question?

   b. If the corporation decides to use a cafeteria plan, why might it want a minimum level of core benefits?

5. What does it mean to self-insure and have the stop-loss programs for workers' compensation and for group health insurance?

6. Jan Czyrmer, the employee benefits manager at Ludlow Enterprises, wants to restructure the leave policy for the company. He is concerned that employees abuse the sick leave policy, taking sick leave time for personal reasons not related to illness. He wants to abolish particular types of leave (such as sick leave, vacation leave, personal leave) and give employees a certain number of general leave days per year to use as they choose.

   a. What advantages might Jan cite to convince upper management that consolidating leave time may be helpful for Ludlow Enterprises?

   b. If upper management rejects Jan's idea of a major restructuring of leave time, what can he do to prevent abuse of the current sick leave policy? What steps can be taken to reduce moral hazard within the traditional leave system?

7. Knowledge Networking, Inc., provides a growing business of high-tech and electronics equipment and software. It is a specialty retail and online business that has tripled its revenues in the past seven years. The company started fifteen years ago and includes fifty outlets on both the East and West coasts. In 2005, the company went public and now, despite the major financial crisis, it is doing very well with innovation and creative offerings. The company has 5,600 full-time employees and 1,000 part-time employees. Knowledge Networking, Inc., provides all the social insurance programs and offers its employees a cafeteria plan with many choices. Employees have generous choices of health, life insurance, and disability coverages; dental and vision care; premium conversion plan; and flexible spending accounts as part of the cafeteria plan. Each employee receives $5,500 a year from the employer to pay for the benefits.

   a. Describe in detail your understanding of the structure of the cafeteria plan of Knowledge Networking, Inc. (design this cafeteria plan). What are the advantages and disadvantages of this cafeteria plan?

   b. Knowledge Networking, Inc., follows the federal laws: FMLA, ADA, Civil Rights Act, and Age Discrimination in Employment Act. If you were the employee benefits manager, how would you explain the impact of each of these acts on the employee benefits of the employees?

   c. How would the group insurance rates be computed (what factors play into the computation) for such a company?

   d. Why might Knowledge Networking, Inc., prefer to self-insure their workers' compensation and health insurance rather than buy insurance?

8. Yolanda Freeman is evaluating whether federal nondiscrimination laws have helped or hurt employees.

   a. Which federal laws particularly affect employee benefits? Which workers are particularly affected by each law?

b. Who pays the cost of requiring that benefits be paid on a nondiscriminatory basis? Do additional benefit costs have any effect on employee wage levels?

c. If federal laws did not require coverage for certain employees and their dependents, who would pay for benefits for these individuals? Do you think that social welfare is maximized by mandating coverage for certain workers and their dependents through these nondiscrimination laws?

ENDNOTES

1. Employee Benefit Research Institute, *EBRI Databook on Employee Benefits*, ch.2: Finances of the Employee Benefit System, updated September 2008. http://www.ebri.org. More information can also be found in the U.S. Chamber of Commerce Survey at uschamber.com at http://www.uschamber.org/Research+and+Statistics/Publications/Employee+Benefits+Study.htm (accessed April 12, 2009).

2. Includes paid holidays, vacations, and sick leave taken.

3. Consists of payments for medical services for dependents of active duty military personnel at nonmilitary facilities.

4. Employee Benefits Research Institute, "Tax Expenditures and Employee Benefits: Estimates from the FY 2009 Budget," February 2008, http://www.ebri.org/pdf/publications/facts/0208fact.pdf (accessed April 12, 2009).

5. Rebecca Auerbach, "Your Message to Employers: Manage FMLA with Other Benefit Programs," *National Underwriter, Life & Health/Financial Services Edition*, April 22, 2002.

6. This case, *Ragsdale v. Wolverine worldwide*, No. 00-6029 (U.S. March 19, 2002), hinged on the extent that employers are obligated to inform employees of their rights when they begin a leave of absence. Wolverine had given Tracy Ragsdale time off for cancer treatment, but when she was unable to return to work after thirty weeks, Wolverine ended her employment. Ragsdale filed suit, citing a FMLA regulation that a leave of absence counts against the employee's FMLA allowance only if the employer specifically designated it as FMLA leave. She claimed she was still entitled to her twelve weeks of FMLA leave. The Court disagreed and declared that regulation invalid. One of the Court's reasonings was that Ragsdale had not been harmed—she would not have been better off if Wolverine had designated her original leave as FMLA. See Steven Brostoff, "U.S. High Court Ruling Helps RMs," *National Underwriter Online News Service*, March 20, 2002.

7. Jerry Geisel, "COBRA Subsidy Could Increase Beneficiaries: Survey," *Business Insurance*, August 30, 2002.

CHAPTER 21

Employment-Based and Individual Longevity Risk Management

As noted earlier in this text, individuals rely on several sources for income during retirement: Social Security, employer-sponsored retirement plans, and individual savings (depicted in our familiar three-step diagram). In Chapter 18, we discussed how Social Security, a public retirement program, provides a foundation of economic security for retired workers and their families. Social Security provides only a basic floor of income; it was never intended to be the sole source of retirement income.

Employees may receive additional retirement income from employer-sponsored retirement plans. According to the Employee Benefit Research Institute (EBRI), of the $1.5 trillion in total employee benefit program outlays in 2007, employers spent $693.9 billion on retirement plans. Retirement obligations, mostly in the form of mandatory social insurance programs, made up the largest portion of employer spending on benefits in 2007.[1] Private retirement benefits are an important component of employee compensation, especially because many large employers are transitioning from providing a promise at retirement through a defined benefits plan (as explained later) into helping employees invest in 401(k) plans. Big corporations such as IBM froze their promise for defined benefits plans for new employees entering employment with the company. Watson Wyatt Worldwide found that seventy-one Fortune 1,000 companies that sponsored defined benefits plans froze or terminated their defined benefits plans in 2004, compared with forty-five in 2003 and thirty-nine in 2002. An example is Hewlett Packard where, effective 2006, newly hired employees and those not meeting certain age and service criteria are covered by 401(k) with matching only.[2]

These issues and more will be clarified in this chapter as we discuss the objectives of group retirement plans, how plans are structured and funded, and the current retirement crisis for the baby boomers (U.S. workers born between 1946 and 1964) who are entering their golden retirement years.[3] The chapter covers the following topics:

1. Links

2. The nature of qualified pension plans

3. Types of qualified plans, defined benefits plans, defined contribution plans, other qualified plans, and individual retirement accounts (IRAs)

4. Annuities

5. Pension plan funding techniques

1. LINKS

In our search to complete the risk management puzzle of Figure 21.1, we now add an important layer that is represented by the second step of the three-step diagram: employer-sponsored pension plans. The pension plans provided by the employer (in the second step of the three-step diagram) can be either defined benefit or defined contribution. Defined benefit pension plans ensure employees of a certain amount at retirement, leaving all risk to the employer who has to meet the specified commitment. Defined contribution, on the other hand, is a promise only to contribute an amount to the employee's separate, or individual, account. The employee has the investment risk and no assurances of the level of retirement amount. Defined benefit plans are insured by the Pension Benefit Guaranty Corporation (PBGC), a federal agency that ensures the benefits up to a limit in case the pension plan cannot meet its obligations. The maximum monthly amount of benefits guaranteed under the PBGC in 2009 for a straight life annuity at 65 percent is $4,500 and for joint and 50 percent survivor annuity (explained later) is $4,050.[4] The employee never contributes to this plan. The prevalence of this plan is on the decline in the new millennium. The PBGC protects 44 million workers and retirees in about 30,000 private-sector defined benefit pension plans.

Another trend that became prevalent and has received congressional attention is the move from the traditional defined benefit plans to cash balance plans, a transition that has slowed down in the first decade of the 2000s due to legal implications. Cash balance plans are defined benefit plans, though they are in a way a hybrid between defined benefit and defined contribution plans. More on cash balance plans, and all other plans, will be explained in this chapter and in the box "Cash Balance Conversions: Who Gets Hurt?"

The most common plans are the defined contribution pension plans. As noted above, under this type of plan, the employer provides employees with the money and the employees invest the funds. If the employees do well with their investments, they may be able to enjoy a prosperous retirement. Under defined contribution plans, in most cases, employees have some choices for investments. Plans such as money purchase, profit sharing, and target plans are funded by employers. In another type of defined contribution plan, employees contribute toward their retirement by forgoing their income or deferring it on a pretax basis, such as into 401(k), 403(b), or 457 plans. There are also Roth 401(k) and 403(b) plans, where employees contribute to the plans on an after-tax basis and never pay taxes on the earnings. These plans are sponsored by employers, and an employer may match some portion of an employee's contribution in some of these deferred compensation plans. Because it is the employees' savings, they can say that it belongs in the third step of Figure 21.1. However, because it is done through the employer, it is also part of the second step. The pension plans discussed in this chapter are featured in Figure 21.2.

FIGURE 21.1   Links between Holistic Risk Puzzle Pieces and Employee Benefits—Retirement Plans

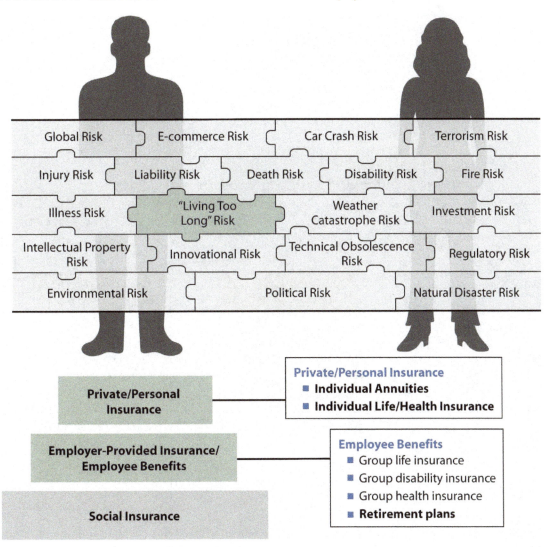

FIGURE 21.2   Retirement Plans by Type, Limits as of 2009

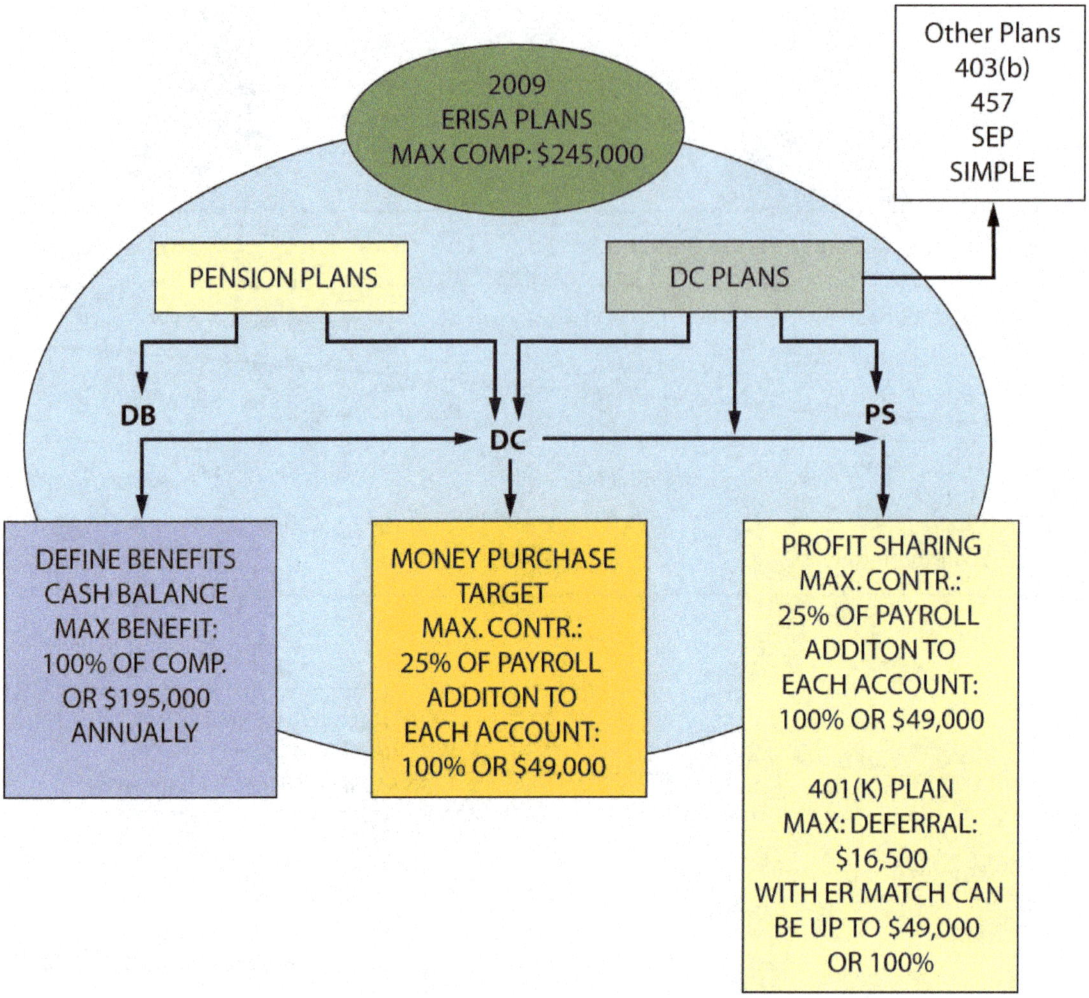

As you can see, we need to know what we are doing when we invest our defined contribution retirement funds. During the stock market boom of the late 1990s, many small investors put most of their retirement funds in stocks. By the summer of 2002, the stock market saw some of the worst declines in its history, with a rebound by 2006. Among the reasons for the decline were the downturn in the economy; the terrorist attacks of September 11, 2001; and investors' loss of trust in the integrity of the accounting numbers of many corporations. The fraudulent behavior of executives in companies such as Enron, WorldCom, and others led investors to consider their funds not just lost but stolen.[5] On July 29, 2002, President George W. Bush signed a bill for corporate governance or corporate responsibility to rebuild the trust in corporate America and punish fraudulent executives.[6] "The legislation, among other things, brought the accounting industry under federal supervision and stiffened penalties for corporate executives who misrepresent company finances."[7] Congress also worked on legislation to safeguard employee 401(k)s in an effort to prevent future disasters like the one suffered by Enron employees, who were not allowed (under the blackout period) to diversify their 401(k) investments and lost the funds when Enron declared bankruptcy. In May 2005, lawyers filed suits on behalf of AIG 401(k) participants, alleging that AIG violated the Employee Retirement Income Security Act by failing to disclose improper business practices and by disseminating false and misleading financial statements to investors that led to reductions in AIG stock prices.[8] The reform objective is intended to give more oversight and safety measures to defined contribution plans because these plans do not enjoy the oversight and protection of the PBGC. The 2007–2008 economic recession has brought about a plethora of new problems and questions regarding the merits of defined contribution plans, which will be the subject of the box, "Retirement Savings and the Recession."

In this chapter, we drill down into the specific pieces of the puzzle that bring us into many challenging areas. But we do need to complete the holistic risk management process we have started. This chapter delivers only a brief insight into the very broad and challenging area of pensions. Pensions are also featured as part of Case 2 in Chapter 23.

2.   THE NATURE OF QUALIFIED PENSION PLANS

LEARNING OBJECTIVES

In this section we elaborate on distinguishing aspects of qualified retirement plans:

- **Legislation affecting qualified retirement plans and their key provisions**
- **Eligibility criteria for qualified plans**
- **Determination of retirement age**
- **What is meant by vesting**
- **Nondiscrimination tests for qualified plans**
- **Treatment of plan distributions**
- **Loan provisions**

A retirement plan may be qualified or nonqualified. The distinction is important to both employer and employee because qualification produces a plan with a favorable tax status. In a **qualified plan**, employer contributions to an employee's pension during the employee's working years are deductible as a business expense but are not taxable income to the employee until they are received as benefits. Investment earnings on funds held by the trustee for the plan are not subject to income taxes as they are earned.

Most **nonqualified** plans do not allow employer funding contributions to be deducted as a business expense unless they are classified as compensation to the employee, in which case they become taxable income for the employee. Investment earnings on these nonqualified accumulated pension funds are also subject to taxation. Retirement benefits from a nonqualified plan are a deductible business expense when they are paid to the employee, if not previously classified as compensation. Most nonqualified plans are for executives and designed to benefit only a small number of highly paid executives.

2.1   ERISA Requirements for Qualified Pension Plans

To be qualified, a plan must fulfill various requirements. These requirements prevent those in control of the organization from using the plan primarily for their own benefit. The following requirements are enforced by the United States Internal Revenue Service, the United States Department of Labor, and the Pension Benefit Guaranty Corporation (PBGC).

- The plan must be legally binding, in writing, and communicated clearly to all employees.
- The plan must be for the exclusive benefit of the employees or their beneficiaries.
- The principal or income of the pension plan cannot be diverted to any other purpose, unless the assets exceed those required to cover accrued pension benefits.
- The plan must benefit a broad class of employees and not discriminate in favor of highly compensated employees.
- The plan must be designed to be permanent and have continuing contributions.
- The plan must comply with the Employee Retirement Income Security Act and subsequent federal laws.

qualified plan

Type of retirement plan where employer contributions to an employee's pension during the employee's working years are deductible as a business expense, are not taxable income to the employee until they are received as benefits, and investment earnings on funds held by the trustee for the plan are not subject to income taxes as they are earned.

nonqualified plan

Type of retirement plan that does not allow employer funding contributions to be deducted as business expenses unless classified as compensation to the employee (in which case they become taxable income for the employee), investment fund earnings are also subject to taxation, and retirement benefits are deductible business expenses when paid to the employee (if not previously classified as compensation).

Employee Retirement Income Security Act (ERISA) of 1974

Federal law that regulates the design, funding, and communication aspects of qualified retirement plans; specifically, protects the benefits of plan participants and prevents discrimination in favor of highly compensated employees (those who control the organization).

Economic Growth and Tax Relief Reconciliation Act (EGTRRA) of 2001

Federal law that regulates the design, funding, and communication aspects of qualified retirement plans; allows increases in retirement savings limits and mandates faster participant vesting in employers' matching contributions to defined contribution plans.

Pension Protection Act of 2006

Federal law that regulates the design, funding, and communication aspects of qualified retirement plans; specifically, added permanency to EGTRRA 2001 laws and provides greater portability, increases in flexibility in plan funding and design, and administrative simplification.

The **Employee Retirement Income Security Act (ERISA) of 1974** and subsequent amendments and laws—in particular, the Tax Reform Act of 1986 (TRA86)—are federal laws that regulate the design, funding, and communication aspects of private, qualified retirement plans. The most recent amendments include the **Economic Growth and Tax Relief Reconciliation Act (EGTRRA) of 2001** and the **Pension Protection Act of 2006**. In practice, the term ERISA is used to refer to the 1974 act and all subsequent amendments and related laws. The purpose of ERISA is twofold: to protect the benefits of plan participants and to prevent discrimination in favor of highly compensated employees (that is, those who control the organization).[9]

Within the guidelines and standards established by ERISA and subsequent federal laws, the employer must make some choices regarding the design of a qualified retirement plan. The main items covered by ERISA and subsequent laws and amendments are the following:

- Employee rights
- Reporting and disclosure rules
- Participation coverage
- Vesting
- Funding
- Fiduciary responsibilities
- Amounts contributed or withdrawn
- Nondiscrimination
- Tax penalties

ERISA and all subsequent laws provide significant protection to plan participants. Over time, however, the nature of the work force changed from stable and permanent positions to mobile and transient positions, and it appeared that ERISA failed to address portability issues when employees changed jobs. ERISA and subsequent laws are also considered to have administrative difficulties and to be a burden on employers. While the percentage of the working population covered is still unchanged since 1974, the number of defined benefit plans has dropped significantly, from a high of 175,000 plans in 1983, and more employees are now covered under defined contribution plans. ERISA has a safety valve for defined benefit plans with the insurance provided by the PBGC. Plans such as 401(k)s do not have such a safety valve. Information on how to protect your pensions is available from the Department of Labor and is featured in the box "Ten Warning Signs That Pension Contributions Are Being Misused" in Chapter 20.

In 2001, EGTRRA addressed some of ERISA's shortfalls and the 2006 Pension Protection Act provided some permanency to some of the EGTRRA laws. The new laws offer employers that sponsor plans more flexibility in plan funding and incentives by allowing greater tax deductions. The major benefits of EGTRRA are the increases in retirement savings limits and mandates of faster participant vesting in employers' matching contributions to 401(k) plans. These changes became permanent with the adoption of the Pension Protection Act of 2006. Also, all employers' contributions are now subject to faster vesting requirements. The new laws provide greater portability, increased flexibility in plan funding and design, and administrative simplification. The EGTRRA ten-year sunset provision was eliminated with the 2006 act.[10]

2.2 Eligibility and Coverage Requirements

eligibility criteria

Determines who participates in employer pension plans, subject to ERISA, the Age Discrimination in Employment Act, and other federal requirements.

A pension plan must establish **eligibility criteria** for determining who is covered. Most plans exclude certain classes of employees. For example, part-time or seasonal employees may not be covered. Separate plans may be set up for those paid on an hourly basis. Excluding certain classes of employees is allowed, provided the plan does not discriminate in favor of highly compensated employees, meets minimum eligibility requirements, and passes the tests noted below.

Under ERISA, the minimum eligibility requirements are the attainment of age twenty-one and one year of service. A year of service is defined as working at least 1,000 hours within a calendar year.[11] This is partly to reduce costs of enrolling employees who cease employment shortly after being hired, and partly because most younger employees attach a low value to benefits they will receive many years in the future. The Age Discrimination in Employment Act eliminates all maximum age limits for eligibility. Even when an employee is hired at an advanced age, such as seventy-one, the employee must be eligible for the pension plan within the first year of service if the plan is offered to other, younger hires in the same job.

In addition to eligibility rules, ERISA has **coverage requirements** that are designed to improve participation by nonhighly compensated employees. All employees of businesses with related ownership (called a **controlled group**) are treated for coverage requirements as if they were employees of one plan.

2.3 Retirement Age Limits

To make a reasonable estimate of the cost of some retirement plans, mainly defined benefit plans, it is necessary to establish a retirement age for plan participants. For other types of plans, mainly defined contribution plans, setting a retirement age clarifies the age at which no additional employer contributions will be made to the employee's plan. The **normal retirement age** is the age at which full retirement benefits become available to retirees. Most private retirement plans specify age sixty-five as the normal retirement age.

Early retirement may be allowed, but that option must be specified in the pension plan description. Usually, early retirement permanently reduces the benefit amount. For example, an early retirement provision may allow the participant to retire as early as age fifty-five if he or she also has at least thirty years of service with the employer. The pension benefit amount, however, would be reduced to take into account the shorter time available for fund accumulation and the likely longer period that benefits will be paid out.

Early retirement plans used to be very appealing both to long-timers and to employers who saw replenishment of the work force. In 2001, companies such as Procter & Gamble, Tribune Company, and Lucent Technologies used early retirement as an alternative to layoffs. Since the decline of old-fashioned defined benefit pensions, employees have less incentive to take early retirement. With defined contribution plans, employees continue to receive the employer's contribution or defer their compensation to a 401(k) plan as long as they work. The benefits are not frozen at a certain point, as in the traditional defined benefit plans. Mandatory retirement is considered age discrimination, except for executives in high policy-making positions. Thus, a plan must allow for late retirement. Deferral of retirement beyond the normal retirement age does not interfere with the accumulation of benefits. That is, working beyond normal retirement age may produce a pension benefit greater than would have been received at normal retirement age. However, a plan can set some limits on total benefits (e.g., $50,000 per year) or on total years of plan participation (e.g., thirty-five years). These limits help control employer costs.

2.4 Vesting Provisions

A pension plan may be contributory or noncontributory. A **contributory plan** requires the employee to pay all or part of the pension fund contribution. A **noncontributory plan** is funded only by employer contributions; that is, the employee does not contribute at all to the plan. ERISA requires that if an employee contributes to a pension plan, the employee must be able to recover all these contributions, with or without interest, if she or he leaves the firm.

Employer contributions and earnings are available to employees who leave their employment only if the employees are vested. **Vesting**, or the employee's right to benefits for which the *employer* has made contributions, depends on the plan provisions. The TRA86 amendment to the original ERISA vesting schedule and EGTRRA 2001 established minimum standards to ensure full vesting within a reasonable period of time. The Pension Protection Act of 2006 provides that the minimum vesting requirements for employers' contributions matches those that were required for 401(k)s by EGTRRA. For defined contribution plans, the employer can choose one of the two minimum vesting schedules (or better) as follows:

- Cliff vesting: full vesting of employer contributions after three years, as was the case for top-heavy plans and the employer-matching portion of 401(k) plans.
- Graded vesting: 20 percent vesting of employer contributions after two years, 40 percent after three years, 60 percent after four years, 80 percent after five years, and 100 percent after six years, as was the case in top-heavy plans and the employer-matching portion of 401(k) plans.

For defined benefit plans, the employer can choose one of the two minimum vesting schedules (or better) as follows:

- Cliff vesting: full vesting of employer contributions after five years, as was the case for top-heavy plans and the employer-matching portion of 401(k) plans.
- Graded vesting: 20 percent vesting of employer contributions after three years, 40 percent after four years, 60 percent after five years, 80 percent after six years, and 100 percent after seven years.

coverage requirements

ERISA provisions designed to improve participation in qualified pension plans by nonhighly compensated employees.

controlled group

Employees of businesses with related ownership; treated for coverage requirements as if employees of one plan.

normal retirement age

The age at which full retirement benefits become available to retirees; age sixty-five in most private retirement plans.

contributory plan

Pension plan that requires the employee to pay all or part of pension fund contributions.

noncontributory plan

Pension plan funded only by employer contributions.

vesting

In pension plans, specifies the extent of employee's right to benefits for which the employer has made contributions, subject to ERISA, EGTRRA 2001, TRA86, and other federal requirements.

top-heavy plans

Pension plans in which the owners or highest-paid employees hold over 60 percent of the value of the plans.

Top-heavy plans are those in which the owners or highest-paid employees hold over 60 percent of the value of the pension plan. The dollar limitation under Section 416(i)(1)(A)(i) concerning the definition of *key employee* in a top-heavy plan has increased from $150,000 in 2008, to $160,000 in 2009.[12] If an employer has a top-heavy defined benefit plan, the minimum vesting schedule is as of the defined contribution plans.

2.5 Nondiscrimination Tests

The employer's plan must meet one of the following coverage requirements:

- Percentage ratio test: The percentage of covered nonhighly compensated employees must be at least 70 percent of highly compensated employees who are covered under the pension plan. For example, if only 90 percent of the highly compensated employees are in the pension plan, only 63 percent (70 percent times 90 percent) of nonhighly compensated employees must be included.

- Average benefit test: The average benefit (expressed as a percentage of pay) for nonhighly compensated employees must be at least 70 percent of the average benefit for the highly compensated group.

The limitation used in the definition of highly compensated employee under Section 414(q)(1)(B) has increased from $105,000 in 2008 to $110,000 in 2009.[13] Although the objective of coverage rules is to improve participation by nonhighly compensated employees, the expense and administrative burden of compliance discourages small employers from having a qualified retirement plan.

2.6 Distributions

Distributions are benefits paid out to participants or their beneficiaries, usually at retirement. Tax penalties are imposed on plan participants who receive distributions (except for disability benefits) prior to age fifty-nine and a half. However, the law requires that benefits begin by age seventy and a half, whether retirement occurs or not. Depending on the provisions of the particular plan, distributions may be made (1) as a lump sum, (2) as one of several life annuity options (as explained in the settlement options in Chapter 19), or (3) over the participant's life expectancy. At age seventy and a half, the distribution requirements under ERISA direct the retiree to collect a minimum amount each year based on longevity tables.[14] Because of recent census data, Congress directed changes in the required minimum distribution calculations under EGTRRA 2001.[15]

     The longest time period over which benefits may extend is the participant's life expectancy. ERISA requires that pension plan design make spousal benefits available. Once the participant becomes vested, the spouse automatically becomes eligible for a qualified **preretirement survivor annuity**. This provision gives lifetime benefits to the spouse if the participant dies before the earliest retirement age allowed by the plan. Once the participant reaches the earliest retirement age allowed by the plan, the spouse becomes eligible for benefits under a **joint and survivor annuity** option. This qualifies the spouse for a lifetime benefit in the event of the participant's death. In most cases, the spouse receives 50 percent of the annuity. Upon the employee's retirement, the spouse remains eligible for this benefit. These benefits may be waived only if the spouse signs a notarized waiver.

preretirement survivor annuity

Provision made possible once a participant becomes vested in a pension plan that gives lifetime benefits to the spouse if the participant dies before the earliest retirement age allowed by the plan.

joint and survivor annuity

Provision made possible once a participant reaches the earliest allowed retirement age that qualifies the spouse for a lifetime benefit in the event of the participant's death (in most cases, 50 percent of the annuity).

2.7 Loans

Employees who need to use their account balances are advised to take a loan rather than terminate their employment and receive distribution. The distribution results not only in tax liability but also in a 10 percent penalty if the employee is younger than 59½ years old. The loan provisions require that an employee can take only up to 50 percent of the vested account balance for not more than $50,000. A loan of $10,000 may be made even if it is greater than 50 percent of the vested account balance. The number of loans is not limited as long as the total amount is within the required limits. Some employers do not provide loan provisions in their retirement plan.

KEY TAKEAWAYS

In this section you studied qualified employee retirement plans, which allow tax-deductible contributions for employees and tax deferral for employees:

- Requirements are set forth by ERISA, EGTRRA 2001, TRA86, the Pension Protection Act, the IRS, and the PBGC for plans to meet qualified status.
- Eligibility criteria establish which employees are covered under a plan, and the eligibility criteria must comply with ERISA coverage requirements and the Age Discrimination in Employment Act regarding the rights of older workers.
- Normal retirement age is stipulated by employers; if allowed, early retirement reduces benefits; late retirement increases benefits.
- TRA86, ERISA, EGTRAA 2001, and the Pension Protection Act of 2006 establish minimum vesting standards regarding employees' rights to employers' contributions to retirement plans.
- Qualified plans must meet either the percentage ratio or average benefit nondiscrimination tests.
- The IRS imposes tax penalties on participants who receive distributions from retirement plans prior to age fifty-nine and a half and requires that benefits begin by age seventy and a half (regardless of retirement occurring).
- Spouses are entitled to preretirement survivor and joint and survivor annuity options once participants are vested or reach the earliest allowed retirement age.
- Some plans allow a participant to take loans in amounts of up to 50 percent of a vested account balance, for no more than $50,000, at a 10 percent tax penalty if the participant is under 59½ years old.

DISCUSSION QUESTIONS

1. What is the PBGC? Why is it an important agency?
2. List ERISA requirements for qualified pension plans.
3. If an employer has 1,000 employees with 30 percent made up of highly compensated employees and 70 percent made up of nonhighly compensated employee, would the employers pass the ratio test
   a. if 200 nonhighly compensated employees are in the pension plan and all highly compensated employees are in the pension plan? Explain.
   b. if 200 nonhighly compensated employees are in the pension plan and only 50 percent of the highly compensated employees are in the pension plan? Explain.
4. Why was the ratio test created for qualified pension plans?
5. Explain briefly the changes brought about by the Pension Protection Act of 2006.
6. What happens to an employee's retirement benefits if he or she leaves a job after five years?
7. An employer is considering the following vesting schedules. Determine if these schedules comply with the laws governing qualified retirement plans:
   a. In a defined benefit plan, full vesting after six years.
   b. In a defined benefit plan, 60 percent vesting after six years and 100 percent vesting after seven years.
   c. In a defined contribution plan, 40 percent vesting after three years and 100 percent vesting at six years
   d. In a defined contribution plan, 100 percent vesting after two years.
8. There has been a proposal that all private pension plans be required to provide full vesting at the end of one year of participation. If you were the owner of a firm employing fifty people and had a qualified pension plan, how would you react to this proposal? Explain your answer.
9. Under what circumstances would an employee elect to take a loan out of his or her defined contribution plan, rather than ask for the money?

3. TYPES OF QUALIFIED PLANS, DEFINED BENEFIT PLANS, DEFINED CONTRIBUTION PLANS, OTHER QUALIFIED PLANS, AND INDIVIDUAL RETIREMENT ACCOUNTS

LEARNING OBJECTIVES

In this section we elaborate on the various qualified plans available through employers or on an individual basis:

- **Defined benefit pension plans: traditional defined benefit plan, cash balance plan**
- **Defined contribution retirement plans: cash balance plan, 401(k), profit sharing**
- **Special types of qualified plans: 403(b), Section 457, Keogh, SEP, SIMPLE**
- **Individual retirement accounts (IRAs): traditional IRA, Roth IRA, Roth 401(k), Roth 403(b)**

3.1 Types of Qualified Plans

As noted above and as shown in Figure 21.2, employers choose a pension plan from two types: defined benefit or defined contribution. Both are qualified plans that provide tax-favored arrangements for retirement savings.

Figure 21.2 displays the different qualified retirement plans. Defined benefit (DB) and defined contribution (DC) pension plans are shown in the first two left-hand squares. The defined contribution profit-sharing (PS) plan is shown in the third left-hand rectangle. The leftmost square represents the highest level of financial commitment by an employer; the profit-sharing rectangle represents the least commitment. The profit-sharing plan is funded at the discretion of the employer during periods of profits, whereas pension plans require annual minimum funding. This is why the employer is giving greater commitment to pension plans—contributions are required even in bad years. Among the pension plans, the traditional defined benefit plan represents the highest level of employer's commitment. It is a promise that the employee will receive a certain amount of income replacement at retirement. The benefits are defined by a mathematical formula, as will be shown later. Actuaries calculate the amount of the annual contribution necessary to fund the retirement promise given by the employer. As noted above, the PBGC provides insurance to guarantee these benefits (up to the maximum shown above) at a cost to the employer of $34 per employee per year (since 2009). Because the traditional defined benefit pension plan is the plan with the greatest commitment, usually a high level of contribution is allowed for older employees. The annual compensation limit under IRS sections 401(a)(17), 404(l), 408(k)(3)(C), and 408(k)(6)(D)(ii) has increased from $230,000 in 2008 to $245,000 in 2009, and the limitation on the annual benefit under a defined benefit plan under Section 415(b)(1)(A) has increased from $185,000 to $195,000 in 2009 or 100 percent of compensation.[16] These are shown in Figure 21.2.

Another defined benefit plan is the cash balance plan. As discussed above, it is a hybrid of the traditional defined benefit plan and defined contribution plans. In a cash balance plan, the employer commits to contribute a certain percentage of compensation each year and guarantees a rate of return. Under this arrangement, employees are able to calculate the exact lump sum that will be available to them at retirement because the employer guarantees both contributions and earnings. This plan favors younger employees. It is currently the topic of court cases and debate because many large corporations such as IBM converted their traditional defined benefits plans to cash balance, grandfathering the older employees' benefits under the plan.[17] See the box, "Cash Balance Conversions: Who Gets Hurt?"

A cash balance plan is considered a hybrid plan because the contributions are guaranteed. The benefits are not explicitly defined but are the outcome of the length of time the employee is in the pension plan. Because both the contributions and rates of return are guaranteed, the amount available at retirement is therefore also guaranteed. It is an insured plan under the PBGC, and all funds are kept in one large account administered by the employer. The employees have only hypothetical accounts that are made of the contributions and the guaranteed returns. As noted above, it is a defined benefit plan that looks like a defined contribution plan.

The simplest of the defined contribution pension plans is the money purchase plan. Under this plan, the employer guarantees only the annual contribution but not any returns. As opposed to a defined benefit plan, where the employer keeps all the monies in one account, the defined contribution plan has separate accounts under the control of the employees. The investment vehicles in these accounts are limited to those selected by the employer who contracts with various financial institutions to administer the investments. If employees are successful in their investment strategy, their retirement benefits will be larger. The employees are not assured an amount at retirement, and they have the investment risk, not the employer. This aspect is illuminated by the 2008–2009 recession and discussed in the box "Retirement Savings and the Recession." Because the employer is at less of an investment risk here and the employer's commitment is lower, the tax benefit is not as great (especially for older employees). The limitation for defined contribution plans under Section 415(c)(1)(A) has increased from $46,000 in 2008 to $49,000 in 2009 or 100 percent of the employee's compensation.[18]

Another defined contribution plan is the target pension plan, which favors older employees. This is another hybrid plan, but this is actually a defined contribution plan (subject to the $49,000 and 100 percent limitation in 2009) that looks like a traditional defined benefits plan in its first year only. Details about this plan are beyond the scope of this text.

For employers seeking the least amount of commitment, the profit-sharing plan is the solution. These are defined contribution plans that are not pension plans. There is no minimum funding requirements each year. As of 2003 and onward, the maximum allowed tax deductible contribution by employer per year is 25 percent of payroll. This is also a major change in effect after the enactment of EGTRRA 2001. The level used to be only 15 percent of payroll, with limits of an annual addition to each account of $35,000 or 25 percent in 2001. The additions to each account are up to the lesser of $49,000 or 100 percent of compensation in 2009.[19] The 401(k) is part of the tax code for a profit-sharing plan, but it is not designed as an employer contribution. Rather, it is a pretax-deferred compensation contribution by the employee with possible matching by an employer. See Tables 21.6 and 21.7 later in this chapter for the limits if the employer meets the discrimination testing or falls under certain safe-harbor provisions. As shown, EGTRRA 2001 increased the permitted deferred compensation under 401(k) plans gradually up to $16,500[20] (in 2009) from the level of $10,500 in 2001. On January 1, 2006, Internal Revenue Code (IRC) §402A providing for Roth 401(k)s and Roth 403(b)s (discussed later) became effective. This also is an outcome of EGTRRA 2001 with a delayed effective date. Roth 401(k) and Roth 403(b) means that the contributions are after-tax, but earnings are never taxed. EGTRRA 2001 has catch-up provisions. The explanation of the 401(k) plan includes an example of the average deferral percentage (ADP) discrimination test used for 401(k) plans. When an employer adds matching, profit sharing, or any other defined contribution plans, the amount of annual additions to the individual accounts cannot exceed the lesser of $49,000 or 100 percent of compensation, including the 401(k) deferral in 2009.[21] The combination of 401(k) and any other profit-sharing contributions cannot exceed 25 percent of payroll. Nearly two-thirds of all U.S. large employers consider the 401(k) as the main retirement plan for their employees.[22]

An employee stock ownership plan (ESOP) is another type of profit-sharing plan. An ESOP is covered only briefly in this text. This section also provides a brief description of other qualified plans such as 403(b), 457, Savings Incentive Match Plan for Employees (SIMPLE), Simplified Employee Pension (SEP), traditional IRA, and Roth IRA. EGTRRA 2001 made major changes to these plans, as well as to the plans discussed so far. Traditional IRA and Roth IRA are not sponsored by the employer, but require employee compensation through employment.

Cash Balance Conversions: Who Gets Hurt?

Over the past two decades, a number of employers have switched their traditional defined benefit pension plans to cash balance plans. Employers like cash balance plans because they are less expensive than traditional plans, in part, because they do not require the high administrative cost and large contributions for employees who are near retirement. Also, cash balance benefit plans may pay out less because they base their benefits on an employee's career earnings, while defined benefit plans are based on the final years of salary, when earnings usually peak.

In November 2002, Delta Airlines joined the cash balance trend, citing the soaring costs of its underfunded traditional pension plan as the reason. Like Delta, many companies have implemented cash balance plans by converting their old defined benefit plans. In doing so, they determine an employee's accrued benefit under the old plan and use it to set an opening balance for a cash balance account. While the opening account of a cash balance account can end up being less than the actual present value of the benefits an employee has already accrued (called wear away), cash balance plans have the advantage of portability. The traditional defined benefits plan is not portable because an employee who leaves a job may need to leave the accrued and vested benefits with the employer until retirement. Cash balance plans are considered very portable. The plan is similar to defined contribution plans because the employee knows at any moment the value of his or her hypothetical account that is built up as an accumulation of employer's contributions and guaranteed rate of return. For this reason, cash balance plans are advertised as advantageous for today's mobile work force. Also, cash balance plans are considered best for younger workers because these employees have many years to accumulate their hypothetical account balances.

However, these conversions have not been free of major controversies. Older employees, who do not have a long enough time to accumulate the account balance, in most cases are granted continuation under the old plan, under a grandfather clause. Midcareer employees in their forties have most to risk because it is uncertain whether the new cash balance plans can actually catch up to the old promise of defined benefits at age sixty-five. Plan critics have repeatedly charged that pay credits discriminate against older employees because the credits they receive would purchase a smaller annuity at normal retirement age than would those received by younger employees. Numerous lawsuits alleging discrimination have been filed against employers offering the plans.

IBM's conversion in 1999 provides a notorious example of the pitfalls of conversion for midcareer employees. When IBM announced the conversion, it was inundated with hundreds of thousands of e-mails complaining about the change, so the company repeatedly tweaked its plan. Still, many employees are not satisfied when they compare the new plan with the defined benefit plan they might otherwise have received. A federal court gave a final approval to partial settlement between IBM and tens of thousands of current and former employees about the conversion. Under one part of the settlement, IBM has to pay more than $300 million to plan participants in the form of enhanced benefits. Since the partial settlement was proposed, IBM had frozen its cash balance plan, with employees hired as of January 1, 2005, receiving pension coverage under an enriched 401(k) plan.

The 2005 U.S. Government Accountability Office (GAO) report regarding cash balance pension plans concluded that cash balance plans do cut benefits. In July 2005, congressional committees passed legislation to make clear that cash balance plans do not violate age discrimination law, but the measures do not apply to existing plans. This relates to a court case that provided victory for employers. The judge dismissed a case against PNC Financial Services Group that was brought on behalf of its employees and retirees in connection with the company's switch to a cash balance plan. The Pittsburgh-based PNC replaced its traditional defined benefit plan in 1999. The plaintiffs filed suit against the company and its pension plan in December 2004, arguing that the plan was age discriminatory, among other allegations. Judge D. Davis Legrome of the U.S. District Court in Philadelphia dismissed all the charges against the company in his decision (*Sandra Register v. PNC Financial Services Group, Inc.*).

To soften the effects of cash balance conversion, many companies offer transitional benefits to older employers. Some companies allow their workers to choose between the traditional plan and the cash balance plan. Others offer stock options or increased contributions to employee 401(k) plans to offset the reduction in pension benefits.

Questions for Discussion

1. Who actually is the beneficiary of the conversions? The employer? All employees? Or only some? Is it ethical to change promises to employees?

2. Are conversions to cash balance plans a reflection of the lowering of the noncash compensation (pension offering) of employers in the last two decades? Or are they just a smart move to accommodate the mobile work force? Is it ethical to make a noncash compensation reduction without reaching an agreement with employees?

3. Is the fact that many employers are trying to get away from the traditional defined benefits plans that are similar to the current Social Security system a signal that Social Security will be privatized? Would it be ethical to make changes that may not be clear to employees (see Chapter 18)?

Sources: Jerry Geisel, "Delta's New Pension Plan to Generate Big Savings," Business Insurance, November 25, 2002, http://www.businessinsurance.com/ cgi-bin/article.pl?articleId=12013&a=a&bt=delta's+new+pension+plan (accessed April 17, 2009); Jonathan Barry Forman, "Legal Issues in Cash Balance Pension Plan Conversions," Benefits Quarterly, January 1, 2001, 27–32; Lawrence J. Sher, "Survey of Cash Balance Conversions," Benefits Quarterly, January 1, 2001, 19–26; Robert L. Clark, John J. Haley, and Sylvester J. Schieber, "Adopting Hybrid Pension Plans: Financial and Communication Issues," Benefits Quarterly, January 1, 2001, p. 7–17; "Cash Balance Plans Questions & Answers," U.S. Department of Labor, November 1999, https://www.dol.gov/ebsa/publications/cb_pension_plans.html (accessed April 17, 2009); Jerry Geisel, "Proposed Rules Clarify Cash Balance Plan Status," Business Insurance, December 10, 2002; Jerry Geisel "Court Gives Final Approval in IBM Pension Case," Business Insurance, August 15, 2005, http://www.businessinsurance.com/cgi-bin/article.pl?articleId=17389&a=a&bt=court+gives+final+approval+ibm (accessed April 17, 2009); Jerry Geisel, "Effort to Dispel Cash Balance Doubts Criticized for Ignoring Existing Plans," Business Insurance , August 1, 2005, http://www.businessinsurance.com/cgi-bin/article.pl?articleId=17312&a=a&bt=effort+to+dispel+cash+balance (accessed April 17, 2009); Judy Greenwald, "Court Ruling Favors Cash Balance Conversions," Business Insurance, November 23, 2005, http://www.businessinsurance.com/cgi-bin/ news.pl?newsId=6781, accessed April 17, 2009; Jerry Geisel "Cash Balance Plan Conversions Cut Benefits: GAO," Business Insurance, November 4, 2005.

Defined Benefit Plans

A **defined benefit (DB) plan** has the distinguishing characteristic of clearly defining, by its benefit formula, the amount of benefit that will be available at retirement. That is, the benefit amount is specified in the written plan document, although the amount that must be contributed to fund the plan is not specified.

Traditional Defined Benefit Plan

In a defined benefit plan, any of several benefit formulas may be used in the following:

- A flat dollar amount
- A flat percentage of pay
- A flat amount unit benefit
- A percentage unit benefit

Each type has advantages and disadvantages, and the employer selects the formula that best meets both the needs of employees for economic security and the budget constraints of the employer.

The defined benefit formula may specify a flat dollar amount, such as $500 per month. It may provide a formula by which the amount can be calculated, yielding a flat percentage of current annual salary (or the average salary of the past five years or so). For example, a plan may specify that each employee with at least twenty years of participation in the plan receives 50 percent of his or her average annual earnings during the three consecutive years of employment with the highest earnings. A flat amount unit benefit formula assigns a flat amount (e.g., $25) with each unit of service, usually with each year. Thus, an employee with thirty units of service at retirement would receive a benefit equal to thirty times the unit amount.

The most popular defined benefit formula is the percentage unit benefit plan. It recognizes both the employee's years of service and level of compensation. See Table 21.1 for an example. Tables 21.1 through 21.5 feature different qualified retirement plans for the Slone-Jones Dental Office. The dental office is used as an example to demonstrate how each plan would work for the same mix of employees.

TABLE 21.1 The Slone-Jones Dental Office: Standard Defined Benefit Pension Plan (Service Unit Formula, 2009)

Employees	(1) Current Age	(2) Current Salary	(3) Allowable Compensation	(4) Years of Service	(5) Years of Service to Age 65	(6) Maximum Allowed Benefit	(7) Expected Benefit at Age 65 2% × (3) × (5)
Dr. Slone	55	$250,000	$245,000	20	30	$195,000	$90,000
Diane	45	$55,000	$55,000	10	30	55,000	$11,000
Jack	25	$30,000	$30,000	5	45	30,000	$3,000

When the compensation base is described as compensation for a recent number of years (e.g., the last three or highest consecutive five years), the formula is referred to as a **final average formula**. Relative to a **career average formula**, which bases benefits on average compensation for all years of service in the plan, a final average plan tends to keep the initial retirement benefit in line with inflation.

defined benefit (DB) plan

Type of pension plan that assures employees of a certain amount at retirement, leaving all risk to the employer to meet the specified commitment; accumulated funds for all participants are managed in one account.

final average formula

Sets the compensation base as compensation for a recent number of years (e.g., the last three or highest consecutive five years) in computing the retirement benefit in a defined benefit plan; tends to keep the initial benefit in line with inflation.

career average formula

Bases benefits on average compensation for all years of service under the plan in computing the retirement benefit in a defined benefit plan.

supplemental liability

In a retirement benefit formula, past service liability giving credit to employees' service prior to the adoption of a defined benefits plan; can be amortized over a certain number of years.

cash balance plan

Defined benefit plan that is a hybrid of the traditional defined benefit plan and a defined contribution plan where the employer commits to contribute a certain percentage of compensation each year and guarantees a rate of return such that employees can calculate the exact lump sum that will be available at retirement (since the employer guarantees both contributions and earnings).

Two types of service are involved in the benefit formula: past service and future service. Past service refers to service prior to the installation of the plan. Future service refers to service subsequent to the installation of the plan. If credit is given for past service, the plan starts with an initial past service liability at the date of installation. To reduce the size of this liability, the percentage of credit for past service may be less than that for future service, or a limit may be put on the number of years of past service credit. Initial past service liability may be a serious financial problem for the employer starting or installing a pension plan. Past service liability or **supplemental liability** can be amortized over a certain number of years, not to exceed thirty years for a single employer.

Cash Balance Plan

The **cash balance plan** does not provide an amount of benefit that will be available for the employee at retirement. Instead, the cash balance plan sets up a hypothetical individual account for each employee, and credits each participant annually with a plan contribution (usually a percentage of compensation). The employer also guarantees a minimum interest credit on the account balance. For example, an employer might contribute 10 percent of an employee's salary to the employee's plan each year and guarantee a minimum rate of return of 4 percent on the fund, as shown in Table 21.2. If investment returns turn out to be higher than 4 percent, the employer may credit the employee account with the higher rate. The amount available to the employee at retirement varies, based on wage rates and investment rates of return. Although the cash balance plan is technically a defined benefit plan, it has many of the same characteristics as defined contribution plans. These characteristics include hypothetical individual employee accounts, a fixed employer contribution rate, and an indeterminate final benefit amount because employee compensation changes over time and interest rates may turn out to be well above the minimum guaranteed rate.

TABLE 21.2   **The Slone-Jones Dental Office: Standard Cash Balance Plan (2009)**

Employees	(1) Current Age	(2) Current Salary	(3) Allowed Compensation	(4) Maximum Benefit	(5) Contribution Year (10%)	(6) Years to Retirement	(7) Future Value of $1 Annuity at 4%	(8) Lump Sum at Age 65 (7) × (5)
Dr. Slone	55	$250,000	$245,000	$195,000	$24,500	10	12.006	$294,147
Diane	45	$55,000	$55,000	55,000	$5,500	20	29.778	$163,779
Jack	25	$30,000	$30,000	30,000	$3,000	40	95.024	$285,072

Features of Defined Benefit Plans

All defined benefit plans may provide for adjustments to account for inflation during the retirement years. A plan that includes a **cost-of-living adjustment (COLA)** clause has the ideal design feature. Benefits increase automatically with changes in a cost-of-living or wage index.

Many plans integrate the retirement benefit with Social Security benefits. An **integrated plan** coordinates Social Security benefits (or contributions) with the private plan's benefit (or contribution) formula. Integration reduces private retirement benefits based on the amount received through Social Security, thus reducing the cost to employers of the private plan. On the other hand, integration allows employees with higher income to receive greater benefits or contributions, depending on the formula. The scope of this text is too limited to explore the exact mechanism of integrated plans. There are two kinds of plans. The offset method reduces the private plan benefit by a set fraction. This approach is applicable only to defined benefit plans. The second method is the integration-level method. Here, a threshold of compensation, such as the wage base level shown in Chapter 18, is specified, and the rate of benefits or contributions provided below this compensation threshold is lower than the rate for compensation above the threshold. The integration-level method may be used for defined benefit or defined contribution pension plans.

cost-of-living adjustment (COLA)

Increases retirement benefits automatically with changes in a cost-of-living or wage index to account for inflation during retirement years.

integrated plan

Defined benefit plan that coordinates Social Security benefits (or contributions) with the benefit (or contribution) formula, thus reducing private retirement benefits based on the amount received through Social Security and lowering employer costs.

As noted above, defined benefits up to specified levels are guaranteed by the **Pension Benefit Guarantee Corporation (PBGC)**, a federal insurance program somewhat like the Federal Deposit Insurance Corporation (FDIC) for commercial bank accounts, and like the Guarantee Funds for Insurance. All defined benefit plans contribute an annual fee (or premium) per pension plan participant to finance benefits for members of insolvent terminated plans. The premium amount takes into account, to a degree, the financial soundness of the particular plan, measured by the plan's unfunded vested benefit. Thus, plans with a greater unfunded vested benefit pay a greater PBGC premium (up to a maximum amount), providing an incentive to employers to adequately fund their pension plans. Despite this incentive, there is national concern about the number of seriously underfunded pension plans insured by the PBGC. If these plans were unable to pay promised retirement benefits, the PBGC would be liable, and PBGC funds may be insufficient to cover the claims. Taxpayers could end up bailing out the PBGC. Careful monitoring of PBGC fund adequacy continues, and funding rules may be tightened to keep the PBGC financially sound.

Defined Benefit Cost Factors

Annual pension contributions and plan liabilities for a defined benefit plan must be estimated by an actuary. (Actuaries with pension specialties are called enrolled actuaries.) The time value of money explained in Chapter 4 is used extensively in the computations of pensions. The defined amount of benefits becomes the employer's obligation, and contributions must equal whatever amount is necessary to fund the obligation. The estimate of cost depends on factors such as salary levels; normal retirement age; current employee ages; and assumptions about mortality, turnover, investment earnings, administrative expenses, and salary adjustment factors (for inflation and productivity). These factors determine estimates of how many employees will receive retirement benefits, how much they will receive, when benefits will begin, and how long benefits will be paid.

Normal costs reflect the annual amount needed to fund the pension benefit during the employee's working years. **Supplemental costs** are the amounts necessary to amortize any past service liability, which is explained above, over a period that may vary from ten to thirty years. Total cost for a year is the sum of normal and supplemental costs. Under some methods of calculation, normal and supplemental costs are estimated as one item. Costs may be estimated for each employee and then added to yield total cost, or a calculation may be made for all participants on an aggregate basis.

Defined benefit plan administration is expensive compared with defined contribution plans because of actuarial expense and complicated ERISA regulations. This explains in part why about 75 percent of the plans established since the passage of ERISA have been defined contribution plans.

Defined Contribution Plans

A **defined contribution (DC) plan** is a qualified pension plan in which the contribution amount is defined but the benefit amount available at retirement varies. This is in direct contrast to a defined benefit plan, in which the benefit is defined and the contribution amount varies. As with the defined benefit plan, when the defined contribution plan is initially designed, the employer makes decisions about eligibility, retirement age, integration, vesting schedules, and funding methods.

The most common type of defined contribution plan is the **money purchase plan**. This plan establishes an annual rate of employer contribution, usually expressed as a percentage of current compensation; for example, a plan may specify that the employer will contribute 10 percent of an employee's salary, as shown in the example in Table 21.3. Separate accounts are maintained to track the current balance attributable to each employee, but contributions may be commingled for investment purposes.

Pension Benefit Guaranty Corporation (PBGC)

Federal agency that ensures the benefits of defined benefit plans up to annual limits in case the pension plan cannot meet its obligations.

normal costs

In defined benefit plans, the annual amount needed to fund pension benefits during an employee's working years.

supplemental costs

In defined benefit plans, the amounts necessary to amortize any past service liability over a period that may vary from ten to thirty years.

defined contribution (DC) plan

Type of pension plan that promises only to contribute an amount to the employee's separate or individual account; the employee has the investment risk and no assurances of the level of retirement amount; has separate accounts under the control of each participant.

money purchase plan

In this simplest of the defined contribution plans, the employer guarantees only the annual contribution to an employee's retirement account, but not any returns.

TABLE 21.3   The Slone-Jones Dental Office: Standard Money Purchase Plan (2009)

Employees	(1) Age	(2) Current Salary	(3) Allowed Compensation	(4) Service	(5) Maximum Contribution Allowed	(6) Contribution at 10.00% (3) × 0.10	(7) Years to Retirement	(8) Future Value of $1 Annuity at 10%	(9) Lump Sum at Retirement (6) × (8)
Dr. Slone	55	$250,000	$245,000	20	$49,000	$24,500	10	15.937	$390,457
Diane	45	$55,000	$55,000	10	$49,000	$5,500	20	57.274	$315,007
Jack	25	$30,000	$30,000	5	$30,000	$3,000	40	442.58	$1,327,740

The benefit available at retirement varies with the contribution amount, the length of covered service, investment earnings, and retirement age, as you can see in Column 9 of Table 21.3. Some plans allow employees to direct the investment of their own pension funds, offering several investment options. Generally, retirement age has no effect on a distribution received as a lump sum, fixed amount, or fixed period annuity. Retirement age affects the amount of income received only under a life annuity option.

From the perspective of an employer or employee concerned with the adequacy of retirement income, the contributions that typically have the longest time to accumulate with compound investment returns are the smaller ones. They are smaller because the compensation base (to which the contribution percentage is applied) is lowest in an employee's younger years. This is perhaps the major disadvantage of defined contribution plans. It is also difficult to project the amount of retirement benefit until retirement is near, which complicates planning. In addition, the speculative risk of investment performance (positive or negative returns) is borne directly by employees.

From an employer's perspective, however, such plans have the distinct advantage of a reasonably predictable level of pension cost because they are expressed as a percentage of current payroll. Because the employer promises only to specify a rate of contribution and prudently manage the plan, actuarial estimates of annual contributions and liabilities are unnecessary. The employer also does not contribute to the Pension Benefit Guaranty Corporation, which applies only to defined benefit plans. Most new plans today are defined contribution plans, which is not surprising given their simplicity, lower administrative cost, and limited employer liability for funding.

Other Qualified Defined Contribution Plans

Employers may offer a variety of defined contribution plans other than money purchase plans to assist employees in saving for retirement. These may be the only retirement plans offered by the organization, or they may be offered in addition to a defined benefit plan or a defined contribution money purchase plan, as you can see in Case 2 of Chapter 23. One such defined contribution plan is the **target plan**, which is an age-weighted pension plan. Under this plan, each employee is targeted to receive the same formula of benefit at retirement (age sixty-five), but the benefits are not guaranteed. Because older employees have less time to accumulate the funds for retirement, they receive a larger contribution as a percentage of compensation than the younger employees do. The target plan is a hybrid of defined benefits and defined contribution plans, but it is a defined contribution pension plan with the same limits and requirements as defined contribution plans.

Profit-Sharing Plans

All **profit-sharing plans** are defined contribution plans. They are considered incentive plans rather than pension plans because they do not have annual funding requirements. Profit-sharing plans provide economic incentives for employees because firm profits are distributed directly to employees. In a **deferred profit-sharing plan**, a firm puts part of its profits in trust for the benefit of employees. Typically, the share of profit allocated is related to salary; that is, the share each year is the percentage determined by the employee's salary divided by total salaries for all participants in the plan. Per EGTRRA 2001, the maximum amount of contribution is 25 percent of the total payroll of all employees.

Table 21.4, featuring again the Slone-Jones Dental Office, shows an allocation of profit sharing should the employer decide to contribute $30,000 to the profit-sharing plan. The allocation is based on the percentage of each employee's pay from total payroll allowed (see Column 4 in Table 21.4). The maximum profits to be shared in 2009 cannot be greater than an allocation of $49,000 for top employees.[23] If the maximum compensation allowed is $245,000 and the maximum contribution is $49,000, in essence the contribution to the account of an employee making $245,000 or more would not be more than 20 percent.

target plan

Hybrid age-weighted defined contribution plan in which each employee is targeted to receive the same formula of benefit at retirement, but the benefits are not guaranteed; older employees receive a larger contribution as a percentage of compensation than younger employees since they have less time to accumulate funds to retirement.

profit sharing plans

Incentive defined contribution plans whereby employers may voluntarily elect to annually distribute a specified portion of company profits among employees in relation to salary.

deferred profit-sharing plan

Profit sharing plan in which the employer puts part of its profits in trust for the benefit of employees.

TABLE 21.4 The Slone-Jones Dental Office: Standard Profit Sharing Plan (2009)

	(1)	(2)	(3)	(4)	(5)
Employees	Current Age	Salary	Maximum Allowed Compensation	Percentage of Pay from Total Adjusted Payroll (3)/330,000	Allocation of $30,000 Profits (4) × 30,000
Dr. Slone	55	$250,000	$245,000	74.24%	$22,272
Diane	45	$55,000	$55,000	16.67%	$5,001
Jack	25	$30,000	$30,000	9.09%	$2,727
Total			$330,000	100.00%	$30,000

Employee Stock Ownership Plans

An **employee stock ownership plan (ESOP)** is a special form of profit-sharing plan. The unique feature of an ESOP is that all investments are in the employer's common stock. Proponents of ESOPs claim that this ownership participation increases employee morale and productivity. Critics regard it as a tie-in of human and economic capital in a single firm, which may lead to complete losses when the firm is in trouble. An illustration of the hardship that can occur when employees invest in their company is Enron, a case we noted earlier.

An ESOP represents the ultimate in investment concentration because all contributions are invested in one security. This is distinctly different from the investment diversification found in the typical pension or profit-sharing plan. To alleviate the ESOP investment risk for older employees, employers are required to allow at least three diversified investment portfolios for persons over age fifty-five who also have at least ten years of participation in the plan. Each diversified portfolio contains several issues of nonemployer securities, such as common stocks or bonds. One option might even be a low-risk investment, such as bank certificates of deposit. This allows use of an incentive-type qualified retirement plan without unnecessarily jeopardizing the future retiree's benefits.

employee stock ownership plan (ESOP)

Special type of profit sharing plan where all investments are in employer's common stock.

401(k) Plans

Another qualified defined contribution plan is the **401(k) plan**, which allows employees to defer compensation for retirement before taxes. Refer to the example of deferral in Table 21.5. As you can see, contributions to a 401(k) plan are limited per the description in Figure 21.2 and Tables 21.6 and 21.7. The total contribution amount to a 401(k) plan, by both employee and employer, cannot exceed $49,000 or 100 percent of the employee's income. In 2009, the deferral by the employee cannot exceed $16,500, unless the employee is over age fifty.[24]

401(k) plan

Defined contribution plan that allows an employee to defer before-tax compensation toward a retirement account, which may be matched or supplemented by employer contributions.

TABLE 21.5 The Slone-Jones Dental Office: ADP Tests for 401(k) Plan (2009)

	(1)	(2)	(3)	(4)	(5)
Employees	Current Age	Salary	Allowable Compensation	Voluntary 401(k) Contribution	Contribution as a Percentage of Compensation (4)/(3)
Dr. Slone	55	$250,000	$245,000	$16,500	5.92%
Diane	45	$55,000	$55,000	3,000	5.45%
Jack	25	$30,000	$30,000	1,200	4.00%
ADP Test 1: Average Jack's and Diane's contributions ([5.45% + 4.00%]/2) = 4.73%; multiply 4.73% × 1.25 = 5.91%. This figure is less than Dr. Slone's contribution. **Failed**.					
ADP Test 2: 4.73% × 2 = 9.46%. 4.73% + 2 = 6.73%. The lesser of these is more than Dr. Slone's contribution. **Passed**.					

TABLE 21.6 Limits for 401(k), 403(b) [also Roth 401(k) and 403(b)], and 457 Plans

Taxable Year	Salary Reduction Limit
2005	$14,000
2006	$15,000
2007	$15,500
2008	$15,500
2009	$16,500

TABLE 21.7 Additional Limits for Employees over 50 Years of Age for 401(k), 403(b) [also Roth 401(k) and 403(b)], and 457 Plans

Taxable Year	Additional Deferral Limit (Age 50 and Older)
2005	$4,000
2006	$5,000
2007	$5,000
2008	$5,000
2009	$5,500
2010	Indexed to inflation

To receive the tax credits for 401(k), employers have to pass the average deferral percentage (ADP) test, unless they either (1) match 100 percent of the employee contribution up to 3 percent of compensation and 50 percent of the employee contribution between 3 percent and 5 percent of compensation or (2) make a nonelective (nonmatching) contribution for all eligible nonhighly-compensated employees equal to at least 3 percent of compensation. These employers' contributions are considered a safe harbor. The ADP test is shown in Table 21.5 for a hypothetical elective deferral of the employees of the Slone-Jones Dental Office.

As you can see, the ADP has two parts:

- Average the deferral percentages of the nonhighly-compensated employees. Multiply this figure by 1.25. Is the result greater than the average for the highly compensated employees? If it is, the employer passed the test. If it is not, proceed to the next test.

- Take the average of the deferral percentages of nonhighly-compensated employees. Double this percentage or add two percentage points, whichever is less. Is the result greater than the average for the highly compensated employees?

If the answer is no, the employer did not pass the ADP test and the highly compensated employees have to pay taxes on the amounts they cannot defer. Most employers give incentives to employees to voluntarily defer greater amounts.

As noted, strict requirements are put on withdrawals, such as allowing them only for hardships (that is, heavy and immediate financial needs), disability, death, retirement, termination of employment, or reaching age fifty-nine and a half. As in all other qualified retirement plans, a 10 percent penalty tax applies to withdrawals made by employees before age fifty-nine and a half. The penalty undoubtedly discourages contributions from employees who want easier access to their savings. Most employees would rather take loans.

Other Qualified Plans

Tax-deferred programs for employees include individual retirement accounts (IRAs); employer-sponsored Internal Revenue Code (IRC) Section 401(k) savings/profit-sharing plans, discussed above; IRC Section 403(b) tax-sheltered annuity (TSA) plans for employees of educational and certain other tax-exempt organizations; and IRC Section 457 plans for state and local government employees. The TSA is a retirement plan of tax-exempt organizations and educational organizations of state or local governments.

403(b) and 457 Plans

Employees of tax-exempt groups, such as hospitals or public schools, can elect to defer a portion of their salaries for retirement in what are called **403(b) plans**. They are similar to 401(k) plans. **Section 457 plans**, offered to employees of state and local governments and nonprofit, noneducational institutions, were created in 1978. They are similar to 401(k) and 403(b) plans because the money in the plan must be held separately from employer assets, in a trust, custodial account, or annuity contract. The 457 plan may be offered in conjunction with another defined-contribution plan such as a 401(k) or 403(b) or a defined benefit pension plan. EGTRRA 2001 changed the 457's unique features and made it more comparable to the 401(k) and 403(b). Employees of governmental educational institutions can defer compensation in both 403(b) and 457 plans up to the maximum of each. Tables 21.6 and 21.7 show the new maximums for the plans under EGTRRA 2001.

Self-employed workers can make tax-deferred contributions through a Keogh plan or a simplified employee plan (SEP). Small employers also can establish a SEP or a savings incentive match plan for employees of small employers (SIMPLE).

Keogh Plans

Keogh plans (also known as HR-10 plans) are for people who earn self-employment income. Contributions can be made based on either full- or part-time employment. Even if the employee is a retirement plan participant with an organization that has one or more qualified defined benefit or defined contribution plans, the employee can establish a Keogh plan based on self-employment earned income. For example, the employee may work full-time for wages or salary but part-time as a consultant or accountant in the evenings and on weekends. Saving part of net income from self-employment is what Keogh is all about. Proprietors, partners, and employees can be covered in the same plan. The Keogh plan may be designed as either a regular defined benefit or money purchase plan with the same contribution limits.

Simplified Employee Pension Plans

A **Simplified Employee Pension (SEP)** is similar to an employer-sponsored individual retirement account (IRA). With a SEP, the employer makes a deductible contribution to the IRA, but the contribution limit is much higher than the annual deduction limit of the typical IRA (explained in the next section). The SEP contribution is limited to the lesser of $49,000 or 25 percent of the employee's compensation in 2009.[25] Coverage requirements ensure that a broad cross section of employees is included in the SEP. Employers are not locked into an annual contribution amount, but when contributions are made, they must be allocated in a way that does not discriminate in favor of highly compensated employees. The main advantage of the SEP is low administrative cost.

SEPs allow employers to establish and make contributions to IRAs. The two critical differences between SEP-IRAs and other IRAs are that SEP contributions are generally made by employers, not employees, and that the limits of SEP are substantially larger.

SIMPLE Plans

Savings Incentive Match Plan for Employees (SIMPLE) plans are for employers with one hundred employees or less. This plan was authorized by the Small Business Job Protection Act of 1996. Small businesses comprise over 38 percent of the nation's private work force. The maximum contributions under EGTRRA 2001 are shown in Tables 21.8 and 21.9. Under the new limits, eligible employees can contribute up to $11,500 in 2009[26] through convenient payroll deductions. Employers offer matching contributions equal to employee contributions (up to 3 percent of employee wages) or fixed contributions equal to 2 percent of employee wages. This plan, like SEP, eliminates many of the administrative costs associated with larger retirement plans. The employees who can participate are those who earned $5,000 or more during the preceding calendar year. This plan cannot be established with other qualified plans. As in all other defined contribution plans, the employee may make the initial choice of financial institution to receive contributions.

TABLE 21.8 SIMPLE Plan Limits

Taxable Year	Salary Reduction Limit
2005	$10,000
2006	$10,000
2007	$10,500
2008	$10,500
2009	$11,500

403(b) plans

Allows employees of tax-exempt entities to defer compensation toward retirement accounts, similar to 401(k) plans.

Section 457 plans

Allows employees of state and local governments and nonprofit, noneducational institutions to defer compensation toward retirement accounts, similar to 401(k) plans; the money must be held separately from employer assets in a trust, custodial account, or annuity contract.

Keogh plans

Allow tax-deferred retirement contributions toward retirement savings for self-employed persons.

simplified employee pension (SEP)

Allows employers to make deductible contributions to employee individual retirement accounts (IRAs) at higher limits than the traditional IRA.

Savings Incentive Match Plan for Employees of Small Employers (SIMPLE)

Allow employees of small businesses who meet income eligibility to make retirement savings contributions through payroll deductions that can be supplemented by employer contributions.

TABLE 21.9 SIMPLE Plan Limits for Employees Age Fifty or Older

Taxable Year	Additional Deferral Limit (Age 50 and Older)
2005	$2,000
2006	$2,500
2007	$2,500
2008	$2,500
2009	$2,500
2010	Indexed to inflation

Individual Retirement Accounts (IRAs)

Traditional IRA and Roth IRA

traditional IRA

Individual retirement account that allows individuals to defer taxes on account contributions and earnings on contributions until the account is withdrawn, subject to annual income and contribution limits; also the vehicle for rolling over employers' sponsored retirement accounts in order to avoid penalties and tax issues.

Roth IRA

Individual retirement account funded with after-tax dollars, but earnings on the account are never taxed, even when drawn upon at retirement, subject to annual income and contribution limits.

When discussing other retirement plans, we include **traditional IRA** and **Roth IRA** despite the fact that these programs are not provided by the employer. But they do require some level of income for participation. An employee cannot make contributions to an IRA without some level of compensation. An employee who is not part of an employer's program can defer compensation by establishing an individual retirement account (IRA) or Roth IRA. This is also the vehicle for rolling over employers' sponsored retirement accounts in order to avoid penalties and tax issues. An employee who participates in the employer's retirement plans but earns a low income can open an IRA or a Roth IRA. A traditional IRA allows the employee to defer taxes on the contributions and the earning on the contributions until the accounts are withdrawn. A Roth IRA is funded with after-tax dollars, but the earnings on the account are never taxed, even after the employee retires and begins drawing from the account. The Roth IRA is considered a wonderful program from a taxation planning point of view, especially during low earning years when the tax rate is very low. The maximum allowed contributions to the traditional IRA and Roth IRA are featured in Table 21.10 and Table 21.11.

TABLE 21.10 Traditional IRA and Roth IRA Limits

Taxable Year	Maximum Deductible Amount
2002–2004	$3,000
2005	$4,000
2006–2007	$4,000
2008	$5,000
2009	$5,000
2010	Indexed to inflation

TABLE 21.11 IRA and Roth IRA Limits for People Age Fifty and Older

Taxable Year	Maximum Deductible Amount (Age 50 and Older)
2002-2004	$3,500
2005	$4,500
2006-2007	$5,000
2008	$6,000
2009	$6,000
2010	Indexed to Inflation

Who is eligible to make tax-deferred IRA contributions? An employee who does not participate in an employer-sponsored retirement plan in a particular year can make contributions up to the amount shown in Tables 21.10 and 21.11 (or 100 percent of the employee's earned income if he or she is making less than that shown in Tables 21.10 and 21.11). If the employee participates in an employer-sponsored retirement plan (that is, an employer makes contributions or provides credits on the employee's behalf), the maximum amount of tax-deferred IRA contribution depends on income earned from work, but not from investments, Social Security, and other nonemployment sources. The maximum contributions for the following income levels in 2009 are the following:[27]

- Single people earning $55,000 or less and married couples filing a joint income tax return earning $89,000 or less adjusted gross income (AGI) are eligible not to pay current income taxes on IRA contributions up to the contribution limits.

- Single people earning $65,000 or more and married couples earning $109,000 or more have zero tax-deferred contributions.
- Single people and married couples with earnings between the eligible and ineligible thresholds have a partial deduction on contributions

The advantage of making tax-deferred contributions to any of the several tax-deferred, qualified programs is the deferral of income taxes until the employee withdraws the funds from the annuity (or other tax-deferred plan such as a mutual fund). Ideally, withdrawal takes place in retirement, many years in the future. If the employee had not made the qualified contributions, a significant portion would have gone to government treasuries in the years they were earned. When contributions are made to qualified plans, the money that would otherwise have gone to pay income taxes instead earns investment returns, along with the remainder of the employee's contributions.

A 10 percent federal penalty tax applies to premature withdrawals (those made prior to age fifty-nine and a half). The penalty does not apply to the following:

- Withdrawals due to death
- Withdrawals due to disability
- Payments taken in essentially equal installments over the employee's life expectancy (or the joint life expectancy of the employee and the employee's spouse)
- Withdrawals allocated to contributions made before August 14, 1982
- Withdrawals from a structured settlement contract

The Roth IRA is a program for retirement without tax implication upon distribution, but the contributions are made with after-tax income. The Roth IRA was instituted on January 1, 1998, as a result of the Taxpayer Relief Act of 1997. It provides no tax deduction for contributions, which is not a great incentive to save, but instead it provides a benefit that is not available for any other form of retirement savings. If certain earning requirements are met, all earnings are tax-free when withdrawn. Other benefits included under the Roth IRA are avoiding the early distribution penalty on certain withdrawals and avoiding the need to take minimum distributions after age seventy and a half. Roth IRA is not a pretax contribution type of retirement savings account, but it is the only plan that allows earnings to accumulate without tax implication ever. A regular IRA provides a pretax saving, but the earnings are taxed when they are withdrawn.

Eligibility for the Roth IRA is available even if the employee participates in a retirement plan maintained by the employer. The contribution limits are shown in Tables 21.10 and 21.11. There are earning requirements: (1) for the maximum contribution, the income limits are less than $105,000 for single individuals and less than $166,000 for married individuals filing joint returns; (2) the amount that can be contributed is reduced gradually and then completely eliminated when adjusted gross income is $120,000 or more (single) and $176,000 or more (married, filing jointly).[28]

A regular IRA can be converted to a Roth IRA if (a) the modified adjusted gross income is $100,000 or less, and (b) the employee is single or files jointly with a spouse.[29] Taxes will have to be paid in the year of the conversion.

The Pension Protection Act of 2006 allows IRA owners who are age seventy and a half and over to make tax-free distributions of up to $100,000 directly to tax-exempt charities. Otherwise, if no distribution has been taken, the owner is required to take minimal distribution and pay taxes on that amount as noted above.

The brief description presented here is introductory, and you are advised to consult the many sources for each pension plan on the Internet and in the many books written on the topic.

Roth 401(k) and Roth 403(b) Plans

On January 1, 2006, the IRS provided for **Roth 401(k) and Roth 403(b)**—a new after-tax contribution feature that is part of the EGTRRA 2001 (with a delayed effective date). The same limits that apply to regular 401(k) and 403(b) plans apply to both Roth plans. Thus, if an employee decides to contribute to 401(k) and Roth 401(k), the maximum combined for 2009 is $16,500, plus $5,500 for an employee over the age fifty.[30] Both Roth 401(k) and Roth 403(b) work like a Roth IRA. The deferral is on an after-tax basis and the account is never taxed if it is held for five years. Distributions are allowed after age fifty-nine and a half and after five years in the program. There are no income limits and no coordination limits between a Roth IRA and a Roth 403(b) or Roth IRA and Roth 401(k). ERISA 401(k) plans must include the Roth contributions in the ADP test, but ADP tests do not apply to 403(b) plans, as you already know. The IRS provides ample explanation about these new accounts.[31]

The 2006 act also permanently extended the Roth 401(k) and 403(b) features that were introduced in 2006 and were scheduled to sunset in 2010. Under these provisions, employees are allowed to make after-tax contributions to those accounts. Like the Roth IRA, there is never tax on the earnings for the Roth contributions. This is subject to keeping the money in the account for five years or at least until the account holder reaches age fifty-nine and a half.

Roth 401(k) and Roth 403(b)

After-tax contribution plans created from EGTRRA 2001 that work like the Roth IRA subject to a five-year waiting period and attainment of age fifty-nine and a half for distributions; have no income limits and no coordination limits.

Retirement Savings and the Recession

The prevalence of defined contribution plans, while not preferred by many Americans compared to the security of defined benefit plans, has at least come to be accepted as the way of the world. Individuals understand that the extent to which they are able to accumulate funds for retirement is largely a matter of their own design. A study by the Employee Benefit Research Institute (EBRI) indicates that 67 percent of workers considered defined contribution plans their primary retirement vehicle in 2006, over twice the percentage reported twenty years prior. Conversely, about 31 percent of workers had defined benefit plans as their primary retirement option in 2006 compared to almost 57 percent in 1988. In times of economic prosperity, retirement savings from defined contribution plans can be a boon to employees. In return for accepting the greater risk associated with individual responsibility for funding retirement, employees are rewarded. On the other hand, the negative aspects of shouldering more of this risk are brought into play during economic downturns. The 2008–2009 recession is perhaps the first large-scale test of the resiliency of defined contribution retirement plans under significant market pressures.

The S&P 500 lost 37 percent of its value in 2008. This decline just barely trailed the S&P's worst-ever year of 1937 (during the Great Depression). Many managed funds such as mutual funds, exchange traded funds, and pension funds are made up of investments that are representative of the S&P 500 index's performance. Consequently, proportionate losses were recorded in many individuals' retirement funds, particularly those in defined contribution plans. Even before the negative stock returns could be quantified for the year, the director of Congressional Budget Office, Peter Orszag, reported in October 2008 that retirement savings plans had lost $2 trillion over the previous fifteen months alone. Defined benefit plans lost 15 percent of their assets, and defined contribution plans eroded slightly more. According to EBRI, account balances for 401(k) plans fell between 7.2 and 11.2 percent. Public pension plans (like the 403[b] and Section 457 plans discussed in this chapter) have also been hit hard, losing $300 billion between the second quarter of 2007 and the first quarter of 2008. Investments in equities, like those in the S&P 500, are primarily to blame for these widespread losses and are due to the overall depreciation in stock prices. Also of note are institutional investments by fund managers in mortgage-backed securities (MBSs) that defaulted (as detailed in the box "Problem Investments and the Credit Crisis" in Chapter 7), which in turn devalued portfolios designed for retirement savings.

Those with defined benefit plans may be somewhat comforted by the fact that these plans are insured by the Pension Benefit Guaranty Corporation (PBGC), as discussed in this chapter. Defined benefit recipients will at least get something in the event of private pension fund insolvency. Defined contribution plan participants, however, are largely left to fend for themselves. As a direct consequence of the recession, these employees have seen their account balances shrink and their employers who contributed funds go out of business. EBRI reports that 401(k) account balances in excess of $200,000 have lost 25 percent of their value. This most affects workers between the ages of thirty-six and forty-five who have long tenures with their employers. Much of the growth they have directly contributed to and actively managed over years or decades has been erased in short order—and these employees have less time until retirement to rebuild their accounts than do younger workers. EBRI posits several scenarios under which diminished account balances could be replenished in the future. At a 5 percent return-on-equity rate, for example, workers aged thirty-six to forty-five who incurred moderate losses would need close to two years to restore accounts to their 2008 end-of-year positions. Workers in this age range with the most severe losses would need five years.

Burdens of the recession affecting other areas of workers' lives have also had carryover effects on retirement plans. Individuals struggling to make ends meet are turning to savings, including withdrawals from retirement accounts. Prudential Retirement reports that hardship withdrawals from defined contribution plans increased at a rate of 45 percent throughout 2007 and most of 2008. The short-term benefit of using such funds today produces a long-term shortfall in the form of a future needs funding gap, but for many Americans, this is the only option left. The American Association for Retired Persons (AARP) reports that 20 percent of baby boomers had stopped making voluntary contributions altogether as a consequence of the recession. On the other side of this issue, many employers too announced they were suspending (at least temporarily) matching contributions to employees' 401(k) plans. Such employers include companies like Coca-Cola Bottling, Motorola, UPS, General Motors, and (ironically enough) the AARP. The end result of all these problems is that more and more U.S. workers are choosing to delay their retirement plans. History is bearing this pattern out, and the recession will only serve to accelerate it.

In 1990, 22 percent of individuals aged fifty-five and older were working full-time; by 2007, this had increased to 30 percent. By 2016, it is not inconceivable to speculate that 80 percent of persons fifty-five and older will remain in the work force. As further proof, an AARP poll indicates that 65 percent of workers over age forty-five believe they will need to work for a longer period of time if the economic trend is not soon reversed. When employees do retire, they have little confidence that retirement income will be sufficient to maintain their standards of living, as suggested by the 69 percent of respondents who anticipate cutting back on spending during retirement. Continuing to work beyond one's normal retirement age buys more time to accumulate income for nonworking years and increases the benefit amounts from Social Security and individual retirement options. Working longer may mean putting plans and dreams on hold, but for many Americans looking forward to enjoying any retirement at all, it is the most practical solution. If there's any good news, it's that workers today are in the best position to afford this luxury, with life expectancies (and quality of life) of the population substantially improved over previous generations (as discussed in Chapter 17).

Employees unaccustomed to making long-term investment decisions have understandably found the shift to defined contribution plans jarring. There is some evidence that employers could do a better job of informing workers about the realities of their responsibilities. EBRI found that one in four workers in the fifty-six to sixty-five age range had more than 90 percent of their 401(k) account balances in equities at year-end 2007; two in five had more than 70 percent in equities. This degree of risk is alarming to see for individuals so close to retirement. Rather than dazzling their workers with the array and complexity of investment options available to defined contribution plan participants, employers could instead emphasize sound, basic principles of financial planning. How many employees are guided by the notion that investments should become more conservative over time to preserve accumulated earnings and reduce risk? For example, subtracting one's age from one hundred is a general rule of thumb that could be used to give a rough estimate as to the proportion of retirement assets that should be invested in stocks (with the remainder in lower-risk investments). The financial planning community also stresses the importance of diversification not just to balance risk between bonds and equities, but across different investment sources to ensure that one's savings will not be spoiled because it was concentrated in only a few funds that performed badly. A family needs analysis, incorporating projected future income requirements against earnings from Social Security, personal savings, investments, and employer plans (like the hypothetical cases in Chapter 23 and Chapter 17, Section 6), is another component of responsible retirement planning.

Sources: Nancy Trejos, "Retirement Savings Lose $2 Trillion in 15 Months," Washington Post, October 8, 2008, http://www.washingtonpost.com/wp-dyn/content/article/2008/10/07/AR2008100703358.html?sid=ST2008100702063&s_pos=, accessed March 10, 2009; "New Research from EBRI: Defined Contribution Retirement Plans Increasingly Seen as Primary Type," Reuters, February 9, 2009, http://www.reuters.com/article/pressRelease/idUS166119+09-Feb-2009+PRN20090209, accessed March 10, 2009; Jack VanDerhei, "The Impact of the Recent Financial Crisis on 401(k) Account Balances," Employee Benefit Research Institute (EBRI), February 2009, http://ebri.org/publications/ib/index.cfm?fa=ibDisp&content_id=4192, accessed March 10, 2009; Jim Connolly, "Pru Panelists: Recovery May Be Slow," National Underwriter Life/Health Edition, January 7, 2009, http://www.lifeandhealthinsurancenews.com/News/2009/1/Pages/Pru-Panelists—Recovery-May-Be-Slow.aspx, accessed March 13, 2009; "AARP to Stop Matching 401(k) Contributions," All Things Considered (National Public Radio), March 11, 2009, http://www.npr.org/templates/story/story.php?storyId=101751588, accessed March 13, 2009; Chris Farrell, "Why You'll Work Through Your Retirement," BusinessWeek, January 21, 2009, http://www.businessweek.com/investor/content/jan2009/pi20090121_749273.htm, accessed March 10, 2009; Peter Grier, "Fallout of Stock Market's Plunge: Retirement Woes," Christian Science Monitor, October 17, 2008, http://www.csmonitor.com/2008/1017/p01s06-usec.html, accessed March 10, 2009.

KEY TAKEAWAYS

In this section you studied the types and features of qualified defined benefit plans and defined contribution plans:

- Defined benefit plans require the greatest degree of employer commitment by guaranteeing specified retirement benefits for employees.
    - Defined benefit plans use a benefit formula based on a flat dollar amount, flat percentage of pay, amount unit benefit, or percentage unit benefit.
    - The cash balance plan sets up hypothetical individual retirement accounts for employees and credits participants annually with plan contributions and guarantees minimum interest credit (similar to defined contribution plans, making it a hybrid plan).
    - Defined benefit plans may be integrated with Social Security, they provide cost-of-living adjustments, and all are insured by the PBGC.
    - Salary levels, normal retirement age, employee ages, mortality assumptions, and more influence employer funding obligations, as actuarially determined.
- Defined contribution plans require less employer commitment by guaranteeing only contribution amounts toward employees' retirement accounts
    - Money purchase plan—most common, establishes rate of annual employer contributions such that the benefit at retirement varies with the contribution amount, length of participation, investment earnings, and retirement age
    - Profit-sharing plans—distribute a portion of company profits among participants in relation to salary
    - 401(k) plans—allow employees to defer compensation for retirement before taxes, but employers must pass ADP test to receive tax credits
- Other qualified plans allowing tax-deferred contributions include 403(b), Section 457, Keogh, SEP, and SIMPLE
    - 403(b)—for employees of tax-exempt organizations
    - Section 457—for employees of state and local governments and nonprofit, noneducational institutions
    - Keogh plans—for the self-employed
    - SEP—individual retirement accounts (IRAs) that employers can contribute toward on a tax-deductible basis
    - SIMPLE—for employees of small businesses
- Contributions toward qualified plans and benefits are subject to annual IRS limits, and tax penalties are imposed for taking early distributions
- Individual Retirement Accounts (IRAs)
    - Traditional IRA—allows individuals to defer taxes on account contributions and earnings on contributions until account is withdrawn, subject to annual income and contribution limits; also the vehicle for rolling over employers' sponsored retirement accounts in order to avoid penalties and tax issues
    - Roth IRA—funded with after-tax dollars, but earnings on the account are never taxed, even when drawn upon at retirement, subject to annual income and contribution limits
    - Roth 401(k) and Roth 403(b)—after-tax contribution plans created from EGTRRA 2001 that work like the Roth IRA subject to a five-year waiting period and attainment of age fifty-nine and a half for distributions; have no income limits and no coordination limits

1. As an employee with a defined benefit pension plan, which would you prefer: a flat amount benefit formula that specifies $1,000 per month, or a percentage unit benefit formula that figures your benefit to be 1.5 percent per year times your average annual salary for your highest three consecutive years of employment? Explain your answer.

2. As an employer, would you prefer a defined contribution pension plan or a defined benefit plan? Explain your answer.

3. What are the primary differences between a defined benefit plan and a defined contribution plan? Create a matrix and include discussion about:

   a. Who bears the risk of investment?

   b. What are the actuarial complexities?

   c. What is fixed, contributions or benefits?

   d. Are there separate accounts?

   e. Is the plan insured?

   f. Is the plan better for older or for younger employees?

4. What is a cash balance plan? What is a cash balance conversion and what employees does it favor?

5. What are the different types of deferred compensation plans available to employers?

6. Some employers have deferred profit-sharing plans instead of defined benefit or defined contribution money purchase plans. Why?

7. As an employee, would you prefer a deferred or an immediate (cash at the end of the year) profit-sharing plan? If your income doubled, would your choice change? Explain your answer.

8. Compare the traditional IRA with the Roth IRA.

9. What conditions need to be met for an employer to receive tax credits for a 401(k) plan?

10. What type of pension benefit plan best meet the needs of small employers? What are its advantages over other types of plans?

4. ANNUITIES

LEARNING OBJECTIVES

In this section we elaborate on the following key features of annuities:

- **Parties to an annuity**
- **Mechanics of annuities**
- **Annuity settlement options**
- **The use of annuity contracts**
- **Tax treatment of annuities**

The discussion of employer-provided pensions and IRAs in the previous section emphasized the importance of selecting the right investment vehicle for the individual. This is even prevalent as employers are opting to provide more enhanced 401(k) plans rather than the traditional defined benefits plans. Annuities, which offer features not available in any other investment products, are provided by insurance companies to help individuals accumulate funds for retirement. During preretirement years, annuities are primarily investment vehicles. During retirement years, the product provides a periodic payment that continues throughout a fixed period and/or for the duration of a life or lives. Although annuities are frequently used to save for retirement, their unique function is the scientific (actuarially computed) liquidation of a principal sum, usually during retirement years. During this period, they protect against the risk of outliving the financial resources invested earlier in the annuity. If the duration of payment from an annuity depends upon the expected length of a life or lives, the contract is known as a **life annuity**.

life annuity

Contract in which the duration of payment from an annuity depends upon the expected length of a life or lives.

4.1 Parties to an Annuity

The person or entity that purchases an annuity is the **owner**. The person on whose life expectancy payments are based is known as the **annuitant**. For annuities sold directly to individuals, the owner and annuitant are usually the same person. The **beneficiary** is the person or entity who receives any death benefits due at the death of the annuitant.

4.2 Mechanics of Annuities

Accumulation versus Liquidation

The time during which premiums are being paid and benefits (distribution) have not begun is called the **accumulation period**. The value of the contract during this period consists of premiums plus investment earnings minus expenses and is called the **accumulation value**. The time during which the accumulation value and future investment returns are being liquidated by benefit payments is called the **liquidation period**.

Premium Payments

Annuities may be bought either on the installment plan or with a single premium. Most people use the installment plan. Usually, the owner chooses a flexible plan in which premiums may vary in amount and frequency. In the event the annuitant dies before benefit payments begin, deferred annuities sold to individuals promise to return the accumulation value at the time of death.

Deferred annuity on the installment plan is a savings program during the accumulation period. There is no protection (insurance) element involved—not any more than would be the case with monthly deposits in a savings account at the bank. The insurance or mortality element is only part of the distribution over the life of the annuitant. The payments are promised to last for the life of the annuitant even in cases of living longer than the life expectancy.

Commencement of Benefits

Annuities may be classified as either immediate or deferred, reflecting when benefit payments begin. An **immediate annuity** begins payments at the next payment interval (e.g., month, quarter, or year) after purchase. They require a single premium. A **deferred annuity** begins payments sometime in the future as elected by the owner, such as at age sixty-five. Deferred annuities may be funded by a single premium; equal installments; or, more commonly, by flexible premiums.

owner
The person or entity that purchases an annuity.

annuitant
The person on whose life expectancy payments are based.

beneficiary
The person or entity who receives any death benefits due at the death of the annuitant.

accumulation period
The time during which premiums are being paid toward an annuity and benefits (distribution) have not begun.

accumulation value
The value of the annuity contract during the accumulation period; consists of premiums plus investment earnings minus expenses.

liquidation period
The time during which the accumulation value and future investment returns of an annuity contract are being liquidated by benefit payments.

immediate annuity
Begins payments at the next payment interval (e.g., month, quarter, or year) after purchase; requires a single premium.

deferred annuity
Begins payments sometime in the future as elected by the owner, such as at age sixty-five; may be funded by a single premium, equal installments, or, more commonly, by flexible premiums.

Level of Benefits

During the accumulation period and the liquidation period, the annuity is classified as either a fixed-dollar annuity or a variable annuity. A **fixed-dollar annuity** earns investment returns at rates guaranteed by the insurer, subject to periodic changes in the guaranteed rate for the next period. A set amount of benefit per dollar of accumulation (varying also by life expectancy when benefits begin) is paid during the liquidation period. **Variable annuity** returns vary with the investment performance of special investment accounts. The amount of benefit payment may vary from month to month or at another interval.

4.3 Settlement Options

Generally, an annuity owner does not set a precise retirement income goal in advance. The retirement benefit is whatever amount has accumulated by retirement time. Further, the amount accumulated is a function of the amount of contributions, their timing, and the rates of investment return credited to the account over time. This concept is illustrated in Figure 21.3. If the annuitant dies before beginning the annuity payments, the accumulation value is returned to the beneficiary. When the annuitant lives until the liquidation period and selects an income option based on the life expectancy of the annuitant alone, it is considered a **single life annuity**.

FIGURE 21.3 Hypothetical Values for the Flexible Premium, Deferred Annuity Concept

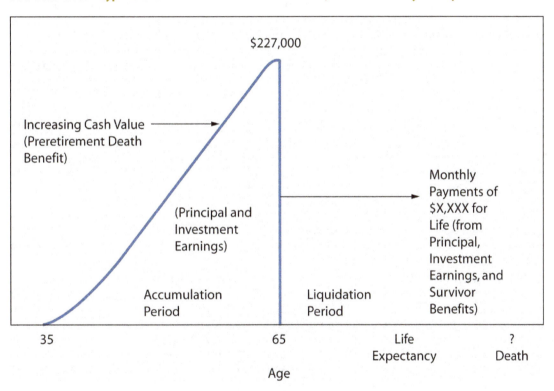

The originally specified retirement date can be changed after the annuity is purchased. Upon retirement, there are several options for settlement, similar to the ones shown in Chapter 19 for life insurance proceeds:

- Lump-sum cash payment
- Fixed period payment
- Fixed amount payment
- Life annuity
- Refund annuity
- Temporary life annuity
- Period-certain life annuity
- Joint life annuity
- Joint-and-survivor annuity

fixed dollar annuity

Earns investment returns at rates guaranteed by the insurer, subject to periodic changes in the guaranteed rate for the next period; a set amount of benefit per dollar of accumulation (varying also by life expectancy when benefits begin) is paid during the liquidation period.

variable annuity

Returns vary with the investment performance of special investment accounts; the amount of benefit payment may vary from month to month or at another interval.

single life annuity

When the income option is based on the life expectancy of the annuitant alone, assuming the annuitant lives until the liquidation period.

fixed period annuity

Makes payments for a specified period, such as twenty years, and then ceases.

fixed amount annuity

Pays benefits of a set amount per period until the accumulation value at the time benefits begin plus investment earning during the liquidation period are exhausted.

The typical options include taking cash in a lump sum equal to the accumulation value of the contract. A **fixed period annuity** makes payments for a specified period, such as twenty years, and then ceases. A **fixed amount annuity** pays benefits of a set amount per period until the accumulation value at the time benefits begin plus investment earning during the liquidation period are exhausted. The amount paid under these three options is not influenced by anyone's life expectancy.

As with whole life or universal life policies, there are mortality factors and investment return factors that are guaranteed. The mortality guarantee is in case a person lives longer than expected. Unlike a regular savings account, where the recipient of the money gets only the total amount in the account, in annuities, the payments are promised for the duration of the annuitant's life. The insurance company is taking the risk of paying more to someone who lives longer than expected according to mortality tables. This is the mortality guarantee.

An annuity in which benefit payments are guaranteed for life but then cease and the premium is considered fully earned upon the death of the annuitant is known as a life annuity. In this case, no beneficiary will receive any more payments even if the annuitant dies very early. While this annuity pays the maximum periodic benefit per dollar accumulated at the time benefits begin (or per immediate single premium), far more common is the selection of a payment option that provides continuation of payments to beneficiaries for a certain amount of time, such as ten or twenty years following the death of the annuitant. Most people do not like the idea that they might die shortly after beginning to receive benefit payments from an annuity in which they have made a large investment. Therefore, insurers have made available refund annuities, period-certain life annuities, and annuities like joint-and-survivor that reflect the life expectancies of more than one person.

temporary life annuity

Combination of a fixed period annuity and a life annuity; payments stop at the end of a specified period or at the death of the annuitant, whichever comes first.

period-certain option

Guarantees a minimum number of annuity payments whether the annuitant lives or dies.

refund annuity

Guarantees that the annuitant and/or beneficiary will receive, during the liquidation period, minimum payments equal to the single premium in an immediate annuity or the accumulation value in a deferred annuity.

joint annuity

Names two annuitants and payments stop when the first joint annuitant dies.

joint-and-survivor annuity

Names two annuitants and continues payments as long as at least one annuitant is alive.

A **temporary life annuity** is a combination of a fixed period annuity and a life annuity. Payments stop at the end of a specified period or at the death of the annuitant, whichever comes first. A **period-certain option** guarantees a minimum number of annuity payments whether the annuitant lives or dies. Thus, a person can purchase a life annuity with five years certain, ten years certain, or some other period certain. If the annuitant dies before the end of the specified period, payments continue to a beneficiary for at least the period specified. A cash payment may be available to the beneficiary equal to the present value of the remaining payments. If the annuitant lives through the period certain, payments continue until death.

A **refund annuity** guarantees that the annuitant and/or beneficiary will receive, during the liquidation period, minimum payments equal to the single premium in an immediate annuity or the accumulation value in a deferred annuity. For example, assume an accumulation value of $250,000 at the time of annuitization and that the annuitant receives $100,000 before death. The beneficiary would receive a lump-sum payment of $150,000. The annuitant is also promised lifetime benefits. Consequently, benefits can far exceed the accumulation value of $250,000 at the time of annuitization plus future investment earnings on this amount. The annuitant pays for the refund feature by taking a reduced amount of periodic benefit compared to what he or she would receive for a life annuity. He or she would also pay for any other options to guarantee certain payments to beneficiaries are paid with a reduced amount of periodic payments.

With a **joint annuity**, two people are named, and payments stop when the first joint annuitant dies. In contrast to the joint annuity, a **joint-and-survivor annuity** continues payments as long as at least one annuitant is alive. You may recall that the joint-and-survivor annuity is the mode required in pensions unless the spouse relinquishes this benefit. In annuities sold by insurers, husbands and wives are the typical users of the joint-and-survivor option. They can decide at the time of annuitization whether payments should continue at the same amount after one spouse dies or if the amount should be reduced (perhaps to one-half or two-thirds of the original amount). Some annuitants want the full refund guaranteed by the refund option, while others are satisfied with a period-certain guaranteed. Others select a joint or joint-and-survivor option because of concern for another person, possibly over their lifetime. The effect of such guarantees is to reduce the monthly installments that can be purchased with any given sum of money. The option selected depends on one's situation and viewpoint.

4.4　Types of Contracts

Annuities commonly used to help fund retirement include the following:

- Flexible premium annuity
- Single premium deferred annuity
- Single premium immediate annuity

All are available with fixed-dollar guarantees, as a variable or as index annuities.

The **flexible premium deferred annuity** allows you to change the amount of contributions, stop contributions, and resume them at will. For example, you may use a payroll deduction plan in which you authorize your employer to transfer $100 per pay period to the insurer. For a period of time, you may want to discontinue these contributions and later resume them at $200 per pay period. Without payroll deductions, you might prefer to submit premiums on a monthly, quarterly, annual, or some other basis. Earlier in the chapter, we referred to this as the installment plan.

For fixed-dollar annuities, the insurer guarantees a minimum rate of interest. Initially, a current rate of return is promised on funds in your account for a certain time (e.g., two years) during the accumulation period. Returns vary over time on your insurer's investments that support fixed-dollar annuities, so the guarantee for future periods is likely to change. The degree of change may, in part, reflect the need for your insurer to remain competitive with annuity returns offered by other insurers, bank certificates of deposit, and other competing investment vehicles. Often, two or more interest guarantees are made by the insurer. One set of guarantees applies to funds contributed to the account in past periods. The other rate applies to funds contributed during a future period.

The **single premium deferred annuity** differs from a flexible premium deferred annuity primarily in the manner of premium payments. As the name implies, only one premium is paid. The motivation for purchase usually is driven more by the tax deferral of interest on earnings than by the promise of lifetime income during retirement. Another difference between the single premium deferred annuity and its flexible premium cousin is the longer period to which the current rate of interest is guaranteed

Many insurers have either a low or no sales load, which is basically a surrender charge (a percentage attached to withdrawals) that applies during the first five or more years. For example, 7 percent of the amount withdrawn can be retained by the insurer if the contract is surrendered for its cash value in the first year. The penalty decreases 1 percent per year, disappearing at the end of the seventh year. The surrender charge has two purposes. First, it discourages withdrawals. Second, it allows the insurer to recover some of its costs if the contract is terminated early.

The agent or broker may receive a normal level of sales commission on no-load and low-load annuities, but the commission is not deducted directly from the contributions. Annual expense charges levied on all assets are usually around 2 percent. Part of this charge is used to pay marketing expenses.

The **single premium immediate annuity** is best understood by emphasizing the word *immediate*. Benefit payments to the annuitant begin on the next payment date following the premium payment, usually a large sum. The primary purchase motive would typically be interest in lifetime income. A primary source of funds for these annuities is lump-sum distributions from corporate retirement plans, as discussed in the next section. Other sources of funds include various forms of personal investment and life insurance death benefits.

Another use of annuities arises out of legal liability judgments. Liability insurers are increasingly interested in making periodic payments to the plaintiff, to lower the total cost of the liability. A **structured settlement annuity** is a special type of single premium immediate annuity that achieves the goal. Issued by a life insurer, its terms are negotiated by the plaintiff, the defendant, their attorneys, and a structured settlement specialist. The market for structured settlement annuities is highly competitive. Consequently, the successful insurer in this market is likely to have a high rating for financial soundness, a competitive assumed rate of investment return, and a mortality assumption that reflects the plaintiff's life expectancy.

Variable Annuities

Variable annuities are more complicated than fixed-dollar annuities and are similar in concept to variable life insurance, which is discussed in Chapter 19. They are available as single premium annuity or immediate or deferred annuities.

In the variable annuity, two types of units are employed: accumulation units and annuity units. Some accounts invest primarily in variable-dollar assets such as common stocks and real estate. Investments are made in accounts that are kept separate from the insurers' general funds. These are called separate accounts in the insurer's annual statement, and their significance will be covered in the next section. The value of each unit varies with the current market value of the underlying investments in the portfolio.

As premiums are paid, the account is credited with a number of **accumulation units**, the number to be determined by (1) the amount of premium and (2) the current market value of an accumulation unit. For example, if the monthly premium after expenses is $50 and the current value of a unit is $10, the account is credited with five units. If the current value of a unit has changed to $9.52, the account is credited with 5.25 units. The surrender value, or maximum withdrawal, at a specific point in the accumulation period is:

(Total number of units × Current market value per unit) − Surrender charge, if any = Surrender value

flexible premium deferred annuity
Allows owners to change the amount of contributions, stop contributions, and resume them at will.

single premium deferred annuity
Requires payment of a single premium and a stipulates a longer period to which a current rate of interest is guaranteed.

single premium immediate annuity
Begins benefit payments to the annuitant on the next payment date following the premium payment, usually as a large sum.

structured settlement annuity
Makes periodic payments to a plaintiff in a legal liability judgment to lower the total cost of liability.

accumulation units
Credits variable annuity accounts when premiums are paid, as determined by the amount of premium and current market value.

This same calculation determines the death benefit received by the beneficiary in case of the annuitant's death during the accumulation period.

During the liquidation or distribution period, **annuity units** are exchanged for accumulation units. The determinants of the dollar income are (1) the current market value of each unit; (2) an assumed investment return, such as 4 percent; and (3) the number of units considering the age, gender, and settlement option of the annuitant. Because women live longer, gender is important in determining the periodic amount paid. Women of the same age as men will receive a smaller periodic payment for an equal accumulated account. If the investments perform better than the assumed return, the income will be greater. Many variable annuities offer a choice of investment mediums. The choices are similar to those for a family of mutual funds. In fact, some variable annuities are funded by a family of mutual funds rather than by separate accounts maintained by the insurer. For example, your variable annuity might offer the following separate accounts:

- Money market
- Long-term commercial bond fund
- High-grade common stocks
- Balanced fund with bonds and stocks
- Growth stocks

The funds can be divided among two or more accounts in a manner that reflects your personal risk propensity.

Guaranteed Minimum Withdrawal Benefits[32]

A special type of variable annuity providing a guaranteed minimum withdrawal benefit (GMWB) has become problematic for annuity companies throughout the 2008–2009 recession. GMWB annuities promise fixed minimum income benefits, and they are attractive to consumers because of their expected provision for growth of future benefits based on positive investment returns (as mentioned above). However, with upfront investments in stocks, real estate, and mutual funds rapidly eroding—or performing poorly due to low interest rates—over the course of the 2008–2009 recession, companies are struggling to provide even the minimum guaranteed withdrawal rate to holders of GMWB annuities. The opportunity for growth of future income streams, therefore, seems a far-off prospect to annuitants.

As a hedge against the falling value of GMWB annuities, insurers are required to increase their reserves to assure customers of solvency. Consequently, more liability must be added to companies' books (which may also be contaminated by bad debt taken on during the credit crisis), forcing them to draw upon and deplete working capital as a recourse. This was one of the reasons that the three major rating agencies downgraded numerous life and annuity companies in late 2008 and early 2009 (see the box, "The Life/Health Industry in the Economic Recession of 2008–2009" in Chapter 19). The industry has petitioned the National Association of Insurance Commissioners (NAIC) to lower reserve requirements, a request already denied once. Even if the NAIC does revise its position on reserves, the effect would be only a superficial appearance of improved net worth. The rating agencies typically do not modify ratings in response to accounting changes. Therefore, the future solvency of carriers offering GMWB annuities remains an important concern to both the industry and consumers.

Index Annuities

Equity indexed annuities are annuities with returns linked to the S&P 500, with guarantees of investment or to some fixed interest rate indexes. Some index annuities have several so-called buckets of investment mixes, including one that has a fixed interest rate. The appeal of these annuities is the opportunity to earn more returns yet retain the minimum guarantees.

4.5 Taxation of Annuities

The first major tax question is, Can individuals deduct annuity contributions (premiums) from adjusted gross income each year? Generally, premiums are not deductible. The exception is when annuities are invested in any of the pension plans described in this chapter.

When an annuity is purchased separately from any pension plan by individuals, the premiums paid are from after-tax income. During the accumulation period with these annuities, no income taxes are due on the returns unless the annuitant is making withdrawals or surrenders. When the annuity is distributed to the annuitant, only the earnings (not the premiums) are subject to income tax. When annuities are used as investment instruments in pensions or in IRAs, they are considered tax-deferred annuities. The premiums are paid with before-tax income. Distributions from tax-deferred annuities are subject to income taxation on the whole account. All payments from a tax-deferred annuity are subject to ordinary income taxes during the liquidation period.

annuity units

Exchanged for accumulation units during an annuity's liquidation or distribution period, as determined by current market value, assumed investment return, and key features of the annuitant.

For annuities that are bought with after-tax money by individuals, ordinary income taxes are paid on the return of (previously untaxed) investment earnings. The amount of each payment returned during the distribution of the annuity represents previously taxed contributions. These are not taxed again. Therefore, each payment is divided between taxable and nontaxable amounts at the beginning of the payout period by calculating an **exclusion ratio**. The ratio is then multiplied by each periodic payment to determine the amount of each annuity payment that is excluded from gross income. The exclusion ratio is the following:

$$\frac{\text{Investment in contract}}{\text{Expected return}}$$

exclusion ratio

Expression of annuity payments during distribution as taxable and nontaxable portions and calculated as investment in contract divided by expected return.

KEY TAKEAWAYS

In this section you studied different types of annuities, which are retirement investment and distribution vehicles:

- Annuities can be purchased on either an installment plan or a single premium.
- Annuities are classified as immediate or deferred, depending on when benefit payments begin.
- Annuities are classified as either fixed-dollar or variable during accumulation and liquidation.
- Settlement options for annuities include lump-sum cash payment, fixed-period payment, fixed-amount payment, life annuity, refund annuity, temporary life annuity, period-certain life annuity, joint life annuity, and joint-and-survivor annuity.
- Mortality and investment return factors are guaranteed in annuities, adding to the issuer's risk.
- The following annuities are commonly used to fund retirement, all available with fixed-dollar guarantees, as variable or index annuities: flexible premium, single premium deferred, and single premium immediate.
- Variable annuities are available in single premium, immediate, or deferred options and employ accumulation units and annuity units.
- Index annuities have returns linked to the S&P 500 with guarantees of investment, or to fixed interest rate indexes.
- Premiums invested in qualified pension plans are tax-deductible.
- Distributions from annuities funded with after-tax dollars are not taxable; distributions from annuities funded with tax-deferred, before-tax dollars (as in pension plans) are taxable.
- The exclusion ratio is used to determine the taxable (investment earnings) and nontaxable (return of after-tax principal) portions of annuity payments during distribution.

DISCUSSION QUESTIONS

1. Why might an individual purchase a single premium annuity if he or she can just invest the money and live off the proceeds?
2. Meg Cohen is about to turn sixty-five and retire from her job as a school librarian. When she retires, she will receive a lump-sum pension disbursement of $320,000. She plans to place the money in an annuity, but she is having trouble deciding among three different annuity options:

    - Option 1: fixed period annuity
    - Option 2: single life annuity
    - Option 3: refund annuity

    What are the advantages and disadvantages of each option?
3. Explain the differences among a fixed-dollar annuity, a variable annuity, and an indexed annuity.
4. Why do you suppose the flexible premium annuity is the most popular form of deferred annuity?
5. Who assumes the investment risk in variable annuities? Does the same party assume mortality and operating expense risk?

5. PENSION PLAN FUNDING TECHNIQUES

LEARNING OBJECTIVES

In this section we elaborate on the employer's pension plan funding options, which include the following:

- **Noninsured trust plans**
- **Insured plans: group deferred annuity, deposit administration, immediate participation guarantee (IPG) contract, separate account plans, guaranteed investment contract (GIC)**

ERISA requires advance funding of qualified pension plans. An advance funded plan accumulates funds during the period in which employees are actively working for the organization. Pension expense is charged against earned income while pension obligations are accumulating instead of being deferred until employees have retired. Pension plans are funded either through noninsured trust plans or insured plans.

The Pension Protection Act of 2006 includes provisions to strengthen the funding of defined benefits plans. Plans are required to be fully funded over a seven-year period.

5.1 Noninsured Trust Plans

noninsured trust plan

Pension plan funding technique whereby the employer creates a trust to accumulate funds and disburse benefits; the trustee may be an individual, a bank, a trust company, an insurer, or some combination of cotrustees whose responsibilities are to invest funds contributed by the employer to the trust (and by employees, if contributory); accumulate earnings; and pay benefits to eligible employees.

With a **noninsured trust plan**, the employer creates a trust to accumulate funds and disburse benefits. The trustee may be an individual, a bank, a trust company, an insurer, or some combination of cotrustees. The duties of the trustee are to invest the funds contributed by the employer to the trust (and by the employees, if contributory), accumulate the earnings, and pay benefits to eligible employees. The trustee makes no guarantee with regard to earnings or investments.

Under a defined benefit trust plan, a consulting actuary is employed to estimate the sums that should be put into the trust. The employer is, in effect, a self-insurer. The consulting actuary does not guarantee that the estimates will be accurate. There is also no guarantee as to the expense of operating the plan. Thus, the employer that chooses a noninsured trust to fund a defined benefit plan should be large enough and financially strong enough to absorb differences between actual experience and past estimates of mortality, investment returns, and other cost factors.

5.2 Insured Plans

Several insurer options are available for funding pension plans. These are group deferred annuity contracts, group deposit administration contracts, immediate participation guarantee contracts, separate accounts, and guaranteed investment contracts.

Group Deferred Annuity Contracts

group deferred annuity

Insured pension funding option that is a contract between insurer and employer to provide for the purchase of specified amounts of deferred annuity for employees each year.

The **group deferred annuity** is a contract between the insurer and the employer to provide for the purchase of specified amounts of deferred annuity for employees each year. For example, an annuity that would pay retirees $50 per month beginning at age sixty-five might be purchased by the employer from the insurer each year for each employee. The employer receives a master deferred annuity contract, and certificates of participation are given to individuals covered by the plan. Group plans usually require some minimum number of participants to lower administrative expenses per employee.

Under this plan, all actuarial work is done by the insurer, which also provides administrative and investment services. Neither the employees nor the employer are subject to the risks of investment return fluctuations. The only risk is the possible failure of the insurers. The employer's only responsibilities are to report essential information to the insurer and to pay the premiums.

Group Deposit Administration Contracts

The **deposit administration** arrangement requires the employer to make regular payments to the insurance company on behalf of employees, and these contributions accumulate interest. An actuary estimates the amount of annual employer deposits necessary to accumulate sufficient funds to purchase annuities when employees retire. The insurer guarantees the principal of funds deposited, as well as a specified minimum rate of interest. However, the insurer has no direct responsibility to employees until they retire, at which time an annuity is purchased for them. Before retirement, the employee's position is similar to that under an uninsured trust plan. After retirement, the employee's position is the same as it would be with a group deferred annuity contract.

Immediate Participation Guarantee Contracts

The **immediate participation guarantee (IPG) contract** plan is a form of deposit administration; the employer makes regular deposits to a fund managed by the insurance company. The insurer receives deposits and makes investments. An IPG may be structured like a trust plan in that the insurer makes no guarantee concerning the safety of investments or their rate of return. However, some IPGs may guarantee the fund principal and a minimum rate of return.

The IPG is distinct from other deposit administration contracts and attractive to employers because it gives employers more flexibility after an employee retires. The employer has the option to pay retirement benefits directly from the IPG fund rather than locking into an annuity purchased from the insurer. This gives the employer control over the funds for a longer period. The employer can also purchase an annuity for the retired employee.

Separate Accounts

Separate account plans are another modification of deposit administration contracts and are designed to give the insurer greater investment flexibility. The contributions are not commingled with the insurer's other assets and therefore are not subject to the same investment limitations. At least part of the employer's contributions is placed in separate accounts for investment in common stocks. Other separate accounts pool money for investment in bonds, mortgages, real estate, and other assets. Usually, the funds of many employers are pooled for investment purposes, although a large firm may arrange for a special, separate account exclusively for its own funds. Separate accounts may be used to fund either fixed-dollar or variable annuity benefits.

Guaranteed Investment Contracts

Guaranteed investment contracts (GICs) are arrangements used by insurers to guarantee competitive rates of return on large, lump-sum transfers (usually $100,000 or more) of pension funds, usually from another type of funding instrument. For example, an employer may terminate a trust plan and transfer all the funds in the trust to an insurer who promises to pay an investment return of 7 percent for each of the next ten years. At the end of the specified period, the GIC arrangement ends and the fund balance is paid to the original investor, who may decide to reinvest in another GIC.

deposit administration

Insured pension funding arrangement that requires the employer to make regular payments (as determined by actuaries) to the insurance company on behalf of employees, and these contributions accumulate at interest.

immediate participation guarantee (IPG) contract

Insured pension funding plan that is a form of deposit administration whereby the employer makes regular deposits to a fund managed by the insurance company and the insurer receives deposits and makes investments.

separate account plans

Insured pension funding plans that are a modification of deposit administration contracts designed to give the insurer greater investment flexibility; contributions are not commingled with the insurer's other assets and not subject to the same investment limitations.

guaranteed investment contracts (GICs)

Insured pension funding arrangements used by insurers to guarantee competitive rates of return on large, lump-sum transfers (usually $100,000 or more) of pension funds, usually from another type of funding instrument.

KEY TAKEAWAYS

In this section you studied the methods of funding retirement benefit plans, as required by ERISA:

- The employer assumes all retirement plan funding and benefit obligations in noninsured trust plans; the trustee makes no guarantee regarding earnings or investments and may be an individual, bank, trust company, insurer, or combination of cotrustees.
- Funding of pension plans can be insured through several options.
    - Group deferred annuity—insurer handles all actuarial, administrative, and investment services
    - Deposit administration—insurer guarantees the principal and a specified rate of interest, but has no direct responsibility to retirees
    - Immediate participation guarantee (IPG) contract—form of deposit administration that may be structured like a trust plan
    - Separate account plans—form of deposit administration contract giving the insurer greater investment flexibility
    - Guaranteed investment contracts (GICs)—used to guarantee competitive rates of return on large transfers of pension funds from another type of funding instrument

DISCUSSION QUESTIONS

1. Under what circumstances might an employer fund retirement plans through a noninsured trust plan?
2. What makes an IPG contract more attractive to employers?
3. Explain the difference between a group deferred annuity contract and a deposit administration contract. Which offers more protection to employers against the risk of inadequate funding of a promised, defined benefit?
4. Compare variable annuities with index annuities.

6. REVIEW AND PRACTICE

1. Which is preferable from an employee's point of view: a defined contribution or a defined benefit pension plan? Explain your answer.

2. Henry Wooster meets with the employee benefits manager to discuss enrolling in the company's 401(k) plan. He finds that if he enrolls, he must choose the amount of salary to defer and also direct his fund investment. Having no college education and no business experience, Henry lacks confidence about making these decisions.

    a. Should Henry enroll in the 401(k) plan? Do the advantages outweigh the difficulties he may have in managing the plan?

    b. What would you recommend that Henry do to educate himself about fund management? How can the benefits manager help?

    c. Is it appropriate for the employer to establish a plan that requires employees to take so much responsibility for retirement planning? Explain your answer.

3. As an employee benefits manager, you must recommend to the firm's CEO a defined contribution plan to add to the existing defined benefit retirement plan. First, describe a hypothetical firm, giving the size of the firm, its profitability, and the stability of its work force. Then explain your choice of a deferred profit-sharing plan, a 401(k), a money purchase plan, or some combination of these.

4. The law firm of Dunham, Chapman, & Hart has five employees. Following is information regarding these employees:

Employee	Age	Salary	Position
Dunham	57	$240,000	Partner
Chapman	34	$180,000	Partner
Hart	58	$110,000	Partner
Perez	38	$60,000	Associate
McCall	27	$40,000	Paralegal

The partners talked to Rollings Benefits Consultants about the best-qualified pension plan for the firm in light of their major success in and anticipated growth in profits in the coming years. Rollings Benefits created a presentation of a possible plan that showed the maximum possible contributions for the highly paid employees (the partners). Under this proposal, what qualified plan do you think Rollings Consultants suggested to Dunham, Chapman, & Hart? The objective is to give highly paid employees the highest possible contributions. Explain the proposal.

5. Cash balance plans have become increasingly popular in recent years. Why do employers like cash balance plans relative to other types of defined benefit plans?

6. The VA Regional Bank employs 5,300 full-time employees. It is a privately owned corporation that was established in 1972 and has been very successful, despite the recession, because of the conservative investments of the owners. All employees work at least thirty hours a week. The management team has expanded and now includes 830 highly compensated employees. The VA Regional Bank has had an established traditional integrated defined benefit plan for the past twenty years. Despite its major success, management decided to follow the lead of converting traditional defined benefit plans to cash balance plans. There are many good reasons to do so, but management is worried about the impact on some segments of its work force. In a survey they conducted, they saw a high level of resistance by many employees. The case has been a topic of much discussion in the media and in Congress, and it is under the jurisdiction of the 2006 Pension Protection Act. Respond to the following:

   a. Design the formula for the traditional integrated defined benefit plan that you think the company currently provides based on what you learned in this chapter.

   b. Design the formula for the cash balance plan that you think the company is contemplating for its employees.

   c. Who benefits most from each of these plans? Compare your answers in (a) and (b). Why do you think so many employees expressed resistance to the possibility of a cash balance plan?

7. What are the ramifications of terminating a defined benefits pension plan? (Refer to the box, "Cash Balance Conversions: Who Gets Hurt?" and the PBGC Web site.)

8. The following table shows the five employees of the law firm of Tayka, Mooney & Ruhn, plus some information about each.

Employee	Age	Salary	Position
Tayka	37	$210,000	Partner
Mooney	34	$160,000	Partner
Ruhn	28	$110,000	Partner
Davies	38	$60,000	Associate
Edmundsen	27	$40,000	Paralegal

   a. Rollings Consultants explain to the owners of Tayka, Mooney & Ruhn the problems that may occur with 401(k) plans. They show an example of how the company can fail the ADP test and how highly paid employees would not be able to take all the deductions they want. Pretend you are the Rollings consultant. Show such an example and give the firm some methods to overcome this problem. Use the table above to calculate an example and explain your answer.

   b. If the company decides to start a profit-sharing plan with $35,000 the first year, how much will be allocated to each employee?

9. The Children Dentistry Place is a successful fifteen-year-old professional firm with five employees. Following is information regarding these employees (note their ages):

Employees	Age	Salary	Years of Service	Position
Marie	55	$320,000	15	Part owner
Stan	55	$220,000	15	Part owner
Dan	35	$70,000	5	Assistant
Elli	30	$70,000	13	Assistant
Shannon	50	$60,000	12	Office manager

The firm is interested in establishing a defined contribution pension plan. Because the business is doing so well, the top employees want to maximize the contribution for themselves but not for the other employees.

    a. Given the age of the top employees, what defined contribution pension plan would you suggest?

    b. Using the plan you think will work best for them, show the contribution for each employee. Explain your answer.

    c. What types of loans and distributions are permitted under the plan you designed?

    d. Describe ERISA requirements regarding survivors.

10. Prepare a matrix comparing the differences among the following:

    a. IRA and Roth IRA

    b. 401(k) and ESOP

    c. 403(b) or 457 (select one of the two plans)

    d. SEP or SIMPLE plans (select one of the two plans)

Make sure to include the following:

- Who or what organizations should use each plan? What are the limitations?
- What are the unique characteristics of each plan?
- Who is eligible?
- What are the provisions for loans and distributions?

11. Jackson Appliances has twelve employees. The owner, Zena Jackson, is considering some system to reward them for their loyalty and to provide some funds to help them with their living expenses after they retire. Explain why a SEP might be a good choice for the company and explain how it works. Are there other alternatives Zena should consider?

12. What is the primary way in which a single premium deferred annuity differs from a flexible premium deferred annuity? How might the typical motivations for purchase differ for investors in these two types of annuities?

ENDNOTES

1. Employee Benefits Research Institute, *EBRI Databook on Employee Benefits*, ch. 2: "Finances of the Employee Benefit System," updated September 2008, http://www.ebri.org (accessed April 17, 2009).

2. Judy Greenwald, "Desire for Certainty, Savings Drives Shift from DB Plans," *Business Insurance*, September 19, 2005, http://www.businessinsurance.com/cgi-bin/article.pl?articleId=17551&a=a&bt=desire+for+certainty,+savings (accessed April 17, 2009); Jerry Geisel, "HP to Phase out Defined Benefit Plan," *Business Insurance*, July 25, 2005, http://www.businessinsurance.com/cgi-bin/article.pl?articleId=17263&a=a&bt=hp+to+phase+out (accessed April 17, 2009); Jerry Geisel, "Congress Responds to Pension Failure Stories," *Business Insurance*, July 11, 2005, http://www.businessinsurance.com/cgi-bin/article.pl?articleId=17156&a=a&bt=pension+failure+stories (accessed April 17, 2009).

3. Matt Brady, "ACLI: Bush Is Right About the Boomers," *National Underwriter Online News Service*, February 1, 2006, http://www.lifeandhealthinsurancenews.com/News/2006/2/Pages/ACLI--Bush-Is-Right-About-The-Boomers.aspx?k=bush+is+right+about+the+boomers (accessed April 17, 2009).

4. Pension Benefit Guaranty Corporation (PBGC) News Division, "PBGC Announces Maximum Insurance Benefit for 2009," November 3, 2008, http://www.pbgc.gov/media/news-archive/news-releases/2008/pr09-03.html (accessed April 17, 2009).

5. Kara Scannell, "Public Pensions Come Up Short as Stocks' Swoon Drains Funds," *Wall Street Journal*, August 16, 2002.

6. Elisabeth Bumiller, "Bush Signs Bill Aimed at Fraud in Corporations," *New York Times*, July 30, 2002.

7. Greg Hitt, "Bush Signs Sweeping Legislation Aimed at Curbing Business Fraud," *Wall Street Journal*, July 21, 2002.

8. Jerry Geisel, "Senate Finance Committee Passes 401(k) Safeguards," *Business Insurance*, July 11, 2002; "401(k) Participants File Class-Action Suit Against AIG," *BestWire*, May 13, 2005; "Lawyers File Suit on Behalf of AIG Plan Members," *National Underwriter Online News Service*, May 13, 2005.

9. ERISA defines highly compensated and nonhighly compensated employees based on factors such as employee salary, ownership share of the firm, and whether the employee is an officer in the organization.

10. See information about the Pension Protection Act of 2006 at http://www.dol.gov/ebsa/pensionreform.html. For information about the pension laws, see many sources from the media, among them Vineeta Anand, "Lawyer Steven J. Sacher Says That for the Most Part ERISA Has Performed 'Smashingly Well,'" *Pensions & Investments*, September 6, 1999, 19; Barry B. Burr, "Reviewing Options: Enron Fallout Sparks Much Soul-Searching; Experts Debate Need for Change Following Huge Losses in 401(k)," *Pensions & Investments*, 30 (2002): 1; William G. Gale et. al, "ERISA After 25 Years: A Framework for Evaluating Pension Reform," *Benefits Quarterly*, October 1, 1998; Lynn Miller, "The Ongoing Growth of Defined Contribution and Individual Account Plans: Issues and Implications," *EBRI Issue Brief*, no. 243 (2002), http://www.ebri.org/publications/ib/index.cfm?fa=ibDisp&content_id=160, accessed April 17, 2009; Martha Priddy Patterson, "A New Millennium for Retirement Plans: The 2001 Tax Act and Employer Flexibility," *Benefits Quarterly*, January 1, 2002.

11. The service requirement may be extended to two years in the small minority of plans that have immediate vesting. Vesting is defined later in the chapter.

12. Internal Revenue Service (IRS), "IRS Announces Pension Plan Limitations for 2009," IR-2008-118, October 16, 2008, http://www.irs.gov/newsroom/article/0,,id=187833,00.html, accessed April 17, 2009.

13. Internal Revenue Service (IRS), "IRS Announces Pension Plan Limitations for 2009," IR-2008-118, October 16, 2008, http://www.irs.gov/newsroom/article/0,,id=187833,00.html, accessed April 17, 2009.

14. April K. Caudill, "More Clarity and Simplicity in New Required Minimum Distribution Rules," *National Underwriter*, Life & Health/Financial Services Edition, May 13, 2002.

15. The regulations state that the new method can be used to calculate substantially equal periodic payments under Section 72(t)—distributions of retirement funds after age seventy and a half.

16. Internal Revenue Service (IRS), "IRS Announces Pension Plan Limitations for 2009," IR-2008-118, October 16, 2008, http://www.irs.gov/newsroom/article/0,,id=187833,00.html (accessed April 17, 2009).

17. For more information, see coverage of this topic in the following sample of articles: "Sun Moves to Cash Balance Pensions," *Employee Benefit Plan Review* 45, no. 9 (1991): 50–51; Arleen Jacobius, "Motorola Workers Embrace New Hybrid Pension Plan," *Business Insurance* 34, no. 45 (2000): 36–37; Karl Frieden, "The Cash Balance Pension Plan: Wave of the Future or Shooting Star?" *CFO: The Magazine for Chief Financial Officers* 3, no. 9 (1987): 53–54; September 1987; Avra Wing, "Employers Wary of Cash Balance Pensions," *Business Insurance* 20, no. 39 (1986): 15–20; September 29, 1986; Arleen Jacobius, "60 percent of Workers at Motorola, Inc. Embrace Firm's New PEP Plan," *Pensions & Investment Age* 28, no. 19 (2000): 3, 58; Jerry Geisel, "Survey Aims to Find Facts About Cash Balance Plans," *Business Insurance* 34, no. 21 (2000): 10–12; "American Benefits Council President Discusses Cash Balance Plans, Pension Reform," *Employee Benefit Plan Review* 55, no. 4 (2000): 11–13; Donna Ritter Mark, "Planning to Implement a Cash Balance Pension Plan? Examine the Issues First," *Compensation & Benefits Review* 32, no. 5 (2000): 15–16; Vineeta Anand, "Young and Old Hurt in Switch to Cash Balance," *Pensions & Investment Age* 28, no. 20 (2000): 1, 77; Vineeta Anand, "Employees Win Another One in Cash Balance Court Cases," *Pensions & Investment Age* 28, no. 19 (2000): 2, 59; Regina Shanney-Saborsky, "The Cash Balance Controversy: Navigating the Issues," *Journal of Financial Planning* 13, no. 9 (2000): 44–48.

18. Internal Revenue Service (IRS), "IRS Announces Pension Plan Limitations for 2009," IR-2008-118, October 16, 2008, http://www.irs.gov/newsroom/article/0,,id=187833,00.html (accessed April 17, 2009).

19. Internal Revenue Service (IRS), "IRS Announces Pension Plan Limitations for 2009," IR-2008-118, October 16, 2008, http://www.irs.gov/newsroom/article/0,,id=187833,00.html (accessed April 17, 2009).

20. Internal Revenue Service (IRS), "IRS Announces Pension Plan Limitations for 2009," IR-2008-118, October 16, 2008, http://www.irs.gov/newsroom/article/0,,id=187833,00.html (accessed April 17, 2009).

21. Internal Revenue Service (IRS), "IRS Announces Pension Plan Limitations for 2009," IR-2008-118, October 16, 2008, http://www.irs.gov/newsroom/article/0,,id=187833,00.html (accessed April 17, 2009).

22. "New Research from EBRI: Defined Contribution Retirement Plans Increasingly Seen as Primary Type," Reuters, February 9, 2009, http://www.reuters.com/article/pressRelease/idUS166119+09-Feb-2009+PRN20090209, accessed March 10, 2009.

23. Internal Revenue Service (IRS), "IRS Announces Pension Plan Limitations for 2009," IR-2008-118, October 16, 2008, http://www.irs.gov/newsroom/article/0,,id=187833,00.html (accessed April 17, 2009).

24. Internal Revenue Service (IRS), "IRS Announces Pension Plan Limitations for 2009," IR-2008-118, October 16, 2008, http://www.irs.gov/newsroom/article/0,,id=187833,00.html (accessed April 17, 2009).

25. Internal Revenue Service (IRS), "IRS Announces Pension Plan Limitations for 2009," IR-2008-118, October 16, 2008, http://www.irs.gov/newsroom/article/0,,id=187833,00.html (accessed April 17, 2009).

26. Internal Revenue Service (IRS), "IRS Announces Pension Plan Limitations for 2009," IR-2008-118, October 16, 2008, http://www.irs.gov/newsroom/article/0,,id=187833,00.html (accessed April 17, 2009).

27. Internal Revenue Service (IRS), "2009 IRA Contribution and Deduction Limits—Effect of Modified AGI on Deduction if You Are Covered by a Retirement Plan at Work," January 13, 2009, http://www.irs.gov/retirement/participant/article/0,,id=202516,00.html (accessed April 17, 2009).

28. Internal Revenue Service (IRS), "2009 Contribution and Deduction Limits—Amount of Roth IRA Contributions That You Can Make for 2009," February 16, 2009, http://www.irs.gov/retirement/participant/article/0,,id=202518,00.html (accessed April 17, 2009).

29. Internal Revenue Service (IRS), "Individual Retirement Arrangements (IRAs)," Publication 590 (2008), http://www.irs.gov/publications/p590/ch01.html#en_US_publink10006253 (accessed April 17, 2009).

30. Internal Revenue Service (IRS) "COLA Increases for Dollar Limitations on Benefits and Contributions," February 18, 2009, http://www.irs.gov/retirement/article/0,,id=96461,00.html (accessed April 17, 2009).

31. For frequently asked questions regarding Roth 401(k) and Roth 403(b), visit the IRS Web site at http://www.irs.gov/retirement/article/0,,id=152956,00.html#1 (accessed April 17, 2009).

32. Jane Bryant Quinn, "Boost Your Variable Annuity's Future Benefit," *Washington Post*, December 14, 2008, F01.

CHAPTER 22
Employment and Individual Health Risk Management

The costs of health care and health insurance have been of major social concern in the United States in the last three decades. The U.S. Department of Commerce Centers for Medicare and Medicaid Services reported that national health care expenditures were $2.1 trillion in 2006, up 6.7 percent from 2005. National health care expenditures made up 16 percent of gross domestic product (GDP) in 2006; by 2017, they are projected to rise to 19.5 percent.[1] The 1980s were a decade of double-digit rate increases in health insurance cost, which was the impetus for the birth of managed-care plans such as preferred provider organizations (PPOs) and for the boom in health maintenance organizations (HMOs). The newest innovation of the new millennium is the defined contribution health plan, also called consumer-driven health plans (CDHPs) and high-deductible health plans (HDHPs) in the forms of health savings accounts (HSAs) and health reimbursement accounts (HRAs). The CDHPs and HDHPs intend to transform the defined benefits approach to health insurance into defined contribution plans as part of an ownership society paradigm. Because managed-care plans no longer limit the spiraling health care costs, the defined contribution health plans with large deductibles emerged as a solution, albeit with their own problems. The issues of high cost and the impact on benefits are discussed in more detail in the box "What Is the Tradeoff between Health Care Costs and Benefits?" later in this chapter.

Most nongovernmental health insurance is provided through employer groups. Health insurance is a substantial percentage of an employer's total benefits expenditures. According to the Employee Benefit Research Institute (EBRI), of the $1.5 trillion in total employee benefit program outlays in 2007, employers spent $623.1 billion on health benefit plans. After retirement plans, health care was the second largest employer expenditure for employee benefits in 2007.[2] Health insurance is a substantial expense for employers and a major concern of society. Just consider your own situation. Do you have health insurance coverage? If you responded yes, you probably feel very comfortable. If you do not have coverage, you are probably making a note to yourself to check how you can get coverage and be able to afford the cost. This chapter will touch upon that subject, too, because individual contracts are an important source of insurance for people without employer-sponsored benefits, or those employed but with inadequate employee benefits. Some of the policy characteristics of individual contracts are similar to those of group contracts; however, there are differences worthy of discussion. Thus, we explore the individual contract and also investigate various health policies, such as individual dental and cancer policies, individual long-term care insurance, and Medigap insurance. In this chapter, you will gain an understanding of the choices an employee has to make when given the option to select among various health plans such as PPOs, HMOs, HSAs, or HRAs, or the individual alternatives available when he or she does not have these options.

A practical application of the concepts discussed is provided in Cases 1 and 2 of Chapter 23. Thus, this chapter covers the following:

1. Links

2. Group health insurance: an overview, indemnity health plans, managed-care plans, and other health plans

3. Individual health insurance contracts, cancer and critical illness policies, and dental insurance

4. Disability insurance, long-term care insurance, and Medicare supplementary insurance

1. LINKS

Among the risks shown in the holistic risk puzzle, the risk of illness or injury is the leading personal risk. The desire to mitigate this risk—a cause of major expense—is why many employees would not take a job without health insurance as part of the compensation package. In the big picture of risk management in our lives, taking care of health insurance is ranked very high. If you have surveyed your friends or classmates, you have probably learned that those who do not have health insurance coverage are not comfortable about it. They are likely aware that a serious accident or severe illness could cause them serious financial trouble.

We believe that we are entitled to the best health care possible to protect our health and keep us well. While in the distant past, the town's doctor visited a patient's home to provide help and accepted any payment, today's medical care is an impersonal business wherein doctors and emergency rooms require patients to show proof of capacity to pay. Health care coverage is expensive and deserves careful consideration in completing our holistic risk management. In Figure 22.1, the connection between the health risk and the possible coverage available from the employer is depicted. It is important to note that if health care coverage is not available from an employer, it is the responsibility of the individual to obtain individual coverage. With the added individual products discussed in this chapter, we provide the final step in the three-step diagram shown in Figure 22.1 and complete our study of holistic risk management. Individual arrangements for health, dental, disability, life, and pensions are necessary when all other programs represented in the bottom two steps do not complete the risk management program of a family. Case 1 of Chapter 23 presents the risk management portfolio of the hypothetical Smith family, and group health is covered in the overview of a sample employee benefits handbook in Case 2 of Chapter 23.

It is no wonder that health care issues have been high on the agendas of Congress and the new administration of President Barack Obama. The most notable issue is the proposed guarantee of health insurance for the 48 million Americans who are currently uninsured. Significant issues in health care over the years are discussed in the box "What Is the Tradeoff between Health Care Costs and Benefits?"

FIGURE 22.1   Links between Health Risks and Insurance Products

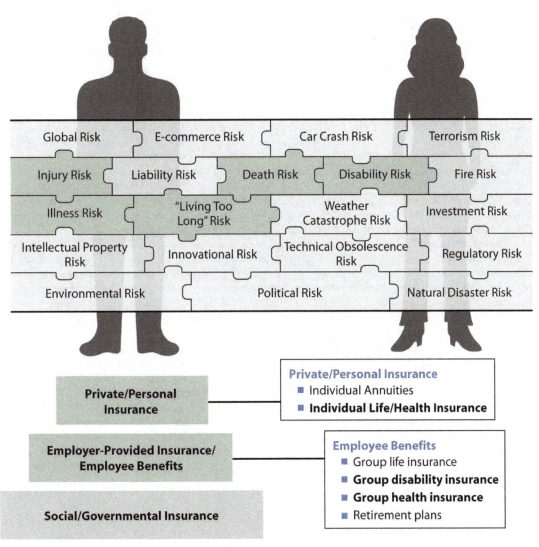

2. GROUP HEALTH INSURANCE: AN OVERVIEW, INDEMNITY HEALTH PLANS, MANAGED-CARE PLANS, AND OTHER HEALTH PLANS

LEARNING OBJECTIVES

In this section we elaborate on the following topics regarding group health insurance plans:

- **Changes with respect to employer-sponsored health coverage over time**
- **Indemnity health insurance plans—traditional fee-for-service plans: features, coordination of benefits, and cost containment initiatives**
- **The transition to managed care: indemnity plans with networks, HMOs, PPOs, POSs, HSAs, and HRAs**

2.1 Group Health Insurance: An Overview

Today, health insurance is very different from what it was two or three decades ago. Most of us do not pay providers of health care directly and submit an insurance form for reimbursement. In addition, most of us do not have complete freedom in choosing our physicians but must select from a list of in-network providers. The days of seeing any doctor and being reimbursed for any procedure the doctor orders are gone. We live in an era of receiving health care under managed care: controlled access to doctors, procedures, and medicines. While limited access is the disadvantage of the managed-care systems, there are many advantages. The most important is cost containment through efficiency. Another advantage is that most patients no longer have to deal with paperwork. Insureds simply make a copayment to the health care provider, and the remaining reimbursements are done behind the scenes. Additional advantages include preventive care and higher standards for quality care.

Costs are no longer controlled because the underlying issues that created medical cost inflation never disappeared. The main underlying factors are medical technology development, medical malpractice lawsuits, drug and medication development, the aging population, and the fact that a third party pays for the cost of obtaining medical services. People made the transition from the open choice of indemnity plans into the more controlled managed-care plans such as PPOs, point of service (POS) plans, and the various types of HMOs, but medical technology improvements, introduction of new medications, aging of the population, and medical malpractice continued in full swing. The cost-control factors of managed care that eased medical cost inflation during the transition period are not as effective as they once were. Once most of the U.S. population enrolled in managed-care plans, the cost saving factors no longer surpassed medical cost inflation factors. The situation in the health market is discussed in the box "What Is the Tradeoff between Health Care Costs and Benefits?"

The old managed-care plans are no longer viable and new ideas have emerged to supplement them. While the old systems are considered defined benefit health programs, the new ideas call for defined contribution health plans in which the consumer/employee receives a certain amount of money from the employer and then selects the desired health care components. Rather than employers negotiating with insurers or managed-care organizations for the group health plans, consumers are encouraged to negotiate directly with providers because these new plans are considered consumer-driven health plans. In some form, these are the HSAs and the HRAs.

Table 22.1[3] describes the managed health care plans prevalent in the marketplace today. Note, however, that the various health plans are no longer as distinct from one another as they appear in the table. Since these plans were introduced, changes in health care regulations, coupled with new laws concerned with patients' rights, have eliminated some of the differences among the plans and they now overlap greatly. (For example, it is no longer true that HMOs are necessarily cheaper than PPOs and HMOs with open access.) Figure 22.2 provides the five most prevalent health insurance plans on a continuum of choice and cost. There are other health care plans, such as exclusive physician organizations (EPOs), where doctors have created their own networks in response to the competitive environment, specifically, hospital chains, medical centers, and insurance companies acquiring group practices. These networks do not provide access to out-of-network providers.

TABLE 22.1 Spectrum of Health Plans

	Indemnity	Indemnity with Network	PPO	POS	health savings accounts	HMO
Choice Level	Highest					Lowest
Cost Level	Highest					Lowest
Main Characteristics	Comprehensive medical coverage with deductibles and coinsurance. Open access to providers.	Comprehensive medical coverage with deductibles and coinsurance. Access to providers in large networks and outside the network (with penalty).	Comprehensive medical coverage with deductibles, copayments, and coinsurance. Access to providers in networks and outside the network (with penalty).	Comprehensive medical coverage with deductibles, copayments, and coinsurance. Access to providers in networks and outside the network (with penalty). A gatekeeper.	Any type of health plan with a high deductible of at least $1,050 for a single individual and $2,100 for a family (in 2006). Rollover savings account with maximum of $2,700 for a single individual or $5,450 for a family—or up to the amount of the deductible (2006). Employer and employee contributions.	Comprehensive medical coverage with low copayments. Access to providers only in networks (except for emergencies). A gatekeeper.
Access to Providers	Access to any provider—no restriction.	Access to any provider in a large network and outside the network (with penalty).	Access to any provider in a large network and outside the network (with penalty).	Same as PPO, but required to see primary care physician (PCP) first. Referral from PCP to see a specialist. (PPO+PCP)	Depending on the underlying health plan	Staff model: facility only. Other models: in networks only, with PCP as a gatekeeper.
Methods of Reimbursing the Providers	Fee-for-service: patient pays total fee directly to the doctor for service rendered.	Fee-for-service, subject to usual, customary, and reasonable (UCR) limits.	Discounted fee-for-service.	PCPs by capitation; specialists by discounted FFS.	Depending on the underlying health plan after the high deductible.	Staff model: salaries. Other models: capitations. Individual practice association: capitation for PCP, discounted FFS for specialists.
What Is Required of the Patient?	Patient files claim forms; insurer reimburses coinsurance after the deductible, up to a maximum.	Same as indemnity, but reimbursement is only for UCR.	Copayments[4] in networks; out of networks are similar to indemnity with penalties, up to a maximum.	Same as PPO.	Encourage participants to make more informed, cost-conscious decisions about their health care. Patient has to open a savings account, pay deductible and other coinsurance, and copays up to a maximum.	Copayment only; traditionally, no out-of-network reimbursement except for emergency care.

	Indemnity	Indemnity with Network	PPO	POS	health savings accounts	HMO
The Benefits—Levels of Preventive Care[5]	Comprehensive medical package with minimal preventive care.	Comprehensive medical package with minimal preventive care.	Same as indemnity, with increased preventive care and well baby care.	Same as PPO.	Preventive care required by law is covered, as in other comprehensive plans (deductible does not apply).	Same as PPO with most preventive care, well-being, baby, physical exams, immunizations, extended dental, vision, and prescription plans.[6]
Prevalence	Lowest	Low	High	high	Growing (newest)	High

FIGURE 22.2 Continuum of Health Plans

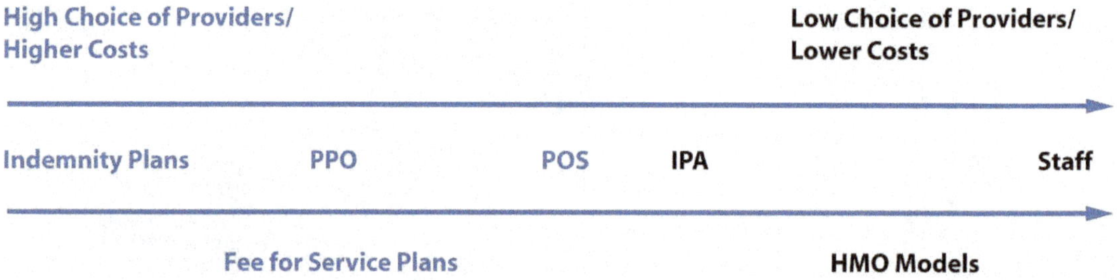

High Choice of Providers/ Higher Costs   **Low Choice of Providers/ Lower Costs**

Indemnity Plans   **PPO**   **POS**   **IPA**   **Staff**

                    Fee for Service Plans   **HMO Models**

The student who is new to this topic might best comprehend the changes of the past three decades by first learning about the profiles of HMOs and the indemnity plans of the late 1970s and early 1980s. These two types of plans were truly far apart. Patients had unlimited provider choice in the indemnity plans and the least choice in the HMOs. The HMOs supplied a person's medical needs for about $5 a visit. The subscriber to the staff model HMO would visit a clinic-like facility and see a doctor who was paid a salary. Baby, eye, and dental care were included. A new baby would cost a family very little. On the other side of the spectrum, the subscribers of the indemnity plans could see any provider, pay for the services, and later apply for reimbursement. The premiums for HMOs were substantially lower than those for the indemnity plan. In most cases, the employer paid the full premium for an HMO and asked the employee to supplement the higher cost of the indemnity plan.

Of these two extremes, who would select the HMO and who would select the indemnity plan? You answered correctly if you said that young and healthy employees most likely selected the HMOs. It turned out that there was adverse selection against the indemnity plans, which saw the more mature and less healthy employees. The managers of the indemnity plans began looking at the other extreme of the continuum for help in reducing costs. This is how managed care in traditional indemnity plans began. First, there were indemnity plans with large networks limiting access to providers and reimbursing only for **usual, customary, and reasonable (UCR)** costs for that area based on studies of the appropriate cost for each medical procedure. But this was only the first step. The low copayment (copay) that HMOs asked was very desirable. The newly formed **preferred provider organizations (PPOs)** adopted the copay method and used managed-care organizations to negotiate with doctors and all providers for large discounts, with some more than 50 percent off the usual, customary, and reasonable charges. The next step was to bring the gatekeeper, the primary care physician (which the HMOs used in most of their models and is discussed later in this chapter), into the structure of the PPO. When a gatekeeper was introduced, the new plan was called a **point of service (POS)** plan. This new plan is the PPO plus a gatekeeper, or the individual practice association (IPA) HMO model discussed later in the chapter.

The HMOs include various models: the model of one facility with doctors on staff (the staff model), the group model, the network model of doctors, and the **individual practice association (IPA)** of many doctors in one practice. The doctors in an IPA could see HMO and non-HMO patients. In many cases, the POS and IPA are very similar from the point of view of the patients, except that when the POS is based on a preferred provider organization rather than an HMO, there is more access to out-of-network providers (but with penalties). These days, many IPAs allow some out-of-network access as well, especially in cases of emergencies. In both the PPO and IPA-based networks with a gatekeeper (POS), the provider specialists receive discounted fees for service, while the gatekeepers (primary care physicians) receive **capitation** (a set amount paid to each provider based on the number of subscribers in the plan). These are the areas where the distinctions among the plans become fuzzy. HMOs were forced to give more choices and services. Their subscribers, originally young, healthy employees, had become aging baby boomers who needed more quality care. Many states have passed bills requiring HMOs to loosen many of their restrictions. With all these changes came a price. HMOs became more expensive; with the best practices widely emulated, the offerings of all plans converged. The pendulum of choice versus cost has probably moved to be somewhere in the middle of the continuum shown in Figure 22.2. For learning purposes, this chapter will regard HMOs as the plans with minimal access to out-of-network providers. A comparison of the actual benefits under the various plans is available in the employee benefits portfolio in Case 2 of Chapter 23.

What Is the Tradeoff between Health Care Costs and Benefits?

Health care coverage costs are growing at a faster pace than almost any other segment of the economy. One of the nation's largest benefits purchasing groups, the California Public Employee Retirement Systems, saw its PPO rates rise 20 percent and its HMO plans increase 26 percent. Many other employers saw similar increases. To balance their books, employers have to either pass these additional costs along to employees, find ways to cut benefits or transition into health savings accounts (HSAs).

HMOs were once seen as the saviors of the health insurance system. Offering lower costs, they often attracted younger, healthy workers. But now, as their costs are rising, even HMOs no longer look like good deals. Many of the benefits they once offered are being cut. For many older individuals, or those with greater health needs, HMOs do not provide the level of care and flexibility they desire. The PPOs they prefer, however, are becoming more and more expensive. And even with PPOs, benefits such as low copayments for drugs are now being reduced. With the creation of HSAs, it appears that the satisfaction level is lower than that of comprehensive health coverage. A survey conducted by the Employee Benefit Research Institute (EBRI) and discussed in its December 2005 conference revealed that patients who are using the consumer-driven health plans and high-deductible health plans, in the form of HSAs and HRAs, said that they (1) were less satisfied, (2) delayed seeing a health care provider, and (3) behaved in a more cost-conscious way.

At the same time, doctors are also feeling the pinch. Pressured by insurance companies to cut costs, they are forced to see more patients in less time, which can lead to medical mistakes. Insurance companies are also questioning expensive tests and medical procedures and refusing to pay doctors the full amount submitted. Soaring medical malpractice costs are causing some doctors to leave the profession. President George W. Bush called for tort reform to alleviate this problem during his State of the Union address on January 31, 2006.

---

usual, customary, and reasonable (UCR)

The costs of health care services that insurers generally agree to cover in fee-for-service or managed care arrangements, based on studies of the appropriate cost for each medical procedure.

preferred provider organizations (PPOs)

Groups of hospitals, physicians, and other health care providers that contract with insurers, third-party administrators, or directly with employers to provide medical care to members of the contracting group(s) at discounted prices.

point of service (POS)

A preferred provider organization (PPO) that includes a primary care physician to serve as a gatekeeper, keeping costs contained.

individual practice associations (IPAs)

HMO model where contractual arrangements are made with physicians and other providers in a community who practice out of their own offices and treat both HMO and non-HMO members.

capitation

As in the case of managed care, a set amount paid to each health care provider based on the number of subscribers in the provider's plan.

In the United States, those individuals who have insurance, primarily through their employers, are the lucky ones. Some 47 million Americans have no insurance at all. Those who earn too much to qualify for Medicaid but not enough to purchase private health insurance often find themselves paying huge out-of-pocket bills. Often, uninsured patients neglect treatment until their condition becomes an emergency. When they cannot pay, hospitals and doctors pick up the cost, and they make up for it by increasing prices elsewhere, which contributes to escalating health care costs.

Is rationing health care the answer? Canada and many European countries have adopted systems of universal coverage, but such coverage comes with a price. Benefits, while universal, may be lower. It may be difficult to see specialists, especially about nonemergency conditions. Long waiting times are not uncommon. A universal health care system proposed during the first Clinton administration never got off the ground. Legislation aimed at giving patients a greater voice in determining what procedures health insurers would cover under a patients' bill of rights did not materialize. However, the advent of HSAs is an attempt to allow patients to carefully choose their own coverage and allocate the appropriate costs.

In addition to the defined contribution health plans, some employers are looking to cut costs through disease management programs. With the majority of costs resulting from chronic conditions, such as asthma, diabetes, heart disease, and arthritis, human resource executives believe that they can reduce costs by developing better ways to manage the health care of employees with such conditions.

In an effort to alleviate the strain of unaffordable medical bills on the 48 million Americans without insurance, President Barack Obama brought renewed focus to the issue of health care reform throughout his 2008 presidential campaign. President Obama advocates universal health insurance and expressed his desire to see such a system implemented in the United States by the end of his four-year term. The Obama proposal emphasizes cost reductions to guarantee eligibility for affordable health care through measures such as insurance reform, abolishing patent protection on pharmaceuticals, and requiring that employers expand group coverage. A National Health Insurance Exchange would also be established for individuals not covered under employer arrangements, giving them access to plans pooled by private insurers and limited coverage through the government (in an arrangement similar to Medicare). Anyone, regardless of preexisting conditions, would have access to coverage at fixed premiums. Although more specific details have yet to emerge, President Obama says that this plan would reduce premiums by $2,500 for the typical family and would cost $60 billion to provide annually.

Critics contend that the Obama initiative would add a new government entitlement program whose funding, like Social Security and Medicare, would impose severe burdens because it does not resolve the fundamental issues responsible for escalating medical costs (discussed previously in this chapter). The eligibility requirements could also encourage adverse selection, leading to large deficits if an allowance for this is not built into the premiums. Employers might view the plan as a substitute for employee benefit options that they sponsor and a justification for discontinuing certain types of group coverage. Finally, nationalized health insurance risks alienating individuals who are content with their existing coverage and might resent having to finance a program they could not see themselves utilizing. This, of course, invites discussion about the merits of government intervention to such an extent in an individualistic society such as the United States. Still, the insurance industry finds the concept of cooperating with a national exchange preferable to the alternative of having to compete with a wholly public health insurance plan.

In his speech before a joint session of Congress on February 25, 2009, President Obama reiterated his position, stating, "Health care reform cannot wait, it must not wait, and it will not wait another year," and he called for comprehensive reform efforts by the end of 2009. Shortly thereafter, the White House Forum on Health Reform was hosted on March 5. It presented findings from the group reports of over 30,000 participants in all 50 states who held HealthCare Community Discussions in December 2008. Once the forum had concluded, the Obama administration launched the Web site HealthReform.gov, detailing intended reform efforts. A preliminary health budget prepared by the Department of Health and Human Services was also made available on the site. Highlights of the budget include the following:

- Accelerated adoption of electronic health records
- Expanded research comparing the effectiveness of medical treatments
- $6 billion investment for National Institutes of Health cancer research
- $330 million in spending to increase the number of health professionals in areas with personnel shortages
- Additional outlays for affordable, quality child care
- Fortifications to Medicare

The interested student is invited to go to healthreform.gov for complete details of the health budget. Ongoing developments can be tracked at the interactive Web site, which also features the formal report from the HealthCare Community Discussions presented at the White House Forum and group reports from discussions in all states.

In March 2009, Senate Finance Committee chair Max Baucus (D-Mont.) published a white paper highlighting the proposals that have been floated since President Obama took office. A consensus is forming in terms of reform priorities: containing medical costs, decreasing the number of uninsured people, and producing better results for patients. Cost containment emphasizes better value for health care dollars—streamlined payment systems and elimination of redundancies. A greater insured population, it is reasoned, contributes to increased use of primary and preventive care so that people do not suffer severe, debilitating, and expensive-to-treat ailments by the time they seek medical intervention.

Lawmakers are focused on providing the best possible health care experience at the lowest possible cost. Such a balancing of the scales may not be possible, as pointed out by Congressional Budget Office (CBO) director Douglas Elmendorf. Elmendorf explained, "The available evidence suggests that a substantial share of spending on health care contributes little if anything to the overall health of the nation, but finding ways to reduce such spending without also affecting services that improve health will be difficult." To reconcile this problem, the CBO director stressed changing the incentives within the current health care system, such as moving Medicare payments out of the fee-for-service realm, altering tax exclusions on employer-based coverage, and requiring greater transparency regarding the quality of services and treatments by care providers.

Despite the burdens of the economic recession, health reform has remained on the frontlines of President Obama's first-term agenda. The stimulus authorized by the American Recovery and Reinvestment Act of 2009 (discussed in the box "Laws Affecting Health Care" in Chapter 20) included over $20 billion in health-related targeted spending consistent with recent reform measures. In February 2009, President Obama signed a bill expanding the State Children's Health Insurance Program to guarantee coverage of 11 million children, at a cost of $33 billion. How these actions and proposals affect the quality of care remains to be seen, but Americans can certainly expect changes in the days, weeks, and months ahead.

Questions for Discussion

1. Who should be responsible for individuals' health care coverage? The employer? The individual? The government?
2. How would it be possible to solve the health care crisis under the current health care system in the United States? Should it be socialized, as it is in many European countries and Canada?
3. Where do you stand with respect to President Obama's proposed National Health Insurance Exchange?

Sources: Lucette Lagnado, "Uninsured and Ill, a Woman Is Forced to Ration Her Care," Wall Street Journal, November 12, 2002, A1; Allison Bell, "Group Health Rates Still Rocketing," National Underwriter, Life & Health/Financial Services Edition, August 19, 2002; Lori Chordas, "Multiple-Choice Question: Disease Management, Cost Shifting and Prescription-Drug Initiatives Are Some of the Strategies Insurers Are Using to Stabilize Health-Care Expenses," Best's Review, August 2002; Barbara Martinez, "Insurer Software Shaves Bills, Leaves Doctors Feeling Frayed," Wall Street Journal, July 31, 2002, A1; Frances X. Clines, "Insurance-Squeezed Doctors Folding Tents in West Virginia," New York Times, June 13, 2002; Mary Suszynski, "Survey: HMO Rate Increases Are Highest in 11 Years," Best Wire, July 2, 2002, http://www3.ambest.com/Frames/FrameServer.asp?AltSrc=23&Tab=1&Site=bestweekarticle&refnum=19513 (accessed April 22, 2009); "Dueling Legislation on Patients' Rights in the House and Senate," Washington Post, August 5, 2001, A5; Mark Hofmann, "Senators, White House Deadlock on Patient Rights," Business Insurance, August 2, 2002; John A. MacDonald "Survey of Consumer-Driven Health Plans Raises Key Issues," EBRI Notes 27, No. 2 (2006), http://www.ebri.org/publications/notes/index.cfm?fa=notesDisp&content_id=3618 (accessed April 22, 2009); President G. W. Bush, State of the Union address, January 31, 2006; Victoria Colliver, "McCain, Obama Agree: Health Care Needs Fixing," San Francisco Chronicle, October 1, 2008, http://www.sfgate.com/cgi-bin/article.cgi?f=/c/a/2008/09/30/MNLG12Q79L.DTL, accessed March 4, 2009; Kevin Freking, "Coverage Guarantee Can Hit Young The Hardest: Obama Health Plan Follows Where Some States Have Struggled," Associated Press, September 11, 2008, http://www.usatoday.com/news/politics/2008-09-11-2075765460_x.htm, accessed March 4, 2009; HealthReform.Gov, http://healthreform.gov/, accessed March 13, 2009; Department of Health and Human Services, Proposed Health Budget, http://www.whitehouse.gov/omb/assets/fy2010_new_era/Department_of_Health_and_Human_Services1.pdf, accessed March 13, 2009; Ruth Mantell, "Meaningful Health-Care Reform Getting Closer: Outline of Changes Likely to Be Enacted Begins to Take Shape," Wall Street Journal (MarketWatch), March 16, 2009, http://www.marketwatch.com/news/story/story.aspx? guid=%7B6723EF15%2D7E92%2D4118%2D928A%2DF9FCA8DB592D%7D&siteid=djm_HAMWRSSObamaH, accessed March 17, 2009.

We will now give more detailed descriptions of the plans featured in Table 22.1 and Figure 22.2. Following these descriptions, additional plans such as dental and long-term care plans will be discussed.

2.2   Indemnity Health Plans: The Traditional Fee-for-Service Plans

The traditional method for providing group medical expense benefits has been by paying health care providers a fee for services rendered. **Health care providers** include health professionals, such as physicians and surgeons, as well as health facilities, such as hospitals and outpatient surgery centers. Medical expense benefits may be provided on an indemnity, service, or valued basis.

health care providers

Include health professionals, such as physicians and surgeons, and health facilities, such as hospitals and outpatient surgery centers.

indemnity benefits

Reimburse insureds for actual costs incurred for health care up to covered limits in traditional fee-for-service plans.

fee-for-service

Medical expense insurance providing hospital, surgical, and medical expenses, plus major medical and comprehensive coverage.

basic health care benefits

The hospital, surgical, and medical expenses of a fee-for-service plan.

Indemnity benefits apply the principle of indemnity by providing payment for loss. The insured (the covered employee or dependent) would receive, for example, the actual costs incurred up to but not exceeding $300 per day for up to ninety days while confined in a hospital. Other dollar limits would be placed on benefits for other types of charges, such as those for ancillary charges (such as X-ray, laboratory, and drugs) made by the hospital.

There are five major classifications of traditional **fee-for-service** medical expense insurance: (1) hospital expense, (2) surgical expense, (3) medical expense, (4) major medical, and (5) comprehensive medical insurance. The first three types are called basic coverage and provide a limited set of services or reimburse a limited dollar amount. As the names suggest, major medical and comprehensive medical insurance provide coverage for large losses.

2.3 Basic Health Care Benefits

Basic health care benefits cover hospital, surgical, and medical expenses. These coverages are limited in terms of the types of services (or expenditure reimbursements) they provide, as well as the dollar limits of protection. As Figure 22.3 shows, basic medical coverage generally provides first-dollar coverage instead of protection against large losses.

FIGURE 22.3 Basic Medical Coverage

* Basic coverage excludes some expenses, and some policies have a small deductible.

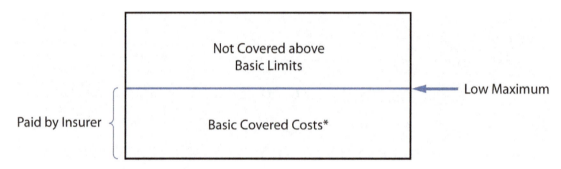

basic hospital policy

Basic health care benefit for room and board (for a specified number of days) and hospital ancillary charges, such as for X-ray imaging and laboratory tests.

basic surgical policy

Basic health care benefit that usually pays providers according to a schedule of procedures, regardless of whether surgery is performed in a hospital or elsewhere.

basic medical expense policy

Basic health care benefit for all or part of doctors' fees for hospital, office, or home visits due to nonsurgical care.

The **basic hospital policy** covers room and board (for a specified number of days) and hospital ancillary charges, such as those for X-ray imaging and laboratory tests. The basic hospital policy primarily provides benefits during a hospital confinement. In addition, it covers outpatient surgery and limited emergency care in case of an accident. Many policies have a small deductible. Ancillary charges may be covered on a schedule basis, or more commonly on a blanket basis for all X-rays, laboratory work, and other ancillary charges, with a maximum limit such as $5,000 for all such charges. Maternity coverage is included in group medical expense insurance policies because the Civil Rights Act forbids employer-sponsored health insurance plans from treating pregnancy differently from any other medical condition.

The **basic surgical policy** usually pays providers according to a schedule of procedures, regardless of whether the surgery is performed in a hospital or elsewhere. The policy lists the maximum benefit for each type of operation. A second approach sometimes used by insurers is to pay benefits up to the UCR surgical charges in the geographical region where the operation is performed. UCR charges are defined as those below the ninetieth percentile of charges by all surgeons in a geographical region for the same procedure.

A **basic medical expense policy** covers all or part of doctors' fees for hospital, office, or home visits due to nonsurgical care. Often a plan only provides benefits when the insured is confined to a hospital. Most policies have an overall limit of a daily rate multiplied by the number of days in the hospital. Common exclusions are routine examinations, eye examinations, X-rays, and prescription drugs.

Basic health care coverage has been criticized for encouraging treatment in the hospital, the most expensive site for medical care delivery. For example, both the basic hospital and medical policies cover services primarily delivered on an inpatient basis. Newer basic policies provide better coverage for outpatient services. For example, some provide X-ray and laboratory benefits on an outpatient basis (up to a small maximum benefit) and cover the cost of preadmission tests done on an outpatient basis prior to hospital admission.

2.4 Major Medical and Comprehensive Insurance

The hospital, surgical, and medical expense insurance policies previously discussed are basic contracts in the sense that they provide for many of the medical expenses on a somewhat selective basis and with rather low limits. They are weak in the breadth of their coverage as well as their maximum benefit limits. Two health insurance plans have been developed to correct for these weaknesses: major medical insurance and comprehensive medical insurance.

Major Medical Insurance

Major medical insurance covers the expense of almost all medical services prescribed by a doctor. It provides coverage for almost all charges for hospitals, doctors, medicines, blood, wheelchairs, and other medically necessary items. Major medical policies have four fundamental features: high maximum limits (such as $1 million) or no limits, a large deductible, coverage of a broad range of different medical services, and coinsurance provisions.

Maximum limits apply to the total amount the insurer will pay over the insured's lifetime. It may apply to each injury or illness separately, but it typically applies to all injuries and illnesses regardless of whether they are related.

Internal policy limits often apply to specified services. Hospital room and board charges are usually limited to the hospital's most prevalent semiprivate rate. All charges are subject to a usual and customary test.

As Figure 22.4 shows, the deductible in policies is large, ranging from $300 to $2,000. The purpose of the deductible is to eliminate small claims and restrict benefits to the more financially burdensome expenses, thus making possible high limits and broad coverage at a reasonable premium rate. A new deductible must be satisfied each **benefit period**. In group insurance, the benefit period is usually a calendar year. The deductible applies to each individual; however, many policies require only that two or three family members meet the deductible each year. This reduces the possibility of deductibles causing financial hardship when several family members have serious illnesses or injuries during the same year.

The **coinsurance provision** gives the percentage of expenses the insurer will pay in excess of the deductible. It may vary from 70 to 90 percent; 80 percent is common. The insured bears the remainder of the burden up to a **stop-loss limit**, for example, $3,000, after which 100 percent of covered charges are reimbursed. Some group contracts include the deductible in the stop-loss limit and others do not. Figure 22.4 shows the deductible included in the stop-loss limit.

FIGURE 22.4 Major Medical Insurance

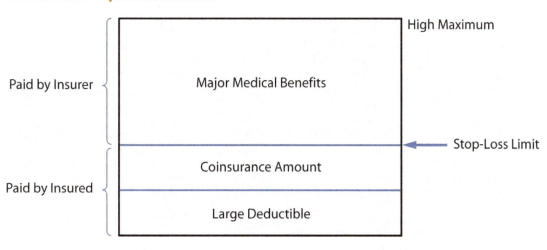

Deductibles and coinsurance requirements are **cost-sharing** provisions that increase the personal cost to the insured of using medical services. When insureds pay part of the cost, they tend to use fewer unnecessary or discretionary medical services. That is, deductibles and coinsurance provisions reduce moral hazard and help keep group insurance premiums affordable. The stop-loss limit protects the insured from excessive cost sharing, which could be financially devastating.

---

major medical insurance

Covers virtually all charges for hospitals, doctors, medicines, blood, wheelchairs, and other medically necessary items in a fee-for-service arrangement and has four fundamental features: high maximum limits (or no limits), a large deductible, coverage of a broad range of different medical services, and coinsurance provisions.

maximum limits

In major medical insurance, apply to the total amount the insurer will pay over the insured's lifetime.

internal policy limits

In major medical insurance, apply to specified services such as hospital room and board charges.

benefit period

Term for which premiums, deductibles, copayments, and limits on insurance apply; in group insurance, usually a calendar year.

coinsurance provision

Gives the percentage of expenses the insurer will pay in excess of the deductible, usually between 70 and 90 percent.

stop-loss limit

Amount above which an insured is no longer responsible for paying on a covered loss, regardless of any coinsurance provision.

cost sharing

Provisions such as deductibles and coinsurance requirements that increase personal costs to insureds, reducing overall costs and moral hazard.

Comprehensive Medical Insurance

comprehensive medical insurance

Reduces financial burdens of major medical policies on insureds by providing smaller deductibles and broad coverages in a single policy.

With major medical policies, the insurer pays most of the cost for medical services. However, major medical policy cost sharing may still be sizeable, putting a heavy financial burden on the insured. **Comprehensive medical insurance** deals with this problem by providing smaller deductibles, typically $100 to $300 per individual per calendar year (see Figure 22.4). Comprehensive medical insurance is designed as a stand-alone policy that provides broad coverage for a range of in-patient and out-patient services. Except for the smaller deductible, the provisions of a comprehensive plan are usually the same as those in a major medical plan. The comprehensive policy is sold mainly on a group basis.

2.5 Coordination of Benefits

coordination of benefits provision

Establishes a system of primary and secondary insurers specifying the order and terms of payment when an insured has coverage under two separate insurance plans.

Many employees and their dependents are eligible for group medical expense coverage under more than one plan. For example, a husband and wife may each be eligible on their own employer's plan as well as their spouse's. Children may be eligible under both the father's and the mother's plans. Workers with more than one permanent part-time job may be eligible for coverage with more than one employer. Coordination is needed to prevent duplicate payment of medical expenses when employees or their dependents are covered under more than one group policy.

The **coordination of benefits provision** establishes a system of primary and secondary insurers. The primary insurer pays the normal benefit amount, as if no other insurance were in force. Then the secondary insurer pays the balance of the covered health care expenses. The total payments by the primary and secondary insurers are limited to 100 percent of the covered charges for the applicable policies. Estimates are that coordination of benefits reduces the total cost of health insurance by over 10 percent by reducing duplicate payment.

An employee's group plan is always considered primary for expenses incurred by the employee. For example, a husband's primary coverage is with his employer, a wife's with her employer, and each has secondary coverage through the spouse's plan. When a child is insured under both parents' plans, the policy of the parent whose birthday falls first in the year is the primary policy. However, in the case of separation or divorce, the primary coverage for the child is through the custodial parent. Secondary coverage is through stepparents, and coverage through the noncustodial parent pays last. In some cases, these rules may not establish a priority of payment, and then the policy in effect for the longest period of time is primary. Any group plan that does not include a coordination of benefits provision is considered the primary insurer by all insurers that have such provisions. This encourages almost universal use of the coordination of benefits provision.

Allowing insureds to be covered under more than one policy means that these insureds may not have to meet deductible or coinsurance requirements. However, group policies sometimes stipulate that the secondary payer cannot reimburse the deductible amounts required by the primary policy. This is designed to preserve the effect of the cost-sharing requirement, namely, to control the use of unnecessary or excess services by the insured and to reduce moral hazard.

Following is an example of a dependent insured who has double coverage. Sharon and John Shank are both covered by indemnity health plans under their respective employers. They also cover their three children. Sharon is born on October 1, 1970, and John on November 30, 1968. On January 3, 2009, their son, Josh, was hurt in a soccer tournament and had to have surgery on his ankle. The cost of the procedure was $5,000. John's plan provides for a $250 deductible and 90 percent coinsurance, while Sharon's plan has a $400 deductible with 80 percent coinsurance. Because Sharon's birthday is earlier in the year, her insurer is the primary carrier. The reimbursement under her carrier is ($5,000 – $ 400) × −0.80 = $3,680. The out-of-pocket cost would be $1,320, but because the family is covered by both parents' health plans, the amount will be covered in full under the plan of John's employer. John's employer, as a secondary payer, does not impose the deductibles and coinsurance. Note that if Sharon's health plan were self-insured, her plan would not be the primary insurer, regardless of her birthday.

Cost Containment Initiatives for Traditional Fee-for-Service Policies

cost containment techniques

Methods of controlling costs in traditional fee-for-service policies through plan design, administration/funding, and utilization review.

As noted above, escalating medical costs propelled high-cost plans to look for effective methods to control costs. These **cost containment techniques** can be categorized as follows:

1. Plan design techniques
2. Administration and funding techniques
3. Utilization review

Plan Design Techniques

Plan design techniques relate to deductibles, coinsurance, limits on coverage, and exclusions such as experimental procedures or purely cosmetic surgeries. Most of the plans charge extra for coverage of routine eye examinations, eyeglasses, hearing examinations, and most dental expenses.

Administrative and Funding Techniques

When employers decide to self-insure their employees' group coverage, insurers continue to have an administrative role. The insurers enroll the employees, pay claims, and reinsure catastrophic claims. Through self-insurance, employers may be able to avoid state premium taxes (usually 1 or 2 percent of premiums) levied on insurance; eliminate most of the insurers' potential profits; and, in some cases, earn higher investment returns on reserves for health claims than those normally earned by group insurers. In addition, self-insured plans do not have to comply with state laws mandating coverage of medical care benefits (e.g., alcoholism and infertility benefits). A small percentage of employers administer their plans themselves, eliminating any insurer involvement. The overall effect of these changes on the cost of health care can be characterized as significant in absolute dollar savings yet minor as a percentage of total costs.

Utilization Review

Efforts to control costs include utilization review techniques developed by insurers and employers to reduce the use of the most costly forms of health care—hospitalization and surgery. Some of these techniques are listed in Table 22.2. Most group plans use some or all of these methods to control costs. The first ten are discussed briefly in this section, and the others are described later in more detail.

Insurers will pay full coverage when the insured seeks a second surgical opinion before undergoing elective or nonemergency surgery and a lower percentage or no coverage if the insured proceeds with surgery after obtaining only one opinion. Second surgical opinions do not require that two surgeons agree that surgery needs to be done before the insurer will pay for the procedure. A **second surgical opinion provision** requires only that the insured get a second opinion to increase the information available before making a decision about whether to have the surgery.

Insurers encourage patients to use ambulatory surgical centers or have outpatient surgery at the hospital or surgeon's office rather than opt for a hospital stay. The reimbursement rates also encourage **preadmission testing**, where patients have diagnostic tests done on an outpatient basis prior to surgery to reduce the total time spent in the hospital.

second surgical opinion provision

Requires that an insured seeks a second opinion to increase information available before making a decision about whether to have the surgery; does not require that two surgeons agree as to the need for surgery.

preadmission testing

Diagnostic tests done on an outpatient basis prior to a patient's surgery to reduce the total time spent in the hospital.

TABLE 22.2 Health Care Cost Containment Methods

- Second surgical opinions
- Ambulatory surgical centers
- Preadmission testing
- Preadmission certification
- Extended care facilities
- Hospice care
- Home health care
- Utilization review organizations
- Statistical analysis of claims
- Prospective payment
- Business coalitions
- Wellness programs
- Health maintenance organizations
- Preferred provider organizations
- Managed-care plans

Most group fee-for-service plans require **preadmission certification** for hospitalization for any nonemergency condition. The insured or the physician of the insured contacts the plan administrator for approval for hospital admission for a specified number of days. The administrative review is usually made by a nurse or other health professional. The recommendations are based on practice patterns of physicians in the region, and an appeals process is available for patients with conditions that require admissions and lengths of stay outside the norm.

preadmission certification

In fee-for-service plans, requires the physician of the insured to contact the plan administrator for approval of hospital admission for a specified number of days.

Extended care facilities or nursing facilities, hospice care for the dying, or home health care following hospital discharge may be recommended to reduce the length of hospitalization. **Extended care facilities** provide basic medical care needed during some recoveries, rather than the intensive and more expensive medical service of a hospital. With **hospice care**, volunteers and family members help to care for a dying person in the hospital, at home, or in a dedicated hospice facility. **Home health care** is an organized system of care at home that substitutes for a hospital admission or allows early discharge from the hospital. The insurer covers the cost of physicians' visits, nurses' visits, respiratory therapy, prescription drugs, physical and speech therapy, home health aids, and other essentials. Cancer, diabetes, fractures, AIDS, heart ailments, and many other illnesses can be treated as effectively and less expensively with home health, hospice, and extended care.

Employers or their insurers often contract for reviews by an outside utilization review organization, sometimes called a professional review organization (PRO). **Utilization review organizations**, run by physicians, surgeons, and nurses, offer peer judgments on whether a hospital admission is necessary, whether the length of the hospital stay is appropriate for the medical condition, and whether the quality of care is commensurate with the patient's needs. When problems are identified, the utilization review organization may contact the hospital administrator, the chief of the medical staff, or the personal physician. When treatment deviates substantially from the norm, the physician may be asked to discuss the case before a peer review panel. The medical insurance policy may refuse to pay for care considered unnecessary by the reviewing organization.

Utilization review organizations, third-party administrators, and many large employers collect and analyze data on health care claims. This **statistical analysis of claims** has the purpose of identifying any overutilization or excessive charges by providers of medical care. These studies usually establish standard costs for a variety of **diagnostic-related groups (DRGs)**. Each DRG is a medical or surgical condition that recognizes age, sex, and other determinants of treatment costs. By looking at each provider's charges on a DRG basis, the analyses can identify high- and low-cost providers.

Another cost containment technique using DRGs is **prospective payment**. In 1983, the federal government adopted the practice of paying a flat fee for each Medicare patient based on the patient's DRG. Prospective payment provided an economic incentive to providers, specifically hospitals, to minimize the length of stay and other cost parameters. Use of prospective payment proved effective, and other insurers and employers now use similar methods. But the downside is that the level of reimbursement is too low and many providers do not accept Medicare patients. Assignment of incorrect or multiple DRGs to obtain higher fees can be problematic, and monitoring is necessary to keep costs as low as possible.

Another cost containment initiative by employers has been to sponsor **wellness programs** designed to promote healthy lifestyles and reduce the incidence and severity of employee medical expenses. The programs vary greatly in scope. Some are limited to educational sessions on good health habits and screening for high blood pressure, cholesterol, diabetes, cancer symptoms, and other treatable conditions. More extensive programs provide physical fitness gymnasiums for aerobic exercise such as biking, running, and walking. Counseling is available, usually on a confidential basis, as an aid in the management of stress, nutrition, alcoholism, or smoking.

---

extended care facilities

Provide basic medical care needed during some recoveries rather than the intensive and more expensive medical service of a hospital.

hospice care

Arrangement where volunteers and family members help to care for a dying person in the hospital, at home, or in a dedicated hospice facility.

home health care

Organized system of care at home that substitutes for hospital admission or allows early discharge from the hospital.

utilization review organizations

Run by physicians, surgeons, and nurses, offer peer judgments on whether hospital admission is necessary, whether the length of hospital stay is appropriate for the medical condition, and whether quality of care is commensurate with the patient's needs.

statistical analysis of claims

Has the purpose of identifying any overutilization or excessive charges by providers of medical care.

diagnostic related groups (DRGs)

A medical or surgical condition that recognizes age, sex, and other determinants of treatment costs.

prospective payment

Practice of paying a flat fee for patient care based on a patient's DRG; provided an economic incentive to providers, specifically hospitals, to minimize length of stay and other cost parameters.

wellness programs

Designed to promote healthy lifestyles and reduce the incidence and severity of employee medical expenses.

2.6 Managed-Care Plans

The central concept in the area of health care cost containment is managed care. The concept of managed care has grown in the last fifteen to twenty years, and several characteristics are common across health care plans. **Managed-care** plans control access to providers in various ways. Managed-care fee-for-service plans control access to procedures through provisions such as preadmission certification, PPOs control access by providing insureds with economic incentives to choose efficient providers, and HMOs control access by covering services only from HMO providers. Managed-care plans typically engage in utilization review, monitoring service usage and costs on a case-by-case basis. In addition, managed-care plans usually give economic incentives to stay in networks by charging penalties when nonpreferred providers are seen.

Preferred Provider Organizations

Preferred provider organizations (PPOs) were first formed in the 1980s as another approach to containing costs in group health insurance programs. PPOs are groups of hospitals, physicians, and other health care providers that contract with insurers, third-party administrators, or directly with employers to provide medical care to members of the contracting group(s) at discounted prices. They provide a mechanism for organizing, marketing, and managing fee-for-service medical care.

Unlike most HMOs, PPOs give employees and their dependents a broad choice of providers. The insured can go to any provider on an extensive list, known as the in-network list, supplied by the employer or insurer. The insured can also go to a provider not on the list, known as going out of network. If the insured goes to a preferred provider, most PPOs waive most or all of the coinsurance, which is a percentage of the fee paid to the doctor by the insurer. PPOs always charge a copay that can range from $10 to $30 or more depending on the specialty or the contract the employer negotiated with the insurance company. Providers such as doctors and hospitals are in abundant supply in most urban areas. Most operate on a fee-for-service basis and are concerned about competition from HMOs. To maintain their market share of patients, providers are willing to cooperate with PPOs. The income that they give up in price discounts they expect to gain through an increase in the number of patients. Employers and insurers like PPOs because they are not expensive to organize and they direct employees to low-cost providers. The primary incentives for employees to use preferred providers are being able to avoid deductibles and coinsurance provisions and only having to make copayments.

Cost effectiveness would not be achieved, even with discounts, if providers got insureds to accept more service(s) than necessary for the proper treatment of injury or illness. Therefore, many PPOs monitor their use of services.

Health Maintenance Organizations

Health maintenance organizations (HMOs) have been around for over sixty years. In the 1970s, they gained national attention for their potential to reduce health care costs.

History of HMOs

The HMO concept is generally traced back to the Ross-Loos group, which was a temporary medical unit that provided medical services to Los Angeles construction workers building an aqueduct in a California desert in 1933. Henry J. Kaiser offered the same service to construction workers for the Grand Coulee Dam in the state of Washington. During World War II, what is now called the Kaiser Permanente plan was used for employees in Kaiser shipyards.[7]

The major turning point in popularity for HMOs occurred with the passage of the Health Maintenance Organization Act of 1973. This act required an employer to subscribe exclusively to an HMO or to make this form of health care available as one of the options to the employees, provided an HMO that qualified under the act was located nearby and requested consideration. By the time this requirement was retired, employers were in the habit of offering HMOs to their employees. Sponsors of HMOs include insurance companies, government units, Blue Cross Blue Shield, hospitals, medical schools, consumer groups, unions, and other organizations.

Nature of HMOs

As noted above and featured in Table 22.1, HMOs provide a comprehensive range of medical services, including physicians, surgeons, hospitals, and other providers, and emphasize preventive care. The HMO either employs providers directly or sets up contracts with outside providers to care for subscribers. Thus, the HMO both finances care (like an insurer) and provides care (unlike an insurer).

The scope of HMO coverage is broader than that of most fee-for-service plans. For example, HMOs cover routine checkups even when the employee is not ill. Copayments apply only to minor cost items, such as physician office visits and prescription drugs (e.g., a $10 copayment may be required for

managed care

Controlled access to doctors, procedures, and medicines through a variety of plans.

preferred provider organizations (PPOs)

Groups of hospitals, physicians, and other health care providers that contract with insurers, third-party administrators, or directly with employers to provide medical care to members of the contracting group(s) at discounted prices.

health maintenance organizations (HMOs)

Provide a comprehensive range of medical services, including physicians, surgeons, hospitals, and other providers, emphasizing preventive care; either employs providers directly or sets up contracts with outside providers to care for subscribers.

each of these services). The employee has lower cost-sharing requirements than with traditional fee-for-service plans.

Two basic types of HMOs are available. Some of the oldest and largest plans are the not-for-profit **group practice association** and the staff model. In this arrangement, HMO physicians and other providers work for salaries or capitation. In **individual practice associations (IPAs)**, which can be either for-profit or not-for-profit organizations, contractual arrangements are made with physicians and other providers in a community who practice out of their own offices and treat both HMO and non-HMO members. A physician selected as an HMO member's primary physician is often paid a fixed fee per HMO member, known as capitation fee.[8] When a physician is paid by salary or per patient, the primary physician acts as a gatekeeper between the patient and specialists, hospitals, and other providers. The group association, the staff model, and the individual practice association all pay for and refer subscribers to specialists when they consider this necessary. However, if the HMO subscriber sees a specialist without a referral from the HMO, the subscriber is responsible for paying the specialist for the full cost of care. HMOs either own their own hospitals or contract with outside hospitals to serve subscribers.

Cost-Saving Motivation

Because HMO providers receive an essentially fixed annual income and promise to provide all the care the subscriber needs (with a few exclusions), they are financially at risk. If the HMO providers overtreat subscribers, they lose money. Consequently, no economic incentive exists to have subscribers return for unnecessary visits, to enter the hospital if treatment can be done in an ambulatory setting, or to undergo surgery that is unlikely to improve quality of life. This is the key aspect of an HMO that is supposed to increase efficiency relative to traditional fee-for-service plans.

A major criticism of HMOs is the limited choice of providers for subscribers. The number of physicians, hospitals, and other providers in the HMO may be quite small compared with group, staff, and individual practice models. Some individual practice plans overcome the criticism by enrolling almost every physician and hospital in a geographic region and then paying providers on a fee-for-service basis. Paying on a fee-for-service basis, however, may destroy the main mechanism that helps HMOs control costs. Another concern expressed by critics is that HMOs do not have proper incentives to provide high-quality care. A disadvantage for many of the baby boomers is the inability to seek the best health care possible. As noted in the Links section of this chapter, health care is a social commodity. Every person believes that he or she deserves the best health care. Thus, if M.D. Anderson in Houston, Texas, were the best place to receive cancer treatment, everyone would want to go to Houston for such treatment. Under HMOs, there would not be any reimbursement for this selection. Under a PPO or POS plan, the insured may use the out-of-network option and pay more, but at least he or she would receive some reimbursement. However, a recent national survey of 1,000 insureds under age sixty-five revealed that customer dissatisfaction with HMOs is lessening.[9] The explanation may be the narrowing gap in services and access to out-of-network providers that has resulted from an increased concern for patient rights, such as the 2002 Supreme Court decision that allows the states to challenge HMOs' treatment decisions.[10] Many states have subsequently created independent boards to review coverage decisions.[11]

group practice association

Not-for-profit HMO model where physicians and other providers work for salaries or capitation.

individual practice associations (IPAs)

HMO model where contractual arrangements are made with physicians and other providers in a community who practice out of their own offices and treat both HMO and non-HMO members.

2.7   Other Health Plans

Health Savings Accounts (HSAs)

Health savings accounts (HSAs) were created by the Medicare bill signed by President Bush on December 8, 2003, and are designed to help individuals save for future qualified medical and retiree health expenses on a tax-free basis. HSAs are modeled after the **medical savings accounts (MSAs)**. MSAs were used for small employers and the self-employed only and were not available to individuals or large employers. Employers or employees could contribute to the MSA but in limited amounts relative to HSAs. The annual insurance deductible for MSAs ranged from $1,650 to $2,500 for individuals, of which no more than 65 percent could be deposited into an MSA account. The range for families was $3,300 to $4,950, of which no more than 75 percent could be deposited in an MSA.

The Treasury Department created a document explaining the features of HSAs, some of which are described here. An HSA is owned by an individual, and contributions to the account are made to pay for current and future medical expenses. The most important requirement is that an HSA account can be opened only in conjunction with a **high-deductible health plan (HDHP)**, as was the case with MSAs. Only preventive care procedures are not subject to the high deductible. The HSA can be part of an HMO, PPO, or indemnity plan, as long as it has a high deductible. Eligibility is for individuals who are not covered under other comprehensive health plans or Medicare. Children cannot establish their own HSAs, and there are no income limits to open an account. Contributions to the account are made on a pretax basis, and the monies are rolled over from year to year, unlike the flexible spending account explained in Chapter 20. Health coverages that are eligible for HSAs include specific disease or illness insurance; accident, disability, dental care, vision care, and long-term care insurance; employee assistance programs; disease management or wellness programs; and drug discount cards.

In 2009, a high-deductible plan that qualifies for the HSA is a plan with a $1,050 deductible for a single person and a $2,300 deductible for a family. The maximum allowed out-of-pocket expense, including deductibles and copayments, cannot exceed $5,800 for single person coverage and $11,600 for family coverage. These amounts are indexed annually for inflation.[12] The benefits are designed with limits. Not all expenses are added toward the out-of-pocket maximum. For example, the extra cost of using providers who charge more than the usual, customary, and reasonable (UCR) amounts is not included in the maximum annual out-of-pocket expense. Preventive care is paid from first dollar and includes the required copayment. If the individual goes out of the network, out-of-pocket expenses can be higher because the limits apply to in-networks costs. Deductibles apply to all plan benefits, including prescription drugs.

Contribution to an HSA can be made by the employer or the individual, or both. If made by the employer, the contribution is not taxable to the employee. If it is made by the individual, it is a before-tax contribution. Maximum amounts that can be contributed in 2009 are $3,000 for single individuals and $5,950 for families or up to the deductible level. The amounts are indexed annually. For individuals age fifty-five and older, additional catch-up contributions are allowed (up to $1,000 in 2009).[13] Contributions must stop once an individual is enrolled in Medicare. Any amounts contributed to the HSA in excess of the contribution limits must be withdrawn or be subject to an excise tax.

HSA distributions are tax-free if they are taken for qualified medical expenses, which include over-the-counter drugs. Tax-free distributions can be taken for qualified medical expenses of people covered by the high deductible, the spouse of the individual, and any dependent of the individual (even if not covered by the HDHP). If the distribution is not used for qualified medical expenses, the amount of the distribution is included in income and there is a 10 percent additional tax, except when taken after the individual dies, becomes disabled, or reaches age sixty-five. Distributions can be used for COBRA continuation coverage (discussed in Chapter 20), any health plan coverage while receiving unemployment compensation, and for individuals enrolled in Medicare who encounter out-of-pocket expenses. It can also be used for the employee share of premiums for employer-based coverage but not for Medigap premiums (discussed later in this chapter). HSA distributions can be used for qualified long-term care insurance (see later in this chapter) and to reimburse expenses in prior years.

HSAs are owned by the individual (not the employer), and the individual decides whether he or she should contribute, how much to contribute, and how much to use for medical expenses. The employer has no right to restrict the employee or not allow rollover from year to year. The money is to be put in accounts with an HSA custodian or trustee. The custodian or trustee can be a bank, credit union, insurance company, or entity already approved by the IRS to be an IRA or an MSA trustee or custodian. Trustee or custodian fees can be paid from the assets in the HSA without being subject to tax or penalty, and the HSA trustee must report all distributions annually to the individual (Form 1099 SA). The trustee is not required to determine whether distributions are used for medical purposes.

HSAs are not "use it or lose it," like flexible spending arrangements (FSAs). All amounts in the HSA are fully vested (see Chapter 21), and unspent balances in an account remain in the account until they are spent. The objective of the HSAs is to encourage account holders to spend their funds more

health savings accounts (HSAs)

Designed to help individuals save for future qualified medical and retiree health expenses on a tax-free basis by providing participants in high deductible health plans with personal accounts funded by employer or employee contributions with before-tax dollars to put toward out-of-pocket medical expenses.

medical savings accounts (MSAs)

Allowed limited contributions from employers and employees of small businesses and self-employed persons to help cover out-of-pocket medical expenses.

high deductible health plan (HDHP)

Any health insurance plan that requires deductibles up to the amounts established by the IRS annually.

wisely on their medical care and to shop around for the best value for their health care dollars. The idea is to allow the accounts to grow like IRAs (see Chapter 21). Rollovers from HSAs are permitted, but only once per year and within sixty days of termination from the plan.

A survey by the Employee Benefit Research Institute (EBRI; featured in the box "What Is the Tradeoff between Health Care Costs and Benefits?") pointed out that owners of HSAs are less satisfied than those in comprehensive health care plans. They also found that the owners delay seeking care and are making cost-conscious decisions as intended, but lack of information makes those decisions very difficult.

The *Wall Street Journal* reported in its February 2, 2006, issue that many large employers are adopting the HSAs for their employees. They regard it as giving the employees an opportunity to open a tax-free account. Among the companies that offer HSAs to their U.S. workers are Microsoft Corporation, Fujitsu Ltd., Nokia Inc., General Motors Corporation, and DaimlerChrysler.[14] Most major banks offer HSA services.

Health Reimbursement Arrangements

health reimbursement arrangement (HRA)

Plan similar to the Health Savings Account (HSA), with the distinction that the employer controls plan contributions.

The move to consumer-driven health care plans described in "What Is the Tradeoff between Health Care Costs and Benefits?" includes another plan that can be provided by the employer only. This plan is also a defined contribution health program accompanied by a high-deductible plan. It is the **health reimbursement arrangement (HRA)** in which employees use the accounts to pay their medical expenses or COBRA premium, and they have their choice of health care providers. Under the IRS ruling, accounts funded completely by the employer are not taxable to the employees and can be carried over from year to year. At the time, this IRS ruling was considered an important step toward creating the innovative ideas of defined contribution health plans.[15]

As noted, HRA plans are funded by the employer with nontaxable funds. While these funds can be rolled over from year to year, the amount of carryover and the way in which the plan operates is determined by the employer. This is the exact opposite of what happens with HSAs. Because the funds are the employer's, any amount in an HRA usually reverts back to an employer if the employee leaves the company, although employers may fold HRA funds into a retiree benefit program. HRA funds cannot be used to pay for health insurance premiums pretaxed though a cafeteria plan (as described in Chapter 20). The only exceptions to this rule are that COBRA premiums or premiums for long-term care can be paid for from an HRA.

KEY TAKEAWAYS

In this section you studied the evolution of group health insurance and the components of different group plans:

- Employers have transitioned from traditional defined benefit health insurance arrangements to defined contribution plans that shift costs and responsibilities to employees.
- Factors responsible for the rising cost of medical care include technological advances, malpractice lawsuits, and drug/medication development.
- Traditional fee-for-service indemnity plans provided open access to subscribers, required high premiums, and reimbursed patients for care received (less deductibles).
- Basic coverages of fee-for-service plans include the following:
    - Basic hospital policy—covers room and board for a set number of days and hospital ancillary charges
    - Basic surgical policy—pays providers according to a schedule of procedures, regardless of where the surgery is performed
    - Basic medical expense policy—covers all or part of doctors' fees for hospital, office, or home visits related to nonsurgical care
- Additions to basic coverages in fee-for-service plans are the following:
    - Major medical insurance—covers the expense of nearly all services prescribed by doctors, subject to maximum and internal policy limits
    - Comprehensive medical insurance—covers a broad range of in-patient and out-patient services for a small deductible
- Coordination of benefits specifies the order and provisions of payment when individuals have coverage through two different group plans.
- Fee-for-service cost containment techniques focus on plan design, administration and funding, and utilization review.
- Managed-care plans control access to providers as a way to deal with escalating costs in the traditional fee-for-service system.
    - Health maintenance organizations (HMOs)—negotiate large discounts with health care providers and require low copays, but they limit access to in-network providers
    - Preferred provider organizations (PPOs)—provide more freedom of choice when it comes to providers (for somewhat higher costs than HMOs) and provide incentives for in-network coverage
    - Health savings accounts (HSAs)—available only in high-deductible health plans, accounts owned by individuals funded by employer or employee contributions of before-tax dollars to use for out-of-pocket medical costs
    - Health care reimbursement arrangements (HRAs)—similar to HSAs, but accounts are owned by employers

preferred provider organizations (PPOs)

Groups of hospitals, physicians, and other health care providers that contract with insurers, third-party administrators, or directly with employers to provide medical care to members of the contracting group(s) at discounted prices.

health maintenance organizations (HMOs)

Provide a comprehensive range of medical services, including physicians, surgeons, hospitals, and other providers, emphasizing preventive care; either employs providers directly or sets up contracts with outside providers to care for subscribers.

DISCUSSION QUESTIONS

1. What is the purpose of including deductible and coinsurance provisions in group medical insurance policies?
2. What characteristics should be contained in a managed-care plan?
3. What problem was managed care supposed to help solve? Did it succeed?
4. What are some of the health care cost containment methods that an insurer might utilize?
5. Explain how second surgical opinion provisions work to control health care costs.
6. What services are provided by a home health service? How do home health services reduce overall health care expenses?
7. How do PPOs differ from group practice HMOs? Is there much difference between a PPO and an individual practice HMO that pays its providers on a fee-for-service basis?
8. How does a PPO differ from a POS?
9. Describe health savings accounts (HSAs).
10. Jenkins Real Estate provides its employees with three health plan options:

   - An indemnity plan with a $200 deductible and 80 percent copayment for all medical care and prescriptions ($70 a month + $70 for spouse and dependents).
   - A **PPO**, with a $200 deductible and a $10 copay within the network, a 70 percent copay out of network, and a $15 copay for prescriptions ($50 a month for an individual, $75 for an entire family).
   - An **HMO** with no deductible and a $10 copay for all visits within the network and a $10 copay for prescriptions; no coverage out-of-network (free for employees, $20 a month for spouse and dependents).

   Which plan do you think the following employees would chose? Why?

   a. Marty Schmidt, real estate agent (age thirty-six, married, two children, wife is a stay-at-home mom, earned $80,000 last year). Neither he nor his wife have any health problems. The family is not particularly attached to any doctor.
   b. Lynn Frazer, real estate agent (age forty-five, not married, no children, earned $75,000 last year) suffers from diabetes and has a longtime doctor she would like to keep seeing (who is not in either the PPO or HMO network).
   c. Janet Cooke, receptionist (age twenty-two, single, earns $18,000 a year). She has chronic asthma and allergies, but no regular doctor.

3. INDIVIDUAL HEALTH INSURANCE CONTRACTS, CANCER AND CRITICAL ILLNESS POLICIES, AND DENTAL INSURANCE

LEARNING OBJECTIVES

In this section we elaborate on the following:

- **Individual health coverage**
- **Cancer and critical illness policies**
- **Individual and group dental insurance**

3.1 Individual Health Insurance Contracts

The individual health insurance products closely mirror the group market products. Because most of these policies are very close to the structure of the group health, we provide here examples of individual health policies available to twenty-two-year-old male and female college students in Richmond, Virginia. Table 22.3 shows examples of the plans available to the male student from some insurers using the Web site eHealthInsurance; the plans were retrieved for a start date in April 2009. Table 22.4 shows the equivalent information for the female student.

TABLE 22.3 Individual Health Insurance Option for a Full-Time Male Student, Age Twenty-Two, Residing in Richmond, Virginia, Starting April 1, 2009

Company/Plan	Monthly Premium	Plan Type	Deductible	Office Visit	Coinsurance
Anthem Individual KeyCare Preferred	$188.00	PPO	$300	$20	20%
UnitedHealthOne Saver 80	$71.43	Network	$1,000	Not covered	20%
Anthem Individual KeyCare HSA	$77.00	PPO	$1,200	$20	20% after deductible

Source: eHealthInsurance.com, http://www.ehealthinsurance.com, accessed March 17, 2009 (a registered trademark of ehealthinsurance.com).

TABLE 22.4 Individual Health Insurance Option for a Full-Time Female Student, Age Twenty-Two, Residing in Richmond, Virginia, Starting April 1, 2009

Company/Plan	Monthly Premium	Plan Type	Deductible	Office Visit	Coinsurance
Anthem Individual KeyCare Preferred	$227.00	PPO	$300	$20	20%
UnitedHealthOne Saver 80	$74.99	Network	$1,000	Not covered	20%
Anthem Individual KeyCare HSA	$93.00	PPO	$1,200	$20	20% after deductible

Source: eHealthInsurance.com, http://www.ehealthinsurance.com, accessed March 17, 2009 (a registered trademark of ehealthinsurance.com).

As you can see, one of the offers includes an HSA. Despite the high deductible of Saver 80, the plan is not HSA-compatible. While the above figures provide merely an overview, eHealthInsurance allows detailed comparisons among all available plans, and the reader is invited to take advantage of this feature. It is important to compare the policies based on the benefit package; cost sharing (such as copays, coinsurance, and deductibles); and other factors, including gender. Most of all, the comparison should include what the student assumes his or her needs may be.

In Case 2 of Chapter 23, the most noticeable difference between the individual plan and the group plan regards maternity benefits. Maternity benefits are available as a rider, or optional coverage, in the individual policy, but they cannot be optional in group insurance because of the Civil Rights Act described in Chapter 20. The act requires employers to treat pregnancies as any other medical condition.

3.2 Cancer and Critical Illness Policies

Some health policies reimburse only for specific illnesses (such as cancer), pay only a per diem amount for medical expenses, or are otherwise very limited in coverage. The consumer needs to read individual policies carefully. These policies are not for reimbursement of medical services.

"Critical illness insurance is one of those product areas that is almost guaranteed to spark a spirited debate when insurance folks get together and talk about sales," said *National Underwriter* reporter Linda Koco in "Critical Illness Insurance: Real or Gimmick?"[16] "Some producers call it a brand-new kind of policy—the fourth leg of the living benefits stool (life, health, and disability insurance being the other three). But others aren't so kind. They sniff at it and walk away baffled about why it's even here. Some dismiss it outright, as a gimmick or some sort of warmed-over cancer insurance." A **cancer or critical illness policy** is designed to pay for the extra expenses incurred during the period of medical treatment. It does not pay the doctors or any of the medical bills that are paid by health insurance. It is not a disability income policy for lost time at work (discussed later in this chapter) or accelerated benefits available in a life insurance policy. It is meant to cover the travel expenses associated with the illness, such as parents staying at a hotel next to the hospital of the child if the hospital is far away from home. It will also pay for adaptive equipment expenses such as reconfiguration of a bathroom. One of the attributes that makes this coverage interesting to buyers is the critical illness policy's lump-sum payment upon diagnosis of a dread or critical illness. Insureds believe that the coverage helps them cope with the health crisis and recovery.[17] But, like all coverages, a detailed need analysis should accompany the decision to buy such coverage.

Critical illness policies were introduced in the United States in the mid-1990s. Numerous insurance companies offer the product. One that you may be familiar with is AFLAC. The products are vastly different across the states because of varying regulations, but typically the policy pays a lump sum when the insured is diagnosed with a qualified illness. Individual contracts usually require insurability evidence. Several important questions should be asked when evaluating a critical illness policy,

cancer or critical illness policy

Pays for the extra expenses incurred during the period of medical treatment for a covered illness; used to supplement medical coverage.

including how many illnesses it covers and whether the definitions of illness are precise. The American Cancer Society regards these policies as supplementing medical coverage. The coinsurance and deductibles of a major medical policy are a major source of financial burden to families inflicted with a critical illness because such policies have no limits on out-of-pocket expenses.[18] The supplemental expense policies are available to ease this hardship. They are not to replace the health insurance but rather to help with catastrophic out-of-pocket costs. The policy also provides an initial sum of money to help cope with a critical illness. The reader is advised not to use such a policy in lieu of health insurance because a critical illness policy does not provide medical insurance, and the debate about the real need for such policies has never subsided.

3.3   Dental Insurance

Group Dental Insurance

dental insurance policies

Available in both the individual and group market, typically pay for normal diagnostic, preventive, restorative, and orthodontic services, as well as services required because of accidents.

Most medical insurance policies do not cover dental expenses. **Dental insurance policies**, available in both the individual and group market, typically pay for normal diagnostic, preventive, restorative, and orthodontic services, as well as services required because of accidents. Diagnostic and preventive services include checkups and X-rays. Restorative services include procedures such as fillings, crowns, and bridges, and orthodontia includes braces and realignment of teeth.

Group dental insurance is available from insurance companies (under fee-for-service plans); dental service plans; Blue Cross and Blue Shield; and managed-care dental plans such as dental HMOs, dental PPOs, and dental POSs. The rules under these plans are similar to that of medical expense plans. Most of the dental plans cover all types of treatment, with a schedule of maximum benefits for each procedure, such as no more than $2,000 for orthodontic treatment. Benefits are subject to coinsurance and deductibles, and the limitation may be for a calendar year maximum ($500 to $2,000) or a lifetime maximum ($1,000 to $5,000), or both. Teeth cleaning may be paid for once every six months. COBRA rules apply to dental plans. An example of a dental plan is available in Case 2 of Chapter 23.

Individual Dental Insurance

Most individual medical insurance policies do not cover dental expenses. Dental plans are offered on an individual basis as separate policies, although they can be offered as an option attached to individual health policies, too. Table 22.5 shows the dental plans offered to our twenty-two-year-old male and female students residing in Richmond, Virginia, close to school. Gender made no difference in the cost of coverage for these individual policies. In many ways, there is no difference between the individual dental plans featured here and the group dental plan featured in Case 2 of Chapter 23.

TABLE 22.5   Dental Plans for a Full-Time Male or Female Student, Age Twenty-Two, Residing in Richmond, Virginia, as of April 1, 2009

Company/Plan	Monthly Premium	Plan Type	Deductible	Annual Maximum Benefit	Coinsurance
Anthem Individual and Family Dental Plan	$32.25	PPO	$50	$1,000 per person	0% to 50%
Security Life Plan I	$18.64	Indemnity	$50	$750 per person	30% to 80%

Source: eHealthInsurance.com, http://www.ehealthinsurance.com, accessed March 17, 2009 (a registered trademark of ehealthinsurance.com).

Dental insurance policies encourage better dental health by not applying a deductible or coinsurance to charges for checkups and cleaning. By having first-dollar coverage, insureds are more likely to seek routine diagnostic care, which enables early detection of problems and may reduce total expenditures. Dental policies not only cover routine care but also protect insureds against more expensive procedures such as restorative services. For restorative and orthodontic services, insureds usually pay a deductible or coinsurance amount. A fee schedule limits the amount paid per procedure, so the insured may also pay out-of-pocket for the cost of services above the scheduled amount. Policy maximums are specified on an annual and lifetime basis, such as $2,000 per year and $50,000 during a lifetime.

Many dentists consult with the insured in advance of the procedure to determine what will be paid by insurance. The dentist lists what needs to be done and then the dentist or the insured checks with the insurer to determine coverage. Most policies exclude coverage for purely cosmetic purposes, losses caused by war, and occupational injuries or sickness.

KEY TAKEAWAYS

In this section you studied individual health policies, cancer and critical illness policies, and dental insurance:

- The features of individual health policies closely mirror those of group policies
- Special health policies called cancer and critical illness policies cover expenses related to specific illnesses and pay a lump sum upon diagnosis of a covered disease to cope with high out-of-pocket expenses (unlimited in the case of major medical coverage)
- Group dental insurance is available under fee-for-service arrangements, Blue Cross and Blue Shield plans, and managed-care options, and rules (coverage limits, coinsurance, deductibles, etc.) are very similar to health plans
- Individual dental plans can be purchased separately or as part of individual health coverage

DISCUSSION QUESTIONS

1. How do individual and group medical insurance policies differ regarding maternity benefits?
2. What kinds of expenses are cancer and critical illness policies intended to cover?
3. How does cancer and critical illness coverage differ from health insurance, disability income, or accelerated benefits from life insurance?
4. Why are cancer and critical illness policies viewed as supplementing medical coverage?
5. What types of services are covered by dental insurance contracts?
6. Why are individuals given first-dollar coverage for some dental services but not for others?

4.   DISABILITY INSURANCE, LONG-TERM CARE INSURANCE, AND MEDICARE SUPPLEMENTARY INSURANCE

LEARNING OBJECTIVES

In this section we elaborate on the following:

- **Group and individual short-term and long-term disability income insurance**
- **Group and individual long-term care (LTC) insurance**
- **Medigap supplementary insurance**

4.1   Disability Insurance

Disability income insurance replaces lost income when the insured is unable to work. Income replacement is especially critical with disability because the individual faces not only the risk of reduced earnings but also the risk of additional expenses resulting from medical or therapeutic services. In Chapter 18, we discussed the Social Security disability program, which covers most employees in the United States. However, qualifying under the Social Security definition for disability is difficult. Workers' compensation is another source of disability insurance, but only for disability arising from employment-related injury or illness (see Chapter 16). Disability income insurance, available on a group or individual basis, closes the coverage gap that arises due to nonoccupational injury or illness interrupting one's employment.

Group Disability Insurance

Group disability income coverage provides economic security for employees who are unable to work due to illness or injury. An extended disability may result in greater economic hardship for the family than does the premature death of the employee. Employers, however, are less likely to provide group disability insurance than group life or medical expense insurance.

Disability income may be provided on a short- or long-term basis. The uninterrupted flow (without gaps) of coverage of group disability income is shown in Table 22.3. Employers used to offer only sick leave and long-term disability, leaving employees without coverage for a period of time. Consultants and employee benefits specialists urge employers to close the gap and provide seamless coverage, as noted in Table 22.6.

TABLE 22.6 Seamless Coverage of Group Disability

Coverage	Salary Continuation/ Sick Leave	Short-Term Disability (STD)	Long-Term Disability (LTD)
Length of coverage	7 or more days paid time off	From 7 days up to 3, 6, 12 months or 2 years (flexibility)	From expiration of STD to age sixty-five or to lifetime
Replacement of income	100% of pay	May be as high as 100% of pay, but 70% is more common	Usually 60% to 70% of pay coordinated with Social Security and workers' compensation
Definition of disability	Inability to do your own job	Inability to do your own job or a job for which you are qualified by education and training, nonoccupational	Inability to do a job for which you are qualified by education and training, or inability to work at all, occupational and nonoccupational

Group Short-Term Disability Plans

The first step in short-term disability coverage is sick leave plans (also called salary continuation plans). With **sick leave plans**, employees accumulate leave, typically at a rate of one day per month of work up to a maximum of twenty-six weeks. In the event of illness or disability, the employee uses sick leave and receives 100 percent income replacement beginning on the first day of illness or disability. Today, many employers do not offer sick leave separately from vacation. The combined time off is called **paid time off (PTO)**. Under PTO, there is less incentive to abuse sick leave and more reward to employees who never use sick leave. PTO consolidates sick leave, personal leave, and vacation leave into a total number of personal days off each year.

Short-term disability (STD) income replacement through insured plans generally includes all full-time employees after meeting some probationary period, such as three months. Unlike sick leave, these plans do not pay benefits until after an **elimination period**, typically from one to seven days of absence from work due to disability. The employee may be required periodically to provide medical evidence of continuing disability. These plans pay for the duration stipulated in the employer's policy, usually ranging from three months to two years (although the majority pays for one year at most). Group short-term disability insurance plans do not provide full income replacement but instead pay 65 to 75 percent of salary. This provision reduces moral hazard and encourages employees to return to work.

---

sick leave plans

Allow employees to accumulate leave time that can be used in the event of injury or illness at 100 percent income replacement, typically at a rate of one day per month of work up to a maximum of twenty-six weeks.

paid time off (PTO)

Consolidates sick leave, personal leave, and vacation leave into a total number of personal days off each year to reduce employee incentive to abuse sick leave and reward those who never use sick leave.

short-term disability (STD) income replacement

Pays employees between 65-75 percent of salary from three months to two years in the event of nonoccupational injury or illness that interrupts employment.

elimination period

The one- to seven-day absence from work often required before employees qualify for benefits from short-term disability; in the case of long-term disability, may be the benefit period under short-term disability.

The **definition of disability** determines when the employee is eligible for benefits. Short-term disability insurance policies generally define disability as the inability of the employee to perform any and every duty of the job. This liberal definition allows disabled workers to qualify for benefits relatively easily when compared with the definition of disability used by most group long-term disability insurance policies. Some STD policies require a more stringent definition of disability, especially those that provide coverage for a year or more. Under this definition, the employee will receive benefits only if unable to perform a job for which he or she is qualified by education and training. Generally, group short-term disability policies pay only for nonoccupational disability, and workers' compensation benefits cover employees for short-term occupational income loss.

Group Long-Term Disability Plans

The eligibility criteria for group **long-term disability (LTD) insurance** are often different from those for short-term insured plans. Unlike short-term insured plans, which generally cover all full-time workers, long-term disability plans usually cover mostly salaried workers after they meet a probationary period lasting from three months to one year. Long-term disability plans also have an elimination period prior to payment of benefits, ranging from three to six months. The elimination period is often equivalent to the benefit period for the short-term disability plan. If the elimination period is longer than the period covered by short-term income replacement, the employee may have a gap in coverage.

The definition of disability used for long-term plans is generally more restrictive than for short-term plans. Most contracts pay only if the employee is unable to engage in the material duties of the job. Under this definition, the employee receives benefits only if he or she cannot perform a job for which he or she is qualified by education, experience, and training. For example, a surgeon who can no longer perform surgery because of a hand injury may be able to manage the surgery room. This employee will not be eligible for LTD.

Some group STD and LTD policies use a dual definition of disability. For example, benefits are payable while the own-occupation definition applies for a relatively short period of time, perhaps two or three years. After that, long-term benefits are paid only if the employee is unable to engage in any reasonable occupation for which he or she is or can become qualified. Use of both definitions provides economic security to the employee and an economic incentive to find reasonable, gainful employment.

The benefit period for LTD policies can vary greatly. Employees may be covered only for five or ten years, or they may be covered until retirement age or for life. Typically, group LTD plans pay no more than 60 to 70 percent of salary to disabled employees. In addition, a maximum dollar benefit amount may apply. Group disability benefits are usually coordinated with other disability income from Social Security or workers' compensation to ensure that the overall benefits are still below the level earned prior to disability. Employees may be able to obtain additional nongroup disability insurance in the individual market to increase their total amount of protection, although seldom to the level of full income replacement. This ensures that the disabled person has an economic incentive to return to work.

Most group LTD contracts include a rehabilitation provision. This allows insureds to return to work on a trial basis for one or two years while partial long-term disability benefits continue. If disabled employees are unable to perform in the new job, long-term disability benefits are fully restored. By providing this safety net, insurers encourage disabled workers to attempt to return to work through rehabilitative employment. Insurers may also assist with training and rehabilitation costs because these can be far less than continuing benefit payments for those who do not return to work.

LTD benefit amounts may also be affected by supplemental benefits made available to employees through payroll deductions. Cost-of-living adjustments can be added to prevent the erosion of purchasing power of the disability income benefit. Survivors' benefits can protect an employee's dependents after the death of the disabled employee.

Group LTD contracts contain several important exclusions. Benefits are not paid unless the employee is under a physician's care. Benefits are not paid for self-inflicted injuries, and **preexisting condition clauses** may restrict coverage. Generally, benefits are not paid if the employee is gainfully employed elsewhere.

In the past, long-term disability claims experience (both frequency and duration) for hourly workers has been especially unfavorable (relative to salaried employees). This may be because hourly workers are more likely to be in jobs that are monotonous and produce lower satisfaction, factors that do not help keep employees at work or encourage them to return quickly. Disability claim frequency among hourly workers has risen, especially during periods of economic recession, when job security is threatened. Hourly employees may choose to make a disability claim rather than to be laid off with temporary and minimal unemployment benefits. Because of unfavorable claims experience, employers and insurers are reluctant to provide hourly workers with long-term disability insurance.

For salaried workers, too, there has been a shift in long-term disability claims experience in the last few years. The frequency and duration of claims by salaried employees and highly paid professionals, particularly physicians, have increased significantly. The rise in claims among physicians may be due in

definition of disability

Determines when an employee is eligible for short-term disability insurance benefits, generally stated as the inability of the employee to perform any and every duty of the job; long-term disability definitions are more restrictive.

long-term disability (LTD) insurance

After satisfying an elimination (generally equivalent to the benefit period in short-term disability), pays employees between 60 and 70 percent of salary for a five to ten years or longer in the event of nonoccupational injury or illness that interrupts employment.

preexisting condition clauses

Restrict coverage of named preexisting conditions in the case of disability benefits.

part to an increasingly litigious environment for practicing medicine and to health care financing reform initiatives that threaten the traditional practice of medicine, factors that can negatively affect physician job satisfaction. Among nonmedical professionals, the increased incidence may be due to a more stressful business environment characterized by firm downsizing, especially among mid- and upper-management employees. Employers and insurers are paying attention to the increased incidence of claims among salaried employees and in some cases are limiting the amount of benefits payable for long-term disability to reduce any potential moral hazard problems.

Whether group disability benefits are taxable income to the employee depends on who pays the premiums. If the employer pays the premiums, the employee is taxed on the benefits. If the employee pays with after-tax income, the employee does not have to pay taxes on the benefits. If the employee pays with before-tax income, the employee pays taxes on the benefits in case of disability. Thus, many employers advise their employees to pay for this coverage themselves with after-tax income through payroll deductions.

Traditionally, disability insurance has never been easy to sell. However, the need for such a product is always clearer during hard times. It is known that financial planners look at the lack of disability coverage as a gap in the complete coverage for a person. A downturn in the economy is actually helpful in pushing the sales of disability income policies.[19]

Individual Disability Income Insurance Contracts

Group disability income insurance is an employee benefit less commonly offered than life, medical, and retirement benefits. If it is offered, it may not be sufficient to replace lost income. Individuals may want to purchase disability coverage on their own, in case they are not eligible for Social Security, workers' compensation, or private employer-sponsored plans, or simply because they want additional protection. Again, it is important to perform a needs analysis to determine whether a layer of individual coverage is necessary over any employer-provided disability and Social Security.

Definition and Cause of Disability

Definitions of disability vary more among individual policies than among group policies. **Total disability** may be defined as the complete inability to perform "any and every duty" of the individual's own job. Alternatively, it may be defined as the inability to engage in any "reasonable and gainful occupation" for which the individual is (or could become) qualified by education, training, or experience. Some policies combine these two definitions, with the more liberal (from the insured's point of view) "own occupation" definition satisfying the requirement for total disability during an initial short-term period (e.g., two years) and the more stringent definition being used thereafter. Partial disability is even more difficult to define than total disability. **Partial disability** is usually measured in terms of the inability to perform some of the important duties of the job. Some policies pay partial disability only if partial disability follows total disability, or only if a loss of income results.

Some contracts provide income benefits for disability caused by accident only, others for both accident and sickness. It is necessary to distinguish between losses caused by accident and those caused by sickness because the benefits can differ. Some policies provide that income losses resulting from injuries due to accident must start within ninety days after the injury. Losses resulting from injuries that begin after the ninety-day period are deemed to have resulted from sickness. A loss is not considered caused by accident unless it results "directly and independently of all other causes." This provision is designed to eliminate from the definition of accidental bodily injury those income losses actually caused by illness. For example, a person who suffers a heart attack and is injured when falling to the ground would not qualify for accident benefits but would qualify for sickness benefits.

The debate about the definition of disability is an old one. It is not always clear which definition best serves the individual policyholder. In reality, it is desirable to have a true needs assessment of the individual in this market.

Benefits

As with group insurance, both short-term disability and long-term disability policies are available for individuals. Short-term disability (STD) policies are those with benefits payable up to two years. Short-term plans may restrict benefits to periods as short as thirteen or twenty-six weeks. Individual STD plans may limit benefit duration to six months for the same cause of disability, sometimes requiring the insured to return to work for up to ninety days before establishing a new maximum benefit period for disability from the same cause.

Long-term disability (LTD) policies are those that pay benefits for longer periods, such as five years, ten years, until a set retirement age, or for life. Long-term disability policies often assume that the insured will become eligible for retirement benefits from Social Security or private retirement plans at age sixty-five. To coordinate benefits, the disability policy defines the maximum duration as age sixty-five. LTD benefits for any shorter period would expose the insured to a potentially devastating income loss because neither disability nor retirement income would be provided for this period.

---

total disability

Definitions vary across different disability policies, but generally: the complete inability to perform "any and every duty" of the individual's own job; alternatively, the inability to engage in any "reasonable and gainful occupation" for which the individual is (or could become) qualified by education, training, or experience.

partial disability

Usually measured in terms of the inability to perform some of the important duties of one's job; paid in some disability policies only if partial disability follows total disability or only if a loss of income results.

Long-term benefits do not cost proportionately more than short-term coverage. From the consumer's point of view, the longer term policy is a better buy. It protects against an unbearable risk: the long-term loss of income. This is a good example of the large loss principle, where an insurance purchase should be governed by the potential severity of loss rather than the frequency of loss. The large loss principle should govern disability income insurance purchases even though most disabilities are of relatively short duration.

Policies pay benefits after an elimination or waiting period. The elimination period, like a deductible in medical insurance, reduces moral hazard. For STD policies, the elimination period typically extends from a few days to two weeks; for LTD policies, the period extends from one month to one year. Here, as in group coverage, the insured may be covered during the LTD waiting period by benefits from the STD policy or a salary continuation plan (such as sick leave).

Individual contracts generally state the amount of the benefit in terms of dollars per week or month, unlike group policies that state benefits as a percentage of the insured's basic earnings. In either case, the insurer is wary of having the benefit equal to anything approaching full earnings. Typically, the amount is limited to about two-thirds of earned income because benefits under individual disability policies are typically not taxable. The benefits are not taxable because the premiums are paid from after-tax income. As with group disability, the purpose of this limitation is to reduce moral hazard by providing an economic incentive for employees to return to work.

Benefits may differ for disabilities resulting from accident rather than sickness. Benefits for sickness are not as generous as those for accidents. For example, a policy may provide benefit payments for five years if disability is caused by accident but only two years if caused by sickness. Some long-term policies pay to age sixty-five for sickness but for life when the cause of disability is accidental. Benefits for partial disability, which are more likely to be provided by individual contracts rather than group contracts, are often only for disability caused by accident. Some policies pay no benefits if the sickness or accident is work-related and the employee receives workers' compensation benefits. Such policies are called nonoccupational. Others supplement workers' compensation benefits up to the point at which the insured gets the same payment for occupational and nonoccupational disabilities. Some individual policies specify a maximum combined benefit for Social Security and the private policy. The insured can purchase a plan with a **social insurance substitute**, which replaces Social Security benefits if the individual does not qualify under their strict definition of disability.

Often, individual policies are not coordinated with other disability income benefits. The relatively few individual policies that coordinate disability benefits use the **average earnings provision**. This provision addresses the problem of overinsurance, which may occur when a person has more than one policy. (In group insurance, coordination of benefits provisions addresses the problem of overinsurance.) For example, a person whose salary is $2,000 per month may have two disability income policies, each of which provides $1,200 of income benefits per month. In the event of total disability, assuming no coordination provision, the insured loses $2,000 per month in salary and receives $2,400 in benefits. This reduces the incentive to return to work and may lead to benefit payment for a longer time than anticipated when the premium rate was established.

The average earnings clause provides for a reduction in benefit payments if the total amount of income payments under all insurance policies covering the loss exceeds earnings at the time disability commences, or exceeds the average earnings for two years preceding disability, whichever is greater. The amount of the reduction is the proportion by which all benefits would have to be reduced to prevent total benefits from exceeding average earned income. In the example above about the worker whose salary is $2,000 per month, total insurance payments exceeded income by one-fifth, in which case the benefits of each policy containing an average earnings clause would be reduced so that disability benefits do not exceed predisability earnings. A reduction of the payment provided by each policy from $1,200 to $1,000 per month eliminates the excess.

The insured may have policies in place that do not have an average earnings clause, and he or she could receive benefits in excess of predisability earnings. This provides an income advantage during a period of disability. As noted above, a further advantage to the insured is the absence of federal income taxes on disability benefits from individual policies (as well as employee-paid group policies). In addition, the disabled insured has few, if any, work expenses, such as clothing and transportation costs. Insurance underwriters recognize these advantages, as well as the potential for moral hazard, and may be unwilling to issue a large policy when benefits are otherwise available.

4.2 Long-Term Care Insurance

Group Long-Term Care Insurance

A significant risk that individuals face later in life is the risk of insufficient resources to pay for nursing home services. This risk applies also to a need for nursing home or skilled nursing facilities in case of an injury that requires lengthy recovery time for any age group, not only the elderly. Generally, wealthy

social insurance substitute

Disability policy provision that replaces Social Security benefits if the individual does not qualify under the strict definition of disability in Social Security.

average earnings provision

Coordinates benefits under different disability policies by providing for a reduction in benefit payments if the total amount of income payments under all insurance policies covering the loss exceeds earnings at the time disability commences or exceeds the average earnings for two years preceding disability, whichever is greater.

individuals are able to pay these expenses from their private income or savings. Those with few resources may qualify for Medicaid and public assistance. Long-term care services can be very expensive. According to the U.S. General Accounting Office (GAO), the national average annual cost for one's nursing home care is $55,000 and more in some areas. Nursing home costs are likely to increase dramatically over the next thirty years and are estimated to reach $190,000 annually per person.[20] Some people mistakenly think that long-term nursing care is covered by Medicare; as you learned in Chapter 18, Medicare covers only a limited number of days of skilled nursing care after a period of hospitalization. Group long-term care insurance is being offered by an increasing number of employers, but it is still only a small part of the long-term care insurance market. HIPAA (discussed in Chapter 20) gave tax incentives to employers offering group LTC.

group long-term care (LTC) insurance

Up to maximum daily benefits, covers the costs of skilled nursing care, intermediate care, custodial care needed to handle personal needs, home health care, and adult day care for individuals whose ability to perform a certain number of activities of daily living is impaired.

activities of daily living (ADL)

Activities such as bathing, dressing/undressing, eating, and grooming that, once unable to be performed independently, qualifies a person for long-term care insurance.

Group long-term care (LTC) insurance covers the costs of the following levels of care:

- Skilled nursing care
- Intermediate care
- Custodial care help needed to handle personal needs
- Home health care
- Adult day care

Generally, benefits are expressed as a maximum daily benefit, such as $50 or $100 per day, with an overall policy limit such as five years of benefits or a $100,000 lifetime maximum. Waiting or elimination periods are not uncommon; for example, a policy may not pay the first ninety days of nursing home expenses.

Eligibility for benefits usually is based on the inability to perform a certain number of **activities of daily living (ADL)**, such as getting out of bed, dressing, eating, and using the bathroom. Some LTC policies recognize cognitive impairment. Most cover skilled nursing care, which requires medical professionals to treat the patient on a twenty-four-hour basis under the direction of a physician. Patients typically need this type of attention for a relatively short period of time, immediately after hospitalization or following an acute illness. However, some individuals may require skilled nursing care for longer periods. Skilled nursing care is the most expensive kind of long-term care. Intermediate nursing care is for those not requiring around-the-clock assistance by medical professionals. This type of care typically extends for longer periods than skilled nursing care does.

Custodial care provides individuals with assistance in activities of daily living, such as bathing, dressing, and eating. Medical staff is not required. Although it is the least intensive kind of care, custodial care is often needed for the longest period of time and thus can be the most costly care overall. Coverage of custodial care varies across policies. Some contracts cover custodial care only if a doctor states that it is medically necessary. Others cover it only if the insured is unable to perform a certain number of activities of daily living.

Group LTC insurance typically covers skilled, intermediate, and/or custodial nursing care in a nursing home facility. Some group policies also cover home health care, in which all or a portion of these services are provided in the insured's own home. Coverage of home health care is becoming increasingly common because insureds generally prefer to be at home and total costs may be lower than if care is provided in a medical facility.

If an employer offers group LTC, eligibility may be restricted to active employees and their spouses, although sometimes retired employees up to age eighty are included. In most cases, employers do not pay for or contribute to this benefit, and the premiums paid by the employee cannot be included in a cafeteria plan or flexible spending account (explained in Chapter 20). Thus, the premiums cannot be paid with before-tax income. But HIPAA provides some tax relief if the group plan meets stringent qualification with regard to the benefits. If the employer pays the premiums, the amount is not taxable to the employees because the premiums for health insurance are not included in taxable income. Under the act, the benefits are tax-free, as are the benefits of health insurance, as long as the benefit payment per day does not exceed a certain amount. At the time of enactment of HIPAA, the amount per day was limited to $190. The qualification requirements, according to HIPAA, are that the group LTC policies cover only what is considered LTC service, benefits are paid to chronically ill people who cannot perform two out of five or six daily living activities, and the services of an LTC facility is required because of substantial cognitive impairment. These factors make the group LTC policies that qualify for the tax break very stringent and undesirable. These factors may be the main reason for the slow growth of the group LTC market. Individual LTC policies are not so limiting in the definition of the qualified recipient of the benefits.

Individual Long-Term Care Insurance

Long-term care insurance is one type of coverage that is more prevalent in the individual market because a greater number of older people are interested in such coverage than are younger working individuals. As noted previously, the inability to perform the regular daily living activities are never covered by health insurance or Medicare. The gap in coverage is closed by the development of LTC policies.

The American Association of Retired Persons (AARP) helps to promote long-term care and provides information regarding the coverage on its Web site. The site notes, "Typically, policies reimburse the insured for long-term care expenses up to a fixed amount, such as $100 per day for nursing home care and $50 per day for home care. To receive benefits, however, the insured must meet the policy's disability (long-term care) criteria. For example, some policies require the individual to be severely cognitively impaired or to need help in performing two 'activities of daily living' (such as bathing and dressing)." Other policies will pay benefits based on the loosely defined term "medical necessity."[21]

Long-term care insurance began as a basic form of nursing care insurance in the 1960s, and it expanded into custodial and home care in the 1980s. During the 1990s, the product began developing into today's LTC insurance. Contemporary policies expand the coverage and differentiate themselves.[22] Today's LTC policies include favorable changes, such as the following:

- Adding assisted living facility (ALF) coverage to policies that had nursing home and home care coverage
- Broadening the definitions of activities of daily living to include stand-by assistance
- Expanding bed reservation coverage to include reasons beyond hospitalization
- Lowering existing premiums
- Removing restrictions such as three-day prior hospitalization as well as inorganic mental and nervous exclusions
- Adding home care coverage and assisted living facility coverage[23]
- Many of these changes have pricing consequences.

The cost of individual long-term care insurance is based on cohorts of individuals. The factors for the costs are duration of benefits, the length of waiting periods, and the types of triggers of benefits. Compared with group long-term care, the definition of the triggers is not as stringent in individual LTC policies. Many policies provide for inflation protection. Cost factors vary by age, as would be expected.

The passage of HIPAA (see Chapter 20) also affected individual long-term care policies. Only the more stringent, federally qualified long-term care policies meet the favorable tax treatment of health policies. Those who use these policies can deduct the premiums up to a maximum (provided the taxpayer itemizes deductions and has medical costs in excess of 7.5 percent of adjusted gross income).

LTC Annuities

In the world of insurance, change and new products are constants. There is a new interest in **LTC annuity** products.[24] The product is similar to life insurance with an LTC rider. This rider covers the costs of nursing home stays, home health care treatment, and other LTC services typically covered by stand-alone LTC policies.[25] The tax implications of the portion of the premiums attributed to LTC are not yet determined. The LTC risk and living too long risk are inversely related because those needing LTC are expected to have a shorter life span. This provides the insurer a type of hedge.

LTC Acceleration Life Rider

Like living benefits, accelerated LTC benefits fit well with life insurance. LTC benefits are provided to the needy insureds while still living, like living benefits. Traditional life insurance policies are considered best suited for LTC riders because of the guarantees.

Insurers such as National Life and Interstate entered this market with various universal and variable life insurance products. The development activity is more pronounced in the variable universal life. These integrated VUL/LTC products pose many challenges because LTC requires more guarantees than those provided by universal variable life products. To overcome some of the challenges, the LTC benefits are designed as a percentage of the death benefit or other specified amount.[26] Some products provide a minimum death benefit guarantee, and the LTC monthly maximum benefit reflects the death benefit guarantee.

LTC annuity

Life insurance rider that covers the costs of nursing home stays, home health care treatment, and other long-term care services typically covered by stand-alone long-term care insurance policies.

4.3 Medicare Supplementary Insurance

Medigap insurance

Private individual health contracts used to supplement the coverage provided by Medicare that represent a range of benefits and premiums; ten standard Medigap insurance policies are approved for use.

Medicare health insurance is provided through the Social Security system for covered persons over age sixty-five, those under sixty-five with kidney disease, and those eligible to receive Social Security disability benefits. Medicare, however, does not completely cover the cost of all medical services needed by elderly people. Private individual health contracts, known as **Medigap insurance**, supplement the coverage provided by Medicare. Various Medigap policies are available, representing a range of benefits and premiums. In the past, the wide variety of products, as well as unethical sales practices by agents, made it difficult for consumers to understand policy provisions or compare contracts. Lengthy preexisting-condition requirements limited the protection offered by many policies. Many people purchased duplicate coverage, not realizing that the additional policies provided no extra protection. Many of the policies were not good buys, returning less than 60 cents in benefits for each dollar of premium.

In 1990, legislation required standardization of Medigap policies to make it easier for consumers to understand and compare various policy provisions. Ten standardized policies (developed by the National Association of Insurance Commissioners) are now approved for sale in the individual Medigap market. Preexisting-condition clauses cannot exceed six months. In addition, loss ratios, the ratio of benefits paid to premiums received, are required to be at least 60 percent. Legislation outlawed the sale of duplicate policies, and agents can be fined for deceptive sales practices.

The ten standard Medigap plans range from Plan A to Plan J. Plan A, the least expensive contract, is the basic policy and covers a core of benefits. Benefits increase as one moves toward Plan J, which provides the most coverage and has the highest premium. Comparing the ten standardized policies on the basis of benefits and price is straightforward, and the insured can simply decide what to purchase based on need for coverage and willingness or ability to pay. However, not all insurers selling Medigap coverage sell all of the plans.

Like long-term care insurance, Medigap insurance can provide an important element of economic security for elderly people. Given the current funding shortfalls of Medicare and the national concern with the federal budget deficit (discussed in Chapter 18), additional public funding of medical care for the elderly is unlikely. Thus, the importance of Medigap insurance is not likely to diminish anytime soon.

Every state provides Medicare supplements booklets to educate the public. The booklets provide rate comparisons and details about the differences among the various policies. Many can be found online at your state's department of insurance.[27]

KEY TAKEAWAYS

In this section you studied group and individual disability insurance, long-term care insurance, and Medicare supplemental insurance:

- Group and individual disability insurance are available to provide short-term (STD) or long-term (LTD) partial income replacement for insureds in the event of nonoccupational illness or injury.

  - The definition of disability is usually less stringent in STD than in LTD and varies more among individual policies than group policies.

  - Some policies cover disability caused by accidents only; others cover both accidents and sickness.

  - In group plans, STD might be offered as a basic coverage, with an option to purchase supplemental LTD coverage; on an individual basis, both are separate policies.

  - STD usually provides higher income replacement than LTD.

  - Group policies state benefits as a percentage of earnings, while individual contracts state benefits in terms of dollars per week.

  - STD may provide coverage for up to a year, beyond which LTD takes over.

  - Employees are taxed on disability benefits when employers pay the premiums or when premiums are paid with before-tax income; benefits from individual policies are nontaxable because premiums are paid with after-tax dollars.

  - Individual policies are often not coordinated with other disability income benefits.

- Group long-term (LTC) care insurance covers skilled nursing care, intermediate care, custodial care, home health care, and adult day care

  - Group LTC is much more popular on an individual basis than as a group coverage.

  - Group LTC benefits are expressed as a maximum daily limit subject to the overall policy limit.

  - Group LTC eligibility is based on an inability to perform a certain number of activities of daily living (ADL); individual LTC eligibility varies widely across different policies.

  - Employers rarely contribute to LTC premiums, and premiums cannot be paid with before-tax income by employees.

  - HIPAA provides tax-free benefits of group LTC if the coverage meets strict cost requirements and allows deduction of premiums up a maximum for individual policies.

  - The cost of individual LTC is based on cohorts of individuals.

  - LTC can be added as a rider to individual life insurance policies in various forms.

- Medigap insurance policies are private, individual health contracts that supplement coverage provided by Medicare.

- Ten standard Medigap plans are approved for use, offering basic to broad coverages.

DISCUSSION QUESTIONS

1. Why do most group disability insurance plans limit income replacement to no more than 70 percent of salary, even if employees are willing to pay more to get 100 percent coverage?

2. In what ways does group disability insurance differ from individual disability insurance?

3. Why would someone purchase disability income insurance when Social Security disability and workers' compensation benefits are available?

4. Explain the following statement: "The benefits of a disability income policy are no better than the definition of disability."

5. In what ways does group long-term care insurance differ from individual long-term care insurance?

6. What is a LTC annuity?

7. What are Medicare Supplement (Medigap) policies? Why are they needed?

5. REVIEW AND PRACTICE

1. What are the advantages and disadvantages of managed-care plans?

2. Anna Claire's Costumes, Inc., has experienced medical benefit cost increases of 16 and 19 percent over the last two years. The benefits manager believes that high hospitalization rates and unnecessarily long hospital stays may explain these increases. The company wants to control costs by reducing hospitalization costs.

   a. What cost control methods could be implemented to achieve this objective?

   b. Would employees still have adequate protection with these new techniques in place?

3. Marguerite Thomas, a Canadian, and Margaret Phythian, a Minnesotan, each tried to convince the other that the health care system in her respective country was superior. In Canada, Marguerite enjoys nationalized health care, where everyone is covered. She does not worry that she may need care she can't afford. She is willing to pay the taxes necessary to support the system. She doesn't mind waiting several weeks to get certain elective procedures done because she knows that everyone is getting the care they need and she is willing to wait her turn. Margaret, however, likes the high-quality, high-tech care available to her in the Twin Cities area through her employer-provided HMO. She gets high-quality care and never needs to wait for treatment. She also likes the lower tax rate she pays, partly because the U.S. government isn't funding a nationalized health care system.

   a. If Marguerite and Margaret were unemployed or had low income, which system might they prefer? Would this change if they were in high income tax brackets? Explain your answer.

   b. Which system would you prefer? What tradeoffs are you willing to make to have this type of health care system?

4. How do employees gain in the long run if the company contains medical benefit costs?

5. Knowledge Networking, Inc., is a growing business of high-tech and electronics equipment and software. It is a specialty retail and online business that has tripled its revenues in the past seven years. The company started fifteen years ago and includes fifty outlets on both the East and West coasts. In 2005, the company went public and now, despite the financial crisis, it is doing very well with innovation and creative offerings. The company has 5,600 full-time employees and 1,000 part-time employees. Knowledge Networking, Inc., provides all the social insurance programs and offers its employees a cafeteria plan with many choices.

   For the health coverage, Knowledge Networking employees have a choice among the following:

   5.1. An IPA type HMO (fully insured) at a cost of $250 for the employee only per month

   5.2. One PPO and one POS administered by a TPA (self-insured) at a cost of $300 and $320 respectively

   5.3. An HSA with an underlying PPO plan (fully insured) at a cost of $150 per month.

Employees also have generous choices of group disability coverages, dental and vision care, premium conversion plan, and flexible spending accounts as part of the cafeteria plan.

a. Use the table below to describe what you think Knowledge Networking's group disability insurance plans look like.

Knowledge Networking, Inc. Group Short-Term and Long-Term Disability Insurance	
	Current
Definitions and amounts	
Supplements	
Additions	
Eligibility	
Financing/cost and who pays	
Tax implication	
Insured and by whom?	

b. Give an example of the benefit plan choices that the following two employees would make:

- Shawn Dunn, a young, unmarried healthy employee who makes $100,000 a year
- Dan Rohm, a forty-five-year-old man with four school-age children who makes $125,000 a year

6. Describe long-term care insurance.

7. If custodial care is the least expensive type of service covered by long-term care insurance, is it important to make sure your contract covers this type of care?

8. Your grandmother is sixty-five years old. She has begun to receive benefits through Medicare and has just enrolled in Medicare Part B. She wants to know why she should purchase a Medigap insurance policy. Explain this predicament to her.

9. The Meridian Advertising Agency has 1,340 employees in six states. The main office is in Richmond, Virginia. Fifty percent of the employees are women in their childbearing years. Most employees are in good health. The major medical losses last year occurred because of Jack Denton's heart surgery, fifteen baby deliveries, and four cases of cancer treatment. Jack Denton is the creative director of the agency.

Meridian is using EB-Consulting to assist in choosing health care and dental coverages. Currently the agency fully insures six options of health plans:

- A staff model HMO available only in Richmond (premium per employee is $145 per month)
- An IPA HMO available in many but not all locations ($155 per month)
- A POS available in all locations ($160 per month)
- A PPO available in all locations ($175 per month)
- An indemnity plan available in all locations ($190 per month)
- An HSA plan with an underlying PPO ($70 per month premium; the employer contributes into the account at $100 per month)

The Meridian Agency provides $145 each month. The rest is paid by the employee using a premium conversion plan.

a. Compare the current health care programs that are used by the Meridian Agency in terms of the following:

- Benefits provided under each plan
- Possible out-of-pocket expenses for the employees and their families for illnesses and injuries
- Choice of providers
- The ways providers are being reimbursed

b. Jack Denton (the employee who had heart surgery) has two children. He lives twenty miles west of Richmond in a rural community of one hundred people and farms his land on the weekends. His wife is expecting another baby in four months. Before his surgery, Jack and his wife evaluated the plans and selected the one that best fit their needs.

- Which health plan do you think they selected? Explain your answer.
- Do you think now, after his surgery, Jack is still happy with this choice? Explain your answer.

c. Meridian is considering adding a dental plan.

- What type of dental plan do you think EB-Consulting would suggest?
- Why are dental insurance plans more likely than medical expense plans to include benefits for routine examinations and preventive medicine?

d. EB-Consulting is trying to convince the Meridian Agency to add long-term care insurance to their employee benefits package. Explain long-term care coverage.

ENDNOTES

1. Insurance Information Institute, *The Insurance Fact Book*, 2009, 13–14.

2. Employee Benefit Research Institute, *EBRI Databook on Employee Benefits*, ch.2: "Finances of the Employee Benefit System," updated September 2008, http://ebri.org/pdf/publications/books/databook/DB.chapter%2002.pdf (accessed April 22, 2009).

3. Not all types of plans are included in the table. Exclusive physician organization (EPO) is another plan that does not permit access to providers outside the network. Also, HRA is not featured here.

4. Copayments can run from $10 for PCP to $35+ for specialists. Each plan is negotiated, so copayments may differ. See examples later in this chapter.

5. All plans are required to provide preventive care such as mammography screenings and Pap tests.

6. The distinction among the managed care plans—PPOs, POSs, and HMOs—has become more fuzzy in recent years because HMOs are required to provide emergency benefits outside the network and more choice. HMOs have begun unbundling the preventive care services and charge additional premiums for more benefits such as vision and dental care.

7. Today, Kaiser Permanente is one of the largest HMOs in the United States, with operations scattered across the country.

8. An example of the calculation of capitation provided by the American Society of Dermatology is featured in "Develop a Realistic Capitation Rate" at the society's Web site: http://www.asd.org/realrate.html.

9. "HMOs Tightening Consumer Satisfaction Gap: Survey," *National Underwriter Online News Service*, July 15, 2002.

10. Robert S. Greenberger, Sarah Lueck, and Rhonda L. Rundle, "Supreme Court Rules Against HMOs on Paying for Rejected Treatments," *Wall Street Journal*, June 21, 2002.

11. Steven Brostoff, "High Court Upholds States' HMO Rules," *National Underwriter Online News Service*, June 20, 2002.

12. Internal Revenue Service (IRS), "Health Savings Accounts and Other Tax-Favored Health Plans," Publication 969 (2008), http://www.irs.gov/publications/p969/ar02.html#en_US_publink100038739 (accessed April 22, 2009).

13. Internal Revenue Service (IRS), "Health Savings Accounts and Other Tax-Favored Health Plans," Publication 969 (2008), http://www.irs.gov/publications/p969/ar02.html#en_US_publink100038739 (accessed April 22, 2009).

14. Sarah Rubenstein, "Is an HSA Right for You? President Proposes Sweetening Tax Incentives As More Companies Offer Latest Health Benefit," *Wall Street Journal Online*, February 2, 2006, http://online.wsj.com/public/article/SB113884412224162775-jMcNHLtKsbwT1_WhQ90yKd2FDfg_20070201.html?mod=rss_free (accessed April 22, 2009).

15. "Hewitt Praises New IRS Health Account Rules," *National Underwriter Online News Service*, July 2, 2002. The IRS has posted more information about the HRA guidelines on the Internet at http://www.ustreas.gov/press/releases/po3204.htm.

16. Linda Koco, "Critical Illness Insurance: Real or Gimmick?" *National Underwriter*, Life & Health/Financial Services Edition, January 1, 2002.

17. Patrick D. Lusk, "Critical Illness Insurance Ideal for Worksite," *National Underwriter*, Life & Health/Financial Services Edition, August 31, 1998.

18. IEEE Financial Advantage Program, insurance articles of interest at http://www.ieeeinsurance.com (accessed April 22, 2009).

19. Sadler, Jeff. "Down Economy Can Push DI Sales Up," *National Underwriter*, Life & Health/Financial Services Edition, February 25, 2002.

20. From TIAA-CREF Web Center, "How Much Does Long-Term Care Cost, and Who Pays for It?" at http://www.tiaa-cref.org/ltc/ltcosts.html.

21. AARP, http://www.aarp.org/research/longtermcare/insurance/, accessed April 22, 2009.

22. Mary Madigan and Cheryl McNamara, "Insuring an Independent Lifestyle," *Best's Review*, April 1, 2002, http://www3.ambest.com/Frames/FrameServer.asp?AltSrc=23&Tab=1&Site=bestreview&refnum=16718, accessed April 22, 2009.

23. Claude Thau, "Surveying Industry Practices on Changes to In-Force LTCI Policies," *National Underwriter*, Life & Health/Financial Services Edition, March 29, 2002.

24. Chelsea K. Bachrach and Craig R. Springfield, "LTC-Annuities: Two Birds, One Stone," *National Underwriter Life & Health/Financial Services Edition*, September 2, 2002.

25. Cary Lakenbach, "Traditional Life: A Chassis for LTC Riders," *National Underwriter Life & Health/Financial Services Edition*, September 13, 1999.

26. Cary Lakenbach, "Integrated VL/LTCs Pose Some Challenges," *National Underwriter Life & Health/Financial Services Edition*, February 21, 2000.

27. For examples, see the Texas Department of Insurance Web site at http://www.tdi.state.tx.us/; the North Dakota Department of Insurance Web site at http://www.state.nd.us/; or the Nebraska Department of Insurance Web site at http://www.state.ne.us/. Details are also provided at the AARP Web site at http://www.aarp.org/.

CHAPTER 23
Cases in Holistic Risk Management

By this point, you have gained an understanding of the life cycle risks associated with mortality, longevity, and health/disability. You have learned about the social insurance programs such as Social Security and Medicare that help counter these risks. We have delved into life, health, and disability insurance products in Chapter 19 and Chapter 22 and discussed pensions in Chapter 21. The availability and features of these products in group (employer-sponsored) or individual arrangements were also discussed. On the property/casualty side, we covered all the risks confronted by families and enterprises. We discussed the solutions using insurance for the home, automobile, and liability risks. Thus, you now have the tools needed to complete the holistic risk puzzle and the steps representing each layer of the risk management pyramid, from society on up to you as an individual.

With that said, this chapter is a departure from most, but it is vitally important. Our final lesson focuses on applying your knowledge and skills in the complete holistic risk management picture. In other words, you will now learn how to use your new tools. Practical case studies featuring hypothetical families and companies—some designed by fellow students—are utilized to fulfill this objective. The situations posed by these cases are ones that you may encounter in the roles you serve throughout your life, and they incorporate the insurance products and risk management techniques discussed throughout this text.

We begin first with a sample family risk management portfolio involving home, auto, life, health, and disability insurance coverage and planning for retirement. This case is for the personal needs of families. The second case focuses on the employer's provided employee benefits package. It is designed as the benefits handbook of a hypothetical employer who provides more benefit options than current practices. In the last case, we broaden our understanding of enterprise risk management (covered in Part I of the text) by exploring the concept of alternative risk financing and the challenges faced by a risk manager in selecting among insurance products for commercial risk management needs.

At the conclusion of this chapter, your knowledge of risk management concepts will be reinforced and expanded. The chapter is structured as follows:

1. Links

2. Case 1: The Smith Family Insurance Portfolio

3. Case 2: Galaxy Max, Inc., Employee Benefits Package

4. Case 3: Nontraditional Insurance Programs and Application to the Hypothetical LOCO Corporation

1. LINKS

1.1 Losses Paid to Hypothetical Victims' Families

To understand the spectrum of personal losses to the families, we introduce two hypothetical families who were directly affected by the World Trade Center catastrophe. The families are those of Allen Zang, who worked as a bond trader in the South Tower of the World Trade Center, and his high school friend Mike Shelling, a graduate student who visited Allen on the way to a job interview. Both Mike and Allen were thirty-four years old and married. Mike had a six-year-old boy and Allen had three young girls.

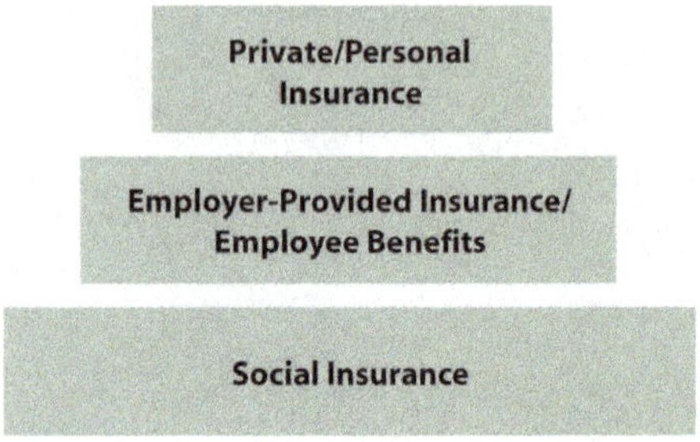

FIGURE 23.1 Structure of Insurance Coverages

Private/Personal Insurance

Employer-Provided Insurance/ Employee Benefits

Social Insurance

Both Allen and Mike were among the casualties of the attack on the World Trade Center. But their eligibility for benefits was considerably different because Mike was not employed at the time. In the analysis of the losses or benefits paid to each family, we will first evaluate the benefits available under the social insurance programs mandated in the United States and in New York. Second, we will evaluate the benefits available under the group insurance programs and pensions provided by employers. Third, we will evaluate the private insurance programs purchased by the families (as shown in Figure 23.1). We will also evaluate the ways that families might attempt to collect benefits from negligent parties who may have contributed to the losses.

Recall from Chapter 18 that social insurance programs include Social Security, workers' compensation, and unemployment compensation insurance (and, in a few states, state-provided disability insurance). In the United States, these programs are intended to protect members of the work force and are not based on need. The best-known aspect of Social Security is the mandatory plan for retirement (so-called old-age benefits). But the program also includes disability benefits; survivors' benefits; and Medicare parts A, B, C, and D.

Table 23.1 shows the benefits available to each of the families. It is important to note that both Mike and Allen were employed for at least ten years (forty quarters). Therefore, they were fully insured for Social Security benefits, and their families were eligible to receive survivors' benefits under Social Security. Each family received the allotted $255 burial benefit. Also, because both had young children, the families were eligible for a portion of the fathers' Primary Insurance Amount (PIA). The Social Security Administration provided the benefits immediately without official death certificates, as described by Commissioner Larry Massanari in his report to the House Committee on Ways and Means, Subcommittee on Social Security.[1]

You learned in Chapter 16 that workers' compensation provides medical coverage, disability income, rehabilitation, and survivors' income (death benefits). Benefits are available only if the injury or death occurred on the job or as a result of the job. Because Allen was at the office at the time of his death, his family was eligible to receive survivors' benefits from the workers' compensation carrier of the employer.

TABLE 23.1 Benefits for Two Hypothetical Losses of Lives

	Mike's Family	Allen's Family
Social insurance		
Death benefits (survivors' benefits) from Social Security	Yes	Yes
Workers' compensation	No	Yes
State disability benefits	No	No
Unemployment compensation	No	No
Employee benefits (group insurance)		
Group life	No	Yes
Group disability	No	Yes
Group medical	No	Yes (COBRA)
Pensions and 401(k)	Yes (former employers)	Yes
Personal insurance		
Individual life policy	Yes	No

The New York Workers' Compensation Statute states, "If the worker dies from a compensable injury, the surviving spouse and/or minor children, and lacking such, other dependents as defined by law, are entitled to weekly cash benefits. The amount is equal to two-thirds of the deceased worker's average weekly wage for the year before the accident. The weekly compensation may not exceed the weekly maximum, despite the number of dependents. If there are no surviving children, spouse, grandchildren, grandparents, brothers, or sisters entitled to compensation, the surviving parents or the estate of the deceased worker may be entitled to payment of a sum of $50,000. Funeral expenses may also be paid, up to $6,000 in Metropolitan New York counties; up to $5,000 in all others."

The maximum benefit at the time of the catastrophe was $400 per week, less any Social Security benefits, for lifetime or until remarriage.[2] Thus, Allen's family received the workers' compensation benefits minus the Social Security amount. Recall from Chapter 16 that under the workers' compensation system, the employee's family gives up the right to sue the employer. Allen's family could not sue his employer, but Mike's family, not having received workers' compensation benefits, may believe that Allen's employer was negligent in not providing a safe place for a visitor and may sue under the employer's general liability coverage.

In Mike's case, the New York Disability Benefits program did not apply because the program does not include death benefits for "non-job-injury." If Mike were disabled rather than killed, this state program would have paid him disability benefits. Of course, unemployment compensation does not apply here either. However, it would apply to all workers who lost their jobs involuntarily as a result of a catastrophe.

Because Allen was employed at the time, his family was also eligible to receive group benefits provided by his employer (as covered in Chapter 20, Chapter 21, and Chapter 22). Many employers offer group life and disability coverage, medical insurance, and some types of pension plans or 401(k) tax-free retirement investment accounts. Allen's employer gave twice the annual salary for basic group term life insurance and twice the annual salary for accidental death and dismemberment (AD&D). The family received from the insurer death benefits in an amount equal to four times Allen's annual salary, free from income tax (see Chapter 19 and Chapter 21). Allen earned $100,000 annually; therefore, the total death benefits were $400,000, tax-free.

Allen also elected to be covered by his employer's group short-term disability (STD) and long-term disability (LTD) plans. Those plans included supplemental provisions giving a small amount of death benefits. In the case of Allen, the amount was $30,000. In addition, his employer provided a defined contribution plan, and the accumulated account balance was available to his beneficiary. The accumulated amount in Allen's 401(k) account was also available to his beneficiary.

Mike's family could not take advantage of group benefits because he was not employed. Therefore, no group life or group STD and LTD were available to Mike's family. However, his pension accounts from former employers and any individual retirement accounts (IRAs) were available to his beneficiary.

Survivors' medical insurance was a major concern. Allen's wife did not work and the family had medical coverage from Allen's employer. Allen's wife decided to continue the health coverage the family had from her husband's employer under the Consolidated Omnibus Budget Reconciliation Act (COBRA) of 1986. The law provided for continuation of health insurance up to 36 months to the wife as a widow for the whole cost of the coverage (both the employee and the employer's cost) plus 2 percent (as covered in Chapter 22).

For Mike's family, the situation was different because Mike was in graduate school. His wife covered the family under her employer's health coverage. She simply continued this coverage.

The third layer of available coverage is personal insurance programs. Here, the families' personal risk management comes into play. When Mike decided to return to school, he and his wife consulted with a reputable financial planner who helped them in their risk management and financial planning. Mike had made a series of successful career moves. In his last senior position at an Internet start-up company, he was able to cash in his stock options and create a sizeable investment account for his family. Also, just before beginning graduate school, Mike purchased a $1 million life insurance policy on his life and $500,000 on his wife's life. They decided to purchase a twenty-year level term life rather than a universal life policy (for details, refer to Chapter 19) because they wanted to invest some of their money in a new home and a vacation home in Fire Island (off Long Island, New York).

The amount of insurance Mike bought for his wife was lower because she already had sizeable group life coverage under her employer's group life insurance package. Subsequent to Mike's death, his wife received the $1 million in death benefits within three weeks. Despite not having a death certificate, she was able to show evidence that her husband was at the World Trade Center at the time. She had a recording on her voice mail at work from Mike telling her that he was going to try to run down the stairs. The message was interrupted by the sound of the building collapsing. Thus, Mike's beneficiaries, his wife and son, received the $1 million life insurance and the Social Security benefits available. Because the family had sizeable collateral resources (non–federal government sources), they were eligible for less than the maximum amount of the Federal Relief Fund created for the victims' families.

Allen's family had not undertaken the comprehensive financial planning that Mike and his family had. He did not have additional life insurance policies, even though he planned to get to it "one of these days." His family's benefits were provided by his social insurance coverages and by his employer. The family was also eligible for the relief fund established by the federal government, less collateral resources.

1.2 Losses Paid to a Hypothetical Business

To see how the catastrophe affected nearby businesses, we will examine a hypothetical department store called Worlding. In our scenario, Worlding is a very popular discount store, specializing in name-brand clothing, housewares, cosmetics, and linens. Four stories tall, it is located in the heart of the New York financial district just across from the World Trade Center. At 9:00 A.M. on September 11, 2001, the store had just opened its doors. At any time, shoppers would have to fight crowds in the store to get to the bargains. The morning of September 11 was no different. When American Airlines Flight 11 struck the North Tower, a murmur spread throughout the store and the customers started to run outside to see what happened. As they were looking up, they saw United Airlines Flight 175 hit the South Tower. By the time the towers collapsed, all customers and employees had fled the store and the area. Dust and building materials engulfed and penetrated the building; the windows shattered, but the structure remained standing. Because Worlding leased rather than owned the building, its only property damage was to inventory and fixtures. But renovation work, neighborhood cleanup, and safety testing kept Worlding closed—and without income—for seven months.

The case of insurance coverage for Worlding's losses is straightforward because the owners had a business package policy that provided both commercial property coverage and general liability. Worlding bought the Causes of Loss—Special Form, an open perils or all risk coverage form (as explained in Chapter 11 and Chapter 15). Instead of listing perils that are covered, the special form provides protection for all causes of loss not specifically excluded. Usually, most exclusions found in the special form relate to catastrophic potentials. The form did not include a terrorism exclusion. Therefore, Worlding's inventory stock was covered in full.

Worlding did not incur any liability losses to third parties, so all losses were covered by the commercial property coverage. Worlding provided regular inventory data to its insurer, who paid for the damages without any disputes. With its property damage and the closing of the neighborhood around the World Trade Center, Worlding had a nondisputable case of business interruption loss. Coverage for business interruption of businesses that did not have any property damage, such as tourist-dependent hotel chains and resort hotels,[3] depended on the exact wording in their policies. Some policies were more liberal than others, an issue described in Chapter 15.

Because Worlding was eligible for business income interruption coverage, the owners used adjusters to help them calculate the appropriate amount of lost income, plus expenses incurred while the business was not operational. An example of such a detailed list was provided in Chapter 15. The restoration of the building to Worlding's specifications was covered under the building owners' commercial property policy.

1.3 Importance of the Loss Cases

As these examples show, complete insurance is a complex maze of varying types of coverage. This introduction is designed to provide a glimpse into the full scope of insurance that affects the reader as an individual or as a business operator. In our business case, if Worlding had not had business insurance, its employees would have been without a job to return to. Thus, the layer of the business coverage is as important in an introductory risk and insurance course as are all aspects of your personal and employment-related insurance coverages.

In addition, emphasis is given to the structure of the insurance industry and its type of coverage and markets. Emphasis is given to the new concept of considering all risks in an organization (enterprise risk management), not just those risks whose losses are traditionally covered by insurance.

The text has been designed to show you, the student, the width and variety of the field of risk management and insurance. At this stage, the pieces needed for holistic risk management now connect. As noted above, current events and their risk management outcomes have been clarified for you, whether the losses are to households or businesses. Furthermore, you now have the basic tools to build efficient and holistic risk management portfolios for yourself, your family, and your business.

The risk puzzle piecing together the risks faced by individuals and entities is presented one final time in Figure 23.2, which brings us full circle.

FIGURE 23.2 Complete Picture of the Holistic Risk Puzzle

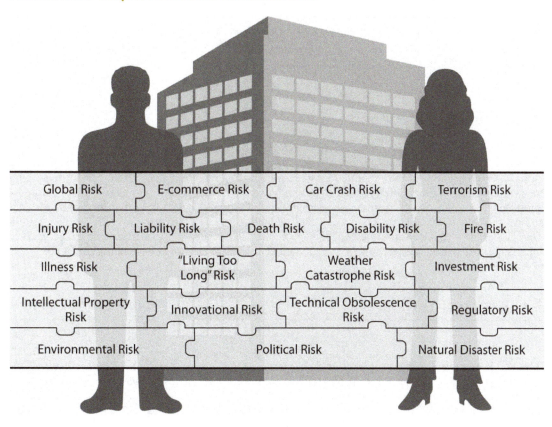

2.   CASE 1: THE SMITH FAMILY INSURANCE PORTFOLIO

LEARNING OBJECTIVES

In this section we elaborate on insurance and employee benefits selections of the hypothetical Smith family based on their specific needs:

- **Homeowners insurance**
- **Auto insurance**
- **Long-term disability**
- **Life insurance**
- **Health insurance**
- **Retirement planning**

2.1   Preface

The purpose of this project is to build a portfolio of risk management and insurance coverages for a hypothetical family. This report is typical of those produced by students as a group project in the author's risk and insurance classes. The students present sections of the types of coverage they design throughout the semester and submit the complete project at the end of the semester as part of their final grade. The students live the project during the semester and provide creativity along with hands-on knowledge and information about the best risk management for their fictional families. Many groups develop special relationship with helpful agents who volunteer to speak to the class. The help that agents provide receives high marks from most students.

This report, as all the others produced by the students, considers property, auto, disability, life, health, and long-term care insurance, as well as retirement planning. The group project presented here does not involve the agent-customer relationship. Many other reports do include the relationship as a reason to buy from a specific company.

2.2 Introduction

We[4] examined different types of insurance and selected the best coverage for our hypothetical family—the Smith family. Several insurance quotes were found through Insweb.com, and others were benefits offered by Virginia Power, a utility company in Richmond, Virginia. We also talked to some agents.

2.3 Family Description

John is a thirty-five-year-old nuclear engineer who has been working for Virginia Power since 1999. His wife, Karen, is a thirty-year-old homemaker. They have been married for five years. John and Karen have a nine-month-old infant named Tristian. John and Karen are in good health. They are looking forward to having another child, but Karen has high pregnancy risk. This has to be taken into consideration when selecting health insurance coverage for the family. Their annual net income is $72,000 (John's salary of $100,000, less taxes and other deductions). They own two cars. John drives a 1996 Toyota Corolla and Karen drives a 1997 Toyota Camry. They need good insurance coverage because John is the only one who is working. All the insurance providers examined have ratings of "A" or better in A.M. Best ratings.

2.4 Insurance Coverage

Homeowners Insurance

John and Karen purchased a two-story single home for $150,000 in 1996. The house is located on 7313 Pineleaf Drive in Richmond, Virginia. The total footage is 2,014 square feet. There is a two-car attached garage. John and Karen decided not to renew their homeowners insurance with AllState Insurance because of the expensive premium and unacceptable customer service they experienced in the past. John did research on the Internet and found quotes from different companies. He was asked to give detailed information on the house. The house is located within 1,000 feet of a fire hydrant and it is one hundred feet away from a fire station. John promised to install a security system to prevent theft. Karen wanted extra protection on her precious jewelry worth $10,000, Ming china worth $5,000, and antique paintings valued at $7,000. They need scheduled personal property endorsements. Over the last five years, John and Karen's house has appreciated by $10,000. They want to insure the home to 100 percent of its estimated replacement cost, which is $160,000, rather than 80 percent. In case of a total loss, the insurer will replace the home exactly as it was before the loss took place, even if the replacement exceeds the amount of insurance stated in the policy. Table 23.2 summarizes the coverage quoted by three insurance companies.

TABLE 23.2 Homeowners Insurance Plan Options

	Geico Insurance	Travelers Insurance	Nationwide Insurance
Coverage A: dwelling replacement	$160,000.00	$160,000.00	$160,000.00
Coverage B: other structures	$ 16,000.00	$ 16,000.00	$ 16,000.00
Coverage C: personal property	$112,000.00	$112,000.00	$112,000.00
Coverage D: loss of use	$ 48,000.00	$ 48,000.00	$ 48,000.00
Coverage E: personal liability	$300,000.00	$300,000.00	$300,000.00
Coverage F: guest medical	$ 2,000.00	$ 2,000.00	$ 2,000.00
Deductible	$ 500.00	$ 250.00	$ 500.00
Endorsements for collectibles and inflation guard	Yes	Yes	Yes
Annual premium	$ 568.00	$ 512.00	$ 560.00
S&P rating	AAA	AA	AA–

The Smith family decided to choose the insurance coverage provided by Travelers because of the company's good rating and low premium, and because the premium includes a water-back coverage. Under this HO 3 (special form), dwelling and other structures are covered against risk of direct loss to property. All losses are covered except certain losses that are specifically excluded.

Auto Insurance

John drives a 1996 Toyota Corolla, which he purchased new for $18,109. He had one accident in the past four years in which he was hit by another driver. His estimated driving mileage within a year is 10,000. He drives 190 miles weekly to work. His car is not used for business purposes. Karen bought a new Toyota Camry in 1997 for $20,109. She has never had an accident. Her estimated mileage within a year is 7,500 and the weekly driving is 100 miles.

The Smiths used Insweb.com and found several quotes from various insurance companies that fit their needs. Table 23.3 summarizes the results of their research.

TABLE 23.3   Auto Insurance Plan Options

Companies	Harford	Integon Indemnity	Dairyland
A.M. Best Rating	A+	A+	AA+
Liability	100,000/300,000/ 100,000	100,000/300,000/ 100,000	100,000/300,000/ 100,000
Medical payments	$5,000	$5,000	$5,000
Uninsured/underinsured motorist	100,000/300,000/ 100,000	100,000/300,000/ 100,000	100,000/300,000/ 100,000
Collision	$250 deductible	$250 deductible	$250 deductible
Other than collision	$500 deductible	$500 deductible	$500 deductible
Monthly premium	$160	$210	$295

The Smith family decided to choose the insurance coverage provided by Harford Insurance Company. Harford has an A+ rating, the coverage is more comprehensive, and the premium is significantly lower than the other two companies.

Loss Scenario 1

John has had this auto insurance for almost half a year. On the way to a business meeting one day, he is hit by an uninsured motorist. John's car is badly damaged and he is rushed to the emergency room. Luckily, John has only minor cuts and bruises. John reports this accident to the police and notifies his insurer. The insurance company inspects and appraises the wrecked car. The Smiths' uninsured motorists coverage covers John's medical expenses (under bodily injury) and property damages caused by the accident. Harford Insurance considers John's car a total loss and pays him $14,000 (fair market value less the deductible).

Long-Term Disability

The Smith family decided to purchase long-term disability (LTD) insurance for John because he is the only breadwinner in the family. In the event of an accident that would disable John and leave him unable to work, the family would need adequate coverage of all their expenses. The LTD benefit provided by John's employer, Virginia Power, would pay 50 percent of John's salary in case of his total disability; however, the family would like to have more coverage.

TransAmerica, an insurance broker that prepares coverage for Erie and Prudential Life, prepared two plans for the Smiths as shown in Table 23.4. Both plans provided benefits to age sixty-five with a ninety-day waiting period. Both plans offer the same level of optional benefits, including residual disability and an inflation rider.

TABLE 23.4   Long-Term Disability Plan Options

	Erie	Prudential
Benefit period	To age sixty-five	To age sixty-five
Waiting period	90 days	90 days
Monthly benefit	$2,917.00	$3,700
Base annual premium	$1,003.49	$1,262.10
Total annual premium	$1,414.88	$1,783.92
Optional benefits		
Residual disability	$183.25	$232.43
Inflation rider	$228.14	$289.38

The Smith family chose additional disability coverage provided by Erie because of the lower premium, lower residual disability cost, and lower inflation rider cost.

Life Insurance

The Smith family realized they needed to invest in additional term life insurance for John because his employer provided only term life coverage in the amount of one times his salary, $100,000. They did not need to worry about life insurance for Karen because her parents bought a ten-year level term coverage in the amount of $250,000 on Karen's life when Tristian was born. They told Karen that an untimely death would mean an economic loss to the family because John would likely have to hire help for housekeeping and child care.

As noted above, John is thirty-five years old and in very good health. He enjoys working out at the gym after work at least three days a week and has never been a smoker. John's family history shows no serious health problems, and most of his relatives have lived well into their seventies.

To decide how much life insurance is needed for John, he and Karen worked on a needs analysis with some friends who are familiar with financial planning. They came to the conclusion that he will need to purchase $300,000 additional coverage. The following breakdown shows why they believe they need this amount of coverage:

Cash needs		
Funeral expenses	$12,000	
Probating will and attorney fees	$3,000	
Income needs		
To get Karen and Tristian on their feet	$192,000	($4,000 monthly for 4 years)
Special needs		
Balance on mortgage	$120,000	
College fund for Tristian	$50,000	
Emergency fund	$75,000	
Total family needs		**$452,000**
Current financial assets		
Savings balance	$20,000	
401(k) current balance	$32,000	
Group term insurance	$100,000	
Total current financial assets		**$152,000**
Additional coverage needed		**$300,000**

Virginia Power offers additional life insurance that their employees can purchase through North American Life. The Smiths wanted to compare prices of additional coverage, so they looked on the Internet. They found that the Western-Southern Life and John Hancock plans to fit their budget and their needs. All three plans are compared in Table 23.5.

TABLE 23.5 Life Insurance Plan Options

	North American (VA Power)	Western-Southern Life	John Hancock
Amount	$300,000	$300,000	$300,000
Term period	20 years	20 years	20 years
Initial monthly premium	$21.00	$19.95	$18.50
Initial rate guarantee	5 years	20 years	20 years
S&P rating	AA	AAA	AA+

The Smith family decided to go with Western-Southern Life because of its higher rating, low premiums, and guaranteed initial rate for twenty years. John will have to prove evidence of his insurability when he purchases the coverage (unlike the group life coverage provided by the employer). This is not a major issue to John because he is in excellent health. If John were to leave the company, his life insurance would terminate, but he could convert it to an individual cash-value policy at that time.

Health Insurance

Virginia Power offers its employees two preferred provider organization (PPO) options and one health maintenance organization (HMO) option. The Smith family decided to choose one of the PPO plans as opposed to an HMO plan because Karen and John are planning to have another child and, considering her high-risk status, prefer to have more choices and out-of-network options if necessary.

A PPO is a network of health care providers who have agreed to accept a lower fee for their services. A PPO plan gives one the flexibility to select a network provider without having to select a primary care physician to coordinate care or to go out-of-network with higher copayments. All of Virginia Power's benefit coverage is provided by Anthem, a Blue Cross/Blue Shield company with A++ rating. Employees of Virginia Power and their family members are covered on the date employment begins. Benefits will be provided at the in-network level to an employee who lives outside the network's geographic area. In-network participants must receive preventative care benefits from PPO providers. Participants who live outside the network's geographic area may receive these services from PPO and non-PPO providers. Table 23.6 compares the benefits of the two PPO options.

TABLE 23.6 Health Insurance Plan Options

Feature	Medical Plan 1	Medical Plan 2
	In-Network/Out-of Network	In-Network/Out-of Network
Annual deductible	$572	$1,146
Monthly premiums (employee's portion for the whole family)	$91.41	$41.13
Out-of-pocket maximum	$2,288/$4,004	$4,584/$8,022
Lifetime maximum benefits	Unlimited	$1,000,000
Participant coinsurance	20%/40%	20%/40%
Preventative care	100% after $10 copay for generalist; $20 copay for specialist	
Prescription drugs		
—Deductible	None	None
—Participant coinsurance	20%	20%
—Out-of-pocket maximum	$700	$700
Out-patient mental health	After deductible, next 20% of $500 of expenses, then 50% of the balance for the remainder of the plan year; no out-of-pocket maximum	
In-patient mental health	Up to 30 days per person per year; 60 days maximum per person, per lifetime, for substance abuse	
Chiropractic	Maximum benefits $500 per person per year	

The Smith family chose Plan 1 because of the lower deductible and lower out-of-pocket maximum compared to Plan 2. Also, the lifetime maximum benefit is unlimited.

Loss Example 2

While vacationing with his family in Orlando, Florida, John keeps up his morning jogging routine. On the third day of the vacation, John suffers chest pains while running and collapses. John is rushed by ambulance to a nearby hospital where he is diagnosed with a bronchial infection. X-rays and lab work total $300. The family pays 20 percent of the bill because they had met their deductible for the year. Their total out-of-pocket expenses for the visit are $60. Though disappointed that he can't jog for a week or two, John is thankful that, even out of state, he is able to have expert medical care and return to his family to enjoy the remainder of his vacation.

Long-Term Care

John and Karen are very young, so they do not perceive the need for investing in long-term care. Virginia Power doesn't offer this option. However, John has heard rumors that long-term care might be offered next year. If Virginia Power does begin offering long-term care, John will consider participating in it.

Retirement

The Smiths decided to invest in the 401(k) plan offered by Virginia Power. Virginia Power matches contributions at 50 percent. John chose to defer 4 percent of his salary ($240 monthly). When added to

Virginia Power's 2 percent, or $120, the monthly total is $360. The contribution is invested in mutual funds. John's 401(k) current balance is $32,000 and he hopes he will be able to invest it wisely. He can begin withdrawing his retirement benefits at age fifty-nine and a half with no penalties if he wishes.

2.5   Annual Budget and Net Assets

Table 23.7 and Table 23.8 depict the Smith family's finances. Figure 23.3 shows the costs of insurance premiums in reference to the Smiths' income.

TABLE 23.7 **Smith Family Income Statement**

Monthly salary after taxes		$6,000
Mortgage	$1,200	
Utilities	$350	
Homeowners insurance	$42.67	
Car insurance	$160	
Life insurance	$19.95	
Health insurance	$91.41	*
	$401(k) plan	$240
Disability insurance	$117.91	
Baby needs	$300	
Groceries	$500	
College fund	$100	
Entertainment	$400	
Other expenses	$200	
Possible expenses	$800	
Total	$4,522	
Potential savings		$1,478.07

* Health premiums are paid on a pretax basis into a premium conversion plan.

TABLE 23.8 **Smith Family Net Worth**

Assets	
Savings	$20,000
401(k) current balance	$32,000
House	$160,000
Collectibles	$22,000
Total assets	**$234,000**
Liability	
Mortgage payable	$120,000
Net assets	**$114,000**

FIGURE 23.3 Monthly Cost Allocation

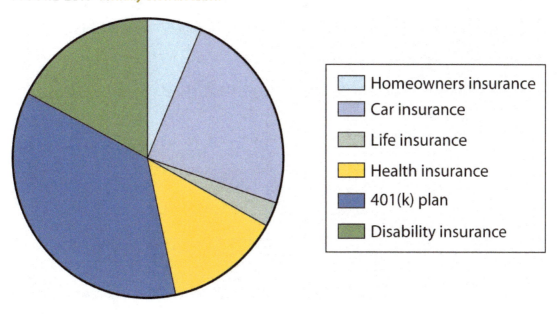

2.6 Conclusion

With the help from all group members working on the project, the Smith family is able to choose the best coverage they can get from various insurance plans. Their homeowners insurance is provided by Travelers Insurance Company; their auto is covered by Harford Insurance Company. They bought additional life insurance from Western-Southern Life Company and additional long-term disability from Erie. Virginia Power provides good health care coverage, term life insurance, a 401(k) retirement plan, and long-term disability. The Smith family chose insurance plans that best fit their needs.

KEY TAKEAWAYS

In this section you studied how the needs of a hypothetical family affect the selection of insurance coverage and employee benefits:

- Value of real and personal property, loss provisions, premiums, and deductibles, and company financial strength ratings all influence the amounts and types of homeowners coverage as well as the selection of the insurer.

- In the underwriting of auto insurance, insurers consider the accident history, age of the driver, market value, utility, and purpose of the vehicle.

- Employers may offer basic life and disability insurance benefits, but a family should consider supplemental coverage if its income is provided by a sole breadwinner.

- Family planning, desire for flexibility, and the overall health of family members are important considerations in the choice of health insurance.

- Employer-sponsored retirement options can be adequate to meet a family's retirement needs if the family saves and invests wisely in relation to their age and expected retirement.

- A family needs analysis should include a family income statement including monthly income less insurance premiums, retirement savings, utility bills, and other monthly expenses to assess the feasibility of the plan.

DISCUSSION QUESTIONS

1. What provision in homeowners insurance allows John and Karen to have their home replaced at 100 percent of its value rather than 80 percent?

2. Why was the family asked to give detailed geographic information about the home when they were obtaining insurance quotes?

3. What does it mean to schedule personal property? Why would Karen choose to do this?

4. Why must John provide evidence of insurability for his supplemental life insurance coverage but not his basic group coverage?

5. What does liability listed as "100,000/300,000/100,000" in the Smiths' auto insurance policy refer to?

6. What needs should be considered when determining the amount of life insurance coverage?

7. Do you think the ten-year level term life insurance coverage on Karen is appropriate?

8. What features make a PPO plan preferable to an HMO for the Smiths?

3. CASE 2: GALAXY MAX, INC., EMPLOYEE BENEFITS PACKAGE

LEARNING OBJECTIVES

In this section we elaborate on the benefits and plan structure that can be expected in a sample employee benefits portfolio:

- **Features of each employee benefit (eligibility, costs, exclusions, etc.)**
- **Group life insurance and any supplemental options**
- **Group disability insurance and any supplemental options**
- **Group health insurance plans**
- **Flexible benefits**
- **Defined benefit and/or defined contribution retirement plans**

3.1 Preface

This case, like Case 1, is a group project that is part of employee benefits classes taught by the author of this textbook. Following is the employee benefits portfolio of a compilation of the ten groups of the fall 2002 class (and some of the fall 2000 class), in the words of the students.[5] The case is a typical project that lasts for the students throughout the semester. The students present portions of the case as the material is covered in class. In most cases, the whole employee benefits portfolio of the hypothetical company created by the students is presented at the conclusion of the semester as part of the final grade. This case does not provide a long-term care coverage plan. Most of the retirement plans offered by the hypothetical employers of these projects are not realistic in terms of the amounts and variety. The students are requested to provide a defined benefit plan, a defined contribution plan, and a 401(k) plan in order to experience the workings of these plans. The students did not offer a complete cafeteria plan—only a flexible spending account.[6]

3.2 Welcome, Galaxy Max Employees

The Board of Directors and the corporate executives of Galaxy Max, Inc., have developed a comprehensive benefits package to meet the needs of our employees and their families. This handbook includes a brief overview of the organization and its structure and a detailed description of benefits related to group life insurance, health care, dental and vision coverage, flexible spending accounts, and retirement benefits. The information provided will enable you to understand your benefits. General information may be secured from the company's Web site, www.galaxymax.com. Additional questions may be addressed to the Human Resources Department, 7500 Galaxy Max Road, Richmond, VA 23228; telephone 1-800-674-2900; e-mail hrgalaxymax@vcu.edu. Suggestions are always welcome as we continue to improve customer service.

Background and Current Information

- Galaxy Max, Inc. (the "Company"), is a multimillion-dollar business equipment retail chain established in 1985 to service the needs of companies and consumers.

- The company specializes in direct sales and e-commerce of office equipment, business accessories, and computer hardware and software, and provides technical support for all facets of the industry involved in maintaining the business environment. The company plans to expand its service capabilities throughout the global marketplace.

- The corporation is headquartered in Richmond, Virginia, and has one retail outlet and two regional stores in northern Virginia and the Tidewater area (see Figure 23.4).

FIGURE 23.4 Galaxy Max, Inc., Organizational Structure

Employee Description

Galaxy Max employs 758 staff members: 338 full-time salaried and 420 hourly employees. Our rapid growth in size and value allows us to provide a substantial benefit package to salaried and full-time employees.

Employee Benefits

Galaxy Max has developed a competitive and comprehensive benefits package for our employees because we value their service to the organization and we want to maintain a healthy, motivated, and high-quality staff. Our commitment to employees is to support their personal needs and financial goals for retention and to reward dedicated individuals. The benefits package is summarized in Table 23.9.

TABLE 23.9 Galaxy Max Benefits Package

Full-Time Salaried Employees (32 or More Hours per Week)	Hourly and Part-Time Employees
Group term life insurance	None
Short- and long-term disability	None
Health	Optional
Dental	Optional
Flexible spending account	Flexible spending account
Defined benefit plan	Defined benefit plan available for those working more than 1,000 hours per year
Profit-sharing plan	Profit-sharing plan available for those working more than 1,000 hours per year
401(k) plan with matching	401(k) plan with matching available for those working more than 1,000 hours per year

Mission Statement

Galaxy Max is committed to providing superior customer satisfaction in administering sales and service to consumers while maintaining competitive prices, quality products, and active growth within the international business community. We strive for technological advancement and excellence in the delivery of services, and we promote partnerships.

3.3 Part I: Group Insurance Benefits

Life Insurance

Galaxy Max provides you with basic life insurance at one times your annual base pay (1 × annual salary) at no cost to you. Benefits are rounded to the next higher $1,000. The minimum benefit is $5,000. You may purchase supplemental coverage. The maximum benefit is five times your current annual base pay or $1,000,000, whichever is less. Table 23.10 outlines the main features of the company's life insurance plan. The cost of supplemental life insurance coverage is shown in Table 23.11.

TABLE 23.10   Group Term Life Insurance: Major Plan Provisions

Benefits	Basic life insurance is equal to one times your annual base pay—employer pays Additional coverage up to five times your annual base pay as supplemental coverage—you pay (see costs in Table 23.11)
	Added coverage for dependents—you pay (see costs in Table 23.11)
	Accidental death and dismemberment (AD&D)—employer pays
	Waiver of premium in case of disability (life coverage continues without charge)—part of the basic coverage
	Convertibility (in case of termination of the term life, you can convert the policy to whole life policy without evidence of insurability)—part of basic coverage Accelerated benefits (living benefits)—in case of becoming terminally ill, you can collect up to 50 percent of the policy benefits while still living—part of basic coverage
Eligibility	Regular, full-time employees (working 32 hours per week or more) who are active at work
Enrollment	Coverage is automatic
When coverage begins	30 days after employment date
Cost	The company pays the full cost of basic life insurance; you pay for any additional coverage (supplements of 2×, 3×, 4×, or 5× annual salary, and for dependent coverage)
Evidence of insurability	For basic coverage paid by the employer, no evidence of insurability is required
	For supplemental amounts greater than $150,000, evidence of insurability is required
Provider, A.M. Best Rating	Minnesota Life (Minnesota, USA), A++ Rating
Taxes	Premiums on coverage greater than $50,000 are taxable income to you (based on IRS Table PS-58)
	Death benefits paid to the beneficiary are not taxed

TABLE 23.11   Costs for Supplemental Life and Dependent Life

Supplemental Term Life			
Age	**Cost per Month per $1,000 of Coverage**	**Age**	**Cost per Month per $1,000 of Coverage**
29 and under	$0.06	50–54	$0.42
30–34	$0.07	55–59	$0.69
35–39	$0.09	60–64	$1.10
40–44	$0.15	65–69	$2.00
45–49	$0.25	70 and over	$3.60

Dependent: Rates for Spouse	
Amount	**Cost**
$5,000	$0.58
$10,000	$1.15
$15,000	$1.73
$20,000	$2.31
$25,000	$2.88

Beneficiary

The employee names the beneficiary. It cannot be the employer.

Termination

Coverage shall terminate automatically when any of the following conditions exist:

- The employee terminates employment.
- The employee ceases to be eligible.
- The policyholder terminates the master contract.

- The insurer terminates the master contract.
- Contributions have not been made.

Important Features of Your Life Insurance Plans

- Wavier of the payment of your premium if you become disabled
- The right to convert to an individual policy if you terminate your employment
- Accelerated benefits if you become terminally ill

Accelerated Benefits

If a covered employee is diagnosed with a qualifying condition, the employee may request that an accelerated benefit be paid immediately. The amount payable is 50 percent, up to a maximum benefit of $50,000. Qualifying conditions include the following:

- The diagnosis of a terminal illness that is expected to result in death within six to twelve months
- The occurrence of a specified catastrophic illness, such as AIDS, a stroke, or Alzheimer's disease

Dependent Life Insurance

Life insurance on a spouse can be purchased by full-time employees in increments of $5,000 up to $25,000. Life insurance on children can be purchased in the amount of $5,000 per child.

Accidental Death and Dismemberment

Benefits under the accidental death and dismemberment (AD&D) plan are in addition to any benefits payable under the life insurance plan. AD&D benefits are payable in the event of an accident resulting in the following:

- Your death
- Loss of one or more of your body parts (such as hand or foot)
- Loss of sight in one or both eyes

Table 23.12 outlines the main features of the Company's AD&D plan. If you survive an accident but sustain certain injuries, AD&D benefits would be payable as shown in Table 23.13.

TABLE 23.12 AD&D Plan Provisions

Benefit	In case of accidental death, the basic and supplemental amounts are doubled (in case of a loss, see Table 23.13)
Eligibility	Regular, full-time employees (working 32 hours per week or more) who are active at work
Enrollment	Coverage is automatic
When coverage begins	30 days after employment date
Cost	The company pays the full cost of basic AD&D insurance; you pay for any additional coverage (supplements of 2×, 3×, 4×, or 5× annual salary)
Evidence of insurability	Same as for regular group term life
Provider, A.M. Best Rating (periods as elsewhere)	Minnesota Life, A++ Rating

TABLE 23.13 AD&D Loss Provisions

If You Have This Loss	You Will Receive This Percentage of Your AD&D Coverage
Loss of hand	50%
Loss of foot	50%
Loss of eye	50%
Multiple loss	100%

Life insurance will not pay out if you survive an accident; it pays only in the event of your death. Losses not covered under AD&D include the following:

- Bodily or mental infirmity
- Disease, ptomaine, or bacterial infection, unless resulting directly from the injury or any resulting surgery

- Medical or surgical treatment, unless resulting directly from the injury or any resulting surgery
- Suicide or attempted suicide while sane or insane
- Intentionally self-inflicted injury
- War or any act of war, whether declared or undeclared

Provider

Life insurance is provided by Minnesota Life Insurance Company, which is rated A++ by A.M. Best.

Life Insurance Loss/Benefit Examples

Life Insurance Example 1

A forty-year-old employee making annual base salary of $45,000 dies in an automobile accident. He had chosen to purchase supplemental insurance for both life (one times salary) and AD&D (one times salary).

Beneficiary will receive the following:

- 1 times pay or $45,000 from Minnesota Life for basic life
- 1 times pay or $45,000 from Minnesota Life for AD&D
- 1 times pay or $45,000 for his supplemental life
- 1 times pay or $45,000 for his supplemental AD&D

Total received is $180,000.

Life Insurance Example 2

A life insurance claim was filed by Mary Jones after the death of her husband, Robert, in June 2002. He died after a short battle with cancer. He was a full-time employee at Galaxy Max for five years and his salary at the time was $55,000 annually. He has life insurance in the amount of three times his salary: $55,000 × 3 = $165,000. Therefore, his benefit is $165,000, payable to his beneficiary, which is his spouse, Mary Jones. Mrs. Jones filed the claim within two weeks of Mr. Jones's death. Mrs. Jones had to present a copy of his death certificate and fill out the required forms. She was informed that she would receive her benefit within sixty days from the date of the claim.

Mrs. Jones has chosen to receive the life insurance benefit in a lump-sum payment. She received this payment fifty-eight days from the date of the claim.

Internal Revenue Service Code Section 101 provides that the death benefits are not counted toward taxable income.

Sick Leave, Short-Term Disability, and Long-Term Disability

Table 23.14 summarizes all the disability plans provided by Galaxy Max.

TABLE 23.14 Sick Leave, Group Short-Term Disability, and Group Long-Term Disability—Major Plan Provisions

Benefits	Sick leave—7 days, 100% of pay
	STD (7 days to 6 months)—80% of pay up to $5,000 benefit per month
	LTD (6 months to age sixty-five)—60% of pay up to $6,000 benefit per month coordinated with workers' compensation and Social Security
Eligibility	Regular, full-time employees (working 32 hours per week or more) who are active at work
Enrollment	Coverage is automatic
When coverage begins	30 days after employment date
Cost	The company pays the full cost of STD; employee pays for LTD through payroll reduction
Definition of disability	Sick leave and STD—unable to do your own job due to nonoccupational injury or illness
	LTD—from 6 months to 2 years, unable to do any job relating to your training and education; after two years, unable to do any job
Evidence of insurability	Required if joining after open enrollment
Provider, A. M. Best Rating	Sick leave and STD—self-insured
	LTD—Aetna (rated "A" for excellent by A.M. Best)
Taxes	Employees do not pay taxes on premiums paid by employer for STD; but in the case of receiving benefits, taxes will be paid on the benefits
	For LTD, employee pays the premium from income after taxes, and benefits in the case of disability are nontaxable

Sick Leave

Benefits

The employee will receive regular pay for time missed due to illness or injury (nonoccupational) up to seven days per calendar year.

Cost of Sick Time

Galaxy Max pays for sick leave from its operating budget.

Short-Term Disability

Definition of Disability

"Disability" is the total and continuous inability of the employee to perform each and every duty of his or her regular occupation.

Benefits

Short-term disability (STD) benefits are 80 percent of salary up to $5,000 per month after a seven-day waiting period. The maximum length of the benefit is six months. There is no integration of benefits under short-term disability.

Premium

Galaxy Max pays STD premiums and deducts such as normal business expense. Galaxy Max will continue to pay premiums for disabled employees.

Exclusions

An employee cannot collect STD benefits under the following conditions:

- For any period during which the employee is not under the care of a physician
- For any disability caused by an intentionally self-inflicted injury
- If the employee is engaged in any occupation for remuneration
- If the disability was incurred during war, whether declared or undeclared
- If the disability was incurred while participating in an assault or felony
- If the disability is mental disease, alcoholism, or drug addiction

Termination

Disabled employees will not be considered terminated and, when able to return to work, will not have to satisfy any waiting period for coverage.

Long-Term Disability

Definition of Disability

Long-term disability (LTD) is defined as the total and continuous inability of the employee to engage in any and every gainful occupation for which he or she is qualified or shall reasonably become qualified by reason of training, education, or experience for the first two years. After two years, it is the inability to engage in any gainful employment.

Benefits

LTD provides for the following:

- LTD benefit amount is 60 percent of your basic monthly earnings, to a maximum monthly benefit of $6,000.
- Monthly LTD benefit will be reduced by amounts received from other benefit programs such as Social Security, workers' compensation, and any other coinciding retirement plan. However, your monthly benefit can never be less than 10 percent of the gross benefit or $100, whichever is greater.
- LTD benefit is 60 percent of your basic monthly earnings to a maximum benefit of $6,000 per month. Your benefit is coordinated with (that is, reduced by) other income benefits received.

"Basic monthly earnings" means your monthly salary in effect just prior to the date disability begins. It includes earnings received from commissions and incentive bonuses but not overtime pay or other extra compensation. Commissions and incentive bonuses will be averaged for the thirty-six-month period of employment just prior to the date disability begins.

Cost of Coverage

The employee will pay the full cost through payroll deduction. The Human Resources representative will advise of the contribution amount, which is based on a rate per $1,000 of your annual base pay. The cost of coverage is determined by the insurance company, Aetna (rated "A" for excellent by A.M. Best). Galaxy Max will notify you in advance in the event of a rate change.

LTD Exclusions

An employee cannot collect LTD benefits under the following conditions:

- Any disability caused intentionally
- Any period not under the care of a physician
- Active participation in a riot
- War, declared or undeclared, or any act of war

Taxation

Because the employee pays the entire premium from income after taxes, benefits are not taxable to the employee.

Rehabilitation

A disabled employee may enter a trial work period of up to two years in rehabilitative employment. During this time, benefits will be reduced by 50 percent. If the trial is unsuccessful, original long-term benefits will resume without penalty.

Termination

Disabled employees will not be considered terminated and, if able to return to work, will not have to satisfy any waiting period for coverage. Long-term disability coverage cannot be converted upon termination of employment.

Health Insurance Coverage

Galaxy Max offers two plans for health insurance, an HMO and PPO. The broad benefits are described in Table 23.15. The medical plans pay the cost of necessary and reasonable medical expenses for non-work-related illness or injury and are completely optional.

TABLE 23.15 Health Plan Provisions

Benefits	You have a choice between an HMO and a PPO.
Eligibility	Regular, full-time salaried and part-time employees scheduled to work at least 32 hours per week and their eligible dependents: spouse; unmarried dependent child under age 19, or under age 25 in school full-time; disabled dependent child; eligible child with qualified medical child support order.
Enrollment	You may enroll when eligible. You may elect to enroll eligible dependents for extra charges provided they meet the qualifications of a "dependent."
	Annual open enrollment period for current plan participants is October 1 to November 1 every year. Changes made during open enrollment become effective January 1 the following year.
Waiting period	30 days after the first day of employment
Coverage categories	Employee only
	Employee and child(ren)
	Employee and spouse
	Employee and family
Cost	You and Galaxy Max share the cost of coverage (see Table 23.17)
What is covered	Medically necessary services and supplies
	Inpatient and outpatient hospital care
	Doctors' care and treatment
	Home or office visits
	Prescription drugs
	In-patient and out-patient mental health care
	Routine physical exams and preventive care (in network only)

Insurers

Galaxy Max has chosen Healthkeepers, Inc., for HMO coverage. Healthkeepers' most recent A.M. Best rating is "A" (excellent). Cigna Healthcare of Virginia, Inc., is Galaxy Max's PPO provider and has also earned A.M. Best's rating of "A." Benefits paid are at the discretion of the insurance companies.

Benefits

The benefits under each plan are explained in Table 23.16.

TABLE 23.16 HMO and PPO Plan Benefits

	HMO	PPO in Network	PPO out of Network
Annual Deductible			
	None	None	$300/individual, $600/family
Outpatient Care			
	Copay per Visit ($)	Coinsurance (%) or Copay ($) per Visit	Coinsurance (%) per Visit
Primary care physician	$10	$15*	30%
Diagnostic labs/X-rays	Fully covered	10%	30%
Preventive care	$10	$15†	30%
Well-baby care	$10; no age limit	$15 plus 10% of screening and diagnostic tests; through child's seventh birthday†	30%
Maternity care for all routine pre and postnatal care of mother rendered by ob/gyn	Routine care fully covered; $10 for diagnostic testing	$15 for initial visit if doctor submits one bill after delivery	30%
Mammogram screenings	$20	20%	30%
Ob/gyn visit (includes pelvic exam, breast exam, and pap smear)	$10	$15	30%
Specialist office visit	$20 with PCP referral	$15	30%
Emergency services	$50 (waived if admitted)	$50 plus 20%; $15 for doctor's services	30%
Annual vision exams	$10	no	
Out-patient surgery	$75	$50 plus 20%; $15 for doctor's services	30%
Out-patient nonsurgical services	$20	$50 plus 20%; $15 for doctor's services	30%
Mental health and substance abuse	$20	26 visits per calendar year: $15 for visits 1–13; 50% for visits 14–26	30%
Home health care	Fully covered	Fully covered	30%
Out-patient physical, speech, and occupational therapy	$20 (90 days maximum) §	limits per calendar year: physical, $2,000; speech, $750; occupational, $2,000	30%
In-Patient Care (Preauthorization Required)			
	Copay per Visit ($)	Coinsurance (%) or Copay ($) per Visit	Coinsurance (%) per Visit
Hospital care for illness, injury, or maternity in a semiprivate room	$250 per admission	$250 plus 10% per admission	30%
In-hospital physician's services	Fully covered	10%	30%
In-patient mental health and substance abuse	$250 per admission§	$250 plus 10% per admission	30%
Skilled nursing facility care	Fully covered (limited to 100 days per illness or condition)§	20% (limited to 100 days per illness or condition)	30%

* Primary care physician or specialist visit.

† Coverage includes annual checkups, annual gynecological exam and pap smear, prostate specific antigen (PSA) test and prostate exams for men age forty and over, one baseline mammogram for women ages thirty-five to thirty-nine, annual mammogram for women age forty and over, and annual colorectal cancer screening; up to $200 per calendar year for family members age seven and older for all other routine immunizations, labs, and X-rays done in connection with annual checkups whether received in-network or out-of-network.

† No coinsurance for immunizations.

	HMO	PPO in Network	PPO out of Network
Durable medical equipment and supplies	Fully covered up to $1,000 per calendar year§	10%; limited to $5,000 per calendar year§	30%
Hospice services	Fully covered for patients diagnosed with a terminal illness with a life expectancy of 6 months or less	Fully covered for patients diagnosed with a terminal illness with a life expectancy of 6 months or less	30%
Annual Out-of-Pocket Expense Limit Through Deductibles, Coinsurance, and Copayments for Covered Services			
Individual	$1,000	$2,000	$4,000
Family	$2,000	$4,000	$8,000
Lifetime Maximum			
	$500,000	$750,000	$750,000
* Primary care physician or specialist visit.			
† Coverage includes annual checkups, annual gynecological exam and pap smear, prostate specific antigen (PSA) test and prostate exams for men age forty and over, one baseline mammogram for women ages thirty-five to thirty-nine, annual mammogram for women age forty and over, and annual colorectal cancer screening; up to $200 per calendar year for family members age seven and older for all other routine immunizations, labs, and X-rays done in connection with annual checkups whether received in-network or out-of-network.			
† No coinsurance for immunizations.			

Financing

Galaxy Max will pay a generous 85 percent of the health care premiums. Table 23.17 lists employee obligations.

TABLE 23.17 Employee Premiums

Plan	HMO	PPO
Biweekly premium per insured	$35.67	$51.09
Each additional dependent	$12.00	$18.00

Coverage Area

The PPO is comprised of specific in-network offices. Consult your Benefits Liaison for a complete list of providers in your area. All employees residing in Virginia are considered in-area.

Exclusions

The items listed below, among others, are not covered in any of the plans. If you have any questions regarding the coverage of a treatment or service, you must contact the appropriate provider.

- Treatment that is not medically necessary in accordance with the designated insurers
- Experimental drugs or investigative procedures
- Chiropractic services

Termination of Coverage

Coverage is terminated at the following times:

- The date on which employment terminates
- The date on which the employee becomes ineligible
- The end of the last period for which the employee has made any required contributions
- Dependent coverage is terminated in the following cases:
- The date on which the dependent ceases to meet the definition of a dependent
- The date on which the dependent receives the maximum benefit of major medical coverage

Conversion

The employee may convert to individual health coverage within thirty-one days of losing eligibility. Galaxy Max complies with all local, state, and federal legislation with regard to group health plans.

COBRA

The Consolidated Omnibus Budget Reconciliation Act (COBRA) extends coverage for eighteen to thirty-six months following a qualifying event[7] that causes the employee to lose eligibility. The employer does not have to pay the premium, and the premium may be increased to a maximum of 102 percent of the group rate. The employee may elect COBRA within sixty days of the qualifying event. As noted above, the thirty-one-day period of conversion may be applied after COBRA coverage. COBRA does *not* protect an employee who is fired for cause.

HIPAA

The Health Insurance Portability and Accountability Act (HIPAA) forbids insurers from imposing preexisting-condition exclusions when an eligible individual transfers from one plan to another. After you have been covered in a health plan for twelve months, preexisting-condition exclusions are no longer in effect. Prior coverage would not qualify if there is a break in health insurance coverage for more than sixty-three days.

Group Dental

Group dental provides coverage for any dental work you may incur. Like group medical, group dental has many variations, and coverage can be obtained from two different providers. However, there are some clear differences between the two plans. For example, group dental plans are more likely to provide benefits on a fee-for-service basis but provide the benefits under a managed-care arrangement.

Eligibility

Full-time (thirty-five hours or more per week) and salaried employees are eligible to enroll for group dental coverage. You may enroll your spouse and child(ren) for an additional premium.

Waiting Period

You may enroll when eligible. Coverage becomes effective the first day of the month following employment. For example, if you start employment on the first of the month, coverage begins immediately.

Plan Highlights

Table 23.18 summarizes the key features of the dental plan, including benefits, types of service, and cost information.

TABLE 23.18 **Major Dental Plan Provisions**

Annual deductible		$30 per person, with $90 family maximum
Cost		You and the company share the cost
Plan maximums		$1,000 per person per year
		$1,000 lifetime under age 19 for orthodontics
Coverage	**Examples of Items Covered**	**Plan Pays Up To ...**
Preventive	Nonorthodontics X-rays, oral exams, and cleaning of teeth	100% of reasonable and customary fees (R&C) for cleanings, X-rays, exams, fluoride treatments
Restorative	Fillings, extractions	80% R&C fillings, extractions
Prosthodontics	Replacement of natural teeth with bridgework or dentures	50% R&C for bridgework
Orthodontics	Straightening of teeth with braces	50% of R&C for orthodontic services

Conversion

Dental coverage cannot be converted to an individual policy if employment terminates. You, your spouse, or your dependent children may elect to continue coverage under the company's dental plan as provided by COBRA if the original coverage ends because of one of the following life events:

- Termination of employment by employee
- Retirement
- Disability
- Death
- Reduction in hours to less than full-time

Provider

Galaxy Max has chosen Cigna Corporation for dental coverage because the company has a strong presence in the insurance business and has been one of the leaders in coverage. Cigna's A.M. Best rating is NR-5, meaning that they have not been formally evaluated for the purpose of assigning a rating opinion.

Flexible Spending Account

To accommodate the needs of our diverse work force, Galaxy Max has created a flexible spending account (FSA) plan to help employees to meet expenses that are not covered under any benefit plan. Money deposited in these accounts is not taxed when it goes into the accounts or when it is paid back to you. Employees can use these pretax dollars to pay for miscellaneous items such as eyeglasses or unreimbursed medical/dental expenses. This plan also allows employees to pay dependent care expenses with pretax dollars. Any amount not spent at the end of the plan year is forfeited by the employee (use it or lose it). See Table 23.19 for details. In addition, a premium conversion plan is offered to employees for payment of health insurance premiums on a pretax basis.

TABLE 23.19 Summary of FSA: Major Plan Provisions

Eligibility	Regular, full-time salaried employees and part-time employees scheduled to work 1,000 hours or more during a year
When coverage begins	Employment date; or
	Each January, following annual open enrollment; or
	Date of life event
When coverage ends	Employment termination or your pay ceases for any reason (death, retired, or disabled)
	You or your survivors may continue to submit claims expenses incurred prior to the date you left the payroll
Contributions	Your selected contributions will be deducted from each pay before federal income tax and, in most cases, state income tax and Social Security tax are withheld
	Minimum annual contribution: health care and/or dependent day care: $120
	Maximum annual contribution: health care and/or dependent day care: $5,000
Accounts	Health care accounts for tax-deductible health care expenses
	Dependent day care accounts for work-related dependent day care expenses
Maximums	Health care: $5,000 per year to each account
	For dependent day care:
	Amount of spouse's earnings, if less than $5,000
	Maximum of $2,500 if married and filing separate returns
Reimbursement	Eligible claims paid monthly
	Minimum claim of $10/month
	Claims must be received by administrator by April 1 for prior year's expenses
	Unclaimed account balances must be forfeited

3.4 Part II: Pension Plan

Galaxy Max offers to its eligible employees a defined benefit pension plan. The pension plan is designed to provide you or your beneficiary with monthly benefit payments at retirement. The pension plan is funded entirely by the company; employees do not contribute. In addition, Galaxy Max offers a 401(k) plan and a profit-sharing plan.

Defined Benefit Plan

A defined benefit plan explicitly defines the amount of benefit available at retirement. Table 23.20 summarizes the major pension program provisions.

TABLE 23.20 Defined Benefit Plan

Benefit formula	(1.3% of your final average salary up to the Social Security–covered compensation level) + (1.8% of your final average salary in excess of the Social Security–covered compensation level, if any) × (years of creditable service). See example in Table 23.21.
Eligibility	Full- or part-time employees who are scheduled to work or who actually work at least 1,000 hours in a twelve-month period are eligible
	Participation begins on your date of hire or your twenty-first birthday, whichever is later
Normal retirement	You may retire and receive normal retirement benefits the first day of the month on or after your sixty-fifth birthday
Early retirement	You may retire and receive an early retirement benefit on or before you reach age sixty-five
	You are eligible for early retirement on the first day of the month on or after your fifty-fifth birthday with three years of vesting service
Insured	Plan is insured by the Pension Benefit Guaranty Corporation
Vesting	You become fully vested when you complete three years of vesting service (including vesting service with an acquired company) or reach age sixty-five
	Vesting credit begins when you are eligible for the pension program

Payments

Your pension benefit is paid to you in monthly installments at the end of the month. Your benefits will be paid as a lump-sum payment if the present value of your pension is $5,000 or less. The normal form of benefit paid by the retirement plan is based on your marital status. Unless you elect a different option, you will receive your benefit in one of the following forms, which are actuarially equivalent:

- If you are single, you will receive a single life pension.
- If you are married, you will receive a 50 percent survivorship pension with your spouse as the beneficiary. If you are married and would like to receive your benefit in another form, you will need to provide your spouse's written consent.

The survivorship option pays you for as long as you live. When you die, benefits continue to be paid to your designated beneficiary, assuming your beneficiary survives you. Written spousal consent is required before you can designate a beneficiary other than your spouse. Benefits are reduced for the survivorship option because payments will be made over two lives rather than one. Payments depend on your age and your beneficiary's age when you begin receiving payments. If you choose the survivorship option and your beneficiary dies before you do, your payment will be increased to the amount that you would have received under the single life option. Additionally, you may choose the amount (50 percent, 75 percent, or 100 percent) your surviving beneficiary will receive after you die.

Formula and Calculations

The traditional formula used in calculating your retirement benefit is based on your final average salary, your creditable service, and the Social Security–covered compensation level based on your age. Your retirement pension benefit may not be more than 100 percent of your final average salary, or $160,000 in 2002. These formula components are outlined below. See Table 23.21 for an example of how the formula works.

TABLE 23.21 Example of Defined Benefit Formula

Suppose Joe, a sales representative for Galaxy Max, was born in 1942 and retired after thirty years of service to Galaxy Max with a final average salary of $40,000. At the time of Joe's retirement, the Social Security–covered compensation level is $37,212. To calculate Joe's benefit:	
1. Multiply Joe's final average salary, up to Social Security–covered compensation level, by the benefit percentage	$37,212 × 1.3% = $484
2. Multiply Joe's final average salary in excess of Social Security–covered compensation level by the excess benefit percentage	($40,000 – $37,212) × 1.8% = $50
3. Add amounts calculated	$448 + $50 = $534
4. Multiply by years of service to calculate Joe's annual retirement benefit	$534 × 30 = $16,018
Thus, Joe's annual pension benefit from Galaxy Max is $16,018.	

Final Average Salary

Your final average salary is your highest average annual compensation during any consecutive sixty-month period. It includes base pay, commission payments, bonuses, and overtime.

Creditable Service

Your service with Galaxy Max, including approved leaves of absence up to six months, certain periods of military and public service, and periods in which you are totally disabled (as defined in the LTD plan), is considered your creditable service. Service for part-time work is reduced to the equivalent portion of the year worked.

Social Security Compensation Level

The average of the Social Security wage bases (maximum amount on which you pay Social Security taxes) for the thirty-five years before the date of your retirement is the Social Security compensation level that is used to calculate your benefits. These amounts change each year according to the Covered Compensation Table provided by the Social Security Administration.

Vesting

We at Galaxy Max chose to use a cliff vesting option. You become 100 percent vested after three years of creditable service. Our plan provides you with a cash settlement option if your employment at Galaxy Max is terminated. The cash settlement option is effective on your termination date. This distribution is considered taxable income in the year the distribution is made. The only exception to this rule is if you choose to shift this payment into an IRA.

Loans

Loans are not available under the retirement plan

Distributions

As a valued employee of Galaxy Max, you or your beneficiaries may choose one of the following distribution options:

Guaranteed Payment

You may choose to have your pension payments guaranteed for a certain period of time after retirement. The payment options include either five or ten years for a single life pension or five years for a survivorship pension benefit.

Lump-Sum Payment

You may request a lump-sum payment of $1,000 or more (in $100 increments) to your designated beneficiary from your pension benefit, payable after you die.

Level Income Payment

If you retire early and want to start receiving benefits before age sixty-two, you may choose this payment feature. You will receive larger benefit payments prior to age sixty-two and then receive lower benefit payments upon reaching age sixty-two. At age sixty-two, you will be eligible to receive Social Security benefits. The intent of this plan is to provide level retirement income before and after Social Security payments begin at age sixty-two.

So ... When Can I Retire and Receive Benefits?

Depending on your age and length of service, you may choose normal retirement or early retirement. Normal retirement is when you retire at or after age sixty-five. If you choose this option, you will receive normal retirement pension benefits.

Early Retirement

You become eligible for early retirement benefits when you reach age fifty-five with three years of vested service. You can retire on the first day of any month on or after your fifty-fifth birthday. If you retire before you reach age sixty-five, the date you retire will be known as your early retirement date.

Benefits for early retirement are less than normal retirement benefits because the plan adjusts the payment amount to allow the benefits to be paid over a longer period of time. The amount of your normal retirement benefit is available to you, without reduction, if you retire early on or after your sixtieth birthday. If you retire on or after your fifty-fifth birthday and before your sixtieth birthday, your pension benefit will be reduced, as explained in Table 23.22.

TABLE 23.22 **Early Retirement Reduction in Defined Benefit Plan**

If you retire between the ages of fifty-eight and sixty, your pension benefit will be reduced by 0.25% for each month that remains until your sixtieth birthday. For example, if you retire on your fifty-eighth birthday, your pension will be reduced by (24 months × 0.25% per month) = 6%. If you retire between the ages of fifty-five and fifty-eight, your pension will be reduced by that 6% plus an additional 0.50% for each month that remains until your fifty-eighth birthday. For example, if you retire on your fifty-sixth birthday, your benefit will be reduced by (6% + [24 months × 0.50% per month]) = 18%. This table shows the percentage your benefit would be reduced if you retired on your birthday.	
Retirement Age	**Benefit Reduction**
60 or older	None
59	3%
58	6%
57	12%
56	18%
55	24%

The benefit in Galaxy Max's defined plan is protected by the Pension Benefit Guaranty Corporation (PBGC). The cost of $19 per year per employee is paid by Galaxy Max.

401(k) Plan

Galaxy Max offers you a Section 401(k) plan, hereinafter referred to as the Galaxy Max 401(k) Plan, as a supplement to the retirement plan. You have the opportunity to put aside salary dollars on a pretax basis, and Galaxy Max makes employer-matching contributions to help build retirement savings more quickly. You can choose your own level of deferral, if any. The plan also offers you several investment options with varying portfolios to allow your savings to grow over time. Taxes are deferred on employer matching contributions, your pretax deferral, and investment returns until you withdraw the funds from your account.

Eligibility

All full-time and part-time employees are eligible. You become eligible for the Galaxy Max 401(k) Plan after completing one year of continuous service and must complete at least 1,000 hours of service during the year. Your enrollment commences on the first day of the month following the completion of that first year of service. You are *not* eligible to participate in the plan if you are no longer an employee as of fiscal year end or if you are a temporary employee.

Maximum Contributions

For employees under the age of fifty, the 2009 contribution limit is $16,500. If you are fifty years old or older, this limit is $22,000 in 2009.

Employer Matching

During each of your first five years of service, Galaxy Max will match 80 percent ($0.80 for every $1.00) that you contribute to the plan, up to 6 percent of your salary. After five years of service, our matching increases to 100 percent ($1.00 for every $1.00) that you contribute to the plan, up to 6 percent of your salary.

Vesting

Vesting is your right to the money in your 401(k) account. You are always 100 percent vested in the value of your own contributions and the earnings on your investments. You are vested on Galaxy Max's matching contributions at the rate of 20 percent each year of service, and thus fully vested after five years. For example, if you left Galaxy Max three full years after joining the 401(k) plan, you would have the right to all your investments and their earnings and to 60 percent of the matching funds plus their earnings. The vesting schedule for the 401(k) matching contribution is summarized in Table 23.23 below.

TABLE 23.23 Galaxy Max 401(k) Matching Contribution Vesting Schedule

Completed Years of Service	Percentage Vested on Employer's Match
1	20%
2	40%
3	60%
4	80%
5	100%

Withdrawals

In-service withdrawals for certain hardships are permitted under the Galaxy Max 401(k) Plan, as long as two conditions are met:

1. The withdrawal must be necessary and follow severe financial hardships. Examples include the following:
   - Purchasing your primary residence
   - Preventing foreclosure or eviction from your primary residence
   - Paying for major uninsured medical expenses for you or your eligible dependents
   - Paying tuition, room and board, and related education expenses for the next twelve months for you or your eligible dependents to attend college

2. The funds are not reasonably available from any other resources. The requirements are met if the following circumstances exist:
   - The distribution does not exceed the amount of the severe financial hardship
   - The employee has obtained all other forms of distributions other than hardship distributions

Contributions will be suspended twelve months after the distribution and the maximum contribution in the next year will be reduced by the amount contributed in the prior year.

Loans

The minimum loan amount is $1,000. The maximum loan amount is the lesser of $50,000 or 50 percent of your vested balance. The following two types of loans are available under the plan.

General-Purpose

You can take between six and sixty months to repay a general-purpose loan.

Primary Residence

You can take between sixty-one and 180 months to repay this loan. Eligible residences include house, condominium, co-op, mobile home, new home construction, or land for new construction or mobile home.

Investment and Investment Risk

You bear the risk of investments in your Galaxy Max 401(k) Savings Account. However, you can choose from several investment funds through the SunTrust Classic Funds Family, commonly referred to as the STI Classic Funds. This will enable you to select your own desired level of risk.

Investment funds range from a fixed income fund (with very low risk and corresponding low return potential) to higher risk equity funds with higher return potential. The funds that you may choose from are as listed:

- Galaxy Max Stock Fund
- STI Classic Small Cap Growth Stock Fund
- STI Classic Mid-Cap Equity Fund
- STI Classic Appreciation Fund
- SunTrust 500 Index Fund
- STI Classic Growth and Income Fund
- STI Classic Value Income Stock Fund
- STI Classic Investment Grade Bond Fund

- STI Classic Short-Term Bond Fund
- STI Classic Prime Quality Money Market Fund

Termination

You will be terminated from the Galaxy Max 401(k) Plan if you cease to be employed by Galaxy Max.

Profit-Sharing Plan

Over the past five years, Galaxy Max has been financially successful because of the dedication and talent of our valued employees. We started the profit-sharing program to give you the opportunity to share in the success of our wonderful company. The primary purpose of this plan is to help you build retirement income. Along with the Galaxy Max 401(k) Plan and the defined benefit plan, the profit-sharing plan can provide you with the foundation for a financially secure retirement.

A profit-sharing plan is a qualified, defined contribution plan that features a flexible contribution by us. When you become eligible to participate, Galaxy Max will set up an individual account in your name. In other words, you do not need to enroll in the plan. Participation in the plan is automatic and you are not required or permitted to contribute personal funds into the plan.

Eligibility

The eligibility requirements for the Galaxy Max Profit-Sharing Plan are the same as the Galaxy Max 401(k) Plan. Please refer to that section.

Contributions

Each year, Galaxy Max will contribute a portion of its pretax income for profit-sharing purposes. The contribution is made after the end of each fiscal year. The amount allocated to your account is based on a formula that includes your compensation during the fiscal year. This contribution is made at the discretion of Galaxy Max and cannot be guaranteed every year.

Profit-Sharing Formula

Here is how the allocation formula works. Once you become a participant, we evaluate your eligible compensation (base pay, commissions, and bonuses) and the eligible compensation of all Galaxy Max employees. Your portion of the amount of profits we contribute is the proportion of your eligible compensation to that of all employees. For example, suppose that Galaxy Max will contribute $200,000 to the profit-sharing plan, your eligible compensation is $35,000, and the eligible compensation of all employees is $950,000. Your share would be $35,000/$950,000, or 3.68 percent, of $200,000. Therefore, the allocation to your account would be $7,368.42. These numbers are used only as an example. (The total contribution from Galaxy Max and eligible compensation from all employees is much larger.)

Investing Your Profit-Sharing Account

The plan's trustee, SunTrust Bank, will invest contributions to your account. At the end of each fiscal year, investment earnings are allocated to your profit-sharing account. Because the value of your investments will fluctuate, you will assume the investment risk. Therefore, your account balance will increase or decrease in value from year to year.

Profit-Sharing Account Balance

Once all accounts have been reconciled for the fiscal year, you will receive an annual statement of your account. It will include your beginning balance, allocation of investment income, contributions, and ending balance. These statements are typically distributed to you four to five months after the fiscal year end.

Vesting

You begin earning ownership rights to your account once you complete three continuous years of service. After your second full year, you are 20 percent vested, and you earn another 20 percent each year. Once you complete six years of service, you are fully vested. If your employment ends because you become permanently disabled, die, or leave Galaxy Max after age sixty-five with at least five years of service, you and your beneficiary will be entitled to receive the full value of your account, regardless of your vesting. The vesting schedule for profit-sharing plan contributions is presented in Table 23.24 below.

TABLE 23.24 Galaxy Max Profit-Sharing Contribution Vesting Schedule

Continuous Vesting Service	Vested Percentage
Less than 2 years	0%
2 years	20%
3 years	40%
4 years	60%
5 years	80%
6 years or more	100%

Loans

You may borrow from your profit-sharing account under the same provisions that apply to 401(k) loans. Please refer to that section for details.

Distributions

You can receive the vested portion of your account after you leave Galaxy Max, retire, or become permanently and totally disabled. Your designated beneficiary will receive your vested account balance if you die before receiving your benefit.

If your vested account balance is $6,000 or less, you or your beneficiary will receive the payment in a single lump sum. If your account balance is more than $6,000, you or your beneficiary can take a single lump sum, receive annual installments for up to five years, or delay receiving distributions until a later time. Generally, you can roll over the vested portion of your account balance into another qualified retirement account or individual retirement account (IRA) so that you can defer paying federal income taxes.

Termination from Plan

You will be terminated from the plan if you cease to be employed by Galaxy Max.

Limitations on Contributions

For all three plans, certain legal limits are placed on contributions to your account. The combined annual contributions to your retirement plans cannot exceed $40,000 or 100 percent of your compensation, whichever is lower. This limit applies to both your and Galaxy Max's contributions to your 401(k), profit-sharing, and defined benefit plans, unless the defined benefit plan requires (under the minimum required annual contribution) a greater annual contribution. Thus, in summary, all qualified retirement plans combined cannot exceed the $40,000 or 100 percent of compensation annual limit, unless more contribution is necessary to meet the minimum requirements under the defined benefit plans.

3.5 Conclusion

The management of Galaxy Max hopes that the benefits we offer are clear to you. Our studies indicate that our benefits package far exceeds the norms of our industry. We are very interested in your well-being, and this has motivated us to exceed our peer group's offerings. Should you have questions, please contact the Human Resources Department, 7500 Galaxy Max Road, Richmond, VA 23228; telephone 1-800-674-2900; e-mail hrgalaxymax@vcu.edu. Suggestions are always welcome as we continue to improve service to our employees.

KEY TAKEAWAYS

In this section you studied the employee benefits package of a hypothetical company (Galaxy Max, Inc.):

- Each group benefit option in an employee benefits program is explained in terms of benefits, eligibility, enrollment requirements, waiting periods, employee costs, coverage exclusions, benefit providers, tax implications, and plan termination provisions.
- Employees are able to add beneficiaries and dependents (subject to eligibility requirements) for applicable benefits.
- Life insurance at one-time employees' annual salary is a typical group benefit, with options to purchase supplemental coverage wholly funded by employees.
- Sick leave and short- and long-term disability options may be partially subsidized by employers, with options for employees to purchase supplemental long-term coverage.
- Group health insurance usually includes a mix of HMO, PPO, or high-deductible options provided at costs shared by employer and employee.
- Flexible spending accounts are offered within a cafeteria plan or as a stand-alone option to help employees pay for qualified out-of-pocket costs with pretax dollars.
- Retirement plans can be a combination of a traditional defined benefit plan and various defined contribution plans.
- A benefits package should explain the benefit or contribution formula of retirement plans, include payment options, clarify the requirements of early withdrawals or loans, define normal retirement age (and implications of early retirement), and stipulate vesting provisions.
- Limits apply to retirement plan contributions by employers and employees; benefit plans should give an understanding of employees' contributions and investment options.

DISCUSSION QUESTIONS

1. Why are employee benefits limited for part-time (versus full-time) employees?
2. What is the purpose of a waiting period in employee benefits?
3. Why would an employer enforce a minimum benefit limit on life insurance?
4. Why is the definition of disability stricter in the case of LTD than in STD?
5. When employees pay the LTD premiums, why aren't benefits taxable as income?
6. Why are long-term disability benefits coordinated with Social Security? What effect does this have?
7. How is the survivorship pension payment option made equitable to the retiree in the event that his or her beneficiary dies first?
8. How do vesting provisions protect employers?

4. CASE 3: NONTRADITIONAL INSURANCE PROGRAMS AND APPLICATION TO THE HYPOTHETICAL LOCO CORPORATION

LEARNING OBJECTIVES

In this section we elaborate on alternative risk-financing techniques using real-world case studies and a hypothetical example:

- **The evolution of sophisticated, nontraditional insurance arrangements**
- **Integrated risk management programs**
- **Finite risk management techniques**
- **Actual applications of alternative risk financing**
- **Utilization of alternative risk financing by hypothetical LOCO Corporation**

From Academy of Insurance Education
    Written by Phyllis S. Myers, Ph.D., and Etti G. Baranoff, Ph.D.
    Edited by Gail A. Grollman

Formerly a video education program of the National Association of Insurance Brokers
Copyright: The Council of Insurance Agents and Brokers[8]

4.1 Preface

Case 3, unlike Cases 1 and 2, is designed for risk management students who are interested in the more complex types of insurance coverage designed for large businesses. It is provided here to enhance Chapter 6 and the material provided in the textbook relating to different types of commercial coverage.

4.2 Introduction

alternative risk financing

Risk-funding arrangements that typically apply to losses above a firm's primary self-insurance retentions or losses above the primary insurance layer.

Alternative risk financing (sometimes referred to as alternative risk transfer) are risk-funding arrangements that typically apply to losses that are above the primary self-insurance retentions or losses above the primary insurance layer. Because of the complexities in designing these programs, they are utilized for solving the problems of large clients, and they merit substantial premiums.

Alternative risk transfer is an evolving area of risk finance where programs are often tailored for the individual company. Insurers have been expanding their offerings and creativity in designing methods of financing corporate risk. This new generation of financing risk is becoming more and more mainstream as more experience is gained by insurers, brokers, and risk managers.

An analogy between alternative medicine and alternative risk financing is made to demonstrate the importance of such insurance programs. The evolution of alternative risk transfer holds a striking parallel to that of alternative medicine. Individuals and the medical community began turning to alternative medicine when conventional methods failed. Alternative risk transfer is not much different. Risk managers looked for alternatives when the conventional insurance markets failed to satisfy their needs. When availability and affordability issues became prevalent in the insurance markets,[9] risk managers resorted to higher retention levels and creative methods of risk financing. In this process, corporations' risk tolerance levels increased, as did the expertise and comfort level of risk managers in managing risk. Consequently, they did not rush back into the market when it softened. Many of today's risk managers are protecting themselves from being at the mercy of the insurance industry. A long period of softness in the 1990s also put the buyers in the driver's seat and the buyers have been demanding products that align more closely with their company's needs. No longer was alternative risk financing created to heal availability and affordability problems. It has also been adopted to improve cash flows and effectively handle all risks in the organization. As in alternative medicine, the new methods have been seen as viable options for the improved (financial) health of the organization.

Risk managers began taking and maintaining long-term control of the process. They have been looking for cost, accounting, and tax efficiencies. Thus, in addition to using captives and risk retention groups (discussed in Chapter 6 and Chapter 8), they have been establishing customized finite risk programs, multiyear, multiline integrated risk programs, and they have been insuring risks that previously were once considered uninsurable. We will first delve into explaining these new-generation products before working on the LOCO case. The explanation of each program includes examples from real companies.

4.3 Nontraditional Insurance Products: The New Generation

New-generation risk-financing programs have emerged in response to the needs of large and complex organizations. These new-generation products blend with an orchestrated structure of self-insurance, captives, conventional insurance, and excess limits for selected individual lines. These more sophisticated methods of financing risk are being driven by a new breed of strategic-thinking risk managers who have an increased knowledge of risk management theory. They come to the table with a good understanding of their company's exposures and the financial resources available to handle risk. They are seeking risk-handling solutions that will improve efficiency, be cost-effective, and stabilize earnings.

integrated risk management

Coordinated alternative risk-financing approach of identifying, measuring, and monitoring diverse and multiple risks that require effective and rapid response to changing circumstances.

Increasingly, today's risk managers are practicing a holistic approach to risk management in which all of the corporation's risks—business, financial, and operational—are being assessed (as noted in Chapter 6). This concept, sometimes referred to as **integrated risk management**, is a coordinated alternative risk-financing approach of identifying, measuring, and monitoring diverse and multiple risks that require effective and rapid response to changing circumstances.[10] Nontraditional risk transfer programs, combined with traditional coverages, are being used to meet the needs of this holistic and strategic risk management approach.[11] Two of the nontraditional transfer programs available to risk managers that are covered in this case are integrated risk and finite insurance programs.

Integrated Risk Programs

The discussion of integrated risk programs includes responses to the following questions:

- What attracts corporations to the new integrated program?
- What is the response of the insurance industry and the brokerage community?
- How do you determine the coverages to include in an integrated program?
- What limits are appropriate?
- How do deductibles operate?
- Why do you need a reinstatement provision?
- What are three overall advantages to the integrated risk concept?

What Attracts Corporations to the New Integrated Programs?

The traditional approach of a tower of monoline coverages, each with a separate policy limit, has not been meeting the needs and operations of many corporations. Companies have been looking to integrated programs that combine lines of coverages in one aggregate policy—generally for a multiyear term. These integrated programs also go by names such as concentric risk and basket aggregates. The features that are attracting corporations to these programs include the following:

- Less administration time and cost
- Less time and cost for negotiations with brokers and underwriters
- Elimination of the need to build a tower of coverages
- One loss triggers just one policy
- Elimination of gaps in coverage (seamless coverage)
- Elimination of the need to buy separate limits for each type of coverage

Judy Lindenmayer's[12] program for FMR (Fidelity Investments) was one of the earliest integrated programs. She referred to it as concentric risk. She explained how she lowered her cost through the use of an aggregate limit. Under traditional coverage, an insured may be purchasing limits that are $50 million per year, but it is unlikely that there would be a major loss every year; thus, the full limit would not be used. Therefore, there is a waste of large limits in many of the years while the insured continues to pay for them. The solution to the redundancy and the extra cost is "the integrated program, with one aggregate limit over the three-year period. You buy one $50 million limit." Obviously, this is going to cost the insured less money. Judy Lindenmayer claimed that cost reductions could be as much as 30 or 40 percent.

Norwest, a bank with assets of $71.4 billion and 43,000 staff members in 3,000 locations (in 1997) across the United States, Canada, the Caribbean, Central and South America, and Asia was another company that could provide an example of what attracts corporations to the new concept. Until 1994, Norwest had traditional coverages. Each class of risk had an individual limit of self-insurance, a layer of commercial insurance, and an excess coverage. There were many risks that were not covered by insurance because of lack of availability.

K. C. Kidder, Norwest's risk manager, established a new integrated risk-financing program for simplicity and efficiency. In addition, she opted for the multiyear integrated approach. Kidder's other objectives for the major restructuring included the following:

- Provide aggregate retentions applicable to all risks
- Develop a long-term relationship with the insurer
- Stabilize price and coverage
- Provide catastrophe protection
- Reduce third-party costs significantly
- Use the company's captive insurer
- Maximize cash flow and investment yields
- Include previously uninsured risks.

Coca-Cola was another major company that was motivated to use an integrated program.[13] Allison O'Sullivan, Coca-Cola's director of risk management, was looking for a program that would do the following:

- Provide long-term stability
- Recognize the company's financial ability to retain risk
- Create value through attaining the lowest sustainable cost

- Increase administrative efficiencies
- Provide relevant coverage enhancements
- Strengthen market relationships
- Enhance options for hard-to-insure business risks worldwide

multitrigger contract

Insurance in which coverage is triggered by the occurrence of more than one event happening within the same time period.

Another attractive integrated product of limited use is the multitrigger contract. A **multitrigger contract** is insurance in which claims are triggered by the occurrence of more than one event happening within the same time period. The time period is defined in the contract and could be periods such as calendar year, fiscal year, season, or even a day. In a traditional single-trigger policy, a claim is based on the occurrence of any one covered loss, such as an earthquake or a fire. In the multitrigger contract, a claim can be made only if two or more covered incidents occur within that defined contract period. This coverage costs less than individual coverages because the probability of the two (or more) losses happening within the contract time period is lower than the probability of a single loss occurring. In the multitrigger policy, the insurer recognizes this lower probability in the pricing of the product. Thus, it would cost more to buy the earthquake insurance on a stand-alone basis than it would cost to buy earthquake insurance contingent on some other event taking place within that contract time period, such as a shift in foreign exchange or a shift in the cost of a key raw material to the client. Insureds who are concerned only with two very bad losses happening at the same time are those who would be interested in a multitrigger program.

What Is the Response of the Insurance Industry and the Brokerage Community?

Market conditions are contributing to insurers' responsiveness to risk managers. The insurance industry and brokerage community have created a new concept of bundling risks into one basket, under one limit, for multiple years. David May of J&H Marsh and McLennan, Inc.,[14] reported that "many insurance markets have lined up behind this new approach, offering close to $1 billion in capacity."[15] The industry provides large capacity for these types of programs. Two observations of their use include the following: (1) the corporations that use them are large with substantial financial strength and (2) the multiyear term of the programs promotes long-term relationships.

The U.S., European, and Bermuda markets all have been actively participating in various program combinations. XL and CIGNA were among the first players when they teamed up to combine property and casualty lines of coverage. The market demanded broader coverage, and the two insurers, in a very short time, have expanded their offerings. Another active player is Swiss Re with its BETA program. AIG, Chubb, and Liberty Mutual are active in the U.S. market.

Most of this capacity is not dependent on reinsurance. Some insurers offer one-stop shopping, while in other cases the structure uses a number of insurers. Coca-Cola's program, for example, was provided ultimately by several carriers.

How Do You Determine What Coverages to Include in an Integrated Program? What Limits Are Appropriate?

Integrated programs may include different combinations of coverages and may be designed for different lengths of time and different limits. Insurers provide many choices in their offerings. Programs are put together based on each corporation's own risk profile. These products are individualized and require intensive study to respond to the client's needs.

The typical corporations looking into these types of programs are Fortune 200 corporations—companies needing $100 million to $200 million or more in coverage.[16] These are corporations that have much larger and complex risks and need to work with a few carriers.

Judy Lindenmayer of Fidelity Investments explained the process of determining which coverages to combine the following:

- Review loss history
- Consider predictability of losses
- Review annual cost of coverage and coverage amount by line
- Consider risk tolerance level
- Select an aggregate limit that exceeds expected annual losses for all coverages

FMR had two separate integrated programs, as shown in Figure 23.5.[17] FMR's program for its mutual funds combines the government mandated fidelity bonds and E&O liability insurance. FMR took a very conservative approach, with a separate program to protect its mutual funds clients from employees' dishonesty or mistakes. For the other part of the company, the corporate side, the coverage included consolidated financial institutions bond coverage, which protects the employee benefits plans and protects against employees' dishonesty. The other coverages were Directors & Officers (D&O), stockbrokers Errors & Omissions (E&O), corporate E&O, E&O liability for charitable gifts, partnership liability, and electronic and computer crime. The corporate program was designed to respond to the risk management needs of the corporate side, which was "on the cutting edge on a lot of things" and therefore less conservative than the mutual funds' concentric program.

FIGURE 23.5 Fidelity Investments Integrated Risk Program

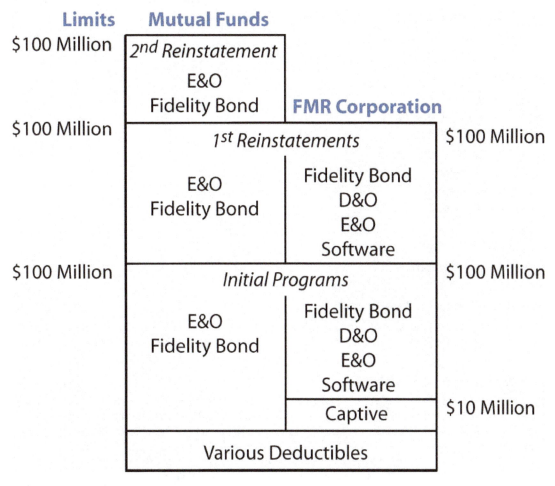

Integrated programs include coverages such as D&O, fiduciary liability, crime, E&O, and employment practices liability. The following are examples of the coverages that may be included in an integrated program under one aggregate limit:

- Property
- Business interruption
- General, products, and automobile liabilities
- Workers' compensation
- Marine liabilities and cargo
- Crime
- D&O liability
- E&O liability

For specific companies, it may also include the following:

- Product recalls
- Product tampering
- Political risks
- Environmental liabilities

Both Coca-Cola's and Norwest's programs combined a very broad array of coverages. Coca-Cola's program combines over thirty different risks in one contract. Although Coca-Cola did not do so in 1997, Allison O'Sullivan, then-director of risk management for Coca-Cola, said that she was open to the idea of blending financial risks like interest rate and currency exchange fluctuations. Norwest's program had a layer of true integrated insurance, with an aggregate of $100 million limit over a five-year period. It combined the following coverages in its program:

- Aircraft liability (nonowned)
- Automobile liability
- D&O (corporate reimbursement)
- Employers' liability
- Fiduciary liability
- Foreign liability
- Foreign property
- General liability
- Mail and transit
- Mortgagee E&O
- Professional liability
- Property
- Repossessed property
- Safe deposit
- Workers' compensation

Understanding the loss history of each line of coverage is very important to selecting the appropriate limits. The aggregate limit must be adequate to cover losses of all combined lines for the entire multi-year period.

How Do Deductibles Operate?

Programs may be structured with one aggregate deductible for the term of the policy or with separate, per occurrence deductibles. Norwest's integrated program had a $25 million aggregate retention over a five-year term. They had another five-year aggregate retention that was covered by its Vermont-based captive, Superior Guaranty Insurance Company. Above their retention, they had a finite risk layer (explained in the next section of this case) of $50 million. Fifty percent of this layer was covered by the captive. The other 50 percent was covered by American International Group (AIG).

The FMR aggregate programs are also structured over retentions. As discussed previously, FMR had two separate programs. The mutual funds program had multiple deductibles and the captive was not used.[18] For the corporate concentric program, FMR's captive, Fidvest Ltd., wrote up to $10 million in aggregate limits, as shown in Figure 23.5. Fidvest's retention included most of the risks except for the trustees' E&O. The captive retained only $5 million of this risk.

The decision about the appropriate retention levels forces the risk manager to look at risks and risk tolerance.

Why Do You Need a Reinstatement Provision?

As noted previously, selecting the limit that will cover all included losses over the entire multiyear period is an estimate based on a number of factors. But that estimate can prove to be wrong. The insured could use up his or her entire aggregate limit before the end of the term. For that reason, it is important to include one or more reinstatement provisions. Negotiating a reinstatement provision on the front end is critical to provide the following:

- Additional limits if the initial limits are exhausted
- A guarantee of coverage when needed
- Coverage at the right price

The FMR program contained reinstatement provisions in the event its aggregated limits were exhausted. Figure 23.5 illustrates that FMR had one reinstatement on the corporate program and an option to purchase two additional reinstatements for the funds' program.

What Are the Overall Advantages of the Integrated Risk Concept for Insureds?

The integrated risk programs are reported to produce in excess of 25 percent savings. This savings results from the following:

- Large premium decreases as a result of utilizing fewer carriers

- Flexibility of mixing the most appropriate risks (i.e., customized plans)
- Comprehensive coverage
- More efficient operation of the captives and retentions
- Reduced administrative costs and greater efficiency regarding renewals

The risk manager does not need to shop every year and prepare for renewals. The worry about the volatility of the traditional, cyclical insurance market is also reduced. These programs are expected to increase in prevalence. They have been combined with other new-generation products, such as finite risk, which is discussed next.

Finite Risk Programs

Finite risk programs are a way to finance risk assumptions that have their origins in arrangements between insurers and reinsurers. Premiums paid by the corporation to finance potential losses are placed in an experience fund that is held by the insurer. The insured is paying for its own losses through a systematic payment plan over time. Thus, it not subjected to the earnings volatility that can occur through self-insuring. **Finite risk programs** allow the insured to share in the underwriting profit and investment income that accrues on its premiums if loss experience is favorable and to recognize the individual risk transfer needs of each corporation. Consequently, each contract is unique. Generally, finite programs have the following characteristics in common:

- Multiyear term—at least three years, but may be five or even ten years
- Overall aggregate limit—often one limit applies; thus all losses of any type and line will be paid until they reach the aggregate limit
- Experience fund is established for the insured's losses—monies are paid into the fund and held by the insurer over the time period
- Interest earned on funds—a negotiated interest is earned on the funds that the insured has on deposit with the insurer
- Element of risk transfer—often includes some traditional risk transfer for the program to be recognized as insurance by the IRS
- Designed for each insured individually using manuscripted policy forms

Differences between Finite Protection and Traditional Insurance

The key difference between the finite risk program and traditional insurance coverage is that the funds paid to the insurer

- earn interest, which is credited to the insured, and
- are refundable to the insured.

An Example of How the Finite Risk Program Can Be Structured

Figure 23.6 shows an example of how a finite risk program operates. In this example, the insured has implemented a three-year program with a $100 million aggregate coverage limit for the entire period, with annual premium payments of $20 million. Thus, the insured has promised to pay $60 million over the three-year period, as denoted by increasing increments for each year on the graph. Actual risk transfer—that is, the conventional insurance layer of the finit eprogram—exists between the $60 million that the insured pays in and the $100 million limit. Thus, there is $40 million in risk transfer. This risk transfer layer is shown in dark blue on the graph.

At the end of the three-year period, the deposits may be returned to the insured with interest, less any losses. As will be discussed later, a return of funds constitutes a taxable event and the insured may choose to roll the funds over to the next term.

finite risk programs

Allow insureds to share in the underwriting profit and investment income that accrues on premiums if loss experience is favorable and recognize firms' individual risk transfer needs.

FIGURE 23.6 Finite Risk Program of Fidelity Investments, $100 Million Coverage Limit

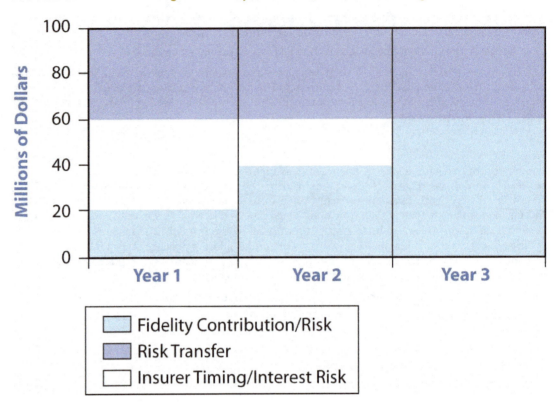

What If Losses Exceed the Funds Paid to Date?

In the example in Figure 23.6, the insured has paid in $20 million in the first year. But what if losses exceed $20 million in the first year? This is the timing risk that the insurer takes—the risk that losses will exceed the insured's deposit—in which case, the insurer has to pay for them prior to having received the funds from the insured. The graph shows the timing risk in white. It is the difference between the insured's accumulated payments into the fund and the total amount the insured promises to pay into the fund over the entire time period (in this example, $60 million over a three-year period). The timing layer is similar to a line of credit for the insured. The insured must still pay the insurer for the losses that were paid out in advance, or "loaned" to the insured.

The FMR Corporation structured its finite program around its integrated risk program. Figure 23.7 displays how FMR's finite program fits around the two integrated programs described previously. The finite program is outlined with dotted lines. An important part of its program was the inclusion of risks that are traditionally uninsurable. If a loss occurs under the finite program that is also covered by its underlying integrated coverage, the finite program acts as a layer above the integrated limit. Thus, the finite risk protection is pierced when the integrated limit is exhausted—no deductible is incurred under the finite program. If a loss occurs under the finite program and it is not covered by the integrated program, a $100,000 aggregate deductible applies. Such losses are paid if and when aggregate losses under the finite program reach $100,000.

A finite program can fit into a corporation's risk-financing structure in other ways as well. It can be used to fund primary losses. It can also be used in intermediate layers to stabilize infrequent but periodic losses.[19]

FIGURE 23.7   Structure of Fidelity Investments' Finite Risk and Integrated Risk Programs

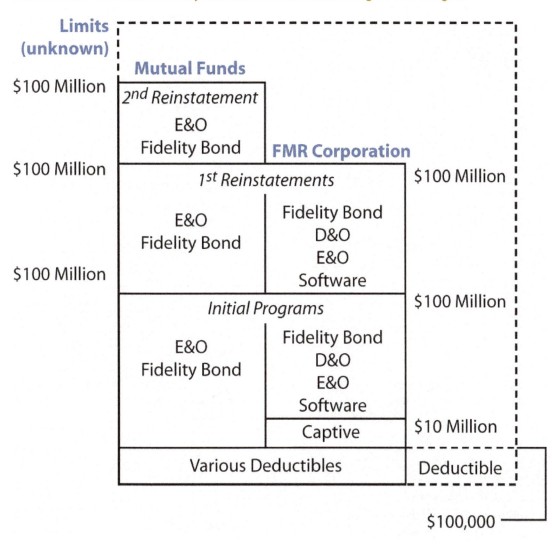

An Example of How the Experience Fund Operates

Now, let us show an example of how the experience fund works. Table 23.25 displays a chart of an experience fund with annual deposits of $20 million for a three-year term. Assume an annual interest rate of 6 percent is credited quarterly to the fund. Also assume that the interest accrues on a tax-free basis, as would be the case if the fund is placed with an offshore insurer where investment income is not subject to taxation. In this example, the insured incurs a $5 million loss in year two. At the end of the term, the insured's balance is $62,120,260. The funds may be returned to the insured or rolled over to another contract term.

TABLE 23.25 Finite Risk Experience Fund

Date	Credit/Debit to Fund	Fund Balance at Beginning of the Period	Interest Earned
Jan. 1, 1997	$20,000,000	$20,000,000	
March 31, 1997		$20,300,000	$300,000
June 30, 1997		$20,604,500	$304,500
Sept. 30, 1997		$20,913,568	$309,068
Dec. 31, 1997		$21,227,271	$313,704
Jan. 1, 1998	$20,000,000	$41,227,271	
March 31, 1998		$41,845,680	$618,409
March 31, 1998	($5,000,000)	$36,845,680	
June 30, 1998		$37,398,365	$552,685
Sept. 30, 1998		$37,959,340	$560,975
Dec. 31, 1998		$38,528,730	$569,390
Jan. 1, 1999	$20,000,000	$58,528,730	
March 31, 1999		$59,406,661	$877,931
June 30, 1999		$60,297,761	$891,100
Sept. 30, 1999		$61,202,227	$904,466
Dec. 31, 1999		$62,120,260	$918,033

Pricing

Pricing of the product will vary. There can be an additional premium to pay for the risk transfer and timing risk elements. Alternatively, the insurer's risk can be paid for by the spread between the interest it expects to earn on the funds and the interest credited to the insured.

Suitability of Finite Risk

Finite programs typically are used by large corporations with one or more of the following characteristics:

- High retention levels
- Unique or difficult to insure risks
- Risks where adequate limits are not available
- Ability to make large cash outlays

Advantages of a Finite Risk Program

Finite risk programs offer a number of benefits to corporations:

- Improves the balance sheet—by including risks for which noninsurance reserves had been established, it allows the company to remove these reserves from its balance sheet.
- Reduces volatility in earnings—instead of paying unpredictable losses out of current earnings, the insured is paying equal payments to the insurer to cover losses; if losses exceed the payments, the insurer pays them and the insured can work out an arrangement to pay them back up to the agreed-on amount that should be paid into the fund.
- Allows for profit sharing if the loss experience is favorable—the insured earns interest on the payments that it pays to the insurer. In addition, these payments can be structured as tax deductible, whereas reserves on the balance sheet are not deductible until losses are paid.
- Helps secure insurance for uninsurable risks—because the losses are paid by the insured, a program can be structured without limitations on what types of risk can be included.
- Accesses new capacity for catastrophic risks—finite programs can be structured so they are layered over a very large retention level, a captive, or other insurance program, such as integrated risk programs or conventional insurance.

Determining the Risks to Include in a Finite Program

Finite risk programs can be structured to include any type of risk, contingent on approval by the company's auditors.[20] They are touted as a means of financing traditionally uninsurable risks. Thus, a corporation looks at its own risk profile to determine the appropriate risks to include in the program. A corporation can do this in one or more of the following ways:

- Examine the balance sheet for reserves—reserves are established for risks on which there is no insurance coverage. The size of these reserves reflects the potential impact of the risk.

- Examine insurance policies for existing exclusions—this exercise reveals important risks that currently are uninsured.

- Ask senior managers what keeps them awake at night—in addition to potentially identifying previously unidentified risks, the process reveals the firm's tolerance for risk by determining what is important to senior managers.

Potential Disadvantages of a Finite Risk Program

Finite risk programs are becoming increasingly popular. But they are not without disadvantages:

- Tax and accounting questions—accounting and tax rules say that there must be more than timing and interest rate risk for the insurer in order for the insured's payments to be tax deductible. The tax code requires that the finite financing arrangement involve real underwriting risk transfer with a reasonable expectation of loss. Transactions that do not meet tax and accounting rules regarding risk transfer will be treated as deposits. The main requirement is that the insurer (or reinsurer) must stand to realize a significant loss from the transaction. Judy Lindenmayer mentions a general rule of thumb that has developed, whereby 10 to 15 percent of the estimated exposure should be transferred to the insurer, and the risk so transferred must have a 10 to 20 percent chance of loss. Actuaries, however, caution against specifying probability thresholds because they do not allow for the differences in frequency and severity of various exposures.[21] Evaluation of the risk transfer element is a complex process that requires a complete understanding of the transaction, the details of which are beyond the scope of this course.

- The premiums should not be construed as a deposit for accounting purposes. The risk transfer element must be verified by outside auditors. It is permissible to base the tax and accounting for the finite program on two different foundations. However, doing so may draw the attention of income tax auditors.

- Any monies that are returned to the insured at the end of the period constitute taxable income. To avoid a taxable event, the insured can roll the funds over to the next term.

- Time-consuming and complex to develop—although finite programs can save considerable time once they are in place, they can take up to a year to develop.

- Frictional costs may be greater than perceived benefits—these costs are estimated to range from 5 to 10 percent. A fee is paid to the insurer, and a federal excise tax applies to premiums paid for programs that are domiciled offshore.

- Opportunity cost of committed funds—the programs entail large outlays of cash each year of the term. These large outlays, and the fact that they tie up the funds, can overshadow the net cost efficiencies that might have been obtained. Generally, these cash outlays require the involvement of the company's CFO or other senior manager. Often, the cash outlays form the obstacle to obtaining senior management approval of the program.

4.4   Loco Corporation Case Study: Part I

Background Information

Since its formation in 1945, LOCO Corporation has been a leader in the investment banking field. Its largest and best known subsidiary is Loyalty Investment, an investment advisory and management company for a family of one hundred funds. Through a network of thirty-two principal offices in twenty-two countries, LOCO and Loyalty Investment offer a complete range of financial services, including online trading and research assistance to corporations, institutions, and individuals throughout the world. LOCO, through another subsidiary called Loyalty Brokerage Group, engages in sales and trading on a discounted fee basis. It uses the most advanced technologies available in the market. Approximately 50 percent of trades (for both the direct funds and through the brokerage firm) are handled online, another 40 percent are handled over the telephone, and 10 percent are handled in person at sales offices around the world.

LOCO also provides financial underwriting services and advice to corporations and governments around the world regarding their capital structures. Its products and services include corporate finance, real estate, project finance and leasing, debt and equity capital markets, mergers and acquisitions, and restructuring.

Under Loyalty Investment are three subsidiaries:

- The Loyalty Brokerage Group (formerly the Kendu Financial Group acquired in 1994)—a stock brokerage firm that handles $4 billion annually in trades for retail and institutional clients on a discounted fee basis.
- The Loyalty Financial Services Group—an insurance, estate planning, and investment advisory organization for high net worth individuals operating only in the United States and the United Kingdom. The nonsupport staff is licensed to sell insurance and securities.
- Loyalware—a financial services software producer.

LOCO has offices in Europe, the Middle East, the Far East, South Africa, Australia, and South America and is expanding into Russia and China. LOCO's financial highlights are shown in Table 23.26, which provides information on LOCO's size, liquidity, and debt positions in 1995 and 1996. Although LOCO has been enjoying increased revenues, LOCO's profit margins have decreased from 1995 to 1996. Return on equity has remained stagnant for the last two years.

TABLE 23.26 LOCO Corporation Financial Highlights

For the Years Ended September 30 (in Millions)	1996	1995
Cash and marketable securities	$ 73,259	$ 93,325
Real estate	$ 45,464	$ 35,217
Other assets	$ 20,000	$ 18,000
Total assets	$138,723	$146,542
Liabilities	$115,050	$116,046
Reserves for losses	$ 300	$ 250
Long-term borrowing	$ 9,114	$ 8,891
Stockholders' equity	$ 23,259	$ 21,355
Total liabilities and equity	$138,723	$146,542
Net revenue	$ 4,356	$ 3,480
Net income	$ 696	$ 634
Net profit margin (net income/net revenue)	15.98%	18.2%
Return on equity (net income/stockholder's equity)	2.99%	2.97%
Shares outstanding	173,924,100	163,239,829
Number of employees	14,987	14,321

Recently, Dan Button, director of risk management, was appointed director of global risk management, a newly created position to reflect the integration of domestic and international risk management operations. LOCO has a separate operating officer both for its domestic operations and its international operations. Most likely, the separation of operations was the reason that the risk management operations were handled separately as well. Dan and his chief financial officer (CFO), Elaine Matthews, were instrumental in effecting a change. They knew that economies of scale could be realized by consolidating the risk management function on a global basis. Elaine believes in the holistic approach to risk management and involves Dan in the management of all the risks facing the corporation, be they financial, business, or event-type risks that were traditionally under the authority of the risk manager.

LOCO has a rather large amount of reserves on its balance sheet. A considerable portion of the reserves are attributable to the expected E&O losses that were assumed from Kendu Financial Group when it was acquired in 1994. Another big chunk of the reserve amount is attributable to self-insured workers' compensation losses. LOCO has self-insured its domestic and international workers' compensation risk since the early 1980s. Even though claims were handled by a third-party administrator, two individuals on Dan's staff have devoted their full-time work to workers' compensation issues. Prompted by soft market conditions, Dan decided to insure the risk. He secured Foreign Voluntary Workers' Compensation coverage for U.S. workers abroad and for foreign nationals, as well as workers' compensation coverage for the domestic employees. The company has built up fairly significant loss obligations from self-insuring.

LOCO's business has been changing rapidly over the last several years. It has become more global, more dependent on technology, and more diversified in its operations. This changing risk environment, along with the corporation's cost-cutting efforts, has compelled Dan to embark on a comprehensive assessment of his risk management department and the corporate risk profile.

4.5 Loco Corporation Case Study: Part II

Background Information

The following are some of the actions taken by Dan's team:

- Restructuring of all coverages to save money on administration and to provide streamlined and sufficient coverage for all the risks faced by LOCO and its subsidiaries
- Finding ways to take the 1991 losses of the Gulf War off the balance sheet and insure risks that previously were uninsured

The hypothetical LOCO Corporation was created to help you apply the concepts of alternative risk financing that you studied in this chapter. Familiarize yourself with the features of LOCO Corporation, then answer the discussion questions that follow the Key Takeaways section below.

KEY TAKEAWAYS

In this section you studied integrated risk management and finite risk management programs, two types of alternative risk-financing arrangements:

- Alternative risk-financing arrangements are complex arrangements used by large commercial clients that apply to losses above the primary self-insurance retentions or losses above the primary insurance layer.
- Alternative risk-financing arrangements are tailored to clients' diverse needs and blend self-insurance, captives, conventional insurance, and excess limits.
- Integrated risk management identifies, measures, and monitors multiple business, financial, and operational risks to satisfy holistic risk management objectives.
  - An integrated risk program combines lines of insurance coverage into an aggregate, multitrigger contract for a multiyear term for improved efficiency and cost savings.
  - A company's loss history, predictability of losses, costs of coverage, and risk tolerance influences the determination of coverages to combine in integrated programs.
  - Integrated programs may be structured with one aggregate deductible for the term of the policy or with separate per occurrence deductibles.
  - Savings from integrated risk programs result from premium decreases, customization, comprehensive coverage, more efficient operations, and reduced administrative costs.
- In a finite risk program, the insured pays for its own losses through premiums placed in an experience fund held by an insurer
  - Finite risk programs allow insureds to share in the underwriting profit and investment income that accrues on premiums, if loss experience is favorable.
  - Finite risk programs are associated with multiyear terms, overall aggregate limits, risk transfer elements, and so forth.
  - The insurer assumes timing risk because losses can exceed funds paid to date by the insured, resulting in liability for the insurer.
  - Finite risk programs can be used in conjunction with integrated risk management.
  - Companies suited for finite programs have high retention levels, unique and/or difficult to insure risks, inadequate availability of traditional coverage, and high liquidity.
  - Finite programs can improve the balance sheet, reduce earnings volatility, secure insurance for previously uninsurable risks, and access new capacity for catastrophic risks.
- Fidelity Investments, Norwest, and Coca-Cola have successfully implemented integrated risk and/or finite risk management programs

DISCUSSION QUESTIONS

1. What is alternative risk financing? How has it evolved over time?
2. What attracts corporations to integrated risk management products?
3. How does integrated risk management improve efficiencies and reduce costs?
4. Why is the cost of coverage in multitrigger contracts less than in single-trigger contracts?
5. What are two reasons that the insurance industry provides large capacity for insurance products designed for integrated risk management?
6. What is the main difference between finite risk programs and traditional insurance coverage?
7. What is meant by timing risk in finite risk programs? How is this like a line of credit for the insured?

   For questions 8 and 9, refer to the information in Part I of the LOCO Corporation hypothetical case study.

8. Assume you are LOCO Corporation's major insurance broker. Assist director of global risk management Dan Button in identifying the risks that LOCO faces. Use your knowledge from this chapter as well as the risk-mapping concepts of Chapter 4 and Chapter 5.
9. Take each risk that you identified in question 8 and discuss whether you expect aggregate frequency and severity of losses to be low, medium, or high.

   For question 10, refer to the actions taken in Part II of the LOCO Corporation hypothetical case study.

10. Current consolidation and diversification in the industry has resulted in an across-the-board corporate mandate to cut costs. Like other department heads, Dan is under pressure to increase efficiency. Dan wants to investigate the feasibility of an integrated risk management approach. What advantages would an integrated program have for LOCO? What characteristics about LOCO make it conducive to starting an integrated program?

5. REVIEW AND PRACTICE

1. Refer to Table 23.3. Other than the fact that the policies are provided by different companies, what could account for the significant differences among premiums presented in the table?
2. What is the purpose of the waiting period in LTD insurance? How does the Smith family make certain there are no gaps in coverage in the event of disability?
3. Examine the insurance premiums allocation shown in Figure 23.3. Why do you think auto insurance has the highest insurance allocation and life insurance the lowest?
4. Do you agree with the Smith family's assessment of its insurance needs? Are there other relevant facts about the family that should be factored into the decision?
5. How might accelerated benefits in a life insurance policy be triggered? What does this provide?
6. Which of the hypothetical Galaxy Max, Inc., health plans do you personally find preferable? Explain your reasoning.
7. In what way does use of a flexible spending account and premium conversion plan reduce health care costs to employees?
8. How can employees continue to have life and health insurance coverage without providing new evidence of insurability in the event of termination from a group plan?
9. What should employees consider when selecting among 401(k) investment options?
10. What employee benefits of the hypothetical Galaxy Max, Inc., are unrealistic and impossible to find in today's world?
11. How does a reinstatement provision provide an additional layer of protection in an integrated risk program?
12. What are the potential disadvantages of a finite risk program?
13. Explain how to determine which types of coverage to include in a multiyear integrated risk program and the appropriate limits to select.
14. It is said that traditionally uninsurable risks are insurable under finite risk programs. Explain why this is possible.

15. Refer to the information in Part I of the LOCO Corporation hypothetical case study and respond to the following:

    a. Draw a risk map graph (as described in Chapter 4) and place your estimates of the risks faced by the company in the appropriate quadrant.

    b. For each risk, indicate what risk-handling method is suggested by your estimates.

16. Refer to the actions taken in Part II of the LOCO Corporation hypothetical case study and respond to the following:

    a. Briefly explain what a finite risk management program is.

    b. Why might a finite risk program be appropriate for LOCO Corporation?

6. CHAPTER BIBLIOGRAPHY

Aldred, Carolyn. "Alternative Financing of Primary Interest to Risk Managers: Expected to Become More Familiar with Nontraditional Products." *Business Insurance*, September 3, 1997.

Banham, Russ. "When Insurance Really Is a Total Risk Package." *Global Finance*, February 1997, 11–12.

Doherty, Neil A. "Corporate Insurance: Competition from Capital Markets and Financial Institutions." *Assurances*, April 1997, 63–94.

Helbting, Carolyn P., Georg Fallegger, and Donna Hill. *Rethinking Risk Financing*. Zurich, Switzerland: Swiss Reinsurance Company, 1996.

Herrick, R. C. "Exploring the Efficient Frontier." *Risk Management*, August 1997, 23–25.

Koral, Edward S. "A Tug of War Accounting Rules and Finite Risk Programs." *Risk Management*, November 1995, 45–47.

Lenckus, Dave. "Concentric Risk Programs Means Big Saving: Innovative Programs to Save FMR Time, Money." *Business Insurance*, April 14, 1997, 98.

Lenckus, Dave. "FMR Corp." *Business Insurance*, April 14, 1997, 98.

Lenckus, Dave. "Reinsurance Program Strives to Find the Right Blend of Risks." *Business Insurance*, April 14, 1997, 100.

May, David G. "All-in-One Insurance." *Financial Executive*, no. 3 (1997): 41–43.

May, David G. "Integrated Risk; Reaching Toward Risk Management Heaven." *Viewpoint Quarterly*, Marsh & McLennan Companies, Winter 1996.

May, David G. "The Real Thing." *Financial Executive* 13, no. 3 (1997): 42.

Mello, John P. Jr., "Paradise, or Pipe Dream?" *CFO: The Magazine for Chief Financial Officers* 13, no. 2 (1997): 73–75.

Myers, Gregory K. "Alternative Risk Financing in the Traditional Insurance Marketplace." *John Liner Review* 10, no. 3 (1996): 6–16.

Nottingham, Lucy. "Integrated Risk Management." *Canadian Business Review* 23, no. 2 (1996): 26–28.

Teach, Edward. "Microsoft's Universe of Risk." *CFO: The Magazine for Chief Financial Officers*, March 1997, 68–72.

"What Is Risk Transfer in Reinsurance? Comments on Financial Accounting Standard 113," *Contingencies*, September/October 1997, 50–53.

ENDNOTES

1. Social Security Testimony Before Congress, "House Committee on Ways and Means, Subcommittee on Social Security (Shaw) on SSA's Response to the Terrorist Attacks of September 11, Larry Massanari, Commissioner," http://www.ssa.gov/legislation/testimony_110101.html (accessed April 16, 2009).

2. Daniel Hays, "Workers' Compensation Losses Might Top $1 Billion," *National Underwriter*, Property & Casualty/Risk & Benefits Management Edition, September 2001, 10; See also New York State Workers' Compensation Board at http://www.wcb.state.ny.us/ (accessed April 16, 2009).

3. John D. Dempsey and Lee M. Epstein, "Re-Examining Business Interruption Insurance" (part one of three), *Risk Management Magazine*, February 2002.

4. This project was prepared by Kristy L. Blankenship, Crystal Jones, Jason C. Lemley, and Fei W.Turner, students in the author's fall 2000 class in risk and insurance. Many other groups also prepared excellent projects, which are available upon request from the author.

5. The work of the following students is reflected in this case: Donna Biddick, Lavonnia Bragg, Katrina Brand, Heather Cartes, Robert Cloud, Maria Conway, Thomas Dabney Clay, Lillian Dunlevy, Daniel Fleming, Shannon Fowlkes, Caroline Garrett, Barbara Guill, Steven Hall, Georgette Harris, Shirelle Harris, Tyron Hinton, Tiffany Jefferson, Tennille McCarter, Pamela Nicholson, Hiren Patel, Susan Shaban, Carolyn Shelburne, Gaurav Shrestha, Stephanie Soucy, Christopher Speight, Cassandra Townsend, Geoff Watkins, and Tresha White, from fall 2002. Also included is the work of Margaret Maslak and Shelisa Artis from fall 2000.

6. The students used information from the following companies and sources: Dominion Co., www.dominion.com; Dominion Virginia Power, http://www.dom.com/; Phillip Morris, USA, http://www.philipmorrisusa.com/en/cms/Home/default.aspx; Virginia Retirement System, www.state.va.us/vrs/vrs-home-htm; Henrico County, Virginia, www.co.henrico.va.us.; Minnesota Life, www.minnesotalife.com; A. M. Best Company, ambest.com; Federal Reserve Board, http://www.federalreserve.gov/; Stanley Corp.; Ethyl Corporation, http://www.ethyl.com/index.htm; Aetna, www.aetna.com; Anthem, http://www.anthem.com/; CIGNA, www.cigna.com; and more.

7. A qualifying event is a marriage or divorce, adoption of a child, death of a covered dependent, a change in status or eligibility of a dependent, and so forth.

8. The Council of Insurance Agents and Brokers assumed all National Association of Insurance Brokers (NAIB) copyrights when the two organizations merged. The Council gave permission to use the material. The Council of Insurance Agents and Brokers is located in Washington, D.C. This case is based on the video education series created for continuing education of brokers in 1996 and 1997. Five video education modules were created. The material used in this case is from video number 5. Some modifications to the original material were necessary when making the transition to a print format.

9. Recall the explanation of the underwriting cycles described in Chapter 8 of the text. Also, remember that this case was prepared in 1996–1997 during the end tail of a long soft market condition.

10. Lucy Nottingham, "Integrated Risk Management," *Canadian Business Review* 23, no. 2 (1996): 26.

11. Carolyn Aldred, "Alternative Financing of Primary Interest: Risk Managers Expected to Become More Familiar with Nontraditional Products," *Business Insurance*, September 3, 1997.

12. Judy Lindenmayer was one of the experts contributing to the creation of this video education segment.

13. David G. May, "The Real Thing," *Financial Executive* 13, no. 3 (1997): 42.

14. Today, the company name is simply Marsh. During the period of the case, many brokerage houses merged. The large mergers and the decrease in the number of brokerage houses prompted the consolidation of the brokers and agents organizations into the Council of Insurance Agents and Brokers.

15. David G. May, "All-in-One Insurance," *Financial Executive* 13, no. 3 (1997): 41.

16. John P. Mello, Jr., "Paradise, or Pipe Dream?" *CFO: The Magazine for Chief Financial Officers* 13, no. 2 (1997): 73.

17. Dave Lenckus, "Concentric Risk Programs Means Big Saving—Innovative Programs to Save FMR Time, Money," *Business Insurance*, April 14, 1997, 98.

18. Dave Lenckus, "Reinsurance Program Strives to Find the Right Blend of Risks," *Business Insurance*, April 14, 1997, 100.

19. Gregory K. Myers, "Alternative Risk Financing in the Traditional Insurance Marketplace," *John Liner Review* 10, no. 3 (1996): 13.

20. Types of risks included in the program may be restricted by the corporation's external auditors.

21. "What is 'Risk Transfer' in Reinsurance? Comments on Financial Accounting Standard 113," *Contingencies*, September/October 1997, 50–53. (Based on a report of the American Academy of Actuaries Committee on Property and Liability Issues.)

CHAPTER 24

Appendix A

SAMPLE HOMEOWNERS SPECIAL FORM (HO-3) HO 00 03 05 01

Copyrighted material of Insurance Services Office, Inc., with its permission

FIGURE 24.1

HOMEOWNERS 3 – SPECIAL FORM

AGREEMENT

We will provide the insurance described in this policy in return for the premium and compliance with all applicable provisions of this policy.

DEFINITIONS

A. In this policy, "you" and "your" refer to the "named insured" shown in the Declarations and the spouse if a resident of the same household. "We", "us" and "our" refer to the Company providing this insurance.

B. In addition, certain words and phrases are defined as follows:

1. "Aircraft Liability", "Hovercraft Liability", "Motor Vehicle Liability" and "Watercraft Liability", subject to the provisions in **b.** below, mean the following:

a. Liability for "bodily injury" or "property damage" arising out of the:

(1) Ownership of such vehicle or craft by an "insured";

(2) Maintenance, occupancy, operation, use, loading or unloading of such vehicle or craft by any person;

(3) Entrustment of such vehicle or craft by an "insured" to any person;

(4) Failure to supervise or negligent supervision of any person involving such vehicle or craft by an "insured"; or

(5) Vicarious liability, whether or not imposed by law, for the actions of a child or minor involving such vehicle or craft.

b. For the purpose of this definition:

(1) Aircraft means any contrivance used or designed for flight except model or hobby aircraft not used or designed to carry people or cargo;

(2) Hovercraft means a self-propelled motorized ground effect vehicle and includes, but is not limited to, flarecraft and air cushion vehicles;

(3) Watercraft means a craft principally designed to be propelled on or in water by wind, engine power or electric motor; and

(4) Motor vehicle means a "motor vehicle" as defined in **7.** below.

2. "Bodily injury" means bodily harm, sickness or disease, including required care, loss of services and death that results.

3. "Business" means:

a. A trade, profession or occupation engaged in on a full-time, part-time or occasional basis; or

b. Any other activity engaged in for money or other compensation, except the following:

(1) One or more activities, not described in **(2)** through **(4)** below, for which no "insured" receives more than $2,000 in total compensation for the 12 months before the beginning of the policy period;

(2) Volunteer activities for which no money is received other than payment for expenses incurred to perform the activity;

(3) Providing home day care services for which no compensation is received, other than the mutual exchange of such services; or

(4) The rendering of home day care services to a relative of an "insured".

4. "Employee" means an employee of an "insured", or an employee leased to an "insured" by a labor leasing firm under an agreement between an "insured" and the labor leasing firm, whose duties are other than those performed by a "residence employee".

5. "Insured" means:

a. You and residents of your household who are:

(1) Your relatives; or

(2) Other persons under the age of 21 and in the care of any person named above;

b. A student enrolled in school full time, as defined by the school, who was a resident of your household before moving out to attend school, provided the student is under the age of:

(1) 24 and your relative; or

(2) 21 and in your care or the care of a person described in **a.(1)** above; or

FIGURE 24.2

c. Under Section **II**:

(1) With respect to animals or watercraft to which this policy applies, any person or organization legally responsible for these animals or watercraft which are owned by you or any person included in **a.** or **b.** above. "Insured" does not mean a person or organization using or having custody of these animals or watercraft in the course of any "business" or without consent of the owner; or

(2) With respect to a "motor vehicle" to which this policy applies:

(a) Persons while engaged in your employ or that of any person included in **a.** or **b.** above; or

(b) Other persons using the vehicle on an "insured location" with your consent.

Under both Sections **I** and **II,** when the word an immediately precedes the word "insured", the words an "insured" together mean one or more "insureds".

6. "Insured location" means:

a. The "residence premises";

b. The part of other premises, other structures and grounds used by you as a residence; and

(1) Which is shown in the Declarations; or

(2) Which is acquired by you during the policy period for your use as a residence;

c. Any premises used by you in connection with a premises described in **a.** and **b.** above;

d. Any part of a premises:

(1) Not owned by an "insured"; and

(2) Where an "insured" is temporarily residing;

e. Vacant land, other than farm land, owned by or rented to an "insured";

f. Land owned by or rented to an "insured" on which a one, two, three or four family dwelling is being built as a residence for an "insured";

g. Individual or family cemetery plots or burial vaults of an "insured"; or

h. Any part of a premises occasionally rented to an "insured" for other than "business" use.

7. "Motor vehicle" means:

a. A self-propelled land or amphibious vehicle; or

b. Any trailer or semitrailer which is being carried on, towed by or hitched for towing by a vehicle described in **a.** above.

8. "Occurrence" means an accident, including continuous or repeated exposure to substantially the same general harmful conditions, which results, during the policy period, in:

a. "Bodily injury"; or

b. "Property damage".

9. "Property damage" means physical injury to, destruction of, or loss of use of tangible property.

10. "Residence employee" means:

a. An employee of an "insured", or an employee leased to an "insured" by a labor leasing firm, under an agreement between an "insured" and the labor leasing firm, whose duties are related to the maintenance or use of the "residence premises", including household or domestic services; or

b. One who performs similar duties elsewhere not related to the "business" of an "insured".

A "residence employee" does not include a temporary employee who is furnished to an "insured" to substitute for a permanent "residence employee" on leave or to meet seasonal or short-term workload conditions.

11. "Residence premises" means:

a. The one family dwelling where you reside;

b. The two, three or four family dwelling where you reside in at least one of the family units; or

c. That part of any other building where you reside;

and which is shown as the "residence premises" in the Declarations.

"Residence premises" also includes other structures and grounds at that location.

FIGURE 24.3

DEDUCTIBLE

Unless otherwise noted in this policy, the following deductible provision applies:

Subject to the policy limits that apply, we will pay only that part of the total of all loss payable under Section I that exceeds the deductible amount shown in the Declarations.

SECTION I – PROPERTY COVERAGES

A. Coverage A – Dwelling

1. We cover:

   a. The dwelling on the "residence premises" shown in the Declarations, including structures attached to the dwelling; and

   b. Materials and supplies located on or next to the "residence premises" used to construct, alter or repair the dwelling or other structures on the "residence premises".

2. We do not cover land, including land on which the dwelling is located.

B. Coverage B – Other Structures

1. We cover other structures on the "residence premises" set apart from the dwelling by clear space. This includes structures connected to the dwelling by only a fence, utility line, or similar connection.

2. We do not cover:

   a. Land, including land on which the other structures are located;

   b. Other structures rented or held for rental to any person not a tenant of the dwelling, unless used solely as a private garage;

   c. Other structures from which any "business" is conducted; or

   d. Other structures used to store "business" property. However, we do cover a structure that contains "business" property solely owned by an "insured" or a tenant of the dwelling provided that "business" property does not include gaseous or liquid fuel, other than fuel in a permanently installed fuel tank of a vehicle or craft parked or stored in the structure.

3. The limit of liability for this coverage will not be more than 10% of the limit of liability that applies to Coverage A. Use of this coverage does not reduce the Coverage A limit of liability.

C. Coverage C – Personal Property

1. **Covered Property**

   We cover personal property owned or used by an "insured" while it is anywhere in the world. After a loss and at your request, we will cover personal property owned by:

   a. Others while the property is on the part of the "residence premises" occupied by an "insured"; or

   b. A guest or a "residence employee", while the property is in any residence occupied by an "insured".

2. **Limit For Property At Other Residences**

   Our limit of liability for personal property usually located at an "insured's" residence, other than the "residence premises", is 10% of the limit of liability for Coverage C, or $1,000, whichever is greater. However, this limitation does not apply to personal property:

   a. Moved from the "residence premises" because it is being repaired, renovated or rebuilt and is not fit to live in or store property in; or

   b. In a newly acquired principal residence for 30 days from the time you begin to move the property there.

3. **Special Limits Of Liability**

   The special limit for each category shown below is the total limit for each loss for all property in that category. These special limits do not increase the Coverage C limit of liability.

   a. $200 on money, bank notes, bullion, gold other than goldware, silver other than silverware, platinum other than platinumware, coins, medals, scrip, stored value cards and smart cards.

   b. $1,500 on securities, accounts, deeds, evidences of debt, letters of credit, notes other than bank notes, manuscripts, personal records, passports, tickets and stamps. This dollar limit applies to these categories regardless of the medium (such as paper or computer software) on which the material exists.

   This limit includes the cost to research, replace or restore the information from the lost or damaged material.

FIGURE 24.4

c. $1,500 on watercraft of all types, including their trailers, furnishings, equipment and outboard engines or motors.

d. $1,500 on trailers or semitrailers not used with watercraft of all types.

e. $1,500 for loss by theft of jewelry, watches, furs, precious and semiprecious stones.

f. $2,500 for loss by theft of firearms and related equipment.

g. $2,500 for loss by theft of silverware, silver-plated ware, goldware, gold-plated ware, platinumware, platinum-plated ware and pewterware. This includes flatware, hollowware, tea sets, trays and trophies made of or including silver, gold or pewter.

h. $2,500 on property, on the "residence premises", used primarily for "business" purposes.

i. $500 on property, away from the "residence premises", used primarily for "business" purposes. However, this limit does not apply to loss to electronic apparatus and other property described in Categories **j.** and **k.** below.

j. $1,500 on electronic apparatus and accessories, while in or upon a "motor vehicle", but only if the apparatus is equipped to be operated by power from the "motor vehicle's" electrical system while still capable of being operated by other power sources.

Accessories include antennas, tapes, wires, records, discs or other media that can be used with any apparatus described in this Category **j.**

k. $1,500 on electronic apparatus and accessories used primarily for "business" while away from the "residence premises" and not in or upon a "motor vehicle". The apparatus must be equipped to be operated by power from the "motor vehicle's" electrical system while still capable of being operated by other power sources.

Accessories include antennas, tapes, wires, records, discs or other media that can be used with any apparatus described in this Category **k.**

4. **Property Not Covered**

We do not cover:

a. Articles separately described and specifically insured, regardless of the limit for which they are insured, in this or other insurance;

b. Animals, birds or fish;

c. "Motor vehicles".

  (1) This includes:

    (a) Their accessories, equipment and parts; or

    (b) Electronic apparatus and accessories designed to be operated solely by power from the electrical system of the "motor vehicle". Accessories include antennas, tapes, wires, records, discs or other media that can be used with any apparatus described above.

    The exclusion of property described in (a) and (b) above applies only while such property is in or upon the "motor vehicle".

  (2) We do cover "motor vehicles" not required to be registered for use on public roads or property which are:

    (a) Used solely to service an "insured's" residence; or

    (b) Designed to assist the handicapped;

d. Aircraft meaning any contrivance used or designed for flight including any parts whether or not attached to the aircraft.

We do cover model or hobby aircraft not used or designed to carry people or cargo;

e. Hovercraft and parts. Hovercraft means a self-propelled motorized ground effect vehicle and includes, but is not limited to, flarecraft and air cushion vehicles;

f. Property of roomers, boarders and other tenants, except property of roomers and boarders related to an "insured";

g. Property in an apartment regularly rented or held for rental to others by an "insured", except as provided in **E.10.** Landlord's Furnishings under Section **I** – Property Coverages;

h. Property rented or held for rental to others off the "residence premises";

i. "Business" data, including such data stored in:

  (1) Books of account, drawings or other paper records; or

  (2) Computers and related equipment.

We do cover the cost of blank recording or storage media, and of prerecorded computer programs available on the retail market;

FIGURE 24.5

j. Credit cards, electronic fund transfer cards or access devices used solely for deposit, withdrawal or transfer of funds except as provided in **E.6.** Credit Card, Electronic Fund Transfer Card Or Access Device, Forgery And Counterfeit Money under Section I – Property Coverages; or

k. Water or steam.

D. Coverage D – Loss Of Use

The limit of liability for Coverage **D** is the total limit for the coverages in **1.** Additional Living Expense, **2.** Fair Rental Value and **3.** Civil Authority Prohibits Use below.

1. Additional Living Expense

If a loss covered under Section I makes that part of the "residence premises" where you reside not fit to live in, we cover any necessary increase in living expenses incurred by you so that your household can maintain its normal standard of living.

Payment will be for the shortest time required to repair or replace the damage or, if you permanently relocate, the shortest time required for your household to settle elsewhere.

2. Fair Rental Value

If a loss covered under Section I makes that part of the "residence premises" rented to others or held for rental by you not fit to live in, we cover the fair rental value of such premises less any expenses that do not continue while it is not fit to live in.

Payment will be for the shortest time required to repair or replace such premises.

3. Civil Authority Prohibits Use

If a civil authority prohibits you from use of the "residence premises" as a result of direct damage to neighboring premises by a Peril Insured Against, we cover the loss as provided in **1.** Additional Living Expense and **2.** Fair Rental Value above for no more than two weeks.

4. Loss Or Expense Not Covered

We do not cover loss or expense due to cancellation of a lease or agreement.

The periods of time under **1.** Additional Living Expense, **2.** Fair Rental Value and **3.** Civil Authority Prohibits Use above are not limited by expiration of this policy.

E. Additional Coverages

1. Debris Removal

a. We will pay your reasonable expense for the removal of:

(1) Debris of covered property if a Peril Insured Against that applies to the damaged property causes the loss; or

(2) Ash, dust or particles from a volcanic eruption that has caused direct loss to a building or property contained in a building.

This expense is included in the limit of liability that applies to the damaged property. If the amount to be paid for the actual damage to the property plus the debris removal expense is more than the limit of liability for the damaged property, an additional 5% of that limit is available for such expense.

b. We will also pay your reasonable expense, up to $1,000, for the removal from the "residence premises" of:

(1) Your tree(s) felled by the peril of Windstorm or Hail or Weight of Ice, Snow or Sleet; or

(2) A neighbor's tree(s) felled by a Peril Insured Against under Coverage **C**;

provided the tree(s):

(3) Damage(s) a covered structure; or

(4) Does not damage a covered structure, but:

(a) Block(s) a driveway on the "residence premises" which prevent(s) a "motor vehicle", that is registered for use on public roads or property, from entering or leaving the "residence premises"; or

(b) Block(s) a ramp or other fixture designed to assist a handicapped person to enter or leave the dwelling building.

The $1,000 limit is the most we will pay in any one loss regardless of the number of fallen trees. No more than $500 of this limit will be paid for the removal of any one tree.

This coverage is additional insurance.

2. Reasonable Repairs

a. We will pay the reasonable cost incurred by you for the necessary measures taken solely to protect covered property that is damaged by a Peril Insured Against from further damage.

FIGURE 24.6

b. If the measures taken involve repair to other damaged property, we will only pay if that property is covered under this policy and the damage is caused by a Peril Insured Against. This coverage does not:

    (1) Increase the limit of liability that applies to the covered property; or

    (2) Relieve you of your duties, in case of a loss to covered property, described in **B.4.** under Section I – Conditions.

3. Trees, Shrubs And Other Plants

We cover trees, shrubs, plants or lawns, on the "residence premises", for loss caused by the following Perils Insured Against:

    a. Fire or Lightning;

    b. Explosion;

    c. Riot or Civil Commotion;

    d. Aircraft;

    e. Vehicles not owned or operated by a resident of the "residence premises";

    f. Vandalism or Malicious Mischief; or

    g. Theft.

We will pay up to 5% of the limit of liability that applies to the dwelling for all trees, shrubs, plants or lawns. No more than $500 of this limit will be paid for any one tree, shrub or plant. We do not cover property grown for "business" purposes.

This coverage is additional insurance.

4. Fire Department Service Charge

We will pay up to $500 for your liability assumed by contract or agreement for fire department charges incurred when the fire department is called to save or protect covered property from a Peril Insured Against. We do not cover fire department service charges if the property is located within the limits of the city, municipality or protection district furnishing the fire department response.

This coverage is additional insurance. No deductible applies to this coverage.

5. Property Removed

We insure covered property against direct loss from any cause while being removed from a premises endangered by a Peril Insured Against and for no more than 30 days while removed.

This coverage does not change the limit of liability that applies to the property being removed.

6. Credit Card, Electronic Fund Transfer Card Or Access Device, Forgery And Counterfeit Money

    a. We will pay up to $500 for:

        (1) The legal obligation of an "insured" to pay because of the theft or unauthorized use of credit cards issued to or registered in an "insured's" name;

        (2) Loss resulting from theft or unauthorized use of an electronic fund transfer card or access device used for deposit, withdrawal or transfer of funds, issued to or registered in an "insured's" name;

        (3) Loss to an "insured" caused by forgery or alteration of any check or negotiable instrument; and

        (4) Loss to an "insured" through acceptance in good faith of counterfeit United States or Canadian paper currency.

    All loss resulting from a series of acts committed by any one person or in which any one person is concerned or implicated is considered to be one loss.

    This coverage is additional insurance. No deductible applies to this coverage.

    b. We do not cover:

        (1) Use of a credit card, electronic fund transfer card or access device:

            (a) By a resident of your household;

            (b) By a person who has been entrusted with either type of card or access device; or

            (c) If an "insured" has not complied with all terms and conditions under which the cards are issued or the devices accessed; or

        (2) Loss arising out of "business" use or dishonesty of an "insured".

    c. If the coverage in **a.** above applies, the following defense provisions also apply:

        (1) We may investigate and settle any claim or suit that we decide is appropriate. Our duty to defend a claim or suit ends when the amount we pay for the loss equals our limit of liability.

        (2) If a suit is brought against an "insured" for liability under **a.(1)** or **(2)** above, we will provide a defense at our expense by counsel of our choice.

        (3) We have the option to defend at our expense an "insured" or an "insured's" bank against any suit for the enforcement of payment under **a.(3)** above.

FIGURE 24.7

7. **Loss Assessment**

a. We will pay up to $1,000 for your share of loss assessment charged during the policy period against you, as owner or tenant of the "residence premises", by a corporation or association of property owners. The assessment must be made as a result of direct loss to property, owned by all members collectively, of the type that would be covered by this policy if owned by you, caused by a Peril Insured Against under Coverage **A**, other than:

   (1) Earthquake; or

   (2) Land shock waves or tremors before, during or after a volcanic eruption.

   The limit of $1,000 is the most we will pay with respect to any one loss, regardless of the number of assessments. We will only apply one deductible, per unit, to the total amount of any one loss to the property described above, regardless of the number of assessments.

b. We do not cover assessments charged against you or a corporation or association of property owners by any governmental body.

c. Paragraph **P.** Policy Period under Section **I** – Conditions does not apply to this coverage.

This coverage is additional insurance.

8. **Collapse**

a. With respect to this Additional Coverage:

   (1) Collapse means an abrupt falling down or caving in of a building or any part of a building with the result that the building or part of the building cannot be occupied for its current intended purpose.

   (2) A building or any part of a building that is in danger of falling down or caving in is not considered to be in a state of collapse.

   (3) A part of a building that is standing is not considered to be in a state of collapse even if it has separated from another part of the building.

   (4) A building or any part of a building that is standing is not considered to be in a state of collapse even if it shows evidence of cracking, bulging, sagging, bending, leaning, settling, shrinkage or expansion.

b. We insure for direct physical loss to covered property involving collapse of a building or any part of a building if the collapse was caused by one or more of the following:

   (1) The Perils Insured Against named under Coverage **C**;

   (2) Decay that is hidden from view, unless the presence of such decay is known to an "insured" prior to collapse;

   (3) Insect or vermin damage that is hidden from view, unless the presence of such damage is known to an "insured" prior to collapse;

   (4) Weight of contents, equipment, animals or people;

   (5) Weight of rain which collects on a roof; or

   (6) Use of defective material or methods in construction, remodeling or renovation if the collapse occurs during the course of the construction, remodeling or renovation.

c. Loss to an awning, fence, patio, deck, pavement, swimming pool, underground pipe, flue, drain, cesspool, septic tank, foundation, retaining wall, bulkhead, pier, wharf or dock is not included under **b.(2)** through **(6)** above, unless the loss is a direct result of the collapse of a building or any part of a building.

d. This coverage does not increase the limit of liability that applies to the damaged covered property.

9. **Glass Or Safety Glazing Material**

a. We cover:

   (1) The breakage of glass or safety glazing material which is part of a covered building, storm door or storm window;

   (2) The breakage of glass or safety glazing material which is part of a covered building, storm door or storm window when caused directly by earth movement; and

   (3) The direct physical loss to covered property caused solely by the pieces, fragments or splinters of broken glass or safety glazing material which is part of a building, storm door or storm window.

FIGURE 24.8

b. This coverage does not include loss:

    (1) To covered property which results because the glass or safety glazing material has been broken, except as provided in **a.(3)** above; or

    (2) On the "residence premises" if the dwelling has been vacant for more than 60 consecutive days immediately before the loss, except when the breakage results directly from earth movement as provided in **a.(2)** above. A dwelling being constructed is not considered vacant.

c. This coverage does not increase the limit of liability that applies to the damaged property.

10. Landlord's Furnishings

We will pay up to $2,500 for your appliances, carpeting and other household furnishings, in each apartment on the "residence premises" regularly rented or held for rental to others by an "insured", for loss caused by a Peril Insured Against in Coverage **C,** other than Theft.

This limit is the most we will pay in any one loss regardless of the number of appliances, carpeting or other household furnishings involved in the loss.

This coverage does not increase the limit of liability applying to the damaged property.

11. Ordinance Or Law

a. You may use up to 10% of the limit of liability that applies to Coverage **A** for the increased costs you incur due to the enforcement of any ordinance or law which requires or regulates:

    (1) The construction, demolition, remodeling, renovation or repair of that part of a covered building or other structure damaged by a Peril Insured Against;

    (2) The demolition and reconstruction of the undamaged part of a covered building or other structure, when that building or other structure must be totally demolished because of damage by a Peril Insured Against to another part of that covered building or other structure; or

    (3) The remodeling, removal or replacement of the portion of the undamaged part of a covered building or other structure necessary to complete the remodeling, repair or replacement of that part of the covered building or other structure damaged by a Peril Insured Against.

b. You may use all or part of this ordinance or law coverage to pay for the increased costs you incur to remove debris resulting from the construction, demolition, remodeling, renovation, repair or replacement of property as stated in **a.** above.

c. We do not cover:

    (1) The loss in value to any covered building or other structure due to the requirements of any ordinance or law; or

    (2) The costs to comply with any ordinance or law which requires any "insured" or others to test for, monitor, clean up, remove, contain, treat, detoxify or neutralize, or in any way respond to, or assess the effects of, pollutants in or on any covered building or other structure.

       Pollutants means any solid, liquid, gaseous or thermal irritant or contaminant, including smoke, vapor, soot, fumes, acids, alkalis, chemicals and waste. Waste includes materials to be recycled, reconditioned or reclaimed.

This coverage is additional insurance.

12. Grave Markers

We will pay up to $5,000 for grave markers, including mausoleums, on or away from the "residence premises" for loss caused by a Peril Insured Against under Coverage **C.**

This coverage does not increase the limits of liability that apply to the damaged covered property.

SECTION I – PERILS INSURED AGAINST

A. Coverage A – Dwelling And Coverage B – Other Structures

  1. We insure against risk of direct physical loss to property described in Coverages **A** and **B.**

  2. We do not insure, however, for loss:

    a. Excluded under Section I – Exclusions;

    b. Involving collapse, except as provided in **E.8.** Collapse under Section I – Property Coverages; or

    c. Caused by:

       (1) Freezing of a plumbing, heating, air conditioning or automatic fire protective sprinkler system or of a household appliance, or by discharge, leakage or overflow from within the system or appliance caused by freezing. This provision does not apply if you have used reasonable care to:

          (a) Maintain heat in the building; or

FIGURE 24.9

(b) Shut off the water supply and drain all systems and appliances of water.

However, if the building is protected by an automatic fire protective sprinkler system, you must use reasonable care to continue the water supply and maintain heat in the building for coverage to apply.

For purposes of this provision a plumbing system or household appliance does not include a sump, sump pump or related equipment or a roof drain, gutter, downspout or similar fixtures or equipment;

(2) Freezing, thawing, pressure or weight of water or ice, whether driven by wind or not, to a:

(a) Fence, pavement, patio or swimming pool;

(b) Footing, foundation, bulkhead, wall, or any other structure or device that supports all or part of a building, or other structure;

(c) Retaining wall or bulkhead that does not support all or part of a building or other structure; or

(d) Pier, wharf or dock;

(3) Theft in or to a dwelling under construction, or of materials and supplies for use in the construction until the dwelling is finished and occupied;

(4) Vandalism and malicious mischief, and any ensuing loss caused by any intentional and wrongful act committed in the course of the vandalism or malicious mischief, if the dwelling has been vacant for more than 60 consecutive days immediately before the loss. A dwelling being constructed is not considered vacant;

(5) Mold, fungus or wet rot. However, we do insure for loss caused by mold, fungus or wet rot that is hidden within the walls or ceilings or beneath the floors or above the ceilings of a structure if such loss results from the accidental discharge or overflow of water or steam from within:

(a) A plumbing, heating, air conditioning or automatic fire protective sprinkler system, or a household appliance, on the "residence premises"; or

(b) A storm drain, or water, steam or sewer pipes, off the "residence premises".

For purposes of this provision, a plumbing system or household appliance does not include a sump, sump pump or related equipment or a roof drain, gutter, downspout or similar fixtures or equipment; or

(6) Any of the following:

(a) Wear and tear, marring, deterioration;

(b) Mechanical breakdown, latent defect, inherent vice, or any quality in property that causes it to damage or destroy itself;

(c) Smog, rust or other corrosion, or dry rot;

(d) Smoke from agricultural smudging or industrial operations;

(e) Discharge, dispersal, seepage, migration, release or escape of pollutants unless the discharge, dispersal, seepage, migration, release or escape is itself caused by a Peril Insured Against named under Coverage **C**.

Pollutants means any solid, liquid, gaseous or thermal irritant or contaminant, including smoke, vapor, soot, fumes, acids, alkalis, chemicals and waste. Waste includes materials to be recycled, reconditioned or reclaimed;

(f) Settling, shrinking, bulging or expansion, including resultant cracking, of bulkheads, pavements, patios, footings, foundations, walls, floors, roofs or ceilings;

(g) Birds, vermin, rodents, or insects; or

(h) Animals owned or kept by an "insured".

Exception To c.(6)

Unless the loss is otherwise excluded, we cover loss to property covered under Coverage **A** or **B** resulting from an accidental discharge or overflow of water or steam from within a:

(i) Storm drain, or water, steam or sewer pipe, off the "residence premises"; or

FIGURE 24.10

(ii) Plumbing, heating, air conditioning or automatic fire protective sprinkler system or household appliance on the "residence premises". This includes the cost to tear out and replace any part of a building, or other structure, on the "residence premises", but only when necessary to repair the system or appliance. However, such tear out and replacement coverage only applies to other structures if the water or steam causes actual damage to a building on the "residence premises".

We do not cover loss to the system or appliance from which this water or steam escaped.

For purposes of this provision, a plumbing system or household appliance does not include a sump, sump pump or related equipment or a roof drain, gutter, down spout or similar fixtures or equipment.

Section I – Exclusion **A.3.** Water Damage, Paragraphs **a.** and **c.** that apply to surface water and water below the surface of the ground do not apply to loss by water covered under **c.(5)** and **(6)** above.

Under **2.b.** and **c.** above, any ensuing loss to property described in Coverages **A** and **B** not precluded by any other provision in this policy is covered.

B. Coverage C – Personal Property

We insure for direct physical loss to the property described in Coverage **C** caused by any of the following perils unless the loss is excluded in Section I – Exclusions.

1. Fire Or Lightning

2. Windstorm Or Hail

This peril includes loss to watercraft of all types and their trailers, furnishings, equipment, and outboard engines or motors, only while inside a fully enclosed building.

This peril does not include loss to the property contained in a building caused by rain, snow, sleet, sand or dust unless the direct force of wind or hail damages the building causing an opening in a roof or wall and the rain, snow, sleet, sand or dust enters through this opening.

3. Explosion

4. Riot Or Civil Commotion

5. Aircraft

This peril includes self-propelled missiles and spacecraft.

6. Vehicles

7. Smoke

This peril means sudden and accidental damage from smoke, including the emission or puffback of smoke, soot, fumes or vapors from a boiler, furnace or related equipment.

This peril does not include loss caused by smoke from agricultural smudging or industrial operations.

8. Vandalism Or Malicious Mischief

9. Theft

a. This peril includes attempted theft and loss of property from a known place when it is likely that the property has been stolen.

b. This peril does not include loss caused by theft:

  (1) Committed by an "insured";

  (2) In or to a dwelling under construction, or of materials and supplies for use in the construction until the dwelling is finished and occupied;

  (3) From that part of a "residence premises" rented by an "insured" to someone other than another "insured"; or

  (4) That occurs off the "residence premises" of:

    (a) Trailers, semitrailers and campers;

    (b) Watercraft of all types, and their furnishings, equipment and outboard engines or motors; or

    (c) Property while at any other residence owned by, rented to, or occupied by an "insured", except while an "insured" is temporarily living there. Property of an "insured" who is a student is covered while at the residence the student occupies to attend school as long as the student has been there at any time during the 60 days immediately before the loss.

10. Falling Objects

This peril does not include loss to property contained in a building unless the roof or an outside wall of the building is first damaged by a falling object. Damage to the falling object itself is not included.

11. Weight Of Ice, Snow Or Sleet

This peril means weight of ice, snow or sleet which causes damage to property contained in a building.

FIGURE 24.11

12. **Accidental Discharge Or Overflow Of Water Or Steam**

   a. This peril means accidental discharge or overflow of water or steam from within a plumbing, heating, air conditioning or automatic fire protective sprinkler system or from within a household appliance.

   b. This peril does not include loss:

   (1) To the system or appliance from which the water or steam escaped;

   (2) Caused by or resulting from freezing except as provided in Peril Insured Against **14.** Freezing;

   (3) On the "residence premises" caused by accidental discharge or overflow which occurs off the "residence premises"; or

   (4) Caused by mold, fungus or wet rot unless hidden within the walls or ceilings or beneath the floors or above the ceilings of a structure.

   c. In this peril, a plumbing system or household appliance does not include a sump, sump pump or related equipment or a roof drain, gutter, downspout or similar fixtures or equipment.

   d. Section I – Exclusion **A.3.** Water Damage, Paragraphs **a.** and **c.** that apply to surface water and water below the surface of the ground do not apply to loss by water covered under this peril.

13. **Sudden And Accidental Tearing Apart, Cracking, Burning Or Bulging**

   This peril means sudden and accidental tearing apart, cracking, burning or bulging of a steam or hot water heating system, an air conditioning or automatic fire protective sprinkler system, or an appliance for heating water.

   We do not cover loss caused by or resulting from freezing under this peril.

14. **Freezing**

   a. This peril means freezing of a plumbing, heating, air conditioning or automatic fire protective sprinkler system or of a household appliance but only if you have used reasonable care to:

   (1) Maintain heat in the building; or

   (2) Shut off the water supply and drain all systems and appliances of water.

   However, if the building is protected by an automatic fire protective sprinkler system, you must use reasonable care to continue the water supply and maintain heat in the building for coverage to apply.

   b. In this peril, a plumbing system or household appliance does not include a sump, sump pump or related equipment or a roof drain, gutter, downspout or similar fixtures or equipment.

15. **Sudden And Accidental Damage From Artificially Generated Electrical Current**

   This peril does not include loss to tubes, transistors, electronic components or circuitry that are a part of appliances, fixtures, computers, home entertainment units or other types of electronic apparatus.

16. **Volcanic Eruption**

   This peril does not include loss caused by earthquake, land shock waves or tremors.

SECTION I – EXCLUSIONS

A. We do not insure for loss caused directly or indirectly by any of the following. Such loss is excluded regardless of any other cause or event contributing concurrently or in any sequence to the loss. These exclusions apply whether or not the loss event results in widespread damage or affects a substantial area.

1. **Ordinance Or Law**

   Ordinance Or Law means any ordinance or law:

   a. Requiring or regulating the construction, demolition, remodeling, renovation or repair of property, including removal of any resulting debris. This Exclusion **A.1.a.** does not apply to the amount of coverage that may be provided for in **E.11.** Ordinance Or Law under Section I – Property Coverages;

   b. The requirements of which result in a loss in value to property; or

   c. Requiring any "insured" or others to test for, monitor, clean up, remove, contain, treat, detoxify or neutralize, or in any way respond to, or assess the effects of, pollutants.

   Pollutants means any solid, liquid, gaseous or thermal irritant or contaminant, including smoke, vapor, soot, fumes, acids, alkalis, chemicals and waste. Waste includes materials to be recycled, reconditioned or reclaimed.

   This Exclusion **A.1.** applies whether or not the property has been physically damaged.

2. **Earth Movement**

   Earth Movement means:

   a. Earthquake, including land shock waves or tremors before, during or after a volcanic eruption;

FIGURE 24.12

b. Landslide, mudslide or mudflow;

c. Subsidence or sinkhole; or

d. Any other earth movement including earth sinking, rising or shifting;

caused by or resulting from human or animal forces or any act of nature unless direct loss by fire or explosion ensues and then we will pay only for the ensuing loss.

This Exclusion **A.2.** does not apply to loss by theft.

3. **Water Damage**

Water Damage means:

a. Flood, surface water, waves, tidal water, overflow of a body of water, or spray from any of these, whether or not driven by wind;

b. Water or water-borne material which backs up through sewers or drains or which overflows or is discharged from a sump, sump pump or related equipment; or

c. Water or water-borne material below the surface of the ground, including water which exerts pressure on or seeps or leaks through a building, sidewalk, driveway, foundation, swimming pool or other structure;

caused by or resulting from human or animal forces or any act of nature.

Direct loss by fire, explosion or theft resulting from water damage is covered.

4. **Power Failure**

Power Failure means the failure of power or other utility service if the failure takes place off the "residence premises". But if the failure results in a loss, from a Peril Insured Against on the "residence premises", we will pay for the loss caused by that peril.

5. **Neglect**

Neglect means neglect of an "insured" to use all reasonable means to save and preserve property at and after the time of a loss.

6. **War**

War includes the following and any consequence of any of the following:

a. Undeclared war, civil war, insurrection, rebellion or revolution;

b. Warlike act by a military force or military personnel; or

c. Destruction, seizure or use for a military purpose.

Discharge of a nuclear weapon will be deemed a warlike act even if accidental.

7. **Nuclear Hazard**

This Exclusion **A.7.** pertains to Nuclear Hazard to the extent set forth in **M.** Nuclear Hazard Clause under Section I – Conditions.

8. **Intentional Loss**

Intentional Loss means any loss arising out of any act an "insured" commits or conspires to commit with the intent to cause a loss.

In the event of such loss, no "insured" is entitled to coverage, even "insureds" who did not commit or conspire to commit the act causing the loss.

9. **Governmental Action**

Governmental Action means the destruction, confiscation or seizure of property described in Coverage **A**, **B** or **C** by order of any governmental or public authority.

This exclusion does not apply to such acts ordered by any governmental or public authority that are taken at the time of a fire to prevent its spread, if the loss caused by fire would be covered under this policy.

B. We do not insure for loss to property described in Coverages **A** and **B** caused by any of the following. However, any ensuing loss to property described in Coverages **A** and **B** not precluded by any other provision in this policy is covered.

1. Weather conditions. However, this exclusion only applies if weather conditions contribute in any way with a cause or event excluded in **A.** above to produce the loss.

2. Acts or decisions, including the failure to act or decide, of any person, group, organization or governmental body.

3. Faulty, inadequate or defective:

a. Planning, zoning, development, surveying, siting;

b. Design, specifications, workmanship, repair, construction, renovation, remodeling, grading, compaction;

c. Materials used in repair, construction, renovation or remodeling; or

d. Maintenance;

of part or all of any property whether on or off the "residence premises".

FIGURE 24.13

SECTION I – CONDITIONS

A. Insurable Interest And Limit Of Liability

Even if more than one person has an insurable interest in the property covered, we will not be liable in any one loss:

1. To an "insured" for more than the amount of such "insured's" interest at the time of loss; or

2. For more than the applicable limit of liability.

B. Duties After Loss

In case of a loss to covered property, we have no duty to provide coverage under this policy if the failure to comply with the following duties is prejudicial to us. These duties must be performed either by you, an "insured" seeking coverage, or a representative of either:

1. Give prompt notice to us or our agent;

2. Notify the police in case of loss by theft;

3. Notify the credit card or electronic fund transfer card or access device company in case of loss as provided for in **E.6.** Credit Card, Electronic Fund Transfer Card Or Access Device, Forgery And Counterfeit Money under Section I – Property Coverages;

4. Protect the property from further damage. If repairs to the property are required, you must:

   a. Make reasonable and necessary repairs to protect the property; and

   b. Keep an accurate record of repair expenses;

5. Cooperate with us in the investigation of a claim;

6. Prepare an inventory of damaged personal property showing the quantity, description, actual cash value and amount of loss. Attach all bills, receipts and related documents that justify the figures in the inventory;

7. As often as we reasonably require:

   a. Show the damaged property;

   b. Provide us with records and documents we request and permit us to make copies; and

   c. Submit to examination under oath, while not in the presence of another "insured", and sign the same;

8. Send to us, within 60 days after our request, your signed, sworn proof of loss which sets forth, to the best of your knowledge and belief:

   a. The time and cause of loss;

   b. The interests of all "insureds" and all others in the property involved and all liens on the property;

   c. Other insurance which may cover the loss;

d. Changes in title or occupancy of the property during the term of the policy;

e. Specifications of damaged buildings and detailed repair estimates;

f. The inventory of damaged personal property described in **6.** above;

g. Receipts for additional living expenses incurred and records that support the fair rental value loss; and

h. Evidence or affidavit that supports a claim under **E.6.** Credit Card, Electronic Fund Transfer Card Or Access Device, Forgery And Counterfeit Money under Section I – Property Coverages, stating the amount and cause of loss.

C. Loss Settlement

In this Condition **C.**, the terms "cost to repair or replace" and "replacement cost" do not include the increased costs incurred to comply with the enforcement of any ordinance or law, except to the extent that coverage for these increased costs is provided in **E.11.** Ordinance Or Law under Section I – Property Coverages. Covered property losses are settled as follows:

1. Property of the following types:

   a. Personal property;

   b. Awnings, carpeting, household appliances, outdoor antennas and outdoor equipment, whether or not attached to buildings;

   c. Structures that are not buildings; and

   d. Grave markers, including mausoleums;

   at actual cash value at the time of loss but not more than the amount required to repair or replace.

2. Buildings covered under Coverage **A** or **B** at replacement cost without deduction for depreciation, subject to the following:

   a. If, at the time of loss, the amount of insurance in this policy on the damaged building is 80% or more of the full replacement cost of the building immediately before the loss, we will pay the cost to repair or replace, after application of any deductible and without deduction for depreciation, but not more than the least of the following amounts:

      (1) The limit of liability under this policy that applies to the building;

      (2) The replacement cost of that part of the building damaged with material of like kind and quality and for like use; or

      (3) The necessary amount actually spent to repair or replace the damaged building.

FIGURE 24.14

If the building is rebuilt at a new premises, the cost described in **(2)** above is limited to the cost which would have been incurred if the building had been built at the original premises.

b. If, at the time of loss, the amount of insurance in this policy on the damaged building is less than 80% of the full replacement cost of the building immediately before the loss, we will pay the greater of the following amounts, but not more than the limit of liability under this policy that applies to the building:

(1) The actual cash value of that part of the building damaged; or

(2) That proportion of the cost to repair or replace, after application of any deductible and without deduction for depreciation, that part of the building damaged, which the total amount of insurance in this policy on the damaged building bears to 80% of the replacement cost of the building.

c. To determine the amount of insurance required to equal 80% of the full replacement cost of the building immediately before the loss, do not include the value of:

(1) Excavations, footings, foundations, piers, or any other structures or devices that support all or part of the building, which are below the undersurface of the lowest basement floor;

(2) Those supports described in **(1)** above which are below the surface of the ground inside the foundation walls, if there is no basement; and

(3) Underground flues, pipes, wiring and drains.

d. We will pay no more than the actual cash value of the damage until actual repair or replacement is complete. Once actual repair or replacement is complete, we will settle the loss as noted in **2.a.** and **b.** above.

However, if the cost to repair or replace the damage is both:

(1) Less than 5% of the amount of insurance in this policy on the building; and

(2) Less than $2,500;

we will settle the loss as noted in **2.a.** and **b.** above whether or not actual repair or replacement is complete.

e. You may disregard the replacement cost loss settlement provisions and make claim under this policy for loss to buildings on an actual cash value basis. You may then make claim for any additional liability according to the provisions of this Condition **C.** Loss Settlement, provided you notify us of your intent to do so within 180 days after the date of loss.

D. Loss To A Pair Or Set

In case of loss to a pair or set we may elect to:

1. Repair or replace any part to restore the pair or set to its value before the loss; or

2. Pay the difference between actual cash value of the property before and after the loss.

E. Appraisal

If you and we fail to agree on the amount of loss, either may demand an appraisal of the loss. In this event, each party will choose a competent and impartial appraiser within 20 days after receiving a written request from the other. The two appraisers will choose an umpire. If they cannot agree upon an umpire within 15 days, you or we may request that the choice be made by a judge of a court of record in the state where the "residence premises" is located. The appraisers will separately set the amount of loss. If the appraisers submit a written report of an agreement to us, the amount agreed upon will be the amount of loss. If they fail to agree, they will submit their differences to the umpire. A decision agreed to by any two will set the amount of loss.

Each party will:

1. Pay its own appraiser; and

2. Bear the other expenses of the appraisal and umpire equally.

F. Other Insurance And Service Agreement

If a loss covered by this policy is also covered by:

1. Other insurance, we will pay only the proportion of the loss that the limit of liability that applies under this policy bears to the total amount of insurance covering the loss; or

2. A service agreement, this insurance is excess over any amounts payable under any such agreement. Service agreement means a service plan, property restoration plan, home warranty or other similar service warranty agreement, even if it is characterized as insurance.

G. Suit Against Us

No action can be brought against us unless there has been full compliance with all of the terms under Section I of this policy and the action is started within two years after the date of loss.

FIGURE 24.15

H. Our Option

If we give you written notice within 30 days after we receive your signed, sworn proof of loss, we may repair or replace any part of the damaged property with material or property of like kind and quality.

I. Loss Payment

We will adjust all losses with you. We will pay you unless some other person is named in the policy or is legally entitled to receive payment. Loss will be payable 60 days after we receive your proof of loss and:

1. Reach an agreement with you;

2. There is an entry of a final judgment; or

3. There is a filing of an appraisal award with us.

J. Abandonment Of Property

We need not accept any property abandoned by an "insured".

K. Mortgage Clause

1. If a mortgagee is named in this policy, any loss payable under Coverage **A** or **B** will be paid to the mortgagee and you, as interests appear. If more than one mortgagee is named, the order of payment will be the same as the order of precedence of the mortgages.

2. If we deny your claim, that denial will not apply to a valid claim of the mortgagee, if the mortgagee:

    a. Notifies us of any change in ownership, occupancy or substantial change in risk of which the mortgagee is aware;

    b. Pays any premium due under this policy on demand if you have neglected to pay the premium; and

    c. Submits a signed, sworn statement of loss within 60 days after receiving notice from us of your failure to do so. Paragraphs **E.** Appraisal, **G.** Suit Against Us and **I.** Loss Payment under Section I – Conditions also apply to the mortgagee.

3. If we decide to cancel or not to renew this policy, the mortgagee will be notified at least 10 days before the date cancellation or nonrenewal takes effect.

4. If we pay the mortgagee for any loss and deny payment to you:

    a. We are subrogated to all the rights of the mortgagee granted under the mortgage on the property; or

    b. At our option, we may pay to the mortgagee the whole principal on the mortgage plus any accrued interest. In this event, we will receive a full assignment and transfer of the mortgage and all securities held as collateral to the mortgage debt.

5. Subrogation will not impair the right of the mortgagee to recover the full amount of the mortgagee's claim.

L. No Benefit To Bailee

We will not recognize any assignment or grant any coverage that benefits a person or organization holding, storing or moving property for a fee regardless of any other provision of this policy.

M. Nuclear Hazard Clause

1. "Nuclear Hazard" means any nuclear reaction, radiation, or radioactive contamination, all whether controlled or uncontrolled or however caused, or any consequence of any of these.

2. Loss caused by the nuclear hazard will not be considered loss caused by fire, explosion, or smoke, whether these perils are specifically named in or otherwise included within the Perils Insured Against.

3. This policy does not apply under Section I to loss caused directly or indirectly by nuclear hazard, except that direct loss by fire resulting from the nuclear hazard is covered.

N. Recovered Property

If you or we recover any property for which we have made payment under this policy, you or we will notify the other of the recovery. At your option, the property will be returned to or retained by you or it will become our property. If the recovered property is returned to or retained by you, the loss payment will be adjusted based on the amount you received for the recovered property.

O. Volcanic Eruption Period

One or more volcanic eruptions that occur within a 72 hour period will be considered as one volcanic eruption.

P. Policy Period

This policy applies only to loss which occurs during the policy period.

Q. Concealment Or Fraud

We provide coverage to no "insureds" under this policy if, whether before or after a loss, an "insured" has:

1. Intentionally concealed or misrepresented any material fact or circumstance;

FIGURE 24.16

2. Engaged in fraudulent conduct; or

3. Made false statements;

relating to this insurance.

R. Loss Payable Clause

If the Declarations show a loss payee for certain listed insured personal property, the definition of "insured" is changed to include that loss payee with respect to that property.

If we decide to cancel or not renew this policy, that loss payee will be notified in writing.

SECTION II – LIABILITY COVERAGES

A. Coverage E – Personal Liability

If a claim is made or a suit is brought against an "insured" for damages because of "bodily injury" or "property damage" caused by an "occurrence" to which this coverage applies, we will:

1. Pay up to our limit of liability for the damages for which an "insured" is legally liable. Damages include prejudgment interest awarded against an "insured"; and

2. Provide a defense at our expense by counsel of our choice, even if the suit is groundless, false or fraudulent. We may investigate and settle any claim or suit that we decide is appropriate. Our duty to settle or defend ends when our limit of liability for the "occurrence" has been exhausted by payment of a judgment or settlement.

B. Coverage F – Medical Payments To Others

We will pay the necessary medical expenses that are incurred or medically ascertained within three years from the date of an accident causing "bodily injury". Medical expenses means reasonable charges for medical, surgical, x-ray, dental, ambulance, hospital, professional nursing, prosthetic devices and funeral services. This coverage does not apply to you or regular residents of your household except "residence employees". As to others, this coverage applies only:

1. To a person on the "insured location" with the permission of an "insured"; or

2. To a person off the "insured location", if the "bodily injury":

a. Arises out of a condition on the "insured location" or the ways immediately adjoining;

b. Is caused by the activities of an "insured";

c. Is caused by a "residence employee" in the course of the "residence employee's" employment by an "insured"; or

d. Is caused by an animal owned by or in the care of an "insured".

SECTION II – EXCLUSIONS

A. "Motor Vehicle Liability"

1. Coverages **E** and **F** do not apply to any "motor vehicle liability" if, at the time and place of an "occurrence", the involved "motor vehicle":

a. Is registered for use on public roads or property;

b. Is not registered for use on public roads or property, but such registration is required by a law, or regulation issued by a government agency, for it to be used at the place of the "occurrence"; or

c. Is being:

(1) Operated in, or practicing for, any prearranged or organized race, speed contest or other competition;

(2) Rented to others;

(3) Used to carry persons or cargo for a charge; or

(4) Used for any "business" purpose except for a motorized golf cart while on a golfing facility.

2. If Exclusion **A.1.** does not apply, there is still no coverage for "motor vehicle liability" unless the "motor vehicle" is:

a. In dead storage on an "insured location";

b. Used solely to service an "insured's" residence;

c. Designed to assist the handicapped and, at the time of an "occurrence", it is:

(1) Being used to assist a handicapped person; or

(2) Parked on an "insured location";

d. Designed for recreational use off public roads and:

(1) Not owned by an "insured"; or

(2) Owned by an "insured" provided the "occurrence" takes place on an "insured location" as defined in Definitions **B. 6.a., b., d., e.** or **h.**; or

e. A motorized golf cart that is owned by an "insured", designed to carry up to 4 persons, not built or modified after manufacture to exceed a speed of 25 miles per hour on level ground and, at the time of an "occurrence", is within the legal boundaries of:

(1) A golfing facility and is parked or stored there, or being used by an "insured" to:

(a) Play the game of golf or for other recreational or leisure activity allowed by the facility;

FIGURE 24.17

(b) Travel to or from an area where "motor vehicles" or golf carts are parked or stored; or

(c) Cross public roads at designated points to access other parts of the golfing facility; or

(2) A private residential community, including its public roads upon which a motorized golf cart can legally travel, which is subject to the authority of a property owners association and contains an "insured's" residence.

B. "Watercraft Liability"

1. Coverages **E** and **F** do not apply to any "watercraft liability" if, at the time of an "occurrence", the involved watercraft is being:

a. Operated in, or practicing for, any prearranged or organized race, speed contest or other competition. This exclusion does not apply to a sailing vessel or a predicted log cruise;

b. Rented to others;

c. Used to carry persons or cargo for a charge; or

d. Used for any "business" purpose.

2. If Exclusion **B.1.** does not apply, there is still no coverage for "watercraft liability" unless, at the time of the "occurrence", the watercraft:

a. Is stored;

b. Is a sailing vessel, with or without auxiliary power, that is:

(1) Less than 26 feet in overall length; or

(2) 26 feet or more in overall length and not owned by or rented to an "insured"; or

c. Is not a sailing vessel and is powered by:

(1) An inboard or inboard-outdrive engine or motor, including those that power a water jet pump, of:

(a) 50 horsepower or less and not owned by an "insured"; or

(b) More than 50 horsepower and not owned by or rented to an "insured"; or

(2) One or more outboard engines or motors with:

(a) 25 total horsepower or less;

(b) More than 25 horsepower if the outboard engine or motor is not owned by an "insured";

(c) More than 25 horsepower if the outboard engine or motor is owned by an "insured" who acquired it during the policy period; or

(d) More than 25 horsepower if the outboard engine or motor is owned by an "insured" who acquired it before the policy period, but only if:

(i) You declare them at policy inception; or

(ii) Your intent to insure them is reported to us in writing within 45 days after you acquire them.

The coverages in **(c)** and **(d)** above apply for the policy period.

Horsepower means the maximum power rating assigned to the engine or motor by the manufacturer.

C. "Aircraft Liability"

This policy does not cover "aircraft liability".

D. "Hovercraft Liability"

This policy does not cover "hovercraft liability".

E. Coverage E – Personal Liability And Coverage F – Medical Payments To Others

Coverages **E** and **F** do not apply to the following:

1. Expected Or Intended Injury

"Bodily injury" or "property damage" which is expected or intended by an "insured" even if the resulting "bodily injury" or "property damage":

a. Is of a different kind, quality or degree than initially expected or intended; or

b. Is sustained by a different person, entity, real or personal property, than initially expected or intended.

However, this Exclusion **E.1.** does not apply to "bodily injury" resulting from the use of reasonable force by an "insured" to protect persons or property;

2. "Business"

a. "Bodily injury" or "property damage" arising out of or in connection with a "business" conducted from an "insured location" or engaged in by an "insured", whether or not the "business" is owned or operated by an "insured" or employs an "insured".

This Exclusion **E.2.** applies but is not limited to an act or omission, regardless of its nature or circumstance, involving a service or duty rendered, promised, owed, or implied to be provided because of the nature of the "business".

b. This Exclusion **E.2.** does not apply to:

(1) The rental or holding for rental of an "insured location";

FIGURE 24.18

(a) On an occasional basis if used only as a residence;

(b) In part for use only as a residence, unless a single family unit is intended for use by the occupying family to lodge more than two roomers or boarders; or

(c) In part, as an office, school, studio or private garage; and

(2) An "insured" under the age of 21 years involved in a part-time or occasional, self-employed "business" with no employees;

3. Professional Services

"Bodily injury" or "property damage" arising out of the rendering of or failure to render professional services;

4. "Insured's" Premises Not An "Insured Location"

"Bodily injury" or "property damage" arising out of a premises:

a. Owned by an "insured";

b. Rented to an "insured"; or

c. Rented to others by an "insured";

that is not an "insured location";

5. War

"Bodily injury" or "property damage" caused directly or indirectly by war, including the following and any consequence of any of the following:

a. Undeclared war, civil war, insurrection, rebellion or revolution;

b. Warlike act by a military force or military personnel; or

c. Destruction, seizure or use for a military purpose.

Discharge of a nuclear weapon will be deemed a warlike act even if accidental;

6. Communicable Disease

"Bodily injury" or "property damage" which arises out of the transmission of a communicable disease by an "insured";

7. Sexual Molestation, Corporal Punishment Or Physical Or Mental Abuse

"Bodily injury" or "property damage" arising out of sexual molestation, corporal punishment or physical or mental abuse; or

8. Controlled Substance

"Bodily injury" or "property damage" arising out of the use, sale, manufacture, delivery, transfer or possession by any person of a Controlled Substance as defined by the Federal Food and Drug Law at 21 U.S.C.A. Sections 811 and 812. Controlled Substances include but are not limited to cocaine, LSD, marijuana and all narcotic drugs. However, this exclusion does not apply to the legitimate use of prescription drugs by a person following the orders of a licensed physician.

Exclusions **A.** "Motor Vehicle Liability", **B.** "Watercraft Liability", **C.** "Aircraft Liability", **D.** "Hovercraft Liability" and **E.4.** "Insured's" Premises Not An "Insured Location" do not apply to "bodily injury" to a "residence employee" arising out of and in the course of the "residence employee's" employment by an "insured".

F. Coverage E – Personal Liability

Coverage **E** does not apply to:

1. Liability:

a. For any loss assessment charged against you as a member of an association, corporation or community of property owners, except as provided in **D.** Loss Assessment under Section II – Additional Coverages;

b. Under any contract or agreement entered into by an "insured". However, this exclusion does not apply to written contracts:

(1) That directly relate to the ownership, maintenance or use of an "insured location"; or

(2) Where the liability of others is assumed by you prior to an "occurrence";

unless excluded in **a.** above or elsewhere in this policy;

2. "Property damage" to property owned by an "insured". This includes costs or expenses incurred by an "insured" or others to repair, replace, enhance, restore or maintain such property to prevent injury to a person or damage to property of others, whether on or away from an "insured location";

3. "Property damage" to property rented to, occupied or used by or in the care of an "insured". This exclusion does not apply to "property damage" caused by fire, smoke or explosion;

4. "Bodily injury" to any person eligible to receive any benefits voluntarily provided or required to be provided by an "insured" under any:

a. Workers' compensation law;

FIGURE 24.19

b. Non-occupational disability law; or

c. Occupational disease law;

5. "Bodily injury" or "property damage" for which an "insured" under this policy:

   a. Is also an insured under a nuclear energy liability policy issued by the:

      (1) Nuclear Energy Liability Insurance Association;

      (2) Mutual Atomic Energy Liability Underwriters;

      (3) Nuclear Insurance Association of Canada;

      or any of their successors; or

   b. Would be an insured under such a policy but for the exhaustion of its limit of liability; or

6. "Bodily injury" to you or an "insured" as defined under Definitions 5.a. or b.

This exclusion also applies to any claim made or suit brought against you or an "insured":

   a. To repay; or

   b. Share damages with;

another person who may be obligated to pay damages because of "bodily injury" to an "insured".

G. Coverage F – Medical Payments To Others

Coverage **F** does not apply to "bodily injury":

1. To a "residence employee" if the "bodily injury":

   a. Occurs off the "insured location"; and

   b. Does not arise out of or in the course of the "residence employee's" employment by an "insured";

2. To any person eligible to receive benefits voluntarily provided or required to be provided under any:

   a. Workers' compensation law;

   b. Non-occupational disability law; or

   c. Occupational disease law;

3. From any:

   a. Nuclear reaction;

   b. Nuclear radiation; or

   c. Radioactive contamination;

all whether controlled or uncontrolled or however caused; or

   d. Any consequence of any of these; or

4. To any person, other than a "residence employee" of an "insured", regularly residing on any part of the "insured location".

SECTION II – ADDITIONAL COVERAGES

We cover the following in addition to the limits of liability:

A. Claim Expenses

We pay:

1. Expenses we incur and costs taxed against an "insured" in any suit we defend;

2. Premiums on bonds required in a suit we defend, but not for bond amounts more than the Coverage **E** limit of liability. We need not apply for or furnish any bond;

3. Reasonable expenses incurred by an "insured" at our request, including actual loss of earnings (but not loss of other income) up to $250 per day, for assisting us in the investigation or defense of a claim or suit; and

4. Interest on the entire judgment which accrues after entry of the judgment and before we pay or tender, or deposit in court that part of the judgment which does not exceed the limit of liability that applies.

B. First Aid Expenses

We will pay expenses for first aid to others incurred by an "insured" for "bodily injury" covered under this policy. We will not pay for first aid to an "insured".

C. Damage To Property Of Others

1. We will pay, at replacement cost, up to $1,000 per "occurrence" for "property damage" to property of others caused by an "insured".

2. We will not pay for "property damage":

   a. To the extent of any amount recoverable under Section **I**;

   b. Caused intentionally by an "insured" who is 13 years of age or older;

   c. To property owned by an "insured";

   d. To property owned by or rented to a tenant of an "insured" or a resident in your household; or

   e. Arising out of:

      (1) A "business" engaged in by an "insured";

      (2) Any act or omission in connection with a premises owned, rented or controlled by an "insured", other than the "insured location"; or

      (3) The ownership, maintenance, occupancy, operation, use, loading or unloading of aircraft, hovercraft, watercraft or "motor vehicles".

FIGURE 24.20

This exclusion **e.(3)** does not apply to a "motor vehicle" that:

(a) Is designed for recreational use off public roads;

(b) Is not owned by an "insured"; and

(c) At the time of the "occurrence", is not required by law, or regulation issued by a government agency, to have been registered for it to be used on public roads or property.

D. Loss Assessment

1. We will pay up to $1,000 for your share of loss assessment charged against you, as owner or tenant of the "residence premises", during the policy period by a corporation or association of property owners, when the assessment is made as a result of:

   a. "Bodily injury" or "property damage" not excluded from coverage under Section II – Exclusions; or

   b. Liability for an act of a director, officer or trustee in the capacity as a director, officer or trustee, provided such person:

   (1) Is elected by the members of a corporation or association of property owners; and

   (2) Serves without deriving any income from the exercise of duties which are solely on behalf of a corporation or association of property owners.

2. Paragraph I. Policy Period under Section II – Conditions does not apply to this Loss Assessment Coverage.

3. Regardless of the number of assessments, the limit of $1,000 is the most we will pay for loss arising out of:

   a. One accident, including continuous or repeated exposure to substantially the same general harmful condition; or

   b. A covered act of a director, officer or trustee. An act involving more than one director, officer or trustee is considered to be a single act.

4. We do not cover assessments charged against you or a corporation or association of property owners by any governmental body.

SECTION II – CONDITIONS

A. Limit Of Liability

Our total liability under Coverage **E** for all damages resulting from any one "occurrence" will not be more than the Coverage **E** limit of liability shown in the Declarations. This limit is the same regardless of the number of "insureds", claims made or persons injured. All "bodily injury" and "property damage" resulting from any one accident or from continuous or repeated exposure to substantially the same general harmful conditions shall be considered to be the result of one "occurrence".

Our total liability under Coverage **F** for all medical expense payable for "bodily injury" to one person as the result of one accident will not be more than the Coverage **F** limit of liability shown in the Declarations.

B. Severability Of Insurance

This insurance applies separately to each "insured". This condition will not increase our limit of liability for any one "occurrence".

C. Duties After "Occurrence"

In case of an "occurrence", you or another "insured" will perform the following duties that apply. We have no duty to provide coverage under this policy if your failure to comply with the following duties is prejudicial to us. You will help us by seeing that these duties are performed:

1. Give written notice to us or our agent as soon as is practical, which sets forth:

   a. The identity of the policy and the "named insured" shown in the Declarations;

   b. Reasonably available information on the time, place and circumstances of the "occurrence"; and

   c. Names and addresses of any claimants and witnesses;

2. Cooperate with us in the investigation, settlement or defense of any claim or suit;

3. Promptly forward to us every notice, demand, summons or other process relating to the "occurrence";

4. At our request, help us:

   a. To make settlement;

   b. To enforce any right of contribution or indemnity against any person or organization who may be liable to an "insured";

FIGURE 24.21

c. With the conduct of suits and attend hearings and trials; and

d. To secure and give evidence and obtain the attendance of witnesses;

5. With respect to **C.** Damage To Property Of Others under Section **II** – Additional Coverages, submit to us within 60 days after the loss, a sworn statement of loss and show the damaged property, if in an "insured's" control;

6. No "insured" shall, except at such "insured's" own cost, voluntarily make payment, assume obligation or incur expense other than for first aid to others at the time of the "bodily injury".

D. Duties Of An Injured Person – Coverage F – Medical Payments To Others

1. The injured person or someone acting for the injured person will:

    a. Give us written proof of claim, under oath if required, as soon as is practical; and

    b. Authorize us to obtain copies of medical reports and records.

2. The injured person will submit to a physical exam by a doctor of our choice when and as often as we reasonably require.

E. Payment Of Claim – Coverage F – Medical Payments To Others

Payment under this coverage is not an admission of liability by an "insured" or us.

F. Suit Against Us

1. No action can be brought against us unless there has been full compliance with all of the terms under this Section **II.**

2. No one will have the right to join us as a party to any action against an "insured".

3. Also, no action with respect to Coverage **E** can be brought against us until the obligation of such "insured" has been determined by final judgment or agreement signed by us.

G. Bankruptcy Of An "Insured"

Bankruptcy or insolvency of an "insured" will not relieve us of our obligations under this policy.

H. Other Insurance

This insurance is excess over other valid and collectible insurance except insurance written specifically to cover as excess over the limits of liability that apply in this policy.

I. Policy Period

This policy applies only to "bodily injury" or "property damage" which occurs during the policy period.

J. Concealment Or Fraud

We do not provide coverage to an "insured" who, whether before or after a loss, has:

1. Intentionally concealed or misrepresented any material fact or circumstance;

2. Engaged in fraudulent conduct; or

3. Made false statements;

relating to this insurance.

SECTIONS I AND II – CONDITIONS

A. Liberalization Clause

If we make a change which broadens coverage under this edition of our policy without additional premium charge, that change will automatically apply to your insurance as of the date we implement the change in your state, provided that this implementation date falls within 60 days prior to or during the policy period stated in the Declarations.

This Liberalization Clause does not apply to changes implemented with a general program revision that includes both broadenings and restrictions in coverage, whether that general program revision is implemented through introduction of:

1. A subsequent edition of this policy; or

2. An amendatory endorsement.

B. Waiver Or Change Of Policy Provisions

A waiver or change of a provision of this policy must be in writing by us to be valid. Our request for an appraisal or examination will not waive any of our rights.

C. Cancellation

1. You may cancel this policy at any time by returning it to us or by letting us know in writing of the date cancellation is to take effect.

2. We may cancel this policy only for the reasons stated below by letting you know in writing of the date cancellation takes effect. This cancellation notice may be delivered to you, or mailed to you at your mailing address shown in the Declarations. Proof of mailing will be sufficient proof of notice.

    a. When you have not paid the premium, we may cancel at any time by letting you know at least 10 days before the date cancellation takes effect.

    b. When this policy has been in effect for less than 60 days and is not a renewal with us, we may cancel for any reason by letting you know at least 10 days before the date cancellation takes effect.

FIGURE 24.22

c. When this policy has been in effect for 60 days or more, or at any time if it is a renewal with us, we may cancel:

   (1) If there has been a material misrepresentation of fact which if known to us would have caused us not to issue the policy; or

   (2) If the risk has changed substantially since the policy was issued.

   This can be done by letting you know at least 30 days before the date cancellation takes effect.

d. When this policy is written for a period of more than one year, we may cancel for any reason at anniversary by letting you know at least 30 days before the date cancellation takes effect.

3. When this policy is canceled, the premium for the period from the date of cancellation to the expiration date will be refunded pro rata.

4. If the return premium is not refunded with the notice of cancellation or when this policy is returned to us, we will refund it within a reasonable time after the date cancellation takes effect.

D. Nonrenewal

We may elect not to renew this policy. We may do so by delivering to you, or mailing to you at your mailing address shown in the Declarations, written notice at least 30 days before the expiration date of this policy. Proof of mailing will be sufficient proof of notice.

E. Assignment

Assignment of this policy will not be valid unless we give our written consent.

F. Subrogation

An "insured" may waive in writing before a loss all rights of recovery against any person. If not waived, we may require an assignment of rights of recovery for a loss to the extent that payment is made by us.

If an assignment is sought, an "insured" must sign and deliver all related papers and cooperate with us.

Subrogation does not apply to Coverage **F** or Paragraph **C.** Damage To Property Of Others under Section **II** – Additional Coverages.

G. Death

If any person named in the Declarations or the spouse, if a resident of the same household, dies, the following apply:

1. We insure the legal representative of the deceased but only with respect to the premises and property of the deceased covered under the policy at the time of death; and

2. "Insured" includes:

   a. An "insured" who is a member of your household at the time of your death, but only while a resident of the "residence premises"; and

   b. With respect to your property, the person having proper temporary custody of the property until appointment and qualification of a legal representative.

FIGURE 24.23   ISO Endorsement, Homeowners HO04270402: Limited Fungi, Wet or Dry Rot, or Bacteria Coverage

POLICY NUMBER: **HOMEOWNERS**
                                                                            HO 04 27 04 02

THIS ENDORSEMENT CHANGES THE POLICY. PLEASE READ IT CAREFULLY.

LIMITED FUNGI, WET OR DRY ROT, OR BACTERIA COVERAGE
FOR USE WITH FORMS HO 00 03 AND HO 00 05

SCHEDULE*

These limits of liability apply to the total of all loss or costs payable under this endorsement, regardless of the number of "occurrences", the number of claims-made, or the number of locations insured under this endorsement and listed in this Schedule.	
1. Section I – Property Coverage Limit Of Liability for the Additional Coverage "Fungi", Wet Or Dry Rot, Or Bacteria	$
2. Section II – Coverage **E** Aggregate Sublimit of Liability for "Fungi", Wet Or Dry Rot, Or Bacteria	$

*Entries may be left blank if shown elsewhere in this policy for this coverage.

DEFINITIONS

The following definition is added:

"Fungi"

     a. "Fungi" means any type or form of fungus, including mold or mildew, and any mycotoxins, spores, scents or by-products produced or released by fungi.

     b. Under Section **II**, this does not include any fungi that are, are on, or are contained in, a good or product intended for consumption.

SECTION I – PROPERTY COVERAGES

E. Additional Coverages

     Paragraph **10.k.(2)(d)** is deleted in Form **HO 00 05** only.

The following Additional Coverage is added:

     13. "Fungi", Wet Or Dry Rot, Or Bacteria

         a. The amount shown in the Schedule above is the most we will pay for:

            (1) The total of all loss payable under Section **I** – Property Coverages caused by "fungi", wet or dry rot, or bacteria;

            (2) The cost to remove "fungi", wet or dry rot, or bacteria from property covered under Section **I** – Property Coverages;

            (3) The cost to tear out and replace any part of the building or other covered property as needed to gain access to the "fungi", wet or dry rot, or bacteria; and

            (4) The cost of testing of air or property to confirm the absence, presence or level of "fungi", wet or dry rot, or bacteria whether performed prior to, during or after removal, repair, restoration or replacement. The cost of such testing will be provided only to the extent that there is a reason to believe that there is the presence of "fungi", wet or dry rot, or bacteria.

         b. The coverage described in **13.a.** only applies when such loss or costs are a result of a Peril Insured Against that occurs during the policy period and only if all reasonable means were used to save and preserve the property from further damage at and after the time the Peril Insured Against occurred.

FIGURE 24.24

c. The amount shown in the Schedule for this coverage is the most we will pay for the total of all loss or costs payable under this Additional Coverage regardless of the:

(1) Number of locations insured under this endorsement; or

(2) Number of claims-made.

d. If there is covered loss or damage to covered property, not caused, in whole or in part, by "fungi", wet or dry rot, or bacteria, loss payment will not be limited by the terms of this Additional Coverage, except to the extent that "fungi", wet or dry rot, or bacteria causes an increase in the loss. Any such increase in the loss will be subject to the terms of this Additional Coverage.

This coverage does not increase the limit of liability applying to the damaged covered property.

SECTION I – PERILS INSURED AGAINST

In Form **HO 00 03:**

A. Coverage A – Dwelling And Coverage B – Other Structures

Paragraph **2.c.(5)** is deleted and replaced by the following:

(5) Caused by constant or repeated seepage or leakage of water or the presence or condensation of humidity, moisture or vapor, over a period of weeks, months or years unless such seepage or leakage of water or the presence or condensation of humidity, moisture or vapor and the resulting damage is unknown to all "insureds" and is hidden within the walls or ceilings or beneath the floors or above the ceilings of a structure.

Paragraph **2.c.(6)(c)** is deleted and replaced by the following:

(c) Smog, rust or other corrosion;

B. Coverage C – Personal Property

12. **Accidental Discharge Or Overflow Of Water Or Steam**

Paragraph **b.(4)** is deleted and replaced by the following:

(4) Caused by constant or repeated seepage or leakage of water or the presence or condensation of humidity, moisture or vapor, over a period of weeks, months or years unless such seepage or leakage of water or the presence or condensation of humidity, moisture or vapor and the resulting damage is unknown to all "insureds" and is hidden within the walls or ceilings or beneath the floors or above the ceilings of a structure.

In Form **HO 00 05:**

A. Under Coverages **A, B** and **C:**

Paragraph **2.d.** is deleted and replaced by the following:

d. Caused by constant or repeated seepage or leakage of water or the presence or condensation of humidity, moisture or vapor, over a period of weeks, months or years unless such seepage or leakage of water or the presence or condensation of humidity, moisture or vapor and the resulting damage is unknown to all "insureds" and is hidden within the walls or ceilings or beneath the floors or above the ceilings of a structure.

Paragraph **2.e.(3)** is deleted and replaced by the following:

(3) Smog, rust or other corrosion;

SECTION I – EXCLUSIONS

Exclusion **A.10.** is added.

10. **"Fungi", Wet Or Dry Rot, Or Bacteria**

"Fungi", Wet Or Dry Rot, Or Bacteria meaning the presence, growth, proliferation, spread or any activity of "fungi", wet or dry rot, or bacteria.

This exclusion does not apply:

a. When "fungi", wet or dry rot, or bacteria results from fire or lightning; or

b. To the extent coverage is provided for in the "Fungi", Wet Or Dry Rot, Or Bacteria Additional Coverage under Section I – Property Coverages with respect to loss caused by a Peril Insured Against other than fire or lightning.

Direct loss by a Peril Insured Against resulting from "fungi", wet or dry rot, or bacteria is covered.

SECTION I – CONDITIONS

Condition **P. Policy Period** is deleted and replaced by the following:

P. Policy Period

This policy applies to loss or costs which occur during the policy period.

FIGURE 24.25

SECTION II – CONDITIONS

Condition **A. Limit Of Liability** is deleted and replaced by the following:

A. Limit Of Liability

Our total liability under Coverage **E** for all damages resulting from any one "occurrence" will not be more than the Coverage **E** limit of liability shown in the Declarations. This limit is the same regardless of the number of "insureds", claims-made or persons injured. All "bodily injury" and "property damage" resulting from any one accident or from continuous or repeated exposure to substantially the same general harmful conditions will be considered to be the result of one "occurrence".

Our total liability under Coverage **F** for all medical expense payable for "bodily injury" to one person as the result of one accident will not be more than the Coverage **F** limit of liability shown in the Declarations.

However, our total liability under Coverage **E** for the total of all damages arising directly or indirectly, in whole or in part, out of the actual, alleged or threatened inhalation of, ingestion of, contact with, exposure to, existence of, or presence of any "fungi", wet or dry rot, or bacteria will not be more than the Section **II** – Coverage **E** Aggregate Sublimit of Liability for "Fungi", Wet Or Dry Rot, Or Bacteria. That sublimit is the amount shown in the Schedule. This is the most we will pay regardless of the:

1. Number of locations insured under the policy to which this endorsement is attached;

2. Number of persons injured;

3. Number of persons whose property is damaged;

4. Number of "insureds"; or

5. Number of "occurrences" or claims-made.

This sublimit is within, but does not increase, the Coverage **E** limit of liability. It applies separately to each consecutive annual period and to any remaining period of less than 12 months, starting with the beginning of the policy period shown in the Declarations.

With respect to damages arising out of "fungi", wet or dry rot, or bacteria described in **A.** Limit Of Liability of this endorsement, Condition **B. Severability Of Insurance** is deleted and replaced by the following:

B. Severability Of Insurance

This insurance applies separately to each "insured" except with respect to the Aggregate Sublimit of Liability described in this endorsement under Section **II** – Conditions, **A.** Limit Of Liability. This condition will not increase the limit of liability for this coverage.

All other provisions of the policy apply.

CHAPTER 25

Appendix B

SAMPLE PERSONAL AUTOMOBILE POLICY (PAP) PP 00 01 01 05

Copyrighted material of Insurance Services Office, Inc., with its permission

FIGURE 25.1

AGREEMENT

In return for payment of the premium and subject to all the terms of this policy, we agree with you as follows:

DEFINITIONS

A. Throughout this policy, "you" and "your" refer to:

   1. The "named insured" shown in the Declarations; and

   2. The spouse if a resident of the same household.

If the spouse ceases to be a resident of the same household during the policy period or prior to the inception of this policy, the spouse will be considered "you" and "your" under this policy but only until the earlier of:

   1. The end of 90 days following the spouse's change of residency;

   2. The effective date of another policy listing the spouse as a named insured; or

   3. The end of the policy period.

B. "We", "us" and "our" refer to the Company providing this insurance.

C. For purposes of this policy, a private passenger type auto, pickup or van shall be deemed to be owned by a person if leased:

   1. Under a written agreement to that person; and

   2. For a continuous period of at least 6 months.

Other words and phrases are defined. They are in quotation marks when used.

D. "Bodily injury" means bodily harm, sickness or disease, including death that results.

E. "Business" includes trade, profession or occupation.

F. "Family member" means a person related to you by blood, marriage or adoption who is a resident of your household. This includes a ward or foster child.

G. "Occupying" means:

   1. In;

   2. Upon; or

   3. Getting in, on, out or off.

H. "Property damage" means physical injury to, destruction of or loss of use of tangible property.

I. "Trailer" means a vehicle designed to be pulled by a:

   1. Private passenger auto; or

   2. Pickup or van.

It also means a farm wagon or farm implement while towed by a vehicle listed in **1.** or **2.** above.

J. "Your covered auto" means:

   1. Any vehicle shown in the Declarations.

   2. A "newly acquired auto".

   3. Any "trailer" you own.

   4. Any auto or "trailer" you do not own while used as a temporary substitute for any other vehicle described in this definition which is out of normal use because of its:

      a. Breakdown;

      b. Repair;

      c. Servicing;

      d. Loss; or

      e. Destruction.

This Provision (**J.4.**) does not apply to Coverage For Damage To Your Auto.

K. "Newly acquired auto":

   1. "Newly acquired auto" means any of the following types of vehicles you become the owner of during the policy period:

      a. A private passenger auto; or

      b. A pickup or van, for which no other insurance policy provides coverage, that:

         (1) Has a Gross Vehicle Weight Rating of 10,000 lbs. or less; and

         (2) Is not used for the delivery or transportation of goods and materials unless such use is:

            (a) Incidental to your "business" of installing, maintaining or repairing furnishings or equipment; or

            (b) For farming or ranching.

   2. Coverage for a "newly acquired auto" is provided as described below. If you ask us to insure a "newly acquired auto" after a specified time period described below has elapsed, any coverage we provide for a "newly acquired auto" will begin at the time you request the coverage.

FIGURE 25.2

a. For any coverage provided in this policy except Coverage For Damage To Your Auto, a "newly acquired auto" will have the broadest coverage we now provide for any vehicle shown in the Declarations. Coverage begins on the date you become the owner. However, for this coverage to apply to a "newly acquired auto" which is in addition to any vehicle shown in the Declarations, you must ask us to insure it within 14 days after you become the owner.

If a "newly acquired auto" replaces a vehicle shown in the Declarations, coverage is provided for this vehicle without your having to ask us to insure it.

b. Collision Coverage for a "newly acquired auto" begins on the date you become the owner. However, for this coverage to apply, you must ask us to insure it within:

(1) 14 days after you become the owner if the Declarations indicate that Collision Coverage applies to at least one auto. In this case, the "newly acquired auto" will have the broadest coverage we now provide for any auto shown in the Declarations.

(2) Four days after you become the owner if the Declarations do not indicate that Collision Coverage applies to at least one auto. If you comply with the 4 day requirement and a loss occurred before you asked us to insure the "newly acquired auto", a Collision deductible of $500 will apply.

c. Other Than Collision Coverage for a "newly acquired auto" begins on the date you become the owner. However, for this coverage to apply, you must ask us to insure it within:

(1) 14 days after you become the owner if the Declarations indicate that Other Than Collision Coverage applies to at least one auto. In this case, the "newly acquired auto" will have the broadest coverage we now provide for any auto shown in the Declarations.

(2) Four days after you become the owner if the Declarations do not indicate that Other Than Collision Coverage applies to at least one auto. If you comply with the 4 day requirement and a loss occurred before you asked us to insure the "newly acquired auto", an Other Than Collision deductible of $500 will apply.

PART A – LIABILITY COVERAGE

INSURING AGREEMENT

A. We will pay damages for "bodily injury" or "property damage" for which any "insured" becomes legally responsible because of an auto accident. Damages include prejudgment interest awarded against the "insured". We will settle or defend, as we consider appropriate, any claim or suit asking for these damages. In addition to our limit of liability, we will pay all defense costs we incur. Our duty to settle or defend ends when our limit of liability for this coverage has been exhausted by payment of judgments or settlements. We have no duty to defend any suit or settle any claim for "bodily injury" or "property damage" not covered under this policy.

B. "Insured" as used in this Part means:

1. You or any "family member" for the ownership, maintenance or use of any auto or "trailer".

2. Any person using "your covered auto".

3. For "your covered auto", any person or organization but only with respect to legal responsibility for acts or omissions of a person for whom coverage is afforded under this Part.

4. For any auto or "trailer", other than "your covered auto", any other person or organization but only with respect to legal responsibility for acts or omissions of you or any "family member" for whom coverage is afforded under this Part. This Provision (B.4.) applies only if the person or organization does not own or hire the auto or "trailer".

SUPPLEMENTARY PAYMENTS

We will pay on behalf of an "insured":

1. Up to $250 for the cost of bail bonds required because of an accident, including related traffic law violations. The accident must result in "bodily injury" or "property damage" covered under this policy.

2. Premiums on appeal bonds and bonds to release attachments in any suit we defend.

3. Interest accruing after a judgment is entered in any suit we defend. Our duty to pay interest ends when we offer to pay that part of the judgment which does not exceed our limit of liability for this coverage.

FIGURE 25.3

4. Up to $200 a day for loss of earnings, but not other income, because of attendance at hearings or trials at our request.

5. Other reasonable expenses incurred at our request.

These payments will not reduce the limit of liability.

EXCLUSIONS

A. We do not provide Liability Coverage for any "insured":

1. Who intentionally causes "bodily injury" or "property damage".

2. For "property damage" to property owned or being transported by that "insured".

3. For "property damage" to property:

   a. Rented to;

   b. Used by; or

   c. In the care of;

   that "insured".

   This Exclusion **(A.3.)** does not apply to "property damage" to a residence or private garage.

4. For "bodily injury" to an employee of that "insured" during the course of employment. This Exclusion **(A.4.)** does not apply to "bodily injury" to a domestic employee unless workers' compensation benefits are required or available for that domestic employee.

5. For that "insured's" liability arising out of the ownership or operation of a vehicle while it is being used as a public or livery conveyance. This Exclusion **(A.5.)** does not apply to a share-the-expense car pool.

6. While employed or otherwise engaged in the "business" of:

   a. Selling;

   b. Repairing;

   c. Servicing;

   d. Storing; or

   e. Parking;

   vehicles designed for use mainly on public highways. This includes road testing and delivery. This Exclusion **(A.6.)** does not apply to the ownership, maintenance or use of "your covered auto" by:

   a. You;

   b. Any "family member"; or

   c. Any partner, agent or employee of you or any "family member".

7. Maintaining or using any vehicle while that "insured" is employed or otherwise engaged in any "business" (other than farming or ranching) not described in Exclusion **A.6.**

   This Exclusion **(A.7.)** does not apply to the maintenance or use of a:

   a. Private passenger auto;

   b. Pickup or van; or

   c. "Trailer" used with a vehicle described in **a.** or **b.** above.

8. Using a vehicle without a reasonable belief that that "insured" is entitled to do so. This Exclusion **(A.8.)** does not apply to a "family member" using "your covered auto" which is owned by you.

9. For "bodily injury" or "property damage" for which that "insured":

   a. Is an insured under a nuclear energy liability policy; or

   b. Would be an insured under a nuclear energy liability policy but for its termination upon exhaustion of its limit of liability.

   A nuclear energy liability policy is a policy issued by any of the following or their successors:

   a. Nuclear Energy Liability Insurance Association;

   b. Mutual Atomic Energy Liability Underwriters; or

   c. Nuclear Insurance Association of Canada.

B. We do not provide Liability Coverage for the ownership, maintenance or use of:

1. Any vehicle which:

   a. Has fewer than four wheels; or

   b. Is designed mainly for use off public roads.

   This Exclusion **(B.1.)** does not apply:

   a. While such vehicle is being used by an "insured" in a medical emergency;

   b. To any "trailer"; or

   c. To any non-owned golf cart.

2. Any vehicle, other than "your covered auto", which is:

   a. Owned by you; or

   b. Furnished or available for your regular use.

3. Any vehicle, other than "your covered auto", which is:

   a. Owned by any "family member"; or

   b. Furnished or available for the regular use of any "family member".

FIGURE 25.4

However, this Exclusion (**B.3.**) does not apply to you while you are maintaining or "occupying" any vehicle which is:

   a. Owned by a "family member"; or

   b. Furnished or available for the regular use of a "family member".

4. Any vehicle, located inside a facility designed for racing, for the purpose of:

   a. Competing in; or

   b. Practicing or preparing for;

any prearranged or organized racing or speed contest.

LIMIT OF LIABILITY

A. The limit of liability shown in the Declarations for each person for Bodily Injury Liability is our maximum limit of liability for all damages, including damages for care, loss of services or death, arising out of "bodily injury" sustained by any one person in any one auto accident. Subject to this limit for each person, the limit of liability shown in the Declarations for each accident for Bodily Injury Liability is our maximum limit of liability for all damages for "bodily injury" resulting from any one auto accident.

The limit of liability shown in the Declarations for each accident for Property Damage Liability is our maximum limit of liability for all "property damage" resulting from any one auto accident.

This is the most we will pay regardless of the number of:

1. "Insureds";

2. Claims made;

3. Vehicles or premiums shown in the Declarations; or

4. Vehicles involved in the auto accident.

B. No one will be entitled to receive duplicate payments for the same elements of loss under this coverage and:

1. Part **B** or Part **C** of this policy; or

2. Any Underinsured Motorists Coverage provided by this policy.

OUT OF STATE COVERAGE

If an auto accident to which this policy applies occurs in any state or province other than the one in which "your covered auto" is principally garaged, we will interpret your policy for that accident as follows:

A. If the state or province has:

1. A financial responsibility or similar law specifying limits of liability for "bodily injury" or "property damage" higher than the limit shown in the Declarations, your policy will provide the higher specified limit.

2. A compulsory insurance or similar law requiring a nonresident to maintain insurance whenever the nonresident uses a vehicle in that state or province, your policy will provide at least the required minimum amounts and types of coverage.

B. No one will be entitled to duplicate payments for the same elements of loss.

FINANCIAL RESPONSIBILITY

When this policy is certified as future proof of financial responsibility, this policy shall comply with the law to the extent required.

OTHER INSURANCE

If there is other applicable liability insurance we will pay only our share of the loss. Our share is the proportion that our limit of liability bears to the total of all applicable limits. However, any insurance we provide for a vehicle you do not own, including any vehicle while used as a temporary substitute for "your covered auto", shall be excess over any other collectible insurance.

PART B – MEDICAL PAYMENTS COVERAGE

INSURING AGREEMENT

A. We will pay reasonable expenses incurred for necessary medical and funeral services because of "bodily injury":

1. Caused by accident; and

2. Sustained by an "insured".

We will pay only those expenses incurred for services rendered within 3 years from the date of the accident.

B. "Insured" as used in this Part means:

1. You or any "family member":

   a. While "occupying"; or

   b. As a pedestrian when struck by;

a motor vehicle designed for use mainly on public roads or a trailer of any type.

2. Any other person while "occupying" "your covered auto".

FIGURE 25.5

EXCLUSIONS

We do not provide Medical Payments Coverage for any "insured" for "bodily injury":

1. Sustained while "occupying" any motorized vehicle having fewer than four wheels.

2. Sustained while "occupying" "your covered auto" when it is being used as a public or livery conveyance. This Exclusion **(2.)** does not apply to a share-the-expense car pool.

3. Sustained while "occupying" any vehicle located for use as a residence or premises.

4. Occurring during the course of employment if workers' compensation benefits are required or available for the "bodily injury".

5. Sustained while "occupying", or when struck by, any vehicle (other than "your covered auto") which is:

   a. Owned by you; or

   b. Furnished or available for your regular use.

6. Sustained while "occupying", or when struck by, any vehicle (other than "your covered auto") which is:

   a. Owned by any "family member"; or

   b. Furnished or available for the regular use of any "family member".

   However, this Exclusion **(6.)** does not apply to you.

7. Sustained while "occupying" a vehicle without a reasonable belief that that "insured" is entitled to do so. This Exclusion **(7.)** does not apply to a "family member" using "your covered auto" which is owned by you.

8. Sustained while "occupying" a vehicle when it is being used in the "business" of an "insured". This Exclusion **(8.)** does not apply to "bodily injury" sustained while "occupying" a:

   a. Private passenger auto;

   b. Pickup or van; or

   c. "Trailer" used with a vehicle described in **a.** or **b.** above.

9. Caused by or as a consequence of:

   a. Discharge of a nuclear weapon (even if accidental);

   b. War (declared or undeclared);

   c. Civil war;

   d. Insurrection; or

   e. Rebellion or revolution.

10. From or as a consequence of the following, whether controlled or uncontrolled or however caused:

    a. Nuclear reaction;

    b. Radiation; or

    c. Radioactive contamination.

11. Sustained while "occupying" any vehicle located inside a facility designed for racing, for the purpose of:

    a. Competing in; or

    b. Practicing or preparing for;

    any prearranged or organized racing or speed contest.

LIMIT OF LIABILITY

A. The limit of liability shown in the Declarations for this coverage is our maximum limit of liability for each person injured in any one accident. This is the most we will pay regardless of the number of:

   1. "Insureds";

   2. Claims made;

   3. Vehicles or premiums shown in the Declarations; or

   4. Vehicles involved in the accident.

B. No one will be entitled to receive duplicate payments for the same elements of loss under this coverage and:

   1. Part **A** or Part **C** of this policy; or

   2. Any Underinsured Motorists Coverage provided by this policy.

OTHER INSURANCE

If there is other applicable auto medical payments insurance we will pay only our share of the loss. Our share is the proportion that our limit of liability bears to the total of all applicable limits. However, any insurance we provide with respect to a vehicle you do not own, including any vehicle while used as a temporary substitute for "your covered auto", shall be excess over any other collectible auto insurance providing payments for medical or funeral expenses.

FIGURE 25.6

PART C – UNINSURED MOTORISTS COVERAGE

INSURING AGREEMENT

A. We will pay compensatory damages which an "insured" is legally entitled to recover from the owner or operator of an "uninsured motor vehicle" because of "bodily injury":

  1. Sustained by an "insured"; and

  2. Caused by an accident.

The owner's or operator's liability for these damages must arise out of the ownership, maintenance or use of the "uninsured motor vehicle".

Any judgment for damages arising out of a suit brought without our written consent is not binding on us.

B. "Insured" as used in this Part means:

  1. You or any "family member".

  2. Any other person "occupying" "your covered auto".

  3. Any person for damages that person is entitled to recover because of "bodily injury" to which this coverage applies sustained by a person described in **1.** or **2.** above.

C. "Uninsured motor vehicle" means a land motor vehicle or trailer of any type:

  1. To which no bodily injury liability bond or policy applies at the time of the accident.

  2. To which a bodily injury liability bond or policy applies at the time of the accident. In this case its limit for bodily injury liability must be less than the minimum limit for bodily injury liability specified by the financial responsibility law of the state in which "your covered auto" is principally garaged.

  3. Which is a hit-and-run vehicle whose operator or owner cannot be identified and which hits:

    a. You or any "family member";

    b. A vehicle which you or any "family member" are "occupying"; or

    c. "Your covered auto".

  4. To which a bodily injury liability bond or policy applies at the time of the accident but the bonding or insuring company:

    a. Denies coverage; or

    b. Is or becomes insolvent.

However, "uninsured motor vehicle" does not include any vehicle or equipment:

  1. Owned by or furnished or available for the regular use of you or any "family member".

  2. Owned or operated by a self-insurer under any applicable motor vehicle law, except a self-insurer which is or becomes insolvent.

  3. Owned by any governmental unit or agency.

  4. Operated on rails or crawler treads.

  5. Designed mainly for use off public roads while not on public roads.

  6. While located for use as a residence or premises.

EXCLUSIONS

A. We do not provide Uninsured Motorists Coverage for "bodily injury" sustained:

  1. By an "insured" while "occupying", or when struck by, any motor vehicle owned by that "insured" which is not insured for this coverage under this policy. This includes a trailer of any type used with that vehicle.

  2. By any "family member" while "occupying", or when struck by, any motor vehicle you own which is insured for this coverage on a primary basis under any other policy.

B. We do not provide Uninsured Motorists Coverage for "bodily injury" sustained by any "insured":

  1. If that "insured" or the legal representative settles the "bodily injury" claim and such settlement prejudices our right to recover payment.

  2. While "occupying" "your covered auto" when it is being used as a public or livery conveyance. This Exclusion **(B.2.)** does not apply to a share-the-expense car pool.

  3. Using a vehicle without a reasonable belief that that "insured" is entitled to do so. This Exclusion **(B.3.)** does not apply to a "family member" using "your covered auto" which is owned by you.

C. This coverage shall not apply directly or indirectly to benefit any insurer or self-insurer under any of the following or similar law:

  1. Workers' compensation law; or

  2. Disability benefits law.

D. We do not provide Uninsured Motorists Coverage for punitive or exemplary damages.

FIGURE 25.7

LIMIT OF LIABILITY

A. The limit of liability shown in the Declarations for each person for Uninsured Motorists Coverage is our maximum limit of liability for all damages, including damages for care, loss of services or death, arising out of "bodily injury" sustained by any one person in any one accident. Subject to this limit for each person, the limit of liability shown in the Declarations for each accident for Uninsured Motorists Coverage is our maximum limit of liability for all damages for "bodily injury" resulting from any one accident.

This is the most we will pay regardless of the number of:

1. "Insureds";

2. Claims made;

3. Vehicles or premiums shown in the Declarations; or

4. Vehicles involved in the accident.

B. No one will be entitled to receive duplicate payments for the same elements of loss under this coverage and:

1. Part **A** or Part **B** of this policy; or

2. Any Underinsured Motorists Coverage provided by this policy.

C. We will not make a duplicate payment under this coverage for any element of loss for which payment has been made by or on behalf of persons or organizations who may be legally responsible.

D. We will not pay for any element of loss if a person is entitled to receive payment for the same element of loss under any of the following or similar law:

1. Workers' compensation law; or

2. Disability benefits law.

OTHER INSURANCE

If there is other applicable insurance available under one or more policies or provisions of coverage that is similar to the insurance provided under this Part of the policy:

1. Any recovery for damages under all such policies or provisions of coverage may equal but not exceed the highest applicable limit for any one vehicle under any insurance providing coverage on either a primary or excess basis.

2. Any insurance we provide with respect to a vehicle you do not own, including any vehicle while used as a temporary substitute for "your covered auto", shall be excess over any collectible insurance providing such coverage on a primary basis.

3. If the coverage under this policy is provided:

a. On a primary basis, we will pay only our share of the loss that must be paid under insurance providing coverage on a primary basis. Our share is the proportion that our limit of liability bears to the total of all applicable limits of liability for coverage provided on a primary basis.

b. On an excess basis, we will pay only our share of the loss that must be paid under insurance providing coverage on an excess basis. Our share is the proportion that our limit of liability bears to the total of all applicable limits of liability for coverage provided on an excess basis.

ARBITRATION

A. If we and an "insured" do not agree:

1. Whether that "insured" is legally entitled to recover damages; or

2. As to the amount of damages which are recoverable by that "insured";

from the owner or operator of an "uninsured motor vehicle", then the matter may be arbitrated. However, disputes concerning coverage under this Part may not be arbitrated.

Both parties must agree to arbitration. If so agreed, each party will select an arbitrator. The two arbitrators will select a third. If they cannot agree within 30 days, either may request that selection be made by a judge of a court having jurisdiction.

B. Each party will:

1. Pay the expenses it incurs; and

2. Bear the expenses of the third arbitrator equally.

C. Unless both parties agree otherwise, arbitration will take place in the county in which the "insured" lives. Local rules of law as to procedure and evidence will apply. A decision agreed to by at least two of the arbitrators will be binding as to:

1. Whether the "insured" is legally entitled to recover damages; and

2. The amount of damages. This applies only if the amount does not exceed the minimum limit for bodily injury liability specified by the financial responsibility law of the state in which "your covered auto" is principally garaged. If the amount exceeds that limit, either party may demand the right to a trial. This demand must be made within 60 days of the arbitrators' decision. If this demand is not made, the amount of damages agreed to by the arbitrators will be binding.

FIGURE 25.8

PART D – COVERAGE FOR DAMAGE TO YOUR AUTO

INSURING AGREEMENT

A. We will pay for direct and accidental loss to "your covered auto" or any "non-owned auto", including their equipment, minus any applicable deductible shown in the Declarations. If loss to more than one "your covered auto" or "non-owned auto" results from the same "collision", only the highest applicable deductible will apply. We will pay for loss to "your covered auto" caused by:

    1. Other than "collision" only if the Declarations indicate that Other Than Collision Coverage is provided for that auto.

    2. "Collision" only if the Declarations indicate that Collision Coverage is provided for that auto.

  If there is a loss to a "non-owned auto", we will provide the broadest coverage applicable to any "your covered auto" shown in the Declarations.

B. "Collision" means the upset of "your covered auto" or a "non-owned auto" or their impact with another vehicle or object.

  Loss caused by the following is considered other than "collision":

    1. Missiles or falling objects;

    2. Fire;

    3. Theft or larceny;

    4. Explosion or earthquake;

    5. Windstorm;

    6. Hail, water or flood;

    7. Malicious mischief or vandalism;

    8. Riot or civil commotion;

    9. Contact with bird or animal; or

    10. Breakage of glass.

  If breakage of glass is caused by a "collision", you may elect to have it considered a loss caused by "collision".

C. "Non-owned auto" means:

    1. Any private passenger auto, pickup, van or "trailer" not owned by or furnished or available for the regular use of you or any "family member" while in the custody of or being operated by you or any "family member"; or

    2. Any auto or "trailer" you do not own while used as a temporary substitute for "your covered auto" which is out of normal use because of its:

      a. Breakdown;

      b. Repair;

      c. Servicing;

      d. Loss; or

      e. Destruction.

TRANSPORTATION EXPENSES

A. In addition, we will pay, without application of a deductible, up to a maximum of $600 for:

    1. Temporary transportation expenses not exceeding $20 per day incurred by you in the event of a loss to "your covered auto". We will pay for such expenses if the loss is caused by:

      a. Other than "collision" only if the Declarations indicate that Other Than Collision Coverage is provided for that auto.

      b. "Collision" only if the Declarations indicate that Collision Coverage is provided for that auto.

    2. Expenses for which you become legally responsible in the event of loss to a "non-owned auto". We will pay for such expenses if the loss is caused by:

      a. Other than "collision" only if the Declarations indicate that Other Than Collision Coverage is provided for any "your covered auto".

      b. "Collision" only if the Declarations indicate that Collision Coverage is provided for any "your covered auto".

    However, the most we will pay for any expenses for loss of use is $20 per day.

B. Subject to the provisions of Paragraph **A.**, if the loss is caused by:

    1. A total theft of "your covered auto" or a "non-owned auto", we will pay only expenses incurred during the period:

      a. Beginning 48 hours after the theft; and

      b. Ending when "your covered auto" or the "non-owned auto" is returned to use or we pay for its loss.

    2. Other than theft of a "your covered auto" or a "non-owned auto", we will pay only expenses beginning when the auto is withdrawn from use for more than 24 hours.

  Our payment will be limited to that period of time reasonably required to repair or replace the "your covered auto" or the "non-owned auto".

FIGURE 25.9

EXCLUSIONS

We will not pay for:

1. Loss to "your covered auto" or any "non-owned auto" which occurs while it is being used as a public or livery conveyance. This Exclusion (**1.**) does not apply to a share-the-expense car pool.

2. Damage due and confined to:
   a. Wear and tear;
   b. Freezing;
   c. Mechanical or electrical breakdown or failure; or
   d. Road damage to tires.

   This Exclusion (**2.**) does not apply if the damage results from the total theft of "your covered auto" or any "non-owned auto".

3. Loss due to or as a consequence of:
   a. Radioactive contamination;
   b. Discharge of any nuclear weapon (even if accidental);
   c. War (declared or undeclared);
   d. Civil war;
   e. Insurrection; or
   f. Rebellion or revolution.

4. Loss to any electronic equipment that reproduces, receives or transmits audio, visual or data signals. This includes but is not limited to:
   a. Radios and stereos;
   b. Tape decks;
   c. Compact disk systems;
   d. Navigation systems;
   e. Internet access systems;
   f. Personal computers;
   g. Video entertainment systems;
   h. Telephones;
   i. Televisions;
   j. Two-way mobile radios;
   k. Scanners; or
   l. Citizens band radios.

   This Exclusion (**4.**) does not apply to electronic equipment that is permanently installed in "your covered auto" or any "non-owned auto".

5. Loss to tapes, records, disks or other media used with equipment described in Exclusion **4.**

6. A total loss to "your covered auto" or any "non-owned auto" due to destruction or confiscation by governmental or civil authorities.

   This Exclusion (**6.**) does not apply to the interests of Loss Payees in "your covered auto".

7. Loss to:
   a. A "trailer", camper body, or motor home, which is not shown in the Declarations; or
   b. Facilities or equipment used with such "trailer", camper body or motor home. Facilities or equipment include but are not limited to:
      (**1**) Cooking, dining, plumbing or refrigeration facilities;
      (**2**) Awnings or cabanas; or
      (**3**) Any other facilities or equipment used with a "trailer", camper body, or motor home.

   This Exclusion (**7.**) does not apply to a:
   a. "Trailer", and its facilities or equipment, which you do not own; or
   b. "Trailer", camper body, or the facilities or equipment in or attached to the "trailer" or camper body, which you:
      (**1**) Acquire during the policy period; and
      (**2**) Ask us to insure within 14 days after you become the owner.

8. Loss to any "non-owned auto" when used by you or any "family member" without a reasonable belief that you or that "family member" are entitled to do so.

9. Loss to equipment designed or used for the detection or location of radar or laser.

10. Loss to any custom furnishings or equipment in or upon any pickup or van. Custom furnishings or equipment include but are not limited to:
    a. Special carpeting or insulation;
    b. Furniture or bars;
    c. Height-extending roofs; or
    d. Custom murals, paintings or other decals or graphics.

    This Exclusion (**10.**) does not apply to a cap, cover or bedliner in or upon any "your covered auto" which is a pickup.

11. Loss to any "non-owned auto" being maintained or used by any person while employed or otherwise engaged in the "business" of:
    a. Selling;
    b. Repairing;

FIGURE 25.10

c. Servicing;

d. Storing; or

e. Parking;

vehicles designed for use on public highways. This includes road testing and delivery.

12. Loss to "your covered auto" or any "non-owned auto", located inside a facility designed for racing, for the purpose of:

   a. Competing in; or

   b. Practicing or preparing for;

   any prearranged or organized racing or speed contest.

13. Loss to, or loss of use of, a "non-owned auto" rented by:

   a. You; or

   b. Any "family member";

   if a rental vehicle company is precluded from recovering such loss or loss of use, from you or that "family member", pursuant to the provisions of any applicable rental agreement or state law.

LIMIT OF LIABILITY

A. Our limit of liability for loss will be the lesser of the:

   1. Actual cash value of the stolen or damaged property; or

   2. Amount necessary to repair or replace the property with other property of like kind and quality.

   However, the most we will pay for loss to:

   1. Any "non-owned auto" which is a trailer is $1500.

   2. Electronic equipment that reproduces, receives or transmits audio, visual or data signals, which is permanently installed in the auto in locations not used by the auto manufacturer for installation of such equipment, is $1,000.

B. An adjustment for depreciation and physical condition will be made in determining actual cash value in the event of a total loss.

C. If a repair or replacement results in better than like kind or quality, we will not pay for the amount of the betterment.

PAYMENT OF LOSS

We may pay for loss in money or repair or replace the damaged or stolen property. We may, at our expense, return any stolen property to:

   1. You; or

   2. The address shown in this policy.

If we return stolen property we will pay for any damage resulting from the theft. We may keep all or part of the property at an agreed or appraised value.

If we pay for loss in money, our payment will include the applicable sales tax for the damaged or stolen property.

NO BENEFIT TO BAILEE

This insurance shall not directly or indirectly benefit any carrier or other bailee for hire.

OTHER SOURCES OF RECOVERY

If other sources of recovery also cover the loss, we will pay only our share of the loss. Our share is the proportion that our limit of liability bears to the total of all applicable limits. However, any insurance we provide with respect to a "non-owned auto" shall be excess over any other collectible source of recovery including, but not limited to:

   1. Any coverage provided by the owner of the "non-owned auto";

   2. Any other applicable physical damage insurance;

   3. Any other source of recovery applicable to the loss.

APPRAISAL

A. If we and you do not agree on the amount of loss, either may demand an appraisal of the loss. In this event, each party will select a competent and impartial appraiser. The two appraisers will select an umpire. The appraisers will state separately the actual cash value and the amount of loss. If they fail to agree, they will submit their differences to the umpire. A decision agreed to by any two will be binding. Each party will:

   1. Pay its chosen appraiser; and

   2. Bear the expenses of the appraisal and umpire equally.

B. We do not waive any of our rights under this policy by agreeing to an appraisal.

FIGURE 25.11

PART E – DUTIES AFTER AN ACCIDENT OR LOSS

We have no duty to provide coverage under this policy if the failure to comply with the following duties is prejudicial to us:

A. We must be notified promptly of how, when and where the accident or loss happened. Notice should also include the names and addresses of any injured persons and of any witnesses.

B. A person seeking any coverage must:

   1. Cooperate with us in the investigation, settlement or defense of any claim or suit.

   2. Promptly send us copies of any notices or legal papers received in connection with the accident or loss.

   3. Submit, as often as we reasonably require:

      a. To physical exams by physicians we select. We will pay for these exams.

      b. To examination under oath and subscribe the same.

   4. Authorize us to obtain:

      a. Medical reports; and

   b. Other pertinent records.

   5. Submit a proof of loss when required by us.

C. A person seeking Uninsured Motorists Coverage must also:

   1. Promptly notify the police if a hit-and-run driver is involved.

   2. Promptly send us copies of the legal papers if a suit is brought.

D. A person seeking Coverage For Damage To Your Auto must also:

   1. Take reasonable steps after loss to protect "your covered auto" or any "non-owned auto" and their equipment from further loss. We will pay reasonable expenses incurred to do this.

   2. Promptly notify the police if "your covered auto" or any "non-owned auto" is stolen.

   3. Permit us to inspect and appraise the damaged property before its repair or disposal.

PART F – GENERAL PROVISIONS

BANKRUPTCY

Bankruptcy or insolvency of the "insured" shall not relieve us of any obligations under this policy.

CHANGES

A. This policy contains all the agreements between you and us. Its terms may not be changed or waived except by endorsement issued by us.

B. If there is a change to the information used to develop the policy premium, we may adjust your premium. Changes during the policy term that may result in a premium increase or decrease include, but are not limited to, changes in:

   1. The number, type or use classification of insured vehicles;

   2. Operators using insured vehicles;

   3. The place of principal garaging of insured vehicles;

   4. Coverage, deductible or limits.

If a change resulting from **A.** or **B.** requires a premium adjustment, we will make the premium adjustment in accordance with our manual rules.

C. If we make a change which broadens coverage under this edition of your policy without additional premium charge, that change will automatically apply to your policy as of the date we implement the change in your state. This Paragraph **(C.)** does not apply to changes implemented with a general program revision that includes both broadenings and restrictions in coverage, whether that general program revision is implemented through introduction of:

   1. A subsequent edition of your policy; or

   2. An Amendatory Endorsement.

FRAUD

We do not provide coverage for any "insured" who has made fraudulent statements or engaged in fraudulent conduct in connection with any accident or loss for which coverage is sought under this policy.

LEGAL ACTION AGAINST US

A. No legal action may be brought against us until there has been full compliance with all the terms of this policy. In addition, under Part **A**, no legal action may be brought against us until:

   1. We agree in writing that the "insured" has an obligation to pay; or

   2. The amount of that obligation has been finally determined by judgment after trial.

FIGURE 25.12

B. No person or organization has any right under this policy to bring us into any action to determine the liability of an "insured".

OUR RIGHT TO RECOVER PAYMENT

A. If we make a payment under this policy and the person to or for whom payment was made has a right to recover damages from another we shall be subrogated to that right. That person shall do:

1. Whatever is necessary to enable us to exercise our rights; and

2. Nothing after loss to prejudice them.

However, our rights in this Paragraph **(A.)** do not apply under Part **D,** against any person using "your covered auto" with a reasonable belief that that person is entitled to do so.

B. If we make a payment under this policy and the person to or for whom payment is made recovers damages from another, that person shall:

1. Hold in trust for us the proceeds of the recovery; and

2. Reimburse us to the extent of our payment.

POLICY PERIOD AND TERRITORY

A. This policy applies only to accidents and losses which occur:

1. During the policy period as shown in the Declarations; and

2. Within the policy territory.

B. The policy territory is:

1. The United States of America, its territories or possessions;

2. Puerto Rico; or

3. Canada.

This policy also applies to loss to, or accidents involving, "your covered auto" while being transported between their ports.

TERMINATION

A. Cancellation

This policy may be cancelled during the policy period as follows:

1. The named insured shown in the Declarations may cancel by:

   a. Returning this policy to us; or

   b. Giving us advance written notice of the date cancellation is to take effect.

2. We may cancel by mailing to the named insured shown in the Declarations at the address shown in this policy:

   a. At least 10 days notice:

   (1) If cancellation is for nonpayment of premium; or

   (2) If notice is mailed during the first 60 days this policy is in effect and this is not a renewal or continuation policy; or

   b. At least 20 days notice in all other cases.

3. After this policy is in effect for 60 days, or if this is a renewal or continuation policy, we will cancel only:

   a. For nonpayment of premium; or

   b. If your driver's license or that of:

   (1) Any driver who lives with you; or

   (2) Any driver who customarily uses "your covered auto";

   has been suspended or revoked. This must have occurred:

   (1) During the policy period; or

   (2) Since the last anniversary of the original effective date if the policy period is other than 1 year; or

   c. If the policy was obtained through material misrepresentation.

B. Nonrenewal

If we decide not to renew or continue this policy, we will mail notice to the named insured shown in the Declarations at the address shown in this policy. Notice will be mailed at least 20 days before the end of the policy period. Subject to this notice requirement, if the policy period is:

1. Less than 6 months, we will have the right not to renew or continue this policy every 6 months, beginning 6 months after its original effective date.

2. 6 months or longer, but less than one year, we will have the right not to renew or continue this policy at the end of the policy period.

3. 1 year or longer, we will have the right not to renew or continue this policy at each anniversary of its original effective date.

C. Automatic Termination

If we offer to renew or continue and you or your representative do not accept, this policy will automatically terminate at the end of the current policy period. Failure to pay the required renewal or continuation premium when due shall mean that you have not accepted our offer.

If you obtain other insurance on "your covered auto", any similar insurance provided by this policy will terminate as to that auto on the effective date of the other insurance.

FIGURE 25.13

D. Other Termination Provisions

1. We may deliver any notice instead of mailing it. Proof of mailing of any notice shall be sufficient proof of notice.

2. If this policy is cancelled, you may be entitled to a premium refund. If so, we will send you the refund. The premium refund, if any, will be computed according to our manuals. However, making or offering to make the refund is not a condition of cancellation.

3. The effective date of cancellation stated in the notice shall become the end of the policy period.

TRANSFER OF YOUR INTEREST IN THIS POLICY

A. Your rights and duties under this policy may not be assigned without our written consent. However, if a named insured shown in the Declarations dies, coverage will be provided for:

1. The surviving spouse if resident in the same household at the time of death. Coverage applies to the spouse as if a named insured shown in the Declarations; and

2. The legal representative of the deceased person as if a named insured shown in the Declarations. This applies only with respect to the representative's legal responsibility to maintain or use "your covered auto".

B. Coverage will only be provided until the end of the policy period.

TWO OR MORE AUTO POLICIES

If this policy and any other auto insurance policy issued to you by us apply to the same accident, the maximum limit of our liability under all the policies shall not exceed the highest applicable limit of liability under any one policy.

CHAPTER 26

Appendix C

SAMPLE STATE FARM WHOLE LIFE INSURANCE POLICY BASIC PLAN DESCRIPTION

Used with permission

FIGURE 26.1

STATE FARM LIFE INSURANCE COMPANY

HOME OFFICE, ONE STATE FARM PLAZA, BLOOMINGTON, ILLINOIS 61710

STATE FARM INSURANCE®

Insured	
Age	
Policy Number	
Policy Date	
Basic Plan Amount	$50,000
Total Initial Amount	Re-Issued As Requested

This Policy is based on the Application and the payment of premiums to the Policy Anniversary shown under the heading Premiums Payable on page 3 while the Insured lives. State Farm Life Insurance Company will pay the Proceeds to the Beneficiary when due proof of the Insured's death is received.

30-Day Right to Examine this Policy. This Policy may be returned within 30 days of its receipt for a refund of all premiums paid. Return may be made to State Farm Life Insurance Company or one of Our agents. If returned, this Policy will be void from the Policy Date.

Read this Policy with care. This is a legal contract between You and State Farm Life Insurance Company.

Kim M. Brunner
Secretary

Edward B. Rust Jr.
President

BASIC PLAN DESCRIPTION

Whole life insurance with premiums payable to the Policy Anniversary shown under Premiums Payable on page 3 while the Insured is alive. Insurance is payable when the Insured dies. The Basic Plan is eligible for annual dividends.

07000-43 PAGE 1 20061005

FIGURE 26.2

CONTENTS

General
The Contract.   Error in Age or Sex.
Transaction Delay.   Incontestability.
Cash Surrender.   Limited Death Benefit.
Assignment.

Owner.   Change of Owner/Successor Owner.

Payment of Premiums.   Automatic Premium Loan.
Grace Period.   Reinstatement.
Nonpayment of Premium.   Premium Adjustment When the Insured Dies.
Accumulations to Avoid Lapse.

Annual Dividends.   Dividend When the Insured Dies.
Dividend Options.

Guaranteed Values.   Extended Term and Paid-up Insurance.
Cash Value.   Basis of Computation.

Loan.   Loan Interest Rate.
Loan Value.   Loan Repayment.

Beneficiary Designation.   Order of Payment on the Insured's Death.
Change of Beneficiary Designation.   Methods of Payment.

The Application and any Riders and Endorsements follow page 12.

FIGURE 26.3

PRINTED IN U.S.A.

IMPORTANT NOTICE	AVISO IMPORTANTE
To obtain information or make a complaint:	Para obtener informacion o para someter una queja:
You may call State Farm's toll-free telephone number for information or to make a complaint at:	Usted puede llamar al numero de telefono gratis de State Farm's para informacion o para someter una queja al:
1-800-252-1932	1-800-252-1932
You may contact the Texas Department of Insurance to obtain information on companies, coverages, rights or complaints at:	Puede comunicarse con el Departamento de Seguros de Texas para obtener informacion acerca de companias, coberturas, derechos o quejas al:
1-800-252-3439	1-800-252-3439
You may write the Texas Department of Insurance:	Puede escribir al Departamento de Seguros de Texas:
P.O. Box 149104 Austin, TX 78714-9104 Fax: (512) 475-1771 Web: http://www.tdi.state.tx.us E-mail: ConsumerProtection@tdi.state.tx.us	P.O. Box 149104 Austin, TX 78714-9104 Fax: (512) 475-1771 Web: http://www.tdi.state.tx.us E-mail: ConsumerProtection@tdi.state.tx.us
PREMIUM OR CLAIM DISPUTES: Should you have a dispute concerning your premium or about a claim, you should contact the company first. If the dispute is not resolved, you may contact the Texas Department of Insurance.	**DISPUTAS SOBRE PRIMAS O RECLAMOS:** Si tiene una disputa concerniente a su prima o a un reclamo, debe comunicarse con la compania primero. Si no se resuelve la disputa, puede entonces comunicarse con el departamento (TDI).
ATTACH THIS NOTICE TO YOUR POLICY: This notice is for information only and does not become a part or condition of the attached document.	**UNA ESTE AVISO A SU POLIZA:** Este aviso es solo para proposito de informacion y no se convierte en parte o condicion del documento adjunto.

FORM 8636366.1   20070301

FIGURE 26.4

POLICY IDENTIFICATION

Insured		Age	
Policy Number	LF-	Basic Plan Amount	$50,000
Policy Date	May 20, 2009	Total Initial Amount	Re-issued As Requested
Issue Date	May 27, 2009	Policy Class	1
Owner			

SCHEDULE OF BENEFITS

Form	Description	Initial Amount	Benefit Period Ends	Annual Premium	Premiums Payable
07000	Basic Plan (Whole Life Paid-up at Age 100) Class of Risk: Standard Female Non-Tobacco	$50,000	With Life	$565.50	To 2081
07200	Waiver of Premium *Shown below for each life insurance benefit Class of Risk: Standard Female Non-Tobacco		In 2041	*	To 2041
	Basic Plan			$12.00	

SCHEDULE OF PREMIUMS

Beginning	Annual	Semi-Annual	Quarterly	Monthly
May 20, 2009	$577.50	$295.69	$149.58	$50.25
May 20, 2041	565.50	289.54	146.47	49.20

If the premium paid is not the annual premium, the total amount of premium due each year is greater than the annual premium. Premiums other than the annual premium are increased to reflect the time value of money. Monthly premiums must be paid under one of the monthly payment plans made available.

Form 07000 Page 3 20090527

FIGURE 26.5

SCHEDULE OF INSURANCE AND VALUES

- Insurance Amount -			Guaranteed Values		
On Insured	May 20,	End of Policy Year	Cash Value Dollars	Paid Up Insurance Dollars	Extended Term Ins Yrs Days
$50,000	2009				
50,000	2010	1	.00	0	0 0
50,000	2011	2	.00	0	0 0
50,000	2012	3	263.00	1,650	6 215
50,000	2013	4	630.00	3,750	13 195
50,000	2014	5	1,009.50	5,750	18 58
50,000	2015	6	1,401.50	7,700	21 78
50,000	2016	7	1,806.50	9,600	23 156
50,000	2017	8	2,224.00	11,400	25 60
50,000	2018	9	2,655.00	13,100	26 213
50,000	2019	10	3,100.50	14,800	27 278
50,000	2020	11	3,561.50	16,400	28 269
50,000	2021	12	4,038.50	17,950	29 195
50,000	2022	13	4,531.50	19,500	30 64
50,000	2023	14	5,041.00	20,950	30 247
50,000	2024	15	5,567.00	22,350	31 23
50,000	2025	16	6,109.50	23,650	31 125
50,000	2026	17	6,668.00	24,950	31 196
50,000	2027	18	7,243.00	26,200	31 241
50,000	2028	19	7,833.00	27,400	31 262
50,000	2029	20	8,438.50	28,550	31 262
50,000	2030	21	9,025.50	29,550	31 212
50,000	2031	22	9,625.50	30,500	31 144
50,000	2032	23	10,239.00	31,400	31 59
50,000	2033	24	10,864.00	32,300	30 324
50,000	2034	25	11,501.00	33,100	30 212
50,000	2035	26	12,150.00	33,900	30 90
50,000	2036	27	12,810.00	34,650	29 323
50,000	2037	28	13,481.50	35,400	29 185
50,000	2038	29	14,162.50	36,100	29 38
50,000	2039	30	14,854.00	36,750	28 251
50,000	2040	31	15,556.50	37,400	28 90
50,000	2041	32	16,271.00	38,000	27 287
50,000	2042	33	16,997.50	38,600	27 114
50,000	2043	34	17,736.00	39,150	26 300
50,000	2044	35	18,487.00	39,700	26 118
50,000	2045	36	19,250.50	40,200	25 296
50,000	2046	37	20,026.50	40,750	25 112
50,000	2047	38	20,814.00	41,200	24 290
50,000	2048	39	21,612.50	41,700	24 105
50,000	2049	40	22,421.50	42,100	23 285

Continued on Next Page
Page 4

Form .07000   20090527

FIGURE 26.6

SCHEDULE OF INSURANCE AND VALUES

Continued from Page 4

| - Insurance Amount - | | | ------------------Guaranteed Values-------------- | | |
On Insured	May 20,	End of Policy Year	Cash Value Dollars	Paid Up Insurance Dollars	Extended Term Ins Yrs Days
50,000	2041	Age 60	16,271.00	38,000	27 287
50,000	2043	Age 62	17,736.00	39,150	26 300
50,000	2046	Age 65	20,026.50	40,750	25 112
50,000	2051	Age 70	24,067.50	42,950	22 275

Guaranteed values at the end of any policy year presume payment of all specified premiums to the end of such policy year. The interest rate for guaranteed values and single premiums is 4.0% a year. The mortality table used is the 2001 CSO mortality table.

FIGURE 26.7

LIFE INSURANCE BUYER'S GUIDE

This guide can help you when you shop for life insurance. It discusses how to:

– Find a Policy That Meets Your Needs and Fits Your Budget

– Decide How Much Insurance You Need

– Make Informed Decisions When You Buy a Policy

Prepared by the National Association of Insurance Commissioners

The National Association of Insurance Commissioners is an association of state insurance regulatory officials. This association helps the various insurance departments to coordinate insurance laws for the benefit of all consumers.

Reprinted by
State Farm Life Insurance Company
Home Office:
Bloomington, Illinois 61710-0001

03900.1   PAGE 1   20080222

FIGURE 26.8

IMPORTANT THINGS TO CONSIDER

1. Review your own insurance needs and circumstances. Choose the kind of policy that has benefits that most closely fit your needs. Ask an agent or company to help you.

2. Be sure that you can handle premium payments. Can you afford the initial premium? If the premium increases later and you still need insurance, can you still afford it?

3. Don't sign an insurance application until you review it carefully to be sure all the answers are complete and accurate.

4. Don't buy life insurance unless you intend to stick with your plan. It may be very costly if you quit during the early years of the policy.

5. Don't drop one policy and buy another without a thorough study of the new policy and the one you have now. Replacing your insurance **may be costly.**

6. Read your policy carefully. Ask your agent or company about anything that is not clear to you.

7. Review your life insurance program with your agent or company every few years to keep up with changes in your income and your needs.

Buying Life Insurance

When you buy life insurance, you want coverage that fits your needs.

First, decide how much you need—and for how long—and what you can afford to pay. Keep in mind the major reason you buy life insurance is to cover the financial effects of unexpected or untimely death. Life insurance can also be one of many ways you plan for the future.

Next, learn what kinds of policies will meet your needs and pick the one that best suits you.

Then, choose the combination of policy premium and benefits that emphasizes protection in case of early death, or benefits in case of long life, or a combination of both.

It makes good sense to ask a life insurance agent or company to help you. An agent can help you review your insurance needs and give you information about the available policies. If one kind of policy doesn't seem to fit your needs, ask about others.

This guide provides only basic information. You can get more facts from a life insurance agent or company or from your public library.

What About the Policy You Have Now?

If you are thinking about dropping a life insurance policy, here are some things you should consider:

-- If you decide to replace your policy, don't cancel your old policy until you have received the new one. You then have a minimum period to review your new policy and decide if it is what you wanted.

-- It may be costly to replace a policy. Much of what you paid in the early years of the policy you have now, paid for the company's cost of selling and issuing the policy. You may pay this type of cost again if you buy a new policy.

-- Ask your tax advisor if dropping your policy could affect your income taxes.

-- If you are older or your health has changed, premiums for the new policy will often be higher. You will not be able to buy a new policy if you are not insurable.

FIGURE 26.9

-- You may have valuable rights and benefits in the policy you now have that are not in the new one.

-- If the policy you have now no longer meets your needs, you may not have to replace it. You might be able to change your policy or add to it to get the coverage or benefits you now want.

-- At least in the beginning, a policy may pay no benefits for some causes of death covered in the policy you have now.

In all cases, if you are thinking of buying a new policy, check with the agent or company that issued you the one you have now. When you bought your old policy, you may have seen an illustration of the benefits of your policy. Before replacing your policy, ask your agent or company for an updated illustration. Check to see how the policy has performed and what you might expect in the future, based on the amounts the company is paying now.

How Much Do You Need?

Here are some questions to ask yourself:

-- How much of the family income do I provide? If I were to die early, how would my survivors, especially my children, get by? Does anyone else depend on me financially, such as a parent, grandparent, brother or sister?

-- Do I have children for whom I'd like to set aside money to finish their education in the event of my death?

-- How will my family pay final expenses and repay debts after my death?

-- Do I have family members or organizations to whom I would like to leave money?

-- Will there be estate taxes to pay after my death?

-- How will inflation affect future needs?

As you figure out what you have to meet these needs, count the life insurance you have now, including any group insurance where you work or veteran's insurance. Don't forget Social Security and pension plan survivor's benefits. Add other assets you have: savings, investments, real estate and personal property. Which assets would your family sell or cash in to pay expenses after your death?

What is the Right Kind of Life Insurance?

All policies are not the same. Some give coverage for your lifetime and others cover you for a specific number of years. Some build up cash values and others do not. Some policies combine different kinds of insurance, and others let you change from one kind of insurance to another. Some policies may offer other benefits while you are still living. Your choice should be based on your needs and what you can afford.

There are two basic types of life insurance: **term insurance** and **cash value insurance**. Term insurance generally has lower premiums in the early years, but does not build up cash values that you can use in the future. You may combine cash value life insurance with term insurance for the period of your greatest need for life insurance to replace income.

FIGURE 26.10

Term Insurance covers you for a term of one or more years. It pays a death benefit only if you die in that term. Term insurance generally offers the largest insurance protection for your premium dollar. It generally does not build up cash value.

You can renew most term insurance policies for one or more terms even if your health has changed. Each time you renew the policy for a new term, premiums may be higher. Ask what the premiums will be if you continue to renew the policy. Also ask if you will lose the right to renew the policy at some age. For a higher premium, some companies will give you the right to keep the policy in force for a guaranteed period at the same price each year. At the end of that time you may need to pass a physical examination to continue coverage, and premiums may increase.

You may be able to trade many term insurance policies for a cash value policy during a conversion period—even if you are not in good health. Premiums for the new policy will be higher than you have been paying for the term insurance.

Cash Value Life Insurance is a type of insurance where the premiums charged are higher at the beginning than they would be for the same amount of term insurance. The part of the premium that is not used for the cost of insurance is invested by the company and builds up a cash value that may be used in a variety of ways. You may borrow against a policy's cash value by taking a policy loan. If you don't pay back the loan and the interest on it, the amount you owe will be subtracted from the benefits when you die, or from the cash value if you stop paying premiums and take out the remaining cash value. You can also use your cash value to keep insurance protection for a limited time or to buy a reduced amount without having to pay more premiums. You also can use the cash value to increase your income in retirement or to help pay for needs such as a child's tuition without canceling the policy. However, to build up this cash value, you must pay higher premiums in the earlier years of the policy. Cash value life insurance may be one of several types; whole life, universal life and variable life are all types of cash value insurance.

Whole Life Insurance covers you for as long as you live if your premiums are paid. You generally pay the same amount in premiums for as long as you live. When you first take out the policy, premiums can be several times higher than you would pay initially for the same amount of term insurance. But they are smaller than the premiums you would eventually pay if you were to keep renewing a term policy until your later years.

Some whole life policies let you pay premiums for a shorter period such as 20 years, or until age 65. Premiums for these policies are higher since the premium payments are made during a shorter period.

Universal Life Insurance is a kind of flexible policy that lets you vary your premium payments. You can also adjust the face amount of your coverage. Increases may require proof that you qualify for the new death benefit. The premiums you pay (less expense charges) go into a policy account that earns interest. Charges are deducted from the account. If your yearly premium payment plus the interest your account earns is less than the charges, your account value will become lower. If it keeps dropping, eventually your coverage will end. To prevent that, you may need to start making premium payments, or increase your premium payments, or lower your death benefits. Even if there is enough in your account to pay the premiums, continuing to pay premiums yourself means that you build up more cash value.

Variable Life Insurance is a kind of insurance where the death benefits and cash values depend on the investment performance of one or more separate accounts, which may be invested in mutual funds or other investments allowed under the policy. Be sure to get the prospectus from the company when buying this kind of policy and STUDY IT CAREFULLY. You will have higher death benefits and cash value if the underlying investments do well. Your benefits and cash value will be lower or may disappear if the investments you chose didn't do as well as you expected. You may pay an extra premium for a guaranteed death benefit.

FIGURE 26.11

PRINTED IN U.S.A.

DEFINITIONS

We, Us, and **Our** refer to State Farm Life Insurance Company.

You and **Your** refer to the Owner.

Application. Includes any life insurance application, medical history, questionnaire, and other documents from You or any other person proposed for insurance which are made a part of this Policy.

Basic Plan Amount. The amount of insurance on the Insured provided by the Basic Plan shown on pages 1 and 3.

Benefit Period Ends. The coverage for the benefit extends to, but does not include, the Policy Anniversary in the year shown on page 3 under this heading.

Cash Value. Sum of the Cash Values provided by the Basic Plan and any Riders.

Cash Surrender Value. Cash Value plus the Cash Value of any Paid-up Additions plus any Dividend Credits less any Loan and accrued Loan Interest.

Class of Risk. The underwriting class of the person insured.

Code. The U.S. Internal Revenue Code, as amended from time to time.

Dividend Credits. Any Dividend Accumulation or any current dividend under Dividend Option 1 or 3.

Dollars. Any money We pay, or which is paid to Us, must be in United States dollars.

Effective Date. Coverage starts on this date.

Initial Amount. The amount of coverage on the Effective Date of each benefit shown on page 3 under this heading.

Initial Payment. The amount shown on page 3 You must pay before this Policy becomes effective.

Insurance Amount. The amount of life insurance provided by the Basic Plan and any Rider on the dates shown on page 4 under this heading.

Issue Date. The date this Policy is issued shown on page 3.

Officer. The president, a vice president, the secretary, or an assistant secretary of State Farm Life Insurance Company.

Payee. On the Insured's death, the Beneficiaries shown in the Application, unless changed. If You surrender this Policy while the Insured is alive, the persons that You have named to receive the Cash Surrender Value. A Payee can be other than a natural person only if We agree.

Policy Class. The classification of the Basic Plan shown on page 3 used to determine eligibility for Extended Term or Paid-up Insurance if this Policy lapses.

Policy Date. The Effective Date of this Policy shown on pages 1 and 3.

FIGURE 26.12

| DEFINITIONS (CONTINUED) |

Policy Month, Year, or Anniversary. A policy month, year, or anniversary is measured from the Policy Date.

Premiums Payable. Premiums are payable until the Policy Anniversary shown on page 3 under this heading.

Proceeds. The sum of the insurance amounts payable under
(1) the Basic Plan,
(2) any Paid-up Additions, and
(3) any Rider on the Insured
plus any Dividend Credits, any dividend payable at the Insured's death, and any premium paid for part of the Payment Period beyond the Insured's date of death less any Loan, any accrued Loan Interest, and any part of a premium due.

Request. A written request signed by the person making the Request. Such Request must be received by Us and be on Our request form; or if such Request is not on Our request form, it must include the information required by Our request form.

Rider. Any benefit, other than the Basic Plan, made a part of this Policy.

Successor Owner. May be named in the Application or later by Request.

Total Initial Amount. The amount of life insurance on the Insured provided by the Basic Plan and any Rider on the Policy Date shown on pages 1 and 3.

| GENERAL PROVISIONS |

The Contract. This Policy contains the Basic Plan, any amendments, endorsements, any Riders, and a copy of the Application. This Policy is the entire contract. We have relied on the statements in the Application in issuing this Policy. We reserve the right to investigate the truth and completeness of those statements. In the absence of fraud, those statements are representations and not warranties. Only material misstatements in the Application will be used to contest this Policy or deny a claim within the time period specified in the Incontestability provision.

Only an Officer has the right to change this Policy. No agent has the authority to change the Policy or to waive any of its terms. All endorsements, amendments, and Riders must be signed by an Officer to be valid.

We may modify this Policy after We notify You to assure continued qualification of this Policy as a life insurance contract under any section of, regulation or ruling under, the Code, as amended from time to time. If We modify this Policy, We will send You the appropriate endorsement to be placed with this Policy. Such endorsement is subject to regulatory approval. If any provision of this Policy conflicts with the law of a jurisdiction that governs this Policy, the provision is deemed to be amended to conform to such law.

FIGURE 26.13

PRINTED IN U.S.A.

GENERAL PROVISIONS (CONTINUED)

Transaction Delay. Any payment of the Cash Surrender Value or Loan will usually be made within 7 days of receipt of the Request for payment. We may defer payment of any Cash Surrender Value or Loan for up to 6 months from the date We receive Your Request. However, a Loan to pay a premium on other policies with Us will not be deferred.

If We defer any such payment for 30 days or more, We will pay interest in addition to such payment. Such interest accrues from the date the payment becomes payable to the date of payment at 2% per year or the interest rate and time required by law, if greater.

Cash Surrender. You may surrender this Policy at any time by Request. All coverage ceases on the date We receive the Request or later date if You so indicate in Your Request. We will pay You the Cash Surrender Value as of the date coverage ceases plus any premium paid for the Payment Period beyond that date. We may defer paying You the Cash Surrender Value for up to 6 months after receiving Your Request.

Assignment. You may assign this Policy or any interest in it. We will recognize an assignment only if it is in writing and filed with Us. We are not responsible for the validity or effect of any assignment. An assignment may limit the interest of any Beneficiary.

Error in Age or Sex. If the Insured's date of birth or sex is not as stated in the Application, We will adjust each benefit on the Insured to that which the premium paid would have bought at the correct age and sex. Such adjustment will be based on the premium rates in effect on the issue date of the benefit.

Incontestability. Except for nonpayment of premiums, We will not contest the Basic Plan after it has been in force during the Insured's lifetime for 2 years from the Policy Date.

Except for nonpayment of premiums, We will not contest any reinstatement after it has been in force during the lifetime of the Insured for 2 years from the Effective Date of the reinstatement.

Any contest of the Basic Plan or reinstatement will be limited to material misstatements contained in the Application for the Basic Plan or reinstatement.

Each Rider has its own incontestability provision.

Limited Death Benefit. If the Insured dies by suicide while sane or self-destruction while insane within 2 years from the Policy Date, the Basic Plan Amount will not be paid. The Proceeds in this case will be limited to the premiums paid on the Basic Plan less any Loan, accrued Loan Interest, and any dividends paid on the Basic Plan.

Each Rider has its own limited death benefit provision.

OWNERSHIP PROVISIONS

Owner. The Owner is as named in the Application, unless changed. You may exercise any policy provision only by Request and while the Insured is alive, subject to the rights of any assignee that We have on record and to the rights of any irrevocably designated Beneficiary. The Successor Owner will become the Owner of this Policy if You die while this Policy is in force.

Change of Owner/Successor Owner. You may change the Owner or Successor Owner by Request while the Insured is alive and this Policy is in force. The change will take effect the date You sign the Request, but the change will not affect any action We have taken before We receive the Request. A change of Owner or Successor Owner does not change the Beneficiary Designation.

FIGURE 26.14

PREMIUM PROVISIONS

Payment of Premiums. You may pay premiums at Our Home Office or to one of Our agents. We will give You a receipt signed by one of Our Officers, if You request one.

The first premium is due on the Policy Date. All other premiums are payable on or before their Due Dates. A Due Date is the first day of each Payment Period. A Payment Period may be 1 month, 3 months, 6 months, or 12 months, starting on the same date of the month as the Policy Date. If the Payment Period is 1 month, the monthly premium is due at the start of each 1-month Payment Period. If the Payment Period is 3 months, the quarterly premium is due at the start of each 3-month Payment Period. If the Payment Period is 6 months, the semi-annual premium is due at the start of each 6-month Payment Period. If the Payment Period is 12 months, the annual premium is due at the start of each 12-month Payment Period. If the Due Date does not appear in a calendar month's days, the Due Date will be the last day of that same month. You may change the Payment Period on any Due Date by paying the premium for the new period, but You cannot change the Payment Period if premiums are being waived.

Grace Period. Except for the first premium, 31 days are allowed for the payment of a premium after its Due Date. During this time, the policy benefits continue.

Nonpayment of Premium. If any premium has not been paid by the end of its Grace Period, the Accumulations to Avoid Lapse and, if chosen, the Automatic Premium Loan provisions will apply. If neither of these provisions apply, this Policy will lapse as of the Due Date of any unpaid premium. With such lapse, coverage ceases unless continued as Extended Term or Paid-up Insurance.

Accumulations to Avoid Lapse. If any premium has not been paid by the end of its Grace Period, any Dividend Accumulation will be used to pay all or part of that premium. The unpaid balance of that premium will be due the day after the end of the partial Payment Period. A new Grace Period will be allowed for the payment of this unpaid balance.

We will send You a notice if any Dividend Accumulation is used to pay part of any premium. We will not use any Dividend Accumulation if You choose an available Guaranteed Values Provision within 90 days after the premium Due Date. Your choice will take effect as of the premium Due Date.

Automatic Premium Loan. This provision will apply if You chose it on the Application or later by Request. This provision will apply if there is enough Loan Value less any existing Loan and accrued Loan Interest to pay the unpaid premium for the current Payment Period and there are no Dividend Accumulations. Any premium or part of any premium that is not paid by the end of its Grace Period will be paid by Loan. Loan Interest will be charged from the due date of the unpaid premium. You may cancel this provision at any time by Request. We must receive Your Request to elect or cancel this provision before this Policy lapses.

Reinstatement. If You have not surrendered this Policy for cash, You may apply to reinstate it within 5 years after lapse. You must give Us proof of the Insured's insurability that is satisfactory to Us. You must pay all unpaid premiums with compound interest from their Due Dates. The interest rate is 6% a year. You must repay or restore any Loan at the time of lapse with compound interest, based on the Loan Interest Rates in effect during the period of lapse, to the date of reinstatement. The amount restored cannot be greater than the Loan Value on the date of reinstatement. Reinstatement will take effect on the date We approve the Insured's insurability.

Premium Adjustment When the Insured Dies. If the Insured dies during a Grace Period, any part of a premium due will be paid from the Proceeds. Any premium paid for the Payment Period beyond the Insured's death will be part of the Proceeds.

FIGURE 26.15

PRINTED IN U.S.A.

DIVIDEND PROVISIONS

Annual Dividends. We may apportion and pay dividends each year. Any such dividends will be paid only at the end of a Policy Year. There is no right to a partial or pro rated dividend prior to the end of a Policy Year. Such dividends will not be paid if all premiums due have not been paid or if the Basic Plan is in force as Extended Term Insurance.

Dividend Options. You may choose to have Your dividend used under one of these options:

1. **Premium Payment.** We will apply it toward payment of a premium then due.

2. **Paid-up Additions.** We will use it to buy a paid-up life insurance addition to the Basic Plan. Each addition is bought at the single premium rate for the Insured's sex and attained age at that time. We may also pay an annual dividend on these Paid-up Additions. You may surrender Paid-up Additions for their Cash Value at any time. The Cash Value of Paid-up Additions is based on the single premium rate for the Insured's sex and attained age on the date surrendered. If surrendered prior to the end of the Policy Year, there is no right to a partial or pro rated dividend. Paid-up Additions in force at the Insured's death will be part of the Proceeds.

3. **Dividend Accumulation.** We will hold it at interest. We will credit interest at a rate not less than 3% a year. Such interest will be paid only at the end of the Policy Year. You may withdraw all or part of the dividend accumulation at any time. If withdrawn prior to the end of the Policy Year, there is no right to a partial or pro rated credit of such interest. The dividend accumulation plus interest to the Insured's death will be part of the Proceeds.

4. **Cash.** We will pay it to You in cash.

If You do not choose a Dividend Option on the Application or the Dividend Option chosen is not available, We will use Dividend Option 2. You may change the Dividend Option by Request. The change will apply only to dividends paid after We receive Your Request.

Dividend When the Insured Dies. We may pay a dividend when the Insured dies. Such dividend will be a partial or pro rated amount based on the period from the start of a Policy Year to the Insured's death.

FIGURE 26.16

GUARANTEED VALUES PROVISIONS

Guaranteed Values. The Guaranteed Values shown on page 4 are based on Your payment of all premiums when they are due. These values are as of the end of the Policy Years shown. They do not include the Cash Value of any Paid-up Additions and will be adjusted for any Dividend Credits or Loan on this Policy. If requested, We will furnish You with any values not shown.

Cash Value. The Cash Value is the sum of the Cash Value of the Basic Plan and any Riders. Any Cash Values on the Basic Plan not shown on page 4 will be calculated as specified in the Basis of Computation provision. If any amount of premium is due and not paid, the Cash Value for the 90 days after that Due Date is the same as on such Due Date.

If the Basic Plan has been in force for more than 90 days as Extended Term or Paid-up Insurance, the Cash Value is the single premium for the insurance remaining. The Cash Value of such insurance will not decrease during the 31 days after a Policy Anniversary.

Extended Term and Paid-up Insurance. If this Policy lapses and there is a Cash Surrender Value, We will continue the Basic Plan as Extended Term or Paid-up Insurance. Extended Term Insurance is available only if this Policy is in Policy Class 1 or 2. Extended Term Insurance will be used at the time of lapse unless You choose to continue this Policy as Paid-up Insurance or surrender this Policy. If this Policy is in Policy Class 3, Paid-up Insurance will be used at the time of lapse unless You surrender this Policy.

You may choose by Request to have the Basic Plan continued as Paid-up Insurance or, if this Policy is not in Policy Class 3, as Extended Term Insurance. To be effective on the Due Date of any unpaid premium, Your Request must be received by Us within 90 days after that date.

The amount of Extended Term Insurance will be the Basic Plan Amount plus the amount of any Paid-up Additions plus any Dividend Credits less any Loan and accrued Loan Interest. The amount will stay level. The extended term period will be determined by applying the Cash Surrender Value as a single premium at the Insured's sex and attained age on the Due Date of any unpaid premium. If there is more value than needed to provide Extended Term Insurance for life, We will promptly pay You the excess in one sum. Extended Term Insurance has no Loan Value and will receive no dividends.

The amount of Paid-up Insurance will be determined by applying the Cash Value plus the Cash Value of any Paid-up Additions less any Loan and accrued Loan Interest as a single premium at the Insured's sex and attained age on the Due Date of any unpaid premium. The amount will stay level. Paid-up Insurance has Loan Value and may be eligible for dividends. Any Dividend Accumulation at the time this Policy is continued as Paid-up Insurance will not be affected.

Basis of Computation. The Guaranteed Values in this Policy are at least as large as those required by law in the state where it is delivered. The insurance authority there has a statement of how these values are determined.

The Guaranteed Values and single premiums are based on the Insured's age last birthday and sex. It is assumed that premiums are paid continuously and claims are paid immediately. The interest rate and the mortality table that We use are shown on page 4. The Cash Values for the Basic Plan for Policy Anniversaries not shown on page 4 are equal to the reserves which are calculated using the Commissioners Reserve Valuation Method. The Cash Value on any date between Policy Anniversaries is determined by interpolating between the Cash Value on the Policy Anniversary immediately before and after that date for the time period from the previous Policy Anniversary to that date.

FIGURE 26.17

PRINTED IN U.S.A.

POLICY LOAN PROVISIONS

Loan. You may borrow against this Policy by Request, unless the Basic Plan is in force as Extended Term Insurance. This Policy is the sole security for such Loan. We may defer a Loan for up to 6 months after receiving Your Request unless the Loan will be used to pay premiums on this or other policies with Us.

You may borrow the Loan Value less any existing Loan, accrued Loan Interest, and unpaid premiums. If Your unpaid Loan plus accrued Loan Interest exceeds the Cash Value of this Policy plus the Cash Value of any Paid-up Additions, We will send You a policy termination notice. This Policy will terminate 31 days after We have mailed that notice to You and to any assignee of record. If this occurs and is the result of a change in the Loan Interest Rate, this Policy will terminate at the later of the end of the Policy Year or 31 days after mailing of the notice. At policy termination, We will then pay You any Dividend Accumulation.

Loan Value. The Loan Value is the Cash Value of this Policy and the Cash Value of any Paid-up Additions on the next premium Due Date discounted at the Loan Interest Rate from the next Policy Anniversary to the date of the Loan. If premiums are no longer payable, the Loan Value will be the Cash Value of this Policy and the Cash Value of any Paid-up Additions on the next Policy Anniversary discounted at the Loan Interest Rate from that Policy Anniversary to the date of the Loan.

Loan Interest Rate. The Loan Interest Rate is an adjustable rate. We determine the rate each calendar quarter. Such rate will take effect the first day of January, April, July, and October after the date We determine it. Such rate will apply to any new and existing Loan under this Policy.

Any change in the rate will be subject to the following:
(1)   The rate will be lowered to be equal to or less than the legal maximum rate if such legal maximum is ½% or more a year lower than Our rate then in effect.
(2)   The rate may be increased by at least ½% a year if the legal maximum is ½% or more a year higher than Our rate then in effect. Such rate cannot exceed the legal maximum.

The legal maximum interest rate cannot exceed 15% a year nor the higher of the following:
(1)   The Moody's Corporate Bond Yield Average - Monthly Average Corporates as published by Moody's Investors Service, Inc. for the calendar month ending 2 months prior to the date the Loan Interest Rate is to go into effect; or
(2)   The interest rate used to calculate Cash Values under this Policy during the period for which the Loan Interest Rate is being determined plus 1% a year.

If the Moody's Corporate Bond Yield Average - Monthly Average Corporates is no longer published, the rate used in its place will be set by law or regulation of the insurance supervisory official in the jurisdiction where this Policy was delivered.

We will:
(1)   Notify You of the initial Loan Interest Rate at the time a Loan is made, unless it is an Automatic Premium Loan;
(2)   Notify You of the initial Loan Interest Rate as soon as practical after an Automatic Premium Loan is made; and
(3)   Give You advance notice of any increase in the Loan Interest Rate, if You have a Loan at that time.

We charge interest each day on any Loan. Loan Interest is due at the end of each Policy Year or at the time the Loan is repaid, if earlier. Loan Interest is added to the Loan if not paid when due.

Loan Repayment. You may repay all or part of a Loan at any time before the Insured dies or this Policy is surrendered. Any Loan that We deducted when the Basic Plan was placed on Extended Term or Paid-up Insurance may be repaid or restored only if the Basic Plan is reinstated.

FIGURE 26.18

PAYMENT OF BENEFITS PROVISIONS

Beneficiary Designation. This is as shown in the Application, unless You have made a change by Request. It includes the name of the Beneficiary. If You name "estate" as a Beneficiary, it means the executors or administrators of the last survivor of You and all Beneficiaries. If You name "children" of a person as a Beneficiary, only children born to or legally adopted by that person will be included. We may rely on an affidavit as to the ages, names, and other facts about all Beneficiaries. We will incur no liability if We act on such affidavit.

Change of Beneficiary Designation. You may make a change by Request while the Insured is alive and this Policy is in force. The change will take effect on the date the Request is signed, but the change will not affect any action We have taken before We receive the Request.

Order of Payment on the Insured's Death. When the Insured dies, We will make payment in equal shares to the primary Beneficiaries living when payment is made. If the last primary dies, We will make payment in equal shares to the successor Beneficiaries living when payment is made. If, at any time, no Beneficiary is living, We will make a one sum payment to You, if living when payment is made. Otherwise, We will make a one sum payment to the estate of the last survivor of You and all Beneficiaries. You may change this order of payment by Request while the Insured is alive.

Methods of Payment. We will pay the Proceeds or the Cash Surrender Value under the One Sum Method unless You choose another method then available. If the Payee is other than a natural person, We will make payment under the One Sum Method.

All payment intervals are measured from the date this Policy is surrendered or from the date the Insured dies.

After the Insured's death, a Payee who has the right to make a withdrawal may change the method of payment. This Payee may also appoint a successor payee. The successor payee may be the Payee's estate.

We must receive a Request for payment of the Proceeds and due proof of the Insured's death. Due proof of the Insured's death is evidence satisfactory to Us:
  (1)   to establish the date and fact of the Insured's death;
  (2)   to permit Us to determine whether Proceeds are payable; and
  (3)   such other items and information as may be necessary for Us to comply with laws and regulations related to payment of the claim or administration of the business of insurance.

Method 1 (One Sum Method). We will pay the Cash Surrender Value or the Proceeds in one sum. Interest will be paid from the date of the Insured's death to the date of payment. The interest rate will be the greater of 2% a year or the interest rate required by law, if applicable.

Method 2 (Other Method). Payment by any other method may be made if We agree.

FIGURE 26.19

PRINTED IN U.S.A.

WAIVER OF PREMIUM BENEFIT RIDER

General. This Rider is part of this Policy. It is based on the Application for this Rider and the payment of premiums. The premiums for this Rider are shown on page 3. Only certain policy provisions are a part of this Rider. They are "Definitions," "Ownership," "Premium," "The Contract," "Assignment," and "Error in Age or Sex."

Waiver of Premium Benefit. We will waive each premium due under this Policy if the Insured becomes totally disabled while this Rider is in force and such Total Disability has existed for 6 continuous months during the lifetime of the Insured. We will waive each premium due under this Policy as long as the Total Disability continues. We will only waive premiums due on and after Total Disability starts. No premium will be waived which was due more than one year prior to the date We receive notice of claim. While premiums are waived, all benefits continue as though You had paid the premiums.

A recurrence of a Total Disability for which We had been waiving premiums will be deemed a continuation of the prior period of Total Disability if the recurrence:
   (1)   results from the same injury or disease that caused the previous Total Disability;
   (2)   starts within 6 months of the date the previous Total Disability ended; and
   (3)   starts while this Rider is still in force.
Such recurrent Total Disability will not be subject to a new requirement that the Total Disability must first exist for 6 continuous months during the Insured's lifetime.

Total Disability Defined. Total Disability is a condition caused by injury or disease. During the first 24 months after Total Disability starts, this condition must prevent the Insured from performing substantially all of the work of the Insured's regular occupation. After the first 24 months after Total Disability starts, the condition must prevent the Insured from performing substantially all of the work in any occupation for which the Insured is, or becomes, reasonably qualified based upon education, training, or experience. The Insured's total and irrecoverable loss, caused by injury or disease, of any of the following will be considered Total Disability even if the Insured is able to work:
   (1)   sight in both eyes.
   (2)   use of both hands.
   (3)   use of both feet.
   (4)   use of one hand and one foot.

Disabilities Not Covered. We will not waive premiums if Total Disability:
   (1)   starts before the Effective Date of this Rider unless such disability was disclosed in the Application,
   (2)   starts before the Policy Anniversary when the Insured is age 5,
   (3)   results from an intended self-injury, or
   (4)   results from any act due to war whether or not the Insured is in the military service. "War" means declared or undeclared war or conflict involving the armed forces of one or more countries, governments, or international organizations.

Notice and Proof of Total Disability. We must receive notice of a claim and due proof of Total Disability while the Insured is alive and totally disabled and within 91 days after such total disability starts. If this is not done, You should submit such notice and proof as soon as reasonably possible. We may also require You to submit proof of the Insured's continuing Total Disability at reasonable intervals. You have at least 91 days after the date requested to submit such proof. If You do not submit proof when we require it, no further premiums will be waived. We will not require proof more than once a year after the Total Disability has lasted more than 2 years.

Premium Payments. If the Insured's Total Disability starts during a Grace Period, the unpaid premium must be paid before a claim will be approved. We may charge interest on that premium from the end of the Grace Period to the date paid at 6% a year. You must pay all premiums that come due until We approve the claim. We will refund any premium that You paid after Total Disability starts which is later waived. If the Insured dies before such refund is made, We will include that amount in the Proceeds.

07200-43   20061005

FIGURE 26.20

WAIVER OF PREMIUM BENEFIT RIDER (CONTINUED)

Termination. This Rider will terminate on the Policy Anniversary shown on page 3 under Benefit Period Ends. We will terminate this Rider before that date when:
  (1)   this Policy is terminated by surrender or lapse or
  (2)   the Basic Plan is continued as Extended Term or Paid-up Insurance.

You may terminate this Rider by Request. This Rider will terminate on the date We receive Your Request. We will revise page 3 of this Policy to show this change. Any premium paid for the payment period beyond the date this Rider terminates will be paid to You.

Termination will not affect any claim for Total Disability which starts before termination.

Incontestability. Except for nonpayment of premiums, We will not contest this Rider after it has been in force during the lifetime of the Insured for 2 years from the Effective Date of this Rider unless the Insured becomes totally disabled within that period.

Effective Date of This Rider. This is the date coverage starts. It is the same as the Policy Date of this Policy unless a different date for this Rider is shown on page 3.

State Farm Life Insurance Company

Kim M. Brunner
Secretary

Edward B. Rust Jr.
President

07200-43   20061005

FIGURE 26.21

BASIC PLAN DESCRIPTION
Whole life insurance with premiums payable to the Policy Anniversary shown under Premiums Payable on page 3 while the Insured is alive. Insurance is payable when the Insured dies. The Basic Plan is eligible for annual dividends.

07000

20050821

FIGURE 26.22

Life Insurance Illustrations

You may be thinking of buying a policy where cash values, death benefits, dividends or premiums may vary based on events or situations the company does not guarantee (such as interest rates). If so, you may get an illustration from the agent or company that helps explain how the policy works. The illustration will show how the benefits that are not guaranteed will change as interest rates and other factors change. The illustration will show you what the company guarantees. It will also show you what **could** happen in the future. Remember that nobody knows what will happen in the future. You should be ready to adjust your financial plans if the cash value doesn't increase as quickly as shown in the illustration. You will be asked to sign a statement that says you understand that some of the numbers in the illustration are not guaranteed.

Finding a Good Value in Life Insurance

After you have decided which kind of life insurance is best for you, compare similar policies from different companies to find which one is likely to give you the best value for your money. A simple comparison of the premiums is not enough. There are other things to consider. For example:

- Do premiums or benefits vary from year to year?

- How much do the benefits build up in the policy?

- What part of the premiums or benefits is not guaranteed?

- What is the effect of interest on money paid and received at different times on the policy?

Remember that no one company offers the lowest cost at **all** ages for **all** kinds and amounts of insurance. You should also consider other factors:

- How quickly does the cash value grow? Some policies have low cash values in the early years that build quickly later on. Other policies have a more level cash value build-up. A year-by-year display of values and benefits can be very helpful. (The agent or company will give you a policy summary or an illustration that will show benefits and premiums for selected years.)

- Are there special policy features that particularly suit your needs?

- How are nonguaranteed values calculated? For example, interest rates are important in determining policy returns. In some companies increases reflect the average interest earnings on all of that company's policies regardless of when issued. In others, the return for policies issued in a recent year, or a group of years, reflects the interest earnings on that group of policies; in this case, amounts paid are likely to change more rapidly when interest rates change.

FIGURE 26.23

IMPORTANT TAX INFORMATION CONCERNING YOUR LIFE INSURANCE POLICY

Money that is deemed removed ("distributed") from or grows within some life insurance policies may be taxed. The following briefly describes examples of how this could occur. Your tax advisor must determine the taxation of your specific situation.

What is a "distribution" from the policy?

The term distribution is used in the tax laws to describe the deemed withdrawal of values from the policy. Typical withdrawals include: withdrawals of cash value, loans, assignments of contract values to another person, or crediting of a dividend, unless it is used to purchase additional insurance or to pay a premium.

How are policies normally taxed?

Generally, death benefits are not subject to income tax. Values inside the policy grow tax-free. Loans are tax-free until you surrender the policy or allow it to lapse. Other distributions are tax-free until all premiums are returned, and distributions above that amount are taxed as "gain."

What is "gain"?

Gain simply means your policy has a larger value than the total amount of premiums you have paid, net of some amounts such as premiums that have been returned through dividends. The gain is the difference between the value of your policy and the premiums paid. For example, if a policy has a value of $1,000.00 and premiums of $800.00 have been paid, the gain is $200.00. It is only the $200.00 gain that would be subject to tax.

When might my policy be taxed differently?

Certain actions that you take may result in various situations where your policy may be taxed differently, including but not limited to the following:

- Pay premium above the limits specified in the tax laws
- Change the amount of insurance, including paid-up additions, such as through partial withdrawals
- Add, cancel, or change rider coverage or amounts

Also certain distributions are taxable - but only to the extent of the gain in your policy. Any gain is considered to be the first - rather than the last - amount withdrawn; so, any distribution is taxed until the amount of the gain is reached. After that, the remainder of the distribution is not taxed.

If the distribution occurs before age 59½, the IRS may impose a 10% additional tax on the amount of the distribution that is taxable.

In extreme situations, the policy may be disqualified as "life insurance" for tax purposes. That means the policy's internal cash value growth could be taxable.

How will I know for certain how my policy is taxed?

Prior to taking actions such as those listed above, you may wish to contact your tax advisor to find out for certain how your policy will be taxed. In some cases the tax consequences of these actions may be irreversible.

Policyholder Information Service

State Farm Life Insurance Company
Home Office:
Bloomington, Illinois 61710-0001

03911   Printed in U.S.A.   20030126

FIGURE 26.24

STATE FARM LIFE INSURANCE COMPANY

IMPORTANT INFORMATION ABOUT COVERAGE UNDER THE TEXAS LIFE, ACCIDENT, HEALTH AND HOSPITAL SERVICE INSURANCE GUARANTY ASSOCIATION

Texas law establishes a system, administered by the Texas Life, Accident, Health and Hospital Service Insurance Guaranty Association (the "Association"), to protect Texas Policyholders if their life or health insurance company fails. Only the policyholders of insurance companies which are members of the Association are eligible for this protection, which is subject to the terms, limitations, and conditions of the Association law. The law is found in the **Texas Insurance Code**, Chapter 463.)

It is possible that the Association may not cover your policy in full or in part due to statutory limitations.

Eligibility for Protection by the Association

When a member insurance company is found to be insolvent and placed under an order of liquidation by a court or designated as impaired by the Texas Commissioner of Insurance, the Association provides coverage to policyholders who are:
— Residents of Texas at that time **(irrespective of the policyholder's residency at policy issue)**
— Residents of other states, ONLY if the following conditions are met:
  1. The policyholder has a policy with a company based in Texas;
  2. The policyholder's state of residence has a similar guaranty association; and
  3. The policyholder is **not eligible** for coverage by the guaranty association of the policyholder's state of residence.

Limits of Protection by the Association

Accident, Accident and Health, or Health Insurance;
— For each individual covered under one or more policies: up to a total of $500,000 for basic hospital, medical-surgical, and major medical insurance, $300,000 for disability or long term care insurance, and $200,000 for other types of health insurance.
Life Insurance:
— Net cash surrender value or net cash withdrawal up to a total of $100,000 under one or more policies on any one life; or
— Death benefits up to a total of $300,000 under one or more policies on any one life; or
— Total benefits up to a total of $5,000,000 to any owner of multiple non-group life policies.
Individual Annuities:
— Present value of benefits up to a total of $100,000 under one or more contracts on any one life.
Group Annuities:
— Present value of allocated benefits up to a total of $100,000 on any one life; or
— Present value of unallocated benefits up to a total of $5,000,000 for one contractholder regardless of the number of contracts.
Aggregate Limit:
— $300,000 on any one life with the exception of $500,000 health insurance limit, the $5,000,000 multiple owner life insurance limit, and the $5,000,000 unallocated group annuity limit.

Insurance companies and agents are prohibited by law from using the existence of the Association for the purpose of sales, solicitation, or inducement to purchase any form of insurance. When you are selecting an insurance company, you should not rely on Association coverage.

Texas Life, Accident, Health, and Hospital Service Insurance Guaranty Association 6504 Bridge Point Parkway, Suite 450 Austin, Texas 78730 800-982-6362 www.txlifega.org	Texas Department of Insurance P.O. Box 149104 Austin, Texas 78714-9104 800-252-3439 www.tdi.state.tx.us

Appendix D

SAMPLE UNIVERSAL LIFE INSURANCE POLICY BASIC PLAN DESCRIPTION

Used with permission

FIGURE 27.1

STATE FARM LIFE INSURANCE COMPANY

HOME OFFICE, ONE STATE FARM PLAZA, BLOOMINGTON, ILLINOIS 61710

Insured

Age

Policy Number   _   ‾   6 /

Policy Date   March 26, 2009

Initial Basic Amount $50,000

This Policy is based on the Application and the payment of premiums, as specified in this Policy, while the Insured lives. State Farm Life Insurance Company will pay the Proceeds to the Beneficiary when due proof of the Insured's death is received.

30-Day Right to Examine the Policy. This Policy may be returned within 30 days of its receipt for a refund of all premiums paid. Return may be made to State Farm Life Insurance Company or one of Our agents. If returned, this Policy will be void from the Policy Date.

Read this Policy with care. This is a legal contract between the Owner and State Farm Life Insurance Company. In the event You need to contact someone about this Policy for any reason, please contact Your State Farm agent. If You have additional questions, You may contact Us at Our Home Office or (970) 395-5330 or www.statefarm.com.

Secretary

President

BASIC PLAN DESCRIPTION

Flexible premium adjustable life insurance. A death benefit is payable when the Insured dies. Flexible premiums are payable while the Insured is alive prior to the Policy Anniversary when the Insured is age 121. The Basic Plan is eligible for Annual Dividends.

FIGURE 27.2

CONTENTS

The Contract.	Assignment.
Transaction Delay.	Error in Age or Sex.
Annual Report.	Incontestability.
Minimum Values.	Limited Death Benefit.
Changes in Rates and Charges.	Conformity with Interstate Insurance Product
Annual Dividends.	Regulation Commission Standards.
Projection of Benefits and Values.	

Owner.	Change of Owner/Successor Owner.

Death Benefit.	Change in Basic Amount.
Death Benefit Options.	Change of Death Benefit Option.

Payment of Premiums.	Grace Period.
Premium Charge.	Reinstatement.
Rejection of Premium Payments for Tax Purposes.	

Account Value.	Monthly Expense Charge.
Monthly Deduction.	Monthly Issue Charge.
Cost of Insurance.	Interest Credited.
Monthly Cost of Insurance Rates.	Surrender Charge.

Surrender.	Withdrawals.

Loan.	Loan Interest.
Loan Value.	Loan Repayment.

Beneficiary Designation.	Methods of Payment.
Change of Beneficiary Designation.	Interest on Delayed Payment of Proceeds.
Order of Payment on the Insured's Death.	

The Application and any Riders and Endorsements follow page 16.

ICC07 08030   PAGE 2   20070515

FIGURE 27.3

PRINTED IN U.S.A.

IMPORTANT NOTICE

To obtain information or make a complaint:

You may call State Farm's toll-free telephone number for information or to make a complaint at:

1-800-252-1932

You may contact the Texas Department of Insurance to obtain information on companies, coverages, rights or complaints at:

1-800-252-3439

You may write the Texas Department of Insurance:

P.O. Box 149104
Austin, TX 78714-9104
Fax: (512) 475-1771
Web: http://www.tdi.state.tx.us
E-mail: ConsumerProtection@tdi.state.tx.us

PREMIUM OR CLAIM DISPUTES: Should you have a dispute concerning your premium or about a claim, you should contact the company first. If the dispute is not resolved, you may contact the Texas Department of Insurance.

ATTACH THIS NOTICE TO YOUR POLICY: This notice is for information only and does not become a part or condition of the attached document.

AVISO IMPORTANTE

Para obtener informacion o para someter una queja:

Usted puede llamar al numero de telefono gratis de State Farm's para informacion o para someter una queja al:

1-800-252-1932

Puede comunicarse con el Departamento de Seguros de Texas para obtener informacion acerca de companias, coberturas, derechos o quejas al:

1-800-252-3439

Puede escribir al Departamento de Seguros de Texas:

P.O. Box 149104
Austin, TX 78714-9104
Fax: (512) 475-1771
Web: http://www.tdi.state.tx.us
E-mail: ConsumerProtection@tdi.state.tx.us

DISPUTAS SOBRE PRIMAS O RECLAMOS: Si tiene una disputa concerniente a su prima o a un reclamo, debe comunicarse con la compania primero. Si no se resuelve la disputa, puede entonces comunicarse con el departamento (TDI).

UNA ESTE AVISO A SU POLIZA: Este aviso es solo para proposito de informacion y no se convierte en parte o condicion del documento adjunto.

FORM 8636366.1

20070301

FIGURE 27.4

IMPORTANT INFORMATION

In the event You need to contact someone about this Policy for any reason, please contact Your State Farm agent. If You have additional questions, You may contact Us at www.statefarm.com or the phone number shown on page 1.

If You have been unable to contact or obtain satisfaction from your State Farm agent or Us, You may contact the insurance supervisory official where this Policy was issued. The phone numbers are shown below:

Alaska	907-269-7900	Maryland	410-468-2090	Rhode Island	401-222-5466
Colorado	303-894-7499	Massachusetts	617-521-7794	South Carolina	803-737-6131
Georgia	404-656-2056	Michigan	517-373-0220	Tennessee	615-741-6007
Hawaii	808-586-2790	Minnesota	651-296-5769	Texas	512-463-6464
Idaho	208-334-4250	Nebraska	402-471-2201	Utah	801-538-3800
Indiana	317-232-2385	New Hampshire	603-271-2261	Vermont	802-828-3301
Iowa	515-281-5523	North Carolina	919-733-3058	Virginia	804-371-9694
Kansas	785-296-3071	Ohio	614-644-2658	Washington	360-725-7000
Kentucky	502-564-6027	Oklahoma	405-521-2828	West Virginia	304-558-3354
Louisiana	800-259-5300	Pennsylvania	717-783-0442	Wisconsin	800-236-8517
Maine	207-624-8401	Puerto Rico	787-722-8686	Wyoming	307-777-7401

When contacting Your State Farm agent, Us, or the insurance supervisory official, please have the Policy Number for this Policy available.

ICC07 07904

20090310

FIGURE 27.5

POLICY IDENTIFICATION

Insured   xP   Age

Policy Number   ___   Initial Basic Amount $50,000

Policy Date   March 26, 2009

Issue Date   April 27, 2009

SCHEDULE OF BENEFITS

Universal Life Basic Plan:
  Death Benefit Option 1 (Basic Amount includes the Account Value)
  Basic Amount: $50,000
  Class of Risk: Standard Male Non-Tobacco
  Basic Amount Minimum until the policy anniversary when the insured is age 55: $50,000
  Basic Amount Minimum on and after the policy anniversary when the insured is age
  55: $25,000
  Minimum Amount of Increase: $25,000
  Minimum Amount of Decrease: $10,000
  Minimum Withdrawal: $500

Riders:

Form Description	Insurance Amount	Benefit Period Ends	Monthly Charge Deductible
08251 Guaranteed Insurability Option	$25,000	In 2035	To 2035
Option Years: 2011, 2014, 2017, 2020, 2023, 2026, 2029, 2032, 2035.			
08206 Waiver of Monthly Deduction Class of Risk: Standard Male Non-Tobacco		In 2046	To 2046

SCHEDULE OF PREMIUMS

Initial Premium: $41.80
Planned Premium: $27.80
Payment Period: Monthly

Beginning	Total Premiums For Policy Year
March 26, 2009	$347.60
March 26, 2010	333.60

Continued on Next Page
Page 3

FIGURE 27.6

Continued from Page 3

INTEREST RATES

Guaranteed Interest Rate: 4%

CHARGES AND FEES

Deduction Date: 26th of each month

Maximum Premium Charge Percentage: 5%

Maximum Monthly Expense Charge in Policy Years 1-5: $8.00
Maximum Monthly Expense Charge in Policy Years 6 and later: $10.00

For the Initial Basic Amount, the Monthly Issue Charge in first 24 Policy Months
starting on the Policy Date:
    $.10 per $1000, subject to a maximum of $50.00 per month.
For each increase in Basic Amount, the Monthly Issue Charge in first 24 Policy Months
starting on the Effective Date of the increase:
    $.10 per $1000, each subject to a maximum of $50.00 per month.

ANNUAL DIVIDENDS

This Policy is eligible for annual dividends; however, we do not expect to pay dividends on
this Policy. Dividends are not guaranteed. See the Dividend Provision on page 7.

****

NOTE: The Planned Premium shown may not continue this Policy in force to the Policy
       Anniversary when the Insured is age 121 even if this amount is paid as scheduled. The
       period for which this Policy will continue will depend on (1) the amount, time, and
       frequency of premium payments, (2) changes in Premium Charge Percentage, (3) changes
       in the Basic Amount and Death Benefit Option, (4) changes in interest in excess of the
       Guaranteed Interest rate, (5) changes in Monthly deductions including Monthly Expense
       Charge and Monthly Issue Charge, and (6) withdrawals and Loans.

       This Policy may not qualify as life insurance under federal tax law after the Policy
       Anniversary when the Insured is age 100 and may be subject to adverse tax
       consequences. A tax advisor should be consulted before the Owner chooses to continue
       this Policy after the Policy Anniversary when the Insured is age 100.

****

ICC07 08030   Page 3 Continued   20090529

FIGURE 27.7

SCHEDULE OF SURRENDER CHARGES

Beginning Policy Year	Policy Month	Surrender Charge	Beginning Policy Year	Policy Month	Surrender Charge
1	1	$5.00	2	8	$100.00
1	2	10.00	2	9	105.00
1	3	15.00	2	10	110.00
1	4	20.00	2	11	115.00
1	5	25.00	2	12	120.00
1	6	30.00	3	1	120.00
1	7	35.00	4	1	120.00
1	8	40.00	5	1	120.00
1	9	45.00	6	1	120.00
1	10	50.00	7	1	108.00
1	11	55.00	8	1	96.00
1	12	60.00	9	1	84.00
2	1	65.00	10	1	72.00
2	2	70.00	11	1	60.00
2	3	75.00	12	1	48.00
2	4	80.00	13	1	36.00
2	5	85.00	14	1	24.00
2	6	90.00	15	1	12.00
2	7	95.00	16	1	0.00

Additional surrender charges will apply for each increase in Basic Amount for 15 years starting on the effective date of the increase.

COST OF INSURANCE RATES AND MONTHLY CHARGES

Maximum Monthly Cost of Insurance Rates
Per $1000

Class of Risk: Standard Male Non-Tobacco

Age	Rate	Age	Rate	Age	Rate	Age	Rate	Age	Rate
23	.0800	41	.1376	59	.7125	77	4.4247	95	27.0677
24	.0809	42	.1510	60	.7890	78	4.9534	96	29.0947
25	.0834	43	.1668	61	.8825	79	5.5501	97	31.3129
26	.0867	44	.1844	62	.9914	80	6.2211	98	33.7487
27	.0884	45	.2036	63	1.1105	81	6.9572	99	36.4325
28	.0867	46	.2228	64	1.2349	82	7.7445	100	39.0835
29	.0859	47	.2387	65	1.3645	83	8.6135	101	41.5109
30	.0850	48	.2512	66	1.4961	84	9.5913	102	44.1763
31	.0842	49	.2671	67	1.6339	85	10.6935	103	47.1103
32	.0850	50	.2880	68	1.7796	86	11.9242	104	50.3318
33	.0875	51	.3148	69	1.9435	87	13.2765	105	53.8699
34	.0892	52	.3475	70	2.1352	88	14.7403	106	57.8027
35	.0934	53	.3851	71	2.3686	89	16.3061	107	62.1940
36	.0976	54	.4329	72	2.6423	90	17.8976	108	67.1272
37	.1034	55	.4865	73	2.9318	91	19.4964	109	72.7010
38	.1109	56	.5419	74	3.2440	92	21.2072	110	79.0454
39	.1176	57	.5956	75	3.5855	93	23.0525	111-120	83.3333
40	.1268	58	.6494	76	3.9724	94	25.0443	121 & over	0.000

Continued on Next Page
Page 4

ICC07 08030   20090529

FIGURE 27.8

COST OF INSURANCE RATES AND MONTHLY CHARGES

Continued from Page 4

The Maximum Monthly Cost of Insurance Rates are based on the Insured's age last birthday at the start of the Policy Year, sex, and tobacco use as shown above. The Commissioners 2001 Standard Ordinary Nonsmoker Ultimate Age Last Birthday Mortality Table applies. Modifications are made if the Class of Risk is other than Standard.

Monthly Charges Per $1000 for Guaranteed Insurability Option

Age	Monthly Charge	Age	Monthly Charge	Age	Monthly Charge	Age	Monthly Charge
23	.06	30	.08	37	.13	44	.20
24	.07	31	.09	38	.14	45	.21
25	.07	32	.09	39	.15	46	.22
26	.07	33	.10	40	.16	47	.23
27	.07	34	.11	41	.17	48	.24
28	.07	35	.11	42	.18		
29	.08	36	.12	43	.19		

Monthly charges for this Rider are based on the Insured's age last birthday at the start of the Policy Year.

Monthly Charges Per $1 of Monthly Deductions for Waiver of Monthly Deduction

Class of Risk: Standard Male Non-Tobacco

Age	Monthly Charge	Age	Monthly Charge	Age	Monthly Charge	Age	Monthly Charge
23	.0192	33	.0312	43	.0644	53	.1598
24	.0202	34	.0340	44	.0682	54	.1790
25	.0212	35	.0375	45	.0739	55	.2060
26	.0216	36	.0410	46	.0805	56	.2288
27	.0222	37	.0445	47	.0900	57	.2534
28	.0232	38	.0480	48	.1015	58	.2843
29	.0243	39	.0515	49	.1129	59	.3589
30	.0254	40	.0550	50	.1231		
31	.0269	41	.0585	51	.1336		
32	.0289	42	.0618	52	.1448		

Monthly charges per $1 of monthly deduction are based on the Insured's age last birthday at the start of the Policy Year.

FIGURE 27.9

PRINTED IN U.S.A.

DEFINITIONS

We, Us, and **Our** refer to State Farm Life Insurance Company.

You and **Your** refer to the Owner.

Application. Includes any life insurance application, any application for change in this Policy, medical history, questionnaire, and other documents from You or any other person proposed for insurance which are made a part of this Policy.

Basic Amount. The Initial Basic Amount plus any Basic Amount Increases less any Basic Amount Decreases shown on page 3.

Basic Amount Minimum. Shown on page 3.

Benefit Period Ends. For any Rider, the coverage for the benefit extends to, but does not include, the Policy Anniversary in the year shown on page 3 under this heading.

Cash Surrender Value. The Cash Value less any Loan and accrued Loan Interest. This amount will not be less than zero.

Cash Value. The Account Value less any Surrender Charge. If this Policy is surrendered within 31 days after a Policy Anniversary, this amount will not decrease within that period except for any Withdrawals.

Class of Risk. The underwriting class of the person insured. A Class of Risk will be determined for the Initial Basic Amount and each Basic Amount Increase.

Code. The United States Internal Revenue Code, as amended from time to time.

Deduction Date. The Policy Date and each monthly anniversary of the Policy Date.

Dollars. Any money We pay, or which is paid to Us, must be in United States dollars.

Effective Date. Coverage starts on this date.

Initial Basic Amount. The amount of coverage on the Insured provided by the Basic Plan on the Policy Date shown on page 3.

Initial Net Premium. The Initial Premium less any Premium Charge.

Initial Premium. The amount shown on page 3 You must pay before this Policy becomes effective.

Insurance Amount. The amount of coverage on the Effective Date of each Rider shown under this heading on page 3. For the Insured, see the Death Benefit Options provision on page 9.

Issue Date. The date this Policy is issued shown on page 3.

Monthly Charge Deductible. A monthly charge for any Rider is deducted as part of the Monthly Deduction until the Policy Anniversary in the year shown on page 3 under the heading Benefit Period Ends.

Net Premium Payment. Your premium payment less any Premium Charge.

Officer. The president, a vice president, the secretary, or an assistant secretary of State Farm Life Insurance Company.

FIGURE 27.10

DEFINITIONS (CONTINUED)

Payee. On the Insured's death, the Beneficiaries shown in the Application, unless changed. If You surrender this Policy while the Insured is alive, the persons that You have named to receive the Cash Surrender Value. A Payee can be other than a natural person only if We agree.

Planned Premium. The premium amount shown on page 3 that You have chosen. This amount is for the payment period that You have chosen.

Policy Date. The Effective Date of this Policy shown on pages 1 and 3.

Policy Month, Year, or Anniversary. A policy month, year, or anniversary is measured from the Policy Date.

Proceeds. The amounts payable on the death of the Insured.

Request. A written request signed by the person making the Request. Such Request must be received by Us and be on Our request form; or if such Request is not on Our request form, it must include the information required by Our request form.

Rider. Any benefit, other than the Basic Plan, made a part of this Policy.

Successor Owner. May be named in the Application or later by Request if You are not the Insured.

GENERAL PROVISIONS

The Contract. This Policy contains the Basic Plan, any amendments, endorsements, any Riders, and a copy of the Application. A copy of any Application for a change to this Policy will be sent to You to be placed with this Policy. Such Applications become part of this Policy. This Policy is the entire contract. We have relied on the statements in the Application in issuing this Policy. We reserve the right to investigate the truth and completeness of those statements. In the absence of fraud, those statements are representations and not warranties. Only statements in the Application will be used to rescind this Policy or deny a claim within the time period specified in the Incontestability provision.

Only an Officer has the right to change this Policy. No agent has the authority to change this Policy or to waive any of its terms. All endorsements, amendments, and Riders must be signed by an Officer to be valid.

We may modify this Policy after We notify You to assure continued qualification of this Policy as a life insurance contract under any section of, regulation or ruling under, the Code as amended from time to time. If We modify this Policy, We will send You the appropriate endorsement to be placed with this Policy. Such endorsement is subject to regulatory approval. If any provision of this Policy conflicts with the law of a jurisdiction that governs this Policy, the provision is deemed to be amended to conform to such law.

Transaction Delay. Any payment from the Account Value or for a Loan will usually be made within 7 days of receipt of the Request for payment. We may defer payment of any Cash Surrender Value, withdrawal, or Loan for up to 6 months from the date We receive Your Request. However, a withdrawal or a Loan to pay a premium on other policies with Us will not be deferred.

If We defer any such payment for 30 days or more, We will pay interest in addition to such payment. Such interest accrues from the date the payment becomes payable to the date of payment at 2% per year or the interest rate and time required by law, if greater.

FIGURE 27.11

PRINTED IN U.S.A.

GENERAL PROVISIONS (CONTINUED)

Annual Report. Each year, We will send You a report. This report will show:
  (1) the Account Value, the Cash Surrender Value, any Loan and accrued Loan Interest, and the amount of the death benefit as of the date of the last report and this report and
  (2) any premiums paid, any deductions made, and any Withdrawals made since the last report.

Minimum Values. The Cash Values are at least as large as those required by the Interstate Insurance Product Regulation Commission, which has a statement of how these values are calculated. We base minimum Cash Values, Maximum Monthly Cost of Insurance Rates, and reserves on the Insured's age last birthday, sex and tobacco use, if applicable. The Guaranteed Interest Rate is shown on page 3. The mortality table used is shown on page 4. Modifications are made for each Class of Risk other than Standard.

Changes in Rates and Charges. Prior to the Policy Anniversary when the Insured is age 121, Monthly Cost of Insurance Rates, Monthly Charges for any additional insured's level term life insurance benefit rider, the Premium Charge Percentage, the Monthly Expense Charge, and the interest rate applicable to the Account Value can change at any time, subject to the limitations in this Policy. We will determine each based on future expectations as to investment earnings, mortality, expenses, and persistency.

Annual Dividends. We do not expect to pay dividends on this Policy; however, We may apportion and pay dividends each year. Any such dividends will be paid only at the end of a Policy Year. There is no right to a partial or prorated dividend prior to the end of a Policy Year.

You may choose to have Your dividend used under one of these Dividend Options:
  (1) Cash. We will pay it to You in cash.
  (2) Addition to Account Value. We will add it to the Account Value at the end of the Policy Year.

If You do not choose a Dividend Option on the Application or by Request or the Dividend Option chosen is not available, We will use Dividend Option 2. You may change the Dividend Option by Request. The change will apply to dividends paid after We receive Your Request.

Projection of Benefits and Values. If you send Us a Request, we will provide You with a projection of death benefits, account values, and cash surrender values each year. An additional projection can be provided if You send Us a Request. We may charge no more than a $25 fee for providing each additional projection.

Assignment. You may assign this Policy or any interest in it. We will recognize an Assignment only if it is in writing and filed with Us. We are not responsible for the validity or effect of any Assignment. An Assignment may limit the interest of any Beneficiary.

FIGURE 27.12

GENERAL PROVISIONS (CONTINUED)

Error in Age or Sex. If the Insured's date of birth or sex is not as stated in the Application, We will adjust each benefit on the Insured to the benefit payable had the Insured's age and sex been stated correctly. Such adjustment will be based on the ratio of the correct deduction for the Cost of Insurance or Monthly Charge for the most recent Deduction Date for that benefit to the deduction for the Cost of Insurance or Monthly Charge that was made. For the Basic Plan, the adjustment is made to the amount of insurance less the Account Value.

Incontestability. We will not contest the Initial Basic Amount after the Basic Plan has been in force during the Insured's lifetime for 2 years from the Policy Date. We will not contest any Basic Amount Increase or reinstatement after it has been in force during the lifetime of the Insured for 2 years from the Effective Date of the Basic Amount Increase or reinstatement. We will not contest a Basic Amount Increase due to a change to Death Benefit Option 1. Any contest will be based on statements made in the Application that are material to the risk or the hazard assumed by Us. Each Rider has its own incontestability provision.

Limited Death Benefit. If the Insured dies by suicide while sane or insane within 2 years from the Policy Date, the Initial Basic Amount will not be paid. The Proceeds in this case will be limited to the premiums paid on the Basic Plan less any Loan, accrued Loan Interest, any withdrawals from the Account Value, and any dividends paid on the Basic Plan. Any Basic Amount Increase or amount reinstated will not be paid if the Insured's death results from suicide while sane or insane within 2 years from the Effective Date of such Basic Amount Increase or reinstatement. The Proceeds of the Basic Amount Increase will be limited to the Monthly Deductions for the Basic Amount Increase. This does not apply to a Basic Amount Increase due to a change to Death Benefit Option 1. The Proceeds of a reinstated policy will be limited to the premiums paid on the Basic Plan since reinstatement less any Loan, accrued Loan Interest, any withdrawals from the Account Value, and any dividends paid on the Basic Plan. Each Rider has its own limited death benefit provision.

Conformity with Interstate Insurance Product Regulation Commission Standards. This Policy was approved under the authority of the Interstate Insurance Product Regulation Commission and issued under the Commission standards. Any provision in this Policy that on the provision effective date is in conflict with Interstate Insurance Product Regulation Commission standards for this type of product is hereby amended to conform to the Interstate Insurance Product Regulation Commission standards for this type of product as of the provision's effective date.

OWNERSHIP PROVISIONS

Owner. The Owner is as named in the Application, unless changed. You may exercise any policy provision only by Request and while the Insured is alive, subject to the rights of any assignee that We have on record and to the rights of any irrevocably designated Beneficiary. The Successor Owner will become the Owner of this Policy if You die while this Policy is in force.

Change of Owner/Successor Owner. You may change the Owner or Successor Owner by Request while the Insured is alive and this Policy is in force. The change will take effect the date You sign the Request, but the change will not affect any action We have taken before We receive the Request. A change of Owner or Successor Owner does not change the Beneficiary Designation.

FIGURE 27.13

DEATH BENEFIT AND DEATH BENEFIT OPTIONS PROVISIONS

Death Benefit. The amount of Death Benefit is an amount of insurance based on the Death Benefit Option shown on page 3 plus any insurance amounts payable under any Riders on the Insured and the part of the Cost of Insurance for the part of the Policy Month beyond the Insured's death less any Loan, accrued Loan Interest, and, if the Insured dies during the Grace Period, the Monthly Deductions from the start of the Grace Period.

Death Benefit Options. There are two Death Benefit Options. If You do not choose an option, We will use Option 2. The Account Value on the date of death is used in determining the amount of insurance. If the Death Benefit Option is Option 2 on the Policy Anniversary when the Insured is age 121, the Death Benefit Option will automatically be changed to Option 1.

Option 1. The amount of insurance will be the greater of:
(1) the Basic Amount plus Net Premium Payment received since the last Deduction Date plus interest earned on that Net Premium Payment or
(2) a percentage of the Account Value based on the Insured's age at the start of the current Policy Year, as indicated in the table shown below.

Option 2. The amount of insurance will be the greater of:
(1) the Basic Amount plus the Account Value or
(2) a percentage of the Account Value based on the Insured's age at the start of the current Policy Year, as indicated in the table shown below.

Percentage of Account Value Table							
Age	Percentage	Age	Percentage	Age	Percentage	Age	Percentage
0-40	250%						
41	243%	51	178%	61	128%	71	113%
42	236%	52	171%	62	126%	72	111%
43	229%	53	164%	63	124%	73	109%
44	222%	54	157%	64	122%	74	107%
45	215%	55	150%	65	120%	75-90	105%
46	209%	56	146%	66	119%	91	104%
47	203%	57	142%	67	118%	92	103%
48	197%	58	138%	68	117%	93	102%
49	191%	59	134%	69	116%	94	101%
50	185%	60	130%	70	115%	95 & up	100%

The percentages in the table are those in effect on the Policy Date. We reserve the right to change the percentages if the table becomes inconsistent with any section of, regulation or ruling under, the Code, as amended from time to time.

FIGURE 27.14

> ### DEATH BENEFIT AND DEATH BENEFIT OPTIONS PROVISIONS (CONTINUED)

Change in Basic Amount. You may change the Basic Amount once each Policy Year by Request. The minimum amount of change is shown on page 3. For any change in Basic Amount, We will send You revised pages 3 and 4 to be placed with this Policy.

For a Basic Amount Increase, an Application must be completed, evidence of insurability satisfactory to Us must be furnished, and there must be enough Cash Surrender Value to make a Monthly Deduction which includes the Cost of Insurance for the Basic Amount Increase. No Basic Amount Increase will be allowed after the Policy Anniversary when the Insured is age 80. The revised pages 3 and 4 will show the amount of the Basic Amount Increase, its Effective Date, Maximum Monthly Cost of Insurance Rates for the Basic Amount Increase if the Class of Risk for the Basic Amount Increase is different, the additional Surrender Charges, and any change in Planned Premium.

For a Basic Amount Decrease, the Basic Amount remaining after the decrease cannot be less than the Basic Amount Minimum. We reserve the right to not accept a Request for a Basic Amount Decrease if such decrease could result in this Policy being disqualified as a life insurance contract under any section of, regulation or ruling under, the Code, as amended from time to time. Any decrease will first be used to reduce the most recent Basic Amount Increase. Then, the next most recent Basic Amount Increases will be reduced. Finally, the Initial Basic Amount will be reduced. The revised pages 3 and 4 will show the amount of decrease, its Effective Date, and any change in Planned Premium and Surrender Charges. The Basic Amount Decrease will take effect on the date We receive the Request.

Change of Death Benefit Option. You may change a Death Benefit Option once each Policy Year by Request prior to the Policy Anniversary when the Insured is age 121. The change will take effect the date We receive Your Request. For a change in Death Benefit Option, We will send You a revised page 3 to be placed with this Policy. The revised page will show the new Death Benefit Option and the Effective Date of the change.

If the change is to Death Benefit Option 1, the Basic Amount will be increased by the amount of Account Value on the Effective Date of the change. We reserve the right to not accept Your Request for a change to Death Benefit Option 1 if such change could result in this Policy being disqualified as a life insurance contract under any section of, regulation or ruling under, the Code, as amended from time to time.

If the change is to Death Benefit Option 2, the Basic Amount will be decreased by the Account Value on the Effective Date of the decrease.

> ### PREMIUM PROVISIONS

Payment of Premiums. You may pay premiums at Our Home Office or to one of Our agents. We will give You a receipt signed by one of Our Officers, if You request one. The Initial Premium, shown on page 3, is due on the Policy Date. All other premiums may be paid in any amount and at any time prior to the Policy Anniversary when the Insured is age 121 if:

    (1)   the amount is at least $25;

    (2)   in a Policy Year, the total premiums, excluding the Initial Premium, do not exceed without Our consent, the total Planned Premiums for a Policy Year; and

    (3)   no premium or part of any premium paid would be rejected for tax purposes.

On and after the Policy Anniversary when the Insured is age 121, no premium will be accepted other than premiums required to keep this Policy in force under the Grace Period.

FIGURE 27.15

PRINTED IN U.S.A.

PREMIUM PROVISIONS (CONTINUED)

Premium Charge. The Premium Charge Percentage times the amount of the premium received is the Premium Charge. The actual premium charge percentage will be determined as described in the Changes in Rates and Charges provision. Such percentage cannot exceed the Maximum Premium Charge Percentage shown on page 3.

Rejection of Premium Payments for Tax Purposes. We reserve the right to reject any premium or part of any premium paid if such premium amount would result in this Policy being disqualified as a life insurance contract under any section of, regulation or ruling under, the Code, as amended from time to time. We will promptly return any rejected premium. No Premium Charge will be deducted from the rejected premium. No premium will be rejected if it is necessary to continue coverage.

Grace Period. A Grace Period is 61 days and starts on a Deduction Date as specified below. We will mail a notice to You and to any assignee of record at least 31 days prior to the end of the Grace Period. The notice will state:
  (1)   this Policy will remain in force until the end of the Grace Period,
  (2)   the date the Grace Period ends, and
  (3)   this Policy will terminate and lapse without value unless the required amount is paid prior to that date.
Prior to the Policy Anniversary when the Insured is age 121, the Grace Period will start on any Deduction Date if the Cash Surrender Value is not enough to cover the Monthly Deduction on that Deduction Date. On and after the Policy Anniversary when the Insured is age 121, the Grace Period will start on any Deduction Date if the Account Value is less than the Loan plus accrued Loan Interest. If the Grace Period ends prior to the Policy Anniversary when the Insured is age 121, the required amount is a premium large enough to provide an increase in the Cash Surrender Value to cover the Monthly Deductions for the Grace Period and any increase in the Surrender Charges. If the Grace Period ends on or after the Policy Anniversary when the Insured is age 121, the required amount must be a payment large enough to cover the Loan plus accrued Loan Interest that is in excess of the Account Value at the end of the Grace Period. Any premium payment sent by U.S. mail with a postmark before the end of the Grace Period will be considered paid during the Grace Period.

Reinstatement. If this Policy is terminated at the end of the Grace Period, You may apply to reinstate it within 5 years after lapse. You must give Us proof of the Insured's insurability that is satisfactory to Us. You must pay an amount as specified below:
  (1)   If reinstatement is applied for prior to the Policy Anniversary when the Insured is age 121, the premium must be large enough to provide an increase in the Policy Account Value over the amount We reinstate so that the Cash Surrender Value will cover the Monthly Deductions for the Grace Period and keep this Policy in force for 2 months following the date the reinstatement takes effect.
  (2)   If reinstatement is applied for on or after the Policy Anniversary when the Insured is age 121, that amount must be large enough to cover the accrued Loan Interest in excess of the Account Value less the Loan on the date the reinstatement takes effect.
Reinstatement will take effect on the date We approve the Application for reinstatement. The amount of any Loan Amount on the date of lapse will be reinstated when reinstatement takes effect. No interest from the date of lapse to date of reinstatement is included in that amount. We will reinstate the amount of the Policy Account Value equal to the Policy Account Value on the date of lapse less any decrease in the amount of any Surrender Charge between the date of lapse and the date of reinstatement.

FIGURE 27.16

GUARANTEED VALUES PROVISIONS

Account Value. The Account Value on the Policy Date is the Initial Net Premium less the Monthly Deduction for the first Policy Month.

The Account Value on any Deduction Date after the Policy Date is the Account Value on the prior Deduction Date:
(1) plus any Net Premium Payments received since the prior Deduction Date,
(2) less the deduction for the Cost of Insurance and the Monthly Issue Charge for any Basic Amount Increase and the Monthly Charges for any Riders that became effective since the prior Deduction Date,
(3) less any Withdrawals since the prior Deduction Date,
(4) less the current Monthly Deduction,
(5) plus any dividend paid and added to the Account Value on the current Deduction Date, and
(6) plus any interest accrued since the prior Deduction Date.
The Account Value on any other date is the Account Value on the prior Deduction Date:
(1) plus any Net Premium Payments received since the prior Deduction Date,
(2) less the deduction for the Cost of Insurance and the Monthly Issue Charge for any Basic Amount Increase and the Monthly Charges for any Riders that became effective since the prior Deduction Date,
(3) less any Withdrawals since the prior Deduction Date, and
(4) plus any interest accrued since the prior Deduction Date.

Monthly Deduction. This deduction is made on each Deduction Date prior to the Policy Anniversary when the Insured is age 121, whether or not premiums are paid, as long as the Cash Surrender Value is enough to cover that Monthly Deduction. Each Monthly Deduction includes:
(1) the Cost of Insurance,
(2) the Monthly Charges for any Riders,
(3) the Monthly Expense Charge, and
(4) the Monthly Issue Charge, if applicable.
No Monthly Deduction will be made on or after the Policy Anniversary when the Insured is age 121.

Cost of Insurance. This cost is calculated each Policy Month prior to the Policy Anniversary when the Insured is age 121. The cost is determined separately for the Initial Basic Amount and each Basic Amount Increase. The Cost of Insurance is the Monthly Cost of Insurance Rate times the difference between **(1)** and **(2)** where:

>**(1)** is the amount of insurance attributable to the Initial Basic Amount of Insurance or Basic Amount Increase, as applicable, on the Deduction Date at the start of the month divided by 1.0032737, and
>**(2)** is the Account Value attributable to the Initial Basic Amount or Basic Amount Increase, as applicable, on the Deduction Date at the start of the month after the deduction of the part of the Monthly Deduction that does not include the Cost of Insurance and the Monthly Charge for any waiver of monthly deduction benefit rider.

Until the Account Value exceeds the Initial Basic Amount, the Account Value is part of the Initial Basic Amount. Once the Account Value exceeds that amount, if there have been any Basic Amount Increases, the excess will be part of the increases in the order in which the increases occurred.

Monthly Cost of Insurance Rates. These rates for each Policy Year are based on the Insured's age on the Policy Anniversary, sex, and applicable Class of Risk. A Class of Risk will be determined for the Initial Basic Amount and for each Basic Amount Increase. The rates shown on page 4 are the Maximum Monthly Cost of Insurance Rates for the Initial Basic Amount. Maximum Monthly Cost of Insurance Rates will be provided for each Basic Amount Increase. The actual Monthly Cost of Insurance Rates will be determined as described in the Changes in Rates and Charges provision. Such rates cannot exceed the Maximum Monthly Cost of Insurance Rates and cannot be changed more than once a calendar year.

FIGURE 27.17

PRINTED IN U.S.A.

GUARANTEED VALUES PROVISIONS (CONTINUED)

Monthly Expense Charge. The Maximum Monthly Expense Charge is shown on page 3. The actual Monthly Expense Charge will be determined as described in the Changes in Rates and Charges provision. The actual Monthly Expense Charge cannot exceed the maximum.

Monthly Issue Charge. The Monthly Issue Charge is shown on page 3. A Monthly Issue Charge is determined separately for the Initial Basic Amount and each Basic Amount Increase.

Interest Credited. We guarantee to credit interest to the Account Value. The actual effective annual rate will be determined as described in the Changes in Rates and Charges provision. Such rate will not be less than the Guaranteed Interest Rate shown on page 3. The rate applied to the Account Value up to the amount of any Loan may differ from the rate applied to the Account Value in excess of the amount of the Loan.

On and after the Policy Anniversary when the Insured is age 121, the Guaranteed Interest Rate will be credited to the Account Value.

Surrender Charge. The Schedule of Surrender Charges is shown on page 4. For each Basic Amount Increase, additional Surrender Charges will apply. The revised page 4 will show a revised Schedule of Surrender Charges which includes those additional charges.

Upon reinstatement, the Surrender Charges will be adjusted for any Surrender Charge deducted at the time of lapse. The revised page 4 will show a schedule of the adjusted Surrender Charges.

FIGURE 27.18

SURRENDER AND WITHDRAWAL PROVISIONS

Surrender. You may surrender this Policy at any time by Request. This Policy will terminate on the date We receive Your Request or later date if You so request it. We will pay You the Cash Surrender Value as of the date coverage ceases plus the Monthly Deduction for the part of the Policy Month beyond that date. See the Surrender Charge provision regarding the Surrender Charges applicable.

Withdrawals. You may withdraw part of the Cash Surrender Value by Request at any time while this Policy is in force. No more than 4 Withdrawals can be made in any Policy Year. The Minimum Withdrawal Amount is shown on page 3. The withdrawal is effective on the date We receive Your Request or a later date, if You so request it. As of that date, the Account Value is reduced by the amount of the withdrawal.

If You request a Basic Amount Decrease or a Change in Death Benefit Option at the same time You request a withdrawal, We will process the withdrawal before processing either the Basic Amount Decrease or the Change in Death Benefit Option.

If Death Benefit Option 1 is in effect, then the Basic Amount will be reduced by the amount of the withdrawal. The effective date of the reduction will be the date of the withdrawal. The reduction will be made as if a Basic Amount Decrease had been requested.

We reserve the right to reject Your Request for a withdrawal if Your Request would reduce the Basic Amount below the Basic Amount Minimum. We reserve the right to reject Your Request for a withdrawal if the withdrawal would result in this Policy being disqualified as a life insurance contract under any section of, ruling or regulation under, the Code, as amended from time to time.

POLICY LOAN PROVISIONS

Loan. You may borrow against this Policy at any time while this Policy is in force. This Policy is the sole security for such Loan. You may borrow the Loan Value less any existing Loan and accrued Loan Interest and Monthly Deductions for the next 2 months. If Your unpaid Loan plus accrued Loan Interest exceeds the Loan Value on any Deduction Date, the Grace Period provision will apply.

Loan Value. The Loan Value is the Cash Value of this Policy.

Loan Interest. Interest accrues and is payable each day at a rate of 8% a year in Policy Years 1-10, 7% a year in Policy Years 11-20, and 6.5% a year in Policy Years 21 and later. Any interest not paid is added to the Loan on each Policy Anniversary.

Loan Repayment. You may repay all or part of a Loan at any time before the Insured dies or this Policy is surrendered or terminated. Prior to the Policy Anniversary when the Insured is age 121, You must tell Us that a payment is for repayment or We will assume it is a premium payment. If this Policy has a Loan on or after the Policy Anniversary when the Insured is age 121, only a repayment of a Loan will be accepted.

FIGURE 27.19

PAYMENT OF BENEFITS PROVISIONS

Beneficiary Designation. This is as shown in the Application, unless You have made a change by Request. It includes the name of the Beneficiary. If You name "estate" as a Beneficiary, it means the executors or administrators of the last survivor of You and all Beneficiaries. If You name "children" of a person as a Beneficiary, only children born to or legally adopted by that person will be included. We may rely on an affidavit as to the ages, names, and other facts about all Beneficiaries. We will incur no liability if We act on such affidavit.

Change of Beneficiary Designation. You may make a change by Request while the Insured is alive and this Policy is in force. The change will take effect on the date Your Request is signed, but the change will not affect any action We have taken before We receive the Request. To change a named irrevocable Beneficiary, the Request must include a written statement from the irrevocable Beneficiary who is being changed.

Order of Payment on the Insured's Death. When the Insured dies, We will make payment in equal shares to the primary Beneficiaries living when payment is made. If the last primary dies, We will make payment in equal shares to the successor Beneficiaries living when payment is made. If, at any time, no Beneficiary is living, We will make a one sum payment to You, if living when payment is made. Otherwise, We will make a one sum payment to the estate of the last survivor of You and all Beneficiaries. You may change this order of payment by Request while the Insured is alive.

Methods of Payment. We will pay the Proceeds or the Cash Surrender Value under the One Sum Method unless You choose another method then available. If the Payee is other than a natural person, We will make payment under the One Sum Method.

All payment intervals are measured from the date this Policy is surrendered or from the date the Insured dies.

After the Insured's death, a Payee who has the right to make a withdrawal may change the method of payment. This Payee may also appoint a successor payee. The successor payee may be the Payee's estate.

We must receive a Request for payment of the Proceeds and due proof of the Insured's death. Due proof of the Insured's death is evidence satisfactory to Us:
  (1) to establish the date and fact of the Insured's death;
  (2) to permit Us to determine whether Proceeds are payable; and
  (3) such other items and information as may be necessary for Us to comply with laws and regulations related to payment of the claim or administration of the business of insurance.

  Method 1 (One Sum Method). We will pay the Cash Surrender Value or the Proceeds in one sum. Interest will be paid from the date of the Insured's death to the date of payment. The interest rate will be the greater of 2% a year or the interest rate applicable to Proceeds left on deposit with Us.

  Method 2 (Other Method). Payment by any other method may be made if We agree.

Interest on Delayed Payment of Proceeds. Additional interest at the rate of 10% a year will be credited to Proceeds if the payment of Proceeds is delayed more than 31 calendar days after the earliest of the following dates:
  (1) the date We receive due proof of the Insured's death;
  (2) the date We receive sufficient information to determine Our liability, the extent of the liability, and the appropriate Beneficiary legally entitled to the Proceeds; and
  (3) the date legal impediments to payment of the Proceeds that depend on the action of parties other than Us are resolved and sufficient evidence of the same is provided to Us. Legal impediments to payment include, but are not limited to, (a) the establishment of guardianships and conservatorships; (b) the appointment and qualification of trustees, executors and administrators; and (c) the submission of information required to satisfy state and federal reporting requirements.

FIGURE 27.20

FIGURE 27.21

GUARANTEED INSURABILITY OPTION BENEFIT RIDER

General. This Rider is part of this Policy. It is based on the Application for this Rider and the deduction of the Monthly Charges for this Rider. The Monthly Charges for this Rider are shown per $1000 on page 4 of this Policy and are not subject to change. Only certain policy provisions are a part of this Rider. They are "Definitions," "Ownership," "Payment of Benefits," "Grace Period," "Reinstatement," "Monthly Deduction," "The Contract," "Assignment," and "Error in Age or Sex." The provisions of this Rider apply in lieu of any other Policy provisions to the contrary. This Rider does not increase the Cash Value or Loan Value of this Policy.

Guaranteed Insurability Option Benefit. Option Years for this Benefit are shown on page 3 of this Policy. An Option Date is the Policy Anniversary in an Option Year. On each Option Date before termination, You may increase the Basic Amount by Request. We must receive Your Request for the Basic Amount Increase within the 60-day period that ends on the Option Date. No evidence of insurability is required. The Basic Amount Increase will become effective on the Option Date if the Insured is alive on the Option Date.

The Basic Amount Increase will be subject to the following conditions on the Option Date:
  (1) The amount of Basic Amount Increase must be at least $25,000 but can be no more than the amount for this Rider shown under the heading Insurance Amount on page 3 of this Policy.
  (2) The monthly cost of insurance rates for the Basic Amount Increase will be based on the Insured's attained age, sex, and standard class of risk then available.
  (3) All limitations that apply to this Policy on this Effective Date of this Rider will apply to the Basic Amount Increase. Any limitations that We place on such policies then being issued will apply to the Basic Amount Increase.
  (4) We will not contest the Basic Amount Increase after this Rider has been in force during the lifetime of the Insured for 2 years from the Effective Date of this Rider.
  (5) If the waiver of monthly deduction benefit is then a part of this Policy and a Monthly Deduction is then being waived, the Monthly Deduction for the Basic Amount Increase will be waived while the Insured's total disability continues.

There is a 90-day period of term life insurance on the Insured. It starts when a Named Event occurs. A Named Event is:
  (1) the Insured's marriage or legally-sanctioned civil union or domestic partnership,
  (2) a live birth of a child of the Insured, or
  (3) the effective date of a legal adoption of a child by the Insured.
The term life insurance provided is equal to the initial amount of this Rider. If a multiple birth occurs, this amount is multiplied by the number of live children born at that time. The amount will be paid when due proof is received that a Named Event occurred and the Insured died within the 90-day period and before this Rider terminated. The amount will be paid as part of the Proceeds.

Advance of Option Date. When such term insurance is in effect, the next available Option Date may be advanced to the day after the end of the 90-day period. The amount of the Basic Amount Increase can be no more than the amount of term insurance then provided. If a Basic Amount Increase becomes effective, the Option Date that is advanced will be canceled. To advance the Option Date, We must receive due proof that a Named Event occurred.

Termination. This Rider will terminate on the Policy Anniversary shown under the heading Benefit Period Ends shown on page 3 of this Policy. We will terminate this Rider before that date when this Policy is terminated by surrender or lapse.

You may terminate this Rider by Request. This Rider will terminate the date We receive Your Request. We will revise pages 3 and 4 of this Policy to show this change.

ICC08 08251

20080415

FIGURE 27.22

GUARANTEED INSURABILITY OPTION BENEFIT RIDER (CONTINUED)

Incontestability. We will not contest this Rider after it has been in force during the lifetime of the Insured for 2 years from the Effective Date of this Rider.

Limited Death Benefit. If the Insured dies by suicide while sane or insane within 2 years from the Effective Date of this Rider, the Benefit will be limited to the charges paid for this Rider.

Effective Date of This Rider. This is the Policy Date unless a different date for this Rider is shown on page 3 of this Policy.

State Farm Life Insurance Company

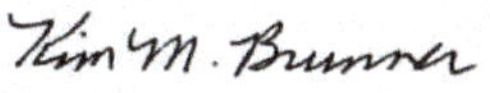

Kim M. Brunner
Secretary

Edward B Rust Jr.
President

FIGURE 27.23

PRINTED IN U.S.A.

WAIVER OF MONTHLY DEDUCTION BENEFIT RIDER

General. This Rider is part of this Policy. It is based on the Application for this Rider and the deduction of the Monthly Charges for this Rider. Only certain policy provisions are a part of this Rider. They are "Definitions," "Ownership," "Death Benefit and Death Benefit Options," "Grace Period," "Reinstatement," "Monthly Deduction," "The Contract," "Assignment," and "Error in Age or Sex." The provisions of this Rider apply in lieu of any other Policy provisions to the contrary. This Rider does not increase Cash Value or Loan Value of this Policy.

Monthly Charge for This Rider. The Monthly Charge is (1) times (2) where:
    (1) is the total Monthly Deduction to which this benefit applies before the Monthly Charge for this Rider is added, and
    (2) is the Monthly Charge for this Rider per dollar of Monthly Deduction.
The Monthly Charges per dollar of Monthly Deduction are shown on page 4.

Waiver of Monthly Deduction Benefit. We will waive Monthly Deductions for this Policy as defined below if the Insured becomes totally disabled while this Rider is in force and such Total Disability has existed for 6 continuous months during the lifetime of the Insured. We will waive those Monthly Deductions until the Policy Anniversary when the Insured is age 65 as long as the Total Disability continues. If the Insured is totally disabled as defined below on the Policy Anniversary when the Insured is age 65, we will waive all future Monthly Deductions. We will only waive Monthly Deductions on Deduction Dates on and after Total Disability starts. Any Monthly Deductions made after the Total Disability starts will be added to the Account Value, with interest; however, no Monthly Deduction will be included which was deductible more than one year prior to the date We receive notice of the claim. If Death Benefit Option 1 is in effect, it will be automatically changed to Death Benefit Option 2. The change in Death Benefit Option will be effective the date We start to waive Monthly Deductions. On the Policy Anniversary when the Insured is age 121, the Death Benefit Option will be changed to Death Benefit Option 1.

Any increase in the Surrender Charges that would occur while the Total Disability continues will be waived.

A recurrence of a Total Disability for which We had been waiving Monthly Deductions will be deemed a continuation of the prior period of Total Disability if the recurrence:
    (1)   results from the same injury or disease that caused the previous Total Disability;
    (2)   starts within 6 months of the date the previous Total Disability ended; and
    (3)   starts while this Rider is still in force.
Such recurrent Total Disability will not be subject to a new requirement that the Total Disability must first exist for 6 continuous months during the Insured's lifetime.

While Monthly Deductions are waived, all benefits provided under this Policy continue in force.

Total Disability Defined. Total Disability is a condition caused by injury or disease. During the first 24 months after Total Disability starts, this condition must prevent the Insured from performing substantially all of the work of the Insured's regular occupation. After the first 24 months after Total Disability starts, the condition must prevent the Insured from performing substantially all of the work in any occupation for which the Insured is, or becomes, reasonably qualified based upon education, training, or experience. The Insured's total and irrecoverable loss, caused by injury or disease, of any of the following will be considered Total Disability even if the Insured is able to work:
    (1)   sight in both eyes.
    (2)   use of both hands.
    (3)   use of both feet.
    (4)   use of one hand and one foot.

ICC07 08206

20071201

FIGURE 27.24

WAIVER OF MONTHLY DEDUCTION BENEFIT RIDER (CONTINUED)

Disabilities Not Covered. We will not waive Monthly Deductions if Total Disability:
(1)   starts before the Effective Date of this Rider unless such disability was disclosed in the Application,
(2)   starts before the Policy Anniversary when the Insured is age 5,
(3)   results from an intended self-injury, or
(4)   results from any act due to war whether or not the Insured is in the military service. "War" means declared or undeclared war or conflict involving the armed forces of one or more countries, governments, or international organizations.

Notice and Proof of Total Disability. We must receive notice of a claim and due proof of Total Disability while the Insured is alive and totally disabled. If this is not done, You should submit such notice and proof as soon as reasonably possible. We may also require You to submit proof of the Insured's continuing Total Disability at reasonable intervals. If You do not submit proof when We require it, no further Monthly Deductions will be waived. We will not require proof more than once a year after the Total Disability has lasted more than 2 years. We will not require proof after the Policy Anniversary when the Insured is age 65.

Premium Payments. If the Insured's Total Disability starts during a Grace Period, before We will approve a claim, a premium must be paid which is large enough to cover the Monthly Deductions plus any increase in the Surrender Charge from the start of the Grace Period through the Policy Month in which Total Disability starts.

Premiums, sufficient to keep this Policy in force until We approve the claim, are payable.

Termination. This Rider will terminate on the Policy Anniversary shown on page 3 under Benefit Period Ends. We will terminate this Rider before that date when this Policy terminates by surrender or lapse or by Your Request.

You may terminate this Rider by Request. This Rider will terminate the date We receive Your Request. We will revise pages 3 and 4 of this Policy to show this change.

Termination will not affect any claim for Total Disability which starts before termination.

Incontestability. We will not contest this Rider after it has been in force during the lifetime of the Insured for 2 years from the Effective Date of this Rider unless the Insured becomes totally disabled within that period.

Effective Date of This Rider. This is the Policy Date unless a different date for this Rider is shown on page 3.

State Farm Life Insurance Company

Kim M. Brunner

Secretary

Edward B. Rust Jr.

President

ICC07 08206

20071201

FIGURE 27.25

BASIC PLAN DESCRIPTION

Flexible premium adjustable life insurance. A death benefit is payable when the Insured dies. Flexible premiums are payable while the Insured is alive prior to the Policy Anniversary when the Insured is age 121. The Basic Plan is eligible for Annual Dividends.

ICC07 08030

20070515

FIGURE 27.26

LIFE INSURANCE BUYER'S GUIDE

This guide can help you when you shop for life insurance. It discusses how to:

– Find a Policy That Meets Your Needs and Fits Your Budget

– Decide How Much Insurance You Need

– Make Informed Decisions When You Buy a Policy

Prepared by the National Association of Insurance Commissioners

The National Association of Insurance Commissioners is an association of state insurance regulatory officials. This association helps the various insurance departments to coordinate insurance laws for the benefit of all consumers.

Reprinted by
State Farm Life Insurance Company
Home Office:
Bloomington, Illinois 61710-0001

03900.1 PAGE 1 20080222

FIGURE 27.27

IMPORTANT THINGS TO CONSIDER

1. Review your own insurance needs and circumstances. Choose the kind of policy that has benefits that most closely fit your needs. Ask an agent or company to help you.

2. Be sure that you can handle premium payments. Can you afford the initial premium? If the premium increases later and you still need insurance, can you still afford it?

3. Don't sign an insurance application until you review it carefully to be sure all the answers are complete and accurate.

4. Don't buy life insurance unless you intend to stick with your plan. It may be very costly if you quit during the early years of the policy.

5. Don't drop one policy and buy another without a thorough study of the new policy and the one you have now. Replacing your insurance may be costly.

6. Read your policy carefully. Ask your agent or company about anything that is not clear to you.

7. Review your life insurance program with your agent or company every few years to keep up with changes in your income and your needs.

Buying Life Insurance

When you buy life insurance, you want coverage that fits your needs.

First, decide how much you need–and for how long–and what you can afford to pay. Keep in mind the major reason you buy life insurance is to cover the financial effects of unexpected or untimely death. Life insurance can also be one of many ways you plan for the future.

Next, learn what kinds of policies will meet your needs and pick the one that best suits you.

Then, choose the combination of policy premium and benefits that emphasizes protection in case of early death, or benefits in case of long life, or a combination of both.

It makes good sense to ask a life insurance agent or company to help you. An agent can help you review your insurance needs and give you information about the available policies. If one kind of policy doesn't seem to fit your needs, ask about others.

This guide provides only basic information. You can get more facts from a life insurance agent or company or from your public library.

What About the Policy You Have Now?

If you are thinking about dropping a life insurance policy, here are some things you should consider:

-- If you decide to replace your policy, don't cancel your old policy until you have received the new one. You then have a minimum period to review your new policy and decide if it is what you wanted.

-- It may be costly to replace a policy. Much of what you paid in the early years of the policy you have now, paid for the company's cost of selling and issuing the policy. You may pay this type of cost again if you buy a new policy.

-- Ask your tax advisor if dropping your policy could affect your income taxes.

-- If you are older or your health has changed, premiums for the new policy will often be higher. You will not be able to buy a new policy if you are not insurable.

FIGURE 27.28

- You may have valuable rights and benefits in the policy you now have that are not in the new one.

- If the policy you have now no longer meets your needs, you may not have to replace it. You might be able to change your policy or add to it to get the coverage or benefits you now want.

- At least in the beginning, a policy may pay no benefits for some causes of death covered in the policy you have now.

In all cases, if you are thinking of buying a new policy, check with the agent or company that issued you the one you have now. When you bought your old policy, you may have seen an illustration of the benefits of your policy. Before replacing your policy, ask your agent or company for an updated illustration. Check to see how the policy has performed and what you might expect in the future, based on the amounts the company is paying now.

How Much Do You Need?

Here are some questions to ask yourself:

- How much of the family income do I provide? If I were to die early, how would my survivors, especially my children, get by? Does anyone else depend on me financially, such as a parent, grandparent, brother or sister?

- Do I have children for whom I'd like to set aside money to finish their education in the event of my death?

- How will my family pay final expenses and repay debts after my death?

- Do I have family members or organizations to whom I would like to leave money?

- Will there be estate taxes to pay after my death?

- How will inflation affect future needs?

As you figure out what you have to meet these needs, count the life insurance you have now, including any group insurance where you work or veteran's insurance. Don't forget Social Security and pension plan survivor's benefits. Add other assets you have: savings, investments, real estate and personal property. Which assets would your family sell or cash in to pay expenses after your death?

What is the Right Kind of Life Insurance?

All policies are not the same. Some give coverage for your lifetime and others cover you for a specific number of years. Some build up cash values and others do not. Some policies combine different kinds of insurance, and others let you change from one kind of insurance to another. Some policies may offer other benefits while you are still living. Your choice should be based on your needs and what you can afford.

There are two basic types of life insurance: **term insurance** and **cash value insurance**. Term insurance generally has lower premiums in the early years, but does not build up cash values that you can use in the future. You may combine cash value life insurance with term insurance for the period of your greatest need for life insurance to replace income.

FIGURE 27.29

Term Insurance covers you for a term of one or more years. It pays a death benefit only if you die in that term. Term insurance generally offers the largest insurance protection for your premium dollar. It generally does not build up cash value.

You can renew most term insurance policies for one or more terms even if your health has changed. Each time you renew the policy for a new term, premiums may be higher. Ask what the premiums will be if you continue to renew the policy. Also ask if you will lose the right to renew the policy at some age. For a higher premium, some companies will give you the right to keep the policy in force for a guaranteed period at the same price each year. At the end of that time you may need to pass a physical examination to continue coverage, and premiums may increase.

You may be able to trade many term insurance policies for a cash value policy during a conversion period--even if you are not in good health. Premiums for the new policy will be higher than you have been paying for the term insurance.

Cash Value Life Insurance is a type of insurance where the premiums charged are higher at the beginning than they would be for the same amount of term insurance. The part of the premium that is not used for the cost of insurance is invested by the company and builds up a cash value that may be used in a variety of ways. You may borrow against a policy's cash value by taking a policy loan. If you don't pay back the loan and the interest on it, the amount you owe will be subtracted from the benefits when you die, or from the cash value if you stop paying premiums and take out the remaining cash value. You can also use your cash value to keep insurance protection for a limited time or to buy a reduced amount without having to pay more premiums. You also can use the cash value to increase your income in retirement or to help pay for needs such as a child's tuition without canceling the policy. However, to build up this cash value, you must pay higher premiums in the earlier years of the policy. Cash value life insurance may be one of several types; whole life, universal life and variable life are all types of cash value insurance.

Whole Life Insurance covers you for as long as you live if your premiums are paid. You generally pay the same amount in premiums for as long as you live. When you first take out the policy, premiums can be several times higher than you would pay initially for the same amount of term insurance. But they are smaller than the premiums you would eventually pay if you were to keep renewing a term policy until your later years.

Some whole life policies let you pay premiums for a shorter period such as 20 years, or until age 65. Premiums for these policies are higher since the premium payments are made during a shorter period.

Universal Life Insurance is a kind of flexible policy that lets you vary your premium payments. You can also adjust the face amount of your coverage. Increases may require proof that you qualify for the new death benefit. The premiums you pay (less expense charges) go into a policy account that earns interest. Charges are deducted from the account. If your yearly premium payment plus the interest your account earns is less than the charges, your account value will become lower. If it keeps dropping, eventually your coverage will end. To prevent that, you may need to start making premium payments, or increase your premium payments, or lower your death benefits. Even if there is enough in your account to pay the premiums, continuing to pay premiums yourself means that you build up more cash value.

Variable Life Insurance is a kind of insurance where the death benefits and cash values depend on the investment performance of one or more separate accounts, which may be invested in mutual funds or other investments allowed under the policy. Be sure to get the prospectus from the company when buying this kind of policy and STUDY IT CAREFULLY. You will have higher death benefits and cash value if the underlying investments do well. Your benefits and cash value will be lower or may disappear if the investments you chose didn't do as well as you expected. You may pay an extra premium for a guaranteed death benefit.

FIGURE 27.30

Life Insurance Illustrations

You may be thinking of buying a policy where cash values, death benefits, dividends or premiums may vary based on events or situations the company does not guarantee (such as interest rates). If so, you may get an illustration from the agent or company that helps explain how the policy works. The illustration will show how the benefits that are not guaranteed will change as interest rates and other factors change. The illustration will show you what the company guarantees. It will also show you what could happen in the future. Remember that nobody knows what will happen in the future. You should be ready to adjust your financial plans if the cash value doesn't increase as quickly as shown in the illustration. You will be asked to sign a statement that says you understand that some of the numbers in the illustration are not guaranteed.

Finding a Good Value in Life Insurance

After you have decided which kind of life insurance is best for you, compare similar policies from different companies to find which one is likely to give you the best value for your money. A simple comparison of the premiums is not enough. There are other things to consider. For example:

— Do premiums or benefits vary from year to year?

— How much do the benefits build up in the policy?

— What part of the premiums or benefits is not guaranteed?

— What is the effect of interest on money paid and received at different times on the policy?

Remember that no one company offers the lowest cost at **all** ages for **all** kinds and amounts of insurance. You should also consider other factors:

— How quickly does the cash value grow? Some policies have low cash values in the early years that build quickly later on. Other policies have a more level cash value build-up. A year-by-year display of values and benefits can be very helpful. (The agent or company will give you a policy summary or an illustration that will show benefits and premiums for selected years.)

— Are there special policy features that particularly suit your needs?

— How are nonguaranteed values calculated? For example, interest rates are important in determining policy returns. In some companies increases reflect the average interest earnings on all of that company's policies regardless of when issued. In others, the return for policies issued in a recent year, or a group of years, reflects the interest earnings on that group of policies; in this case, amounts paid are likely to change more rapidly when interest rates change.

FIGURE 27.31

STATE FARM LIFE INSURANCE COMPANY

IMPORTANT INFORMATION ABOUT COVERAGE UNDER THE TEXAS LIFE, ACCIDENT, HEALTH AND HOSPITAL SERVICE INSURANCE GUARANTY ASSOCIATION

Texas law establishes a system, administered by the Texas Life, Accident, Health and Hospital Service Insurance Guaranty Association (the "Association"), to protect Texas Policyholders if their life or health insurance company fails. Only the policyholders of insurance companies which are members of the Association are eligible for this protection, which is subject to the terms, limitations, and conditions of the Association law. The law is found in the **Texas Insurance Code, Chapter 463.)**

It is possible that the Association may not cover your policy in full or in part due to statutory limitations.

Eligibility for Protection by the Association

When a member insurance company is found to be insolvent and placed under an order of liquidation by a court or designated as impaired by the Texas Commissioner of Insurance, the Association provides coverage to policyholders who are:

– Residents of Texas at that time **(irrespective of the policyholder's residency at policy issue)**
– Residents of other states, ONLY if the following conditions are met:
  1. The policyholder has a policy with a company based in Texas;
  2. The policyholder's state of residence has a similar guaranty association; and
  3. The policyholder is **not eligible** for coverage by the guaranty association of the policyholder's state of residence.

Limits of Protection by the Association

Accident, Accident and Health, or Health Insurance;
– For each individual covered under one or more policies: up to a total of $500,000 for basic hospital, medical-surgical, and major medical insurance, $300,000 for disability or long term care insurance, and $200,000 for other types of health insurance.

Life Insurance:
– Net cash surrender value or net cash withdrawal up to a total of $100,000 under one or more policies on any one life; or
– Death benefits up to a total of $300,000 under one or more policies on any one life; or
– Total benefits up to a total of $5,000,000 to any owner of multiple non-group life policies.

Individual Annuities:
– Present value of benefits up to a total of $100,000 under one or more contracts on any one life.

Group Annuities:
– Present value of allocated benefits up to a total of $100,000 on any one life; or
– Present value of unallocated benefits up to a total of $5,000,000 for one contractholder regardless of the number of contracts.

Aggregate Limit:
– $300,000 on any one life with the exception of $500,000 health insurance limit, the $5,000,000 multiple owner life insurance limit, and the $5,000,000 unallocated group annuity limit.

Insurance companies and agents are prohibited by law from using the existence of the Association for the purpose of sales, solicitation, or inducement to purchase any form of insurance. When you are selecting an insurance company, you should not rely on Association coverage.

Texas Life, Accident, Health, and Hospital Service Insurance Guaranty Association 6504 Bridge Point Parkway, Suite 450 Austin, Texas 78730 800-982-6362 www.txlifega.org	Texas Department of Insurance P.O. Box 149104 Austin, Texas 78714-9104 800-252-3439 www.tdi.state.tx.us

03906-43.3

20080226

FIGURE 27.32

IMPORTANT TAX INFORMATION CONCERNING YOUR LIFE INSURANCE POLICY

Money that is deemed removed ("distributed") from or grows within some life insurance policies may be taxed. The following briefly describes examples of how this could occur. Your tax advisor must determine the taxation of your specific situation.

What is a "distribution" from the policy?

The term distribution is used in the tax laws to describe the deemed withdrawal of values from the policy. Typical withdrawals include: withdrawals of cash value, loans, assignments of contract values to another person, or crediting of a dividend, unless it is used to purchase additional insurance or to pay a premium.

How are policies normally taxed?

Generally, death benefits are not subject to income tax. Values inside the policy grow tax-free. Loans are tax-free until you surrender the policy or allow it to lapse. Other distributions are tax-free until all premiums are returned, and distributions above that amount are taxed as "gain."

What is "gain"?

Gain simply means your policy has a larger value than the total amount of premiums you have paid, net of some amounts such as premiums that have been returned through dividends. The gain is the difference between the value of your policy and the premiums paid. For example, if a policy has a value of $1,000.00 and premiums of $800.00 have been paid, the gain is $200.00. It is only the $200.00 gain that would be subject to tax.

When might my policy be taxed differently?

Certain actions that you take may result in various situations where your policy may be taxed differently, including but not limited to the following:

- Pay premium above the limits specified in the tax laws
- Change the amount of insurance, including paid-up additions, such as through partial withdrawals
- Add, cancel, or change rider coverage or amounts

Also certain distributions are taxable - but only to the extent of the gain in your policy. Any gain is considered to be the first - rather than the last - amount withdrawn; so, any distribution is taxed until the amount of the gain is reached. After that, the remainder of the distribution is not taxed.

If the distribution occurs before age 59½, the IRS may impose a 10% additional tax on the amount of the distribution that is taxable.

In extreme situations, the policy may be disqualified as "life insurance" for tax purposes. That means the policy's internal cash value growth could be taxable.

How will I know for certain how my policy is taxed?

Prior to taking actions such as those listed above, you may wish to contact your tax advisor to find out for certain how your policy will be taxed. In some cases the tax consequences of these actions may be irreversible.

Policyholder Information Service

State Farm Life Insurance Company
Home Office:
Bloomington, Illinois 61710-0001

Index

CPSIA information can be obtained
at www.ICGtesting.com
Printed in the USA
LVHW061057100320
649504LV00007B/69